LEGAL PROBLEM SOLVER

READER'S DIGEST

LEGAL PROBLEM SOLVER

A Quick-and-Easy Action Guide to Canadian Law

The Reader's Digest Association (Canada) Ltd.
Montreal

Project Editor
Alice Philomena Rutherford

Designers
Cécile Germain
Andrée Payette

Senior Editor
Sandy Shepherd

Research Editor
Wadad Bashour

Editorial Assistant
Elizabeth Eastman

Copy Editor
Joseph Marchetti

Art Supervisor
John McGuffie

Production Coordinator
Susan Wong

Production Manager
Holger Lorenzen

Consultants and Contributors

**Chief Legal
Consultant and Contributor**
Nelson Brott of Borenstein,
Duquette, Brott & Shea

Legal Researchers
Kelley Harvey
Kevin MacNeill
Damon Park

Special Contributors
Pierre Duquette
Ebie Weizfeld

Copy Preparation
Françoise Bibor

Indexer
Jane Broderick

Spot Illustrations
Beth Krommes

Copyright © 1994 The Reader's Digest Association (Canada) Ltd.
215 Redfern Avenue, Montreal, Que., H3Z 2V9

Canadian Cataloguing in Publication Data

Main entry under title:
    Reader's Digest Legal problem solver
Includes index.
ISBN 0-88850-230-3

1. Law—Canada—Popular works.   I. Rutherford,
Alice Philomena . . . II. Reader's Digest Association
(Canada) . . . III. Title: Legal problem solver

KE447.R425 1994   349.71   C94—9000197-X

Printed in Canada

94 95 96 97 98 / 5 4 3 2

▪ CONTENTS ▪

About This Book

"Knowledge is power," goes an old saying, and nowhere is that truer than in the field of law. Armed with the right facts, you can avoid legal pitfalls, bail yourself out of trouble, minimize potential losses, become a wiser consumer, and take full advantage of your rights and benefits as a citizen. LEGAL PROBLEM SOLVER shows you how to do all these things.

Throughout this book, you will find valuable information on hundreds of law-related topics, as well as advice on how to deal with the kinds of legal problems that an average person is likely to encounter in daily life. With nearly 700 major entries encompassing virtually every area of everyday law, this legal action guide is one of the most comprehensive—and comprehensible—books of its kind. It contains reliable information and sound advice on everything from false advertising to false arrest, from dating to divorce, from pawnbrokers to stockbrokers,

This book is not intended to be a substitute for a lawyer, but it can serve as a trusted legal adviser. For instance, it will help you determine whether you need a lawyer in the first place. Fighting a traffic ticket or getting a document notarized may not require a lawyer, while buying real estate or signing an important contract usually should not be undertaken without one.

If you do hire a lawyer, LEGAL PROBLEM SOLVER will make you a better-informed client. Before consulting a lawyer, first see what this book has to say about your particular situation. Chances are, it will answer some of your questions, help you formulate others, and give you a sense of how serious or complex your problem is. Then, when you do meet with a lawyer, these few minutes of preparation will have saved you both time and money (most lawyers bill by the hour). More important, you will be better equipped to understand the lawyer and better able to help him serve you effectively.

LEGAL PROBLEM SOLVER is a user-friendly reference tool. Entries are arranged in alphabetical order, and the information you need is readily accessible. If you do not see the topic you are looking for, check the comprehensive index at the back of the book.

The typical LEGAL PROBLEM SOLVER entry begins with a clear definition of the topic. It then goes into a fuller explanation of how the subject can affect your life. It assesses the relative risks you assume by taking certain actions, and it explains how the law affects different people in different situations. In most entries, straightforward examples give the reader a clear idea of how legal principles apply in everyday circumstances.

Often, hypothetical problems are introduced to illustrate a topic. In many articles, numbered "Steps to Take" outline specifically what you need to do to resolve the issue. When a topic is related to other entries, cross-references are included to help you locate them. You will also find cross-references to the *Useful Addresses* and *Everyday Legal Forms* that appear at the back of the book.

Special supplementary features add to the reader's understanding of a given subject. Convenient *Checklists* serve as reminders about what not to overlook when you must take action or need to solve a problem. *ABC's* boxes simplify and summarize the essentials of a topic. And the features called *Real Life, Real Law* offer pertinent examples of how the law has been applied in actual court cases.

As you dip into LEGAL PROBLEM SOLVER, you will notice that it is refreshingly free of legal jargon. No matter how lofty or abstract the principles involved, you will find no turgid, technical legalese in this book. Instead, you will find clear, concise explanations of the facts, written in plain English and illustrated with concrete, down-to-earth examples. On the few occasions when legal terminology must be used, it is clearly defined. In addition, the *Glossary* defines and clarifies more than 300 legal terms.

Of course, no book—no matter how large—can cover every aspect of the law or answer every conceivable question. LEGAL PROBLEM SOLVER provides neither the last word on every subject nor the only word. Although every effort has been made to ensure that the information provided is as complete, accurate, and up-to-date as possible (including last-minute changes made up to press time), the reader must keep in mind that laws change over time, often vary from province to province, and—in the case of bylaws—town to town.

LEGAL PROBLEM SOLVER is first and foremost an action guide. Its purpose is to help you help yourself. But without doubt some situations call for a lawyer, not a layman. So if you are going to take any legal action that you believe may have serious consequences, be sure to consult a lawyer first.

— The Editors

A

FROM

ABANDONED PROPERTY

TO

AUTOPSY

ABANDONED PROPERTY

You are on your way to the bus stop when you see it—a beautiful blue bicycle, the very kind your daughter wants. But it is not in the window of a bicycle shop; it is piled on top of the garbage set at the curb for pickup. The bike has a flat tire and a broken chain but otherwise is in good condition. Is it all right to take it home?

The answer depends on whether or not the bike has been abandoned.

To be considered abandoned, a piece of property must have been left behind purposely by the owner, who must have no intention of reclaiming it later on. The law involved here applies to personal property only, not to real estate. (For a discussion of abandoned real estate, see ADVERSE POSSESSION.)

In this instance, the bicycle seems to be abandoned. The garbage is where much abandoned property ends up, and the bicycle's condition suggests that it has been thrown away.

Before claiming it, however, consider a couple of other possibilities. First, the bike may have been stolen and left with the garbage by the thief. If that is so, the true owner has not voluntarily given up ownership, and may want the bike back.

Second, even if the bike was not stolen, the owner may not have intended it to go out with the garbage. In that event, the bicycle is considered lost, not abandoned. Fortunately, there is a solution to your problem.

STEPS TO TAKE

1. If you have any doubt about whether the bicycle was truly abandoned, try to find out whether someone living in a nearby building abandoned it.

2. If this proves futile, take the bicycle to the police station and get a receipt. Local authorities may take charge of lost or stolen property and dispose of it after enough time has passed for the owner to claim it.

3. If the bicycle is not claimed within a prescribed period (usually about 90 days), you can claim it. If there are storage costs, you may have to pay these to prevent municipal authorities selling the bicycle.

ABANDONMENT

When lawyers use the word *abandonment*, it has the dictionary meaning of "relinquishing" or "giving something up

completely." However, laws are very specific about what a person must do in order to abandon something.

A person may abandon a legal claim, for example, by failing to bring a lawsuit within the time prescribed by law. See STATUTE OF LIMITATIONS.

A tenant may abandon her apartment before her lease is up by leaving it vacant and allowing the landlord to reclaim it. Goods left by a tenant who has abandoned the premises, or left in a dwelling after the lease has expired, may also be considered abandoned goods. See TENANTS' RIGHTS.

If you forget your umbrella in a restaurant, you have not abandoned it. But if you leave your shoes at the shoe repair shop for six months, the owner can assume that you have abandoned them. Your claim check, or receipt, usually states the time period during which you can claim your goods before they are considered abandoned.

Even a motor vehicle that has remained unclaimed at an airport (other than one that allows long-term parking) for at least 30 days may be considered abandoned. See ABANDONED PROPERTY.

If a wife disappears and fails to communicate with her husband within a reasonable period of time, she is said to have abandoned her spouse. See DIVORCE.

To willfully neglect a child in your care or to deal with a child in a manner that exposes it to risk without protection is also abandonment and constitutes a criminal offense.

ABDUCTION

One of the most painful things that can happen is to have one's child abducted. It is common knowledge that when the abductor is a stranger, he or she can be charged with kidnapping. Less well known is the fact that even a parent can be charged with abduction. For example, when a couple is separated or divorced and their child ordinarily resides with one or the other, it is a criminal offense for either parent to deprive the other of the child, *even if there is no custody order*. So even if there have been no court proceedings, one parent may not legally keep the other from seeing their child.

Even a parent who has custody of a child may not lawfully stop the other parent visiting the child, unless the court has expressly denied that parent visiting rights. Abducting a child for whom a custody order exists makes the abducting parent liable to imprisonment for up to 10 years. Even when there is no custody order, the abducting parent could be sentenced to 10 years in jail. However, such prosecution requires prior approval by the attorney general.

INTERNATIONAL ABDUCTIONS

Since The Hague Convention on International Child Abduction (1980), it has been easier to have an abducted child returned to Canada. But this convention only applies to signatories—the United States,

Israel, and most Western European countries. Moslem countries and most African and South American countries have not yet signed the convention.

When children are abducted to non-signatory countries, a parent faces immense difficulty in having them returned to Canada. External Affairs does not usually intervene, even if the children are Canadian citizens. However, the Canadian Red Cross Society, International Social Service Canada, and the Missing Children's Network (le Réseau Enfants Retour) do help locate abducted children. See USEFUL ADDRESSES at back of book.

ABORTION

Abortion is the deliberate, intentional and premature termination of a pregnancy. Parliament has not passed any laws to regulate abortion since 1988, when the Supreme Court declared Canada's abortion laws unconstitutional. Prior to that, abortions were prohibited unless a hospital's therapeutic abortion committee agreed that a woman's life, or her mental or physical health, would likely be endangered by continuing the pregnancy. Having an abortion without the approval of such a committee was punishable by up to two years' imprisonment; the person who performed the abortion could be imprisoned for life.

SUPREME COURT RULINGS

In the *Morgentaler* case of 1988, however, the Supreme

Court found that this section of the Criminal Code violated a woman's right to life, liberty, and the security of the person, rights enshrined in our Charter of Rights and Freedoms. In the *Daigle* case a year later, the Supreme Court declared a fetus had no rights until it was born alive, a view it reaffirmed in 1991, when it said a fetus was not "a person."

In the landmark *Daigle* case, the Supreme Court said a prospective father could not force his partner to continue a pregnancy. This ruling overturned a Quebec Court of Appeal injunction given to a Montreal man who tried to stop his former girlfriend from having an abortion. The Supreme Court held that the woman's right to control her own body overrode the man's interest in the fetus or unborn child.

QUALIFIED PRACTITIONER

Only a qualified medical practitioner may carry out an abortion. A person other than a physician who supplies a drug or other instrument to help someone have an abortion could be imprisoned for up to two years.

ABUSIVE LANGUAGE

If someone showers you with unflattering words, tells you where to go, or otherwise berates you, you might want to see her arrested, and fined or imprisoned. Objectionable as it is, however, verbal abuse is not a crime and usually does not provide sufficient cause for a civil lawsuit.

Suppose, however, that a neighbor repeatedly curses you and your family in an outrageous manner over a period of time. As a result, you suffer mental anguish, become ill, and miss work. You may be able to sue your neighbor for inflicting emotional distress, and if you win, you may be able to collect both your lost wages and additional money as punishment.

When combined with lies, racial slurs, sexual innuendo, or threats, abusive language enters an entirely different realm of the law, and lawsuits may be appropriate. See DEFAMATION; HATE CRIME; LIBEL AND SLANDER; SEXUAL HARASSMENT.

ACCESS TO INFORMATION

In the early 1980s, the federal government and a number of provinces enacted freedom-of-information legislation. These laws give individuals the right to examine and copy unpublished records compiled by public institutions and agencies such as hospitals, universities, and government boards and departments.

The information may be in the form of reports, photographs, films, microfilms, and even letters, memos, and computerized data. The subject matter is wide-ranging, everything from reports on the economy or environment to the results of tests conducted on various products.

Cabinet meeting documents, trade secrets, and any information that might threaten an individual's safety or public security are exempt. As a result, journalists, students, and others conducting research under freedom-of-information legislation do not have access to certain military information and details of ongoing police investigations.

Most laws specify that the information be provided within a reasonable time and for a nominal fee—usually about $5.

HOW TO GET ACCESS

Agencies subject to access-to-information legislation are published in the *Access Register,* a book the size of a metropolitan telephone directory, found in most public libraries and many post offices. It gives the name and address of the person in charge of each agency or department. This is the individual to whom you should send your request for information.

Both the *Access Register* and the access request forms tell you how to get help filling out the form or identifying information sources appropriate to your needs. The agency or institution in question must provide the information within 30 days. If this is impossible, you must be advised of the delay.

Applicants who feel that requests for information were denied or incompletely answered without valid reason, or that the fees were too high, can file a complaint with the Information Commissioner. If the commissioner does not resolve the matter to your sat-

isfaction, you can ask the Federal Court (provincial court in the case of provincial documents) to investigate. If the court finds in your favor, it can order the particular agency to give you the information.

One such case occurred in Montreal, where the Royal Victoria Hospital refused to release a patient's entire medical file. The patient sued, and even though the hospital argued that such files are confidential, the court ruled the confidentiality applied only to third parties, not to the patient himself. It is worth noting, however, that even under freedom-of-information legislation, information about an individual is rarely provided to a third party, even when such information is available to the individual himself.

ACCESSORY

A person who helps someone else commit a crime but is not present while the crime is being committed is known as an accessory. There are two kinds of accessories:

◇ An accessory before the fact helps prepare for or plan a crime—for example, he supplies a gun to a bank robber but does not participate in the robbery itself.

◇ An accessory after the fact helps the criminal avoid capture and trial after the crime has been committed. For example, a person who throws the robber's gun into the river or who allows him to hide from the police in the attic is an accessory after the fact.

However, a person who helps a spouse who has committed a crime to escape the law is not generally regarded as an accessory after the fact since our law places great importance on spousal loyalty and support.

When the crime is punishable by life imprisonment, murder for example, the accessory after the fact could be imprisoned for up to 14 years; when the crime is punishable by 14 years or less, the accessory is liable to be jailed for half the term meted out to the actual perpetrator. An accessory after the fact is usually treated more leniently by the courts because his actions relate more to the obstruction of justice than to the crime itself. See also ACCOMPLICE.

ACCIDENTS

The word accident has no special legal meaning. Life insurance policies, laws regarding workers' compensation, disability insurance policies, and the like often provide their own definitions of what constitutes an accident. Laws and lawyers focus on who is responsible for causing the accident or allowing it to happen. For more information on your legal responsibility in preventing accidents, and your rights if you are an accident victim, see also ACCIDENTS ON GOVERNMENT PROPERTY; ACCIDENTS IN THE HOME; ACCIDENTS IN PUBLIC PLACES; ACCIDENTS ON PUBLIC TRANSPORTATION; ACCIDENTS AT WORK; ACT OF GOD; BOATING; NEGLIGENCE.

ACCIDENTS ON GOVERNMENT PROPERTY

As you are cruising along the highway on a gorgeous spring day, you see a pothole the size of a small crater ahead. You swerve, but your wheel hits it anyway. Afterward, you realize your car has developed an ominous shimmy. Can you sue the province for the damage?

At one time a private individual could not sue a government for injuries and damages. Now, however, most governments can be sued—provided that the circumstances are appropriate and that the correct procedures are followed.

City, provincial, and federal property must be kept in reasonably safe condition. For example, floors in government buildings must not be slippery, public roads must have a well-maintained surface, and trees in public parks must be kept free of rotting branches that could fall and hit someone.

Should you be injured as a result of the government's failure to meet these standards, you can file a lawsuit. But be aware that the procedures differ somewhat from other lawsuits.

SPECIAL RULES FOR SUING GOVERNMENTS

In most situations, before you can file suit against the city, provincial, or federal government, you have to file a claim with the appropriate government office. For example, if you are hurt by a falling branch in a city park, you can file a claim with the city clerk's office. If you are hurt on provincial or federal property, you must file your claim with the agency responsible for that particular building, park, or other property.

Usually you have a very short period of time after the accident to file your claim—the delay to give notice may be as little as 15 days. If it is rejected, you have another short period to file your lawsuit—this delay may be as short as three months. (In 1987, the courts declared unconstitutional a section of the Ontario Municipal Act requiring claims for injuries caused by ice or snow on public sidewalks to be made within seven days—10, in rural areas. The Ontario Court of Appeal found the section made a "discriminatory distinction" between injury caused by non-repair of roads and injury sustained because of icy sidewalks.) Keep in mind that these times may be extended if you can show that an injury or circumstances beyond your control prevented you from filing on time.

If your claim is relatively small, you can file suit in small-claims court. But if it is large, you should seek the help of a lawyer experienced in filing claims against the government. That way you will be sure to meet all the requirements necessary to keep your claim alive.

LIMITED LIABILITY

Whether or not you can sue a local or provincial government or a government agency often depends on that government's precise duty—what exactly it is charged with doing. For example, is the government responsible for keeping the roads in good repair?

A British Columbia cyclist, injured when his bicycle hit a pothole, learned just how important this particular point can be. He took his case to court, but finally lost when the B.C. Supreme Court ruled that although the municipality in question may have had the power to maintain roads, it did not, however, have the statutory duty to do so.

Since 1993, Quebec municipalities are not liable for some types of damage to vehicles caused by road conditions.

ACCIDENTS IN THE HOME

Suppose a guest in your home hurts her back when she sits on a wobbly chair that collapses beneath her. Or suppose the plumber slips on your freshly mopped kitchen floor and injures his knee. Can you be held responsible?

It depends on the circumstances. If visitors are clearly warned about existing dangers, such as a weak chair or a slippery floor, the homeowner generally will not be held responsible.

HOMEOWNER'S OBLIGATION

The law recognizes that no home is 100 percent accident-proof. Nevertheless, it requires the occupant to take certain precautions to ensure that visitors are not hurt. Such

phrases as "duty of care" and "reasonable care" are used to describe a homeowner's obligation to protect visitors from harm. Of course the amount of care required largely depends on the visitor's reason for being in the home.

THREE TYPES OF VISITORS

All provinces other than Quebec recognize three categories of visitors to your home —invitees, licensees, and trespassers. The amount of reasonable care that you must show toward each varies.

Invitees come into your home for both their own benefit and yours. They include babysitters, plumbers, appliance repair personnel, potential home buyers, and letter carriers. You owe invitees the greatest duty of care. For example, to prevent your babysitter from tripping over a loose floorboard, either repair it or temporarily cover it with boxes, perhaps with a note attached, and clearly warn the sitter of the danger in advance.

Licensees enter your home for their own benefit or convenience. They include sales people, relatives, guests, people asking for directions and, in some cases, fire fighters and police. The duty of care you owe to licensees is generally less than that owed to invitees. If a cosmetics salesperson visits your home, for example, you do not have to cover your loose floorboard with boxes, but you should warn her of the danger.

Trespassers enter a property without permission—for

example, burglars and mischievous children. Understandably, they are owed the least amount of protection by homeowners. If a burglar trips over your loose floorboard, he gets what he deserves. One exception to the law's unsympathetic view of trespassers involves children who harmlessly walk on your property. If you are aware of a hazard, such as a broken swing or rickety tree house on which they might unwittingly hurt themselves, you must correct the condition or, at least, warn about the danger. See also ATTRACTIVE NUISANCE; TRESPASS.

STEPS TO TAKE

Prevent costly lawsuits by using "reasonable care":

1. Inspect your property for hidden dangers (wobbly railings, rotten stairs, and the like) and make appropriate repairs.

2. If repairs cannot be made before visitors come into your home, warn them explicitly about the dangers.

3. When someone is on your property, take extra care when performing dangerous tasks, such as moving ladders or using power tools.

4. Put signs up to warn trespassing children (or adults) of any hazards that exist on your property, and if possible, remove the danger.

5. Remember that certain things—an empty swimming pool for example, or a hole in the ground—may be more dangerous at night than during daylight, and lights, fences, or other appropriate markers should be used to clearly indicate the danger at nighttime.

ACCIDENTS IN PUBLIC PLACES

Stores, restaurants, theaters, and other businesses have a responsibility to their patrons to protect them from accidents. But by law, they are not expected to ensure the complete safety of people who enter their premises, which are regarded as public places.

REASONABLE CARE

According to law, shop owners must exercise "reasonable care" in seeing that no one gets hurt. To fulfill this obligation, the owner should take the following precautions:

◇ Inspect his property periodically to eliminate potential risks to customers.

◇ Make sure that floors are not slippery and rugs are not torn, wrinkled, or loose.

◇ See that entrances and exits are not blocked and are easy to find.

◇ Mark clear glass doors in some way to keep people from walking into them.

◇ Keep rooms well lit.

◇ Post warnings about hazards that are not easily noticeable, such as unexpected steps or low ceilings.

HIDDEN DANGERS

The duty to warn is not limited to dangers that the proprietor is aware of. For example, if a customer in a lighting store gets a shock from a defective lamp, the owner may be responsible even if she did not know the hazard existed. The assumption is that if the owner had shown reasonable care by periodically inspecting the premises, she would have been aware of the danger.

The duty to use reasonable care also applies to establishments that maintain parking lots, garages, and restrooms for customers, but not to storerooms, kitchens, and other areas closed to the public.

MERCHANDISE DISPLAYS

A store must display merchandise in a way that minimizes the risk of injury. Because displays are designed to attract the customer's attention, they may become a hazard. If a customer walking down an aisle is distracted by a motorized cardboard clown waving a tube of toothpaste back and forth, and as a result trips over a case of sardines left in the aisle, the store may be responsible. In most situations, however, the person who tripped over an obvious obstruction would have no complaint.

ROLLER COASTERS AND FOUL BALLS

Owners and managers of amusement parks, stadiums, hockey arenas, ski resorts, golf courses, zoos, harness racing tracks, and other recreational areas are also subject to the duty of reasonable care and must warn of dangers that are not apparent. People who visit a pony ride at a country fair, for example, should be warned about a pony that kicks.

In amusement parks, rides that have a potential for serious injury, such as roller coasters, require more care, warnings, and inspections than safer rides like merry-go-rounds. In ballparks all seats must be inspected periodically for safety, and screens must be put up around home plate to protect spectators from being hit by foul balls and flying bats.

Sometimes the behavior of other patrons creates hazards that could lead to injuries. If a gang of reckless teenagers at a skating rink is not kept under control by supervisory personnel, for example, the management may be responsible for any injuries that result.

However, certain activities such as football or hockey are by their very nature dangerous; so in certain cases no one may be held responsible for injuries that were caused unintentionally and were a foreseeable risk. The Latin saying *volenti non fit injuria* ("harm is not caused to he who consents") sums it up.

STEPS TO TAKE

If you are injured in a public place, do as follows:

1. Report the accident to the management right away.

2. If the person in charge writes a report of the accident, get a copy. If he does not, write to the management yourself, giving details of the accident.

3. Get the names and addresses of witnesses.

4. Ask your physician to keep a record of your injuries.

5. Obtain photos of your injuries if possible.

6. The management or its insurer may ask you to sign a release. Do not sign anything until you have talked to your lawyer. He will probably advise you to wait until you know the full extent of your injuries. What at first seems like a minor injury may get worse later.

7. If your injury is clearly due to the owner's negligence, he may be willing to settle out of court. If not, you can file a lawsuit seeking compensation for certain medical bills not covered by Medicare, disability or disfigurement, lost wages, and pain and suffering.

8. If you are injured in a publicly owned place, such as a city park or sidewalk, or a provincial or federal building, you must sue the city, province, or federal government as the case may be. Note that special rules may apply when suing municipal or other governments.

You must submit written details of the accident to the government in question within a short time (15 days in some cases). Legal action must be commenced within a shorter period than that allowed when suing an individual or corporation. In Ontario, for example, you have only three months in which to sue a municipality for certain actions arising from nonrepair of roads. See ACCIDENTS ON GOVERNMENT PROPERTY.

ACCIDENTS ON PUBLIC TRANS- PORTATION

The companies that run buses, taxis, trains, planes, and ferries, which charge money to take people from one place to another, are called common carriers. Since the accidents that can occur are potentially serious, common carriers are required to use what the law calls the highest degree of care for their passengers' safety. This means that they are responsible for any injuries resulting from even the slightest carelessness on their part. In addition, responsibility for such carelessness may rest not only on the common carrier but also on the person who operates the vehicle—the driver, engineer, pilot, or captain.

The high degree of care expected of common carriers begins when passengers are boarding and ends when they are safely off. Buses, trains, and taxis must stop long enough to allow passengers to get in and out safely. Suppose a woman is getting out of a cab and the driver takes off suddenly and injures her arm. The driver and the cab company can be held responsible for her injury.

Common carriers must provide help in boarding and getting off when (1) a passenger is disabled or frail, (2) the stopping place is unsafe, or (3) the step to the vehicle is high.

Common carriers and their employees must also use the highest degree of care in selecting, maintaining, and operating vehicles. When passengers are on board, the aisles and floors must be kept clear, and baggage must be carefully secured in racks. Drivers must obey all traffic, navigation, and aviation laws and must not make sudden starts or stops.

Where the common carrier operates a motor vehicle as opposed to a train or airplane, Alberta, British Columbia, Ontario, Quebec, and Saskatchewan have instituted government insurance boards to handle most claims involving bodily injury.

PASSENGERS' RESPONSIBILITIES

Common carriers must warn passengers of dangers they are not likely to see for themselves, such as unexpected steps. But they cannot be expected to warn about hazardous situations that appear out of nowhere. For example, if an elderly man suddenly goes berserk on a train and whacks a fellow passenger with his umbrella, the railway is not to blame. But if the man had been waving the umbrella madly and bellowing threats toward other passengers, and the train crew did nothing to stop him, the railway would most likely be held responsible.

Passengers have a duty to be reasonably careful too. Suppose a passenger on a speeding train ignores signs warning people not to stand between cars and is injured as a result. Because he was largely responsible for the injury, he probably could not win a suit against the carrier.

However, if a passenger and a carrier share responsibility for an accident, the passenger may be partially compensated for his injuries.

PLATFORMS AND WAITING ROOMS

A common carrier's responsibility for its buildings and other facilities, such as stations, platforms, and waiting areas, is one of reasonable care (not the highest degree of care). The same standard applies to carriers as to stores and restaurants. See ACCIDENTS IN PUBLIC PLACES.

STEPS TO TAKE IF YOU ARE INJURED

If you are the victim of an accident on public transportation, follow the steps outlined in the entry ACCIDENTS IN PUBLIC PLACES, plus the following:

1. If you are injured on a bus or taxi, get the driver's name, license plate number, and the vehicle identification number.

2. Try to get a copy of any written report of the accident made by the police or anyone other than the common carrier.

3. If your province has provincial automobile insurance, give the agency a detailed account of the accident.

See also AIRLINE ACCIDENTS.

ACCIDENTS AT WORK

Every year, thousands of Canadians are injured in work-related accidents. Whether the injury is as minor as a dislocated finger or is permanently disabling, a worker is entitled by law to compensation for injuries caused by someone else's action or negligence. Occupational Health and Safety (OHS) laws require most employers to join provincial or federal work accident insurance plans. This way injured workers can be compensated for lost wages and permanent incapacity. In return, employers are assured that an employee who suffers an injury will not be allowed to sue. See also OCCUPATIONAL HEALTH AND SAFETY COMMISSION.

If you are injured on the job, notify your employer immediately. This will help to protect your legal rights and will also protect other employees from a potentially dangerous condition. If your employer does not respond, seek legal advice.

The various OHS laws require employers to ensure the workplace, as well as its tools, machinery and procedures, is safe. Government inspectors see that safety standards are met. Workers (usually defined as anyone who performs work or supplies services for a fee; the definition includes officers of a company, full- or part-time workers, consultants, and temporary workers) have the right to refuse hazardous work, and their employers may not retaliate by reducing employees' salaries, or changing their jobs, or firing them. Worker complaints to OHS commissions are kept confidential.

Self-employed workers are excluded from OHS coverage. If you are self-employed, buy disability insurance to provide income in case you are injured and unable to work.

REAL LIFE, REAL LAW

The Case of the TTC Transfer

Howard showed his transfer to the driver when he boarded the Toronto Transit Commission (TTC) bus, but when he asked to get off at his stop, the driver refused to open the back doors. Howard went to the front and asked if the back doors were not working, but the driver ignored him. No other passengers wanted to get on or off at the next stop and, still ignoring Howard, the driver passed that one too.

Howard finally got off the bus at a third stop, a transfer point on the line. Perspiring and shaking with anger and outrage, he waited an hour for a bus inspector to come by. But when his complaint did not result in an apology from the driver, Howard sued the TTC for false imprisonment and emotional distress.

The case was heard in small-claims court. The judge awarded Howard $750 plus costs for false imprisonment, distress, loss of liberty, and the time lost pursuing his complaint.

ACCOMPLICE

An accomplice is someone who helps another commit a serious crime. Many times an accomplice is considered just as accountable as the person who actually committed the crime. The accomplice may or may not be present at the crime scene, and his assistance may be provided before, during, or after the crime itself.

One type of accomplice is known as an "accessory before the fact." He or she provides assistance before the crime but is not at the scene when it is committed. See ACCESSORY.

An accomplice who is present during a crime is usually referred to as an aider and abettor. An abettor is one who encourages another to commit a crime and is not the same as one who aids the principal criminal in committing the crime. Such a person may serve as a lookout while a burglar breaks into a store. Or he may assist a mugger by watching for potential victims and signaling when one is near.

Someone forced, by threats for example, to help a criminal may not be considered an accomplice, by definition one who forms a genuine common intention with the criminal to carry out the crime. Neither is a person an accomplice simply because he witnesses a crime.

For example, suppose you are in a jewelry store and see a stranger steal a watch from one of the displays. Even if you fail to report the crime, you are not an accomplice to the act, since you do not know the thief and you and he have not planned the crime together.

ACKNOWLEDG-MENT

Sometimes a court requires that the person who wrote a will or other legal document make a formal declaration that the document is authentically his. This declaration, called an acknowledgment, is usually made in the presence of a notary public or officer of the court, such as a lawyer. A form (also called an acknowledgment) is then completed as evidence. In Quebec, certain documents, such as marriage contracts, or deeds of sales of land or buildings, must be drawn up before a notary. For an example of an acknowledgment, see EVERYDAY LEGAL FORMS at back of book.

ACT OF GOD

Flash floods, tidal waves, earthquakes, hurricanes, incapacitating disease, and death are all considered acts of God—accidents of nature that cannot be foreseen or prevented in any way. In such circumstances standard legal obligations do not apply.

Some insurance policies contain clauses that exclude payment for damages caused by acts of God. For example, your insurance company may not reimburse you for flooding to your basement if the flood was caused by an unforeseeable torrential downpour and if no reasonable means could have been taken to avoid the flooding. For an additional premium, most companies offer insurance even for damage caused by an act of God.

ACTUAL CASH VALUE

The fair price on the open market for any kind of property—such as a house, car, land, or furniture—is known as its actual cash value. The term means the same as fair market value, market value, market price, cash value, and the like, but it is quite different from book value. See BOOK VALUE.

Actual cash value is the amount a buyer would be willing to pay in the normal course of business. It is not, for example, the price paid when the buyer has an urgent need to buy or the seller has to raise money quickly.

For insurance purposes, actual cash value is the cost of replacing damaged or lost property with an item of equal value, less depreciation. For example, a five-year-old refrigerator would not be replaced by a new one; the settlement is more likely to be about half the cost of a new fridge. Items such as antiques, however, may become more valuable with time and should be insured separately.

ADOPTION

Adoption is a legal proceeding that severs a person's legal ties to his or her biological parents and substitutes new parents.

Anybody can be adopted as the child of someone else. Stepparents can adopt stepchildren, an aunt and uncle can adopt a niece or nephew, an adult can adopt another adult, and, of course, a couple (or a single adult) can adopt a child unrelated and previously unknown to them.

Often certain requirements are set out in the adoption laws of the various provinces. For example, one province may

CHECKLIST

Legal Steps in an Adoption

Although adoption can be complicated and time-consuming, the formal legal steps are straightforward and relatively simple.

■ **NOTICE.**
Notice of adoption proceedings is given to everyone legally interested in the case, including the child if he or she is 10 years of age (12 years in some provinces) or older. Even when the parents are not married, the father must usually be notified as well as the mother.

■ **PETITION.**
The adopting parents ask the court's permission to adopt the child. This petition gives their names and addresses, and those of the child, and of the natural parents if known, as well as the child's sex and age.

■ **WRITTEN CONSENT.**
Whenever possible, the written consent of the child's natural parents must accompany the petition.

■ **QUALIFYING PERIOD.**
Most provinces have "a qualifying period of residence," during which the child lives with the adopting parents while a provincial agency checks to see how the relationship develops. If everyone is happy with the situation, the court issues a permanent adoption order.

■ **HEARING.**
A court hearing examines the qualifications of the prospective parents and grants or denies the petition accordingly. Because adoption proceedings are confidential, the hearing takes place in camera (in a courtroom closed to the public), and its records are usually available for examination only by court order.

■ **BIRTH CERTIFICATE.**
A new birth certificate is issued for the child, giving his new family name, the date and place of his birth, and the occupation of his adopting parents at the time of his birth. The old birth certificate is sealed and filed away, after which it can usually be opened only by a court order.

Saskatchewan also provide that, as far as is practical, the child and the adoptive parents should be of the same religion.

In Alberta, Manitoba, and Ontario, the culture and heritage of aboriginal children must be respected and protected wherever possible. For example, Ontario adoption agencies must consult with Indian bands and native communities before Indian or Inuit children are adopted.

Once an adoption is final, the new parents have the same rights, duties, and responsibilities toward the adopted child that they would have toward a child born to them. When an adoption is complete, a new birth certificate is prepared and filed, reflecting that the child has the same legal standing as a natural child of the adoptive parents.

METHODS OF ADOPTION

Traditional adoptions were done through adoption agencies, but increasingly people are finding and adopting through private placement.
Private placement
When the child's natural parents (also known as the birth parents) choose the adoptive parents for their child, the adoption process is referred to as private placement.

At the time of writing, British Columbia is planning to make it illegal to charge a fee for arranging a private adoption. If enacted, such legislation could slow down private placements, which are usually completed more quickly than adoptions done through provincial agencies. The latter can take up to

specify that the adopting parents be at least 18 years older than the person they adopt; another, that a child 10 years of age or older agrees to his or her own adoption. Legislation in Manitoba and Ontario specifically allows common law spouses to adopt children.

Most provinces have special rules concerning stepparent adoptions. Because family ties

◆ have already been established, such adoptions are easier than those where neither spouse is the biological parent. In Alberta, British Columbia, Manitoba, New Brunswick, Ontario, Saskatchewan, and Yukon, the parent of the child being adopted must consent to his or her spouse adopting the child. Alberta, Newfoundland, Ontario, Prince Edward Island, and

five years, whereas private adoptions take half that time.

Manitoba, New Brunswick, Newfoundland, and Ontario limit private adoptions to certain circumstances. For example, Ontario and New Brunswick permit them only when the adoptive parent is a relative or a stepparent.

All provinces insist that a child welfare agency approve adoptive parents. Newfoundland, Manitoba, and Ontario require this approval before the child is placed in the adoptive home. In Alberta, British Columbia, Nova Scotia, Prince Edward Island, and Yukon, the minister or director of child welfare services must be notified within a short period (it varies from 14 to 30 days) after the child has been placed with the prospective parents. The child welfare agency may then investigate the family. In some cases, such as the adoption by a relative or stepparent, no investigation is required.

Once a child is placed with his or her prospective parents, there is a "qualifying period of residence." This varies from one province to another, but in most cases is six months. During this period, the child may be removed at any time if the child welfare agency decides the placement is not in the best interests of the child.

Once the qualifying period has passed to the satisfaction of the child welfare authorities, the court may proceed with the adoption. These hearings are generally informal, and often held in camera (with no one other than the parties involved present).

WHO MUST CONSENT TO AN ADOPTION?

Most problems in adoption proceedings involve the question of consent.

Since an adoption order cuts all ties between the child and its biological parents, ordinarily the latter must consent in writing to the adoption. However, the presiding judge has considerable discretion in deciding whether consent is needed from either one. The guiding principle in these matters is "the best interest of the child."

Abandoning a child, for example, would be grounds for dispensing with parental consent in British Columbia, Manitoba, and Quebec; the disappearance of the biological father or his refusal to consent on "grounds that the judge considers insufficient" would be adequate cause in the Northwest Territories.

Parental consent can be waived in Nova Scotia if the child has been placed with a child welfare agency for more than two years or if the biological parent is divorced, does not have custody of the child, and is not contributing to its support. Manitoba and New Brunswick do not require consent from a parent who is incapable of caring for the child.

In adoption proceedings, the rights of the biological parents are the same whether or not they are married. Therefore the natural father, as well as the birth mother, must consent to the adoption of a child born out of wedlock.

Anyone over the age of 10 (12 years in some provinces) must consent in writing to being adopted. In special cases, however, the court may dispense with the child's consent.

In a British Columbia adoption for example, the birth parents had separated before the child was born, and the mother had lived with his stepfather since he was two years old. The mother had two more children with this man, whom she married shortly before the adoption proceedings. None of the children knew that the child's stepfather was not his biological father nor that their parents had recently married. For all intents and purposes, all three children thought they had the same father and mother.

In view of these facts, the court decided it would not be in the child's best interest to seek his consent.

INTERNATIONAL ADOPTION

Sometimes, for humanitarian reasons, or to get a baby or young child, couples decide to adopt a child from overseas.

The availability of these children varies from one country to another. In war zones, for example, children orphaned in the fighting are often put up for adoption.

Before attempting to adopt a child born in another country, consult the appropriate government authorities. Such adoptions must comply with all provincial legislation on adoption, as well as with federal immigration law.

Since the adoption will begin in a foreign country, you must also comply with that country's laws. Be sure that it has the approval of local authorities and the Canadian consulate or embassy there. Otherwise you might find yourself cheated out of a large sum of money, or even charged with kidnapping. At best, international adoption is a risky business, which can be costly, time-consuming, and often ends in heartbreak. If, however, you are intent on adopting a child from overseas, a good first step would be to contact either the Canadian Red Cross or International Social Services. See USEFUL ADDRESSES at back of book.

ADULTERY

Voluntary sexual intercourse between a married person and a person other than his or her spouse constitutes adultery.

Although adultery is one of the grounds for divorce, it is seldom used now that a divorce can be obtained by a couple simply not living together for at least one year prior to the divorce hearing. Unlike some other countries and a number of U.S. states, adultery is not a crime in Canada.

ADVERSE POSSESSION

It is possible for someone to gain ownership of your property simply by occupying or using it. This process is called adverse possession. The theory behind it is that by failing to challenge another person's use and possession of your property, you abandon your own claim to ownership.

Even a homeowner can lose title to his property by adverse possession. Suppose your neighbor has built a circular driveway that juts onto your land for several feet. To keep the peace, you have said nothing. When he sells the property, you plan to hire a lawyer and notify the new owner that part of the driveway is yours. But depending on how long you have let the situation continue, you could lose ownership of that piece of property forever.

Adverse possession is known as acquisitive prescription in Quebec. If you own land there, and someone uses it for 30 years without interruption or challenge from you, he will become the owner. In Quebec also, if, in good faith, you obtain a deed or title to land for which the "seller" is not the true owner, and you use the land for 10 years, the previous owner loses his rights to the land and you become the legal owner.

ELEMENTS OF POSSESSION

Fortunately for whoever is the true owner, a number of important elements must be present before another person can successfully claim ownership by adverse possession.

◇ Possession must be, in legal terminology, "open" and "notorious"—that is, it must be obvious to the other members of the community.

◇ The person claiming ownership by adverse possession must also show that he has actual possession of the property. In the case of real estate, actual possession could be shown by erecting a fence around the property and planting crops, or by building a house on the land and occupying it. In the case of personal property, the neighbor with whom you stored some furniture could show possession of it by furnishing her living room with it for all to see, or by wearing the ring you gave to her for safekeeping and telling people that it is hers.

◇ Note that the period for acquiring personal property (anything other than land or buildings) by adverse possession is shorter than for real estate. Sometimes it can be a mere two or three years. A suit to recover personal property is called an action for replevin. Your chances of recovering personal property are slim if the possessor says he acquired them as a gift, and you cannot prove otherwise.

◇ The possession must be hostile to the owner's interest. A tenant who pays rent has open, notorious, and actual possession of your property, but he does not dispute your right of ownership. Therefore he cannot claim ownership by adverse possession.

◇ The possession must be uninterrupted and continue for a period specified by provincial law—10 years in Alberta, Manitoba, Ontario, and Saskatchewan, 12 years in Yukon and Northwest Territories, 20 years in the

Maritime provinces—but not necessarily by the same person. Possession is considered continuous, for example, if the land passes from a father to his son. If the true owner retakes possession of the property during this period, however, the adverse possession comes to an end. In British Columbia and Manitoba, the registration of an indefeasible title would stop adverse possession as a means to ownership.

Suppose Jim owns a piece of land in the country, to which he used to drive every fall to go hunting. His interests changed, however, and he stopped going there. One day a concerned neighbor calls to tell Jim that a stranger has been camping on the land several weekends every fall. Will the stranger be able to claim the land by adverse possession?

Because the camper's "possession" is only intermittent, Jim need not fear losing his land to him. He does not even need to visit his property to restate his claim. But he should recognize the possibility that someone else might take open, notorious, hostile, and continuous possession of his land, and make sure this does not happen.

If, during an adverse possession, the possessor writes to the "true owner" for permission to plant trees or cultivate the land, or otherwise acknowledges that the land belongs to another, the adverse possession is interrupted. The possessor would have to reoccupy the land and, depending on the province, act as owner for another 10 to 30 years before gaining ownership.

STEPS TO TAKE

If you are in danger of losing your property by adverse possession, this is what you can do:

1. Determine the length of time the person has been occupying or using your property.

2. Find out how long your province says that adverse possession must exist before you lose title to your property.

3. Notify the occupant in writing that he is trespassing and demand that he end the trespass. If possible have your notice served by a court official or process server. Failing that, use registered mail.

4. If he refuses, or if the provincial time limit is near, contact a lawyer immediately.

AFFIDAVIT

An affidavit is a written statement of facts, signed and sworn to before a notary public or other official authorized to take oaths. Generally an affidavit is made voluntarily.

Often someone with knowledge of facts that are pertinent to a business transaction or a lawsuit is asked to write an affidavit of what he knows. For example, if you were the accountant for a boutique whose owner put it up for sale, you might be asked to make an affidavit attesting to the accuracy of the store's financial records. Or if you witnessed an accident, you might sign an affidavit in which you described what you saw. If you make a statement that you know to be untrue in an affidavit, you are guilty of perjury.

A sample affidavit is included in EVERYDAY LEGAL FORMS at back of book. See also DEPOSITION; OATH AND AFFIRMATION; PERJURY.

AFFIRMATIVE ACTION

The Canadian Charter of Rights and Freedoms states that: "Every individual is equal before and under the law and has the right to the equal protection and equal benefit of the law without discrimination and, in particular, without discrimination based on race, national or ethnic origin, color, religion, sex, age or mental or physical disability." The charter also points out that these guarantees do not preclude any law, activity, or program designed to further the rights or ameliorate conditions of individuals or groups "disadvantaged because of race, national or ethnic origin, color, religion, sex, age or mental or physical disability."

Such measures are called affirmative action and are used by federal and provincial governments (most provincial human rights legislation reflects the federal charter) and by corporations to redress unfair practices. Under one such program, Canadian National Railways now hires a specific number of women for jobs, such as welding, that previously were held almost exclusively by men. Affirmative action programs have opened doors for the many women seen today as bus drivers, airline pilots, police officers, and in countless other positions that were considered "men's jobs" a few years ago.

Critics of affirmative action claim that such programs discriminate against the majority in allowing women or members of minority groups to obtain jobs, even when they are less qualified than other applicants. But the courts generally uphold such programs since they are expressly allowed by law, and are intended to remedy certain historic social inequities.

AGE OF CONSENT

The minimum age at which a person may legally marry is called the age of consent. It is 18 years in most provinces, 19 in a few. A young man or woman who wants to marry before then must first obtain his or her parents' consent.

An adult who has sex with a person under the age of consent may be convicted of sexual assault. See SEXUAL ABUSE.

The age of consent is not the same as the age of majority which, again depending on the province, is also 18 or 19 years of age. The age of majority is the age when you can legally enter into a contract.

AGE DISCRIMINATION

The boss comes bearing bad news. Because of cutbacks at the company, you are being let go, even though your performance on the job has always been more than satisfactory. This is tough news to take at

the age of 50. It gets worse when you find out two months later that you have been replaced by someone 15 years younger, earning half your salary. If this should in fact ever happen to you, you may have been a victim of age discrimination—a practice prohibited by law in most instances.

DISCRIMINATION IN EMPLOYMENT

The Canadian Charter of Rights and Freedoms and most provincial human rights legislation prohibit discrimination because of age. Unless the employer can show that an employee's age may affect the health or safety of the public, as in the case of an airline pilot, for example, age may not be a factor in hiring an employee.

It is also illegal for an employer to deny employees certain benefits, sickness insurance for example, because of their age. In 1991, a 48-year-old student complained to the B.C. Council of Human Rights when she was refused work in a government job training program. The program was open only to students aged 15-24 years. The tribunal that reviewed the case said this age requirement violated the B.C. Human Rights Act. The employer had to drop it, and pay the 48-year-old $1,200 for injury to her feelings.

MANDATORY RETIREMENT

Government, corporate, and institutional rules requiring employees to retire when they reach a certain age are currently subject to great controversy.

Except where mandatory retirement is expressly prohibited by federal law, or by human rights legislation, as is the case in Alberta, Manitoba, New Brunswick, and Quebec, court judgments have not been consistent. In some cases, the courts upheld mandatory retirement; in others, they declared it discriminatory and illegal.

A Winnipeg deputy police chief, ordered to retire at 60, won his case because the court felt a person that age could carry out the functions of the job. A University of Alberta policy requiring professors to retire at age 65 was declared illegal, even though the contract of the professor who challenged the policy clearly stated that she was obliged to retire at that age. The tribunal noted that the university was unable to show that a person's abilities decline at age 65, and that there were procedures for dismissal for incompetence.

A similar decision was reached by the B.C. Council of Human Rights in a case by a University of British Columbia professor, who was forced to retire at 65. Claiming that UBC had discriminated because of age, the tribunal ordered the professor reinstated with full back pay. This decision was reversed, however, on appeal to the Supreme Court of Canada, which held that the law only protected people between 45 and 65 years of age.

The Supreme Court also ruled that the University of Guelph and three other Ontario universities could establish a mandatory retirement age. It reasoned that "the benefit to society of the preservation of academic freedom and excellence in higher education outweighed the detriment to those who were forced to retire."

These Supreme Court decisions were not unanimous. The dissenting judges felt that mandatory retirement should be illegal. But as a result of the rulings, people in British Columbia, Newfoundland, Nova Scotia, Ontario, Prince Edward Island, and Saskatchewan are still subject to mandatory retirement.

STEPS TO TAKE

If you believe your employer has discriminated against you because of your age, here are some things you can do:

1. Register a complaint with your company's human resources department.

2. File a formal complaint with your provincial human rights office.

3. Consult a lawyer experienced in employment-discrimination law. The various deadlines for filing a claim are complicated, however, and you may lose out if you are not careful to comply with them exactly.

AGENT

A person who is authorized to act on behalf of another person or for a business is an agent. An agent is more than a mere employee, because he often is required to exercise independent judgment in the performance of his duties. Unlike an employee, he can make agree-ments with others that legally bind the party he serves (the principal); for example, he can enter into contracts or manage property.

However, an agent is always under the control of the principal, even if it is not always used. Let us say you have hired an agent to manage the rental of a house that you own. You can tell the agent not to rent to Ms. X, because you know that she has a habit of defrauding landlords. But if you do not give him those instructions, and he thinks her credentials are satisfactory, you cannot object if he rents your house to her.

When a principal ends his agent's employment, he is no longer bound by the agent's actions.(In Quebec an agent is called a mandatary, the person he works for is the mandator. The contract between them is called a mandate.) See also INDEPENDENT CONTRACTOR; INSURANCE AGENT AND BROKER; POWER OF ATTORNEY; REAL ESTATE AGENT AND BROKER.

AIDS

Acquired immune deficiency syndrome, or AIDS, is a fatal disease caused by infection with a virus known as HIV, the human immunodeficiency virus. AIDS is a communicable disease, usually transmitted by sexual contact or by injection into the bloodstream.

The latter type of infection often results from contaminated needles that are shared by intravenous drug users. When the disease first appeared, however, and before adequate blood screening was in place, many other people, especially hemophiliacs, contracted AIDS from contaminated blood transfusions. Alberta, British Columbia, Manitoba, Nova Scotia, and Quebec were among the first provinces to approve compensation programs for hemophiliacs who contracted the HIV virus in this way.

Understandably, a disease as deadly as AIDS causes widespread fear. Many people believe they have the right to know if they are being exposed to the virus. On the other hand, because the disease is fatal and is associated with male homosexuals and intravenous drug users, people with AIDS are often reluctant to admit it for fear of being stigmatized. But AIDS is increasingly being contracted from an infected partner in a heterosexual relationship. Clearly the disease has entered the general population.

In June 1993, the World Health Organization estimated that14 million people worldwide had the HIV virus. Compared to parts of the world where the disease is of epidemic proportions, AIDS is still relatively rare in Canada: about 10 percent of the 30,000 Canadians with the virus have full-blown AIDS.

A person who has the virus may still function normally for many years—up to 10 in some cases—before the symptoms of AIDS appear. Once AIDS develops, however, the patient becomes incapacitated in a short time. As a result, many face financial impoverishment.

Through a plan developed for such victims, a person with AIDS may sell his or her life insurance policy for a percentage of its value. Thus a patient who has a life insurance policy for $50,000, payable upon death to his estate, could name another person, or company, the beneficiary, in exchange for, say, an immediate $35,000.

Of course insurance companies would only honor policies obtained in good faith before the insured knew he had AIDS. A policy taken out by someone who knew he had AIDS but did not inform the insurance company would be canceled for fraudulent misrepresentation.

Diagnosis of full-blown AIDS is based on positive results to blood tests for HIV along with infections and tumors characteristic of the disease. Transmission is by sexual contact, blood to blood, and from woman to fetus. There have been rare instances of infection through artificial insemination, kidney transplants, and accidental needle injury. Casual spread does not occur: the virus is not transmitted by a hug or a handshake,.

AIDS AND THE LAW

In the 1990s, well over a decade after AIDS was identified, the laws concerning AIDS remain in a state of flux. How they will finally take shape depends to some extent on whether science finds a cure.

Although both the federal and provincial governments want to protect the public from AIDS, they also have a duty to protect persons infected with the disease from unwarranted discrimination. It is illegal to discriminate in employment or housing against someone who has AIDS. Nevertheless, sufferers are often dismissed from their jobs or refused housing. Such victims can sue for damages before the various human rights tribunals.

At present there is no specific criminal charge that expressly deals with knowingly transmitting the HIV virus to another person. So in order to criminalize this potentially catastrophic behavior, people who do so are charged with a variety of offenses.

People who have contracted AIDS through sexual intercourse may sue for damages, including mental distress and anguish, if their partners did not disclose they were infected. An Alberta man who had sex without disclosing that he had AIDS was charged with aggravated assault; for a similar offense, an Ontario man was charged with criminal negligence causing bodily harm.

An Ottawa man, charged with common mischief for donating infected blood to the Red Cross, was sentenced to 15 months' imprisonment. In upholding the sentence, the Supreme Court of Canada stated that the HIV-infected man "endangered the life, safety, and health of the public."

INDIVIDUAL PRIVACY VS. PUBLIC HEALTH

Because a person's right to have his medical files confidential and his right to security of the person (that is, his right not to be touched by another unless allowed by law) conflict at times with the public's right to be protected against harm, several important questions have been raised in court. In one case, a Quebec court ruled that a sexual assault victim cannot force her accused attacker to undergo an AIDS test unless he consents.

AIRLINE ACCIDENTS

Although the risk of being killed in a plane crash is less than one-tenth the risk of being killed in an auto accident, when airline accidents do occur, the consequences are often dire. The extent to which an airline can be held financially responsible, or liable, depends to a large degree on whether the flight is domestic or international. If a flight begins and ends within Canada, the airline can be held liable for all damages that result from injuries or death due to a plane crash.

If an international flight begins or ends in Canada, or stops at an airport in Canada, the airline's liability is strictly limited. The maximum amount that can be awarded is US$75,000, including legal fees. This limited liability was established by an international treaty known as the Warsaw Convention.

If the flight does not touch down within Canada, the extent of an airline's liability depends on which version of the Warsaw Convention its country of origin ratified. If the country follows the original treaty of 1929, the maximum liability is US$10,000. If it

REAL LIFE, REAL LAW

The Case of the Harrowing Holiday

Maryla, a day-care worker, had long dreamed of vacationing in Paris. Finally the magic day arrived and she happily settled into the aisle seat she had requested on the charter flight. She had chosen this flight over one offered by the scheduled airlines because the fare was so much less—a major consideration for someone earning a modest income.

The voyage was pleasant but uneventful—until the plane landed. When it did, Maryla was dismayed to learn she was in Brussels, not Paris: the charter company did not have landing rights there.

The Brussels-to-Paris bus provided by the charter company did little to mollify Maryla and her copassengers. So they parlayed their collective anger into a class-action suit against the company that sold them the flight.

The judge ruled in favor of the disgruntled passengers. Each received a one-week holiday at the charter company's expense, plus $400 compensation for the original, aborted flight.

follows the amended version of 1955, liability is limited to US$20,000. And if it follows the 1975 treaty, the maximum is US$140,000.

The International Civil Aviation Organization (ICAO) has attempted to update the Warsaw Convention, the most recent developments being the Guatemala and Montreal protocols of 1971 and 1975 respectively. But by 1993, only about 15 percent of ICAO's members had signed these agreements to increase compensation.

You may, however, be able to sue for amounts that exceed these limits. If the accident was due to gross negligence or willful misconduct by the airline or its employees—for example, if the ground crew failed to secure and lock the doors or if the pilot was not qualified to fly

♦ that particular aircraft—the Warsaw Convention limitations do not apply and you can sue for greater amounts. Of course air carriers from poor countries, such as those in Eastern Europe, cannot afford to pay the same compensation as carriers from North America and Western Europe.

The wisest course is probably to take out private flight insurance. For a few dollars, you can generally get several thousand dollars of insurance.

Some credit card companies provide automatic accident insurance as an incentive for people to use their cards to purchase tickets. If someone dies in a plane crash, that person's next of kin should find out how the ticket was paid for. Insurance benefits of $100,000 or more may be payable to the

♦ dead person's estate. See also ACCIDENTS ON PUBLIC TRANSPORTATION.

AIRLINE CHARTER

You spot an ad in the travel section of the Sunday paper offering a bargain-basement price for a flight to Honolulu. Somewhat incredulous, you call the number listed. The person who answers confirms the low price but informs you that the flight is a charter, rather than a flight on a regularly scheduled airline. You have never heard of the charter company, but the low price is hard to resist. Is it too good to be true?

Most charter flights are arranged by charter operators, who buy a number of seats from an air carrier at a heavily discounted price, and then resell them to the public. Charter companies try to keep their prices below rates offered by regularly scheduled airlines, but you cannot assume that a charter is always the cheapest way to fly.

Still, a charter flight can save you money, and it could be the only way to fly to your destination nonstop. But you may have to sacrifice some comfort and convenience. It is possible, for example, that the flight will be (1) on a carrier you have never heard of, (2) scheduled at an inconvenient time, (3) on a plane with tight seating arrangements, or (4) preceded by long check-in lines at the airport.

In the past some charter operators have either failed

to provide the services promised, or suddenly gone out of business. Many people were stranded for days in Mexico and the Caribbean in 1993, when Nationair, then Canada's biggest charter airline, first experienced the financial problems that put it out of business.

If your schedule is flexible, flying "stand-by" may be the cheapest way to go. However, you will only get a seat if the plane is not fully booked about two hours before takeoff.

STEPS TO TAKE

Before you fly on a charter, be sure to do the following:

1. Shop around for the lowest air fares to make sure the charter price is really a bargain.

2. Find out from Transport Canada or your provincial consumer protection office whether the charter operator has put up a bond to cover losses to passengers in case of canceled flights or bankruptcy.

3. Ask your provincial consumer affairs office if any complaints have been filed against the charter operator and the air carrier.

4. Be sure you know your rights and obligations as a passenger before you sign a contract with a charter operator.

AIRLINE PASSENGER RIGHTS

You are one of those people who hate to fly—but for reasons that have nothing to do with safety. In the past you have been bumped from flights, the airlines have lost your luggage, and you have missed connecting flights. What are your rights?

BUMPING

Being bumped, or not being allowed to board the flight you booked, is the result of the airlines' traditional practice of accepting reservations for more seats than are on the plane. It is not against the law, and the airlines state they must overbook because many travelers who make reservations for flights never show up.

When a flight is overbooked, the airline is legally required to ask for volunteers who are willing to give up their seats and take a later flight. As an inducement, the airline usually offers some kind of compensation, such as a free round-trip ticket to a destination of one's choice. If not enough volunteers come forward, some passengers will have to stay behind against their will. Usually, the passengers who checked in last are bumped.

If you are bumped, you may be angry and inconvenienced, but you still have certain rights:

◇ Usually the airline must put a passenger who has been bumped on the next available flight to his destination, even if it means reserving a seat for him on another airline.

◇ If a bumped passenger arrives at his destination between one and two hours late, the airline must pay him either the price of a one-way ticket or about $200, whichever is less.

◇ If the passenger arrives more than two hours late, the amount to be paid is doubled.

◇ You also have rights to a free telephone, fax, or telex message to your destination and, depending on how long you have to wait for a new flight, meals and refreshments. When the delay is overnight, you are entitled to hotel accommodation.

◇ You may even get more benefits if you sue. A Quebec court held that overbooking is not a risk characteristic of air travel and therefore an airline could not rely on the limitation of liability as set out in the Warsaw Convention.

European carriers such as Alitalia, British Airways, Lufthansa, KLM, and Air France operate under regulations adopted by the European Economic Community in the early 1990s. If you are denied boarding because of overbooking, you are entitled to reimbursement of your ticket, rerouting at the earliest opportunity or a flight at your convenience. You would also be entitled to a cash compensation, the amount varying according to the length of your flight.

If the arrangements were made with a tour operator, then the tour operator would compensate you and later be reimbursed by the carrier.

LOST OR DAMAGED LUGGAGE

Many of the complaints about air travel concern lost or damaged luggage. An airline's responsibility to compensate you for luggage is limited. At present, airlines do not have to pay you more than $1,250 for luggage lost on domestic flights and $9.07 per pound for international flights, even if your luggage is worth more.

Moreover, an airline will reimburse you only for the depreciated value of your luggage and its contents. If, for example, you bought a suitcase for $125 and used it for a year, you might get only half that amount from the airline.

Some airlines limit their liability even further. For example, some small airlines refuse to take responsibility for damage to soft luggage or for the loss of wheels from suitcases. A few such airlines even demand that passengers file a written claim within four hours of arrival, and provide written documentation of the contents of lost baggage within 45 days. People who do not follow these rules forfeit any claims for reimbursement.

Protect yourself by packing your luggage so that you can carry it on board or buy some form of insurance. You may buy "excess valuation" insurance directly from the airline, or your homeowners' insurance may provide "off-premises" coverage for lost or damaged items. This is known as a "floater." Some credit card companies provide baggage insurance if you use their card to purchase your ticket.

SMOKING

For several years, Transport Canada has prohibited smoking on all Canadian carriers, whether on domestic or international flights. Even restrooms have smoke detectors, and anyone caught smoking there or elsewhere in the plane is subject to fines from $50 to $100.

Anyone who persists in smoking after being warned not to may be obliged to leave the aircraft at the next landing, even if it is not his or her destination. An aircraft owner who makes no attempt to stop a passenger from smoking is liable to fines of $1,000 (for a first offense) to $10,000.

CONDITIONS OF CARRIAGE

The conditions that govern the legal relationship between an airline and its passengers are spelled out in each airline's contract of carriage.

These conditions, which vary from one airline to the next, relate to canceled flights, missed connections, reservations, check-in times, and restrictions on which kinds of passengers they will accept. For example, an airline may refuse to accept a passenger who is sick, on drugs, behaving erratically, or unable to fasten his seat belt.

This information does not appear on the ticket and is not always made readily available. To get a copy of an airline's "conditions of carriage," as these rules are called, write to the airline's office of consumer affairs, to Transport Canada if it is a Canadian carrier, or to Air Transport Association of America in the case of an American carrier. See USEFUL ADDRESSES at back of book.

STEPS TO TAKE

The following may help if you have problems with an airline:
1. Ask at the ticket counter for the address and phone number of the airline's office of consumer affairs, or call the airline's central reservation number.

2. Make your complaint in writing. Be sure that you include the flight number, the flight time, and a clear description of the problem and what you want done about it. Include copies of boarding passes and ticket receipts if you can.

3. If you do not get a satisfactory response or you feel that the company has not resolved your problem in a fair way, you can sue the airline in small-claims court.

ALCOHOL

Both federal and provincial laws regulate the manufacture and sale of alcoholic beverages, an important source of revenue for the provinces and the federal government.

The federal Excise Act and Excise Tax Act set out licensing requirements for distillers and breweries. The federal government issues permits to manufacturers and wholesalers, supervises imports, and enforces standards for safety and quality. For example, the Consumer Products Branch of Consumer and Corporate Affairs requires that labels include not only the alcohol content of each beverage but also prohibits brewers and distillers from making any claims about the intoxicating effects of their products.

In most provinces alcoholic beverages are only available at government-run outlets. In Quebec, beer and wine can be

REAL LIFE, REAL LAW

The Case of the Pugilistic Partygoers

Richard invited his friend Ross to a bush party to which the guests were to bring their own liquor. After much carousing, a fight broke out between Ross and Steve, another guest who taunted Ross by calling him bad names. Ross, who was severely injured in the altercation, eventually sued both Steve and Richard for several million dollars.

As the "social host," the owner of the property where the fight took place, Richard was liable under the Ontario Occupiers' Liability Act. Cases against social hosts (as opposed to hotel and tavern keepers) are still rare in Canada but a growing trend in the United States. There is no reason why actions against social hosts should not follow the same route here.

In Richard's case, his insurance company settled out of court, paying Ross some $600,000 in damages and about $100,000 in costs. Obviously the insurer did not want to risk the court ruling that Ross was not the author of his own misfortune and so awarding him even more money.

---

bought at local food stores. Provinces also regulate the hours of business for those places that serve alcohol; no sale of alcohol may take place after 1 a.m. in Ontario, but is legal until 3 a.m. in Quebec.

Although it may be tolerated in some cases, strictly speaking, alcohol in any form may not be consumed at park or beach picnics, or other public places. Alcoholic beverages, in descending order of alcohol content, are alcohol, spirits, wine, cider, and beer. Liquor laws do not apply to candies or chocolates that contain small amounts of spirits.

Some provinces allow local communities to decide for themselves how to regulate alcohol, as long as their ordinances do not conflict with provincial law. The result is that a "dry" municipality, whose citizens have banned the sale of liquor, may be situated next to one where liquor can be sold.

UNDERAGE DRINKING

Each province regulates the sale of alcohol. The legal age for having and consuming alcohol is 19 years in Nova Scotia, 18 years in all other provinces.

An adult who gives alcohol to a minor may be subject to prosecution, fines, and imprisonment. Any business that serves alcohol to a minor may have its liquor license revoked.

A parent who regularly lets his minor children drink to excess may be charged with contributing to the delinquency of minors. The children may be taken away and put in the care of the Children's Aid Society.

DRUNKEN BEHAVIOR

Alcohol and the law often rub elbows when crimes are committed by people "under the influence." Suppose a man, after leaving a party, goes on a rampage and smashes all the glass windows on a city street. Can he be held responsible?

It depends. If he deliberately got drunk, he would probably be held responsible, because voluntary intoxication is not considered an acceptable defense. However, if the man is a teetotaler who never touches alcohol because it makes him berserk, and he was told the punch being served contained only fruit juice, there is a good chance he would not be held responsible for the damage.

A relatively new trend in the law is to hold the owners of bars, restaurants, and liquor stores responsible for injuries inflicted by their patrons as a result of drunkenness. In one Ontario case, a woman and her family, injured in an auto accident caused by a drunken driver, sued both the driver of the vehicle and the owner of the restaurant that had served him drinks. At trial it was shown that the defendant was so drunk in the restaurant that he passed out. Restaurant employees found the man's car keys, put him into his car, threw the keys in after him, and watched as he drove away.

The court awarded $401,000 damages, 22 percent of this against the driver, 78 percent against the restaurant for continuing to serve alcohol to an apparently intoxicated patron, and for not ensuring the customer got home by means other than driving his own car.

Such laws, called dramshop acts, apply only if the person selling the liquor knew the patron was already drunk.

But what about hosts of private parties who continue to serve drinks to guests who are already under the influence?

Everyone who owns or rents premises owes a duty of care to those who lawfully gather there for a party or otherwise. The golden rule in measuring responsibility is that of the "reasonable person": what degree of care would a reasonable person give? A wise host would ensure that his guests do not drink to excess, and if they do, should arrange rides home with other guests or by taxi.

If you serve liquor to someone who is already showing signs of intoxication, you could be held responsible for damages and injuries the drunken guest causes to himself or others. Or a court might split the damage award on grounds your guest allowed himself to get intoxicated, in which case you would be responsible for part of the damages. A court in British Columbia held a college fraternity responsible for 50 percent of damages awarded to a 20-year-old guest who fell through a window at a fraternity party. The man had five to six ounces of vodka before the event, then had two beers at the party.

STEPS TO TAKE WHEN YOU ARE A HOST

If you are hosting a party at which liquor will be served, it is worth your while to take the following precautions:

1. Try to limit the amount of alcohol being served. Offer a variety of soft drinks and fruit juices as well as beer, wine, and hard liquor.

2. Close the bar an hour or so before the party ends.

3. Serve snacks and coffee or nonalcoholic beverages to give people time to sober up before they drive home.

4. If a guest appears to be "under the influence," do not let him drive. Have someone drive him home or offer him a bed for the night. See also ALCOHOLISM; DRUNK DRIVING.

ALCOHOLISM

The problems associated with alcoholism are many, but those that concern the law center primarily on the workplace and the public roads. In recent years more and more employers are requiring employees to submit to alcohol and drug testing, especially when their jobs affect the safety of others.

Although the law in this area is far from settled, the trend is to permit such testing, except when it is discriminatory—for instance, if only employees that belong to a minority are tested.

Because an employer has a duty to maintain the safety of his workplace, he can usually discipline or fire employees who abuse alcohol in a way that threatens the general safety.

Sometimes, however, an employee may be able to challenge an employer's hasty actions. Let us say that Jack is frequently late for work or absent altogether. His eyes are bloodshot and his hands often

tremble, but this does not seem to affect his work. One day Jack shows up late for the third time in one week, and his employer tells him he is fired.

If Jack's company normally warns employees before firing them, or if it usually refers workers to an employee assistance program or some other counseling program aimed at rehabilitation, Jack might be able to have his dismissal reversed because his company failed to follow standard procedures. See also DRUG TESTING.

The nature of the work and the worker's position can be important when assessing alcohol-related misconduct. For example, if a general worker or store cashier was found drunk at a party, this would rarely be a valid cause for dismissal. However, it might be valid in the case of a bank manager or company executive, since such drunkenness may reflect badly on his or her employer.

ALIMENTARY PENSION

When a couple separates or divorces, the payments made by one spouse to support the other are called alimentary pension or support payments. In the past, courts made men responsible for family support upon divorce or separation. Husbands paid alimentary pensions to their former wives and child support for their children.

Since women increasingly contribute to family income, the delegation of financial responsibility after marriage breakup has changed (with women often assuming a greater share than previously), and so has the terminology. "Alimentary pension" is being replaced in legal usage by the terms "spousal support" and "maintenance." See also DIVORCE.

ALLEGATION

An accusation that serves as the basis for a civil lawsuit or criminal prosecution is called an allegation. In order for the accuser to win his case, he must prove his allegation. For example, in a suit for damages resulting from a fall in the aisle of a supermarket, the claim that the store owners caused the plaintiff's injuries is an allegation that must be proved before the plaintiff can be compensated for injuries suffered.

In referring to cases in which allegations have been made but not proved, reporters, attorneys, and others must use the word "alleged" to avoid defaming people who have been accused but not found guilty. In keeping with our legal system's presumption of innocence, they will resort to statements such as: "the alleged robber was found a block from the scene of the crime."

ALTERNATIVE DISPUTE RESOLUTION

Hoping to save yourself time and trouble, you buy an expensive tractor mower to cut your lawn. But what you get instead is trouble of another kind: the machine digs up the lawn, will not shift into reverse, and repeatedly conks out. The company refuses to replace it, and you cannot afford an expensive, time-consuming lawsuit. Do you have another choice?

You certainly do. More and more people are using alternative dispute resolution (ADR), which bypasses the clogged and costly courts and may well be the wave of the future.

ADR is an umbrella term that encompasses several different ways of resolving disputes: negotiation, conciliation, mediation, and arbitration. In negotiation, the two parties try to come to an agreement by themselves. Conciliation and mediation rely on an impartial third party, or referee, to find a fair solution. Arbitration uses a referee too, but it is a more formal process, in which the decision of the third party is often legally binding.

See ARBITRATION; CONCILIATION; MEDIATION.

ADR is generally cheaper, faster, and less stressful than litigation, and it is often more effective. Used for years in labor disputes, it is now a common way of resolving neighborhood disputes and consumer battles with manufacturers, insurers, doctors, home contractors, and others. Both Alberta and Ontario have successful programs offering arbitration services.

STEPS TO TAKE

To find out whether or not your dispute is one that ADR can help settle, and which of the several types is best for you, do one or more of the following:

1. Call your Better Business Bureau and ask their advice. They may direct you to a mediator or arbitrator.

2. Look in the Yellow Pages under "Arbitration" or "Mediation" for the name of a local company, lawyer, or retired judge who practices ADR.

3. Ask the Canadian Bar Association or your provincial legal society for the names of lawyers or retired judges in your area who are experienced in arbitration. Your business associates may also be able to suggest names of possible arbitrators.

See also ARBITRATION; CONCILIATION.

AMNESTY

In granting amnesty a government provides a large number of people with immunity from prosecution for a past criminal offense or other infraction. From that time forward, however, those who were given amnesty must obey the law.

Amnesty is usually invoked when it presents the most workable solution to a problem.

In the early 1980s, for example, the Department of Immigration responded to a vast overload of cases involving refugees and illegal immigrants by declaring an amnesty. For humanitarian and administrative reasons, it set aside many lengthy and expensive claimant procedures. As a result, applicants from countries such as Haiti and Lebanon, who had entered Canada before a specific date, could apply directly for landed immigrant status.

More recently, the government declared an amnesty for unregistered guns and dangerous weapons. People who surrendered them to police during this amnesty period were not charged with illegal possession.

ANIMALS

Although animals provide us with food, clothing, transportation, hard work, and companionship, they are also capable of creating a nuisance, destroying property, causing injury, and even taking people's lives. As a result, laws have been enacted to protect the public from animals. And since animals are often on the receiving end of injury and harm, other laws have been passed to protect animals from people.

Animals are divided into two categories by law: (1) wild animals, which cannot be completely tamed, such as lions, tigers, bears, and alligators; and (2) domestic animals, which are tame by nature or have been tamed by humans. Sheep, cattle, horses, chickens, and other farm animals, as well as pets such as cats and dogs, are domestic animals. See Dog Law; Pets.

FARM ANIMALS

Local zoning laws often prohibit keeping farm animals in residential neighborhoods. Some ordinances limit the number of chickens, ducks, and pigeons that one may keep on one's property. Some cities may restrict not only the number of pigeons one can keep but also where the pigeon coop can be located in relation to neighbors. Large farm animals are usually forbidden within city limits.

UNWANTED VISITORS

When an animal wanders onto your property, you are entitled to take reasonable measures to remove it. If you cannot simply shoo it away, you can try calling the owner.

If you do not know who the owner is, you can call your local animal control department, which will send someone to remove it. Unless the animal is vicious, you cannot kill it. If you do, the owner can sue you for the animal's value and possibly extra compensation too.

ANIMAL OWNERS' RESPONSIBILITIES

If your neighbor's sheep, cow, or other domestic animal dines on the flowers in your garden or traipses across your freshly cemented patio, the animal's owner is responsible for the damage, whether or not he knew the animal was likely to do such mischief.

Oddly enough, however, if a domestic animal kicks, bites, pecks, or otherwise injures you—whether on your property or anyone else's—its owner usually cannot be sued, unless he knew the beast had a history of inflicting such injuries or of being temperamental.

Different laws apply to wild animals. The owner of a wolf, bear, tiger, monkey, raccoon, or other wild animal is responsible for any injuries it may cause—even if the owner did his best to keep the animal from doing any harm.

Even a zoo or circus, where animals are caged, can be sued if someone is injured as a result of getting too close to an animal.

REAL LIFE, REAL LAW

The Case of the Stress-Causing Squawking

A bird fancier living in a residential area of a midsize town got into the business of raising large tropical birds. He got a license to raise birds from his town council and installed double-paned windows and extra insulation to cut down on any noise resulting from his bird business.

Despite these precautions, the birds' squawking and screeching did not sit well with the man's neighbors, especially since the cacophony was loudest at 5 a.m. They claimed the noise increased their stress levels to the point where they developed certain physical ailments. Some declared they were at their "wit's end" because of the noise. When they finally sought an injunction against the birds, the court ordered the bird lover to restrict his collection to three. He was also instructed to keep the birds inside at all times other than 9 a.m. to 3 p.m.

CRUELTY TO ANIMALS

Although beatings come to mind first, domestic animals may be victims of many forms of mistreatment: failing to provide enough food or water; keeping an animal in unhealthy surroundings; not caring for an animal when it is sick; or abandoning it to the elements. Cock fighting and dog fighting are also considered forms of cruelty and are against the law. A person who is convicted of cruelty may have his animal taken from him and may also be subject to fines or imprisonment.

Contact your local branch of the Canadian Society for the Prevention of Cruelty to Animals about mistreated animals or abandoned pets.

FAIR AND UNFAIR GAME

Laws strictly regulate the hunting and capturing of wild animals. The federal Endangered Species Act protects many animals that are declining in numbers from being killed, captured, or otherwise threatened.

Deer and other game animals are protected by provincial laws that require hunters to be licensed. These laws restrict the equipment hunters can use and limit the times and the places in which they can hunt.

ANNUITY

One way for a person to have money available after retirement is through an annuity, which is a type of investment typically obtained from an insurance company. An annuity is a contract by which you pay an amount of money (either in a lump sum or over a period of years) to the insurance company, which invests the money. In return, the company agrees that on a specified date it will begin to pay you a regular sum each month, usually for the rest of your life.

The payment is actually a repayment of the amount you contribute, plus interest. Depending on the terms of your contract, the annuity may end when you die, or the balance may be paid to someone you name as a beneficiary.

Like any other contract, an annuity can be broken—at a price. If you decide to terminate it, you will probably have to pay a penalty, most likely a percentage of the amount you have already paid into the annuity. The exact terms of the penalty are spelled out in your contract. Read it carefully and be sure you understand it before you sign.

ANNULMENT

An annulment is a legal action that declares a marriage void. Unlike a divorce, which legally ends a marriage, an annulment asserts that the marriage never existed in the first place.

How can it be, you may ask, that a marriage never existed if a hundred people watched the couple get married? Just as divorce recognizes flaws in a marriage that caused it not to work, annulment recognizes flaws that existed prior to a marriage which, if known, would have prevented a legal marriage from taking place.

WHY AN ANNULMENT

Annulments are far less common than they were in the past, largely because divorces are easier to obtain. The Catholic Church considers annulment the only way to end a marriage. If a couple are granted a church annulment, a legal civil annulment or divorce is nevertheless required before either may remarry.

Sometimes annulment may be the only choice, because the union was considered void to begin with—for instance, a marriage between a boy and a girl who are underage.

GROUNDS FOR ANNULMENT

If Jane and John meet on vacation in Hawaii, get married after a quick courtship, and within a week have second thoughts, they probably will not be able to have the marriage annulled. The grounds for annulment are many, but a hasty marriage is not one of them.

Laws vary from one province to another, but the following are the most common grounds for an annulment:

◇ If one or both were underage when they married.

◇ If one or both were forced to marry because of some threat, as in the classic "shotgun wedding." In this case the annulment would be based on the fact that at least one of the parties did not freely consent to the marriage.

◇ If either partner was mentally ill, drunk, or otherwise unable to understand the implications of the wedding or to give valid consent.

◇ If one party hid some important fact, such as a criminal record, a serious disease, sexual impotence, a previous marriage, or an intention not to have children. In most cases an annulment must be obtained relatively soon after the deceived party learns the hidden fact: otherwise he or she could be said to have accepted and condoned the behavior or fact, thus eliminating ground for the annulment.

ANTIQUE

When does something that is old become an antique? What is the difference between junk and collectibles? In law, there is no cut-and-dried definition and no set age at which an object becomes an antique. Virtually anything that is old—whether a rug, a statue, a car, or a doll—can be called an antique.

A rule of thumb for furniture is that an object becomes an antique when it is 100 years old. To be insured as antiques, automobiles usually must be at least 25 years old. According to the Criminal Code, an antique firearm is one that was manufactured before 1898 and does not fire modern ammunition.

EVALUATING ANTIQUES

Putting a value on antiques can be as hard as defining what they are. An item's worth depends on its scarcity, its condition, who made it, the materials used, the workmanship, its historical significance, and its current popularity.

One way to find out what an antique is worth is by consult-ing collectors' guides, which list the prices of similar items sold at auction. Another way is to consult an appraiser, dealer, or other expert who knows the current market price.

If you hire an appraiser, make sure that he is a specialist in the kinds of items you are having appraised—Turkish rugs, 18th-century Chippendale furniture, or early Quebec furniture, for example.

To make the appraisal go more smoothly, gather together in advance all the documents that relate to your antique, such as bills of sale and previous appraisals. If you have a lot of items, provide an inventory for the appraiser.

Appraisers bill you for their services in different ways. Some charge a flat fee, some an hourly rate, and some a percentage of the value of the collection. To avoid an unpleasant surprise, be sure you understand in advance how the appraiser will charge you. See also APPRAISAL.

LET THE BUYER BEWARE

Suppose you go to an auction and pay a high price for a musket used during the War of 1812. At home, while cleaning your new acquisition, you find the words "Made in Taiwan" on the stock. Will you be able to sue the auction house? The answer depends on how the item was represented at the time of purchase.

Dealers often provide a written description of the piece they are selling. It includes the age of the item, its condition, the materials used in its manufacture, and the name of the artisan. Antiques of great value or historical significance usually come with a *provenance*—a document that includes the names of all of the item's previous owners. These documents serve as the dealer's warranty that the item is genuine.

If these documents are provided, and the item later turns out to be a reproduction or forgery, as was the case with the musket, the dealer could be held responsible for breach of warranty or for fraud. However, if no documents or guarantees are provided at the time of sale, the buyer must assume the risk of his purchase.

Note however that verbal misrepresentation may contravene provincial consumer protection legislation. So your case may hinge on whether the auctioneer guaranteed the musket was an authentic War of 1812 artifact, or simply said it might be a replica of one used in the War of 1812.

APPEAL

A court trial usually ends with a winner and a loser. The loser may have lost only temporarily, however, if he is able to file an appeal—a procedure in which he claims the lower court made the wrong decision and asks a higher court to review the case in hopes of a ruling that is more favorable to him. For more information on the different kinds of courts, see COURTS.

APPEAL LIMITATIONS

Usually appeals are restricted to cases involving a certain amount of money, for example judgments for more than $15,000. Also, appeals are often limited to cases where the judge made an error in law or a *gross* error in the appreciation of fact.

Different provinces have various names for their appeal courts. In Quebec and British Columbia, appeals are brought to the Appeal Court; in Nova Scotia, to the Appeal Division of the Supreme Court. Ontario has an intermediate Court of Appeal known as the Divisional Court. In Alberta, Saskatchewan, and Manitoba appeals from the provincial superior court, which is called the Court of Queen's Bench, are heard by the Court of Appeal.

The highest appeal tribunal in the land, the Supreme Court of Canada, is made up of nine judges. It hears only cases involving important principles of national interest and concern. Its judgments are binding on all provinces.

See COURTS (The Canadian Court System), page 145.

HOW AN APPEAL IS MADE

An appeal usually begins when the appellant (the person who brings the appeal) files a notice of appeal. This notice, which states that some aspects of the lower court decision were in error, is sent to the appellate court and to the respondent (the person against whom the appeal is brought). Both the appellant and the respondent then file documents, called briefs, with the appellate court.

The briefs (factums) present the facts of the case, questions that the appellate court is being asked to consider, and the arguments about these questions. The purpose of the appellant's brief is to point out the errors that he claims were made by the lower court. The respondent's brief tries to show that the decision of the lower court was correct. The appellate court reviews these briefs along with the record of the lower court. No trial takes place, and neither new evidence nor witnesses are introduced.

The lawyers for both sides are then permitted to present short oral arguments that allow them to address questions outlined in the briefs and to answer questions asked by the appellate judges. Appellate courts have three, five, and sometimes even seven judges.

POSSIBLE APPEAL OUTCOMES

After hearing the oral arguments and reviewing the trial court record and briefs, the appellate court renders its decision. Appellate court decisions are of four kinds:

◇ The appellate court may affirm the lower court's decision, having found that no errors were made during the original trial.

◇ It may reverse the lower court's decision—the loser in the lower court is declared the winner.

◇ It may modify the lower court's decision by agreeing with parts of the decision but disagreeing with others.

◇ It may remand the case— send it back to the lower court for a new trial—because it finds that some facts were not resolved.

APPRAISAL

The determination of the value of a home, furniture, antiques, jewelry, art, coin or stamp collection or other property is called an appraisal. This should be done by a professional appraiser who has no personal interest in the property. A real estate appraisal is usually required when you apply for a mortgage. The most common method for gauging the worth of a house or land is by comparing it with similar properties.

There are also occasions when you may want personal property appraised. Insurance companies, for example, need appraisals to determine how much coverage to offer for most household items of value.Very expensive items may require more coverage than a standard homeowners' policy provides. For a few extra dollars, you can buy additional coverage based on the property's appraised value. See also ANTIQUE.

If you need an appraisal for mortgage purposes, make sure the lender approves the appraiser you have in mind.

An appraiser is judged on his reputation and creditation. An appraisal by a reputable jeweler or a member of a licensed appraisal board carries far more weight than one by someone who claims to be highly informed about the value of certain items.

Many insurance contracts specify that disputes concerning the company's liability for damages be submitted to the appraisal. In such cases both the insured and the insurer may appoint appraisers who in turn appoint a disinterested party known as an umpire. The umpire's decisions are usually binding.

ARBITRATION

You bought an expensive car six months ago. Because it has been in the repair shop four times already, you want a new car, but the dealer does not want to give you one. You don't want to file a lawsuit and the amount is too big for small-claims court. What can you do?

You can take your dispute to arbitration. It is one way, along with mediation and conciliation, to solve disputes without going to court.

In mediation and conciliation the two parties in a dispute turn to a third person, who serves as an adviser and helps them settle their difference. In arbitration, the disputing parties place the decision entirely in the hands of a third person or persons. The arbitrator's decision is final and binding (except for court-ordered arbitration, which can be appealed).

Proposals for a national arbitration plan have been presented to all provinces by representatives of Canada's automobile industry. The plan's advocates hope to have it operating in at least two provinces by mid 1994.

The national plan is modeled on the Ontario Motor Vehicle Arbitration Plan (OMVAP), which has existed since 1986. Rather than suing the manufac-

turer, Ontario car owners can ask OMVAP to resolve their disputes with manufacturers over alleged defects in vehicles less than four years old. Trained arbitrators take three to six weeks to resolve disputes.

Although the program is financed by the car companies, the arbitrators are independent of the industry. The service is free to consumers. See also COLLECTIVE BARGAINING; CONCILIATION; MEDIATION.

HOW ARBITRATION WORKS

When there is no formal plan, such as OMVAP, in place, arbitration begins when the parties to a dispute agree to have one or more impartial persons decide the matter. Each side then appoints an arbitrator and together the arbitrators appoint a third arbitrator (called an umpire), who actually hears and decides the case.

In a matter of weeks a hearing is scheduled. The arbitrator listens to the facts and examines documents and other evidence presented by both sides. Although he may be (and often is) a lawyer, he does not have to base his decision on legal considerations. He may use fairness or common business practice as a basis for his decision, called an award.

Once the award is made, usually in a matter of days or weeks, it may be confirmed in a court. Confirmation converts the award into a judgment, or decision of the court. This means that the winning party can use legal means to collect the money or otherwise enforce the award. In some cases, to

avoid going to court to collect, each party posts a bond for the amount in dispute.

ADVANTAGES

Arbitration is usually cheaper than court proceedings, and you can put limits on the amount you will spend. Arbitration is also much faster, as lawsuits can take months or years.

Another benefit is that voluntary arbitration settlements are not likely to be appealed. For one thing, grounds for appeal are usually restricted to cases where bias or lack of respect for the rules of natural justice can be proven.

TYPES OF DISPUTES

Almost any dispute can be arbitrated—landlord and tenant disputes, medical malpractice, insurance claims, accident cases, contract disputes, sales agreements, to name a few. Matters of family law such as divorce, custody, and alimentary pension are rarely put to arbitration because the courts like to keep an eye on these matters. But even that situation may be changing. In two recent cases, the divorce arbitration of a rabbinical court and the custody and support recommendations of a family law expert were upheld by Ontario courts.

Mediation on the other hand is often recommended in family matters. A mediator, whose recommendations are not binding, helps people find their own solutions. Many contracts, such as auto sales agreements, have arbitration clauses. Or you can draw up an arbitration agreement after the dispute arises.

See EVERYDAY LEGAL FORMS at back of book.

Some industries, including auto and major household appliance makers, moving companies, stock brokerage firms, and funeral homes, have their own arbitration systems. The arbitrator's decision is usually not binding on the consumer.

ARBITRATION SERVICES

Many provinces have legislation encouraging citizens to use arbitration whenever possible. Ontario's Arbitration Act and Labour Relations Act are some examples. Your local Better Business Bureau, your provincial legal society, or the Canadian Bar Association can give you the names of qualified arbitrators in your area.

STEPS TO TAKE

Suppose you bought a $3,000 dining room set, but when it was delivered the upholstery was in the wrong color. You chose the same pattern in another color. The furniture dealer says the existing color is close enough. What do you do?

1. Get the furniture dealer to agree to arbitration.

2. Select an arbitrator. Look in the Yellow Pages or get references from lawyers, from business people, or from the arbitration service if you are using one. Try to find out if the arbitrator has decided similar cases in a way that would be favorable to you.

3. Obtain the rules of arbitration from the arbitrator and make sure you understand them. You and your opponent can usually agree to change them if you wish.

4. When you present the facts of the case at the arbitration hearing, explain the applicable law as you understand it and traditional business or professional practices in your area. For instance, it may be customary for merchants to provide buyers with a swatch of the material they ordered.

5. Be ready to supply eyewitnesses or expert witnesses. Perhaps a friend was there when you placed your order and heard you say you wanted pink, not peach.

6. Find out whether the other side will be represented by a lawyer. If so, consider hiring your own.

7. Even though arbitration hearings are less formal than court proceedings, be businesslike in your dress and overall demeanor.

ARMED SERVICES

In many ways the armed services represent a world different from that of civilians. They have their own customs and codes of behavior—even their own laws and courts.

WHO THEY ARE

The Canadian Armed Forces—the world's first unified armed service—came into being in 1968 when the army, navy, air force, coast guard, and militia were combined. Except for short periods during the two world wars, membership in what were then called the Canadian Army, Royal Canadian Navy, and Royal Canadian Air Force was always on a voluntary basis: conscription has always been a thorny issue in Canada.

Canada's armed services are charged with patrolling our air space and coasts to protect our sovereignty and providing emergency services and rescue missions. Internationally, our armed services are most visible as members of United Nations peacekeeping forces.

Because of the prohibition against discrimination for reason of sex, the Canadian armed services are made up of both men and women, and many women are now aircraft pilots and officers as well as regular army members.

Before becoming full-fledged members of the armed services, many young people join the cadets, open to anyone 13 to 18 years of age. Cadet involvement gives these young people a taste of military life and provides them with training, discipline, and some income.

Young people educated by the armed services attend university under a program subsidized by the armed services or attend the royal military colleges in Kingston, Ont., or St. Jean, Que.

ARRAIGNMENT

At an arraignment a person accused of a crime appears before the court to hear the charges against him, and to enter a plea of not guilty, guilty, or "autrefois acquit" (previously acquitted on the same charge), "autrefois convict" (previously convicted on the same charge), or pardon (having received a pardon for this same charge).

If the accused person enters a plea of not guilty, a trial date is set. If the accused pleads guilty, a sentence will be imposed. If the crime is a minor one, the judge may impose the sentence right away, but if the crime is more serious, he will have to set a later date for the sentencing. This delay gives court staff time to prepare a presentence report on the history of the accused and the circumstances of his arraignment. Taking such particulars into account should help the judge render a just sentence.

If the court finds that an "autrefois acquit," "autrefois convict," or "pardon" plea is valid, the charges are dismissed. One cannot be charged twice with the same offense.

ARREARS

A debt is in arrears when part of the amount due remains unpaid. For example, suppose you take out a loan for $500 in January and agree to make payments of $60 a month to pay off the principal and interest. You make your payments in February and March, but miss the one for April. In May you are $60 in arrears. Depending on the terms of the loan, you may be charged a penalty based on both the amount owed and the length of time you are in arrears.

Most contracts for the loan of money have what is known as

CHECKLIST
What to Do If You Are Arrested

If you are a solid citizen, being arrested is an unlikely event. But if the unthinkable happens, remember these points.

■ **DO NOT RESIST ARREST.** Resisting arrest, if you are innocent, is not in itself an offense. But if you do so, someone may be injured. You will have ample time to prove your innocence.

■ **ASK TO SEE A COPY OF THE ARREST WARRANT, OR ASK WHAT THE CHARGES ARE.** The police officer should have an arrest warrant stating the charges against you, and you are entitled to a copy. If there is no warrant, the officer must tell you what he is arresting you for and that you have a right to a lawyer. Strictly speaking, the police need not tell you of your right to be silent, but a confession made without such warning might be disallowed.

■ **IDENTIFY YOURSELF.** You are not obliged to answer any questions, even about your name or where you live. But there is rarely any advantage in not disclosing this information.

■ **MAKE NO STATEMENTS UNTIL YOU SEE YOUR LAWYER.** You will be booked—searched for weapons, drugs, or any evidence related to the charge, fingerprinted, and photographed. You may fear that remaining silent suggests you have something to hide, and your natural impulse may be to tell your side of the story. Resist the temptation, lest you inadvertently implicate yourself in a crime. If you are innocent and were elsewhere

with other people at the time of the alleged crime, you may say so. But it is wiser to consult your lawyer before giving your alibi.

If police try to question you, tell them you want to speak with a lawyer first. You will then be allowed to call your lawyer. If you do not have one, you will be given one, but this could take a few days. You probably *do not* have to appear in an identification lineup and should never do so without consulting a lawyer.

■ **BAIL HEARING.** Bail cannot be denied without just cause. If the judge sets a cash bail, the money must be deposited in court before your release. Anyone can put up your bail, but no one can charge a fee for this. Sometimes a surety—a signed agreement to pay the specified sum if you do not show for trial, or violate a bail condition—must be pledged. A cash bail may be set if an accused lives 200 km from the court. Apart from serious charges, however, most accused are released on their own recognizances—their promises to appear for trial.

■ **OBEY BAIL CONDITIONS.** Bail is a conditional release given an accused until trial. The condition might be to abstain from alcohol or stay away from certain individuals. Follow the conditions to the letter: otherwise your bail could be revoked, and you will have to await your trial in jail.

an acceleration clause. This means that the entire balance owing becomes payable immediately the borrower is in arrears—in effect once he defaults on a payment.

ARREST

An arrest occurs when a police officer detains a person and takes him into custody to answer for a crime. In most cases an arrest is made with a warrant issued by a magistrate or judge directing the police to take someone into custody. A copy of the warrant is given to the accused at the time of the arrest. An arrest or detention implies some element of coercion. If the police officers simply ask you to accompany them to the police station, and you go, it would be difficult to claim later that you were illegally arrested or detained.

ARREST WARRANTS

Warrants serve to protect the rights of innocent people. Before the warrant is issued, a judge or magistrate (such as a justice of the peace) reviews the evidence against the accused person to ensure that he or she is not arrested on insufficient evidence or for arbitrary reasons. The magistrate or judge must be assured that there is some reasonable ground for believing that a crime has been committed and that the person named has committed it.

Let us say a police officer wants to obtain a warrant to arrest a man for holding up a liquor store. Although the man was masked at the time of the crime, the store owner reported that he had a crescent-shaped scar on his left hand, just like one on the hand of a notorious neighborhood thug. When the police officer presents this evidence to the judge, he is issued a warrant for the man's arrest.

ARRESTS WITHOUT WARRANTS

Police officers can arrest a person without a warrant only under special circumstances. For example, an officer may arrest a person who commits an offense right before his eyes, if he believes a crime is about to be committed, or if he has reasonable and probable grounds to believe a person has committed a crime and there is no time to procure a warrant.

ARRESTING THE WRONG PERSON

If a police officer arrests the wrong person for a crime as a result of misidentification, he will usually not be responsible for false arrest. As long as he acts in good faith, and had reasonable and probable grounds for believing the person arrested was guilty of a crime, the police department cannot be sued for an honest mistake. See also CITIZEN'S ARREST; WARRANT.

ARSON

Arson is the act of intentionally setting fire to a building or other property (whether completed or not), or to crops, building materials, woods or forests. It is an indictable offense, punishable by up to 14 years' imprisonment. If someone sets fire to a house, and a person in the house is burned to death, the person who set the fire may be charged with murder as well as arson.

Setting fire to one's personal property (things other than buildings) in order to collect insurance is punishable by up to five years' imprisonment. Unless there is evidence to the contrary, the law presumes fraudulent intent whenever the person willfully setting the fire stands to benefit. Neither is drunkenness an excuse: one can still be charged with "willfully setting" the fire, since voluntary intoxication is not a defense to this charge.

Recently the Supreme Court of Canada ruled in favor of an insurance company that refused payment to a client once charged with arson. Because the man did not give this information on his insurance application, the company declined payment on his claim.

ARTIFICIAL INSEMINATION

When a woman cannot conceive a child because the husband is not fertile, the couple may turn to artificial insemination. In this procedure sperm is collected from a donor, who is usually anonymous. A doctor then inserts the sperm into the woman's uterus to fertilize her egg and produce a child. (Although artificial insemination is still relatively rare among people, it is extensively used in animal breeding.)

BIOLOGICAL VERSUS LEGAL FATHERHOOD

Sometimes a relative provides the sperm for fertilization, but more often the donor is anonymous, and the sperm is obtained from a sperm bank. Even though the donor is the biological father of a child conceived by artificial insemination, he gives up all the rights and responsibilities of parenthood before the procedure begins. For example, the donor cannot be asked to provide financial support for the child, nor is he permitted visitation rights. In most instances, the donor never knows whether a child was conceived from his sperm or even whether the sperm was used.

The husband of the woman who has been artificially inseminated is considered the legal father of the child, provided that he consents to the procedure in writing. Neither the adoption process nor other legal proceedings are required, and the husband's rights and responsibilities as a parent are the same as they would be if the child were his own. See also IN VITRO FERTILIZATION.

SURROGATE MOTHERS

When the wife is unable to conceive, a couple may decide to use the husband's sperm to impregnate another woman, who agrees to serve as a surrogate mother. When she bears the child, she turns it over to the couple with whom she made the arrangement. See SURROGATE MOTHER.

At this time there is little legislation on the subject, and the legality of having children by this method is far from a settled issue. The possibilities for abuse and exploitation are immense. Concern about the effects and legal implications prompted the setting up of the Royal Commission on New Reproductive Technologies. Its observations and recommendations should provide a framework for future legislation.

ASSAULT AND BATTERY

Although the two terms are often used together, assault and battery are actually two separate acts.

◇ *Assault.* A deliberate act that puts another person in fear of immediate physical harm. Even if no attack follows, the reasonable belief that an attack was intended is all that is necessary to constitute an assault. No actual physical contact is required in committing an assault, but there must be the justified fear that some sort of attack is about to take place.

For example, a man who raises his hand and threatens to strike someone is guilty of assault. But a person who says something like, "If I had a gun, I'd shoot you," is not guilty of assault since there is no threat of immediate harm.

◇ *Battery.* An intentional physical contact committed by one person against another. Accidental contact, like bumping against a fellow passenger in a crowded subway car, is not battery. Even slight contact that is offensive and intentional can be considered battery.

Assault and battery are civil wrongs (torts) as well as criminal acts. You can sue for injuries you suffer as the result of an assault or battery. See TORT.

Recently a Saskatchewan baseball player sued an opponent for intentionally and recklessly striking him with full force. During a game, the batter hit a pop fly to the infield. As the player was about to catch the ball, he was struck in the ribs by the defendant who was running from third base to home plate. His injuries included broken ribs, bruises, and a punctured lung.

At trial it was shown that the defendant could have avoided the other player but purposefully ran into him to cause him to drop the ball. The judge held the hit was intentional, outside the purview of the sport, and caused by excessive competitive zeal and frustration over the probable loss of the game. He awarded the injured player more than $8,000 damages.

ASSEMBLY, RIGHT OF

The Charter of Rights and Freedoms (see pages 88 to 92) grants every Canadian citizen and resident the right to associate and assemble freely. As with most rights, however, the right of assembly has some limits.

A government, for example, can regulate the use of public places under its control. Therefore, a city council or other municipal authority may legally require a group to obtain a permit before holding a meeting or demonstration in a public place.

The size of the group is an important factor in granting permits, as the government has to deal with such tangles as traffic flow problems. If 60,000 people want to protest in midtown Toronto during rush hour, for example, they are sure to cause traffic problems.

But there are no set rules for how many people constitute a crowd, or assembly. Three people do not need a permit to gather at a street corner, but if those three people start a party and the number swells to 30, the police might consider the gathering a disturbance rather than an exercise in the right of assembly.

The government, however, cannot deny a permit because of the nature of the meeting or the kind of group. It cannot, for example, refuse a permit to a group that wants to remove the mayor from office or a group composed of left-wing radicals. Also, if the government denies the use of a public place to one particular group, it must do so to all groups.

Governments can impose reasonable requirements for granting permission to assemble. For example, a city may deny permission to hold a demonstration on the busiest downtown street at the height of rush hour. The city may require a bond or charge a fee to help defray the costs to the public of additional police, cleanup, and other expenses it incurs because of the meeting. Any conditions placed on one group must be applied to all. See also UNLAWFUL ASSEMBLY.

ASSIGNMENT

The transfer of property, rights, or responsibilities from one person to another is called an assignment. You could assign the rent you receive from a house you own to your daughter, for example.

Generally you can assign duties and responsibilities you assume, but contracts often specifically prohibit such assignments. Suppose you have agreed to write an article for a magazine. As the deadline nears, you have all the research done, but you suddenly have writer's block and you cannot complete the article on time. Whether you can ask your friend who is a journalist to do it for you depends on the terms of your contract with the magazine's publisher.

ASSIGNMENT OF LOANS

A common form of assignment is the assignment of debts, such as mortgages and other types of loans. Many financial institutions assign their loans, including mortgages, to other companies; the debtor is then obligated to pay the new holder of the loan.

If the lender from whom you received your loan assigns it to another financial institution, he will inform and will also notify you of the new lender's name and address. You will then be required to make payments to the new holder of the loan. The new holder cannot change the terms of the mortgage.

Sometimes a dispute between a landlord and the mortgage holder can cause problems to tenants. For example, a mortgage holder, claiming your landlord has defaulted in his payments, may notify all tenants to pay the rent to him. Your landlord, claiming this notice of assignment of rents is not valid, may demand that you continue paying him.

In such cases, your best course is to deposit your rent in court, get a receipt, and notify both parties of your action. That way your lease cannot be canceled for nonpayment of rent and you will not be forced to pay your rent twice. See EVERYDAY LEGAL FORMS section at back of book.

ATTACHMENT

Attachment is a legal procedure that brings the property of a debtor under the control of a court while he is being sued by his creditor. Attachment is used to keep the debtor from destroying, hiding, or otherwise disposing of property that could be used to satisfy a judgment, or court decision, that the creditor might win against the debtor.

Suppose Joseph files a lawsuit to collect a debt of $5,000 that Miles owes him. Miles has a bank account of $15,000. To prevent Miles from giving the money to his mother and thus putting it out of Joseph's reach, Joseph can ask the court to attach Miles's bank account for the amount of $5,000.

Before a court authorizes an attachment, it must be satisfied that the alleged debtor will try to hide or otherwise dispose of his property or money before a final judgment is rendered. In Quebec, an attachment is known as a *scizure before judgment*.

The word *attachment* is sometimes used erroneously to describe a garnishment (a court order that lets the creditor obtain his money). See GARNISHMENT.

ATTORNEY

An attorney is an agent, a person authorized to act on another's behalf. An *attorney-at-law* is an officer of the court, licensed by the province, who can be appointed by others to act on their behalf in legal matters. See LAWYER.

An *agent* is someone authorized by a power of attorney to act for another person in conducting business matters, in transferring property, or for other purposes. The actions of an agent are binding on the person who gave him the power of attorney (the principal). See POWER OF ATTORNEY. In Quebec the agent who acts on behalf of the person who gave him the power of attorney is called the mandatory, his principal is called the mandator and the contract is known as a contract of mandate.

In Canada, the terms attorney, barrister, lawyer, counselor-at-law, and solicitor are interchangeable. In Great Britain, there are distinctions between barristers (who plead cases in court) and solicitors (who also plead cases, but mostly draw up legal documents and instruct barristers).

ATTRACTIVE NUISANCE

An attractive nuisance is an object or condition on someone's property that is both potentially hazardous and attractive to children—something that might entice children to wander onto the property and become exposed to danger. A swimming pool, a tree house, or a concrete foundation could each be considered an attractive nuisance. An attractive nuisance is also known as an allurement.

In general, a property owner is not legally responsible if an adult is injured while trespassing on her property. But if the trespasser is a child, most provinces, under the so-called doctrine of allurement, hold a landowner responsible for injuries suffered. To prevent an accident—as well as to avoid possible prosecution—the owner must try to minimize any risks to children playing on his or her property.

PONDS VERSUS SWIMMING POOLS

An attractive nuisance or allurement may differ from one case to another. Generally, ponds, forests, streams, and other naturally occurring features are not characterized as allurements. Man-made things such as a trench, a construction site, heavy equipment, or swimming pools would fall into this category, however. Since it is reasonable to expect young children to play in or with these things, simply placing a sign or

two or erecting a wire fence around the object would not usually be enough to ensure the owner was not liable.

DETERMINING RESPONSIBILITY

In deciding whether a property owner is to blame for a trespassing child's injuries, the courts consider several factors.

◇ Did the landowner know that children might trespass on the property? If, for example, she had previously asked children to leave, she would more likely be held responsible.

◇ Did the owner know that the object presented a risk of serious injury? No landowner can make her property completely safe for children. Nor can an owner be held responsible for certain conditions, such as cliffs or fires, that create obvious dangers.

◇ What is the child's age? The younger a child is, the less likely he is to understand the risks he may be taking, and the more likely an owner is to be held responsible for the child's injuries. Children 12 years old and under have a better chance of being financially compensated for their injuries than do teenagers.

◇ What is the likelihood of injury compared to the effort needed to prevent it? A house under construction in a secluded area, for example, is not likely to be noticed by many children, and injuries received from playing around the building site would probably not be serious. Therefore, it would be unfair to expect the landowner to fence in the site. Electrical towers, in contrast, are very hazardous. If they are located in a populated area, it would not be unreasonable to expect the power company to erect fences around the towers.

Note that it is not only the owner who is liable for damages caused by an allurement; the person who had the care and control of the thing—the occupier—is also liable.

AUCTION

An auction is a public sale at which items are sold by competitive bidding. Although auctions are popular with collectors and bargain hunters alike, they can present pitfalls for those who are ignorant of the basic procedures.

Most of the time, items to be auctioned are on view before the auction takes place. If you are going to bid on an item, you should first look it over to determine its value. In the case of real estate, the auctioneer usually announces a time and date prior to the auction for inspection of the property.

TERMS OF THE AUCTION

By law, the rules and conditions that apply to an auction must be announced at the sale before the bidding begins. An auctioneer may require that payment be in cash only, or the seller may offer no guarantees about the quality or authenticity of the property being sold. The high bidder must honor those terms, even if he was not aware of them at the time that he made his bid.

A seller can refuse to sell an item below a certain minimum price, called the upset or reserve price. He can even bid on his own property, as long as the other bidders are notified before the bidding begins. But if an auction is "without reserve," the seller can neither withdraw an item because bids are too low nor drive them up by bidding on his own property.

THE BIDDING PROCESS

Bidding may be by voice, in writing, or by a nod or hand signal. Secret signals between bidder and auctioneer are not permitted, but an auctioneer may be on the alert for a particular bidder's signal, which may be so discreet that it is not apparent to other bidders.

When offers appear to have stopped, the auctioneer usually warns bidders of their last chance to bid by saying: "Going once, going twice…" before he strikes a block with his hammer and says, "Sold!"

Once a high bid has been accepted, both buyer and seller are bound by the agreed price. The seller cannot accept a higher price from someone else after the auction, and the buyer cannot withdraw the bid. A buyer who defaults and does not want to conclude the sale can be sued.

Although by law anyone can bid at an auction, the auctioneer may exercise discretion. For example, he does not have to accept bids from minors, people who are not mentally competent, or people he thinks will not honor a bid.

When a debtor's goods are sold by a court officer to satisfy a judgment, the sale is final and no guarantees are given as to the nature and quality of the object sold. On the other hand, a person who buys something at a judicial sale buys it free of all liens that may have been related to the object, when it was in the prior owner's possession.

AUCTION SCAMS

At an auction the seller wants the highest price, while the bidders are looking for a bargain. These two opposing interests sometimes prompt unscrupulous behavior.

It is illegal for a seller to fraudulently inflate bids. Suppose a seller, determined to get the highest possible price for his Chippendale-style furniture, hires two people to make bids. These accomplices, or "puffers," know they will not be bound by their offers, and as the auction proceeds, cast a higher bid whenever there is a lull in the bidding.

When a bona fide buyer finally does win the bid, he may pay much more than the item is worth. If the buyer later discovers the scam, a court may void the sale and order the buyer's money returned.

In another common scam a potential buyer who wants to get a good deal at an auction pretends to represent a charity. The other buyers, believing they are performing a public service by letting the charity pay a lower price, are reluctant to outbid the impostor, who then gets a bargain price. If the seller discovers the buyer's ruse, he can void the sale.

However there is nothing illegal in a serious buyer approaching another person bidding on the same object, and giving him a small sum, say $50, to stop bidding against him. If the other party accepts, the serious bidder may save hundreds of dollars.

For a discussion of real estate auctions, see FORECLOSURE.

AUTOMOBILE ACCIDENTS

Some automobile accidents are unavoidable, and no one can be blamed. But when the owner or operator of a motor vehicle is negligent, he will be held liable, or legally responsible, for any damages resulting from the accident.

NEGLIGENCE

With regard to automobile accidents, negligence means the failure to use ordinary or reasonable care in operating a vehicle. Under ordinary conditions, just obeying all traffic and safety laws would constitute ordinary care. But sometimes obeying the law is not enough. For example, when the roads are wet or icy, extra caution is required. The same is true when someone drives through a residential area or a school zone.

SHARED RESPONSIBILITY

Suppose an accident is due to the negligence of both drivers. For example, Jane backs out of her driveway carelessly and runs into a car driven by Judy, who has just run a red light. While both drivers are at fault, Judy is more at fault than Jane.

Because of situations like this the doctrine of contributo-ry negligence was developed. Under this, the degree of responsibility is divided between the parties concerned according to the percentage of fault or negligence committed by each person.

In this instance, Jane obtains more compensation than Judy, because the court figured she was only 25 percent at fault, in contrast to Judy's 75 percent. In 1991, the British Columbia Court of Appeal held a passenger partially liable for his injury because he knew the driver had been drinking.

PEDESTRIANS AND PASSENGERS

The amount of care drivers must show toward pedestrians depends on who the pedestrians are. Drivers must use more care around a child, for example, and the younger the child the greater the care, because young children may not understand the dangers associated with moving vehicles.

In the case of adults and older children, a driver can reasonably expect that they will not step off the curb into traffic. But if the person is aged or handicapped in some way, a driver must use special care.

A driver is also obligated to the passengers in his car. The degree of care often depends on whether the passenger is an invited guest or is paying. In the past there was a clear-cut distinction between the rights of a guest passenger and those of someone who paid for the transportation. Until 1967, for example, it was impossible for a guest passenger to sue the host driver. From 1967 to 1977 the guest passenger could only sue the host if "gross negligence" was proved. By 1977 this distinction was abolished in most provinces.

In Quebec, *all* claims for bodily injury in auto accidents are paid through the Quebec Automobile Insurance Society.

CAR OWNER'S RESPONSIBILITY

Although the driver of a car can always be held responsible for negligence, the owner may be at fault too, even if he was not in the car at the time of the accident. Most provinces hold the owner jointly responsible for any damages, but not for criminal offenses, such as speeding, reckless driving, or driving while intoxicated, committed by the driver.

Since virtually every province and territory requires that the vehicle owner carry third-party liability insurance, the owner rarely has to pay for damages from his own pocket. However, his insurance premiums would likely increase after an accident, regardless of who was driving.

The insurance company could sue a driver who was grossly negligent if he was a friend or acquaintance of the owner, but not someone who lived under the same roof.

See also DAMAGES; NEGLIGENCE.

SEAT BELTS

All provinces and the Northwest Territories require automobile drivers and passengers to wear seat belts. Persons caught not doing so are liable for fines ranging from $25 to $100 for a first infraction.

In one court challenge to Alberta's seat belt law, the province's Court of Appeal unanimously refused the plaintiff's claim that obligatory use of a seat belt infringed his liberty as guaranteed by the Charter of Rights and Freedoms. The law was valid because it saved lives and often reduced the severity of bodily injury, the court ruled. See also SEAT BELT LAWS.

STEPS TO TAKE IF YOU ARE IN AN ACCIDENT

It is not easy to think clearly right after an auto accident. But if you remember these steps, you may avoid trouble later on:

1. Do not move injured people until medical help arrives. Moving them can make their injuries worse.

2. If no one is injured, move the cars out of traffic to prevent another accident.

3. Call the police, who will make out a report describing how the accident happened.

4. Get the other driver's name, address, phone number, license number, and the name of his insurance company.

5. Get the names, addresses, and telephone numbers of witnesses.

6. Do not say anything to the other driver about how the accident happened, such as "Oh, it was all my fault." Such a statement may not be true, and more important, it may be used against you in court.

7. If the other driver offers to give you a cheque for the damages to your car in exchange for your not telling the police, say no. The amount offered may not cover the damages, or the cheque may bounce. In addition, by keeping silent you may be breaking a provincial law requiring damages over a specified amount to be reported.

8. Call your insurance agent. He will start processing your claim, and if you are out of town he may be able to get you a rental car and a place to stay.

9. If you are injured, do not sign anything until the full extent of your injuries is known. Some serious injuries do not show up until later.

AUTOMOBILE INSURANCE

Automobile accidents account for thousands of deaths and injuries each year, and the resulting medical costs, property damage, and lost wages add up to billions of dollars. An auto insurance policy is an agreement between you and an insurance company stating that, in return for a specific amount of money (the premium), the insurance company will pay for certain types of damages you sustain or cause with your automobile.

All provinces require you to have a specified minimum amount of insurance coverage, generally at least $200,000. If you get into an accident and you do not have insurance, you may lose your license for a year or more, and you may also be fined. Most provinces demand proof of coverage when your car is registered.

INSURANCE POLICIES

All provinces require car owners to carry auto insurance, and insurance companies offer collision insurance; comprehensive insurance; and liability insurance.

No-fault insurance

In recent years, government-run "no fault" insurance plans have been established by British Columbia, Saskatchewan, Manitoba, Ontario, and Quebec. The Quebec plan is notable in that it prohibits anyone from ever suing another for bodily injuries suffered in an auto accident.

Under government "no fault" insurance, anyone injured in a motor vehicle accident, whether he be the driver, passenger, driver of another vehicle or even a pedestrian, is entitled to certain benefits from the agency administering the plan, but cannot sue except in certain cases.

An injured person may be compensated for some loss of income (for example, 80 percent in Ontario, 90 percent in Quebec) up to a stated amount per week ($600 say). He or she would also be compensated for supplementary medical care and rehabilitation and long-term care, as well as compensation for permanent disability or disfigurement. Death benefits are paid to heirs or surviving spouses.

The Quebec plan provides all these benefits but the injured

person cannot sue even if his loss is greater than the prescribed benefits. In British Columbia, Saskatchewan, Manitoba, and Ontario, however, the injured person can sue for losses not covered by the government plan.

Ontario's plan originally allowed a victim to sue only if the accident caused death, permanent serious disfigurement, or permanent, serious, physical impairment. Psychological trauma was not included. Modified in 1993, the plan now permits legal action for psychological as well as physical injuries, and has dropped the requirement that such injuries be permanent. Victims may sue for "serious disfigurement," or "serious impairment of an important physical, mental or psychological function."

The Manitoba and Saskatchewan plans pay income replacement benefits for those totally disabled (up to a certain amount), medical and rehabilitation expenses, funeral expenses, and death benefits.

Supplemental insurance

If you want to be covered for amounts greater than those offered by the government plans, you can buy more insurance from a private insurance company. Because court awards in bodily injury cases have been increasing, you would be wise to purchase an extra $1 million to $2 million liability insurance. You might want to consider purchasing extra income replacement insurance as well, in case the person at fault has not enough insurance to pay for injuries you incur.

REAL LIFE, REAL LAW

The Case of the Invalid Insurance

Robert's late-model Camaro was stolen on one of his regular business trips to New York. To his surprise, his insurance company declined to pay his claim for $13,000, the depreciated value of the car. In checking Robert's driving record before approving payment, the company discovered that his driver's permit was suspended once in the previous three years, that he had had numerous prior accidents, that he went to New York regularly, and that other insurance companies had refused to insure him in the past. His present insurer claimed Robert should have disclosed all this on his application.

Robert sued and lost. The court ruled the insurance company did not have to pay him since he did not disclose important facts. Had the company known these facts, it would not have insured him in the first place. An insurance contract is one of the "utmost good faith"(*uberimmae fidei*), so all facts that may affect the premium must be disclosed. Robert should have informed the insurer of his driving record even if the insurance agent did not ask about it. Therefore his insurance contract was declared null and void from the time it was issued. His $575 premium was refunded. It was all he got for his stolen automobile.

Robert's case was heard in Quebec, but the principles involved apply in all provinces. An insured must tell the insurer all facts that could have a bearing on the the premium or which might cause the insurer to refuse an insurance policy in the first place.

Family protection insurance, known as SEF 44 endorsement, provides coverage if a motorist does not have enough coverage to pay a claim. An SEF 44 endorsement would make up the shortfall between what was recovered from the insurer of the no-fault motorist and your own liability coverage.

For example, Ralph and his wife Judy, injured in an auto accident, might have combined injuries calculated to cost them $1 million in loss of salary, extra medical, rehabilitation, and child-care expenses. But the person who caused their injury might only have $200,000 worth of insurance. In that case, Ralph and Judy would be able to collect the $800,000 difference through their SEF 44 endorsement.

By and large, supplemental insurance is relatively inexpensive. One reason is that bodily injury claims exceeding $200,000, amounts common in United States, are comparatively rare here since Medicare covers most medical expenses.

Collision and comprehensive insurance

Collision insurance covers the repair of your car if it is damaged in a collision with another vehicle or object, even if the collision was your fault or was intentionally caused by the other driver. If someone with a grudge against you purposely crashes into your car as you pull out of your driveway, collision insurance will compensate you for any damage to your car.

Comprehensive coverage protects you against incidents not covered by collision insurance—from theft and from property damage caused by falling objects, vandalism, riots, earthquakes, fires, floods, tornadoes, hurricanes, lightning, and explosions. Many comprehensive policies specifically exclude jewelry, documents, and other personal items stolen from the car. A car stereo may be regarded as equipment that is part of the car, and so may be covered by the policy.

Both collision and comprehensive coverage include a "deductible" clause, which specifies an amount, usually $250 or $500, that you must pay from your own pocket. If the cost to your broken windshield is $279 and the deductible is $250, your insurance company will give you only $29 to pay for the windshield; the rest is your responsibility.

INSURANCE RATES

When fixing rates for drivers, insurance companies consider such factors as: (1) their age and marital status; (2) the make, model, and year of the car; (3) the ages of additional drivers (especially teenagers); (4) the driving records of the persons to be insured; (5) how the car will be used; and (6) the car owner's place of residence.

Insurance rates are higher or lower according to the driver's "risk group" and how much protection is desired. A $50,000 liability policy for a male teenager costs much more than the same coverage for a 50-year-old woman, because statistical data show that the male teenager is much more likely to have an accident.

Insurance companies may raise their rates after a claim is filed, even if the insured was not at fault. They base their rate increases on the number of claims filed by the driver, not just the dollar amounts they might have to pay out. The insurance rates for someone who has had five "fender benders" will probably be raised more readily than those of a person who has made a claim for only one serious accident.

AUTOMOBILE PURCHASE

Buying an automobile, whether new or used, usually means spending a lot of money. For this reason and because a number of things can go wrong in the process, you should know your legal rights.

BUYING A NEW CAR

When you buy a new car, you enter into a contract. As is the case with any other contract, the best time to prevent a problem is before you put your signature on the dotted line.

Financing

Determine in advance how much you can afford to pay. Most lenders will help you figure out this amount. The rule of thumb they use is that your total monthly debt payments should amount to no more than 20 percent of your income after taxes. Many lenders pre-approve car loans so that you know before you shop how much you can pay. A dealer, knowing what your limits are, may decide to give you a better price on the car.

Never sign the contract to purchase a car or take possession of a car until you have arranged the financing. If your financing falls through and you have to return the car, your purchase contract may require you to pay a fee for each day you have possession of the car plus an additional amount for each mile you have driven it. If this happens, you could lose a considerable amount of money.

STEPS TO TAKE WHEN TAKING DELIVERY

1. Before you accept a car, inspect it and take it for a test drive. Do this even if you have driven the same or a similar model before, because every single automobile is different.

2. Be particularly careful if your car was specially ordered from the factory. If you notice any defects, or if the car you receive is not exactly what you ordered, you have the right to reject it. But the dealer has the right to modify the car to the proper specifications within a reasonable time, and if he does so, you must accept it.

3. If the dealer does not

deliver in a reasonable time, you may have the right to cancel the order and get back your down payment. It is the dealer's duty to deliver your car within a "reasonable time" of the delivery date specified on the purchase order. A reasonable time for delivering a standard inexpensive car might be a week after the date specified but much longer for a limited-production import. If the dealer knew when he took your order that he could not deliver the car on time, you may be able to sue him for fraud as well.

NEW CAR WARRANTY

Every new car sold in Canada comes with a manufacturer's warranty, which the dealer must give you. A typical manufacturer's warranty covers defects in materials and workmanship for 12 months or 20,000 kilometres, with a longer period of coverage for such major components as the engine, the transmission, and the power train.

Most provinces have laws stating that new cars come with an implied (unwritten) "warranty of merchantability." This type of warranty assures a consumer that the product he is buying meets certain minimum standards of quality and safety. If it does not meet these standards, the dealer or manufacturer may be held responsible. See WARRANTY AND GUARANTEE.

The consumer protection laws are intended to protect consumers from new and even used cars that have to be repaired often because of defects in the workmanship, manufacture or parts.

BUYING A USED CAR

You should handle the purchase of a used car differently from that of a new car.

Inspection

Before you agree to buy a used car, arrange for an independent inspection. A reputable dealer will have no objection. If the dealer does object, it is likely that he has something to hide.

Have the car inspected by a mechanic you trust. He may see mechanical problems that would otherwise have been overlooked. The dealer may then correct minor problems or lower the price. If the problems affect the engine, transmission, or other major components, look for another car.

Other precautions

If the dealer tells you that major work was done on the car, such as installing a new engine, ask to see the receipts. Give these to your mechanic so that he can make certain that the work was actually completed.

Although the practice is illegal, a dishonest used-car dealer may set back the odometer on a car to lower the mileage, thus increasing its apparent value. You should check carefully to see if all the numbers are level. If, for example, the dial shows 33250 kilometres, but the 2 is not in perfect alignment with the other numbers, someone probably tampered with the odometer.

Consumer protection legislation requires that the mileage be written on a certificate. If the mileage is not the true figure, the purchaser can sue for a price reduction or sometimes cancellation of the sale with

complete reimbursement. Ask your mechanic to check if the car's overall condition seems to match the figures on the odometer. If you have any reason to believe the odometer has been adjusted, look for another dealer and another car.

USED CAR WARRANTIES

Consumer protection legislation requires used-car dealers to display a sticker in the window of each car being sold indi-

---

■ **ABC's** ■

OF ILLEGAL AUTO DEALER PRACTICES

Consumer protection laws prohibit new- and used-car dealers from making certain claims and engaging in fraudulent practices. It is illegal for an auto dealer to:

■ Refuse to show you a car that has been advertised at a low price unless it has already been sold; or substitute a car that has less equipment than the advertised car.

■ Knowingly conceal the fact that a car has been repainted, repaired, rebuilt, or damaged in shipment, or that it was a police car or a taxi.

■ Advertise a car it does not have in its possession, unless the ad clearly states when the car will become available.

■ Sell a used car that does not display the provincially required warranty information sticker on the window.

cating what kind of warranty applies to the vehicle. If there is no warranty, the sticker must clearly state that the car will be sold "as is"—that is without any guarantee.

"As is" sales usually involve older cars, or cars that are obviously damaged or otherwise in poor shape. Generally the cars are purchased for parts and such sales are legal.

If a warranty is offered with the car, the dealer must indicate on the sticker whether it is a full warranty or limited warranty, how long it will last, and what parts and systems are covered. If the buyer will have to pay part of the repair costs, the sticker must indicate the amount.

For example, the warranty might cover only half the cost of transmission repairs for a certain period of time. If the transmission should break within the specified period, the dealer will repair it, but the owner will have to pay 50 percent of the bill.

Used-car dealers sometimes offer optional warranties, but these are often expensive, cover things that rarely go wrong, and have a short duration. Before buying such a warranty, check its contents carefully so that you do not spend good money for something that is essentially worthless.

Buying a car from the owner
Buying a used car from a private individual poses a different problem. Unless he sells cars on a regular basis, an owner is not considered a car dealer and will not be bound by the standard laws that protect consumers. If the car falls

apart even one day after you purchase it, you may have no recourse.

On the positive side, keep in mind that private sales often yield good bargains. Many car owners would rather sell quickly than spend time and effort looking for the highest price.

Have the car inspected by a mechanic you know and trust. Ask to see the owner's repair bills and the car's maintenance history. Check that it was not used as a taxi. In that case, even a recent model may be near collapse.

Most important, make sure that there are no liens on the car. If the seller has not fully paid for repairs to the car or for the car-purchase loan, either creditor may seize the car. This only applies to private sales, not to purchases from a reputable car dealer who will be insured against such events.

Since all provinces now have a central automobile registry, it is easy to check the vehicle's ownership history.

Ask pointed questions about the car's problems. Many people would rather tell the truth and risk losing a sale than be accused of misrepresentation.

PUTTING THE AGREEMENT IN WRITING

Whether you are buying a new or a used car and whether the purchase is from a dealer or a private individual, it is essential to get any oral promises from the seller included in a written contract. For example, if the salesperson at a dealership promises to include stereo speakers in the back as well as the front of the car or to pro-

vide rustproofing at no extra cost, you may not be able to collect on these promises unless they are written into your contract. See also CONSUMER PROTECTION.

AUTOMOBILE REGISTRATION

The purpose of automobile registration is to give the province some measure of control over the vehicles that operate on its roads and highways. Through registration, automobiles and their owners are identified in public records, and this enables car sales, thefts, and accidents to be monitored.

In all provinces you must obtain a registration certificate and license plates in order to drive your car on public roads.

If you move to another province, you will have to register your car in the new province when the registration expires.

If your vehicle is not properly registered, you can be fined, and your vehicle may be towed and impounded if it is parked on a public street. You may have to pay the towing and storage charges in order to reclaim your car.

AUTOMOBILE RENTAL

Rental car companies are allowed to make their own rules about who can rent a car. Some of their restrictions seem discriminatory, but they are not against the law.

CHECKLIST

How to Sell Your Car

The easiest way to sell your car is to take it to a dealer and accept whatever he offers. If you want the best price, however, you will have to sell it privately, and that means doing a little work. These guidelines will help you through the process:

■ **FIND OUT WHAT YOUR CAR IS WORTH.**
Before you set a price, find out the approximate value of your car. Look in one of the used-car price books, called "red books," or take your automobile to used-car dealers and ask what they would give you.

■ **MAKE YOUR CAR LOOK ITS BEST.**
People tend to judge a book by its cover, so wash and wax your car, clean the inside, and be sure the horn, lights, and doors work.

■ **BE SURE THE CAR WILL PASS INSPECTION.**
A car that meets your province's standards for safety is a much more attractive buy than one that needs work.

■ **ADVERTISE.**
Place a classified ad in your local newspaper and post ads on community bulletin boards, such as the ones in supermarkets. The ad should include the car's make, model, year, options, condition, mileage, and your asking price. State that the sale is "by owner" and give your phone number. Also place a for-sale sign in the window of the car, with your phone number and the price.

■ **GET THE PAPERS TOGETHER.**
Ask your provincial motor vehicle department what forms to use and what procedure to follow when you transfer ownership of your car. Be sure you have the car's title, registration, warranties, and service records on hand.

■ **PREPARE A BILL OF SALE.**
The bill of sale should include the following: your name and address and that of the buyer, the date of sale, a description of the automobile, the vehicle identification number, the license plate number, the odometer reading, and the price. Also, state that the car is being sold without any guarantees.

■ **DON'T LIE TO THE BUYER.**
In most provinces, you are not legally required to tell the buyer about your car's defects, but if he asks, you must either tell him the whole truth or decline to say anything. If you lie or tell only half the truth, the buyer may sue you.

■ **ALLOW A TEST DRIVE.**
Test drives are customary, but be sure the buyer has a valid driver's license before he gets behind the wheel. Ride along with him to be sure he does not steal your car.

■ **DON'T TAKE RISKS WHEN GETTING PAID.**
Ask the buyer to pay by certified cheque, cashier's cheque, money order, or cash. If he pays by personal cheque, keep the automobile until the cheque clears.

Most companies will not rent to a person under 21 years of age, and some charge higher rates for drivers under 25. One common requirement is that renters must present at least one major credit card, even though the company will accept payment by cash or traveler's cheque when the car is returned.

COLLISION INSURANCE

When renting a car, you will be offered the chance to buy collision insurance, often called a collision-damage waiver or loss-damage waiver, usually costing $10 or more per day. This insurance will protect you from financial responsibility for any damage to the rental car.

If you refuse collision coverage you can be held responsible for damage up to the full value of the car, no matter how the damage was caused—even if a drunken driver hit the automobile while it was parked or a police car hit it while running a red light.

ALTERNATIVE COLLISION INSURANCE

If you have an automobile insurance policy, you may find that it automatically extends collision coverage to include a rented car. Be sure to read your policy, however, as some policies exclude this coverage.

Many credit card companies provide free collision insurance if you use their card when you rent a car. But you may be required to seek reimbursement from your primary insurer before they will pay a claim, or to pay the damages out of your own pocket before they will reimburse you.

AUTOMOBILE REPAIR

Few things are anticipated with as much dread as having to take your car to the repair shop. For one thing, you expect it will cost twice or 10 times what it should. And what will you do if the car still does not run properly?

Most of the problems that come with auto repairs can be avoided by taking a few precautions. If a dispute arises about the work done or the cost of repairs, you are in a better position when you can offer written documents as evidence of your agreement with the repair shop. The most important documents are the written estimate and the work order.

THE WRITTEN ESTIMATE

In many provinces an auto repair shop is legally required to provide a written estimate. The estimate should list the cost of each part and note whether the parts are used, reconditioned, or rebuilt. A separate list should indicate the estimated cost of labor. Ask for a written estimate even if your province does not require it and, if possible, get two or more additional estimates from different repair shops.

A written estimate can be important if the final bill is considerably higher. Although it is not unusual for the estimate to be less than the final figure on your bill, a wide gap between the two amounts raises some questions about the repair shop's reliability.

Some auto repair shops stoop to the unscrupulous practice of giving an extremely low estimate to attract a customer, while knowing full well that the final bill will be much higher. This is called lowballing and is a type of fraud. If you are a victim of lowballing, you can file a lawsuit to recover the cost of the repairs. With a written estimate it is much easier to prove in court that lowballing occurred. The court may award you extra money— called punitive damages—in addition to the cost of repairs, to discourage the shop from repeating the practice in the future.

Most courts would limit repair overruns to 10 percent of the written estimate. Some garages advertise that they honor their estimates. Whether such advertisements are made on television, radio or in the newspaper, they form part of your repair contract.

THE WORK ORDER

The work order—the document you sign giving the auto repair shop authority to repair your automobile—is every bit as important as the estimate. In most provinces a repair shop can legally charge a customer only for the work that appears on the work order.

It is important, though, that you have the repair shop indicate the price of the work to be done as specifically as possible on the order. In the case of a lowball, for example, the mechanic may tell you the work will cost $200, write out a work order with no specific price, and then charge you $800.

In this situation, if you refuse to pay, the repair shop can legally put a lien on your car. The best thing to do is pay the bill and then take the case to small-claims court.

In a dispute, the work order, which is a contract, can be used by either party as evidence for its claims. Because it has such legal importance, you should fully understand what you are signing. Make sure that any vague or incorrect items on a work order are clarified and corrected. Never sign a blank work order, since it gives the garage the authority to make whatever repairs it wants to your vehicle, then charge you for them.

WARRANTIES AND PARTS

Before you choose a repair shop, find out what kinds of warranties, or guarantees, it provides for parts and labor. The warranties should be included on the work order or put in writing somewhere else.

Ask that any parts removed from your car be saved and returned to you. These parts could be useful evidence if a dispute develops over the work performed. Unless the parts are under warranty and have to be returned to the manufacturer, you have a right to keep them. If necessary, have another mechanic see if they really needed to be replaced. See WARRANTY AND GUARANTEE.

UNSATISFACTORY WORK

If you are dissatisfied with the repair work on the car, you can respond in several ways. You can give the repair shop the chance to redo the job, or if that does not work, you can take the car to another place.

Although you will have to pay another repair bill by taking your car elsewhere, the second bill can be used to show that the work was not done properly by the first shop. You may then be able to get the original shop to give you a

refund. If they will not do so, you can file a lawsuit in small-claims court to recover your loss or try to resolve the dispute through arbitration.

RIGHTS OF THE REPAIR SHOP

Just as you have the right to expect proper repair work, the shop has the right to be paid for work well done. If the customer does not pay, most provinces will give the shop a mechanic's lien, which allows the shop to keep the car until payment has been made. In some provinces the lien is automatically created when the repair work is completed—the shop owner does not have to file a document with the court.

While a lien is in effect, the shop may charge a customer fees for storing the car until the repair bill is paid. To avoid the lien and the additional storage cost, you should consider paying a contested bill first and then look into other legal alternatives that may be able to resolve the dispute. See also ALTERNATIVE DISPUTE RESOLUTION; ARBITRATION; MECHANIC'S LIEN; SMALL-CLAIMS COURT.

AUTOPSY

When a person dies, a dissection of the body is sometimes performed to find out the cause of death. This procedure is

called an autopsy and is legally required only when a coroner decides it is necessary.

A coroner usually requests an autopsy when a death is unexplained, unexpected, suspicious, or violent. If a body is discovered in a car at the bottom of a river, an autopsy is needed to establish the cause of death. It is important to know whether the death was caused by a heart attack, or by a malicious act committed before the automobile entered the water. The results of an autopsy are kept on file in the coroner's office and can be used as evidence in a trial.

A family may object for religious or other personal reasons to having their loved one's body subjected to an autopsy. But when one is required by law, it must be performed regardless of family objections.

Usually the family would rather have an autopsy performed than remain ignorant about the cause of death. If the cause of death proves to be a physical ailment, such as an unsuspected heart condition, family members can benefit by knowing about it. Such knowledge may put them on the alert to seek treatment for the same condition in themselves. In the event that there is any suspicion of murder or other foul play, the family can be satisfied that the police will have the necessary information to pursue justice.

If an autopsy is performed without the family's permission and for reasons that do not conform to provincial law, the family will have substantial grounds to initiate a lawsuit.

FROM BABYSITTER TO BUYER'S CLUB

BABYSITTER

Someone who is temporarily entrusted with the care of another person's child—usually just for an evening but sometimes for a few days or more—is known familiarly as a babysitter. The sitter must follow the parents' instructions in regard to meals, bedtimes, and the like, and is legally required to use reasonable precautions to protect the child's safety.

But if your child gets sick or is injured while in the care of a sitter, the sitter does not have the legal authority to obtain medical treatment. Suppose your child starts vomiting and has a fever and the sitter takes him to the hospital. Unless the staff consider his condition a medical emergency, they will not treat him without your permission.

Such a situation has obvious risks, especially if you leave your child in the care of a baby-sitter for an extended period of time—for example, while you attend an out-of-town wedding. One solution is to grant the babysitter medical power of attorney, authorizing her to consent to treatment if it becomes necessary. In such a situation the babysitter must be an adult, because power of attorney cannot be granted to minors.

If you are leaving your child in the care of a minor, consider giving special power of attorney to a neighbor or a relative who lives nearby. A sample form for special power of attorney is included in the section titled EVERYDAY LEGAL FORMS. See also DAY CARE.

BAD FAITH

Fraud or dishonesty in dealing with another person, either by misleading him or by refusing to fulfill a contractual obligation, is known as bad faith. When a dealer sells a reconditioned television set, claiming it is new, he is acting in bad faith.

Although acting in bad faith is not a crime, it can affect the opinion of a judge or jury that is deciding a lawsuit. Because our society values fairness (good faith), a person who is found to have acted in bad faith is unlikely to win his suit.

Good faith, or bad faith, can be the basis of a legal defense. Suppose John has a beautiful work of art, which he promises to sell to Peter. They draw up an agreement and Peter arranges to pick up the painting the following week. In the meantime, Mary comes along, falls in love with the work, and decides to buy it for even more money than Peter agreed to pay. John accepts her bid, and she takes the painting away.

Whether Mary has good title to the painting depends on whether she is acting in good or bad faith—whether she knows of the previous sale. If she knows nothing of it, she has good title to the painting. John, however, has sold something that does not belong to him.

The concepts of good faith and bad faith apply equally to buyers and sellers. A shopper who buys a party dress can expect that its quality is reasonably good and that she will not have to return it because of defects. The retailer can assume the customer is honestly buying the dress and does not plan to return it once the party is over.

BAIL

In our system of justice, a person accused of a crime is considered innocent until proved guilty. Bail, or judicial interim release, is the release of an accused person awaiting trial if he promises that he will appear in court on the trial date, and, in some cases, a sum of money, or bail bond. Under the Charter of Rights and Freedoms, "any person charged with an offense has the right . . . not to be denied reasonable bail without just cause."

BAIL BOND

In cases other than those involving serious crimes such as murder or armed robbery, the accused is released on his own recognizance, that is, he is released upon his promise alone to appear for trial. It is rare that an accused is asked to pay a bail bond. However, an accused who lives more than 200 kilometres from the court may have to put up sureties. For example, he may be obliged to deposit $500 or even $5,000 before being released.

Although it seldom happens, the court may require a witness to deposit a bail bond to ensure his or her presence in court at a later date.

The amount of bail depends on the nature of the crime and the accused person's links to the community. Factors such as steady employment, property ownership, and family ties help a court assess the likelihood that a defendant will appear for trial and not "jump bail." If the accused shows up as required, the bail is returned to the person who put it up.

When bail is granted, a court may impose restrictions that will also help to ensure the appearance of the accused in court. For example, a court may restrict his freedom to travel, the kind of people with whom he associates, or his living arrangements. Failure to observe such conditions imposed by the court constitutes a separate violation of the law. The accused may find his bail revoked, and he may have to spend additional time in jail.

BAIL BONDSMEN

It is illegal in Canada for anyone to act as a professional bail bondsman. In the United States, however, such money-lenders are legal and, for a fee, they will guarantee to pay in full if the accused jumps bail. When a Canadian court sets bail, a friend of the accused, or anyone else, can deposit the money into court on the accused's behalf, but no fee may be charged for doing so.

BAILMENT

When you lend your lawn mower to your neighbor, have your car parked by a lot attendant, or take your VCR to the shop for repair, you create a type of contract known as a bailment. In each of these and many other situations, property, and the responsibility for it, passes from the hands of one person (the bailor) to another (the bailee). Every consumer who makes such a transaction should know when a bailment is created and the responsibilities of the parties concerned.

The concept of bailment does not exist in Quebec, where the Civil Code provides for certain contracts instead. For example, there is the contract of loan, contract of loan for use, simple deposit, necessary deposit, and pledge and pawning. Each contract has its own rules on its formation, what elements it contains, and the liabilities of those involved.

In a pledge, a debtor may grant his creditor the right to keep certain things as security for his loan. A pledge of movables (accounts receivable, or stocks and bonds) is often used in commercial matters. Pledging movables, such as jewelry, is known as pawning.

Provincially licensed pawnshops deal with this type of contract. When an immovable (a building) is pledged, the pledge is known as a hypothec, and the contract is similar to what is known as a mortgage in the rest of Canada.

HOW BAILMENT IS CREATED

Three steps are required for a bailment to exist. First, the property must be delivered to the bailee, who then has charge of it. This happens, for example, when you let your neighbor borrow your lawn mower.

Sometimes the property itself may not actually be delivered to the bailee, but the bailee may obtain possession and control of it. This is called constructive delivery, and occurs, for example, when a bank gives a customer the key to a safe-deposit box. Although the box remains with the bank, the customer has control because he has the key.

Second, the bailee must know that the property is being delivered and agree to receive it. If you deliver your VCR to the repair shop without informing a clerk that you are doing so, the shop will not be responsible if someone steals it.

Third, because bailment is a type of contract, there must be some "consideration"— something of value given or relinquished by one person to induce the other to agree to the contract. The bailor's temporary loss of possession of his property in exchange for the bailee's promise to return it later is all the consideration required for a bailment.

THREE KINDS OF BAILMENT

Depending on the type of bailment, the person to whom you entrust your property has varying degrees of responsibility. Three kinds of bailment can be created.

◇ When you deliver your VCR to the repair shop and the owner agrees to repair it for a price, you have created a bailment for mutual benefit. Your benefit is getting the machine fixed; the shop owner benefits by getting paid. In this type of bailment, the bailee must exercise ordinary care while the property is in his possession. If he leaves the VCR on the edge of the table and accidentally knocks it off, he is responsible for damage to the VCR. But if an armed robber steals the machine at gunpoint, the shop owner is not responsible.

◇ When you leave your wristwatch in the safe provided by your athletic club (provided no fee is charged for this service), you create a bailment for the sole benefit of the bailor—you. The club is not responsible for loss or damage to your watch unless its employees are grossly negligent. If the safe alarm fails suddenly and someone walks in and takes your watch, the club is not responsible for your loss. But if the safe keeper simply leaves the door open and goes out for coffee, the club is responsible for the loss.

◇ Lending your lawn mower to your neighbor creates a bailment for the sole benefit of the bailee. You gain nothing by relinquishing your property to her. In this situation your neighbor must be very careful not to lose or damage the lawn mower. If she runs your mower over a metal sprinkler head and destroys the mower blade, she is responsible for repairing it.

Sometimes the type of bailment and the liability that goes with it are not clear-cut. For example, if you leave your car in a parking lot but take the keys with you, the contract may be one of license and not bailment. In that case the parking lot could argue that it was not liable for subsequent loss or damage to your car, since it contracted only to rent you a parking space.

Cases involving property lost or damaged in parking lots, marinas, and in coat checks depend upon the particular circumstances. Was a fee charged for the service or given as a courtesy? Were signs posted stating the owner was not responsible for loss? Did the owner take adequate precautions to safeguard the property? Did he or she maintain the high standard of care normally required in cases of bailment?

However, the courts have held parking lots responsible for damages caused to parked cars, even when there were signs stating that the parking lot owner was not responsible for any loss or damage.

BAIT AND SWITCH

The ad in Wednesday's newspaper sounds tempting. Steaks, roasts, and chops are all priced below your local supermarket's prices for ground beef. When you arrive at the store to take advantage of the bargain, the clerk seems less than eager to sell you the advertised special. "That meat's tough and fatty," she tells you. "Why not buy our Manager's Special? It costs more, but the quality is good."

When you find that the Manager's Special is twice what you had expected to pay, you tell the clerk you will take your chances with the advertised special. "Sorry," she says, "but the special is all sold out."

If this happens, you have been subjected to a technique known as bait and switch, in which an item (the bait) is advertised at a bargain price to lure you into the store. Once there, you are told that the advertised item is inferior or unavailable, and you are urged to buy the more expensive version (the switch).

When confronted with such sales tactics, your best step is out the door. You may also wish to file a complaint with your local department of consumer affairs, or with the director of Investigation and Research of Industry Canada's Bureau of Competition Policy. See USEFUL ADDRESSES at back of book.

The bait-and-switch technique is illegal in Canada and merchants who engage in it can be fined and required to make restitution to victimized consumers.

If, on the other hand, the store offers a rain check so that you can buy the same product at the same price at a later date, then they can be said *not* to be involved in bait-and-switch selling.

BALLOON LOAN

In a balloon loan, the final payment is significantly larger than each of the previous payments. If not properly understood, a balloon loan can cause trouble for the unwary buyer.

Balloon mortgages are often used when a seller finances the purchase of his home for the buyer. The buyer makes monthly payments of principal (the money borrowed) and interest as though the loan extended over a 15- or 30-year period. However, the principal becomes due as a lump sum much earlier—for instance, after three or five years—and at that time the buyer must pay off the balance (the balloon payment). Because the monthly payments usually consist primarily of interest, very little principal is repaid before the balloon payment becomes due. The buyer may therefore owe almost as much as he did originally. See also MORTGAGE.

BANK ACCOUNT

When you have a bank account, you have an agreement with the bank; you can deposit money with it and, in return, the bank will pay you interest or let you draw cheques against the money, or both.

General deposits

Most bank accounts—including chequing, savings, money market accounts, and certificates of deposit—consist of what are called general deposits. When you make a general deposit, you transfer ownership of your money to the bank, which can use it to make loans or investments or to help run the bank.

When you make a general deposit, you are essentially giving the bank a loan. It gives you a deposit slip as proof of the loan and creates a credit in your account against which you can withdraw funds. As your debtor, the bank is legally obliged to pay out money from your account according to your instructions.

Special deposits

Unlike general deposits, special deposits do not become the property of the bank. The bank merely holds the money and, upon the depositor's demand, returns the money to the depositor or pays it to someone else. The most common types of special deposits are money held in escrow (for example, a deposit on a home), items placed in a safe-deposit box, and money put in a trust fund.

Special deposits represent a kind of bailment—that is, you have delivered your personal property to the temporary custody of another person or organization. You retain ownership of the property and the bank must either return it to you or deliver it to someone else according to your instructions. See also BAILMENT; ESCROW; SAFE-DEPOSIT BOX; TRUST.

WHAT THE DIFFERENCE MEANS TO YOU

Knowing the differences between general and special deposits is important, because the way your money is deposited can affect you legally and financially. Since funds in a general deposit are under the control of the bank, for example, the bank must bear the responsibility for any loss. If the bank pays $500 to a thief who has stolen your passbook, it must replace your money.

But if a special deposit is lost, stolen, or destroyed, and the bank has exercised reasonable care over the money, it will not be held responsible for the loss. Suppose, for example, that a bank holds a trust account for Paul, with Paul's nephew Earl as the trustee. Earl withdraws $500 from the account, ostensibly to benefit Paul, but uses it to buy himself a suit. The bank is not responsible for the loss, and Paul must seek repayment from the trustee.

Banks almost always limit their liability for safety-deposit boxes, in the event that the contents of a box should be lost or stolen.

Loans

General and special deposits are treated differently with respect to loans. Suppose you take out a loan at the bank where you have your savings account, which is a general-deposit account. If you are unable to pay the full amount of the loan when it falls due, the bank is allowed to dip into your savings account to make up the difference. However, the bank is forbidden to take money from a special-deposit account.

Term and demand deposits

If you have a certificate of deposit, Christmas Club account, or vacation-fund account, you

CHECKLIST

Tips for Safe Banking

A simple trip to the bank can sometimes be more dangerous than you might think. Here are a few ways to protect yourself:

■ DO NOT ENDORSE CHEQUES YOU ARE TAKING TO THE BANK FOR DEPOSIT.
If you do, write "for deposit only" next to your signature. A cheque with only your signature on the back is a blank endorsement; anyone can cash the cheque if you happen to lose it. The inscription "for deposit only" or "pay only to" beside your name is called a restrictive endorsement. This should prevent a thief who steals your cheque from cashing it or passing it to another person.

■ WHEN YOU GET CASH FROM A TELLER, COUNT IT RIGHT AWAY.
Count your cash with your hands on top of the counter, so that they are in full view of the teller. Then, if you are shortchanged, it will be much simpler to prove.

■ DO NOT LEAVE THE BANK WITH CASH IN YOUR HAND.
Put it out of sight first, and be wary of anyone who is watching you, who jostles you, or who follows you. If you are robbed even while inside the bank, the bank is not responsible because the money was in your possession when it was taken.

■ FOLLOW YOUR BANK'S INSTRUCTIONS WHEN YOU PUT CASH IN A DEPOSIT BOX.
Your money could disappear if, for example, the envelope in which you place your deposit is not sealed properly, does not contain a deposit slip, or is put in the wrong slot.

■ BE CAUTIOUS WHEN YOU USE AN ATM.
Do not use an automatic teller machine (ATM) in a dark or isolated area, and be on the lookout for people loitering nearby. Also, when using an ATM, shield your personal identification number (PIN) from people standing behind you, and do not walk away until you have put away your money.

■ ASK FOR DIRECT DEPOSIT OF GOVERNMENT CHEQUES.
Direct deposit is the best way to ensure certain government cheques are not stolen. Canada and Quebec Pension Plan and Old Age Security cheques are among those that can be sent directly to your bank for deposit in your account. Check with your bank or the appropriate government agency for details.

Most general-deposit accounts are demand-deposit accounts: you can withdraw some or all of your money at any time. Chequing and savings accounts are demand-deposit accounts, but are subject to federal regulations regarding the availability of funds.

BANKING SERVICES

Because of the competition between the chartered banks, trust companies, credit unions, and the foreign banks that may now operate in Canada, today's consumers have a wide variety of banking options.

As well as filling their traditional roles—taking deposits, dealing with negotiable instruments such as bills of exchange and promissory notes, and lending money—banks have expanded into new areas. They often act as mortgage lenders, handle Registered Retirement Saving Plans (RRSPs) and other savings plans, and have even entered into security trading: today you can buy or sell shares at a bank or a bank subsidiary. That trail was blazed by the Toronto-Dominion Bank, the first Canadian bank to offer a discount brokerage service (1983). Its lead was quickly followed by other banks.

As well as administering a customer's mortgage portfolio, banks may also sell public transit tickets and government-sponsored lottery tickets. A bank subsidiary may also act as a factor in relation to accounts receivable, that is, it may lend money to a business and receive as security the company's accounts receivable, and/or its merchandise, or

have what is known as a term deposit. You lend your money to the bank for a specified length of time and you cannot withdraw money from the account before the time has gone by. The advantage of time de- ◆ posits is that the bank usually gives you a higher return. The disadvantage is that your money is tied up for the specified time and you have to pay substantial penalties if you ◆ withdraw it prematurely.

inventory. A bank subsidiary may also engage in financial leasing, for example buying a fleet of automobiles and leasing them to its customers.

One of the most common activities of banks is issuing and administering credit cards, usually Visa or Mastercard.

The Bank Act prohibits banks from managing trust funds for investment purposes. Such services are offered by trust and insurance companies. Banks do, however, set up trust accounts.

JOINT ACCOUNTS

Bank accounts can be set up for one person or more. The signature card of the account indicates who is entitled to withdraw the funds.

Unless the terms of the account state otherwise, each person listed on the signature card owns the funds and has access to the account. If one of the account holders dies, the funds belong to the surviving owner or owners. Heirs of the deceased owner will have no claim to the money unless they are owners of the account.

Sometimes joint accounts are set up for the convenience of one of the owners during his lifetime, and not to give the other person ownership. Suppose you want to name another person on your account so that she can make deposits and withdrawals for you, but you do not want the money to become her property in the event of your death. To make sure the bank understands your intentions, include careful instructions on the signature card when you open the account.

In most cases, the bank "freezes" the account as soon as it learns that one of the owners of a joint account has died. The surviving co-owner cannot withdraw any money until the rightful owner of the funds is ascertained by probate of the will and settlement of the estate.

YOUR BANK STATEMENT

Your bank is required to provide you with a periodic statement—a document that shows the status of your account. You should check the statement carefully and report any errors as soon as possible. If you do not, you may not be able to recover any money you lose owing to a bank error.

But if the bank makes a mistake in your favor and credits your account with $5,000, for example, you must report the error to the bank. If you withdraw the money you may have to face criminal charges. See also CHEQUE; ELECTRONIC FUND TRANSFERS.

STEPS TO TAKE

Here are some suggestions that might be useful to you if you have a problem with your bank account:

1. Talk to a bank officer or someone in the bank's customer service department. Most banks will make an effort to resolve your problem as quickly as possible.

2. If the problem cannot be resolved satisfactorily, write to the Canadian Bankers' Association or to the Office of the Superintendent of Financial Institutions Canada. See USEFUL ADDRESSES at back of book.

BANKRUPTCY

Federal bankruptcy laws provide a legal procedure by which a debtor obtains relief from the demands of his creditors. (The constitution gives Parliament the right to make bankruptcy laws to be administered by a provincial superior court.)

The most recent amendments to the Bankruptcy and Insolvency Act (1992) made bankruptcy, for individuals owing $75,000 or less, easier and cheaper. The legislation allows an honest but unfortunate debtor to be discharged of his liabilities on reasonable conditions, and provides for the equitable distribution of his assets among creditors.

Although bankruptcy was once a source of personal shame, changes in the law and a shift in public sentiment have made it more common and acceptable. Nevertheless, you should examine all your options. Make bankruptcy your last resort since it can remain in your credit history for up to seven years after discharge. As a result, you may find it hard to get credit.

There is a also a cost for filing a bankruptcy. In even the simplest case, where the individual has no assets, the bankrupt has to pay about $1,000 to the trustee. For even the simplest corporate case, the costs can easily be $10,000 to $15,000 or more. And although society has changed its attitude toward bankruptcy, business people are still sensitive about dealing with a former bankrupt.

ALTERNATIVES TO BANKRUPTCY

If your financial troubles are only temporary, get in touch with your creditors and try to renegotiate payments until such time as your financial situation improves. The creditor may be willing to accept a smaller total amount to settle the outstanding debt.

Under Part X of the Bankruptcy Act, a creditor may consolidate his debts, and pay a certain amount of his revenue into court. Only individual consumers may take advantage of this "orderly payment of debts" (OPD), which is not available to companies or commercial partnerships, nor in cases where the creditor is deceased.

Once your OPD proposal has been approved by the appropriate court official, no creditor is allowed to sue you or seize your property or salary, so long as you fulfill your obligations under the plan. (Quebec's voluntary deposit plan, known as the Lacombe Law, gives the debtor benefits similar to those of OPD.)

If you cannot work out an arrangement with your creditors, you may have no choice but to declare bankruptcy. If you owe less than $75,000, you are eligible for a consumer bankruptcy. Contact a trustee in bankruptcy to help you through the various steps. Because amendments to the legislation have simplified consumer bankruptcy procedures considerably, you will rarely need the services of a lawyer in such a situation.

BANKRUPTCY OPTIONS

The Bankruptcy and Insolvency Act provides a troubled debtor with two relief mechanisms, bankruptcy and proposal. Under a proposal, a debtor proposes a repayment plan to his creditors—perhaps a reduction of the amount owed, or a longer repayment period.

Part III of the act deals with proposal. The process is open to anyone with total debts, excluding the mortgage on a principal residence, of less than $75,000. Part II of the act also provides a consumer proposal for individuals, but not for corporations or partnerships, even those owing less than $75,000. Refusal of a proposal no longer means automatic bankruptcy, as was once the case.

WHAT YOU CAN KEEP

In bankruptcy, the debtor's property is divided among the creditors, who take their share according to law. Under provincial laws, certain properties are exempt—ones the debtor holds in trust for another, and some of his own properties, such as his work tools and items needed for survival.

In Alberta, for example, the debtor is allowed to keep:

◇ Furniture and household goods up to a value of $4,000.

◇ An automobile used for business up to a value of $8,000.

◇ Tools, books and instruments necessary to carry on a trade or profession up to a value of $7,500.

◇ Necessary clothing and fuel required by the debtor and his family.

◇ Things for religious worship.

◇ Family papers, portraits, medals, and other decorations.

◇ A certain amount of livestock and feed.

◇ Periodic disability pensions and Old Age pensions and supplements.

A bankrupt is entitled to his salary from his employer. Depending on his family responsibilities, the court may order that part of it be given to the trustee to pay his creditors.

DEBTS YOU CANNOT DISCHARGE

The only debts that are not affected by a bankruptcy are those owed to a former spouse for alimentary pension, child support, debts that were fraudulently incurred, and fines.

At one time, the Bankruptcy Act did not eliminate debts incurred for basic necessities such as food. This was to ensure that suppliers did not withhold these items for fear of nonpayment. Under 1992 amendments, however, debts for food, dental services, electricity, rent, and other such necessities can be wiped out. So, too, can money owing because of a court judgment against you, for example, for accidentally burning down someone's property. If you owe money for unpaid income tax or other taxes, these debts *can* be discharged. Even student loans can be discharged by bankruptcy if, after sincere attempts to pay them back, you are unable to do so.

The first step in declaring a bankruptcy is to contact a trustee in bankruptcy. You will find a list of trustees in the Yellow Pages. The bankruptcy trustee, usually a chartered accountant licensed by the federal government to administer a bankruptcy, acts for both the creditors and the person or company filing for bankruptcy.

In the case of an individual, the trustee will file a petition.

FILING FOR BANKRUPTCY

A bankruptcy begins when you file a petition for bankruptcy. On the form you must list what property you own, your income, your living expenses, debts, and exempt property.

Once the petition is filed, the trustee whose appointment is confirmed by the bankruptcy court assumes legal control of your nonexempt property. His principal job is to obtain as much of your property as possible to satisfy creditors' claims.

For example, he must challenge all unjustified claims, and claim back properties improperly disposed of before bankruptcy. This could occur through fraudulent settlements, fraudulent preferences, and reviewable transactions.

◇ *Fraudulent settlements.* These involve the disposal of property for the benefit of the beneficiary. Any settlement made within one year before bankruptcy is void against the trustee, who has power to take action for any irregularity. If the trustee can prove that at the time of settlement the debtor was insolvent, *or* the bankruptcy petitioner retained an interest in the property, the period is extended to five years before bankruptcy. So if John makes a gift to his friend Mary

---

CHECKLIST

Six Bad Reasons for Filing Bankruptcy

Bankruptcy has become an increasingly common way for Canadians to get out from under the burden of debt and the problems that come with it, but bankruptcy is not always the best solution for credit problems. Filing for bankruptcy may not be necessary or advisable under the following circumstances:

■ **IF YOU ARE THREATENED WITH GARNISHMENT OR A WAGE ASSIGNMENT.**
All provinces and territories have laws restricting how much salary can be claimed by a trustee in the case of bankruptcy. Usually there is an initial exemption of about $110 per week, and some 30 percent of what remains can be seized from your *gross* salary.

■ **IF YOUR DEBTS ARE PRIMARILY FOR FINES, ALIMENTARY PENSION, CHILD SUPPORT, OR DEBTS INCURRED BY FRAUD.**
Bankruptcy does not relieve you of these obligations.

■ **IF YOUR DEBTS ARE SECURED BY YOUR HOME OR OTHER PROPERTY.**
To eliminate a secured debt, such as a mortgage, through bankruptcy, you are usually required to allow your creditor to repossess the property and sell it. You may be better off trying to renegotiate your payment schedule with the creditor, or selling the property yourself and paying off the debt before the property is repossessed.

■ **IF YOU ARE BEING HARASSED BY COLLECTION AGENCIES.**
Most provinces have legislation prohibiting a creditor from calling you or your family once your lawyer gives instructions to communicate only with him concerning your debt. Some laws limit the hours, or number of times per week, that a creditor may call.

■ **IF YOU RECENTLY INCURRED A LOT OF DEBT.**
Anyone who carelessly incurs a lot of debt thinking a bankruptcy is an easy solution may be unpleasantly surprised. Bankruptcy judges are quite severe in imposing payments when the debts are incurred in an irresponsible manner.

■ **IF YOU RECENTLY TRANS-FERRED PROPERTY TO ANOTHER PERSON.**
If you put your house in your mother's name, for example, so that it would be beyond the reach of your creditors, you have committed a fraud, and the transfer of property could be annulled by the trustee.

---

in the year preceding his bankruptcy, the gift is void and Mary must return it to the trustee.

◇ *Fraudulent preferences* These occur when John, knowing that he will declare bankruptcy in three months' time, pays off his debts to his buddy Peter, by giving him his property. If Peter and John are related, the review period is extended to 12 months.

◇ *Reviewable transactions.* These cover all dealings of the previous year between the debtor and someone not at "arm's length," in other words a relative. If the price given for the property is very different from its fair market value, the buyer has to pay the trustee the difference. So if Barry sells his $30,000 BMW to his brother Paul for $1,000 in the year before bankruptcy, Paul must pay the trustee $29,000.

The court notifies all creditors named in the bankruptcy petition. From this time forward, all collection efforts, foreclosures on your home mortgage, and garnishments of wages are stopped by a procedure known as the automatic stay. A date is set for you to meet creditors, usually several weeks after the petition is filed. At this meeting, you are questioned about your debts, assets, and other facts relating to the bankruptcy.

Creditors who want to participate in the first meeting must provide the trustee with proof of their claim beforehand. At this meeting, creditors vote to accept the initial trustee, or to appoint a new one, and (in individual bankruptcies) they elect inspectors. The inspectors' job is to ensure that the trustee is acting in the creditors' interest.

Unless a bankruptcy is opposed, the first-time bankrupt's debts are automatically discharged nine months after he files for bankruptcy. In all other cases, the trustee prepares a report of the bankrupt's conduct and applies to the court for a discharge.

A bankrupt corporation cannot be discharged of its debts unless it pays creditors in full. In reality, it will never be discharged: instead, the corporation owner will reincorporate under a new name and start afresh.

CONSUMER BANKRUPTCY

This is available to debtors owing up to $75,000. Since it may be combined with the estate of a related person, a husband and wife may file a joint bankruptcy.

The bankruptcy covers all debts other than fines, alimentary pension, child support payments, and debts obtained through fraud. (Up to 1992, debts for food, medical and dental bills, and essential furniture were not wiped out by bankruptcy.)

In a consumer bankruptcy, inspectors are not usually appointed.

If there is no opposition to the discharge of debt, the first-time bankrupt is automatically discharged after nine months without having to go to court.

FILING A PROPOSAL

Individuals (but not corporations or partnerships) who owe $75,000 or less, *excluding* a mortgage on their principal residence, may seek either a consumer summary bankruptcy, or a consumer proposal. The procedures for filing a proposal are essentially the same as filing for bankruptcy (see the steps outlined on facing page).

With a proposal governed by Part III of the Bankruptcy Act, a trustee is appointed and a meeting of creditors is held

shortly after. In the case of a consumer proposal, as outlined in Part II of the Act, an administrator is appointed, but unless a creditor requests a meeting, none takes place. In either case, once a proposal is filed, creditors must halt any court proceedings until the proposal is refused, if such is the case.

A consumer proposal must be made to all creditors, designed so that all terms can be met within five years. For example, you might offer to pay them back 25 cents on the dollar within three years. Certain debts, such as expenses and fees relating to the proposal, its administration, and counseling the debtor must get priority.

The administrator must investigate the consumer debtor's property and financial affairs in order to assess the reasonableness and fairness of the proposal. If creditors reject the proposal, the proposer is not automatically bankrupt, as was the case at one time.

Once a proposal is filed, all unsecured creditors must stop court proceedings against their debtor. Secured creditors (people who hold something belonging to the debtor, for example a Canada Savings Bond, as security for his loan) may still deal with their security unless the court orders otherwise.

Preferred claims (funeral expenses, legal fees, three months' rent and other claims given priority in law) must be paid in full before payment is made to unsecured creditors. Under the latest amendments, most debts owed to the Crown (federal or provincial) are no longer preferred claims, and are paid in the same manner as debts owing to other unsecured creditors.

No creditors' meeting is required for a Part 11 consumer summary bankruptcy, unless a creditor rejects the proposal, or creditors owed at least 25 percent of the debt request a meeting. Any meeting called must be held within 21 days. If no meeting is called, the proposal is deemed accepted. If there is a meeting, acceptance depends on approval by a majority of creditors in value.

If neither the Official Receiver nor a creditor requests a court review within 30 days, the proposal will not be subject to court review.

The court can annul the proposal if it is later shown that its approval was obtained by fraud or that the proposal's terms would result in continuing injustice. A debtor whose proposal is annulled may not make another proposal.

SPOUSES AND COSIGNERS

If you are married, it is usually best to file a joint bankruptcy petition. Otherwise, the spouse who does not file will be completely responsible for any joint debts. Similarly, a person who has cosigned (guaranteed) a loan for you can be held responsible for repaying the loan if you file for bankruptcy. Before you file, you should consider how your bankruptcy will affect any relatives or friends who may end up paying the debt that you are having discharged. See also COSIGNING.

SOME RECENT CHANGES IN THE LAW

1. A supplier has 30 days from delivery to demand repossession of his unpaid goods, and 10 days from the time his right to the goods has been acknowledged by the trustee to reclaim these goods. This does not apply if the goods were sold to a purchaser who paid for them in good faith.

2. Creditors who are farmers and fishermen have a special priority in respect of unpaid amounts of inventory supplied within 15 days of the debtor declaring bankruptcy.

3. Employees who are owed salary have a priority claim against the bankrupt for $2,000 in wages or commission and $1,000 for expenses incurred within six months of their employer filing for bankruptcy. (Formerly the figures were $500 in wages and $300 for expenses.) A House of Commons committee continues to study the possibility of a government fund to pay unpaid employees up to $2,000.

STEPS TO TAKE TO AVOID BANKRUPTCY

Although the bankruptcy laws are designed to give an overextended debtor a fresh start, it is better to avoid the problems of bankruptcy altogether. These are some ways to help keep your debts under control:

1. Make a realistic budget. Be sure to include a fund for emergency expenses, such as sickness, home repairs, or unemployment, so that you will not have to rely on expensive credit to meet them.

2. Keep your mortgage or rent payments at no more than one-third of your monthly gross income.

3. Keep your monthly payments on personal debt at no more than 20 percent of your take-home pay.

4. When you do need credit, shop for the best terms and interest rates available. Interest rates on bank credit cards can vary by as much as 8 percent, depending on the issuer.

5. If you have a savings account at a bank or with a credit union, you may be able to obtain a better interest rate by financing purchases through those institutions.

BAR ASSOCIATION

A bar association is a provincial or national organization of lawyers. The word *bar* comes from the traditional wooden railing that separates the general public from those concerned with the trial.

A bar association usually makes rules that govern the professional conduct of its members and the procedures for disciplining for misconduct. Such rules are generally enforced by the bar's administrative board. If you have dealings with a lawyer who you think is behaving unethically, you should report the problem to the local bar association. Penalties for misconduct may include fines, conditions regarding future conduct, and even disbarment. Since only bar members may practice law, a disbarred lawyer cannot practice his profession. Disbarment is subject to review by the bar association and can be appealed to the courts.

The Canadian Bar Association, as well as all provincial bar associations (also known as legal societies), has published rules of conduct and ethics to govern the profession.

BARGAIN AND SALE DEED

In real estate, deeds of various kinds are used to transfer title, or ownership, from one person to another. One of these, a bargain and sale deed, does not contain any explicit guarantees that the property is free and clear of liens or mortgages. Even so, courts have held that the seller is responsible for any actions that he has knowingly taken to cause title problems (such as allowing a lien to be placed on the property). So if you are buying property, protect yourself against such actions by making sure there is a clause (called a covenant against the grantor's acts) in the deed that holds the seller responsible for them. To protect yourself further, have a title search conducted on the property before you buy.

Bargain and sale deeds as a method of transferring property have generally become obsolete in Canada. However, such deeds are common in some U.S. states, Florida being one. Canadians buying property there through a bargain and sale deed should protect themselves with title insurance. See also REAL ESTATE.

BATTERED WOMEN

Violence in the home is one of the most serious problems our society faces. Newspapers regularly carry stories about women being gravely injured and often killed by present and former spouses and boyfriends. In cases of interspousal violence, some 80 percent of the victims are women; 53 percent of all women killed in 1991 were slain in their own homes.

For a long time, court and law enforcement officials downplayed domestic violence often considering it a "private affair." In the last decade, however, the public's attitude has changed considerably, and this has been reflected in the policies of police departments across Canada. Spousal violence is no longer seen as normal or acceptable.

It has even been suggested that domestic violence may be passed on from one generation to the next. Children who see violence in the home may imagine it portrays normal behavior; when they get older they may imitate their parents either by being violent toward their own wives and girlfriends or, in the case of girls, tolerating abuse.

When a woman has been repeatedly abused, physically and psychologically, by her spouse or lover, she may develop the "battered wife syndrome." This relatively new concept entered Canadian case law in 1990, when the Supreme Court of Canada set aside a judgment of the Manitoba Court of Appeal and acquitted a woman who killed her common-law spouse. The court judgment was based on the woman's subjective state of mind.

The accused had pleaded self-defense. Her lawyer argued that a woman who is repeatedly beaten by her spouse or another man with whom she is living may come to fear that her life is in danger. The apprehension is real for such victims, even if "ordinary reasonable men" would feel no such fear in the circumstances.

The Supreme Court found that it may strain one's credibility to imagine what the "ordinary man" might do in such circumstances, since men rarely find themselves in the position of a battered woman. So rather than the standard of the "reasonable man," the court employed that of the woman who was the victim of violence, and considered how she could reasonably be expected to act given a particular set of circumstances.

DOMESTIC VIOLENCE: AN OFFENSE

Every victim of spousal abuse is the victim of a crime, just as if she had been assaulted by a stranger. Any woman who is subjected to physical abuse, whether from her spouse or from anyone else, has the right to call the police and demand the arrest and prosecution of the offender.

MANDATORY ARREST

To address the problems of reluctant victims and escalating violence, some communities have instituted policies that require the arrest of the offender in any domestic assault. By transferring the responsibility of pressing charges from the victim to the state, these laws relieve victims from any pressure they may feel to drop charges against their attackers.

If officers are called to the scene of domestic violence, they must arrest the offender. After charges are filed, the prosecutor may proceed with the case even if the victim does not want to do so. More and more prosecutors are reluctant to drop charges under such circumstances. A victim who refuses to cooperate in the criminal prosecution of her violent mate may be subpoenaed to testify and may even be held in contempt of court.

Once an arrest is made, the victim has the right to be kept informed about developments in the case, such as court hearings and the prosecutor's plans to plea-bargain or drop the charges for lack of evidence. See Plea Bargaining.

ORDERS OF PROTECTION

Anti-stalking legislation, in effect since August 1993, makes it a crime for anyone to persistently follow or watch another person, even if no threats are made.

The Criminal Code prohibits intimidation through persistent following or threats against a person or that person's relatives. The offense is punishable by a $2,000 fine and up to six months in jail. But intention, a crucial element of this crime, is difficult to prove. For example,

it is difficult to prove that the person persistently following another is doing so in order to compel that person to abstain from doing something she is entitled to do, or to force her to do something she does not want to do. (The 1993 anti-stalking law was enacted to offset this shortcoming.)

If you have reasonable and probable grounds to fear that someone will injure you or damage your property, you can ask the court to issue a "surety to keep the peace" against the offending party. In issuing such a restraining order, the judge who hears the complaint can order the accused to keep the peace for up to a year or risk imprisonment.

Filing criminal charges against your attacker, even if it is your spouse, does not prevent you from also suing for damages before the civil courts.

In most cases the court gives the victim temporary possession of the family residence and requires the offender to stay away from her home, place of business, or anywhere else she may be. See Contempt of Court.

SHELTERS

Many battered women feel that a restraining order will not prevent the abuser from returning to harm them further, and sometimes their concerns are justified. For women who have nowhere else to turn, a nationwide network of shelters and safe houses exists, the locations of which are kept secret. The phone numbers of these shelters can be obtained from the police, courts, and workers

at victim-advocacy programs.

The shelters provide temporary housing and counseling for women and children fleeing abusive homes. They may also offer emotional support to victims, put them in touch with lawyers who specialize in these types of cases, and arrange for staff members to appear with them in court to give emotional support during the criminal prosecution.

STEPS TO TAKE IF YOUR SPOUSE OR COMPANION BEATS YOU

1. Call the police and give details of the incident.

2. Get medical help if you need it. Tell the doctor truthfully what happened. She will understand that you are not to blame for the abuse: your partner is.

3. Save all evidence of the abuse, such as torn clothing. Take photos of injuries and damaged property if you can.

4. Move out with your children. If you do not have a place to go, call the police for the name of a battered women's shelter near you.

5. Take all important documents with you. You should have your driver's license; social insurance card; birth certificates and Medicare cards for you and your children; school records; utility bills (for establishing identity); credit cards; passports; and any documents that will take time to duplicate. If you cannot leave your abuser right away, store the documents and some money in a safe place where you can get them quickly once you do decide to leave.

6. Get in touch with a lawyer and find out more about your legal recourses. Can you get a divorce or a separation, or sue your abuser for damages?

7. All provinces and territories have crime victim compensation boards which have funds available for victims who suffered injuries because of a crime. You may be compensated for loss of earnings, disfigurement, pain and suffering, dental expenses, and sometimes even for property damage. Contact your provincial criminal injuries fund, or ask your local police department or crown attorney's office for more informations. See also VICTIM'S RIGHTS.

BETTER BUSINESS BUREAU

The Council of Better Business Bureaus is a voluntary association of business people that provides various free or low-cost services to consumers. Better Business Bureau (BBB) offices are to be found in virtually every Canadian city. Services include the following.

◇ *Reliability reports*. The BBB maintains records on thousands of companies across the country, on the basis of which the firms are rated "satisfactory" or "unsatisfactory."

◆ A satisfactory rating means either that a firm has responded to all complaints by the bureau or else that no complaints have been recorded against it. An unsatisfactory rating may mean the company fails to answer complaints, uses questionable business practices, or refuses to stop deceptive advertising.

◇ *Consumer complaint services*. Written complaints about businesses are forwarded to companies by the bureau, which asks for a written response from a company official.

◇ *Arbitration*. Consumers and companies may be able to have the bureau arbitrate certain disputes. The arbitrations are conducted by specially trained volunteers. No lawyers are required. See ARBITRATION.

◇ *Autoline*. This service handles consumers' disputes with auto manufacturers through mediation.

Although the bureau has no legal authority, it reports any illegal activities it finds to law enforcement officials. It provides referrals to other organizations and agencies that deal with matters the BBB does not handle. See also CONSUMER PROTECTION.

BEYOND A REASONABLE DOUBT

The standard of proof required to convict someone of a crime is very high. You need proof beyond a reasonable doubt; that amounts to almost absolute certainty.

◆ Because punishment is much more severe for crimes than for civil wrongdoings (such as breach of contract or civil fraud), the law requires that there be no "reasonable doubt" that the accused is guilty of committing the offense. The facts in the case must be such that any other explanation for the crime is extremely unlikely.

See also BURDEN OF PROOF; EVIDENCE.

BIGAMY

You commit bigamy if you go through a form of marriage with one person while still married to another. Even if you stopped living with your first spouse years ago, you cannot enter a marriage with another unless the first marriage is legally dissolved.

This applies even if you marry outside the country. A married Canadian resident who leaves Canada to get married to another person in a country where polygamy or polyandry are allowed, for example, would be guilty of bigamy in Canada.

When you enter into a marriage, it remains valid until the death of your spouse or until the marriage has been dissolved by divorce or legal annulment. You cannot marry someone else unless your first marriage has ended for one of these reasons.

If you marry someone who you know is already married, you too might be charged with bigamy. The punishment can be up to five years in prison.

IF YOU THOUGHT YOU WERE DIVORCED OR WIDOWED

In early cases, the courts found a person guilty of bigamy, even if that person thought that he was divorced before remarrying. More recently the courts have accepted a person's honest belief that he is divorced as a defense against bigamy, and have acquitted people if they had reasonable grounds to believe that they were divorced or that the first marriage was annulled.

Finding out that your spouse has remarried is grounds for divorce. However, if you are married to someone who did not previously get divorced from his or her first spouse, then the second "marriage"— yours— would not be valid.

If your spouse has disappeared and has not been in touch with you or other family members for a long while, you may have good reason to think that she is dead. If you really believe that your spouse is dead when you enter into another marriage, you have a valid defense against bigamy charges. See also DEATH.

IF YOUR RELIGION PERMITS BIGAMY

Some religions have traditionally allowed marriages to more than one partner. If you follow such a religion however, Canadian law would recognize as valid only your marriage to your first spouse. The courts have held that right to freedom of religion is not absolute, and religious practices are still regulated by the Criminal Code.

BILL OF LADING

A bill of lading is the contract used when goods are transported from one location to another. Moving companies and railways, as well as other shipping companies, write a bill of lading as proof of their agreement with the owner of the property. The bill of lading also serves as a receipt, listing the goods or personal property that are being shipped.

BILL OF SALE

A bill of sale is a document that transfers ownership of a piece of personal property from one person to another in exchange for money. Suppose that your neighbor wants to buy your lawn mower. Once you agree on a price, you should prepare a bill of sale identifying the buyer, the seller, the date of sale, and the lawn mower, and stating the price. After you receive full payment, you turn the mower over to your neighbor, along with the bill of sale, which is his proof of ownership.

If a bill of sale is prepared properly, it can prevent the buyer from claiming that the seller misrepresented the item he purchased. If you state on the bill of sale that the mower is being sold "as is," you have proof that you made no special claims regarding its condition.

Not everything you sell requires a bill of sale, but you should write one up for valu-

able items, such as video and audio equipment, antiques, automobiles, and jewelry. Rules for selling guns and automobiles are regulated by either federal or provincial laws on registration.

A sample bill of sale is provided in the EVERYDAY LEGAL FORMS section of this book.

BINDER

A binder, also known as an interim agreement, is a written agreement used in some kinds of transactions until a final contract is prepared. An insurance binder provides temporary protection until a formal policy is issued. For example, when Anne applies for a homeowners' policy, the insurance agent covers her with a binder while the company reviews her application to determine the value of the house, its susceptibility to fire, and other risks the insurance will cover. If Anne's home is damaged while the binder is in effect, the insurance company must pay any legitimate claims she makes, even if her insurance application is ultimately rejected. See also HOMEOWNERS' INSURANCE; INSURANCE.

REAL ESTATE

In real estate a binder or an interim agreement with earnest between the buyer and the seller of property indicates the buyer has paid a sum of money, called an earnest money deposit, in return for the right to purchase the property. The binder serves as a preliminary agreement until the fully

65

detailed formal sales contract is completed.

Suppose Ralph wants to buy a house in a new development and makes an offer that is accepted. Ralph and the owner sign a simple paper identifying them as buyer and seller, describing the property and stating its price, and specifying the amount (usually from $100 to $1,000) that Ralph is paying as proof of his serious intention. Ralph gives the money to the owner, who then takes the property off the market.

A binder is not a purchase agreement (a legal obligation to buy the house), nor is it a down payment (a percentage of the price of the property payable at the closing). Depending on the conditions of the binder or interim agreement, Ralph can choose not to buy the house after he has paid the earnest fee, but in most cases his money will not be returned.

If the seller refuses to sell his property he must refund Ralph's earnest deposit plus an equal compensatory amount for backing out of the sale.

For a sample binder, see the EVERYDAY LEGAL FORMS section. See also HOME BUYING AND SELLING.

BIRTH CERTIFICATE

A birth certificate is an official record of a person's birth. It contains particulars of the time, date, and place of birth, and the parents' names and occupations. (The short form of the certificate simply shows the person's name, and the date and place of birth.) The information is recorded in whichever province that the child is born.

There is no legal requirement that a child be given his father's last name, and the choice of another last name, such as the mother's maiden name, does not affect the father's rights or duties.

It is important to have a copy of your child's birth certificate. You may be asked to present it when he first enters school, and he will need it when he applies for a driver's license, a passport, a social insurance number, and any type of government assistance.

ADOPTION

When an adoption is granted by a court, copies of the adoption decree are forwarded to the bureau of vital statistics in the province where the adopted child was born. The bureau then prepares a new birth cer-

REAL LIFE, REAL LAW

The Case of the Hesitant Home Buyer

Just days after Irene and Jerry Conway put their house on the market, Joe and Dora made an offer to purchase. The offer was conditional on two things: getting financing within 12 days and selling their own house. So eager were Joe and Dora to buy that they told the Conways they would waive their conditions if higher offers came in.

In fact, the Conways did receive a higher offer and informed Joe and Dora who, as promised, agreed to drop their conditions. Thinking that the sale was a sure thing, Irene bought a condominium and packed all the furniture and belongings in preparation for the move.

On the 11th day after the offer, Dora told the Conways that she was unable to obtain financing and could therefore not buy the house. Irene suffered a nervous collapse at the news and was unable to go to work. She remained at home among her packed boxes and disconnected appliances. News that the condominium owners were suing her and Jerry to complete the sale did not improve her condition. So Jerry, who had counted on the proceeds of the house sale to pay business debts, had to remortgage the house to pay for the condo.

The Conways sued Joe and Dora for breach of contract, and the court awarded $5,000 to Irene for mental distress, $1,000 to Jerry for trouble and inconvenience. Mental distress, said the court, was as much a result of the breach of contract as mental distress resulting from a wrongful dismissal or the sufferings of a vacationer on a holiday that fell far short of the travel agent's promises.

tificate with the adoptee's new name, the names of the adoptive parents, their occupations, and the date when the adoptee was born. Information about the adoptee's natural parents becomes confidential and does not appear on the new birth certificate.

ILLEGITIMACY

When a child is born out of wedlock, the mother often gives the child her last name. If later the father acknowledges the child as his, or if the parents marry, the name on the birth certificate can usually be changed.

All provinces have procedures whereby illegitimate children may, in certain circumstances, be legitimized. Children born during a marriage that was later annulled retain the status of legitimate children. British Columbia, Manitoba, New Brunswick, Ontario, Prince Edward Island, Quebec, Yukon and the Northwest Territories make no distinction between children born inside or outside marriage. In Alberta, Nova Scotia, and Newfoundland, however, the word "child" in statutes or in wills means a legitimate child.

In most provinces, a child born to a married couple is presumed to be their legitimate child. However, there is no presumption of legitimacy in British Columbia, where biological parenthood is the only type recognized by provincial law. As a result, it is easier for a biological father in that province to prove his paternity, even if the child's mother is married to another man, than it is elsewhere in Canada.

The rights of illegitimate children to inherit property where there is no will vary from province to province. All children, legitimate or not, can inherit from their parents. However, problems can arise in inheriting from other family members, such as grandparents, uncles, and aunts. Inheritance problems may also arise when the person who dies lives in a country where the rights of illegitimate children are not recognized. For example, suppose grandfather Sam, who lives in Austria, wills one half of his estate to his grandchildren. But his Canadian grandson Mark, who was born outside of marriage, may be deprived of inheritance, since Austria may not consider him to be Sam's grandchild.

NAME CHANGES

If, as an adult, you decide to change your name, you can do so in a court proceeding and have your birth certificate amended to reflect your new legal name. See NAME CHANGE.

HOW TO OBTAIN YOUR BIRTH CERTIFICATE

To request a copy of your birth certificate, call the bureau of vital statistics or the keeper of the register of births in your birth province. Be ready to provide the following information:
   ◇ Your name as it appears on the birth certificate.
   ◇ Your date of birth.
   ◇ Your place of birth.
   ◇ Your mother's maiden name.
   ◇ Your father's name.

In most provinces you have to make your request in writing and pay a fee. The bureau of vital statistics will tell you what the charges are and where to write for your copy.

BIRTH CONTROL

For generations of Canadian couples, abstinence from sex and the rhythm method (limiting sex to the woman's least fertile period) were the only family-planning methods used. Until relatively recent times, birth control devices were not sold for that specific purpose, but rather for reasons of health.

Today the use of birth control and contraceptives is widespread, but several related issues continue to spark controversy and litigation.

MINORS

Medical personnel usually will not treat minors or give them medical advice without parental consent, except in emergencies. But cases vary depending on the minor's age. For example, a doctor may be more hesitant in treating a 12-year-old without advising his or her parents than someone who is 17 years of age. However, some provinces have laws that allow minors to obtain birth control counseling and even prescriptions without parental consent. Some provinces also permit minors to obtain medical treatment for sexually transmitted diseases without their parents' consent or knowledge. "Consider first the well-being of the patient" is one of seven principles of ethical behavior for physicians set out in the code of ethics of the Canadian Medical Association. "Protect the patient's secrets" is another.

Physicians who treat children are expected to discuss their findings with the parents. Ordinarily this is possible without infringing the medical code. But inevitably children mature to the point where their confidences merit the same respect as those of adult patients.

Sometimes parents and physician disagree on where the child's request for confidentiality overrides the parents' right to receive information or approve a medical procedure. In one such case, a British Columbia couple took their daughter's doctor to court. Even though the 15-year-old had been fitted with a contraceptive device without parental consent, the court held that the doctor, concerned for his patient's well-being, had merely carried out a normal medical procedure.

Should a doctor refuse certain contraceptive devices to a minor, the minor can ask the youth court's permission for the procedure without the knowledge of her parents. Similarly, she may ask permission to have an abortion.

CONTRACEPTIVE FAILURES

Contraceptives do not provide 100 percent protection against pregnancy or disease. The statistical chances for the failure of a particular type of contraceptive are available from the doctor who prescribes it or the pharmaceutical company that makes it. If a woman becomes pregnant as a result of the failure of a contraceptive device or medicine, she has no cause for suing her doctor or the pharmaceutical company.

Some 20,000 female sterilizations are performed each year in Canada. Failure rates for the procedure are very low—about 0.05 pregnancies per 100 women years of use, that is, the number of pregnancies among 100 women using the method for one year. When a New Brunswick woman gave birth to a child three years after undergoing a tubal ligation, she sued her doctor. But the court held he had not guaranteed a 100 percent success rate, agreeing only to "faithfully exercise his skill, knowledge, and judgment" in carrying out the operation; all of this he had done.

Vasectomy, a surgical procedure that sterilizes a man, has a near-zero failure rate. However, sometimes the operation is performed incorrectly, and the man makes a woman pregnant. In such a case the couple can file a lawsuit for negligence. Generally, they can recover only the expenses of prenatal care and cost of items such as baby clothes and crib.

The courts rarely view the birth of a child as a "fault" that would give rise to an action for damages. This is true even when the child results because a contraceptive technique fails. The birth of a new child is considered to be in the public interest.

See WRONGFUL LIFE.

SIDE EFFECTS

The side effects of contraception have become a major area of litigation. One of the most famous cases involved the Dalkon Shield, an intrauterine birth control device (IUD). By 1991 nearly 100,000 claims had been filed against the A.H. Robins Company by women injured by the device. The injuries were due to a design flaw that caused infections resulting in pelvic inflammation, sterility, and sometimes death. Because of the large number of claims, the manufacturer filed for bankruptcy, and claims against the company are being settled through a trust fund established for that purpose.

Medical researchers are currently investigating possible links between vasectomies and prostate cancer but no cases linked to this have come before the courts. (Two 1993 Harvard University studies found that men who have vasectomies are more likely to develop prostate cancer than those who do not have this surgery.)

MANDATORY BIRTH CONTROL

Unlike Canada, birth control can be ordered in the United States for persons who are unable to care for themselves and have been declared legally incompetent. As well, contraceptives have featured in sentencing in some U.S. courts. For example, a California woman found guilty of child abuse was sentenced to a year in jail and three years of probation. Upon her release from prison, she was ordered to use

Norplant, a long-acting contraceptive that is implanted under the skin and is effective for up to five years.

Because Canada's Charter of Rights and Freedoms (see pages 88 to 92) grants every citizen and resident the right to life, liberty and security of the person, declares every individual equal before the law, and prohibits discrimination because of mental or physical disability, mandatory birth control would be unconstitutional.

Compulsory sterilization of those convicted of sexual crimes or suffering severe mental impairment would also be considered an infringement of individual rights and, as such, illegal. Even so, it is still not a settled area of law if a mentally impaired person, who is unable to express his or her consent, must submit to mandatory birth control authorized by a guardian or curator.

BLACKLISTING

Dan Watson, an employee at the Big Brass Button factory, is fired after reporting a safety violation to the Occupational Health and Safety Commission (OHSC). He sues his company for a handsome sum and wins. The company's executives then place Dan's name on a list of former employees who have caused problems. Five years later, when Dan applies for work with a manufacturer in the same town, he is turned down.

Dan is the victim of blacklisting, the practice of making a list of certain people who are to be denied some opportunity, usually employment. Blacklisting is most commonly done by employers to prevent former employees from obtaining jobs elsewhere. Sometimes employers exchange blacklists or buy them from companies who compile lists of undesirable workers, such as employees who have filed for workers' compensation.

Although blacklisting is an illegal practice, these laws can be hard to enforce. The former employee may be required to show that the employer's actions were willful or malicious or that the employer misrepresented the truth.

Saying unfavorable things about a former employee when questioned by the man's prospective employer is not an offense, provided of course such information is true. In cases where the employer/ employee relationship was difficult, however, it would be best for the employer to give—and the employee to ask for—a simple attestation. This would simply state the length of service, a list of duties, and a statement of salary and benefits. See also REFERENCE, EMPLOYEE; WHISTLE-BLOWER.

LABOR UNIONS

Labor unions have also practiced blacklisting, circulating lists of employees who refused to join the union or of members who did not take part in a strike or refused to follow union rules. They have also blacklisted subcontractors with whom they have had a dispute, passing the list to the general contractors who employ them.

LEGAL BLACKLISTING

Not all backlisting is illegal. For example, each month the Consumer Affairs Branch of Industry Canada publishes several editions of a "Misleading Advertising Bulletin." Available to the public, these bulletins list companies that have been found guilty of false advertising and other fraudulent marketing practices forbidden by the Competition Act. The bulletin describes the offense and the penalties levied.

BLACKMAIL

The crime of illegally exacting money from someone by using a threat is called blackmail. The blackmailer typically threatens to destroy property, cause injury, or reveal a damaging secret unless money or something else of value is given to him. See EXTORTION.

BLOOD TESTING

Blood testing is required in a variety of legal circumstances. You may have to take a blood test before you get married or if you are a man involved in a paternity suit. Blood tests are used more and more often to screen people for HIV. In addition, if you happen to be stopped for drunk driving in situations involving death or bodily injury, you may be required to take a blood-alcohol test.

Before issuing a marriage license, Prince Edward Island

requires a couple to take a blood test to determine whether either is infected with a communicable disease, such as syphilis. If the test is positive, the license is withheld. Such tests may also be required in Manitoba, Northwest Territories, and Yukon.

PATERNITY SUITS MAY CALL FOR TEST

In a lawsuit for child support, a man may claim he is not responsible for the child's support since he is not his father. To establish paternity, courts in provinces such as Ontario, New Brunswick, and British Columbia may require him, as well as the child, to take a blood test. However, in a paternity suit, the Quebec Court of Appeal upheld a man's right to refuse a blood test, since it would infringe his right to security of the person, guaranteed by the province's human rights charter.

Until recently, the only blood test available for helping to prove paternity could determine merely that a man was *not* a particular child's father. The test used, the ABO test, was based on the fact that children inherit their blood types from their parents. If Mary and John both have type A blood, their children will never have type B blood. Therefore, if Mary has a child with type B blood, John (and the courts) can be sure that it is not his. However, this does not mean that Jack, who also has type B blood, and who has been living with Mary and John, is the father. Any man with type B blood could be the father.

The newer, human leukocyte antigen (HLA) test is more telling than the ABO test. The test is based on the fact that these antigens, which are present in every person's blood cells, are inherited and unique to that person (except for identical twins). Some experts believe that the test is more than 95 percent accurate.

Another development involves deoxyribonucleic acid (DNA) typing. All living organisms contain DNA, and the DNA molecule which carries the coded messages of heredity is different from one organism to another. Some experts claim the Restriction Fragment Length Polymorphism (RFLP) process used to examine DNA molecules is so accurate that the chance of a random duplication of a molecule is 1 in 70 billion.

In Canada, DNA testing was first admitted as evidence in 1986 and was used in a New Brunswick court that convicted Allan Legere of murdering four people. It has since been used in a number of paternity and immigration cases and in the trial of Toronto janitor John Carlos Terciera for the murder of a six-year-old girl.

AIDS TESTING

Because of the increasing incidence of AIDS, insurance companies now ask applicants for health or life insurance policies if they have the human immunodeficiency virus (HIV). Policies are not issued to those who have the virus.

See also AIDS.

BLOOD-ALCOHOL TESTING

A police officer who suspects you of driving under the influence of alcohol may ask you to take a blood-alcohol test, which measures the amount of alcohol present in your blood. A breath test or a blood test may be used although you have to take only one of the two. See also BREATH TEST; DRUNK DRIVING.

Most impaired driving convictions are based on excessive blood-alcohol levels (over 0.08, or more than 80 milligrams of alcohol per 100 millilitres of blood). In most cases the readings are taken by police, who measure a sample of the driver's breath. According to the Criminal Code, a blood-alcohol level of 0.08 is enough to be considered legally intoxicated. Since the apparatus for measuring the alcohol content from a person's breath is not always 100 percent accurate, a person who has a blood-alcohol level of 0.09 or even 0.10 may sometimes be acquitted of drunk driving.

In certain circumstances, the driver may have to submit to a blood test, and these results are more difficult to challenge in court. Such a test might be required of the drivers in a motor vehicle accident causing bodily harm or death. The blood sample must be taken by a qualified medical practitioner and the act must not endanger the driver's life or health. The driver must be informed of these details. According to a 1992 ruling by the Supreme Court of Canada, a driver not given this information cannot be charged with refusing a blood test.

A blood sample must be taken within two hours of being stopped by the police if the justice authorizing the blood sample and the medical practitioner believe the person's mental and physical condition makes him incapable of consenting to a blood sample or unable to provide a breath sample.

The laws concerning impaired driving and the right to counsel are among the most complex criminal laws in Canada. They have given rise to hundreds of decisions concerning "care and control" of a vehicle, the validity of random police checks, being detained by police, and the right to counsel. For more on this subject see DRUNK DRIVING.

In recent cases, the Supreme Court declared that random stops were valid, and that one must be advised of the right to a lawyer before undergoing a Breathalyzer test. However, the police need not advise you of this right if they stop and ask you to do a preliminary roadside test, such as walking a straight line, or taking either the Alcohol Level Evaluation Roadside Tester (ALERT) or Alcotest. Of course, if you fail the roadside test, the police have good reason to insist on a Breathalyzer test. (Ontario suspended use of the ALERT in 1993 because the manufacturer modified the machine without prior government approval.)

REFUSING A BLOOD-ALCOHOL TEST

You cannot refuse a breath test unless you have a reasonable excuse, which is hard to come up with. Penalties for refusing a breath sample, or in some cases a blood sample, are similar to those for driving while intoxicated. For anyone already convicted of drunk driving, being found guilty of refusing a breath test carries the same penalties as a second impaired driving conviction.

Under the Criminal Code, a person who is found guilty of a first drunk driving charge is usually fined $300 (the minimum) plus costs, and is forbidden to drive for at least three months. You could lose your license for an even longer period if charges are laid under one of the various provincial highway safety codes rather than the Criminal Code. See also DRUNK DRIVING.

BLUE LAW

A law that forbids certain kinds of businesses to be open on Sunday is called a blue law. Blue laws are also called Sunday or Sabbath Day laws, but their primary purpose is no longer religious. It is rather to give workers a day of rest and to promote the general welfare of the community.

For example, some municipalities ban the sale of liquor on Sunday. This prohibition is meant to ensure that at least one day of the week will see a reduction in the purchase (and perhaps the consumption) of alcohol. Other blue laws prohibit the sale of most goods, but not necessities such as food.

In recent years the trend has been against the enactment or enforcement of blue laws.

Blue laws derive their name from the legal code drawn up in the mid 17th century in the New Haven Colony in the United States. The laws were printed on blue paper.

BLUE-SKY LAW

Provincial laws that regulate the sale of securities such as stocks and bonds in order to protect consumers from fraud are referred to as blue-sky laws. In order to offer securities for sale within a province, a company must reveal the risks related to the purchase of its stocks and bonds, and the company is not allowed to overstate the potential return on an investment. The term *blue-sky law* is supposed to have originated when a judge ruled that a particular stock "had as much value as a patch of blue sky." The sale of stocks and bonds is regulated by various provincial securities commissions.

See also SECURITIES REGULATION; STOCKS AND BONDS.

BOATING

Just as drivers must obey the rules of the road, boaters must follow the laws that pertain to boating. Speed limits, safety equipment, proper lighting, and right-of-way rules are some of the subjects the laws cover.

Failure to observe the nautical "rules of the road" can lead to lawsuits as well as criminal charges. If your boat does not have proper lights and you collide with another craft, you can be held responsible for injuries and damages. You can also be held responsible for accidents that occur if you operate a boat under the influence of drugs or alcohol, fail to keep a lookout for other boats, water-skiers, or swimmers, or neglect to warn of approaching danger.

You should never allow your boat to be used by someone who is not qualified to operate it. If an accident occurs, you can be held responsible even if you were nowhere near the scene of the accident.

The Canadian Government Publishing Centre produces many nautical charts and boating publications such as Safe Warning Regulations, Sailing Directions for Canadian Waters, Code of Navigation Practices and Procedures, Rules of the Road for the Great Lakes. These can be purchased from federal government bookstores and are also available in libraries.

BOND

There are many types of bonds but they all have the same general purpose: they are documents that represent a promise by one party to pay another party after a specified length of time. Some bonds, such as savings and corporate bonds, are used to borrow money. Others, such as bail bonds and performance bonds, serve as a guarantee that money will be paid if a certain promise—to appear in court or to complete a job, for example—is not kept.

See also BAIL; CONTRACTOR; STOCKS AND BONDS.

BOOK VALUE

If you own stock in a corporation, you may hear a reference to the stock's "book value." This is the value of a share of stock, as determined by subtracting the company's liabilities from its assets and then dividing that amount by the total number of shares that the company has issued.

For example, suppose there are 1,000 shares of Wonderful Widget Works, Inc. The company's assets, including its factory, its office equipment, and the money owed to it, equal $1 million. The company's liabilities, such as unpaid invoices from suppliers, transportation costs, and salaries, amount to $200,000. The company's theoretical worth—its assets minus its liabilities—equals $800,000.

Dividing this amount by the 1,000 shares of ownership in the company, the book value of each share is $800. It is important to compare a stock's book value with its price to determine whether the stock is sound or overpriced.

BORROWED PROPERTY

Your car refuses to start, and you need to get to an important meeting. Your neighbor, seeing your predicament, suggests you borrow his car for the day. You accept his generous offer.

Borrowing a car or any other kind of personal property creates what is known as a bailment. As the borrower, you become a bailee of your neighbor's property. Because your neighbor does not gain anything of value in allowing you to borrow his car, this bailment is considered to be for your sole benefit. As a result, you are legally required to exercise extraordinary care while using the car, and you must return it on demand in the same condition in which you received it. If someone sideswipes the car and scratches the fender while you are borrowing it, you are responsible for the damage despite the fact that you were not at fault.

But suppose your neighbor lends you his car knowing that it needs a brake job. If you have an accident because you cannot stop the car in time to avoid a collision, your neighbor could be held at least partially responsible for the accident.

Be wary of lending objects that may be dangerous to the user. For example, do not lend a power saw to someone who does not know how to use it, an automobile to someone who does not know how to drive, or either object to someone not in a physical or mental condition to use it properly.

Commenting on one such case that came before the Supreme Court of Canada in 1993, Justice Peter Cory wrote: "It is an application of common sense that one who has the care and control of a vehicle should not permit another person that he or she knows, or should know, is unfit to drive, to take over control of his or her vehicle." In that instance, the court upheld an injuries' claim for $120,000 against a man who lent his car to a drunken buddy. Even though the lender was also drunk, the court ruled he should have exercized his legal "duty of care" in refusing to let his drunk friend drive. See also BAILMENT.

BOUNCED CHEQUE

The day before your car payment is due you realize that you do not have enough money to pay it. But since your paycheque is due at the end of the week, you write a cheque and mail it to the loan company. You are sure that by the time the company presents the cheque to your bank, you will have received and deposited your paycheque. However, the cheque you wrote reaches the bank first. In other words, your cheque has "bounced," or been returned to the loan company. Now you are in legal trouble as well as financial trouble.

Unless you have arranged for overdraft protection, the bank has no obligation to honor a cheque written on an account with insufficient funds. Writing a cheque on an account that you know has insufficient funds to cover the cheque is a crime and may be punishable by fine or imprisonment.

Even if the overdraft was unintentional and you escape criminal prosecution, the cost of this mistake can mount up considerably. Unless you have an agreement with the bank permitting overdrafts (a service that has become increasingly popular in recent years), the bank usually imposes a service charge on your account to compensate it for the added cost of handling.

Aside from the financial penalty imposed by the bank, writing a bad cheque can adversely affect your credit rating. This can happen if the person or company to whom you mailed the cheque reports it to a company that keeps credit records.

See also CHEQUE.

BOUNDARY LINE

The border where one piece of real estate ends and another begins is known as a boundary line. The lines may be imaginary ones that exist only on maps, or they may be indicated by objects such as stakes, stone monuments, fences, rivers, trees, cliffs, or any other physical markers. Most property owners have only a rough idea where their boundary lines are because most of the time it is not necessary to know the exact location. However, if you or your neighbor want to chop down a tree, put up a fence, or build a new garage near the edge of your property, you need to know precisely where your boundary line is in order to avoid possible legal troubles.

SURVEY IN ORDER WHEN BOUNDARY LINES ARE IN DOUBT

Your deed should describe your boundary lines, or you should be able to find them on the town map. If neither of these documents divulges their location, you may have to call a surveyor to make a survey of your property. Unfortunately, a survey can be expensive, ranging from several hundred dollars to more than $1,000. If nothing more is at stake than a bed of shrubbery, you and your neighbor may be able to agree on where the boundary is. It is often a good idea to make your offer to purchase land conditional on the seller providing a survey prior to closing. Specify that the survey—a sketch or description of the land—be done by a licensed surveyor according to accepted practices in your province.

If two or more people own a parcel of land, in most cases one of the owners can order that the property be divided and his or her share sold.

In most provinces, a neighbor has the right to build a fence or other boundary marker between the two properties, and the costs for such a boundary fence will be borne by both neighbors equally.

WHEN OTHERS BUILD ON YOUR LAND

Suppose you come home from work one day and see a bulldozer clearing a strip of your land to make way for your neighbor's tennis court. What should you do?

Take action right away. Most of the time you can solve the problem on the spot by explaining to your neighbor that he is on your property. If he does not cooperate, you can threaten to call the police or sue. If he still refuses, your lawyer can have a judge order him to stop work until you can bring a suit against him for trespassing on your property.

If you do not take action, the consequences can be worse than you might think. First, if you wait until your neighbor completes his tennis court before you sue, the judge will be reluctant to have it destroyed. Second, if you try to sell your house, the insurance company may not insure your land as long as a neighbor is occupying part of it. Third, if the neighbor uses your land long enough, he may obtain a permanent right to do so. See ADVERSE POSSESSION; EASEMENT; FENCE BUILDING; TRESPASS.

BOYCOTT

If you refuse to patronize a company or attempt to prevent others from doing so, you are imposing a boycott. The word originated in 1880 during the Land League movement in Ireland, when land agent Charles Boycott was ostracized by local farmers who would not harvest his land.

In recent years, some civil rights activists have encouraged a boycott of California grapes because of alleged abuses of the rights of fruit pickers in California. Another boycott that originated in the United States and spread to Canada involved South African wines and was designed to draw attention to civil rights abuses in South Africa. Boycotts, or threats of boycott, are often an effective way to make a foreign country or large corporation respond to certain community values or needs. See also LABOR UNION.

BREACH OF CONTRACT

The colors have been picked, the contract has been signed, the advance payment made. But on the appointed day your house painter fails to show up. When he does arrive, three days later, the paint he applies is not the one you had chosen. Then, halfway through the job, he demands an extra $100 to finish. When you refuse, he stomps out of the house, never to return. Each of these actions is a breach of the painter's contract with you. Breach of contract occurs when, without any justification, one of the parties fails to complete his or her part of the bargain.

WAYS A CONTRACT CAN BE BREACHED

You can breach a contract by not keeping your promises; by not paying for the work done; by delivering defective merchandise, by not completing a job,or by not doing it correctly.

Preventing the other person from fulfilling his side of the bargain, such as refusing to let in the painter on the day he is scheduled to work, is a breach of contract, as is canceling your paint job the day before the painter is due to begin.

SUBSTANTIAL PERFORMANCE

Not every broken promise is a breach of contract. Suppose the painter told you he was going to use the Blue Giant brand, but you notice that the cans are labeled Mighty Midget. He assures you that the quality and color of the substituted paint are equal to the one specified. If this is true, he has given you essentially the same product that you agreed to accept. This is known as substantial performance, and you have no grounds for legal complaint unless you can prove that you suffered some loss because of the change.

MONEY DAMAGES

When you suffer loss resulting from a breach of contract, you can sue to be compensated. For example, in the case of the unreasonable painter, the three-day delay in itself would probably not have caused you any real loss. But you can sue for the cost of buying paint to cover the poorer-quality coat he applied and for any additional expenses you incur by hiring another painter to finish the job. These money losses to you are known as damages.

But note that when you sue, a court will expect you to show that you tried to minimize your loss and the resulting damages. Let us say that on the day the painter was supposed to arrive you missed a day of work and were docked for it. However, your mother-in-law was at your home that day and could have called you when the painter arrived. In this instance, you would probably not be entitled to have the painter reimburse you for lost wages.

WHAT IS MEANT BY SPECIFIC PERFORMANCE

Sometimes money is neither what you want nor what you are entitled to when you suffer a breach of contract.

Suppose you are browsing in a secondhand shop and come across the silver coffee service you have always wanted. You pay for it immediately, but leave it behind to be cleaned. When you come to pick it up, the owner tells you that in the meantime he has learned it is worth much more money than what you paid for it and he offers you a refund.

You have a right to demand the coffee set at the price you paid. This is called specific performance and is the remedy you would sue for.

One very important exception to the specific performance remedy is personal services. Let us say you sign a contract with an interior decorator to redo your living and dining rooms. Just before her first scheduled visit, she tells you she is too busy and cannot do your work. You cannot ask a court to force her to decorate your home, although you could sue her for damages.

On the other hand, where a public official has a duty to perform, say to issue a license to sell goods on the street once certain conditions are met, a person who has satisfied all the conditions can sue by way of a "writ of mandamus" to force the official to issue such a licence.

STEPS TO TAKE FOR A BREACH OF CONTRACT

If you believe you are the victim of a breach of contract, here are some steps to take in your search for redress:

1. In writing, notify the person with whom you have the contract of the breach. Tell him what you expect him to do to correct it. Give him a firm deadline for taking action (such as 10 days or two weeks).

2. Send the letter by certified mail, return receipt requested. Keep a copy of the letter, along with the written contract, if there is one.

3. If you do not receive a satisfactory response by your deadline, you may want to take legal action. If the amount in question is relatively small, your best bet may be to go to small-claims court. But if the amount is large, if money damages alone will not compensate you adequately, or if the offender lives in some other province, you may have to file a lawsuit. In this event, you should hire a lawyer to advise and assist you.

4. Try to keep things in perspective. If the breach is insignificant, consider whether the matter is worth pursuing legally. For example, suppose your contract called for you to receive three hand-painted china figurines. If you find that one of them has a minor blemish, you must decide if the cost, in time and money, of pursuing your right to a perfect figurine will exceed the amount that a court would award you.

See also CONTRACT.

BREACH OF THE PEACE

Anything that violates the order and tranquillity of a community may be considered a breach of the peace. For example, setting off fireworks, playing very loud music, or using obscene language in public have all been considered to be breaches of the peace.

A person who breaches the peace can be charged with disorderly conduct or disturbing the peace. These offenses are usually considered minor or summary conviction offenses, punishable by fines or short terms of imprisonment. See DISORDERLY CONDUCT; DISTURBING THE PEACE.

BREACH OF PROMISE

The right to sue for breach of promise or, more precisely, breach of marriage promise, was a time-honored way for a jilted fiancée (or fiancé) to be avenged. Suppose that Tom and Wanda become engaged and set a date. During the following months Wanda makes the wedding preparations—buying gowns, hiring a hotel and caterer, ordering flowers. But when the big day comes, Tom is nowhere to be found.

Legally, Tom is guilty of breach of promise and could be

REAL LIFE, REAL LAW

The Case of the Noisy Neighbor

Moe liked to collect things, which his neighbor Phil described as junk. With time, Moe's collection filled his backyard. However it was not until Moe started to run some of the motors he collected that Phil's nerves snapped.

From across the street, he yelled obscenities and unflattering epithets at Moe, who called the police. Phil was charged with causing a public disturbance and convicted, a conviction upheld by the Nova Scotia Court of Appeal.

Phil was finally acquitted on appeal to the Supreme Court of Canada. In deciding what constitutes "a disturbance of the peace," its seven justices studied cases back to 1869. Taking into account "the proper goals and limits of the criminal law," and striking a balance between individual liberty and the public interest in going about its affairs in "peace and tranquillity," it held that Phil did not disturb the peace. To do so, behavior must be "overtly manifested" in such a way that it interferes with the "ordinary and customary use of the public place in question."

A mere emotional upset could not be construed as "disturbing the peace," said the Supreme Court of Canada.

---

sued for the costs Wanda incurred because of his promise. This could include the costs of the gown, the hotel, the caterers, and the flowers. In some cases, Tom might even have to pay for the mental distress and humiliation suffered by Wanda. See also ENGAGEMENT, BROKEN.

BREATH TEST

If a police officer suspects you of driving under the influence of alcohol, he can ask you to take a sobriety test on the spot, or he can take you to the police station to take a blood-alcohol test from a breath sample or, in the case of an accident involving death or bodily injury, from a blood sample.

♦ If you agree to take a breath test, you will be told to blow into a tube connected to a Breathalyzer, a device that measures the concentration of blood alcohol in your breath. You can refuse to take the test, but if you do, you will be charged with refusal to take a Breathalyzer test. If convicted, the penalty will be the same as for driving with more than 0.08 alcohol in your blood. For a first offense you will probably be fined at least $300 and lose your license for at least three months.

WHAT YOU SHOULD KNOW

If the machine registers a blood-alcohol level over the legal limit (0.08, or 80 mil-

♦ ligrams of alcohol in 100 millilitres of blood), you will be arrested for drunk driving.

YOUR OPTIONS IF YOU FAIL

Breath tests are the least accurate method of measuring blood-alcohol concentration, and are often successfully challenged in court. A lawyer who is experienced in defending drunk-driving cases can be very helpful if you are arrested for failing a Breathalyzer test.

See also BLOOD-ALCOHOL TESTING; DRUNK DRIVING.

BRIBERY

Ed, who has been barreling down the highway at 140 kilometres per hour, meekly pulls over to the curb when his rearview mirror reveals a police car gaining on him, rooftop lights flashing. When the officer comes forward and announces that he is ticketing Ed for speeding, Ed pulls out a $100 bill and offers it to the officer if he will "just forget the whole thing." The officer counters with a charge of attempted bribery. But if the officer accepted Ed's offer, he too would be guilty of bribery.

In legal terms bribery is a gift—money, trips, merchandise, or tickets to sporting events—offered to a public official in exchange for favors within the scope of the official's duties. The list of people who qualify as public officials is long and includes sheriffs and other peace officers, jurors, witnesses, school-board members and school officials, public prosecutors, and income tax inspectors. If a public official seeks payment for taking an official action, he is guilty of soliciting a bribe. This is an indictable offense, punishable by up to five years' imprisonment in the case of municipal officials, and up to 14 years in the case of police officers or members of parliament.

BRIEF

No matter what kind of lawsuit you pursue, you or your lawyer may be required to prepare a written statement for the court to support your case. This brief, as it is called, usually contains a summary of the facts of the case, cites the law that you believe governs the dispute, and explains how the law should be applied. The brief concludes with a statement of the decision you are requesting from the court. The collection of documents—copies of the court proceedings, transcripts of testimony and arguments—published in book form and filed before an appeal court is called a factum.

BRITISH NORTH AMERICA ACT

The British North America (BNA) Act, passed by the British Parliament in 1867, gave effect to the confederation scheme worked out by the Fathers of Confederation at conferences held between 1864 and 1866 in Charlottetown, Quebec, and London. The act united Canada, Nova Scotia, and New Brunswick. (On Confederation, Upper Canada became Ontario; Lower Canada, Quebec.) It also set out the principles for governing Canada—a federal parliament consisting of an elected house of commons, an appointed senate, a governor-general to represent the Crown; provincial legislatures and lieutenant-governors; and a judiciary.

The federal parliament got legislative authority for armed forces, banking, navigation and shipping, issuing paper money and coinage, bankruptcy, copyrights and patents, criminal law, the postal service, interest rates, marriage and divorce, and matters such as naturalization. The provincial legislatures got exclusive jurisdiction, within their boundaries, for education, civil and property rights, and for operating provincial courts, jails, reformatories, and hospitals. They could also raise taxes, appoint provincial officials, administer justice in the province, and license businesses, including any concerned with developing roads, railways, and telegraph lines, so long as these companies operated only within the province and did not cross provincial or international borders.

Legislative power not granted directly to the provinces fell into the domain of the federal parliament, which would be responsible for what lawyers and political scientists now call POGG, the peace, order, and good government of Canada. Wide ranging powers were given to the governor general, who, on the advice of cabinet, can declare certain provincial legislation invalid.

The BNA Act was amended numerous times by both the British and Canadian parliaments, and provincial legislatures. Some amendments admitted other provinces into Confederation (Manitoba, 1870; British Columbia, 1871; Prince Edward Island, 1873; Alberta and Saskatchewan, 1905; Newfoundland, 1949).

The Supreme Court of Canada and an Exchequer Court (predecessor of today's Federal Court) were established in 1875. Until the Supreme Court of Canada became the court of last resort in 1949, Supreme Court decisions were appealed to the Judicial Committee of the Privy Council of Great Britain. One famous appeal was the *Persons* case of 1929 when, on appeal by Alberta magistrate Emily Murphy, the Privy Council ruled that, under the BNA Act, women were indeed persons.

Many constitutional cases heard by the Supreme Court of Canada down the years concerned federal and provincial jurisdiction: whether laws were *ultra vires* (beyond the powers) of a particular government. Were airport personnel bound by federal or provincial labor laws? Were truckers subject to provincial or federal transport legislation? When Quebec outlawed the dissemination of communist propaganda in the 1930s, the Supreme Court ruled this was *ultra vires*: making such an act an offense was tantamount to making criminal law, a federal domain. At the time of writing, Montreal is appealing a judgment that a bylaw intended to add some $500 million to city coffers is *ultra vires*. Under the bylaw, owners of commercial and multi-unit residential properties must pay a surtax on their properties, vacant or otherwise, such tax to be passed on to their tenants as increased rent. (In the first court action, lawyers for the property owners had the bylaw declared invalid on grounds it was *ultra vires* municipal or provincial powers. They argued that provinces may only legislate direct taxation, but that the Montreal tax is indirect, being paid by the owner of premises rather than the person using them.)

Since 1982, the Supreme Court of Canada has dealt less with matters of jurisdiction and more with issues surrounding the Charter of Rights and Freedoms. In 1982 then Prime Minister Pierre Trudeau "patriated" (brought under Canadian control) the BNA Act. The act and the Charter of Rights and Freedoms were incorporated into the Constitution Act 1982. This act ended the British Parliament's role in approving Canadian legislation.

BROKER

In general, a broker is a person who is retained to arrange sales for other people. Unlike agents who represent either the buyer or the seller, the broker serves as a middleman in the transaction, bringing the parties together and helping them reach a mutual agreement.

For example, an insurance agent generally represents a single company and offers only the products of that company. An insurance broker offers the products of several companies and can therefore provide clients with a selection of insurance products. See also INSURANCE AGENT AND BROKER; REAL ESTATE AGENT AND BROKER; STOCKBROKER.

BURDEN OF PROOF

You have sued the manufacturer of a hair dryer that caught fire while you were using it, burning your hands and face. Efforts to settle the suit have failed, and the case is set for trial. It is up to you (the plaintiff) or your lawyer to convince the court to rule in your favor.

To do so, you will have to meet the "burden of proof." This means that it is your responsibility to prove that the facts of the case weigh in your favor. Because you have begun the lawsuit, the initial burden of proving that the hair dryer was defective falls on you.

If the manufacturer claims your injuries resulted from your own negligence, the manufacturer will have to bear the burden of proving its allegation that you were negligent.

Courts use one of two different standards in determining whether a party has met its burden of proof:

◇ *Preponderance of the evidence*. This standard is the easiest to meet and is used in most lawsuits, as for breach of contract and personal injury. It involves weighing the evidence of both parties to see which side is more believable. If the evidence is found to be even, the party bearing the burden of proof cannot win; but if it is more convincing toward the party who has the burden of proof, that side will prevail.

◇ *Beyond a reasonable doubt*. This last standard is required in criminal cases. A person cannot be convicted of a crime unless the judge or jury is convinced of that person's guilt beyond a reasonable doubt. If there is any reasonable uncertainty about the defendant's guilt based on the evidence presented, no conviction can take place.

BURGLARY

Someone enters your home and stealthily moves around. You call the police, who take him away. Will the prowler be charged with burglary?

Burglary, also known as breaking and entering, originally meant forcibly entering a home at night with the intention of committing a crime, usually theft. Today, the law on burglary extends to commercial buildings, kennels, stables, and barns and does not limit the act to nighttime.

However, the penalties for breaking and entering a dwelling are greater than for a business. Intoxication is not a defense for breaking in and committing a crime (for example stealing something), but drunkenness could be a defense for breaking in to commit a crime, then not doing so. For example, someone who breaks into a store, and is so drunk he falls asleep before he can steal anything, may not be guilty of burglary, but may be guilty of the lesser offense of trespassing. However, if someone is found in a dwelling without lawful excuse, he is *presumed* to have entered with a criminal intent and is liable to imprisonment for up to 10 years. This is true even if he did not actually break in, but entered through an open door or window. See also TRESPASS.

BUSINESS TAXES

Operating a business involves paying taxes and fees to local, provincial, and federal governments. If you have employees, you must contribute to the Workers' Compensation Fund, the Unemployment Insurance Commission, and the Canada (Quebec) Pension Plan. You must also deduct at source all federal income taxes, as well as provincial income taxes where applicable. In some cases, you must collect and pay other taxes, too.

You may have to pay for a municipal business license and possibly municipal real estate and water taxes. You will have to get a building permit whether you are renovating premises or building a new place of business. If you are a manufacturer, you will have to comply with the packaging and labeling requirements set out by Consumer and Corporate

Affairs Canada, and respect all patents, trademarks, industrial designs, and copyrights.

If you are incorporated, you must file company tax returns; if you are in a partnership or registered company, your income from that source must be included with your personal income tax return.

The Canadian Federal Business Development Bank, found in all major cities, can advise you about setting up a business, and may even help you to find government funding. For a nominal fee, it also provides new entrepreneurs with counseling from retired successful businessmen. See also CORPORATION; LIMITED LIABILITY COMPANY; PARTNERSHIP; SMALL BUSINESS.

BUYER'S CLUB

You are asked to join a buyer's club, which promises big savings on merchandise bought through its catalog. Do such clubs really save you money?

Some do offer merchandise or services at reduced prices and for reasonable membership fees, but others cost you more in time, money, and frustration than they will ever save you through lower prices.

With some clubs you shop in warehouselike stores for discounted household goods and food, which must be purchased in large quantities. If the membership fee is modest, and you have storage space to accommodate bulk buying, this type of club may be worth considering. Other clubs offer discounted shopping through

catalogs or with coupons. Be wary of coupon clubs. The coupons may be valid under limited circumstances or useless because the stores are no longer in business.

To determine whether a buyer's club will actually save you money, do some comparison shopping in local stores. Check its record with your local Better Business Bureau or consumer protection agency. Take membership and renewal fees into account. If your membership fee is $250 for example, and you save 25 percent on each purchase, you will have to spend $1,000 before you begin to realize any savings.

You do not always have to join a buyer's club to get goods or services at a discount. If your home and your neighbor's are heated by oil, for example, you could form an informal association, agree to buy your heating oil from one company, then approach a number of oil heating companies seeking a collective discount. Because of the group volume, one or more dealers will probably be willing to sell oil at a discount to your group. A similar approach could work for lawn care services, snow removal, or house painting. One such nonprofit group, the Canadian Transfer Association of Barrie, Ont., has been listed with the Toronto Better Business Bureau since 1989. It concentrates on getting its members the best possible deals on moving and real estate agents' fees.

Before joining a buyer's club, first check its record with your local Better Business Bureau or consumer protection agency.

CALENDAR

When lawyers refer to the calendar, they mean the court calendar—a list of cases awaiting a trial or a hearing in court.

In discussing your case, your lawyer may also refer to a "calendar call." This is a court session during which the judge determines the progress of cases awaiting trial—depositions that must be taken and motions that must be made before trial. Sometimes the judge sets the date for a trial at that time. See also DEPOSITION.

CANADA CUSTOMS

Customs and Excise, a subdepartment of the federal Ministry of Revenue, exists in order to fulfill several func-tions. Perhaps the best known deal with regulating the flow of goods into Canada. Customs Canada controls the importation of prohibited goods such as drugs, firearms, and pornography, and is responsible for enforcing commercial laws and regulations concerning the flow of commodities between Canada and other nations.

For most Canadians, contact with Customs involves declaring personal purchases, made out of the country, for which duty may have to be paid. Duty is a form of tax on the merchandise. Suppose you buy a cashmere coat in Ireland for $600, but a similar coat made here costs $1,000. To protect Canadian clothing companies, the federal government may impose a duty on the foreign coat to narrow the gap between the two prices. The amount of the tariff will probably not raise the Irish coat's price to that of the Canadian coat, but it will make the foreign purchase less attractive financially.

The kinds of goods subject to duties and the amounts owed for each kind of item are listed in federal tariff schedules. The amount to be paid not only varies from item to item, but also depends on the country from which the item is being imported.

EXEMPTIONS

In many cases, you do not have to pay duty if you qualify for a personal exemption. And whether you pay duty or not also depends on the length of time you were out of the country, the type of goods you brought back, your age (in the case of alcohol and tobacco), and how often you use your personal exemption. Duty rates and exemption amounts change from time to time. Look in the blue pages of your telephone directory for the phone number of Customs and Excise in your area and call them for up-to-date information.

At the time of writing, if you have been out of the country for 24 or more hours, you may bring $20 worth of goods (but not tobacco and alcohol) into Canada without paying duty. After 48 hours' absence, you may return with goods valued up to $100. For both the 24- and 48-hour exemptions, you may be required to make a written declaration. These exemptions may be used any number of times in a year.

Once a year, if you are gone for seven days or more, you may bring back $300 worth of merchandise without paying duty. For this exemption, you must declare your purchases in writing. Exemptions may not be added together or saved up to gain a larger exemption.

Duty-free purchases of alcohol and tobacco may be included in the 48-hour or seven-day exemptions only. All tobacco and alcohol products must be in your hand or checked luggage when you come into Canada. Anyone 16 years of age and over may bring in up to 200 cigarettes and 50 cigars (or cigarillos), and 400 tobacco sticks and 400 grams of manufactured tobacco. If you meet the age requirements of the province where you enter Canada, you may bring up to 1.14 litres (40 imperial ounces) of wine or liquor or up to 8.5 litres of beer or ale (48 12-ounce bottles, for example).

Even if you exceed your regular personal exemption, you may benefit from what is known as a "special duty rate" for goods other than tobacco and alcohol, which you take back after an absence of 48 hours or more. Suppose you bring back $600 worth of merchandise after being out of Canada for one week. As outlined above, $300 of your purchases are exempt from duty. The other $300 will be assessed at about 15 percent. In other words, on the total $600, you would pay only $45 duty. Goods covered under the Free Trade Agreement between Canada and the United States are subject to even more favorable special duty rates.

PAYING DUTY

If you do not qualify for an exemption, you will have to pay a percentage of the purchase price of the commodities you bring into Canada. The rates vary over time and according to the product you bring back, but generally run to about 30 percent. In the case of luxury items, such as jewelry, you may pay even more. Most forms of payment (cash, certified cheque, credit card, traveler's cheque or, in the case of less than $500 duty, a personal cheque) are accepted at Customs offices in Canada.

FALSE DECLARATION

If goods are falsely declared or not declared at all, then they may be seized and forfeited to the government. In addition, severe penalties may be imposed on offenders according to the law and the facts of each case. Included in the penalties that may be imposed is confiscation of the vehicle used to smuggle goods across the border. Depending on the type of goods you are caught smuggling, you will have to pay an administrative cost of up to 100 percent of the penalty applied to the goods in order to get your vehicle back.

CANADA DEPOSIT INSURANCE CORPORATION

The Canada Deposit Insurance Corporation (CDIC), a Crown corporation, was created in 1967 to protect money deposited in member financial institutions—banks, trust companies and loan companies. (The Quebec Deposit Insurance Board fills a similar function in Quebec.) For a list of insured member institutions, pick up a pamphlet on the CDIC at any bank.

The CDIC insures the following types of deposits made at member institutions: savings and chequing accounts; term deposits such as guaranteed investment certificates (GICs) and debentures issued by loan companies; money orders; bank drafts; certified cheques and drafts; and traveler's cheques issued by members.

To be insurable, the deposit must be payable in Canada in Canadian currency, and must be repayable no later than five

REAL LIFE, REAL LAW

The Case of the Cross-Border Caper

Returning to Canada from the United States, Irene was stopped by Customs and Excise and asked about her citizenship and if she had anything to declare. She said "No." The Customs official then asked her to park her car a short distance away in order to fill out some forms and have her vehicle inspected. Irene complied, but after waiting several minutes, she became frustrated and left. She was subsequently charged and convicted of failing to undergo an inspection under the Customs Act.

Irene appealed and won her case. The section of the act under which she was charged applied only to a person importing things. Since she was not involved in importation, and had truthfully answered the questions asked by the Customs officer, she could not be convicted.

You should never count on running scot-free from border checks, however. Irene may have got away with it on a technicality, but you would be foolish to take a similar risk.

REAL LIFE, REAL LAW

The Case of the Hapless Husband

Even though Marilyn and Richard were separated for several months, they did not make a settlement agreement or otherwise legalize their *de facto* separation. As the months went by, it became clear they would never reconcile. When Richard found himself in financial straits, he decided to use the situation and a little legal knowledge to his advantage. Knowing that the Canada Evidence Act prohibited one spouse from becoming a Crown witness against the other, he forged his wife's name on a cheque payable to them both, then cashed the cheque.

Unfortunately for Richard, the Supreme Court of Canada decided that the rule that one spouse could not testify against another did not apply if there was an irreconcilable separation. The old rule, which was meant to preserve family harmony, had to give way to the modern view of women being free and equal, said the court. The old Canada Evidence Act rule was not consistent with the values enshrined in the charter of rights.

Richard had once thought of making a name for himself in law. He never imagined it would be as an unsuccessful appellant in a criminal case before the Supreme Court.

years from the time of deposit. Thus, the CDIC does not insure foreign currency deposits, debentures issued by chartered banks, government and corporate bonds and debentures, treasury bills, mortgages, stocks, and mutual funds.

Except for joint deposits, trust deposits, and registered retirement savings plans (RRSPs), the maximum insurance you will get is $60,000 for each bank branch you have deposits with. Depositors of large amounts therefore have to spread their wealth over several institutions to make sure that it is all insured. However, in doing this, the advantages of doing all one's business at one bank may be lost. Moreover, the depositor will spend more time completing transactions. In the case of joint deposits, trust deposits, and RRSPs, however, you could have $60,000 insured in each of the above categories of deposit at one institution, making a total of $240,000 in insured deposits.

If a member institution fails, you need not make a claim with the CDIC. Payments will automatically be made to you, usually within a month. Reforms are being considered to guarantee only the deposits of individuals and not of businesses.

CANADA EVIDENCE ACT

The Canada Evidence Act applies to all criminal and civil proceedings that fall under federal jurisdiction. The act sets out rules of evidence dealing with the competence or expertise of witnesses to be heard in court. Rules on cross-examination of written or oral statements are also provided. Moreover, there is a section in the act that regulates the giving and taking of oaths in a courtroom context. Lastly, the act extensively deals with evidentiary rules pertaining to documents. See also EVIDENCE; OATH AND AFFIRMATION.

CANADA MORTGAGE AND HOUSING CORPORATION

The Canada Mortgage and Housing Corporation, a Crown corporation, was established in 1946 to study and improve housing conditions in Canada. It is involved in several programs concerning aboriginal housing, housing safety, home repair subsidies for needy families, technical innovation, and adaptable housing for seniors and people with disabilities.

The CMHC is responsible for developing certain government-owned lands, and overseeing construction of residential properties for a variety of home buyers. It administers National Housing Act (NHA) loans and grants, and insures mortgages borrowed from private lenders.

The CMHC publishes housing statistics and publications relating to housing. Some 60,000 research reports, journals, and audiovisual materials in the Canadian Housing Information Centre of its Ottawa headquarters are available to the public.

MORTGAGE LOAN INSURANCE

The CMHC's main involvement in housing is through its mortgage loan insurance program. Because the CMHC insures loans, lenders face a reduced risk and will approve loans to more people than they would otherwise. Consequently, an increased number of Canadians have access to mortgage financing.

In order to get mortgage loan insurance through the CMHC, you must deal with a lender that has been authorized by the corporation. Most banks, trust companies, credit unions, life insurance companies and *caisses populaires* are CMHC-approved lenders. You will have to pay an application fee, as well as an insurance premium, which varies from 0.5 to 2.5 percent, depending on the size of your loan. More information is readily available from any approved lender or from any CMHC branch office.

The CMHC's First Home Loan Insurance plan enables first-home buyers to buy a house with a down payment of as little as 5 percent; ordinarily the minimum down payment is 10 percent of the purchase price. The CMHC also administers the Home Buyer's Plan, which permits buyers to use their registered retirement savings plan (RRSP) funds as a down payment. See also INSURANCE; MORTGAGE.

CANADIAN RADIO-TELEVISION AND TELECOMMUNICATIONS COMMISSION

The Broadcasting Act established the Canadian Radio-Television and Telecommunications Commission (CRTC) to supervise the broadcasting industry, and to implement policies designed to promote Canadian culture.

The commission issues, amends, reviews, suspends and revokes broadcasting licences, and regulates the holders of such licences, whether for radio, television, telecommunications or cable stations. It also regulates the character and amount of time allotted to advertising, and the time given to partisan political announcements, and must ensure that all political parties receive fair access to the medium. To make sure it uses its powers fairly, CRTC decisions are subject to review by the governor-general in council, that is, the cabinet.

The Broadcasting Act requires the CRTC to hold public hearings before a new licence is issued, or before an existing one is suspended or revoked. Hearings, though informal, must be conducted in a judicial manner—expert witnesses must be allowed, and the right to cross-examination, as well as the right of parties to be heard in a fair and impartial manner, must be observed. As

well as being subject to review by the federal cabinet, CRTC decisions may be appealed to the Federal Court of Appeal.

Public radio and television is but one area of CRTC responsibility. The commission also regulates private broadcasters and local radio stations, as well as telephone company rates and services.

Part of the CRTC's mandate is to ensure that radio and television programs do not encourage stereotyping of the sexes, races or cultures that make up Canadian society. Its rulings sometimes conflict with the Charter of Rights and Freedoms' guarantees of free expression. As a result, the limits of CRTC decisions in this respect are often ultimately decided by the courts.

CANADIAN SECURITY INTELLIGENCE SERVICE

The Canadian Security Intelligence Service (CSIS) investigates suspected subversion, terrorism, foreign espionage and sabotage, and conducts background investigations on public servants whose work gives them access to sensitive national security information. The agency was created in 1984 to provide services that were formerly the responsibility of the Royal Canadian Mounted Police (RCMP). Even though many CSIS members are former RCMP officers, CSIS is a civilian agency, not a police force.

Nevertheless, it can obtain warrants to conduct searches and electronic surveillance, such as wiretapping.

The agency has headquarters in Ottawa, field officers in major Canadian cities, and liaison officers in many capital cities around the world.

CAPITAL GAINS TAX

The tax you pay on the profit you make from the sale of a capital asset is called a capital gains tax. Almost everything you sell can be considered a capital asset, except your home, which is not subject to a capital gains tax. Your car, boat, jewelry, works of art, and stocks and bonds are all considered capital assets.

HOW THE TAX WORKS

Suppose you bought a 1976 Cadillac convertible several years ago for $10,000. The car is now a collector's item, and because you have kept it in mint condition, you are able to sell it for $35,000 today. Your capital gain is $25,000, of which 75 percent is taxable at the rate of tax you pay. If your income is taxed at 25 percent, for example, you would pay $4,687.50 on your capital gain (25 percent of $18,750, which is 75 percent of $25,000).

$100,000 EXEMPTION

Up to spring 1994, you were allowed to make $100,000 in capital gains over a lifetime without paying tax. Under 1992 legislation, that $100,000 exemption could be reduced in

some cases. For example, if you paid $10,000 interest on your loan to acquire real estate, that $10,000 was tax deductible. But the $100,000 you would otherwise be allowed as a one-time capital gains exemption would be reduced accordingly.

The $100,000 exemption was abolished, however, under the terms of Finance Minister Paul Martin's spring 1994 budget. Canadians who had not already claimed the exemption could do so in their 1994 tax returns (to be filed by April 30, 1995). Under the phasing-out provisions, for tax purposes, you can treat a property or investment as if you sold it, designating its sale price. This must be more than the purchase price, but cannot exceed its market value on budget day (Feb. 22, 1994).

A $500,000 capital gains exemption for small businesses and farms was not affected by the February 1994 changes.

In calculating your liability for capital gains tax, consult an accountant or tax lawyer. Not only is the Income Tax Act extremely complex but it is constantly revised, and changes with every new budget. See CLOSING, REAL ESTATE.

SELLING YOUR HOME

If you own a home in the city and another in the country, you may consider either one your principal residence and will not pay capital gains tax on the profits of the sale. However, if you sell your principal home and move into your second home, capital gains tax will have to be paid on the difference between the purchase price of your second home and

its current market value when you sell it, or at the time of your death, at which time your second home is deemed to be sold.

CASH SURRENDER VALUE

If you decide to cancel your life insurance policy, you may receive a sum of money from your insurance company. This is called the cash surrender value—the amount of money you receive when you surrender, or give up, the policy.

Not all life insurance policies have a cash value when surrendered. Your policy (which is a contract) states whether you are entitled to cash it in before your death. See LIFE INSURANCE.

Whole-life insurance policies and endowment policies both accumulate cash values. The premiums you pay include not only the cost of the actual life insurance (the death benefit) but an additional amount invested by the insurance company. This investment, plus the money it earns, is considered the cash value of the policy.

With a policy that accumulates cash value, you can borrow against it at a relatively low interest rate. Many policies also contain a provision that allows you to use the cash value to pay past due premiums. In both cases, if you do not repay the loan, the amount you borrowed is deducted from the death benefit, and what remains is paid to the beneficiary.

Term insurance, which offers the greatest amount of coverage for the smallest premium, does not have a cash surrender value. In some cases where the cash value is considerable, an older policyholder may convert the cash value to a monthly retirement pension.

CASHIER'S CHEQUE

A cheque issued by a bank against its own account and signed by a bank officer is known as a cashier's cheque. Because it is drawn against the bank itself and not against a private depositor's account, a cashier's cheque often is accepted by a party (such as an auction house or an antiques dealer) that will not take a personal cheque.

You can buy a cashier's cheque from your bank either with cash or by having money transferred to the bank from your account.

CASUALTY INSURANCE

Automobile collision insurance, homeowners' insurance, and business insurance are some of the various kinds of casualty insurance. They provide financial protection against injuries or loss you cause someone else, as well as injuries or loss suffered by you and by others covered by the policy. For example, a business casualty policy provides liability coverage for another person's loss or injury due to the negligence of the business or its employees. It may also protect a business against loss due to theft or damage by its own employees. See also AUTOMOBILE INSURANCE; FLOOD INSURANCE; HOMEOWNERS' INSURANCE.

CAUSE OF ACTION

Your neighbor slips on the icy sidewalk in front of your house, and sues you for compensation for her injuries. The legal papers you are served state that she is charging you with negligence for failing to keep the sidewalk safe. Your alleged negligence is the cause of action—the claim that serves as the basis for filing a lawsuit.

Failure to come up with a legitimate cause of action usually leads to the dismissal of a lawsuit. Suppose your neighbor drops a banana cream pie on your sidewalk and slips on that. Although the accident takes place on your property, it is caused by your neighbor's negligence rather than yours. In this event, she has no cause of action—in other words, no legally acceptable reason to initiate a lawsuit against you.

CENSORSHIP

Suppose you write a pamphlet about the corruption you have discovered at a government agency. As the pamphlet is about to be published, the agency seeks a court injunction to halt its publication.

You have become the victim of attempted censorship, an effort to prevent information from reaching the public. It is a violation of freedom of speech and freedom of the press, both of which are guaranteed by the Charter of Rights and Freedoms and by most provincial human rights legislation. Also known as prior restraint (because the information is suppressed before it can reach the public), censorship can apply to any medium, including film, television, outdoor signs, and even works of art.

WHEN CENSORSHIP IS LEGAL

Although the Charter of Rights and Freedoms guarantees the right to freedom of expression and freedom of the press, these freedoms are limited by other considerations in extreme situations, especially in times of war. In wartime, factory workers, scientists, soldiers, and other people connected with the war effort can be prevented legally from talking or writing about their work. During a war, newspaper, radio, and television reporters may not be allowed to give out information about troop movements and locations and the weapons being used in combat.

The Canadian Official Secrets Act and the Canadian Security and Intelligence Service (CSIS) Act may also limit one's right to express oneself freely, especially when national security or national interest may be endangered by such free expression.

CONTROVERSIAL MATERIAL

The Canada Evidence Act and various access-to-information laws state that a person or government official may refuse to disclose certain information to a court, if she feels such disclosure may harm the public interest or otherwise be injurious to international relations or national defense or security.

The Criminal Code also forbids seditious writings, defined as any writing that advocates the illegal use of force to bring about a change of government. (Publishing or circulating such writing is an offense; having it in your possession is not.)

The courts have the power to ban publication of evidence in certain trials (for example those involving small children) when they feel the administration of justice or the accused's well-being may be at stake. During the manslaughter trial of Karla Homolka in St. Catharines, Ont., in June 1993, Ontario Court General Division Judge Francis Kovacs closed the courtroom to the general public and prohibited the media from publishing or broadcasting any details of the deaths of teenagers Leslie Mahaffey and Kristen French. Since Homolka's estranged husband, Paul (Bernardo) Teale, was facing first-degree murder charges in the case, the judge ruled that Teale's right to a fair trial took precedence over freedom of expression.

Material depicting sexual activity often presents problems for the courts, since what some people may consider art, others may consider pornographic. Displaying obscene material is prohibited by the Criminal Code, but different courts have reached different interpretations of obscenity. One criterion of what is obscene, and so subject to censorship, is whether the item offends community standards. In 1992, the Supreme Court of Canada maintained that portraying explicit sex that is neither violent nor degrading nor dehumanizing is not obscene, but that portraying sex coupled with violence is nearly always unduly exploitative and therefore subject to censorship. See also OBSCENITY; PORNOGRAPHY; PRESS, FREEDOM OF; PRIOR RESTRAINT; SPEECH, FREEDOM OF.

CERTIFIED CHEQUE

Sometimes a person will ask for payment with a certified cheque, which you can get from your bank. By certifying the cheque, the bank guarantees the person to be paid (the payee) that the money needed to cash the cheque is in your bank account. This amount is frozen in your account until the payee collects it from the bank. Unlike a cashier's cheque, which is written on the bank's account, a certified cheque is written on your own account.

A certified cheque will have *certified* or *accepted* stamped on it, along with the signature of a bank officer. You cannot stop payment on a certified cheque. Because the bank has guaranteed payment, it must honor the cheque; if it does not, you can sue for wrongful conduct. See also CASHIER'S CHEQUE; CHEQUE.

CHANGE OF VENUE

When a trial is moved from one district or county to another, the move is called a change of venue, or location. Bias is the most common reason for such moves. Lawyers may claim they cannot find an impartial jury because of media coverage of a case in the original locale. But just because a case has been publicized does not mean the trial will inevitably be moved. It will probably remain in its original location if the court is convinced that jurors will decide the case solely on the evidence presented in court and not on what is reported by the media.

Bias on the part of the presiding judge—if he has a financial interest in the case, or happens to be a friend, relative, or even an acquaintance of one of the parties in the case—is another reason to move a trial, if another judge in the same district is not available.

Sometimes a trial is moved to promote the cause of justice — to enable the jury to view the scene of the crime or accident, or to be closer to important documents and witnesses.

CHARACTER EVIDENCE

Evidence presented during a trial about a person's traits and overall conduct is called character evidence. It is used to help the judge and jury decide if the person's alleged actions as they relate to the case are consistent with his behavior in the past. Usually offered by a "character witness," the evidence may be the statement of a close friend or of someone familiar with the person's reputation in the community.

Character evidence is not a substitute for factual proof. A judge will allow it only if a person's character has some bearing on the case — for example, in a child-custody suit.

After a conviction in criminal cases, character witnesses are sometimes called to help the court decide what sentence should be imposed. A person convicted of embezzlement may call witnesses to testify the crime was out of character for him—that it resulted from a nervous breakdown, devastating financial loss, or some other difficulty—and that he was otherwise a model citizen. The purpose of this kind of character evidence is to convince the court to impose a more lenient sentence. See also EVIDENCE; EXTENUATING CIRCUMSTANCES.

CHARITABLE DONATION

Hundreds of charitable organizations in Canada help the poor, the sick, the elderly, and the homeless. Funds are also raised for many other causes, ranging from sports to the arts.

Because charitable organizations relieve the government of some of its burden, Revenue Canada and most provinces give charities special treat-

ment. Charities often pay a lower rate of income tax or sometimes no tax at all, and may be exempt from provincial and local property taxes.

Donations to qualified charities are tax deductible. Revenue Canada or the charity organization itself can tell you if a charity has tax-exempt status.

The amount you can claim as a contribution depends on whether you received anything in return. If you make a $50 contribution to your local public television station, you can claim a $50 deduction. But if you attend a benefit concert, you must deduct the amount of money you would have paid for tickets at the box office. Or suppose you attend a benefit auction and pay $300 for a camel hair coat donated by a local boutique. If the coat costs $300 in the shop, you cannot claim the $300 as a deduction. But if you pay $450 for the coat, the extra $150 is a tax-deductible contribution.

If you give clothes, furniture, toys, or other personal property to a tax-exempt charitable organization, you can include the fair market value as a tax deduction. (The fair market value is what a willing buyer would pay a willing seller.) Get a receipt to prove your donation if your tax return is audited. See also INCOME TAX AUDIT.

CHARITY SCAMS: STEPS TO TAKE

Most charities are legitimate, but some are scams run by people who put the money they collect into their own pockets. By the time the authorities find

CHECKLIST
When a Charity Telephones

Although many legitimate charities solicit contributions by telephone, some callers who claim to represent charities are confidence artists who seek donations (often to fake organizations) in order to fill their own pockets. Below are some tips to help minimize troubles when a fund-raiser calls.

■ **NEVER GIVE YOUR CREDIT CARD NUMBER TO A FUND-RAISER WHO CALLS YOU.** Make contributions by cheque, payable to the charity only—not to a person's name.

■ **DON'T ALLOW YOURSELF TO BE PRESSURED TO MAKE AN ON-THE-SPOT CONTRIBUTION.** Legitimate charities will be as happy to take your money tomorrow as today. If the caller intimidates you, report the call to the police and your provincial office of consumer affairs.

■ **ASK HOW MUCH OF YOUR DONATION WILL ACTUALLY GO TO THE CHARITY.** Some telephone fund-raising organizations keep as much as 90 percent of the contributions that they solicit.

■ **IF YOU ARE IN DOUBT ABOUT THE CHARITY, ASK FOR WRITTEN INFORMATION.** This will not only give you more time to think, it will also enable you to make a more informed judgment.

out about the deception, the bogus charities have vanished from the community, only to start up again somewhere else.

Protect yourself from scams with these precautions.

1. Be suspicious of an organization with a name resembling that of a well-known charity. For example, the "Salvation Union" could be a fraudulent outfit trading on the name of the Salvation Army.

2. If an unknown charity claims to be affiliated with a recognized one, call the latter to confirm the relationship.

3. Be wary of solicitations made over the telephone or door-to-door. (See CHECKLIST on previous page.)

4. Beware of any appeal disguised as an invoice or a bill.

5. Before sending money to an unfamiliar charity, call your provincial ministry of consumer affairs. Most provinces require charities to register with Revenue Canada. If the charity is not legitimate, you can help end its activities by reporting it to the police.

6. If a charity sends you a gift that you did not request, you are not obligated to make a donation or to return the item.

CHARTERED ACCOUNTANT

The exam by which one qualifies as a chartered accountant (CA) varies from province to province, but is based on a national model set by the Canadian Order of Chartered Accountants. Once an applicant passes the exam, he is licensed by the province.

Aside from such work as preparing tax returns and auditing, CAs may examine and report on individual and corporate financial records. Unlike a non-certified accountant, a CA has a fiduciary relationship (one of trust) with his client and must hold his client's business in strict confidence. If the directors of a corporation hire him to examine the corporation's books, he is responsible to the directors and not to the corporation's management. He is also obliged to report any erroneous information he finds in financial statements he reviews.

A CA who fails to meet the standards of his profession may have his license suspended or revoked and may be expelled from the order. In addition, he may be held responsible for any financial loss he has caused his client.

CHARTER OF RIGHTS AND FREEDOMS

In 1982, the British Parliament passed the Canada Act, ratifying a resolution of the Canadian Parliament to finally sever the legal ties binding Canada to the United Kingdom. This cleared the way for "patriating the constitution," a term coined by Canadians to describe bringing the British North America Act under Canadian control. With patriation, only the Canadian Parliament has the power to make laws concerning Canada.

The Constitution Act 1982 that marked Canada's coming-of-age contained a 34-part

Charter of Rights and Freedoms. This document set out the basic human rights and fundamental freedoms that apply to all governments, citizens, and residents of Canada. The charter had an immediate and far-ranging effect on the Canadian way of life: one by one, long-standing laws, regulations, and customs were struck down when they were found to conflict with the charter. The process continues today.

Before the charter was drawn up, Canadian rights and freedoms were derived from various sources, principally the common law of England. This guaranteed such rights as freedom of expression, freedom of association, freedom of religion, and such democratic freedoms as the right to a fair trial and to be free from unreasonable search and seizure.

As well as the traditions and customs of English common law, Canadian rights were also enshrined in the 1960 Canadian Bill of Rights, a legacy of Prime Minister John Diefenbaker. They were also expressed in various provincial human rights laws, and in such international treaties and conventions as the Universal Declaration of Human Rights, adopted by the United Nations in 1948.

The Charter of Rights and Freedoms, however, not only incorporated into one document the most important rights and freedoms already backed by the courts, but it created further rights, and established the charter as the supreme law of the country. Laws by all levels of government are subject to the charter, which overrides any law or regulation that conflicts with its provisions. Companies and institutions must also abide by the charter. As a result, private clubs that once restricted membership to men have had to admit women, as the charter forbids discrimination based on sex.

But since asserting one's rights can infringe on those of another, no rights are absolute. For this reason, an avalanche of such conflicts has had to be resolved by the courts, and the results have redefined the Canadian legal landscape.

THE CHARTER IN ACTION

These case law examples are a minute sample of the charter's effects on everyday life since its enactment in 1982.

◇ A law prohibiting a business from operating on Sunday, a legally established religious day of observance, was declared invalid, since it contravened the right of freedom of religion (1985);

◇ A municipal bylaw prohibiting people from wearing bathing suits in a public park and other public places was declared invalid (1986);

◇ The charter was found to apply to laws and regulations affecting individuals but not to relations between individuals (1986);

◇ A law requiring new physicians to open a practice away from large urban centers was declared unconstitutional (1989);

◇ The immunity of the Crown, of the Crown prosecutors and of the attorney general is not absolute and these parties may be sued if malicious

prosecution is proven (1989);

◇ The requirement that a person be a Canadian citizen in order to practice law and become a member of the bar was declared invalid (1989);

◇ Evidence obtained by a policeman posing as a coprisoner with an accused was declared inadmissible (1990);

◇ A section of the Unemployment Insurance Act granting 15 weeks' insurance benefits to both parents in the case of adoption, but not in the case of natural birth, was ruled discriminatory (1990);

◇ Because the Ontario Business Practices Act is of a regulatory rather than a criminal nature, the courts found that inspectors do not have to have search warrants when carrying out their duties (1990);

◇ A penitentiary officials' refusal to allow a homosexual prisoner to have conjugal visits with his partner of six years

was ruled discriminatory (1990);

◇ The refusal of medical treatment because of the age of the patient, the severity of the condition, and the poor quality of life likely if that person should recover, was declared wrong and illegal (1990);

◇ The fact that the Income Tax Act does not permit a woman to deduct all her day-care expenses was found to be not discriminatory because of sex (1993);

◇ A section of the unemployment insurance law that denied benefits to anyone 65 years of age or older was invalid (1991);

◇ A law prohibiting public servants from working for a federal political party was declared invalid (1991);

◇ The section of the Canada Election Act prohibiting federal prisoners from voting in a federal election was declared invalid (1993).

REAL LIFE, REAL LAW

The Case of the Confiscated Craft

Jerry bought a lovely powerboat while vacationing in Florida. On his return to Canada, he told Customs officials he had paid U.S.$22,000 for his purchase. Becoming suspicious of what appeared an exceptionally good deal, the Customs officers questioned Jerry further, and he confessed that he had actually paid U.S.$36,000 for the boat. Once Jerry confessed to breaking the law, Customs seized the boat and its trailer.

Jerry had to pay some Can$18,000 in penalties to get his goods back. Then, feeling that his rights to counsel and silence, guaranteed by the Canadian Charter of Rights and Freedoms, had been violated, he appealed his fine. Unfortunately, the Federal Court did not look kindly on this case and Jerry was stuck with the whole amount.

The Charter of Rights and Freedoms

Whereas Canada is founded upon principles that recognize the supremacy of God and the rule of law:

GUARANTEE OF RIGHTS AND FREEDOMS

1. The *Canadian Charter of Rights and Freedoms* guarantees the rights and freedoms set out in it subject only to such reasonable limits prescribed by law as can be demonstrably justified in a free and democratic society.

FUNDAMENTAL FREEDOMS

2. Everyone has the following fundamental freedoms: (a) freedom of conscience and religion; (b) freedom of thought, belief, opinion and expression, including freedom of the press and other media of communication; (c) freedom of peaceful assembly; and (d) freedom of association.

DEMOCRATIC RIGHTS

3. Every citizen of Canada has the right to vote in an election of members of the House of Commons or of a legislative assembly and to be qualified for membership therein.

4. (1) No House of Commons and no legislative assembly shall continue for longer than five years from the date fixed for the return of the writs at a general election of its members. (2) In time of real or apprehended war, invasion or insurrection, a House of Commons may be continued by Parliament and a legislative assembly may be continued by the legislature beyond five years if such continuation is not opposed by the votes of more than one-third of the members of the House of Commons or the legislative assembly, as the case may be.

5. There shall be a sitting of Parliament and of each legislature at least once every twelve months.

MOBILITY RIGHTS

6. (1) Every citizen of Canada has the right to enter, remain in and leave Canada. (2) Every citizen of Canada and every person who has the status of a permanent resident of Canada has the right (a) to move to and to take up residence in any province; and (b) to pursue the gaining of a livelihood in any province. (3) The rights specified in subsection (2) are subject to (a) any laws or practices of general application in force in a province other than those that discriminate among persons primarily on the basis of province of present or previous residence; and (b) any laws providing for reasonable residency requirement as a qualification for the receipt of publicly provided social services. (4) Subsections (2) and (3) do not preclude any law, program or activity that has as its object the amelioration in a province of conditions of individuals in that province who are socially or economically disadvantaged if the rate of employment in that province is below the rate of employment in Canada.

LEGAL RIGHTS

7. Everyone has the right to life, liberty and security of the person and the right not to be deprived thereof except in accordance with the principles of fundamental justice.

8. Everyone has the right to be secure against unreasonable search or seizure.

9. Everyone has the right not to be arbitrarily detained or imprisoned.

10. Everyone has the right on arrest or detention (a) to be informed promptly of the reasons therefor; (b) to retain and instruct counsel without delay and to be informed of that right; and (c) to have the valididy of the detention determined by way of *habeas corpus* and to be released if the detention is not lawful.

11. Any person charged with an offence has the right (a) to be informed without unreasonable delay of the specific offence; (b) to be tried within a reasonable time; (c) not to be compelled to be a witness in proceedings against that person in respect of the offence; (d) to be presumed innocent until proven guilty according to law in a fair and public hearing by an independent and impartial tribunal; (e) not to be denied reasonable bail without just cause; (f) except in the case of an offence under military law tried before a military tribunal, to the benefit of trial by jury where the maximum punishment of the offence is imprisonment for five years or a more severe punishment; (g) not to be found guilty on account of any act or omission unless, at the time of the act or omission, it constituted an offence under Canadian or international law or was criminal according to the general principles of law recognized by the community of nations; (h) if finally acquitted of the offence, not to be tried for it again and, if finally found guilty and punished for the offence, not to be tried or punished for it again; and (i) if found guilty of the offence and if the punishment for the offence has been varied between the time of commission and the time of sentencing, to the benefit of the lesser punishment.

12. Everyone has the right not to be subjected to any cruel and unusual treatment or punishment.

13. A witness who testifies in any proceedings has the right not to have any incriminating evidence so given used to incriminate that witness in any other proceedings, except in a prosecution for perjury or for the giving of contradictory evidence.

14. A party or witness in any proceedings who does not understand or speak the language in which the proceedings are conducted or who is deaf has the right to the assistance of an interpreter.

EQUALITY RIGHTS

15. (1) Every individual is equal before and under the law and has the right to the equal protection and equal benefit of the law without discrimination and, in particular, without discrimination based on race, national or ethnic origin, colour, religion, sex, age or mental or physical disability. (2) Subsection (1) does not preclude any law, program or activity that has as its object the amelioration of conditions of disadvantaged individuals or groups including those that are disadvantaged because of race, national or ethnic origin, colour, religion, sex, age or mental or physical disability.

OFFICIAL LANGUAGES OF CANADA

16. (1) English and French are the official languages of Canada and have equality of status and equal

rights and privileges as to their use in all institutions of the Parliament and government of Canada. (2) English and French are the official languages of New Brunswick and have equality of status and equal rights and privileges as to their use in all institutions of the legislature and government of New Brunswick. (3) Nothing in this Charter limits the authority of Parliament or a legislature to advance the equality of status or use of English or French.

17. (1) Everyone has the right to use English or French in any debates and other proceedings of Parliament. (2) Everyone has the right to use English or French in any debates and other proceedings of the legislature of New Brunswick.

18. (1) The statutes, records and journals of Parliament shall be printed and published in English and French and both language versions are equally authoritative. (2) The statutes, records and journals of the legislature of New Brunswick shall be printed and published in English and French and both language versions are equally authoritative.

19. (1) Either English or French may be used by any person in, or in any pleading in or process issuing from, any court established by Parliament. (2) Either English or French may be used by any person in, or in any pleading in or process issuing from, any court of New Brunswick.

20. (1) Any member of the public in Canada has the right to communicate with, and to receive available services from, any head or central office of an institution of the Parliament or government of Canada in English or French, and has the same right with

respect to any other office of any such institution where (a) there is significant demand for communications with and services from that office in such language; or (b) due to the nature of the office, it is reasonable that communications with and services from that office be available in both English and French. (2) Any member of the public in New Brunswick has the right to communicate with, and to receive available services from, any office of an institution of the legislature or government of New Brunswick in English or French.

21. Nothing in sections 16 to 20 abrogates or derogates from any right, privilege or obligation with respect to the English and French languages, or either of them, that exists or is continued by virtue of any other provision of the Constitution of Canada.

22. Nothing in sections 16 to 20 abrogates or derogates from any legal or customary right or privilege acquired or enjoyed either before or after the coming into force of this Charter with respect to any language that is not English or French.

MINORITY LANGUAGE EDUCATIONAL RIGHTS

23. (1) Citizens of Canada (a) whose first language learned and still understood is that of the English or French linguistic minority population of the province in which they reside, or (b) who have received their primary school instruction in Canada in English or French and reside in a province where the language in which they received that instruction is the language of the English or French linguistic minority population of the province, have the right to have their children receive primary and secondary school instruction in that language in that province. (2) Citizens of Canada of whom any child has received or is receiving primary or secondary school instruction in English or French in Canada, have the right to have all their children receive primary and secondary school instruction in the same language. (3) The right of citizens of Canada under subsections (1) and (2) to have their children receive primary and secondary school instruction in the language of the English or French linguistic minority population of a province (a) applies wherever in the province the number of children of citizens who have such a right is sufficient to warrant the provision to them out of public funds of minority language instruction; and (b) includes, where the number of those children so warrants, the right to have them receive that instruction in minority language educational facilities provided out of public funds.

ENFORCEMENT

24. (1) Anyone whose rights or freedoms, as guaranteed by this Charter, have been infringed or denied may apply to a court of competent jurisdiction to obtain such remedy as the court considers appropriate and just in the circumstances. (2) Where, in proceedings under subsection (1), a court concludes that evidence was obtained in a manner that infringed or denied any rights or freedoms guaranteed by this Charter, the evidence shall be excluded if it is established that, having regard to all the circumstances, the admission

of it in the proceedings would bring the administration of justice into disrepute.

GENERAL

25. The guarantee in this Charter of certain rights and freedoms shall not be construed so as to abrogate or derogate from any aboriginal treaty of other rights or freedoms that pertain to the aboriginal peoples of Canada including (a) any rights or freedoms that have been recognized by the Royal Proclamation of October 7, 1763; and (b) any rights or freedoms that now exist by way of land claims agreements or may be so acquired.

26. The guarantee in this Charter of certain rights and freedoms shall not be construed as denying the existence of any other rights or freedoms that exist in Canada.

27. This Charter shall be interpreted in a manner consistent with the preservation and enhancement of the multicultural heritage of Canadians.

28. Nothwithstanding anything in this Charter, the rights and freedoms referred to in it are guaranteed equally to male and female persons.

29. Nothing in this Charter abrogates or derogates from any rights or privileges guaranteed by or under the Constitution of Canada in respect of denominational, separate or dissentient schools.

30. A reference in this Charter to a province or to the legislative assembly or legislature of a province shall be deemed to include a reference to the Yukon Territory and the Northwest Territories, or to the appropriate legislative authority thereof, as the case may be.

31. Nothing in this Charter extends the legislative powers of any body or authority.

APPLICATION OF CHARTER

32. (1) This Charter applies (a) to the Parliament and government of Canada in respect of all matters within the authority of Parliament including all matters relating to the Yukon Territory and Northwest Territories; and (b) to the legislature and government of each province in respect of all matters within the authority of the legislature of each province. (2) Notwithstanding subsection (1), section 15 shall not have effect until three years after this section comes into force.

33. (1) Parliament or the legislature of a province may expressly declare in an Act of Parliament or of the legislature, as the case may be, that the Act or a provision thereof shall operate notwithstanding a provision included in section 2 or sections 7 to 15 of this Charter. (2) An Act or a provision of an Act in respect of which a declaration made under this section is in effect shall have such operation as it would have but for the provision of this Charter referred to in the declaration. (3) A declaration made under subsection (1) shall cease to have effect five years after it comes into force or on such earlier date as may be specified in the declaration. (4) Parliament or a legislature of a province may re-enact a declaration made under subsection (1). (5) Subsection (3) applies in respect of a re-enactment made under subsection (4).

CITATION

34. This Part may be cited as the *Canadian Charter of Rights and Freedoms*.

CHATTEL MORTGAGE

A chattel is an item of personal property—a car, boat, bond, or any other property except real estate. A chattel mortgage is a loan that is guaranteed by pledging the borrower's chattel as collateral. She keeps the item that he puts up as collateral, while the lender files an agreement with a local public office specifying the amount of the debt and the property used as collateral. If the borrower does not repay the loan as agreed, the lender can take the property and sell it to satisfy the amount of the loan.

In recent years most chattel mortgages have been replaced by documents that are known as security agreements.

Except for merchants and farmers who may pledge their machinery, rolling stock, crops, and animals while still retaining them, chattel mortgages did not exist in Quebec up to 1994. However, a form of chattel mortgage was among Civil Code revisions that went into effect in January 1994. See also SECURITY AGREEMENT.

CHEQUE

Strictly speaking, a cheque is a bill of exchange that is drawn on a bank. Since the Bill of Exchange Act states that a bank is "an incorporated bank or savings bank carrying on business in Canada," a "cheque" drawn on a trust company, *caisse populaire*, credit union, or other financial institution is a bill of exchange, not a cheque. However, the difference between the two has now all but disappeared.

Most of us write cheques routinely, unaware that their use and misuse have a number of legal consequences. The basic process is simple: the person who writes a cheque (the drawer) directs his bank (the drawee) to pay a specified sum of money from his account to a third party (the payee).

Banks are usually required to cash a cheque when the payee presents it to the drawer's bank, provided the payee is one of its customers. If he is not, the bank may refuse to cash the cheque. The payee then may take the cheque to his own bank or to a business that offers cheque-cashing services.

CASHING CHEQUES

A bank may be reluctant to cash a cheque when the payee is not one of its depositors because the bank has no protection if the drawer's account does not have sufficient funds to cover the cheque. In contrast, when one of its own depositors presents a cheque, the bank can protect itself by putting a temporary hold, or lien, on that person's account until the cheque clears.

If a cheque "bounces"—if it is returned by the bank because of insufficient funds in the account, the payee must try to collect the money from the person who wrote the cheque. For example, suppose someone buys a television set from you at a garage sale and pays with a cheque that bounces. You should first try to talk to the purchaser and attempt to arrange for payment in cash. If your attempt at negotiation fails, you can always take the case to the small claims court to get your money or recover the set. See also BOUNCED CHEQUE.

STOP-PAYMENT ORDERS

Suppose you suddenly realize you do not have enough money in your account to cover a cheque you have mailed, or for some reason you do not want a certain cheque to be cashed by the bank—a cheque to a charity that you subsequently find is bogus, for example. What can you do? One solution is to tell your bank to stop payment on the cheque.

The bank will ask for your account number, the number of the cheque, the amount, the date, and the name of the payee. You can stop payment by telephone, but the bank will generally require written authorization within a few days. Unless the cheque was certified or was already paid, a bank usually honors a stop-payment order. It does, however, charge a fee to cover the cost of the paperwork involved.

FORGED CHEQUES

If you discover that a cheque has been forged in your name, notify your bank immediately. Since it has your correct signature on file, the bank is responsible if it allows the forged cheque to go through and must replace the money taken from your account to pay it. It is the bank's responsibility to recover the money from the forger.

However, if your own negligence contributes to the forgery, the responsibility may be placed on you. If you do not notify the bank when your chequebook is lost or stolen, for example, you may not be able to recover the money that is lost to a forger. If you notice a forged cheque when reviewing your bank statement, notify the bank right away. Otherwise, you could lose your right to get your money back. Remember that you are responsible for examining the bank's monthly statement against your own records and canceled cheques.

A Saskatchewan man agreed in writing to notify the Toronto Dominion Bank of any errors in his bank statements or attached cheques and vouchers, but failed to do so within the agreed 30 days. Unfortunately, the bank had honored several bad cheques; his signature had been forged on some, and the sums payable had been altered on others. The customer sued, but the court dismissed his action. It ruled the signed agreement was clear and unambiguous: therefore the customer had no right of action for breach of contract.

ALTERED CHEQUES

Will you be out of pocket if a crook alters the amount on one of your cheques? It all depends.

Suppose you write a cheque for $5 to Harvey Potts, an unscrupulous antiques dealer. By adding two zeros and the word *hundred* to your cheque, he collects $500 from your account. If you wrote the cheque so carelessly that Harvey could easily alter it, you could be con-

sidered negligent and responsible for the full amount. But if you made the cheque out properly, your bank is the unlucky party. It can deduct from your account the $5 you intended to pay in the first place, but it will have to get the other $495 from Harvey Potts.

To discourage any alteration of your cheques:

◇ When writing the amount in numerals, leave no space between the printed dollar sign on the cheque and the numbers you enter alongside. Write the cents numbers raised above the line and underline them twice.

◇ When writing the amount in words, use capital letters (they are harder to alter than script) and draw a line between the amount and the word *dollars* printed on the cheque.

◇ Never give anyone a "blank cheque" (one you have signed without filling in the amount). The bearer might lose the cheque or turn out to be untrustworthy and fill in a higher sum than you intended.

ENDORSING CHEQUES

Be careful when endorsing cheques for deposit. If you sign your name on the back without any other statement, you have made a "blank endorsement," authorizing the bank to pay the funds to anyone who presents the cheque—even a thief who steals it after you endorse it. (But the bank is responsible if it cashes a cheque on which your endorsement was forged, because it has a duty to verify each depositor's signature.)

To avoid the risk of a blank endorsement you can instruct the bank to deposit funds

directly into your account. To do this, simply write the words "for deposit only" on the back of the cheque next to your signature. This prevents anyone else from cashing the cheque.

You can also direct the bank to cash the cheque for a third party. If the endorsement reads "Jane Witherspoon—pay only to Derek Davis," the bank can give the money only to Derek Davis unless Derek in turn endorses the cheque to another person. However, some banks will not honor cheques with third-party endorsements.

If you want to endorse a cheque over to a third person, but you do not want to be responsible if the cheque should bounce, you can protect yourself by the way you write the endorsement. Suppose you owe Bob $200, and Abe has just given you a cheque for that amount. You sign the cheque over to Bob, including the words "without recourse" in the endorsement. If the cheque is no good, Bob cannot hold you responsible for the money. He will have to seek it from Abe, who initially wrote the cheque. See BANK ACCOUNT; CASHIER'S CHEQUE; CERTIFIED CHEQUE; ELECTRONIC FUNDS TRANSFER; FLOAT; KITING.

CHILD ABUSE AND NEGLECT

Under normal circumstances, parents have the right to the custody of their children, the right to control and discipline them, and the right to make decisions with regard to their health and welfare.

Parents who abuse or neglect their children may forfeit some or all of these rights. Sometimes the state, through its youth or family courts, must step in and assume the parents' responsibilities. Provincial laws define child abuse and declare when the province may take action to protect the child.

Corporal punishment

In most provinces, parents have the right to use corporal punishment, as long as it is not excessive. The average spanking (which many experts believe is wrong) does not legally constitute child abuse. But 50 blows with a leather belt definitely does. (Quebec's new Civil Code prohibits all corporal punishment.)

Any injury requiring medical attention that a parent or other adult inflicts is child abuse. So are actions that, even if they produce no visible wounds, amount to torture, such as holding a child's head under water or confining a child to a closet or basement. Increasingly, courts are holding parents responsible if their child is harmed by another person, such as the mother's boyfriend.

Sexual and emotional abuse

Sexual behavior toward a child, including intercourse, fondling for a sexual purpose, or making a child watch sexual acts, calls for legal action when discovered. But hugging and kissing a child in an affectionate, non-sexual way is not sexual abuse, nor is taking photos of your child nude in the bathtub, as long as the pictures are not suggestive or provocative.

Physical and sexual abuse cause emotional damage, but emotional abuse can also be inflicted by words or actions. If a mother dresses her young son in skirts and parades him around as a girl, or a father repeatedly calls his teenage daughter a slut, the humiliation the child suffers amounts to emotional abuse and may be grounds for removing the child from the parents' custody.

REDRESSING THE PAST

Several provinces have allowed children to sue parents who have sexually abused them in the past. The Supreme Court of Canada has also held that the usual prescription or limitation of action (the period of time allowed in which to sue) does not apply in these tragic cases.

A Manitoba court ordered a young woman's father to pay her $170,000 damages for sexually abusing her as a child. Of this, $20,000 was allotted for therapy, $100,000 for psychological trauma, and $50,000 for aggravated damages.

An Ontario court (General Division) ordered a mother to pay her daughter $135,000 for failing to protect the young girl from sexual abuse by the mother's common law spouse. Mr. Justice Rutherford said that the mother, "faced with known circumstances . . . failed . . . to protect the best interests of her daughter . . . but enabled the abuse and sexual exploitation at the hands of the defendant stepfather to continue."

PREVENTIVE MEASURES

In June 1993, an all-party Commons Committee recommended a series of measures to better protect abused children.

Among their recommendations were:

1. The prosecution of child sexual abuse cases should be speeded up and given high priority, since it is damaging to a child to have to wait up to two years for the case to be heard.

2. More programs should be set up to "demystify" the criminal law process so that young victims should not have to suffer the stress and fear that a court hearing can cause.

3. Police, prosecutors and judges should receive special training on how to respond better to complaints involving the sexual abuse of children.

4. The same prosecutor should handle all aspects of the case, from arraignment to preliminary hearing to trial.

5. The "formality and intimidating environment" of courtrooms should be relaxed for child witnesses.

6. Victims younger than 14 years should be able to testify before a screen or in a room away from the accused, unless the judge orders otherwise.

7. A code of ethics should be developed for the benefit of defense lawyers so that they are not allowed to intimidate or harass child witnesses during cross-examination.

CHILD NEGLECT

Extreme neglect of a child is a crime that warrants court intervention. It can take a number of forms.

When a parent leaves his or her children without making arrangements for their supervision, care, or support, the parent is guilty of abandonment. If the abandonment continues for a long time, the child may be taken from the parents and put up for adoption.

Failure to provide

Not giving a child adequate food, shelter, supervision, or medical care is also considered neglect. Anyone guilty of this can be charged with abandonment and refusing to provide the necessities of life, a crime punishable by fine, or imprisonment up to two years, or both.

Generally the state would not remove children from their homes if their parents' failure to provide for them is due solely to poverty. If a family is living in a camper with no electricity, and local service agencies cannot provide other shelter, the state does not have grounds to remove the children from the home against the parents' will.

However, if resources are available that the family refuses to use to their advantage, the state may intervene to protect the children. If low-income housing is available to a single mother who insists on living in a public park with her infant child, she could be charged with neglect and her child placed in a foster home. An employed father, who has the means to support his family but fails to do so, could be charged with failing to provide the necessities of life for his wife and child, even if they were receiving these from the welfare authorities.

The failure of parents to provide their children with adequate medical care is usually grounds for court intervention. The courts have consistently held that whenever certain medical procedures are not permitted by a person's faith, for example the receiving of a blood transfusion by the child of Jehovah's Witnesses, the child's right to life overrides the parents' right to freedom of religion.

The Supreme Court has also upheld a conviction of involuntary homicide against the parents of a diabetic child who died for want of insulin. The parents refused to allow the child to receive insulin on grounds that such a medical procedure was incompatible with their religious beliefs.

If parents refuse, for whatever reason, to provide the medical care needed to save a child's life, the court will not hesitate to appoint a guardian, who would have authority to permit medical treatment.

MANDATORY REPORTING OF SUSPECTED ABUSE

In an effort to stop child abuse, many provinces have enacted mandatory reporting laws. They require professionals such as doctors, nurses, teachers, social workers, therapists, and police officers to report any suspected child abuse to the child-protection service.

Professionals who fail to report the suspected abuse may be charged with a crime. Those who do report child abuse are granted immunity in the event that they make an honest mistake. For example, a doctor who discovers multiple bruises on a child suspects child abuse and files a report. Later it turns out the bruises were due to a fall. The child's parents cannot sue the doctor for making a false report, nor can they sue her for slander, libel, breach of confidentiality, or invasion of privacy.

VOLUNTARY REPORTING

Even if you are not a professional legally required to report child abuse, you should report abuse if you have a good (preferably concrete) reason for suspecting it. Although you may be wrong in your suspicions, it is better to put the interests of the child first. Do not assume that someone else will report the abuse, or that it is none of your business. The child could be suffering great harm and have no way to protect himself. Do not worry about retaliation, because your report will be kept confidential.

Many communities have child-abuse hotlines. If you do not have this service in your area, call your local police or child-welfare agency. For a child in immediate danger of injury or death, call the general emergency number, 911.

CHILD-ABUSE INVESTIGATIONS

When a local child-welfare agency receives a report of child abuse or neglect, it is required by law to conduct a prompt investigation. The kind of action taken depends on the severity of the abuse. In cases of serious abuse or neglect, the child is removed from the custody of his parents immediately. If crimes such as sexual assault or beating have been committed, the parents may be arrested and charged. The child-welfare agency then makes arrangements for the child to

Declaration of the Rights of the Child

On Nov. 20, 1959, the General Assembly of the United Nations unanimously adopted the Declaration of the Rights of the Child. It affirmed to all children—without distinction of race, color, sex, language, religion, political or other opinion, national or social origin, property, birth, or other status—the fundamental human rights promulgated by the U.N.'s 1948 Universal Declaration of Human Rights. The Declaration calls on mankind to grant children the following:

PRINCIPLE 1. The child shall enjoy all the rights set forth in this Declaration. All children, without any exception whatsoever, shall be entitled to these rights, without distinction or discrimination on account of race, color, sex, language, religion, political or other opinion, national or social origin, property, birth or other status, whether of himself or his family.

PRINCIPLE 2. The child shall enjoy special protection, and shall be given opportunities and facilities, by law and by other means, to enable him to develop physically, mentally, morally, spiritually and socially in a healthy and normal manner and in conditions of freedom and dignity. In the enactment of laws for this purpose the best interests of the child shall be the paramount consideration.

PRINCIPLE 3. The child shall be entitled from his birth to a name and nationality.

PRINCIPLE 4. The child shall enjoy the benefits of social security. He shall be entitled to grow and develop in health; to this end special care and protection shall be provided both to him and to his mother, including adequate prenatal and postnatal care. The child shall have the right to adequate nutrition, housing, recreation and medical services.

PRINCIPLE 5. The child who is physically, mentally or socially handicapped shall be given the special treatment, education and care required by his particular condition.

PRINCIPLE 6. The child, for the full and harmonious development of his personality, needs love and understanding. He shall, wherever possible, grow up in the care and under the responsibility of his parents, and in any case in an atmosphere of affection and of moral and material security; a child of tender years shall not, save in exceptional circumstances, be separated from his mother. Society and the public authorities shall have the duty to extend particular care to children without a family and those without adequate means of support. Payment of state and other assistance toward the maintenance of children of large families is desirable.

PRINCIPLE 7. The child is entitled to receive education, which shall be free and compulsory, at least in the elementary stages. He shall be given an education which will promote his general culture, and enable him on a basis of equal opportunity to develop his abilities, his individual judgment, and his sense of moral and social responsibility, and to become a useful member of society. The best interests of the child shall be the guiding principle of those responsible for his education and guidance; that responsibility lies in the first place with his parents.

The child shall have full opportunity for play and recreation, which should be directed to the same purpose as education; society and the public authorities shall endeavor to promote the enjoyment of this right.

PRINCIPLE 8. The child shall in all circumstances be among the first to receive protection and relief.

PRINCIPLE 9. The child shall be protected against all forms of neglect, cruelty and exploitation. He shall not be the subject of traffic, in any form.

The child shall not be admitted to employment before an appropriate minimum age; he shall in no case be caused or permitted to engage in any occupation or employment which would prejudice his health or education, or interfere with his physical, mental or moral development.

PRINCIPLE 10. The child shall be protected from practices which may foster racial, religious and any other form of discrimination. He shall be brought up in a spirit of understanding, tolerance, friendship among peoples, peace and universal brotherhood and in full consciousness that his energy and talents should be devoted to the service of his fellow man.

stay with relatives, a foster family, in a shelter, or, if necessary, a hospital. Within a few days a court hearing is held and a judge decides whether it is necessary to remove the child from his parents' custody permanently.

In less serious situations, when the child is not in immediate danger, he cannot be removed from the family home. The court may, however, require the parents to undergo counseling or take parenting lessons. If they refuse to cooperate or the situation gets worse, the court may remove the child from the home.

If abuse or neglect is minor or unlikely to recur—if a parent left her child unattended in the park for five minutes, for example—the welfare agency and the parents may agree to work together informally. Sometimes the investigation produces no evidence of wrongdoing, and the case is closed.

COURT PROCEEDINGS

Cases of serious abuse or neglect are referred to the youth court or family court, which determines who should have jurisdiction, or authority, over the child—the parents or the youth protection agency. If there is sufficient evidence that the child is in danger, the court assumes authority and may take any one of a number of measures for his protection. The court may:

◇ Allow the child to remain at home under the supervision of the child-protection agency.

◇ Order the child to be

placed in a foster or group home until the family situation has improved.

◇ Temporarily suspend all contact between the parents and the child.

◇ In extreme cases, take away the parents' rights to the child and have the child placed in an adoptive home or in long-term foster care.

Removing a child from his parents' custody, temporarily or permanently, is a drastic move. Most of the time, therefore, the child will be returned to the family home when the family cooperates with authorities to rectify the problems that led to the abuse or neglect. See also FAMILY COURT; YOUNG OFFENDER.

CHILD CUSTODY

Child custody means much more than having your children live in your home. It includes the right to guide and discipline them and to make important decisions about their education, religious training, and medical care.

Every parent has the right to the custody of his or her children, unless that right has been restricted or taken away by a court. The following are typical circumstances under which a parent must give up custody:

◇ When a youth or family court finds that the parent has neglected or abused his child. See CHILD ABUSE AND NEGLECT.

◇ When a parent voluntarily gives his custodial rights to another person in an adoption proceeding. See ADOPTION.

◇ When a parent loses some or all of his custodial rights in a separation or divorce. See DIVORCE.

Most questions affecting custody arise in cases of divorce. While the parents are married, they have equal custody of their children. When they separate, hard decisions must be made. The parents must try to agree on a custody arrangement that is in the best interests of their children. If they cannot agree, the court must make the decision for them.

JOINT CUSTODY

These days, courts are quite likely to grant parents who are divorcing joint custody of their children. This has psychological benefits for all concerned. Neither parent is made to feel that he or she has "lost" the child or children, and often the relationships between the parents themselves and between the parents and the child or children are more comfortable as a result. Section 16 (1) of the Divorce Act (1985) says that: "The court shall give effect to the principle that a child of the marriage should have as much contact with each spouse as is consistent with the best interests of the child."

Joint custody means parents share responsibility for important decisions, such as their children's education and medical care. It does not necessarily mean that the children spend half their time in their mother's home and half in their father's.

The physical custody of the children can be handled in a number of ways. Usually, children live with one parent most of the time and regularly visit the other. Sometimes, parents who live in the same school district switch the children's residence every few months, or the children may spend part of the week with each parent. Whatever the arrangements, joint custody is most successful when parents cooperate to do what is best for their children.

SOLE CUSTODY

On the surface, sole custody resembles joint custody since the noncustodial parent is usually given visitation rights— even for extended periods, such as the Christmas holidays or the entire summer. The major difference is that the custodial parent has the main responsibility for making important decisions about the children's lives.

Sometimes the court may limit visitation rights. If the judge knows a father is likely to harm his son if they are left alone, she can order that a third person be present during the visit. If she feels a mother may try to abduct her children, she may order that the visit take place within the city limits. If the judge finds a parent is often too drunk to care for a child overnight, she can order that visits be arranged in the day. In extreme cases, such as when a parent is known to be a constant danger to the children, the judge can deny visitation rights altogether.

In a recent and important case, the Ontario Court of Appeal unanimously ruled that the custodial parent, in this case the mother, could not move from Ontario to British Columbia with her young son. To do so would deprive the child of his right to see his father with whom he enjoyed a good relationship. The mother wanted to make the move because her new husband had better business prospects out west. The Appeal Court, maintaining the earlier decision of the Ontario Supreme Court, and acknowledging that the father did not have the financial means to travel to British Columbia, ruled that removing the child from Ontario "would negatively affect the close relationship between the respondent (the father) and his child."

SPECIAL CIRCUMSTANCES

Several factors affect court decisions in custody cases.

Tender-years doctrine

In the past, most courts presumed that young children (children of "tender years") belonged with their mother. If there was a contest between parents for custody, they gave custody to the mother unless she was shown to be unfit.

The modern trend, however, is for the courts to regard both parents as equally fit to care for the children and to grant custody to the parent who can provide the better care for them.

Wishes of the child and third-party custody

Many courts consider the wishes of the child before deciding who gets custody, especially in the case of a teenager. However, the judge has the authority to go against those wishes, if they are not in the child's own best interests. If the judge determines that neither parent is fit to have custody, she may grant it to someone else, such as a grandparent or other relative. Parents may also agree between themselves to place their children with another person.

Grandparents' rights

After the divorce proceedings, the Divorce Act allows grandparents to file a petition for their own visitation rights. This ensures that their opportunities for seeing their grandchildren are not subject to the whims of the custodial parent. See also GRANDPARENTS' RIGHTS.

Modification

A custody order can always be modified by the court if circumstances warrant the change. For example, a judge may alter a custody arrangement if the custodial parent interferes with the other parent's visitation rights, makes plans to move out of the province, or suffers from a debilitating illness that makes caring for the child virtually impossible. In any judgment that varies from the original custody order, the court always considers the best interests of the child, and the goal that the child should have the maximum desirable contact with both parents. If the custodial parent tries to frustrate the other parent's right to visit the child, the court may very well order the custody to be transferred to the other parent.

CHILD EMPLOYMENT

Both the federal and provincial governments have strict laws to protect children from overwork, hazardous jobs, and dangerous, unhealthful, or immoral working conditions.

Federal law is embodied in the Canada Labour Code. This applies to banks, air transport and airports, bus companies, trains and truck companies operating interprovincially or internationally, telephone and cable systems, radio and television broadcasting, Crown corporations, and certain operations such as grain elevators, uranium mining and processing, and flour and feed mills.

Provincial labor laws deal with companies that operate completely or at least very substantially within the province.

MINIMUM AGE

The Canada Labour Code prohibits anyone under 17 years of age from working between 11 p.m. and 6 a.m. Other federal laws, such as the Explosives Act and Regulations, and the Atomic Energy Act and Regulations, make it illegal to hire anyone under age 18 (21 in some cases), for certain jobs.

Some provincial laws, such as the British Columbia Mines Act and the Alberta Coal Mines Safety Act, prohibit young people from certain jobs, such as working underground, unless they are 18 years old or older.

All provinces also have laws making education compulsory until the age of 16; in Ontario,

Newfoundland, Yukon, and the Northwest Territories, a 16-year-old must attend school until the end of the school year. As well, most provinces prohibit anyone under age 16 from engaging in employment that is "likely to be unwholesome or harmful to health and prejudicial to school attendance."

New Brunswick prohibits children under 14 from working in industry, including the construction and forest industries. Nor may they work in hotels, restaurants, theaters, dance halls or garages.

Newfoundland, on the other hand, specifically allows 12- to 14-year-olds to work as messengers, newspaper sellers, pinboys, and shoeshine boys, but not after 8 p.m. in winter, 9 p.m. the rest of the year.

Ontario prohibits anyone under 14 from working in industry, and prohibits anyone under 16 from engaging in a trade or occupation in a place that has public access between the hours of 9 p.m. to 6 a.m. However, they can be employed in public entertainment if the Children Aid Society has no objection.

Alberta prohibits 15- to 18-year-olds from working from 9 p.m. to midnight in retail stores, hotels, and restaurants, unless supervised by an adult. They are absolutely prohibited from working between midnight and 6 a.m. Children 15 to 18 may work in other businesses after midnight provided they are supervised and have written permission from their parent or guardian.

British Columbia prohibits work for children under 15,

except with the permission of the director of the Employment Labor Standards Commission, and in the case of students in a work experience or occupational training program. Children under 15 may, however, work as baby-sitters, attendants for disabled people, and as artists and musicians.

Quebec prohibits any school child from working during school hours unless an exemption has been obtained from the school board. Exemptions will only be given for carrying out urgent work, and for no more than six weeks.

WORK HOURS

The employment standards legislation of all provinces and territories limits how many hours people under 16 years of age may work, and what times of day that they may work. Even though the limits vary greatly, the situation across Canada has vastly improved since the Ontario Factory, Shop and Building Act of 1913 was passed. Progressive at the time, it still allowed a 10-hour day and a 60-hour workweek.

Most provinces now restrict people of 16 or under from working more than three hours during a school day and six to eight hours on other days. People under 16 are usually also prohibited from working after about 10 p.m. unless they receive special permission from their provincial Labour Standards Commission.

The usual workweek today is about 40 hours, but the length of the workweek may vary, depending on the particular industry. For example, tradesmen in Quebec work a 40-hour week, whereas employees of the garment industry in both Ontario and Quebec work 36 to 37 ½ hours.

OVERTIME

Work done after the standard workweek is considered overtime. In New Brunswick, Newfoundland, and Nova Scotia, overtime is calculated at 1½ times the minimum wage; in the other provinces overtime is paid at 1½ times the employee's rate of pay.

In British Columbia, double pay must be paid for any work that exceeds 11 hours in one day or 48 hours in one week.

Overtime pay scales for unionized workers are spelled out in the collective agreements of their organizations.

There are numerous exceptions to rules on overtime, especially in the case of farm workers, fishermen, students, professionals, domestics, and managerial staff.

WAGES

At the time of writing, the minimum wage for students and inexperienced workers ranges from $4 per hour (federal) to $5.90 per hour in Ontario for students under 18 who are employed for 28 hours per week or less.

EMPLOYER VIOLATIONS

An employer who violates his provincial labor standards is subject to fines of up to $10,000, and in some cases imprisonment for up to one year. The decision to prosecute usually lies with the attorney general of the province. If an employer refuses to pay the salary owed, the employee can sue before the courts, usually before the small-claims court.

Most provinces also have another procedure for recovering wages, including overtime pay and any outstanding vacation pay: an employee can have the Labour Standards Commission investigate his claim. If the employer contests the claim, the matter can be appealed to an umpire or another administrative board whose decision is binding.

CHILD SUPPORT

With so many children living in homes headed by single parents, child support has become a major issue. When a couple with children separates or divorces, an important aspect of the separation agreement or divorce judgment involves payments by the noncustodial spouse to the other for support of the couple's children. Child support applies whether or not the parents are married.

Even in cases involving the breakup of a second marriage, some courts have required the new spouse to support children of his spouse's first marriage. In the court's view, the new spouse stands *in loco parentis* (in the place of the parent), and parents are always obliged to support their children.

"The position that a new spouse bears no financial or other responsibility with respect to his or her partner's children by another marriage is truly outdated in today's world," said Mr. Justice Mason of the Alberta Queen's Bench in March 1993. The judge ordered a stepparent to support his spouse's children from a previous marriage, a judgment under appeal at the time of writing.

Parents' obligations toward their adopted children and their biologically conceived offspring have always been identical. Children born to parents who are not married to each other, and stepchildren in some cases, also have the same right to support as legitimate children.

The Ontario Child Welfare Act defines a "child" as someone "born within or outside marriage, and includes a person whom the parent has demonstrated a settled intention to treat as a child of his or her family . . . ."

HOW CHILD SUPPORT IS CALCULATED

When parents divorce or separate, they can agree between themselves, and with their lawyers' help if necessary, what the absent parent should pay the one with whom the child lives. If the couple cannot agree, or if the noncustodial parent refuses to contribute, the custodial parent must go to court to obtain a child support order. A judge can then order the absent parent to pay the custodial parent a certain sum for child's support, usually on a monthly or weekly basis.

How much one spouse must pay the other for child maintenance depends on the needs of the child, and the capacity and means of the spouse to pay such support. By law, the spouses have a joint financial obligation to maintain the child. So, even if the spouse with custody of the children is a multimillionaire, and the other earns only $250 per week, both are legally obliged, according to their respective means, to pay toward raising the children.

Factors to be considered in arriving at a fair contribution are the age of the children; the cost of their housing, food and clothing; educational costs, such as school fees, uniforms, and fees for extracurricular activities; dental and eye care; special medical needs not covered by Medicare; day care and baby-sitters; transportation; sports equipment; reasonable entertainment expenses such as movies, concerts, and restaurant meals; and special needs the children may have for such things as psychological counseling or orthodontic expenses.

These needs vary from one case to another. The financial support required by a two-year-old child, for example, is often different from that of a teenager. The courts try to order support that will maintain the child's standard of living as close as possible to what it was before the divorce or separation of the parents.

There is no age deadline for ending support payments. Parents are obliged to support their children even after the age of 18, if these children are unable to support themselves because of a mental or physical handicap, or if the children are still students.

AMICABLE SETTLEMENT

Divorcing or separating parents who mutually agree on child support arrangements avoid the considerable expense of a lengthy court battle. They would be wise to get the advice of lawyers experienced in family law. These will be knowledgeable of court judgments in comparable situations and can help the couple reach an agreement that is fair to both sides.

In some separation or divorce settlements, one spouse makes a lump sum payment, say $150,000, to the other in lieu of any future support. The courts usually accept any such agreement that is arrived at in a fair manner. A judge would be most unlikely to grant additional support to a spouse who agrees to such a court-approved settlement, then spends the money and finds himself or herself destitute, and seeks further support payments from the ex-spouse.

In the case of child support, however, a lump sum in lieu of periodic payments would most probably not be valid. Such an agreement would violate a minor child's right to future support. It probably would violate also provisions of the Divorce Act and provincial family law statutes, which declare parents' obligations to their children cannot be extinguished except in the most exceptional circumstances.

Although child support is almost always calculated in terms of money, the Northwest Territories recently passed a law whereby support payments may in some cases be made in kind. It may be an amount of meat or fish obtained from hunting or fishing.

MODIFICATIONS

How much alimentary pension you pay depends on the financial situation of you and your spouse when you made the agreement, or the court ordered the support. If either of your circumstances changes, one or other of you can ask the court to increase, decrease, or even cancel the alimentary pension. No modification is likely unless you can prove that circumstances have changed substantially.

Such would be the case, however, if one of you got, or lost, a job. That could substantially alter the ability of one spouse to pay, or the financial needs of the other. Or if you are contributing to the support of three children, two of whom have begun full-time jobs since the court judgment, a judge may agree to reduce your support obligation.

Of course if you have increased your debts by buying a new car, or by spending too much on new housing or vacations, the courts would not look favorably on your request to reduce your child support, considered to be one of your most important obligations.

A child's needs may increase as he or she grows older. This may be considered reason enough for increasing the amount of the child support.

Most jurisdictions have laws whereby alimentary pensions may be indexed annually according to the rate of inflation. Although the Divorce Act does not expressly provide for this indexation, it would be a good idea to include such a clause in any agreement submitted to the courts in divorce proceedings.

HOW THE COURTS ENFORCE CHILD SUPPORT ORDERS

Getting a support order from the courts is relatively easy: enforcing it is a different matter especially if the person responsible for the support is self-employed. The federal government and most provinces have agencies to help you get the support awarded to you. In Alberta, Prince Edward Island, Saskatchewan, and Quebec, the director of maintenance enforcement can enforce a court order by seizing the debtor's salary or other property, and will also take measures to find a debtor who has disappeared. In most cases the director of maintenance enforcement (in Quebec known as *le Percepteur des pensions alimentaires*) will try to recover support that is up to three years in arrears; in Alberta, he will try to get up to 10 years of missed payments.

In Ontario, under a Family Support Plan introduced in 1992, deductions are automatically made from the debtor's salary when there is a court order for him to pay support.

At the time of writing, Quebec is considering suspending the driver's license of anyone who defaults on support payments. This would strengthen the province's hand against self-employed debtors, such as taxi drivers or others

who could hide their assets from seizure.

In Manitoba, the person required to pay alimentary support must send post-dated cheques to the director of the maintenance orders program. The program checks payments or defaults by computer. Upon default, the director may seize the debtor's salary, property, and any retirement pension, accident or other insurance payments he receives. The debtor must also appear before a court officer or judge to explain why he defaulted. Anyone receiving support may register with this program by calling the clerk of the Provincial or Queen's Bench Court.

The Federal Family Orders and Agreements Enforcement Assistance Act gives the federal Department of Justice authority to help the creditors of court judgments find defaulters. If the defaulters are federal employees, members of the public service or armed forces for example, the justice department may seize any federal monies, such as income tax rebates, unemployment insurance benefits, and federal pensions, or salaries, owing to the debtor. (See USEFUL ADDRESSES at back of book.)

Even if the debtor declares bankruptcy, alimentary support debts will not be affected. He or she will owe the same amount plus interest and any new arrears even when liberated from other debts.

As a final measure, the courts sometimes imprison a defaulting debtor. Disobeying a court order to pay support

may constitute contempt of court, which is punishable by a fine, imprisonment, or both. Also, if the person who has custody of the child or children has no revenue other than the support payments ordered by the court, or that person is receiving social welfare assistance, the defaulting debtor may be guilty of "non support" — a criminal act punishable by jail.

SUPPORT ACROSS PROVINCIAL BORDERS

All provinces and territories have reciprocal agreements to enforce maintenance and support orders made by each other's courts. This Reciprocal Enforcement of Maintenance Orders (REMO) Agreement helps a creditor in, say, British Columbia, seize the salary or property of an ex-spouse who has moved to, say, Ontario.

If you have a judgment from your province, and the person who owes you support lives in another, contact the clerk of the court that rendered the order, or your lawyer. The provincial attorney general will notify his counterpart in the province where your ex-spouse lives, and execute your judgment. Make sure you have a certified copy of your judgment and some information about your ex-spouse's whereabouts.

Some provinces also have reciprocal arrangements with certain American states (Alberta, for example, has agreements with over 35 states), and even with other countries. For example, Quebec and France enforce each other's support judgments. See also DIVORCE.

If you have a support order for a child in your custody but are not receiving these payments from your former spouse, the following steps may help you secure them:

1. Get the help of a lawyer or a provincial child support enforcement agency. Keep in mind that although the federal government charges a small fee for enforcing support orders, most of the provincial enforcement agencies offer their services free.

2. Determine the precise amount you are owed. Since some support payments are made through the clerk of the court, his records may show how much has been paid and how much is still owing to you. If no such records exist, review your bank statements or deposit slips for the period in question to find out exactly what has been paid.

3. Make copies of important documents. Your lawyer will need to see the original court order setting the amount of child support and any further orders that have altered that amount. If payments have come through the court, she must have a copy of the current court ledger to see how much has been paid.

4. Gather whatever information your lawyer will need to make your case. For instance, if she intends to issue garnishment orders, she must know a few things about the noncustodial parent, such as where his bank is, who owes him money, and where he works. Other helpful information is his Social Insurance Number, last address, last employer, and car license number.

TRACING A DEFAULTER

If a defaulting parent has moved and you do not know where to, the federal Department of Justice will take steps to find him or her. You could try the following:

◇ Call or write to his most recent employer. Your spouse may have left a forwarding address, or his new employer may have contacted his former company for a reference.

◇ Ask unions or his social organizations for an address.

◇ Call his former utility and phone companies to see if he left a forwarding address.

◇ Ask his former associates, relatives, and friends where he is. Someone is likely to feel sympathetic toward you and tell you. See also DIVORCE.

CHILD TAX BENEFIT

In January 1993, the Child Tax Benefit replaced the former Family Allowance, Child Tax Credit, and the Credit for Dependent Children. A tax-free benefit based on family income, it is meant to redirect child benefits toward the neediest modest-income families. It provides a supplement to low-income working families, and payments are reduced when family income exceeds a certain figure ($25,921 in 1992).

Since the amount of the benefit depends on your revenue, you have to file an income tax return in order to receive payments. Monthly benefits are payable for all children as soon as they are born or adopted.

To be eligible, you must reside with a child under 18 years of age, and must be a citizen or permanent resident of Canada, a refugee (as determined by the Geneva Convention, 1951, see IMMIGRATION), or be a visitor or hold a Minister's Permit under the Immigration Act and have resided in Canada for at least 18 months.

You must apply for the benefit for a child born or adopted after January 1993. (Families that received a family allowance for December 1992 were automatically included in the program.) At the time of writing, the basic annual amount per child is $1,020 ($85 a month) for each child under 18, with supplements of $75 ($6.25 a month) for a third or any additional children, and additional supplements of about $213 ($17.75 a month) for each child under seven years of age, and up to $500 ($41.67 a month) for low-income working families. These amounts are adjusted annually.

Quebec and Alberta residents receive slightly different amounts, as these provinces have set different standards for determining the amount of the benefit. Alberta's are related to the age of the children, increasing from $933 for children under seven to $1,002 for children seven to 11, $1,131 for 12- to 15-year-olds, and $1,203 for 16- to 17-year-olds. In Quebec, payments vary according to the number of children.

Parents receive $869 for a first child, $1,000 for a second, and $1,597 for a third or any additional children.

The child tax benefit is payable even if you are absent from Canada, so long as your absence is for less than six months in any one year. Payments, made to the parent who is the primary care-giver, stop when the child turns 18, no longer lives with you, when you stop being a resident of Canada, or when your family income increases to the point that you are no longer entitled to the child tax benefit.

The money can be deposited directly into your bank account. Simply fill out the Direct Deposit Request available from Revenue Canada.

CHILDREN'S RIGHTS

Because of their immaturity, children do not have the same rights as adults. Our laws are written to protect children from the consequences of their acts and to prevent them from doing things that require a certain maturity. Except for acts specifically prohibited by law, children are under their parents' control and protection.

A child becomes an adult when she reaches the age of majority—18 to 19 years of age, depending on the province. A child may also be considered an adult for some purposes, such as driving, but not for others, such as voting.

Parents have the duty to provide medical care for their children and the right to make the decisions relating to this care. A universal exception to this right is when a child's life or health is in danger. If neither parent is available to give consent in an emergency, medical care can be provided without it. If a child's life is endangered, either because parents refuse to provide medical treatment or are providing inappropriate treatment, the state will intervene, and a court can appoint a guardian to make medical decisions for the child.

In some provinces, minors can obtain birth-control information, contraceptives, abortions, and treatment for venereal disease and drug and alcohol abuse, without the consent of their parents. See also ABORTION.

ADOPTION

In some provinces, children over a certain age, usually 10, must give their consent before they can be adopted.

A minor who has a child may consent to the child's adoption without her parents' approval. All provinces require the minor to obtain independent legal advice regarding the consequences of surrendering her rights to the child. See also ADOPTION.

MARRIAGE AND SEX

A minor usually may not marry without the consent of at least one parent. If she does, the marriage may later be declared void and annulled. When parents refuse permission to marry, minors in some provinces may petition the court for permission. Once married, a minor is considered to be an emancipated minor and has the same rights as an adult. In most provinces, if minors enter into marriage without their parents' consent and a child is born, the marriage cannot be annulled.

CONSENTING TO SEX

The age at which a minor can consent to sex is a complex issue. Because a young person does not always know the consequences of his acts, the Criminal Code has attempted to set certain guidelines.

The law clearly states that no person under 12 years of age can validly consent to having sex. For minors aged 12 to 14 the law is a bit more flexible. It considers sex between two such minors not criminal so long as the older one is not more than 16 years of age.

In all cases, the older adolescent cannot be more than two years older than his partner. If a person who is, say, 18 has sex with another aged 15, then the 18-year-old can be in deep trouble. A person over 14 years of age but under 18 may consent to having sex. However, this person's consent would not be considered valid if the other partner, even one who is less than two years older, is in a position of authority or confidence to the younger partner.

Sexual consent is not valid if the younger person is dependent upon the older one. If a 16-year-old runaway lived with a 20-year-old who provided food and shelter for the younger one, sex between the two would be illegal, since the 16-year-old could be considered dependent on the other.

The penalty for having sex with a minor varies with the circumstances. If found guilty, the accused could be given probation, a suspended sentence, a fine with or without imprisonment, or in the most serious cases, imprisonment for life.

Buying sex from a person under 18 years of age is punishable by five years' imprisonment. It is not a defense to say you thought the prostitute was older than 18; the accused must prove to the court that he took every reasonable measure to ascertain that the prostitute was over 18. See also AGE OF CONSENT; SEXUAL ASSAULT.

DRIVING AND WORKING

Minors can apply for a driver's license when they reach the age specified by provincial law. Some provinces require the parent's consent.

Children under 14 have no legal right to work except in "casual employment," such as delivering newspapers and baby-sitting. Federal and provincial laws regulate both the types of employment open to minors of 14 years and over, and the number of hours they may work. Parents have the right to keep the money earned by their minor children who are not emancipated.

CONTRACTS

If an adult enters into a contract with a minor, the adult can be held to the contract but the minor cannot.

Suppose 16-year-old Johnny signs an agreement to buy a television on an installment plan. If, after making only one payment, he decides he cannot

afford it and calls the dealer to tell him to pick up the television, there is nothing else the dealer can do. Furthermore, if the television should be destroyed in a fire, Johnny, unlike an adult, could not be required to make any additional payments, and the dealer would be out of luck.

In most provinces the legal age for making a contract is 18. But most provinces allow minors to enter into binding contracts for "necessaries"— food, clothing, and shelter.

DRINKING, SMOKING, AND PORNOGRAPHY

Every province prohibits the sale of alcohol and tobacco to anyone under 18 years of age. Federal laws also prohibit the sale of obscene or pornographic materials to minors. Both the minor using the alcohol, tobacco, or obscene material, and the adult who supplies it, face criminal prosecution. See also ALCOHOL.

INHERITANCES AND WILLS

Minors may inherit property but cannot manage or dispose of their inheritance until they reach the age of majority.

Depending on the province, you must be 18 or 19 years of age to make a valid will. If a minor dies and has property, it will be distributed according to provincial laws, generally to the next of kin. See DYING WITHOUT A WILL; WILL.

YOUTH COURT

Children who have been accused of crimes are tried in a youth court, a distinct and

separate system from adult criminal courts.

Children generally do not have a right to trial by jury, and the youth court proceedings are closed and confidential so that they will not stigmatize a child in later life.

Nevertheless they do have many of the same rights as adult criminal defendants— the right to be represented by a lawyer, to confront their accusers in open court, to cross-examine witnesses, to remain silent, and to be presumed innocent until found guilty. See YOUNG OFFENDER.

EMANCIPATION

When a child is emancipated, he is freed of parental control and his parents no longer have any legal duties toward him. He has the right to be employed, to keep his wages, and to live apart from the family home. He can also make contracts, write a will, and get a driver's license without his parents' consent.

Emancipation occurs automatically when a child reaches the age of majority—18 or 19 years, depending on the province—but it can take place earlier if he gets married.

CHURNING

Just about every week, the stockbroker Louise hired six months ago calls her with investment advice. The advice is usually the same. A stock she bought last month is about to go down, but another is poised to skyrocket. Now is the time to sell the old stock and buy the new one.

Louise follows her broker's advice, but despite all the buying and selling she never seems to make any money. Whatever profit she makes gets eaten up by the broker's commissions.

Louise may be the victim of churning—excessive unjustified transactions by a broker in an investor's account, usually to generate commissions.

A stockbroker is considered a fiduciary, and so he must act in the best interest of his client. Churning violates this duty, and a broker who is found guilty of this may have his license suspended or revoked.

STEPS TO TAKE

If you think your broker may be churning your account, you should do the following:

1. Call or write to the nearest office of your provincial securities commission, which licenses most stockbrokers. The commission has the authority to investigate both individual brokers and brokerage firms.

2. Call your provincial office of consumer protection. It may investigate your complaint and may advise you if it would be worthwhile to sue your stockbroker for losses caused to you by churning.

3. If you can do without investment advice, consider doing business through discount brokers such as DISNAT, the Green Line Service of the Toronto Dominion Bank, or Marathon Brown. A discount broker's rates may be as much as 75 to 80 percent less than those of a regular broker.

4. Remember, you have the final say in buying or selling stocks, and if you think your stockbroker is trading too often, get him to reduce the number of transactions.

See also SCAMS AND SWINDLES; STOCKBROKER; STOCKS AND BONDS.

CIRCUMSTANTIAL EVIDENCE

Facts that indirectly establish other facts, or from which other facts can be inferred, are known as circumstantial evidence. When Evelyn disappeared from home one day, her husband, Jack, called the police to report her as a missing person. Weeks later the police found Evelyn's dead body; she had been shot.

In investigating Evelyn's death, the police discovered Jack had recently taken out a large insurance policy on his wife's life, and purchased an automatic pistol, which he told the police he had lost. The police also learned that Jack had been having an affair with a co-worker. Although no one saw Jack shoot Evelyn, and the police never found the gun that killed her, Jack was charged with her murder, based on the circumstantial evidence.

In this situation, the facts that (1) Jack owned a pistol, (2) had insured his wife's life, and (3) was having an affair could all be proved. These facts were enough to lead the police to the conclusion that Jack had murdered his wife. In this case, the circumstantial evidence also convinced the jury that convicted him.

Circumstantial evidence is just as useful in court as direct evidence. Its strength lies in its logic. It can be used in civil lawsuits—such as those involving contracts and wills—as well as in criminal cases.

Although it is always dangerous to convict someone on circumstantial evidence alone, the high standard of proof required in a criminal case, that is, proof "beyond a reasonable doubt," acts as a restraint on the use of such evidence.

CITIZEN'S ARREST

Private citizens have the right to arrest any person who commits a crime in their presence. For example, if you are in a car accident and the other driver, obviously intoxicated, tries to leave the scene, you may legally detain him until the police arrive. Although the police will take the driver into custody and make the formal charge of drunk driving, your action in holding him for the police constitutes an arrest.

Before you make a citizen's arrest, be very sure the person you are arresting has committed a crime. The law grants the police immunity from civil lawsuits if they make an honest mistake when arresting someone, but there is no such immunity for private citizens.

Unlike a policeman who can arrest a person when he has

reasonable and probable grounds to believe a crime was committed, a private citizen cannot act on suspicion. You must actually see the other person commit a crime before you can make a citizen's arrest. See also FALSE ARREST; FALSE IMPRISONMENT; SHOPLIFTING.

CITIZENSHIP

Other than the aboriginal peoples, everyone else in Canada is either an immigrant or the descendant of immigrants. But whether your Canadian citizenship has roots going back many generations or just one, the Charter of Rights and Freedoms guarantees you equality under the law.

You become a Canadian citizen in one of two ways: by being born in Canada or by being "naturalized." Unlike countries such as Germany and Japan, where citizenship is not granted by virtue of being born there, Canada says any person born on Canadian soil is automatically a Canadian citizen. As does the United States, we follow the principle of *jus solis* (law of the soil), which says the territory in which you are born determines your citizenship.

Aside from children born in Canada, and children born outside the country to Canadian parents temporarily employed abroad (these children automatically being Canadian citizens), citizenship is available to all other Canadian residents who meet certain criteria.

If, for example, you are over 18 years of age and have legally resided here as a landed immi-

---

ABC's
OF YOUR RIGHTS ABROAD

As a Canadian citizen you have the right to advice and assistance from Canadian consulates and embassies in other countries you visit. You are subject to the laws of the lands that you visit, however, so keep these points in mind when you travel.

■ If a country on your itinerary requires a visa or proof of inoculation against smallpox or other diseases, you must obtain the visa or vaccinations at home.

■ Canadian passports cannot be renewed. When your passport expires you must get a new one, and this could be a problem if you are in another country. Avoid needless hassles by making sure your passport will be valid for your entire trip.

■ If you break the laws of the country you are visiting, you will be subject to the same court procedures and penalties as the local citizens. Remember that what may be a minor offense in Canada — possession of a small amount of marijuana, say, or buying currency on the black market — may be punishable by years in prison elsewhere.

■ Canadian consular and embassy officials can offer only limited service in another country. They may take steps to see that the laws of the country you are visiting are applied fairly to you, give you the name of a

local lawyer if you need one, and lend you money to return to Canada if you lose your funds or are affected by civil disruption or a natural disaster. In countries where there are no Canadian diplomatic or consular offices, the British embassy may act on your behalf, provided Canada has so arranged.

■ If you are a resident of Canada but not a citizen — a landed immigrant, say, or a refugee — and you stay away for more than six months, immigration authorities may decide on your return that you have voluntarily abandoned your immigrant status. So if you plan to stay away from Canada for more than six months, avoid complications by asking immigration authorities for a "returning resident permit" before you leave.

■ In certain cases, you may not have the right *to leave* Canada. Such would be the case if you are under court order to remain here pending the disposition of criminal charges against you.

---

grant for three of the last four years, you may apply for Canadian citizenship. In calculating your three years' residence, each day from the time you became a landed immi-

grant counts as one day, and any day you resided in Canada prior to being granted landing counts as half a day. So if you came to Canada as a student on Jan. 1, 1988, and became a landed immigrant on Jan. 1, 1992, you could apply for citizenship on Jan. 1, 1993. The four years from Jan. 1, 1988, to Dec. 31, 1991, would count for two years' residency, and the year from Jan. 1, 1992, to Dec. 31, 1993, would count as a full year, thus completing your three-year residency requirement.

APPLYING FOR CITIZENSHIP

Once you meet the eligibility requirements, contact the offices of the Citizenship Court in your area, or apply to the Registrar of Citizenship, Department of Citizenship and Immigration. See USEFUL ADDRESSES at back of book.

You must provide a birth certificate or other satisfactory proof of date and place of birth as well as proof that you have legally resided in Canada for the required period of time.

You should also have at least two other documents, such as your social insurance and Medicare cards, and/or your driver's license, to establish your identity, as well as two black-and-white passport-type photos, and the required fee.

Once the application has been filled out, signed by you before a notary public or commissioner for oaths, and mailed together with the fee, you will be ready for the next stage, an interview or hearing before a citizenship judge. The judge will ask you general questions about Canada and determine if you have sufficient English or French to integrate into Canadian society (exceptions are made for older people).

Booklets such as *A Look at Canada* and *The Canadian Citizen* are available free from Citizenship and Immigration Canada. So too is information on Canada's government, geography and history, and on citizen responsibilities, topics the judge will question you about. See USEFUL ADDRESSES at back of book. Citizenship classes are also available for prospective new Canadians.

Finally you take the oath of citizenship ("I swear/affirm that I will be faithful and bear allegiance to Her Majesty Queen Elizabeth the Second, Queen of Canada, Her Heirs and Successors, according to law and that I will faithfully observe the laws of Canada and fulfil my duties as a Canadian citizen"), receive your citizenship certificate, and are declared a citizen.

Should you be denied citizenship, you will be told why. You may then appeal to the Federal Court, or simply reapply for citizenship.

RIGHTS AND PRIVILEGES

Although all residents of Canada are protected by and are equal under law and no one has to endure discrimination based on race, religion, sex, age, color, national or ethnic origin, or mental or physical disability, citizens have additional rights and privileges.

Citizens may vote, and be candidates, in all federal and provincial elections (some provinces and municipalities grant voting privileges to noncitizens), may enter and leave the country, work and reside anywhere in Canada, and hold jobs as judges and diplomatic and immigration officers, posts not open to noncitizens.

Citizens may have priority for certain programs, such as student aid, and only citizens may get certain grants and scholarships. Citizens taught in English or French have the right to have their children taught in that language, where numbers permit.

Sponsoring certain foreign members of your family may be easier as a citizen than as a landed immigrant.

DUAL CITIZENSHIP

Canada's laws permit a Canadian to be a citizen of one or more other countries. Thus, a person born in England may remain a British citizen even if he becomes Canadian. Citizenship laws vary from one country to another and some countries may consider you have renounced their citizenship when you become Canadian. Greece and Turkey on the other hand would still consider you a Greek or Turkish citizen.

Dual citizenship can be both positive and negative. A naturalized Canadian citizen of Greek origin vacationing in Greece may be obliged to do his military service in that country. Canadian consular officials may be unable to help such a person, especially if he traveled on his Greek passport.

Holding dual citizenship may be advantageous if you wish to work in a country that considers you a citizen. You may even qualify for certain social programs there. Weigh the pros and cons carefully. In some circumstances you may wish to retain citizenship in another country, in others you may be better off renouncing it. See also IMMIGRATION.

CIVIL RIGHTS

The term *civil rights* refers to the rights everyone in Canada is entitled to have. Those rights are guaranteed by the Canadian Charter of Rights and Freedoms (see pages 90 to 92), now part of Canada's Constitution Act 1982. Since the charter became law (1982), the courts have led the way in recognizing our rights and seeing they are respected.

Most provinces also have human rights acts and other laws that recognize certain civil rights. Ontario, for instance, now guarantees the right to a civil trial in French, a right formerly reserved for trials involving criminal charges.

British Columbia's human rights legislation stipulates one cannot be refused a job simply because of a criminal record, if the criminal record is not related to the job. A bank would probably be justified in refusing you work as a teller if you had been convicted of fraud, but not if your conviction was for drunk driving. A British Columbia woman was compensated for her lost wages, humiliation, and loss of self-esteem after she was fired from her truck-driving job because of a prior drug conviction.

Human rights laws are also helping stamp out sexual harassment, expressly prohibited by many provinces and under sections 14(1) (c) and 14(2) of the Canadian Human Rights Act. (Provinces that do not specifically prohibit sexual harassment forbid discrimination on the basis of sex, which includes sexual harassment.)

In prohibiting sexual harassment, the Canada Labour Code also obliges employers to deal with and prevent such acts. Employers must have policies on ridding their workplaces of sexual harassment, and programs for dealing with victim complaints.

See also CHARTER OF RIGHTS AND FREEDOMS; DUE PROCESS OF LAW; EQUAL PROTECTION OF THE LAWS; PRESS, FREEDOM OF; RELIGION, FREEDOM OF; SPEECH, FREEDOM OF.

CIVIL SERVICE

Nonmilitary employees of a national, provincial, or municipal government who carry out its day-to-day operations are called the civil, or public service. A police officer in Toronto is a civil servant, as is a secretary to the lieutenant governor of Manitoba or an expert on political developments with the Department of Foreign Affairs in East Africa. The rules by which civil servants are hired, fired, paid, and promoted constitute the civil service system.

Civil service jobs, and even upgradings to higher classifications, are usually obtained in competitions: applicants who pass certain examinations qualify. Jobs in the civil service, though not as secure as in the past, are usually more secure than in the private sector. Unfortunately, certain higher posts are still obtained through patronage or favoritism toward certain persons by government ministers.

Government employees are expected to serve with impartiality and loyalty, and this was one reason why they were once forbidden to participate in political campaigns. In 1988, however, the Supreme Court of Canada held that all government employees can run for political office and/or participate in political campaigns.

The matter of police officers and public office is not yet fully resolved. Some say that those who enforce the law should not be involved in making it. Ontario police officers can run for political office, but they cannot work as police officers while doing so. Quebec police officers are forbidden to run for public office, but efforts to abolish that law are under way.

CLASS ACTION

Normally, anyone involved in a lawsuit must have a chance to appear in court and present her side of the case. This is a sensible rule for most lawsuits. But if a case involves hundreds of plaintiffs, allowing each one to appear would quickly exhaust court officials and cause unnecessary delays in resolving the suit. To overcome this problem, a judge may allow one or more plaintiffs to bring a class action, a lawsuit on behalf of many others who have the same claim against the defendant. Such a suit permits all similar claims to be heard in a single trial, thus saving a lot of time and expense for the courts and the people bringing the actions.

Class actions are most useful when many people have, for instance, been hurt because of a manufacturer's defective product. They could also be used to sue food and pharmaceutical manufacturers, financial institutions, and even condominium corporations, when a number of people have been hurt by their wrongdoing.

Before someone can undertake a class action, he must give notice to the public that he is bringing the action to court on behalf of those affected. If you fall within the class, but wish to opt out, you can do so.

Only Quebec (where they have been successfully used for several years) and Ontario permit class actions. Until relatively recently, they were difficult to get under way in Ontario. Owners of defective Firenza automobiles, for example, were not allowed to bring a class action against General Motors of Canada Ltd. because not everybody suffered the same amount of damages, and because the contracts of purchase for the automobiles were all different.

Problems that had previously prevented class actions were overcome in 1992 when the province passed the Class Proceedings Act, and the Law Society Amendment Act (Class Proceedings Funding). The Class Proceedings Act allows one person in a class action to represent the interests of many people. But first, certain criteria have to be met: this kind of action must be the most efficient and expedient way of settling the case, and it must fairly represent the interests of all the members of the class.

At the time of writing, the Borrowers' Action Society, a consumers' group, is suing Canadian Tire Ltd. in the first test of the act, and the first in several suits planned by the group against credit card issuers. The plaintiffs are claiming the card issuers misled the public about the rate of interest charged on overdue accounts. At stake is what the group estimates to be about $435 million in overpayments.

Anyone bringing a class action in Ontario may seek financial assistance from the class proceedings fund toward court costs and expenses such as the cost of bringing in expert witnesses. If the plaintiff wins, such funds may have to be repaid, at least in part.

When the plaintiff wins, the court must decide how much to order the defendant to pay. Not all the plaintiffs are in the courtroom, so the court does not know exactly how much money will be needed to cover all the claims. It must estimate how many people have been hurt by the defendant's actions and try to estimate how much the damages should be. In order to claim money from the judgment, you may have to have proof that you are entitled to a portion of the money awarded.

CLOSING, REAL ESTATE

The final step in the sale and purchase of a house or other real estate is known as the closing. This usually takes place at a meeting at which the buyer pays the seller, the seller gives the deed to the buyer, and the final mortgage transactions take place. Buyers are often apprehensive about closings because they must pay large sums of money, sign imposing documents, deal with lawyers and bankers, and be sure that all the cumbersome paperwork is done correctly. Some of these fears are unwarranted, however, because the buyer's lawyer or financing representative (or both) usually takes care of most of the paperwork, and has as great a stake as the buyer in seeing that nothing goes wrong.

In the period before the closing, the buyer must arrange for financing, have the property inspected, and have a title search made to ensure the seller truly owns (has title to) the property and that it is free of liens. The buyer is then ready to complete (close) the transaction.

The closing date is set in the sales contract. If either party is not ready to close the sale on that date, he must arrange for a postponement and may have to pay a penalty. Not showing up for a closing can mean forfeiting the deposit and being sued for damages or for the transfer of the property.

CHECKLIST

Your Real Estate Closing

When you buy a house or other real estate, you will have to examine a number of documents, including the ones listed below, when ownership of the property is finally transferred from the seller to you.

■ **SALES CONTRACT.**
You should see both the original sales contract and any changes made in it subsequently.

■ **CLOSING STATEMENT.**
Be sure the items in the closing statement agree with the sales contract, and that any changes made to it are correct.

■ **DEED TO THE PROPERTY.**
This is the document that transfers title (or ownership) of the property from the seller to you, the buyer.

■ **SELLER'S AFFIDAVIT.**
This document proves that no liens or mortgages are outstanding on the property.

■ **MORTGAGE DOCUMENTS.**
These will depend on the nature of your mortgage agreement.

■ **PRORATING AGREEMENTS.**
These documents specify how you and the seller will divide such ongoing expenses as property taxes, insurance, and utilities.

■ **HOMEOWNERS' INSURANCE.**
You and the seller must both have proof that the property is insured.

■ **SELLER'S WARRANTIES.**
Be sure to obtain warranties on the roof, plumbing, heating system, and appliances, and a guarantee that the insulation does not include urea formaldehyde foam, a toxic compound.

■ **OTHER DOCUMENTS.**
These may include a property survey; a bill of sale for the seller's personal property (such as furniture or appliances); and a termite inspection report.

Often closings are held in the office of the buyer's lawyer. Although not all closings require a lawyer, it is a good idea to hire one experienced in real estate transactions to review the closing documents.

TRANSFER OF OWNERSHIP

At the closing, the seller and buyer, their real estate agents, and the bank's representative meet to complete the transac-tion. After all the documents are signed, the seller gets his money and the buyer gets the deed and keys to the house.

The buyer should make sure that the deed is signed by all the owners, dated, and certified by a notary public. If a corpora-tion (such as a real estate development company) owns the property, it must submit documents, such as a resolu-tion of the company, to show it had authority to sell it.

Notaries are usually involved in real estate transactions in Quebec. In that province, they are the only people legally allowed to prepare valid deeds of sale for immovable proper-ties. Notaries can also help you arrange financing, check the title, and register the deed of sale and mortgage (hypothec as it is called in Quebec).

Since the sale of real estate is often your largest financial transaction, you would be wise to hire your own lawyer (notary in Quebec) rather than relying on the one used by the buyer. Your lawyer may check certain things such as whether there are easements (servi-tudes in Quebec), and may include a clause excluding the guarantee against hidden defects in the property. This way you will have no concerns about possible future court actions. Of course, as a buyer, you would object to a clause in the deed excluding liability for hidden defects unless you were adequately compensated for this possible problem.

CLOSING COSTS

What complicates a closing and puts dread in the heart of a pro-spective buyer are the closing, or settlement, costs. They con-sist of items beyond the actual price of the property: appraisal fees, notary fees, lender's fees, lawyer's fees, plus money for insurance, taxes, and other miscellaneous expenses. As well, some municipalities charge a "welcome tax," a small percentage of the purchase price, which nevertheless may add up to several hundred dollars.

Closing costs are generally about 5 percent of the purchase price, but can be higher. It is best to add them up ahead of time to be sure you have the cash on hand to cover them at the closing. Your lawyer or notary should prepare these figures for you.

CLOSING STATEMENT

Both parties receive copies of the closing statement—a complete financial accounting of the real estate transaction. It lists the purchase price, the amount already paid toward it, any outstanding mortgages on the property, how the money paid by the buyer is to be applied to those mortgages, and the closing costs. The statement also indicates how the insurance costs and real estate taxes will be apportioned between the buyer and seller, and what part of the purchase price has been applied to the seller's obligations, such as real estate commissions, mortgage taxes, surveying costs, and outstanding utility bills.

Finally, the closing statement shows the total balance due to the seller after all payments have been deducted. Both parties should review this document carefully to be sure the money paid for the property is distributed according to the terms of the contract.

AFTER THE CLOSING

As soon as possible after the closing, the buyer (or his representative) should record his deed to the property, usually at the local courthouse.

See also HOME BUYING AND SELLING.

CODICIL

A legal document that changes or amends your last will and testament is known as a codicil. If your will names your uncle as an executor and he dies, you can write a codicil naming a new executor, rather than writing a new will. To be valid, a codicil must be drawn up with the same formalities as the will itself. For example, if the law in your province requires two people to witness a will, the codicil also must be witnessed by two people.

Many lawyers advise their clients not to use codicils, because as separate documents they can become lost or separated from the will, which would then be carried out without the changes in the codicil.

Remember, too, that even in provinces that recognize the validity of handwritten or holograph wills, these must meet certain requirements to be valid. A Manitoba court, for example, accepted some handwritten and initialed changes made on the will itself, but rejected all alterations to the will that were written on a note found in the same envelope.

If you are not absolutely sure if your codicil will be considered valid, consult your lawyer. See also ESTATE PLANNING; WILL.

COHABITATION

Living together as husband and wife without being married is known legally as cohabitation. Since 1992, the federal government and the Quebec government regard cohabiting couples the same as married couples for tax purposes. The change in the tax law came about to ensure that, if you were married, you did not pay more in taxes than if you were simply living with someone, as was sometimes the case.

To qualify on your tax return as the equivalent of a married couple, you and your partner must cohabit for 12 months or have a child together. You will then be entitled to some tax benefits of married couples.

You can claim for spousal registered retirement savings plan contributions. Or you can claim a married tax credit if the person you are living with makes little or no money. You can also share medical expenses, and charitable contribution claims. Revenue Canada will use information on both your returns to calculate your child tax benefit.

If your common-law spouse dies, you will benefit from the same tax deferral rule to which married couples are entitled.

If you separate, all spousal and child support payments made or received must be reported to Revenue Canada.

Since 1993, cohabiting couples are also subject to the rules governing income and capital gains. You must report any transfer of assets such as stocks, bonds, money or buildings to your cohabiting partner.

If two people have cohabited for more than a year, or have had a child together, neither can claim the "equivalent to married credit" for dependent children or parents.

Ironically, as the law stands, you could be living with one person, and be married to another, and be considered married to both those people for income tax purposes. See COMMON-LAW MARRIAGE; LIVING TOGETHER; ROOMMATES; ZONING.

COLLATERAL

Collateral is property pledged to ensure that a debt will be paid. Suppose you want to apply for a bank loan in order to expand your business. The bank may ask you to pledge your accounts receivable (the money owed to you for your goods or services) as collateral for the loan. Or if you need a loan in order to send your child to college, you might pledge stocks and bonds you own as collateral or take out a second mortgage on your home. If you fail to repay the loan, you will have to forfeit, or give up, the collateral. See also MORTGAGE.

COLLECTION AGENCY

A collection agency is a company hired by creditors to collect overdue debts. The agency receives a percentage of the amount it recovers, 10 to 50 percent or more.

By the time a business gives your overdue bill to a collection agency, you will have received

CHECKLIST

Illegal Collection Agency Practices

Although laws concerning collection agencies differ from one province to another, certain practices are prohibited by most provinces. An agency bill collector is forbidden:

■ To communicate with your neighbors, employer, or anyone else for any reason except to ask where you live.

■ To tell anyone that he is trying to collect a bad debt from you.

■ To add collection charges to the amount of your debt, or use documents that look like court documents to intimidate you.

■ To phone you before 8 a.m. or after 9 p.m.

■ To phone you at work if you or your employer objects to your receiving calls there.

■ To use obscene, profane, or threatening language.

■ To make your name public as a person who fails to pay his bills.

■ To fail to identify himself as a bill collector when he calls you, or pretend to be a lawyer, law enforcement officer, or other government official.

■ To obtain information by claiming that he is taking a survey or that you have committed a crime.

■ To write or call you personally if you have told him that you are represented by a lawyer.

■ To communicate with you in any manner once you notify the agency in writing to contact only your legal representative.

several letters or telephone calls requesting payment. You may be frightened, particularly if you cannot pay the bill and you do not want your neighbors or employer to know about your financial position. At one time bill-collecting agencies were able to play on these fears. They made threatening phone calls in the middle of the night and at your job, and burly collectors claiming to be law enforcement officers might have knocked on your door demanding payment.

To counter such practices, several provinces have enacted laws regulating the way debts are collected. Collection agencies are licensed by the provinces, and can lose their licenses for serious or repeated violations of the relevant laws.

Creditors, such as banks, department stores, and finance companies, who do their own collecting do not need licenses. Neither do lawyers who collect money on their clients' behalf.

COLLECTION AGENCY PRACTICES

Once a collection agency receives a bill to collect, its chief goal is to get from you as much money as possible, as quickly as possible. As a result, bill collectors continue to use a variety of unethical, even illegal, collection tactics. For example, a bill collector might tell you that the original creditor will accept a partial payment to settle the account in full. You make the payment, only to find later that you are being sued for the remainder of the debt. If a collection agency makes such an offer, be sure the original creditor has agreed to the terms.

Another common unethical practice is to ask you to write a series of postdated cheques. The collector promises not to deposit them until the dates written on them, and assures you that your bank cannot cash the cheques ahead of time. Do not fall into this trap. Cheques are now processed electronically, and there is a good chance that no person will ever see what date you have written. The agency will deposit the cheques immediately, and you may end up with an overdrawn account, bank fees, bounced cheques, and a lot more trouble than you started with. If the collection agency agrees to accept payment in installments, do not send them before they are due.

STEPS TO TAKE

If you think a collection agency has been acting illegally, you can take the following steps:

1. Notify the collection agency in writing (by certified mail, return receipt requested) that you do not wish to hear from it anymore. Its next step must be to take you to court.

2. If the collection agency is using threats or foul language, record the conversation to use as proof in future actions.

3. Call or write to the consumer protection division of your provincial attorney general's office.

In British Columbia, the Debt Collection Act specifically allows a debtor to sue for damages from any creditor who used tactics prohibited by law. Even if your province's laws do not specify whether victims of unfair collection tactics will be eligible for compensation, you can sue for damages if the illegal tactics caused you psychological problems or other loss.

COLLECTIVE BARGAINING

Collective bargaining is the legal process of negotiating an agreement between an employer and his employees' authorized representative (usually a labor union) on wages, hours, and other conditions of employment.

Freedom of association— the right to form unions, to be a member of a union, and the freedom to negotiate— is guaranteed by the Charter of Rights and Freedoms. It could be argued that this also includes the right to bargain collectively and the right to strike. In 1987, however, the Supreme Court of Canada ruled otherwise. The government of Alberta had asked if the public service employees' right to strike could be replaced by compulsory arbitration. The Court decided that, although Canadians do

have the right to strike and to bargain collectively, these rights are not protected by the charter.

You may ask whether you can be forced to be a part of the union, and whether you should have to pay union dues simply because you are employed by a company whose employees are all union members. This question was settled in 1991 by a Supreme Court decision involving the Ontario Public Service Employees' Union. One employee objected to paying union dues because he did not support some of the organizations to which the union contributed. Forcing him to do so, he argued, violated his right to associate only with those organizations he chose to associate with. The Court disagreed, saying the employee was not being forced to support these organizations just because he paid union dues: it would be different if he had been forced to take part in activities he did not wish to participate in. If people could opt out of paying union dues, workers might be encouraged to opt out of organized labor altogether, said Mr. Justice LaForest, and this would "seriously undermine unionism's financial base." See BOYCOTT; LABOR UNION; STRIKE.

COLLEGE ADMISSIONS

No one has a legal right to a college education, and colleges can set their own standards for admission. They can require that students have a specified high school grade average and a specified score on college entrance exams, such as the Scholastic Aptitude Test (SAT). They may also choose to admit someone based on other kinds of achievements, as in sports, the arts, or community service. The school is not required to tell applicants why they have been rejected.

Since colleges and universities (and this includes most schools) receive federal funding, they cannot discriminate against students on the basis of race, religion, or ethnic origin. In fact, many schools have adopted affirmative action programs to provide increased educational opportunities to students from racial and ethnic minorities. (See AFFIRMATIVE ACTION.) Colleges are often required to admit every student who meets their admission standards, but standards vary greatly. Your high school guidance counselor will know the admission policies for the university of your choice.

Colleges may charge a non-refundable application fee to offset the cost of examining applicant qualifications. This practice is legal, as long as you are told when you pay that the fee will not be refunded. Some colleges waive the fee for students who can show financial hardship, or may charge foreign students higher fees.

COLLEGE SCHOLARSHIP

A scholarship is an amount of money awarded to a student for his support or to pay his tuition while he studies. Stu-

dents may be selected for college scholarships on the basis of ability, previous school record, or financial need. There are many federal and provincial programs, as well as bursaries by colleges and universities to help students financially.

Universities and colleges often offer entrance scholarships for students who have high academic achievements and/or students who are in financial need. Some scholarships are provided for members of minority groups, and those who are disabled. Most universities and colleges have scholarship and financial aid departments on campus, and they will have information on sources of funding within the school, and from outside institutions. You can visit the school, or ask that the information be included in your application package.

Student loans are also offered by the federal and provincial governments. Many programs offered by colleges, universities and even specialized training schools are eligible for student loan funding. The eligible programs are usually listed in the application package the government sends you. To get an application package, contact the student aid branch in your province, or contact a university or college near you—the packages are often available at the scholarship and financial aid departments on campus.

So that your financial needs can be assessed properly, your parents' income must ordinarily be included on student loan and scholarship applications.

However, New Brunswick, Ontario, and Quebec do not require this information if you are married, if you have been working for two years without returning to school, or if you hold an undergraduate degree. Instead, you will have to report your own earnings, as well as any income you receive from other sources.

Generally, the maximum annual student loan is $3,000 to $4,000. If your assessment shows you need more than the maximum available, you may receive an additional sum in the form of a bursary. Unlike a loan, a bursary does not have to be repaid. Ordinarily, student loans are interest-free while you are at school—the governmen pays the bank the interest. Once you have completed your studies, you must begin repaying the loan and the interest. Some provinces, New Brunswick and Quebec, for example, do not require repayments to begin until six months after you complete your studies.

If you receive student loans one year, but do not apply for assistance the next year even though you are still a student, make sure your school notifies your bank and the government that you are still in school. Otherwise your loan becomes payable.

There may also be other types of programs to help you with your studies. In Quebec, for example, you can get a student loan to buy a computer. But unlike "regular" student loans, you must make interest payments on the loan even while you are still in school.

See also STUDENT LOAN.

Below are some pointers on applying for a scholarship:

1 . If you are a high school student, talk to your guidance counselor. She should have information about scholarships in general and those available in your chosen field.

2. If you are employed, ask about company-sponsored scholarships. Many large firms offer scholarships to employees or their children.

3. Write to the college of your choice and ask for information on scholarships. Find out what policy the institution has on both need-based and merit scholarships.

4. Apply for any scholarships for which you might qualify on merit. Do this regardless of your family income. Apply early, before funds run out.

5. Beware of companies that charge to locate "hidden scholarships." You can probably get the same information on your own for no cost at all.

COLLUSION

A secret agreement between two or more parties to break the law or defraud a third party is known as collusion. Suppose you buy a new car, which turns out to be a lemon with multiple problems that no mechanic seems able to correct. The car is also heavily insured. You make an agreement with your friend Steve to take your car and dispose of it in the river. You report the car as stolen,

collect the theft insurance, and split it with Steve. You and he are guilty of collusion.

Or suppose several construction companies are bidding for a contract. Alpha Corporation, the lowest bidder, makes a secret pact with Beta Corporation, the second-lowest bidder, to withdraw from the competition if Beta promises lucrative subcontracts to Alpha. The two are guilty of collusion.

A couple would be guilty of collusion if, with no intention of separating, they seek a divorce so as not to be considered married for income tax purposes (so one could claim for sums paid for child support). If the court discovers the collusion, the divorce will be refused.

COMMERCIAL PAPER

Commercial paper (also called negotiable instrument) is a document that represents one person's obligation to pay money to another. The most important thing about commercial paper is that it is negotiable. A negotiable document must be in writing and signed by the person making the promise to pay. That promise must be unconditional and for a specific sum. The money is either payable on demand or at a time stated in the document.

The four types of commercial paper are cheques, bank drafts (such as cashier's cheques), promissory notes, and bills of exchange.

See also BANK ACCOUNT; CASHIER'S CHEQUE; CHEQUE; PROMISSORY NOTE.

COMMON CARRIER

Bus lines, airlines, railways, taxicabs, moving companies, and trucking lines—businesses that transport the general public or personal property for hire (for a fee)—are called common carriers. They are distinguished from private carriers, such as charter bus companies and air cargo companies, which transport people or property only by special arrangement.

By publicly declaring themselves to be in the transportation business, common carriers are legally required to carry any and all passengers or freight, assuming that there is enough space for them and the fee has been paid. If they do not, they could face a lawsuit.

Depending on where they operate, common carriers are regulated either by the provincial or the federal government. Intraprovincial companies (those that operate entirely within one province) are subject to provincial laws, whereas interprovincial companies and those that do business out of the country are regulated by federal law. See also ACCIDENTS ON PUBLIC TRANSPORTATION; MOVING; TAXICAB.

COMMON LAW

Canada's legal system consists of statute and common law. Statutes are laws enacted by Parliament and provincial legislatures; common law is the body of laws that have arisen from judge-made decisions. Because common law evolves case by case, it is often referred to as case law.

Common law has been described as "the common sense of the community, crystallized and formulated by our forefathers." Its origins are so old that even the Magna Carta, signed by King John at Runnymede in 1215, refers to it.

Common law originated with decisions made by judges in England who interpreted the customs that prevailed in their jurisdictions, and whose then unwritten decisions were cited as precedents in future cases where the facts were similar. By use of analogy, logic, and experience, a body of case law was developed, which gradually covered the entire range of human activity. It is still not uncommon for a lawyer to cite a judgment rendered several hundred years ago and preserved for us by some unknown court reporter.

A judgment by the Court of King's Bench in 1732 (the case of *Holt* v. *Ward Clarencieux* 93 E.R.954) stated a principle of common law that still applies today. The court held that contracts with a minor except for the necessaries of life are voidable at the minor's option, but the other party to that contract is bound by its terms. In rendering that decision centuries ago, Lord Redmond stated: "The law so far protects him (the minor) as to give him an opportunity to consider it when he becomes of age: and it is good or voidable at his election . . . . But though the infant has this privilege, yet the party

with whom he contracts has not; he is bound in all events."

Common law was introduced to Canada and the United States by British immigrants and is the basis for the laws of all provinces except Quebec. The law of Quebec is the Civil Code, which traces its origins to Roman law, as do the laws of France and Spain, and even California and Louisiana.

Quebec law derives from certain codifications of various regional customs in France, especially the *coutumes de Paris* (customs of Paris). Napoleon codified French law in the Napoleonic Code, which is the origin of Quebec's Civil Code. This was first passed as law in 1866 just before Confederation, and extensively overhauled in 1994. Much of the family law of Quebec derives from canon or religious law and thus differs in certain aspects from the common law of the other provinces. Quebec, for example, does not recognize common-law marriages.

COMMON-LAW MARRIAGE

Common-law marriages are recognized by law in certain provinces only, and for certain purposes. In Ontario, you would be considered common-law spouses once you have lived together for three years, or once you have a child together. If you separate from your common-law spouse, you can claim support for yourself and your children. Similar legislation exists in the provinces of Alberta and Manitoba.

When an Ontario couple separated, the man was ordered to support the woman with whom he had lived with for eight years. Even though the woman was not employed during the course of the relationship, she was compensated for helping maintaining their home, and for helping out at the man's business. Under Ontario's Family Law Act she was entitled to the same support a married woman would receive.

Common-law marriages are not recognized in Quebec except under specific legislation, such as the Quebec Pension Act, the Automobile Insurance Act, the Crime Victims Indemnity Act, and the law governing work-related accidents and illnesses. Under these laws, you can get compensation if someone is killed and you and that person:
a) lived together as if you were husband and wife;
 b) have been living together for a year, or have been living together and have had a child;
 c) have been publicly acknowledged as husband and wife.

The Civil Code lets you claim child support from someone you lived with and from whom you are separated if he or she is the biological parent of your child or children. You can be entitled to custody of your children, or the right to visit them, even if you are not married to their other parent.

ENDING A COMMON-LAW MARRIAGE

A common-law spouse is often at a great disadvantage because he or, more usually, she can spend years caring for children and maintaining the family's home, and yet have no right to any property when the couple separate. In a landmark 1993 case, the Supreme Court of Canada awarded a British Columbia woman compensation for her 12 years as the homemaker in a common-law relationship. In granting her a portion of the assets her partner had acquired over the years, the court acknowledged her contribution to the relationship, and to preserving and maintaining her common-law spouse's property.

If you are in a common-law relationship, it may be a good idea to draw up a cohabitation agreement that stipulates what you will receive if the relationship comes to an end. You can specify how your property and other assets are to be divided. The matter of support—what you would give, or receive—would be particularly important if you have children.

The fact that a man and woman live together does not automatically mean they are in common-law marriage. For that, they must have the intention to live as husband and wife. A man and a woman could live together simply to share expenses. Since a common-law marriage is not technically a marriage, it can be dissolved by one party leaving the other. Divorce is not necessary. See also ANNULMENT; DIVORCE; MARRIAGE.

COMMUNITY PROPERTY

The rules that apply to the division of your property when you divorce depend on where you were married, the laws of your province, and whether you have a marriage contract.

In most provinces, you are entitled to a portion of the family assets—the property and other items in which you and your spouse have rights and which can be divided between you—even if you did not work during your marriage. How long you were married and how many children you have can be important factors in determining what portion of the assets you receive.

If you and your spouse have a separation agreement and your share of the assets is already "fixed" under the agreement, this does not mean that you cannot receive a larger share of the assets. In many cases the court can alter the separation agreement if it is not fair, and give you a larger portion of the family assets. British Columbia's Family Relation Act, for instance, expressly allows a judge to change the terms of such agreements.

To be entitled to share in the family assets you must have contributed to the maintenance of the home and to the marriage. Your contribution does not necessarily have to be financial. A spouse who has dedicated his or her life to raising children and taking care of the house could be entitled to the same portion of the family's

assets as a spouse whose salary supported the family.

Many provinces have laws designed to protect the family assets in the event of separation or divorce. The family home is usually considered a family asset, even if it is not in your name, and even if your spouse made the payments. Section 21 of Ontario's Family Law Act prevents one spouse from taking a mortgage on the family home without the consent of the other spouse—whether or not the home is in both spouses' names. An Ontario court held that a husband could not even use the home to guarantee a personal loan without his wife's consent.

Quebec has laws to prevent your spouse from ending a lease on rented accommodation. Your lease and the contents of your apartment will be protected if you register a declaration of family residence with the court.

COURT JUDGMENTS

Section 5(6) of Ontario's Family Law Act permits an unequal division of property if, for instance, the marriage did not last very long, or one spouse made little contribution to the marriage. Because her husband did not contribute to the care or the financial upkeep of the home, an Ontario woman was awarded the entire family home when she and her husband divorced after 11 years of marriage. Another Ontario woman got a larger share of the family assets than her husband, because he had lied to her about his debts, a large portion of which she had to pay.

Courts in British Columbia and Ontario have ruled that RRSPs, old age pension plans, and retirement plans are part of the family assets.

British Columbia courts have held that a life insurance policy was a family asset, as was a trust fund established in favor of the husband when he was an infant. His wife got a 40 percent share in the trust upon divorce. An inheritance received by a British Columbia man during marriage and a country cottage used by the couple were also declared family assets: the court awarded the wife 20 percent of the inheritance and a 25 percent share of the cottage.

The Ontario Court of Appeal ruled income from a wife's trust fund is a family asset subject to division if a marriage breaks down. And so, too, are a husband's frequent flyer "air miles," according to the Nova Scotia Court of Appeal.

COMPETENCY

In law, a person is deemed competent if he is legally qualified to perform a specific function and has all the requirements for doing so. If a person is declared incompetent, he cannot take part in any legal proceedings or be legally bound to a contract. Incompetent people include children, senile or mentally retarded people, and in some cases, drug addicts and alcoholics.

COURT PROCEEDINGS

Before a criminal case can be tried, the judge must make sure that the defendant under-

REAL LIFE, REAL LAW

The Case of the Widower's Will

Three years before making his will, Mr. Munny suffered a stroke. Following the stroke, he was hospitalized in a psychiatric ward and his doctors filed reports to the effect that he was incompetent to manage his own affairs. The public trustee took care of his finances until his death. Prior to his death however, Mr. Munny left hospital and resumed farming. He also made some real estate transactions and bought a car. During this time, he met a woman of whom he grew quite fond, and for whom he bought expensive gifts.

When he died, Mr. Munny left property to six of his 12 children. The other six contested the will, saying he was incompetent when he made it. They cited the gifts to his female friend as an example of incompetency. The children who were left out of the will also claimed that after the stroke their father was confused, childish, and unkempt. Other evidence showed that Mr. Munny, always eccentric, was not greatly changed by the stroke.

The court found it understandable that Mr. Munny would give his female friend gifts. It also felt that Mr. Munny knew what he was doing when he made his will, since he had already provided for his late wife from whom he had separated and six of his children at the time of separation, and he knew that the six children excluded from the will were not dependent upon him.

The court held the will was valid.

stands why he is being brought to court and what will happen there. The defendant should be able to cooperate with his attorney and assist in his own defense. If the defendant does not understand his situation and cannot participate at his trial, he is considered incompetent and cannot be tried for the offense.

The issue of competency also arises in court when a person is called as a witness. Before being allowed to testify, the witness must show that he comprehends the significance of taking the oath to tell the truth and is reasonably able to

answer questions about what he saw or heard.

Whether a witness is competent is especially important when dealing with child witnesses who may be victims of sexual assault. In 1992, appeal courts in Alberta and Nova Scotia ruled that trial judges had erred in refusing to hear the testimony of children aged five and two. The appeal court held the trial judges were wrong in not conducting an adequate inquiry into the competency of the older child, and in conducting an inadequate one in the case of the younger child. Commenting on the principles involved in such dilemmas, Madame Justice Beverly McLachlin of the Supreme Court of Canada said: "Every person giving testimony in court, of whatever age, is an individual whose credibility and evidence must be assessed by reference to criteria appropriate to her mental development, understanding and ability to communicate."

WILLS

In order for a will to be valid, the testator, or person who makes it, must be competent: he must understand what it means to make a will, realize what property he has, be able to identify the people who could benefit from property he might leave them, and be able to dispose of his property according to a plan.

Many wills are contested on the basis of the testator's competency, which is hard to establish after he dies. If you suspect that a senile relative has made a will, you should see a lawyer before he dies.

See also INCOMPETENCY.

COMPLAINT

The document that initiates a civil lawsuit is called the complaint in some provinces; in others it is the statement of claim, or the declaration. It serves as notice to the defendant that he is being sued; it sets forth the facts that the person suing him (the plaintiff) will use to support his lawsuit; and it states the remedy that the complainant seeks from the defendant.

COMPOSITION WITH CREDITORS

An agreement in which a debtor agrees to pay a portion of what he owes, and his creditors accept his partial payment as a full settlement of the debt, is called a composition with creditors.

Suppose Jim owes $10,000 to a rug company and $3,000 to a computer dealer. He gets into financial trouble and cannot pay his debts. Instead of filing for bankruptcy, he makes what the Bankruptcy Act calls a proposal: he arranges a deal with the two companies in which he agrees to pay them a percentage of the original debt.

The two companies agree to accept 40 cents for every dollar Jim owes them and to forgive the rest. Jim ends up paying $4,000 to the rug company and $1,200 to the computer dealer. He will not have to pay the balance of the debt.

Since the Bankruptcy Act was amended in 1992, individuals who make such proposals to their creditors in consumer bankruptcies (where the bankrupt's debts are $75,000 or less) will not be forced into bankruptcy if the proposal is rejected. This would not apply, however, in the case of a proposal by a corporation.

See also BANKRUPTCY.

THE CONTRACT

A composition with creditors is a contract, and its terms must be met exactly. The contract must state the total settlement

agreed upon and the payment plan to be implemented. The money can be due immediately or at a specified later date, and it may be paid in a lump sum or in installments.

Jim should make quite sure that the contract also has a clause stating that the agreed amount will satisfy the debts completely.

RIGHTS OF EACH SIDE

If Jim makes a payment late, both the rug company and the computer dealer can sue for breach of contract and make a claim for all the original debt.

Once the contract has been signed, Jim's creditors cannot claim any more money than the amount stated. For example, the rug company cannot accept the $4,000 from Jim, then put a lien on his car for the remaining sum.

COMPROMISE AND SETTLEMENT

A compromise and settlement is an agreement by which two disputing parties settle for less than what is specified in the contract. Suppose the contractor whom you hired to put a new roof on your house has finished the job, but you are not satisfied with the work. Some shingles are already coming loose and the gutters are poorly fastened. The roofer, however, thinks the job is fine and wants to be paid for it. You could take this dispute to court and possibly end up spending more money than it would cost to hire someone to finish the job properly. Or you might do better if you propose a compromise and settlement.

For example, after discussing the problem with the contractor, you might agree not to pursue any further claims against him for his poor workmanship. In return, he forgives the final payment due him under the terms of the contract. The agreement can be either written or verbal, but it is better to put it in writing. Your written proof will be important if the contractor later sues you for not making the final payment on the roof.

CONCEALED WEAPON

"Carrying" a concealed weapon does not necessarily mean the weapon must actually be in your hand: it could be in your purse, or briefcase, or even in your automobile. Of course in Canada, it is illegal to carry a weapon, concealed or otherwise, unless you have a special permit to do so. But if you conceal a weapon under the carpet of a vehicle, say, you could be charged with carrying a concealed weapon. In some circumstances, the penalty can be up to five years in jail.

Offenses related to concealed weapons are not just confined to firearms. Also prohibited are certain oriental martial arts devices, such as nunchaku (two hard sticks or pipes connected by a short wire or chain), brass knuckles, spiked bracelets, metal star-shaped throwing disks with

sharp points, razors, switchblades and other knives that open automatically. Depending on the circumstances, even having a bread knife on your person could make you liable for this criminal charge.

CONCILIATION

Conciliation is one of several ways to solve a dispute without going to trial. In court, just before a trial is about to begin, the parties may try to hammer out a compromise that will avert the need for a long and costly trial. This process is called conciliation. The term is often used interchangeably with mediation but the two are not the same. See also ALTERNATIVE DISPUTE RESOLUTION; MEDIATION.

CONDOMINIUM

A condominium, or "condo," may be a multiple-unit building (an apartment house) or complex (a group of town houses) in which each unit is separately owned. If you buy a unit in a condominium, not only do you own the unit you purchased, but you become a part owner of the common areas, such as sidewalks, elevators, gardens, laundry rooms, swimming pools, and parking areas. Together with the other condo owners, you are financially responsible for maintaining these common areas. Moreover, the larger your unit, the greater the percentage of common area you may have to maintain.

As a condominium owner, you are a member of the condo-

minium association, which consists of the owners of the individual units. Members pay a monthly fee to provide common-area maintenance. You also elect the association's officers and directors, who make day-to-day decisions on maintenance of the condominiums.

FINANCING

A mortgage to purchase your condominium is like the mortgage on a single-family house. It becomes a lien against your property until you have made all the required payments. If you should default, the bank or other lender can foreclose on your property, just as it would on a house. See FORECLOSURE; MORTGAGE.

OWNERSHIP

When you buy a condominium, you receive at least three documents: a deed, a declaration of condominium, and a copy of the bylaws. At the time of writing, Ontario is considering legislation that would also require developers to provide disclosure statements setting out condominium relationships where the owner of the condo does not own the land upon which it is built. Toronto's Queen's Quay Terminal is such a condominium since the land is not part of the condo.

Condo deed
The deed, which is recorded at the county courthouse, includes a detailed description of your condominium unit, with the apartment number, size, location, and any other pertinent information. It also states the dollar value of your unit at the time of purchase, the percent-

CHECKLIST

For Condominium Buyers

If you are thinking of buying a condominium, you will want to take these steps before you sign a purchase contract.

■ **REVIEW THE CONDOMINIUM DEVELOPER'S PROSPECTUS.**
This document should contain information about the developer's background and financial history, the plans for the condominium project and timetables for completion, and the amount of interest the developer will keep in the project once it is completed. A call to your local Better Business Bureau or consumer protection agency can tell you if there are any complaints outstanding against the developer.

■ **EXAMINE THE OPERATING BUDGET OF THE COMPLEX.**
You will want to know how monthly assessments for the maintenance of common areas are computed, as well as the amount of reserves that the condominium has set aside to cover major building repairs.

■ **READ THE CONDOMINIUM ASSOCIATION'S DEED, COVENANTS, AND BYLAWS.**
What restrictions are there on the way you can use your condominium? Will you be prohibited from placing a flower box on your windowsill, or will you be limited in the number and kind of pets you may keep? Some condo associations enforce their rules strictly, right down to the colors you can paint your window sills.

■ **TALK TO THE PEOPLE WHO LIVE IN THE COMPLEX.**
Current residents should be able to tell you if they are happy with their purchase, if common areas are kept clean and maintained properly, if noise or traffic is a problem, and if security and police protection are adequate.

■ **CHECK THE STABILITY OF THE CONDO WITH LOCAL REAL ESTATE AGENTS.**
If there is a high turnover of residents, or if many units are rented out by their owners, the building may not be well run.

■ **EXAMINE THE PUBLIC RECORDS AT THE OFFICE OF THE RECORDER OF DEEDS.**
The recorder of deeds can tell you the value of units that have recently been purchased in the condo. If the value of the condominium is not rising as fast as other real estate in the area, you may want to reconsider buying.

■ **CHECK THE ENGINEER'S REPORT AND THE MANAGEMENT AGREEMENT**
The engineer's report will describe the physical condition of the condo—the structure itself, the roof, the plumbing and the electrical wiring. The management agreement will spell out how the condo management is organized.

■ **CHECK OUT LOCAL SERVICES**
If your condo is in a new development, see what plans exist for schools, churches, shops, and public transport.

age amount of your responsibility for maintaining the common areas, and a list of these common areas. It includes any covenants that dictate the ways in which you can use your condominium. The deed should not have any provisions that contradict either the declaration of condominium or the condominium bylaws.

Declaration
Provincial law requires that the declaration of condominium contain a description of the whole condominium complex; the exact details of each unit; a description of the common areas; and the rules, restrictions, and responsibilities that apply to the owners. It may also specify the number of votes that each unit wields in the association, the procedures for assessing and paying maintenance fees, and the procedures for assessing payments for major repairs or improvements.

Bylaws
The bylaws give the procedures for electing officers and directors to the condominium association and for meetings. They also cover rules for maintenance and insurance. A condominium owner must adhere to his association's bylaws. See also COOPERATIVE APARTMENT; HOME BUYING AND SELLING.

CONFESSION

A confession is a voluntary admission of guilt by a person accused of a crime and his description of the events and circumstances under which he committed it. To be admissible in a criminal trial, a confession

REAL LIFE, REAL LAW

The Case of the Improper Interrogation

The police suspected that Ralph robbed a convenience store one day in late October. Two days after the robbery, the police arrested him, and searched his car, where a gun, a knife, and a sweatshirt fitting a description given by a witness to the robbery, were found. At the time of the arrest, Ralph was read his rights after which he scoffed "Prove it. I ain't saying nothing until I see my lawyer. I want to see my lawyer."

Despite this request, however, one constable continued to question Ralph before allowing him to see his lawyer. During the questioning, Ralph slipped up and confessed to the crime. The confession led to Ralph's conviction.

Ralph appealed the conviction, on grounds that his right to a lawyer, guaranteed by the Charter of Rights and Freedoms, was violated. At the end of a long process, the Supreme Court of Canada found that this was indeed so. When Ralph asked to see his lawyer, the police should have stopped their questions. Because they did not, Ralph won his case.

---

must be voluntary. If a confession occurs during questioning by the police, the accused must be advised of his rights against self-incrimination.

Some recent judgments concerning confessions illustrate the complexity of the law. In 1991 the Supreme Court of Canada ruled that confessions made to a clergyman or religious adviser are not automatically inadmissible in criminal cases. A British Columbia Court of Appeal ruled the same year that the confession of an intoxicated man was inadmissible because he was too drunk to understand the policeman's advice on his right to a lawyer.

A confession made to a policeman who pretended to be a fellow prisoner was ruled inadmissible as it violated the accused's right to remain silent.

CONFESSION OF JUDGMENT

A confession of judgment is a clause in a financing contract for items such as automobiles, houses, or television sets. The clause states that if you, the buyer, miss a payment, even for a legitimate reason, the seller can go to court and obtain a judgment against you. The judgment could be for as much as the entire amount due, or perhaps for the property itself, depending on the terms of the contract. You will not be permitted to defend yourself. Moreover, you will have to pay the seller's lawyer for representing you.

If you find a clause in a contract that sounds like a confession of judgment, do not sign the contract. Confessions of judgment are illegal or highly restricted in most provinces.

A confession of judgment could also refer to a court document in which the defendant agrees to pay a certain amount of the sum for which he is sued, or the full amount claimed. Judgment rendered on a confession of judgment would save the defendant a lot of money in court and lawyer's costs.

CONSENT FORM

Increasingly, we are asked to give our consent—to agree actively and voluntarily to someone else's action—so much so that consent forms have become a part of daily life. You will be asked to sign one before you receive certain medical treatments, when you request payment from your insurer, and under many other circumstances.

CONFIDENTIAL INFORMATION

Doctors, lawyers, and other professionals, as well as such institutions as hospitals and drug treatment centers must keep all their records confidential. Anyone who attempts to secure your confidential records or releases them without your permission is breaking the law. If you want to have confidential information divulged—for example, if your insurance company wants to examine your hospital records before it reimburses you for damages, you must give written consent. Your medical insurance claim form includes a "blanket release," a type of consent form that allows the release of all records pertinent to your medical condition.

In other situations, such as when you want to provide medical records to your lawyer, you can create your own consent form. It should:

◇ Identify precisely which records you want released.

◇ Name the person or persons who are authorized to receive the records.

◇ Specify the period of time for which the release will remain in effect.

AGENTS

In order to designate someone to sign a contract for you as your agent, you must execute a consent form called a power of attorney. Suppose your company wants to transfer you to another city, and you do not have time to sell your house. Your best friend, Alma, agrees to run ads in the local paper for you, and sell your house at a price you set. If she finds a buyer, Alma cannot sign a contract to sell your house unless she has your written authorization. The authorization should identify Alma as your agent, limit her authority to the sale of your house, and spell out any other terms, such as a minimum price and the fact that payment is due in full before the new owner moves in. See POWER OF ATTORNEY.

MEDICAL TREATMENT

A doctor may not treat you without your permission, and your permission must be based on an understanding of the essential facts. This is called informed consent, and it is the cornerstone of your rights as a patient, whether in a hospital or other medical facility or in the doctor's office. Although you should always understand what is written in the consent form (or what you are agreeing to verbally—for example, when you accept a prescription), hospitals and physicians are still responsible for giving you the appropriate medical advice and treatment. See INFORMED CONSENT; PATIENT'S RIGHTS.

The only time that a patient's informed consent is not required is in an emergency. If you are in a train wreck and rescuers rush you unconscious to the nearest hospital, the law assumes that you would like to have whatever medical procedures are needed to save your life. You cannot object later on religious or other grounds.

WHEN CONSENT IS NOT VALID

It is essential when signing a consent form to be fully aware of the relevant facts and understand the consequences of giving consent. For this reason, consent by minors and incompetent people or consent forms signed as the result of a trick or fraud are invalid.

You cannot claim fraud easily or arbitrarily, however, as the courts presume that a competent adult who signs a form has read and understood it. Make sure you read any consent form carefully; never rely on someone else to tell you what it says.

A consent form signed under duress or coercion is not enforceable. If a father gives consent to the adoption of his child because the mother has threatened him with false child-abuse charges, his consent is not valid.

CHILDREN'S ACTIVITIES

Parents are often asked to sign consent forms for their children so that they are able to participate in certain activities. Generally these forms release the school board, church, scout troop, or other organization from liability if a child is injured in an accident.

Many courts will not allow such consents to be used to bar a lawsuit, and hold that no person can, by means of a consent form, release another party from liability for negligence that has not yet occurred. See also LIABILITY; NEGLIGENCE.

IMPLIED CONSENT

Sometimes, written consent is not practical or possible, as in a medical emergency. In such situations, consent is said to be implied. Suppose a passerby sees a dog threatening your child and rushes onto your property to protect her. In this instance the law assumes you want him to do this—that is, that he has your implied consent—and you will not be able to accuse him of trespassing.

CONSIGNMENT

When you ask a merchant to sell goods for you in exchange for a commission, you have entered into a consignment sales agreement. You retain ownership of the articles until they are sold, and the merchant becomes your agent. She is obliged to get the best deal possible, account for the merchandise, and forward payment for any goods that are sold within a reasonable time, after first deducting her commission.

Consignment is a time-honored practice for wholesalers and manufacturers. Individuals also sell personal items such as antiques, artwork, rare books, stamp collections and even clothing and furniture on consignment.

Take care when signing a consignment agreement. Most merchants have standard forms that serve their own interests. The form may allow the merchant to reduce the price of your merchandise without your consent, for example. Your agreement should clearly state the amount of the merchant's commission, allow you to reclaim unsold goods whenever you like, and hold her responsible for any loss of your property due to theft or accident while it is in her hands. If you cannot convince the merchant to change her standard agreement, look for someone who will agree to your terms.

For a sample consignment sales agreement, see EVERYDAY LEGAL FORMS at back of book.

CONSPIRACY

When two or more people agree to commit an illegal act or to accomplish a legal objective by illegal means, they are guilty of conspiracy. Suppose Simon, an official at the provincial lottery office, and

his neighbor, Irma, agree that Simon will forge winning numbers on losing lottery tickets and pay out winnings to Irma, who will turn over half the money to Simon later on. In addition to being charged with the crime of fraud, Simon and Irma can be charged with conspiracy to commit fraud, which is a separate crime.

CONSUMER PROTECTION

Years ago the Canadian consumer had little choice but to be guided by the old Latin saying *caveat emptor* ("let the buyer beware"). Consumers had very few options when a product turned out to be unsafe, defective, or unsatisfactory in some way.

Today most provinces have consumer protection legislation in place to guard you from nefarious marketplace practices. Some laws are aimed at unfair trade practices or any instance where the seller misrepresents the product or service; others at defective merchandise.

Many provinces impose minimum standards for merchandise, or have legislation that stipulates the products must be fit for the purpose for which they were intended. Even so, some transactions may be outside the scope of existing laws. You should be especially cautious, for example, when buying used articles or items that are drastically reduced in price. The law may not protect you if you had the opportunity to inspect the merchandise and

did not do so. This is true in Manitoba, New Brunswick, Nova Scotia, Ontario, Quebec, and Saskatchewan.

Many provinces have legislation specifying that the nature and quality of goods must meet certain minimum standards, and prohibiting sellers from excluding such warranties. Therefore a merchant cannot simply evade the law by putting a disclaimer into the sales contract. If you find you have purchased damaged merchandise, ask yourself: Did you inspect the product? If you had, would you have discovered the damage? Was the condition of the product reasonable given the price you paid for it? Your answers will help determine whether you are entitled to have the contract rescinded and a full refund, whether you are entitled to have the damage repaired free of charge or to be given a replacement, or whether you are stuck with the merchandise "as is."

Certain purchases are treated very differently, and are regulated by different legislation. In Ontario, British Columbia, Quebec, and Alberta, for example, there is specific legislation which deals exclusively with the purchase of automobiles.

Most legislation affords protection to written and oral contracts. See also FALSE ADVERTISING; MAIL-ORDER SALES.

DEFECTIVE MERCHANDISE

That a warranty of serviceability is implied in any purchase is central to most consumer protection legislation: in Quebec,

CHECKLIST

Where to File Consumer Complaints

These federal agencies handle complaints about:

■ **FOODS, DRUGS, COSMETICS**
Department of Health
Health Protection
Health Protection Building
Tunney's Pasture
Ottawa, Ont. K1A 0L2

Agriculture Canada
Food Production and Inspection
Sir John Carling Building
930 Carling Ave.
Ottawa, Ont. K1A 0C6

■ **MAIL FRAUD**
Canada Post Corporation
720 Heron Road
Ottawa, Ont. K1A 0B1

RCMP, local offices, or
1200 Vanier Parkway
Ottawa, Ont. K1A 0R1

■ **UNSAFE PRODUCTS**
Industry Canada
Consumer Products
Place du Portage 1
50 Victoria St.
Hull, Que. K1A 0C9

Department of Health
Health Protection (see above)

■ **ADVERTISING, LABELING, WARRANTIES, DOOR-TO-DOOR SALES, CREDIT AND COLLECTION PRACTICES**
Industry Canada
Consumer Products (see above)
RCMP (See above)

■ All provinces also have consumer protection bureaus.

the principle is included in the recently revised Civil Code. It would be wise nonetheless to examine all merchandise.

Saskatchewan consumers, for example, benefit from an implied or express warranty of quality and fitness for purpose only if the defect was not pointed out to the consumer in the store, or the consumer would not have discovered the defect even if she had inspected the product in the store.

Other factors and circumstances surrounding a sale may also be relevant. If, for example, a product is offered at a greatly reduced price, the consumer would be wise to inquire why the seller is making such a "sacrifice." In many provinces this is particularly important, since the legislation is meant to ensure that you get what you paid for.

PRODUCT LIFE EXPECTANCY

When you buy something, you have a right to expect it will fulfill the basic minimum requirements of the job for which it is intended—that a lawn mower will cut grass, for example, or a lamp provide light—for a reasonable length of time. In other words, there is an implied warranty of durability after purchase.

A number of factors such as the price of the particular item, the type of product, the reasonable life expectancy of similar merchandise, and the way that you have used the product are fundamental in determining the extent to which the warranty of durability will apply.

Most important, therefore, would be the condition the product was in, or supposed to be in, when it was purchased, and whether it lasted for a "reasonable period of time."

Implied warranties are not confined to merchandise. In some provinces, the same warranty applies to services performed on your merchandise. If you have a stereo repaired, and it breaks down a week after the repairs were done, then you may be entitled to have the work done again, or to have your money refunded.

Any oral promises made to you when you purchased the product may enable you to get a refund or have repairs done if your merchandise is not what the seller says it is. Oral statements, including televised statements by the seller or the manufacturer, may be binding on the merchant or manufacturer. It would nonetheless be prudent, and make things easier, to have the promises in writing. Otherwise it could be your word against the seller's.

REPAIRS OR REFUND?

Whether or not you have recourse against a seller or a manufacturer depends on several things, including the damage to the merchandise, the terms of the warranty, and whether the warranty was implied or was an express warranty. If the seller does not sell that particular merchandise in "the ordinary course" of his business, and the merchandise has a latent or hidden defect, you may only be entitled to a refund, a replacement or repairs from the manufacturer.

This is the case in New Brunswick, for instance. But in Quebec, the consumer can expect the same remedies from the merchant or the manufacturer, even if the retailer was not dealing exclusively with the merchandise in question.

In certain cases, if you purchased the merchandise, not from a retailer, but rather from a friend, you may not be able to get a refund or repair from the store where your friend bought the product. Nonetheless, you still may be entitled to benefit from the manufacturer's warranty on the product.

Depending on the nature and extent of the damage, you may be able to return the merchandise for a full refund within a reasonable time after the purchase. In Saskatchewan, if merchandise is returned after a somewhat lengthy period of time, you can get a refund, less a reduction for the length of time you had use of the product. Sasketchewan is also one of the provinces where the seller must be given a chance to either replace or repair the product if the damage is not major, and if the work can be done without causing you undue inconvenience.

If the seller refuses to refund your money or repair the merchandise, you can have it repaired elsewhere, then attempt to recover the cost of the repairs from the seller.

YOUR OBLIGATION

Many provinces give retailers the opportunity to remedy the situation so long as the damage to the merchandise and the inconvenience to you are not substantial. In most provinces, you are entitled to a refund or repairs only if you act within a specific period of time. Check with a consumer protection agency in your province.

Most consumer legislation also covers sales made at your home by itinerant merchants. In all provinces you have a "cooling-off" period of two to 10 days, in which you can cancel the contract and return the goods. Do not rely on canceling the contract by telephone. If you are within the cooling-off period allowed by your provincial consumer legislation, send back the cancellation form (if one is included) or send a cancellation letter by registered mail. Keep a photocopy of your letter and the post office receipt. Do not rely on the salesman's word that he will accept the cancellation after the cooling-off period. Also, do not accept the excuse that the salesman is not available but will call you back. He may not call until the cooling-off period has expired. Act immediately and do not be intimidated or feel guilty for "wasting" the salesman's time.

Contracts that offer ongoing services, such as memberships in health clubs or vocational schools, may also be canceled, although you may be obliged to pay for the classes that you have already taken, as well as a penalty.

Consumer protection laws prevent goods being seized once a certain percentage of the cost has been paid. In Quebec, for example, an item cannot be repossessed by the merchant if you have paid half the price; it cannot be repossessed in British Columbia if you have paid two-thirds.

A merchant may never go to your home to get back something he sold you unless you agree or he has a court order that allows him to do so.

Merchants are also obliged to disclose the real cost of credit when your purchase is not fully paid for at the time of sale. The real cost may include handling fees, commissions, storage costs, interest, and other items that may greatly increase the real cost of an item.

Some clauses in certain consumer contracts are illegal, especially some of the conditions in contracts of loan with finance companies. These are not valid, even if you sign them.

Some consumer legislation allows for exemplary damages against the seller if he violates the consumer protection laws. See ARBITRATION; BETTER BUSINESS BUREAU; DAMAGED MERCHANDISE; FOOD AND DRUG LAWS; SMALL-CLAIMS COURT; WARRANTY AND GUARANTEE.

CONTEMPT OF COURT

Any action that undermines the court's authority, dignity, or ability to administer justice, is contempt of court.

Someone who ignores a subpoena or insults a judge in the courtroom will be held in contempt of court. Parties to a lawsuit who destroy court records, or who open documents that the court has ordered to remain sealed, can be held in contempt. So can witnesses who commit perjury, anyone who refuses to obey a court order, and jurors who ignore court instructions not to discuss the case with the press. Lawyers show contempt of court when they make disrespectful comments, assist a client in defrauding the court, or violate the rules of the court.

CIVIL VERSUS CRIMINAL CONTEMPT

Contempt of court can have civil and criminal aspects. The distinction between the two is hard to define, as the consequences, whether fine or imprisonment, may be the same in either case.

The Supreme Court tried to make a distinction between the two in 1992 in hearings involving the United Nurses of Alberta versus the attorney general of Alberta. It defined criminal contempt as being found in the concept of public defiance that "transcends the limits of any dispute between particular litigants and constitutes an affront to the administration of justice as a whole . . . . The gravamen of the offense is . . . the open continuous and flagrant violation of a court order without regard for the effect that it may have on the respect accorded to edicts of the court."

In civil and criminal contempt cases, the procedural rules and the standards of proof are the rigorous standards used in criminal law. Destroying court records or bribing a witness are examples of criminal contempt. Disobeying a court order may be civil *and* criminal contempt.

REAL LIFE, REAL LAW

The Case of the Drunk Defendant

Alfred was charged with two counts of contempt of court. It all began when he was charged with committing mischief to private property. He appeared at court without a lawyer and his case was postponed to the afternoon. When he appeared in court after lunch, he was so drunk that he could not stand trial and the judge charged him with being in contempt of court. He was ordered to return at another date to explain why he should not be charged with contempt.

On the appointed day, Alfred did not show up, and a warrant was issued for his arrest. When brought to court by the police, the judge concluded that Alfred was drunk once again, and charged him with another count of contempt. Alfred was sentenced to jail terms of 30 days and 60 days respectively. He appealed both sentences.

The British Columbia Court of Appeal allowed Alfred's appeal, and set aside the convictions. The appeal court felt the trial judge erred in requiring Alfred to defend himself of the charge of contempt when he was drunk, since his condition did not allow him to make a fair and proper defense, as was his right.

CONTINGENT FEE

When a lawyer agrees to be paid for his services only if he wins an award or settlement in the case, any money he gets is called a contingent fee. It is figured as a percentage of the amount his client obtains in the lawsuit. The contingent fee has been called the "key to the courthouse" for people with legitimate cases who cannot afford to pay hourly legal fees.

Contingent fees, once illegal in Canada, are now allowed in all provinces. Often, they are the only way a person of modest means can afford a lawyer. They are allowed for the lawyer's fee only: the person who hires the lawyer must pay court stamps, services costs, costs of expert witnesses, depositions, and all other such expenses. If a lawyer paid these costs, he would be involved in "champerty and maintenance," an arrangement that would be illegal for him, or for any third party who stood to benefit from your winning the case. This rule prevents court cases from becoming a form of gambling.

The various legal societies set a 15 to 30 percent ceiling on the contingency fee percentage a lawyer may charge. The lawyer's experience, the complexity of the case, the amount of money involved, the time spent, and the result obtained are all considered.

If a client complains, courts, as well as law societies, can adjust legal fees that are out of line. The Supreme Court of British Columbia cut a law firm's bill to $272 from $17,000, a 98 percent reduction. The case involved the settlement of an estate the judge estimated to be valued at $13,610. The court felt that 3 percent of the estate value divided between two lawyers and a third party would be a fair and reasonable fee. Legal fees for settling an estate are usually estimated as a percentage of the estate value, usually 5 percent.

Contingent fees may be most appropriate where the outcome is unpredictable, accident cases, for example. They should not be considered in matrimonial cases that involve the family home and other valuable trust funds or business assets. Before agreeing to a contingent fee arrangement, however, calculate what the case would cost if you pay on an hourly basis as opposed to a percentage of your settlement. See also LAWYER.

CONTINUANCE

When a trial or part of a trial is postponed, the procedure is called a continuance. It is up to the presiding judge to decide whether to grant a continuance, but he will usually do so if it is requested in good faith.

Suppose the prosecuting lawyer in a criminal case wants to call a crucial witness, but she is in the hospital recovering from an appendectomy. In this instance the prosecutor's request for a continuance will be granted. But if a lawyer asks for a continuance merely to delay the trial, it will be refused.

A continuance is automatically granted when a trial cannot be held as scheduled. For example, if a lawsuit comes before a court near the end of its term and, because of delays in other cases, it cannot be heard in the current term, it will be continued into the court's next term. See COURTS.

CONTRACT

Whether we realize it or not, most of us enter into contracts every day. Whenever you buy lunch at a restaurant, subscribe to a magazine, take a ride in a taxi, or get a haircut, you are making a contract.

A contract is a legally enforceable agreement between two or more people. It can be implied (with the terms of the contract evident from the circumstances, as when you order a pizza) or express (with the terms specifically laid out orally or in writing, as when you agree to buy a camera from a friend). Not all contracts are enforceable, however, because the law requires some to be in writing.

CONTRACTS THAT MUST BE IN WRITING

In 17th-century England a law known as the Statute of Frauds required that certain kinds of contracts (especially those subject to fraud) must be in writing. Today, some version of the Statute of Frauds is on the books in all provinces. Usually the kinds of contracts that must be in writing include:

◇ Contracts for the sale of goods worth more than about $500 (the amount varies from one province to another).

◇ Contracts for the sale of real estate.

◇ Contracts that cannot be completed within a year of being made, such as a lease that lasts longer than a year.

◇ Contracts promising to pay another person's debts, such as an executor's agreement to pay the debts of an estate out of his own pocket.

◇ Contracts made in consideration of marriage, such as prenuptial agreements. See PRENUPTIAL AGREEMENT.

WHAT MAKES A CONTRACT ENFORCEABLE

Almost any adult can enter into a contract, but certain requirements must be met before a contract can be enforced in a court of law. These include:

Mutual agreement
The parties must have a "meeting of the minds" regarding the details of the contract, so that they are clearly understood. This mutual agreement is the result of an offer by one party and its acceptance by another.

Suppose a co-worker offers to sell you his stereo system for $350, and you agree to buy it. He delivers a CD player, a cassette deck, and a receiver, but does not include the speakers that you assumed were part of the deal. If you decide not to go through with the purchase and your co-worker sues you in the small-claims court for breach of contract, you can legitimately

REAL LIFE, REAL LAW

The Case of the Haphazard Holes

Robert entered a tournament in which the sponsoring golf club promised to give an automobile valued at $18,000 to the first golfer scoring a "hole in one" in hole No. 2. Since the golf course had only nine holes, and the tournament was an 18-hole game, each participant had to play the course twice.

Because there were a great many entrants, Robert was told to tee off from hole No. 3 and play through twice. On the 17th hole, which technically was hole No. 2, he scored a "hole in one." But the scorekeeper entered it as hole No. 11, the hole number when played as an 18-hole course if one teed off at the outset toward hole No. 1. When the club refused to hand over the car, Robert took the club to court, but lost his case.

The court of appeal, however, reversed the decision and ordered the club to give Robert the prize. By the rules of the Royal Canadian Golf Association he had scored a hole in one at hole No. 2. The court held that the tournament committee had breached the rules of the contract since it did not authorize a change in the numbering of the holes, and if it did, it did not properly publicize this fact. By starting from hole No. 3 and making a "hole in one" at his 17th hole, Robert in fact scored at hole No. 2 on his second time around the course.

---

argue that there was no contract in the first place, since the two of you made different assumptions about a key part of it, and therefore had no mutual agreement.

In written contracts, clear and precise wording is important. If a contract happens to contain wording that is confusing or ambiguous, it probably cannot be enforced. Furthermore, the contract would probably be interpreted by a court in favor of the person who did not write it.

For example, an IOU may show that someone owes you money, but does not say when that money should be paid or if interest is to be charged. It would be better to prepare a promissory note, which would show that something or some amount of money was given as consideration for the loan, and would state when the loan is to be repaid, and what interest would be charged either from the time the money was lent or from the time the loan was to be repaid.

Consideration

Consideration is a legal term that refers to something of value that each person hopes to get out of the contract. In the example on the facing page, the consideration for your co-worker's stereo is the sum of $350. The consideration for your $350 is the stereo itself.

A promise without consideration is unenforceable. Suppose your co-worker had said, "I'm going to deliver my stereo to you on Sunday," and then failed to show up. Without consideration you could not require him to deliver it. But if you had said, "Great, and I will give you $350 for it," there would be consideration—and an oral contract.

Competence

The parties to a contract must be legally competent—that is, they must be considered by law to be capable of handling their own affairs. This excludes people who are underage, intoxicated, or mentally unsound.

For example, suppose Oscar, who has Alzheimer's disease, enters into a contract for two years' worth of dance lessons. When he does not pay, the dance studio sues Oscar for the money. Oscar's lawyer can use the defense that the contract is not valid because of Oscar's illness, which renders him incompetent.

Legality

The purpose of the contract must be legal. For example, a hired killer cannot go to court to demand payment from the person who hired him to commit the murder. In some provinces, gambling debts fall into the category of contracts that cannot be enforced. See GAMBLING.

A contract that goes against public order would not be valid, either. In Quebec, a will was declared invalid because the testator specified that his son could inherit only if he married a woman of the same religion as he was. At trial, the courts declared that this part of the will was void because it was discriminatory and against public order.

Time limit

A contract must specify a time period for completion. If you enter into a contract to plant trees on a neighbor's farm but fail to indicate when the job will be done, your contract may not be enforceable.

Proper form

As discussed earlier, certain types of contracts must be in writing. If they are not, they will not be enforceable.

In Quebec, for example, pre-nuptial or marriage contracts, as well as deeds of sale for immovables, must be made by notaries in order to be valid. Also bulk sales, being a sale by a merchant of all his inventory and interests in his lease, must be accompanied by an affidavit of the seller, listing all his creditors and the amounts he owes to each. If the bulk sales contract does not have this affidavit, the contract could be canceled.

BREAKING A CONTRACT

If you fail to meet any of the terms of a legally enforceable contract, you are breaking, or breaching, the contract. Selling defective merchandise, not doing work that was promised, and not paying someone the money you owe him are all breaches of contract.

A breach of contract can be partial (as when you move out of an apartment a month before your lease is up without making the last rent payment) or total (deciding not to move in after you have signed the lease).

♦ The victim of a breach of contract is entitled to seek reimbursement. The amount of money that can be awarded will depend on both the nature of the contract and the nature of the breach. For further discussion, see BREACH OF CONTRACT. See also CONTRACTOR; DAMAGES; HOME BUYING AND SELLING; HOME IMPROVEMENT AND REPAIR; SCAMS AND SWINDLES.

CONTRACTOR

As commonly used, the term *contractor* refers to a person who is in the business of home building, home improvement, and home repair. Contractors are usually hired by homeowners, and the work they agree to do is laid out in a legal contract.

HIRING A CONTRACTOR

Although most contractors are honest and reputable, many are not. It therefore pays to be cautious when hiring a contractor. Ask your friends and neighbors who have had work done on their homes for recommendations, and interview several contractors before you decide on the one you want.

Ask the contractors you interview for references from satisfied customers, and follow up on the information by talking to the customers themselves. Also, ask the contractor (or one of his customers) if you can see a recently completed job. If your provincial law requires contractors to be licensed or certified, make sure that those you are considering have the proper credentials. Ask to see them.

♦ Request a written bid from each contractor, and be sure that all the bids call for the same quality and the same kinds of construction materials.

THE CONTRACT

Have your agreement with the contractor put in writing and make sure it is as specific as possible. Your lawyer should review contracts for major jobs, such as an addition to your home or an in-ground pool. At the minimum, the contract should describe the work to be done, the materials that will be used, the proposed completion date, the warranties provided on the work, and the schedule for the contractor's payments.

Since most cities now require permits for remodeling work as well as for building jobs, your contract should require the contractor to obtain these permits and give you copies of them. If inspections are required, you should also receive copies of the inspectors' reports.

Ask for a provision (called liquidated damages) that penalizes the contractor if he misses the completion date by more than one or two weeks. And insist the contractor give you a list of the suppliers and subcontractors who will be working with him. Then you will know who can file a lien against your home if the contractor does not pay them. You should also ask for proof that the contractor is covered by workers' compensation and liability insurance.

The payment schedule you receive should specify that, when the job is done, you will withhold 10 to 20 percent of the final payment until the contractor has cleaned up the work area, until you have written proof that you are no longer subject to mechanic's liens from suppliers and subcontractors, and you are assured that the job has been done right.

Provincial legislation entitles you to withhold a certain percentage of the value of the services or materials supplied in order to satisfy any builders' liens or claims. If the work has been completed and the head contractor has been paid but does not pay the subcontractors or suppliers he dealt with, they can make a claim for payment against the owner of the property. In such a case, the funds held back will be available to satisfy these claims.

Ontario's Construction Lien Act permits 10 percent of the ordinary payment to be withheld, whereas the Builders' Lien acts of Alberta and British Columbia stipulate 15 percent. Keep the holdback for about 45 days after the head contractor has notified you the work is done, then check your local land registry office to see if any liens are registered against your property. If none appear, make the final payment to the head contractor. If there is a lien registered, talk to a lawyer.

See also MECHANIC'S LIEN.

MONITORING THE WORK

Keep an eye on the work, and question anything that seems wrong or does not match your expectations. It is a lot easier to correct a plumbing mistake before the drywall goes up than after the job is done.

♦ Suppose you change your mind in the middle of a project. You want a picture window where an ordinary-size window has just been installed; or you decide you want flagstones on your patio or your front path rather than the brick you specified at first. In such a case, you should submit a written request, called a change order, to the contractor. He, in turn, will give you the adjusted cost and the revised completion date in writing.

Make the payments as required by your contract, but do not make them earlier than scheduled. When the job is done, make a list of any items that you find unsatisfactory or incomplete and give it to the contractor. Do not make the final payment until they are corrected.

WHEN SOMETHING GOES WRONG

Suppose that the new tile floor in your kitchen has begun to crack, or the wooden beams in your new family room already show signs of warping. Most reputable contractors provide warranties on their materials and workmanship and will correct the situation without cost to you.

If you hired a contractor without demanding written warranties, however, you may have to rely on a court to decide whether the contractor was at fault and you are therefore entitled to compensation.

Or suppose the contractor you hired works for two days and then disappears after you have given him a substantial down payment. Or the contrac-

♦ tor's helper trips over a small end table, sending an expensive vase crashing to the floor. Predicaments like these have spurred a number of provinces and cities to require contractors to be licensed, insured, and to post a bond. If the contractor does not finish the job or pay for the damage, the bond can be used to satisfy your claims.

STEPS TO TAKE

If a dispute develops between you and your contractor that you cannot resolve, here are some steps you can take to bring about a resolution:

1. Call your local consumer protection agency to report the problem. In many parts of the country, this agency will talk to the contractor and try to work out a solution.

2. Check the terms of your contract; they may include a clause that requires arbitration. If your contractor is a member of your local Better Business Bureau or a trade organization such as the Canadian Home Builders Association, you may be able to resolve your dispute by mediation or arbitration.

See ARBITRATION; MEDIATION.

3. If your contractor refuses to cooperate with you in an effort to settle the dispute, you may have to sue him. If you do, be sure to hire a lawyer who has experience in disputes with contractors.

See also HOME IMPROVEMENT AND REPAIR.

COOLING-OFF PERIOD

It sounds good when the salesman appears at your door. He promises that just for letting him demonstrate his new vacuuming system, you will receive a set of steak knives and a chance to win a trip to Hawaii. Three hours later you find yourself agreeing to buy the system for $500—just to get him to leave. In the light of morning, however, you realize you don't need a new vacuuming system for your studio apartment. But you have signed a contract. Is there anything you can do?

In all provinces, you are entitled to a short grace period, or "cooling-off" time, during which you may cancel the contract. At the time of writing, Ontario allows you two days and is proposing to extend this, Quebec lets you have 10 days. British Columbia, Newfoundland, Nova Scotia, Prince Edward Island, and Yukon each allow seven days. Alberta's Direct Sales Cancellation Act allows four days' grace.

These laws apply primarily to door-to-door sales, not sales negotiated in a store or regular place of business. In some cases the laws do not apply to sales involving less than $25, or to dealings at auctions, trade fairs or exhibitions.

Never assume that any contract you are about to sign is covered by this type of legislation. Inquire first with your local department of consumer and corporate affairs or your consumer protection agency. Most provinces require door-to-door salespeople and other itinerant vendors to supply a cancellation form with the contract. In Quebec, vendors covered by these laws must tell customers they have up to 10 days to cancel their contracts.

COOPERATIVE APARTMENT

In some parts of the country, especially in eastern cities, many apartment buildings are run as cooperatives. When you buy an apartment in a cooperative building (called a co-op for short), you enter into a form of ownership different from that of either a house or a condominium. See CONDOMINIUM.

When you own a house, you usually own the entire structure and the land. When you own a condominium, you own the space your apartment occupies. When you own a co-op, you own shares in a corporation. The corporation is the cooperative, which owns the building and all the apartments in it. When you "buy" a cooperative apartment, you are not buying the apartment itself. You are buying shares in the corporation, which gives you the right to occupy your apartment.

Your monthly payments, called maintenance, will ordinarily include your share of the building's mortgage payments, its property taxes, and a building maintenance fee, which covers such expenses as doormen, gardeners, and repairs. If one of your fellow co-op owners does not make his maintenance payments, the remaining owners (including you) are responsible for them. Your maintenance might be increased or you might have to pay a special assessment to make up for the default.

Buying a co-op presents a unique set of problems. Financing is sometimes more difficult to obtain than for a home, because a co-op loan is secured by shares in a corporation rather than by real estate. In addition, co-ops have rules, called bylaws, that you agree to obey when you buy. You may find, for example, that you cannot have a certain kind of pet or a washing machine in your apartment. You may also find that the co-op's board of directors has veto power if you decide to move and want to sell your shares.

Given these potential problems, it is essential that you consult a lawyer who knows your local real estate law. Ask him to review the purchase agreement before you buy. See also HOME BUYING AND SELLING; REAL ESTATE.

COPYRIGHT

Copyright is the protection given by federal law to people who create original works of various kinds, such as books, magazines, plays, poems, movies, songs, records, tapes, paintings, sculptures, computer programs, and board games. The holder of a copyright has the primary right to market, distribute, display, perform, or reproduce a work. By copyrighting his work, the creator guards himself against theft—that is, he protects his work from those who would reproduce it for their own gain without compensating him.

CANADIAN COPYRIGHT LAWS

First enacted in 1924, the Copyright Act has been significantly reformed to keep it abreast of technological advances in such areas as satellite communication, computers, and sound recording. Computer software, piracy, and moral rights were included in 1988 revisions. The act now recognizes computer programs as literary works entitled to copyright protection.

Ruling in *Apple Computer Inc.* v. *Macintosh Computer Ltd.* in 1990, the Supreme Court of Canada held that computer programs transferred onto silicon chips are protected by copyright laws. The penalties for copyright infringement can be up to $1 million in fines, and/or up to five years' imprisonment. (You do not infringe copyright by making one reproduction of a software to make it compatible with a computer, if it is solely for personal use, and if the reproduction is destroyed as soon as the user is no longer the owner of the program. A copy may also be made for backup purposes.)

The 1988 revisions placed strong emphasis on moral rights—rights which permit the creator of a work to prevent subsequent buyers from distorting or mutilating the work, or from using it "in association with a product, service, cause

or institution." For instance, when selling the rights to a hit song, the artist can stipulate that buyers will not be allowed to grant a license to use the song in a radio or television commercial. Moral rights cannot be sold, but may be waived.

Copyright generally lasts for the life of the author or creator, plus 50 years following his or her death. There are exceptions in cases of unknown authors, Crown copyrights, mechanical contrivances such as records and tapes, photographs, works published after an author's death, and works that have more than a single author.

It is not necessary to indicate on a work that you are the copyright holder. However, if you want to receive international protection, you should follow the steps set out in various international agreements. On the back of the title page, put the copyright symbol "©," the name of the copyright

owner and the year of first publication. Keep in mind that if you create a work while employed by someone else, the copyright may belong to the employer. Check your employment contract for conditions attached to what you create.

COPYRIGHT ISSUES

In time, advances in biotechnology may present a whole range of problems concerning copyright and patents. For example, can one patent a new life-form, or one created from DNA of an extinct species, as was the premise of the 1993 hit movie *Jurassic Park*?

In 1977, the U.S. Patent Office granted a patent on a living microorganism, and one can even patent higher life forms in parts of Australia, Europe, and Japan. Here, however, the Supreme Court of Canada has yet to rule on such matters, although an Ontario court of appeal has ruled that life-forms are not patentable.

REAL LIFE, REAL LAW

The Case of the Prisoner's Painting

When Bill was in prison, he took advantage of the leisure programs provided for inmates, one of which was painting. Bill eventually produced an immense picture, a four-by-eight-foot representation of a British Columbia mountain. It took him almost 400 hours to complete his painting. The finished work of art was framed and hung in the prison itself. After Bill's release from prison, he built a successful career as an artist. But something was missing. He wanted his painting, and took the government to court to get it. Unfortunately for Bill, he lost. Since the painting had been paid for by the institution and was created under the institution's program, the trial judge held that the copyright rested with the government, not the artist.

One new problem, software piracy, is especially difficult to control. The unauthorized copying of computer programs is said to have cost the computer industry U.S.$15 billion in 1992 alone. To combat such infringement, leading software companies began the Business Software Alliance (BSA) in 1988. Most software litigation is now conducted through this association, which is active in 37 countries.

Copyrights, along with patents, trademarks, and industrial designs, fall into the category of intellectual property, a field of law that has grown considerably in recent years. Although books, poems, plays, records, tapes, computer software, video recordings and even photographs can be copyrighted, names, titles, ideas, themes and catch phrases or other short word combinations cannot.

Be aware that if your school puts on a play by a living playwright, or one whose copyright is still valid, the school must pay a royalty to the author. This is not the case when the copyright has expired. When a copyright expires, the work enters the "public domain." Therefore the works of Mark Twain, William Shakespeare, Robert Service and other long-deceased writers are not subject to royalty payments.

WHAT CAN, AND CANNOT, BE COPYRIGHTED

Only an original work can be copyrighted. This does not mean that everything about it must be brand-new, but the work must include some form

---

REAL LIFE, REAL LAW

The Case of the Garlanded Geese

Artist Michael Snow once created a sculpture called *Flightstop*, consisting of 60 geese in mid-flight. Mr. Snow subsequently sold his work to Toronto's Eaton Centre. During the 1982 Christmas season, the Eaton Centre decorators decided to festoon the geese with ribbons in order to heighten the mall's Christmas atmosphere. This was done without consulting the artist.

Upset with what he considered a distortion of his work and an infringement of his moral rights, Mr. Snow applied to the court for an injunction to force the Eaton Centre to remove the ribbons. The internationally renowned artist claimed that placing ribbons on his geese was like hanging earrings from the *Venus de Milo*, and that, in addition, this unwanted and unauthorized transformation of his work was prejudicial to his reputation.

In order to reach a decision, the judge relied on the opinions of other well-known artists and people familiar with the subject matter. They all agreed that Mr. Snow was right. The court ordered that the ribbons be removed.

---

of original expression. Originality is necessary because copyright laws protect the expression of ideas, not the ideas themselves or the facts underlying the ideas.

Suppose you intend to write a western novel, and you do extensive research on posses and cattle rustlers in the Old West. Then you concoct a plot in which the main character is saved from lynching by a band of gun-toting barmaids. Neither your research (which consists of facts) nor your plot (which consists of ideas) can be copyrighted. Only your novel itself can, because it alone qualifies as an expression of ideas.

To be copyrighted, a work must also be put down on paper, film, magnetic tape, canvas, or another "tangible medium." A songwriter who

never records her songs on tape or on paper cannot claim any copyright.

Suppose you decide to write an article analyzing the Battle of the Bulge and obtain a copyright for it. This does not prevent someone else from writing his own article on the subject, using the same facts. Historical facts and statistics, which are available to the general public, cannot be copyrighted.

Other examples of what cannot be copyrighted are:

◇ Names, titles, and symbols (except trademarks).

◇ Ideas, systems, processes, devices, and discoveries. But note that these may qualify for patent protection. See PATENT.

◇ Blank forms and blank cheques, address books, tape measures, height and weight charts, and score cards.

CROWN COPYRIGHT

A looming problem in copyright law is the possible enforcement of what is known as the Crown copyright. Government publications, as well as statutes and regulations and perhaps even the judgments of the courts, could technically be covered by the copyright laws. In that case you would be forbidden to reproduce these materials unless you paid a royalty. Should that happen, it would of course drive up the cost of the legal process, even the costs of law school, and would limit the legal information available to the public.

UNPUBLISHED MATERIAL

An original work does not have to be published to have copyright protection, because protection begins automatically when the work is created. Nor does a copyright notice have to appear on unpublished work in order for it to be protected. However, it is wise to put a copyright notice on work that is being released to the public, simply because it shows that the author is aware of his rights and wants to deter possible infringement.

STEPS TO TAKE TO OBTAIN A COPYRIGHT

If you have produced a work for which you wish to have copyright protection, here are the steps you should take:

1. Place a copyright notice on the work. The notice consists of three pieces of information: the copyright symbol (©); the name of the person who owns the copyright; and the year in which the work was produced—for example: "Copyright © John Smith 1995." The copyright notice must be easy to read and quite visible.

If you are publishing a book with a reputable publisher, all you need to do is put this notice on the manuscript. The publisher will take care of the steps that follow.

For information and permission to use Crown copyrighted material write to: Permissions Officer, Canadian Government Publications Centre. The center can also supply you with a copy of the Copyright Act and Rules. See USEFUL ADDRESSES at back of book.

To file an application for registration of copyright in a published work, or even for a work in manuscript form, write to: Copyright and Industrial Design Branch. See USEFUL ADDRESSES at back of book.

Failing any proof to the contrary, the first person to register a copyright is considered to own the rights to such work. There is a fee for registration, which may take six to eight weeks.

Once the copyright office has received your application and other materials, and it has determined that the work can be copyrighted, you will get a certificate of registration.

The National Library Act provides that two copies of every book published in Canada, or one copy of every sound recording with Canadian content, which was manufactured in Canada, must be sent to the National Library in Ottawa.

CORPORAL PUNISHMENT

Corporal punishment usually refers to the kinds of bodily discipline, such as spanking or paddling, sometimes administered in schools. School board policy determines whether a public school may administer corporal punishment. Many boards strictly prohibit any form of such punishment; others allow teachers and school officials to use it. But even where corporal punishment is permitted, there are restrictions on its use.

Under the Criminal Code, schoolteachers may use force to correct a pupil as long as it is reasonable under the circumstances. If charges are laid in such a case, the court will examine the nature of the offense committed by the pupil, the child's age and character, the severity of the punishment and its possible effect on the pupil, as well as any other relevant considerations. This provision of the Criminal Code also applies to parents and the punishment that they administer to their children.

ABUSE OF PUNISHMENT

The right to administer corporal punishment is sometimes abused. Suppose seven-year-old Bobby disrupts his class by making animal noises, and he continues to do so after his teacher, Mr. Dawson, asks him to stop. Mr. Dawson loses his temper, and instead of giving Bobby a light spanking with a wooden paddle as prescribed by the school board, he beats the boy across the back with a wire coat hanger, drawing blood.

Bobby's parents can file a lawsuit and also bring criminal charges of assault against both Mr. Dawson and the school. A teacher who oversteps the legal bounds on corporal punishment may be disciplined, or even fired.

STEPS TO TAKE

If your child has been subjected to corporal punishment, which you believe was unjust or excessive, you can:

1. Arrange a meeting with the school principal.

2. Ask the principal if the local school board permits corporal punishment in its schools. Discuss the pupil's behavior and the punishment with the principal in order to better understand the circumstances of the incident that caused cor-

poral punishment to be used.

3. If you suspect there is no justification for the punishment, consult a lawyer to help you decide what legal action you can take against the school.

CORPORATION

A corporation is a business or organization formed by one or more persons, and it has rights and liabilities separate from those of the individuals involved. It may be a nonprofit organization engaged in activities for the public good; a municipal corporation, such as a city or town; or a private corporation (the subject of this article), which has been organized to make a profit.

In the eyes of the law, a corporation has many of the same rights and responsibilities as a person. It may buy, sell, and own property; enter into leases

and contracts; and bring lawsuits. It pays taxes. It can be prosecuted and punished (often with fines) if it violates the law. The chief advantages of a corporation are that it can exist indefinitely, beyond the lifetime of any one member or founder, and that it offers its owners the protection of limited personal liability.

LIMITED LIABILITY

If you own shares in a corporation that cannot pay its debts and is sued by its creditors, the assets of the company may be seized and sold. But although you can lose your investment, the creditors cannot attach your personal assets (such as cars, houses, or bank accounts) to satisfy their claims.

There are some important exceptions to this rule, however. If the business affairs of a corporation and its shareholders are so entangled that they are, in effect, one and the same, an opponent in a lawsuit may be able to convince a court to "lift the corporate veil" and impose personal liability, or responsibility, on the active shareholders. (This issue was first raised in Britain in 1897 in the case of *Salomon* v. *Salomon & Co.* The court dismissed allegations of fraud levied against a corporation's major shareholder who creditors claimed was using the corporation only as a means to escape all personal liability.)

Personal liability may also be imposed if the corporation does not comply with required legal formalities, fails to keep proper records, transfers funds from one corporation to another

REAL LIFE, REAL LAW

The Case of the Punished Pupil

Three Saskatchewan students were on their way home from school on a bus when they spotted the school's vice-principal in the school yard. They began shouting at him and called him a variety of names. The next school day, the vice-principal accosted the boys and slapped each of them on the face as punishment for their previous behavior. One of the boys claimed that he had not been a party to the name-calling and, therefore, assault charges were laid against the vice-principal.

The trial judge found the accused guilty. Because slapping the boy had no corrective purpose, the vice-principal was convicted of assault. On appeal, however, the conviction was overturned. The appeal judge found that the accused had reasonable and probable grounds to apply corrective force, and the punishment was not unduly severe.

simply to prevent liability, or if the corporation is nothing more than a subsidiary or shell, which makes all its decisions based on directives issued by its controlling corporation.

The veil may also be lifted if there is uncertainty regarding who the creditor is actually dealing with, or if a partnership incorporates without notifying previous creditors.

There is a significant amount of legislation that imposes liability on directors and officers of corporations for certain acts and omissions, in both the civil and criminal domains, even without lifting the corporate veil. The case of the 1993 Westray Mines disaster in Nova Scotia is an example where directors were charged with criminal offenses for actions of the corporation.

FORMING A CORPORATION

Every province, as well as the federal parliament, has laws that govern the formation of corporations. The Canada Business Corporations Act, the Ontario Business Corporations Act, and the Quebec Companies Act are just a few examples.

If a corporation is to be involved in matters coming under federal jurisdiction, such as banking, it must apply to incorporate under the Canada Business Corporation Act. Corporations wanting to do business in more than one province may also find it useful to incorporate under federal legislation. Such a corporation, however, would not be immune to provincial law.

REAL LIFE, REAL LAW

The Case of the Treasured Timepiece

Ms. Lee took her valuable wristwatch for repair to a jeweler named Mr. Diamond. She returned to the store several times to pick up the watch, but each time she was told the work was not yet completed. At one point the jeweler told her he had lost certain parts of the watch, and this was the cause of the delay.

One day, after having worked on the watch, Mr. Diamond left it overnight on a workbench instead of placing it in his safe. Unfortunately, that night a fire destroyed the store, and the watch was seriously damaged. The fire had started in an adjacent building and was clearly not the fault of Mr. Diamond.

Ms. Lee sued Mr. Diamond personally for the value of her watch. At the trial, the jeweler claimed the contract of repair was between the client and an incorporated business, namely Diamond Credit Jewellers Ltd. Consequently, he argued, there should be no personal liability.

The court examined the claim ticket issued by the jeweler, and found the name Diamond Credit Jewellers Ltd. printed on it. The court held, however, that while the contract may have been with Diamond Credit Jewellers Ltd., there was no evidence that Ms. Lee was made aware she was dealing with a limited corporation, since all her dealings were with Mr. Diamond on a personal basis. For these reasons, the court ruled that the jeweler was personally liable to his client.

You must decide on the following points, and include them on your application, when you apply to be incorporated:

◇ *Choose a name for your corporation.* This can be difficult, mainly because there are thousands of registered corporations, and no two may use the same name. When you submit an application, the authorities will check that your name is not the same as, or deceptively similar to, the name of another corporation.

According to federal, and some provincial laws, you may simply use a number to identify your corporation, "64932

Alberta Inc.," for example. Quebec corporations must set out both a French and an English name.

◇ *Decide where the head office will be located.* The place must be within the jurisdiction of the relevant legislation. Choosing this site is an important decision, since the head office is where the corporation's financial and corporate records must be kept, and where corporate meetings will generally be held.

◇ *List names and addresses of all incorporators.* Depending on the jurisdiction, the incorporators may or may not be required to hold shares, and existing corporations may also serve as incorporators. Incorporators become the first directors of the corporation, although new directors are often chosen once the corporation commences operations.

◊ *Set out the object of the incorporation.* At one time, all Canadian corporations were required to state their object, or proposed sphere of activity. If a corporation carried on business in an area outside its stated object, contracts that it had entered into could be declared illegal. Today, this requirement applies only in the Maritime provinces.

◊ *Decide what shares to issue.* The application to incorporate must describe the type and number of shares in the corporation. For example, it is possible to have different categories of shares, each with its own rights and preferences. Small corporations normally issue only common shares.

The application may also include provisions regarding matters of organization such as the voting rights of shareholders, the replacement of directors and the ability of the corporation to buy back its own common shares.

In modern corporation legislation, the information contained in the application is referred to as the articles of incorporation. They must be sent, along with the required fee, to the director of financial institutions for the particular jurisdiction (federal or provin-

cial), who will then issue a certificate of incorporation. Some corporations are begun by letters patent issued by either the federal or provincial government.

You can buy books that tell you how to form your own corporation, but they may not cover all the steps required in your province. It is best to get the help of a lawyer when you incorporate or at least have him review your articles of incorporation before you file.

PROFESSIONAL CORPORATIONS

A professional corporation, or PC, is formed much like a regular corporation, but the stockholders must be licensed professionals, such as doctors or engineers, or, in some provinces, lawyers.

A professional who has incorporated as a PC cannot use the corporation to shelter himself from a charge of malpractice, but otherwise receives the same protection from personal liability as any other corporate shareholder. For example, Jane, a patient of Dr. Grimes, who is a PC, breaks her ankle when she trips on the waiting room carpet and sues. She is awarded $5 million in compensation because she happens to be a prima ballerina. But Jane can collect only from the assets of Dr. Grimes's practice, which has only $2 million in assets, and not from him personally—even if he is worth $10 million himself.

Not all Canadian jurisdictions permit the establishment of PCs. Under Ontario law, a corporation may practice a pro-

fession only when the law governing the profession allows it. In Alberta, professional associations—the Law Society of Alberta, for example—must approve the articles of incorporation of members wishing to set up PCs. Lawyers in Quebec cannot form professional corporations, whereas lawyers in Ontario may do so. Before setting up a PC, check the relevant incorporation legislation, or speak to a lawyer.

MAINTAINING A CORPORATION

Once your certificate of incorporation is issued, the incorporators must meet to elect directors and pass the corporation's bylaws, the rules by which the corporation is run. The directors then become responsible for managing the corporation, although they can appoint officers to supervise day-to-day operations. In small corporations, the incorporators, directors, and officers are often the same people.

A corporation needs money to operate, and its initial financing generally comes from the sale of stock. In many small corporations, the incorporators, family members, and friends buy and own most of the stock. This type of corporation is called a closed corporation, because its stock is not for sale to the general public.

Other companies raise money by selling shares through a public offering. Since public offerings are closely regulated by the provinces, incorporators should get competent legal advice before offering shares for public sale.

TYPES OF SHARES

Shares in a corporation usually fall into one of two classes, common and preferred. Most common stock entitles owners to vote at the company's annual meeting, although some common stock can be nonvoting. If you own common stock, you will receive dividends from the corporation whenever it declares them. The corporation does not have to declare a dividend on common stocks.

Owners of preferred stock are usually not entitled to vote at corporate meetings, and typically they receive a fixed dividend payment every year, whether the company earns a profit or not. Sometimes the dividends are accumulated, for example, if the company does not pay a dividend in any one year. Preferred shareholders' dividends must be paid before dividends to holders of common shares.

Laws require corporations to keep adequate records and make them available to shareholders. Officers and directors who unreasonably refuse a shareholder's request to see company records can be fined. See STOCKS AND BONDS.

DISSOLVING A CORPORATION

Most corporations are set up to exist indefinitely. However, a majority of the shareholders can vote to dissolve the corporation (some legislation requires a two-thirds majority). If a minority of the shareholders think a corporation is being mismanaged, they can bring a lawsuit to dissolve it. And the company's creditors can petition to have it dissolved in bankruptcy court if they are not being paid.

If a corporation is dissolved, it goes through a "winding-up" period. It collects whatever assets it has (such as bills that are owed to it), pays off the legitimate claims of its creditors, and distributes any money left over to the shareholders. Once this process is complete, the corporation files a certificate of dissolution with the director specified under the relevant legislation and the corporation's existence ends.

COSIGNING

When you sign a contract, you may be required to have it cosigned (signed by you and someone else) in order to guarantee that the terms of the contract will be met.

For example, when Dick decided to buy a new car, he was told he could not qualify for an auto loan unless he had a cosigner. He asked his cousin Elmer to cosign his loan, and Elmer agreed, out of a sense of family loyalty. Six months later Elmer received a notice from Dick's bank. Dick had failed to make the required payments on the car, and now the lender wanted payment in full from Elmer. When Elmer called Dick for an explanation, he discovered his cousin had moved away without leaving a forwarding address. Elmer ended up having to pay off Dick's sizable car loan. The reason: the cosigner of a loan agreement or any other contract assumes the same legal responsibilities as the original signer.

If you are ever asked to cosign someone else's loan, remember that there is more involved than just helping a friend to borrow some money. You will be legally committed to pay the entire sum if your friend cannot, and the lender can file a lawsuit against you to collect what is owed. Moreover, in some provinces the lender can collect the debt from you without first trying to collect it from the borrower. You should also be aware that most lenders do not require a cosigner unless they lack confidence in the borrower's ability to repay.

STEPS TO TAKE

If you do decide to act as a cosigner, you should be sure to:

1. Get a copy of the loan agreement.

2. Make sure you receive a separate document that identifies the debt being guaranteed and explains the cosigner's rights and obligations. Consumer protection rules and the law in most provinces entitle you to such a document.

3. If the borrower has not kept up the payments, and the lender demands payment in full from you, contact the lender immediately. You may be able to arrange a repayment plan, rather than having to pay the total amount as a lump sum.

4. Get the help of a lawyer with experience in consumer credit cases. If the lender has failed to give you all the documents he is required to give you by law, you may not have to repay the debt.

COUNTERFEIT MONEY

Making a false copy of something for the purpose of passing it off as the real thing is the crime known as counterfeiting. While almost anything from stamps to theater tickets can be illegally duplicated, the word "counterfeiting" most often applies to money.

In general, counterfeit bills are of poorer quality than genuine ones, and you should be able to recognize this at a glance. Compare a suspected banknote with a genuine one of the same denomination. Check for differences, not similarities.

Most counterfeit money is the printed kind. In the past, counterfeiters used engraved metal plates to print money. But with the recent advances in photographic reproduction techniques, their job has been made much simpler. In fact, the new color processing machines are making it easier for criminals to counterfeit not only currency but stock and bond certificates, tickets to high-priced events, valuable stamps, and travelers' cheques.

IF YOU HAVE A BOGUS BILL

What should you do if you find that you have a counterfeit bill? Once money is recognized as counterfeit, the last person to possess it before the discovery will suffer the loss. So if you try to deposit the bill in your bank account and the bank notices it is counterfeit, the deposit will not be credited to your account. Moreover, the bank is required by law to inform the police.

However, if you make a withdrawal and the bank inadvertently gives you a counterfeit bill it accepted from another customer, it must reimburse you. To be on the safe side, examine all bills as soon as you receive them.

Suppose Jill has a counterfeit bill and, rather than getting stuck with it, she passes it along to someone else, such as the cashier in a grocery store. One of several things may happen. If the cashier fails to notice the phoney bill, Jill will probably get away with it. But if he does notice it, he may call the police and Jill may be arrested.

Now, suppose that after getting caught trying to pass the bogus bill, Jill claims she didn't know it was counterfeit. Can she be prosecuted? It depends. If the bill is an obvious forgery, one the average person would be likely to notice, she may be in trouble. Moreover, even if Jill offers to take it back when she is caught, her offer will not remove the possibility of her being prosecuted.

If, on the other hand, Jill receives and passes along counterfeit money that she believes is genuine, and it also looks genuine to the average person, she would not be convicted of violating the law.

COURT-MARTIAL

As its name suggests, a court-martial is a court established under military law to hold trials and to punish military personnel for criminal activity. Behavior that is not criminal in civilian law, such as being absent without leave, may violate military regulations and make a serviceman or woman subject to a court-martial. The punishments a court-martial may impose include reduction in rank, imprisonment, dishonorable discharge, or any combination of these.

Surprisingly enough, while capital punishment has been abolished under the Criminal Code, it still exists under military law for the crime of treason. However, it has not been applied by a military court since its removal from the civilian criminal law.

Defendants in a court-martial do not have a right to a trial by jury. They are judged by a panel of five to nine senior officers who are assisted by a legal officer known as a judge advocate. The rules for appointing the panel members and the prosecutor have recently been revised to meet the requirements of the Canadian Charter of Rights and Freedoms. In 1992, the Supreme Court of Canada held that the previous rules (under which the prosecutor and panel were chosen by the same military authorities) were unacceptable. In addition, the fairness of the trial could not be guaranteed because the panel members, not having financial or job security, were not sufficiently independent.

Aside from a jury trial, military personnel have most of the same rights as civilian defendants, including the right to legal counsel, to call defense witnesses, and to confront and cross-examine accusers. If convicted, a defendant may appeal the verdict.

The rules for conducting courts-martial are set out in the Code of Service Discipline, which forms part of the National Defense Act. If convicted, an accused person may appeal to the Court-Martial Appeal Court, composed of Federal Court judges as well as judges from the criminal division of the superior courts. It is also possible to appeal a case from the Court-Martial Appeal Court to the Supreme Court of Canada.

COURTS

Courts serve as impartial forums to which opposing parties can bring their disputes for resolution. The role of the courts is to interpret and apply the law to the facts of each case in order to bring about justice. Courts are of all different kinds: provincial and federal courts, criminal and civil courts, small-claims and supreme courts, and many others. Which type of court hears a particular case depends on its jurisdiction.

JURISDICTION

A court's authority to hear certain cases and not others, as determined by law, is known as its jurisdiction. Jurisdiction may be based on one or more things, such as geographical area, the subject of the case (taxes or young offenders, for example), civil versus criminal matters, or the amount of money at stake in a lawsuit.

The broadest of all the divisions that determine jurisdiction is the division between the provincial and the federal court systems, which are separate but have much in common. See THE CANADIAN COURT SYSTEM, page 145.

PROVINCIAL COURTS

Courts administered by the provinces are of two types: provincial courts and superior courts. Provincial court judges are appointed by the provincial government, and in general, they deal with most criminal offenses, except for such serious offenses as murder and conspiracy. Provincial small-claims courts handle civil cases involving small amounts of money, although in some jurisdictions provincial courts may hear cases involving up to $15,000. Provincial courts in some provinces administer youth and family cases.

Superior courts
Superior court judges are appointed by the federal government. Superior courts are normally divided into two levels: a trial court and an appeal court. Depending on the province, the superior court trial level is often called the Superior Court, the Supreme Court, or the Court of Queen's Bench. In Ontario it is called the Ontario Court of Justice,

General Division. The trial level of the superior court is responsible for hearing cases involving serious criminal and civil matters for which the provincial courts do not have jurisdiction.

Whether provincial or superior, trial courts are known as courts of original jurisdiction, because they are where cases begin. A trial court will hear the evidence, decide the facts of the case, and apply the law to those facts. Juries of six persons are allowed in certain provinces for certain civil cases. They are seldom used nowadays because of the expense involved.

The appeal courts hear appeals from the trial level. They do not decide the facts of a case, but accept the facts as decided by the trial court and look at the applicable law and procedural rules to see if they were properly applied. The appeal (or appellate) court may affirm the lower court's decision, reverse it, or modify it. In some instances, the case will be sent back to the trial court for further proceedings. Appeal courts are usually called just that, such as the Alberta Court of Appeal. In some provinces, however, it may be the Supreme Court, Appeal Division. Ontario has an intermediate appeal court called the Divisional Court. For information on the court system in your province, contact the attorney general's office.

THE SUPREME COURT OF CANADA

The general court of appeal for all of Canada, the Supreme Court of Canada, was estab-lished in 1875. It hears appeals from the Federal Court (Appeal Division) and from the appeal courts in the various provinces involving controversial legal issues of national importance. Appeals to the Supreme Court of Canada are guaranteed only in certain criminal cases.

FEDERAL COURTS

The Federal Court of Canada is divided into a Trial Division and an Appeal Division. The court deals with specialized matters such as maritime law and copyrights, and also reviews decisions made by federally appointed administrative bodies, such as the Immigration Appeal Board and the National Parole Board.

Other federal courts include the Court-Martial Appeal Court and the Tax Court of Canada. See FEDERAL COURTS.

COURT REFORM IN ONTARIO

At the time of writing, the Ontario government has proposed changes to the province's legal system. The Ontario Judicial Council, responsible for hearing complaints about provincial judges, is to become more accessible to the public. In this way the government hopes to make the judicial process more accountable, while maintaining the independence of the judiciary.

The United Family Court will also be affected by the Courts of Justice Statute Law Amendment Act 1993. Judges in this Hamilton-Wentworth area court are specialists in the field of family law and young offend-ers. The hope is to expand this specialized tribunal to more and more centers in the province, thus bringing about an increasingly efficient and issue-sensitive administration of family law cases.

COURT DELAYS

The court system across Canada is presently plagued by serious problems of backlog and delay. It is not unusual for five or 10 years to pass before a case reaches the Supreme Court of Canada.

This issue was central to the case of *Regina* v. *Askov*, in which the Supreme Court of Canada ruled that because the accused had to wait two years for his initial trial, his constitutional right to be tried within a reasonable time had been infringed. The court's decision meant that the case could proceed no further.

Many lower courts subsequently followed the Supreme Court's lead, resulting in tens of thousands of cases being thrown out. A Newfoundland Supreme Court judge decided that serious delays at the appeal level also infringe this constitutional right. But the Supreme Court of Canada recently ruled that the delays for appeal do not infringe upon the individual's right to a trial within a reasonable time.

Several provinces have been attempting to remedy the matter of delays. As part of reforms to Ontario's court system, judges in Metropolitan Toronto instituted a case management system to deal more rapidly with criminal cases. The Law Reform Commission of Canada

THE CANADIAN COURT SYSTEM

Our court system consists of trial courts, appeal courts, and the court of last resort, the Supreme Court of Canada. Because each province administers justice in its own territory, the names and jurisdictions of trial and appeal courts may vary from province to province. For example, courts of similar jurisdiction are known as Court of Queen's Bench in Manitoba and New Brunswick, as Supreme Court in Ontario, and as Superior Court in Quebec.

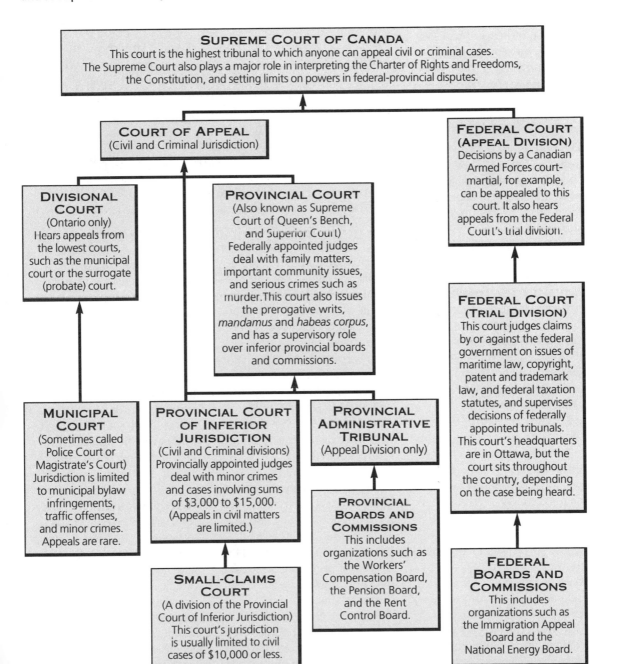

SUPREME COURT OF CANADA
This court is the highest tribunal to which anyone can appeal civil or criminal cases. The Supreme Court also plays a major role in interpreting the Charter of Rights and Freedoms, the Constitution, and setting limits on powers in federal-provincial disputes.

COURT OF APPEAL
(Civil and Criminal Jurisdiction)

FEDERAL COURT (APPEAL DIVISION)
Decisions by a Canadian Armed Forces court-martial, for example, can be appealed to this court. It also hears appeals from the Federal Court's trial division.

DIVISIONAL COURT
(Ontario only)
Hears appeals from the lowest courts, such as the municipal court or the surrogate (probate) court.

PROVINCIAL COURT
(Also known as Supreme Court of Queen's Bench, and Superior Court)
Federally appointed judges deal with family matters, important community issues, and serious crimes such as murder. This court also issues the prerogative writs, *mandamus* and *habeas corpus*, and has a supervisory role over inferior provincial boards and commissions.

FEDERAL COURT (TRIAL DIVISION)
This court judges claims by or against the federal government on issues of maritime law, copyright, patent and trademark law, and federal taxation statutes, and supervises decisions of federally appointed tribunals. This court's headquarters are in Ottawa, but the court sits throughout the country, depending on the case being heard.

MUNICIPAL COURT
(Sometimes called Police Court or Magistrate's Court)
Jurisdiction is limited to municipal bylaw infringements, traffic offenses, and minor crimes. Appeals are rare.

PROVINCIAL COURT OF INFERIOR JURISDICTION
(Civil and Criminal divisions)
Provincially appointed judges deal with minor crimes and cases involving sums of $3,000 to $15,000. (Appeals in civil matters are limited.)

PROVINCIAL ADMINISTRATIVE TRIBUNAL
(Appeal Division only)

PROVINCIAL BOARDS AND COMMISSIONS
This includes organizations such as the Workers' Compensation Board, the Pension Board, and the Rent Control Board.

SMALL-CLAIMS COURT
(A division of the Provincial Court of Inferior Jurisdiction)
This court's jurisdiction is usually limited to civil cases of $10,000 or less.

FEDERAL BOARDS AND COMMISSIONS
This includes organizations such as the Immigration Appeal Board and the National Energy Board.

has advocated the creation of a unified court structure in each province to deal exclusively with criminal justice. And in cases of routine appearances and pleas, the commission has also proposed that people should be able to "appear" in writing, by telephone or by fax.

The Supreme Court of Canada now hears appeals via satellite, thereby reducing costs, and making the justice system more accessible to many more Canadians.

HOW COURTS ARE RUN

The purpose of the courts is to settle disputes. How they go about doing so varies somewhat from court to court, but the general procedures are often similar.

Court rulings

If the case is tried before a jury, the jury must decide on the facts in the case, based on the evidence. It must, according to the judge's instructions, apply the law to those facts to arrive at a verdict. In criminal trials the jury's verdict must be unanimous. If there is no jury, the judge decides what the facts are, applies the law to those facts, and renders a judgment.

The decisions of the panel of judges on an appeal court are generally determined by a simple majority vote, although some rules specify that a certain number of judges (three, five, or seven)—known as a quorum—must be present to render a valid judgment. Judgments of the Appeal Court are rendered by a simple majority of the judges present.

When an appeal court makes a decision on a case, its

REAL LIFE, REAL LAW

The Case of the Tiring Trial

The jury in Pat's drug trafficking case deliberated for quite some time following the end of a very long trial. At 11:43 p.m., it was still deadlocked. The judge was very tired, indeed annoyed, that jury members had not yet come to a verdict. He complained it was a "shame" some of them were "not doing their duty." Moreover, as the record of the trial would later show, the judge stressed over and over during the hearings that it would be "fine" if the jury could come to a verdict that evening so that jurors would avoid being "locked up" overnight in a hotel one more time. Shortly after the judge's admonishment, the jury brought in a guilty verdict.

The accused's lawyer appealed, charging the trial judge had coerced the jury into a hasty verdict. The court of appeal looked at the record of the judge's comments to the jury, and ruled that these had not been prejudicial to the accused.

The appeal was dismissed and the conviction stood.

---

explanation for reaching that decision is called the court's opinion. When the judges agree on the outcome of the case but base their decisions on different reasons, the reasoning that has been adopted by the majority is given first, and other judges write what are called concurring opinions. Judges who disagree with the decision may write dissenting opinions.

Court records

A record of the court's proceedings is made by the clerk of the court. Written opinions are often published in bound volumes that become part of law libraries. They are used by lawyers in preparing cases and by other courts for guidance in deciding similar cases.

Access to court records is not restricted to people involved in a case. Court records are public records, but the right

to inspect them is governed by law. Requests to examine or copy court records may be granted to people with a legitimate interest in the case, but requests made simply out of curiosity, or for the purpose of publishing embarrassing information, may be refused.

Some records may be sealed by the court—for example, to protect the identities of juveniles or victims of sexual assault. However, court judgments are available to anyone.

Court personnel

The clerk of the court makes notes about the proceedings in each case and receives all papers filed with the court, which then become part of the court record and are reviewed by the judge. Other court personnel include law clerks (who do legal research for the judge), court attendants, or bailiffs (who maintain order in the courtroom), and stenographers (who take down a word-for-word record of court proceedings). Interpreters may be available to assist people who do not fully understand English, or French in some cases, or who are hearing-impaired. Lawyers are also officers of the courts.

Terms and sessions

By law, a court is authorized to perform its judicial functions, including the conduct of trials, during a certain time period. This is often referred to as the "term of court." Typically, a term of court runs from early September to the end of June. Within a given term, sessions are held. These are the times during which the judge or judges actually hear cases.

Court procedure

Specific rules and procedures must be followed in presenting a case in court. The federal and provincial court systems have their own rules of procedure regarding jurisdiction, parties, pretrial motions, evidence, judgments, and appeals.

Courts also have the authority to control all judicial proceedings and to ensure that the dignity of the court is maintained. For example, a court may prohibit photographs of an accused person, or it may control the admission of the public to the courtroom.

As a general policy, the public has the right to attend court proceedings because public access is designed to assure that a hearing or trial is conducted fairly. However, a judge may limit public access to protect a witness's identity, to maintain order, or to ensure that the proceedings are just. See also APPEAL; FEDERAL COURT; JURISDICTION.

CREDIT

Your credit is your ability to borrow money now and pay it back later, or to purchase items now and pay for them later. Because lenders collect interest on the money they provide in advance, credit is big business. Every year, banks, credit unions, trust companies, loan associations, and merchants extend billions of dollars of credit to consumers for major purchases, such as homes, automobiles, and appliances.

To decide whether you are a good credit risk, lenders need information about your income, expenses, and bill-paying history. Rather than spending the time and money to conduct their own investigations, lenders turn to credit bureaus for this information. See CREDIT BUREAU AND CREDIT RATING.

Establishing credit can be a study in frustration. Suppose you have never had a credit card or taken out a loan, and now you want to establish credit. You go to a bank to take out a small loan, well within your means, which you expect to repay month by month. You find out, however, that you cannot get a loan until you have established some kind of credit record. What can you do?

One way might be to apply for a credit card at a local department store. Always pay your bills on time, and after a few months apply for another card at another store. After another few months apply for a national credit card, such as Visa or Mastercard. Once you have been granted a national card, you are considered a good credit risk.

Another way to establish credit is to take out a secured loan at your bank. With this kind of loan, you pledge a savings bond or other security as collateral for a personal loan. If you make the scheduled payments on time, the bank will report you to credit bureaus as a reliable customer, and you will have established a credit record that lenders can look to when you next apply for loans.

CREDIT BUREAU AND CREDIT RATING

A credit bureau is a private company that collects data about your employment, earnings, and debts. It passes this information to institutions that subscribe to its service—banks, credit card companies, and department stores—and that want to find out whether you are a good financial risk.

Usually there is only one bureau in a town. This will be registered with the Associated Credit Bureaus of Canada.

Contrary to popular belief, your credit history (the information collected by a credit bureau) does not contain a judgment about your character or your general reliability as a person. A credit bureau reports facts, not judgments, and those

ABC's
OF YOUR CREDIT RIGHTS

Although no one has a right to obtain credit from a bank, merchant, finance company, or other credit grantor, neither may the company granting credit refuse to do so if their decision is based on considerations other than your credit history and ability to pay. Some of the credit grantors' obligations and the consumers' rights are listed below:

■ No company can refuse credit on the basis of race, religion, color, sex or marital status.

■ Most credit reporting laws and consumer protection laws require that the entire cost of credit be clearly shown. Any credit that is loaned at a cost of over 60 percent of the original amount is illegal.

■ Most provinces have laws governing the procedures and tactics that creditors may use. Threats, harassment, contacting neighbors and friends, or calling too early or late in the day, or too often, in order to collect are usually considered abusive practices forbidden by law.

■ If you are the victim of threats or harassment by telephone, make a tape recording of the conversation for possible use in court. You may record a telephone conversation if you are one of the parties in the telephone conversation.

■ In most provinces, the consumer is allowed to consult his file, have the codes used explained to him, and is entitled to a copy of the credit report either free or for a nominal charge. Consumers have the right to correct errors in their file.

■ In provinces with "seize or sue" laws, as in Alberta, British Columbia, Newfoundland, Quebec, and Saskatchewan, the creditor may either retake possession of the object sold or sue. In these provinces, he cannot retake possession and sue for the balance, as once the merchant has taken back the item, the contract is canceled and no balance remains to be paid. See CONSUMER PROTECTION.

amount of these loans, payment records, credit card debts, the status of charge accounts, and other credit transactions. Moreover, any bankruptcies, judgments, summonses and changes of name that could affect a credit rating will be included.

The term *credit rating* derives from the fact that credit bureaus use a point system, on a scale from 0 to 9, to describe your payment history. For a given debt, 0 indicates "paid within 30 days," the most favorable rating. Things get worse the higher the number goes.

In certain cases, credit bureaus may have the wrong credit information about a given person. Despite great care, an error may occur because of the sheer amount of records kept by credit bureaus, and the constant updating that takes place. This can have serious consequences. For example, John took out a loan six years ago to buy a car, which has been paid off for three years now. By a stroke of bad luck, the record of the final 10 months of payments was either lost or never added to John's file. So, when John tried to take out a loan on a house, his loan was denied because of an apparently bad credit rating.

At one time, the type of information that could be in a credit file, or to whom that information could be shown, was not regulated. As well, the person on whom a given file was made could even be unaware of its existence or

facts include statistical information received from stores, banks, and other sources. It is up to an individual lender to review your record and decide whether you are a good risk.

WHAT YOUR CREDIT FILE CONTAINS

Usually, a credit record includes a person's name, address, occupation, employer's name and address, his or her spouse's name, and an indication of the length of time that the person being rated has spent at a given address or job. A detailed itemization of the person's credit history is also included in the file. This involves a history of the loans that have been taken out, the

denied access to it. Concerns about accuracy and privacy eventually led to several provincial laws being enacted to regulate these matters.

LEGAL PROTECTION

Apart from Alberta and New Brunswick, all provinces have laws regulating the collection and reporting of credit information. While the substance of these laws may vary from one province to another, the core provisions are similar. Most require credit bureaus to be licensed by the government and supervised by a government agency. They must keep the most accurate files possible, by using the best sources of credit information available. Files may not include a person's race, color, ethnic origin or political convictions.

A credit bureau cannot merely say that a civil judgment was registered against John. Details of the trial, who was involved, and the reasons for the judgment must be included. The bureau cannot give a false impression about someone because of what is not said anymore than by what is said.

Credit file access is restricted to whoever is the subject of the file and those with a legitimate interest in seeing it. That might include someone evaluating applications for credit, employment, insurance, and equipment or housing rentals. If credit is denied because of a credit report, the consumer must be told where the information was obtained. In some cases, a person must be told before or after a credit report about him is obtained.

CHECKING YOUR FILE

Because of the problems you can face if your credit record is inaccurate, it is a good idea to check your rating once a year, or at least before you apply for a significant loan. Under legislation regulating credit bureaus, you are entitled to see what information your file contains. If there are inaccuracies, the bureau must correct them. If you cannot mutually agree on what must be changed, you can take your dispute to court.

CREDIT CARD AND CHARGE ACCOUNT

Credit cards and charge accounts are handy ways to purchase items now and pay for them over time. Indeed, there are some 2.3 cards for every adult Canadian over the age of 18. In the 1980s, the number of Mastercard and Visa cards doubled, from 12 million to 24.3 million. By 1991, there were more than 857,000 Canadian businesses that accepted one or both of these cards.

Many of the nationally recognized cards (such as Visa, Mastercard, and American Express) carry interest rates that hover around the 20 percent mark, as do the charge cards offered by department stores and other merchants.

The interest rate is not important if you pay your credit card bill in full each month. But if you make only partial payments, finding a card with a lower interest rate can save you hundreds of dollars each year.

DISPUTED BILLS

If you use a credit card, always look carefully at your monthly statement as soon as it arrives. If you see a charge for an item you did not buy, or an amount that is greater than what you actually paid for a particular purchase, inform the issuer right away.

Usually, you will have to contest such items directly with the merchant who claims you made the purchase. According to most credit card contracts, you will be responsible to whoever issued your credit card for the amount on your statement. If you can prove that you did not buy the contested item, that you were overcharged for it on your bill, or that you never received delivery of an item, the issuer will probably make the necessary correction. If not, you can take the matter to court.

Consumer protection legislation generally requires that credit contracts be in writing. So, if you really signed for an amount lower than what you are charged, and if you have a copy of the bill, you cannot be held responsible to the merchant for the amount overcharged. Moreover, the offending merchant will have to reimburse you for your expense and trouble. See also CHEQUE; CREDIT BUREAU AND CREDIT RATING.

LOST OR STOLEN CARDS

In 1991, nearly 625,000 credit cards were reported lost or stolen. As well, 54,000 credit cards were used fraudulently. This resulted in losses of over $45 million. The obvious question: Are you responsible for unauthorized charges when your credit card or charge card is lost or stolen?

The answer depends on the applicable consumer protection legislation in your province. Usually, if you notify the card issuer as soon as you discover your card is missing, you are not responsible for any charges made after you report the loss. If charges are made on your card before you report it missing, you are liable only for the first $50. Some credit card agreements hold you responsible for all charges made on your card that use your personal identification number (PIN), up to the time that you report the card stolen.

Call the card issuer immediately you find that your card has been lost or stolen. Get the name of the person you speak to and follow up your telephone call with a letter. Since the credit card company is responsible for any unauthorized charges over $50, you can be sure your problem will be treated expeditiously. The company will cancel your present account right away and issue you a new card.

If your credit card company sends you a letter urging you to buy "credit card protection," a kind of insurance against unauthorized use of your card, think twice about it. After a couple of years, the fees you pay for this "protection" will probably exceed the $50 you might have forfeited after a loss or theft.

UNAUTHORIZED USE BY SOMEONE YOU KNOW

Under the terms of your credit card agreement, you are not responsible for any unauthorized charges, no matter who makes them.

Suppose your teenage daughter uses your credit card to buy a portable compact disc player. If you did not authorize the charge, you are not obliged to pay it. But your daughter must return the machine, and she may also face charges of theft by fraud. However, if you have allowed her to use your card in the past, you may have a hard time convincing the credit card issuer that the charge was unauthorized.

Your cooperation in the investigation of your daughter's actions will probably be required in order to give substance to your claim of unauthorized use. This does not mean you will have to watch your child go to jail, but more likely that you will have to make sure that the item is returned, and perhaps compensate the merchant for wear and tear on the machine.

CREDIT COUNSELING

You have been unable to keep up with your debts—your car has been repossessed, your credit cards have been canceled, and now you are getting strongly worded letters from collection agencies. Friends suggest you file for bankruptcy, but you find the idea too humiliating. What can you do? You may want to consider the alternative provided by credit counseling.

There are several credit counseling agencies in Canada that may help you find alternatives to bankruptcy. Moreover, if you have been declared bankrupt already, federal law requires you to undergo credit counseling before you can be absolutely discharged from bankruptcy.

Credit counseling will provide you with a number of possible solutions to your debt problems. If your creditors see your good faith in taking steps to pay off debts, they may be open to participating in one of these solutions. As one example, you may be able to convince your creditors to allow you to pay off debts by a scheme of debt pooling instead of resorting to collection agencies and the courts.

A debt pool may be set up whereby each of your creditors is paid a percentage of your monthly income until your debts are paid off. Imagine, for example, that you owe $1,000 to X, and $500 to Y. And say that your monthly payments would regularly be $50 and $25 respectively. However, you can afford only $50 of the total $75 of monthly payments. You could thus meet your obligations to either X or Y, but not to both creditors. Under a debt pooling plan, you could propose to pay $35 to X and $15 to Y until your debt is repaid or until you can afford more.

Beyond debt pooling, credit counselors may also suggest that you try to reach an agreement with your creditors that you pay a lump sum, less than the total owed, to relieve you of your debt. Some creditors might prefer to get partial payment than to get nothing from a bankrupt customer. In some cases, creditors may even agree to suspend interest charges while you are making payments.

Many provinces have debt counseling agencies, such as the Ontario Association of Credit Counselling and the British Columbia Debtor Assistance Branch of the Ministry of Housing, Recreation and Consumer Services. See USEFUL ADDRESSES at back of book. See also BANKRUPTCY; COMPOSITION WITH CREDITORS.

CREDIT UNION

A credit union is a nonprofit, provincially incorporated, financial cooperative that functions much like a bank. Historically, credit unions have been organized by people sharing a common bond, membership of a trade union, say, or belonging to an ethnic group.

Members of a credit union are not merely customers, as in the case of a regular bank. They are also shareholders of the corporation, with a voice in how it is operated and a share in the annual dividends paid, if any. Instead of a straight cash payment, dividends may be allotted in the form of low-interest loans or higher-interest savings accounts.

In some parts of Canada, particularly Quebec, credit unions (*caisses populaires*) have been so successful that they are virtually as common as banks. Healthy credit unions are able to offer virtually all the same services as banks and often at more favorable rates of interest. See BANK ACCOUNT.

CRIME

While everyone knows what crime is generally, the particularities of a given crime are probably not as well understood. For example, suppose Jim knowingly takes a compact disc from a store without paying for it. He is guilty of the crime of theft. But, if Louise absentmindedly walks out of the store with a compact disc, would this be considered a crime? According to the principles of Canadian criminal law, it would not. For a crime to exist, there has to be a mental component, sometimes referred to as a guilty mind, or *mens rea*, and an unlawful act or omission, called the *actus reus*. A Crown prosecutor who proves there was *actus reus* and *mens rea* wins a conviction, unless of course the plaintiff has a valid defense.

There are exceptions to this principle. Some crimes, called strict liability offenses, do not require the existence of a knowing mind. Driving while impaired is such an offense.

In legal terms, a crime is an act which is prohibited by the federal Criminal Code. But not all conduct that contravenes the law is criminal. A civil wrong, called a tort (delict, in Quebec), is not a crime. Offenses determined by provincial governments, although dealt with in a manner similar to crimes, are not crimes either, because only the federal Parliament can make criminal laws.

Criminal offenses are classified as indictable, summary conviction, or hybrid. Serious offenses, such as murder and kidnapping, come to trial by indictment and can result in life imprisonment. Summary conviction offenses are less serious and are punishable by a $2,000 fine or six months' imprisonment, or both. The classification is important, because of the different manner in which these two types of offenses are brought to trial and prosecuted. For example, a person accused of a summary conviction offense does not have the right to request a jury trial. In some cases, the legislation will specify that the Crown may proceed by indictment or on summary conviction. These are known as hybrid offenses.

CRIMINAL INJURIES COMPENSATION

If you are the victim of a crime, you may get compensation from your province for any injury you sustained as a result of a criminal act against you.

If you are robbed and valuable property has been stolen from you, or if you are attacked and injured, there are two ways that you could get compensation for your lost property or for your injury: either the criminal could be ordered to pay you money or replace your property, or you could apply to your provincial criminal (victims) injuries compensation board for compensation for bodily injury and lost wages.

In most cases, it is impossible to get compensation from the criminal. Even if the court orders the wrongdoer to return your property, this may be impossible: your stolen car, stereo, or television may already have been taken apart and sold piece by piece. In such cases, the court could order that the wrongdoer pay you money for your loss.

Similarly, the court could order the criminal to pay you money for the injury you suffered as a result of the criminal act. But the court cannot order the criminal to pay you unless the criminal can afford to do so. Given that the criminal usually cannot pay, the bottom line is that you may recover little, if anything, from the criminal. You would be lucky if you got even your legal costs.

Another problem with court-ordered compensation is that the kinds of losses you can claim are limited. If, for example, your daughter is attacked and you take time off work to care for her, you probably cannot claim for the wages you lose as a result. The court will usually order only that the criminal compensate the victim for her lost wages and her pain, suffering, and trauma.

It does not seem right that victims of crime suffer substantial losses and are never compensated. It may be for this reason that every province and territory has criminal injuries compensation schemes.

CRIMINAL INJURIES COMPENSATION SCHEMES

Whether or not the criminal can afford to pay you, or even if he is never caught, any compensation is actually paid by the province. A victim who cannot get compensation from the criminal himself can apply to the provincial criminal (victims) injuries compensation board. In paying you, the province gets the right to sue the criminal in your place.

As a rule, you cannot claim for lost or damaged property. The one exception is in Alberta, where you can claim for property destroyed or damaged by the police while they were preventing a crime or apprehending a criminal.

Most provinces limit compensation to certain offenses. Only victims of those offenses are eligible for compensation. For example, if you are injured by a drunk driver, and cannot work because of your injuries, you may qualify for criminal injuries compensation only in the Northwest Territories. Elsewhere in Canada, dangerous driving and impaired driving are not offenses for which you can receive criminal injuries compensation. Most likely, this is because many provinces have separate legislation that deals with compensation for automobile-related injuries. In Alberta and Manitoba, for example, there is other legislation which stipulates that a victim's spouse will be compensated if the spouse is killed by an impaired or a dangerous driver.

If you are the victim of an offense for which your province compensates victims, but also somehow involved in the crime, Prince Edward Island is the only province that will compensate you. If you get into a fight with someone, for instance, and your arm is broken, it is not likely that you could receive compensation. New Brunswick will not compensate the relatives of a criminal. A woman who is beaten by her husband, for example, may not be able to claim damages.

Under the criminal injuries compensation schemes you are entitled to the money you lose as a result of being injured—lost wages, for example. In some provinces, you are also entitled to compensation for such things as the pain and suffering caused by your injury. This varies from province to province. Manitoba, for instance, will not compensate you for your pain and suffering.

If you were not physically injured, yet suffer psychologically from, for instance, witnessing a crime, you are unlikely to be compensated for your trauma. Most provinces and territories will only compensate you for any trauma you suffer as a result of a crime directed at you.

In most cases, once your compensation claim is approved, you are paid in one lump sum. In British Columbia and Quebec, however, your claim can be reassessed and an additional sum paid if other costs come up after your claim has been settled. This would be the case, for example, if after you receive compensation for the wages you lost when you were first injured, you need to take more time off work because of medical complications arising from your injury.

Your claim under the criminal injuries compensation scheme may be reduced if your employer, or your insurance company, compensates you for wages you lost as a result of your injury.

To make a claim, apply to the criminal (victims) injury compensation board in the province where the offense occurred. (You do not have to reside there.) Check the Blue Pages of your telephone book, or get the address from your local police department. See USEFUL ADDRESSES at back of book. See also VICTIM'S RIGHTS.

CRIMINAL LAW

You look in the rearview mirror and see the flashing red lights of a police car. Pulling over to the side of the road, you wait for the officer to approach. He says you were speeding, asks for your license and proof of insurance, and returns to his patrol car to check them out.

Several minutes pass before the police officer returns, gun drawn, and orders you out of the car. Before you know what has happened, you are being searched, handcuffed, and placed in the back of the patrol car. The officer tells you that

you are wanted for armed robbery. You know you are innocent, but how will you convince the police, a judge, or a jury?

If, as in this alarming scenario, you find yourself charged with a crime, you have certain basic rights that are designed to protect you from being convicted of an offense you did not commit. These rights are guaranteed by the Charter of Rights and Freedoms and are fundamental to Canadian justice.

However, they are subject to interpretation, and no rights are absolute. Section 1 of the Charter allows certain individual rights to be violated by the government under lawful authority, which can be reasonably and demonstrably justified in a free and democratic society. Section 33, moreover, allows the federal or provincial governments to pass laws that may violate certain individual rights, without having to justify themselves to the courts. In criminal matters, sections 7 to 15 of the charter are of crucial importance.

RIGHT TO FUNDAMENTAL JUSTICE

Section 7 of the charter guarantees the rights to life, liberty and security of the person. At the same time, it provides that these rights cannot be deprived except when done in accordance with the principles of fundamental justice, which perhaps is best described as fairness. The law and all its procedures must be applied as fairly as possible to all parties in a given dispute.

Dr. Henry Morgentaler, who was charged under sections of

the Criminal Code that made abortion illegal, argued that his section 7 rights had been violated. Under the Criminal Code, an exception was created to the offense whereby hospital committees, in theory, could permit "therapeutic abortions," where to do otherwise would endanger the life of the pregnant woman. The defendant argued that this exception to the crime of abortion did not work in practice. Finally, in 1988, the Supreme Court of Canada held that the abortion law should be struck down since it violated a pregnant woman's right to security of person and liberty. See also CRIMINAL PROCEDURE; DUE PROCESS OF LAW.

RIGHT TO EQUAL PROTECTION OF THE LAWS

The law may not be enforced in a way that discriminates against you on the basis of race, national or ethnic origin, color, religion, sex, age or mental or physical inability. A proposal to prohibit discrimination because of sexual orientation came before Parliament in 1993, but was not passed into law before that year's general election.

Criminal statutes must be applied evenhandedly, with no one group being singled out for prosecution. This does not mean that prosecutors do not have some latitude in deciding whom to prosecute; you cannot use equal protection of the laws as a defense simply because another person who committed an identical crime was not charged. See also EQUAL PROTECTION OF THE LAWS.

RIGHT TO A SPEEDY TRIAL

Section 11(b) of the federal charter guarantees that any person charged with an offense has a right to a trial within a reasonable time. It is important to note that the courts will consider delays only from the time an accused is charged, not from the time the police begin a criminal investigation about someone. If the court finds that a pretrial delay is unreasonable and therefore against the charter, the charges against an accused will be dropped.

In 1990, the Supreme Court found a pretrial delay of two years unreasonable. For a number of reasons, trial courts took the Supreme Court's words very literally and, as a result, nearly 47,000 cases pending trial were thrown out of court. Included were 10,000 impaired driving charges, 1,000 assaults and 500 sexual assaults. The Supreme Court stated later that it had been misunderstood. From now on, what is a reasonable pretrial delay is not fixed. Each case will be decided on its merits according to a number of criteria: the length of delay; whether the delay is the fault of the prosecution or the accused; and the possible prejudice to the accused by allowing a given pretrial delay.

RIGHT TO A TRIAL BY JURY

Section 11(f) of the charter guarantees a right to a trial by jury where the punishment is five years in prison or a more severe punishment. There are exceptions. Those who are to be tried by a military tribunal and those who have been charged with contempt of court (which may carry prison terms of more than five years upon conviction if the penalty is repeatedly re-imposed) have no guarantee of a jury trial. Corporations, too, are not guaranteed a right to trial by jury. At a certain stage before trial, for certain offenses, the accused may also opt for trial by judge alone, thus waiving his right to trial by jury.

The jury must be drawn from a cross-section of the community where the trial is being held, and neither the prosecution nor the defense may intentionally exclude any group. But a jury need not proportionally represent all the racial groups in a given area.

To be fair and impartial, the jury must remain free of outside influences. Members of the jury should not be subjected to excessive pretrial publicity (what is considered excessive is determined case by case) or to publicity during the trial, and they should not communicate with witnesses.

Contrary to popular belief, juries do not always have to be composed of 12 people. Certain sections of the Criminal Code allow for less (as few as 10) where circumstances so merit. The courts have found that this does not violate the accused's right to a jury trial under the charter. See also JURY.

RIGHT TO BE PRESENT AT YOUR TRIAL

You have the right to be present at any stage of the trial that will affect you. This includes the selection of the jury, presentation of evidence, arguments by lawyers, judge's instructions to the jury, announcement of the verdict, and judge's sentence. If you do not show up for your trial, you have waived your right to be present, and the court may try the case without you.

RIGHT NOT TO INCRIMINATE YOURSELF

It is not entirely clear whether a court can compel you to be a witness against an accused in a trial when you are simultaneously up for charges in a separate but related offense. For example, John is accused of stealing a radio; Janet, of stealing a video camera. There are two separate offenses of theft, but both may have occurred from one break-in in which both persons were supposedly involved.

By testifying as to her knowledge of John's theft, Janet may incriminate herself, even though she is not in jeopardy at the time she testifies against John. However, even if Janet's testimony may be compelled by the court, Section 13 of the charter states that anyone who gives evidence in any proceedings may not have that evidence used against him or her in other proceedings except in a prosecution for perjury.

The Supreme Court of Canada has ruled that a co-accused does not have to testify against the other accused in the same supposed crime, as that would infringe upon his right not to incriminate himself.

The right not to incriminate yourself is often called the right to silence. Yet this right is more than the mere legal power to say nothing. It probably also allows you to refuse to be part of a lineup for suspect identification. In some cases you may also refuse to have your photo or your fingerprints taken. This is typically so for summary offenses, such as common assault, shoplifting, or certain gambling offenses.

This right extends even to the early stages of a criminal investigation, before any charges have been filed. For example, you have the right to refuse to speak with the police about a crime of which you may be accused. At the trial, the prosecution may not make comments to the jury suggesting your failure to talk to the police or to testify at the trial implies you are guilty.

RIGHT TO CONFRONT ACCUSERS

Generally you have the right to hear and cross-examine witnesses who testify against you. But there are exceptions. If one of your witnesses cannot be present at the trial, in some cases you may be able to introduce testimony from him or her that was recorded previously. See DEPOSITION.

There are special rules, too, to protect sexual assault victims. In the case of child witnesses, the courts have allowed a screen to be placed before the child who is giving testimony, to avoid traumatizing her. In some child sex assault prosecutions, videotaped testimony by children could also be allowed, depending on the facts of the case. See HEARSAY.

In sexual assault charges involving children, the accused is no longer allowed to personally question the victim.

The "rape shield" section of the Criminal Code also provides another form of exception to the general right to confront your accusers in a criminal trial. For example, evidence of the complainant's past sexual conduct cannot be introduced to prove that she consented to sex. Nor can it be presented to discredit her as a witness. (Many defense lawyers claim this law, passed in 1992, denies the accused the chance of a fair trial.)

RIGHT TO COUNSEL

Section 10(b) of the Charter of Rights and Freedoms guarantees an accused person, upon arrest or detention, the right to be represented by a lawyer.

When arrested, the police must inform you of that right without delay. Where legal aid is available, those under arrest must also be informed of their right to financial assistance for obtaining a lawyer, though the right to be represented by the lawyer of your choice is not required by the charter.

If it appears that an arrested person does not understand his rights merely by being informed of them verbally, then the police are obliged to take steps (such as providing an interpreter) to make sure the person who has been arrested does understand the situation.

Even though you have a general right to a lawyer, you may forfeit it by unreasonably refusing to contact a legal representative. One accused could have

called his lawyer the afternoon he was arrested, but chose to wait until the next day. The Supreme Court of Canada found this delay was unreasonable, and so the accused was considered to have waived his right to a lawyer at the arrest stage of the case.

The right to assistance of counsel means your lawyer must meet you, advise you of your rights, and propose various defenses. If you are being held in jail before or during your trial, you have the right to communicate freely and in private with your lawyer.

No court will force a defendant who does not want a lawyer to have one. You also have the right to dispense with a lawyer you have and represent yourself. If you do, the court may appoint a lawyer to help you prepare and present your own case, even if you do not use him.

If the police fail to inform you of your right to a lawyer, or if they deny you that right, then serious problems may arise for the prosecution. Any evidence, such as a confession, obtained after the accused's right has been violated, will be rejected by the court. Often, this may result in an acquittal.

RIGHT TO PRESUMPTION OF INNOCENCE

If you are accused of a crime, under the law you are presumed innocent until proved guilty. The burden of proof is on the prosecution, which must establish your guilt beyond a reasonable doubt in order to obtain a conviction. See also BURDEN OF PROOF.

CRIMINAL PROCEDURE

The Criminal Code sets out a number of rules designed to ensure the fair and orderly prosecution of criminal charges. These procedures will vary depending on these questions: Has the accused already been arrested? Is the offense a summary conviction offense or an indictable offense? Must the offense be tried by the Superior Court (with federally appointed judges) or a provincial court? Will there be a preliminary hearing?

It would be impossible to explain in a few paragraphs what the Criminal Code takes hundreds of pages to do. Set out here are just some of the broad themes in this area of the law. In any case, a competent criminal lawyer is your best bet for finding your way through the criminal justice system.

CLASSIFICATION OF OFFENSES

Generally, summary offenses tend to be less serious (though this is not always the case), and the trial procedure speedier and much less formal. For example, preliminary hearings and jury trials are not held in summary conviction offenses. The reverse is true of indictable offenses, which tend to be more serious and involve longer and more formal preliminary and trial procedures.

How a trial will proceed also depends on the mode of trial that has been chosen or is required by law. In some cases, the accused may stand before a judge alone, and in others, before a judge and jury. Sometimes, the accused may choose whether she or he wants a jury or not. For example, those accused of murder can choose to have a trial by judge and jury or to have the case heard by a judge alone. In other cases, procedural rules require that the case be heard before judges of a certain court regardless of the accused's choice. Someone charged with driving while his license is under suspension may be tried before a provincial court judge even if he would rather be tried by a superior court with federally appointed judges.

CHARGE, INFORMATION, AND INDICTMENT

Charges can be laid against a person before or after an arrest. When charges are pressed before an arrest, usually a police officer (although anyone can do so) will lay an information before a justice of the peace. An information is a document that must contain a sworn claim that the accused person has committed a certain offense at a given time and date. If the justice believes there is sufficient sworn evidence, she will issue a summons or a warrant for arrest. Often, such arrests are made without a warrant, and charges are typically laid within 24 hours of the arrest.

Charges can also be laid by way of indictment, which has virtually the same purpose as an information. The prosecutor may opt for an indictment when the accused has chosen to be tried by judge with no jury for an indictable offense. The prosecutor may also add charges (or provide substitutes for earlier ones) to those on the original indictment, following evidence from the preliminary inquiry.

BAIL

A person who has been both arrested and charged with offenses carrying a maximum penalty of less than five years' imprisonment may be released upon his promise to appear for trial. This usually happens after he has been issued an appearance notice or summons.

The accused may be detained if he poses a threat to the public, or if it is necessary to identify him, preserve evidence, or to ensure that he will show up for court. If the police officer making this initial decision feels it best not to release the accused, then the prisoner must be brought to the officer in charge who will change or confirm the original decision. If the accused still is not released, then he must be brought before a judge within 24 hours or as soon as possible. Even if the judge decides that there are valid reasons to continue the detention until trial, this decision is open to review by an appeal court.

If an accused is released by the officer in charge or a judge, special conditions such as a money deposit (commonly known as bail), or restrictions on his movements, may be imposed depending on what the circumstances require.

PRELIMINARY HEARING

In 1980, the Department of Justice estimated that preliminary hearings took place in only about 5 percent of cases. Most often, this procedure is implemented for the most serious offenses, such as murder or robbery, as a final step in determining whether the accused should be committed to trial. The preliminary hearing also gives the prosecution a chance to include other charges for which sufficient evidence did not previously exist.

The Supreme Court of Canada has held that the prosecution has a duty to disclose all information relevant to the trial, since its job is not always to win cases, but rather, to see that justice is done.

See ARREST; BAIL.

PURPOSE OF PRELIMINARY HEARING

At the preliminary hearing, the prosecution must present enough evidence to convince the court that a crime has occurred and that there is "probable cause" to believe you committed it. Probable cause is not as strict a standard as "beyond a reasonable doubt," which represents the level of proof required for a conviction.

You have the legal right to be present at your preliminary hearing, where you can cross-examine witnesses and present your own evidence. If the court is not convinced that there is probable cause a crime occurred or that you committed it, the charges will be dismissed. However, charges dismissed at the preliminary

hearing stage can sometimes be refiled if additional evidence comes to light later.

If the court does find probable cause to believe you committed the crime, you will be required to stand trial. Before your trial, you will have to appear for an arraignment.

Once it is clear that you will be committed to trial and a date is set, a few procedural matters may remain before the trial. If you have chosen a trial by jury, it must be selected. Lastly, pretrial motions may be made for such things as a request for particulars or for a change of venue. Particulars help to let the defense know more about the Crown's case. A motion for a change of venue—that is, the change of place where the trial will be held—may be requested in cases where widespread media coverage or the nature of the trial would prejudice the accused's right to a fair trial.

At a preliminary hearing, if there is a doubt about the accused's guilt, the doubt is in favor of the prosecution, and the accused will be sent to trial.

ARRAIGNMENT

At the arraignment you will enter your plea: guilty, not guilty, or a special plea. Special pleas are made where the accused has been previously convicted, acquitted, or pardoned in respect to a given set of events.

For example, if John was acquitted of manslaughter for the beating death of Fred, he could not later be tried for that crime again. John could also not be tried for the lesser offense of assault, which is a

component part of manslaughter. The rationale underlying these legal rules is that an accused should not be subject to double jeopardy; namely, to be in danger of double punishment for the same offense.

Another special plea, in the case of defamatory libel, is that of justification for speech or actions that are claimed to be slanderous. If a special plea is successful, the trial will end there. If the accused enters no plea or does not clearly utter it, a plea of not guilty will automatically be entered. If a guilty plea is entered, then the judge will proceed to sentencing. If the plea is not guilty, then the trial will finally commence.

TRIAL

If you choose a jury trial, the proceedings will begin with the selection of a jury. Far more jurors than necessary will be summoned, and the defense and prosecution will then pick a jury from those called. They will question the potential jurors to find out whether they know any facts about the case, have any particular prejudices about it, are acquainted with you or any of the witnesses, or are in some way unlikely to be fair and impartial.

Once the jury has been chosen, the trial can proceed. The prosecution presents evidence and questions witnesses, and your lawyer cross-examines those witnesses and tries to show that they are mistaken or are not telling the truth. You may testify on your own behalf, but you cannot be forced to testify, because it would violate your charter rights. If you choose not to testify, the jury is told not to assume that your silence is a sign of guilt.

When both sides have presented their case, the judge instructs the jury on the law. For example, in a first-degree murder case, the judge will inform the jury about which elements (such as willful killing and premeditation) must be proved in order to obtain a murder conviction. The jury then retires to a separate room, where it must try to determine what happened on the basis of the evidence alone. Once the jury decides what the facts are, it must apply the law to them as instructed by the judge, and determine if you committed the crime. When the jurors reach their verdict (they must be unanimous in the decision), they return to the courtroom and announce it to the court.

If the jury finds you not guilty, you will be let go. If it finds you guilty, the judge will set a date for sentencing. A jury that cannot agree on a verdict is called a "hung jury." The judge may discharge such a jury and order that a new one be chosen, or he may ask the jury to try again to reach a verdict. If it is found that the judge unduly pressures the jury to come to a unanimous decision, an appeal court may allow a new trial. See MISTRIAL.

SENTENCING

Before your sentence is determined, the court may order an investigation of your background, education, work history, criminal record, and family situation.

The Criminal Code allows victims to address the court with a "victim impact statement," to explain the harm done to them. The court will review this victim impact statement as part of the process of arriving at an appropriate sentence. See VICTIM'S RIGHTS.

The sentence must be within the guidelines set by law for your particular crime. You may be fined, sent to prison, or both. Or you may be released on probation, which means you will not go to jail as long as you follow certain rules. See DEATH PENALTY; PROBATION.

APPEAL

If you believe that mistakes during your trial—for example, if you believe the judge did not instruct the jury properly —resulted in your conviction, you can file an appeal.

A higher court reviews the proceedings of the trial court to find out if there were mistakes that would justify a reversal of the trial court's decision. While awaiting a decision about your appeal, you may either be freed on bail or start serving your sentence. If the appeals court reverses your conviction, you must be released or given a new trial. See APPEAL.

CRIMINAL RECORD

If you are convicted of an offense under a federal regulation or act, such as the Criminal Code or the Narcotic Control Act, you will receive a criminal record. This is also the case if you were convicted in another

country and have been transferred to Canada under the Transfer of Offenders Act. Information regarding your conviction is stored in the RCMP's Canadian Police Information Centre computer.

A criminal record can jeopardize your attempts to find employment, purchase car insurance, or visit the United States and other countries. However, offenses such as impaired driving—a crime in Canada—may be only a "traffic offense" in the United States and would not bar you visiting that country. In some cases, you can get a waiver from U.S. Immigration if you would otherwise not be admitted into that country. To make sure a criminal record does not create problems in other countries, before leaving Canada, contact the consulates of any countries you plan to visit.

After a certain period of time you may apply for a pardon, which will erase your criminal record as far as federal records are concerned. See PARDON.

CROSS-EXAMINATION

Cross-examination, the process of questioning the opposing party's witness in a court proceeding, is a mainstay of fictional courtroom dramas. A Crown attorney calls a witness to the stand. After a few minutes of testimony that makes the defendant look hopelessly guilty, the Crown attorney turns from the witness stand and says, "No further questions, Your Honor." Then his opponent rises to cross-examine the witness and, with a series of deftly phrased questions, pummels what moments ago had seemed like rock-solid evidence into a fine dust of half-truths, hazy memories, and pitiful lies.

PURPOSES

Although cross-examination is rarely so dramatic in real-life courtrooms, it is fundamental to our judicial system. In typical court procedure, the cross-examination follows the initial questioning—the "direct examination"—of a witness by the party that has called him. The opposing lawyer may then cross-examine the witness to clarify testimony given previously, to discredit the witness, to test whether the witness is telling the truth, or to develop points that will be helpful to the lawyer's client.

A judge cannot deny the right of cross-examination in either civil or criminal cases, because this would be a denial of the right to a fair trial. If a witness is unavailable for cross-examination for some reason, such as illness, the testimony he gave during direct examination may be removed, or struck, from the record. Or if a witness refuses to answer questions during cross-examination, the court may strike the testimony he gave on direct examination. If there is a jury, members are instructed to ignore anything the witness said during direct examination.

LIMITATIONS

In civil cases, as a general rule, neither a witness in a civil case nor a party to the lawsuit can refuse to answer questions during a cross-examination. In criminal cases, however, there is one exception to this rule: a defendant or witness may refuse to answer a question if it violates his right against self-incrimination.

Questions may be asked to get more details from a particular witness or to point out inconsistencies or weaknesses in his testimony. For example, the exchange may go something like this:

LAWYER: Under direct examination, didn't you say that you saw the defendant strike Mr. Smith?

WITNESS: Yes.

LAWYER: And where were you when you saw this take place?

WITNESS: At the end of the alley.

LAWYER: What time did you say it was?

WITNESS: Just after midnight.

LAWYER: Wasn't it awfully dark out?

WITNESS: Well, yes.

LAWYER: So let me ask you how you can be so sure the defendant was the person who struck Mr. Smith?

WITNESS: Well, I guess I'm not sure, but I think it was him.

LEADING QUESTIONS

Leading questions are prohibited during direct examination. However, they are allowed during cross-examination to enable the opposing lawyer to get the answers he wants from a witness. A leading question is usually worded so that the witness need answer only yes or no—for example, "Didn't you see the defendant strike his wife?" Such questions enable the lawyer to limit what a witness can say and thus to shape the testimony to fit his case.

While the court must give each side the chance to cross-examine witnesses called by the other side, in some cases the lawyer chooses not to do so. If a witness's story is air-tight and unassailable, cross-examination might do more harm than good. Or a lawyer may forgo cross-examination in order to indicate to the jury that a witness has nothing to say that is of importance to the case. See also CRIMINAL PROCEDURE.

CROWN

The Canadian political system consists of a federal state, which acts in a symbolic way in partnership with a monarchy. The Constitution states that the Queen is the head of Parliament and that "The Executive Government and Authority of and over Canada is hereby declared to be vested in the Queen."

The Crown is represented at the federal level by the governor general, and in the provinces by the lieutenant governors. Therefore, it can be said that in Canada there are 11 crowns, one federal and 10 provincial. It is for this reason that the government and its various branches are often called the Crown in right of Canada, whereas provincially we speak of the Crown in right of Manitoba, or any other province.

CROWN ATTORNEY

A Crown attorney, sometimes called a Crown prosecutor, is an agent of the government responsible for the prosecution of persons accused of criminal offenses. Crown attorneys appointed and paid by the provincial governments prosecute only offenses under the Criminal Code and provincial penal statutes. Federal prosecutors deal with offenses not found in the Criminal Code and are employees of the Department of Justice. The Crown attorneys in Canada fulfill a similar duty to district attorneys in the United States.

CROWN CORPORATION

Corporations that are owned entirely by the federal or provincial governments are referred to as Crown corporations. They have been created to fulfill the need for various goods and services that cannot suitably be provided by the private sector, often because of Canada's immense geography and relatively small population, other times because the public interest would best be served by a government organization.

Crown corporations such as the Canadian Broadcasting Corporation, Air Canada, and the Canadian National Railway are examples of what many feel to be necessary government participation in commercial activity. Other Crown corporations are more involved in regulatory, administrative, or advisory activities: bodies such as the Canadian Wheat Board and the Canadian Dairy Commission.

In general, Crown corporations are freer of government control than ordinary government departments. Nevertheless, the federal Financial Administration Act makes Crown corporations accountable to Parliament. The act also permits the Treasury Board to set out the manner in which annual financial reports of Crown corporations are to be submitted, and enables Parliament to participate in creating Crown subsidiaries.

CROWN LIABILITY

Historically, you had to obtain the permission of the King, and later the government, if you wished to sue the Crown. However, as equality before the law came to be seen as an important concept, laws permitting citizens to sue the government were passed.

Today, you can sue the Crown in contract and in tort, just as you would sue a person. As is usually the case, there are exceptions: you will not be granted an injunction against the Crown, and in some jurisdictions the time for bringing an action against the Crown is shorter than for actions against individuals.

There are also restrictions on evidence that may be detrimental to the public interest. The legislation in some jurisdictions also provides a measure of Crown immunity, or protection from liability, in tort. Public corporations do not benefit from Crown immunity unless they are found to be agents of the Crown.

In the case of Nurse Susan Nelles, wrongly charged with murdering four young patients at Toronto's Hospital for Sick Children, the Supreme Court of Canada ruled that even the attorney general and his prosecutors are not immune from civil suits. This is particularly true if the wronged party can show that the attorney general used his office in a deliberate and malicious manner that was in the words of the chief justice of the Supreme Court, the Hon. Mr. Justice Antonio Lamer: "improper and inconsistent with the traditional prosecutional function."

In 1982, Susan Nelles' case was thrown out of court at the preliminary hearing stage because of a total lack of proof against her.

CRUEL AND UNUSUAL PUNISHMENT

The charter of rights prohibits the government from using "cruel and unusual punishment." This term is usually defined as punishment that is grossly out of proportion to the crime or punishment that shocks the moral sensibility of reasonable people.

For example, in Canadian prisons, the torture and ill-treatment of prisoners is prohibited because it is considered cruel and unusual punishment.

The "cruel and unusual" prohibition would also apply to too harsh sentences for minor crimes and substandard prison conditions caused by overcrowding.

See also DEATH PENALTY.

D

FROM

DAMAGED MERCHANDISE

TO

DYING WITHOUT A WILL

DAMAGED MERCHANDISE

Sometimes when you unwrap your purchases, you find damaged items. How you go about getting a refund or replacement depends largely on how you bought the merchandise and the way it was sent to you.

MAIL-ORDER PURCHASES

If the damaged goods were bought by mail order, keep the shipping carton and all the packing materials, as they may be needed to substantiate the cause of the damage. A dented box, for example, may prove the package was damaged in transit. If the merchandise was broken because it was packed improperly or the delivery company mishandled it, you are entitled to a replacement from the mail-order company.

Check the company's catalog for instructions on returning damaged goods. Or call the customer service department to find out how they want you to return the merchandise and whether you will be reimbursed for postage or shipping costs.

Companies that deliver merchandise by a private delivery or courier service may have the company pick up the damaged goods at no cost to you. Companies that send merchandise through Canada Post will probably require you to pay the shipping costs when you send something back.

If you return the merchandise by mail, insure the package and keep the receipt as proof that you sent it. If you return the merchandise through a private courier service, your package will probably be automatically insured up to a certain amount. If the item is particularly valuable, you can buy additional coverage.

IN-STORE PURCHASES

Before you buy something in a store and take it home, ask about the company's return policy. Does the store accept returns of damaged goods? Is there a time limit? If possible, watch the item being packed and inspect the package before leaving the store. If the merchandise is sealed in a manufacturer's carton, do not accept a carton that looks poorly wrapped, badly dented, or otherwise damaged.

Some stores sell floor models or slightly damaged merchandise at reduced prices. Be cautious in buying such items. Even though you can some-

times get a bargain, damaged goods are usually sold "as is." This means you probably cannot get a refund or replacement under any circumstances.

If a salesclerk assures you that "We guarantee all our merchandise," ask for a written guarantee of the item you are buying. Keep in mind, however, that according to most provincial consumer legislation, any oral statement by a salesclerk or anyone else working for the vendor, as well as any advertisement broadcast on radio or television—statements such as "money refunded if not completely satisfied"—are part of the contract.

GOODS THAT BREAK AFTER YOU RECEIVE THEM

Often, merchandise proves inferior or defective only after you have had it at home for a while. In such circumstances, you will have to go to either the store owner or the manufacturer for repair or replacement. Many merchants will not accept responsibility after you have kept an item for a certain length of time.

In the case of small appliances, such as toasters and clock radios, the manufacturer, not the merchant, is usually responsible for repairing or replacing damaged goods, and you will have to contact the manufacturer directly. If neither the seller nor the manufacturer takes responsibility for the damaged goods, you may have to take action in small-claims court to recover your money. See also SMALL-CLAIMS COURT.

Sometimes your method of purchasing an item adds protection. Certain credit cards—the Gold Mastercard and the Gold American Express Card for example—will double the manufacturer's warranty if you use these cards to make your purchase. Be sure to keep the credit card sales slip, proof of purchase, and guarantee if you wish to take advantage of this "extra" warranty.

DAMAGES

The money awarded in a lawsuit to someone who has been harmed or injured because of another person's wrongful conduct (whether in the form of some action or of negligence) is known as damages. If Mary falls over a brick that Harry left on the path to his house, and is left with a limp, Harry cannot make her leg straight again. If Mary sues Harry for negligence and wins, the jury will award her damages that express in money the harm Harry's act did to her. The award is not intended to make Mary so rich that she will be able to hire limousines to carry her around, nor to punish Harry by leaving him so poor that he will have to sell his house.

You are entitled to damages only for particular types of injury or loss that are recognized by law. For example, you may win damages if someone destroys your property, causes you personal injury, or causes you financial loss by breaking a contract. But the law does not give you the right to collect damages for hurt feelings, for a single trespass (a neighbor's use of your yard once for a shortcut) or for your lack of sleep (due to noise from a nearby railway). Successful lawsuits may result in an award of one or more of three categories of damages: compensatory, nominal, and punitive.

COMPENSATORY DAMAGES

Compensatory damages consist of money that will repay someone for a loss or injury. Suppose the transmission of Ray's car is ruined and his hand broken when he drives over a large pothole on a city street. Ray sues and wins. The court orders the city to reimburse him for the cost of the transmission and the physiotherapy needed for his broken hand, nothing more. These are called compensatory damages.

But suppose Ray is a carpenter and cannot work for six weeks after the accident. His loss of wages is a direct consequence of the accident, and he could therefore expect to be reimbursed for this loss as part of his compensatory damages.

Some forms of personal injury, such as pain and suffering, or mental anguish, are real and merit compensation, but attaching specific dollar amounts may be difficult. Suppose you suffer a minor injury in an accident, and as a result you become nervous, irritable, and have trouble sleeping. Your suffering is very real, but it may be impossible to place an exact monetary value on it, especially if you are able to work at your regular job and do not incur a loss of income.

The Ontario Court of Justice (General Division) recently ordered the manufacturer of a defective infant car seat to pay $3.6 million in damages for injuries to a young child. Of this sum, $400,000 was for general damages; $1,200,000 for care up to the age of 21; $1,300,000 for care after age 21; $300,000 for lost wages. The child's mother was awarded $28,000 in general damages, $127,000 for loss of income, and $75,000 in damages under provisions of the Ontario Family Law Act (see page 164).

Breach of contract
Compensatory damages are also awarded when there has been a breach of contract. If you have a contract with Country Landscapers to plant your yard for $3,000 and they never show up, your damages would be the difference between the $3,000 and any higher amount you have to pay another contractor for the job. Therefore, if you had to pay another landscaper $3,500, your damages would be $500. See BREACH OF CONTRACT.

Duty of the injured person
When you are harmed or injured as a result of someone else's wrongful act or breach of contract, you have a duty to minimize your loss or suffering. Suppose Nancy's upstairs neighbor Jerry goes out late one night and leaves the sink faucets running. The sink overflows and the water drips into Nancy's living room. Nancy is at home, but because she is angry with Jerry, she does not call the superintendent to enter Jerry's apartment and turn off the water; nor does she put a

bucket under the drip. Instead, she later sues Jerry not only for the damage to her ceiling, but for a new carpet. Because Nancy did nothing to mitigate, or lessen, her damages, she would probably be reimbursed only for repairs to her ceiling.

NOMINAL DAMAGES

The small sum of money known as nominal damages, awarded as recognition of a wrongful act, is the law's way of recognizing that a person's rights have been violated, even when he has not suffered any real loss.When a judge (or jury) imposes nominal damages, he symbolically places blame on the defendant (the person sued). A trespasser, for example, might be ordered to pay his neighbor $1 for repeatedly taking a shortcut through his lawn.

A person who suffers damage to himself or his property, but fails to demonstrate the exact loss, may receive nominal damages only. For example, if Ray fails to document the cost of repairing his automobile or having his hand treated by a physiotherapist, the judge or jury, with no basis for deciding the extent of his loss, can award nominal damages only.

A person arrested because of mistaken identity may receive only nominal damages, especially if he was in custody only briefly and was released as soon as the mistake was discovered.

PUNITIVE DAMAGES

A plaintiff may get punitive (also known as exemplary) damages to punish a defendant for his actions. Punitive dam-

ages also serve to warn others that certain conduct will not be condoned. They are typically awarded in lawsuits where a defendant has acted in a willful, wanton, or malicious way, or has otherwise demonstrated a total indifference or reckless disregard for the consequences of his act. If Bill's reckless driving causes him to hit and injure a bicyclist, he might be required to pay both compensatory and punitive damages. This award is meant to send Bill and others a strong message to drive more carefully.

Article 1619 of Quebec's updated Civil Code states: "Where the awarding of punitive damages is provided for by law, the amount of such damages must not exceed what is reasonably sufficient to fulfill their preventive purpose."

ASSESSING DAMAGES

Typically, it is the judge who determines the types of damages a plaintiff may recover. Mr. Justice John H. Gomery of Quebec Superior Court felt $2,000 in punitive damages was justified when "the behavior of the offender displays an antisocial or particularly reprehensible attitude." He awarded this sum to the client of a leasing company that had failed to repair the client's car for four months after an accident, then billed the client for the balance of the contract, more than $37,000. The judge also canceled the contract, an 8½- by 14-inch document covered on both sides with fine print that "would take a well-educated person about half an hour to read. . . . "

A court may also decide damages should be limited because the plaintiff could have avoided a loss or injury. Suppose that after Ray drove over the pothole, he lost control of his car and crashed through the window of the nearby liquor store. If the owner fails to board up the window or post a guard after the incident, Ray cannot be held responsible for losses the store incurs when looters arrive later and steal the merchandise.

In jury trials, the jury decides how much money should be awarded, but the judge may increase or reduce the amount. In some contract cases, it may be difficult to determine the exact amount of damages caused by one party's failure to fulfill its part of the bargain. Suppose, as part of its fringe-benefit pay package, a company makes an agreement with a law firm to provide legal services to its employees. If the law firm decides to back out of the agreement and the matter is brought to court, a judge or jury might not be able to decide how much extra the company would have to pay to replace the law firm's services—and so it might not award any damages.

"Liquidated damages" clause
To avoid such a situation, contracts often include a "liquidated damages" clause that specifies how one party is to be compensated if the other breaks the contract. Such a clause sometimes specifies that you are entitled to a fixed sum if services or obligations are not performed. Beware that

this type of clause may make it impossible for you to invalidate the agreement before a court, because the court may not want to interfere with the parties' freedom to contract. It might intervene if the agreed-on sum is unreasonably low or high, but if it does, it may not rule in your favor.

Say, for example, you have a dispute with a builder who fails to complete your house. Even if your contract stipulates that, in case of such failure, he will pay you the cost of completing the work plus 50 percent of the contract price, a court may find the extra 50 percent agreed upon unreasonable and award you much less.

Personal injuries

If you are physically injured because of somebody else's actions, you may be able to get compensation for a number of different things. In most circumstances, you will be entitled to damages for the injuries you suffered, and to other kinds of damages for such things as pain and suffering. If your injury is so serious that it affects your ability to work, you may also be entitled to damages for future pain and suffering, your loss of earning capacity and the costs of any future care.

Should your injury be such that your future earning capacity is adversely affected, you will be entitled to compensation for that. The judge will take into account your current earnings and what your earnings would have been had you not been injured. The sum awarded could also include an allowance for lost retirement income, including retirement income that would have been payable by your employer or under the Canada (Quebec) Pension Plan. In the case of a student, the courts will take into account what her earning capacity would have been had she been able to complete her program.

The court will also look at your specific injury and grant whatever monies you may need to adapt to everyday living with your new needs. If you suffered a loss of hearing, for example, you would be awarded funds to furnish your home with equipment specially designed for the hearing impaired. If you are bedridden or otherwise unable to carry out normal household chores, the court may award you funds for future costs for household help and/or medical in-home care. If you have been rendered paraplegic or quadriplegic and require a wheelchair, the court will award you enough money to renovate your home for your new needs and to purchase any special equipment you may need for recreational activities.

Pain and suffering

In most provinces, you are entitled to damages for both present and future physical and mental pain. If seriously injured, you may receive compensation for loss of enjoyment of life and diminished life expectancy. There is a maximum amount you can get for these types of damages: the figure (set at $100,000 in 1978 by the Supreme Court of Canada) is fixed annually against the Consumer Price Index, Canada's most widely used measure of the rate of inflation. Today, the ceiling amount would be about $250,000.

Personal injuries to dependents and relatives

If a spouse, parent, or other relative is hurt or killed as a result of another's wrongdoing, or dies from injuries before he or she can take action against the culprit, you may be able to recover certain damages. Your recourses are more limited than those available to the actual victim, since many provinces have laws that limit the damages recoverable by children, spouses, and relatives.

In most provinces, if a person is killed, his dependents are entitled to whatever contribution that person would have made to them had he or she still been alive. Under section 61 of the Ontario Family Law Act and article 1457 of the Quebec Civil Code, certain relatives can claim financial losses. In Ontario, as in many other provinces, some spouses, children, and relatives may be entitled to compensation for "loss of guidance, care, and companionship."

But the Ontario act also specifies several other categories of recoverable damages. These include travel expenses to visit the relative while his or her injuries are being treated, actual expenses incurred for the benefit of the deceased, and funeral expenses. You can also claim any loss of income incurred for taking time off work to care for the victim, or for the value of your services in providing care.

The damages can easily add up to very large sums of money. Most insurance policies, both home and automobile, allocate a certain amount for damages to another person. This is called personal liability insurance. If you are ever involved in an accident and are responsible for the injuries suffered by the other party, your insurance may not cover the damages you are ordered to pay. If, for example, you injure a 40-year-old woman who was earning $40,000 a year and she is no longer able to work following the accident, the damages for loss of salary alone could amount to $1 million. If your insurance does not cover this amount, you are personally liable for its payment.

STATUTORY REMEDIES

In certain cases, there may be legislation in your province affecting the amount of damages you can recover, and whom, or where, you can get them from. Your provincial motor vehicle legislation may only allow a fixed amount of damages for injuries suffered in an automobile accident. Or if you are injured at work, you may have to make your claim through your provincial workers' compensation board. If you are the victim of a crime, you may be eligible for compensation from the Criminal Injuries (Victims) Compensation Board of the province where the crime occurred.

If you are seeking damages for breach of a consumer sales contract, your local consumer protection office can tell you what options you have.

Keep in mind that, if you receive compensation under one kind of program, you may not be able to make other claims for damages. If you receive workers' compensation, you probably could not sue your employer for damages. Should your former employer be ordered to pay you damages for unjustified dismissal, unemployment insurance (UI) benefits you receive following your dismissal could be taken into account in assessing damages—the amount awarded by the court would be reduced by the amount received from UI.

Whether you can collect welfare benefits, insurance benefits, or UI benefits as a result of being injured, and still recover damages from the person responsible for your injury depends largely on where you live. In some provinces you can collect both from your private insurance company as well as from the person responsible for your loss.

See AUTOMOBILE INSURANCE.

DATE RAPE

Date rape, or acquaintance rape, is the term used for rape committed by a man whom the victim knows socially. The term also applies to non-dating situations, such as rape by a classmate, co-worker, or neighbor. Date rape is said to account for 70 percent of all rapes.

For victims, prosecution of such rapes (the criminal charge is aggravated sexual assault) presents a distinctive set of problems. Because the rapist knows the victim, he may try to coerce her into not reporting the crime. If the rapist is a boyfriend, the victim may feel guilty about subjecting him to prosecution. Or she may fear being accused of having seduced the rapist, or of having consensual sex and later claiming she was raped, or of bringing rape charges as a retaliation for being jilted.

Because women realize that if they are raped their behavior will be scrutinized and their character might be questioned, many victims decide not to report the crime. To make it easier for sexual assault victims both to come forward and to prosecute those guilty of sexual assault offenses, Parliament enacted in 1983 what was commonly known as the "rape shield law." This made the prior sexual history of a rape victim inadmissible as evidence at trial. But in the *Seaboyer* case of 1991, the Supreme Court of Canada struck down the law. The Court ruled that under sections 7 and 11(d) of the Charter of Rights and Freedoms, the law violated the accused's right to be presumed innocent, and the right to provide a full answer and defense.

Under recent legislation, an alleged rapist could not easily escape prosecution by saying that he was so drunk that he believed the woman consented. He would have to show that he acted reasonably to ensure she had consented.

Many legal authorities point out that this law, too, could potentially violate an accused's rights and so may be struck down. But it is an encouraging sign of legislators' acknowledgment of the problems in rape cases and their commitment to finding remedies.

As with all violent crimes, date rape or any form of sexual assault should be reported immediately. Because a victim's delay in reporting the crime may be due to psychological trauma, some courts allow the prosecution to present expert evidence to that effect. See also RAPE; SEXUAL ASSAULT.

DATING

Even the ritual of dating can lead to legal problems, sometimes at such time-honored events as the high school prom. As prom celebrations have grown more and more elaborate, participation has become more expensive. Some young women who invested in dresses and coiffures for the event and were "stood up" by their dates on prom night have filed lawsuits, usually in a small-claims court, against the young men.

A much more serious consequence of dating is date rape, when the woman is sexually assaulted by a man whom she knows and has no reason to fear. See DATE RAPE.

Another area of concern is the workplace. When co-workers date, the potential for sexual harassment increases, especially if one is a supervisor and the subordinate wishes to end the romance or stop further advances. Some companies try to prohibit dating between supervisors and subordinates and sometimes between co-workers, too.

♦ Some years ago, the Toronto Branch of the Multiple Sclerosis Society put on a bachelor auction, in which about 50 bachelors strutted down a runway and women in the audience bid for dates with them. A Toronto doctor paid $1,700 for an evening out with one of the participants, but he never showed up. The reason: in between the auction and the date, he had been charged with attempted murder and, on the night of the date, his bail conditions forbade him from leaving the neighboring city of Hamilton, where he lived.

The doctor was able to get her money back.

Dating sometimes leads to marriage and at one time it was possible to get damages if someone promised to marry you and did not. The court could compensate you for mental distress and loss of reputation. Ontario and Quebec have abolished damages for breach of promise to marry and other provinces may follow suit.

See BREACH OF PROMISE; DATE RAPE; SEXUAL HARASSMENT.

DAY CARE

During the last 20 years or so, the traditional family in which the woman stayed home with her children has changed dramatically. For economic and personal reasons many women with young children also have business careers, a trend that will most likely continue.

Some large corporations have day-care centers in or near their offices or factories for the benefit and convenience ♦

♦ of their employees. Numerous studies show that day-care facilities at the workplace reduce absenteeism and increase motivation.

REGULATION

Standards for day care and child care are set by provincial law. These standards and their enforcement vary widely.

Most day-care providers, those who take children into their homes, are unlicensed and, therefore, unregulated. Even those that are licensed are rarely monitored. Day-care centers are more closely regulated, but government regulations and periodic inspections do not provide sufficient guarantees that a child will be properly cared for in a clean and safe environment or offered a variety of stimulating, healthy activities. You can help ensure your child's well-being by following the suggestions in "ABC's of Choosing Day Care" on page 167.

CHILD CARE IN YOUR HOME

If you plan to hire someone to come into (and perhaps live in) your home, you will have to make certain arrangements.

◇ You will have to withhold from your employee's pay an amount for the Canada (Quebec) Pension Plan, income tax, and unemployment insurance, and you will have to pay the employer's portion toward these programs.

◇ Make sure your home insurance policy covers the caregiver for any injuries she may incur in your home or while employed by you. ♦

◇ if she will be using your car, be sure that your automobile insurance will cover her as a member of your household.

◇ If your caregiver is not a citizen or permanent resident, make sure she has the proper work authorization.

See also HOMEOWNERS' INSURANCE; HOUSEHOLD HELP.

TAX CREDIT

At the time of writing, you can claim an annual $4,000 per child for child care. In 1991, the Federal Court of Appeal ruled that a Toronto lawyer was not entitled to deduct the $50,000 salary she paid her full-time nanny from 1982 through 1985. The trial judge (whose decision was overruled by the Court of Appeal) felt the woman should be able to deduct the full cost of child care and that the Income Tax Act discriminated against working mothers by limiting it to $4,000. In late 1993, despite dissenting views by its two women members, the Supreme Court of Canada ruled child-care costs were not a legitimate business expense.

LEGAL PROTECTION

Although each province has its own laws on the number of children allowed at a day-care center and regulations on day care generally, most address the following concerns.

Training

Some provinces will license only caregivers who have had some child-care training— workshops, college courses, or reading courses in child development. Some provinces require program directors of day-care centers to have

ABC's
OF CHOOSING DAY CARE

In trying to find the best day care for your child, you should gather all the information you can about the available options and investigate each one before entrusting your child to someone else.

■ Look for a recommended center or provider with a valid license whose location, hours, and fees match your needs. Ask if there are penalties if you are late picking up your child.

■ Ask for references from both former and current clients, and talk to them by telephone. Ask former clients why they left. If you get even a whisper of negative feedback, look elsewhere.

■ Visit the center to make sure it is clean, spacious, and safe. Take a close look at toys, bathroom facilities, playground equipment, and conditions for daytime naps. Are windows and stairwells fitted with toddler-proof screens or bars? Ask to see fire exits, extinguishers, and smoke detectors. Is there reliable transportation for field trips? Who checks vehicle safety? Are the drivers bonded?

■ Check the staff-to-child ratio. A rule of thumb is that each adult caregiver can be responsible for no more than four infants, five preschoolers, or six older children. Ask how many caregivers are graduates of child development or early childhood education programs.

■ Ask how long the staff has been there. Child care is a low-paying job with a high turnover. Long-term workers suggest that a place is well managed.

■ Ask how employees are screened and how carefully workers' backgrounds are investigated. Observe staff interactions with children. Do they get on the floor and engage in activities? Do they speak directly to the children and seem to enjoy being with them? Are the activities structured and age-appropriate?

■ Find out how medical needs and emergencies are handled. The day-care provider should maintain medical records of children with special needs as well asconsent forms from all parents to ensure medical treatment if parents cannot be reached. Be sure that emergency procedures are posted and that at least one caregiver with CPR and first-aid training is always present.

■ Spend some time observing daily activities. Are these appropriate for the children's ages? Do the children look happy? Is there regular activity, or do the children (and staff) simply sit around watching television? Are meals, naps, and playtimes well organized?

■ Can you visit at any time your child is there, or must your visits be prearranged? If so, look for another provider. Day-care facilities are not schools and should not restrict parental visits.

appropriate academic credentials and teaching experience.

Health tests

Day-care providers must prove that they have been vaccinated against tuberculosis and other communicable diseases.

Physical facilities

Some provinces require day-care centers to have at least 2.3 square meters (25 square feet) of play space per child; an adequate number of toilets and sinks (about one toilet per 14 children) for the number of youngsters, and at appropriate heights for their size; fire extinguishers and smoke alarms; covered garbage containers; guards on stairways and heating elements; safety caps on electrical outlets; an accessible telephone with emergency numbers posted nearby; bathrooms with doors that unlock from both sides; a refrigerator; and locked storage cabinets for medications.

Activities

Some provinces specify that the children must have a certain number of hours of supervised outdoor play, rest periods, and snacks daily. A few provinces require day-care providers to prepare written activity plans designed to develop children's creativity, self-confidence, coordination, and intellectual growth.

Consent forms

Caregivers should keep health data on each child, as well as medical consent forms in case a child needs medical care and neither parent can be reached.

Child abuse registry

Caregivers should keep a register with the name, address, and birth date of everyone who works in a day-care center or lives in a provider's home, and should screen the register for the names of anyone reported to have abused children or to have been convicted of child abuse or neglect.

Emergency plans

Centers may be required to develop and post emergency plans for earthquakes, fires, floods, and storms, and to practice and record fire drills.

Admissions

A day-care center should have a written, nondiscriminatory admission policy, and it should tell parents if religious training is included in its program.

To obtain more information about the laws regulating day care in your province, call or write to your province's child welfare agency.

DEATH

Death is the cessation of life, but the medical community has not formulated any precise definition of when life ends, and courts have been forced to define for themselves the moment of death. The definition is important, because life-support systems can sustain a person's bodily functions for extended periods of time. The growing demand for organ transplants has further focused the need for objective standards regarding the moment of death. The sooner the heart, kidneys, liver, and other vital organs are taken from the donor after death, the better the chance for a successful transplant. Therefore, the moment of death must be clearly defined so that a terminally ill person is not declared dead prematurely.

Physicians use the following criteria to establish death: a permanent vegetative state (the person is unconscious and cannot perform such vital activities as eating); absence of movement, breathing, or reflexes; no response to stimuli; a flat electroencephalogram (a recording of brain waves that shows no brain activity); and the failure of a vital organ.

RIGHT TO DIE

Since medical technology makes it possible to sustain life, the question arises whether a patient has the right to die, when there is no hope of a cure or improvement. (For a related, but quite different issue, see the Right to Refuse Medical Care on facing page.) Resolving this question involves balancing the patient's wishes against society's interest in preserving life. The state's interest is evident in federal laws prohibiting not only murder, but also euthanasia. See EUTHANASIA.

Suicide is not a crime in Canada, but (under section 241 of the Criminal Code) assisting someone to commit suicide is. Assisted suicide and euthanasia have been the subjects of controversy for years. A 1989 Gallup poll revealed that 77 percent of Canadians would not object to lethal injections being administered to dying patients and lawmakers have tried to fashion legislation that would permit physicians to administer death-hastening (as opposed to death-inducing) drugs to the terminally ill.

Of course the professionals in these situations have rights too. Hastening a person's death, even if it were legal and desired by the sick person, would challenge the integrity of the medical profession; asking a doctor or nurse to do so would amount to asking her to violate her professional ethics—to "do no harm."

ASSISTED SUICIDE

Regardless of the circumstances, assisting someone to commit suicide is illegal. So the Supreme Court of Canada ruled in 1993, in deciding the case of Susan Rodriguez. The 42-year-old British Columbia woman suffered from amyotrophic lateral sclerosis (Lou Gehrig's disease), a motor neuron disease of the brain and spinal cord. Although intellect and awareness are not affected, victims of the disease gradually lose control of all muscle functions (including the ability to eat and breathe without assistance). There is no known cure. Because Ms. Rodriguez did "not wish to face the indignity of a mentally agonizing death," she sought permission to have a doctor help her end her life when her life became unbearable.

Although all nine justices agreed that the law prohibiting assisted suicide was unfair in Ms. Rodriguez's case (a mentally competent person, physically unable to take her life), five justices sided with the greater societal interest in protecting "the vulnerable, who might be induced in moments of weakness to commit suicide."

RIGHT TO REFUSE MEDICAL CARE

The state is obliged to seek the extension of life, unless there is clear and convincing evidence that doing so would violate the sick person's wishes. A competent adult generally has the right to refuse medical treatment if, without duress, he clearly expresses his wishes orally or in writing. In Nova Scotia and Quebec, for example, you write a "living will," spelling out the circumstances under which no extraordinary measures should be taken to preserve your life. In any province, you can execute a durable power of attorney for health care, designating a third party to make medical decisions for you if you are unable to do so.

The right to refuse medical treatment is a different issue from the right to die (see facing page) in that it does not involve committing suicide, but rather removing artificial devices or ceasing to administer drugs that are prolonging a person's life, or postponing death.

Refusing medical treatment is not as controversial as assisted suicide, and the right has been widely acknowledged. Complications arise, however, when the right cannot be exercised by the individual being treated, and the decision must be made by physicians, a spouse, or other family members. Making such a decision can be emotionally devastating for family members. Physicians who order an end to life-sustaining treatments may leave themselves open to civil or criminal proceedings.

See LIVING WILL; POWER OF ATTORNEY.

PRESUMPTION OF DEATH

Sometimes there is no way of knowing if a missing person is alive or dead. If someone has disappeared, his property cannot be distributed to his heirs, nor can they receive benefits from his life insurance, until he is declared dead. Also, his spouse cannot remarry.

In most provinces the courts will make the presumption that a person is dead after seven years of continued and unexplained absence. If there is evidence that the person was seen or heard from within that seven-year period, he cannot be presumed dead.

If some event or incident in a missing person's life might explain his disappearance, the court is less likely to declare him dead. For example, if he was wanted by the police, if he had an unhappy marriage or family situation, or if a threat had been made against his life, then his continued absence can be reasonably explained.

Before declaring a missing person dead, courts want proof that his family or others made a "diligent search" for him. After a search has been conducted, the court will examine the evidence and decide whether to issue an order declaring the person dead.

When a court declares a missing person dead, the official date of death is usually set at seven years from the date of disappearance. In some cases, however, it is important to presume that death took place earlier. For example, death benefits or inheritance may be contingent on an earlier date of death. Suppose Enoch disappears in 1989, and his father dies in 1992. The father's will left everything to Enoch, but it also provided that if Enoch died before his father, everything would go to Enoch's cousin Elizabeth.

Elizabeth has evidence that Enoch may have died soon after his disappearance. She could ask the court to declare the date of Enoch's death as occurring before his father's, so that she would receive the estate right away.

Courts are sometimes willing to presume an earlier date of death if the missing person was exposed to some danger that makes his death likely, such as fire, war, or hazards at sea. See also DYING WITHOUT A WILL; FUNERAL AND BURIAL; WILL.

The presumption of death is often important in insurance law, since the beneficiaries must obtain a "declaration of death" from the courts before they can collect the proceeds of an insurance policy.

STEPS TO TAKE IF YOUR SPOUSE HAS DISAPPEARED

Suppose your husband or wife mysteriously disappears, and you wonder whether your partner is living or dead. Here are a few suggestions on what to do:

1. Tell your friends and family members about the disap-

pearance and ask them to let you know if they hear anything from your spouse.

2. File a missing person's report with your local police department. You will need to provide them with a recent picture of your spouse, a physical description, and the names of people he or she may contact.

3. Check with hospitals to see if they have admitted any unidentified accident victims.

4. Contact the issuers of your spouse's credit cards and ask whether any meals, hotel rooms, or other purchases have been charged to the cards.

5. If much time has elapsed and your search has failed, find a lawyer who can help you petition the surrogate (probate) court for a declaration of death.

DEATH PENALTY

In Canada at one time even theft could be punished by execution. Now the trend is toward sentences that will deter crime, rehabilitate criminals, and reintegrate them into society.

Although Canada's last execution occurred in 1962, capital punishment was not abolished until 1976. (It is still permitted under the National Defense Act for cowardice, desertion, spying for the enemy, and unlawful surrender.)

Although some people advocate reintroducing the death penalty for certain offenses, capital punishment has never been found to be effective in cutting crime.

DEBT

Most Canadians have debts of some kind. Debt in the form of consumer loans and mortgages enables most people to own a home and a car. And credit card debt allows people to buy from department stores, gas stations, restaurants, and other retail outlets and pay for their purchases later.

TYPES OF DEBT

Debts fall into two categories: secured and unsecured. Secured debts, such as auto loans and home mortgages, are those in which the borrower offers collateral to the lender—that is, the borrower gives the lender an interest in the house or the car until he pays his debt. Unsecured debts, such as credit card purchases, are ones in which the lender depends entirely on the borrower's promise to pay him back. See also COLLATERAL; CREDIT CARD AND CHARGE ACCOUNT; MORTGAGE.

If you owe money that you cannot repay, the type of debt you have incurred affects the lender's ability to collect. For example, if you default on your mortgage, which is secured by your home, the lender has the right to go to court, seek foreclosure, obtain ownership of your house, and sell it. If your debt is unsecured, the lender must ask the court for permission to appropriate any assets you have, such as wages or money in your bank account, which can be used to satisfy the debt.

Every province and territory has laws that limit how much of your salary or assets a creditor may seize once he has obtained a judgment against you. In Alberta, for example, a creditor must leave you household furniture and appliances up to a value of $4,000 (this is depreciated value, not the value of the things when new), tools you need for your trade up to a value of $7,500, and a vehicle used for business up to a value of $8,000.

A creditor must also leave untouched $40,000 of equity for each name on the title of the house you live in. Equity is the difference between the value of the house and how much you owe on it. For example, if Wendell and Jola own a $120,000 house, both their names are on the deed of sale, and they have $40,000 left to pay on their mortgage, their equity is $80,000. Since the Alberta Exemptions Act makes $40,000 equity unseizable for Wendell, and $40,000 unseizable for Jola, neither Wendell's creditor nor Jola's can seize their house. Property a creditor cannot take is called unseizable or exempt property.

A creditor who seizes part of your salary for debt (garnishees your salary) must also leave a certain amount untouched. In Alberta, for example, a married person can keep $700 per month, an unmarried person $525 per month. An additional $140 per month for each child is also exempt from garnishment.

In all provinces it is illegal for a creditor to garnishee more than is allowed by law, even if you have signed a form permitting him to do so. Such an agreement, whether part of the original contract or made as a separate agreement, is illegal and unenforceable. The one exception to this rule arises if your debt is for an alimentary pension ordered by the court for maintenance of your ex-spouse or children. In the case of alimentary debts, the creditor is allowed to garnishee a greater part of your salary.

Each province and territory also has laws that regulate how seized articles are sold. Usually the debtor has a short period after seizure to pay off the debt and so prevent having his goods sold by the sheriff or bailiff. See COLLECTION AGENCY; FORECLOSURE; GARNISHMENT.

UNMANAGEABLE DEBT

If you are unable to reduce the balance on your credit cards, or if you are using cash advances on your credit cards to pay your everyday living expenses, then you are probably living beyond your means. If so, you may want to seek the help of a credit counseling service.

Many counseling services are affiliated with your provincial consumer affairs office and their services are often free. Beware of private companies that promise to reduce or cancel your debts for a fee. There is no magic or simple way out of indebtedness.

Legitimate counseling services may help you prepare a budget, and in some cases may make special arrangements with creditors—for example, to reduce or cancel interest while you are making payments according to an agreed-upon schedule.

Remember, most creditors would rather get their money, even if it takes longer, than incur the extra trouble and costs involved in suing and then seizing and selling your property.

If your debts are totally unmanageable and would require many years of living on the edge of poverty to repay, you can always opt for a bankruptcy. Under the rules that went into effect in late 1992, consumer bankruptcy has been greatly simplified and most people who apply are discharged from bankruptcy after nine months, without ever having to go to court. See BANKRUPTCY; CREDIT COUNSELING; GARNISHMENT.

DEED

The written document that transfers title to (ownership of) real estate is called a deed. A deed must accurately identify the property being transferred, the names of the people or the organization making the transfer, and the names of those receiving ownership. Typically, the deed must be signed by the person making the transfer in the presence of witnesses who can attest to the fact that the transferer's signature is valid and that he or she transferred it voluntarily.

In most provinces, certain other formalities must be observed. The deed must be delivered to the new owner, he must accept it, and the deed must be recorded.

Recording the deed involves delivering it to the recorder's office in the county where the property is located. The deed is then photocopied, and the copy is inserted into a chronological record of property transfers. In this way, an official record exists, putting the public on notice of the transfer of property and of the new owner.

If you fail to record a deed, you will have difficulty transferring ownership when you want to sell the property. With modern real estate closing procedures, however, it is unlikely that a deed would not be recorded. A title insurance policy also protects your ownership. See also CLOSING, REAL ESTATE; TITLE INSURANCE.

After the deed is copied and recorded, it will be returned to you. Keep it in a safe place, such as a bank safe-deposit box or a fireproof box in your home. Before the era of photocopying, a lost deed meant trouble if you wanted to sell or mortgage the property it covered. These days, however, it is a relatively simple matter to obtain a certified copy of a deed from the recorder's office.

Alberta, British Columbia, and Quebec are among provinces using computers to register immovables and do title searches. The Alberta Land Titles Automation System (ALTA) takes only five seconds to do a title search and less than 15 seconds to print a copy of a pcertificate of title.

Many lawyers and notaries also have computers that are connected to those in registry offices. (Notaries draw up and register deeds in Quebec.) As a result, title searches can be done quickly and economically.

See also BARGAIN AND SALE DEED; QUITCLAIM DEED.

DEED IN LIEU OF FORECLOSURE

A deed in lieu of foreclosure lets a mortgage lender take title to property without going through foreclosure proceedings in the event that the owner cannot make his mortgage payments. The procedure requires the owner to surrender the deed to his home to the mortgage lender. A deed in lieu of foreclosure has certain advantages: the lender saves on foreclosure costs and can resell the house to another buyer, while the debtor avoids the stigma of a foreclosure or bankruptcy.

Generally, where there is only one mortgage, the value of the property is such that the debt is satisfied and the borrower can walk away free if the creditor takes back the property. This is not the case where there is a second mortgage. In that case, the debtor may be liable if proceeds from the sale of the property are insufficient to pay back both mortgage holders. See also BANKRUPTCY; FORECLOSURE.

DEFAMATION

Frank and Mary worked together at the Jimson Company for many years, then had a falling out. Afterward, Mary learned that Frank had been saying things behind her back—not only that she was an incompetent accountant but also that she probably was not above dipping into the petty cash. Mary, hurt and indignant, wants to sue Frank for defamation. Will she win her suit?

Perhaps. Making a false statement that, without lawful justification or excuse, harms someone's good name or reputation, and holds that person up to hatred, contempt, ridicule, or insult, is defamatory libel, a criminal offense. You can even defame someone without words: you could do so in a cartoon, for example, or by portraying a person in a ridiculous manner in a painting.

When a defamatory statement is written or otherwise permanently recorded—as in the newspapers or on television—it is called libel. If the statement is merely spoken but is heard by a third person, it is slander.

LIBEL AND SLANDER

The distinction between libel and slander has been abolished in Alberta, Manitoba, New Brunswick, and the Northwest Territories. Elsewhere the distinction between the two is hard to make.

Some courts consider statements made on radio and television to be slander, whereas others consider them libel. According to the Ontario Libel and Slander Act, "defamatory words in a newspaper or broadcast shall be deemed to be published and to constitute libel." (Proving defamation becomes more complicated in cases involving the media.)

The distinction becomes important when the courts award damages (money to compensate for the harm the defamed person suffered) because some kinds of slander may not be considered to cause the kind of lasting damage that libel does. A Toronto lawyer employed by the Ukrainian-Canadian Committee was awarded $325,000 in damages and a further $140,000 in punitive damages because a Toronto Ukrainian newspaper attacked his honesty and good faith, suggesting deception and underhandedness in the manner he carried on his practice.

In Frank's case, since his statement was made orally (and would therefore be slander), Mary would have to prove she was damaged by it. If Frank's statement was printed (in which case it would be libel), she would not have to prove she was damaged; the law would assume she was, since the defamatory statement was made in a permanent manner.

Of course, mere criticism is not a crime. If Frank had said that in his opinion Mary was not meticulous enough to be a good accountant, Mary could not claim defamation. But even given Frank's outrageous comments, Mary might not win a lawsuit for defamation.

PROVING DEFAMATION

The degree of proof required to be convicted in a criminal court of defamatory libel is higher than that required in a civil suit. (The victim of defamatory libel can also sue before the civil courts for damages.) Mary would be able to win her suit only if she could prove that Frank's statement embodied all the following elements:

◇ The statement was truly defamatory, containing words (such as "thief," "untrustworthy," or "incompetent") that could ruin Mary's good name.

◇ Frank denigrated Mary to other people, such as her co-workers (who need not believe Frank for his words to be considered defamatory). If Frank merely ranted and raved at Mary in private and no one else heard him, Mary's feelings may have been injured but her reputation was not. If someone inadvertently overheard the conversation, it would not be considered defamation, because Frank did not intend his words to be overheard.

◇ The person whom Frank accused of incompetence and theft was indeed Mary. If Frank told a co-worker that the redheaded woman who reports to Jane had been stealing, and Mary is the only person who fits this description, the identification of Mary is sufficient.

◇ Frank's defamatory statement truly harmed Mary. Suppose no one listens to Frank because he is known to be jealous and petty, and Mary even got a raise not long after Frank's accusation. Under such circumstances, she would not be able to prove defamation.

DEFAMATION OF PUBLIC FIGURES

Public figures (such as politicians or celebrities) are normally expected to withstand more criticism than private persons are. Therefore, if a public person sues for libel or slander, the court requires not only proof of the elements noted earlier but also evidence that the defamer acted "falsely and maliciously" in making the defamatory remarks.

Thus, for instance, if Frank and Mary were politicians running against each other for a seat in Parliament, and Frank accused Mary of being dishonest because she did not keep her earlier campaign promises, he would probably not be held liable for defamation. However, if Frank were to accuse Mary publicly of adultery or bribery, simply as a smear tactic with no basis in fact, Mary would have a good case.

DAMAGES

If Mary wins her suit for defamation, Frank will be required to pay damages—that is, to compensate her with money. If Mary establishes that his statement was made with malice, Frank might have to pay her an additional amount, called punitive damages. See DAMAGES.

DEFENSES

The law allows certain defenses to someone facing defamation charges, whether in civil or criminal court.

Justification

One defense is justification. If the defendant can prove his statement was true in all material particulars and in their inferential meanings, or innuendos, he will be found not guilty. However, even a truthful statement, if made maliciously, may not be considered a valid defense. If Frank were to say that Mary's grandfather was a convicted embezzler, he could be sued, because this fact has no bearing on Mary, and was printed in a malicious manner only to tarnish her name.

Absolute privilege

The law grants immunity, or absolute privilege, to people in essential positions in government and the judiciary, so that they can carry out their functions without fear of being sued. Elected members have absolute privilege when speaking in Parliament or a provincial legislature. These assemblies may, however, provide other sanctions, such as expulsion from the house.

A judge trying a case has absolute privilege, a privilege that arguably also applies to lawyers, witnesses, jurors, and other parties to the case, provided the defamatory statement is made during the judicial proceeding. All provinces allow for striking out defamatory allegations in a statement of claim (declaration).

Qualified privilege

Qualified privilege applies to statements made to protect one's interest, for common interest or mutual concern, in the public interest, and where one has a moral or legal duty to protect another's interest. For example, you might not be able to sue a storekeeper who, in good faith, accused you of theft in as discreet and quiet a manner as possible. A citizen who, in good faith, complains to his member of Parliament about a public official, or to police about someone he believes has committed a crime, would also be protected by qualified privilege.

Fair comment

If you make a statement based on facts, and if that statement is for the common good or interest, then you would be protected against liability by the doctrine of fair comment.

In 1979, the Supreme Court of Canada said that freedom to express an opinion on a matter of public interest is protected by fair comment, but only if such opinion honestly represents the view of the person who made or published it.

The dissenting opinion of the Supreme Court's Hon. Mr. Justice Dickson, who was concerned with maintaining "uninhibited debate on every public issue," was reflected in laws later enacted in Ontario and other provinces. They made it legal for a publisher, especially a newspaper publisher, to publish an opinion expressed by another person, so long as any person could honestly hold the opinion, even if the publisher himself did not agree with it. Thus a theater critic could write about a play he saw, and criticize it without his publisher having to fear being sued.

DEFAULT

The failure to perform a duty imposed by law, or keep a contractual promise, is known as a default. A father who fails to make child support payments as required by his divorce decree is in default. So is a person who does not make a minimum payment on his credit card.

The law prefers to see peo-ple make good on their obligations, rather than forcing them to go to court. As a result, most contracts, and even some court orders, include procedures for correcting a default. Suppose you have a contract with a gardening company to mow your lawn every two weeks. If the mowers fail to show up, the company would, strictly speaking, be in default. However, most contracts have a clause giving the company a chance to avoid default by working on a later day, subject perhaps to a small financial penalty.

In most cases where a debtor is in default, the creditor must inform him of his default by letter. This is called a letter in default, or in Quebec, a *mise en demeure*. Most consumer legislation gives the consumer about 30 days to remedy this default and have the contract reinstated without penalty.

DEFAULT JUDGMENT

When one of the parties to a lawsuit fails to appear in court, the opposing party may ask the judge to issue a default judgment. Suppose you file a suit in the small-claims court against a dry cleaner for damaging an expensive evening dress. If, when the day for hearing your case arrives, the cleaner does not show up, you can request the judge to order a default judgment against her. You must then let the dry cleaner know that you have won a default judgment and that she must pay you what the court has ordered.

However, judges prefer to decide lawsuits on their merits, and therefore try to avoid issuing default judgments. If the dry cleaner can show a good reason (such as illness or an accident) for missing the trial, the judge might withdraw (or "vacate") the default judgment and set a new date for trial. In cases involving large sums of money, the judge will not revoke a default judgment unless the defendant can satisfy the court that he had good reasons for not attending the initial hearing.

DEFICIENCY JUDGMENT

When Cori could no longer make her car payments, the loan company repossessed the car and sold it to satisfy the loan. Although Cori owed $7,000 for the car, the sale brought only $4,500. So the lender went to court and obtained a judgment against her for the remaining $2,500.

This type of judgment is called a deficiency judgment. With it, the lender can garnishee Cori's wages, put a lien on her house, or attach other property she owns, such as a bank account.

Not all provinces allow a lender or mortgagee to obtain a deficiency judgment. But if you are notified that someone to whom you owe money is seeking a deficiency judgment for repossessed property, get a lawyer's advice immediately. The court may void the judgment if you can show that the lender did not try to get the

best possible price for your property or that he failed to follow the proper legal procedures, which vary from province to province.

FACTORS IN REPOSSESSION

In some provinces goods cannot be repossessed once a certain percentage of the purchase price is paid (50 percent in Quebec, 66 percent in British Columbia). In Alberta, British Columbia, Manitoba, Newfoundland, Quebec, Yukon, and the Northwest Territories, the contract is canceled and the

seller cannot sue for the balance if he repossesses an article. See CONSUMER PROTECTION.

DEPOSITION

You may be called upon to give a deposition if you are ever involved in a lawsuit—as a plaintiff, a defendant, or a witness. A deposition is sworn testimony taken out of court by a lawyer, weeks or sometimes months before the trial, and recorded by a court stenographer. Depositions are used to gather information and to

---

ABC's OF GIVING A DEPOSITION

If you are called on to give a deposition, try to do the following:

■ **Tell the truth.** When you give a deposition you are placed under oath, just as if you were in court. If you lie, you may face penalties for perjury.

■ **Obey any subpoena.** If you do not appear for a deposition voluntarily, the lawyers in a case can have a subpoena served on you, which legally compels you to appear. A subpoena is an order of the court, and if you do not obey it you may be found in contempt of court. Once found in contempt, you could be fined or put in jail.

■ **Bring any necessary documents.** The lawyers in a case may request that you bring certain documents with you when you appear for your deposition. If these documents are listed in

the subpoena, you have no choice but to bring them along. You should take the original documents, but it is a good idea to take photocopies too.

■ **Listen to the questions** carefully and answer them to the best of your ability. Do not volunteer information that you are not asked for.

■ If you have a good legal reason for not wishing to appear at a deposition or for not producing documents, consult a lawyer. In some cases, you may be able to get the subpoena "quashed," or set aside. Never simply ignore a subpoena. You must go through the proper legal channels and have a judge determine whether or not you must appear.

obtain testimony from a witness who will not be available at the trial.

In many respects, giving a deposition is similar to testifying at a trial, except that no judge or jury is present. If you give a deposition (in which event you will be called the "deponent"), you will be asked by the lawyer for one of the parties to appear at a designated time and place. If you refuse, you could be subpoenaed by the court. The deposition usually takes place in one of the rooms of the courthouse set aside for this purpose, or in a lawyer's office. When you arrive, you will be placed under oath, then asked a series of questions by the lawyer taking your deposition.

Lawyers for both plaintiff and defendant may be present. Each lawyer will have a chance to question you. Just as they would in a trial, the lawyers may object to a question, claiming that it should not be answered. Because no judge is present and objections cannot be ruled on at the time they are made, you may refuse to answer. Later on, the judge will decide if the answer should be disclosed and recorded.

A PRETRIAL FACT-FINDING PROCESS

Lawyers use depositions to gather information. It is part of the pretrial process known as discovery, during which fact-finding and investigating take place. See DISCOVERY.

Lawyers prefer to obtain information from a witness by deposition, even if the same witness will testify at the trial.

♦ Because the witness is under oath, the lawyer can prepare his case with the confidence that the witness will not tell a different story at the trial. If in fact the witness does alter her testimony at the trial, the lawyer can use the deposition to cast doubt on her reliability.

Lawyers also use depositions when a witness cannot be present at the trial—for example, if she is ill, has moved out of the province, or lives far away. If the lawyer has the deposition, it can be read to the judge or jury in place of a testimony.

DEPRECIATION

As property ages and is used, its value diminishes. This loss of value is called depreciation. Just about any kind of property, whether for commercial or domestic use—from filing cabinets and word processors to automobiles and apartment buildings—depreciates in value solely because of age, use, and ordinary wear and tear. For example, by 1995, a computer bought in 1994 will have depreciated through use. Its value may also diminish owing to advances in technology.

Depreciation is important when you borrow money for a car, say, because you may end up owing more than it is worth. Suppose you owe $6,000 on a car you bought for $7,000. Since you cannot make the payments, the lender repossesses the car and sells it for its depreciated value, $5,000, leaving you still owing $1,000.

♦ See DEFICIENCY JUDGMENT.

♦ The depreciating value of certain income-producing property entitles landlords to make tax deductions. Check Revenue Canada's depreciation schedules, which can be obtained at your local Revenue Canada office and at most libraries.

According to the Income Tax Act, immovables may be depreciated by 5 percent per year. However, upon sale of the property, or at the death of the owner, the amount by which the property has depreciated is added to the value of the property as "recaptured depreciation," and taxed.

Not all objects depreciate. Certain automobiles, jewelry, paintings, and some furniture appreciate in value.

DISBARMENT

Once a lawyer is admitted to the bar—that is, allowed to practice law—he usually retains this right for life. However, if he engages in serious professional misconduct, he will be called to account by his peers, who can disbar him. In effect, his license to practice law will be taken away.

Except for the most serious offenses, disbarment is usually temporary. The various provincial legal societies or bar associations determine the ♦ circumstances under which a lawyer may be disbarred, but in general, it is prompted by one or more of the following:

◇ He misappropriated funds or otherwise violated the trust and confidence of his clients.

◇ The fees he charged were excessive or the way he charged them was deceptive.

◇ He represented two or more parties whose interests conflicted.

◇ He conducted himself in a manner that offended judges or obstructed justice.

◇ He represented a client in a matter in which he lacked knowledge. See also LAWYER.

REAL LIFE, REAL LAW

The Case of the Lamentable Lawyer

Harvey, an experienced lawyer, was charged by his provincial law society with professional misconduct. During the law society hearing, he admitted that in virtually all the 423 accounts examined by the investigators, he had billed his provincial legal aid plan for services not rendered, or not rendered according to his statement of account.

Harvey admitted that he charged more than 2,000 extra hours of billing in the three years under investigation. This represented about $200,000 in fees, for which Harvey could not account.

In his defense, Harvey pleaded that the overwhelming pressure of his practice, which consisted of a large number of legal aid and *pro bono* cases, was responsible for his hopelessly inadequate record keeping. He also argued that his past contribution to the legal profession and to society should lessen the penalty if he was found guilty. He also claimed that his practice served a particular segment of society that would not receive legal services if he was disbarred.

Throughout the hearing Harvey marshaled his quite substantial legal skills to produce a pattern of behavior and public utterances to try to show that he was being persecuted.

It turned out, however, that Harvey had been disciplined twice before, once for cheating on his bar admission exams, and another time for making false statements to the court. His disrespect toward the disciplinary committee was also noted.

The discipline committee said Harvey's conduct before them showed a continuing series of dishonest acts and contempt for the committee. The members also felt that accepting his excuse for sloppy bookkeeping would make a virtue of incompetence and ineptitude. They ruled that Harvey demonstrated a pattern of persistent dishonesty that could result only in disbarment, and so he was disbarred.

Harvey's bad luck continued as his appeal was dismissed and his disbarment confirmed.

DISCOVERY

Courtroom dramas on television often include scenes in which an unexpected witness is called to the stand, or new evidence is introduced, surprising everyone in the courtroom and bringing about a dramatic turn in the case.

In real life, however, such surprises rarely happen—on the contrary, they are deliberately avoided.

NO SURPRISES

This lack of surprise is largely due to a process known as discovery. It includes a variety of procedures that are used by both sides to learn as much about the case as possible before the trial begins.

For example, the two sides may want to confirm certain facts, exchange pertinent documents, examine property, or share testimony that has been recorded by witnesses who are unable to appear at the trial.

The purpose of discovery is to provide a faster and fairer trial by allowing access to information that is possessed by the opposing party. Lawyers on both sides can prepare their cases more thoroughly once they learn what evidence exists and which facts are already agreed upon. While discovery is used in both civil and criminal cases, its use is much more extensive in civil lawsuits.

TYPES OF DISCOVERY

A number of different methods for obtaining information are used in the discovery process:

◇ *Depositions.* A deposition is oral testimony given outside the court. It is made under oath, often in the office of the lawyer who requested it, and is recorded by a court stenographer. For example, in a lawsuit filed against a department store by a man who was injured while riding a store escalator, depositions may be requested from witnesses to the mishap who were also riding the escalator, from escalator repair personnel, and from store management. See DEPOSITION.

◇ *Interrogatories.* Unlike depositions, which are given orally, interrogatories are written questions that must be answered under oath and in writing by the opposing party.

◇ *Admissions.* One party may request that the opposing party admit an important fact about the case or affirm that a document to be used at the trial is authentic. Obtaining an admission from the opposing party beforehand saves time and expense at the trial because it eliminates the need to prove those issues that are not actually in dispute.

In the case just described, for example, the injured man may ask the store to admit that the escalator was vibrating badly at the time of the mishap. Or the store may request that the man admit he was taking a type of medication that made him feel dizzy.

◇ *Other requests.* Information is not always obtained by asking people questions. Sometimes a party may ask to look at objects such as documents, photos, or other property that are under the opposing party's control. A physical or mental examination may be ordered by the court if a person's condition is relevant to the lawsuit.

In the department store case, the injured man may ask to have the escalator inspected, and the store's lawyer— perhaps suspecting that the man may have some medical condition that contributed to the accident—may request that he be examined by a doctor.

LIMITATIONS ON DISCOVERY

While discovery is often extensive, it does not permit each side to obtain any and all information from the opposing one. If one party objects to a request made by the other, for example, she may not want to cooperate by giving a deposition. In this event, the court will decide whether the party must supply the requested information.

Discovery will be denied if the information (such as that shared between a social worker and client) is privileged—that is, private and confidential, by law—or if it violates the right of a citizen to protect himself against self-incrimination. A judge will also deny discovery if the information is irrelevant, or if it is used simply to annoy, embarrass, or oppress the opposing side or its witnesses. Usually, expert witnesses are limited to six for each side.

DISCRIMINATION

Many laws have been enacted and constitutional decisions handed down that prohibit discrimination in this country—in housing, schools, the workplace, and elsewhere. However, not all forms of discrimination are illegal. Landlords, for example, may discriminate against potential tenants on the basis of their past records as tenants. See CHARTER OF RIGHTS AND FREEDOMS; EQUAL PROTECTION OF THE LAWS; TENANT'S RIGHTS.

Employers are free to discriminate against job applicants and employees on the basis of age, provided that age is a justifiable bona fide occupational requirement. For example, an air traffic controller may be required to quit at age 55 if it could be shown that his tolerance to stress and reaction and judgment faculties become impaired after that age. See AGE DISCRIMINATION; JOB DISCRIMINATION.

Discrimination based on sex, religion, color, national or ethnic origin or disability is generally prohibited and can lead to a lawsuit if you engage in it.

See RIGHTS, INDIVIDUAL; SEX DISCRIMINATION.

DISINHERITANCE

To disinherit someone is to state in your will that you want to deprive an heir of the right to receive any share of your estate. For example, a mother may want to disinherit a son who has abandoned the family, or a tormented husband may want to disinherit his wife.

Under the law in every province, you have "freedom of willing," and so you have no obligation to leave any part of your estate to your children or your spouse. However, the law makes a presumption against disinheritance, so the mere fact of not mentioning a child or spouse in your will will not usually exclude them. Even if there is an express disinheriting provision in a will, a spouse or heir may be entitled to part of the deceased's estate because of provincial family law legislation, such as the 1986 Ontario Family Law Act, or the relevant dependant's relief legislation.

If you want to remove your child from your will, consult a lawyer experienced in estate planning.

People who have made wills and have later divorced, separated or remarried should check their wills to determine whether or not they wish to make any changes to their will.

See ADOPTION; WILL.

DISORDERLY CONDUCT

What constitutes disorderly conduct is determined by local law, but it usually involves offenses such as disturbing the peace or endangering the public health, safety, or morals. Fighting or swearing in public, vagrancy, loitering, and other similar behaviors are usually considered disorderly conduct.

Often the circumstances determine whether or not an activity amounts to disorderly conduct. For example, picketing may be acceptable in front of a manufacturing plant but not in front of the home of the company president, where it may disturb the peace in the neighborhood.

Disorderly conduct is usually a minor offense, punishable by a fine, imprisonment, or both. See also BREACH OF THE PEACE; DISTURBING THE PEACE.

DISORDERLY HOUSE

A disorderly house is a place where people routinely engage in conduct that is criminal, or one that poses a threat to public health or safety, corrupts public morals, or encourages a breach of the peace. A disorderly house can be a house of prostitution, a shop where drugs are sold from the back room, or a grocery store where liquor is sold without a license. It can even be a boat where illegal gambling is going on, a garage where stolen merchandise is received, or a parking lot where bets are taken.

You can be guilty of maintaining a disorderly house even if you do not own the premises. As long as you are part of the management and know that people are breaking the law there, you can be found guilty of maintaining a disorderly house. The penalty is generally a fine, but if you have several offenses, you may lose your license to operate your club, for example, or other business.

See also BREACH OF THE PEACE.

DISTURBING THE PEACE

If you willfully create a disturbance in a public area, or interfere with the peace and quiet of a family or an individual, you are said to be disturbing the peace. Playing your electric guitar raucously in the middle of the night so that your neighbors can hear it is disturbing the peace. So is drag racing on public streets or engaging in a shouting match on the main street of your town.

Exactly what kind of actions constitute disturbing the peace is determined by the Criminal Code and local laws. In most areas, disturbing the peace is considered a summary conviction and can be punished by a fine, imprisonment, or both. See also BREACH OF THE PEACE; DISORDERLY CONDUCT.

DIVIDEND

The portion of its profits that a corporation passes on to its stockholders is called the dividend. The corporation's board of directors decides how much the allocation for dividends will be, and the rest of the company's profit is reinvested in the business.

Corporations often issue two kinds of stock—common and preferred. The dividends on shares of common stock can vary in amount. When business is good, dividends may be high. But when business is bad, or when the company needs to invest in expensive new equipment or property, dividends can be very low or amount to nothing at all.

When companies issue preferred stock, they guarantee payment of a specified dividend. Owners of the stock usually have the right to receive their dividends before any are paid to owners of common stock. Moreover, most preferred stocks have cumulative rights. This means that if the corporation cannot pay dividends as scheduled, they continue to build up. When the company becomes profitable again, the late dividends must be paid, along with current preferred dividends, before any are paid to owners of common stock.

See also STOCKS AND BONDS.

DIVORCE

Almost one in two Canadian marriages (40 percent) now ends in divorce. Though commonplace, divorce is rarely without emotional strain and difficult tasks for those involved. Nevertheless the process has become more straightforward since the Divorce Act was revised in 1986.

Prior to the revisions, a divorce would not be granted unless one spouse could prove that the other had committed some fault, such as adultery, or treated the partner with physical or mental cruelty. If couples decided not to live together, the spouse who left the home had to wait five years and the abandoned spouse three years before petitioning for divorce.

GROUNDS FOR DIVORCE

Today there is only one ground for divorce—marriage breakdown. According to the Divorce Act, the marriage has broken down if one or more of the following can be proved:

a) for at least a year, you and your spouse have been living separate and apart with no intention of returning to live together;

b) one of you has committed adultery;

c) one of you has treated the other with physical or mental cruelty that renders future cohabitation intolerable.

You need not be legally separated before you apply for a divorce. You can also attempt reconciliation in the year you are apart prior to the divorce, without affecting the one-year separation requirement, provided the time you live together during this "waiting period" does not exceed 90 days. For example, if Robert and Coreen who separated on Jan. 1, 1994, tried to reconcile in the following months, and lived together for 30 days in both March and September and 20 days in November, 80 days in all, either could apply for a divorce on Jan. 2, 1995. Had they lived together for 91 days, they would have had to wait another year before applying.

You do not have to live separately for one year *before filing* for a divorce. It is necessary only that you are not living together when you petition for divorce, and that one year elapses from the time you separate to when the court renders your divorce judgment.

Thus, if Robert and Coreen were married on Jan. 1, 1994, and one week later decided not to live together, either could immediately apply for a divorce. If the application was filed say on Jan. 8, 1994, the petitioner could obtain a divorce on Jan. 7, 1995. At that time, the court could be assured the couple were separated for one year "immediately preceding the determination of the divorce proceedings and were living separate and apart at the commencement of the proceedings."

If marriage breakdown is based on adultery, the maxim that "one cannot profit by one's own moral turpitude" applies: you cannot invoke your own adultery for purposes of divorce. One spouse must prove the other committed the act. If both spouses committed adultery (it does not matter who did it first), then either spouse can use the adultery of the other to prove marriage breakdown.

Mental or physical cruelty encompasses a huge variety of behavior. Since physical cruelty is never justifiable, in most cases it is sufficient grounds for divorce. Unlike criminal cases, the degree of proof required in a divorce is the balance of probabilities, not proof beyond a reasonable doubt. If the violence is such that the police were called, or if medical attention was required, the police or medical reports are often sufficient proof. Evidence by someone who saw marks on the victim, even if the offense is denied by the alleged attacker, would also probably suffice.

Mental cruelty also covers a broad range of behavior and is also hard to define: what one couple may consider "normal" behavior may constitute mental cruelty in the context of another couple's lives.

Extreme jealousy, constant criticism, ridicule, refusing sex on a continuous basis, being rude and insulting to your parents-in-law or family, frequent unjustified absences from home, abusing alcohol or drugs, threats of violence, refusing to work to support the family, excessive gambling, showing disrespect, or refusing to have children, may all be found to be mental cruelty. Case law is almost endless in citing behavior deemed to be "mental cruelty of such a degree as to render future cohabitation intolerable."

Proof of mental cruelty must be established by the testimony of one of the spouses, other family members including children (although the courts deplore situations in which children must testify against their parents), friends, neighbors, or acquaintances.

Behavior that has been condoned or pardoned cannot be used as an example of mental cruelty at a later date.

In a so-called "no fault" divorce, one spouse or both simply show the court that they have been separated for one year with no interest in reconciling.

The certificate giving proof of divorce does not say what led to the marriage breakdown. It lists only the couple's names, date and place of marriage, and date of divorce.

SEPARATION AGREEMENT

Divorce applications are heard by a Superior Court judge, never by a jury. The major issues are custody, visiting rights, alimentary pension, division of property, and in some cases lump sum payments or compensatory allowances.

A wise couple works out an amicable separation agreement that can be made part of the divorce decree. Your lawyer or a mediator (often supplied free of charge by the courts) will assist you. Such an agreement prevents fighting and arguing in the courtroom, thus reducing stress for all involved, especially young children. Your legal expenses, which can cost $100 to $300 an hour, money better spent on the children or reestablishing your own life, will also be reduced.

Most property and maintenance settlements could be made out of court. Working out a reasonable proposal for supporting a spouse and the children will not be a great mystery to an experienced lawyer. She can calculate the amount to be paid, taking into account the ability of one spouse to pay, the needs of the other spouse and children, and the tax consequences of such alimentary pension.

HIRING A DIVORCE LAWYER

Since you and your spouse may have conflicting interests, it is rarely a good idea to have the same lawyer represent both parties in a divorce. If you and your spouse agree on custody, alimentary support, visiting rights, and the division of property, one lawyer may do the job and save you legal costs. It is preferable, however, to consult a lawyer who has your interests only in mind.

Look for a lawyer who specializes in family law. Ask trusted friends who have had experience with a divorce lawyer for help. You can also ask your local legal society or bar association for names.

At your first interview find out what your divorce will cost (you will get only a rough estimate since the cost depends upon many factors). Find out what the hourly rate is. If she takes the case on a contingency basis, ask what percentage she will charge. Get a fee agreement in writing and ask for regular itemized bills. See CONTINGENT FEE.

Remember that your lawyer will charge you traveling time. If the divorce hearing will be in another town or province, you might find it less expensive to hire a lawyer who lives near the court than one from your area.

Also, you must feel comfortable with your lawyer. If, for whatever reason, you find this is not so, or if she does not answer your questions fully or is disrespectful to you in any way, find another lawyer to represent you.

If you cannot afford a lawyer, most provincial legal aid plans will supply one, either free of charge or for a reduced fee.

COUNSELING

Your divorce lawyer is obliged to inquire if there is any possibility that you and your spouse will reconcile and to encourage

CHECKLIST

Getting Through a Divorce

Getting through a divorce means enduring a series of traumatic changes in your life, so try to take them one step at a time. Listed below are a few suggestions on how to make the divorce process go a little more smoothly for you, your spouse, your children, and even your lawyer.

■ WORK OUT AN ACCEPTABLE CUSTODY AGREEMENT.

Unless you have a good reason to believe that contact with your spouse will be harmful to your children, try to work together to create a custody and visitation arrangement that will allow the children to maintain a loving relationship with both parents.

Do not pull the children into your conflict by belittling your spouse in front of them, enlisting them as spies, or using them as messengers. If you do, your children are bound to build up long-term resentments.

■ TRY TO GET A HANDLE ON YOUR FINANCES.

In many marriages, one spouse is in charge of the chequebook, the bill paying, and other financial matters. If you are the other spouse, you may have to educate yourself about your finances.

Find out, for example, how much is in your bank accounts, the cash value of your insurance policies, the amount in your RRSPs or profit-sharing accounts, the value of your stocks and bonds, and the location of your deeds and titles to property. Determine the value of your furniture, antiques, art, jewelry, and special collections (such as stamps) by getting an appraisal.

List your debts, including mortgages on your real estate, liens on your vehicles, or money owed on credit cards. Determine the amount of each debt, the name of the creditor, and the terms of repayment. Your lawyer may ask to review your income tax returns for the last few years, as earning power is an important factor in figuring alimentary pension, child support, and the division of property and debts.

■ COMPLY WITH ALL DISCOVERY REQUESTS AND OBEY ALL TEMPORARY ORDERS.

During your divorce, you and your spouse will probably engage in a great deal of "discovery"— a legal term that means asking each other to produce financial records and other documents and to account for each other's assets and debts.

Do not try to hide assets from your spouse. If the court later finds out that you did so, your case could be reopened and you might be penalized.

Before a full divorce hearing, the court often gives special temporary orders. It might allow one partner the use of the family home, arrange for child custody and support, or restrain the partners from harassing each other. You should obey temporary orders to the letter. If you do not, the judge could find you in contempt of court.

■ KNOW YOUR COSTS.

Whether you are making support payments or receiving them, you should expect to have less money to spend than you had before. When your household breaks up, you will have many of the same expenses but fewer resources to pay them, so plan ahead.

You also have to pay your divorce lawyer. Be certain to get a written fee agreement from him, and do not hesitate to ask for an itemized record of his time and expenses. If you have a question about an item you have been billed for, ask your lawyer about it as soon as possible.

■ BEHAVE YOURSELF.

Even if fault is not an issue in your divorce, your conduct may be when it comes to child custody. If you want the court to find that you are a responsible parent, you must act like one. For example, if you are engaged in a dispute over child custody, do not host a series of wild parties in your home. Assume that your social life is being monitored and will be reported to the court.

■ DON'T TRY TO GO IT ALONE.

Share your feelings with friends and family. If they cannot help, find a professional counselor or support group. Divorce is difficult, but other people can ease you through the process. Although your lawyer will be sympathetic and supportive, talking to a friend will be less expensive. Talking to a professional counselor might be a good idea too.

you to use any guidance facilities or counseling services that might help you do so. She must help you negotiate matters of support and custody with your spouse, and inform you of any mediation services known to her. Many family courts have trained mediators and marriage counselors available free of charge or for nominal fees. Often these services are available from the social welfare agencies of your province. There are also many private agencies that deal with these matters: look in the Yellow Pages under Psychologists, Marriage Counseling, or Mediation Services.

Once the counseling has been completed, however, the partner who opposes the divorce can do little to prevent it.

CONFLICTING DIVORCES

A divorce court has jurisdiction in your case if you have lived in that judicial district for at least 12 months before applying for the divorce, or if your spouse has been residing in that district for 12 months. If it should happen that both spouses file for divorce in two different districts, jurisdiction goes to the court where the first application was filed.

In some cases, one spouse may ask to have the court file transferred to the province or judicial district where she is living. The court will agree if justice is best served by the move, as might be the case when custody is at issue. The court closest to where the children live may be the better court to hear the divorce application.

See also LAWYER; LEGAL AID.

INITIATING THE DIVORCE PROCESS

In the case of Robert and Coreen, for example, the legal proceedings begin when Coreen, say, has a lawyer draft an application, or petition, in divorce. This document contains the couple's names, dates and places of birth, their parents' names, date and place of marriage, and any prenuptial agreements they have. When there are children, the divorce application also gives their names and dates of birth.

The application sets out the reasons for the divorce and the accessory measures sought. Accessory measures refer to alimentary pension, custody, visiting rights, rights to live in the former family home, requests for lump sum or other payments, and requests for the division of the family assets and other property.

This application is then filed with the court and a copy is sent to Robert by a process-server or bailiff. If his address is not known, a notice may be published in the newspaper.

Once the notice of application is served, Robert has 20 to 40 days (depending on how the notice was served) to respond.

Since the divorce hearing may not take place for some time, a motion for interim relief often accompanies the divorce application. Such a motion requests that matters, such as custody, visiting rights, alimentary pension, and use of the former family home, be settled quickly on a temporary basis.

Any interim judgment is very important, especially when

custody is involved. For once the court renders a judgment, even on a provisional basis, that often sets the tone for the final judgment.

You will have to provide a sworn statement of your assets and liabilities with your provisional motion for interim relief. This statement helps the court determine how much support one party should pay the other. The couple may settle such matters between themselves and ask the court to approve their agreement, or the judge may decide after a hearing.

EXAMINATIONS IN DISCOVERY

Before the hearing of the motion for provisional judgment, the lawyers for both sides may hold what are known as examinations on discovery. At these "discoveries," the respective lawyers question the spouses about their assets, debts, relationship with their children, and other relevant matters. The questions and answers are recorded by a stenographer and form part of the court record. The lawyers may also examine such documents as income tax returns, partnership agreements, bank accounts, lists of stocks and bonds, and credit card statements, to get a better picture of the financial and moral standing of the opposite party.

If, at this stage, the parties still refuse to settle at least some of their differences, through mediation and compromise, they may find their legal and expert fees growing quickly. Taking revenge on your spouse by means of the courts and lawyers is an expensive endeavor, and it is far from rare to see two parties to a bitterly contested divorce financially ruined by multiple court proceedings.

CUSTODY AND CHILD SUPPORT

In some cases the couple may agree, or the court may order, that they, or the children, or both, meet psychologists, who could suggest which parent is best suited to have custody. Often each side hires its own psychologist, who generally prepares a report favorable to his client. Some courts may appoint and pay for a psychologist who will report to the court, which must ultimately decide the matter of custody.

The most difficult situations are when both parents want custody and each is equally capable of looking after the children. The court will consider the age and sex of the children, and which parent is more stable and nurturing, and better able to provide the discipline, moral guidance, religious training, and safe environment in which to raise them. The Divorce Act expressly states that the court will not take into consideration the past conduct of any person, unless the conduct is relevant to that person's ability as a parent. The act also states that "a child of the marriage should have as much contact with each spouse as is consistent with the best interest of the child." Where circumstances permit, the courts now frequently award joint custody to both parents.

The court would like the divorce of the parents to have as little impact on the children as possible. In determining support for minor children, the court will look at the income and expenses of each parent, the needs of the children, and the family's accustomed standard of living. In the case of older children, the courts may specify that parents with the means to do so pay for the children's university education.

If either party's circumstances change substantially, judgments concerning custody, alimentary support, and visiting rights can be revised. When the custodial parent is transferred to another province, for example, the courts are faced with a difficult decision. Such a move may deprive the other parent of regular visiting rights. In some cases, the custodial parent has been allowed to take the minor child away from the other parent, and in others ordered not to remove the child from the jurisdiction. There is no easy solution to such problems.

See CHILD CUSTODY; CHILD SUPPORT; GRANDPARENTS' RIGHTS; GUARDIAN AD LITEM.

SPOUSAL SUPPORT

When the marriage ends, the court may order one spouse to pay the other spousal support, consisting of an alimentary pension, or a lump sum, or both. This gives a spouse who cannot provide for her own needs a chance to become self-sufficient. The support may be for a limited time or perhaps until the recipient completes university or job training.

The criteria for spousal support are:

1. It should recognize any advantage or disadvantage to the spouses arising from the marriage or its breakdown.

2. It should relieve any economic hardship caused by the breakdown of the marriage.

3. It should apportion between the spouses any financial consequences arising from the care of any children.

4. It should, as far as practical, try to make each spouse self-sufficient.

The Divorce Act expressly mentions that any misconduct of the spouse within the marriage shall not affect the support order. Thus, support is never to be set in terms of a reward, or denied as a punishment for past behavior, but purely as a means of making the economic playing field a bit more level.

The court will consider the ages of the spouses, how long they were married, whether a spouse spent time and effort raising the children, as well as the condition, means, and needs of that spouse. If both spouses have worked at jobs outside the home, and both can live reasonably well on their own salaries, it is doubtful if the court will order one spouse to support the other.

A support order does not aim to divide the spouses' incomes evenly. Provided both are self-sufficient, the courts will not oblige one spouse who is earning $150,000 per year to pay support to another who is making an annual $50,000. But, if one spouse earned much less than the other because she spent her time raising the children, the court would ensure she was compensated.

The Ontario Court of Appeal ruled that "self-sufficiency" should be defined as "a reasonable standard of living having in mind the circumstances of the marriage." In a case involving an executive who was earning $140,000 annually while his wife made $17,000 a year as a typist, the court ordered the husband to pay his ex-spouse $2,500 per month, indexed to inflation, considering that the marriage lasted 24 years, and the wife gave up her career aspirations for the sake of her husband's career.

Traditional marriage

In the *Moge* v. *Moge* case, the Supreme Court of Canada said in 1992 that self-sufficiency should not be the primary goal of support in the case of traditional marriages, where one spouse, usually the wife, sacrificed her career and future financial security by staying home to raise the children. For such women, who would most probably never become self-sufficient, the support order may continue indefinitely.

In nontraditional marriages, where both spouses pursued their own careers, and child rearing was done by a nanny or day-care center paid for by both spouses, the rules of the *Moge* case would not apply. This is because the economic consequences resulting from a divorce would not be nearly as harsh on either spouse.

In British Columbia, Ontario, and Quebec support orders can be binding on the deceased's estate. See ALIMENTARY PENSION.

DIVISION OF PROPERTY AND DEBTS

Once the grounds for divorce have been proven, and the issues of custody, access rights, and alimentary support for the spouse and children have been decided, the courts must deal with the division of property and the debts incurred during the marriage. All provinces and territories have legislation setting out what is community property—the family assets that are subject to division when the partners separate—and what remains personal property.

Usually, the family home and any secondary residence, furniture in these homes, automobiles that are for family use, and retirement funds such as Registered Retirement Savings Plans (RRSPs) and Registered Retirement Income Funds (RRIFs), and public or private pension funds may be divided between the spouses. In some provinces, savings and investments may also be shared. Inherited property or gifts are rarely divided upon divorce. See COMMUNITY PROPERTY.

Family assets are not always split on a 50-50 basis. Case law is full of instances where the courts have refused to give a half-interest in family assets to one spouse, when it was shown that during the marriage the acquisition of the family assets was almost totally due to the efforts of the other spouse. The test used by the British Columbia Supreme Court is "whether there had been a gross disparity in respective contributions by the parties to the acquisition, preservation, maintenance, improvement, or use of the property, either as a result of the party's failure to contribute or a party's dissipation of assets."

Domestic work in the home would count as preservation, maintenance, and improvement of the property. See also EQUITABLE DISTRIBUTION.

THE DIVORCE DECREE

Depending on whether or not the divorce is contested, the hearing of the divorce petition could be swift, or long and painful. If all the issues—such as custody, alimentary pension, visiting rights, and division of property —are settled, the hearing will proceed ex parte, that is, only one party will provide proof, and judgment will be rendered according to a consent agreement drawn up by the couple's lawyers.

In some jurisdictions, Quebec for example, some divorces may be granted on the strength of affidavits, and no hearing is held.

In any case, once a judgment of divorce decree is rendered, the parties have 30 days in which to appeal. If no appeal is lodged within this period, the divorce becomes final automatically on the 31st day after the first judgment.

ANNULMENT

Because of the separation of church and state in Canada, a divorce judgment granted by the courts dissolves the marriage in the eyes of the law, but the marriage still exists as far as some religions are concerned.

According to religious law, a Roman Catholic or a member of the Jewish faith would still be considered married, by other members of their faith, and so could not be remarried in a religious ceremony, unless a divorce or annulment was granted by the religious authorities.

The Divorce Act (section 21.1) was amended in 1990 to help remedy the situation where one spouse refuses to cooperate in obtaining an annulment or religious divorce, and so remove the barrier to the spouse's religious remarriage. The spouse seeking the religious dissolution may now serve an affidavit on the "recalcitrant" spouse and on the court, indicating a desire for a religious divorce or annulment and the nature of the impediment to be removed, and stating that the other spouse has refused to remove the barrier.

If the recalcitrant spouse's position remains unchanged, the courts could dismiss any application or strike out any other pleading or affidavits of the recalcitrant spouse, unless he or she has genuine religious or conscientious reasons for the refusal.

So, if Mary (a Roman Catholic) was in the process of obtaining a civil divorce from John, and if she wanted to marry Lester in a religious ceremony, she would have to obtain a religious annulment from John first. If John refused to cooperate just for spite, Mary could file the necessary notices and affidavits with the divorce court. The court would then have the power to dismiss any application made by John, such as a request of visiting rights, his divorce contestation, or a request for reduction of alimentary pension, until John agrees to help Mary obtain the religious annulment.

If John was the person asking for the civil divorce in the first place, the court could likewise refuse to hear his application until he complied with Mary's request that he cooperate in seeking a religious annulment. See ANNULMENT.

MARRIAGE CONTRACTS

Before they marry, a couple may determine how their property should be divided in the event of separation or divorce. Such agreements are called marriage or domestic contracts, or prenuptial agreements. This type of contract is usually done by lawyers, although private agreements between the parties themselves are also valid, except in Quebec. In Quebec, marriage contracts must be drawn up by notaries.

A marriage contract could include conditions on support, either specifying that no alimentary pension be paid by either spouse upon divorce, or limiting the amount and duration of support, or stating that support would end upon remarriage. Custody arrangements cannot validly be part of a marriage contract, but the right to direct the education of children may be included.

Although all provinces do not require that marriage contracts be in writing— Saskatchewan, for example, will recognize informal verbal agreements, and British Columbia will recognize the validity of verbal postnuptial agreements—it is always wise to have such an agreement in writing. Some provinces require that marriage contracts be signed and witnessed; others that they be registered with the courts or registry office.

A marriage contract will generally be upheld by the courts. However, the courts will set it aside, or reduce its terms, if one of the spouses has concealed assets, if the contract would result in "manifest unfairness" to either, or if strict adherence to its terms would result in "unconscionable circumstances." The court has immense discretion to make such judgments as it deems "fit and just."

Although it may seem unromantic to consider, prior to the marriage ceremony, how property and support issues should be settled in the event of divorce, it is important to look at a marriage as a form of partnership. Romantic or not, it is often a good idea to have a lawyer draw up a marriage contract before you get married. In the event of divorce, a well drawn up marriage contract would protect your rights and greatly reduce the costs of litigation. See also PRENUPTIAL AGREEMENT.

DO-IT-YOURSELF DIVORCE KITS

If you are thinking about getting a divorce, you may have come across the so-called do-it-yourself divorce kits sold in bookstores. These kits claim to contain all the forms necessary to obtain a legally valid divorce, and they promise to save you hundreds or even thousands of dollars in legal fees.

In reality, the long-term cost of using one of these kits can far exceed the money you save. For example, a kit cannot give specific advice about a couple's unique situation, help you determine if your spouse is disclosing all of his or her assets, or inform you about the subtle differences in court procedures from one province to another.

The forms supplied with these kits can lead to unnecessary delays if they do not meet legal standards or if, later on, you or your spouse want the support orders modified.

Similarly, you should be cautious about lawyers who advertise low-cost divorces. Their fees may cover only the simplest situations and can mount if you and your spouse disagree on important issues.

MAINTENANCE AND TAX

Generally, a lump sum paid as alimentary pension or maintenance is not tax deductible by the spouse who pays, or taxable to the recipient. This is because it is not "periodic."

For example, if a court order or written agreement obliges Ronne to pay Steven $1,000 per month, and she prepays him $12,000 for the coming year, that $12,000 is not deductible by Ronne nor taxable to Steven. Even if the lump sum is paid in more than one instalment, it is still considered to be a lump sum. In a Manitoba case, the judge ruled that because annual payments

by a man to his ex-spouse were not made periodically, three payments totalling $25,000 were not tax deductible for the man and should not be taxed to his ex-spouse.

However, if a lump sum is paid for accumulated arrears, if Ronne, for example, pays Steven $12,000 at the end of the year because she missed 12 periodic payments of $1,000 per month, then this $12,000 would be considered periodic payments, deductible by Ronne.

To control the tax consequence of paying a lump sum or maintenance award, the wording of the judgment must be drafted carefully. For example, if your divorce agreement says that you must pay a certain amount to your spouse, but does not say that the payment is for maintenance or support, this money would probably be considered a lump sum payment or divorce settlement, not deductible by the person who pays nor taxable by the recipient, even if the sum is paid in more than one instalment.

If the sum paid periodically greatly exceeds a person's maintenance requirements, Revenue Canada would likely consider it to be a capital settlement, or lump sum payment, even though the agreement may say it is for maintenance.

Specific-purpose and third-party payments
A key factor in determining whether or not a payment is an alimentary allowance or not is how the agreement or court order says the recipient of this money is to use it.

If the judgment says you will

receive $1,000 per month for food, rent and other necessities, then this $1,000 is taxable to you, because you control how you want to pay for your necessities, and deductible by your ex-spouse. This kind of payment made directly to you is called a specific-purpose payment. But if the judgment says you will receive $500 per month and that another $500 per month will be paid directly to your landlord for your rent, $500 is taxable income for you, and tax deductible by your ex-spouse. However, he cannot claim deductions for the $500 paid to your landlord, since this is a third-party payment.

TAX AND FAMILY ASSETS

Under the Income Tax Act, when property is transferred from one spouse to another, certain taxes may be due, such as capital gains taxes (not on the family residence, however) and recaptured depreciation. For more information, consult your accountant or consult Interpretation Bulletin IT-325, Property Transfers after Divorce and Annulment, available at your district office of Revenue Canada. See also DEPRECIATION.

RRSP, RRIF TRANSFERS

If your divorce judgment or separation agreement requires you to transfer some of your RRSPs or RRIFs to your former spouse, you may do so tax free if at the time of the separation of these funds you are not living with your spouse, and the property is being divided to settle rights arising out of your divorce. These RRSPs or RRIFs are not to be transferred directly to your spouse. To avoid paying tax, the transfer must be made from your RRSP or RRIF plan carrier directly to your spouse's plan carrier.

Canada (or Quebec) Pension Plan credits

Upon divorce, your Canada or Quebec Pension Plan credits will be divided equally between you and your spouse. The division will include those credits accumulated during your marriage and will be paid upon retirement. Either you or your spouse should apply for the division of the CPP credits. The QPP credits are automatically divided upon divorce unless by agreement you expressly renounce the division.

TAX INFORMATION

Although you cannot claim as a deduction money paid to a lawyer to obtain a divorce or separation, you may claim fees paid to a lawyer to enforce an existing court order for maintenance payments that are in arrears.

Keep in mind that tax information that is applicable to legally married people also applies to common-law couples who have lived together for at least one year or who have a child or children.

Tax rules change periodically. For the most up-to-date information, contact your Revenue Canada taxation district office. Ask for the General Inquiries Service.

DNA FINGERPRINT

DNA (deoxyribonucleic acid) is present in the cells of every living thing and carries each individual's unique genetic code. The likelihood of correctly identifying a person on the basis of an analysis of that person's DNA sample is generally thought to be very high, because the possibility of two people having DNA with exactly the same structure (except for identical twins) may be as low as 1 in 70 billion. Thus DNA identifications can help prosecutors identify criminal suspects.

A DNA "fingerprint" is obtained by performing a laboratory analysis of a sample of a suspect's cells—usually from his blood, semen, hair, or skin. If the DNA fingerprint matches the DNA found in similar matter discovered in a criminal investigation—for example, if the skin found under a murder victim's fingernails matches the DNA of the accused person—a prosecutor has powerful evidence for winning her case.

DNA fingerprints are especially useful as tools in prosecutions for crimes such as rape, which are often committed without witnesses and are followed by the contradictory testimony of two individuals. DNA fingerprinting nonetheless has its detractors. Some scientists challenge the reliability of DNA tests, contending that the likelihood of similar DNA results is closer to 1 in 24 than 1 in 70 billion. To some

researchers, DNA fingerprints are no more reliable than lie detector tests, which were once considered scientific but are now widely discredited.

In Canada, DNA evidence has been accepted by the courts since 1989 and has been used in several murder trials, including the widely publicized case of Allan Legere, convicted of murdering four people in New Brunswick.

DOG LAW

You may think of your dog as a member of your family, but the municipality thinks of it as part of your personal property. This is one reason local governments regulate your dog ownership, by requiring you to do things like pay a fee and obtain a license for your dog, have it vaccinated against certain dangerous diseases, such as rabies and distemper, and keep it on a leash when you walk it in public.

If your dog happens to be one of the breeds believed to be especially dangerous, such as a pit bullterrier or a Doberman pinscher, the municipality may impose even stricter laws. For example, in some cities, the owners of certain breeds must prove that they have liability insurance to pay for any injury caused to people by their pets. Moreover, a number of communities across the country have gone so far in their concern to protect their residents as to ban certain kinds of dogs altogether, such as pit bulls or hybrids between dogs and wolves.

DOG BITES

Many people wrongly believe there is a "one-bite rule," which protects them from responsibility the first time their dog bites someone. However, all dog owners are held responsible when their dog bites someone. An owner will be held responsible for his dog biting other people if he knows of the dog's dangerous tendencies—for example, if it growls and barks or tries to escape from restraints when people pass by.

An owner may, however, be able to escape responsibility for dog bites if he can show that the dog bit because it was provoked, or that the person the dog bit was a trespasser. Nevertheless, if the dog presents a real danger to the public because it is consistently vicious toward people, it may be taken away by the local animal control department.

See also ANIMALS; LIABILITY; NEGLIGENCE; PETS; TORT.

BARKING

If Fido barks loudly and consistently, he may be a nuisance in law as well as in fact. If someone complains about your dog's barking and you fail to silence him, you may have to pay a fine or be forced to get rid of him.

Of course, in many communities the police are busy with more serious crimes than persistently barking dogs, and may not have time to follow up on complaints. But if your neighbor cannot get the police to help her solve this problem, she may choose to bring a civil lawsuit against you. In some communities, the local animal control department will mediate a dispute between neighbors about a dog's bad behavior.

See also NEIGHBORS; NUISANCE.

REAL LIFE, REAL LAW

The Case of the Costly Canine

Leo sued Marilyn for injuries received when attacked by one of her two dogs. Marilyn kept her small dog in the house and her large dog tied up on the veranda. Leo had gone to speak to Marilyn's son Raffi, who was the local newspaper boy, and called out Raffi's name. Hearing the shout, the small dog in the house began barking. This inspired the large dog on the veranda to lunge at Leo, clawing his leg. Beating a hasty retreat, Leo lost his balance and fell over a wall, breaking his leg. At the trial, Marilyn was found responsible under the Ontario Dog Owners' Liability Act. The judge stated that the owner of a dog is "almost automotically liable" for any bites by the dog.

Marilyn appealed, but the Court of Appeal dismissed her case. The Appeal Court said, however, that a dog owner was not automatically liable for injuries caused by his or her dog, but the law only created a presumption of liability. If Marilyn had been able to explain why she should not be responsible, she could have won her case, but the facts exonerating her were absent. Leo's hasty retreat had been a reasonable consequence of the actions of Marilyn's two dogs.

DOMICILE

Your domicile is your permanent place of residence, even if you live elsewhere part of the time. For example, if you own a home in Alberta, and you vote and file taxes in Alberta, your legal domicile is Alberta, even though you may spend part of each summer at the vacation cottage you own in Ontario.

The concept of domicile can be important when deciding in which court a case should be brought to trial, or where a will should be administered after a death, or what laws will apply in the case of a contract.

Domicile is not the same as residence. Residence is where you may be on a temporary basis, but domicile is where you have the intention of residing on a permanent basis and from where you conduct your principal activities.

See also LAWSUIT; RESIDENCY LAW; WILL.

DOUBLE JEOPARDY

Section II of the Charter of Rights and Freedoms affirms that once you have been found not guilty of a crime, you can never be tried for it again, even if evidence is later obtained that proves your guilt. Though this sounds relatively straightforward in theory, in practice it is not always easy to determine if double jeopardy applies.

WHAT "TWICE" MEANS

Double jeopardy protects a person only after a court has issued a final judgment in a case. Thus if a judge declares a mistrial (because of a procedural or other problem during trial), or if there is a hung jury (one that cannot decide on a verdict), double jeopardy usually does not apply, because the court was not able to issue a final judgment. If a defendant appeals a case, and the appeal court reverses the lower court and orders that the case be tried again, the double jeopardy clause does not apply.

WHAT "OFFENSE" MEANS

The double-jeopardy rule says that a person may not be "put in jeopardy" twice for the same offense. However, it is important to understand that *offense* has a strict legal meaning. An offense is not necessarily the same as the criminal act itself. Suppose Bob breaks into Jessica's home, forces her into his car, and rapes her. Bob may be tried for burglary, kidnapping, and rape, even though all the offenses occurred at about the same time and seem to be part of the same act. If Bob is tried for burglary and acquitted, he can still be prosecuted for kidnapping and rape.

Suppose he stole the car in which he kidnapped Jessica. The kidnapping verdict would

REAL LIFE, REAL LAW

The Case of the Penalized Prisoner

While Gary was serving time in prison, he was found in possession of a quarter gram of hashish. Brought before a disciplinary prison tribunal, he pleaded guilty to possession of the drug, and prison authorities sentenced him to 45 days' dissociation from the general prison population. Thirty of these days were for the drug offense, possession being against prison regulations, and the other 15 days were for threatening a guard.

But this was not the end of the affair. A few weeks later, Gary found himself in regular court charged by the RCMP for drug possession under the Narcotic Control Act.

When Gary was found guilty, he claimed that no sentence should be handed down by the court. Since he had already been punished for this crime, he said another sentence would put him in double jeopardy.

The judge disagreed, saying a single act (possession of an illegal drug) can have more than one consequence. The hearing by an administrative tribunal of the prison did not constitute criminal proceedings involving the "same offense." The 45-day punishment was for breaking prison rules, whereas a sentence for possession of drugs contrary to the Narcotic Control Act was a sentence "imposed for the purpose of redressing the wrong done to the public at large."

not prevent him from being prosecuted for auto theft, because theft is a different criminal act from kidnapping.

DOWER AND CURTESY

Dower rights go back such a long way that they are even mentioned in the Magna Carta, which was drawn up in 1215. Under English common law, a married person had a right to a part of a spouse's property at the time of death. A widow's right to part of her husband's property was known as her dower; the widower's right to a

share of his wife's property was known as curtesy.

Alberta still maintains a Dower Act, which gives the surviving spouse certain rights to the homestead or a life estate in the personal property of the deceased that is exempt from seizure. In most other provinces, however, dower and curtesy have been replaced by family law and dependant persons acts. Under these, the spouse of a deceased person has certain rights, especially in the matrimonial home, so that he or she is not left penniless even if excluded from the will.

See DISINHERITANCE; DYING WITHOUT A WILL.

DRINKING AGE

The age at which you may legally buy or be served alcohol is determined by provincial legislation. In most provinces it is 18 years of age, but in British Columbia, for example, it is 19. Provincial laws also regulate the distribution and retail sale of alcoholic beverages.

Selling liquor to a minor is a serious offense, and a bar, restaurant or nightclub that does could have its liquor license revoked unless it can prove that the underage customer had documents showing him to be of age. In most provinces, it is illegal for a minor to be in a liquor store, bar, lounge, or pub, even if he is drinking only soft drinks. (This does not apply to restaurants that serve liquor.) It is also illegal to serve liquor to a minor at a private party, although this is seldom enforced, and may even be unenforceable.

Because alcohol is so prevalent in our culture, we tend to forget that it is a drug that impairs judgment and reaction time. When abused, alcohol contributes to marriage breakdown, serious automobile and work accidents, and often financial ruin.

In one Statistics Canada survey of drinking and driving, 27 percent of Canadians aged 16 to 24, 22 percent of those aged 25 to 34, and 10 percent of those aged 45 to 54 have a friend or family member who has been found guilty of a drinking and driving offense in the previous three years.

♦ Some studies suggest that children as young as 12 have begun drinking on a regular basis. It may well be that alcohol is the most abused drug in our society. See also ALCOHOL; DRUNK DRIVING.

DRIVER'S LICENSE

Driver's licenses are issued to enable provincial governments to look out for the health and safety of their citizens and to raise revenue. Each province sets its own rules for obtaining a driver's license, including minimum age, knowledge of the rules of the road, and passing a driving test. In some provinces, the applicant has to pass an eye test and show that he does not have any physical or mental disability that might impair his ability to drive.

A special license—such as one issued to drive a school bus or a truck—usually requires the driver to meet higher-than-normal standards. So a person with frequent traffic violations will probably not be able to get a bus driver's license.

Restricted licenses or learner's permits may be issued to minors before they reach the province's minimum age for a regular license. The occasions when a minor uses the vehicle may be restricted to driving to and from school, or when there is a licensed driver in the car.

RENEWAL AND REEXAMINATION

Driver's licenses expire after a specified number of years. In ♦ most provinces you simply

♦ complete an application form for a new one, which may include questions about your health and criminal record. In some provinces you must pass a vision test.

If you have been involved in certain types of accidents or cited for particular traffic violations, you may be required to take your driver's test again.

In every province authorities can suspend or revoke a driver's license if a person commits many traffic violations. Generally, "moving violations" (driving offenses made while a car is in motion) carry more severe punishments than non-moving violations (such as illegal parking). Most provinces have established especially harsh penalties for drunk driving. See DRUNK DRIVING.

Many provinces use a point system to determine when a license should be suspended or revoked. Point values are assigned to the various traffic violations. If you accumulate a certain number of points in a 12-month period, say, the motor vehicle bureau may suspend or revoke your license.

Statistics show that while drivers between the ages of 16 and 24 account for only 17 percent of all drivers in Canada, they are involved in close to 30 percent of all accidents resulting in personal injury. This has led Ontario, Nova Scotia, and Quebec to consider a three-stage graduated licensing program.

This would begin with a six-month learner's permit; during this time new drivers would have to be accompanied by an ♦ experienced driver. The second stage license would be for two years, but would not be valid from midnight to 6 a.m. unless an experienced driver was present, or the driver had a curfew exemption to get to and from work. Other restrictions would limit the number of passengers and specify zero blood-alcohol level for driver and passengers. To get to a full license, drivers would have to complete a defensive driving course and pass a written test.

DRUG

In everyday usage, the word "drug" refers either to medicine prescribed by physicians or to illegal substances such as cocaine, heroin, or marijuana. All drugs in Canada are regulated either by the Food and Drugs Act (and related regulations) or the Narcotic Control Act (and related regulations). Anyone contravening the Food and Drugs Act is investigated by the Drug Directorate of the Health Protection Branch (HPB) of the Department of Health. Violators of the Narcotic Control Act are prosecuted before the criminal courts.

According to the Food and Drugs Act, a drug is "any substance or mixture of substances manufactured, sold or represented for use in:

a) the diagnosis, treatment, mitigation, or prevention of a disease, disorder, abnormal physical state, or the symptoms thereof in man or animal;

b) restoring, correcting or modifying organic functions in man or animal; or

c) disinfection in premises in which food is manufactured, prepared or kept."

Every drug sold in Canada must have an eight-digit, computerized drug identification number (DIN), that identifies the product. Prescription drugs are licensed for prescription by a physician only. Non-prescription drugs are just that, preparations that can be bought without prescription at pharmacies, supermarkets, or other retail outlets. They fall roughly into three categories: proprietary medicines (or GPs, for general public), over-the-counter drugs (OTCs), and drugs to be used in consultation with a physician.

Proprietary medicines, available at any supermarket or retail store, comprise such products as Rolaids, milk of magnesia, or aspirin. The term "proprietary" is generally applied to the name of a drug product that is registered to a private manufacturer, that is "a proprietor."

Over-the-counter drugs, mostly laxatives, cough and cold remedies, vitamins, sinus and nasal preparations, and other agents for relieving minor self-limiting illnesses, are mostly available in pharmacies.

The smallest group of non-prescription drugs should be used only with the advice of a health professional. These include substances such as insulin, nitroglycerin, muscle relaxants, and antispasmodics.

Drug labels must contain the drug's proper name, the lot number, the DIN or GP number, directions for use, and the expiry date.

DRUG ABUSE

Drug abuse refers to the use of an illegal drug such as LSD, and the improper use of legal prescription drugs, such as Demerol. With drug abuse, problems may arise from adverse effects of the drug, from accidents during intoxication, and from the drug dependence. Commonly abused drugs include amphetamines, alcohol and barbiturates, hallucinogenic agents, and anabolic steroids.

The food and drugs laws regulate the use of such controlled drugs as codeine, diazepam (valium) and Demerol, whereas the Narcotic Control Act regulates the use of drugs such as heroin, morphine and cocaine. Certain illicit drugs, such as LSD and psilocybin, which have a high potential for abuse and no accepted medicinal use, are never prescribable. To have or use such drugs is always illegal. See also DRUG DEALING; DRUG TESTING; FORFEITURE; NARCOTIC CONTROL ACT.

DRUG DEALING

The term "drug dealing" usually refers to the unauthorized and illicit manufacture, sale, or possession (in large quantities) of "controlled substances," or drugs. See DRUG ABUSE.

The Narcotic Control Act and the Food and Drugs Act prohibit drug dealing, or trafficking in controlled drugs or narcotics. Trafficking does not only mean selling; it includes giving the drug away free.

Controlled drugs—those listed in schedule "G" of the Food and Drugs Act—have the potential for abuse, and their use may lead to drug dependence. Included are amphetamines, barbiturates, methylphenidate, methaqualone, and diethylpropion. Anyone in illegal possession of a controlled drug or trafficking in such a drug may be imprisoned for up to 18 months if charged with a summary offense, or up to 10 years if charged by indictment.

A narcotic is described as the opium poppy, its preparations, derivatives, alkaloids and salts, and includes heroin, a drug available to hospitals only, and morphine. These drugs have a potential for abuse, and can lead to serious physical and psychological dependence. Cocaine and marijuana are also prohibited under the Narcotic Control Act, which contains 20 categories of illegal drugs.

The penalties for trafficking in narcotics, as defined by the Narcotic Control Act, are even more severe than for controlled drugs. Anyone possessing narcotics can be fined $1,000, or imprisoned for six months, or both—on a first offense. But, if convicted by indictment, you could be jailed for up to seven years. Conviction for trafficking in one of these drugs, however, makes you liable for imprisonment for life.

DRUG TESTING

Irene has been asked to submit to a drug test at her job, and she feels this is a violation of her privacy. Can she refuse to take the test?

Irene's rights will depend very much upon the kind of job she has and the province where she lives. Although drug tests remain controversial, they are used by many public and private employers.

Concern about invasion of privacy and the possible harm from incorrect results have prompted legislation limiting drug tests. Irene may not have to take a drug test if she works for a private company. In some provinces, drug testing can be conducted only if the employer has "probable cause" to suspect drug use or "reasonable suspicion" that it has occurred. But random testing of employees may be permissible under certain specific conditions—for example, if the employee is a bus or taxi driver, or other worker with the potential to do harm to himself or others.

Although the Charter of Rights and Freedoms does not guarantee privacy, some provincial charters and codes of human rights do. However, some provinces also permit companies to test prospective employees. In recent years, even labor tribunals have acceded that employers can insist on prospective employees undergoing medical examinations that include blood tests as a condition of employment. An employer can also require

an employee returning to work after an illness to submit to a medical examination.

When there is a conflict between a person's right to privacy and the public's safety, the courts tend to favor the public interest. If the employer could demonstrate that he required his employees to undergo drug testing because of the nature of their jobs as airline pilots, air traffic controllers, or bus drivers, for example, drug testing would most likely be permissible. On the other hand, if Irene was applying for a job as a store clerk or cashier, it would be difficult—if not impossible—for the employer to justify such an invasion of privacy.

If an employee acts erratically on the job, an employer may be justified in requesting a drug test. If the employee refuses, the employer would probably be justified in taking disciplinary measures.

Although the U.S. Supreme Court has allowed drug testing in certain federal jobs, at the time of writing the issue has not yet been definitively addressed by the Supreme Court of Canada. See also EMPLOYEE HIRING AND FIRING.

DRUNK DRIVING

Driving or operating a motor vehicle while drunk is a crime in every province. The law refers to drunk driving as driving while intoxicated (DWI) or driving under the influence (DUI). A person will be found guilty of DWI if a prosecutor can establish beyond a reasonable doubt that the accused was: (1) driving, (2) a motor vehicle, (3) on a public road or highway or other area where the public has access; (4) while under the influence of an intoxicating beverage or liquor.

It is not always easy to prove these conditions. Take the first one—driving. Suppose Oliver was found asleep at the wheel of his car on the shoulder of the road. The key was in the ignition, but the engine was not running. According to case law, Oliver could be convicted of drunk driving in this situation because he had the "care and control" of the vehicle. If the police can show that Oliver had a blood alcohol concentration (BAC) of 0.08 or more, his conviction would stand.

The requirement that the accused be operating a "motor vehicle" usually means that he has to be found behind the wheel of a car, truck, motorcycle, moped, or snowmobile. But it can also refer to a boat, or airplane, which strictly speaking you do not "drive." Nevertheless, you can be charged with drunk driving of these vehicles if your BAC is over the legal limit, and you would gain demerit points as well.

The Nova Scotia Court of Appeal held a man guilty of impaired driving after he had been found unconscious under the dash panel of his drifting boat. Although the ignition key was in his pocket, he was considered to have the "care and control" of the boat.

People have been convicted of drunk driving even when the vehicle they were in was out of

gas, or not in running order. Ruling on the *Saunders* case in 1967, the Supreme Court of Canada stated that when the law says no one shall have the care and control of a vehicle while intoxicated, the law refers to the vehicle itself (automobile, boat, plane) and not whether the vehicle is actually operable or not.

Since the Criminal Code does not make a distinction between private and public property, a charge of drunk driving will be laid even if the intoxicated driver is on his own property.

The Criminal Code makes it an offense to drive while your blood alcohol concentration is 0.08 or more, or if your driving is impaired by alcohol or a drug. So, someone who has a low tolerance for alcohol could be convicted of drunk driving even if her BAC was below the legal limit, at say 0.04, if her driving was impaired.

According to the Criminal Code you must provide a breath sample when requested to do so by the police at a roadside test. You do not have the right to see a lawyer before this test. But you may have the right to a lawyer if the roadside test is followed by a sobriety test, such as being asked to walk a straight line. However, if you fail the roadside test, you will be brought to the police station to undergo the more sophisticated Breathalyzer test, and at this second stage you do have the right to have your lawyer present.

In roadside tests, the police may want a suspected drunk driver to walk a straight line from heel to toe, or stand on

one leg while raising the other, or pick up coins from the road. Although no one has to submit to these tests, failure to cooperate or failure in these tests will probably result in a drunk-driving charge.

Ordinarily police do not have the right to stop a motorist unless they have reason to believe he is driving in a dangerous manner, or is intoxicated. Random stopping of vehicles is permitted, however, when there is a special police program to catch drunk drivers. Such road blocks are usually carried out during holidays, to reduce road accidents.

In some cases, usually where someone has been injured in a car accident, the police are able to obtain a warrant for a blood sample instead of a breath sample. Blood samples are more reliable than Breathalyzer tests in proving the BAC. See BLOOD-ALCOHOL TESTING; BREATH TEST.

STEPS TO TAKE

If you are stopped by a police officer who suspects you of drunk driving, here are a few points worth keeping in mind:

1. Don't be hostile or belligerent. Comply with the officer's requests.

2. Ask the officer if you may consult a lawyer before submitting to a breath, blood, or urine test. (A refusal to let you call a lawyer before the Breathalyzer test would probably result in the evidence being inadmissible in court. This does not apply to the roadside test, for which you do not have a right to a lawyer. Police should also inform you of your right to

ABC's

OF DRUNK-DRIVING PENALTIES

The days when police and courts were likely to let a drunk driver off lightly are gone. Today a drunk-driving charge can bring heavy fines and prison sentences. The penalties outlined here are for Criminal Code infractions. Provincial penalties—as far as fines and suspension of a driver's license under their respective highway safety codes and highway traffic acts are concerned—are often more severe. The Criminal Code has six possible offenses related to drunk driving. They are: (1) Impaired driving; (2) BAC over 0.08; (3) refusing to give a breath sample; (4) refusing to give a blood sample; (5) impaired driving causing bodily harm; and (6) impaired driving causing death. The first four are hybrid offenses, in that the police can charge a driver with either a summary conviction offense or by indictment, which is much more serious. Penalties on conviction of those offenses are:

■ **FIRST OFFENSE (1 to 4)**
(Summary conviction)
Prohibition from driving for 3 months to 3 years; fine of $300 to $2,000; imprisonment of up to 6 months.
(Indictment) Prohibition from driving for 3 months to 3 years; fine from $300 to unlimited; imprisonment of up to 5 years.

■ **SECOND OFFENSE (1 to 4)**
(Summary conviction)
Prohibition from driving for 6 months to 3 years; fine from $300 to $2,000; imprisonment of 14 days to 6 months.
(Indictment) Prohibition from driving for 6 months to 3 years; fine from $300 to unlimited; imprisonment of 14 days to 5 years.

■ **SUBSEQUENT OFFENSES (1 to 4)**
(Summary conviction)
Prohibition from driving for 1 to 3 years; fine from $300 to $2,000; imprisonment of 90 days to 6 months.
(Indictment) Prohibition from driving for 1 to 3 years; fine from $300 to unlimited; imprisonment of 90 days to 5 years.

■ **FIRST OFFENSE (5 to 6)**
Impaired driving causing bodily harm or death is always prosecuted by way of indictment. Penalties include prohibition from driving for up to 10 years; unlimited fines; imprisonment for up to 10 years, or up to 14 years if someone is killed.

legal aid, if you cannot afford a lawyer.)

3. If he says no, take the test. Refusing may result in automatic suspension of your driver's license, even if you are later found not to have been under the influence of alcohol.

4. If you are charged with drunk driving and are placed under arrest, call a lawyer as soon as possible to arrange for your release from custody. Or call a friend or family member to make these arrangements for you.

5. Do not make any statements to the police until you have consulted a lawyer. Admissions you make can and will be held against you in court. If you are placed in a holding cell with other prisoners, do not make any statements to them about your drinking habits, either. Some inmates may try to trade this information to the prosecutor in an attempt to obtain a lesser sentence or a reduced charge for themselves.

PUNISHMENT

Usually, a crime is committed only when there is both a wrongful act (*actus reus*) and a wrongful intention (*mens rea*). In 1993, the Supreme Court of Canada ruled that a court does not have to find an accused had the *mens rea*, or "guilty mind," to be convicted of dangerous driving. This new approach to criminal liability may have far-reaching effects, because it seems to impose a strict liability on the accused in regulatory offenses. By using an objective rather than a subjective standard, the courts could convict someone of dangerous driving even if that person did not intend to drive in a dangerous manner, or was unaware that he was so driving. Said the Hon. Mr. Justice Cory: "There is a compelling need for effective legislation which strives to regulate the manner of driving vehicles and thereby lessen the carnage on our highways. It is not only appropriate but essential in the control of dangerous driving that an objective standard be applied."

Critics of this judgment feel that any rear-end collision or running through a red light will automatically result in a conviction for dangerous driving.

In a series of cases that were decided after the *Hundel* case, the Supreme Court unanimously ruled that in crimes of negligence, if *mens rea* was not required, at least an "objective foresight" was the constitutional minimum requirement to be found guilty. This means that if the "ordinary reasonable man" could reasonably foresee that his behavior could cause harm, the accused would be convicted. Chief Justice Antonio Lamer's contention that the ordinary reasonable man standard should be tempered by looking at the accused's education, degree of experience and other personal characteristics gave way in a 5 to 4 decision, whereby the majority of the court ruled that the standard of care should be uniform and not vary from one accused to another.

DRY CLEANER

When you leave your clothes with a dry cleaner, you have created what is known in the law as a bailment. That is, you leave your property with the dry cleaner for servicing, and do so for your mutual benefit: your clothes are cleaned, she is paid, and she returns the clothes to you.

The cleaner is required by law to use "ordinary care" in handling and safeguarding your property while it is in her possession. Nevertheless, you as a customer should do whatever you can to protect your clothes

CHECKLIST

Choosing a Dry Cleaner

When it comes to dry-cleaning problems, an ounce of prevention is worth a pound of cure. Before you risk taking your most valued clothes to a new dry cleaner, find out the following:

■ **HOW LONG THE DRY CLEANER HAS BEEN IN BUSINESS.**
A number of cleaners come and go, but the good ones stay in business for many years.

■ **WHETHER THE DRY CLEANER BELONGS TO THE LOCAL BETTER BUSINESS BUREAU.**
Membership in the Better Business Bureau indicates that the cleaner may be more responsive to consumers. In addition, if a dispute arises, you may be able to settle it by arbitration.

■ **WHETHER THE FEES ARE THE SAME FOR WOMEN'S AND MEN'S CLOTHING.**
Cleaners often charge women twice as much as men for the same type of garment. If the cleaner does this, go elsewhere. You may also want to register a complaint with your provincial attorney general's office or local consumer affairs department.

■ **WHAT KINDS OF SERVICES ARE PROVIDED.**
Ask whether the cleaner gives special attention to stains, checks buttons, and does tailoring.

■ **WHETHER THE CLEANING IS DONE ON THE PREMISES OR IS SENT OUT TO A PLANT.**
Although large plants often do a better job, they may not offer the personalized attention your clothes require. They also lose garments more frequently.

■ **WHETHER THE CLEANER BELONGS TO A LOCAL PROFESSIONAL ASSOCIATION.**
The association can be a useful mediator in the event of disputes.

against any loss or damage that might occur. Get a receipt for the clothing you leave. The receipt should account for each item of clothing, and it may include special instructions for cleaning (as when you request that a grease spot be removed). Be sure to look for any conditions printed on the receipt.

Cleaners often state that they will not be responsible for clothing left beyond a certain period of time, usually 90 days. Although courts do not always

enforce such provisions, you should pick up items within a reasonable time.

When you leave your clothes, the cleaner is expected to handle them responsibly. She must not lose them or clean an item that she knows will be damaged in the process. For instance, if a garment carries a label saying "Hand Wash Only—Do Not Dry-clean," the dry cleaner should not clean it. If she does so and the garment is ruined, she will be obliged to reimburse you for the actual cash value—its original cost minus an amount based on the garment's age and wear and tear.

A dry cleaner usually has a right to try to repair damage to a garment before reimbursing you for its value. Before letting her do so, have another professional look at it. Then, if the dry cleaner does not repair the damage, you will be able to prove the harm that was done.

Occasionally, a garment is damaged because of a flaw in the fabric or because the garment was incorrectly labeled. If this happens, many dry cleaners ask a trade association such as the Canadian Textile Testing Laboratories to analyze the garment. If the damage is due to a manufacturing flaw or improper labeling, the cleaner is not responsible for compensating you, although the manufacturer may be.

In many provinces there are professional associations of dry cleaners, who employ specialized chemists. If they find that the damage is caused by the dry cleaner they will try to mediate a solution to the problem. If the damage occurs because of wrong labeling or defective material, then you should try to get reimbursed by the store that sold you the garment. The store, in turn, will be reimbursed by the manufacturer. If the store refuses to reimburse you, contact the office of Consumer and Corporate Affairs in your area for an explanation of your various recourses. As a final result you can always sue the store and manufacturer in the small-claims court.

You are not obliged to have the garment tested, but if you do not do so, and you subsequently sue the dry cleaner for negligence, your case against her will not be as strong. See also BAILMENT; NEGLIGENCE; WARRANTY AND GUARANTEE.

DUE PROCESS OF LAW

Due process of law is the fundamental justice enshrined in sections 7 to 14 of the Charter of Rights and Freedoms, and applicable to all citizens and residents of Canada, as well as to any visitor or other person on Canadian soil. It also applies to corporations, prisoners, the mentally handicapped, and members of the military.

Due process means there are certain rights that cannot be taken away by the state except in "accordance with the principles of fundamental justice." Those rights are the basic right to life, liberty, and security of the person; the right to be secure against unreasonable search or seizure; the right not to be arbitrarily detained and to be informed promptly of the reasons for one's arrest; and the right to instruct counsel and to be informed of this right.

Other rights that make up due process, or fundamental justice, are the right to remain silent and not incriminate oneself; the right to trial by an impartial tribunal within a reasonable time; the right to be assisted by an interpreter if you cannot understand the language of the (criminal) proceedings. If found guilty of an offense, you have the right not to be treated in a cruel or unusual manner.

In practice, this means that if your property is expropriated, for example, you must be informed of the proposed expropriation, must have a chance to contest it, and be fairly compensated for the loss of your property.

THE *ASKOV* RULING AND ITS AFTERMATH

Due process, or the right to fundamental justice, is most often invoked in the case of criminal law. And so precious is our rule of procedural fairness that from time to time people are acquitted by the courts, not because they were found innocent but because due process or procedural fairness was not followed.

One such example was the *Askov* case, which came before the Supreme Court of Canada in 1990. The defendant had been charged with extortion and several other related offenses in November 1983, detained for almost six months, then released on bail. A July 1984 date was set for the preliminary hearing, but it was not completed until September. A trial date was fixed for October 1985, but the case could not be heard then, and the trial was put over to September 1986—almost two years after the preliminary hearing.

When the trial finally began, the accused and his alleged conspirators requested the case be dismissed since they had been denied their right to trial within a reasonable time. The trial judge agreed, but his decision was overturned by the Ontario Court of Appeal. But the Supreme Court of Canada agreed with the trial judge and ruled the case should be stayed. According to most of the judges, the charter's guarantee of trial within a reasonable time reflects both a community or societal interest in having lawbreakers brought to trial and dealt with according to the law quickly, and a concern that those on trial be treated fairly and justly. A long delay causes prejudice to the accused.

In the wake of the Supreme Court ruling, thousands of cases that had been a long time waiting trial were dismissed by the courts, lest the accused's rights be violated.

The *Askov* decision also helped promote a greater respect for due process and fundamental justice, and inspired the justice departments of most provinces to make their judicial system more efficient.

SUBSTANTIVE DUE PROCESS

Substantive due process, in contrast, focuses on the government and its authority to make or enforce certain kinds of legislation. For example, if the government properly notifies Robert that it wants to expropriate his house for the public good, but Robert is convinced that his house and those of his neighbors are being expropriated for reasons that are suspect, he may bring a lawsuit claiming that his substantive due process rights have been violated.

Substantive due process means that the government cannot enact legislation that is unreasonable and arbitrary. Thus, for example, if Robert can prove that the government is expropriating his home to benefit a private real estate company that owns nearby property, he may have a valid due process lawsuit. Similarly, if the government wants to tear down Robert's house because he uses it for making wine, but making wine is not illegal in his province, he may challenge the law as arbitrary and unreasonable, and therefore a violation of substantive due process.

Laws must be definite and clear enough that a person of ordinary intelligence does not have to guess their meaning. This requirement is especially important in the area of criminal statutes, such as those that apply to loitering and vagrancy. A law that is vaguely worded—for example, "A person cannot be in the street without a purposeful intention"—cannot pass a due process analysis. The courts deem such statutes "void for vagueness" because they give no clear or fair indication to ordinary people of what activity is prohibited.

In criminal law the rule is that the words of the statute must be restrictively interpreted, and be given their ordinary meaning.

If they are not to violate substantive due process, laws—as well as the means provided for their enforcement—must have a legitimate government purpose. Suppose a city government wants to contain the spread of AIDS among its citizens. If it passes a law setting up a plan to educate the public about the disease, this would not violate substantive due process. But a law requiring each new resident to take an AIDS test would both exceed the government's authority and invade individual privacy to such a degree that it would constitute a violation of substantive due process.

If a particular statute affects only a certain portion of the population, the law will meet due process requirements as long as it applies equally to all people who are in a similar situation—for example, a law requiring that all drivers over age 75 take a driving test every two years. A Latin maxim sums it up: *dura lex sed lex* ("it is a hard law, but it is the law").

If a law discriminates between individuals in similar situations, courts apply one of two tests to determine if due process was violated. Courts apply the "compelling state interest" test when constitutionally "suspect" classifications such as age, race, or sex are involved, or when the law affects a fundamental right such as the freedom of religion. This test requires the court to determine whether the classification is needed to further a compelling state interest. For example, the law requiring frequent driving tests for those over 75 has highway safety as its compelling state interest. In this situation the age classification specified in the law does not violate due process.

The other test, called the "rational basis" test, is applied to classifications that are not suspect. This test requires the court to determine whether a law is reasonably related to a legitimate government interest.

For example, a provincial law that requires all drivers and passengers to wear seat belts while they are riding in automobiles applies to the classification of drivers and passengers. But unlike the driving test law mentioned previously, it does not discriminate on the basis of age or any other constitutionally suspect classification (such as sex or race). Since it serves the legitimate government interest of highway safety as well, it passes the rational basis test.

Thus a challenge to the Alberta Seat Belt Law was dismissed because it was demonstrated that the use of seat belts reduced the number and severity of injuries, and thus saved lives and money in the form of reduced medical costs.

DURESS

Duress is the use of pressure or intimidation by one person against another, causing the other person to do something she does not want to do or would not ordinarily do. For example, if Lisa threatens to harm her elderly mother unless she changes her will, leaving all her property to Lisa and her boyfriend, Lisa is guilty of duress.

Since one of the elements in the formation of a contract is the "meeting of the minds"—both parties must give their free and voluntary consent to the contract—proof of duress during the signing of legal documents, such as wills, deeds, or contracts, may invalidate the documents.

DYING DECLARATION

A dying declaration is a statement made by a dying person, who is mentally competent and aware of his imminent death, about a crime or other wrong that has been done by or to him—for example: "Jeremy is the man who shot me," or "I'm the one who stole Meg's ring," or even "I have another wife and family in Winnipeg."

Dying declarations are assumed to be truthful because people who know they are dying usually have no reason to lie. Therefore, a dying declaration, oral or written, may be used as evidence in court, if it can be proved authentic or witnesses can confirm it.

DYING WITHOUT A WILL

If you die without leaving a valid last will and testament, your property will be distributed to your heirs under your province's laws of descent (who will inherit your property) and distribution (what they will inherit). These laws are also referred to as laws of intestate succession.

DESCENT AND DISTRIBUTION LAWS

Descent and distribution laws are meant to give your property to the people whom the law thinks you would most likely have chosen if you had executed a will. As a result, descent and distribution laws are written on the assumption that you would rather leave your property to your immediate family than to more distant family or friends.

These laws vary from province to province, but inherited property usually goes first to the surviving spouse. Next in line are living children, then parents, brothers and sisters and their direct descendants, and finally grandparents and their direct descendants.

The spouse does not inherit everything, however. For example, if you are married, have a child, and die without a will, in many provinces your spouse will inherit only one-third to one-half of your property, with the remainder going to your child.

If you are a widow and you die without a will, all your property will go to your children (or to grandchildren if your own child has died leaving offspring). If you have adopted a child, he or she is entitled to share equally in your estate, but stepchildren you have not legally adopted may not receive anything.

If you die without a spouse and have no children or grandchildren, your parents, if living, will usually get your property, although some provinces also distribute a share to any living brothers or sisters. If your parents die before you, your brothers and sisters will share equally in your estate. And if there are no closer survivors, your cousins, nieces, nephews, and even aunts and uncles may receive your property. If none of these relatives survives you, your property goes to your nearest living blood relative.

When the province takes over

If no blood relative can be found, your property may "escheat," or revert to the state. In short, descent and distribution laws are the province's way of writing a will for you if you neglect to do so yourself.

In such event, there is the risk that the people nearest and dearest to you, such as your spouse and children, will not receive the share you would want them to have. A valid last will and testament, preferably prepared by a lawyer, is your best guarantee that your wishes will be met.

In Quebec, a will drawn up by a notary (a notarial will) does not have to be probated by the courts as do other forms of wills, namely holograph wills (ones entirely handwritten by the testator) or English form wills (wills written, typed or printed, and signed by the testator in the presence of two witnesses, both of whom must also sign the document).

See also WILL.

FROM
EARNED INCOME
TO
EXTRADITION

EARNED INCOME

Salaries, commissions, tips, bonuses, stocks, bonds, and even merchandise received in exchange for work, are considered earned income for tax purposes. So, too, are unemployment insurance and pension benefits, rental income, and royalties. Money you do not work for—such as money you win, inherit, or get from investments—is not considered earned income. However, see *Real Life, Real Law*, p. 299.

EARNEST MONEY

A deposit given to a seller by a buyer as evidence of his intention to follow through with a purchase is called earnest money. In return, the seller promises not to sell the property to someone else.

For important purchases, such as automobiles or real estate, earnest money, along with a document called a binder, takes the property off the market while the buyer obtains financing and investigates the property.

Buyers usually negotiate to make the earnest deposit as small as possible. The accompanying binder should state the amount and purpose of the deposit and specify the circumstances under which it will be refunded. Reasons for a refund include the failure to obtain suitable financing or the discovery of structural flaws in the property.

A buyer may forfeit an earnest-money deposit if she fails to abide by the terms of the binder. For example, if Barbara puts down $1,000 as earnest money to buy Ross's house, she would lose her money if she changes her mind for reasons not allowed under the binder. If Ross changes his mind and decides not to sell, he must give Barbara $2,000—the $1,000 she deposited as well as $1,000 from his own pocket.

See BINDER; HOME BUYING AND SELLING.

EASEMENT

The right to use another person's land for a specific purpose is called an easement. For example, if Maud's property does not extend all the way to the street, her neighbor may grant her an easement, affording her access to the street by allowing her to use a strip of his own land. Easements may also be established for the benefit of either the general public or the government—as when a municipality runs sewer lines under private property.

TYPES OF EASEMENTS

Easements are categorized in several ways. An *easement appurtenant* benefits the person receiving it and becomes part of his estate. It is permanent and can be inherited. The easement Maud acquired through her neighbor's land is an easement appurtenant.

An *easement in gross* is a right acquired by private grant or statute, for example the right of a hydro company to place a power line on a person's property, or the right that one person may give another to harvest crops or cut timber on his property. This type of easement cannot be inherited or assigned to another person.

Easements may be either affirmative or negative. An *affirmative easement* permits someone else to do something on your property; a *negative easement* prohibits you from doing something on your property. For example, if you buy land from an adjacent homeowner who enjoys a scenic view from her backyard, she may insert a negative easement into the sales contract prohibiting you from building anything that would obstruct her view.

CREATING AN EASEMENT

One way of creating an easement is through a provision in a deed, contract, or will. Such an *express easement* is enforceable because the document satisfies the Statute of Frauds,

which specifies that easements must be in writing.

An *easement by implication*, in contrast, is not in writing. It may be created when, for example, property is divided into smaller lots and sold. Suppose Ben installs a water pipeline to water his livestock, then later sells part of his land to Evelyn; however, Ben retains the right to use the pipeline that runs through Evelyn's property, even though this was not specified in their sales contract.

An *easement by prescription* is also an implied easement. It is created by one's continual use of another's land for a specific purpose, even though nothing has been put in writing and the owner has not expressly stated that he agrees to the activity. Suppose Farmer Brown and Farmer Green own two neighboring farms. Farmer Brown's land does not extend to the county road, and he reaches the road by crossing over a small corner of Farmer Green's acreage. If Brown creates a well-worn, visible path across Green's land and continues to use it for a number of years, he may have created an easement by prescription. If he has, Green cannot decide, after several years (the exact length of time varies provincially), to prevent Brown from using the path. The rules on easement by prescription are similar to those on adverse possession.

It is impossible to create an easement by prescription in Alberta, Quebec, Saskatchewan, Yukon, and the Northwest Territories.

See also ADVERSE POSSESSION.

LOSING AN EASEMENT

Farmer Brown and others who enjoy express or implied easements should not assume that they can never be taken away. People can lose their easements if they abuse them. For example, if you have allowed your neighbor to cross a piece of your land to get to a public road, but he later sets up a business that results in numerous customers tracking back and forth over your property, you can take the easement away from him.

An easement may also be lost through abandonment, if it can be shown that it was your intention to abandon the easement.

Since the law does not like to permit waste, the owner of a piece of land which is bordered on all sides by land owned by others would have a right-of-way through one of his neighbor's properties to reach his own land. The right-of-way is usually the shortest and least troublesome route through the property of another, so that the owner of the surrounded lot has access from the public road to his property.

In Quebec, easements are known as *servitudes*, and are acquired by a title deed or in a will or other writing.

ELDER LAW

Older Canadians—a steadily increasing segment of the population—have special needs and unique legal problems. Many lawyers and other professionals offering services to the elderly make a special study of the laws affecting them. Areas of the law identified as being of major concern to older people are abuse and neglect, age discrimination, guardianships, money management, estate planning, long-term health care, and the right to die. If you think you need a lawyer, but are not sure how to find a good one, see LAWYER.

ABUSE AND NEGLECT

Various studies have shown that elderly people are frequently neglected or physically or emotionally abused, often by family members or professional caretakers. Nova Scotia is among the provinces that have enacted legislation to combat this problem. Anyone who knows of a case of elder abuse in that province is obliged to report it to the Minister of Social Service, who in turn must help the victim and take steps to ensure his or her future safety.

In any province, if you suspect that an older person is the victim of abuse or neglect, whether at home or in an institution, tell your local social services office or police department. They will investigate, and your name will be kept confidential. Penalties can be imposed for failing to report a suspected case of elder abuse. See also NURSING HOME; ORDER OF PROTECTION.

AGE DISCRIMINATION

Section 15 of the Charter of Rights and Freedoms and various provincial human rights acts and codes prohibit discrimination on the basis of age.

However, the Ontario legislation permits discrimination against people aged 65 years and over, whereas in Alberta and Quebec this is not the case.

Complaint hearings by human rights tribunals are less formal and less costly than a court proceeding with a charter challenge. However, the protection afforded by these laws is not absolute in the area of employment: an employer may legitimately set age limits in cases of bona fide occupational requirements. See AGE DISCRIMINATION; EMPLOYEE HIRING AND FIRING.

MONEY MANAGEMENT

Some older people have difficulty managing their finances and handling their everyday affairs. If age or illness has impaired someone to the point that she cannot make rational decisions about medical care, the appointment of a guardian may be necessary to protect her and her property. Most provinces have laws that enable a court to appoint a guardian to care for an incompetent older person. This traditional method of guardianship has recently been criticized for dealing primarily with the person's property rather than with the individual, and for granting only full guardianship powers.

Reform is under way, however, with legislation such as in the Dependent Adults Act of Alberta, the Neglected Adults Act of Newfoundland, and the Adult Protection Act of Nova Scotia. Trusted guardians are given the power and authority to perform only those functions that the elderly per-

son cannot adequately perform, so that he or she may continue to live as independently as possible. The appointment of a guardian is a simple process of the Surrogate Court, and there are mandatory provisions for reviewing the court order.

The management of someone's financial affairs could also be handled by using a power of attorney. This allows a friend or family member to write cheques and make sure that bills are paid on time. In the past, powers of attorney were invalid once the person granting the power became incapacitated. British Columbia and Quebec are among provinces that allow enduring powers of attorney: such powers continue to be valid even in the case of incompetency.

In Quebec, guardians (known as tutors or curators) can be appointed to take care of a person's property or person or both. A curator's powers are more extensive that those of a tutor.

The courts can use the common-law doctrine of unconscionability and the civil-law doctrine of lesion to set aside a contract made by an older person, where it was shown that the older person was under duress or abuse by a dominant party. See DURESS; GUARDIAN AND WARD; POWER OF ATTORNEY.

ESTATE PLANNING

Another important area of elder law is estate planning. Judicious estate planning not only helps a person avoid paying taxes unnecessarily but relieves her of the need to be concerned with the management of her property. For example, she can place her assets in a revocable living trust, with herself as the beneficiary and an adult child or another reliable person as cotrustee. See ESTATE PLANNING; LIVING TRUST; NURSING HOME.

LIVING WILLS

Elderly people have special concerns about the costs and complexities of long-term health care. Many people do not want their lives extended by drastic measures such as respirators and feeding tubes; nor do they want to pass on to their families the burden of deciding when to end artificial life support.

One answer may be a living will, written instructions to withdraw or withhold life-support systems if one should become terminally ill and unable to make one's wishes known. See LIVING WILL.

ELECTION LAWS

Fundamental to any democracy is its citizens' right to vote.

Federal elections are regulated by the Canada Elections Act, whereas provincial elections are governed by the provincial elections acts. These acts are, in general, quite similar, although certain aspects may differ from province to province.

THE FREEDOM TO VOTE

If elections are truly to reflect the will of the people, no qualified voter should be prevented from voting. Section 3 of the Charter of Rights and Freedoms states that "Every citizen of Canada has the right to vote in an election of members of the House of Commons or of a legislative assembly." However, the Canada Elections Act lists some exceptions.

Electoral officers, anyone disqualified for participating in illegal or corrupt electoral practices, and people not ordinarily resident in Canada are not permitted to vote in federal elections. Neither are those who do not meet the criteria of age, citizenship or residency. These requirements vary from one province to another. Normally, people of majority age who have lived in a province for one year can vote.

Prisoners have been allowed to vote in federal elections since a 1991 ruling by the Federal Court. By then, provincial appeal courts had granted prisoners in Manitoba and Ontario the right to vote in provincial elections. Restrictions that once prevented federally appointed judges and mentally ill people from voting have also been lifted.

VOTING RIGHTS

To exercise your right to vote you must be registered on the list of voters in your electoral district.

◇ Voters are entitled to absolute secrecy. An election that is conducted in such a way that an individual's vote is identifiable can be invalidated.

◇ If it is proved that a candidate won an election through fraud, bribery, or coercion, he cannot assume office.

◇ Most provinces prohibit electioneering within a specified distance from a polling place, because this practice may intimidate voters.

◇ If any violence or intimidation of voters takes place in a district, all the votes in that district can be invalidated.

EQUALITY OF VOTES

The right to vote has no real meaning if the votes are not weighed equally. "One person, one vote" has long been a basic tenet of our democracy. To ensure the equality of the vote, the principle of representation by population is used in federal elections, where provinces with larger populations are allotted more seats in the House of Commons than less populous provinces. Because the population of each province may increase or decline over the years, it has been necessary to periodically redistribute the number of seats assigned to some provinces.

Redistribution may also occur at the provincial level, to reflect population movement within a province. This has been necessary in the past as a response to urbanization.

It is not necessary to obtain an absolute majority of the votes to win an election, either federally or provincially. The "first-past-the-post" rule means that the candidate with the most votes wins.

ACCESS TO ELECTED OFFICE

The Charter of Rights and Freedoms guarantees citizens the opportunity to become members of the House of

Commons or a provincial assembly. Because our elections are almost always contests between political parties, people seeking to hold office should attempt to secure a party nomination. Candidates with no party affiliation generally receive only a small percentage of the vote.

Legislative restrictions on candidacy are similar to those for voting. In general, people of at least 18 years of age may run for election if they meet citizenship or residency requirements. To represent a particular party, you must be chosen at a nomination meeting attended by party members in that electoral district and be endorsed by the party leader. You will be required to produce a signed list of voters who also endorse your nomination, and you must make a cash deposit.

CAMPAIGN SPENDING

How much a political party can spend during a campaign is limited by law. In federal elections, the limit is about $10 million for a party with a candidate in every riding. Provincial regulations vary. There are also limits on the amount individuals, corporations, and trade unions can contribute to parties or individual candidates. In Ontario, you may contribute up to $4,000 per party and $750 per candidate. This compares with $30,000 per party and $1,500 per candidate in Alberta. Individual candidates who get a significant percentage of the vote in their own ridings may be entitled to at least partial reimbursement of their election expenses.

ABC's
OF YOUR RIGHT TO VOTE

When Canada held its first federal elections in 1867, voting was a privilege accorded only to white male property owners. Today the Canadian Charter of Rights and Freedoms guarantees that right to all Canadians who meet certain age and residency requirements.

MINIMUM VOTING AGE
■ The minimum voting age is 18 in all federal elections. This is also the case for provincial elections, except in Nova Scotia, British Columbia, Yukon, and the Northwest Territories, where only people 19 years of age and over may vote.

SECRET BALLOT
■ Voting secrecy and ballot security are fundamental rights.

RESIDENCY REQUIREMENTS
■ Depending on the province, you must have lived in your district from 6 to 12 months to be eligible to vote in a provincial election.

TIME OUT TO VOTE
■ In federal elections, employees are entitled to four consecutive hours off work to vote. Provincial legislation on this matter varies from 1 to 4 hours.

CONTESTED ELECTIONS

The Controverted Elections Act makes it possible to challenge federal election results in court if fraud or other irregularities are suspected. The challenge may come from any voter or candidate willing to deposit $1,000 within the specified time limit, which varies with the particular election. There is also legislation enabling you to contest provincial elections.

If it is found that illegal practices occurred, the election will be declared void and a new one will be held.

Recounts or challenges would be valid if there was any violation of election laws (for example, through bribery), if legal votes were rejected or illegal ones (votes by unregistered voters or multiple votes by the same voter) accepted, if the ballots were improperly prepared (if party affiliations were misstated), and if the rules of secrecy were violated.

You may also challenge an elected official by way of the writ of *quo warranto*, "by what right." See QUO WARRANTO.

ELECTRONIC FUNDS TRANSFER

The past two decades have seen a rapid increase in the use of computer technology in the areas of banking and consumer transactions. One result is that the bank teller has become less and less important to those of us who now take advantage of automated teller machines (ATMs) and pre-authorized debits on a frequent basis. Personal cheques and even cash are becoming rarer as individuals opt for the speed and convenience of electronic banking and purchasing. It is estimated that Canadians now make ATM transactions more than half a billion times each year. While everyone is aware of the advantages of the electronic medium, not everyone is aware of its legal implications.

USING ATMS

All you need in order to use an ATM is a client card and a personal identification number (PIN). Almost all financial institutions offer this service to their clients, and it is possible for your card to give you access to several accounts, including credit card accounts. You may also use ATMs to pay utility bills, and many institutions do not charge a fee for bills paid through ATMs, whereas you may be charged $1 or more if you pay over the counter.

DEBIT CARD TRANSACTIONS

Debit card transactions are expected to replace the use of cash and cheques in many situations eventually. Essentially the transaction replaces the need for writing a cheque. At the point of purchase, the consumer presents either a debit card or ATM card to the retailer, who verifies that the customer's account

has sufficient funds to cover the purchase. The consumer's PIN is then verified, and the account subsequently debited.

THE CARDHOLDER AGREEMENT

The benefits of electronic banking and purchasing are undeniable, but it is important to understand that financial institutions currently have the upper hand when dealing with cardholders who complain of unauthorized ATM withdrawals. This is because contracts between these institutions and their clients clearly indicate that the client is responsible for the card and is liable for its unauthorized use until the institution is notified that it is lost or stolen.

Some contracts limit cardholder liability to $50, as long as your PIN was kept confidential. However, most institutions hold you completely liable. Besides, when you sign such a contract you normally agree that the bank, trust company or credit union's transaction records are binding and that the institution may change the terms of the agreement whenever it likes. Naturally, financial institutions are reluctant to admit that electronic error or security breaches are possible.

Furthermore, cardholders who claim to have been victims of unauthorized withdrawals have had little success when challenging financial institutions in the courts. A cardholder with such a claim is faced with the onerous task of proving that she kept her PIN confidential. The courts have also refused to acknowl-

edge that the electronic medium may not be foolproof.

Canadian consumer groups have staunchly criticized the one-sided aspect of cardholder agreements and have advocated passing legislation to deal with this problem. These groups point to the greater protection afforded to clients in countries such as the United States, Australia, and New Zealand.

In the meantime, however, you should take steps to protect yourself. Never divulge your PIN to anyone, and do not keep it in close proximity to your card, such as in your wallet. Keep all transaction slips and verify your account statements on a regular basis. If you notice any discrepancy, report it to your financial institution immediately. If you do not do so within 30 days, the institution is not responsible for correcting the error. Lastly, you should be aware that the usual $50 limit of liability on unauthorized credit card purchases does not apply to cash advances received through ATMs.

If you have a complaint, you should first talk to your branch manager. If this proves to be unsatisfactory, contact the institution's regional director or even its national office. If the problem remains unresolved, contact the Office of the Superintendent of Financial Institutions in Ottawa. If you are dealing with a credit union or *caisse populaire*, contact your provincial consumer protection agency.

See USEFUL ADDRESSES at back of book.

PREAUTHORIZED DEBITS

Preauthorized debits (PADs) are withdrawals from your deposit account at periodic intervals made by companies that have your permission to do so. For example, your bank may deduct your monthly mortgage payment from your account, replacing the need for postdated cheques. Insurance and utility companies, rental firms and cable TV suppliers also use PADs. Note that PADs may be used only for amounts that remain relatively constant and recur on a regular basis.

To arrange for a company to make PADs from your account, the company must obtain a signed authorization from you. This authorization should describe the amount and frequency of the debits and the account from which they are to be withdrawn. Never give verbal consent to PAD arrangements. If the company requests a blank cheque, be sure to write "VOID" in ink across the front of the cheque. Ask for a copy of the agreement, and check that it contains an outline of the procedure for canceling the contract.

Notify the company in writing if you change your account or financial institution, or if you wish to cancel the agreement, and keep a copy of your letter. Check your bankbook or account statement on a regular basis to ensure that the withdrawals are being made as agreed to. Upon cancellation or expiry of the authorization, make sure the payments have stopped. You will have 90 days to report any improper withdrawal to your financial institution, which will then return the item and credit your account.

If you do not notice the irregularity within 90 days, you must resolve the problem with the company itself. Always talk to the company before getting your financial institution to rescind the transaction, in case you breach a contract, let an insurance policy lapse, or suffer some disruption in service.

EMBEZZLEMENT

Embezzlement differs from other types of theft in that it involves the violation of a trust. Unlike fraud or swindling, for example, embezzlement does not entail obtaining another's property illegally through false pretenses. Rather, the embezzler has the property lawfully in his possession before he misappropriates (takes) it. The property is misappropriated if the embezzler conceals, converts (sells), or makes away with it without the knowledge of the owner. The difference between ordinary theft and embezzlement is best illustrated by the following.

A used-car salesman told his boss that he had a cash customer for a car on the lot, even though he did not. The dealer entrusted his car to the salesman, who sold it, pocketed the cash, and never showed up for work again. When the salesman was eventually arrested and brought to trial, he was found guilty of theft, not embezzlement, because he took the car illegally, under false pretenses.

The legal circumstances are somewhat different in the second case. Mary accepted Edward's proposal of marriage. When he apologetically told her he could not afford to buy her an engagement ring, she gave him her diamond cocktail ring so that he could have the diamonds removed and reset. But the couple quarreled and broke off their engagement, and Edward sold the ring and kept the money. He was found guilty of embezzlement. Although he received the ring legally, he acted illegally when he sold it for his own gain.

EMPLOYEE

Generally speaking, an employee is anyone who works for someone else. But in the legal sense, whether you are an employee rather than an independent contractor, say, depends on a number of considerations. Each case differs according to its facts and there are never any clear answers in this area of the law. If, on the whole, there are more facts indicating that you are an employee than not, you probably are one, and vice versa.

In general, the difference between an employee and an independent contractor is made up of four elements:

a) there must exist an element of supervision or subordination between the two parties so that one is obliged to follow the instructions of the other. For example, if you hire a plumber to fix your water pipes, you do not tell him exactly what methods he should use, nor how long he should take to do the work, as he is not acting under your direct supervision;

b) an independent contractor would generally use his own tools and materials and would also set out his hours of work;

c) an independent contractor takes on an element of risk. He sets a price for the job, for example, and may make a profit or loss, unlike an employee who would be paid a strict salary for work done. People who share in the profits or losses of an enterprise are usually not considered to be employees.

d) An employee would be entitled to certain benefits to which the employer must contribute, benefits such as unemployment insurance, pension plans (Canada or Quebec or even a private pension plan), workers' compensation, and paid holidays, and would probably have his income tax deducted by the employer. An independent contractor would get only a certain sum of money, either by the hour or the job, with no deductions.

Sometimes, an unethical employer will ask you to sign a form stating that you agree not to be considered an employee, but to work instead as an "independent contractor." The employer does this to avoid making payments for the Canada or Quebec pension plans, Unemployment Insurance, and Workers' Compensation. If you wish, you may contact the government agencies that deal with these matters and anonymously inform them of your employer's refusal to pay into

these plans (check the Blue Pages in your telephone book for local numbers).

If you are truly an independent contractor or freelance worker—that is, if you do not seem to fit the legal test for an employee set out here—you will not be entitled to the legal benefits of an employee. It may be the case as well that you will not be entitled to company benefits that are offered to employees of the business you work for. See also INDEPENDENT CONTRACTOR.

EMPLOYEE HIRING AND FIRING

Employers are governed by a variety of federal and provincial laws regarding the hiring and firing (or "termination," "discharge" or "dismissal") of employees.

The laws that apply to your workplace or prospective workplace depend on the nature of the business. If an enterprise tends to do most of its business in one province, the chances are that the provincial law applies. If a business is involved in international or interprovincial trade, then the chances are that federal law applies. Which law applies is very important, since some jurisdictions have laws that are more favorable to employees than others. To find out about your own situation, ask the provincial or federal Ministry of Labour, human rights commissions, or your union steward. Virtually all provinces and the federal gov-

ernment prohibit discrimination in hiring or firing on the basis of race, sex, age, marital status, mental or physical disabilities. But not all jurisdictions ban discrimination based on political beliefs, previous criminal convictions, language and other grounds.

The various provincial employment standard acts (labor codes and collective agreements for unionized workers) are the most important laws that deal with hiring and firing of employees.

See also AGE DISCRIMINATION; CIVIL RIGHTS.

JOB ADVERTISEMENTS AND JOB APPLICATIONS

The prohibition against discrimination applies equally to job advertisements and job applications. Therefore, an advertisement or application cannot state a preference for candidates of a particular race, color, sex, or age. For example, an employer who ran a newspaper ad that said "Help Wanted, White Male," or "Help Wanted, Asian Female," or employed language such as "young high school graduate," may be subject to discrimination charges.

Advertisements or applications that express a preference based on age, national origin, religion, sex, or the absence of a disability are allowed only if they reflect a legitimate qualification for the job. For instance, a Catholic church may require that applicants for a position as a church administrator or spokesperson be Roman Catholic. Similarly, inquiries about age are legal if the employer can demonstrate that the skills needed for a particular job make it necessary to restrict applicants by age. Courts have recognized that jobs such as fire fighter and police officer, for example, require younger people with the physical stamina to perform the job.

JOB INTERVIEWS

Alice, who is young and wears a wedding ring, was interviewed for a job as a sales representative. At the interview she was asked whether she intended to have children. The employer was concerned because the job required the employee to be on the road a lot. He was afraid that if Alice started having children, she might quit.

No matter how innocent the employer's intentions, this sort of question, while not necessarily prohibited by law, may lead to charges of unfair hiring practices. So may questions about a job candidate's age, marital status, possible pregnancy, number of children, national origin, height, weight, or handicap (except when the handicap might affect job performance). The basic rule is that an employer should ask questions that are relevant only to the applicant's qualifications for the job.

CRIMINAL RECORDS

In some parts of the country, inquiries about arrests or convictions are illegal or may be asked only under limited circumstances. However, in most provinces employers may inquire about convictions (through a question on the application form or a personal interview) if past criminal activity could interfere with a person's ability to perform a job. For example, if Alice is applying for a job as a bank teller, that bank may ask on its application form whether prospective employees have criminal convictions and refuse to hire her if she does. Applicants do not have to make known arrests that did not lead to convictions.

The Ontario Human Rights Code, and similar legislation in Quebec, would permit a person who was convicted of a crime to claim she or he has no criminal record if she or he obtained a pardon under the Criminal Records Act (Canada). Also the question as to whether one has a criminal record or not could be asked only where this would be important because of the nature of the employment. Some companies may have to bond their employees, for example, but cannot obtain a bond for someone with a criminal record.

In British Columbia, a woman was awarded $3,700 by a human rights tribunal when she was fired from her job driving a mobile catering truck because of a previous drug offense conviction. The tribunal gave her $2,200 for lost wages and $1,500 for humiliation and loss of self-esteem.

TESTING JOB APPLICANTS

Alice was asked to take a personality test for the sales representative job. Psychological tests of this kind are permitted if they have been shown to be valuable in predicting job performance. However, tests that are used to discriminate on the basis of race, color, religion, sex, age, or national origin are illegal. For instance, a test full of questions containing Canadian slang might be found to discriminate on the basis of national origin.

Drug tests

Requiring employees to take drug tests may be illegal in certain circumstances. For example, some human rights statutes may regard drug dependency as a handicap. In such cases, drug testing will be considered discriminatory if it singles out those dependent on drugs for disciplinary measures. For jobs such as truck drivers, taxi drivers, pilots, and perhaps jobs in chemical and nuclear industries, drug testing may be considered reasonable (that is not discriminatory) by the courts.

The Ontario Human Rights Commission prohibits employment-related medical examination unless employment has been offered. Such examinations are permissible after an employee has been hired, if there are specific physical requirements for the job. Those failing such tests must be "reasonably accommodated." An Ontario employer cannot legally require employees to undergo drug tests unless he has a reasonable basis for believing that an employee is taking drugs and that this will adversely affect work quality or job safety in the workplace.

See Drug Testing.

Polygraph tests

A polygraph, or lie detector, attempts to measure a person's truthfulness by electronically monitoring physical reactions as the person is being asked various questions.

Only New Brunswick and Ontario explicitly prohibit employers from requiring employees to take lie detector or polygraph tests. Moreover, employers are forbidden to obtain information on such tests an employee may have undergone elsewhere. Should an employee be fired because of such a test, the Director of Employment Standards can either reinstate her with or without compensation (for lost wages and such), or order that she be given lost wages up to $4,000 without reinstatement.

It is possible that your province's human rights legislation on privacy rights protects you from mandatory lie detector tests. Or if you are a member of a trade union, you may be protected under the terms of your collective agreement. See also LIE DETECTOR TEST.

TERMINATION OF EMPLOYMENT

Suppose that, nine months after beginning her job as a sales representative, Alice and her boss have a major disagreement and he fires her. Alice is furious and wants to sue. What rights does she have?

Firing at will

If an employer has "just cause" (in the legal sense) to fire someone (theft, for example, is always "just cause"), then no notice need be given to the employee. She may be fired on the spot. In addition, the employer will not be liable for the consequences of abruptly ending the "justly fired" employee's job. However, if there is no "just cause" for firing, the situation changes. And it depends on the type of employment contract.

There are contracts that clearly specify a period of time for which the contract will last (that is, six months, two years or so on). Or there are contracts that last for an indefinite period of time.

In the case of short-term employment contracts, the party who suffers a breach of contract is entitled to sue for the amount of money that would have been earned had the contract been performed. The complaining party also, out of fairness to the defendant, must try to cut his or her losses—called mitigating damages. However, whoever makes the first move to end an "indefinite term" contract must give reasonable notice to the other party (in order to give a little time to find a replacement worker or, in the case of a terminated employee, to find another job). The length of the required notice varies depending on the employee's years of service, age, and level of specialization.

Some employees with a sufficient amount of service at a given job can be reinstated under employment standards legislation when they are fired for "no just cause." Firings based on racial, sexual, religious or other discriminatory motives are never "just cause." For example, in one case, an employee's supervisor suggested "doing things together" with her. The employee refused and was later discharged from her job. She successfully sued, was awarded $3,000, and got her job back. In British Columbia, a man, fired for lying about what he did on his own time, was likewise awarded one year's salary in lieu of notice because the lie was not at all related to his work and he was under no obligation to explain where he was on his own time.

Whistle-blowers and others

Workers may not be fired from their jobs for exercising their legal right to report hazardous or unhealthy working conditions to the Occupational Health and Safety Commission (OHSC) or to other agencies that monitor the workplace. The courts have also refused to uphold an employee's termination when he has reported illegal activity or when his wages have been garnisheed.

Alberta, Manitoba, Newfoundland, Saskatchewan, Ontario, Prince Edward Island, and Quebec expressly prohibit reprisals against employees serving jury duty. See OCCUPATIONAL HEALTH AND SAFETY COMMISSION; WHISTLE-BLOWER.

Challenging a termination

If the reason given for termination is unsatisfactory work, but the employer or immediate supervisor has never shown any dissatisfaction with the employee's job performance, the worker may have a basis for challenging the dismissal. Some courts have found it unfair to fire an employee without warning him that his job performance is not up to par and without making any suggestions about how he might improve. See DEFAMATION.

Even in provinces where the employer does not have to tell the employee why he was dismissed, the reason may be learned through other sources. For example, if you have the right to see your personnel files, you may uncover the reason by looking carefully at your employment records. Or you may learn why you were fired if you apply for unemployment compensation; an employer is required by law to give a reason for firing you if he disputes your eligibility for unemployment insurance (UI). You may always appeal a decision refusing you UI benefits because you were fired. See EMPLOYEE PERSONNEL RECORDS.

Constructive discharge

The resignation of an employee in order to avoid intolerable working conditions or illegal activities is known as constructive discharge. Suppose Alice's boss touches her "accidentally" at every opportunity and asks her if she really is happily married. Her complaints about his behavior go unheeded, and she sees no way out except to resign. She would then have good reason to sue her employer and would also be eligible for unemployment benefits.

Payment on termination

Employment standards legislation, which dictates when an employee must be paid after termination, varies between provinces. For example, in Alberta, employees must be paid "forthwith." In Ontario, payment must be made within seven days.

To find out which law applies to you, contact your province's Ministry of Labour, Labour Commissioner or other relevant agencies listed in the Blue Pages of your telephone book. See also JOB DISCRIMINATION.

EMPLOYEE PAYCHEQUE DEDUCTIONS

The gross amount of money you earn as an employee is your salary or wage. However, unless you are an independent contractor, your paycheque will be subject to deductions—for Canada (Quebec) Pension Plan, income taxes, unemployment insurance (and sometimes union dues or company pension fund contributions).

Employer's deductions

There are various circumstances in which employers will want to make deductions from pay otherwise owed to an employee.

Suppose Rose is unable to balance her cash register at the end of her shift. Can her boss deduct the missing money from her pay? Or, imagine that Karl has just borrowed $100 from his employer. Can Karl's boss deduct repayment of the loan from the wages owed to him? The general rule in employment standards legislation is that employers may make deductions from wages only where they have a right to do so under statute, court order, collective agreement or with the written consent of the employee. This rule is very strictly followed. There are even cases where an employee has been convicted of stealing from an employer, yet the employer cannot deduct the loss from wages owed. She must take the employee to court to recover the amount stolen. Generally there is no right to deduct wages for inefficient work. However, exceptions have been made where piecework is the basis of payment for work done.

There is no limit on the types of deductions that can be made from an employee's paycheque. However, the law places limits on the amounts of some deductions, such as wage garnishments or deductions to cover cash register shortages. See GARNISHMENT; INDEPENDENT CONTRACTOR; SOCIAL SECURITY.

EMPLOYEE PERSONNEL RECORDS

Arthur suspects that his supervisor has put some negative job-performance evaluations in his file. He asks to see his file, but his request is denied. Arthur argues that it is, after all, his personnel file, and he should be able to see it.

Unfortunately for Arthur, an employee is not automatically entitled to examine his personnel file. Employees are generally not given access to their files because unlimited access might inhibit superiors from making frank evaluations of job performance. In fact, the right to inspect a personnel file is generally available only when established by law. Since your file could contain everything from your job application and performance evaluations to medical records, letters of reference, and other personal information, you may want to find out whether the law permits you to examine it.

GOVERNMENT EMPLOYEES

Federal government employees and employees of provinces that have enacted record-access laws usually have the right to see their personnel files. This often means the employee can not only read the file but also make copies of documents and dispute information contained in it. For example, if Arthur is a federal employee and an insurance company wants certain information from his personnel file, Arthur has the right to inspect it first. If he finds any inaccuracies, he can request that they be corrected. If they are not, his employer must give him a reason.

PRIVATE EMPLOYEES

Employees in the private sector have no general right to see their personnel files held by their employer. However, such rights may exist under collective agreements or individual employment contracts.

PRIVACY

Just because Arthur may not be able to examine his file does not mean that the information is never disclosed. For example, employers must report certain biographical and statistical data to government agencies. The information that can be disclosed to a government agency, however, is generally not of a personal nature. See CONSENT FORM; PRIVACY RIGHTS.

EMPLOYEE RIGHTS

Your rights as an employee are largely determined by the legal restrictions placed on your employer—and they are often few in number. Essentially, employers cannot discriminate in hiring, firing, or promoting employees on the basis of race, color, national origin, religion, sex, age, or disability. But otherwise, the employer-employee relationship is a matter of contract law.

Unless your employment agreement (or union contract) lists special rights that you are entitled to as an employee, or unless you are employed by the government and thus have certain protections spelled out by law, your employer is generally free to set whatever policies he wishes as conditions of employment, even if these policies seem unreasonable. If you are what is known in legal language as an employee at will (one who may terminate his employment at any time)—and most employees are—your employer in turn can fire you at will and does not even have to give a reason for firing you.

EMPLOYEE PRIVACY

You probably regard your privacy as sacred, but your employer may not, depending on the circumstances.

Searching employees
Unreasonable searches and seizures are forbidden by federal and some provincial human rights legislation. Typically these laws prevent only the government or its agents from conducting such searches. But this is not always so. In Quebec, for example, human rights legislation also applies to private employers.

Employers who are burdened with widespread employee theft and illegal drug use in the workplace sometimes claim they must resort to searching employee lockers, purses, lunch boxes, and so on in order to control these problems. However, such searches may not take place unless the right to search was included in the employment contract and the employee agrees to the search. For all practical purposes, employers should not search employees who do not consent to it.

Employers can arrest only an employee they have seen "breaching the peace," committing a crime, or one they have reasonable grounds to believe is being hotly pursued by the police for having committed a crime. Employers who suspect theft should call the police to make the arrest.

Use of company phones
Employers have the right to limit or prohibit the use of company telephones by employees for private calls. However, the Criminal Code makes it an offense for employers to listen in on an employee's telephone conversation.

Candid cameras

Employers may also conduct surveillance of workers by observing them at their desks and installing video cameras that show areas of the workplace. As long as the employer does not create an unnecessary invasion of privacy, such as installing video cameras in the rest rooms, this monitoring activity is permissible.

PROHIBITED ACTIVITIES

Remember that, although all these actions are generally permitted when used for legitimate and legal business purposes, the situation becomes different when the employer exceeds certain limits. For example, an employer may not make physical threats toward an employee or refuse to allow him to leave the premises. Such actions could amount to assault and false imprisonment, and the employer could be sued.

An employer cannot single out employees for search or surveillance or similar activities on the basis of their race, religion, sex, and the like. If, for example, an employer searches the purses and briefcases of Korean-Canadian workers only, the searches would be considered discriminatory and therefore illegal. But if the searches are applied to all employees who consented, they will be allowed.

OUTSIDE THE WORKPLACE

You may think that what you do when you are not at work is strictly your own business, but your employer may think otherwise. Depending on the particular facts, an employer may be justified in firing an employee when there is conflict between her job and what she does in her free time. Sometimes the mere possibility of conflict can justify termination. In one case, a bank employee was fired because she was living with a convicted bank robber, even though there was no proof she had given her companion security secrets.

Employers have also been allowed to fire employees for engaging in conduct that had a negative impact on the employer's reputation or business. In one case, a sales representative made anti-Semitic remarks about a client outside working hours. The client refused to deal with the employer of the sales rep, who was then fired, a firing upheld by the court.

See also AGE DISCRIMINATION; EMPLOYEE; EMPLOYEE HIRING AND FIRING; EMPLOYEE WORKING CONDITIONS; JOB DISCRIMINATION; PRIVACY RIGHTS; REFERENCE.

EMPLOYEE WORKING CONDITIONS

Employers have an obligation to provide employees with a healthy and safe environment in which to work. In addition, they must provide special protection to workers subject to unique hazards. For example, a health-care company may be required by law to provide protective clothing and headgear to technicians who use radioactive materials. An assembly plant whose employees operate heavy machinery may be required to install special safety devices to prevent injuries. And workers at a noisy construction site may be required to wear protective ear coverings.

HEALTH AND SAFETY IN THE WORKPLACE

Industrial accidents are the third leading cause of death in Canada after cancer and heart disease. Therefore there is a great deal of legal regulation of workplace safety, although some critics claim that even this is not enough. Conditions in the workplace are governed primarily by provincial legislation, but also under some federal laws (such as the Canadian Labour Code). Some provinces, such as Ontario and Quebec, have comprehensive statutes dealing with occupational health and safety. Other provinces, British Columbia, for example, have many statutes that regulate health and safety on an industry-by-industry basis (laws such as the Factory Act, the Mines Act, the Gas Safety Act, the Railway Act, etc.). Even where a province has a general occupational health and safety law, regulations are often contained in other related statutes. Some types of work, such as teaching, domestic work and farming, may be exempt from occupational health and safety laws. Check with the appropriate government agencies.

Often, health and safety laws allow workers the right to refuse unsafe work. If you believe you or others are in danger of workplace injury, you should report the safety hazard immediately to your supervisor or job-site safety committee. You cannot be fired for exercising a right under health and safety legislation.

SMOKING

Because governments at all levels now have antismoking laws, and because there is growing concern about the adverse health effects of smoking, many workplaces limit the areas where employees may smoke, or prohibit smoking entirely. See also SMOKING.

EMPLOYMENT AGENCY

The purpose of an employment agency is to bring employers and job seekers together. Employment agencies help job hunters by providing referral and counseling services, and they help employers by locating and screening job candidates. Agencies generally act on behalf of the employer, but they do provide a service to both parties, just as real estate agents do. Before you use an employment agency, you should be aware of your rights and your responsibilities.

SIGNING A CONTRACT

Employment agencies often require you to sign a contract before they will help you to find a job. You should read the contract carefully so that you know whether you will owe the agency money, and if so, when.

Your contract should state the fee to be charged, who will have to pay it (you or the employer), and the conditions of

---

CHECKLIST
Choosing the Right Employment Agency

Looking for a job is hard work, and finding the employment agency that can best help you is not easy either. Listed below are some questions you should ask before you register with an employment agency.

■ HOW LONG HAS THE AGENCY BEEN IN BUSINESS?
Since a number of employment agencies go out of business fairly quickly, be careful to choose one that has a good reputation and a proven track record. To find out whether there have been any complaints about the agency you are considering, call your local Better Business Bureau.

■ IS THE AGENCY EXPERIENCED IN PLACING PEOPLE WITH YOUR BACKGROUND?
Employment agencies are becoming more and more specialized. For example, an agency that primarily places engineers may not be able to help you find a job as a teacher.

■ WILL THE AGENCY HELP YOU IMPROVE OR REFRESH YOUR JOB SKILLS?
Many agencies provide job seekers with access to word processors, computers, printers, and other facilities. If you need such services, find out whether the agency provides them.

■ CAN THE AGENCY HELP ITS CUSTOMERS WITH RÉSUMÉS AND INTERVIEW SKILLS?
Many employment agencies will help you write a résumé and coach you on how to conduct yourself during a job interview. If you need this kind of help, find out how much you can expect before signing a contract. But beware of agencies that charge a fee up front for these services. They may offer little more than a poorly written résumé and a few photocopies.

■ WHAT ARE THE TERMS OF THE CONTRACT?
Employment agencies will often ask you to sign a written contract before they will help you. Read it before you sign, and find out whether you have any financial obligation to the agency and whether the agency is entitled to a finder's fee even if you manage to locate a job on your own. Whether or not you will owe the agency money even if it fails to place you in a job is an important consideration.

---

payment. If you are responsible for the fee, you will usually have to pay it when you accept the job the agency found for you. Should you change your mind and never start work, or even if you quit the job soon after you take it, the agency is

usually still entitled to its fee. Check your contract to see what happens if the agency is only partially responsible for finding you a job. For example, suppose an agency sets up an appointment for you with an employer. Although you are not hired for that particular job, the company keeps your résumé and calls you later about another opening, for which you are hired. Even though the agency's role was indirect, its efforts to some degree resulted in your getting a job. Therefore, you may have to pay the agency's fee.

DISCRIMINATION BY EMPLOYMENT AGENCIES

Employment agencies cannot refuse to refer an applicant to a prospective employer on the basis of age, sex, religion, race, color, national origin, or disability. Employment agencies are also prohibited from sending employers lists of job applicants that classify people according to these categories.

HEADHUNTERS

If you are in a management position, during your career you may be contacted by an executive recruiter, or "headhunter." Headhunters use their contacts in the business world to learn about promising or successful managers, and then try to match these individuals with a company that hires the headhunter to find employees with particular qualifications.

Headhunters are generally legitimate business people, and some of them may be able to help you find a good job. But be wary of any firm that charges a fee. Many of these firms say they are able to "tap the hidden job market," providing access to personnel managers and top executives. In reality, they may offer little more than a résumé service and a list of telephone numbers for you to call.

OTHER CAUTIONS

Be careful, too, about dealing with firms that promise to find you a lucrative job in a foreign country. After the 1991 Gulf War, various companies began to advertise employment opportunities related to the rebuilding of Kuwait. They offered to obtain interviews and jobs in return for fees that sometimes ran into hundreds of dollars. In fact, no jobs were available, and in many cases these companies closed their doors and disappeared before any legal action could be taken against them.

Employment Canada or the personnel departments of the various federal and provincial ministries will have lists of any public service job openings. Check with them periodically.

ENGAGEMENT, BROKEN

After a long-distance courtship, Jessica agrees to marry Brian. To be with him, she quits her job in a large city and then moves to a small town, where she begins working—without pay—as Brian's bookkeeper. Three months after the move, and a month before the wedding, Brian breaks off the engagement, saying he does not love Jessica anymore. He asks her to return the engagement ring and leave.

A few days later, Jessica receives the bill for their wedding invitations and wonders if she should sue Brian for what she feels he owes her. Does Jessica have any right to make Brian pay for a portion of the wedding expenses? Can she keep the ring? What about her moving costs and earnings from the job that she gave up?

RETURN OF ENGAGEMENT GIFTS

Jessica will probably be able to keep her engagement ring, because Brian broke the engagement, and he has no right to expect the return of a gift he gave in contemplation of marriage. Jessica also has the right to ask Brian to return any gifts she gave him, since he broke the engagement. If Brian and Jessica had mutually agreed to break their engagement, they would each be obliged to return the gifts they received from each other. In addition, Jessica can sue for costs incurred by the broken promise under breach of promise. See also BREACH OF CONTRACT; BREACH OF PROMISE.

ENTRAPMENT

Entrapment takes place when law enforcement officers induce a person to commit a crime that he had not planned to commit and then prosecute him for the crime.

One day while walking down the street Karl was approached by Debbie, an undercover police officer. They started talking, and after a few minutes, Debbie said she had some mari-

REAL LIFE, REAL LAW

The Case of the Pressure Police

Shea was approached by undercover police officers who asked him to sell them drugs. Shea refused. The police officers regularly approached Shea over the next six months, asking him over and over to sell them narcotics. Each request was refused. Eventually, the police officers started to threaten Shea. As well, they offered him a large sum of money to comply with their demands. Finally, Shea gave in, sold the officers some drugs, and he was arrested. At trial, he said in his defense that he had been unfairly entrapped by the police.

Shea won his case. Given all the circumstances, the Supreme Court of Canada found that despite society's interest in curbing drug trafficking, Shea had been treated unfairly by the police.

In another case, Joe was standing in front of a mall. The police had earlier begun an investigation following reports that drug trafficking was common in the area. An undercover police officer asked Joe for some drugs. Joe said he had none. The police officer asked again. This time Joe sold the drugs.

At trial, Joe lost. It was found that the police officer had been acting on a reasonable suspicion to ask Joe for drugs (given the reputation of the mall) and that there was no reprehensible inducement in this case.

not believe he was involved in any criminal activity, or else that they suspected he was involved in criminal acts, and induced him to commit an offense. In the first instance, the court will likely decide the accused was a victim of entrapment if the officers were not conducting a legitimate investigation. In the matter of inducement, the courts will look at the type of crime, how many attempts were made to induce the accused into committing the act, what inducements were offered, and whether police took advantage of a vulnerable person (someone with a mental handicap or substance addiction, for example).

Even though entrapment is a legal defense under the Charter of Rights and Freedoms, the Supreme Court of Canada has stated that only in the "clearest of cases" can an accused benefit from it.

juana if Karl wanted it. Karl had never thought of trying marijuana, but he liked Debbie and agreed to take some to please her. Debbie pulled the marijuana out of her jacket and asked Karl to hold it for her. Within minutes, Karl was surrounded by police officers and arrested for possession of marijuana. At his trial, he used entrapment as his defense.

for the person to do so, their actions do not constitute entrapment.

Suppose the police send a female officer dressed in plainclothes into an area where several purse snatchings have occurred. If a man snatches her purse, there has been no entrapment because the police officer did not set up the crime or induce the man to commit it.

WHEN DECEPTION IS FAIR

Courts usually disapprove of trickery on the part of the police but allow it within certain limits. If someone already intends to commit a crime, and the police simply make it easier

HOW THE COURTS DECIDE

To prove entrapment, the accused must show that the police provided him with an opportunity to commit an offense, in effect planned the crime, even though they did

ENVIRONMENTAL PROTECTION

Reflecting an increased public interest in protecting the environment, federal and provincial governments have enacted laws regulating or prohibiting harmful acts and encouraging or developing environmentally friendly activities. Some legislation regulates or prohibits harmful acts, such as industrial pollution, others foster environmentally friendly places, such as picnic areas. Some, such as the Arctic Waters Pollution Prevention Act, the Ontario Water Resources Act, and the British Columbia Mines

CHECKLIST

What You Can Do to Protect the Environment

Much of the job of protecting the environment is up to individuals like you. As a consumer, you can help in a number of ways:

■ **BE ENERGY-CONSCIOUS.**
If you have energy-efficient appliances, a car that gets good mileage, and proper home insulation, you will save energy and a lot of money too.

■ **RECYCLE.**
Glass, newspapers, cardboard, plastic containers, metal cans, and aluminum foil can all be recycled. If you don't have a recycling center in your community, try to get one started.

■ **DISPOSE OF CHEMICAL WASTES WISELY.**
Never dispose of used motor oil, gasoline, or household chemicals by pouring them down a drain or into a sewer. Some communities provide for the pickup of hazardous wastes.

■ **AVOID CONTAINER WASTE.**
Buy reusable containers and, when possible, choose products that are not overpackaged.

■ **REPORT POLLUTERS.**
Report pollution violations to your local environmental agency. If appropriate, file a lawsuit against a company or individual who is causing damage to the environment.

Act deal with specific concerns. The Canadian Environmental Protection Act and various provincial statutes under similar names provide more all-inclusive legislation.

In Ontario, under that province's Environment Bill of Rights, anyone found criminally negligent of causing an environmental disaster is subject to imprisonment and unlimited fines. The act, which also provides for the appointment of an environmental commissioner to monitor government performance on the environment, allows for search and seizure, detention and forfeiture of polluters' property. Polluters' names are available to the public, any member of which may sue a polluter before the courts. In addition, the Ontario Court of Justice confirmed a ruling that the directors of a company fined for pollution cannot be indemnified by the company itself, but must pay the fines from their own pockets.

Environmental law is not just concerned with toxic substances. It also regulates everyday things such as noisy vehicles—aircraft, automobiles, and boats, for example. Public Harbours and Port Facilities acts are among legislation prohibiting the sounding of horns, whistles, and other noisemakers, except under certain circumstances. The various provincial Highway Traffic acts specify permissible noise levels for motor vehicles. The most obvious example of this type of regulation would be the requirement that all cars have proper mufflers.

EQUAL PROTECTION OF THE LAW

The Canadian Charter of Rights and Freedoms states that every individual is equal before and under the law, and mentions that this equality is to be upheld without discrimination based on race, color, national or ethnic origin, religion, sex, age, or mental or physical disability. Exceptions may occur in the case of equal-opportunity laws, programs and activities as well as affirmative action programs.

Suppose that Marleen, an African-Canadian businesswoman, has just moved to Middleton. As an ambitious newcomer she would like to get to know the local business and community leaders, most of whom are members of the Willow Club. Marleen applies for a membership but is turned down. Because the club has no African-Canadian members, Marleen suspects racial discrimination. So she files a lawsuit against the club, claiming she has been denied equal protection of the laws.

If the Willow Club is funded and operated by the province, and Marleen makes a good case that she was denied membership because of her race, she will probably win her lawsuit. However, if the Willow Club is privately run, her lawsuit will probably fail because equal protection of the laws does not apply to private organizations, no matter how discriminatory their rules may be.

Suppose the privately owned Willow Club conducts educational workshops and seminars for the Middleton business community, which are partially funded by the province. In this instance, Marleen's lawsuit would have a good chance of winning, because the charter prohibits discrimination by organizations supported or funded by the government.

The charter is based on the premise that government should benefit everyone, not any particular group of people to the exclusion of others. The provinces may pass laws that apply to one group of persons, only if doing so promotes legitimate governmental purposes. But a province may not classify people in an arbitrary way— the classification must have a rational basis and serve the interests of the public.

GOVERNMENT ACTION ON BEHALF OF SPECIFIC GROUPS

Equal protection does not require that all persons be treated in the same way. But it does require that when a province acts on behalf of a distinct group of people, it does so in order to promote a legitimate purpose.

For example, courts have found that minority job programs do not violate the charter because they serve to develop human resources. Nor is the charter violated when wealthier individuals are taxed at a higher rate than others, because the increased revenue will be used to pay for government needs.

REAL LIFE, REAL LAW

The Case of the Spurned Sportswoman

Deborah was prevented from playing hockey on a boys' team under the rules of the Midville Minor Hockey Association. She felt that she was being discriminated against on the basis of her sex. But the apparent problem was that the association is a private, not a government organization.

On this basis, it seemed that Deborah had no case, since the government would have to be involved with the association— even indirectly—in order to invoke the Charter of Rights and Freedoms

As it turns out, however, the association was relying on a provincial law that allowed discrimination on the basis of sex in certain sporting activities. Since it was the province's own law that allowed Deborah to suffer discrimination, the court found that the charter applied. Deborah won her case, because the charter overrides any conflicting provincial legislation.

Conversely, if a person is denied his constitutional right to legal representation in a criminal proceeding because he cannot pay a lawyer, that person is being denied the equal protection of the laws. As a result, legal aid plays an important role in courtrooms across the country.

PROHIBITED CLASSIFICATIONS

Under the current interpretation of the charter, certain groupings, or classifications, are almost always prohibited as violations of equal protection because they serve no legitimate interest. Other classifications are frequently (but not always) prohibited.

Laws that classify people on the basis of race, color, national origin, or religion are almost always prohibited. Thus if Mary, a Baptist, becomes engaged to

a Roman Catholic, but her application for a marriage license is denied because of a statute against interdenominational marriage, that statute could be invalidated on equal-protection grounds. If Mary became engaged to another woman, however, and her marriage license were denied because of a law prohibiting same-sex marriage, she would have no basis for a lawsuit because such laws apply equally to everyone and are deemed to serve a legitimate interest. (Since laws denying same-sex spousal benefits have recently been overturned by the courts, it is likely that the issue of same-sex marriages will come before the Supreme Court of Canada in the next few years.)

Classifications based on sex are sometimes allowed, but only if they serve an important government objective. For example, suppose Tiffany, a police recruit, fails a demanding physical-agility test and is not appointed to the police force. Stating that women fail the test more often than men and that the test is therefore discriminatory, Tiffany sues the force, claiming that her rights to equal protection have been violated. Her lawsuit will probably fail, because courts have found that the physical demands of police work justify such tests. If, however, Tiffany and other women are passed over for promotions merely because they are women, their claims to being denied equal protection are justified.

AGE DISCRIMINATION

Age is another classification that the court sometimes allows, but age-discrimination claims are always closely examined. For instance, it is not a violation of the charter to require people to reach a certain age before they can vote or serve in the military. This requirement is based on the grounds that a person must achieve a certain level of physical and mental development before he can intelligently elect a public official or undergo the strains of combat. Laws setting minimum-age requirements for drinking alcohol and driving have all been upheld for similar reasons.

The same kind of reasoning applies to classifications based on maximum age. For example, the charter is not violated by a law that requires uniformed police officers, or judges, to retire when they reach a certain age. In cases challenging

these laws, the courts have held that there was a legitimate interest in ensuring that police officers possessed the physical strength and stamina of youth and that judges possessed acute mental powers.

EQUITABLE DISTRIBUTION

Originally, in common law, a married woman had no legal personality. Upon marriage she merged with her husband, and for all practical purposes ceased to exist in the eyes of the law. Her husband became the owner of her property, and only he could sell or otherwise deal with it. The woman's dower rights gave her one-third of her husband's real estate upon his death.

Eventually all provinces except Quebec passed Married Women's Property acts, giving married women the right to own and sell property as if they were single. Thus was created the legal regimes of separation as to property, where each spouse owned and controlled her or his property whether it was obtained through work, inheritance, or as a gift.

FAMILY ASSETS

Although this separation of property worked well enough during marriage, women typically lost out when a marriage broke down. Often the husband

was able to accumulate property while his wife stayed home to raise the family. This was the situation up to the 1960s and 1970s, when all the provinces passed Matrimonial Property and Family Law acts in an attempt to alleviate the difficulties faced by divorced women. Under this legislation, certain assets, such as the matrimonial home, became "family assets" subject to equal partition upon divorce or separation.

Alberta's Matrimonial Property Act declares all property subject to division on dissolution of a marriage except for property owned prior to the marriage or acquired as a gift or through inheritance.

British Columbia's Family Relations Act defines a family asset subject to partition as "property owned by one or both spouses and ordinarily used by a spouse or minor child of either spouse for a family purpose." If one spouse contributed to the other's profession or business, that spouse can also claim an interest in the profession or business. Thus the British Columbia courts have held that a medical practice, in which the wife worked as a receptionist and accountant, was a family asset, of which she was entitled to a 15 percent share, or $30,000.

The Manitoba Marital Property Act has a somewhat similar definition of family assets, but includes saving bonds and savings accounts.

Under Ontario's Family Law Act 1986, other than gifts or inherited property, most property acquired by either spouse after marriage is deemed a family asset subject to equal division at dissolution of marriage. However, the Ontario court could order an unequal partition of family assets in favor of the "innocent" spouse if one of the partners hid some assets, or reduced his equity by taking out debts, or recklessly depleted his assets. Certain property, such as court awards for personal injury, or property acquired by gift or inheritance, is not subject to division.

Quebec's Family Patrimony Law provides for equal division of certain property, such as the matrimonial home, secondary residence, furniture, automobiles used for family purposes, as well as pension and retirement funds.

COMMON-LAW SPOUSES

Common-law spouses are not usually regarded as "spouses" in the various matrimonial property acts. In cases of common-law marriages, however, the courts, including the Supreme Court of Canada, have placed a monetary value on the common-law wife's domestic contribution in raising the family. In this sense she is entitled to a share of her common-law husband's property, since otherwise he would be unjustifiably enriched by his wife's contribution.

JOINTLY OWNED AND SEPARATE PROPERTY

All provinces make a distinction between jointly owned property (family assets) and separate property. Usually, separate property is defined by the way in which it was acquired. Property owned by

---

ABC's

OF EQUITABLE DISTRIBUTION

When you get a divorce, the court must divide your property according to the principles of equitable distribution, contained in your province's family law legislation. The court must try to divide the property as fairly as possible, taking into account various factors, such as the following:

■ You and your spouse's station in life and the standard of living you were accustomed to during the marriage.

■ The particular needs of each of you, taking into account such things as your age, health, and earning skills.

■ How long you were married.

■ The provisions for child custody and child support.

■ The source of jointly held property (whether, for instance, it was originally acquired by or given to one spouse rather than both).

■ The value of your separate property compared to the financial needs of your spouse.

■ The earning capacity of you and your spouse, and whether at any time during the marriage one partner sacrificed education and career opportunities in order to support the other or advance the other's career.

■ Homemaking and child-rearing services rendered by one or both of you during the course of the marriage.

■ Debts incurred or dissipation of assets by one or both of you while you were married.

---

one partner before marriage, or property acquired by gift or inheritance usually remains private property. However, the increased value of such assets during marriage, or interest received on such assets (if money) may be subject to division when the marriage ends.

Often, the courts must take the relevant provincial legislation and the facts of the case into account to determine what is separate property and what is jointly owned. The definitions vary from province to province and often from one judge to another.

MARRIAGE CONTRACT

Although marriage contracts are meant to set out how assets will be distributed in the event of separation or divorce, the courts are rarely bound by these prenuptial agreements. If one partner has hidden assets, or allowed assets to deteriorate, or even if adhering to the terms of such a contract would have an "unfair and unconscionable result," the courts may disregard them.

The British Columbia Court of Appeal in 1993 unanimously ruled that a trial judge can reapportion assets under a "fairly reached" marriage agreement which is unfair in practice. Said Mr. Justice Allen McEachern: "It is not in keeping with contemporary family law, thought or jurisprudence for the court to offer much deference to an agreement which is objectively unfair to its core."

DIVORCE

As the Divorce Act is a federal law, it overrides any conflicting provincial laws when it comes to making a settlement that the court considers fair and just. The divorce court may order a lump sum payment, periodic sums, or both. Also, it "may impose such other terms, conditions, or restrictions in connection therewith as it thinks fit and just," taking into consideration the length of the marriage, the spouses' respective contributions during cohabitation, and any "economic advantages or disadvantages to either one arising from the marriage or its breakdown." In fact, the court is obliged to "relieve any economic hardship of the spouses arising from the breakdown of the marriage."

This wide discretionary power usually allows for a more equitable distribution of assets and support to the spouse in the weaker position.

EQUITY

The word *equity* has two different meanings that pertain to the law. The first and simplest refers to the value of property, minus any amount owed on or secured by that property. For example, suppose your home is worth $100,000, but you owe a mortgage balance of $85,000. Your equity in your home is $15,000.

The second meaning of equity, which will be discussed in more detail, concerns the fairness or impartiality of legal proceedings. It involves a complex set of rules first established in England and later adopted by Canadian courts.

HISTORICAL ROOTS

Originally, there were two different kinds of courts in England—courts of law and courts of equity (also known as courts of chancery). If a person wanted to receive a certain sum of money, he would bring his case to a court of law. If he wanted to right a wrong that could not be satisfied by a money payment, he would bring his case to a court of equity.

Suppose that a century ago Alexander, a famous impresario, signed Natalia, the most famous soprano of her day, to perform in a concert. The day before the concert, the temperamental Natalia had a violent disagreement with Alexander and refused to sing. Alexander sued her in a court of law for the amount he lost in unsold and returned tickets. He also sued her in a court of equity. Although he could not force Natalia to sing, he could ask the court to issue an injunction—an equitable order preventing her from singing for anyone else until she fulfilled her contract with him.

Principles of equity require "clean hands," meaning that Alexander could not sue in a court of equity if he had not acted in a completely fair manner. Thus, if Natalia had canceled because Alexander had contracted to put her in a respected concert hall but at the last minute asked her to sing in a neighborhood pub, his hands would be considered "unclean" and he would be unlikely to get the injunction he requested.

EQUITY TODAY

At present, the courts in all provinces tend to favor awarding money to successful equity claimants. But equitable relief can be granted in many forms.

It could, for example, take the form of an injunction forbidding someone from doing something (such as dumping garbage on a neighbor's land). Injunctions are used when a possible wrong is anticipated and can be nipped in the bud—to limit or ban unions from picketing or launching boycott campaigns during labor disputes, for example, or to forbid ex-spouses from entering the family home during divorce proceedings.

Equity can also void contracts where it can be shown that one party was coerced into making a contract, or where a contract resulted in one party being defrauded.

Equity can also be invoked to force someone to live up to his bargain in the case of a unique property. Suppose Rose contracts with Myron to buy a rare plate collection, but later Myron decides not to sell after all. Rose can claim that suing Myron for money would be inadequate because there are no similar plate collections on the market. Because a specific object is sought, the rare plates themselves, Rose would claim for what is called "specific performance" of the contract.

Lastly, equity does not like the "finders keepers, losers weepers" rules of the playground. When someone has obtained something from another who has lost it, yet the finder has no right to that benefit, the loser may sue for what is termed in legalese as "restitution," the return of the wrongfully obtained property or other benefit.

ESCALATOR CLAUSE

An escalator clause in a contract allows a party to receive more money if certain unpredictable circumstances occur.

Suppose Joe, a contractor, agrees to build an addition to your house. When the contract is signed, Joe estimates that construction will cost $10,000. Because construction estimates are often unreliable, Joe asks for an escalator clause in his contract. If the cost of Joe's building materials suddenly and unaccountably increases, the escalator clause permits him to charge you more. It protects Joe's ability to make a profit under the terms of the contract despite unforeseen cost increases.

An escalator clause may lead to abuses. The best way to protect yourself is to refuse to sign a contract that contains one, or to sign it only if the escalation is limited to a reasonable percentage of the base amount.

Though there are no legal limits on escalator clause increases, the courts will not enforce those that are clearly unconscionable. See also CONTRACT.

ESCROW

Escrow means that money or documents are being temporarily held by a neutral third party until all the conditions of a contract are satisfied. Escrow is most often used in real estate transactions.

Suppose Mary agrees to buy office space from Atlas Realty. Before the contract is signed, she agrees to put her down payment "in escrow," meaning that she gives the money to a third party (or escrow agent), who will hold it in a special account until the closing. Mary does this as a sign of good faith, and, in turn, Atlas lets the escrow agent hold the deed to the property. See HOME BUYING AND SELLING.

ESTATE PLANNING

Your estate is the sum total of what you own when you die. Traditionally, estate planning meant arranging for the transfer of your property to your survivors in ways that minimized high estate taxes. Now that Canada has abolished such taxes, planning has taken on a broader meaning. It involves planning your investments and writing your will with the goal of maximizing the value of what you own for the benefit of your heirs.

ESTATE-PLANNING OPTIONS

Here are some common estate-planning options you can use to reduce probate expenses and delays, as well as help preserve your property:

Joint tenancy

You and your spouse (or someone else) can own your house as a "joint tenancy with right of survivorship." This means that when one of you dies, the house will automatically pass to the other person and will not be subject to probate. See JOINT TENANCY.

Life insurance

Be sure to name your spouse or other family member, not your estate, as the beneficiary on your life insurance policy. In this way, the policy is not considered a part of your estate for probate purposes, and will be paid directly to the named beneficiary.

Trusts

You can create a "living trust" payable to one or more persons. Because the property is held in a trust created during your lifetime, it passes outside your estate to those you have named, and so is not subject to probate and administration costs. See LIVING TRUST.

THE NEED FOR A WILL

Even if you have a comprehensive estate plan, you should still have a will. Most people have property that cannot be provided for by using the estate-planning options outlined above.

Suppose Abe's Aunt Helen dies and leaves her house to him in her will. Abe, a million-

221

aire, dies before he can create a joint tenancy with a right of survivorship for himself and his sister, Diane. As a result, the house becomes a part of his estate, subject to the costs and delays of estate administration. See JOINT TENANCY.

But at least Abe had a will. If he had none, provincial law would determine who would inherit the house, and if he had children or other brothers and sisters, under the laws of most provinces Diane would not have received the whole house as Abe had wished.

See also DYING WITHOUT A WILL.

PLANNING YOUR OWN ESTATE

It may be possible for you to put together a well-rounded do-it-yourself estate plan, particularly since there is an abundance of self-help materials currently available on the subject. However, you should keep in mind that the tax ramifications of estate planning are complex, and for something this important, you may want to seek professional advice.

Also, proper estate planning requires formal legal documents. If the documents are not correctly completed, the consequences could be disastrous for your survivors. For example, if a trust document is incorrectly drafted, you could jeopardize the right of your survivors to receive trust income. If your will is vaguely worded or is not signed according to the requirements of the laws of your province, your estate could be subject to lawsuits challenging its terms.

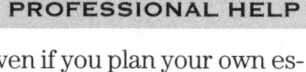

GETTING PROFESSIONAL HELP

Even if you plan your own estate, you should have the plan reviewed by a lawyer with experience in estate planning.

Many insurance agents, financial consultants, and accountants also provide estate-planning services. If you use one of them, you should first find out whether the person has anything to gain by helping you. For example, an insurance agent earns a commission on each policy he sells. This does not mean that the policy he recommends is a bad idea, or that his advice is not helpful. It does mean, however, that the agent is less likely to give you unbiased advice. For this reason you should consult a lawyer, accountant, or other professional who has nothing to gain (except his fee) by examining your estate plan. See also FINANCIAL PLANNER.

ESTIMATE

Because Al's car has been acting up recently, he takes it to Sandy, his mechanic. Sandy listens to the motor for a minute or two but cannot pinpoint the problem. Al agrees to leave the car so that Sandy can examine it more thoroughly and give Al an estimate of the repair cost.

Sandy reports that the car's valves need replacing. She estimates the job will cost $600. Al signs a work order authorizing her to begin work. The next week, however, when Al returns to pick up his car, Sandy hands him a bill for $660.

Can Sandy charge Al more than her estimate? It all depends on the laws that govern contracts for services in her province. In many jurisdictions, the Consumer Protection Act or a similar statute sets certain requirements for a contract to be binding on the buyer of services. Typically, there must be a written contract, which clearly itemizes all work to be done. The itemized work is all the seller of services can charge for once the buyer has accepted the estimate.

Sandy also sent Al a $30 bill for her estimate. Although many businesses offer free estimates as a courtesy, there is no law prohibiting Sandy from charging for her services. As always, the buyer should beware. Some companies take advantage of the widespread belief that estimates are free by offering an estimate for work that needs to be done; then they bill the unwary customer. Unless you have a definite understanding that an estimate is free, you may find yourself harassed by a collection agency and even faced with a lawsuit if you refuse to pay the bill.

To protect yourself, always find out in advance whether an estimate is free and get it in writing. You will then have evidence of your agreement in case the company later tries to charge you. If a company advertises free estimates and then tries to bill you, you have no obligation to pay.

EUTHANASIA

Meaning mercy killing (from the Greek word for "good death"), euthanasia has become an increasingly controversial topic in the past decade. Because modern medical procedures allow life to be prolonged—but not necessarily improved, and sometimes worsened—medical and legal experts have debated whether euthanasia is a valid and merciful method of ending suffering or whether it is a violation of society's prohibition against murder and suicide.

It is a criminal offense to suggest to someone else that he or she should commit suicide. It is also criminal to help someone kill himself, even if the attempted suicide fails. The issue of whether this provision of the Criminal Code may be relaxed in certain circumstances was decided by the Supreme Court in 1993. In a five-to-four decision, the court held that assisted suicide, even in extreme cases where a person is terminally ill and in a vegetative state, is illegal.

EVICTION

Sue is Arnold's tenant. In legal terms, Sue is said to be "in possession of" Arnold's premises. However, if Sue does not pay her rent (or otherwise violates the terms of her lease), Arnold may decide to begin eviction proceedings—the process by which a landlord acts to reclaim possession of his premises.

Eviction is of two kinds: actual and constructive. Actual eviction occurs when the landlord takes direct action to remove the tenant. Constructive eviction occurs when the landlord has willfully created such intolerable conditions that the tenant leaves on his own.

ACTUAL EVICTION

Actual eviction, the forcible removal of a tenant from a landlord's premises, may be lawful or unlawful. If Arnold changes the locks on Sue's apartment, this amounts to breaking the law in most provinces. More commonly, a landlord will begin legal eviction proceedings.

The eviction process
Eviction proceedings begin like other lawsuits. Arnold must file a petition, or complaint, with the court listing his grievances. He must then serve Sue with the petition and with a notice of petition informing her that he has initiated eviction proceedings and stating the time and place of the hearing. Sue has to answer the petition, including any defenses she has to Arnold's charges.

CHECKLIST

Steps Leading to an Eviction

Before a landlord can evict a tenant from a rented house or apartment, he must follow a series of legal steps. Although these steps vary both with the circumstances and with local laws, they tend to follow the same general pattern.

■ **BREACH OF THE LEASE.**
First, you must have breached (violated the terms of) the lease by not paying rent, or by some other serious misconduct.

■ **NOTICE OF THE BREACH.**
The landlord must then give you notice of the breach and an opportunity to remedy the violation (by paying the back rent, for example, if this is the problem). The notice must also state that the landlord intends to evict you if the breach is not remedied within a specified number of days.

■ **EVICTION ORDER.**
If you fail to remedy the breach, the landlord must go to court to get an eviction order.

■ **COURT HEARING.**
You must be given the opportunity to be heard by the court and to raise defenses to the landlord's charges.

■ **COURT DECISION.**
If you are found in breach of the lease, the court may allow yet another period of time for you to remedy the breach and remain in the house, or it may order you to move out within a specified period of time.

■ **EVICTION.**
If you fail to do as the court orders, the landlord may ask the local sheriff to enter the premises and remove your possessions, allowing the landlord to regain control of the property.

There are strict deadlines, which must be respected by both landlord and tenant, regarding notice that a property will be repossessed or vacated.

Defenses

In her answer to Arnold's charges, Sue may present the defense that she understood her lease was renewed automatically, unless she told her landlord she did not wish to renew, and this she had not done. Expiry of a lease is not typically sufficient to allow eviction of a tenant, unless the landlord wants the premises as a residence for himself or a relative, or unless the tenant has bothered the neighbors, or failed to keep the premises clean, pay the rent, or otherwise not respected the terms of the lease. Or Sue may claim that she has not paid her rent because the heating system in Arnold's building is faulty and he refuses to fix it. In this situation, Sue will be more likely to convince the court if she has copies of the letters sent to Arnold about the problem.

Suppose Sue agrees that she owes some but not all the back rent. The court may allow her to pay Arnold and remain in the apartment. However, Sue may be obliged to pay Arnold's court costs for bringing the eviction proceedings.

If the court agrees with Arnold that Sue is unlawfully in possession of Arnold's premises, it will issue an eviction order. The order is used to obtain a warrant that is given to a sheriff or bailiff, who will come to Sue's apartment and see that she gives up the prem-

ises. Prior to eviction, Sue will ordinarily be given several days' notice that a warrant has been issued in order to give her time to get out.

If, after eviction, Sue remains convinced that Arnold wrongfully evicted her from his premises, she can bring a lawsuit against him. In addition to regaining possession, Sue might be able to recover her moving expenses, lost profits (if she happened to be a commercial tenant), and the costs of defending herself in the eviction proceeding.

If the landlord has made an attempt to repossess in bad faith, even if his bid did not succeed, he could be sued for damages, even exemplary damages.

CONSTRUCTIVE EVICTION

Suppose Arnold wants to tear down his building and sell the property to a developer for a princely sum. He deliberately does not repair the heating system and elevator when they break down, hoping to make life so uncomfortable for Sue and the other tenants in the building that they will have to move out. This is known as constructive eviction.

Constructive eviction is any action (or inaction) that violates the basic right of every tenant to have the normal use and "quiet enjoyment" of her property. A landlord's failure to provide heat, water, and lighting or to maintain elevators can also be constructive eviction. In such situations, however, the landlord must be notified, preferably by registered letter, and given a chance to repair

the defect. The tenant should keep a copy of her letter.

Proving constructive eviction

To prove constructive eviction, Sue must show that Arnold intended to deprive her of the normal use and quiet enjoyment of her apartment. She can do this by documenting both his actions and her efforts to have him stop. In addition, she must show that the actions were so intolerable that she was forced to move out.

Surrender

Suppose Arnold tells Sue to move out and, without a word of protest, she does so. This is called surrender. Because Sue voluntarily gave up possession, she cannot later argue that Arnold evicted her. See also LANDLORD; LEASE.

EVIDENCE

Evidence consists of anything (such as records, objects, documents, or testimony from witnesses) that is presented in court to prove a point. The rules of evidence govern what kinds of information may be presented at a trial—that is, whether the evidence is admissible or inadmissible.

ADMISSIBLE EVIDENCE

Relevance determines whether evidence is admissible. Suppose Sam writes a letter to his business partner, Ralph, saying that he intends to substitute sweaters made by another knitwear firm for the 100 jeweled sweaters ordered by Jan's Boutique. The letter would be relevant evidence in a breach of contract suit that Jan files later over the substitution. However, a memo from Ralph to Sam urging him to increase production of jeweled sweaters would not be relevant.

Evidence of past crimes is frequently deemed inadmissible because it is irrelevant. Such evidence forces the defendant to defend himself against past charges, and it tends to divert the jury's attention from evidence relating to the current case.

Direct evidence versus circumstantial evidence

All evidence is either *direct* or *circumstantial*. Direct evidence stands on its own. Suppose the Crown attorney wanted to prove that Frank and Monica were lovers and so had a motive for murdering Frank's wife, Kathy, for the money Frank stood to inherit. At the trial Tod swears he saw Frank having dinner with Monica one evening, and holding her hand across the table. Tod's testimony is direct evidence.

But suppose Tod testifies that Frank, who is always prompt at meetings, showed up at a board meeting one hour late, with his hair tousled and a pink smudge on his collar. In this case, Tod's testimony is circumstantial evidence. It may point to Frank having an extramarital affair, but it does not establish that fact, and it especially does not prove that Monica was involved.

If enough circumstantial evidence accrues, however, it can in some cases decide the issue. Suppose another witness saw Frank and Monica in Frank's car, with Monica applying lip-

stick before stepping out and hailing a taxi. The jury members might conclude that the total circumstantial evidence was enough to convince them.

Other categories of evidence

Admissible evidence can take a number of forms other than the testimony of witnesses under oath. It may be a document, an object, or a demonstration. The letter that Sam wrote to Ralph, for example, is termed *documentary evidence*. So is Kathy's will, if introduced as evidence. But if Kathy's housekeeper found the keys to Monica's apartment in Frank's suit, the keys would be called *real evidence*.

If a chemist testified that the pink stain was salad dressing, not lipstick, and provided scientific evidence showing the difference between the stains, the evidence would be referred to as *demonstrative evidence*.

Character or reputation

Evidence that supports or casts doubt on a person's character or reputation is usually not admissible, since it may divert attention from the facts. If someone has a good reputation, it does not mean that he did not break the law, and vice versa.

In Canada the basic rule is that all relevant evidence is admissible unless barred by a specific exclusionary rule. So *character evidence* is sometimes admitted at trial if such evidence relates to issues other than the accused's character, is probative (that is, can prove something), and the probative value is high enough to outweigh its prejudicial effect.

For example, a witness might be called to testify that Tod, who says he often saw Frank with Monica, has a habit of lying.

In 1993, the Supreme Court of Canada ruled that character evidence was admissible in the case of a man charged with repeated sexual abuse of his niece from the age of 6 to 16. The victim's brothers all testified that the accused brutalized and terrified all the children in the household and held a virtual reign of terror. Evidence of the accused's character was in this case ruled admissible.

However, in allowing character evidence, the trial judge must instruct the jury on how to use such evidence.

Hearsay

Hearsay evidence does not come from the direct personal knowledge of the witness. Suppose that, in the murder proceeding against Frank and Monica, Tod says that Frank's friend Wally told Tod that Frank had said he wished he could get rid of Kathy, the evidence would be hearsay and the judge would not allow it.

Because it is considered unreliable, hearsay evidence was once automatically excluded and even today it is not usually admissible in a trial. For example, Tod could have misunderstood Wally, and Wally himself could have wrongly interpreted Frank's words.

Some years ago, the Supreme Court of Canada reviewed the matter of hearsay evidence, and ruled it admissible if it met two criteria: necessity (is such evidence reasonable and necessary?)

and reliability (is such evidence reliable, taking into account its timing, the demeanor, intelligence and personality of the person giving this evidence, and the absence of any reason to suspect fabrication?).

Both criteria were met in the 1990 *Regina* v. *Smith* trial. As a result, two of three telephone conversations a murder victim had with her mother just prior to being killed were admitted.

Whether to admit hearsay evidence is now decided on a case-by-case basis. If admitted, the jury must be instructed to consider other evidence on the statement's reliability, and cautioned that out-of-court statements have not the same weight as statements made by witnesses in the course of a hearing.

These revised rules on hearsay evidence can be used by both the Crown and the accused. See also HEARSAY.

Expert testimony

The Supreme Court has also overhauled the rules on *expert evidence*. In the *Lavallée* case (1990), for example, the Supreme Court accepted expert testimony on the "battered wife syndrome" from a psychiatrist.

The accused in the case had been abused for years by her common-law husband, and killed him by shooting him in the back after a fight in which he threatened to kill her. Although the expert relied to a certain degree on statements made to him by the accused (hearsay evidence), his psychiatric evidence was deemed admissible nonetheless, and helped win an acquittal for the

woman who had entered a plea of self-defense.

The Supreme Court made it clear that psychiatric evidence was required to help the court determine how a "reasonable" person who lived in an abusive relationship would react if threatened with death by the abuser. The Manitoba Court of Appeal, which heard the *Lavallée* case and from which the appeal to the Supreme Court was made, had dismissed the psychiatric evidence as based on hearsay, and dismissed the accused's plea of self-defense.

Although engineers, pathologists and specialists in the physical sciences often testify as expert witnesses, expert psychiatric evidence is relatively new in Canadian courtrooms.

Also, courts now consider taped and video recorded evidence (provided the tapes are whole and have not been tampered with), and DNA evidence, as admissible.

INADMISSIBLE EVIDENCE

Certain kinds of evidence are prohibited in court—that is, they are termed inadmissible.

Opinion and speculation

Suppose Tod is permitted to testify that he heard Frank and Kathy arguing and that Kathy had stormed out of the room looking very upset. He would probably not be permitted to say that he could tell from her appearance that Frank had just told her he loved Monica. Opinion and speculation are generally not allowed, unless a person testifies as an expert witness.

See EXPERT WITNESS.

EXCLUSIONARY CLAUSE

An exclusionary clause is the part of a contract that restricts what the parties can do to remedy the situation if their contract is broken. Suppose Jay, a dishware merchant, agrees to buy 10,000 coffee cups from Bob. Both sign a contract with an exclusionary clause stating that Jay cannot force Bob to sell if Bob changes his mind before shipping the goods. The day before Bob is to send the coffee cups to Jay, he pulls out of the deal. Because of the exclusionary clause, Jay cannot force Bob to deliver the cups, although other remedies may be available. See BREACH OF CONTRACT; CONTRACT; DAMAGES.

EXECUTOR AND ADMINISTRATOR

When you make out a will, you must name an executor (in Quebec a liquidator) who will handle your estate after your death. If you do not have a will, the court will appoint an administrator to handle your estate.

CRITERIA

You should choose as your executor someone in whom you have absolute trust and confidence. An executor should be someone (or some institution, such as your trust company) that is extremely well organized and reliable. After your death, he will be responsible for paying your debts and for distributing, selling, or otherwise managing your property according to your wishes.

Your executor's actions will be reviewed by a judge or other officials of the surrogate court which has the authority to invalidate an executor's decisions if they are found to be questionable or improper. If necessary, the surrogate court can revoke the executor's authority to act for the estate.

You can require an executor to be bonded to ensure he does not take the property for his own personal gain. But because the cost of the bond is charged to the estate, most people waive the requirement.

See also ESTATE PLANNING; PROBATE; WILL.

NAMING AN EXECUTOR FOR YOUR ESTATE

Legally, you can name just about anyone you want to serve as executor for your estate, provided that you select someone of legal age who is competent to perform the necessary duties (see checklist at right).

Ideally, she should be familiar with your personal and financial affairs. For this reason, many married people name their spouses, adult children, or close personal friends. Although there is no requirement to do so, it is usually wise to pick someone who lives nearby. This makes it easier for the executor to take care of such administrative details as settling the deceased's personal affairs, closing his bank accounts, selling property, and even appearing in court.

CHECKLIST

Your Duties as Executor of an Estate

If you are named as the executor of someone's estate, your list of chores may seem daunting, but keep in mind that you will be permitted to hire lawyers, accountants, and other professionals to help you with the more technical aspects of your duties. Even so, as the executor, you are the one who is ultimately responsible for completing the following tasks:

■ **TAKE THE WILL TO SURROGATE COURT.**
Here you will receive the court's authorization (called letters testamentary) to take control of the deceased person's property and proceed as executor.

■ **OPEN A CHEQUING ACCOUNT IN THE NAME OF THE ESTATE.**
Expenses of the estate will be paid out of this account, and all money owed to the estate will be deposited in it.

■ **TAKE AN INVENTORY.**
Obtain an itemized appraisal of all the real estate and personal property in the estate.

■ **MAKE THE PROPER ANNOUNCEMENTS.**
Notify all the deceased person's known creditors of his or her death, and publish notices in local newspapers announcing your appointment as executor, noting the time limit for filing claims against the estate.

■ **FILE CLAIMS.**
These include claims for life insurance, employee death benefits, and pension benefits.

■ **TRANSFER PROPERTY.**
This may involve transferring personal property to the estate's name and investing or selling assets as necessary to fulfill the terms of the will.

■ **HANDLE UNRESOLVED LAWSUITS.**
You must pursue any claims or lawsuits that were pending at the time the person died.

■ **PAY DEBTS.**
You must pay all the estate's legitimate debts and contest any unjustified claims.

■ **PAY TAXES.**
You will have to prepare federal income tax returns and pay all taxes due out of the assets of the estate.

■ **REPORT TO THE SURROGATE COURT.**
Submit an accounting of your actions as executor to the surrogate court, along with a schedule for distributing the remaining assets to the beneficiaries named in the will.

■ **DISTRIBUTE THE PROPERTY.**
Property must be passed to the beneficiaries, and any property placed in trust must be transferred to the designated trustees.

■ **GET DISCHARGED.**
Petition the surrogate court for a final discharge of your duties as an executor.

CO-EXECUTORS

Sometimes a testator (a person who makes a will) names two individuals, or an individual and a financial institution, as co-executors. Although most provinces permit such an arrangement, it is not usually advisable. If the co-executors disagree on how to administer the estate, they must go to court to have the dispute settled. This will delay the settlement and distribution of the estate. Naming co-executors also means extra fees that must be paid out of the estate.

Better to name an executor and an alternative or substitute executor. The substitute or alternative executor would take over the administration of the estate only if the first executor is unable to fulfill the mandate, because of death or illness for example.

Should this happen and an alternative executor has not been appointed, one will be named by the court. This new executor may not be as scrupulous in preserving your estate, or carrying out your wishes, as one named by you.

EXECUTOR'S CONSENT

Before naming an executor in your will, make sure that he is able and willing to serve. Similarly, carefully consider any request from someone asking you to serve as her executor. If you are not willing to take on the duties, it is better to say so.

Unless you want to keep your intentions private, give your executor a copy of your will. This way he will know in advance what he must do, and he can ask you about any matters that are unclear. If you do not wish to discuss the contents of your will with him, at least let him know where you keep your will.

SPECIAL RESPONSIBILITIES

If you become an executor, you are ultimately responsible for carrying out the terms of the will and for paying all taxes that are due. Should you neglect to pay taxes while you are administering the estate, you may find that you are personally responsible for paying them after the estate is settled. Similarly, if the beneficiaries decide you did not act in the best interest of the estate—if you paid out claims that they thought were unjustifiable, or made unwise investments, for example—they might sue you.

EXECUTOR'S FEES

Provincial laws entitle an executor to get paid for administering an estate. In some provinces the fee is a percentage of the total value of the property. In others, the surrogate court sets a reasonable fee for the executor's services.

Because these fees are deducted from the estate, an executor with close ties to the estate (such as a family member) often waives the right to receive payment for his duties.

ADMINISTRATORS

Most of what has been said about executors also applies to administrators. The principal difference is that, because an administrator is court-appointed when a person dies without a will, and must follow the rules set out in provincial law, she might not distribute your estate as you would have liked. An administrator is also certain to receive a fee, payable from your estate. Thus it is in your best interest both to have a will and to name an executor.

EXPERT WITNESS

An expert witness is someone whose professional or occupational training entitles him to offer a judgment or opinion on what happened in a case, even if he did not witness it. An expert may provide only information within his knowledge or experience. For instance, in a trial involving a car accident, a mechanic might give expert testimony based on his knowledge of and experience with the brake system of a particular model of car. For an expert's report to be admissible, it must be filed in court prior to the hearing and the expert must be available for cross-examination.

EXPROPRIATION

You have just made the final payment on your mortgage when you receive notice from your municipality that your property is being expropriated. The city requires your land as well as that of your neighbors as a site for a new sewage treatment plant.

When the shock wears off you call your lawyer to find out about your rights in this situation. He tells you about the doctrine of eminent domain, the inherent right of federal, provincial, and municipal governments to expropriate private property for public use.

Although property rights are not guaranteed under the Charter of Rights and Freedoms, some limits on expropriation are found in the federal Expropriation Act and similar provincial statutes. Indeed, rules against arbitrary confiscation of property go back to the common law of England. One of the earliest, which mentions that property can be taken through due process only and with compensation, is found in the Magna Carta of 1215. Lines 50-53 read: "If anyone has been dispossessed or deprived by US (the barons) without the legal judgment of his peers, of lands, castles, liberties or rights, WE will immediately restore them to him, and if any dispute shall arise thereupon, the matter shall be decided by judgment of the twenty-five barons."

WHAT CAN BE TAKEN?

Private property can be taken only for such public use as the construction of a government building, park, bridge, railway or port. It can also be taken for urban development or because the property has become a public danger and a risk to health and safety. Part of one's land can be expropriated for the construction of an electrical pylon, electrical cables, or a pipeline.

Whether all your land is taken, or if its value is diminished because of a partial expropriation, you have a right to contest the expropriation. To have it overturned, you will have to convince the expropriation tribunal that the expropriating party does not really need to use your land, or that the purpose of the expropriation is not for the public good, but is done to suit private interests. In any case where your land is adversely affected, you usually—but not always—have the right to be fairly compensated for your loss.

EXPROPRIATION PROCEDURE

If a government decides to expropriate your property, it must serve you with a notice of intent to expropriate. Before the expropriation goes into effect, it must appraise the land, and pay you what the property is worth at that time.

The Supreme Court of British Columbia set aside an expropriation attempt by that province's Minister of Transportation and Highways because the government failed to serve a notice of intention before serving its notice of expropriation. Because expropriation ran against the general common-law rule that a man's home was his castle, any ambiguity in the law was generally to be construed in favor of the property owner, said Mr. Justice Bruce McColl.

The owner of the land is not obliged to accept the appraisal of the land made by the government. In fact it is usually advisable to have your own appraisal made, using the method of appraisal most advantageous to you. By law, the government is obliged to attempt to negotiate a fair price with the owner, but if the parties cannot agree they may go before the courts, or the expropriation commission, which will decide on the fair value. These decisions are appealable by either party to a higher court.

Typically, the "fair market" price is the price that will be deemed acceptable, taking into account the depreciation (if there are buildings on the land), the price you paid and the value of crops, timber, or minerals on the land to be expropriated.

In some cases, expropriation of adjacent land may adversely affect your property, even though your land was not expropriated. Such was the case of an Ontario landowner, who bought land in a quiet rural neighborhood in order to build his retirement home. The Ontario Ministry of Transport and Communications expropriated a strip of land next to this person's home to build a highway. The case was fought all the way to the Supreme Court of Canada. Unfortunately for the landowner, the Supreme Court dismissed his case, stating that the public utility of the highway outweighed the disruption and nuisance the highway may cause. The law of nuisance did not apply in this case.

If you find that the government has expropriated your

land, and has not followed the appropriate procedures or compensated you fairly, you can ask the court for an injunction to stop the process until the issues involved have been settled. See also HABEAS CORPUS.

EXTENUATING CIRCUM-STANCES

Certain facts that make a crime seem less serious or reprehensible are known as extenuating circumstances. For example, Brian, who has no previous criminal record, has been convicted of robbing a grocery store and faces five years in prison. Prior to sentencing, his lawyer argues that Brian should be put on probation instead of serving his jail sentence. The lawyer explains that Brian, who has a wife and six children, recently lost his job and robbed the store in desperation. Brian's lawyer is asking the judge to be more lenient than usual, considering the extenuating circumstances.

The defendant's age, his family obligations, and his standing and reputation in the community are other extenuating circumstances a judge may consider.

EXTORTION

Extortion is the unlawful collection of money from someone through threat or the use of one's influence. Private individuals can be found guilty of extortion, but extortion some-

times also applies to intimidation by public officials. For example, a health inspector who threatens to close a restaurant unless the owner pays him $50 is guilty of extortion when the owner pays up. If the inspector threatens, but the owner does not pay, the inspector is nonetheless guilty of attempted extortion. See also BLACKMAIL.

EXTRADITION

Richard, who lives in Manitoba, has been charged in Illinois with smuggling thousands of pounds of illegal drugs, and Illinois wants to bring him to trial. To obtain custody of Richard, the U.S. authorities must ask Canada for Richard's extradition to Illinois. Such a surrender by one government of someone accused of a crime to another government is possible where countries have signed extradition treaties. In Richard's case, Canada may not comply with the request if authorities here feel his safety will be endangered if he is sent to Illinois. But otherwise, Richard will be arrested and handed over to U.S. officials.

When U.S. citizen Charles Ng, wanted for murder in California, was arrested in Alberta, his lawyers tried to stop his extradition on grounds that this would endanger his life, since California permits the death penalty. Nonetheless, the Supreme Court ordered Ng's extradition lest Canada become a haven for U.S. murderers.

FALSE ADVERTISING
TO
FUTURE INTEREST

FALSE ADVERTISING

Canadians are inundated by countless ads from radio, television, newspapers, magazines, the daily mail, and even the telephone. As a consequence, it is often difficult to differentiate between ads that are false and misleading and ads that merely exaggerate their claims.

Under federal law and the laws of some provinces and municipalities, false advertising—advertising that contains untrue statements—is strictly prohibited. Suppose an ad for a new cold remedy trumpets: "This amazing new discovery cures the common cold." If the manufacturer cannot substantiate this claim, the law could prohibit him from making the statement in an advertisement.

Although it is illegal for advertisers to make false statements, they are permitted to "puff," or make exaggerated claims, and they are allowed to express an opinion about their product. For instance, if the advertiser says that the cold remedy is "the most soothing relief on earth for the common cold," he is not guilty of false advertising, because no reasonable person would take it as a statement of fact.

Omitting vital information can sometimes violate false-advertising laws. For example, a muffler shop ad that claims to install mufflers "for the low, low price of $19.95" would be deceptive if it failed to disclose that the price quoted does not include the cost of clamps or pipes, which usually also need to be replaced. Thus the final price a consumer will pay is considerably more than the advertised figure.

FEDERAL LAWS

The federal government regulates advertising through such laws as the Textile Labelling Act, the Food and Drugs Act, and the Consumer Packaging and Labelling Act among others. Tobacco products must carry warnings of the dangers of smoking. The Competition Act prohibits misrepresentation of any product or business interest.

Suppose Martha, an ardent environmentalist, buys plastic garbage bags because they are marked "biodegradable." She later finds out that the bags are biodegradable only if treated with special chemicals. If Martha complains to the Bureau of Competition Policy that the garbage bag manufacturer made false, deceptive,

and unfair claims about its product, the bureau will investigate. If the complaint is valid, the bureau may attempt to persuade the manufacturer to alter the misleading advertising, or it may prosecute. Costs of such investigations and prosecutions are borne by the federal government, and guilty parties face fines and/or imprisonment. The Competition Act also compensates financially those who have suffered a loss due to false advertising.

A business that is unsure if its advertising might be misleading may contact the Director of Investigation and Research for Consumer and Corporate Affairs. This office will examine your advertisement and give you an opinion on its legality.

PROVINCIAL LAWS

All provinces have legislation for dealing with unfair business practices such as false advertising. The Business Practices Act of Ontario regulates "consumer misrepresentations" that are deemed to be false, misleading or deceptive. Victims may be able to have their transactions or agreements rescinded and recover the losses they have suffered. If this is not possible because, for example, you have already consumed the product, you may get financial compensation.

REAL LIFE, REAL LAW

The Case of the Antiweight Antidote

In the early 1970s a product called "Figure Magic" was offered by a number of outlets throughout Quebec. Advertisements for the product read "Lose by relaxing, smile as you lose! In only 90 minutes you will lose unwanted fat." Clients were measured, wrapped in strips of cloth that had been soaked in a green liquid, then covered with blankets and instructed to lie on a couch for 90 minutes. Afterward, the customer was remeasured and a cream was applied which was to be left on for 24 hours.

Eventually some disgruntled clients took the matter to court. During the prosecution by the federal government, an expert medical witness testified that it was impossible to lose fat by lying on a couch doing nothing. Employees of the outlets testified that they added inches to the initial measurements to convince the client that inches of fat had truly disappeared. The president of the company that sold the product explained that the cloth strips and liquid were only a gimmick intended to increase motivation and lessen nervousness, and perhaps persuade clients to follow a diet also offered by the company. Unfortunately for the president, the court found that the business outlets were guilty of promoting their product with an advertisement that was untrue, deceptive and misleading.

Other laws regulate specific types of businesses. For instance, the travel industry in British Columbia is governed by the Travel Agents Act, and similar legislation exists in Ontario and Quebec.

Victims of false advertising may also sue under the law of contract. Unfortunately, this is often of little help to the average consumer because of the costs and risks involved in going to court.

See also CLASS ACTION; CONSUMER PROTECTION; FRAUD; MAIL; MAIL-ORDER SALES; SCAMS AND SWINDLES; TELEPHONE CALLS.

FALSE ARREST

When a police officer, sheriff, bailliff, or anyone else with legal authority unlawfully detains a person or interferes with her right to liberty without just cause, he is guilty of false arrest.

Suppose Harry goes to the Department of Motor Vehicles to renew his driver's license. While he is waiting in line, a police officer enters the building, makes an unpleasant comment about his appearance, and arrests him. The officer refuses to tell Harry the reason for his arrest, and instead of taking him to the police station, drops Harry off in a vacant lot on the edge of town.

It later turns out that the officer is on a personal crusade against people who, like Harry, have long hair. Because having long hair is not a crime, Harry's arrest was false, and he may be entitled to sue the police officer and the city for interfering with his right to liberty, as set out in Section 7 of the Charter of Rights and Freedoms (see pages 88 to 92).

See also ARREST; FALSE IMPRISONMENT; TORT.

FALSE IMPRISONMENT

Putting someone in jail unlawfully is, as the phrase implies, false imprisonment. But the legal meaning is actually broader. False imprisonment occurs whenever one person restrains another, depriving that person of her freedom without the legal authority to do so.

According to the Charter of Rights and Freedoms, citizens have the right "not to be arbitrarily detained or imprisoned" and are guaranteed the right "on arrest or detention, to be informed promptly of the reasons therefor."

RESTRAINING SUSPECTED SHOPLIFTERS

The issue of false imprisonment often arises when someone suspected of shoplifting is detained by a merchant.

Suppose Linda is shopping at the Mallmart drugstore and buys a lipstick, which she puts into her purse. A security guard named Bud sees her doing this and thinks she is stealing the lipstick. He approaches Linda, takes her to the store's security office, refuses to tell her why he is detaining her, and locks her in the room for an hour. In the meantime, a clerk tells Bud that Linda paid for the lipstick.

When Linda is finally allowed to go, Bud explains the mix-up and apologizes, but she is fuming and threatens to sue. Linda may indeed have a case against Bud and Mallmart for false imprisonment, because she was deprived of her freedom without sufficient reason or legal authority. If Bud had explained to Linda why he was detaining her and quickly proceeded with his investigation, Linda would not be able to claim false imprisonment.

All merchants have the right to take reasonable measures to protect their property, and these include detaining suspected shoplifters. But in Linda's case, the restraint was unreasonable and therefore unlawful.

See also SHOPLIFTING.

FALSE IMPRISONMENT BY THE POLICE

Suppose Bud was a police officer. Although the police have a right to enforce the law when they think it is being violated, they cannot abuse their powers. For instance, even if Linda had taken the lipstick, she could sue Bud for false imprisonment if he locked her in his patrol car and left her there for hours without telling her the reason she was being detained.

Law enforcement officials must exercise their arrest powers in a reasonable fashion. For example, they cannot arrest someone outside their own jurisdiction (area of authority), wrongfully deny someone the opportunity to make bail, or continue to hold someone who is entitled to be released.

The concept of false imprisonment has its limits, however. A criminal defendant who has been acquitted cannot claim that he has been falsely imprisoned merely because he was found not guilty. By the same token, a police officer who acts within the bounds of his lawful authority, even if he arrests an innocent person, cannot be charged with false imprisonment.

See also FALSE ARREST.

FALSE PERSONATION

Pretending to be someone you are not in order to defraud another is known as false personation. Suppose you answer your doorbell and a man in a business suit tells you that his name is John Bailey and that he is collecting donations for the Oakwood Orphans' Hospital, located in your town. You know the cause is worthy, so you give him $50. He thanks you and moves on to the next house.

The following day, you realize that you forgot to ask for a receipt for tax purposes. When you call the hospital to request one, you learn that the hospital has never heard of John Bailey, nor does it solicit door-to-door contributions. You are a victim of false personation.

Fraudulent personation of any person, living or dead, with the intent (a) to gain an advantage for oneself or another person, (b) to obtain property, or (c) to cause disadvantage to the person being personated or another person, is an indictable offense under the Criminal Code and persons found guilty are liable to imprisonment for up to 14 years. The "advantage" mentioned in (a) can be something other than financial gain. The Quebec Court of Appeal has held that pretending to be someone else in order to avoid being arrested constitutes fraudulent personation.

It is also a criminal offense to impersonate a police officer or other public official. If you do so, or even if you simply wear a badge or uniform which is likely to cause others to believe you are a police officer, you may be convicted of false personation.

FALSE PRETENSE

The crime of false pretense, or false representation, involves misrepresenting facts or circumstances so as to defraud someone. Borrowing property with no intention of returning it, declaring that an item is an antique when it is really a reproduction, and paying someone with a cheque drawn on a defunct account or switching price tags on an item that is then purchased, are all typical examples of false pretense.

When Carol sold her car to Kevin, he specifically asked her if it had ever been in an accident. She knew very well that, six months earlier, she had crashed the car, damaging its frame. Nonetheless, she told Kevin that the car had never been in an accident. Kevin paid her $3,000, even though the car was worth only about $500. Carol therefore obtained $2,500 by false pretense.

GETTING PROMISES IN WRITING

You should always ask a seller (whether he is a private individual or a merchant) to put in writing any promises or claims about the merchandise he is trying to sell you. Should you decide to sue him for false pretense, the burden of proof will be on you, and if you do not have his claims in writing, the case will rest simply on your word against his.

See also BURDEN OF PROOF.

CRIMINAL VERSUS CIVIL CASES

In all provinces, it is a crime to sell goods or obtain money by false pretense. However, most criminal courts are overburdened with what prosecutors consider to be more serious matters, and they may not give these cases the highest priority. Therefore, a victim of false pretense may be better off starting a civil lawsuit to recover his loss.

See also FRAUD; LAWSUIT; SCAMS AND SWINDLES; WARRANTY AND GUARANTEE.

FAMILY

There is no all-purpose legal definition of the term *family*, although it generally applies to a person's spouse, children, and parents. When necessary, a statute may define the word. For example, in some places zoning laws and restrictive covenants limit occupants of a home to "family members" and define *family* as people related by blood, marriage, or adoption. These restrictions contained in some zoning laws or condominium bylaws are illegal, as they discriminate because of marital status. By contrast, other localities have extended the definition to include unmarried and homosexual couples.

Various laws recognize the uniqueness of family relationships. For example, under the Canada Evidence Act, spouses are normally not required to disclose to a court the conversation they have had during their marriage.

Family relationships are of such importance that special family courts have been established in some parts of the country, and family law has become an important legal specialty.

See also ADOPTION; CHILD CUSTODY; CHILDREN'S RIGHTS; FAMILY COURT; HOMOSEXUAL RIGHTS; INCEST; LIVING TOGETHER; ZONING.

FAMILY CAR DOCTRINE

The family car doctrine is a principle of negligence law used to impose financial responsibility on the head of a family who owns, provides, and maintains a car for his family's general use. Under this doctrine, if the owner of the car has given members of his fami-

ly explicit or implied permission to use the car, and one of them causes personal injuries or damages property while driving that car, the owner and driver will be responsible for the injuries and damages.

The owner can be held liable, or responsible, even if he was not in the car during the accident. For example, suppose that when Benjy was driving his father's car, he hit a woman on a bicycle, breaking her leg and ruining her bike. Under the family car doctrine, Benjy's father would be responsible for paying the woman damages and for replacing her bike.

When the family car doctrine is applied in a lawsuit, in some instances the court may assign liability to the person who has title to the car, even when he is not actually making the payments or providing the upkeep. If a car is being paid for and used almost exclusively by your son, daughter, or other family member, but its title is in your name, you may want to transfer the title to that person—in order to avoid being sued as the official "owner."

Although the family car doctrine typically applies to family members, it has been known to extend to situations in which a third party is driving with the permission of a family member. If the car is registered in your name, and you lead the insurance company to believe you are the principal driver, when in fact it is your teenage son, you may find that the insurance will not pay if your son causes an accident. It has also been applied to motorcycles as

well as automobiles, but not to bicycles.

See also AGENT; NEGLIGENCE.

FAMILY COURT

In a few provinces, special courts deal with family issues such as adoption, divorce, spousal support, guardianship, custody, and young offenders. These so-called united family courts represent an effort to give a single forum to various family-related legal problems.

These specialized courts exist province-wide only in Manitoba, New Brunswick, and Prince Edward Island. Some urban centers, such as Hamilton, in Ontario, and the Richmond-Surrey-Delta district in British Columbia, have also experimented with this system. In most areas of the country, however, family law matters are dealt with in a variety of settings. For example, in Ontario, these issues are generally resolved either in the Supreme Court, the county courts, the surrogate courts, or the provincial courts (family division). However, the attorney general of Ontario recently announced plans to have unified family courts operating across the province. Certain constitutional issues must be resolved in setting up these courts. At present, for example, provincially appointed judges cannot rule on matters such as divorce.

MARRIAGE AND COHABITATION

Couples seeking a legal separation, annulment, or divorce are in some areas required to go to a united family court, which also handles such related issues as alimentary pension and child support. Cases involving unmarried partners ("palimony" lawsuits in which one person seeks financial support after cohabiting with another) may also be heard in a united family court. If two people want to marry but one or both of them are not of legal age, they may apply to a united family court for permission.

Generally, divorce proceedings must take place in a superior court (with federally appointed judges), known under such names as the Supreme Court of Ontario, or the Court of Queen's Bench. See AGE OF CONSENT; PALIMONY.

CHILD CUSTODY AND SUPPORT

In the absence of a united family court, a divorced parent who wants to receive monthly child support payments from a former spouse, have the amount of support increased, or enforce a payment obligation previously ordered by a court, generally presents the case in the family division of the provincial court. Family courts may also be authorized to decide disputes over a child's legitimacy or parentage and to handle adoption procedures.

NEEDY AND ABUSED CHILDREN

Another important family court responsibility is to protect children. Child abuse and neglect cases, as well as those involving the treatment or placement of mentally ill children, are often handled by the family or youth courts. The court may limit or terminate parents' rights to care for their children, or it may file charges against parents who desert, abandon, or fail to provide support for their children. See also CHILD ABUSE AND NEGLECT.

FAMILY LEAVE

The composition of Canada's work force has changed dramatically over the last few decades, so that today there are many working women and many families in which both parents hold jobs. This has given rise to the need for employees to take extended time off work because of family illness or the birth of a child,

REAL LIFE, REAL LAW
The Case of the Dutiful Dad

At the time Françoise married Bob, she was a widow with two children. She and Bob lived happily together for several years, and had two children, Alexander and Marie. Bob liked all the children and treated his two natural children and the two children from Françoise's first marriage equally. He provided all four children with food, shelter and love.

Unfortunately, the marriage hit rough water and Françoise sued Bob for divorce, claiming support for all the children, even his two stepchildren. Bob countered that he would gladly support Alexander and Marie, but not the children of Françoise's first marriage.

The court did not agree with Bob's offer. Since he stood *in loco parentis* (in place of a parent) to the children of Françoise's first marriage, he could not unilaterally withdraw his support obligation. The family was considered to be made up of four children because of the loving way Bob had treated them all

and to be confident that their jobs will remain secure in the meantime. Family leave legislation now exists at both the federal and provincial levels, although it varies from province to province.

FEDERAL LAW

The Canada Labour Code applies to employees working in federally regulated industries, such as banking, aviation, railways, and broadcasting. An employee who has worked for at least six consecutive months for the same employer may take up to 17 weeks leave of absence for pregnancy. An application must be submitted at least four weeks before the maternity leave is to commence, and must be accompanied by a medical certificate. When she returns to work, the employee must be reinstated into her previously held position or one of a like nature, with the same wages and benefits and in the same location. Employers cannot terminate a worker's job because of a request for pregnancy leave, nor can the employer deny someone the opportunity to receive a promotion or additional training. The Canada Labour Code also provides for 24-week child care, paternity, and adoption leaves under conditions similar to those for maternity leave, and for bereavement leave for up to three days following the death of a family member.

PROVINCIAL LAWS

Depending on the particular province, provincial employment standards regarding leaves of absence for family reasons may not apply to all workers. Some employees have conditions for leave set out in their contracts of employment or in collective agreements with their employers.

With respect to maternity leave it is generally necessary to have worked for the same employer for 12 consecutive months, except in British Columbia, New Brunswick, and Quebec where it may be taken regardless of the duration of employment.

The length of the leave varies from 17 to 20 weeks. Absences due to pregnancy may be extended for up to three weeks in Alberta and for up to six weeks in Quebec and British Columbia.

Paternity, adoption, and bereavement leaves are not covered in the laws of all provinces. For instance, the Employment Standard Act of Newfoundland provides only for maternity leave, whereas Ontario allows for absences in all the above cases, and also permits employees a day off with pay on the occasion of a family wedding.

Contact the nearest office of the Ministry of Labour or the Employment Standards Commission in your province to find out about leave to which you may be entitled.

FAMILY LOAN

Sometimes when a person needs to borrow money—to buy a home or cover funeral expenses, for example—he must turn to a relative or a friend because he cannot get a commercial loan. This type of loan presents its own hazards and, if not properly and legally arranged, can result in a family feud, broken friendship, or the lender losing his money.

If you decide to lend money to a family member or to some other relative or close friend, treat the loan as you would any other business transaction. Have the borrower execute a promissory note or even a mortgage, set an interest rate, and establish a repayment schedule. These arrangements not only protect your right to be repaid but prevent Revenue Canada from considering the transaction a gift and possibly imposing gift taxes. See GIFT.

It is important that the interest rate you set for a family loan is reasonable—that is, close to current consumer rates. If not, Revenue Canada may refuse the borrower deductions that it ordinarily allows on some kinds of business loans or mortgages, and the lender may not be able to take a deduction for a bad debt if the loan is not repaid. As a lender, you must declare any interest you have received on the loan as taxable income.

As with a commercial loan, a lender is legally entitled to take a delinquent debtor to court in order to obtain a judgment for an unpaid loan. See also JUDGMENT.

FEDERAL BUSINESS DEVELOPMENT BANK

If you are experiencing problems starting up or operating a business, the Federal Business Development Bank (FBDB) may be able to help. This Crown corporation deals primarily with small- and medium-sized businesses which have been unable to obtain adequate financing in the financial marketplace.

The FBDB offers a variety of services, such as loans, venture financing, loan guarantees, export receivable financing, and management services.

The FBDB's loan division attempts to cater to the particular needs of each individual or business. Loans may be granted to enable clients to acquire land, machinery or buildings, or even to increase the working capital of an enterprise. Terms of repayment will be arranged to best suit the client. For example, seasonal businesses may have to make payments only during those months in which they are most active. The venture financing program provides business owners with equity capital to facilitate growth, at the same time allowing the owner to retain control over the operation.

The FBDB also provides an extensive counseling assistance to small enterprise (CASE) program. Experienced business people help clients with any marketing, production, accounting, or other business-related difficulties they may have.

To date, the CASE program has helped more than 125,000 Canadian businesses. Management seminars, courses, and publications such as do-it-yourself kits are also available.

The FBDB has branches in over 75 Canadian cities.

FEDERAL COURT

Because Canada is governed both at the provincial and federal levels, the country has federal and provincial court systems. The Supreme Court of Canada and the Federal Court of Canada are established by Parliament. Judicial proceedings may be started at the Federal Court, which has both trial and appeal divisions, but the Supreme Court of Canada is strictly an appellate court; it hears only cases that

REAL LIFE, REAL LAW

The Case of the Countered Court-Martial

Howard, a member of the Canadian Armed Forces, was charged with possession of a narcotic for the purposes of trafficking, and with desertion contrary to the National Defence Act. He was tried and convicted by a general court-martial and his appeal to the Court-Martial Court of Appeal was dismissed. Howard then appealed to the Supreme Court of Canada claiming that he did not receive a fair trial, because the general court-martial was not "an independent and impartial tribunal" as was required by the Charter of Rights and Freedoms. In a split decision, the Supreme Court agreed with Howard and ordered a new trial. The Court held that even though the charter specifically allowed for military tribunals, the charter also required that these tribunals be independent and impartial. The question for the Court was whether an ordinary reasonable person would consider the military tribunal "independent and impartial."

The Supreme Court ruled the answer was no. The courts-martial did not meet the standards for an independent and impartial tribunal because:

1. The judge, advocate, and members of the military tribunal did not enjoy sufficient security of tenure; they were appointed on a case-to-case basis and were not immune to the arbitrary and discretionary interference of the executive.

2. The court members did not enjoy sufficient financial security, since a military officer's pay depended in part on an evaluation of his performance, and thus the way he judged the case before him could be evaluated by a more senior officer.

3. It was unacceptable that the executive, that is the Minister of Defence, who was responsible for the appointment of the prosecutor, was also responsible for naming the judge, advocate and triers of fact (that is the other officers who would judge the case). No one who has an interest in the outcome of a trial should be in such a position of influence.

have already been dealt with at lower levels.

Federal Court authority

Both Federal Court divisions are in Ottawa, but they will conduct hearings or trials anywhere in the country to suit the convenience of the parties.

Lawyers often spend a great deal of time and energy deciding whether they can or should take a case to the Federal Court. In general, the Trial Division shares jurisdiction, or authority, with provincial courts over cases in which the federal government is the plaintiff, or cases where the subject matter includes admiralty and shipping, patents and trademarks, aeronautics and interprovincial undertakings. In order to sue the federal government or appeal rulings involving the Canadian Citizenship Act or the Immigration Act, you must go to Federal Court (Trial Division). Note, however, that the Supreme Court of Canada has recently restricted the jurisdiction of the Federal Court, which has resulted in a great deal of uncertainty and litigation in this area of the law.

A division of the Federal Court, known as the Tax Court, deals with appeals concerning the Unemployment Insurance Act, the Excise Tax Act, and decisions by Revenue Canada.

Appeals

The Federal Court (Appeal Division) hears appeals from judgments of the Trial Division as well as reviewing certain decisions and orders of federal administrative boards and commissions. If you are dissatisfied with a decision by the Federal Court (Appeal Division), you can appeal to the Supreme Court of Canada.

However, because the Supreme Court exists as much to rule on important questions of law and policy that involve national interest as to decide particular disputes, it chooses carefully the cases it hears. Permission to appeal to the Supreme Court may be granted by either the Supreme Court itself or the Federal Court (Appeal Division), although the Supreme Court makes the final determination.

CHECKLIST

How to Talk to the Government

If you want to communicate with a government agency but do not know how to go about it, check the blue pages in your phone directory or call the general inquiries number of the appropriate department. The operator will point you in the right direction. Some federal general numbers are listed below :

■ **REFERENCE CANADA**
Call 613-941-4823 for information on federal programs and services.

■ **HOUSE OF COMMONS**
For inquiries and information, call 613-992-4793
*TDD: 613-995-2266 (D)

■ **STATUS OF WOMEN CANADA**
Call 613-995-7835
*TDD:613-996-1322 (D)

■ **VETERANS AFFAIRS**
Call 613-995-6467

■ **HEALTH**
Call 613-957-2991

■ **BANKRUPTCY INFORMATION**
Call 613-995-2994

■ **PRIVACY COMMISSIONER**
Call 613-995-2410
*TDD: 992-9190 (D)

■ **JUSTICE DEPARTMENT**
Call 613-957-4223/22
*TDD: 613-992-4556 (D)

■ **INDUSTRY (CONSUMER AND CORPORATE AFFAIRS)**
Call 613-997-2938
*TDD: 613-994-0067 (D)

*Telecommunications device for the hearing impaired (TDD)

♦ **Special federal courts**
A few special courts, such as the Court-Martial Court of Appeal and the Tax Court of Canada, hear disputes involving technical subjects. The Tax Court sits throughout the country and deals with appeals of administrative decisions based on federal law, such as the Income Tax Act, the Canada Pension Plan, and the Petroleum and Gas Revenue Tax Act.

FEDERAL INFORMATION

If you need information on federal services, consult the blue pages in your telephone directory. Many departments are listed there, as well as a number to call for general inquiries. Whether you want to know about Canada Savings Bonds, unemployment insurance, or another matter, the operator will either answer your questions or direct you to the appropriate agency.

FENCE BUILDING

As a landowner, you have a legal right to erect a fence or other barrier (such as a hedge) anywhere on your property. However, before building a fence, you should determine the exact location of your boundary line. Building a fence on another person's property, even by mistake, may be considered a trespass, or the fence may become the property of the owner on whose land it is built. See ADVERSE POSSESSION.

It is also worth checking your provincial and municipal laws to find out whether any ordinances restrict the height, location, or type of fence you can build. Some municipalities require you to get a building permit before constructing a fence. If you live in a planned community, find out if your deed restricts the type of material and style of fence you are allowed to erect.

If you want to fence your property, keep in mind that:

◇ Fences that are permanently attached to the land (for instance, those with the fence posts sunk into the ground) may be considered fixtures, and therefore may legally become part of the property. If you move, you cannot take it with you.

◇ If you build a fence that is within your property boundary lines, you can alter or remove it whenever you wish.

◇ If you build a fence right on the boundary between your property and your neighbor's, it is known as a partition fence and is owned by both of you.

PARTITION FENCES

Adjoining property owners usually own partition fences as "tenants in common." In most provinces, tenants in common have equal responsibility for the construction and maintenance of partition fences, and one cannot alter or remove the fence without the other's permission. If you (or your neighbor) do not want to assume responsibility for the fence, you can make a private arrangement that gives sole ownership of the fence to the other person. Such an arrangement is essentially a contract for sale of real estate. It should be in writing and recorded in the county recorder's office, and it is binding on subsequent owners.

In some provinces, tenancy in common is established only when the fence is used by both property owners. Fence use can be difficult to establish; in some areas it may depend on whether you have completely enclosed your property with fences or whether there is a fence on only one side of your property. See TENANCY IN COMMON.

If you have a partition fence and want your neighbor to contribute to its repair, first notify her that you intend to repair the fence and expect her to split the cost. Include a written estimate, but be aware that if you do the work yourself you cannot ask for payment for your labor, only for any materials used. If she does not respond after a reasonable period of time, you can go ahead and do the work, then try to recover the cost from her. Eventually, you may have to take the case to the small-claims court.

SPITE FENCES

If your neighbor builds a fence that serves no reasonable use, but was built simply to annoy you, it is referred to as a spite fence. Suppose Greg has a dispute with his neighbor Sam regarding the appearance of Sam's backyard, where Sam keeps old car parts and tools. Greg feels that the junk constitutes an eyesore. Fed up with Greg's repeated comments and complaints, Sam builds a fence that is nine feet high and made of rough, unpainted lumber. It blocks Greg's view of Sam's messy yard, but it also blocks out the light that falls on Greg's vegetable garden. Greg decides to turn to the courts to compel Sam to alter the fence, or to order Sam to compensate him for the loss of his vegetable garden and a reduction in his property's value.

In order to win his case Greg must show that his neighbor acted unreasonably by building the fence and that his property rights have been significantly affected.

FENCE DISPUTES

It may happen that your neighbor builds a fence that you consider to be too high or that you think is situated on your property. Check with your local government, as municipalities sometimes regulate the size and appearance of fences, or otherwise impose certain restrictions on fence building. If your neighbor starts building a fence that you believe to be unlawful, it is best to notify her as soon as possible in order to remedy the situation before the work proceeds too far.

If you are an Ontario resident, that province's Line Fences Act provides that a committee of fence-viewers will come to your premises to inspect the structure and make a decision regarding its legality. The committee's decision does not affect the title to the land in question.

STEPS TO TAKE

If you believe your neighbor is building a spite fence, here are a few things you can do:

1. First investigate the local laws that restrict fence height or appearance. Try to alert your neighbor to any regulations before the fence is built so that she has time to redesign it.

2. If the fence appears to comply with local restrictions, check to see if there are any spite-fence laws on the books.

3. If you live in a community that is governed by covenants, examine them for restrictions that may prohibit the fence.

4. Check with your homeowners' association or local government representative to determine if mediation services are available. They can help you reach a compromise.

5. If mediation does not work or is not available, you will probably have to hire a lawyer and take the case to court. The burden will be on you to prove malice on the part of your neighbor, as well as to prove that you are in some way harmed by the presence of the fence.

See also BOUNDARY LINE; EASEMENT; MEDIATION; NEIGHBORS; NUISANCE; TRESPASS.

FIDUCIARY

Someone who voluntarily accepts the duty of acting on behalf of another, and in his best interest, is known as a fiduciary. Suppose your elderly father is no longer capable of managing his money—paying his bills, looking after his bank accounts, or reinvesting his certificates of deposit. He asks you to manage his affairs for him, and you agree to do so. You have become your father's fiduciary.

The word *fiduciary* is often used to describe a relationship, such as the one above, in which one person manages money or property for another. But it also describes relationships in which one person trusts another to act in his best interest, such as an executor and the beneficiary of an estate, a guardian and ward, a real estate agent and the seller, a lawyer and a client, a trustee and the beneficiary of a trust.

A trustee, for example, must manage the trust property wisely, follow all provincial and federal laws imposed on trusts, and administer the trust according to its terms. Failure to follow these procedures is considered a breach of fiduciary duty, and the trustee could be held responsible for losses suffered as a result of the breach. A fiduciary cannot use his position for personal gain, although he can be paid for performing his duties.

See also EXECUTOR AND ADMINISTRATOR; GUARDIAN AND WARD; LAWYER; TRUST.

FINANCE COMPANY

Like a bank, trust company, and credit union, a finance company makes loans to consumers for a variety of purposes, including automobile purchases, home improvements, vacation funds, and college expenses. However, finance companies usually charge higher interest rates than other lenders because they often extend credit to people who, because of poor credit standing or another reason, cannot qualify for a loan elsewhere.

Various provincial laws require lenders to disclose the true cost of borrowing, including such things as the interest to be paid, the number of payments, the amount of each payment, the total amount to be repaid, and the total of all finance charges. These types of guidelines are most often found in consumer protection acts or in cost of credit disclosure acts (called the Consumer Credit Transactions Act in Alberta). This legislation normally requires lenders to be registered so that provincial governments may suspend their operations in cases of incompetence and misbehavior. In addition, all provinces have unconscionable transactions acts which prohibit blatantly unfair interest rates and loan costs. For more information, contact your provincial consumer protection agency.

FINANCIAL PLANNER

You have recently left a company where you worked for 20 years, taking with you a hefty lump-sum payment from the company's profit-sharing plan. This is the largest amount you have ever had and you do not know what to do with it. A friend suggests that you go to a financial planner, but you are not sure what that means.

A financial planner is a person who offers personally tailored financial advice. He may make investment suggestions and help you with tax, estate, and retirement planning. A good financial planner can be extremely helpful in creating a budget, directing investments, and recommending adequate amounts of life and disability insurance.

Ultimately, however, it is your responsibility to make decisions about your financial goals and your choice of investments. You should decide for yourself whether to take some risks in hopes of getting higher financial returns. Do not make the mistake of entrusting someone else with the complete authority to make all your financial decisions.

CHECKLIST
Choosing a Financial Planner

If you need the services of a financial planner, interview several candidates before hiring one. As well as asking about their qualifications and fees, be sure to ask the following important questions:

■ **WHAT IS YOUR EXPERIENCE WITH CUSTOMERS LIKE ME?** Find out whether the planner has worked with people whose income and circumstances are similar to yours.

■ **ARE YOUR INVESTMENT PLANS DIVERSIFIED?** A good financial planner will recommend dividing your funds among several different kinds of investments, such as mutual funds, stocks, and investment-grade bonds. Be wary of a planner who favors one kind of investment too heavily—if his advice is wrong, your investment may be depleted or lost.

■ **DO YOU SELL INSURANCE POLICIES OR INVESTMENTS?** If so, find out what they are and what kind of commission the planner gets. If a planner has an interest in particular investments, you should ask what he might gain by recommending them.

■ **WHAT DO YOU CONSIDER A SOLID RATE OF GROWTH?** If a planner promises you unusually high returns, you will almost certainly be taking higher risks. If you cannot afford to take chances with your money, consider settling for smaller returns from safer investments.

■ **MAY I SPEAK TO SOME OF YOUR CURRENT CLIENTS?** A reputable planner will be happy to refer you to his other clients.

■ **WILL YOU PERSONALLY BE AVAILABLE TO ADVISE ME?** You should be aware that large financial-planning organizations may assign accounts to their junior members. On the other hand, using a one-person operation with a large number of clients may mean that the planner will not be readily available.

■ **DO YOU HAVE A BROCHURE AND A SAMPLE FINANCIAL PLAN TO SHOW ME? DO YOU HAVE LIABILITY INSURANCE? WILL A FULL DISCLOSURE STATEMENT ACCOMPANY THE WRITTEN FINANCIAL PLAN?** The more you are able to see in writing, the better you can judge a planner's qualifications.

Alberta and Quebec have enacted legislation to regulate the financial planning industry. The Alberta Financial Consumers Act has resulted in the licensing of financial planners, and guidelines on financial planning documents which now must be in language that is easy to understand. The Quebec Institute of Financial Planning requires industry members to complete a course or studies and take standardized exams. Even though the industry is not regulated in other provinces, financial planners may be subject to codes of ethics of professional associations, such as the Law Society or Securities Commission, to which they belong.

However, not all planners are professionals and almost anyone can claim to be a financial planner, regardless of his background, education, or training. Thus, many insurance agents, stockbrokers, and commodity traders call themselves financial planners, when they are in fact salespeople whose income depends on the commissions they receive from selling you policies and investments. Even though they are constrained by laws relating to negligence, fraud, breach of contract and breach of fiduciary duty, the policies and investments they offer you may not serve your best financial interests.

To avoid such pitfalls, consider using a fee-based financial planner who receives his income from the fee he charges you for your financial plan, rather than from commissions on products he sells. Depending on your income, the kind of property you own, and the complexity of your financial situation, fees can range from a few hundred to several thousand dollars. However, the fees you pay for financial-planning services may be deducted on your federal income tax return, provided that the services are related to your investments or to tax planning.

To find a financial planner, ask friends and advisers, such as your lawyer, or you can call the Canadian Association of Financial Planners, an organization that works to ensure that its members adhere to standards of ethical and professional conduct. The association also recognizes as registered financial planners (RFP) those who have worked for at least two years in the industry and who have passed a six-hour exam. The Canadian Institute of Financial Planning offers a course program as well as certification as a chartered financial planner (CFP).

If your planner has been certified by one of these two organizations, you can have some confidence that she is qualified.

As an extra precaution, you should find out if your prospective planner has ever been disciplined for financial impropriety by a regulatory body, such as your provincial insurance commission or real estate board or the Securities and Exchange Commission.

Because of recent revisions to the federal Bank Act, banks are now authorized to give investment and financial planning advice. Ask at your branch to find out what services are offered.

FINANCIAL RECORDS

Keeping financial records is a necessary chore, but it is often difficult to know which documents to keep and for how long. The following guidelines are designed to help you put your financial records in order and keep them that way.

TAX RECORDS

Because you must document your income for Revenue Canada, keep a home file containing the T4 forms that report income. If you itemize deductions (or if there is a chance that you will), save all records of potential deductions, such as medical expenses, charitable contributions, moving expenses, and any business expenses that are not reimbursed by your employer.

Because Revenue Canada generally keeps tax returns on file for six years, you should do the same, saving copies of your tax returns and all supporting records in the event of an audit. If Revenue Canada's taxation officials suspect fraud, however, their searches may go back as many years as they feel is necessary.

For the same reason, you should also keep your bank statements and your canceled cheques for six years. Store tax-related documents in a safe and accessible place, such as a metal filing cabinet.

STOCKS, BONDS, DEEDS, MORTGAGES

Stock certificates, bonds, deeds, mortgages, and similar documents should be kept in a bank safe-deposit box for extra security. When you buy or sell stocks, bonds, or real estate, put the documents that relate to the sales—such as receipts, canceled cheques, closing documents, and final statements—in your income tax files, because you will have to report any gains or losses you made on those sales to Revenue Canada.

Keep utility bills only until you receive the subsequent bills, verifying that your accounts are up to date. Of course, if you are having a dispute with a company, keep all the bills until the dispute is resolved.

CREDIT INFORMATION

Keep a list of all your credit card and automated teller machine (ATM) account numbers and the telephone number of each issuer so that you can report a lost or stolen card quickly and avoid liability for unauthorized use. Put the list in a safe but accessible place in your home.

INVENTORY OF RECORDS

Prepare a list indicating where you have stored important financial records and documents. You will find a sample personal records inventory form in the EVERYDAY LEGAL FORMS section of this book. Tell trusted relatives and friends where they can find the list in case of emergency. See also PERSONAL RECORDS.

FINE

A fine is a financial penalty imposed on someone who has broken the law. Some offenses, such as parking violations, are usually punishable only by fines. More serious offenses may be punishable by fine or imprisonment or both.

Usually a fine is imposed as a judgment, or decision, of the court, and is determined by the judge. When a fine is imposed by a court, you must pay it or appeal the sentence. The time given for payment is usually set by law; if not, the judge specifies a payment date.

If the penalty for a crime is either a fine or imprisonment, and the law does not specify a period of time allowed for payment, the court has occasionally jailed those who were unable to pay right away.

If you do not pay a fine and are jailed as a result, the law usually limits the length of your imprisonment. Suppose you receive a $100 fine for not curbing your dog and refuse to pay because you feel the fine is outrageous. The judge can order you to be jailed. However, if your local ordinance says that every day you spend in jail reduces the fine by $10, you may have to spend 10 days in jail, but no more.

In most provinces unpaid fines result in a lien, or claim, by the local government upon your property. If you do not pay the fine, you may end up losing your car or house, for example.

If someone dies before paying a fine, his estate does not have to pay the fine. Fines are one of the debts that are not wiped out when you are discharged from bankruptcy, however. See also FORFEITURE; LIEN.

FIRE

The crime of setting fire to property (either yours or another person's) is called arson. See ARSON.

Other kinds of fires, although they may seem innocent, are also against the law. For example, many communities have laws that make it an offense to burn leaves or trash in an open fire, even on your own property. In some cases, if you build a fire on your property and it spreads to a neighbor's, you may be charged with a criminal offense called arson by negligence. In addition, your neighbor can sue you for any damage your fire causes. See also NEGLIGENCE.

In some parts of the country, concerns about air pollution and fire hazards have led communities to ban or restrict the use of wood-burning fireplaces. Some communities offer financial assistance or tax incentives to homeowners who refrain from using their fireplaces or convert them into units that use only nonpolluting electricity or gas.

FIRE INSURANCE

Insurance against a fire that burns part or all of your home or business is usually part of a homeowners' or business owners' insurance policy, which includes insurance against a variety of other hazards as well. Not all contracts of insurance provide the same coverage, but provincial insurance legislation sets requirements as to what must be included. See HOMEOWNERS' INSURANCE; INSURANCE.

If your home or business is damaged by fire, the insurance company will reimburse you, at least in part, for your loss, even if the damage is a result of your own negligence. Suppose you carelessly leave the fire screen open on your fireplace and a spark from the fire sets your rug ablaze. Your homeowners' insurance should cover the loss. Such insurance usually pays for incidental fire damage as well, such as damage caused by smoke, water, and even fire fighters who need to break through windows, doors, or walls to extinguish the fire. Most policies also pay for damage caused by lightning and gas explosions, even if there is no resulting fire.

If a fire occurs after you have left your home or business premises vacant or unoccupied for at least 30 days, you may be excluded from coverage under your contract. The same exclusion applies to the storage of large amounts of flammable substances.

FIREARMS

Unlike the United States and many other countries, anyone resident in Canada, citizen or otherwise, does not have a constitutional right to own weapons. The range of weapons you may have is also restricted. It is difficult to get a permit to carry a handgun, for example, and possession of such a weapon is closely supervised. Rifles for hunting or target shooting are more readily available.

The Criminal Code prohibits the manufacture, sale, or possession of automatic weapons, defined as firearms capable of

◆ "firing projectiles in rapid succession during one pressing of the trigger." It is also illegal to possess a rifle with a barrel shorter than 457 mm or with an overall length shorter than 660 mm.

No one under 16 years of age may own a firearm, defined as any barreled weapon from which any shot, bullet, or other missile can be discharged, and which is capable of causing serious bodily injury or death.

To obtain a firearm, you must be 16 years or older, and have a firearms acquisition certificate issued by a firearms officer who is either an RCMP officer or a member of your provincial police force, or else have a provincial hunting permit issued by a provincial authority.

It is most unlikely that a firearms acquisition certificate would be issued to any person who has been convicted of a weapons offense in the past, or who has been treated for a mental disorder. Such a refusal may be appealed to a provincial court judge.

You must also be 18 years or older to get a restricted weapon, which includes certain semiautomatic weapons and those that can be fired by one hand. To get it you must have a restricted weapons registration certificate, and you must require the weapon for protection of life, or for your lawful occupation, or for use in target practice as a member of a shooting club, or in accordance with such conditions as may be attached to the permit. The weapon must bear distinct
◆ serial numbers.

◆   Any person having a restricted firearm without the required certificate may be charged with an indictable offense punishable by five years' imprisonment, or with a summary conviction offense, punishable by a fine and/or imprisonment of up to two years.

FISHING RIGHTS

Fish, like other wildlife, are owned by the Crown when they are in their natural habitat, even if the fish are in waters on private property. For example, a provincial law that prohibits catching certain species of fish applies even to fish in a stream that passes through private property.

Under most circumstances, the right to catch fish depends on where the body of water is located. If there is a pond or lake that is entirely contained within the boundaries of your property, the right to fish in it is exclusively yours. The same is true for a river or stream that flows through your property— you have exclusive fishing rights on the portion that is on your land. A person who fishes on private property without the owner's permission is guilty of trespassing. When several persons own a lake or pond— because each has property along its shore—they all have fishing rights to the entire lake.

If you own property that adjoins an unnavigable river or stream (one that cannot be used by a boat), you have exclusive fishing rights from the water's edge to the center of the river or stream. If a stream or river passes through your property, the fish still belong to the Crown, and although you can catch them, you cannot otherwise harm them or interfere with their movement (by building a dam, for example).

Everyone has a right to fish in rivers, ponds, and lakes that are navigable. If you own property on such a body of water, you have the same right to fish in it as anyone else. But, once again, you can prohibit anyone from fishing on your land.

The power to regulate fishing on public property rests with the provinces. They may, for example, require you to buy a fishing license; restrict the size, number, and species of fish you may catch; limit the times you can fish; restrict or prohibit the use of nets, spears, and lures; and prohibit the use of explosives or other devices to capture large numbers of fish.

Anyone who violates fishing laws is subject to a fine. A serious or repeated violation of fishing laws is punishable by a fine, or imprisonment, or both.

FIXTURE

A piece of property that is permanently attached to real estate (by being screwed or bolted into a floor or wall, for example) in such a way that it becomes part of the real estate is known as a fixture, and becomes part of the immovable.

When you buy, sell, or rent a building, you should be clear about what constitutes a fix-

ture. For example, if you are buying a house that has a den lined with built-in bookcases that you admire, be sure the sales contract states to whom these will belong. Similarly, if you are selling the house and plan to take the bookcases with you, be sure that this is spelled out in the contract.

If you are a tenant, you can usually take any fixtures you installed with you when you leave, provided you do not do great damage to the real estate. For instance, if you should be so foolish as to install central air-conditioning in a house you rent, you could not remove it. You could, however, take out window air conditioners you install, even if you had nailed brackets into the walls to support them.

To be safe, check your lease before installing any fixtures. It may state that anything you nail or screw into the building, such as shelving, appliances, or cabinets, becomes the property of the landlord.

FLAG, CANADIAN

The Canadian flag, symbol of the country, its people, and our status as a sovereign nation, is a fairly recent addition to the Canadian identity. Although the maple leaf has long been associated with Canada, the red maple leaf, centered on a white square bordered by two red bands, has been our official flag only since Feb. 15, 1965.

Two efforts to adopt a national flag had already failed (in 1925 and 1946), when the

subject was reintroduced in Parliament in 1964. Some members wanted the flag to recall Canada's colonial past and to give pride of place to the Union Jack. Others, including then Prime Minister Lester B. Pearson, felt the nation's sovereignty would be better served by a flag devoid of colonial association, one Canadians could truly call their own.

The design was finally chosen by an all-party 15-member committee appointed by Pearson. After lengthy, and rancorous debate, MPs finally opted for the flag now recognized worldwide as a symbol of Canada.

FLOAT

The period between the time a cheque is written or a credit card charge is made and the time the money is collected from an account is called the float. Suppose you write a cheque to the supermarket on Friday morning. The cheque remains in the cashier's drawer until the end of his shift. It is then turned over to the store's bookkeeper, who deposits it at the supermarket's bank on Saturday morning. The bank processes it on Monday and does not present it to your bank for collection until Tuesday morning. The "float" for your cheque has been four days.

Some people try to "play the float"— that is, even though they do not have enough money in their bank account to cover a cheque, they expect to make a deposit by the time the cheque reaches their bank. Playing the float on a chequing account is a bad idea. If you miscalculate the time, your cheque will not be honored, resulting in financial penalties, administrative hassles, and perhaps even criminal charges.

See also BOUNCED CHEQUE.

FLOATER

An insurance policy that supplements a standard homeowners' policy and gives additional protection to personal property, especially certain valuables, is known as a floater. For example, standard homeowners' insurance does not cover expensive antiques to the full extent of their value or insure your fur coat if it disappears from a restaurant's coatroom, but you can buy a floater that will.

Floaters can be comprehensive and cover all your personal property and the property of those who live with you, or they can be written for specified items only, such as computers, jewelry, cameras, and furs.

For the most part, floaters are "all risk" policies—that is, they cover property against everything except specific exclusions. A standard policy covers only what is specifically named in the policy.

The name *floater* means that the coverage "floats" with the item covered—that is, it ap-

plies whether the item is in the home, in storage, or in transit. Many homeowners' insurance policies include off-premises coverage, but it is generally not as extensive as that provided by floaters. A review of your policy can help you determine the limitations of your present homeowners' coverage.

See also HOMEOWNERS' INSURANCE.

FLOOD INSURANCE

Whether your homeowners' insurance policy covers you in the event of a flood depends on the type of flood. Standard homeowners' policies seldom pay for flood damage caused by severe rain or other unforeseeable causes. However, if you live in an area that has been subject to flooding, you may be able to obtain financial assistance through the federal Disaster Financial Assistance Agreements Program. In this program, the federal government contributes to disaster relief in conjunction with the provinces. Your insurance agent can tell you whether your community qualifies.

If your home is flooded as a result of a burst water pipe, standard homeowners' policies often provide coverage. They will pay for all, or part, of the structural damage and your personal property loss, and may even cover your expenses if you must stay elsewhere until the pipe can be repaired and the water damage cleaned up. See also HOMEOWNERS' INSURANCE.

F.O.B.

F.O.B., or "free on board," is a contractual term meaning that a seller will deliver merchandise at no charge to a particular shipping point. For example, a shipment of Ontario wines going to Manitoba might be sent F.O.B. from the winery to a trucker (or other carrier) in Niagara on the Lake. This means that the seller is responsible for getting the wines onto the truck in Niagara on the Lake at his expense and without breakage. However, once the wine is on the truck, the buyer becomes the owner of the wine, and the seller pays no more delivery charges and is no longer responsible for breakage.

The terms of an F.O.B. contract usually specify that the buyer will pay for goods either before or at the same time that the seller turns them over to the carrier. See also CONTRACT.

FOOD AND DRUGS LAW

Canada's Food and Drugs Act regulates matters as diverse as contraceptive devices, cosmetics, and food, as well as their labeling and packaging, to ensure that such substances and devices are safe and effective when sold to the public.

The act is also designed to restrict the public's access to controlled drugs ("uppers" such as amphetamines and benzphetamines) and restricted drugs (psychedelic substances such as lysergic acid or LSD).

The act provides that no food, drug, cosmetic, or device may be advertised to the general public as a treatment, cure, or preventive medicine for some 40 diseases and conditions, including alcoholism, arthritis, bladder disease, epilepsy, hypotension, and sexual impotence. It prohibits the sale of food containing any harmful substance, or that is adulterated in any way, or that has been prepared, packaged, or stored in unsanitary conditions. The act also forbids labeling or packaging of food in a way that is likely to mislead consumers about the product's character, composition, quantity or quality, and the importation of foods that do not meet regulation standards.

Enforcement measures include comprehensive powers of inspection, penalties of up to 10 years' imprisonment (for trafficking in restricted or controlled drugs), and seizure of property seen as the proceeds of crime. Lesser penalties begin at fines of several hundred dollars.

FORECLOSURE

Losing your home through foreclosure (the forced sale of a home in order to pay back whoever financed it in the first place) can be a nightmare. Foreclosure takes place when a homeowner cannot repay his loan according to the terms of the agreement with the lender. The lender may begin legal proceedings to have the borrower's property sold. Then the proceeds from the sale are used to pay off the outstanding debt. Although foreclosure is a realistic threat to delinquent borrowers, few homeowners actually experience such a nightmare. In fact, most lenders try to avoid foreclosure because it is costly, takes a long time, and does not guarantee complete recovery of the loan.

Foreclosure laws vary from province to province, but proceedings generally follow a series of steps similar to those described below.

FIRST MISSED PAYMENT

When you take out your loan, you will probably sign a mortgage and any other documents that are required by law or your lender. The loan agreement will set out your rights and those of the person or institution that has lent you money, and establish when payments are due, grace periods, and so on. If you miss a payment or fail to pay

---

CHECKLIST

Important Food and Drug Laws

Canada's first law to protect the public from adulterated food, drugs, and drinks was passed in 1875. Today there are several laws to protect consumers and regulate the manufacture and distribution of food and drugs. Some of the most important are:

■ **FOOD AND DRUGS ACT**
Protects consumers from health hazards and fraud in the sale and use of food, drugs, cosmetics, and medical devices.

■ **NARCOTIC CONTROL ACT**
In conjunction with the the Food and Drugs Act, enables Health Department officials to check the potency, purity, and safety of all drugs sold in Canada.

■ **MEAT INSPECTION ACT**
Enables Agriculture Canada officials to inspect meat and meat products for interprovincial and international trade, and to inspect meat-processing facilities.

■ **HAZARDOUS PRODUCTS ACT**
Governs the advertisement, selling, or importation of hazardous materials, such as poisonous, toxic, corrosive, explosive, or reactive products that may pose a health or safety risk. Sets standards for toys, cribs, children's sleepwear, and other objects made of fibers to ensure these materials meet certain standards of flammability and toxicity.

■ **CONSUMER PACKAGING AND LABELLING ACT**
Regulates the packaging, labeling, sale, importation, and advertising of a range of prepackaged products including foods.

your property taxes, your lender or his lawyer will usually remind you by letter and demand a late fee to cover interest on the loan and legal costs. Some provinces legally require grace periods in which the borrower can redeem a default in mortgage payments, and sometimes in property taxes. After a borrower has defaulted on his payments, been given notice of default and any grace periods have expired, only then can the lender commence court action.

THE LAWSUIT

The lender in a foreclosure action will start by suing you for the unpaid balance of your loan, and asking a court to foreclose the mortgage—that is, bar you from redeeming it, or paying it off—and order your property to be sold. You will be named as a defendant in the lawsuit, along with any third parties who may have an interest in your property (such as other creditors who want your property sold to repay them, or government agencies that have claims for unpaid taxes). The lender will have a foreclosure petition delivered to you, either by the sheriff or by certified mail.

If you receive a foreclosure petition, consult a lawyer immediately. If you have a valid defense, such as that you have made all the necessary payments, your lawyer may be able to have the action stopped. If you do not, she may be able to come to some agreement with the lender. Finally, she can advise you whether to seek the protection of a bankruptcy court (which will temporarily stop foreclosure proceedings), especially if you are having trouble paying your other bills. See also BANKRUPTCY.

ABC's
OF BUYING A FORECLOSURE PROPERTY

You may have heard that it is easy and inexpensive to buy a foreclosed home, but actually a good deal of hard work and expense is involved. If you want to undertake such a venture, here are some practical suggestions to guide you:

■ To find out about foreclosure properties, contact a real estate agent or banks in your area.

■ If you are interested in a particular property, visit it before you bid on it at auction, but keep in mind that it may be occupied. You can ask the owners to let you inside, but they have the right to refuse. If the house is vacant, the real estate broker handling the foreclosure may be able to let you in.

■ Conduct a title search in the county records to find out if there are any other liens against the property beside the mortgage, since in some provinces you will have to pay these off if you are the winning bidder.

■ Before deciding how much to bid, ask a real estate broker about the prices of comparable homes in the area.

■ Keep in mind that you may have to make extensive repairs to the house. Sometimes people whose properties have been sold through foreclosure damage the property out of spite, ripping out appliances and knocking holes in plaster walls.

■ Ask about bidding procedures and how to make payment.

■ Do not believe books and television shows that claim to show you how to buy foreclosed properties with no deposit and then resell them for big profits. Lenders who have foreclosed on a home will expect a down payment from you just as from any other buyer. Also, do not count on a bargain basement price for the property. Expect to pay only about 5 or 10 percent less than you would normally pay for a similar property.

■ Finally, where the sale of the immovable is for nonpayment of taxes, be aware that many provincial laws give the former owner the right to redeem his property, or buy it back, within 6 to 12 months. If the owner can come up with the money to pay his taxes and interest, you will get your money back, but you will have to give up the house.

JUDGMENT AND JUDICIAL SALE

If the lender proves his case (that he has lived up to his contractual obligations and that you have defaulted on your mortgage), the court will give him a judgment for the amount due and order that your property be sold. This sale is known as a judicial sale or sheriff's sale—and is a public auction. Most provinces have laws that determine how the notice of a judicial sale is given; often it is published in the local newspaper.

After the notice is published, and before the sale takes place, most lenders will give you one last chance to make good on your loan by paying the amount due plus penalties and court costs. Thus you may be able to save your home even at this late date. If you still cannot pay the lender, your property will be sold to the highest bidder.

DEFICIENCY JUDGMENT

After the sale, the lender of a second mortgage may ask the court to grant approval of the sale and to calculate any "deficiency judgment"—the amount remaining if the sale price of the house does not cover the amount you owe the lender. Armed with this judgment, the lender may then garnishee your wages or seize your assets to redeem his money. See DEFICIENCY JUDGMENT.

On the other hand, if your property is sold for more than you owe, the court determines where the excess funds will go. Usually, other parties who have a lien, or claim, on your property are repaid, and if there is any money remaining, it is given back to you. In a 1993 judgment, the Ontario Court (General Division) ruled that an unsecured creditor (in this case a bank that granted a business loan to a man) could not seize the matrimonial home when the borrower defaulted on the loan because the borrower had not consulted his wife prior to obtaining the loan. Mr. Justice White held that the "unsecured personal guarantee for a business loan, given without the wife's consent, was an impermissible 'encumbrance' of the couple's matrimonial home," which was protected by Ontario's Family Law Act.

The bank was seeking a 50 percent interest in the matrimonial home which had been valued at $285,000 when the loan was issued. This case was being appealed at the time of writing. See LIEN.

REDEMPTION

When a home is sold by judicial sale for nonpayment of taxes, most provinces allow you a period of time (usually 6 to 12 months) after the foreclosure and sale during which you can redeem your home, or buy it back. If you pay the taxes you owe within this period, including the foreclosure costs plus an indemnity of about 10 percent, you can redeem your property. The person who bought your home at the foreclosure sale will be refunded his money. See also MORTGAGE.

FOREIGN BANK ACCOUNT

People who travel abroad, invest in foreign markets, or seek financial privacy, sometimes open a bank account in a foreign country. The process of opening a foreign bank account is not complicated.

CHOOSING A BANK

For a possible source of banks that do business with foreign depositors, contact the embassies of the countries that interest you. Embassies are located in Ottawa, and some countries have consulates in major Canadian cities.

As with a Canadian bank, you should inquire about a foreign bank's services, fees, interest rates, and minimum deposit requirements. Ask how often funds can be transferred out of an account; whether taxes are withheld on interest paid to nonresident accounts; whether you can conduct transactions by mail, telephone, or wire; and whether the account representatives speak English.

GREATER PRIVACY

A primary reason for opening a foreign bank account is privacy. Some government agencies, such as Revenue Canada, have access to information about bank accounts in Canada, but not to foreign accounts, except under special circumstances. For example, Switzerland will provide information to a foreign government only if it is investigating a crime that is also a crime under Swiss law.

In some countries—including Austria, Switzerland, and the Cayman Islands—banks allow accounts to bear a number in place of the owner's name. In Switzerland the identity of the account holder is known only to a few senior bank officials; all other personnel, including the tellers, know only the number. The procedures for setting up numbered accounts vary. Generally, the depositor must visit the bank and show reliable identification, such as a passport.

TAXES AND DISCLOSURE LAWS

Some countries withhold taxes on interest and dividends paid to nonresidents. Income from foreign investments is also taxable in Canada, but you can reclaim foreign taxes you paid if Canada has a tax treaty with that other country. To do so, you must apply for a tax credit on your federal income tax return. It is illegal not to disclose this income on your income tax return.

FORENSIC MEDICINE

Forensic medicine is a medical specialty that focuses on legal problems—especially those involving crime, medical malpractice, and personal injury. (Forensic means "concerned with courts and the law.")

CRIMINAL CASES

Perhaps the best-known use of forensic medicine is in criminal law. Forensic pathologists (doctors who are trained in the various techniques that are necessary for crime detection) often are important witnesses in criminal cases.

A forensic pathologist is specially trained in autopsy techniques. In the case of a suspected murder, he will try to determine the cause of the victim's death, the age and cause

of any wounds, the time of death, and other circumstances surrounding the death. In some cases he may be able to determine the identity of both the victim and the murderer if they are not known.

In addition to conducting autopsies, a forensic pathologist may visit crime scenes, interview witnesses, and perform laboratory experiments. He examines the victim's clothing as well as the body itself and analyzes the hairs, fluids, and body tissues found on a crime victim or at the scene. From such evidence, the forensic pathologist can, for example, tell whether a particular tissue type matches that of the victim or any of the suspects.

FORENSIC PSYCHIATRY IN CRIMINAL CASES

Forensic psychiatrists are often asked to determine whether a particular defendant has the mental ability to distinguish right from wrong, or whether she was unable to control her behavior. Forensic psychiatrists may also determine whether a defendant is mentally able to assist in her defense.

Such questions are important, since a person who cannot distinguish right from wrong or who is suffering from delusions cannot be held legally accountable for her crimes. A person unable to assist in her own defense will not be put on trial until able to do so.

CIVIL CASES

Forensic medicine is used in civil cases too. In medical malpractice and personal-injury

cases, juries may have to decide whether the defendant met a "reasonable standard of care" or was negligent. In order to prove negligence or malpractice, the plaintiff may have to present expert opinions from medical professionals.

FORFEITURE

To forfeit is to lose or be deprived of something because of an offense or failure to act. Fines and penalties are forfeits. Forfeiture also occurs when the government—usually a law enforcement agency—takes possession of property used in illegal activities, without compensating the owner.

For example, suppose Pierre and Lysianne, a married couple, share a family car. Pierre, who sells drugs on the side, regularly uses the car to pick up the drugs and most of his "deals" are done in the car. One day he is arrested on a tip from an informant. If he is convicted, the Criminal Code provides that his (and Lysianne's) car could be forfeited to the government under authority of the Criminal Code.

To seize his property, the prosecutor has to satisfy the judge that the car is more likely than not what is termed a "proceed of crime." A court will hold this to be the case if the total value of Pierre's possessions has increased following his crime, and if his salary from his legal job cannot reasonably account for the increase in his personal wealth. If this is proved, then an order for forfeiture may be ordered.

However, since Lysianne also has a right to the property, she may seek protection from the forfeiture under a provision that relieves innocent parties of this penalty. And so, too, might the bank if Pierre and Lysianne had a lien on the car at the time it was impounded.

Forfeiture may be a penalty under numerous acts other than the Criminal Code. The Canadian Environmental Protection Act and the Food and Drugs Act both permit forfeiture for some offenses. If you fail to declare all your purchases following a visit to the United States, customs agents may seize your car or truck, although this is rarely done. Similarly, you can forfeit your vehicle if you illegally cross the border into either the United States or Canada with an illegal immigrant.

COURT PROCEEDINGS

Although forfeitures are often linked to crimes and criminal prosecutions, forfeiture proceedings are usually viewed as civil. In some cases, they may proceed independently of any criminal prosecution or its outcome. Suppose Jim lends his car to his best friend Carl, who is arrested for speeding while driving it and is found to be carrying bootleg whisky in the trunk. The police seize the car and start forfeiture proceedings. Even if Carl is acquitted of bootlegging, or is never even charged, Jim could still end up losing his car.

In other cases, the property that has been forfeited must be returned to its owner if a criminal defendant is acquitted.

Most forfeiture proceedings are "show cause" hearings. This means an owner must prove to the court why his property should not be forfeited. Since forfeiture is a civil proceeding, the government has to prove its case only by a "preponderance of the evidence"—a much easier task than proving guilt beyond a reasonable doubt, as is required in criminal cases. See also BURDEN OF PROOF; SEARCH AND SEIZURE.

REMISSION

If the forfeiture is allowed by the court, the property owner may be able to have his forfeited property returned by obtaining a "remission" from the the courts.

AVOIDING FORFEITURE

As long as forfeiture laws remain on the books, anyone can be a victim of unfair practices. Reduce your risk by allowing only people you know well to use your property, especially those items you cannot afford to lose.

FORGERY

Creating a false document or substantially altering a genuine one with the intent to defraud is forgery. Someone creates a false document, for example, if he steals a cheque book, fills in all the blanks, and cashes the cheques. If a person changes a provision in another's will, he is guilty of forgery by altering an otherwise genuine document.

A forgery does not have to be handwritten. Engraving, printing, stamping, or typing with

an intent to defraud is forgery. Fraudulently obtaining a legitimate signature is also forgery. Suppose Jim has his elderly father sign a form that Jim claims is needed by Revenue Canada. The father later discovers the form was a quitclaim deed to his own home, transferring the ownership to his son. Jim is guilty of forgery.

ESTABLISHING FORGERY

For a person to be convicted of forgery, three things must be established:

— a document must have been created or altered;

— the document must be able to deceive someone; and

— there must have been an intent to defraud.

Creation and alteration
Creating a document such as a cheque, deed, or promissory note can constitute forgery. So can making changes that substantially alter the meaning or legal effect of a document. Inserting zeros into the amount of a cheque, so that $10 becomes $100, is a common example.

Revising dates on a contract, receipt, or other legal document is another form of alteration. For example, a contract may specify that the Cunningham Crumpet Company will pay all of salesman Barry's expenses to June 15. If Barry changes the date to cover expenses incurred to July 15, he is a forger.

For an alteration to be considered a forgery, it must be "material"—that is, it must substantially change the meaning. Adding a middle name to someone's name in a contract would not be a forgery if it served to further identify that person.

Deceptiveness

To be a forgery a document must look realistic enough to deceive people into believing it is genuine. Someone who photocopies a $20 bill and crudely colors it green, for example, would not be likely to be charged with forgery. See COUNTERFEIT MONEY.

Intent to defraud

By far the most important element of forgery is the intent to defraud, which must be proved beyond a reasonable doubt by the prosecuting lawyer.

Some actions that appear to be forgery are not, because there is no attempt to defraud. Suppose Barry wants to deposit his wife Sarah's paycheque into her account while she is away. He signs her name to endorse the cheque and deposits it into her account. Because he has Sarah's permission to act as her agent, Barry is not guilty of forgery. Or suppose you want to make certain numbers in a contract more legible. If you misread a number and mistakenly change a 3 to an 8, you are not guilty of forgery because you did not intend to defraud anyone.

PUNISHMENT

Forgery is a criminal offense which carries a maximum penalty of 14 years' imprisonment. A forger may also be financially responsible for the loss his forgery causes, as in the case of an altered cheque. See also CHEQUE.

FOSTER HOME

When parents cannot or will not provide proper care for a child, the courts can temporarily transfer custody to a provincial child-welfare agency. The agency may then place the child in a foster home. Sometimes children are placed in foster homes when their parents have voluntarily given them up for adoption. The length of time in a foster home can be as short as one night or as long as several years.

Foster care is not the same as adoption; a foster child's parents usually retain their parental rights, and the child will eventually be either returned to them or adopted by someone else. In some cases, foster parents adopt their foster children, and in certain provinces they are given adoptive preference if the child becomes available for adoption. See also ADOPTION.

THE FOSTER HOME LICENSE

A foster home must be sanctioned by a provincial child-welfare agency. Every province has its own standards for approving and licensing foster homes, but the procedure for licensing is similar in most provinces.

Crucial to the court's decision on whether a child will be placed in a foster home is what is deemed to be the "best interest of the child." In reaching this decision, judges will take religious, linguistic, and cultural factors into account,

as well as the wishes of children of a certain age. The court will also require assurances that prospective foster parents will provide a proper home.

Physical inspection

If you have told your local child-welfare agency that you are interested in becoming a foster parent, you will be visited by an agency social worker. She will check that your home is well kept, has sufficient space for a foster child or children, and meets the agency's minimum standards for health and safety. Typically, homes are required to have smoke detectors, fire extinguishers, and separate beds for each foster child.

Physical exams

Because children who are placed in foster homes often can be exceptionally demanding, their foster parents should be in good health. You may therefore be asked to provide a statement from your family physician concerning your health and to undergo testing for certain communicable diseases, such as tuberculosis.

Background screening

The agency will conduct a background check on all adults in your household. Certain criminal convictions or recorded complaints of child abuse or neglect will rule you out as a prospective foster parent.

Personal evaluation

In the last 20 years the profile of a typical foster home has changed. Increasingly, single women and men become foster parents, and some provinces provide day care for children whose foster parents work outside the home. As the needs of children vary, a social worker will help you determine what type of child would be best suited for your home.

As a prospective foster parent, you should learn how to deal with children who have suffered neglect or abuse. You will need specialized skills to care for a child with great emotional or physical needs. You should also know something about the legal system, to better understand the concerns of the social workers supervising the children in your care.

FOSTER PARENTS' RESPONSIBILITIES

As a foster parent, you should receive a contract that spells out your duties and responsibilities to the child and to the child-welfare agency—as well as those of the agency toward you and the child. Your primary obligation will be to care for and nurture the child who has been placed in your care. You will also have to see that the child attends school and keeps necessary appointments. Although foster parents are responsible for disciplining the foster child, agencies strictly forbid physical punishment.

You will receive a stipend for your foster child's basic needs, such as food, clothing, and toiletries. The agency may be responsible for providing medical, dental, counseling, and special educational services. However, you should be forewarned that the stipend rarely if ever covers all a child's needs; foster care is never a lucrative career.

You will be in frequent contact with the social worker assigned to monitor you and your child, reporting to her on the child's development. The social worker should be able to answer your questions and offer guidance, and she should keep you informed of your foster child's legal status and any future plans for her.

You should not expect that a child living with you will be there forever. The child must return to a permanent living situation, and you will be expected to assist with the process of reintegration.

In some cases, it is not advisable or possible to return a child to her family—for example, if she was severely abused by her parents, if they abandoned her, or if they are chronically mentally ill. The social workers may then want to build a case in order to terminate the parents' rights to the child. In such an instance, you might be asked to report to the court whether the parents visited the child, how they interacted with her, and any other observations you have made about the child.

FOSTER PARENTS' RIGHTS

Foster parents have fewer legal rights than anyone else in the foster-care system. A child in foster care is usually in the legal custody of the province, director of youth protection (or in some cases a private, nonprofit agency). Although there are exceptions, foster parents do not participate in court proceedings relating to their foster child, and a foster child may be removed from the home at any time.

In some provinces foster parents who have cared for a child for a lengthy period are notified before the child welfare agency transfers the child or returns her to her former home, and the foster parents may appeal the decision. In some cases, foster parents can ultimately adopt foster children who become wards of the province.

See also CHILD CUSTODY; CHILDREN'S RIGHTS.

FRANCHISE

A franchise is a special privilege that is granted or sold. There are two basic types. The first is a government franchise, whereby the government gives an individual or corporation a privilege unavailable to the rest of the population. Set up primarily for the benefit of the public, government franchises authorize the operations of such bodies as utility companies, taxi and bus companies, and corporations responsible for building and maintaining bridges, tunnels, and ferries.

The second type of franchise involves the grant of a privilege by a company to an individual or to another company. This grant is usually made by a contract or else by the sale of a license. Nearly always, such a franchise involves the payment of a fee to the company that grants the privilege.

In a private franchise the "franchisor" sells the right to do business using a certain trade name or set of business practices to a "franchisee." This arrangement is especially popular in businesses where a certain level of quality or service is associated with a particular product, such as automobile sales and leasing, fast food, and "brand-name" clothing. Although franchise agreements can be elaborate, they generally specify the methods and procedures a franchisee must follow in exchange for the right to operate the franchised business. This can mean as much as having to rely on the franchisor for all goods and services or as little as promising to maintain a specified level of quality. In any event, the franchisee is solely responsible for the debts, taxes, insurance, and other expenses of the business.

OWNING A FRANCHISE: WHAT YOU SHOULD KNOW

Charlotte has always wanted to run a family-style restaurant. But because she has little experience in managing a business, she decides to look into buying a franchise. This way, she reasons, she will have the benefit of a well-established name, as well as the experience, skills, advertising, and reputation of a national enterprise. Charlotte's reasoning is supported by statistics: 40 percent of newly established businesses fail within one year, but fewer than 5 percent of franchised businesses suffer the same fate. And whether your dream is to own a family-style restaurant, a video outlet, or a clothing store, there is a wealth of franchising opportunities from which to choose.

The pros and cons

As with any other business, operating a franchise has both advantages and drawbacks. Franchisors usually provide training programs and will help with site selection and other important issues—a definite plus for novices who are looking for guidance and structure.

On the negative side, many franchisors have strict policies governing hours of operation,

REAL LIFE, REAL LAW

The Case of the Franchisor's Faulty Figures

Octopus Corporation, an auto parts manufacturer and subsidiary of the World Oil Company, distributed its products through a nationwide network of outlets operated by agents who received a commission on sales. When Octopus Ltd. decided to open a franchise operation in Atlantic Canada, its regional manager drew up a brochure, which he sent to local businessmen and copied to the Toronto head office. The national sales manager, after studying the project, came to the conclusion that the franchise for Yarmouth, N.S., was not feasible as it could count on sales of only about $11,000 per year, and so advised the regional sales manager in Nova Scotia. Despite this assessment, the Nova Scotia regional manager made his own projections for sales, which suggested that a Yarmouth franchise could make $33,000 per year.

Jan, the owner of a local hardware store, thought this was a good sideline to have and entered into the franchise agreement. Within a year Jan was bankrupt and he sued Octopus Ltd. on the strength of the projected sales of $33,000. Octopus Ltd. didn't tell Jan of the previous projection of $11,000 in sales. Although the agreement Octopus drew up contained an exclusionary clause that said that the contract "superceded all prior agreements, understandings, negotiations and discussions," and also contained a clause excluding any warranty as to "volume, profit or sales," Jan was successful in his action.

Even on appeal, the Court of Appeal said Jan was entitled to rely on the projection of sale of $33,000, and the exclusionary clause was "unconscionable." It was unfair because the contract was made by a large national organization on the one hand, and a small businessman on the other, and the large corporation had information that it did not disclose to the franchisee, thus the bargaining position of the parties was not equal.

CHECKLIST

Evaluating a Franchise Opportunity

Before signing an agreement to buy a franchise, carefully read the franchisor's contract and note how the following points have been covered:

■ **EXCLUSIVE RIGHTS.**
Some franchisors offer exclusive rights to territories; others grant many franchises within the same area. Some even may crowd franchisees by operating their own stores nearby.

■ **WRITTEN CONFIRMATION.**
Make sure any spoken promises or agreements made by the franchisor are stated in the contract.

■ **COST OF TRAINING.**
If your franchisor requires a training program, find out whether the cost of travel and other expenses are included in your initial investment fee.

■ **ADDITIONAL SERVICES.**
Find out exactly what services are provided as a part of your franchise agreement—for instance, marketing advice or accounting help, or other assistance.

■ **SUPPLIES AND INVENTORY.**
If the agreement states that you must buy all equipment, supplies, and inventory from the franchisor or a specified supplier, ask why. For instance, is the franchisor or supplier able to give you the best price, or are the goods unavailable elsewhere?

■ **OTHER FRANCHISEES.**
The franchisor should supply you with the names, addresses, and phone numbers of at least 10 franchisees in your area. Visit these investors, to see their operations and to check on claims made by the franchisor.

■ **SELLING YOUR FRANCHISE.**
Your rights to sell or transfer your franchise may be subject to the franchisor's approval. In some cases the franchisor has the right of first refusal to buy the franchise if you later wish to sell it, or if you become disabled or die while you own it.

■ **TERMINATION OF THE FRANCHISE AGREEMENT.**
Make sure any clauses pertaining to the termination of the franchise agreement are consistent with the laws of your province. Find out laws regarding termination by contacting your provincial consumer protection agency.

■ **FRANCHISE PREMISES.**
The franchise contract may require that you construct a building where business is to take place. Be careful to note what consequences you may suffer if a construction deadline is not met. In some cases, the franchisor may own the building and lease it to you. Is the rent unreasonable? Is your lease for a longer period than your franchise agreement? If so you may want to reconsider the franchise deal. Make sure that the proposed building meets all your province's and local government's legal requirements for operating a business.

customer service, use of the company logo, and other business practices. Furthermore, franchise contracts often contain specific guidelines governing a range of concerns from cleanliness to how merchandise is displayed, which are meant to ensure the uniformity of the franchise operations. Although franchisees must be given time to correct problems, noncompliance with these mandatory guidelines can result in the cancellation of the franchise contract.

The cost to you
Starting a franchise requires capital. Franchisees are almost always required to pay an initial fee, usually payable upon signing the contract; this fee can range from less than $1,000 to over $100,000. Ideally, in exchange for the initial fee, the franchisee receives a business package developed by an established organization.

In addition to the start-up fee, the franchisor may charge a royalty of between 2 and 6 percent of total sales (not profit). The amount of royalty will be greater the more services that are provided by the franchisor to the franchisee (accounting, product research, development, advertising and so on). Be careful to account for this royalty charge when determining if a franchise is a viable option for you.

For every dollar the franchisee takes in, the franchisor may be entitled to receive 10 cents. Many businesses operate on a profit margin of less than 5 percent, so it can be hard to turn a profit if the franchisor charges a high royalty.

Most franchisors charge a fee to cover local and national advertising in newspapers and on radio and television. Like the royalty, this fee is usually calculated as a percentage of sales (generally 1 or 2 percent) and is charged on a regular basis. An advertising fund has a distinct advantage for franchisees, since it allows for far more advertising than most small-business owners could afford on their own. Before paying any advertising fees, check that this item is not already covered under royalties to the franchisor.

The franchisor's prospectus should give you the basic information you need to make a reasonable business decision. As well, give careful thought to your own personality and professional goals before signing any agreement. If it will bother you to have others tell you how to use your time and set up your operation, you may not want to buy a franchise.

PROTECTING THE FRANCHISEE

Alberta has enacted legislation on franchising, and Quebec has amended its Securities Act to cover franchising matters. Other than that, there are no specific federal and provincial laws, only general commercial legislation, to deal with franchise issues. For example, the Canadian Business Corporations Act deals with incorporation and business operation, and there are federal laws on patents, trademarks, competition, and trade practices. Some provinces have laws on corporations and partnerships, and all provinces have consumer legislation.

Alberta's franchise law is really a form of consumer protection designed to keep unscrupulous franchisors from taking advantage of those less experienced in the business. Franchisors must file documents with the Securities Commission relating to the viability of the franchise and its history. The franchisor must also make it clear to the franchisee that the business venture does not guarantee profit.

FRAUD

It is a criminal offense to intentionally defraud the public or any person of their land, money, stocks, jewels, or any other form of property, or to alter the market prices of anything offered for sale. Suppose Damon induces Kevin, both of whom live in Ontario, to buy land in British Columbia, where Damon knows there is no such land. He is merely trying to obtain money from Kevin by fraudulent means. Any contract Kevin signed under these circumstances would be voided by the courts.

In fraud cases, it is not necessary for the prosecutor to show that the victim actually lost property. It is enough to show that he was in danger (or at risk) of losing property or money as a result of the fraud.

Proof of fraud requires that the victim was induced into doing something detrimental to himself. For example, imagine that Freddy Freeloader tries to sell what is clearly a bottle of beer as a "miracle lotion" that cures cancer. If the fraud is as blatant as this, you might have a hard time convincing a judge that you relied on it to your detriment.

COURT RULINGS

The elements of fraud were set out in two cases dealt with by the Supreme Court of Canada in 1993. One involved a property developer who claimed in his dealings and advertisements that all prospective purchaser deposits were guaranteed by a financial institution, although this was not the case. The project failed and many deposits were lost. The developer claimed that although he may not have told the truth, he had not intended to defraud anyone and had expected the project to succeed.

The court ruled that in order to sustain fraud the prosecution must prove that the accused (a) knew (had subjective knowledge) that what he said was untrue ; and (b) had subjective knowledge that as a consequence of the prohibited act (the lie about the insured deposits) another person could be deprived of property or money. But if proven, the accused is guilty, whether he actually had the intention to defraud or was reckless as to whether such loss would occur.

In the second case, a businessman obtained goods on credit, but instead of paying the suppliers once he sold the goods, he spent the money gambling. The accused said he had no intention of defrauding his creditors, neither did he mislead or lie to them in obtaining the goods.

The court ruled, however, that although unwise business practices are not fraudulent, dishonest business practices may be. The dishonesty has at its heart, the court said, the wrongful use of something in which another person has an interest.

The accused businessman had a right to use the sale proceeds, but did not have "an unrestricted right to use these funds as he pleased." The test should be whether "a reasonable person would regard as dishonest a scheme involving the acceptance of merchandise for resale without concern for repayment and the diversion of the proceeds to a reckless gambling adventure." Since what the accused did would appear dishonest to a reasonable person, he should be found guilty of fraud.

FRIVOLOUS SUIT

A lawsuit that has no legal merit is called a frivolous suit. Suppose Barney is the owner of Barney's Widgets. His principal competitor, Ace Widgets, has been cutting into his market recently, and Barney is getting worried. He decides to file a lawsuit against Ace, alleging unfair trading practices. Even though Barney knows that Ace has not engaged in any unfair

trading practices, he hopes that the lawsuit will cost Ace time and money, thus eating into Ace's profits. Barney also hopes that Ace will be forced to disclose some trade secrets in the course of the suit.

Barney's lawsuit is frivolous. A lawsuit should be started only if some factual and legal basis warrants it. It should not be based on false or irrelevant claims. And it should not be filed if the plaintiff, or his lawyer, knows (or can easily find out) that similar suits have been rejected by the courts.

Sometimes lawsuits are filed just to harass or embarrass the other party. For example, creditors are notified when a debtor has been declared bankrupt, and they are no longer entitled to pursue him for the debt. If a creditor then files a suit to collect the debt or seeks garnishment of the debtor's wages, he is filing a frivolous suit.

The plaintiff and his lawyer in a frivolous lawsuit may both be subject to sanctions. Barney, for example, may have to pay Ace's lawyer's fees, as well as any other expenses Ace incurs in having to defend against Barney's claim. Barney's lawyer may be subject to serious disciplinary action by the local bar association, and both Barney and his lawyer can be sued by Ace.

FUNERAL AND BURIAL

When you die, decisions about your funeral and burial include such details as the time, place, and manner of your funeral

and burial and the choice of a marker or monument for your grave or tomb. If you have definite ideas about such matters, you should make them clear to your family and friends.

Put your wishes in writing, but not in your will, which may not be read until funeral arrangements have been made or the deceased has been buried. See also EXECUTOR AND ADMINISTRATOR; PROBATE; WILL.

LETTER OF LAST INSTRUCTIONS

To communicate your wishes, prepare a letter of last instructions—a private document (as compared to a will, which becomes public when it is filed with the court) detailing the funeral and burial arrangements you desire. A letter of last instructions can tell how you want your body disposed of (cremation, burial, or donation to medical science) and whether you want flowers or would prefer contributions to your favorite charity.

Leave written instructions if you want to donate your organs or body to medical science. (In the case of underage patients, parental permission will be needed to carry out such directives.) If you die without leaving instructions on organ donation, your closest relative may make any decisions in this matter. In cases of emergency, doctors may remove and use organs of the deceased for life-saving operations such as liver and heart transplants, provided two doctors claim in writing that they could not obtain consent. See ORGAN AND TISSUE TRANSPLANTS.

Give copies of your instructions (which can be updated as you wish) to family members or those who will handle your funeral arrangements. Put the original where it can easily be found upon your death. Do not put it in a safe-deposit box, which may be sealed temporarily when you die.

Your letter of last instructions is not a binding legal document, and your family or the executor of your estate may handle funeral arrangements as they see fit. However, there is generally a duty to carry out the final wishes of the deceased in a fashion consistent with his station in life. If John's father, a millionaire with many friends, dies, he should not simply be buried in a pine box and without a funeral service.

If you do not express your wishes prior to death, the right to decide your funeral and burial arrangements can be made by your spouse or other family members; some provinces specify who has these rights. If no one claims your body, provincial or local laws on such matters will be followed.

WHO PAYS?

Unless you pay in advance for your funeral, the costs are generally deducted from your estate before any other assets are distributed. If your estate cannot cover the cost of a funeral, your spouse may be responsible. If no family member or other person can be identified as responsible for these expenses, the cost may be assumed by your local government, but you may be buried in a pauper's grave.

PREPAYMENT OPTIONS

To spare your family the burden of planning and paying for your funeral, you may decide to make advance arrangements.

Burial societies

One option is to join a burial or memorial society. These cooperative organizations charge a one-time fee, and at your death they make all the arrangements according to your instructions. Since these organizations work with local funeral directors, they receive substantial discounts on funerals and burials.

Burial insurance

Another option is to buy burial insurance. This may cost more than a term life insurance policy for the same benefits. If you buy a term life insurance policy instead, make sure that the beneficiary understands that he is to use the policy proceeds for your funeral expenses. Do not name your estate as the beneficiary, because the benefits may be held up during the process of probate. See also LIFE INSURANCE.

Preneed plans

All funeral homes offer "preneed" plans, enabling you to arrange and pay for your funeral in advance. Usually the money is placed in a trust fund or a life insurance policy. If it is not going into a trust fund regulated by the province, you should probably choose another policy. Choose a plan that is transferable to another funeral home if you move. If you are paying on an installment plan, ask whether your agreement will be good if you die before making all your payments.

Some contracts state that the prearranged price is not locked in until you have paid in full.

Finally, be sure your family or friends know that you have paid for your funeral and burial. In some cases, families have paid for a loved one's funeral only to discover that a prepaid plan was already in place with another funeral home.

You may also prepay for a cemetery plot, but first consider whether you will still be living in the same place at the time of your death.

In many cases, the Canada (Quebec) Pension Plan will pay a certain amount for burial. Money may also be given for burial services when the deceased has been receiving social welfare assistance, and under some workers' compensation plans or auto insurance plans—Quebec's, for example.

EMBALMING

Rules on embalming, a treatment which preserves a corpse from rapid deterioration after death, vary from province to province. Embalming is one of the costliest items on a funeral bill and is not always necessary.

Embalming may not be done without a coroner's permission when death occurred under suspicious or violent circumstances, or when the deceased is being taken out of province for burial.

CREMATION

Cremation is generally seen as a legal and equally acceptable alternative to burial. Provincial law may set requirements on containers (for example, you may not have to have a casket;

an approved cremation container may suffice), and there
may be restrictions on where
the ashes can be scattered.

OUT-OF-PROVINCE DEATHS

Provincial or municipal ordinances may impose certain
requirements before a body
can be moved into or out of a
province. Funeral homes can
usually get the necessary permits to transport the body.

DISINTERMENT

Once a body is buried, it cannot
be removed from its grave or
tomb without legal approval.
The appropriate authority
varies from province to
province, from the Registrar of
Deaths in British Columbia, to
the Director of Vital Statistics
in Alberta, and to the Medical
Officer of Health in Ontario.

The courts will not allow a
body to be moved except out of
necessity or for a justifiable
family purpose. For example,
disinterment may be necessary
if the cemetery has been abandoned or the land is needed for
a public improvement. A
change in burial place may also
be approved if a family wishes
to buy a larger cemetery plot to
accommodate all its members.

The courts allow a body to
be disinterred for the purpose
of performing an autopsy to
gather evidence about the
cause of death. But before a
court will give its permission,
the judge must be satisfied
that disinterment is needed
and that there is a reasonable
likelihood that evidence will
be gained by doing so. See
also AUTOPSY.

MISCONDUCT

Anyone who disturbs a grave
site or disinters or destroys a
corpse may be held in violation
of criminal or provincial laws.
In addition, performing an
unauthorized embalming or
autopsy, or an improper burial
may entitle the heirs of a
deceased person to sue for
money damages.

FUTURE EARNINGS

Future or potential earnings
are often at issue in lawsuits
when damages or other monetary awards are being assessed.
Cases in which future earnings
are disputed often involve
personal injury.

For example, suppose Gene,
a 35-year-old construction
worker, is injured in an automobile accident and is permanently paralyzed from the
waist down. If Gene could have
been reasonably expected to
work in construction for another 25 years, a court might
award damages based on the
loss of 25 years of his average
future earnings as a construction worker. However, Gene
must produce evidence of his
probable future income
(adjusted for inflation) and his
potential for earnings in a different field of endeavor. If he
can get work as a telephone
operator or a bookkeeper, for
instance, his probable salary
as an office worker will be
calculated over the same
time and subtracted from
the total award.

See also DAMAGES.

FUTURE INTEREST

A right to property you do not
currently hold but will obtain at
some future time is known as a
future interest.

Suppose your father dies and
leaves his home to "my friend,
Rita, during her lifetime, and
thereafter to my children." Rita
has a present interest in the
home, which is known as a life
estate. You and your siblings
have a future interest in the
property. Because of your
future interest (or "remainder"), Rita is prohibited from
selling the home or doing anything that intentionally diminishes its potential value to you.
When Rita dies, your future
interest becomes a present
interest. At that point, you and
your siblings will be entitled to
occupy, sell, lease, or otherwise
dispose of the home. Until
then, you have no legal right to
do anything with it.

Another kind of future interest involves a temporary gift.
Suppose your father gives his
home to Rita for 10 years but
reserves the right to occupy it
at the end of that period. He
has what is known as a
reversionary future interest.

In Quebec, ownership and
use divided in this way are
called a usufruct. The person
having use of the property,
Rita, would be considered the
usufructuary, and the person to
become owner after Rita's
rights have expired is called the
bare owner. A usufruct cannot
extend beyond three generations. See LIFE ESTATE; WILL.

G

FROM

GAMBLING

TO

GUARDIAN
AND WARD

GAMBLING

Since many provinces have realized that legalized gambling is a means by which they can obtain additional revenue, they have relaxed some of the prohibitions against various forms of gambling. The proceeds from lotteries and other gambling ventures are in part used to increase provincial revenues. See also LOTTERY.

The general rule in Canada is that it is criminal to run a gambling establishment, to be a "bookie" or to run lotteries. There are exceptions, however. Certain provincially regulated gambling schemes such as lotteries and horse racing are permitted. The federal Minister of Agriculture may also regulate betting on horse racing taking place both in and out of Canada. Certain charitable or religious organizations may obtain licenses for games of

chance which cost no more than $2 per ticket and which have prizes worth no more than $500. Those who hold and award monies to winners of certain types of gambling— anyone working for a provincial lotteries commission, for example, or persons holding money for the winner of a private bet between no more than 10 people—are also not liable to criminal prosecution.

The regulation of gambling varies from province to province. Quebec now licenses Las Vegas-style casinos, and Ontario is moving in the same direction. However, do not plan a gambling venture for your next fund-raiser, until you first check with your local police department or provincial lotteries commission. You will need to know your community's requirements for a gambling license, where gambling may take place, the age at which people may legally gamble, and whether alcohol may be served during the gambling.

Even though private bets between two people are not criminal, unpaid gambling debts are not generally enforced by the courts. Betting is seen as a form of immoral behavior against good public policy. So Sylvie and Marie may bet $50 on the outcome of the Stanley Cup play-offs, but if Sylvie loses and refuses to pay up, Marie has little recourse. Even if she takes Sylvie to the small-claims court, it is almost certain to declare the bet unenforceable.

Exceptions to this legal practice are increasing, nonetheless. In one case, a Toronto

lawyer incurred a $20,800 debt in Atlantic City, N.J., where gambling is legal. When he refused to pay, the casino filed an action against him in Ontario, where he owned property. He argued that he should not have to pay, since the Ontario Gaming Act says gambling debts are not enforceable. But his argument was unsuccessful. The court found that so long as the debt was incurred in a place where it could be enforced legally, then the law of that jurisdiction would be recognized in Ontario. Similar rulings have been made by the Ontario Court of Appeal and by Quebec courts concerning gambling debts incurred where gambling is legal.

Gambling winnings are not subject to income tax, nor are gambling losses tax deductible, unless related to a gambling business. See SWEEPSTAKES.

GARAGE SALE

If your basement and garage are overflowing with old dishes, appliances, and knickknacks accumulated over the years, you can try to sell them at a garage or yard sale. Before going ahead, however, take a few precautions.

◇ Find out if you need a permit from your municipality to hold a sale. Some communities limit how many garage sales you can hold in one year.

◇ If you live in an area that is controlled by a homeowners' association (such as a private housing development or apartment complex), ask the management office if there are any restrictions on garage sales. You may have to conduct the sale during certain hours or on specified days only so that the extra traffic is less likely to disrupt your neighbors.

◇ Inquire about municipal restrictions on signs advertising the sale. Can you post signs on utility poles, for example? How soon after the sale must signs be removed ?

◇ Ask your accountant or local tax office if money from your garage sale is taxable. Generally, it is not, since you do not make a profit when you sell merchandise for less than you paid for it. You are not usually required to collect sales tax unless you conduct garage sales as a regular business.

◇ Be truthful about the condition of items on sale. If you tell a neighbor that a toaster is in working order, he is entitled to a refund if it is not. Put "as is" signs on damaged goods or those that are not in good working condition.

◇ Be prepared to give a bill of sale for expensive items in case of later disputes.

See BILL OF SALE.

GARNISHMENT

Garnishment is a legal measure that a creditor can use to collect money owed to him. But rather than getting the money directly from the debtor, the creditor collects it from a third party, such as the debtor's employer. Suppose Ed borrows $5,000 from his cousin Francine, giving her a promissory note in which he agrees to repay the money in one year.

After two years Francine has not been able to collect any money from Ed. Her lawyer, Dee, suggests that Francine seek to have Ed's wages garnisheed.

Dee's first step is to obtain a court judgment authorizing the garnishment. With this in hand, Dee is able to contact third parties (garnishees) who owe Ed money or have possession of his property. Likely garnishees include the bank that holds his savings, and his employer, whom Dee chose as the most likely garnishee. Ed's employer is required to pay the amount specified in the court order directly to Francine from Ed's wages until the full debt was repaid.

Such an order can be terminated only if Ed's circumstances change—if he loses his job, for example, or if he repays the money.

ATTACHMENT

Only Ed's property that is held by a third party can be taken. Thus, if Ed wears an expensive watch, Francine cannot force him to sell it through garnishment. She can, however, make him sell the watch through an attachment proceeding. See ATTACHMENT.

PROVINCIAL RESTRICTIONS

Provincial legislation restricts the amount and type of assets or property that can be garnisheed. This is particularly the case if the garnishment is of the debtor's wages. Most provinces will not allow pensions to be garnisheed.

PROVINCIAL EXEMPTIONS

Every province has its own rules concerning what a creditor may garnish once he has obtained a judgment against you. However, the various effects and percentage of salary a debtor may keep are relatively similar in all provinces. In Alberta, for example, a single person may keep $525 per month plus another $140 per month for each dependent child. A married person's monthly exemption is $700 plus $140 per dependent child.

The Alberta Exemptions Act also prohibits the seizure of the following articles:

◇ any goods that have been mortgaged to another party (goods under a conditional sales contract for example);

◇ furniture up to a value of $4,000;

◇ tools and equipment up to a value of $7,500 needed for one's trade. This might include a computer and printer, for example;

◇ books required for one's trade or profession;

◇ necessary clothing for one's family;

◇ one car or truck up to $8,000 value needed for trade or agricultural purposes;

◇ the debtor's homestead up to 160 acres;

◇ the debtor's home up to $40,000 equity for each name on the title deed.

PROTECTIONS

Ed's employer cannot fire him from his job because his wages are being garnisheed. In fact, employers who violate this law are subject to penalties. If you are involved in a garnishment proceeding, find out what your province's law requires of you and what protection it offers you, or ask your lawyer.

See also BANKRUPTCY; CREDIT; INCOME TAX.

GIFT

A gift is the voluntary transfer of property from one person (known as the donor) to another (known as the donee). For such a transfer to be a true gift, the donee does not promise anything of value in exchange.

The law distinguishes between a gift made while living, or a gift *inter vivos,* and a gift made while dying, or a gift *causa mortis.* This distinction is important primarily for tax and estate-planning purposes.

GIFTS *INTER VIVOS*

There are three legal requirements for a gift *inter vivos* to be valid. First of all, the donor must intend to make the gift—to transfer ownership permanently. If you tell your nephew that he can use your car for his honeymoon in Niagara Falls, you have not made a gift, because you expect him to return the car to you afterward.

Second, the property must be delivered: a mere promise does not constitute a legal gift. If you promise your niece that you will give her a video player but you change your mind, she cannot require you to turn the player over to her. Delivery can be actual or symbolic. Actual delivery would occur if you put the video player in your niece's

hands. But the delivery would be considered symbolic if you transferred the registration of your car to your nephew.

Third, a gift *inter vivos* is complete only if the donee accepts it. If you decide to leave a kitten on your neighbor's doorstep, she does not have to accept it, even if you intend it as a gift. But if she takes the kitten and begins to feed and care for it as her own, she cannot later force you to take it back. Conversely, if your neighbor takes the kitten and you later decide you want it back, she does not have to return it.

Gifts in the mail

If you receive merchandise in the mail that you did not order, you are not required to pay for it. The law considers merchandise sent to you unsolicited to be a gift. See also UNORDERED MERCHANDISE.

GIFTS *CAUSA MORTIS*

Gifts *causa mortis,* or those gifts given in contemplation of death, also require intention, delivery, and acceptance. However, gifts *causa mortis* can be made only of personal property, not of real estate. Therefore, if your great-uncle Louis turns to you on his deathbed and says, "I want to give you the whole 500-acre ranch," his statement does not fulfill the requirements for a valid gift (he must actually deed the property to you or leave it to you in his will). However, if he says, "I want you to have my prize saddle and tack," he has made a valid gift *causa mortis.*

A gift *causa mortis* could be made orally (so it is helpful to have a witness). If the donor

writes down that he intends to give you a gift, such instructions may be considered a will and thus subject to the strict requirements necessary for a will to be valid. A gift *causa mortis* may also be invalid if the donor was contemplating suicide at the time. See WILL.

A gift *causa mortis* becomes the property of the donee only when the donor dies. If Great-Uncle Louis changes his mind before he dies, or if he recovers and does not give you the saddle, you have no right to claim it. But if you are promised a gift *causa mortis* and do not receive it when the donor dies, you can file a claim against his estate.

GIFTS AND TAXES

If you are giving property as a gift, any money you made from this property may be subject to tax (see your accountant or look in your federal income tax guide under "capital gains and losses"). Gifts may also qualify as income tax deductions, but your occupation—if you are an artist, art dealer or art collector, for example—may affect the way the rules apply. The permissible deduction also varies depending on whether the gift is to a Canadian charity, to Canada or one of the provinces, or whether the gift qualifies as cultural property under the Cultural Property Export and Import Act. Ask your accountant or Revenue Canada (you will find the number in the blue pages of your phone directory), or consult your tax guide. You will need the "fair market value" established by an independent appraiser. There are specific appraisal guidelines for evaluating cultural properties.

You need not claim the deduction the year you make the gift. You have up to five years to do so. It will be to your advantage to claim the deduction whichever year you have most taxes to pay. See ESTATE PLANNING; TRUST.

GIFTS TO MINORS

The law is the same whether the donee is a minor or an adult, but gifts such as real estate must be managed until the minor becomes an adult.

GOOD FAITH

Good faith means honest and fair dealing, with no intent to take advantage of or defraud another person. A seller is acting in good faith when she has no knowledge of facts that would make a transaction unfair or illegal. If you sell your car to someone without knowing that it has a faulty transmission, you are selling it in good faith. But if you misrepresent the condition of the transmission or try to disguise it, you have not acted in good faith and may be guilty of fraud.

If you deal with a seller who is not acting in good faith, you may have to take the matter to court. Suppose James buys a computer from Chips, a computer store. James specifically asks the salesman, George, if the computer has sufficient memory to run his accounting program, and George assures him that it does. When James tries to run the program on his computer, however, he discovers that he will require extra memory components. If Chips refuses to exchange the computer or to give James a refund, James can take the matter to the small-claims court to obtain the money for the components he needs, provided the amount is no greater than the maximum for such courts (usually about $3,000). However, James will have to prove that George knew the computer was inadequate for James's needs. If James wants to have the sale rescinded (to return the computer and get his money back), he may have to see a lawyer.

As Article 1375 of Quebec's Civil Code (revised Jan. 1, 1994), expresses it: "The parties (to a contract) shall conduct themselves in good faith both at the time the obligation is created and at the time it is performed or extinguished."

See also BAD FAITH; FRAUD; SMALL-CLAIMS COURT.

GOOD SAMARITAN LAWS

While skating on a local pond, Françoise falls through the ice. Bob, a stranger, sees her struggling to get out and throws a rope to her. Unfortunately, Françoise cannot reach the rope and, thinking that he cannot save her by himself, Bob runs to a nearby house for help. Meanwhile, Françoise manages to crawl out of the water on her own. Later she sues Bob for negligence in his rescue attempt. Can she win her case?

The answer will differ from province to province.

Quebec's Charter of Human Rights and Freedoms states that anyone whose life is in peril has a right to assistance. This means that Bob must try to aid Françoise, but does not necessarily mean he is obliged to jump in himself to save her. Perhaps he cannot swim or has a heart problem. Where Bob's own life could be in danger or if he reasonably thought help from others was required, he would not be legally bound to try to save Françoise on his own. Calling for competent help would fulfill his obligation.

However, if Bob were a rescue expert, and it was possible for him to rescue Françoise himself, the court might consider he had violated her right to assistance.

In other Canadian provinces, there is generally no legal duty to help someone in distress, and, in most provinces, if you do decide to assist someone in danger, you are liable if you do so negligently. (Thus if Bob shouts to Françoise that he is going to get help although he ends up never doing so, he may be responsible for damages arising out of his actions.) Alberta and Nova Scotia have passed "good samaritan" legislation so that anyone is able to offer help to an injured party without fear of being sued, unless the rescuer acted in a "grossly negligent manner."

REAL LIFE, REAL LAW

The Case of the Medical Misjudgment

Antoinette was severely injured in a car accident and was brought semiconscious to a Toronto hospital. She had sustained abdominal injuries, was vomiting blood, and was bleeding profusely from severe facial lacerations and fractures. An attending nurse found a card in Antoinette's wallet stating that she was a Jehovah's Witness, and so did not want a blood transfusion and realized the consequences of such a decision. Nevertheless, when Antoinette's blood pressure and level of consciousness dropped, Dr. Steve decided to transfuse her, feeling that without fresh blood the patient would die.

When Antoinette recovered, she sued Dr. Steve for battery because he did not follow her written instructions. She won her case and was awarded $20,000 in damages.

On appeal, the award was confirmed. The appeal court maintained that a doctor is not free to disregard a patient's prior written instructions. Although the doctor probably saved the patient's life by transfusing blood, the court said that the doctor had violated the patient's right to control her own body and showed disrespect of her religious values. The state's interest in preserving life had to give way to the patient's stronger right to direct the course of her own life.

Fire fighters, nurses, doctors, and like professionals are expected to provide an especially high standard of care. For example, Steve, a doctor specializing in the emergency treatment of accident victims, is obliged to perform his skills at the average level of competence of doctors in his field. Steve can not decide to give standard first aid treatment, for example, when important surgery is required. If Ronne, a bank employee, arrived at an accident scene, clearly she would not be held to the same standard of care that Steve is.

See also ACCIDENTS IN THE HOME; NEGLIGENCE; TORT; TRESPASS.

GOODS AND SERVICES TAX

Similar to the Value Added Tax (VAT) used in 48 other countries, the Goods and Services Tax (GST) was introduced on Jan. 1, 1991 by the Progressive Conservative government of the day. The 7 percent GST replaced a manufacturer's sales tax that was usually hidden as part of the price one paid for a product, and was sometimes as high as 13 percent. The GST was highly unpopular and its abolition was central to the electoral platform of the Liberal party, which came to power in 1993. On taking office, Finance Minister Paul Martin confirmed the Liberal government would replace the GST with another form of taxation.

EXCEPTIONS

Basic groceries, prescription drugs, most medical devices, most farm produce and livestock, fresh-caught fish and seafood for human consumption, as well as exported goods and services are among the few goods and services not subject to GST. Also exempted are residential rents (over 30 days in duration), most child-care services, financial services, health and dental services, educational services, and services provided by public bodies such as hospitals, colleges and universities, legal-aid services (but not services from private lawyers), as well as most services provided by non-profit organizations and charities.

In many cases it is difficult to know when the GST applies. When purchasing a new house, there is a reduced rate GST (3 percent), but GST is not paid upon the sale or purchase of used housing. If you buy six muffins you do not pay GST, but you do if you buy one or two muffins, or a sandwich, or a prepared salad, since food and beverages sold in a form suitable for immediate consumption are subject to GST.

Used property is not taxable under GST if the sale is not part of a commercial enterprise. So garage sale transactions and money exchanged in the private sale of a used car are exempt.

REGISTRATION

The GST legislation required anyone with annual revenues of more than $30,000 per year from the sale of goods or services to register with the Tax Department and obtain a GST registration number. Taxi drivers and limousine operators had to register regardless of their annual revenue. Partnerships had to register, although the individual partners did not.

By registering, a person conducting a commercial activity became an agent of Revenue Canada and responsible for collecting GST. As a rule, the seller of the taxable service or product had to collect the tax from her customer at the time of payment.

INPUT TAX CREDIT

Under GST legislation registrants can claim input tax credits (ITCs) for the full amount of GST paid in the course of their commercial activities. Such claims could include taxes paid on office furniture, computers, accountant's fees, taxi fares, promotional items, tools, machine repair costs, and other goods and services used in the normal course of your commercial activity. You could also recover the GST paid on meals and entertainment expenses.

You must apply for the ITC when you file your GST return. You have four years in which to do so. For example, registrants have until Oct. 31, 1997 to apply for GST refunds related to purchases that they paid for in September 1993.

GOVERNMENT RECORDS

There are any number of reasons why you might need to obtain such government records as a birth, death, or marriage certificate or a divorce decree. These records are usually available from one or more government agencies. You can generally obtain the records you want at the offices specified below:

◇ *For birth and death certificates.* You may need these in order to collect insurance benefits or to get a clear title to real estate, for example. Write to the province's bureau of vital statistics (in some provinces it may be called the office of vital records or bureau of records and statistics) in the provincial capital. Generally, you must make your request in person or in writing and pay a fee. See ADOPTION; BIRTH CERTIFICATE.

◇ *For marriage records.* Write to the vital statistics bureau or the court clerk in the province where the marriage was registered. In the case of foreign marriage certificates, write to the nearest Canadian embassy and pay the required fee. It may be months before your claim is processed.

◇ *For divorce records.* Write to the clerk of the court that granted the divorce for a true copy of the judgment. If you need information on where and when a divorce was granted or if in fact a divorce has been rendered, write to the Registrar of Divorces in Ottawa. See USEFUL ADDRESSES.

◇ *For records regarding real estate (including deeds or liens).* Call the recorder of deeds in the county where the real estate is located.

◇ *For records about criminal or civil court proceedings.* Contact the clerk of the court where the trial took place. All you need to know is the name of one or more parties in the case, but the records will be found more quickly if you know the case file number. For transcripts of the trial or certified copies of documents used in the trial, you will have to pay a fee in advance.

◇ *For young offender records.* Access to photographs, fingerprints, and other information dealing with crimes by persons 12 to 18 years of age may be disclosed only to the young person, his or her lawyer, the attorney general, or certain other government officials. In some cases—where charges have been dropped, for example—records may not be disclosed unless a judge is satisfied that it is in the interests of justice or that there is some other important reason for allowing access. In such cases, the young person must be given notice by whoever wishes to see the records, and has the right of appeal to the judge in order to stop disclosure of the documents. The courts recently awarded financial damages to a young person who lost his job when police erroneously disclosed his record.

RELEVANT LEGISLATION

The Access to Information Act requires federal agencies to make most of their records available to the public. As well, six provinces and Yukon Territory have enacted legislation giving citizens access to personal files kept by the government as well as other government information. Thus you can check what information the government has compiled on you and whether it is correct. Or you may want the most up-to-date information on government grants for the arts, study or business ventures. In either case, you should contact the access to information commission of your province or that of the federal government.

In addition to the laws mentioned, the federal government, Ontario, and Quebec have privacy legislation governing personal files in government hands. For all three, the general rule is that information about individuals is to be used only for the purposes for which it was gathered. There are only two exceptions. The first is when the person concerned consents to the use of his or her files. The second is when the information will be used in a manner "consistent" with the purpose for which it was originally gathered. Quebec's privacy legislation permits transfer of personal information from one government agency to another without the permission of the person concerned.

There are also privacy clauses in a number of other laws, including the Income Tax Act and the Statistics Act. When information is disclosed without legal authority, those responsible may be sued for damages or fined, depending on the jurisdiction.

In Quebec, private companies may now collect personal information only with the individual's consent, and provided that person can make corrections to his file or have his name deleted from a given list.

See ACCESS TO INFORMATION.

GRAND JURY

The grand jury system has long been abolished throughout Canada. Nova Scotia, the last province to do so, abolished its grand jury in 1985. Grand juries were intended to protect individuals from unreasonable, abusive, or unwarranted prosecutions. The accuser, usually the attorney general, would present the facts on a given case and make an argument that prosecution against a certain person commence. It would be up to the grand jury to decide if there were reasonable grounds to bring a case against the accused. At this stage, the accused's guilt or innocence was not at issue, only the reasonableness of the accusation.

Today, accusations are brought to justices of the peace, who have the power to order an accused to stand trial if the evidence so merits.

GRANDFATHER CLAUSE

A provision in a law, which allows someone to continue a practice that the law otherwise restricts or prohibits, is called a grandfather clause. Such a clause usually applies only to a current activity and to a specific person or organization.

Suppose your province outlaws the incineration of old tires. The law may have a provision that allows a company already operating a tire incinerator to continue doing so, even though no one else can set up a new tire-incinerator business. If the owner of the existing incinerator sells his property or tries to open a new incinerator somewhere else, the clause would probably not apply either to the new owner or the new location.

To obtain a grandfather-clause exemption, contact the regulatory body that oversees the business, such as the zoning board, health department, or environmental agency.

GRANDPARENTS' RIGHTS

When their son was killed in an automobile accident, Mary Jane and Gene Parker took some comfort in the fact that he left behind two beautiful children. The Parkers offered emotional and financial support to their daughter-in-law, who politely but firmly declined.

In the months following their son's funeral, the Parkers saw their grandchildren less and less frequently, and only when they had initiated contact. The Parkers respected their daughter-in-law's need for a little distance, but called weekly to say hello to the children.

A year after their son's accident the Parkers received a letter from their daughter-in-law, explaining that she and the children were moving to another province, and she felt it was in the children's best interests to have no more contact with their grandparents.

The Parkers were stunned. Although they were not close to their son's wife, they never expected to be cut off from their grandchildren. Do they have any legal recourse?

RECOGNIZING GRANDPARENTS' RIGHTS

The Divorce Act and various provincial laws such as the Ontario and Saskatchewan children's law reform acts, Alberta's Provincial Court Act, British Columbia's Family Relations Act, and Yukon's Children's Act provide for visitation rights of grandparents, with the paramount consideration always being "the best interest of the child." But only Quebec's Civil Code expressly forbids parents from interfering with grandparents' rights to see their grandchildren, unless there are valid reasons.

According to a British Columbia Court of Appeal judge: "Courts do not often grant access to a person other than a parent where the child is in a home with good parents. That may be because good parents do not oppose access where it is in the best interests of the child."

Another B.C. court denied the paternal grandparents' request for access to their three-year-old granddaughter because the mother, the custodial parent, believed the grandparents were instrumental in

the marriage breakdown and consequently there were bad feelings between the parties. The judge felt the grandparents "would turn access visits into unhappy occurrences, harmful to the child as being disruptive of the relationship between mother and child."

Several similar judgments have been rendered by the Manitoba Court of Appeal.

The Ontario Provincial Court also denied a grandmother access to her 4½-year-old grandson. Because the grandmother had an unhealthy desire to control her 34-year-old son, there was a great risk she might make derogatory remarks about the child's mother in front of the child, thus scarring the child emotionally, and might attempt to weaken or destroy his parents' marriage. Accordingly, the court felt such visits would not be in the child's best interests.

On the other hand, another Ontario court granted a grandmother and an aunt access to two young children, because they, as well as the children's mother, had performed mothering duties. According to the presiding judge, "to deprive the children of the love of their primary caretakers bordered on deprivation and cruelty."

A Nova Scotia court also refused to rescind a grandmother's visiting rights to her two-year-old grandson. The judge felt objections by the child's mother were unreasonable and immature.

Thus questions of access by grandparents or other non-parents are decided on a case-by-

case basis, depending always upon how the facts of the particular case will affect "the best interests of the child."

GRANT

A grant is a gift of property or legal rights to property. Federal, provincial, and municipal governments, organizations, foundations, and individuals can all be sources of grants.

Grants are offered for many purposes, including scientific research, educational opportunities, renovating real estate, and supporting the arts. Grant donors generally require that interested persons submit an application. The donor is under no obligation to award a grant if no applicant qualifies.

A grant may be conditional— for example, it may stipulate that the recipient use the money for approved purposes only, or that he submit a report at the end of the project for which funds were provided. If a recipient fails to meet the conditions of such a grant, the donor may revoke it and demand the return of grant funds.

For instance, suppose Sylviane, a wealthy patron of the arts, offered a grant for the purpose of setting up a dance studio for underprivileged children. A group of former dancers obtained the grant by promising that they would set up a studio and have the children stage a recital at the end of one year. When the year was up, Sylviane was distressed to learn that not only was no recital scheduled, but the grant recipients had spent almost all the funds on a fact-finding trip to Italy. Sylviane would be entitled to ask that the grant money be returned. See COLLEGE SCHOLARSHIP; GIFT.

GRIEVANCE PROCEDURE

A grievance procedure is a formal means for handling complaints and problems in the workplace. Most labor unions have negotiated grievance procedures as part of their master agreement, whereby the union steward or other intermediary transmits workers' complaints to management. The purpose of these procedures is to bring order to the workplace, promote communication, and minimize or prevent labor disputes.

If your working conditions are regulated by a collective agreement (only for unionized workers), then you may grieve such things as harassment by your superiors, unsafe working conditions, refused transfers or promotions, disciplinary actions, and so on. Talk to your shop steward or call your union local's representative to find out how to set about starting a grievance procedure.

See also LABOR UNION.

GUARDIAN AD LITEM

Appointed by the court, a guardian ad litem ("guardian for the suit") acts on behalf of a minor or for an adult who has been declared physically or mentally incapable of assuming responsibility in a lawsuit. The guardian ad litem's authority extends only to matters pertaining to the lawsuit. See also GUARDIAN AND WARD.

A guardian ad litem's role is to safeguard the rights of the person she represents, the ward. However, she is not entitled to share any award won by the ward. Nor is she responsible if the ward is required to make any compensation or reparation.

CHILDREN AND INCOMPETENT OR MISSING ADULTS

If a lawsuit is started in a child's name, a guardian ad litem must be named in the suit, as well as the child. This guardian is often one of the child's parents but may be any competent adult. If the child is a defendant in a case, the plaintiff will ask the court to appoint a guardian ad litem. Most provinces require youth courts to appoint a guardian ad litem in cases of child abuse or neglect. Sometimes in divorce proceedings involving child custody, the presiding judge may find that the parents are unable to act in the best interests of their children, and he may appoint a guardian ad litem to act as advocate for the children.

When minors are to receive large sums of money (over $5,000 in Ontario, $25,000 in Quebec), a guardian (usually the minor's parents) is appointed to watch over the money.

The court will appoint a guardian ad litem to any lawsuit with an incompetent adult as defendant or plaintiff.

A guardian ad litem may also be appointed in mortgage foreclosures or certain lawsuits involving real estate to represent adults who might have some claim to the property in question but cannot be found.

GUARDIAN AND WARD

Abandoned or orphaned children, as well as insane, elderly, or invalid persons who are unable to care for themselves or their property, are often entrusted to a guardian (called a tutor in Quebec). The court will give this guardian the legal right and responsibility to care for the person (known as the ward) or his property or both.

If 12-year-old Donna's parents die in a car accident and she inherits the family business, a guardian may be appointed to sell the business on her behalf. That guardian must not sell the business, even to a friend or business associate, for less than the market value. In short, the guardian must always act in the ward's interest. A guardian who is negligent may be liable for damages.

GUARDIANS OF MINOR CHILDREN

A child's parents are considered his natural guardians. As such they have the right and responsibility to make important decisions on his behalf—such as where he should go to school, whether he should attend a church, and so on. If the parents are divorced, the custodial parent is considered the guardian. When parents have joint custody, they are both guardians. See also CHILD CUSTODY; CHILDREN'S RIGHTS.

Parents of minor children should draft wills designating a person to be appointed as guardian in the event that they both die. This is known as a testamentary guardianship. Generally, such a guardian will have custody of the children, as well as a duty to manage their property; however, you need not assign the same person both responsibilities. In naming a testamentary guardian, consider the following:

◇ Be sure the person you have named is willing to take on the responsibility of raising your children. If possible, name one or two alternatives in case your first choice becomes unable to do the job.

◇ Choose someone who is prepared to bring up your children in a way that is compatible with your own beliefs, customs, values, and religious practices.

◇ Speak with an estate-planning professional about the best way to provide for your children. For instance, you may wish to set up a trust for your teenage children so that they can receive money in small amounts at a time, rather than leaving them a lump sum that must be managed by their guardian in accordance with a court's directives.

If you do not name a testamentary guardian in your will, any interested party—such as a grandparent or a social service agency—can initiate guardianship proceedings.

In appointing a guardian, courts in Alberta, British Columbia, Manitoba, Ontario, Quebec, Saskatchewan, and Nova Scotia will consider the wishes of a minor 12 to 14 years of age. Alberta, British Columbia, Nova Scotia, Ontario, and Quebec insist the guardian post a bond to faithfully administer the property.

CONSERVATORSHIP

In many provinces, a guardian is a person entrusted with the complete care of another, while a conservator is a person who is appointed to manage property and finances only. Often parents are appointed as conservators of their minor children's inheritance.

Upon her death, Matt's grandmother leaves her 10-year-old grandson a 75-acre farm and $250,000 in cash and securities. His parents want to sell Matt's farm to pay off their own mortgage and use the money to send their older son to college. Can they do so?

Probably not. Even though Matt's parents are the conservators of his property, they are not entitled to sell or dispose of property held in Matt's name, but must manage and conserve it for his benefit—not for that of his brother or themselves.

Courts have the authority to appoint conservators for people who are unable to manage

---

CHECKLIST

Naming a Guardian or Conservator

When appointing guardians or conservators, the courts consider a number of factors, some of which are listed below:

■ **WISHES OF THE PARENT.**
When appointing a guardian for a minor, courts consider the wishes of the parents (such as those expressed in a will). However, courts are not bound by those wishes if they are not in the child's best interests.

■ **WISHES OF THE CHILD.**
Some provincial laws provide that courts must consider the wishes of children who have reached a certain age (10 in many cases) when designating a guardian.

■ **RELATIONSHIP TO THE WARD.**
When naming guardians, courts prefer to appoint close blood relatives whenever possible.

■ **AVAILABILITY OF SUITABLE CANDIDATES.**
If there are no suitable candidates among a ward's close relatives or associates, courts often appoint a government official as the conservator of the ward's property.

■ **FITNESS.**
In determining a candidate's fitness, courts consider his moral character, business competence, stability, health, and age.

■ **RELIGION.**
In appointing a guardian for a minor, courts prefer to name a person with the same religious background as the minor.

their own affairs. However, being forgetful, foolish, naive, or unlucky in business matters is not enough to justify the appointment of a conservator. For example, somebody who invests his family's savings in a new computer software company that quickly goes bankrupt has made an unwise investment. That is not enough to warrant appointing a conservator. If the same person, however, sold the family business for a handful of magic beans, the family could ask a court to appoint a conservator to try to cancel the sale, perhaps, or to handle future property. See also POWER OF ATTORNEY.

POWERS AND DUTIES OF GUARDIAN AND CONSERVATOR

The guardian or conservator is usually responsible for such duties as paying the debts of the ward from her assets, suing to protect her property, taking out loans when necessary, entering into contracts for her, and collecting debts and settling claims relating to her property. Both guardians and conservators may employ accountants, attorneys, real estate agents, and any other person needed to manage the ward's estate. Fees for people so employed are paid from monies under the guardian's or conservator's care.

A guardian or conservator must be reasonable and prudent in his decisions. He may be held responsible for losses if it can be shown that he was reckless or indifferent to his duties, or negligently acted contrary to the ward's inter-

ests, as would be the case, for example, if he sold the property at less than its market value.

If there are funds to be invested, the guardian must make safe, nonspeculative investments that will produce an income for the ward. A court will judge whether a guardian or conservator has acted in the ward's best interests by applying to him the standard of reasonable and prudent behavior.

All guardians and conservators are subject to the supervision and direction of a court. They must provide the court with a regular accounting of their wards' estates and report actions taken on their behalf. Some provinces have laws requiring the guardian to obtain court approval for transactions involving the ward's property, especially immovable property. As an administrator, a guardian or conservator is usually unable to sell his ward's immovable property without the court's permission. A guardian acting with court approval will not be held responsible for any resulting losses.

A guardian or conservator may be removed from his post by the court for neglecting his duty to his ward, disobeying court orders, or misusing the ward's property and funds. If a guardian or conservator fails to put his ward's interests first when conducting the ward's business, the courts will relieve him of his duty.

FROM

HABEAS CORPUS

TO

HOUSEHOLD HELP

HABEAS CORPUS

A Latin term meaning "you have the body," habeas corpus is a writ (court order) directing a warden or other official to produce a prisoner so that the court can decide whether he is being legally detained or imprisoned. The writ of habeas corpus, available to someone who feels he has been illegally detained or imprisoned, is considered one of the great safeguards of personal liberty. Because it charges that a person is being deprived of his constitutional right to liberty as guaranteed by the Charter of Rights and Freedoms, a habeas corpus writ receives prompt attention from the court.

In practice, the general rule is that if there appears to be a case for issuing a writ of habeas corpus, the prisoner will be brought before a superior court judge to hear the merits of the application. The courts are very tolerant about the form of writ, provided it includes an affidavit swearing to the truth of the application. The courts will consider even a handwritten habeas corpus writ.

Writs of habeas corpus are often filed by prisoners or their families, but they can also be used under other circumstances, too. A person who thinks he is being wrongfully confined in a mental institution may try to seek a writ of habeas corpus as a way to force a court to review the legality of his confinement.

A New Brunswick court awarded $2,800 in damages for false imprisonment to a man kept in solitary confinement for 10 weeks. He was placed in quarantine in a federal prison, on transfer there from another prison where there was a case of tuberculosis. There was no evidence that he was ever in contact with the TB victim.

Ruling that his confinement in isolation was oppressive and arbitrary, the court awarded $800 in compensatory damages, $2,000 in punitive damages, and $958 for the habeas corpus application costs.

See also APPEAL; ARREST; BAIL; DEATH PENALTY; IMMIGRATION.

HATE CRIME

Racism and bigotry directed against visible minorities and other vulnerable groups are a serious problem across the world. Canada is not immune. Racism can manifest itself in many ways. It can involve, for example, the painting of a swastika on a synagogue wall, a threatening phone call to a mosque, or an outright physical assault.

As a partial response to these problems, the government has enacted sections in the Criminal Code that make it a crime to advocate genocide or publicly incite hatred against any group of people because of their color, race, religion, or ethnic origin. Calling for people's death on the basis of bigotry carries a sentence of up to five years in jail. Publicly inciting hatred carries a possible two year sentence. Yet, immoral and antisocial though it may be, promoting hate in private conversation does not break the law. For, although the law condemns acts motivated by prejudice, it does not outlaw the prejudice itself. Accordingly, a person who willfully promotes hatred cannot be convicted of hate crimes if his statements are true or are a good-faith opinion on a religious subject. Similarly, if the statements were made on a reasonable belief that they were relevant to a matter of public interest, such as demonstrating how widespread certain racist ideas are in society, then there is no crime.

The validity of hate crime legislation in view of the free speech guarantee in the Charter of Rights and Freedoms has been challenged in the courts. One case involved an Alberta schoolteacher, who was charged with willfully promoting hatred after it was learned that he inculcated anti-Semitism in his students. The Supreme Court of Canada found that the Criminal Code sections dealing with hate crimes did infringe on the teacher's freedom of expression. However, it also held that such limits were reasonable in a free and democratic society such as Canada's. The majority of the judges felt the Criminal Code provisions are justified in light of the serious problems of racism and the experience of the Holocaust (when 6 million Jews were gassed to death in Nazi concentration camps during World War II).

A person, or a group, that is defamed by hate propaganda, may also sue for damages before the civil courts.

See also ASSAULT AND BATTERY; BREACH OF THE PEACE; WRONGFUL DEATH.

HEALTH CLUB

As summer approached, Ned decided to join a health club in an effort to shape up his body. A club near his office offered a "lifetime membership" for only $1,000, so Ned signed a contract in which he agreed to pay $50 monthly until his membership fee was paid up. Two months later, the club owners declared bankruptcy.

Unfortunately, that was not the end of the story. Not realizing that his financial obligation did not end when the club was closed, Ned stopped his payments. Now he is being hounded for the unpaid balance by a finance company to which the club sold Ned's contract before going into bankruptcy. Health clubs and other businesses sell their contracts to obtain immediate cash, rather than waiting for the members to pay all their installments.

THE CONTRACT

Since contracts are generally binding between only the parties who make them, one would expect that Ned would not be obligated to the finance company. However, there are certain contracts that allow one party to promise another that he will do something for a third party (in this case a finance company). This type of contract has what is called a "stipulation for the benefit of a third person" or an "assignable contract," and is legally binding. In Ned's case, it may be that he can claim the contract is "frustrated" (and therefore void), since he will be forced to pay for something he will not receive. Ned, however, has already received some services, and his contract may provide that in such circumstances he is not allowed this defense. Most consumer protection legislation, however, would enable Ned to use the defense of "frustration of contract" against the finance company. Consumer legislation would not give the holder of the contract any more rights than that of the original contracting party, the health club.

Contracts with a health club or other company that supplies its service in a sequential manner rather than all at once may often be canceled by paying a $50 penalty, say, or about 10 percent of the contract.

TAKE PRECAUTIONS

Ned's experience is not uncommon. As many others like him have discovered, health clubs and spas go in and out of business as quickly as promises to diet and exercise are made and broken. Even so, there are ways you can protect yourself from falling into the financial traps associated with them.

You should never sign a long-term contract. Try to find a club that will let you join on a monthly basis, or ask for a two- or three-month trial membership. Even if the club stays in business, your enthusiasm may wane, your financial situation may change, or you may move to another neighborhood. To protect consumers from getting in over their heads, some provinces have passed laws prohibiting health clubs from offering lifetime memberships.

As Ned found out, it can be costly to sign a membership contract without reading the fine print—so scrutinize the contract thoroughly and make sure you understand all your obligations. Never rely on oral assurances from the staff. If a promise is not in writing, it is probably not enforceable.

Find out whether you will be allowed to sell the remainder of your membership or receive a refund, and what penalty, if any, you will have to pay, if you move, change jobs, or simply lose interest.

CHOOSING A CLUB

If you are thinking of joining a health club or spa, do not yield to high-pressure sales pitches or offers that are good "today only." Instead, investigate the club. How long has it been around? Does it have a large membership? Does it make an effort to improve its facilities?

Ask to use the club once or twice to make sure that it does provide the facilities and services it has promised. Visit the club at the time of day you are planning to use it most often. During your visit, talk to other members and note the size of the crowd, the number of staff members, the supply of towels and lockers, and the general level of cleanliness.

CONSUMER PROTECTION

Many provinces have laws that offer some protection to health club members. For example, after signing a contract, you often have the right to cancel the membership and receive a full refund if you cancel the contract before taking any of the classes or before you have received a copy of the contract signed by the health club. You might not be given the contract until your cheque has cleared, thus you have several days to reflect.

In some provinces you must be allowed to put your membership "on hold" if you cannot use it for a while because of injury or illness. See COOLING-OFF PERIOD.

Some provinces require health clubs and spas to buy bonds to protect members from experiences like Ned's if the club goes out of business. If the facility closes, you may file for a refund with the bonding company, but the bond may not be adequate to cover all refund claims.

Your local consumer affairs office will be able to give you details on the laws relating to health clubs and spas in your province. See also BETTER BUSINESS BUREAU; CONSUMER PROTECTION.

HEALTH INSURANCE

An injury or illness, whether short or long term, can cause a temporary loss of income and create a lot of debts. The role of health insurance is to protect people against the high cost of medical care. Both individuals and groups (groups may be composed of businesses, trade groups, or professional associations) can buy health insurance from private companies, such as Blue Cross. It and other insurers offer various plans for dental care, upgrading hospital accommodation to semi-private or private, and treatments such as acupuncture, physiotherapy and chiropractic, not covered by Medicare.

Health insurance coverage can vary widely, but in general most private health insurance policies provide some combination of: (1) basic medical care; (2) hospitalization; (3) items not covered by Medicare—certain drugs, for example, or medical devices such as wheelchairs and hearing aids. Some policies even pay for private nurses round-the-clock when necessary, or pay a nurse to visit you at home. Some private health plans also guarantee a part of your salary when you are unable to work.

See also MEDICARE.

PREMIUMS AND DEDUCTIBLES

Companies that provide health insurance operate by collecting regular payments (premiums) from their customers in exchange for a guarantee to cover certain health-care costs. The insurance company determines the amount of these premiums based on a number of factors, including whether the policy is for a group or an individual and the expectation of how much medical care the policyholders will require. See also INSURANCE.

Most insurers require policyholders to pay a certain part of their health-care costs annually before the company starts paying benefits. This amount, known as a deductible, varies with the amount and type of coverage you hold.

GROUP INSURANCE

Many people receive health insurance through a group plan provided by their employer, by a union, or by some other professional organization. Group policies offer much lower premiums than individual health plans do, largely because the risks are spread out among the group.

Some employers pay the entire premium of the employee's health-care plan. Such plans are termed noncontributory. Other companies deduct a part of the premium from each employee's paycheque. Such plans are called contributory.

With group insurance, the insurance company prepares one master policy, or contract, which is signed by the insurer

and the employer or organization taking it out. Each participant in the group receives a certificate and brochure outlining coverage in general terms. More detailed information about health coverage will be found in the master policy, which is usually available from the company's employee benefits or human resources department.

Family coverage
Most group policies can be extended to cover a member's spouse and children. The premiums and deductibles are usually higher.

INDIVIDUAL POLICIES

Contract (freelance) or part-time workers, employees of small businesses, and others who cannot get health insurance through an employer or other group have the option of buying individual insurance for themselves and their families.

Because premiums are high and coverage is more limited under many individual plans, buyers should carefully review several insurance policies to see which one provides the best protection at the most reasonable rate. For further information, consult the health division of your provincial insurance commission.

DENIAL OF COVERAGE

Insurance companies can deny policies to the ill and to anyone deemed to be a poor risk because of bad health, a previous history of a disease (such as cancer), or employment in a "rated" occupation (one that insurance companies consider dangerous, such as skydiving instruction or working with toxic chemicals). Many companies will, however, insure such people at higher rates.

Experimental treatment

In some cases experimental treatment may be the only option for certain life-threatening diseases. Some insurance companies may allow policyholders to pay an additional premium for coverage of specific experimental treatments should these regimens become necessary in the future.

Preexisting conditions

Most individual health insurance policies contain some provision that allows an insurer to deny coverage for a "preexisting condition" or to terminate coverage after a specified period. A preexisting condition is generally defined as a health problem that existed before (often one to five years before) the coverage was purchased.

In addition, any illness or injury that occurs after the policy was purchased, but which can be traced back to a preexisting condition, will likely be excluded from coverage. Suppose you experience nerve damage and atrophy resulting from a knee injury that was listed as a preexisting condition. Although the nerve damage occurs after you buy the policy, it relates back to the excluded preexisting condition and will probably not be covered.

No duplicate benefits

Most insurance policies include a provision requiring "coordination of benefits." Under this provision, no one can collect from more than one insurance company for the same illness or treatment.

Still, if you and your spouse are both covered by group health insurance provided by your employers, you may want to consider keeping both policies. In this way, you may be able to have complete coverage for illnesses or injuries (after your deductible is paid). For example, if a wife's policy covers 80 percent of a medical bill, her husband's policy will often pay the remaining 20 percent.

If you pursue this course of action, examine both policies to find out which insurer you should submit bills to first. Then submit a claim to the second company for the amount the first insurance company does not pay you. If both you and your spouse are insured by the same company, however, this strategy will not work.

RENEWAL AND CANCELLATION

Most individual health insurance policies are "guaranteed renewable contracts," which means that the policyholder is entitled to renew the policy at the end of its term. If the policy contains a guaranteed renewable provision, you are assured of health protection up to a certain age, commonly 65 years. Guaranteed renewal provisions do not prevent the insurance company from raising its premiums at the beginning of the new term.

If your policy has a noncancellation clause, you are covered throughout the term of the contract at guaranteed rates. However, there are reasons for which any insurance policy can be canceled before its expiry. One common reason

is the failure to pay premiums when they are due. If your policy lapses for this reason, you can be required to prove your insurability again.

Another ground for cancellation is the insured's failure to disclose a medical condition. When you fill out an insurance application, you sometimes have to reveal more than you are asked, and you should be honest about your personal, family, and medical history.

An insurance policy is a contract requiring *uberrima fides* ("the utmost good faith"). If you have a medical condition that would make you uninsurable or for which the company would require a higher premium, you must disclose this fact. Do not be misled by an insurance agent who says such disclosure is not important. If, for example, you are a heavy smoker or drinker, or take certain medication, you should tell this to the insurer so that he can adjust the premium accordingly.

These types of disclosures are known as material facts and must be volunteered if not specifically requested. Remember, the insurance company will likely make an investigation before paying out a large amount. If it finds out that you did not tell the whole truth, it will refuse to pay and most likely you would lose in court if you sued. Be especially careful if asked whether you have ever been hospitalized or if you have consulted a doctor in the last two years. Most women have been hospitalized when giving birth and even a visit to your family doctor when you had a bad cold counts as having consulted a physician.

Individual members cannot be dropped from group plans; the company can only cancel the policy for the entire group.

Travel

Some policies provide health insurance coverage within Canada only. If you are going abroad, find out from your insurer whether you need to purchase additional insurance to cover any medical expenses you incur abroad.

STEPS TO TAKE

If your insurance company denies your claim for reimbursement, or if it pays you less than what you feel you are entitled to, take the following actions:

1. Call the insurer's claims department and ask for a written explanation for denying your claim and a statement of the precise policy terms that allow the company to do so.

2. If you have an individual policy, get in touch with the agent who sold it to you. He may be willing to intercede on your behalf, especially if your claim is being denied on the basis of a questionable interpretation of the policy.

3. File a complaint with your provincial insurance bureau or with the superintendent of insurance in your province. The bureau will investigate your complaint and may be able to exert its influence on the insurer if it decides that your claim has been unreasonably denied.

4. See if your plan contains a clause that provides for compulsory arbitration to settle a dispute over a claim. Arbitra-

tion will avoid the expense and delays of legal action, although you will have to pay arbitration fees. See ARBITRATION.

5. For a large claim, you can hire a lawyer to pursue the matter in court. If your insurer has acted in bad faith by refusing to cover a legitimate claim, you may receive compensatory damages. See also DAMAGES.

HEARING

Conducted much like a trial, a hearing is a proceeding during which evidence is heard for the purpose of deciding a matter of fact or a point of law. During a hearing, opposing sides appear in court or before a provincial or federal agency to present and offer arguments about evidence and about points of law pertaining to the case. Both sides will usually have lawyers present.

A judicial hearing is much like a regular trial, and the outcome can settle a lawsuit, even though the purpose of the hearing may be to decide a preliminary matter before the trial begins. Suppose a preliminary hearing finds that key evidence against the defendant was obtained without a search warrant. Because there is no other evidence sufficient to obtain a conviction, the charges are dismissed—there is no reason to proceed to a trial that will only find the defendant not guilty.

Public administrative agencies (such as housing authorities) and legislative committees (such as those of the House of Commons) hold hearings to investigate issues and resolve disputes. These kinds of hearings tend to be less formal than those conducted by a court of law, and the rules governing admissibility of evidence are not as stringent as those in a criminal or civil trial.

See CRIMINAL PROCEDURE; EVIDENCE; INQUESTS AND INQUIRIES.

HEARSAY

In legal terms, hearsay is secondhand information—something a witness heard another person say. Because the witness has no direct knowledge of the facts, and the original speaker is not under oath or subject to cross-examination, hearsay evidence is usually not admissible in court.

There are exceptions, however, and these have been greatly simplified in recent years by the Supreme Court of Canada. Now, to determine whether a hearsay statement is admissible, it is crucial to ask whether there is any reason to believe it is reliable. To determine reliability, the courts look at the timing of the statement (when it was made out of court) and the demeanor, intelligence, and understanding of the person making it. The fact that a person had no reason to fabricate the statement would also be important.

The closer the hearsay statement is made to the actual event, the more reliable it is, and the rule of "spontaneous declaration" or "the excited utterance" are elements of such timing. For example, if Antoinette ran out of her house exclaiming excitedly: "My brother just threatened to kill me," her spontaneous declaration, as heard by Peter, may be admissible in court if Antoinette is later found dead. This would be so because of Antoinette's demeanor, and the fact that she described the threat in Peter's hearing immediately upon running out of the house.

In any case of hearsay, however, the judge has the duty to inform the jury that hearsay evidence should not be given the same weight as the testimony of a person who is present in court and subject to cross-examination.

See also EVIDENCE.

HEAT OF PASSION

The term "heat of passion" relates to the defense of provocation. By legal definition, provocation is "an illegal act or an insult that is of such a nature as to be sufficient to deprive an ordinary person of the power of self-control," and that "the accused acted on it on the sudden and before there was time for his passion to cool." Whether or not provocation existed is a question of fact that is left to the jury to decide.

According to the Supreme Court of Canada, a reasonable person is "of normal temperament and level of self-control, and is not exceptionally excitable, pugnacious, or in a state

REAL LIFE, REAL LAW

The Case of the Passionately Provoked Professor

In August 1992 a professor at Concordia University in Montreal went to the university armed with three pistols. He killed four engineering professors and wounded a secretary in a massacre that shocked the community.

The professor, Valery Fabrikant, defended himself at his trial, his principal defense being that he acted on provocation. Arguing that his crime was one of passion, caused by the engineering department's alleged improper behavior toward him, he requested that he be found guilty of manslaughter rather than first-degree murder. Fabrikant claimed that much of his research (which he described as of a world-class caliber) was misappropriated, in that he was obliged to include the names of other professors as co-workers on his projects, and he also claimed that he was refused tenure for what he considered improper reasons.

These actions by the university, said the accused, were of such a nature that he suffered from the "battered person syndrome." He claimed that any other normal person who was similarly persecuted by the university would also have been driven to extreme behavior.

Midway through the trial, Mr. Justice Fraser Martin, the presiding judge, held a minitrial to see if the accused was competent to complete his trial. Two psychiatrists testified that although the accused suffered from extreme narcissism and displayed other personality disorders, he was not insane in the legal sense.

After the trial had gone on for 4½ months, the judge put an end to the proceedings, stating that the behavior of the accused made it impossible to continue the trial, and requesting the Crown and the accused to make their final arguments.

The Crown completed its summation in about 30 minutes, but Prof. Fabrikant's submission to the jury, which seemed to have no end, was cut off after three days.

After a few hours' deliberation, the jury convicted Prof. Fabrikant of all four murders and all other charges against him. The jurors did not feel that the university's actions constituted provocation nor did they feel that the accused had acted on the spur of the moment. In fact, the Crown had presented proof at the trial that the accused had made veiled threats to faculty members in the past, and had gone through the process of obtaining a gun, and even taking shooting lessons.

But the matter is still not settled. The professor is presently appealing his conviction on more than 20 grounds.

of drunkenness." Thus the test of heat of passion is twofold:
1) was there provocation in the legal sense of the word?
2) did the accused in fact act on the provocation suddenly before she could regain control and let her passion cool?

Heat of passion is most often used in reference to a crime where mitigating circumstances obscured a person's judgment to the extent that she then acted impulsively. These circumstances may be considered to have so clouded the person's judgment that she cannot be judged according to the same standards as a person whose actions are deliberate and voluntary. As a result, for example, a charge of murder may be reduced to the lesser charge of manslaughter.

Suppose that, upon returning home from work, Lucy finds a man who had previously assaulted her aged mother waiting for her in the driveway. He taunts Lucy, threatening to "beat up" her poor mother "any time he feels like it." Lucy flies into a rage and strikes the man in the face with her heavy briefcase. He falls, hits his head, and later dies of his injuries. Lucy's impulsive act is considered to be a crime committed in the "heat of passion," and therefore she is charged not with murder, but with manslaughter.

See CRIMINAL LAW; MURDER.

HEIR

An heir is a person (often a relative) who is entitled by law to inherit another person's property. Provincial laws (called laws of descent and distribution, or intestate succession) control the distribution of assets if someone dies without a will. So if your grandmother dies intestate and you are her only surviving relative, you are most likely to be her heir.

A child who is not mentioned in a parent's will is known as a pretermitted heir, meaning one who is passed by or omitted. Usually the omission is not intentional and can be rectified. Suppose Jack has three sons—Harry, Barry, and Larry. When Jack wrote his will, Larry had not yet been born. Jack died without revising his will, which states that he is leaving everything to "my sons, Harry and Barry." Larry will probably be entitled to an equal share.

Sometimes, however, a parent intends to disinherit a child by simply not mentioning his name in the will. But wills are interpreted with a "presumption against disinheritance." The mere omission of an heir's name would most likely not result in him being disinherited. Disinheritance requires a clear, precise and probably motivated reason for doing so.

See DYING WITHOUT A WILL; WILL.

HIT-AND-RUN DRIVER

A hit-and-run-driver is the operator of a motor vehicle (including motorcycles and recreational vehicles, or RVs) who strikes a pedestrian, bicyclist, or another vehicle, and then leaves the scene of the accident. Every province has laws requiring persons involved in an accident to stop and identify themselves, and to remain at the scene of the accident until the extent of any damages and injuries can be assessed. Leaving the scene of an accident is a criminal act, and severe penalties will be imposed on the driver. A hit-and-run driver can be charged with vehicular manslaughter or other crimes.

To avoid prosecution as a hit-and-run driver, and to ensure that your insurance claims are settled without delay, you should remain at an accident in which you are involved. If someone has been injured, assist him as best as you can until emergency help arrives. See also AUTOMOBILE ACCIDENTS.

If you strike an empty vehicle and cannot locate the driver, leave a slip of paper under the windshield wiper with your name, telephone number (or your lawyer's telephone number), driver's license number, and information about your insurance coverage.

IF YOU ARE A VICTIM

If you are struck by a hit-and-run driver, try to track down any witnesses who may have noticed the vehicle's license plate number or anything else that could help to identify the driver. If you have collision coverage, your insurance company will compensate you for damage to your vehicle; if you have personal injury protection, you will be compensated for medical expenses. See also AUTOMOBILE INSURANCE.

All provincial auto insurance plans provide compensation

when the victim is injured by a hit-and-run driver. Payment is made by the victim's own insurance company or by the provincial motorist insurance plan. If your injuries are serious, or the damage to your vehicle is extensive, you may seek additional compensation. For example, a hit-and-run victim might be compensated by his province's crime victims' indemnity fund or, as was the case recently in Ontario, by the Superintendent of Insurance.

To get sufficient evidence for a civil suit, you may have to get the help of the police or even hire a private investigator or a lawyer to track down the hit-and-run driver.

HITCHHIKING

Hitchhikers stand by the side of the road hoping to get a free ride from a driver going in the same direction. Hitchhikers, and the motorists who pick them up, sometimes become the victims of crimes ranging from robbery to assault. As a result, hitchhiking is illegal in most provinces, and a hitchhiker can be punished by a fine.

HOLOGRAPHIC WILL

A will that is written and signed entirely in the handwriting of the person making it, but which is unwitnessed, is called a holographic will. Numerous provinces have passed legislation declaring such wills valid.

If any part of a holographic will is written by another hand or typed, then the will may be declared null.

The old common law was suspicious of wills that did not conform to all the legal requirements of a valid will, such as being signed in the presence of two witnesses. This was to prevent fraud. Nowadays, the general trend of the courts is to give effect to one's last will, so long as fraud or undue influence is not shown. An 86-year-old Ontario man, K, made a holograph will that read "I leave my house and my money to J." But J, who visited his elderly friend to dissuade him from an obsession about death, said he did not want the house and tore up the will in front of K, who threw the pieces of paper in the garbage. Shortly after, K committed suicide.

The courts held that the holograph will was valid, as the reasons for throwing the torn paper in the garbage were ambiguous and did not equal an express revocation.

See also WILL.

HOME BUSINESS

Many entrepreneurs begin their business by working out of their homes or apartments. If the business grows, they can then take on the larger commitment of office space and staff. Consulting firms, mail-order suppliers, caterers and bakers, crafts producers, and many other businesses can be run from a desk or kitchen table. Starting a business always involves up-front investment and planning. Yet by starting your business from home, you can minimize your expenses.

For instance, Marian, who has a degree in graphic arts from a local college, has always enjoyed designing clothing for herself. Last Christmas she saved money on gifts by turning a room in her apartment into a small studio and making silk-screen scarves to give as Christmas presents. Her creations were so admired that several of her friends offered to pay her if she would make them some more. Excited by her early success, Marian wonders whether she should leave her full-time job and start her own business at home. Before she hands in her notice, she ought to do some serious planning.

TAX AND FINANCIAL CONSIDERATIONS

If, like Marian, you are thinking about starting a small business, you should contact one of the numerous private sector and government agencies that provide advice and information for people who wish to start businesses. Among these are the Canadian Federation of Independent Business, the Ontario Development Corporation, the Canadian Chamber of Commerce, the Federal Business Development Bank and numerous provincial agencies that serve beginning entrepreneurs.

Talk to an accountant or tax specialist about the financial implications of running a business out of your home. You will have to make deductions and contributions for your employees for such things as Canada Pension Plan, unemployment insurance and worker's compensation. You will also have to pay any applicable taxes.

Your accountant will be able to tell you what type of bank account to open and what kinds of records you need to keep. For example, because the law allows you to deduct a portion of your rent, utilities, and capital costs for equipment and furniture for the business, you should keep all your bills and receipts.

For expenses such as rent, heat, hydro, phone, taxes and so on, Revenue Canada may permit deductions only for that portion of your home which is used mostly for business purposes. For example, if Marian used one out of three bedrooms exclusively as a room for sewing her product, chances are deductions can be made in proportion to the size of the room relative to her home. If her sewing room is one-sixth the size of her home, then one-sixth of certain home expenses are probably deductible as Marian's business expenses. If, however, she occasionally used the sewing room other than for business purposes, then she would have to deduct less of her expenses.

One couple who ran a distributorship out of their home were able to deduct nearly 11 percent of their home expenses. They successfully proved that the space for which they claimed deductions was used "virtually exclusively for business." Similar cases may not always favor the taxpayer, so you would be wise to retain bills and receipts. Then, at tax time, you can back up your claims for deductions.

Insurance

You will also need liability insurance protection beyond that of a usual homeowners' policy, both for yourself and for any employees or visiting clients. And unless you are covered by your spouse's health insurance, you will need to buy an individual health insurance policy. Your insurance agent will be able to tell you what kind of coverage you should have. You may also wish to set up a retirement plan. See ACCIDENTS AT WORK; BUSINESS TAXES; HEALTH INSURANCE; INCOME TAX; INSURANCE; RETIREMENT PLANNING; SOCIAL SECURITY.

LOCAL RESTRICTIONS

Because local laws may affect your home business plans, check with your zoning authority to find out what zoning restrictions apply when you work out of your home. Some zoning ordinances prohibit all home businesses, whereas others merely restrict the hours that you can conduct business with others in your home. If you are going to operate a mail order business, you may have to obtain a post office box rather than receive mail at your home. If you fail to observe zoning laws, the local government can fine you and shut down your business. See also ZONING.

If you rent your home, look at your lease to see whether your home business is subject to any restrictions. If you own your home, check your deed or ask the administrator of your local homeowners' association. If you start a home-catering operation, for instance, and a restrictive covenant in your deed prohibits the operation of a home business, your neighbors may file a lawsuit against you and obtain an injunction forbidding you to continue doing business. See LEASE; RESTRICTIVE COVENANT.

If your business violates a local zoning ordinance, you can request a variance—special permission to operate your business despite the law. You should make a written request to the zoning authority, which will review it and notify the surrounding property owners to see if they have any objections. You may be able to overcome such objections if you can show the zoning authority that there are similar businesses operating in your neighborhood and that your business will not prove disruptive or create a nuisance for your neighbors.

BUSINESS OWNERSHIP

You should decide what form your business will take. The simplest type of ownership is a sole proprietorship, but an accountant or a lawyer may advise you to incorporate the business. If you do incorporate, the corporation, rather than you personally, is responsible for the business's debts and for any lawsuits filed against it. Suppose the dye in Marian's scarves stained Susannah's $5,000 designer suit. Susannah sued her, and the court awarded Susannah $2,500 in damages. If Marian's business is incorporated, Susannah could obtain her money from the corporation only. She could not garnishee Marian's personal bank account or foreclose on her house to collect the money.

Despite its advantages, incorporation is not always recommended for a new business. Incorporating your business may cost you more in taxes (and fees charged by a lawyer or an accountant) than a sole proprietorship. Many businesses begin as sole proprietorships and incorporate when they start to grow. See CORPORATION; SOLE PROPRIETORSHIP.

NAME AND TRADEMARK

You may also want to create a trademarked name and logo that reflect the type of product you are selling. However, you cannot duplicate another company's name if it infringes in any way on the company's conduct of its business. Suppose Marian likes the name Marian's Silks, but a nearby store already uses that name. This store can stop Marian from using its trademark, to prevent loss of business due to customers' confusion over the name. Avoid this problem by hiring a firm that specializes in searching trademark records to perform this service for you. You should also apply for patents to protect any original products or processes. See also PATENT; TRADEMARK.

CAUTIONS

Be cautious in your choice of suppliers, managers, sales representatives, and consultants. Suppose that Marian is selling her scarves at a crafts show when she is approached by a man who claims to know retailers and distributors. He would be happy to sell her products if she gives him a percentage of the sales he arranges. Marian should politely ask the man for his card and tell him that she will be in touch with him. Then she should call her local Better Business Bureau, which will let her know whether any complaints have been filed against the man for unscrupulous business practices. Marian can also ask other clients or suppliers for recommendations.

Never enter into an arrangement with someone without a written contract that clearly spells out your relationship and each of your responsibilities. See also CONTRACT.

Be wary of advertisements offering good wages for simple work such as stuffing envelopes, clipping coupons, or assembling crafts or jewelry. With only their own interests in mind, many of these companies charge you start-up fees for "materials" or "instructions" and then either fail to deliver the materials or send instructions containing so many restrictions that you will never make any money. Be suspicious of any scheme that charges start-up fees. If you suspect that a company may not be legitimate, check with your consumer protection agency or Better Business Bureau. See PYRAMID SALES SCHEME.

PROFESSIONAL CONSIDERATIONS

Be sure to obtain from your local and provincial governments any licenses or permits required in your area, including a business license and a sales tax permit to exempt you from paying any sales tax on items

---

ABC's

OF HOME BUSINESS ZONING LAWS

Zoning laws that pertain to home businesses vary considerably from place to place, so be sure to find out what they are in your area. Typical zoning laws may:

■ Prohibit retail sales or client visits to your home. If client visits are allowed, zoning laws may specify the number of parking spaces you need to provide.

■ Ban signs advertising your business or limit their size, type, and location.

■ Prevent you from hiring employees who are not members of your family.

■ Prohibit or require a separate entrance for your business and your residence.

■ Limit the square footage of your home that can be devoted to business purposes.

■ Prohibit unusual or offensive odors or noises.

■ Restrict the hours during which you can operate your business.

that you will resell, such as the fabric used in making slipcovers or the clay for pottery. Any business that deals with food must meet food-handling and health regulations. A business such as a hair salon, an inn, or a day-care center will require licenses and safety inspections by the appropriate government agency. See also LICENSE.

If you are going to employ others, ask your provincial employment standards commission about your responsibilities to your employees. You will have to withhold taxes from your employees' paycheques and pay Canada (Quebec) Pension Plan, workers' compensation, and unemployment insurance. If you hire only independent contractors or commissioned salespeople, you should give them written work-for-hire contracts and submit the relevant forms to Revenue Canada at the end of the year. You may find the required forms listed in general tax guides, available at the post office. Since tax laws are subject to constant change, inquire annually which forms you must fill out as a business owner. See also INDEPENDENT CONTRACTOR; SELF-EMPLOYMENT; WORKER'S COMPENSATION.

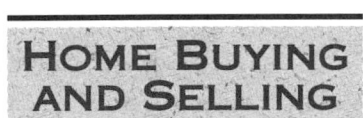

HOME BUYING AND SELLING

Housing is usually the single biggest cost in a family budget, and home ownership is one of the biggest financial responsibilities you will ever have. Even though individually owned single-family homes are still in the majority, you can own another type of home, such as a condominium (in which the owners of each unit also have an interest in the development's common facilities) or a cooperative (where ownership is of shares in a corporation). Whether you are buying or selling a house, condominium, or cooperative, a thorough understanding of the process is helpful. See also CONDOMINIUM; COOPERATIVE APARTMENT; MOBILE HOME.

PROFESSIONAL SERVICES

Many home buyers begin their search at a real estate agency. Typically, the agency will have listings of homes that are for sale. These listings may be exclusive to the agency or "open" listings shared by many agencies. With open listings, more people are likely to be looking at the same properties. If you are a seller, listing a property exclusively with one broker means that you will pay him a full commission. But if you sell the house yourself under an open listing, you are not required to pay the broker.

With an "exclusive right-to-sell" listing, the seller has to pay the broker no matter who sells the house. Although this means that the seller must pay a commission no matter what, the broker has a greater incentive to sell the house.

Many brokers place properties on a special "multiple listing service" so that other brokers can offer the property. If another broker sells the property, she and the original broker split the commission.

If you are a buyer, keep in mind that the agent typically works for the seller (who pays the commission), and as such, represents the seller's interests. In many provinces, buyers who are concerned about this arrangement can engage the services of a "buyer's broker," who works only on their behalf.

As an alternative to a real estate agent, some sellers put their homes up for sale themselves, do their own advertising, and negotiate directly with the buyer. If you want to use this approach, you will not have to pay a real estate agent's fee. However, you will have to find potential buyers and show the house yourself, negotiate your own contract, and risk wasting time with buyers who are unqualified. See also REAL ESTATE AGENT AND BROKER.

OFFER TO PURCHASE

Whatever the procedure, the first step in a real estate transaction is for the buyer to make an offer to purchase. The form of the offer will vary according to local custom. One common approach is to make the offer with a "binder" or "interim agreement" (a document, usually in a standardized form, which is drawn up stating the amount the buyer is offering). If the offer is accepted, the binder has the effect of a sales contract. The binder also contains any contingencies that must be met before the sale is finalized. For instance, most sales are subject to the buyer's ability to obtain suitable financing and to sell his current property. The offer is usually also contingent on a satisfactory appraisal and inspection of the property. For a sample binder or interim agreement, see the EVERYDAY LEGAL FORMS section.

When the binder is drawn up, an "earnest-money deposit" is made by the buyer. This is a cheque (often for $1,000) made out to the real estate broker or to a "trust account" of the seller's lawyer, proving that the buyer seriously intends to buy the house. Provincial law varies on when and where this cheque can be deposited. If you are negotiating a home sale yourself, the cheque should be made out to an impartial party known as the "escrow agent." This agent must hold the funds in trust until a formal contract is drawn up. A buyer should never make an earnest-money cheque payable to the seller. See also ESCROW.

When the seller receives an offer, he can either accept it, reject it outright, or propose a counteroffer. Then the buyer, in turn, can either reject the counteroffer or make one of her own. This process can be repeated until an agreement is reached. At that point the agreement is signed by both parties and a formal contract is drawn up. If the buyer backs out once the agreement is signed, she forfeits her deposit. If the seller changes his mind, the buyer's deposit is returned with an equal amount from the seller's pocket. Be very careful when making a deposit. Specify that the deposit is earnest money and that either party can withdraw from the offer by the buyer forfeiting the deposit or by the seller paying the same amount to the prospective buyer.

If the deposit is made with-out clearly stating in writing that either party can withdraw from the transaction, it may be too late to do so once the offer is accepted. If either the buyer or seller changes his mind once the offer to purchase is accepted, then either party could sue the other for transfer of title or damages.

HIRING A LAWYER

Early in the process, both the buyer and the seller should hire lawyers who are experienced in real estate law. A good real estate lawyer can advise on negotiations, help conduct a title search, and represent the parties at the closing. She can also be of use if there are any problems with inspection, disclosure, and clearing the title. And if either one of the parties changes his mind about the sale, the lawyer will be able to protect her client's rights.

THE CONTRACT

Like the binder or interim agreement, a contract of purchase is usually a standard form. A typical contract states the price of the house, formalizes the deadlines for meeting the contingencies agreed to in the offer to purchase, and sets a date for closing the sale. To avoid disputes, the contract should also specify any furnishings, appliances, and fixtures that are included in the sale.

If the buyer has trouble getting a mortgage, the parties can agree to extend the contract. However, the seller can put the property back on the market if the buyer cannot get a mortgage within the specified time. See also MORTGAGE.

APPRAISAL

Mortgage lenders usually ask the buyer to pay for a professional appraiser to determine the market value of the property (which often differs from its tax assessment value).

It is important that you contact a well-established, professional, real estate appraiser. Beware of using the services of real estate agents as appraisers, especially if you are selling your home. Some real estate agents may artificially inflate the price of your home in order to entice you to list it with their agency. Appraisal costs are typically not exorbitant and therefore your best course is to go with professionals, who may be found in the yellow pages of the phone book. A good appraiser should charge a flat fee for the service and provide a full written report, indicating the method by which the property's value was appraised. See also APPRAISAL.

If the appraisal is significantly lower than the asking price, the lender may not want to give the buyer a mortgage for more than a percentage of the appraised value. The buyer can then try to renegotiate the contract based on the value given by the appraiser; obtain another appraisal and then try to renegotiate the price with the lender; or—as a final option—find financing elsewhere.

INSPECTION

The contract should not only give the buyer the right to have the house inspected; it should also provide that if the inspector finds any serious problems with the roof, house foundation, or the electrical, heating, or plumbing systems, the sale is canceled or the seller has the option of making repairs, after which the sale can proceed.

Newly built homes are usually inspected by the local building inspector. If the buyer of such a home suspects a problem not disclosed by the seller (who is usually a developer), he should have the house inspected privately. If a buyer is purchasing an older home, some mortgage lenders require him to obtain a certificate of noninfestation from a termite inspector and a radon test.

Your real estate agent, your lawyer, the local better business bureau, or the local office of consumer affairs can help you find reputable home and termite inspectors.

In Canada, there are currently no legal guidelines regulating home inspectors. At the time of writing, Canadian counterparts of the American Society of Home Inspectors are taking root in Ontario and Quebec. This organization seeks to act as a private regulatory body to maintain professional standards among home inspectors. Often architects offer their services as home inspectors.

A home inspector should state his fee in advance and provide a full written report of the inspection. However, most inspectors cannot be held liable for any defects that they fail to notice during an inspection so long as they do not perform their inspections negligently or in breach of the provisions of their contract to perform an inspection.

DISCLOSURE

A problem sometimes arises in real estate transactions when the seller knows about a problem with the property but fails to disclose it. Most provinces have laws that require full disclosure by the seller. If the seller hides a problem that substantially reduces the value of the home, the person who buys the home can file a lawsuit in order to get money for repairs or even to have the sale canceled.

The problem of disclosure is complicated, as court records show. The law divides defects into two categories: hidden (or latent) defects, and apparent defects.

A hidden defect is one that a reasonable home inspector could not find after a careful examination. It could be a faulty heating system (hard to detect in a spring or summer), cracks in the foundation, pipes that are so worn that they will leak in a short time, a leaking roof, or dangerous electrical

REAL LIFE, REAL LAW

The Case of the Infested Investment

When Stanley and Helen decided to buy a home, they found Dora's house was just what they were looking for. Stanley looked over the house a few times and, just prior to purchase, had the house professionally inspected. Soon after moving in, they held a party, and during the evening the carpet was removed to allow for dancing. To everyone's horror, it became apparent that the place was infested with termites, which were steadily munching their way through the floor, the beams, and every piece of woodwork.

Stanley and Helen had to almost completely gut the house. Then, with renovations completed, they sued Dora for fraud, claiming she had not disclosed a latent (hidden) defect.

The case, however, was dismissed. The court held that if Dora knew of the termite problem and had not disclosed this to the buyers, then her silence could be misrepresentation. But there was no proof that Dora knew about the termites which, according to evidence, had entered the house only some three years before the sale. The court also held that once the house had been professionally inspected, then reliance for completing the transaction shifted from representations by the vendor to advice of the inspector chosen by buyers. Dora was exonerated by the court since there was no evidence she committed any fraud.

This case illustrates how important it is to have older properties thoroughly inspected before making any offer to purchase. If Stanley and Helen could prove that their inspector was negligent, he might be responsible for damages.

wiring. In some cases, even zoning prohibitions may be a hidden defect. For example, this would be the case if you know the buyer wants to convert your house into a business and you are aware that zoning bylaws prohibit business in your area. If the seller knows about a hidden defect, he could be sued for damages and a reduction of price because hiding, or not disclosing, a known defect is a kind of fraud. If the seller did not know of the defect he can still be sued, but only for cancellation of sale or reduction of price, not for damages.

A seller is not obliged to tell the prospective buyer about apparent defects, such as rotten stairs or balconies, leaking pipes or low water pressure, since these should be obvious to a careful buyer.

NO GUARANTEES

In good faith, a seller could protect himself by specifying in the offer to purchase and the deed of sale that he is making no guarantees as to the quality of the building. Note, however, that a warranty usually applies only to an older building. The law considers new buildings to be automatically guaranteed to serve the purpose for which they were built for a reasonable time without repairs.

If your house has urea formaldehyde foam insulation (UDFI), you must tell the buyer, or risk a future lawsuit. She may still purchase your home, but for a lower price.

Bear in mind that consumer protection legislation rarely covers the sale of real estate.

TITLE

One of the final steps the buyer must take is to determine that the title to (ownership of) the house is free of any liens, fraud, or error. If the seller owns the home in joint tenancy, if he is divorced, or if the house is part of a deceased person's estate, the buyer should make sure that anyone who had an interest in its ownership has relinquished it.

A title company usually conducts the title search. If any problems arise, the sale of the property may not be completed until the matter is resolved. See also TITLE INSURANCE.

Before taking title to the house, the buyer should decide with his lawyer what type of ownership he wants. The house may be owned by only one person, or it may be held in joint tenancy, or some other form of ownership. Finally, the buyer needs to apply for title insurance and homeowners' insurance. See also JOINT TENANCY.

CLOSING

If the buyer obtains financing, the title is clear, and the home and termite inspections show no defects, a closing will take place. At the closing the seller will transfer the deed to the buyer in exchange for the purchase price. Specific closing procedures vary from one place to another, but generally these steps are followed:

◇ Prepaid expenses, such as property taxes and utility bills, are apportioned between the buyer and the seller.

◇ Unless the buyer is paying the full purchase price in cash at the time of the sale, he will sign a mortgage agreement with his lender.

◇ The buyer gives a cheque to a closing agent, who makes the disbursements and gives the remainder to the seller.

◇ The buyer receives the deed and the keys to the house and may now take possession on the agreed date. See also CLOSING, REAL ESTATE; DEED.

HOME EQUITY LOAN

Mortimer's old jalopy is on its last legs, he has mortgage payments to meet, and his son will be going to college next year. Mortimer's savings will not cover all these expenses, so he decides to borrow some money. However, his bank is charging 14 percent interest for personal loans, and the interest rate on his credit card is nearly 20 percent.

One solution Mortimer might consider is a home equity loan (sometimes known as a second mortgage), for which his home is used as collateral to secure the loan. Home equity loans, which are permitted in every province, are either for a fixed amount or for a revolving line of credit (in which the line of credit is reduced as the principal is repaid).

ADVANTAGES

Home equity loans have several advantages over other loans:

◇ *Competitive interest rates.* Because the collateral is Mortimer's home, a home equity loan will probably have a lower interest rate than another kind of loan. The rates are lower because the borrower is more likely to repay the loan in order to keep his home, and because homes are assets with a fairly stable value.

◇ *Low fees.* Mortimer may find a home equity lender who can offer low application fees and finance charges.

DISADVANTAGES

There are some disadvantages to home equity loans, however. First, just as with a regular mortgage, if Mortimer defaults on his payments he could lose his home to the lender, since the loan will be secured by a lien against Mortimer's home. See also FORECLOSURE; LIEN.

Second, most lenders will let you borrow only up to 75 percent of the equity you have in your home. For example, suppose Mortimer's home is appraised at $150,000, and his mortgage balance is $120,000. Since his equity is $30,000, most lenders will give him no more than $22,500. Nonetheless, Mortimer may be able to combine a home equity loan with other kinds of loans to meet his financial needs.

STEPS TO TAKE

Review these steps before taking out a home equity loan:

1. Examine your finances. If you are having difficulty meeting your current expenses, recognize that a home equity loan is not a quick fix. If you fall behind on your payments, you could lose your home.

2. Shop around for a lender. Different home equity lenders may charge different fees when they process such loans. Some

may charge for several services involved in granting a loan. Before choosing a lender, find out who will bill the most for service charges.

3. Ask whether your interest rate is fixed or variable. A lender may advertise an "introductory" interest rate but then increase this rate after an introductory period expires. Find out the maximum rate that can be charged and if your interest rate will change during the lending period.

4. Compare the long-term cost of a home equity loan with other lending options. Most home equity loans offer low interest rates, but they stretch out payments over many years. Thus you can end up paying more in interest over the long haul than if you had settled for a shorter-term personal loan, even one with a higher interest rate. Because a long payment term has high interest costs, a home equity loan often makes the most financial sense if you can promptly repay it. You are unlikely to incur any penalties if you prepay a home equity loan. See also MORTGAGE.

HOME IMPROVEMENT AND REPAIR

This year Eileen plans to make some much-needed improvements and repairs to her house. Specifically, she wants to add a deck, install new carpeting all through the house, and reroute the driveway around the back of the house. Eileen hopes to install the carpet herself and

hire someone to do the other jobs. No matter who does the work, there are some basics she should keep in mind.

PERMITS, LICENSES AND FINANCIAL CONSIDERATIONS

First, Eileen should check with her local government to determine what permits or licenses are required for these jobs. Tasks that do not require structural changes and that will not affect her neighbors, such as installing the new carpet, usually do not require a permit. However, the new deck and the major alterations to her driveway are likely to require a work or building permit.

In most communities any electrical, heating and cooling, or plumbing work must be done by a licensed professional.

Do not try to sidestep the procedures and costs of getting a permit or using licensed contractors where required by law. For instance, if Eileen installs a hot tub on her new deck without checking to see if it is in compliance with local building regulations, she may have to remove the hot tub later if the building inspector finds out about it. And if the work done on the hot tub is faulty, the consequences could be fatal.

Before you begin any work, check with your accountant. You may be able to use the cost of home improvements to reduce any capital gains taxes if you later sell the house. If your property is revenue-producing, such as a duplex in which you rent the upper floor, any work done to the rented premises would be tax deductible.

CONTRACTORS AND SUBCONTRACTORS

If, like Eileen, you are overseeing the work on your house, you are serving as your own general contractor. But you may have to hire subcontractors to work for you.

Before hiring contractors or subcontractors, you should go through the following steps:

◇ Get several estimates from reputable contractors. An estimate that is too low often means that the subcontractor is underestimating the amount of work, and the final price may be significantly higher.

◇ Come to a clear understanding with subcontractors about the work they are to perform and how it is to be done. You should have a contract with each subcontractor. If you are later dissatisfied with his work, you can prove that he failed to follow your instructions. See also CONTRACTOR.

◇ Check both the subcontractor's liability insurance and your own to see if you are covered for any injuries to a worker while he is on your property. If not, speak with your insurance agent about getting this coverage. See also INSURANCE; WORKERS' COMPENSATION.

◇ Go to your local library to look into the lien laws in your province. If a subcontractor fails to pay his employees or suppliers, they may be able to make a claim against you.

◇ Do not pay for the work in advance, not even for materials. If the contractors working for you are reliable, they should have a credit account with a building supply company.

◇ If you are dealing with a general contractor, hold back 15 percent of the contract price as protection against liens put on your property by unpaid workers or unpaid suppliers.

◇ Pay the balance 30-45 days after the work is completed, but only after you have made sure that your contractor has paid all the subcontractors and other bills, and the work has passed inspection from your municipal housing department. See also MECHANIC'S LIEN.

HOME REPAIR AND IMPROVEMENT SCAMS

Home repair and improvement is a big business, and unscrupulous people may try to swindle you. Be on the lookout for these common tactics:

Unsolicited work

One day when Eileen is out mowing her lawn, a man in a truck pulls up. He says that he noticed that she could use a new driveway coating. He says that, as it happens, he just finished a job down the block and has some extra materials available to redo her driveway at a discount for cash payment.

Eileen is a savvy consumer and refuses his offer. Had she agreed, she might have ended up with a driveway resurfaced in a thin coat of motor oil. If you are ever approached by someone under similar circumstances, do not confront him directly, but ask him to produce his construction permit or license, and ask him to wait until you have checked out his credentials with the construction industry. Also ask him for references from customers in your area. If he cannot furnish these proofs, tell him to seek business elsewhere.

The material downgrade

Suppose Eileen had a subcontractor install her carpeting. She agreed to purchase a particular type, but the subcontractor put in an inferior one and then charged her for the more expensive item. Eileen should have checked the carpet before it was installed. After the fact, she may have to sue in a small-claims court for the difference in price or to have the carpet exchanged.

Bait-and-switch tactics

Eileen sees an ad for bargain-priced patio tiles. Tempted by the offer (or "bait"), she calls the contractor, who pays her a visit but says that her job cannot be done at the advertised price. Instead he begins a hard sell to convince her that she should buy more expensive substitute tiles (the "switch"). Eileen insists that she will take the bargain tiles or nothing. See also BAIT AND SWITCH.

The fake inspector

A person claiming to be an inspector for the local public utility knocks on Eileen's door and demands entry to inspect her furnace. Eileen asks him for appropriate identification. When he cannot show this, she closes the door and calls the police.

Impostors sometimes pose as government or utility inspectors to gain entry into homes. Once inside, the fake inspector examines the homeowner's furnace, plumbing, or wiring, and "warns" that they are dangerous. If repairs are not made immediately, the homeowner will have to pay a large fine and the utility company may disconnect service. Luckily, the inspector knows a contractor who can do emergency repairs. Frightened by the prospect of the fine and a service cutoff, the homeowner agrees to have repairs made. In this scam, the so-called inspector usually works for the contractor.

If anyone claiming to be an inspector comes to your door, ask for identification and call the government agency he claims to work for before allowing him in your home. A legitimate inspector will not object to being checked out, while a con artist will quickly disappear if you question his credentials. See also CONSUMER PROTECTION; SCAMS AND SWINDLES.

HOME SCHOOLING

Sarah's parents believe that the school curriculum in their district emphasizes secular values while undercutting biblical teachings. Tunde's father wants his son to learn more about his African heritage and the contributions of African culture. Peter and Ben's mother fears that public schools put a premium on conformity at the expense of creativity. Brittany's mother is concerned about violence in the local schools. Although they have different reasons, these parents have decided to educate their children at home.

ABC's
OF HOME SCHOOLING

Home schooling is legal throughout Canada, but the requirements vary widely from province to province. If you are thinking of educating your children at home, here are a few things you should do:

■ Check with your department of education to find out what qualifications it requires for home school instructors. Most provinces permit only someone with a teaching certificate to instruct children in the home.

■ Find out if there are any circumstances that might entitle you to teach at home. Generally, the province establishes the professional standards for teachers (a certain type and level of training, or a teaching certificate). However, it is not uncommon for exceptions to be made when circumstances so require. Sometimes, teacher shortages or other problems have led to standards being relaxed in certain areas.

■ Ask whether your local school board or department of education must approve the curriculum you have in mind. You will have to teach certain standard subjects.

■ Ask your local school board about the extent of supervision of home schooling in your area. Some boards require children schooled at home to be tested by an independent evaluator. In other areas a representative of the school board must review the students' work. And in some districts, students must take standardized tests.

■ Try to obtain teaching materials from your school board or department of education. Several private organizations also provide workbooks and other aids for course work, curriculum outlines, and computer software.

COMPULSORY EDUCATION LAWS

Because Canada has a future interest in training its young people to be good and productive citizens, every province has compulsory education laws. Children taught at home must receive an education comparable to one they would receive in public schools. Parents who teach their children at home must comply with the compulsory education laws in their province, and provin-cial and local school boards may supervise home schooling. All provinces require students to have instruction in basic subjects, mathematics, social studies, and English or French. If a child's home schooling program does not meet government requirements, his parents may be charged with violating truancy laws.

HOMEOWNERS' ASSOCIATION

If you live in a planned development or subdivision, chances are it has a homeowners' association—a private nonprofit corporation whose purpose is to give residents a voice in how the community is maintained and to keep property values as high as possible.

A homeowners' association is generally organized in accordance with a document known as a community declaration, part of the developer's master plan. The officers and directors of the association are members of the community, elected by their fellow residents. In most planned communities a homeowners' association performs one or more of the following functions:

◇ Enforces the covenants, conditions, and restrictions governing the use and development of community property.

◇ Provides maintenance and upkeep for community property, such as sidewalks, open spaces, and greenbelts.

◇ Manages and maintains community recreational facilities, such as swimming pools, playgrounds, and tennis courts.

To pay for these services, the homeowners in the community are charged a fee. This fee will be stated in your property deed and adjusted according to the community's needs. If a homeowner fails to pay the fee, the association may be entitled to collect late charges and interest, sue the homeowner, and file a lien against his property.

COVENANTS AND RESTRICTIONS

Homeowners' associations try to protect the value of all the property of the community by enforcing the covenants and restrictions in the property owners' deeds. Depending on the community, a homeowner may be required to obtain the association's approval before painting her house, replacing the roof, erecting a television antenna or satellite dish, building a garage, or installing solar panels. Other covenants may prohibit parking certain vehicles on the street. Homeowners may also be prevented from hanging laundry outside to dry, erecting fences, planting trees that interfere with a neighbor's view, or landscaping property in an unusual way.

DISPUTES BETWEEN NEIGHBORS

Homeowners' associations in many communities provide mediation services as a way to help resolve disputes between neighbors. Suppose your next-door neighbor decides to work on his 1967 Dodge Dart in his driveway, and the car sits up on blocks with its parts scattered around for weeks. There is no covenant in his property deed that prohibits him from working on the car, but it is unsightly and you think it is dangerous to local children. You asked your neighbor to hurry up and finish, but to no avail. You may be able to sue him for creating a private nuisance, but first, if you live in a community with a homeowners' association, ask the association to help mediate your dispute. In most instances the mediators will be members of your community who have received special training in resolving problems that arise between neighbors. Their role is not to make a binding rule about the dispute, but to help you and your neighbor work out a solution to it. See also MEDIATION; NEIGHBORS.

DISPUTES WITH AN ASSOCIATION

Suppose you paint your house a color that is unacceptable to the homeowners' association. The association should notify you in writing that you are in violation of the restrictions in your deed and give you a deadline to take corrective action.

You are entitled to a hearing before the association's board of directors. If you cannot resolve your dispute and do not comply with the board's instructions, the association may file suit against you and obtain a court order to require your compliance.

HOMEOWNERS' INSURANCE

Homeowners' insurance is purchased by individuals to protect their homes and possessions against certain risks, including fire, theft, and vandalism. In most cases, mortgage lenders insist that home buyers purchase this insurance when they buy the house. But you should also update your homeowners' insurance policy as the value and replacement cost of your home rise.

Most policies contain several sections indicating the maximum amount of coverage you have for each type of loss. The real-property section covers the primary building and any other structures (such as sheds or garages) on the property. Coverage for structures not attached to, or part of, the home (for example a free-standing garage) is usually about 10 percent of the value of the basic home structure.

The personal-property section covers possessions—furniture, rugs, and the like. Contents or personal property coverage may be up to 50 percent of the value of the structure, and about 10 percent of the value of the insured property away from home. For example, a home valued at $100,000 would have coverage of about $50,000, with up to about $5,000 on property away from home (if you are robbed while on vacation, for instance).

Another section covers loss of use, indicating the amount the company will pay if your house is damaged and you cannot live in it. For example, if a fire forces you to move into a hotel while repairs are made, your policy may cover some of your additional living expenses, but usually runs to 10 or 20 percent of the sum for which the structure is insured.

Most homeowners' policies also include liability insurance, which protects a homeowner if he is sued for having caused bodily damage to someone or for damaging another person's property.

See also NEGLIGENCE; TRESPASS; UMBRELLA INSURANCE.

BASIC COVERAGE

There are many different types of homeowner insurance policies. The most basic, often called HO-1 (for homeowner 1) insures against "fire" and includes extended coverage. This typically includes most types of explosion, but check your policy for excluded risks. Damages caused by smoke, sprinkler, leakage, crashing vehicles, riots, windstorms and hail, and other potential problems such as glass breakage, theft, and vandalism may also be included in an extended coverage policy.

BROAD COVERAGE

For protection against other types of losses, a broad-coverage (or HO-2) policy may be a better choice. In addition to the risks outlined above, HO-2 policies cover six other types of risks, including losses from (1) falling objects; (2) accidental leakage or flow of water or steam from plumbing, air-conditioning, heating systems, or household appliances; (3) the weight of snow, ice, or sleet; (4) sudden accidental cracking, rupture, bulging, or burning of a hot-water or steam heating system, air-conditioning system, or sprinkler system; (5) short circuits or other accidentally generated currents that damage wiring or electrical appliances or fixtures; and (6) freezing of part of a plumbing, heating, or cooling system, or of a household appliance.

SPECIAL COVERAGE

Under an HO-3, or special, policy, the house, but not its contents, is protected against all risks except those specifically excluded by the policy. Normal exclusions include loss resulting from war, nuclear accidents, floods, and earthquakes. Although the contents of the home are not covered from all risks under the HO-3 policy, an "endorsement" may be added (for an additional expense). It gives virtually the same protection to personal property as that provided for the house.

COVERAGE FOR TENANTS AND CO-OP OWNERS

People who live in rental units or cooperative apartments may also purchase home insurance policies. In a cooperative apartment building, the residents lease their apartments from the corporation in which they own shares. The building itself is owned, maintained, and insured by the corporation. Since renters and co-op owners do not own their dwellings, insurance companies have designed HO-4, or tenant, policies to provide coverage for the contents of the home but not for the actual building itself. The protection offered is exactly the same as that provided in an HO-2 broad-coverage policy. Renters and co-op owners can also buy liability insurance. See also COOPERATIVE APARTMENT.

COMPREHENSIVE COVERAGE

The most expensive homeowners' insurance is the comprehensive, or all-risks, policy. It insures the dwelling and its contents against all risks except those specifically excluded by the policy. Typical exclusions include flood, war, nuclear accidents, and earthquakes.

CONDOMINIUM COVERAGE

The common areas of a condominium, such as the lobby, elevators, and lawns, are insured by the condominium corporation. Nevertheless, the owners of the individual units should buy insurance in the event of a fire, flood, or some other incident that destroys the contents of the unit. These homeowners can buy HO-6 policies, which will provide protection similar to that of the HO-4. See also CONDOMINIUM.

EXCLUSIONS

Most insurance policies contain exclusions or restrictions—that is, specific conditions or items that the policy does not cover. Damage that is caused by a flood or an earthquake, for instance, will not be covered by most policies. Theft and vandalism coverage may be limited if you live in a high-crime area or if you are away from your home for more than 30 days at a time. And if you work from your home, you may need additional insurance to cover professional or business liabilities. See also HOME BUSINESS.

AMOUNT OF COVERAGE

How much insurance coverage should you buy? This depends upon how much you need and can afford. In general, most homeowners buy policies that insure between 80 to 100 percent of the replacement value of their property. Eighty percent coverage is sufficient in

most cases, because even rebuilding a house from scratch rarely includes buying land or laying a new foundation.

Nevertheless, the cost of replacing a home often exceeds the price the owner paid for it or its current market value. For this reason, owners can buy replacement cost insurance that exceeds the value of their home. However, homeowners are not allowed to reap a bonus under the replacement cost policy. Let us say that you buy a house for the price of $85,000 and then buy replacement insurance for coverage of up to $100,000. If your home is destroyed and it costs you only $94,000 to rebuild, the insurance company is obliged to pay you just that amount. Even if you hold two separate policies on your house, you cannot collect twice for the same loss. See also FIRE INSURANCE.

ENDORSEMENTS

You may also buy added protection in the form of endorsements (additions to the policy). Since most basic policies limit coverage for personal valuables up to about $1,000, a valuable personal article's endorsement for such items as jewelry, furs, silverware, artwork, and photographic equipment or collections is a good buy. Ask for replacement value insurance, and ask that the valuable articles endorsement contain a "floater," insuring these articles while they are away from the home. Have valuables such as jewelry, watches, and paintings professionally appraised, and also photographed, if possible.

You might also consider an endorsement to cover the replacement cost of the contents of your home. Under standard insurance, the contents are typically covered for their actual value—which is the replacement cost minus depreciation. A replacement cost endorsement provides for the full cost of replacing an item that is stolen from or damaged in your home, and sometimes for losses that occur away from your home.

High-crime areas

Insurers are reluctant to give policies to renters and homeowners who live in areas where burglaries and robberies are frequent. However, you can reduce your theft insurance premiums by 10 percent or more just by installing burglar alarms and outdoor lighting.

Natural disasters

In some areas of the country, homeowners can purchase flood, earthquake, mudslide, tornado, or other insurance to protect against damage caused by rare but potentially catastrophic events.

The cost of flood or earthquake coverage is expensive and is calculated not only on the basis of the location of the home, but also on its construction. For instance, because a brick home is more likely to be damaged during an earthquake, the cost of an endorsement is higher than for a timber-frame house. Before buying extra hurricane insurance, double-check with your broker. Often, damage from windstorms will be covered under your standard homeowners' policy.

MORTGAGE INSURANCE

When you wish to buy a home, you must of course provide some sort of initial payment. The only question is how much are you willing and able to put down on the property.

Usually, a down payment will be 10 to 30 percent of the purchase price of a home. However, with mortgage insurance, a down payment of as little as 5 percent is possible. Typically, the premiums for this insurance are added in with the mortgage payments.

HOMEOWNERS' WARRANTY

Most builders of new homes today offer buyers a homeowners' warranty against structural defects in the house. This type of warranty is almost always a marketing tool to assure the buyer of a home that the house builder and insurer will stand behind the home's quality.

SOME WARNINGS

In most instances homeowners' warranties actually limit a builder's responsibility for construction defects.

For example, a typical warranty may require a builder to repair "excessive" cracks in foundation floors or walls during the first year. The warranty may define "excessive" cracking so narrowly that your foundation would be on the verge of collapse before the warranty covered any repairs.

Even government programs such as the Ontario New Home Warranties Plan have been a disappointment for some homeowners. In one case, it was held that "major structural defects" were to be found only when the home in question was "virtually uninhabitable, uncomfortable beyond reason, unsafe or in a state of imminent collapse."

STEPS TO TAKE

To protect yourself if you buy a home that is covered by a homeowners' warranty, do the following:

1. Read the warranty carefully to be sure you know exactly what it covers.

2. Do not rely on a builder's oral assurances that he will correct problems not covered by the warranty. He should put all his promises in writing.

3. Have an independent inspector look at the house, rather than relying on the local building inspector. You may want higher standards of workmanship than are called for by your local building code.

4. If you think you have a claim under your homeowners' warranty, file it with the warranty company as soon as possible and be persistent. Keep records of your phone calls and correspondence relating to the claim. Then if you are forced to take your claim to court, you can demonstrate that you tried to have the warranty enforced.

5. If your complaint is not handled to your satisfaction, contact your provincial insurance council or the Insurance Bureau of Canada.

See also MORTGAGE; WARRANTY AND GUARANTEE.

HOMICIDE

Homicide is defined as the causing of death of a human being by any means directly or indirectly. Homicide can be culpable (criminal) or not culpable (not an offense).

For example, justifiable homicide (killing someone while trying to protect your life) is not a crime. Nor is homicide committed to protect the life of someone else.

See also MANSLAUGHTER; MURDER; SELF-DEFENSE.

HOMOSEXUAL RIGHTS

Although discrimination based on gender is prohibited under federal civil rights laws, discrimination based on a person's sexual orientation is not. Homosexuals are generally not afforded any special legal protection under federal law. In 1993, then Justice Minister Kim Campbell proposed amending the Charter of Rights and Freedoms to prohibit discrimination based on sexual orientation. The amendment was not passed in the 1993 session of Parliament, and a new government was in power when Parliament reconvened.

Human rights legislation in Manitoba, Ontario, Quebec, and Yukon affords some protection against discrimination based on sexual orientation. Although no province recognizes marriages between homosexuals, several have enacted laws extending spousal benefit

291

coverage to partners of homosexual employees, including family-leave care for seriously ill homosexual partners. See also DISCRIMINATION; HATE CRIME.

Until recently, it was taken as a given that homosexuals were to be afforded no special rights in the military. Indeed, homosexuality was freely treated in a discriminatory manner by military authorities. This has begun to change, however. For example, the Ontario Court of Appeal recently found that the old Canadian Human Rights Act of 1976, which offers no protection based on sexual orientation, was discriminatory and thus offended the Canadian Charter of Rights and Freedoms. The charter guarantees equality before the law, and it would appear that the courts are beginning to apply this thinking even to cases of gays in the military.

One area in which homosexuals have gained greater legal protection is that of child custody. At one time, courts generally refused to grant custody to parents who were admittedly homosexual. Increasingly, however, courts have awarded child custody to homosexual parents when they found it was in the child's best interest. See also AIDS; DISCRIMINATION.

HOSPITAL

Each province has the authority to regulate how many hospitals (whether public or private) may be established in a given area and how they must be maintained. Provincial and fed-

eral laws affecting hospital operation cover a wide range of practices—including everything from billing procedures to the number of beds.

Your insurance company or Medicare may give you coverage for a specific procedure, or only for a certain length of time. For more information, see HEALTH INSURANCE; MEDICARE.

Typically, hospitals are regulated under a province's hospital act or similarly named statute. Depending on where you live, the Minister of Health, a hospital commission, or the Health Services Commission (in the case of Manitoba) administers hospitals in the province. Without approval by the government, an institution cannot operate as a hospital and will receive no funding.

Not all hospitals are obliged to accept you as a patient, except in emergencies. However, hospital bylaws, group health plan provisions, and local laws often restrict a hospital's right to refuse admission to patients who are not in need of emergency care. The general rule is that hospitals shall accept a person for admission so long as it is not against a given hospital's regulations, or if urgent care is required.

EMERGENCY CARE

Generally, hospital emergency rooms are required to accept all patients who seek emergency care. A failure to provide such care could provide the grounds for a lawsuit against the hospital. See also MEDICARE.

In some instances, a hospital's emergency services may not be equipped to give certain

types of care—such as for serious burns. In these situations, provincial law may allow the hospital to transfer patients to another facility if it can be done without jeopardizing the patient's condition. Often, cooperative arrangements exist among hospitals to coordinate specialized emergency care such as this.

DISCHARGES

A hospital may face legal penalties and may be sued if it discharges a patient who requires additional care. See also NEGLIGENCE.

Conversely, suppose you want to leave the hospital, but your doctor feels that you still need medical care. A hospital generally cannot hold you against your wishes, and doing so could lead to a lawsuit for wrongful detention. However, if you have a communicable disease or need further care, and leaving the hospital would endanger your well-being or the health and safety of the community, the hospital may be allowed to detain you. See FALSE IMPRISONMENT; PATIENT'S RIGHTS; PHYSICIAN AND SURGEON.

HOTEL AND MOTEL

Special laws apply to the operation of hotels and motels (and other public accommodations, such as inns and guest houses), and these businesses must be licensed by the province in order to operate.

A hotel or motel may not turn away a guest because of her race, ethnicity, religion, or

ABC's

OF HOTEL AND MOTEL SAFETY

Although accommodations such as hotels and motels must ensure their guests' safety, there are some precautions a guest can take to avoid becoming the victim of a crime:

■ Refuse to accept a room whose door has only a single lock or that has no peephole.

■ Keep the room's doors and windows closed and locked.

■ Don't open the door to anyone unless you know who he is. If someone claims to be from hotel maintenance or security, call the front desk to confirm his identity.

■ If you are returning to your room late at night, use the building's main entrance and ask an employee to escort you to your room.

■ Place your valuables in the hotel's safe. Provincial laws limit the liability of hotels and motels for items missing from your room, and you may have to bear the cost of replacing expensive items stolen from your room.

gender. Nonetheless, hotels and motels are not required to accept every potential guest. Thus a hotel may prohibit families with pets, or require that its guests be at least 18 years old, have a major credit card, and pay a deposit. In addition, in most instances a hotel may, at its own discretion, request a guest to leave if he has been especially rowdy or difficult.

SAFETY STANDARDS

Hotel and motel operators are obliged to keep their guests (and their guests' valuables) reasonably safe. Regulations on fire and building safety, cleanliness, and so on are enforced by the local fire, health, and building departments, which periodically inspect hotels and motels. Operators have to ensure adequate security for guests in their rooms by providing doors that lock, changing keys or locks periodically or when keys are missing, responding to calls for assistance, and removing dangerous, suspicious, or unregistered persons from the hotel premises. Common areas such as lobbies, parking garages and lots, meeting rooms, and hallways must be well lit and safe.

Most provinces also require hotels and motels to provide a secure vault for storing guests' valuables.

SUING FOR NEGLIGENCE

The laws in most provinces allow hotels to limit their liability for losses that their patrons incur. In some cases, however, you may be able to sue. For example, if a hotel knowingly hires an employee who has a criminal record, some courts would consider the hotel responsible for any loss you suffered from the employee's actions. Or, if you are assaulted in a hotel's dimly lit parking area, you may be able to sue if you can prove the hotel knew about the potential danger.

◆ In several instances across the country, hotel guests have successfully sued for damages arising from mistreatment by an hotel or innkeeper's employees, or when they were served too much alcohol and had an accident because the hotel did not ensure that the guest was able to return to his room or home safely.

PAYING THE BILL

If you refuse to pay your bill, the laws in most provinces permit the hotel or motel to hold your luggage until the bill is paid. Also, since many hotels require you to give a credit card number when you register, any outstanding fees can be charged to your credit card. See also LIEN.

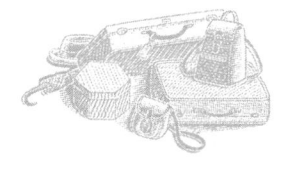

HOUSEHOLD HELP

Domestic employees, including child care providers, cooks, maids, and caretakers, usually do not have the same federal and provincial protection as other workers. Often, the employment standards legislation regarding the number of hours of work, the minimum wage payable, the payment of overtime, as well as statutory holiday pay do not apply to domestic workers in the same way as to other employees, especially when the domestic employee lives in the home of her employer. Even so, there are certain procedures you must follow if you hire someone to work in your home.

Your local tax office or your lawyer or accountant can tell you what tax regulations apply. As an employer, you are responsible for making the appropriate deductions and contributions for your employees. Ordinarily, however, domestic workers are not eligible for unemployment insurance although Revenue Canada may make exceptions. Usually, only employees involved in the employer's principal activity are eligible. A farmer who hires someone to drive machinery will likely have to make unemployment insurance deductions. However, the same farmer who hires a domestic worker will not have to make these deductions, since farming, not housework, is the employer's principal business activity.

In most provinces, you do not have to pay workers' compensation for your household help. Nonetheless, you may be financially responsible for injuries a worker suffers on your property. You should have enough liability insurance to pay for any claims made by employees in your home.

If you hire through an agency, be sure it is licensed, bonded, and insured. Then, if the worker steals or damages your property, the agency can be held liable if you can prove the employee's guilt. See also EMPLOYEE PAYCHEQUE DEDUCTIONS; HOMEOWNERS' INSURANCE; IMMIGRATION; NEGLIGENCE; WORKERS' COMPENSATION.

I FROM ILLEGITIMACY TO IOU

ILLEGITIMACY

Children born to parents who are not married to each other are called illegitimate. The law once tended to treat illegitimate children as second-class citizens, partly because of society's belief in the sanctity of a marriage, and partly because blood relations were used as the basis for inheritance and property rights. Today illegitimate children are, for the most part, entitled to the same legal benefits as legitimate offspring.

British Columbia, Manitoba, Ontario, New Brunswick, Quebec, Yukon, and the Northwest Territories have abolished the distinction between legitimate and illegitimate children in legislation. The Ontario Children Law Reform Act states, for example: ". . . for all purposes of the law of Ontario a person is the child of his or her natural parents and his or her status as their child is independent of whether the child is born within or outside marriage." In those provinces that have preserved the distinction between legitimate and illegitimate children, all children are deemed to be legitimate once their parents have married.

In Canada, all children—whether legitimate or not—may inherit from their parents in the absence of a will. A problem may arise, however, when the testator lived and died outside Canada. For example, if a distinction in law exists in, say, Hungary, that "child" means a legitimate child, and a person who was domiciled in and died in Hungary leaves a will that states his estate shall go to his "children" in Canada, then the deceased's illegitimate child in Canada may be excluded from the inheritance. The same would apply if no will existed.

THE PRESUMPTION OF LEGITIMACY

The following presumptions carry the force of law:

◇ Every person is now presumed legitimate until facts demonstrate otherwise.

◇ Any child born to a married woman is presumed to be the child of her husband and is therefore legitimate—even if the child was conceived before the marriage took place.

◇ Children conceived during a marriage but born after its termination—whether this came about by death, divorce, or annulment—are presumed to be the legitimate children of the husband when the birth took place within 300 days of the termination of the marriage.

LEGITIMATION

The reasons someone may want to prove a child's paternity are many, but the most common is to compel the father to assume financial responsibility for his offspring. Every province has laws regarding legitimizing children.

ESTABLISHING PATERNITY

Acknowledgment of paternity imposes a duty of support on the father and gives him visitation and custody rights. It also gives an illegitimate child the same status as his legitimate brothers and sisters have, as an heir to his father's estate.

In establishing paternity (also known as an action in filiation) any type of proof is permitted, including proof by presumption. If the father does not voluntarily acknowledge his paternity, an action in filiation may be taken by the child or the child's mother. In cases where the mother denies that the father is in fact the father of the child, an action in filiation may be taken by the father to prove his paternity.

Greeting cards such as Father's Day cards, letters or other writings indicating that the man is the father of the child, and even photographic evidence, are admissible to prove paternity. Often, the manner in which a man treats a child, such as buying birthday presents, or publicly acknowledging that he is the child's father, will create a presumption of paternity. The best proof, however, is obtained by blood tests. But not all

provinces or territories can oblige a man to undergo such a test. Blood tests can be ordered only in Ontario, New Brunswick, Prince Edward Island, and Yukon, and then at a judge's discretion. According to a Quebec court of appeal, judgment forcing someone to undergo a blood test would contravene the "inviolability of the person" guaranteed by Quebec's human rights legislation. See also CHILD SUPPORT.

IMMIGRATION

The term "immigration" refers to the process by which non-citizens come to Canada to take up permanent residence. Permanent residents have the right to live and work in Canada, but they do not automatically become citizens. See CITIZENSHIP.

Permanent resident status may also be granted to someone already in Canada, if that person is in a *bona fide* marriage with a Canadian citizen or a permanent resident—especially if children are born of such a marriage—or where the person has lived here for at least five years.

BASIC PRINCIPLES

The essential purpose of our immigration law is to determine and regulate the right of persons to enter and to reside in Canada. According to the BNA Act, immigration is a matter shared between the federal government and the provinces. Nonetheless, only Quebec has a ministry of immigration, although other provinces—

Ontario and British Columbia, for example—also deal with certain immigration matters.

The goal of the federal Immigration Act is to promote Canada's interests nationally and internationally. One objective is to have immigrants settle in the less populous regions of the country. In the past, most congregated in large cities, such as Montreal, Toronto, and Vancouver.

The law also aims to reunify families, stimulate the economy, shelter refugees, and guarantee the health, security, and public order of Canada.

SOME STATISTICS

Canada remains to a large extent a country of immigrants. In just one recent year (1992) about 220,000 immigrants (meaning people who wished to establish permanent residence, not those who came as students, temporary workers, and visitors) came here, compared to 300,000 to 400,000 who came in 1910-1914. Of that 220,000, 41 percent were independent immigrants, 42 percent were closely related to people already established in Canada, and about 17 percent were refugee claimants. Of that 17 percent, 8 percent were selected from refugee camps and elsewhere outside Canada, and 9 percent claimed refugee status once they arrived here.

INDEPENDENT IMMIGRANTS

The first step in immigration is to make an application at a Canadian consulate or embassy. Regardless of whether an applicant wishes to come as an independent worker, investor, or entrepreneur, he must meet the criteria established by the Immigration Act. These criteria are meant to measure an applicant's capacity to integrate into Canadian society and the Canadian work force. Therefore, points or units of assessment are awarded for knowledge of either English or French or both, degree of education, training, and occupation, as well as any job offers the applicant may already have in Canada. A family member, even an uncle or aunt, nephew or niece who is legally resident in Canada, can facilitate the immigration of her relatives. People with criminal records or whose health would pose a public risk or be a burden to our health services are rarely admitted.

Once a person's application is approved, he is issued with an immigrant visa which permits him to enter Canada. From that moment the person has become a permanent resident of Canada.

SPONSORED IMMIGRANTS

A Canadian citizen or permanent resident may sponsor his spouse, fiancée, children, parents, and other family members. In rare cases, the sponsored immigrant may not need as many assessment units as independent immigrants, but other statutory criteria, such as the health of the prospective immigrant or national security, nonetheless apply.

The sponsor must undertake to provide food, clothing, shelter, and other necessities for the proposed immigrant for up to 10 years. The intention is to ensure that the sponsored immigrants will not need public welfare assistance once they have arrived in Canada. Should this happen, the sponsor may have to reimburse the government agency that helped the sponsored immigrants.

REFUGEE IMMIGRANTS

A refugee is a person who fears persecution because of his or her race, religion, nationality, political opinions or membership in a certain social group and who cannot be protected by his or her native country. As a signatory to the Geneva Convention (1951) on refugees, Canada must study any claim for refugee status made by a person in Canada, and may not deport anyone whose claim is accepted. The claim hearing is conducted by two commissioners of the Immigration and Refugee Board, a judicial or quasi-judicial tribunal. The claimant may be represented by a lawyer, and the hearings are usually held in camera, with a government-supplied interpreter if necessary. Except in rare cases, approval by one of the commissioners is sufficient for the claimant to be granted refugee status. If the claim is refused, the claimant may be returned to her country of origin, or the last country where she resided. The board's decisions are subject to review by the Federal Court.

DEPORTATION

Canadian citizens and Indians as defined by the Indian Act cannot be deported from Canada. All others, even permanent residents, may be deported in certain cases. Although most deportations are preceded by an inquiry, a senior immigration officer may order someone deported on the spot in cases involving public security, or if someone arrives at a Canadian point of entry without a passport, visa, or other valid travel document.

A permanent resident who commits a crime or an infraction of the Immigration Act may—following an inquiry—be ordered to be removed from Canada. Such removal might be a deportation order involving permanent exclusion, or the person may be permitted to return after one year. Sometimes a departure notice is issued, which orders the person to leave Canada voluntarily within a certain time. A departure notice does not preclude return at a later date.

SPECIAL POWERS AND STIFF PENALTIES

Immigration officers have the power to make an arrest, or to order someone's detention. They have the right of search and seizure, and even the right of forced entry into a building. They may take fingerprints in certain cases. Fines of up to $500,000 and imprisonment for up to 10 years are among penalties for Immigration Act infractions such as entering Canada at other than at a point of entry, refusing to answer questions asked by an immigration officer during an examination, making a false promise of employment, staying in Canada after one's status as a visitor has expired, helping someone without a valid passport to enter Canada, or hiring someone who is not a citizen or resident and who does not have a valid work permit.

IMMUNITY

Immunity is a special privilege or an exemption from a certain duty (such as paying taxes or serving on a jury) that citizens are usually required to perform. In recent years many of the usual reasons for granting immunity have been rejected by the courts, including the principle of sovereign immunity (which prevented citizens from suing their government).

SUING SPOUSES

Traditionally, spouses could not sue one another for injuries inflicted either intentionally or negligently. For example, a wife could not file suit against her husband for injuries she suffered in a car accident while he was driving. The reason behind this rule was that such lawsuits disrupted "marital harmony" and created opportunities for fraud or collusion.

However, the Charter of Rights and Freedoms now affords equal benefit and protection under law, without discrimination based on marital status, and all provinces will now allow spouses to sue for any injuries caused by intentional wrongful acts (such as assault) and for car accidents.

PARENT-CHILD IMMUNITY

Parents were long immune from lawsuits brought by their minor children. The courts did not want to jeopardize family peace or interfere with the parents' right to discipline their children. Issues of fraud and collusion were also a concern. Today, because of the charter, children can sue any party including their parents for wrongful acts.

Recent case law has abundant examples of children suing one or both parents for sexual abuse, and winning awards in the tens of thousands of dollars. In Ontario, in 1992, an incest victim was awarded $284,000 from her millionaire father, who was also sentenced to four years in prison. The Supreme Court of Canada has also ruled that the usual time limits in which a lawsuit must begin do not apply in cases of sexual abuse. Such actions may be taken no matter how much time has elapsed. See also CHILDREN'S RIGHTS.

SOVEREIGN IMMUNITY

The idea of sovereign immunity was adopted from English common law, which held that the "king can do no wrong." In Canada this has meant that the government could not be sued without its consent.

Today, courts and lawmakers have waived sovereign immunity in a number of cases. For example, a person who is injured through the negligence of a government employee may sue that government department (as long as the employee was on duty at the time of the incident); people injured on government or public property as a result of a dangerous condition may also sue. In fact, the Federal Crown Liability Act and similar provincial legislation expressly set out how and when you can sue the Crown, meaning either the federal or provincial governments. See also ACCIDENTS ON GOVERNMENT PROPERTY.

PUBLIC INTEREST IMMUNITY

It may happen that in some cases, especially those involving public security or national defense, evidence that is relevant and otherwise admissible must be excluded if it would harm the public interest. In those cases, the Crown might decide not to prosecute certain offenders, because a trial might expose state secrets or be against the public interest.

IMPLIED CONSENT

Actions, signs, or silence suggesting that a person has given his permission for something to happen are known as implied consent. Suppose you agree to let your teenage neighbor mow your lawn. For several months you pay him weekly for his services. One week, after he has mowed the lawn, you refuse to pay him, claiming that you did not ask him to do the work. If he takes you to the small-claims court, the court will probably find that your ongoing relationship was a form of implied consent to the mowing, and will order you to pay the bill.

Similarly, suppose that for years you and your family have used your neighbor's yard as a shortcut to the grocery store. Whenever he has seen you, your neighbor has always been quick with a smile and a wave. If he suddenly calls the police and accuses you of trespassing, you would be justified in claiming that his years of friendly acknowledgment implied his consent to the arrangement.

When there is no ongoing relationship, however, silence cannot be taken as a sign of consent. If a merchant sends an article to someone voluntarily, he cannot stipulate that if the recipient does not return the item in 10 days, his silence will be considered as acceptance and he will have to pay for the article.

See also ADVERSE POSSESSION.

INCEST

Incest—the act of sexual intercourse between people who are closely related by blood—is a crime.

According to the Criminal Code, incest is having sexual relations with a parent, child, brother, sister, grandparent or grandchild. Brother and sister also includes a half-brother or half-sister. The maximum penalty for incest is 14 years' imprisonment. According to the Federal Marriage Act (prohibited degrees), all marriages between people in the direct line (grandparents–parents–children) or between brothers and sisters and half-brothers and half-sisters, including brothers or sisters by adoption, are prohibited.

INCOME TAX

Income tax legislation is constantly changing to meet new social realities and public policy goals. As the world becomes more complex, inevitably so does tax law. So, it would be impossible to present a detailed and comprehensive overview of this area of the law in a few pages. Only the broad outlines are set out here. However, if you wish to solve a detailed personal or business income tax problem, you would do best to seek the help of an accountant or lawyer.

FEDERAL AND PROVINCIAL TAXATION

The taxes levied on corporations and individuals in Canada are the major source of federal government revenues. The British North America Act of 1867 allows both the federal and provincial governments the power of taxation. However, the federal government may tax by any method, whereas the provincial governments are restricted to direct taxation in the province. Alberta, Ontario, and Quebec tax corporations under their own corporate tax legislation. Quebec alone collects personal income taxes in the province. For all other provinces, the federal government collects provincial income tax in the form of a surtax on your federal income tax.

THE TERMINOLOGY

By its nature, tax law is very dependent on the interpretation of legal terminology. If the law states that "employees" can deduct certain job-related expenses from their taxable income, we need to know what an "employee" is. The most authoritative interpreter of tax law is the court, and in tax matters this is typically the Tax Court or the Federal Court (Trial Division.) Revenue Canada also issues interpretation bulletins, public statements, information circulars, pamphlets, books and "private advance rulings."

Private advance rulings are best explained by way of an example. Suppose Jacqueline has estimated the cost of expanding her Ontario lumber business into Quebec. If the expenses are not tax deductible, however, she will either stay put or consider some other move. To be on the safe side, she asks for an advance ruling, and Revenue Canada will consider itself bound by any ruling it makes in her favor. That is to say, Jacqueline may make her investments and later deduct the expenses she has been given advance authorization to make, so long as the information she gave to Revenue Canada has not substantially changed.

WHO IS SUBJECT TO INCOME TAX

Canadian tax law is primarily concerned with residents of Canada, that is people who spend 183 or more days a year in the country, and of course Canadian military personnel and diplomatic staff stationed overseas. Corporations who were incorporated in Canada after April 26, 1965, or those whose principal headquarters are in the country are also deemed residents. Nonresidents are liable to be taxed as well for income from Canadian sources, whether from business, employment, or property revenues.

In short, if you are a Canadian citizen who has made no income from a Canadian source and who does not spend at least 183 days in Canada, you will likely not have to file a Canadian income tax return.

WHAT IS TAXABLE INCOME

In Canadian tax law, employment income and business income are treated differently, so it is important to distinguish between employees and employers. While this distinction has been the subject of much litigation, generally, you are an employee if your conditions of work (control over what work is done and how; ownership of tools and raw materials; work schedule, and so on) indicate a subordinate position to an employer, whether this be a person or company. The opposite is true for independent contractors and other business people.

For employees, taxable income is salary, or an hourly wage, or commissions. But it also includes such things as tips, gratuities, traveling allowances, and stock options. From the total of taxable income, employees are allowed to deduct contributions already made to the Canadian Pension Plan, Unemployment Insurance, union dues, and tax deducted at source. Moreover,

an employee may claim deductions for certain items essential for her employment, such as a car, a home office, supplies, and so forth.

In taxing business income, Revenue Canada is concerned primarily with the profit made by any given enterprise. In legal terms, profit is the amount of money remaining after all expenses, including salaries, are deducted. The general rule is that, in order for an expense to be deductible, it must have been made with the view to gaining income from a business venture. Rather than claiming a simple deduction for the cost of machinery, for example, a business must claim a capital cost

allowance instead. In short, a percentage of the machine's value is deducted from the annual taxable income over the course of many years, until the cost of the machine has been completely deducted.

Another form of taxable income is called capital gains. Suppose Nicole buys a printing machine for $35,000 and uses it for one year, then resells it for $36,000, thus realizing a gain of $1,000. This gain has been made on a previous capital investment (thus the term capital gain) and so the $1,000 realized on the sale of the printer is taxable. Capital gains tax is levied on three-quarters of the total gain: in Nicole's case,

REAL LIFE, REAL LAW

The Case of the Stinging Surprise

Ida was ecstatic when she learned that she had won a lottery prize from a local charity, which guaranteed her $1,000 per month for life. This prize was to be given in the form of an annuity administered by an insurance company. As lottery winnings are not taxable, Ida was surprised at the end of the year when she received a T-4 slip showing that $8,155 was to be added to her income for the past year.

Ida objected to Revenue Canada's assessment but was unsuccessful before the Tax Court. However, on appeal to the Federal Court (Trial Division), the judge agreed that her winnings should not be taxable. Revenue Canada then appealed to the Federal Court (Appeal Division). Unfortunately for Ida, the appeal court ruled in favor of Revenue Canada. The court said that as an annuity, the payment was made up of both capital and income. According to the calculations, $8,155 of the $12,000 annual payment was income and taxable, whereas only $3,844 was capital not subject to tax. Had Ida won a lump-sum prize and invested that amount, the lump-sum capital would not have been taxed, but the interest from the capital would have been. The fact that Ida's payments consisted of income and capital did not mean that the total amount she received was not taxable.

on $750. Note, however, that there are a number of exemptions from capital gains and this tax will rarely affect anyone but business people. In Canada, for example, in contrast to the United States, people are allowed an exemption from capital gains tax on the sale of their principal residence.

Depending on the way the capital gain was made (on the sale of farmland, for example) everyone has a life-time capital gains exemption of up to $375,000 on qualifying property. If Jerry sells the family farm and gets back $375,000 more than he paid for it, this money is not taxable.

Corporate taxation is conducted differently from that of individual taxpayers. Corporations are subject to a flat rate rather than a progressive tax. That is, for individuals, the more one makes, the more one is taxed, whereas corporations, depending on their classification, pay a fixed percent of their taxable income regardless of how much that might be.

DISPUTING YOUR TAX ASSESSMENT

If you feel you have been wrongly denied certain deductions on your taxable income, then you may appeal to Revenue Canada by a "notice of objection." Set out all the relevant facts and reasons why your appeal should succeed. If the Minister of Revenue rejects your appeal, you may further contest the decision in the Tax Court or the Federal Court (Trial Division). Both courts hold trial by judge alone—no jury. They can reject

your appeal, quash Revenue Canada's decision, modify it or send the whole case back for a new trial. Beyond this level of appeal, in rare cases you may end up in the Federal Court of Appeal, or finally in the Supreme Court of Canada, which has the last word on any point of law.

INCOME TAX AUDIT

An income tax audit is an official examination of individual or corporate financial records to determine the accuracy of a tax return. Audits are the primary tool available to Revenue Canada to enforce compliance with tax laws. If an audit reveals improper deductions, for instance, you may owe extra taxes, interest, and often a penalty as well. Revenue Canada can do an audit within four years of a return being filed, but in specific circumstances, such as fraud, the time is unlimited.

WHO CAN BE AUDITED

Approximately one out of every 100 tax returns is audited, but there is a greater likelihood that some taxpayers will be audited than others. In particular, someone who has a large income or is self-employed may be subject to an audit. Often, taxpayers who are to be audited are chosen by a Revenue

Canada computer program that is designed to identify anything unusual in a tax return. Your return may be audited for one of the following reasons:

◇ Tax deductions (such as those for charitable contributions) that are disproportionate to your income.

◇ Failure to provide the appropriate information about certain expenses.

◇ Unusual expenses (such as large travel expenditures for a shoe-repair business).

◇ Income that varies widely from year to year.

◇ T-4 forms that do not match those that Revenue Canada has received from your employer.

PREPARING FOR AN AUDIT

If you get an audit notice in the mail, do not panic—a notice does not always mean you have done something wrong. Revenue Canada may have seen something unusual on your tax return.

Read the audit notice carefully; it may be a simple request for you to send additional documents. Most audit notices specifically state the reason for the audit. Suppose you made very large charitable contributions in proportion to your income. Revenue Canada might ask for proof that you made the contributions. Once you send sufficient documentation (such as canceled cheques or receipts) the agency may be satisfied and the audit completed.

In other situations you may be asked to call a Revenue Canada office and make an appointment for the audit to be conducted in person. An audit examiner, or auditor, will either meet you at his office or, if a "field" audit is called for, he will come to your office or that of your lawyer or tax preparer. An auditor is not likely to come to your home unless you operate your business from there, or unless it is inconvenient for you to travel for some reason, such as a disability. An office audit is preferable, since it prevents the auditor from looking through your records for additional information.

The audit notice usually requests that you bring specific documents that relate to the problem that was found with your return (for example, appraisals of property you gave to a charity, canceled cheques, or receipts), as well as any general business records (such as bank statements, brokerage statements, or appointment books) that the auditor wishes to see. Revenue Canada will allow you at least several weeks to prepare for the audit—plenty of time to collect the documents you need. Do not discuss the details of your audit with the auditor on the telephone. Wait until you have all your documents assembled and the examination begins. If you need more time to collect the information, ask for the audit to be rescheduled.

THE AUDIT EXAMINATION

If you prepared your tax forms yourself, or even if you hired someone else, try to become familiar with the laws pertaining to your case by reading the publications produced by Revenue Canada. If you had a preparer do your taxes, have her appear with you at the audit to explain how your return was done. In fact, if your tax return was prepared by a lawyer, a chartered accountant (CA), or a tax professional, she can appear in your place. The main advantage of having a professional represent you is that she should be familiar with tax laws and with Revenue Canada examination procedures. However, you will have to pay for her services, and audits can last a full day or more.

At the audit, the examiner will ask to see any documents he thinks are relevant. With a field audit, be prepared for him to ask questions based on what he sees. For instance, if you claimed that your business only paid you $20,000 last year but you have racing boat trophies on display in your office, an examiner may ask how you could afford such a boat on your salary. You can refuse to answer a question until you get further documentation, particularly if the question concerns an area of your return not specified on the original audit notice. As well, an auditor must ask you for the information he needs—he cannot go through your files without your permission.

The Federal Court of Appeal as well as the Alberta Court of Queen's Bench have ruled in recent years that search warrants issued under the Income Tax Act violate the right to be secure against unreasonable searches and seizures as guaranteed by the Charter of Rights and Freedoms.

Give the auditor your cooperation. If you do not, your resistance may prompt a further examination of your records. And if you lie outright, you can be charged with perjury.

APPEAL PROCEDURES AND DEADLINES

Do not volunteer any information that the auditor has not requested. Simply supply him with the information he needs and answer his questions about it. If you feel that the auditor is unnecessarily rude or unpleasant, ask to speak to his supervisor. You are legally entitled to request another auditor to review your documents.

Some taxpayers receive a refund with interest at the conclusion of an audit, but it is far more likely that you will have to pay additional tax. If you disagree with the auditor's conclusion, you can make an immediate appeal to his supervisor and a further appeal, within 30 days, to the Tax Court. See also INCOME TAX.

If you have intentionally misrepresented your financial situation and made false statements on your return, Revenue Canada or the Justice Department may decide to press charges against you.

In the summer of 1993, the Minister of Finance promised "to go easy" on those people who voluntarily come forth to pay taxes that they evaded in the past, so long as payment or arrangements to pay owed taxes were made within a certain deadline.

See also TAX PREPARATION.

INCOMPETENCY

A person is incompetent if he is mentally or otherwise unable to handle his own affairs. The standard test of competency is to determine whether a person can understand the nature and consequences of his actions. Courts are sometimes asked to decide whether a person is incompetent.

COMPETENCY TO STAND TRIAL

Among the fundamental rights afforded a defendant in criminal proceedings is the right to confront his accusers and to present evidence in his own defense. It is unfair to have someone stand trial if he is so mentally impaired, or suffers from mental illness to such a degree, that he cannot understand the nature of the proceedings, cannot communicate properly with his lawyers, and cannot assist in his own defense. Incompetency proceedings are usually started by the lawyer who is representing the accused.

If a judge declares that the accused is incompetent, he will not be tried for the crime but will often be confined to a mental institution until he can be declared competent. If the condition is permanent or chronic, the trial may never take place.

A person who was found to be mentally disturbed at the time of an alleged crime may nevertheless be competent to stand trial later. For instance, a schizophrenic person may be required to go to court if at the time of the trial his symptoms are being controlled by medication. But his mental condition at the time of the crime may affect the verdict and his sentence. See also INSANITY PLEA.

COMPETENCY TO MANAGE ONE'S AFFAIRS

If a person has a mental illness or defect, or a physical infirmity that renders her unable to manage her daily affairs, a court may declare her incompetent and appoint a guardian to oversee her affairs or to represent her in a civil court case.

Family members usually initiate such incompetency proceedings, but any interested party may do so. Bad judgment, unusual behavior, or eccentricity does not necessarily render a person incompetent, nor does old age or poor health. However, habitual intoxication may do so, especially if the use of alcohol or drugs has permanently impaired a person's ability to reason.

A person who has been declared incompetent loses many rights, among them the right to decide where to live, to choose health care, to marry, to have a driver's license and, in some provinces, the right to vote. But the law prevents others from taking advantage of an incompetent person. For example, she cannot be held accountable for contracts she makes or for damage to property. See also BIRTH CONTROL; MARRIAGE.

NATURE OF INCOMPETENCY PROCEEDINGS

Incompetency proceedings usually take place in the district court where the person whose competence is questioned lives. Anyone who wishes to have the proposed ward judged incompetent must file a petition to the court. The alleged incompetent must then be notified of the proceedings against her and, in most provinces, her close relatives must also be notified. She is entitled to have a lawyer, and she has the right to a court-appointed lawyer if she cannot afford a lawyer herself. She should probably go to the hearing, although her attendance is not required.

At the hearing, the proposed ward has the right to refute evidence of her incapacity and to present her own witnesses. Usually the court requires medical evidence of her incompetence, although other kinds of evidence may also be relevant.

If the judge finds that the proposed ward is incompetent, the court will appoint a guardian or a conservator to assume her custody and manage her affairs. It will arrange for her to stay in her home or be placed in a psychiatric hospital, nursing home, group home, or other institution. The guardian has authority to act for the ward in all matters and to manage her property to ensure that it is preserved. In rare instances, the ward may be restored to competency because the disability or illness is cured. See GUARDIAN AND WARD.

An incompetency action is different from a proceeding for involuntary commitment, by which a mentally ill or disabled person is placed in an institution if a court rules that he is a danger to himself or to others.

INDEPENDENT CONTRACTOR

Not everyone who works for another person is an employee. An independent contractor (also called a freelance worker) provides a service or product for specific clients, but the clients do not directly control the work that is done. Independent contractors perform a service in exchange for money, according to the terms of a contract with the client. They must provide their own place to work, and they determine their own working hours. Some types of work lend themselves to independent contracting. Writers, translators, graphic designers, craftspeople, and other professionals often prefer the flexibility of freelance work.

EMPLOYERS' CONSIDERATIONS

A company that hires an independent contractor does not have to contribute to his Canada (Quebec) Pension Plan, Unemployment Insurance, and workers' compensation insurance, or provide such benefits as health or disability insurance or a retirement plan. As a result, Revenue Canada may scrutinize an independent contractor's written agreements. An employer who tries to falsely characterize employees as independent contractors can be subject to financial penalties.

In addition, employers are responsible for the actions of employees in ways that do not apply to independent contrac-

tors. If an employee makes a mistake at work, the employer may bear the responsibility for lawsuits or claims filed against the company. As an example, even though defects in a car's safety belts can be traced to a single employee on the assembly line who made a mistake, the company has the responsibility to pay compensation to any customers who suffered injuries due to the faulty belts. Of course, the employee may end up losing his job because of his mistake or negligence.

Suppose, however, that a freelance carpenter makes cabinets for a decorating firm. Six months after the firm sells the cabinets to customers, complaints start coming in that the cabinets are warping. If the customers sue the firm, the firm can name the carpenter as a codefendant in the lawsuit.

INDEPENDENT CONTRACTORS' CONSIDERATIONS

As an independent contractor, you have obligations that differ from those of an employee.

Insurance and zoning
If you work from your home, make sure that you have sufficient liability insurance and that you are not violating any local zoning laws and deed or lease restrictions. Because you are not eligible for Unemployment Insurance, you should try to provide for periods when you are out of work. See also HEALTH INSURANCE; HOME BUSINESS; INCOME TAX; SOCIAL SECURITY.

Tax consequences
An accountant can tell you the tax consequences of working

as an independent contractor. You will have to pay Canada (Quebec) Pension Plan premiums and estimated income taxes, usually on a quarterly basis.

The self-employed rate for contributions to the Canada Pension Plan was 4.8 percent of earnings in 1992, and the maximum pensionable earnings were set at $32,200. In 1992, the maximum contribution for an independent contractor, after taking off the basic deduction of $3,200, was $1,392.

Barbers, hairdressers, and manicurists, who operate as independent workers at a barbering or hairdressing establishment where they are not an owner, should also pay Unemployment Insurance premiums so as to be entitled to Unemployment Insurance benefits if they lose their jobs.

Operators of taxis, and passenger vehicles such as buses, are also eligible for Unemployment Insurance benefits, if they pay premiums, are not employees but independent workers, and if they do not own the taxi or bus they are operating. Drivers who rent or lease are not considered to be owners and are eligible for benefits.

You will probably be able to make deductions for business-related expenses, such as travel, entertainment, and certain household expenses, if you work from your home.

If you claim business expenses, you must keep complete records. Some experts say that the tax returns of independent contractors are more likely to be audited, especially if they list home-office deductions.

Rights to your work

Sometimes, freelance work that is done by professionals such as writers or translators is considered "work for hire," and the person who pays for the work obtains the copyright to it. Otherwise, an independent contractor retains the rights to her work (as is often the case with photographers). Your contract should specify who owns the rights to your work. See also CONTRACT; COPYRIGHT.

Getting paid

One of the most difficult tasks that face an independent contractor is trying to collect payment from the companies and individuals for whom she has worked. Generally, independent contractors cannot afford to hire collection agencies to pursue unpaid bills. Furthermore, if the company for whom you were working goes into bankruptcy, you may at best be considered an unsecured creditor. Once again, your best legal defense is a clear contract that spells out the payment terms.

See also SELF-EMPLOYMENT.

INDICTMENT

An indictment is a formal charge, issued by a justice of the peace or a judge, accusing someone of a serious crime. Once the indictment is issued, the accused person may be arrested or arraigned (formally charged before a judge). Sometimes a prosecutor may file reduced charges if the defendant agrees to plead guilty.

◆ A preferred indictment occurs when a prosecutor dealing with a serious crime chooses to proceed directly to trial, bypassing a preliminary hearing. Courts have also allowed for a preferred indictment to be laid on evidence adduced at a preliminary hearing, so that an accused may find himself charged with new offenses that are added to the original charge. See CRIMINAL PROCEDURE; GRAND JURY.

INFORMED CONSENT

Every competent adult has the right to decide whether or not to seek medical care. That decision belongs to the patient, not the doctor, no matter how wise or skillful the doctor may be. Informed consent refers to a physician's duty to explain any treatment, medication, or surgical procedure to a patient beforehand and to obtain his permission to proceed with it.

When you go to the doctor's office or to the hospital, you are usually confronted with a stack of forms to read and sign. They may contain long lists of complications and side effects, ranging from dizziness to death, that are related to your proposed treatment. When you sign these forms, indicating to the doctor that you understand all the information that pertains to your treatment, you are granting your informed consent.

In Canada, patients have the right to refuse medical treatment, except in certain cases involving mental health

patients. Doctors must inform patients of the material risks of a proposed treatment, describe any alternatives, and discuss the consequences of inaction. In the case of a Jehovah's Witness who was badly injured in an accident, the Ontario Court of Appeal ordered a doctor to pay $20,000 in damages because he transfused the patient while she was unconscious, even though a card in her purse stated that she did not want a blood transfusion and that she understood the consequences of her decision. The court held that the doctor had no legal right to administer blood.

This respect of a patient's wishes is a relatively recent departure from the traditional paternalistic approach to medical treatment. At one time, the doctor's idea of what was best was generally accepted by the unquestioning patient. Now a patient is likely to participate with the doctor in deciding what treatment to undergo. In order to give her valid consent, she must be informed of what the treatment entails, and it is in this context that the doctor has a duty to disclose whatever information the patient needs in order to give informed consent or to refuse treatment altogether.

The guidelines were set by the Supreme Court of Canada in the case of *Reibl* v. *Hughes.* The patient (whose understanding of English was poor) suffered a stroke during or shortly after an operation, and was left paralyzed. The Supreme Court held the doctor liable for negligence, not because the operation was negligently performed, but because the patient was not informed of the risk of stroke should such an operation be performed.

The *Reibl* judgment suggests that the physician must answer all the patient's questions completely and honestly. The physician is also obliged to inform the patient of any available alternative treatments, and the difference in risk between the various procedures. If there is an alternative to surgery, for example, the patient has a right to know. The patient also has the right to know what may happen if he decides to avoid treatment.

If the patient does not understand English or French, it is the physician's duty to have the relevant information explained through an interpreter. The interpreter may be a friend or family member who can communicate with the patient. This duty to properly inform a patient of material risks would apply to not only surgical interventions, but also the effects and side effects of prescribed medication. There is an even greater onus on the doctor to disclose information about procedures that are not urgent nor necessarily therapeutic—cosmetic surgery for breast augmentation for example. Since this type of surgery is not absolutely necessary, the patient should completely understand the risks, possible consequences, and alternatives available, so that the decision to embark on this procedure lies more with the patient than with the doctor.

A doctor who ignores a patient's questions, or who does not take time to fully inform her of possible consequences, could be held liable for damages if the operation is unsuccessful. The question the courts would ask would be something like: If the reasonable patient was informed of the risks of the operation and the alternatives available, would she have consented to this type of treatment? If a patient agrees to a procedure without being fully informed, or does not want to be informed of the risks for personal psychological reasons, it would be wise for the doctor to have this waiver of information in writing and signed by the patient.

The duty to inform also applies in cases of medical research where experimental techniques or drugs are used on otherwise healthy people, who are paid a fee to act as "guinea pigs." In these cases, the duty to disclose is very high, and all risks, possibilities, and opinions must be explained to the volunteers, since there is no therapeutic benefit to them.

It would appear that in the case of medical treatment, the signing of a consent form hurriedly given to a patient may not be sufficient to prevent a doctor from avoiding liability. Nor does it mean that the doctor must give a seminar every time he treats a patient.

But the patient has a right to know what is being done and what the risks are, and this information could be given by a nurse, or an assistant, or by providing well-written pam-

phlets on the subject and giving the patient the opportunity to familiarize himself with the material.

INQUESTS AND INQUIRIES

Unlike criminal trials, disciplinary hearings, and malpractice suits, which are adversarial legal proceedings, inquests and inquiries are inquisitional. A coroner or a fire commissioner may hold an inquest to determine the cause of death or destruction and to determine if such death or destruction was criminal in nature.

The judicial proceeding known as an inquiry is carried out by government appointees (often judges) on an issue that does not involve death. A great many matters—the fishing industry or the transportation industry, for example—may be the subject of a judicial inquiry.

Inquests are usually done when the cause of death is unknown or suspicious. In a coroner's inquest (in Alberta, Manitoba, and Nova Scotia the coroner's role is filled by a medical examiner), the coroner will usually interview witnesses, carry out an autopsy and prepare a report of his findings. The inquest attempts to identify the deceased person, establish the time and place of death, report on its probable cause, and perhaps recommend how to avoid similar deaths in future. For example, coroners' inquiries into the deaths of children killed by school buses have recommended that adults accompany children from the bus to the sidewalk, and that certain school buses be redesigned to allow the driver greater visibility.

An inquest is usually open to the public, but may also be held in camera, which means the hearing is closed to the public. The form of an inquest is somewhat similar to a court hearing, in that a Crown attorney conducts an examination in chief, which is followed by cross-examination by the witness or the witness's lawyer. Evidence may be heard by a judge alone or by a jury. The jury may rule on the circumstances of death, but not on who might be legally responsible for the death.

If you are called to testify at a coroner's inquest or public inquiry, you should consider hiring a lawyer to represent you. As a witness at such a proceeding, you are not accused of any crime, and so you do not benefit from all the legal safeguards that are guaranteed an accused at a trial. Also, evidence adduced at an inquest or inquiry could lead to future criminal charges or to a civil lawsuit where fault is found.

Following a 1984 royal commission of inquiry into several deaths at Toronto's Hospital for Sick Children, criminal charges were laid against Nurse Susan Nelles. Even though the judge at the preliminary inquiry dismissed the case against her because of a "total absence of proof," nonetheless, Nurse Nelles suffered greatly because of these unfounded accusations. The public inquiry that preceded the charges received enormous media coverage, and in the eyes of some observers the proceedings were quite adversarial, and sometimes almost took on the atmosphere of a witchhunt.

INSANITY PLEA

The insanity plea is a defense used in criminal trials. In legal usage, the term "insane" refers to someone who is mentally ill and is therefore incapable of distinguishing between right and wrong. An insanity plea will often be based on the M'Naughten rule, which holds that if a person who has committed a crime either could not tell the difference between right and wrong or simply did not know what he was doing, he cannot be found guilty.

The Criminal Code does not allow the defense of diminished responsibility. Even if the accused was ill when he committed the offense, he was technically sane if he was able to distinguish right from wrong. However, the accused's state of mind might come into play where specific intent is an essential factor in a crime. Proof that the accused was mentally ill, but not ill enough to be considered insane, might be used to show he did not have the specific intent to commit a murder, say, and thus a murder charge could be reduced to manslaughter. The Supreme Court has also recognized a defense of non-insane automatism. See MURDER.

In some cases, a defendant can avoid criminal responsibility by proving that he gave way to an "irresistible impulse" —that he could not prevent himself from committing the act. This defense is used when a defendant has endured long-term abuse at someone else's hands or was driven by circumstances to a desperate act.

In order to invoke a plea of insanity, it is not necessary for a defendant to be insane at the time of his trial, nor does the nature of a person's insanity have to conform to a particular medical diagnosis, although medical testimony may be called upon at the trial to help determine the facts of an individual case.

A person can be considered "temporarily insane" due to illness, chronic drug or alcohol abuse, or extreme mental distress—anything that has led to mental impairment or diminishment of reason. However, voluntary intoxication is not a reasonable basis for a temporary-insanity plea.

A defendant who is declared not guilty by reason of insanity is usually committed to a mental institution. If he regains his sanity in the future, the Crown could decide to try him, although this is very unlikely.

See also HEAT OF PASSION; INCOMPETENCY.

INSIDER TRADING

Buying or selling stock because you have information about the company that is not equally available to all stockholders is known as insider trading. Insider trading is illegal when it allows some people (whether employees, outside investors, or stockbrokers) to benefit at others' expense.

Executives of publicly traded companies (companies that are traded on a stock exchange, such as the Toronto Stock Exchange) often purchase their company's stock or they receive it as part of their compensation. Like other stockholders, they have the right to buy or sell the shares they own. However, they are in an advantageous position because they often know, before the public does, of situations that might affect the stock's price. When the company is in a bad situation, they can sell their stock before the price drops, and when things look good, they can buy more stock.

To inform the provincial securities commission of any insider trading, "inside" stockholders are required to report their stock trading to the commission every month. The commission makes those reports available to the public.

If convicted, inside traders stand to lose the profit from their transactions and can be fined by their provincial securities commission or even have criminal charges filed against them.

See also STOCKS AND BONDS.

INSURANCE

Insurance is a way for individuals or groups to protect themselves against losses that could cause serious financial difficulties. In a contract of insurance (called a policy), an insurance company agrees to compensate you (or a beneficiary you have named in the policy) if a specified event, such as a fire or the death of the insured person, takes place. Insurance policies may also provide protection from property loss or lawsuits. A comprehensive automobile insurance policy, for example, will reimburse you if your car is damaged or stolen, and liability insurance will protect you from lawsuits if you have an accident. In return for this coverage, you pay to the insurance company regular amounts of money known as premiums.

The company providing the insurance is called the insurer; the party who buys the insurance is known as the policyholder. Although many people buy insurance policies so that they can protect themselves from loss, far fewer will have to file claims for payment. Thus insurers profit by spreading out the risk of paying claims among all their policyholders.

TYPES OF INSURANCE

The various types of insurance generally fall into three categories: personal insurance, by which a person's life or health is covered; property insurance, by which a person's home, car, or other personal belongings are covered; and liability insurance, by which the insured person is covered for any lawsuits filed against him by others.

The terms of the policy dictate the amount of reimbursement or compensation that the policyholder can receive from the insurer. In the case of life insurance, a specified beneficiary will receive the compensation upon the death of the policyholder. See AUTOMOBILE INSURANCE; CASUALTY INSURANCE; FIRE INSURANCE; FLOOD INSURANCE; HEALTH INSURANCE; HOMEOWNERS' INSURANCE; INSURANCE AGENT AND BROKER; LIABILITY INSURANCE; LIFE INSURANCE.

INSURANCE REGULATION

There are many insurance companies in Canada, all regulated by provincial insurance departments, which grant licenses to insurers, approve insurance claim forms, regulate rates, and try to protect policyholders' interests by investigating complaints made about specific insurers. Because provincial regulations vary, a policy that is approved for sale in one province may be prohibited in another, and rates for virtually identical policies may vary from one province to another.

Most provinces have insurance guaranty funds that pay claims if an insurer becomes insolvent. Your provincial insurance department or the Insurance Bureau of Canada can tell you about protection in your province.

BUYING A POLICY

Before taking out a policy, particularly for life insurance, check out your insurer. Several independent companies regularly rate insurance companies; their reports should be available in the business section of your library. A provincial insurance department can tell you whether it has received complaints about the way an insurer handles claims.

When discussing insurance with a sales agent or broker,

ask him when your policy goes into effect. When you fill out an application, the agent sends it to the insurance company experts (called underwriters), who analyze it and determine the risk the company would assume by accepting it. You are insured only when the company approves your application. If an agent tells you that your policy is in effect from the time you complete the application, the insurance company can be held to this claim. For certain types of insurance, such as a homeowners' policy, the agent who takes your application is authorized by his company to issue a "binder"—in essence, a temporary policy that serves to protect the applicant from loss while the application is being reviewed. See also INSURANCE AGENT AND BROKER.

CANCELLATIONS AND CHANGES

Read a new insurance policy thoroughly, including the cancellation provision. You should be able to cancel a policy whenever you like. Also find out how the company will return to you any premiums that you have paid in advance—for example, if you made a semiannual payment for your homeowners' policy but you are moving after two months and must cancel it.

Provincial laws establish the conditions under which your insurer can cancel or fail to renew your policy. Some typical reasons for doing so are fraudulent or excessive claims, failing to pay premiums, or lying on an application. If you tell a health insurance company that you do not

smoke, for instance, the company could cancel your policy if it later discovers you do smoke.

Most provinces require that policies include an incontestability clause, stating that the insurer cannot cancel your policy after it has been in effect for a certain period—usually two years. Most companies will pay on a life insurance policy, even if the insured committed suicide, providing the policy was in effect for at least two years prior to the suicide. Many insurance companies pay twice the amount of the policy, if the death is caused by accident. This is known as a "double indemnity."

Even though the insurer had never inquired about her psychiatric history, a British Columbia woman had to repay $122,966 disability benefits she was paid because her insurer discovered that two psychiatrists had once diagnosed her as having a mental disorder. The woman claimed she did not agree with the diagnosis and, in any case, the policy's two-year incontestability limit had long since passed. However, the British Columbia Supreme Court ruled that the woman had committed fraud by failing to disclose the psychiatrists' diagnosis and her fraud overrode the two-year contestability period. It ordered her to return all the money she had received.

MAKING A CLAIM

Filing an insurance claim may be as simple as sending copies of your medical report to the insurer. With property insurance, however, there are cer-

tain procedures to follow. If your property is damaged or lost, call your insurer as soon as possible.

You must provide appropriate documentation for your claim—invoices for repairs, appraisals of property that has been lost, or a police report of a theft. In many cases the insurer will ask you to submit an estimate of repairs for damage to a car or other property, or it may want the damage appraised by a company representative. If the repairs exceed the amount authorized by your insurer, the company will probably not pay the difference.

A claims adjuster will investigate your claim and determine how much money you will get. The adjuster cannot reject a legitimate claim and you should not feel obliged to accept the first offer she makes.

If a lawsuit is filed against you, you must gather any information regarding the lawsuit and forward it to your insurer.

STEPS TO TAKE IF YOUR CLAIM IS NOT HANDLED PROPERLY

If you are dissatisfied with the way a claims adjuster is handling your case, here are a few suggestions about what to do:

1. Speak to your adjuster's supervisor, who may be in a position to offer additional money to settle your claim.

2. Hire your own appraiser or an independent adjuster to make an estimate of the damages or loss. The person you hire should be licensed in your province. Send his appraisal to a supervisor at your insurance company.

3. You and your insurer can each hire trained arbitrators to hear your dispute and to propose a fair settlement of your claim. See also ARBITRATION.

4. File a written report with your provincial bureau of insurance. In some provinces this office will intercede for you.

5. If your claim is complicated, your lawyer can negotiate with the insurer for you.

6. Ultimately, you may take your insurer to the small-claims court or have a lawyer file a lawsuit against the company. If it is found that the company or its representative acted in bad faith, you may be awarded money. Remember, however, that you may come out ahead by settling with your insurer, as a lawsuit can be expensive.

INSURANCE AGENT AND BROKER

Most people purchase their insurance policies through an agent or a broker. In general, an insurance agent represents a particular insurance company, while an insurance broker acts as the customer's agent, seeking the best coverage and terms available from a variety of insurance companies. Sometimes a broker may act as an agent. To be sure you are getting impartial information, ask the person from whom you buy a policy about his relationship to the insurer.

Insurance agents and brokers are regulated by the province in which they conduct their business. To become

licensed, they are usually required to pass a written examination and provide evidence of good character. Insurance agents and brokers have an obligation to conduct business in good faith both with their customers and with their insurance companies.

CHECKLIST

Cutting Down Insurance Costs

When you add up the costs of all your insurance coverage, the total may be quite high. Ask your agent or broker about the following ways to reduce your costs:

■ **CONSOLIDATE YOUR POLICIES.** You may get a discount if you purchase your homeowners', auto, and other insurance policies through one company alone.

■ **RAISE THE DEDUCTIBLE.** By raising the amount you will pay out of pocket on your homeowners' and auto insurance, you can reduce your premiums by 10 percent or more.

■ **GET AUTO INSURANCE THAT FAVORS GOOD RISKS.** You may get reduced premiums if you have an antitheft or safety device, if you drive less than 7,500 miles a year, or if you have a good driving record. School-age drivers who have good grades or have completed a driver training course can receive reductions, and drivers over 50 or 55 years old may also receive discounts on their premiums.

■ **BUY "PARTICIPATING" LIFE INSURANCE POLICIES.** Such policies entitle you to receive dividends, which you can use to pay your premiums. Although the premiums may be higher at first, you should save money in the long run.

■ **ASK ABOUT "LIFESTYLE" DISCOUNTS.** Nonsmokers pay lower rates for life and health insurance, and so may people who get regular exercise or who do not drink.

■ **INVESTIGATE HOMEOWNERS' SAFETY DISCOUNTS.** Some homeowners' insurance companies reduce premiums if you have protective devices such as smoke detectors, fire extinguishers, and security alarms, or if your house is built of materials that are fire-resistant.

■ **SHOP FOR COMPARISONS.** Call other companies for price quotes. If you tell your agent that you have been offered a lower rate elsewhere, he may match it. In addition, some companies give long-term policyholders a discount of 5 percent or more. Ask your agent or broker.

◆ ◇ A broker or agent must try to get the terms and amount of coverage that you request. If he cannot do so, he should notify you immediately. Suppose you ask your insurance broker for a $1 million life insurance policy. He presents your application to several companies, all of which reject you because of your previous health problems. Your broker must tell you the status of your application and your chances of obtaining coverage.

◇ If an agent or broker tells you he is obtaining insurance for you and then fails to do so, he may be responsible to you for any loss you suffer. Suppose you file an application for a homeowners' policy and give the agent (or broker) a cheque for the first premium. Instead of sending the form and cheque to the insurance company, he files them away. Weeks pass, and there is a small fire in your kitchen. You call the insurance company's claims department, and discover it has no record of your policy. In this situation the agent could be held liable for the loss you suffered.

◇ If a broker or agent misrepresents the terms, conditions, premiums, or coverage provided by the policy, and as a result you suffer a loss, you may be able to sue him. Written agreements are always easier to prove than oral promises.

◇ If an agent or broker does not properly identify the property, and as a result your claim is denied by the insurance company, he may be responsible for the loss. For instance, when writing a policy for car insurance, the agent must describe the car correctly. Read both your application and your policy to ensure that your property is accurately described.

◇ If the agent agreed to keep your coverage current and the policy expires or is canceled, he may be responsible for any resulting loss. If he does not forward a premium to the company and your policy is canceled for that reason, you can hold him responsible for any loss you suffer. Similarly, he must notify you when your policy is due to be renewed.

◇ If the insurance company becomes insolvent and fails to pay a claim, your agent or broker is generally not personally responsible to you financially —unless he knew that the company would not be able to honor its claims.

◇ An agent must cancel insurance, or lower or limit coverage, when instructed to do so by his company.

◇ When an agent leaves a particular company to work for another, he may solicit his previous customers unless he signed a contract that expressly prohibited this.

See also GOOD FAITH; INSURANCE; NEGLIGENCE.

INTELLECTUAL PROPERTY

Intellectual property is the right that people may have to ideas, designs, and other intellectual creations such as written material. It is important that new ideas and intellectual creations circulate freely, but it is also important that the creator or inventor of these things be protected. Intellectual properties protected by various laws now include:

◇ Patents for inventions and new kinds of technology.

◇ Copyright—protection for literary, artistic, musical, and dramatic works.

◇ Trademarks—words or symbols used to distinguish the goods and services of one person from another.

◇ Industrial designs— shapes, patterns, or ornamentation of an industrially produced object. The shape of a cadillac automobile is an industrial design.

◇ Integrated circuit topographies—the three-dimensional configuration of electronic circuits embodied in integrated circuit products.

◇ Plant breeders' rights— rights to certain new plant varieties made by breeding or by biological technology.

See COPYRIGHT; PATENT; TRADEMARK.

INTENT

Intent is the state of mind a person has when he deliberately commits a criminal offense or a civil wrong. Suppose you get a cheque from someone who bought your son's rickety old bicycle for $10. The buyer mistakenly makes out the cheque for the sum of $100. If you see the mistake and cash the cheque knowing it was written in error, you have acted with intent. Intent is a necessary component of many criminal acts, and prosecutors must prove that there was intent on the part of the defendant in these cases.

Unless a statute says otherwise, prosecutors do not have

to prove intent to obtain a conviction for any crime, such as assault or arson, that is considered inherently wrong. A person who commits such a crime is presumed to be aware that he is doing something wrong.

Canadian criminal law has two general classes of intent: general intent and specific intent. A general intent to commit an illegal act must be proven in all crimes, but to get a conviction for some crimes, the Crown must prove specific intent, and must prove it beyond a reasonable doubt.

For example, in the case of murder, the Crown must prove that the accused intended to kill the victim or at least knew that death could probably result from his illegal action. If the Crown cannot prove specific intent, then the accused may be found guilty of a lesser offense such as manslaughter. An exception to the rule of intent is found in regulatory offenses such as drunk driving and, perhaps, dangerous driving. In these cases, you can be found guilty whether or not you knew you were drunk or knew that your driving was dangerous.

If a defendant committed an unintended illegal act, he may be convicted of a less serious crime. For instance, a homicide is considered murder if the prosecution can prove that the accused intended to kill the victim. If this cannot be proven, the accused may be convicted of a lesser charge, such as manslaughter.

If someone is insane or incapable of forming the criminal intent necessary to commit a crime, he may be found not guilty, but he may also be committed to a mental institution. See also INSANITY PLEA.

The law presumes that most children cannot form the criminal intent sufficient to commit many crimes. Because many youths and even children willfully and knowingly do so, however, a system of youth courts has been established to deal with young lawbreakers.

See also YOUNG OFFENDER.

INTERLOCUTORY DECREE

An interlocutory decree is a temporary or provisional decree issued by a court. Suppose Adele's employer fired her because she refused to relocate to another city and Adele sued him for back wages and reinstatement of her pension and health benefits. Halfway through the trial, the judge issued an interlocutory decree ordering Adele's employer to restore her health benefits to her while the court continued to hear the case on the subject of wages and pension benefits.

If the court ultimately concluded that Adele indeed deserved to have her health benefits continued, the judge would restate the court's decision in his final decree.

IN VITRO FERTILIZATION

In vitro fertilization is a means by which an infertile couple can conceive a child. Despite popular use of the phrase "test tube baby," the child's conception takes place in a petri dish (*in vitro* means "in glass"). The procedure involves extracting an ovum from a woman and fertilizing it in the dish. A resulting embryo is then implanted into her uterus (or that of another woman) so that the pregnancy can continue normally. The service is provided in a private fertility clinic, physician's office, or hospital, and it is usually very expensive.

In vitro fertilization first came to the public's attention when Louise Brown, the first child brought to term as a result of the method, was born in England in 1978. Since that time, this and other reproductive technologies have presented lawmakers and judges with challenging legal and ethical questions, for which there are often no clear-cut solutions.

The procedure often calls for repeated attempts at fertilization, and the chances that a healthy child will result are small. To attract customers, a few clinics have misled would-be parents by exaggerating their success rates. Also, because the overall success rate is so low, health insurance companies generally exclude in vitro procedures from their policies.

The recommendations of a federally financed study of reproductive technologies, completed in 1993, will provide some guidelines for legislation on in vitro fertilization and similar issues. At the time of writing, laws on these matters are quite unsettled in Canada, because few cases on these issues have come before the courts. In one famous U.S. case, a donor contributed an egg that was then fertilized in vitro with her husband's sperm. The fertilized egg was implanted in another woman, who had agreed in writing to carry the child and to relinquish her parental rights to the child. However, her relationship with the couple broke down during the course of the pregnancy, and before she had given birth, she tried to sue for custody of the child. The court ruled against her, holding that the couple were the genetic parents of the child, and that the woman who carried the baby was not its mother.

A similar action would be impossible in Quebec, which expressly prohibits surrogate motherhood.

IOU

An IOU (shorthand for "I Owe You") is a paper given by a borrower to a lender. An IOU will normally contain the amount to be repaid and the borrower's signature. However, a simple IOU may not be adequate proof of a debt if the lender is obliged to seek his repayment in court, as it does not have the characteristics of a proper contract.

In particular, an IOU does not specify what a lender has received in return for his loan or the date by which it must be repaid. Rather than lending money to someone in exchange for an IOU, you should execute a promissory note—a written promise by the borrower to repay you according to specific terms. See PROMISSORY NOTE.

J

FROM
JOB DISCRIMINATION
TO
JUSTICE OF THE PEACE

JOB DISCRIMINATION

A variety of federal and provincial laws prohibit discriminatory practices by employers, trade unions, employee associations, and employment agencies. Human rights legislation in all provinces prohibits discrimination based on sex, race, color, ethnicity, nationality, place of origin, religion, marital status, and physical disability, but prohibitions on discrimination because of age differ from jurisdiction to jurisdiction. For example, mandatory retirement at age 65 is legal in British Columbia, Newfoundland, Nova Scotia, Ontario, and Saskatchewan. Some provinces prohibit discrimination because of sexual orientation, criminal convictions, and political beliefs; others do not.

Apart from human rights laws, there is a variety of legislation dealing with what are called unfair labor practices.

For example, anyone getting a federal contract may not practice job discrimination, and the Unemployment Insurance Act stipulates that government agents must not discriminate when referring jobs to the unemployed.

The Canadian Charter of Rights and Freedoms guarantees all residents certain rights in situations involving federal and provincial governments.

The Supreme Court of Canada has held that sexual harassment in the workplace is one form of sexual discrimination, and that denying a pregnant woman accident and sickness benefits is another.

Under the federal Employment Equity Act, companies with more than 100 employees must ensure that women, aboriginal peoples, the disabled, and visible minorities receive a proportionate level of representation in the work force.

All Canadian governments promote, to some degree, the notion of equal pay for similar work or work of similar value. Pay parity for public servants is the law in Prince Edward Island, New Brunswick, Newfoundland, Manitoba, Nova Scotia, and Ontario, which also obliges private sector employers to implement pay parity. In the other provinces, the requirement of equal pay for work of equal value or similar work is enforced only when someone complains. See also AGE DISCRIMINATION; DISCRIMINATION; SEX DISCRIMINATION.

FILING A COMPLAINT

If you feel you have been the target of a discriminatory practice, you may complain to the appropriate human rights commission. If your job situation is covered by the federal Human Rights Act, file your complaint with the Canadian Human Rights Commission. If it believes you have a valid complaint, it will investigate further and possibly order a human rights tribunal to examine your case.

Similar procedures exist under provincial legislation.

If a human rights commission or tribunal finds discrimination has occurred, it may order your employer to do one or more of the following:

— cease the discrimination;

— hire, rehire, or promote you;

— award you back pay;

— establish an affirmative action program;

— fine, or even fire, the offending party;

— order that the employer make his workplace accessible to the handicapped.

Filing a complaint with a human rights commission may bring results in other ways, too. Employers are reluctant to be accused of discrimination, which can leave them with a bad reputation. Thus even if the commission does not act upon a complaint, the fact that it has been filed may prompt the employer to correct the discriminatory situation.

It is illegal for an employer to retaliate against an employee for filing a complaint with a human rights commission or against someone who cooperates with an ensuing investigation. If you are demoted or fired for your involvement with a job discrimination complaint, you can sue your employer for wrongful treatment.

Note, however, that grievance procedures may be included in your employment contract or collective agreement. In that case, you should attempt to deal with the problem at this level before lodging a complaint with a human rights commission. See also WHISTLE-BLOWER.

WHEN DISCRIMINATION IS ALLOWED

Despite the wide range of legal prohibitions, some types of job discrimination are permitted. When hiring, an employer can claim that the job he is filling has a bona fide occupational qualification (BFOQ). For example, a nursing home administrator may want to hire a certain number of female nurses to attend to the personal needs of women patients. Similarly, a hospital obstetrics ward could employ only female nurses. Courts have upheld this kind of qualification based on gender out of recognition for the patients' personal privacy. However, one provincial board of inquiry held that discrimination existed where male nursing home attendants could not assist female residents who made no objection to male attendants.

Sometimes national origin, religion, or age may be a legitimate criterion—as when a casting company limits actors to certain age groups to cast roles for plays and movies. It would hardly be appropriate, for example, to cast an 80-year-old man as Dennis the Menace.

REVERSE DISCRIMINATION

The issue of reverse discrimination has sometimes been invoked to criticize affirmative action programs, which encourage minority hiring. When tested in court cases, however, affirmative action programs have been upheld in several cases. See also AFFIRMATIVE ACTION.

UNPROVED DISCRIMINATION

Occasionally, what may appear to be discrimination can fail to survive the scrutiny of the courts. Such was the case, for example, when a 60-year-old baker complained to the Nova Scotia Human Rights Commission that he had been laid off because of his age. The baker had worked in the same pastry shop for 40 years, was a faithful employee, and could not understand why younger employees with less seniority were not laid off before him.

The board of inquiry heard evidence from the complainant and his employer, but ruled there was nothing discriminatory in the dismissal. Evidence showed the baker was laid off not because of his age but due to a lack of ability: he was twice as slow as the other employees. Had the complainant been more proficient, he would certainly have been kept on, regardless of his age. See also CIVIL RIGHTS; EMPLOYEE HIRING AND FIRING.

If you think you have been the victim of job discrimination, you can do the following:

1. Before you file your complaint, gather together all the evidence you need. Save all relevant documents given to you by your employer (such as performance evaluations). Keep records of any incidents of discrimination that take place, noting names, dates, and any other pertinent information. Also, compare notes with other employees who may also have been discriminated against. If your information is well documented, your complaint will be taken more seriously.

2. Before filing a complaint, find out if your employment situation is covered by provincial or federal human rights legislation.

3. Find out the proper procedure for filing a complaint. Whichever commission—federal or provincial—is relevant to your case will give you this information. In most instances you must file your complaint within 180 days from the time of the most recent act of discrimination.

JOINT TENANCY

Joint tenancy is a form of ownership by which more than one person holds title to property. Upon the death of one owner, her share passes entirely to the other owner or owners. For example, if you and your brother own your property as joint tenants, you will become the sole

REAL LIFE, REAL LAW

The Case of the Sabbath Sales

Janice, a sales clerk in a large department store, was a member of the Seventh Day Adventists, who observe the Sabbath on Saturday. She told her employer that she would be unable to work on Saturdays as she had to attend church.

Because Saturday was one of the store's busiest days, her employer told her he had no choice but to fire her. Saturday work was essential for his business.

Janice complained to the Ontario Human Rights Commission and when the case reached the Supreme Court of Canada, it ruled that the company had discriminated against her. Because the case involved a large enterprise with many employees, the court felt the company had a duty to accommodate Janice's religious practices. But the court pointed out that a small company would not be similarly obliged if exempting an employee from Saturday work, and having her work another day instead, would cause the company undue hardship

owner when he dies, even if he has tried to leave his interest to someone else. See WILL.

Known more formally as "joint tenancy with right of survivorship" (often abbreviated on bank and real estate records as JTWROS), joint tenancy can be useful as an estate-planning tool. Property owned under joint tenancy does not need to pass through probate when one owner dies, thus enabling the surviving owner or owners to avoid probate costs and delays. See PROBATE.

A word of caution: if you hold a bank account, stocks, bonds, or other personal property in joint tenancy, you or the other owner—whoever holds proof of ownership (such as a passbook or stock certificate)—has access to the whole property. For example, if Jim and Jody jointly own $30,000 worth of

bonds, and then have a falling out, one of them can cash in the bonds without the knowledge or approval of the other.

See also BANK ACCOUNT; TENANCY BY THE ENTIRETY; TENANCY IN COMMON; TRUST.

JUDGE

A judge is a public officer who has been authorized to administer the law in a court. He presides over the court and applies the laws of the nation or province to each case. In cases where there is no jury, the judge decides the outcome.

Federally appointed judges must be lawyers who have been members of a provincial bar association for at least 10 years. Except for Alberta and Newfoundland, judges at the provincial level must be lawyers who have been members of the bar for at least five years. Non-lawyers may become judges in Alberta and Newfoundland, but this is not a common occurrence.

The procedure for choosing a judge depends on the type of court to which he or she is being assigned. Provincial court judges are generally appointed by the provincial attorney general, often after consultation with the province's premier and cabinet. Appointees are selected from lists drawn up by provincial selection committees or judicial councils. These judges usually hold office until the age of 70.

Judges at the superior court and county or district court level in each province are appointed by the federal Minister of Justice from those recommended by assessment committees in which the provinces participate. Supreme Court of Canada judges are chosen by the prime minister and the cabinet. There is no formal procedure for selecting Supreme Court appointees. Such judges are often elevated from positions in lower courts. The Supreme Court Act specifies that at least one-third of the Supreme Court judges be from Quebec. This ensures that the court will be qualified to deal with the civil law system of that province. Depending on the type of court, federally appointed judges face mandatory retirement at age 70 or 75.

Judges may only be removed from office if they contravene standards of good behavior.

Such a breach might occur through abuse of power, improper performance of the duties of the office, criminal convictions, or moral turpitude.

The Canadian Judicial Council (CJC) investigates complaints against federally appointed judges and provides judges with training and continuing education courses. Similar judicial councils exist in each province. Although the CJC can recommend that federally appointed judges be removed from office, such removal can only occur through a joint address of the Senate and House of Commons.

Some provincial judicial councils provide only two sanctions for judges who misbehave—a reprimand or removal from the bench. Because there is no intermediate penalty, such as a suspension, critics claim that disciplinary committees have been too lenient with errant judges in the past.

Though judicial statements and behavior are increasingly under fire, instances of judicial misbehavior are still relatively rare. One of the most glaring occurred in Toronto in 1989 in the case of a man charged with assaulting his wife. After hearing the evidence, the judge claimed the ordeal was the fault of the wife, whom he ordered to be handcuffed and escorted from the court. The Ontario Judicial Council was asked to conduct an inquiry, but before any action was taken the judge resigned.

In a January 1994 interview with Southam News, Chief Justice Antonio Lamer of the Supreme Court of Canada warned that racist or sexist behavior on the bench will not be tolerated. "It's all very well to alert everybody to gender bias, but I want to get rid of those who are biased." He urged those with legitimate complaints to come forward.

Judges are sometimes called justices. The various levels of court are headed by either chief judges or chief justices, depending on the nature of the court.

JUDGMENT

A judgment, the final decision by a court after it has reviewed the evidence presented to it, resolves the issues in dispute and imposes the court's ruling on the parties involved. Unless a judgment is changed by an appeal, the parties have to obey it or face the possibility of a fine or imprisonment.

The judgment handed down to a defendant found guilty in a criminal trial may include a fine or a prison sentence. In civil cases the most common judgment in favor of the plaintiff is an award of compensation, or money damages. In fact, *judgment* and *money damages* are often used synonymously when referring to cases involving personal injury or property damage. See also DAMAGES.

It is one thing to get a court's judgment in your favor, and another to collect that judgment. When you receive a judgment of money damages, the person who lost the case (the judgment debtor) may not pay you right away. In some cases the court imposes a deadline for payment, such as 30 to 45 days after the judgment has been decided upon; in other cases it may specify only the amount to be paid without giving any delay for payment.

If the judgment debtor files an appeal, you may not receive your damages for some time. Some courts require that security or collateral be provided by judgment debtors who appeal and subsequently request that execution be stayed, or postponed.

Ordinarily, the first step in attempting to collect your judgment debt is the filing of a writ of execution. This document contains the details of the judgment and authorizes the sheriff or bailiff to collect the debt on your behalf.

The sheriff or bailiff will formally deliver, or "serve," the writ on the judgment debtor's bank, brokerage house, or mortgage holder. He may even serve the writ on the debtor's employer in order to garnishee his wages. Since your judgment creates a claim, or lien, upon his property, you can seize the amount needed to pay off the judgment. Keep in mind, however, that there may be limits on the amount of wages that can be garnisheed and that cer-

tain property, such as homes, furniture, the tools of one's trade, and vehicles used for business purposes, is often exempted from garnishment. This means that it cannot be seized. See also GARNISHMENT.

If you are awarded damages but receive no payment from the defendant, you can use a legal procedure known as executing a judgment. You may also ask the court to order the defendant to an examination in aid of execution. During the examination, your lawyer will question him about his income and assets and will require him to provide copies of bank and other financial statements, tax returns, and other documents that may disclose the amount and nature of his assets.

If the judgment debtor cannot pay you in a lump sum, you can agree to receive the money in installments. Be sure to get the agreement in writing and have him sign it. Note that you are entitled to receive interest on the judgment from the date it is awarded until the date it is paid in full. The interest rate on court judgments is set by law. The court clerk can tell you the applicable rate.

When the judgment debtor does pay up, he will ask you to sign a form known as a satisfaction of judgment, as proof of payment. Do not sign this form until you have actually received the payment. For example, if you take a personal cheque and it is later returned for insufficient funds, you will have to go back to court to have the judgment reopened. It is better to accept only cash, a money order, or a certified cheque.

Not all judgments in civil cases result in money damages, nor are they necessarily made at the conclusion of a trial.

Summary judgment
When the evidence supporting the position of one of the parties is very clear from the outset, there may be no need for a trial. In such cases the court can issue a summary judgment. Either party to a case has the right to request such a judgment, and the judge will make a decision based on the motions and the supporting documents supplied by the parties.

Default judgment
A default judgment might be issued when one of the parties fails to appear in court or fails to follow court procedure. Because courts prefer to decide disputes on their merits, however, a default judgment can often be overturned if the party in default offers a good reason for the procedural mistake or the failure to appear—such as illness or an accident. See also DEFAULT JUDGMENT.

Declaratory judgment
A declaratory judgment determines the rights of the parties in a case that seeks the court's opinion on a legal question. For example, if the language written in a contract is not clear, the parties may ask the court to decide on the meaning of the contract. They are not seeking money or other property from one another; they are just asking the court to settle a dispute before a wrong is committed.

See also COURTS; CRIMINAL LAW; LAWSUIT.

JURISDICTION

The term *jurisdiction* refers to the extent of a particular court's authority to hear a case and determine its outcome. If a court exceeds its jurisdiction, it cannot enforce its judgment, or decision, in a given case.

A court's jurisdiction is determined by such factors as geographical location, the type of case (such as divorce or bankruptcy), whether the case involves civil or criminal law, and whether the applicable laws are those of the provincial or the federal government.

The categories that determine jurisdiction often overlap. For example, a small-claims court in Kamloops, B.C., has several kinds of jurisdiction: (1) it is a civil (not criminal) court; (2) it serves one region, Kamloops; and (3) it handles only disputes involving relatively minor sums of money. See COURTS.

JURY

A jury is a group of people selected from the community to inquire into the facts of a civil or criminal case and to make decisions about them. The people chosen to sit on a jury are called jurors. They are sworn to hear the evidence presented and to evaluate it according to the instructions that are given to them by the presiding judge.

There are two kinds of juries: criminal and civil. Criminal juries have 12 members and must deliver unanimous ver-

dicts only. Even though the Criminal Code states that criminal juries in the territories may consist of six jurors, this provision has been declared unconstitutional. Civil juries, which are becoming more and more rare, contain six jurors and may deliver a verdict when either five or six members are in agreement.

According to the Canadian Charter of Rights and Freedoms, a person accused of criminal activity "has the right, except in the case of an offence under military law tried before a military tribunal, to the benefit of trial by jury where the maximum punishment for the offence is imprisonment for five years or a more severe punishment." Some Canadian jurisdictions allow accused persons to choose a trial by a jury speaking either English or French. In Canada, criminal juries do not participate in the sentencing of those found guilty. This is strictly the duty of the judge.

In civil cases where private disputes are resolved, however, the jury may have to do more than decide if a party is liable or not. It may also be asked to determine the proportionate liability of two or more parties, or assess the damages owed by one party to another. But, as stated above, civil juries are becoming increasingly rare, and even in instances, such as defamation cases, where a party is entitled to a jury trial, the parties often agree to a trial by judge alone. Besides, a judge may refuse the use of a jury in extremely complex cases.

JURY DUTY

When you receive a notice in the mail summoning you to jury duty, it may raise questions in your mind: Why were you chosen? How long will you serve? Will your boss let you go? Will you have to stay in a hotel room for weeks on end? Will you be allowed to see your family?

Even though such questions concern those who are called to jury duty, they rarely become issues. Employers are usually understanding about absences for jury duty and may not dismiss an employee who is absent due to jury duty. Most cases are settled in days rather than weeks, and jurors are rarely isolated in hotel rooms.

A summons to jury duty represents one of the most important aspects of civil life, for the right to trial by jury is a cornerstone of democracy. In many criminal cases and in certain civil cases, the parties in Canadian courts have the right to have their cases decided by a group of their fellow citizens— a jury of their peers.

HOW PROSPECTIVE JURORS ARE SELECTED

The process of selecting those to be called for jury duty differs from province to province but generally works as follows:

◇ First, public officials such as sheriffs and court clerks determine how many names should be placed on the jury list for each district.

◇ A list of potential jurors is then gathered from various sources such as voter registration lists and provincial lists of Medicare beneficiaries. The selection of names, often done by computer, must be random.

◇ When the court issues an order for a jury to be selected, or "empaneled," a public official selects names at random from the jury list thus creating a jury panel, or array.

◇ Potential jurors will receive a summons to appear for jury duty at a given time and place.

A CIVIC DUTY

Suppose your summons comes during your employer's busiest time. Can you decline to serve? Probably not. In most places, however, you may have your service postponed for a while, and the postponement may be repeated a specified number of times. But sooner or later, unless you fall into one of the categories discussed elsewhere on this page, you must serve.

Jury duty is every citizen's duty, and a summons for jury duty is an order from a court. If you do not obey it, a judge may order you to serve or find you in contempt of court, which is punishable by a jail sentence or fine.

Provincial laws determine how much jurors are paid and what travel allowances they get. Some provinces provide money for child care.

An employer who disciplines an employee for accepting jury duty commits an offense. In some provinces, Manitoba for example, employers must pay the wages or salary of those absent on jury duty. Even in provinces where such laws do not apply, some employers pay their employees absent for jury duty. Even a minister for Employment upheld a ruling of the Unemployment Insurance Commission that penalized a London, Ont., juror for her nine-month jury duty. The commission, and the minister, said juror compensation is a provincial, not a federal, matter, and since the juror was not available for work, she was not eligible for UI benefits.

WHO CAN BE EXCUSED

If you run your own business and have no employees, you may plead economic hardship and be excused from jury duty. You may also be excused if you take care of young children or you have a health problem that makes it hard for you to serve.

Some professionals are automatically excused, sometimes by law. Doctors, fire fighters, and police officers are often excused because their jobs are essential to the public welfare. Lawyers and court officials may be excused because they have professional knowledge that may interfere with their ability to evaluate cases impartially. Depending on the court's rules and provincial law, convicted felons, noncitizens, people who are incompetent, and people who do not speak English or French may also be excluded from jury service. Each province may set its own guidelines for exclusion, as long as it does not discriminate on the basis of race, religion, sex, or national origin.

FORMING A JURY

When you appear for jury duty, there is no guarantee that you will serve on a jury. More people are summoned than will be needed because not all potential jurors will be qualified.

When jurors are needed for a case, prospective candidates are assembled in court, where they swear (or affirm) to answer truthfully any question put to them by the judge or lawyers. In criminal trials, this procedure takes place in the presence of the accused. In such cases, the accused or the prosecutor may object to the entire panel of jurors, claiming that fraud, partiality, or willful misconduct were present when it was selected.

The accused or the prosecutor can also challenge a juror for cause, such as an inability to speak the language of the accused, relationship to one of the parties, or apparent bias toward the accused or one of the witnesses. A challenge for cause may lead to a *voir dire*, or trial of the challenge, during which a potential juror may be asked is she has heard about the case or if she has any preconceived notions about the case's proper outcome or its subject matter. A person may be disqualified from serving as a juror if the *voir dire* uncovers information indicating the person would not be a suitable juror.

If a juror willfully conceals information or lies in order to serve on a jury, he may be guilty of perjury. See PERJURY.

Some jurors may be disqualified because of their profession. If you are an accountant being considered to serve as a juror in a tax-fraud case, a lawyer might feel that your expertise would hinder rather than help your judgment. The lawyer may therefore make a "challenge for cause," protesting that you are unable to serve impartially. If the judge agrees, you will be excused.

After the parties are satisfied that no remaining jurors can be challenged for cause, each side may be allowed peremptory challenges, for which they are not required to give a reason. A peremptory challenge may not be allowed, however, if there is any suspicion that it is being used to exclude a juror solely on the basis of race.

In civil trials, the selection process is much simpler, as only challenges for cause are permitted.

DISCHARGE OF A JUROR

If a juror in a criminal trial cannot continue due to illness or any other reason, he may be discharged by the judge. A legally valid verdict may be rendered as long as there are at least 10 jurors remaining. The judge has the discretion, however, to order the selection of additional jurors.

Recently in Manitoba, a jury spokesperson charged that one juror, claiming to have psychic powers, refused to participate in deliberations. Although the juror in question denied this, he was discharged by the trial judge. The Manitoba Court of Appeal reversed the trial judge's decision, saying that the right to a trial by 12 of one's peers is fundamental to our justice system. Consequently, a more extensive inquiry should have preceded the juror's discharge. But in a recent Montreal murder trial, the judge discharged a juror who was suffering financially because of the length of the trial. The 11 jurors remaining constituted a valid jury, which found the accused guilty.

HEARING THE CASE

After the jury has been sworn in and has received its preliminary instructions, the jurors listen to the lawyers' opening statements. The lawyers then call their witnesses and present evidence. The statements and portions of the evidence may be contradictory. In some courts the jurors may be allowed to take their own notes.

The jurors may not discuss the case among themselves while they are still hearing evidence, and they must avoid all media accounts of the case. In the rare cases that get a lot of press coverage, the jury may be sequestered (confined to a hotel or elsewhere until the proceedings are over).

INSTRUCTIONS FROM THE JUDGE

After all the evidence has been presented, and before the jury leaves to decide on an outcome, the judge instructs the jurors regarding laws that apply to the case. The judge might ask the jury to answer specific questions (for example, "Was the supermarket management negligent by failing to provide safety restraints for children in its shopping carts?"). Or she may ask them to return a general verdict (for example, "We find the defendant guilty").

Although the jury system allows cases to be decided by a cross section of citizens, a jury's verdict will not always stand. For example, a Saskatchewan chiropractor treated a man with a sore neck without first consulting X rays which disclosed a bone fracture, and a jury found him completely liable for the patient's pain and suffering. However, this ruling was overturned by the appeal court which found the jury had permitted its sympathy for the patient to outweigh reason and logic. Since the patient had already been injured, the appeal court found the chiropractor could be responsible for no more than 60 percent of the patient's pain.

IN THE JURY ROOM

Although the procedure for selecting a foreperson varies, his role is always to preside over the jury's deliberations and announce the verdict. Once in the jury room, the jurors discuss the evidence presented during the trial.

When the discussion is over, the jury votes. If the judge has asked the jury to determine several questions (known as counts, in criminal cases), the jury votes on each one separately. Even when the judge has asked for a general verdict, the jury may vote several times before it reaches a verdict.

When the verdict has been reached, the jury returns to the courtroom to announce it. If the jury cannot decide on a verdict, it is said to be hung, or deadlocked. If the jury is hopelessly deadlocked, a new trial will be set (unless the plaintiff and defendant settle, or the prosecutor decides not to retry the case). Before declaring the jury deadlocked, most judges urge members to deliberate longer, in hopes they will reach a decision.

After the verdict is given, the judge gives a judgment (which may be a fine, prison sentence, or money damages).

The Criminal Code forbids jurors from discussing their deliberations with others once the case has concluded on penalty of a fine and/or imprisonment. This rule has recently come under fire for being an unconstitutional restriction on free speech.

JURY TAMPERING

Jury tampering means trying to influence a juror with bribes, threats, suggestions, information, and the like—something other than the evidence that is presented in the courtroom. The crime of jury tampering is considered a form of obstruction of justice and is punishable by a fine or imprisonment.

Perhaps the most common form of jury tampering occurs when a person offers money, makes promises, or threatens jurors, in order to influence the outcome of a case. A juror who solicits bribes in return for rendering a certain decision is also guilty of jury tampering.

Attempting to bribe a court officer, such as the bailiff, who has contact with the jury also constitutes jury tampering.

The jury is charged with reaching a decision based solely on the evidence that is presented in court. It is thus illegal to give information to a juror outside courtroom proceedings. For example, giving a juror news accounts of the case before a decision has been reached constitutes jury tampering.

A nonjuror who tries to talk to a juror about the case during the course of the trial or a juror who discusses the case with another juror before the jury goes into deliberation are both considered to be guilty of jury tampering.

JUSTICE OF THE PEACE

A justice of the peace is a provincial judicial officer with limited authority. Most justices of the peace are not lawyers, but private citizens appointed by the relevant lieutenant governor to act within a given judicial district. Some provinces, such as British Columbia and Quebec, require these officials to undergo formal training.

The most typical duties of a justice of the peace include issuing summonses and warrants, granting bail and conducting civil marriage ceremonies. It is often with the approval of a justice of the peace that a legal process, such as a police search, commences. The role of these officials tends to vary greatly from province to province.

See also COURTS; JUDGE.

K FROM KIDNAPPING TO KITING

KIDNAPPING

Kidnapping is broadly defined as the carrying away of someone against his will by means of force or fraud. Anyone who kidnaps another person against his will and intends to confine him, send him out of Canada, or hold him for ransom or service is liable to life imprisonment. If the person being kidnapped is not transported from one place to another, the offense is deemed forcible confinement. One famous kidnapping case involved two Americans charged in Toronto in 1989. The men, who specialized in tracking down bail jumpers, came to Canada to seize an American fugitive and take him back to the United States. The court held that powers conferred on the accused in their home country did not give them the authority to violate Canadian sovereignty, and they were convicted of kidnapping.

It is of course an offense to abduct children from their parents or legal guardian, and even parents or guardians may be charged with abduction if the act occurs in violation of a custody order of a Canadian court. Penalties for child abduction range from punishment on summary conviction to 10 years' imprisonment.

KITING

Kiting occurs if cheques are written against a bank account that is closed or does not exist, or if the "float" period between the time a cheque is written and it is presented for payment is used illegally. See FLOAT.

Kiting is often used to swindle people out of their money. Suppose Guy writes a $1,000 cheque against an account that he knows does not contain that amount. He goes to a bank in a nearby town, where he opens an account by depositing the $1,000 cheque. He also asks the bank to give him $50 of the face value of the cheque. As a courtesy to its new customer, the bank honors Guy's request, only to have his cheque bounce. By now, Guy has skipped town, leaving the bank $50 poorer.

Kiting schemes are also used to take advantage of merchants or individuals who are making a one-time sale. Suppose you advertise in the local newspa-

per to sell your canoe for $500. In response, Ernest appears at your door, well dressed and personable and offering you your full asking price. But because he says he is short of cash, he offers a cheque for $550 in exchange for the canoe and $50. You call Ernest's bank, where a teller informs you that Ernest's account has sufficient funds to cover the cheque. Happy to have made the sale, you give Ernest his $50 along with the canoe and its paddles.

Next day you deposit the cheque, but within the week it has bounced. Between the time you called Ernest's bank and deposited his cheque, dozens of Ernest's other cheques have passed through the account. Not only have you lost your canoe, you have given an extra $50 to a smooth-talking crook!

STEPS TO TAKE

To protect yourself against the various types of cheque kiting, follow these procedures:

1. Never accept a cheque that is drawn on an account with an out-of-town bank, unless it is from someone you know personally and trust.

2. Sell merchandise for its exact purchase price. Never give extra money to someone in exchange for a cheque.

3. Accept only cash or a certified cheque. If necessary, have your buyer go to the nearest bank to cash his cheque.

4. Hold the merchandise until the buyer's cheque has cleared.

5. If you suspect someone is trying to swindle you by kiting a cheque, notify the police. See CHEQUE; SCAMS AND SWINDLES.

FROM
LABOR UNION
TO
LOTTERY

LABOR UNION

A labor union is an employee organization formed primarily to negotiate employment contracts on behalf of its members, using the process known as collective bargaining. Collective bargaining addresses various employee concerns, including wages, benefits, and working conditions. Labor unions also negotiate insurance and pension plans for their members, and represent their members in disputes with employers. See also COLLECTIVE BARGAINING.

LEGAL AUTHORITY

Although workers in Canada have organized for generations, this was not always the case. In the 1860s, anyone attempting to form a trade union was liable to be charged with criminal conspiracy because trade unionism was seen as restraining trade. However, the Trade Unions Act passed in the late

1800s declared that a union's actions were not illegal simply because they involved the restriction of trade. When labor problems intensified during the 1940s, Parliament passed the Wartime Labour Relations Regulations governing union organization and methods of resolving disputes between unions and employers.

In what is known as collective bargaining, labor unions can now legally represent groups of workers (called bargaining units), in negotiations on wages or salary, working conditions, vacations, and health benefits. The bargaining units must consist of groups of employees whose place of work, job tasks, or employers give them a common interest in such work-related issues.

Today, all provinces as well as the federal government have laws dealing with labor unions and the collective bargaining process. The Canada Labour Code applies wherever the federal government has jurisdiction, such as in the aviation, shipping and banking industries. Provincial legislation, whether British Columbia's Industrial Relations Act or Ontario's Labour Relations Act, applies to matters within the provinces' jurisdiction.

Not all workers are covered by labor legislation. By and large, the various acts do not consider management personnel, independent contractors, industrial relations' personnel acting in a confidential capacity, and many professionals as employees for the purposes of the legislation.

♦ Federal and provincial labor relations boards are responsible for supervising and regulating employer-union negotiations. These boards must also ensure that unions are properly certified and that they adequately represent the interests of their members.

WHY UNIONS WORK

Labor unions achieve success because there is power in numbers. If collective-bargaining negotiations fail, organized workers can force employers to recognize their demands through strikes, slowdowns, and boycotts. These methods would have limited impact if only a few workers participated. See also BOYCOTT; STRIKE.

FORMING A UNION

When employees decide to form or be represented by a union, they usually contact the local division or parent organization of a provincial or national union, such as the United Auto Workers. The union then applies to the relevant labor relations board to become the bargaining agent for that particular unit of employees. If the board is satisfied that a significant portion of employees (about 40 percent) are union members, and that the unit is appropriate for collective bargaining, it will require all employees to vote on whether they want the union as their bargaining agent. The union is certified if a majority votes in its favor.

In Ontario, a union may be certified without all employees voting if 55 percent of them are already union members, or if an ♦

♦ employer has acted improperly, for example by intimidating employees who were promoting union certification.

UNION MEMBERSHIP

In exchange for representation and benefits, union members have certain obligations.
Dues
Members agree to have dues deducted from their paycheques. Dues are used for many purposes: to supply funds for organizing efforts; to provide a strike fund to pay employees if a strike is called; to pay lobbyists to promote legislation favoring issues the union supports; and to pay the union's administrative costs.

Dues usually average about $50 per month, although those who are highly paid may be required to contribute more, and lower-paid workers less. There may also be an initiation fee of several hundred dollars, which often can be paid in installments.

You cannot be forced to join a union if membership conflicts with your religious principles. However, you may still have to pay union dues since every employee benefits in some way from union representation. Most Canadian jurisdictions require that union dues of exempted employees be directed to an approved charity.
Union shops
To continue representing an employee unit, labor unions must retain the support of the employees. For this reason, many collective agreements contain union security clauses that regulate the hiring process as well as continued member-

ship in the union. The most powerful of these clauses creates what is called a closed shop, where only union members may be hired. A more common form of union security is the union shop clause, which permits employers to hire whomever they wish. However, once hired, an employee must become a union member within a specific time period. Certain collective agreements also contain provisions respecting preferential hiring, whereby nonunion workers may be hired only if the supply of union members runs out. The nonunion hirees, however, would be the first to be laid off in a work shortage. Finally, in a modified union shop system, an employee is not obliged to become a union member, but those who are members must remain so in order to retain their employment.

Open shops

In workplaces where there is a union, but which you are not obliged to join, you will nevertheless have to pay union dues: this is known as the Rand formula. At such "open shops," the union must represent you, even if you do not belong to it. Moreover, you have the right to complain to the provincial labor relations board if you feel the union has not been representing your interests.

LANDLORD

Anyone who leases to another person an apartment, house, or other real estate that he owns is a landlord. Landlords have certain legal rights and respon-

sibilities, some of which are prescribed by law. However, it is always best to have a written lease that spells out both the landlord's and the tenant's rights and duties. Most provinces have free pamphlets on these rights and obligations. Residential lease forms may be available from government rental boards in some provinces. See EVERYDAY LEGAL FORMS at back of book. See also LEASE.

Whatever the terms of the lease, you may not—as a landlord—discriminate against potential tenants on the basis of sex, race, nationality, ethnicity, place of origin, color, creed, physical or mental disability, marital status, age, or religion. However, you may make decisions based on a person's past work history or record as a tenant. You have the right to ask an applicant for personal, credit, and income references and you may also have a credit reporting agency run a check on his credit. But, depending on where you live, it may be illegal to refuse to rent to someone because of the person's source of income. In Ontario you cannot refuse to rent to someone solely because he receives social assistance, and Quebec prohibits discrimination based on social condition. Some provinces and even some municipalities outlaw discrimination against families or against those involved in tenants' associations.

SECURITY DEPOSITS

In most provinces, you have a right to demand a security deposit from your tenants,

usually no more than one month's rent. The deposit is to protect the landlord's investment in the event of damages, and it is an incentive to the tenant to care for the place in which he lives.

While security deposits are generally kept in case of damage, some provinces permit the landlord to use the deposit for arrears of rent. In Ontario, the deposit can be used for the last month's rent only, and if there is damage the landlord must take the tenant to court to recover his losses. See SECURITY DEPOSIT.

MINIMUM STANDARDS

All provinces have health and safety standards that require landlords to provide decent living conditions. In general, tenants have the right to adequate light, plumbing, heating, and premises that are structurally sound. If a landlord fails to provide these basic services, tenants have several options, which vary somewhat from province to province. The landlord may be taken to court or required to appear before the rental board. In either case, several outcomes are possible. The lease may be terminated, the rent may be reduced for a certain period to compensate the tenant for lost benefits, or the landlord may be ordered to carry out repairs or to pay the tenant damages. In New Brunswick, Nova Scotia, Manitoba, and Quebec tenants with valid complaints may pay their rent to the government rental board, which will hold the money until the repairs are completed.

Your local department of housing or department of consumer affairs can tell you about local landlord-tenant laws.

PROPER USE

Landlords have a right to expect tenants to use a property for its intended purpose. So if you rent out a house for residential use and your tenant operates a hair salon out of it, you can demand that he close up shop.

Although normal wear and tear can be expected, landlords are entitled to expect tenants to take reasonable care of their property. Standard leases contain clauses obliging tenants to pay for damages that are beyond the usual wear and tear. Other duties (such as mowing the lawn) may also be spelled out. All clauses and restrictions must comply with provincial and local laws and regulations, and tenants who fail to meet them may be evicted. See also EVICTION; RENT STRIKE; TENANT'S RIGHTS.

MAKING REPAIRS

Landlords must make emergency repairs as soon as possible after being notified of the problem. Other repairs must be done within a "reasonable period." Many provinces now allow tenants to make urgent repairs and deduct the cost from the rent. In nonurgent cases, they must first give the landlord written notice of the problems and their intention to "repair and deduct" the expenses from the rent if the landlord does not make the repairs within a reasonable time. A tenant who makes repairs must give his landlord a complete accounting of his costs, including all bills and receipts.

ACCESS TO THE APARTMENT

Landlords must give tenants their privacy. A landlord may enter the house or apartment only after giving the tenant a reasonable amount of notice (usually 24 hours) and only during normal business hours. A landlord may enter an apartment without permission to make emergency repairs. Of course, tenants and landlords may work out their own access arrangements, but a landlord who violates a tenant's privacy can be sued for damages.

Sometimes a landlord may require limited access to an apartment. For instance, if she is trying to sell or rent the property, she may include a clause in the lease specifying which hours she may enter the apartment and for what purpose. However, a clause that infringes unreasonably upon a tenant's right to privacy will probably not be enforceable. Suppose a clause in your lease permits your landlord to enter the apartment at any time to show the property to prospective buyers. Can your landlord then demand access at 6 a.m., or from 9 p.m. to midnight? Probably not. A court or rent tribunal would likely find that such demands are unreasonable and in violation of your privacy.

LANDMARK

Local communities and provincial and federal governments have passed laws that make it possible to preserve historic buildings from destruction or major modification by having them designated as landmarks. To obtain landmark status, a property must meet certain criteria. For example, a building may be so designated because a person who was of historic significance lived or stayed there, or because it was the site of an historic event. Landmark status may also be granted to buildings that typify a style of architecture, such as a log cabin built by early settlers. A group of buildings or an area of town may be worthy of the designation because they represent an era that the community wants to preserve.

Suppose your town has an old house where a famous Canadian was born. The house needs some paint, but it is well constructed and has a distinctive character. A local developer wants to buy it and tear it down to make room for a parking lot. If you want to preserve the house, and if your community has a landmark law, you can petition the local historic- or heritage-preservation commission to designate the house as a landmark.

The commission may hold a hearing to determine whether the building has true historical value. At this point the owner has an opportunity to challenge the designation. One common objection is that landmarking

the building will unfairly
deprive him of his right to do
what he likes with his property.
Since citizens often seek to establish landmarks as much to
prevent change as to preserve
history, an owner may often
prevail on these grounds.

If landmark status is granted,
the building's owner may be
prevented from tearing down
his building or altering it in any
way that is inconsistent with
the original structure. Any
renovations must not affect the
building's historical integrity.
If you are renovating an older
home, for example, a landmark
law might prohibit you from
installing false dropped ceilings
or modern office partitions.

To obtain specific information about landmark designa-
tions and historic preservation
in your community, ask your
local housing or zoning
department, or your provincial
department of culture.

See also ZONING.

LAST CLEAR CHANCE RULE

The last clear chance rule was
developed to soften the effect
of the rule of contributory negligence. That rule held that
even if one person was partly
responsible for an accident, the
other person could be held
totally responsible if he had a
chance to avoid the accident
by being more careful.

Negligence cases are often
not clear-cut, particularly if the
plaintiff (injured party) may
have contributed to his own
accident or injury. It is the
court's job to determine who

bears the responsibility in a
case, and whether the plaintiff's own negligence was a
factor. In cases where the court
reaches such a conclusion,
Canadian law resorts to the
rule of contributory negligence.

Suppose that late one afternoon, at dusk, Don's car begins
to make an odd sound. Don
stops it along a flat stretch of
highway but neglects to turn on
his hazard lights or take any
other steps to warn oncoming
cars that he has stopped. Suddenly, a truck hits Don's car in
the rear, destroying it and injuring Don. Don sues the truck
driver for negligent driving.

The trucker argues—and
the court agrees—that Don is
guilty of contributory negligence because he failed to
warn oncoming traffic of his
predicament, and he did not
drive off the highway. Nonetheless, the judge orders the
truck driver to compensate
Don. Had the driver been more
vigilant, he would have seen
Don's car and thus avoided
the accident. The truck driver
had a "last clear chance" to
prevent the accident.

Because Canadian jurisdictions apply the rule of compar-
ative negligence, whereby
responsibility for accidents is
apportioned between the negligent parties, the last clear
chance rule has relatively little
importance in Canada. However, Alberta, Newfoundland,
and Saskatchewan have laws
stating that the rule applies
when it is beyond dispute
that the most recent negligent
act was the sole cause of the
accident.

See also NEGLIGENCE; TORT.

LAWSUIT

A lawsuit is a legal procedure
begun by one party (an individual or a group) against another
in order to rectify an injustice.
Lawsuits are also called civil
actions, to distinguish them
from criminal actions, or prosecutions by the state. The goal
of many lawsuits is to get
compensation for damages, to
stop someone from creating a
nuisance, or to enforce a
contract. See also CIVIL RIGHTS.

Lawsuits are won due to
a preponderance of the
evidence—that is, one party
must have better evidence than
the other. Suppose Sam and
Diane have an oral agreement
that Sam will sell Diane his
microwave oven for $50. Sam
later changes his mind, and
Diane sues him to enforce the
contract. If the only evidence
is Sam's word against Diane's,
and both are equally credible,
Diane will not be able to prove
her case. However, suppose
Diane has a witness, Rebecca,
who will testify that she heard
Sam make the contract with
Diane. Her testimony backs up
Diane in every way, and she is a
credible witness. Even though
Sam denies that he made the
agreement with Diane, a court
would probably rule in her
favor because of Rebecca's evidence. See also EVIDENCE.

TYPES OF LAWSUITS

Some of the more familiar
categories of lawsuits are
contract actions, tort actions,
and suits against private
nuisances.

Contract actions

When a person fails to meet the terms of a contract, the other party to the contract may file a civil action claiming breach of contract. The lawsuit may ask the court to order the defendant to uphold the contract, to pay compensation for damages resulting from his failure to obey its provisions, or to void the contract. See also BREACH OF CONTRACT; CONTRACT.

Tort actions

Tort actions are lawsuits that seek compensation for a civil wrong (as opposed to a crime) committed by someone against another person. Included are lawsuits for personal injury or property damage due to negligence, as well as suits for libel, false arrest, and other disputes.

Some incidents may result in both civil and criminal actions simultaneously. For example, someone who causes an accident because he drives recklessly not only may be sued by the injured party, but also may be prosecuted under the Criminal Code for criminally negligent behavior. See also DAMAGES; TORT.

Private nuisances

A nuisance interferes with a person's enjoyment of her life or property. Suppose your neighbor's dog stands in the backyard howling all day and night. You have often asked the neighbor to keep his dog quiet, but he has ignored you. You can file a civil lawsuit in court to force your neighbor to do something about his barking dog. See also NUISANCE; PETS.

THE STEPS IN A LAWSUIT

Civil procedure varies from province to province, but most lawsuits follow the same basic steps.

Demand and response

Before a lawsuit is filed, the plaintiff (the person filing the suit) makes a written demand to the defendant (the person he is suing), stating his claim, the remedy he is seeking, and a time limit for the defendant to respond. (This letter of default is known as a *mise en demeure* in Quebec.) For example, suppose Jeff is suing Jennifer for injuries he suffered when he fell down her porch steps. He writes a demand stating his claim (that he fell on her steps, which were negligently maintained, and he suffered injuries as a result). His demand requests a remedy (payment of $20,000 for lost wages, pain and suffering, and medical costs over and above those covered by Medicare), and it must be made within a time limit of 10 days.

If the defendant fails to respond in an acceptable manner (if he does not agree with the amount of money requested or offers a lower amount than the plaintiff might accept), then the plaintiff will file a statement of claim with the court. In some provinces, the statement of claim may be called a declaration or bill of particulars.

The statement of claim describes the dispute as the plaintiff sees it, the legal basis for filing the lawsuit, and the remedy the plaintiff is asking the court to grant. The statement of claim, along with a

---

summons, is delivered by the sheriff (or a process server) to the defendant. The summons notifies the defendant that a suit has been filed and gives him a time limit (usually 10 to 30 days) to give a response, which is known as a statement of defense. In his defense, the defendant may deny some or all of the charges, raise certain defenses, or file a counterclaim for damages that he feels the plaintiff owes him.

If the defendant does not answer the summons and complaint, the plaintiff can ask the court to grant a default judgment. If it is evident that the defendant was properly notified (called proof of service), the default may be granted. See also DEFAULT JUDGMENT.

Gathering evidence

Once the defendant's statement of defense is received, the discovery process can begin. During this process, which takes place before the actual trial, each party can seek information from his opponent to help build and strengthen his case. See DISCOVERY.

In addition to conducting a discovery, each side may file a variety of motions with the court asking it to rule on different issues, such as whether certain evidence is admissible at the trial, or whether a party must respond to a particular discovery request (for documents, for example) made by his opponent. Meanwhile, either side may approach the other with offers of settlement, hoping to avoid the added costs and delays of a trial. The court itself may try to help the opponents reach a settlement.

The trial

If no settlement is reached, a trial is held. Since lawsuits are civil cases, they may be tried with or without a jury, depending on the wishes of the parties and the provisions of the law.

The plaintiff's lawyer may make an opening statement to the court, setting forth all the facts he intends to prove. The defendant's lawyer may then make an opening statement, or he may choose not to make a statement until the plaintiff has presented his entire case.

Because the burden of proof is on the plaintiff, he presents his case first. He calls forth witnesses, who are sworn in and questioned, or examined, by his lawyer. Cross-examination by the defendant's lawyer follows. When the plaintiff has fully presented his case, he is said to "rest his case." See also CROSS-EXAMINATION.

Now it is the defendant's turn. First his lawyer may choose to make a motion for dismissal, claiming that the plaintiff has failed to make a case. If any evidence supports the plaintiff's claim, however, this motion will be refused. The defense now calls its witnesses and questions them under oath, after which the plaintiff may cross-examine them.

After the defense rests, the plaintiff gets a chance to conduct a rebuttal—an opportunity to present new evidence that contradicts that of the defense. Each side then makes closing statements, which reinforce the key points of its case.

The court's decision

At this point, if the case was tried without a jury, the judge retires to consider the evidence before announcing his decision. If the case was tried before a jury, the judge will instruct the members of the jury on the law and how it should be applied to the facts of the case. Then the jury retires to deliberate.

Once the jury's decision is announced, the losing side may ask the judge to grant a "judgment notwithstanding the verdict," or "judgment n.o.v." *(non obstante veredicto)*— that the judge overturn the jury's decision because it is clearly contradicted by the evidence and the law. Such requests are frequently made but rarely granted, and the losing side will have to accept the judgment or file an appeal.

See also COMPLAINT; COMPROMISE AND SETTLEMENT; JURY; SMALL-CLAIMS COURT; STATUTE OF LIMITATIONS.

LAWYER

Maggy, a professional singer, is preparing to sign a recording contract, but she does not understand the fine print. Julie and George are getting married, and they would like to have a prenuptial agreement. Sarah, a department store cashier, has been accused of stealing money from the cash register. Although all these situations are different, the people involved have something in common—all would be well advised to consult a lawyer.

DECIDING WHEN YOU NEED A LAWYER

Sooner or later you will probably need a lawyer to advise you about a problem or to settle a dispute. But you may wonder whether or not your problem requires a lawyer. In general, you should consult a lawyer if your problem is complex, if it involves a lot of money, or if the consequences of not doing so could be severe.

Certain specific situations almost always call for a lawyer. Some of these are:

◇ When you are starting your own business.

◇ When you are buying or selling your home or are threatened with loss of your home.

◇ When you have suffered an injury or your property has been damaged, especially when the damage was due to someone else's negligence.

◇ When you must draw up a will or a trust.

◇ When you must sign a contract, lease, or other important document.

◇ When you are trying to get a divorce, separation, or annulment.

◇ When you adopt a child or would like to obtain custody of one.

◇ When you are accused of a crime or have been the victim of a crime.

FINDING A LAWYER

Waiting until a problem arises before finding a lawyer may mean that you are choosing one under extreme stress. This may be costly to you, both personally and financially. Therefore, it is worth your while to find a lawyer before you actually need one. Here are some tips for conducting your search:

◇ *Shop around.* Getting recommendations from family,

REAL LIFE, REAL LAW

The Case of the Lying Lawyer

After beginning his legal career in Toronto, Sydney Carton moved to London, Ont., to open a practice with a law school colleague. Mr. Carton began practicing as a criminal lawyer, and soon he was involved in a sensational murder case in which his client was acquitted. Before long, he had won a case at the Supreme Court of Canada, and his name appeared in headlines throughout the nation.

After becoming disenchanted with what he felt was an over-abundance of minor criminal cases, he turned his attention to civil practice where he could earn more money. He continued to win important cases, and soon his firm was one of London's largest and most respected. Mr. Carton was also heavily involved in an investment scheme which he controlled, and in which he encouraged his friends and associates to participate. None of them suspected, however, that they would never see their money again.

In reality, Mr. Carton had been orchestrating a massive fraud. By using fake financial documents and share certificates as collateral, he was able to obtain lines of credit from several banks, and as for the investment scheme, it was nonexistent. In the end, his deceit and dishonesty were uncovered and he was sentenced to nine years in prison after pleading guilty to 43 counts of fraud, attempted fraud and forgery. As a result of his actions, several financial institutions and many of his friends and associates lost a total of close to $28 million.

Mr. Carton's inscription in his high school yearbook had been prophetic: "Neither a borrower nor a lender be, just help yourself."

should be to assess the lawyer's competence and to determine whether you find that her personality is compatible with your own. You will also want a lawyer with experience that matches your needs. For example, if you want to have a will drafted and you need help in estate planning, you do not want a lawyer who mainly handles divorce cases.

◇ *Get organized.* If you are hiring the lawyer to help you with a specific problem, show her any useful documents or contracts. Be aware that the lawyer will probably want to give your papers a quick review during the first meeting. See also LEGAL AID.

LAWYERS' FEES

Be sure that you come to a clear understanding with your lawyer about her fees before you hire her. Ask specific questions about acceptable methods of payment. For example, some lawyers require a partial payment (called a retainer) before they begin, and will thereafter bill you at an hourly rate. Some lawyers accept credit cards or let you pay in installments. In personal-injury cases, many lawyers charge a contingent fee, which is based on the amount you are awarded as a result of a settlement or trial. See also CONTINGENT FEE.

Some lawyers will perform certain kinds of standardized legal work—preparing a simple will or representing you in an uncontested divorce—for a flat fee. But if the matter becomes more complicated than the lawyer originally estimated, she

friends, and others whom you trust is probably the best way to find a suitable lawyer. If that fails, call the bar association in your area. Be sure to ask how lawyers are selected for its list. In many places the bar association will accept any lawyer who applies, providing she or he is in good standing with the bar. It is important for you to realize that this screening process may not be particularly thorough, and a listing

with the local bar is not necessarily a guarantee of a lawyer's quality. As a last resort, look under the "Lawyers" entry in the Yellow Pages of your telephone directory.

◇ *Interview before you hire.* Many lawyers will offer a free or low-cost initial consultation. Ask about this charge as well as about the fees for services at the time you schedule an interview. The goals of your interview

may try to add extra charges. Before hiring a lawyer on a flat-fee basis, find out exactly which of her services are covered by the flat fee and what her fee schedule will be for any additional work.

Whether you hire a lawyer on a flat-fee basis or at an hourly rate, ask her to draft a fee agreement detailing all fees and charges. It should include an estimate of how long your project will take, along with a provision that requires her to notify you when she has spent a specified number of hours on your case. Such a provision will help you to monitor your costs.

In addition, the lawyer should explain to you that extra costs, called disbursements, are added to the hourly bill. Disbursements reflect expenses incurred for things such as photocopying, couriers, postage, fees for court filing, searches and registration, fees paid to technical experts and specialists whom the lawyer may need to hire, and travel costs. With regard to photocopying costs, you may be able to save yourself some money by providing extra copies of your documents. Find out if the lawyer will charge extra for phone calls she must make about your case. Ask her to reduce her fee if you think it is too high. Legal fees are open to negotiation, and some lawyers do try to accommodate the different financial situations of their clients.

CHECKLIST

What You Should Expect From a Lawyer

When hiring a lawyer, remember that you are the boss. As such, you should expect the following from your lawyer:

■ **COMPETENCE.**
If your lawyer lacks the skills to handle your case, you have the right to know this as soon as possible. You then should have the option to allow the lawyer to work with someone who does have the needed skills, or to find another lawyer.

■ **RESPECT.**
Your lawyer should speak to you as an equal, take the time to explain strategies he proposes in a way you can understand, answer all of your questions to the best of his ability, and return phone calls promptly. The lawyer's staff should also be respectful and courteous toward you.

■ **PROGRESS REPORTS.**
Although this does not necessarily mean a daily or even weekly update, you do have the right to expect reasonable progress reports, immediate notification about any unexpected developments or settlement offers, and copies of documents filed by your or your opponent's lawyer.

■ **REGULAR, DETAILED BILLING.**
You should be sent an itemized monthly statement that clearly states what the lawyer did, when he did it, and how long it took. Your bill should also itemize all fees for photocopies, messenger and delivery services, long-distance calls, filing fees, and other costs you are expected to pay.

■ **THE TRUTH ABOUT YOUR CHANCES OF SUCCESS.**
If your case is a long shot, your lawyer does you a disservice by telling you that it is a sure thing, and he may be padding his own pocket by keeping a case alive when it would be better to settle or even abandon it.

HELPING YOUR LAWYER HELP YOU

Once you have decided to hire a lawyer, there are some things you can do that will help make her job easier (and that usually mean less worry and fewer costs for you).

◇ *Be candid.* Lying or withholding information about your case from your lawyer never helps. Sooner or later the truth may be revealed, and you will have damaged your lawyer's credibility as well as her ability to represent you effectively.

◇ *Keep your lawyer up to date.* Tell her about any new information you receive or any contact you have had with the opposing party. If you can suggest a helpful witness or locate a misplaced document, let her know.

◇ *Do not expect immediate answers.* Your lawyer will not always know the answers to your questions right away. She may have to do some research. Be wary of a lawyer who tries to give you instant advice on a complicated matter.

◇ *Do not hound your lawyer.* Remember that she has other clients and she cannot devote all her time to your case. Keep phone calls and office visits to a minimum. Calling every day or every week for a progress report is usually not necessary (some cases take months or years to resolve) and can be expensive (most lawyers will charge for phone conferences as well as for visits).

PAYING YOUR BILL

Even if you feel you have been overcharged, pay your lawyer's bill on time. A lawyer who has not received payment can place an automatic lien, or claim, on your case file, documents, and other materials. If she does this, you will have to hire another lawyer and, without the original documents, he may have to duplicate the work that has already been done. Moreover, the original lawyer can sue you to recover the sums you owe her.

If you have a dispute, try to negotiate a settlement. If your lawyer refuses to negotiate, pay the bill under protest. Attach a letter that makes it clear you disagree with the charged amount. Then call or write to your local bar association and lodge a complaint. Bar associations in some provinces have fee-arbitration panels which may help you settle your dispute. In one such instance, a Toronto lawyer saw his $1.7 million fee reduced to zero. Master Basil T. Clark of the Ontario Court of Justice (general division) canceled the fee and allowed for only $12,750 in disbursements. This July 1993 decision was based on the master's belief that the lawyer got too involved with the U.S. case of his client and should have retained U.S. counsel.

Finally, if nothing else works, you can file a lawsuit seeking reimbursement for the amount you feel the lawyer has overcharged you.

PROFESSIONAL CONDUCT

In order to be admitted to the bar, lawyers must swear to observe certain codes of professional conduct. These codes are usually established, interpreted, and enforced by the provincial bar associations. Although the codes vary slightly from province to province, all are based on the Canadian Bar Association's Code of Professional Ethics. A lawyer must swear to represent his or her clients with honesty and integrity and to the best of his or her ability, to preserve client confidences, to deal fairly with the opposing side, and to uphold the law.

Suppose that you have hired a lawyer to negotiate the sale of your house. She does not have the right to reveal to potential buyers the lowest price you will accept for your house. This information is considered privileged—that is, a private matter between client and lawyer.

MALPRACTICE

A lawyer who fails to observe the rules of professional conduct is guilty of malpractice—an unethical or illegal act committed in a professional capacity. For example, a lawyer who misappropriates her clients' funds for her own personal use is guilty of malpractice, as is a lawyer who so neglects his clients' cases that they suffer as a result. A lawyer can also be accused of malpractice if he or she displays an unreasonable lack of skill. Although incompetence is often hard to prove, certain failings are obvious—for example, if a lawyer does not take depositions, interview witnesses, file documents, or meet deadlines.

A lawyer who is successfully prosecuted for malpractice may be disbarred or prohibited from practicing for a period of time. Sometimes complaints are kept on file by the provincial law society or government association in the event that similar or more serious grievances are lodged against the same lawyer. See also DISBARMENT.

STEPS TO TAKE WHEN YOUR LAWYER HAS ACTED IMPROPERLY

If you feel you have been damaged by your lawyer's incompetence or unethical conduct, you might take the following steps:

1. Discuss your concerns with your lawyer and give her a chance to justify her actions. If you still have doubts, get a second lawyer's opinion.

2. Make a written complaint to the provincial bar asssociation. Be as thorough as possible in describing why you feel your lawyer is incompetent or engaging in unethical practices. In most situations an investigator will be appointed to handle your complaint.

3. If you believe your lawyer has stolen money from you or committed some other criminal act, inform your local police. There may be good reason to prosecute her in criminal court.

4. Consult a lawyer who specializes in legal malpractice cases for advice about using arbitration or filing a civil lawsuit. Although suing is time-consuming and expensive, it may be the only way that you can receive financial damages or other compensation. See also LAWSUIT.

LAWYER, ACTING AS YOUR OWN

Even in such legal proceedings as a murder trial, everyone in Canada has the right to act as his own lawyer. Every province has small-claims courts where people can act on their own behalf in lawsuits involving sums of about $1,000 to $4,000 ($10,000 in British Columbia). In fact, lawyers are often not allowed in these courts.

You can perform other legal tasks without a lawyer, too—you can sign a lease or sales contract, make credit purchases, and apply for loans. If you have a relatively small amount of property, you may be able to prepare your will without a lawyer's advice. In many situations, however, you should think carefully before acting as your own lawyer.

By getting legal advice before you make important decisions about financial arrangements, trusts, contracts, wills, and the like, you avoid legal problems. Besides, many legal proceedings, such as a personal-injury or class-action lawsuit, call for a lawyer's expert training and knowledge. See LAWYER.

LAYAWAY PURCHASE

Many stores let their customers purchase merchandise through an installment contract known as a layaway plan. The customer pays a small down payment and then makes additional payments until the full purchase price has been paid. The store keeps the merchandise until it is paid for.

Suppose you want to buy an expensive coat and decide to use the department store's layaway plan. This lets you take up to six months to pay for the coat. After making the down payment and four monthly payments, you are laid off from your job and are unable to make another payment until after the six-month period has expired. Will you lose the coat or your money, or both?

There may be a grace period for redeeming the coat. If so, it will be spelled out in the contract. If there is no grace period, and the store sells the coat to another customer after six months have passed, you will probably receive most of your money back. But depend-

ing on the terms of your contract, the store may keep some of your money as a restocking charge or as compensation for a lost sales opportunity.

Suppose you change your mind after making three payments and decide you do not want the coat after all. Depending on the terms of the contract, you may receive a greater or lesser proportion of your money back. Check the layaway contract terms before you buy anything if you think you might have a change of heart.

As with any other contract, a court can enforce a layaway agreement. If, for example, the store mistakenly sells the coat to someone else and you have been making your payments on time, you could file suit against the store because it has breached its contract. But in most cases your damages would be limited to the money you had already paid and whatever additional amount you had to pay for a similar coat elsewhere. See also CONTRACT.

LEADING QUESTION

During a trial, a lawyer may sometimes ask a witness what is called a leading question—one that is phrased to prompt a particular response, usually a yes or a no. For instance, a lawyer may ask, "Isn't it true that at 8:15 p.m. on October 25 you were standing outside the jewelry store at the time the robbery took place?" The question seems to imply that the witness saw the robbery or that perhaps he was a lookout. By contrast, it would not be considered a leading question if the lawyer asked, "Where were you at 8:15 on the evening of October 25?"

In both civil and criminal trials, leading questions are generally prohibited during direct examination because testimony is supposed to come voluntarily from the witness, not the lawyer who is asking the questions. However, a lawyer may ask leading questions during cross-examination because the witness has already presented his testimony in his own words and the lawyer is now free to shape it in the way that best serves his case. See also CROSS-EXAMINATION; EVIDENCE.

LEASE

A residential or commercial lease is a real estate contract that creates a landlord and tenant relationship and establishes the rights and the duties of both. A written lease is important evidence in the event of a dispute between the parties. A carefully worded one offers legal protection to both landlord and tenant.

The form your lease takes may be standard for housing in your area, or it may be tailored to suit particular circumstances. Either way it should:

◇ Give a clear description of the premises that are being rented. If you are renting an apartment or an entire house, the address will suffice. If the lease is only for a single room or part of a larger space, the lease should describe the space carefully. If storage space,

outdoor space, or garage space is included, the lease should say so clearly.

◇ State the amount of rent to be paid, the date that payments are due, and any penalties for late payments or for bounced cheques.

◇ State the amount of any security deposit and the conditions for its return. Security deposits are governed by provincial laws, which vary widely. See SECURITY DEPOSIT.

◇ Include the names of adult tenants who will live on the premises. The lease should state that they will be "jointly and severally" responsible for the rent. This means that if one tenant cannot pay his share, the others will be responsible.

◇ State the number of tenants who are permitted to live on the premises. Sometimes tenants invite friends or relatives to move in with them, adding to the wear and tear on the property. The landlord has a right to set limits according to the size of the premises leased.

◇ Spell out who is responsible for utility bills, removing garbage, and general maintenance. If a tenant has to mow the grass, shovel snow, or take care of any other upkeep, the lease should state this.

◇ Limit the tenant's right to sublet to someone else. The lease should either require the written permission of the landlord in advance or prohibit subletting entirely. See SUBLEASE.

You may find standard leases at stationery stores. See EVERYDAY LEGAL FORMS at back of book. See also EVICTION; LANDLORD; TENANT'S RIGHTS.

LEGAL AID

Every province and territory has a legal aid plan, and all have a similar purpose: to ensure that people are not denied legal advice because they cannot afford the services of a lawyer. These plans are mostly funded by the federal and provincial governments.

Most legal aid services deal principally with young offenders and with criminal and family law matters such as divorce, custody of and access to children, and child support and welfare. However, other legal matters such as immigration, general litigation, and certain bankruptcy cases may also be dealt with under legal aid plans. Legal aid plans in some provinces also offer education and research services, and assist specific target groups such as the handicapped and environmental organizations.

TYPES OF PLAN

There are three legal aid plans—the staff system, the judicare (fee-for-service) system, and the combined system.

Under the staff system, favored in Alberta and British Columbia, legal aid is provided by salaried employees. In some provinces, people who are not lawyers but who have some legal background, aid staff lawyers. The judicare plan pays private lawyers case by case. Features of both the staff and judicare systems are found in Ontario and Quebec, giving rise to what is termed the combined or mixed delivery system.

Legal aid offices have strict guidelines for verifying whether applicants truly cannot afford to hire a lawyer. If you apply for legal aid, you must be prepared to give detailed information about your income, other financial resources, and expenses. A person receiving social assistance will ordinarily qualify for legal aid.

Financial-eligibility criteria vary widely from province to province. Other than Prince Edward Island and Quebec, all provinces ask clients to repay legal aid costs if they are able to do so. British Columbia and New Brunswick ask clients to pay a standard user fee. In all provinces clients awarded damages in a civil action may be required to contribute to their legal aid costs.

THE RIGHT TO COUNSEL

The issue of the right to counsel has become an important topic in the area of criminal procedure, and the issue is also central to the debate surrounding the escalating costs of legal aid. The Charter of Rights and Freedoms states that "everyone has the right on arrest or detention to retain and instruct counsel." It also declares that "every individual is equal before and under the law and has the right to equal protection and equal benefit of the law."

The courts have applied these charter provisions to various cases. In 1992, the Prince Edward Island Court of Appeal ruled that a province is required to provide 24-hour duty counsel to a person when arrested. A duty-counsel system ensures that a legal aid lawyer is available around the clock. At the time of writing, Prince Edward Island, Nova Scotia, and Manitoba did not have duty-counsel systems.

In Ontario, the caution given to a person under arrest has five clauses. The accused is informed that he has the right to retain and instruct a lawyer without delay; has the right to telephone a lawyer of his choosing; has the right to free advice from a legal aid lawyer; may apply to the Ontario Legal Aid Plan for assistance if charged; and may take advantage of a 1-800 phone number to reach duty counsel, where service will be provided free of charge. A recent Ontario case held that the accused's rights had been violated when a police officer neglected to tell him that duty-counsel service would be provided at no cost.

PRO BONO WORK

To help people who do not qualify for legal aid, but nevertheless cannot afford a lawyer, lawyers sometimes agree to work on a *pro bono* basis, or free of charge. (*Pro bono* is from the Latin phrase *pro bono publico*, "for the public good.") Even if you do not qualify for free services, your local law society may try to help you find a lawyer who will provide services at a price you can afford.

LIABILITY

The term "liability" is generally used to indicate a legal responsibility, duty, or obligation. For example, if you take out a loan to buy a home, you are liable for the debt that is created by the loan. Liability is also created when a person or his property is harmed as a result of someone else's negligence. If your reckless driving causes an accident, for example, you can be held liable for the resulting injury or property damage.

The concept of liability takes a number of different forms under the law, the most important of which are discussed below.

PRIMARY AND SECONDARY LIABILITY

"Primary liability" is a term used to designate who will first be held responsible. When you sign a loan agreement to buy a car, you have the primary liability for the loan. This means that you are responsible for fulfilling the terms of the contract, including making the loan payments on time.

"Secondary liability" creates a duty or obligation only when the person who has primary liability fails to fulfill her responsibilities. Suppose you ask a relative to cosign, or guarantee, your car loan agreement. If you do not meet your obligation to make timely payments, the loan company can turn to the cosigner for payment.

JOINT LIABILITY

Joint liability applies to situations in which more than one person may be held responsible. Because both acted together in causing the damage, each wrongdoer (known as a tortfeasor) shares responsibility for some portion of the loss.

Tort-feasors may be held jointly and severally liable, meaning that the person who has been harmed may sue more than one wrongdoer or just one. For example, if Ed is driving a car owned by Andrea when he injures you in an accident, you may be able to sue both of them together, sue only Ed, or sue only Andrea.

However, if you file suit against Ed only, the amount that you recover from him if you win would represent your full and complete payment for the suit. You cannot later file another suit against Andrea, because that would constitute a double payment for a single wrong. Therefore, you may be advised by a lawyer to sue them both together and individually. See also DAMAGES; TORT.

STRICT LIABILITY

According to the theory of strict liability, a person can be required to compensate another even though no negligence was present. For example, strict liability was imposed in cases where the defendant's attempt to thaw frozen pipes with a blow torch resulted in fire damage, and where injury was caused by poisonous fumes during a fumigation operation. In general, the rule applies to unusual or out of the ordinary activity which requires a great deal of care or prudence. In addition, strict liability is often imposed on

defendants who were acting in a commercial context.

While negligence does not have to be proved, defenses to allegations of strict liability do exist. In one case, a torrential rainstorm caused water to escape from a dam built by the defendant, and resulted in flooding which destroyed bridges on the plaintiff's property. The court held that an unforeseen act of God was the true cause of the damage, and consequently the defendant was not liable. A defense may also be available when the plaintiff either consented to the activity or was at fault himself, or when the accident was caused by the deliberate act of a third party.

VICARIOUS LIABILITY

Vicarious liability means that one party can be held indirectly responsible for the actions of another party. For instance, an employer may be held vicariously liable for the actions of his employees.

Suppose you make a delivery to the Tyler Tool Company and an employee accidentally runs into you with his forklift, injuring your hip. If the accident is due to the worker's negligence, the Tyler Tool Company may be held responsible for your injury.

Similarly, all provinces have laws governing parental liability. When parents fail to control their child, they may be held responsible for damage caused by the child's actions.

See also PARENTAL LIABILITY LAWS.

LIABILITY INSURANCE

Liability insurance pays for injuries or damages caused by the policyholder. Suppose that, while visiting your home, your neighbor is seriously injured by a falling ceiling tile. The money she is awarded by a court to cover any treatments over and above those covered by Medicare and any additional damages will likely be covered by the liability portion of your homeowners' insurance policy.

In general, liability coverage is the most expensive part of any automobile, business, or homeowners' insurance policy. Although coverage is limited, most policies cover liability of up to $1 million. If you feel it is necessary, you can purchase additional coverage.

LIBEL AND SLANDER

Libel and slander are different (but related) forms of defamation. Libel is a false statement about a person's character or reputation that is communicated to others in writing or in some other visual, permanent form. Slander is verbal defamation. Because modern mass communication has made it difficult at times to distinguish libel from slander, Alberta and Manitoba have passed legislation which states that libel and slander both constitute defamation, and are to be treated alike.

See also DEFAMATION; TORT.

LICENSE

A license is the permission granted by a government agency allowing a person or a company to engage in an activity that the government wants to regulate.

Many activities require a license. For example, if you want to operate a barbershop, practice law or medicine, drive a taxi, open a liquor store or restaurant, become an insurance or real estate agent, hunt, fish, marry, own a dog, or drive, you may first have to obtain a license from the appropriate regulatory authority.

The government has an interest in protecting the health, safety, and welfare of its citizens, and the right to do so (by means of its police). By requiring a license, the state can provide some assurance that a licensed person or business meets certain standards. Licensing is also an important source of government revenue.

OBTAINING A LICENSE

To obtain a license, you must first meet the qualifications imposed by law. You will need to complete the required application forms, pay the fees set by the agency, and perhaps provide references or even post bond. For instance, if you want to become a real estate or an insurance agent, you must complete courses that have been approved by the province and perhaps be sponsored by someone who already has a license.

REVOKING A LICENSE

A license is a privilege and can be revoked by a regulatory body if you ignore regulations or violate the law, but you are first entitled to notice and to a hearing. Depending on the license you hold (if, for example, you are a doctor or lawyer), a formal hearing may be required—a process much like a court trial. If a licensing board revokes or suspends your license, you are entitled to appeal its decision.

FILING A COMPLAINT

If you have a complaint about a licensee, call or write to the licensing board responsible for overseeing the licensee's activity or profession. (Many licensing authorities require the complaint to be in writing.) Unfortunately, licensing boards are often underfunded, understaffed, and overworked. Boards often cannot process all the complaints they get and must concentrate on the most serious cases or those that involve a large number of complaints about the same person or business. As a consequence, your complaint may simply be forwarded to the licensee with a request for an explanation.

See also DRIVER'S LICENSE; REAL ESTATE AGENT AND BROKER.

LIE DETECTOR TEST

Also known as a polygraph test, the lie detector test has long been used by police departments and other government authorities in an effort to determine whether a person is telling the truth. A lie detector device measures a person's bodily—and largely involuntary—reactions to stress. To perform the test, galvanized electrodes are attached to the person's skin. These measure and record changes in blood pressure, pulse rate, respiration, and electrical resistance.

The person who is conducting the test first asks neutral questions, such as the subject's name and age, in order to help him relax and to see how he generally responds to this kind of questioning. When questions that are pertinent to the inquiry are asked, the lie detector indicates any changes recorded by the electrodes.

RELIABILITY

Even though the Canadian Police College in Ottawa trains officers to administer polygraph tests, the accuracy of lie detector tests is still being debated. Although a polygraph machine definitely measures the physiological reactions to stress, the chance for inaccurate results is high if the machine is not properly operated and the test is not properly conducted.

USE IN CRIMINAL PROCEEDINGS

The Supreme Court of Canada has ruled that polygraph evidence is not admissible, even to bolster the credibility of the accused. The Court held that the admission of such evidence would only encumber the fact-finding process by misleading the judge or jury, obscuring the main issues in the case, and removing from the jury its traditional role.

In addition, lower courts have held that in instances where the police use lie detector tests during their investigation, they must explain to the suspect that the results of the test cannot be used against him in court. Because suspects often confessed to crimes after submitting to a polygraph test, the courts became worried that these tests were being used to induce confessions. To be admissible as evidence, a confession must have been freely given. See CONFESSION.

USE BY EMPLOYERS

Only New Brunswick and Ontario have legislation prohibiting employers from using lie detector tests. According to employment standards acts in both provinces, an employee cannot be required to take a polygraph test, and employers cannot even ask an employee to undergo such a test. Employers who violate these provisions can be forced either to rehire an employee who was dismissed for refusing to take a lie detector test, or to compensate the employee for lost earnings and benefits.

LIEN

A lien is a claim that is placed against property for the purpose of securing a debt owed by the property's owner. A lien gives the lienholder (the person who obtained the lien) the right to force a sale of the prop-erty in order to satisfy the debt. A home mortgage is one of the most common types of lien.

TYPES OF LIENS

Liens can take several different forms; the most common are equitable liens, judicial liens, statutory liens, and mechanic's liens.

Equitable liens
An equitable lien may be either created by a sales contract or imposed by a court out of fairness. See also EQUITY.

Liens created by a sales contract are called express equitable liens. They are secured by the property you are purchasing. For example, when you borrow money to buy a home or car, the lender who gives you the loan obtains a lien according to the terms of the contract, with the house or the car serving as the collateral for the unpaid amount. If you do not make your payments as specified in the contract, the lender has the right to repossess your property and sell it to recover the money he lent you. See also MORTGAGE.

Judicial liens
Liens imposed by courts are called judicial liens. Suppose Steven sells Frank his boat for $1,000. Frank agrees to make monthly payments of $200, but stops paying after three months. Steven asks the court to impose a lien on the boat. This lien allows him to reclaim the boat or to sell it in order to recover the amount he lost in the deal. It also prevents Frank from selling the boat to someone else without first paying Steven what is owed him.

Statutory liens
A statutory lien is created by law. Generally, statutory liens automatically go into effect when someone does something to improve another person's property or add to its value, and has not yet been paid. Suppose you take your car to the local garage for repairs. Until you pay your bill, the garage may have a statutory lien on your car (depending on where you live), and is not required to return the car until you have paid the bill. If you do not pay, the garage ultimately may be able to sell the car to recover the value of its services, in addition to expenses such as storage charges, court costs, and lawyers' fees.

A lawyer has a statutory lien on documents belonging to her client while they are in the lawyer's possession. If a lawyer has not been paid for her services, she need not return the documents until such time as the bill is settled.

Some statutory liens require the lienholder to obtain court approval before he can sell a debtor's property. Others require only that the lienholder notify the debtor of the date and place of the proposed sale.

Mechanic's liens
A mechanic's lien is a type of statutory lien. However, with this type of lien, the property remains in the debtor's possession while the lien is in effect. The most common example of a mechanic's lien is the claim made by a building contractor when bills for improvements he has made go unpaid. The contractor may be able to foreclose on the property

to collect the money owed him. See MECHANIC'S LIEN.

FILING A LIEN

By filing a lien, you give notice of your claim against property to anyone who might have reason to know of it, such as someone who wants to buy or lease the property. In some provinces liens that are created by contract (such as through a mortgage or by retaining a security interest in a car or other personal property) require that a financing statement or a security agreement, or both, be filed in the appropriate provincial registry office. For mortgages, the office is usually that of the department of land titles or registry office. Documents related to other kinds of property are usually filed in the office of the registrar of movables.

DISCHARGING A LIEN

A lien is discharged, or ended, when the debt is paid or when the lienholder agrees to waive it. In some provinces, a lienholder must take action within a specified period of time—often six months or one year—to enforce the lien. Failure to do so may mean that the lien will be lifted automatically.

Liens may sometimes be discharged if the property they secure is destroyed. For instance, if a contractor has a mechanic's lien on an uninsured house and the house burns down, the lien may be discharged. However, if the house was insured, the insurance company may be directed to pay the lienholder.

If property you own is subject to a lien, get a release of the lien in writing from the lienholder when you pay him. Otherwise, you may face a foreclosure action or repossession if he later claims that he was not paid, or that the payment you gave was insufficient.

See EVERYDAY LEGAL FORMS at back of book. See also DEBT; DEFICIENCY JUDGMENT; JUDGMENT.

LIFE ESTATE

A life estate gives a person the right to use and enjoy property, but only during her lifetime. A person who holds a life estate (usufruct in Quebec) may not sell or give the property away to another or pass it on to her heirs. For example, Neil and Ruth were widowed with grown children when they met. After a few years, Neil asked Ruth to move into his house, and she agreed.

They never married, but Neil wanted to be sure that Ruth would always be able to live in his house, even after he died. He also wanted to be sure that his children, not hers, would ultimately be the owners of the family home. To ensure that Ruth's interest would be protected, Neil left Ruth a life estate in the home when he made out his will. When Ruth dies, the property will belong to Neil's children.

If the house is mortgaged, Ruth is responsible for making the payments as long as she lives in the house. If she cannot make them, Neil's children may arrange to do so. Depending on the circumstances, Neil's children may also choose to sue Ruth if she does anything to endanger the value of the property in which they have a future interest.

See also ESTATE PLANNING; WILL.

LIFE INSURANCE

Life insurance is a contract under which you pay a sum of money (usually in installments called premiums) to an insurance company. In return for your premiums, the insurance company agrees to pay a specified amount of money when you die (a death benefit) to whomever you name as the policy's beneficiary. Life insurance can be an important component of your estate plan, and it serves as a way to provide for your dependents in the event of your death. But buying life insurance can be a dizzying experience because many kinds of policies are offered for sale. Evaluate several policies carefully and do not be pressured into buying one that is not appropriate for your needs.

THE TWO KINDS OF LIFE INSURANCE

There are only two basic types of life insurance—term life insurance and cash value life insurance—but they offer a multitude of options.

TERM LIFE

Term life insurance, the least expensive kind, is designed to protect your family and your estate during your working years. If you outlive the term of the policy, you and your heirs receive nothing. As a result, renewable term life insurance plans are quite common.

Term life premiums are low when you are young, then increase annually or every five years. For example, a company may sell a $100,000 term life policy to a 40-year-old, non-smoking male for an annual premium of $175. When he reaches age 60, his annual premium may be about $650.

CASH VALUE LIFE

Cash value life, or permanent, insurance policies combine insurance and savings components. This type of insurance has two main categories—whole life and universal life insurance.

Whole life

Whole life insurance policies carry much higher premiums than term life policies, but the premiums remain constant for as long as you own your policy. The premiums are higher because the policy builds up a cash reserve, or cash value, against which you may be able to borrow at a relatively low interest rate, or which you may obtain in cash if you cancel your policy. In essence, your premiums become a kind of savings plan. At the same time, you are providing insurance protection for your beneficiary in the event of your death. See also CASH SURRENDER VALUE.

Whole life policies, however, do have disadvantages. The money you pay in premiums, which is held in an investment account, does not pay a high rate of interest, and a large sales commission will be part of your first year's premium. Also, you cannot adjust the amount of the premiums. You may be able to pay the high premium ($1,700 or so for $100,000 of coverage at age 40) when you buy the policy, but the premium cannot be lowered if you suffer a financial setback. If you cannot pay the premiums, you will have to downscale the policy or use the cash value for reduced coverage.

Universal life

To overcome some of the disadvantages of whole life insurance, and to give policies more flexibility, insurance companies have developed universal life insurance, which provides insurance coverage while also allowing you to build up savings. The interest on universal life policies comes from short-term financial investments, such as corporate bonds. Interest rates on such instruments vary: when interest rates go up, their cash value builds up faster, and when interest rates go down, the cash value will build more slowly. In addition, you have the flexibility of increasing or decreasing your premiums as you like, and you can make withdrawals of cash value without having to forfeit your insurance coverage.

Despite their advantages, universal life policies are much more expensive than term insurance policies because the sales commission applies both to the insurance and to the investment elements of the first year's premium.

Participating and nonparticipating

Life insurance can also be either participating or nonparticipating. A participating policy works like this. The insurer issues either a term or cash value policy and adds an overcharge, usually equal to about 30 percent. You are then entitled to receive what insurers call dividends, although these should not be confused with dividends paid to those who invest in stocks. You may use the dividends to purchase more insurance, called a paid-up bonus addition, or they may simply be deposited just as you would deposit funds in a savings account. Interest rates paid in such a situation will be relatively low. Nonparticipating policies do not incorporate this dividend feature.

INSURABLE INTEREST

In order to buy any life insurance policy, you must have an "insurable interest"—that is, you are expected to benefit if the insured person lives and suffer a loss if he or she dies. You have an insurable interest in your own life, and you have an insurable interest in the lives of your spouse and children. Children have an insurable interest in the lives of their parents, and as a result they can take out a life insurance policy on their parents' lives.

Other relationships may lead to the creation of an insurable interest as well. The partners in a business may have an insurable interest in each other's life, and a corporation may have an insurable interest in the lives of key employees who are essential to the conduct of the corporation's business.

ELIGIBILITY

To determine your eligibility for life insurance, your insurer will ask you questions about your age, gender, health, and occupation. If you want a large amount of coverage or you are middle-aged or older, you may be asked to take a physical examination. If you have a serious physical problem, you may have to pay a higher premium or even be denied coverage. Likewise, if you work at a hazardous occupation, or if you have hobbies that involve placing yourself in physical danger (such as skydiving or drag racing), you may be charged an additional premium or be considered ineligible for coverage.

Hiding or misstating significant facts on your application constitutes fraud and allows an insurer to deny you payment of benefits (although the insurer would be required to refund your premium payments). However, life insurance policies generally contain an "incontestability clause." This prohibits an insurer from turning down a claim after the policy has been in effect for a specified period of time, normally two years, even if it was obtained by the policyholder unintentionally misrepresenting facts on the application.

Some policies restrict the amount of benefits you can receive during the early years of your coverage. For example, a policy issued to an older person might only pay a reduced death benefit for the first two or three years if the insured died of a disease (although it may pay a full death benefit if the death was due to an accident). If the insured commits suicide within a specified period after buying the policy (typically two years), the payment is explicitly limited to the return of previously paid premiums.

LIFE INSURANCE AND YOUR ESTATE

When you buy a life insurance policy, you should name a primary beneficiary to receive the policy's death benefit. If you name your children as beneficiaries when they are still minors, you may want to name a trustee to manage the money for them until they reach the legal age of adulthood.

It is also a good idea to name a contingent beneficiary, who will receive your death benefits in case the primary beneficiary dies before or at the same time you do. Without these provisions, the death benefit may be included in your probate estate, and thus payment may be delayed. See also PROBATE.

As the owner of a life insurance policy, you generally have the right to change your beneficiaries, increase or decrease the death benefit, or cancel the policy in order to collect any outstanding cash value. But in some provinces, your spouse has an equal interest in any life insurance you buy after your marriage, and you cannot change the beneficiary on the policy without your spouse's permission. This is known as an irrevocable beneficiary, but the beneficiary may be revoked in case of divorce. See DIVORCE.

Life insurance benefits are not considered taxable income when they are received by the named beneficiary.

LIFE INSURANCE AND THE LAW

The federal government is responsible for the supervision of all foreign-owned companies and federally incorporated companies in Canada. Approximately 90 percent of life insurance companies fall into these categories. The remaining 10 percent are provincially regulated. However, the provinces alone have the power to regulate the wording and interpretation of contracts, licensing and insurance rates.

If you have a question about a life insurance company's stability or a complaint about its sales practices or customer service, you should write to or call the federal office of the Superintendent of Financial Institutions, or your provincial bureau of insurance.

In recent years several large U.S. life insurers have had financial trouble that prevented them from paying benefits to their policyholders. Fortunately, the Canadian insurance industry has been and continues to be financially healthy. As a precautionary measure, it has established a fund to reimburse consumers in the event of an insurance company failure. For savings policies, a policyholder may receive up to $60,000. Death claims are guaranteed for policies with a face value of up to $200,000. See INSURANCE.

LIMITED LIABILITY COMPANY

When someone starts a business, an important decision is how it will be organized. The three main choices are sole proprietorship, partnership, or corporation. This decision is crucial in terms of the tax consequences, the authority given to individuals associated with the company, and the potential liability (that is, the financial responsibility) of each person connected with the business.

SOLE PROPRIETORSHIP

As a sole proprietor of an unincorporated business, you are personally responsible for damages caused by you or your employees in the course of their work. Even if you operate as ABC Registered, for example, you are personally responsible to third parties for all damages caused.

PARTNERSHIPS

Forming a partnership has its benefits and disadvantages. A partnership is less complicated to set up than a corporation, and this form of business avoids the double taxation to which corporations and their dividend recipients are subject.

A major risk inherent in a partnership arrangement, however, is that each partner can be held personally responsible for the debts of the partnership. Another problem is that most partnership laws provide that when one of the partners dies, quits, or declares bankruptcy, the partnership is then dissolved, jeopardizing the continuity of the business. See also PARTNERSHIP.

CORPORATIONS

One of the advantages of a corporation is that stockholders and officers in the business are not personally responsible for its debts. The law recognizes the corporation as a separate legal entity and any claims that are made against the corporation may be paid from corporate assets only. Furthermore, a stockholder can sell his interest in the company without first getting the approval of other stockholders. Another major advantage is that a corporation can continue indefinitely even when investors or owners quit, die, or declare bankruptcy.

The rate at which corporations are taxed by the federal government is a major drawback to this type of business, however. The Income Tax Act requires a corporation to pay taxes on its income before any distribution is made to owners. These individual owners must then pay tax on the income they receive from the corporation. Thus, in essence, corporate income is taxed twice. But the maximum tax rate for a corporation is often lower than the rate paid by individuals. See also CORPORATION.

LINEUP

When the police either arrest or detain a suspect for a crime, they may ask him to appear in a lineup—a group of people who are literally lined up for a witness to view. Those who are grouped in the lineup may share physical characteristics, such as race, approximate age, height, and weight. Sometimes the police might have all participants in the lineup wear clothing that is similar to that described by the witness. Or, if the witness reports that she heard the suspect's voice, the people in the lineup may be asked to speak, perhaps saying the same words that the witness remembers hearing. If the witness identifies a suspect from a lineup, her identification may be sufficient evidence for the police to charge him.

If a suspect is not available for a lineup, the police may ask a witness to look at photographs of suspects. This is known as a photo lineup. The courts recently approved the use of videotapes of people rather than the actual physical lineup.

A lineup must be conducted in a way that does not lead a witness to select a particular member of the lineup. Suppose a woman reports that a bearded man attacked her. It would be improper for the police to put one bearded suspect in a lineup with clean-shaven men. In addition, the police may not tell the witness whether or not the suspect is actually in the lineup.

A criminal suspect has the right to have his lawyer present during a personal lineup.

The Supreme Court of Canada has ruled that evidence obtained because of the accused's participation in a lineup was inadmissible because he was not informed of his right to have the advice of counsel prior to the lineup. It may very well be that one has the right to refuse to participate in a lineup.

LIVING TOGETHER

Today more and more couples are choosing to live together without marrying. But living together (cohabitation) has a number of legal implications you should consider if you are thinking of moving in together.

First you should understand that living together is not the same thing as entering into a common-law marriage. Even in provinces that recognize such marriages, you must have the intent to be married and hold yourselves out to the world as husband and wife in order for the marriage to be valid.

In most cases, it should not be difficult to prove the existence of a common-law marriage. However, these types of marriages are not recognized in Quebec family law. See COHABITATION; COMMON-LAW MARRIAGE.

You may not be discriminated against because you have not chosen to be married. For example, suppose you and your partner find a house that you are interested in renting, but the landlord refuses, saying he wanted to rent to a married couple. You can file a complaint with your provincial human rights commission, since all Canadian jurisdictions outlaw discrimination on the basis of marital status.

CHILDREN

A child is not considered legitimate if his parents are not married unless the father acknowledges paternity. The mother may have to bring a suit against the father in order to establish a child's paternity. Without this status, the child may not be covered by his father's work-related benefits, nor may he have inheritance rights to his father's estate. However, children are eligible for such rights and benefits from their mother.

In the past, a child was denied certain rights unless the parents were married. Illegitimate children were denied the rights of inheritance, and there was no duty to support them financially. While the status of legitimacy has been abolished in most provinces, Alberta and Nova Scotia have retained the distinction. However, for the purposes of maintenance or support in these provinces, the status of the child is immaterial.

If paternity cannot be established, it is possible that a child will not be entitled to support or succession rights. In general, a man will be presumed to be the father of a child if he has been living with the child's mother for a reasonably long time or if the child is born soon after the man and the woman stop living together, or if the man has acknowledged that he is the father. Courts in some provinces can order blood tests in order to prove or disprove paternity. See ILLEGITIMACY.

PROPERTY

Property ownership and inheritance can also be a problem for couples who live together without marrying. For example, a married person is entitled to a share in her spouse's property when he dies, no matter what is contained in his will. But there is no such protection for an unmarried partner. If your partner dies and leaves everything to his mother or his best friend, you will have to rely on various legal principles to persuade a court to grant you a share of his property.

Disputes also arise when partners or cohabitants end their relationships. In a landmark case in 1980, the Supreme Court of Canada held that although the parties had never agreed to joint ownership of their property, the woman was entitled to a share since the property had been acquired by their joint effort and teamwork. The Court found that a constructive trust existed in favor of the woman.

According to the Canada (Quebec) Pension Plan Act, cohabitants are entitled to a survivor's pension as well as a share of the pension plan credits accumulated during cohabitation. Pension plans subject to provincial legislation also grant benefits to cohabitants as do certain provincial laws dealing with workers' compensation, automobile accidents, social welfare, and compensation of crime victims.

A WRITTEN AGREEMENT

Because you and your partner are not married, either of you is free to leave if you should choose to do so. If your partner owns the residence in which you live, he may be able to require you to move out. You do not necessarily have the right to continued support or housing, although your children would be entitled to support if their paternity has been established. Although it is sometimes possible to argue in court that you and your partner had an unwritten contract for the division of property or for continued support, or that it would be unjust for you to be deprived of a proprietary right, proving this can be very difficult. See also PALIMONY.

The most reliable way to protect yourself from such uncertainties is to create a written agreement about the terms of your cohabitation. Such agreements are generally enforceable, provided that nothing in them makes them illegal. For example, a provision that one partner will support the other in exchange for sex would be illegal, because it is against the law to exchange sex for money. Such a provision might also invalidate everything else in the agreement.

Several provinces, including Ontario, British Columbia and New Brunswick, now have laws dealing with agreements between unmarried people who live or plan to live together. Some provinces require that such an agreement be in writing, signed, and witnessed. The following guidelines should ensure that an agreement will be enforced. If your province has no legislation covering cohabitation agreements, follow the rules applicable to marriage contracts. Make your agreement as specific as possible, and deal with all the property that you possess. It is also wise to state the manner in which property will be distributed if the relationship ends. Finally, courts may be more inclined to uphold such an agreement if the partners obtained independent legal advice when drawing it up. It is therefore best to consult a lawyer. See EVERYDAY LEGAL FORMS at back of book.

LIVING TRUST

A living (or *inter vivos*) trust lets you transfer legal title of your property to a trustee, who manages it for you during your lifetime. When you die, he distributes your property to beneficiaries named in the trust.

By law, you can name yourself as the trustee, and name one or more cotrustees to take over if you become incompetent. A living trust may be revocable or irrevocable. Most are revocable—that is, you may be able to cancel or revise it at any time, adding or removing assets as you see fit. When you die, the assets belong to the trust, not you, and they are not subject to probate. See TRUST.

CONSIDERATIONS

A living trust is not for everyone. It is of main benefit to people who own large estates and wish to minimize probate costs and delays, and to people who do not want the distribution of their estate to become public knowledge (as it does with a will). However, although probate is often expensive and time-consuming, especially when the estate is complicated, most provinces have informal, inexpensive probate procedures.

Setting up a living trust is not a simple matter, and it can be very expensive. You must change the title on your bank accounts, automobiles, and deed to your home to reflect the new ownership of the property. You will have to make an inventory of all your property, complete transfer forms at banks and with your stockbroker, execute and record quitclaim deeds, and pay transfer fees or taxes. If you decide to name a financial planner or a bank or other institution as trustee, you must pay annual fees for their services.

A living trust does not eliminate the need for a will, since you may have assets that you do not wish to include in the trust or that you receive after it is established. A will may also be necessary if you want to make specific gifts to your family, your friends, or some charitable organization.

If you are considering a living trust, first talk to a lawyer or estate planner to determine if it is right for you. Be wary of accepting advice from anyone who would profit from serving as your trustee, such as a bank or law firm that promotes living-trust seminars. Also ignore any promise that you can create a valid living trust on your own. Provincial laws on living trusts vary, and a mistake in filling out the forms or a misunderstanding of the explanatory material could be costly.

See ESTATE PLANNING; WILL.

LIVING WILL

A living will is a written document that informs your family, friends, and physicians of your wishes in the event that you are incapacitated by serious illness. Generally it states that you do not want to be kept alive by artificial means or heroic measures if you are suffering from a terminal condition and your death is imminent.

While many people have drawn up living wills, also called advance directives, there is very little Canadian legislation dealing with the matter. At the time of writing, only Nova Scotia and Quebec recognized a form of living will, Ontario was about to pass a law requiring health care professionals to respect an individual's wishes, and Alberta and Manitoba were debating whether to grant legal recognition to living wills.

Even if living wills are not legally recognized in your province, it is still a good idea to make one. Even if there is no legal obligation on others to respect it, your wishes will be known and may help your family and doctor to make difficult decisions in the future. It is also possible that these documents will receive legislative approval in your province in the coming years.

The concept behind living wills differs from that of assist-

REAL LIFE, REAL LAW

The Case of the Debilitating Disease

In June 1989, doctors in Quebec City diagnosed 23-year-old Nancy B's affliction as Guillain-Barré syndrome. Nancy, confined to a hospital bed, could breathe only with the aid of a respirator, without which she would die. About a year later doctors found her nervous system was rapidly deteriorating and, in January 1991, she learned that her condition was incurable. Taking her suffering, her helplessness, and the prognosis into account, she sought a permanent injunction requiring the respirator to be disconnected.

The Quebec Superior Court heard testimony from several doctors, social workers, hospital staff, and from Nancy B's mother. The court learned that Nancy, once a strong, active woman who loved life, had been unable to accept her diminished state since the onset of the disease. It was also established that Nancy's mental faculties were not impaired and that she fully understood the consequences of discontinuing her treatment. Witnesses testified that her desire to die had existed for a significant period of time.

The court noted that both the Civil Code of Lower Canada and the Quebec Code of Medical Ethics required that the free and informed consent of a patient be respected. The court also held that no provision of the Criminal Code could apply to a person who carried out the wishes of a patient in circumstances such as those before the court. The court gave Nancy's doctor permission to disconnect the respirator, but required that Nancy's consent be verified once again before doing so.

In his judgment, Mr. Justice Jacques Dufour said: "I had to state the law on this delicate matter; I have fulfilled my duty. I will continue nonetheless to hope against all hope." Later, he said the decision was one of the most difficult he had had to make.

Nancy B died in 1992, shortly after the Christmas holidays.

---

ed suicide. While a living will expresses a desire that life-sustaining procedures be withheld, assisted suicide involves situations where death is actively brought about. A physician who respects a living will does not break any law. However, this is not so of a physician who assists someone to commit suicide.

A living will instructs doctors and hospitals to withhold or withdraw life-sustaining procedures, taking only the steps necessary to provide for the patient's comfort and minimize any pain as he proceeds toward a natural death. A living will is also meant to relieve families of the burden of making a decision about continuing medical care if a patient is incompetent or otherwise unable to communicate his wishes.

Under the proposed Ontario law, physicians and hospitals will be legally bound to honor a patient's wishes, including those expressed in a living will. Such a document may be rendered invalid, however, if a woman is pregnant when her condition becomes terminal, or if the person making the will was incompetent at the time it was drawn up.

An alternative to a living will is a durable power of attorney for health care, which gives another person authority to make decisions for you respecting life-prolonging treatments. This substitute decision-maker's power does not become effective until the person granting the power becomes incompetent.

Because it is difficult to make provisions for all future circumstances in a living will, a durable power of attorney for heath care may be preferable. For example, the substitute decision-maker will be able to assess the medical situation of the incompetent person once a terminal illness occurs, whereas a living will may not anticipate all possibilities. In addition, living wills do not usually state who is responsible for making the decision to allow a person to die naturally.

Durable powers of attorney for health care are available in Nova Scotia, Ontario, and Quebec. Other provinces have instituted changes permitting powers of attorney to continue in the event of illness or incapacity, although it is unclear at present whether this is restricted to powers over property and finances, or if health care is included.

MAKING A LIVING WILL

If you decide to make a living will, ensure that it is in writing and signed by you and two witnesses. To be valid, you must be of legal age and mentally competent. You should provide copies for your doctor, hospital or health care facility, lawyer, friends and family, and you should also keep one copy in your wallet.

If your province does recognize living wills, there may be requirements pertaining to the form of the will, which may also have to be registered with the public trustee or some other public body. You may also be required to update your living will every few years, thereby indicating that it represents your current wishes. Your living will may be of no value if you travel or move to another province. If you are in doubt about these requirements, contact a lawyer or a notary.

Stationery stores in your area may sell standard forms of living wills. See also EVERYDAY LEGAL FORMS at back of book.

LOAN SHARK

A loan shark makes loans at exceptionally high rates of interest. His clients are often people who cannot get a loan from traditional sources such as banks, credit unions, and finance companies. Despite federal and provincial credit laws (which are designed to protect consumers from illegally high interest rates, threats and intimidation from collectors, and other questionable lending practices), loan sharks continue to thrive. Often they are the only source of loans for the poor, recent immigrants, small-business owners, and many others.

A borrower who falls prey to a loan shark need not fear that he will go to jail if he does not pay. However, it is likely he will be threatened with physical harm by the loan shark's "collector." If you are threatened by a loan shark or his collector, call the police immediately. By doing so, you have a better chance of avoiding harm, and you may help rid your community of this dangerous predator.

A TYPICAL TRANSACTION

Suppose Li Wen needs start-up money for a new business. Because of a poor credit record and no previous business experience, she has been unable to get what she needs. She sees an advertisement offering loans "for good causes" and promising no credit check.

Li Wen answers the ad and is given an appointment at an address in a seedy section of the city. When she arrives for her appointment, the lender agrees to let her have $1,000 on condition she pays back $1,500 within one month. Li Wen is not asked to provide any references or credit information, and there are no papers to sign. The lender says, "It's all a matter of trust, after all." Li Wen gets her money, but the interest is 50 percent, which translates into an annual interest rate of 600 percent. When Li Wen fails to deliver the money at the end of the month, the lender sends a large man called Buddy to "remind" Li Wen of her obligation. As a reminder, Buddy breaks Li Wen's furniture and promises that his next visit will not be so polite. If Li Wen is lucky, she may be able to come up with the money or get police protection. If not, she may have to suffer a further visit from Buddy.

STEPS TO TAKE

If you are looking for a loan and encounter someone who you suspect may be a loan shark because of the exorbitant interest rates he charges, be cautious, and consider dealing with the situation by taking the following steps:

1. Ask the lender if you can see his provincial license. (Finance companies and private lenders are licensed by each province.)

2. Ask if he will give you the names of other borrowers who have used his services.

3. Ask for a written promissory note and loan agreement that you can have your accountant or lawyer review.

4. If you are still suspicious, talk to your local police.

The Criminal Code defines a criminal interest rate as being an effective annual rate of interest which exceeds 60 percent. Anyone found guilty of receiving interest at this rate is subject to a maximum punishment of five years' imprisonment. There are also provincial laws such as Consumer Protection acts, and Cost of Credit Disclosure acts.

Unconscionable Transactions acts deal with the proper form of loan agreements and acceptable methods of loan collection.

LOBBYIST

The Lobbyists Registration Act has been in effect since 1989. It recognizes two principles: lobbying is a legitimate activity that makes legislators aware of certain issues and concerns of individuals and groups; and the decision-making process is best served if there is no mystery surrounding lobbyists or their clients.

The act requires lobbyists to register with Industry Canada's Registrar of Lobbyists. The penalty for not doing so is a $100,000 fine, or two years' imprisonment, or both.

Lobbyists may belong to one of two categories or tiers. Tier 1 lobbyists are professional lobbyists who represent one or more clients. Those in Tier 2 are employees whose jobs are to lobby for their employers.

The public may consult the lobbyist register at the Lobbyists Registration Branch of Industry Canada. It contains the names, titles, and business addresses of all lobbyists, the names of each lobbyist's clients or employers, and each lobbyist's special area of interest. Information on lobbyists is also maintained on a computer database. For a nominal fee you can obtain copies of documents filed with the registrar, or you can use the computer facilities to conduct searches of the computer database.

See also ELECTION LAWS.

LOST AND FOUND PROPERTY

Lost property can be defined as an item that the owner did not intend to give up but can no longer find, owing to neglect, carelessness, or a mistake.

IF YOU FIND LOST PROPERTY

Suppose you find a purse in the street or a shopping bag full of merchandise in a department store dressing room. You cannot legally claim the property as your own—at least not immediately. Your right to eventual ownership is subject to the owner's right to reclaim it, and you have an obligation to make an effort to find the owner.

In some instances it may be easy to locate him. A purse or wallet, for instance, usually contains the owner's name and address. A shopping bag may include a sales slip or price tag with the store's name on it. If you return merchandise to a store, the manager may be able to trace the property's rightful owner through, for example, a credit card number on the sales slip, the cashier's recollection of a familiar customer, or the customer's inquiry.

When there is no information to help identify the owner of lost property, contact the local police. In general, you are required to turn lost property over to the police for a specified period of time, during which the owner may claim it. You may have to file an affidavit with the police describing the property and stating when and where you found it. See AFFIDAVIT.

In some provinces the clerk of the local court is required to publish a notice about found property in local newspapers. Depending on local law, the owner then has from 90 days to a year to reclaim it. If no owner comes forward, the finder usually becomes the owner.

There are certain general rules which apply to the finding of lost property. For example, if an employee finds something while she is working, her employer normally will have a better claim than her. In addition, if you find something on a person's property, that person may have rights superior to yours. You should also be aware that certain legislation may apply to the finding of lost property. For example, police officers are required to deliver found items to the police department, which will then take steps to find the owner or, if this is not possible, sell the objects.

STEPS TO TAKE WHEN YOU LOSE SOMETHING

If you have lost an item that you wish to find, here are some suggestions that may help you track it down:

1. If you lose the item while you are shopping, return to the stores you visited. Leave your name, address, telephone number, and a description of the item with the manager, security office, or cashier.

2. If you lose something during or after your stay in a hotel, notify the hotel management as soon as you miss it.

3. Call the local police and inform them of your loss. Ask what you must do to reclaim your lost item if it is turned in.

4. If all else fails, run an ad in your local newspaper that describes the item and (if appropriate) offers a reward.

5. Keep in mind that if there is a dispute over ownership between you and someone who has found the item, you may have to go to court to resolve it.

See also ABANDONED PROPERTY; REWARD.

LOTTERY

Provincial-sponsored lotteries, one of the more popular forms of legalized gambling, raise a great deal of money for government treasuries. Winnings, however, are not taxable.

Groups of lottery ticket purchasers sometimes pool their money to buy more tickets and thus increase their chances of winning. If you are involved in a lottery pool, make out an agreement in writing and have all participants sign. In general, the law considers the person who signs the lottery ticket the winner. Without such an agreement, if one of the pool participants signs the ticket and claims the money, the others may have to launch a lawsuit to get their winnings.

Remember that lottery laws give you a limited time, ordinarily six months to a year, during which to claim your prize. If you fail to come forward before it expires, you will have to forfeit the money you won.

FROM
MACE
TO
MUTUAL FUND

MACE

A chemical irritant that is typically packaged in a small spray canister, mace is used for self-defense. It causes temporary blindness when sprayed into a person's eyes, in some instances allowing a potential victim to disable an assailant long enough so that she can escape.

In Canada, mace is classified as a prohibited weapon. Those convicted of possession face five years' imprisonment if tried by indictment and 10 years under pending legislation. If the prosecutor decides to try the accused by way of summary proceedings, the maximum sentence is six months' imprisonment and a $2,000 fine.

It is also an offense to be an occupant of a vehicle that you know contains mace or any other prohibited weapon.

Despite being illegal, mace does find its way into the hands of otherwise law-abiding people, who mistakenly regard it as an effective means of protection. Be advised that in many situations mace has been more of a hindrance than a help to the person who is wielding it. Attackers have been known to wrest a can of mace out of the hands of a defender and then use it against her.

See SELF-DEFENSE; WEAPON.

MAGISTRATE'S COURT

If you have ever contested a traffic ticket or been involved in a case concerning a municipal bylaw, the proceedings may have taken place in a magistrate's court, also called a municipal court.

Magistrate's courts deal with lesser criminal offenses and breaches of provincial penal law, such as highway traffic and liquor license offenses. The first step of more serious criminal cases, such as arraignment, may also take place in a magistrate's court, whose judges (magistrates) are appointed by the province.

Magistrate's courts usually have simplified procedures, with no jury trials, or preliminary inquiries. Costs, technicalities, and court delays are thus kept to a minimum. Many accused persons represent themselves in a magistrate's court, especially when they are charged under municipal law (for having deposited their garbage outside earlier than permitted, for example). However, everyone has the right to be represented by a

lawyer. If you plead guilty at the first appearance before a magistrate, you are usually ordered to pay a fine and, if you request it, you will be given time to pay.

You can also plead "guilty with explanation," and the judge may reduce the recommended fine if he finds the explanation credible and reasonable. He cannot acquit you, however, since you have pleaded guilty.

In some cases, the defendant does not have to appear personally before the magistrate's court, but may have his lawyer appear for him instead. Often, companies appear only through lawyers—for example, a bakery charged with not having clean premises as required by municipal or provincial law may plead through its lawyer.

Should you be summoned to appear before the magistrate's court, you would be wise to consult a lawyer. He could advise you of the consequences of the charge, and whether or not it would be advisable to hire a lawyer for the case.

See COURTS.

MAIL

It is a federal crime to interfere with the delivery of mail, and violators can be punished by fines and imprisonment. Mailboxes, particularly those in apartment buildings, can be targets for thieves looking for cheques, cash, or goods.

As with any crime, prevention is better than prosecution. One way to avoid having your cheques stolen is to ask any

person, company, or government agency that sends you cheques regularly to deposit them directly into your bank account. On your part, never send cash through the mail.

Some years ago, three people were arrested for thieving directly from mailboxes. They had been turning the boxes upside down, then stealing valuables from the letters thus released. They were caught red-handed when someone witnessed one of their "jobs" and called the police. When the postbox thieves were arrested, they were found to have wrangled a total of $16.50 that day.

If your mail has been stolen, report the theft to your local postmaster right away so that Canada Post can investigate. Alternatively, you can go directly to the police. See also OBSCENITY; PORNOGRAPHY; SCAMS AND SWINDLES.

MAIL ORDER SALES

Selling products through the mail is big business. In Canada alone, the direct marketing industry employs more than 200,000 people. The millions of pieces of mail sent out annually include catalogs (Canada has more than 600 catalog companies), advertising circulars for countless products, and sweepstakes offers. Indeed mail order offers make up a sizable portion of all mail delivered to Canadian homes, where consumers spend on average $200 per person per year on goods and services purchased by direct

ABC's

OF REMOVING YOUR NAME FROM MAILING LISTS

If you are annoyed by the amount of unsolicited direct mail advertising you receive from mail order companies, advertisers, and other sources, try the following steps to make room in your mailbox:

■ To get your name off several lists at once, write to the Canadian Direct Marketing Association (CDMA), a professional organization of direct mail marketers. Indicate the companies from which you do not wish to receive direct mail—they may be CDMA members. Or ask the CDMA to remove your name from its complete list. The address is: Canadian Direct Marketing Association, 1 Concorde Gate, Suite 607, Don Mills, Ont. M3C 3N6.

■ Write directly to companies that send you mail about products that do not interest you and request that your name be removed from their lists.

■ Place a "No Flyer" sticker or some other written message on your mailbox telling deliverers of flyers to cease delivering such materials to you.

■ To stop mail that consists of erotic or sexually explicit material, go to your local post office. There you can obtain a form that orders the makers of such materials to stop sending them to you. Companies that disregard this order may be subject to penalties and even legal action by Canada Post.

mail. In 1991, for example, Canadians bought some $7.86 billion in goods and services through direct marketing.

Convenience is a major factor in buying by mail. Sometimes, however, packages can be lost, damaged, or stolen, and there may be times when the goods you receive are not what you expected. Reputable businesses, especially major companies with national reputations, are likely to move quickly to resolve problems. Unethical companies on the other hand have no stake in consumer satisfaction. To avoid the few that are deceptive or downright fraudulent,

be wary of "bargains" offered by companies whose reputations are unknown to you. One company, for example, advertised discount vacations at "wholesale prices," when in reality these vacations were not being sold at the bargain price the company claimed they were.

Indeed there are hundreds of examples in court records of companies that intentionally deceive the consuming public in order to make a profit. When it comes to mail orders, remember this: any offer that seems too good to be true probably is.

Mail order companies may be subject to a variety of laws, par-

ticularly consumer legislation. As well, the Canada Post Corporation Act prohibits a company from sending you unordered goods C.O.D. If you receive unsolicited goods, you do not have to return them, and the sender cannot sue you.

If you have problems with a mail order firm, report the matter to the Canadian Direct Mail Marketing Association (CDMA). This self-regulatory body represents 80 percent of Canada's direct mail marketers. Its 800 members include major financial institutions, publishers, catalogers, charities, nonprofit organizations, and advertising agencies.

CDMA members do not transfer customers' names to third parties without the customer's permission and, if requested, will remove consumers' names from their mailing lists. The association will also help customers resolve problems with direct marketers, even those who are not members of CDMA. (See box, this page.)

See also CONSUMER PROTECTION; DAMAGED MERCHANDISE; FALSE ADVERTISING; SCAMS AND SWINDLES.

MAN-SLAUGHTER

A form of "culpable homicide," manslaughter is the criminal offense of causing the death of someone, by way of an unlawful act. There need be no intent to kill the victim, just to commit an unlawful act which caused the death. Suppose Joe engages Harvey in a fistfight. Even though Joe does not intend to kill his adversary, he beats him so severely that Harvey dies as a result of his wounds. If the fight was not consensual, then the actions of Joe were illegal and constituted the offense of assault. This assault in turn was at the root of Harvey's death. Therefore, Joe could be charged with manslaughter. But, if it could be shown that Joe set out to kill Harvey in the fight, then murder would be the more appropriate charge.

The maximum sentence for manslaughter is the same as for murder (25 years' imprisonment); there is no minimum sentence.

See also Homicide; Murder.

MARITAL PROPERTY

Marital property is defined as anything acquired during a couple's marriage, such as automobiles, boats, real estate, bank accounts, certificates of deposit, or stocks and bonds.

OWNERSHIP

There are two ways a couple can jointly own property they acquire during the course of their marriage: through tenancy by the entirety or through joint tenancy.

Tenancy by the entirety means that the marital property is owned in common by both spouses, and neither can sell it without the other's permission. When one spouse dies, the surviving spouse automatically owns the property regardless of the stipula-

tions of a will or of any claims by the heirs of the deceased.

Joint tenancy also offers this right of survivorship, with the difference that either spouse can dispose of the property without the other's permission. Both forms of ownership prevent the property from going through probate court.

IN CASE OF DIVORCE

During a divorce, the court often has to determine how a couple's marital property is to be divided. In some provinces, the court can divide all the property acquired during the marriage, no matter which spouse acquired it. In other provinces, the court will consider only property that was acquired jointly during the marriage. Property owned beforehand or inherited by a spouse during the marriage is usually exempt from partition at the time of divorce. However, the interest or increased value obtained from such property may be subject to division.

See Community Property; Divorce; Equitable Distribution.

MARRIAGE

The institution of marriage grants a couple special legal status, confers certain obligations, and affects the ownership of the couple's property and inheritance rights.

The law recognizes two different types of marriage: legal and common law. A legal marriage is one in which a couple's exchange of vows is presided over by someone the province has authorized to solemnize their marriage, such as a member of the clergy, a justice of the peace, or a judge. In contrast, a common-law marriage is one in which a couple privately agree to live as husband and wife and present themselves to the public as married.

Common-law marriages have not gained universal acceptance across Canada, even though some 10 per cent of Canadian couples have chosen this type of relationship. In Quebec, for example, common-law spouses or *conjoints de fait* do not enjoy the legal privileges of married couples. In some other provinces, there have been examples of common-law marriages being frowned upon by the courts.

Although few people can be prevented from marrying, there are some exceptions. People of the same sex are not recognized as legally married, even if an authorized person performs the ceremony. If you are already married, you will not be granted a marriage license. And people who are mentally incompetent may be prevented from marrying, on the grounds that they are not capable of understanding the nature of the institution. See also Bigamy; Common-Law Marriage; Incompetency.

In the past, religion played a large part in the law of marital relations. Prohibited degrees of marriage were codified in the law, banning marriage between people who were related in various ways by blood or adoption. In 1990, Parliament enacted the Marriage (Prohibited Degrees) Act. This law significantly streamlined the rules of marriage and now holds marriage to be void only where it is between people related in direct line (that is grandparents–parents– children) or between brothers and sisters. These restrictions apply equally to relations by blood or adoption.

MINIMUM AGE

Each province sets its own minimum age for a person to marry legally. Typically this is when one is 18 years or older. The courts can relax this requirement in special cases, allowing marriage at an earlier age. In some cases, the courts will recognize a marriage involving a minor if the couple lived together prior to marriage or if the wife is pregnant or had a child with her spouse.

PROCEDURE

You do not have to be a resident of a province in order to marry there, but you do need to obtain a license from the place where you wish to marry. To get the license, you must usually produce identification, proof of the dissolution of any previous marriages, and in Prince Edward Island you must take a blood test for syphilis or other venereal diseases or undergo a physical examination. You will have to fill out an application and pay a fee, and there may be a waiting period after you have filed the application before the license is granted.

If everything is in order, a clerk will grant you a marriage license that is valid for a limited time only. Marriage licenses are required in all provinces except Quebec.

After your marriage ceremony, a marriage certificate must be signed by each spouse, the person who performed the ceremony, and usually two witnesses. The marriage should be recorded with the county clerk. Unless you get an annulment or a divorce, your marriage will remain legally binding. See also ANNULMENT; DIVORCE.

FINANCIAL CONSIDERATIONS

Usually, the property that a couple bring into a marriage belongs to each partner individually. However, property acquired during a marriage generally belongs to both spouses. This joint ownership can become an issue during divorce proceedings, when marital property must be divided according to provincial laws. Some provinces have community-property laws which stipulate that spouses have equal ownership of any assets acquired during their marriage. Other provinces follow the equitable-distribution rule which considers the contributions and needs of each spouse. Under provincial family law legislation, the court may also grant compensatory allowance to one of the divorc-ing partners for work, such as domestic work or raising children, done during the marriage.

Spouses are required to provide each other with the "necessaries of life," such as food, clothing, and shelter. Similarly, they are expected to provide necessaries for any minor children of their union, both during their marriage and after its termination. See also CHILD SUPPORT; NECESSARIES.

One spouse is not always held responsible for debts incurred by the other spouse, however. For example, if your spouse obtains a credit card without your signature and then charges $5,000 on it, which he cannot repay, you are not liable for his debt.

Usually, spouses inherit each other's property. Even if one spouse tries to disinherit the other, provincial law may require at least some of the inheritance to be distributed to the surviving spouse.

See also MARITAL PROPERTY; PRENUPTIAL AGREEMENT; WILL.

MARTIAL LAW

In times of dire emergency, such as civil unrest or natural disaster, the federal government is empowered to order martial law, or government by the military. The most striking example was when Prime Minister Pierre Trudeau invoked the War Measures Act during the October Crisis of 1970. More recently, during the Oka Crisis of 1990, the military was brought in again, this time to crush native resistance to local authorities over the issue of land claims.

Even though martial law was instituted in 1970 principally to deal with a political problem in Quebec, people as far away as British Columbia were arrested under a nation-wide blanket suspension of civil rights. Many of those arrested were in no way connected to the events taking place in Quebec and, not surprisingly, there was a public outcry.

Ultimately, the War Measures Act was replaced by the Emergencies Act, which places tighter controls on the government's application of martial law.

MATERIAL WITNESS

A material witness is someone whose testimony is essential to the success of a legal action. Typically, a material witness is ordered by the court to appear at a trial and testify against the defendant. If his testimony would implicate him in criminal activities, he may be granted immunity from prosecution. Should his testimony place him in danger, he may have to enter a witness protection program.

See IMMUNITY; WITNESS.

MECHANIC'S LIEN

A mechanic's lien is a legal claim against property, made by someone who has worked to build, repair, or improve the property. Suppose you enter into a contract with Hugh to

REAL LIFE, REAL LAW

The Case of the Library's Liens

The Midville Public Library Board contracted with Fly-by-Nite Construction for a major building project. Work went along smoothly for a while, until Fly-by-Nite found itself in increasing financial hardship. Eventually it had to notify the library that it would be withdrawing from the job.

Before undertaking the contract, Fly-by-Nite had taken out insurance to protect itself from potential liability if it could not meet its contractual obligations. This was in turn paid out to the various subcontractors who properly filed mechanic's liens. The insurance company felt it should not have to make the payouts, since the library had "holdback funds" as allowed by law. However, the court held that even though the library had these funds, they did not have to be used up before the subcontractors could have access to the insurance company's money.

The case of Fly-by-Nite illustrates the way in which various mechanisms are in place to insure the most satisfactory settlement of disputes arising out of claims for mechanic's liens.

have your family room renovated and new windows installed. After the work is done, you pay Hugh, but he fails to pay his supplier, Leo, who provided the windows. You may then find that a mechanic's lien has been placed against your home for the sum of money that Hugh owes Leo for the windows.

Mechanic's liens exist in one form or another in all provinces except Quebec, which has other legal provisions for protecting suppliers of goods and services. (To secure payment, a Quebec subcontractor working for a contractor may exercise a legal hypothec on the property he has worked upon.) These laws permit anyone who provides materials or labor for the construction, repair, or improvement of real estate

to make a claim against the property owner for the money due. See also LIEN.

Whether you can be held responsible for a lien depends on the law of your province and the facts of your case. Suppose you hire a general contractor to build a patio in your backyard. In turn, he hires a subcontractor to provide wood for the project. For unforeseen reasons, the contractor cannot complete the project. In normal contract law, the contractor would be liable to you for breach of contract. However, since the subcontractor never entered into an agreement with you, regular contract rules do not apply.

Suppose the subcontractor has taken a lien on the materials given to the contractor. This would give him what is called a "real" right in the property itself as opposed to a "personal" or contractual right. A real right is enforceable against all people, whereas a personal right binds only the parties to a contract. Therefore the subcontractor has a right to the property used to build the patio instead of payment for it. He can generally enforce his lien on your property regardless of the outcome of the dispute between you and the contractor.

However, when mechanic's lien litigation commences, you can generally file cross claims or counter claims. Thus, if you are sued for x dollars for the lien on the patio, you in turn could sue the contractor for this sum under the breach of your contract.

Some provinces allow you to hold back a sum of money from a contractor's final payment, usually 15 percent—insurance against suits for mechanic's liens in case deals between the contractor and his suppliers go sour. In most provinces, a supplier who files a mechanic's lien must follow through with a lawsuit against you within a specified time, usually within one year. If not, his claim will expire.

A mechanic's lien can affect your credit rating and prevent you from selling your property. In an extreme case it can result in the forced sale of your property in order to satisfy the debt. See also FORECLOSURE.

STEPS TO TAKE

To avoid having a mechanic's lien placed on your property, take the following steps:

1. Deal only with contractors with established reputations.

2. Require the contractor to obtain a surety bond—a guarantee that a third party will pay for any obligations the contractor refuses to honor.

3. Ask the contractor to give you a list of his suppliers and subcontractors.

4. Ask the contractor to give you copies of any receipts that prove he has paid all suppliers and subcontractors.

5. Get a statement from each subcontractor stating that he has been paid in full for his work.

6. Have the contractor give you a notarized affidavit of completion, acknowledging that all bills have been paid.

7. Do not make final payment to the general contractor until you have proof that subcontractors have been paid.

See EVERYDAY LEGAL FORMS at back of book. See also CONTRACTOR; HOME IMPROVEMENT AND REPAIR.

MEDIATION

It is not always necessary to turn to the legal system to resolve a dispute—even one that concerns a legal matter. Mediation is one method used as an alternative to a trial or other court proceeding, or as a way to speed up resolution of issues connected with a court proceeding. Mediation can be useful in resolving personal-injury lawsuits, business disagreements, neighborhood and community conflicts, and divorce cases, particularly those involving children.

For instance, although a couple may have agreed to dissolve their marriage, it may not agree about child custody or support and visitation rights. Rather than bringing these issues to a family court, the couple may turn to mediation.

In divorce cases, lawyers are bound to inform their clients about mediation services. The legal rules of court procedure in some provinces also encourage use of the mediation process, notably in family law matters.

HOW MEDIATION WORKS

In mediation, an impartial person is called upon to help the parties to a dispute reach an agreement. Like arbitration, another method of alternative dispute resolution, mediation offers privacy and informality. Moreover, although each side may retain a lawyer, especially in divorce cases, mediation may be less costly than going to court. In addition, mediation often reduces the tensions and acrimony that can prolong court proceedings. See also ALTERNATIVE DISPUTE RESOLUTION; ARBITRATION; CONCILIATION.

ROLE OF THE MEDIATOR

The parties to a dispute choose the mediator, whose role varies depending on the case. Some mediators prefer to be actively involved and may suggest ways to resolve the matter—for instance, by proposing terms for a settlement or trying to persuade one side to make concessions. Other mediators take a less active role, trying instead to create an atmosphere that fosters communication and allows the parties to reach their own agreement.

Regardless of the mediator's role, the ultimate decision rests with the people involved in the dispute. Unlike an arbitrator, a mediator has no authority to make the participants reach an agreement or accept her solution. Each party may withdraw from mediation at any time. If the parties resolve their differences, they may present their agreement to the court.

STEPS TO TAKE TO FIND A MEDIATOR

Whether it involves a dispute among neighbors or a fight over child custody, mediation can avoid costly legal battles. Here are some tips on finding a qualified mediator in your area:

1. Ask the clerk at your local courthouse for possible leads on mediation services. The local bar association may also help you. Check the Yellow Pages of your phone book under Mediation, Social Service Organizations or Marriage and Family Counselors. In the Yellow Pages you will also find listings for organizations such as the Association de médiation familiale du Québec, the Conciliation Project in Ontario, and the Family Services Bureau of Regina. By tackling your search in this way, you can compile a list of possible mediators.

2. Interview several mediators before deciding on one. Be sure that he or she has experience in mediating the type of dispute you are involved in and that the mediator's personality is compatible with your own.

3. Check the mediator's references. If she declines to provide them, stating her clients' confidentiality as a reason, suggest she ask a few of her former clients to waive their confidentiality. Make it clear that you are not concerned with the details of the cases, but rather with her skills.

4. Although lawyers and former judges often serve as mediators, you should think twice about using them. There is no requirement that mediators have legal training, and a lawyer or a judge may be a bad choice if he has no training in mediation and is more comfortable in adversarial situations.

5. Ask how many meetings the mediator will hold, and how much he charges per hour. Will he meet you and your spouse separately? Will he involve the children in mediation?

MEDICAL MALPRACTICE

When you become ill or are injured, the physician who treats you must make a diagnosis and administer appropriate care. But because medical science is not precise, and every situation is different, doctors can never be sure that the care they give will be successful or that unanticipated side effects or other complications will not develop. The law therefore recognizes that physicians cannot always be held responsible if a treatment is unsuccessful.

However, if a patient is injured because a physician or other health-care professional does not meet minimum standards of care, the patient or her family can file a lawsuit against the practitioner for medical malpractice. Because of the costs involved, these suits are often settled out of court, but they sometimes proceed to trial.

DEFINING MALPRACTICE

Because physicians cannot guarantee the results of medical treatment, a patient's malpractice claim is not valid just because his treatment was not successful. Clear instances of malpractice include cutting off the oxygen supply during surgery, misdiagnosing an injury because routine tests and procedures were not followed, or prescribing an erroneous drug dosage or a drug not approved for the patient's condition. Also, if a physician does not obtain a patient's informed consent before proceeding with treatment, he may be guilty of malpractice, even if the patient improves. See INFORMED CONSENT.

NEGLIGENCE

Most medical malpractice cases are based on the concept of negligence—that is, the patient was harmed because the physician failed to meet the required standards of skill and care. A patient must prove four things in order to recover damages: (1) that the physician owed him a duty, (2) that the physician did not fulfill that duty, (3) that he suffered an injury, and (4) that there was a causal connection between the physician's breach of duty and the patient's injury.

Duty owed

To prove that a physician owed him a duty, the patient simply has to demonstrate that a typical physician-patient relationship existed. Once this has been established, a doctor has an ethical and legal duty to give his patient medical treatment that meets an acceptable standard of care. The physician's agreement to treat the patient would serve as proof of this relationship.

Breach of duty

The second element of a malpractice case requires the patient to prove that the medical treatment he received from his doctor fell below the standard of care he could reasonably expect. For years the courts have struggled to define this concept of "standard of care," but generally a medical professional's conduct is judged in comparison with that of similarly trained professionals in Canada. If the physician in question is a specialist, the standard of care is higher than that required of a general practitioner and is evaluated in comparison with other physicians practicing the same specialty. Likewise, if the defendant in the case is a hospital, its administrative procedures and standard of care will be compared to those of other hospitals.

Injury and cause

Establishing the third element—that the patient has been injured—may not be difficult if the results of the alleged malpractice are readily apparent. For example, if a patient is rendered blind, disfigured, or paralyzed, the injury is obvious.

More difficult to prove is the fourth element, that the injury is directly related to the physician's failure to provide appropriate treatment. Suppose that Theresa claims she developed an infection because her surgeon left a sponge in her stomach after an operation. Theresa must prove specifically that the presence of the sponge, and not some other cause, was the source of her infection. Without expert testimony or other medical evidence that proves this causal connection, Theresa will not be able to win her case. See EXPERT WITNESS.

FILING A LAWSUIT

If you think that you are the victim of medical malpractice, first consult a lawyer who specializes in medical malpractice cases. He can tell you if he thinks you have a potential claim. He will also consult medical experts to help determine the merits of your case. When you meet the lawyer, take along medical records, bills, any notes you have made, and any other documents that relate to your care or injury.

Lawyers often accept medical malpractice cases on contingency—that is, they receive a percentage of any money awarded to the plaintiff. See also CONTINGENT FEE.

If the lawyer agrees to file a lawsuit against your physician, both he and the physician's lawyer will conduct discovery procedures to learn as much as possible about the case. You may be questioned extensively by the physician's lawyer about the circumstances surrounding the alleged malpractice and other aspects of your health and personal life. A pretrial hearing may be held in which both sides present their cases before a judge. This is somewhat like a rehearsal for trial and is used to encourage both parties to reach an out-of-court settlement. If you cannot reach an agreement, your case will proceed to trial. See also DISCOVERY; LAWSUIT.

TIME TO FILE

Each province has a statute of limitations that designates the time within which you should file a medical malpractice claim. The purpose of the statute is to ensure that a claim is made while information relevant to the case is still available. The deadline may be from one to seven years from the time the treatment was given or from the time the patient knew (or should have known) of the alleged malpractice. In the case of a minor, the statute of limitations may not begin until the minor turns 18.

DAMAGES

Damages in a medical malpractice suit may be awarded for medical expenses, pain and suffering, lost wages, and other costs related to the malpractice. Additional, or "punitive," damages may be awarded if the physician was intentionally reckless or incompetent. See DAMAGES.

In 1978, the Supreme Court ruled in three cases that set the tone for damage awards involving malpractice suits. The Court concluded that the patient-victim was entitled to complete compensation for financial losses such as loss of salary and future care costs, but limited the amount she should receive for nonpecuniary costs, such as pain and suffering, to $100,000. Adjusted for inflation, this amount would be approximately $250,000 in 1994.

This ceiling on nonpecuniary costs contrasts with practice in some U.S. states, where awards for pain and suffering often reach into the millions of dollars. Although such awards may enrich the particular patient, they raise the costs of malpractice insurance and may cause doctors to refuse to undertake high-risk operations or avoid certain patients.

As has occurred in other accident cases, structured settlements, or payments over a period of time may be awarded in malpractice cases. The Supreme Court of Canada has noted that a lump-sum award "is subject to inflation, is subject to fluctuation in investment, income from it is subject to tax, after judgment new needs of the plaintiff arise and present needs are extinguished. . . . The difficulties are greatest where there is a continuing need for intensive and long-term care and a long-term loss of earning capacity."

REAL LIFE, REAL LAW

The Case of the Surgeon's Surety

While performing an abortion on a British Columbia woman, a doctor took out part of the placenta but left the fetus. Suspecting she was still pregnant, the woman consulted her family physician who referred her back to the doctor.who performed the abortion. However, he insisted he had performed a complete abortion, and so he did not order a pregnancy test.

In due time a baby girl was born. Unfortunately, the birth was premature and the child suffered various serious medical problems, including brain damage and abnormal physical features. The strain of the unwanted pregnancy and the extra care required for the little girl caused marital problems for the parents, who eventually separated.

When the child was seven years old, she and her mother sued the doctor who performed the surgery for damages, alleging he was negligent in performing an abortion.The British Columbia Supreme Court found the doctor negligent during the attempted abortion as well as in follow-up care. It ruled that he breached his duty of care to the mother and to the little girl, since it was foreseeable that a negligently performed abortion could cause damage to the fetus.

The judge noted that finding the doctor owed a duty of care to the fetus did not confer legal "personhood" on the fetus (the Supreme Court having already ruled that a fetus is not a person). He pointed out that if the abortion had been successful, the girl would of course not be present to sue and would have no rights. Her rights only arose once she was born. She was not suing for "wrongful life," since she was not claiming that she would have been better off dead, but sued for damages caused her by the doctor's negligence.

The court awarded the young girl $395,000 for lost future income and $160,000 for pain and suffering. Her mother was awarded $200,000 for future wage loss, $75,000 for physical pain and emotional distress, and $53,000 for past care of her daughter. Awards for future care, taxes, and a management fee for managing the money received were deferred to a later time.

CHECKING A MALPRACTICE RECORD

Medical malpractice suits are relatively few in Canada. About 1,000 of the Canadian Medical Protective Association's (CMPA's) 55,000 members have court cases pending at any one time. You can ask the CMPA if a medical practitioner has been sued for malpractice, or you can check at the county courthouse for any lawsuits filed against the physician. Sometimes, however, the CMPA will not release this information to the public and your county courthouse will not list actions filed in another district.

Should you discover that your doctor or other health-care provider has a record of malpractice cases, ask him about them. Many doctors, particularly high-risk practitioners, such as obstetricians, have had at least one lawsuit filed against them. However, a repeated history of such lawsuits could indicate that the doctor has in fact been negligent.

SHARED RESPONSIBILITY

Patients as well as doctors have a duty to act reasonably. It is not reasonable to think a doctor will always cure an illness, but you have a right to expect him to do his best to bring about a cure, taking into account his training, his experience, the available equipment, and his degree of skill in comparison with similar physicians.

To succeed in a malpractice suit, you must prove that your doctor was negligent. A mere error of judgment, when there is more than one valid alternative, will rarely lead to the doctor's condemnation. And you must have fulfilled your end of the patient-doctor partnership.

A patient must be honest and frank with the doctor when questioned about a problem. In some cases, you should disclose information that you feel may be important, even if the doctor made no inquiries on the matter. For example, you should disclose an immoderate use of alcohol or drugs, as this may affect your prescribed medication.

You must follow the doctor's advice and not experiment with medication or otherwise deviate from the doctor's instructions. If told not to eat for 12 hours before an operation, do not sneak a large breakfast just before your surgery. The food may interfere with the operation and with your blood and glucose tests. Similarly, if told to avoid certain exercises or movements for a period of time, and you ignore the advice, your doctor is not responsible if your injury worsens or healing is delayed.

It may also be up to you to seek another opinion if your family doctor's advice does not get results. If your doctor says your symptoms seem to indicate a flu, consult her again if the "flu" persists, or ask her to refer you to a specialist.

MEDICAL RECORDS

Medical records—whether kept by the family physician or by a hospital or other health-care facility—provide an account of a patient's care and treatment. For the family physician, a particular patient's medical records represent that patient's medical history. Such records in a hospital let doctors and other health-care professionals know what problems a person has had and what medications were prescribed previously.

All provinces and territories have guidelines on what hospital records must contain and minimum standards for maintaining these records. The latter are set by the Canadian Council on Hospital Accreditation (CCHA). Ontario's Public Hospital Legislation, for example, requires that a medical history, physical examination, and provisional diagnosis be completed and recorded within 72 hours of a patient's admission to hospital. Also, all treatment orders must be in writing and signed by the physician.

Most provinces specify how long hospitals must keep a medical record after a patient's discharge. This ranges from 10 years in British Columbia to two years (for microfilmed records) in Ontario. Newfoundland and Nova Scotia have no time limits.

RIGHT TO PRIVACY

Even though the Supreme Court of Canada ruled in 1928 that a patient's medical records are to be kept confidential, absolute adherence to this rule may be impossible today. The nature of modern medicine is such that many people now treat a patient, and anyone with a legitimate reason for consulting a patient's file may do so.

There are other instances, too, where the right to confidentiality may be sidestepped. A Toronto man accused of first-degree murder was unable to prevent police from obtaining his psychiatric records from British Columbia and Saskatchewan hospitals. Some provincial laws also require health professionals to inform public health authorities when a patient has certain venereal diseases, tuberculosis, polio, and AIDS. And in some provinces, physicians must tell automobile licensing authorities if it would be dangerous for a particular patient to drive a motor vehicle.

Generally speaking, however, your medical records are confidential, and unwarranted disclosure of information they contain would make a hospital, doctor, or nurse liable to a fine or even imprisonment.

ACCESS TO MEDICAL RECORDS

Although medical records belong to the hospital and not the patient, in most cases access-to-information laws give patients the right to copies of their records. The patient must make a written request for the copies or give his lawyer a signed authorization to seek their release.

Access rights are more limited in the case of psychiatric records. Both the Ontario Mental Health Act and the Quebec Mental Patient's Protection Act discourage patient access in such cases. The situation is delicate in that a patient may be harmed by learning the contents of his file, or distressed by finding out who placed him in the psychiatric institution. In the end, an administrative tribunal or the courts may have to resolve matters when a patient persists in requesting records that an institution does not wish to release.

MEDICARE

If there is one social policy of which Canadians are most proud, it is the Canadian Health Care Insurance Plan, commonly known as Medicare. Prior to its introduction, patients had to pay their own medical costs. As a result, many people neglected their health. Thousands of others suffered catastrophic financial problems when illness struck the family.

To offset the hardship, some doctors donated their services free or accepted modest gifts from grateful but poor patients. One such physician was Dr. Norman Bethune, who practiced for most of his professional career at the Sacré-Cœur and Royal Victoria hospitals in Montreal. During the 1930s, Dr. Bethune often spoke out on the need for a national medicare system, but his pleas were largely ignored and his ideas often rejected as being Communist or otherwise farfetched.

In time Canadians came to see the wisdom of a system of national health care insurance. The first provincial public hospital scheme was introduced in Saskatchewan in 1947. By 1961, all 10 provinces and both territories were delivering health-care services in accordance with the federal Hospital Insurance and Diagnosis Services Act. However, it was not until the federal Medical Care Act was passed in 1968 that Dr. Bethune's dream of a nationwide hospital and medical care insurance plan became real.

Medicare, which is jointly funded by the federal and provincial governments, now operates under the Canada Health Act 1984. Although there are minor variations in coverage from one province to another, all provinces must adhere to certain guidelines.

FEDERAL GUIDELINES

Some 50 percent of Medicare's costs are borne by the federal government. For a provincial health plan to receive federal funding it must meet the following criteria:

◇ The plan must be operated by a public authority on a nonprofit basis;

◇ The plan must be comprehensive in that it must insure most health services provided by hospitals and medical practitioners. If these are not available in the province, then arrangements must be made for a patient to be treated elsewhere at public expense;

◇ All residents must be entitled to this care under uniform terms and conditions. This would not cover tourists or people with, say, student visas, as they are not residents. But these people are eligible for emergency treatment and treatment under private medical insurance;

◇ Residents are covered if they are temporarily absent from their province or if they move to another province;

◇ All residents must have reasonable access to the services offered and should not be deterred by special charges or other impediments. This provision would apply to "user fees," currently the subject of much heated discussion.

ELIGIBILITY

As stated above, any legal resident is entitled to Medicare coverage. This is true even if you become ill outside your own province, or even in another country. You are covered up to the amount that would be paid had you received the medical treatment in Canada. Since hospital and medical costs are extremely high in some countries, including the United States, your provincial payments would most likely cover only part of your bill. Therefore, you would be wise to carry supplementary medical insurance when vacationing or traveling abroad.

INSURED SERVICES

Each province is required to set out a tariff of authorized payments to cover the cost of treatment received from hospitals or medical practitioners. Again, what services are covered may vary from one province to another. Some provinces even cover the costs of ambulance services, chiropractors, physiotherapists, and in some cases, orthodontist and optometric services, and cosmetic surgery.

In Quebec, even cosmetic surgery for varicose veins is not covered unless such surgery is necessary because of a medical problem. However, Quebec pays for braces, prostheses, and hearing aids for the handicapped, aids for which Ontario residents must pay 25 percent of the costs, and which are only free to Alberta residents under 18 or over 65 years of age. Alberta, however, provides free wheelchairs to the chronically ill. Seniors in British Columbia pay 75 percent of their out-of-hospital drug costs, and people under 65 years of age must pay the first $325 in prescription costs.

In Newfoundland, the government pays the pharmacists' fee and the first $4 for each prescription. Quebec pays for dental checkups and certain other dental expenses for children up to 15 years of age, costs covered neither by British Columbia nor Ontario.

Despite the variations, all provinces provide certain basic services more or less comparable to the following offered by Ontario. (In 1989 Ontario did away with the premiums paid by residents to the Ontario Hospital Insurance Plan—OHIP. These premiums are now paid out of income tax which automatically makes an OHIP deduction.) In Ontario, Medicare now covers:

◇ Physicians' services in the home, office, hospital or institution;

◇ Services of specialists certified by the Royal College of Physicians and Surgeons of Canada;

◇ Diagnosis and treatment of illness and injury;

◇ Treatment of fractures and dislocations;

◇ Surgery;

◇ Anesthetics;

◇ X rays for diagnosis or treatment;

◇ Prenatal and postnatal obstetrical care;

◇ Laboratory services in most cases;

◇ Necessary nursing services when done in hospital;

◇ Standard ward accommodation;

◇ Drugs prescribed by a physician;

◇ Use of operating and delivery rooms, including surgical supplies.

EXTRA BILLING AND OPTING OUT

Extra billing—charging more for a medical service than the payment authorized by the provincial tariff—has been a subject of great controversy. The Canada Health Act provides that federal Medicare subsidies—about half the total cost of health care—can be denied to provinces that permit physicians to bill extra.

British Columbia and Quebec doctors are barred from extra billing unless they opt out of the government plan and conduct a purely private practice. Doctors in Alberta, New Brunswick, Newfoundland, Nova Scotia, and Prince Edward Island are allowed to bill over and above the Medicare payments they receive. Manitoba and Ontario allow doctors to "opt out" and still receive a part of their Medicare fees. (In 1986, Ontario passed the Health Care Accessibility Act, which prohibited doctors, dentists, and optometrists who did not opt out from the provincial plans from extra billing, and made them subject to a possible $10,000 fine.)

Despite the opportunity to opt out of a provincial health scheme, less than 10 percent of Canadian doctors have done so.

OTHER HEALTH-CARE INSURANCE

Even though Medicare grants every resident basic medical coverage, not all health-care costs are covered. It may be wise to take out supplemental insurance for those services and treatments not covered by the various provincial plans, especially when traveling. A stay in a U.S. hospital could easily cost about $2,000 a day, which is more than any provincial plan will cover. Quebec, for example, will pay no more than $480 a day for out-of-province treatment, British Columbia will pay only $75, and Saskatchewan, only $100.

Private insurance is also useful to upgrade hospital accommodations from public to semiprivate accommodation, or to pay for dental care, nursing home care, prescription drugs, and even salary insurance in case of illness or injury.

MENTAL HEALTH LAWS

Most hospital patients have the right to refuse treatment, to discharge themselves even against their doctors' advice, and to consult their medical files. A person suffering from a mental disorder and whose behavior causes harm to him or others, or is likely to do so, does not enjoy those rights in the same manner.

For example, the British Columbia Health Act, typical of legislation in all provinces, provides that a person can be detained for psychiatric assessment to determine whether he requires medical treatment and "care, supervision and control in a mental health facility for his own protection, or for the protection of others."

A person's mental state is usually assessed by two psychiatrists. If they find the patient

to be a danger to himself or others, they could order his involuntary confinement and treatment. The assessment may be made on request by a family member, or of police officers who come across someone behaving erratically, or a physician who meets the person in an emergency ward, for example.

The Criminal Code allows for involuntary detention in the case of an accused charged with a serious offense, who is unfit to stand trial "on account of a mental disorder." The court would reach this decision on the basis of medical and psychiatric evidence. An accused's fitness to stand trial must be reviewed every two years. Similarly, a person found not guilty of a crime for reason of a mental disorder may likewise be ordered detained in a psychiatric institution until his mental health improves.

In 1991, the Supreme Court of Canada declared lieutenant governor's warrants unconstitutional. Such warrants permitted the courts to detain anyone found not guilty because of insanity indefinitely or, as the Criminal Code states, "until the pleasure of the lieutenant governor of the province is known."

People who voluntarily seek treatment in a mental health facility are normally allowed to refuse treatment or discharge themselves. Nevertheless, such a person can be committed for treatment if two psychiatrists feel the patient would be a danger to himself or society.

Commitals as a result of psychiatric assessment may be

reviewed by a provincial administrative tribunal or, in the case of Nova Scotia and British Columbia, by the courts. If requested, tribunal decisions may also be reviewed by the courts.

PATIENTS' RIGHTS

For the most part, mental patients have the same rights and privileges as any other citizen, and any abridgment of such rights must be justified on medical or security grounds. If the institution cannot justify its actions, this infringement of basic rights would most probably violate either the Charter of Rights and Freedoms or one of the corresponding provincial charters.

The charter's guarantees on the security of the person and the right not to be arbitrarily detained often clash with mental health laws permitting involuntary treatment and detention of people with serious mental disorders.

In 1991, for example, the Ontario Court of Appeal set aside a review board's order that a patient be treated with certain neuroleptic (tranquilizing) drugs against both his wishes and those of his substitute decision-maker. The court felt the order clearly infringed the patient's right to security of the person. But even though a British Columbia woman, held against her will in a psychiatric institution and forcibly injected with medication, successfully sued for false imprisonment, this area of law remains unclear, and may have to be treated on a case-by-case basis.

In most provinces, patients in involuntary detention (also known as "close treatment") are entitled to be informed of their rights. Mental patients in Quebec must be given a written list of their rights and remedies. In Nova Scotia, patients' rights must be posted for patients to read.

Alberta prohibits the opening, examining, or withholding of patients' incoming and outgoing mail.

MINIMUM WAGE LAWS

The Canada Labour Code and the Fair Wages and Hours of Labour Act govern work conditions and salaries of federal government and Crown corporation employees. Apart from professional employees and, in some provinces, management personnel, domestic workers, and students in job-training programs, all other workers are covered by provincial employment standards laws. These regulate hours of work, overtime pay, maternity leave, sick leave, public holidays, severance pay, meal periods, vacation, and redress for discrimination on the job.

Most provinces have two minimum wage rates—one for regular salaried employees, and a lower one for people who receive tips as part of their work. In Ontario, for example, the minimum hourly wage (as of Jan. 1, 1994) is $6.70 for general workers, $6.25 for students under 18, and $5.80 for those working where alcohol is served. Quebec's minimum rate (set Oct. 1, 1993) is $5.85 for general workers and $5.13 for hotel and restaurant workers. Tips received by an employee may not be calculated as part of the minimum wage payable by the employer.

If you have been paid less than the law requires, or if your employer has made illegal deductions—fees for uniform use or cleaning, for example— or exploited you in any way, get in touch with your province's labor standards commission. It may intervene on your behalf to recover all monies due to you; its services are free. An employer who purposely contravenes the law is subject to penalties.

See also EMPLOYEE RIGHTS.

MISSING CHILDREN

Because many cases of missing or runaway children are solved before the police are notified, and because often no report is made of children who run away from abusive homes, exact figures on the frequency of such instances do not exist. Nonetheless, the problem of missing children is a real one in Canada. Children who have run away, and wish to talk to someone sympathetic to their plight, should call the "Kids Help Phone"—1-800-668-6868. This important national service is sponsored by the Canadian Children's Foundation.

INTERFERENCE WITH CHILD CUSTODY

The most typical child abduction is undertaken by parents during a custody battle. There have also been cases of grandparents disappearing with their grandchildren.

It is a criminal offense to abduct your own child if to do so contravenes a court custody order. You may be charged under the Criminal Code with kidnapping. It is no defense to say that the child gave his consent or went along voluntarily.

Alberta's Extra-Provincial Enforcement of Custody Orders Act is typical of legislation in all provinces and territories. Such laws permit each province to enforce a custody order as if it were rendered by the courts where the child is found. As well, a custody order made in divorce proceedings is valid throughout Canada and will be enforced by any superior court judge in any province.

Custody orders are also enforced by most Commonwealth countries and by many American states, which have reciprocal agreements with most Canadian provinces. And, of course, Canada, as well as the United States and most European countries, is a signatory to the Hague Convention (1980), which put in place international procedures for returning abducted children. Unfortunately, this convention has not been signed by many African and most Muslim countries, from which it may be difficult to recover abducted children.

The cost of legal proceedings in the foreign country bound by the Hague Convention is not charged to the parent who applies to have an abducted child returned. The applicant may have to pay the abducted child's airfare home, however.

Even where there is no custody order, it is a criminal offense to abduct your children, or to deny your spouse access to them. Parents should never resort to abduction to "get even" with a former spouse. Being used as a tool to harm a parent is very damaging to children, who too often find themselves the subject of bitter dispute between two people whom they love equally.

For information on what to do if your spouse abducts your child, see "Steps to Take" on this page.

RUNAWAY CHILDREN

Because a runaway is simply defined as a minor child who is away from his home for at least one night without parental permission, it is possible that many cases of runaway children are not reported. Fortunately, the majority of runaways—nearly 75 percent—return home within a week. Those who do not return, however, can face danger and great hardship.

LEGAL STATUS

When a runaway child is located, she may be referred to the youth court system. Being a runaway is a "status" offense—a condition rather than a delinquent act. Status offenders may be taken under the jurisdiction of youth court and placed in a temporary shelter, foster care, a group home, or even a detention center.

Most runaways leave home because of abuse, poor family

communication, or a family crisis. Before returning a child to such a home, social workers with the youth court will try to help family members deal with the problems that caused the child to run away. They will interview parents and siblings and may recommend family counseling to help get the family back together. However, if they suspect that a child has been abused at home, social workers are obliged to make other living arrangements for her until the matter is resolved.

ABDUCTIONS BY STRANGERS

The abduction of a child by a stranger, although rare, strikes fear in parents everywhere. To help find a kidnapped child, parents must cooperate with the police, although they may also act on their own to distribute information through the media or hire private investigators.

Occasionally a newborn is abducted from the hospital. If the kidnapping is due to poor hospital security, the parents can file a lawsuit against the hospital and may recover money damages for their loss and mental anguish. Similarly, if a child is abducted from a school yard or day-care center, the parents may be able to sue the institution for failing to take steps to safeguard their child.

STEPS TO TAKE

If your child runs away or is abducted, you should immediately do the following:

1. Report your child's disappearance to the police. Give them a photo and detailed

description of the child and ask that it be entered in the RCMP's computer. Ask the police to issue a province-wide missing-person bulletin right away. If your child has run away, some police departments might wait, since they know that most runaways come home in a day or two.

2. Describe the abductor, if you can, and tell where he might take your child.

3. If your child has not returned or been found after 48 hours, double-check with the police. If they have not yet notified the RCMP, call the nearest RCMP office yourself.

4. If your child has been abducted by a custodial parent, have a lawyer start court proceedings immediately to transfer custody to you.

5. If your child is found with his parent in another province, send a certified copy of your custody decree to the Family Court in the town or county where they reside. Ask the local court to enforce the decree and return your child.

6. If your child has been abducted to a country that is a signatory of the Hague Convention on the Civil Aspects of International Child Abduction, contact the Legal Advisory Division of the Department of Foreign Affairs and International Trade in Ottawa. Each province also has a central authority for dealing with international abductions. Contact your provincial attorney general's office. See USEFUL ADDRESSES at back of book.

7. If your child is returned from an abducting parent, consult a lawyer about getting an order limiting future contact between the child and his other parent. A family court may suspend or terminate visitation, or allow it only under supervision.

See TEMPORARY RESTRAINING ORDER.

MISTRIAL

A trial that ends before a verdict has been returned by the jury or a judge is called a mistrial. The decision to declare a mistrial is made by the presiding judge, who may do so even before all the evidence has been presented. In other cases, the jury hears all the evidence but fails to reach a decision.

When there is a mistrial, whoever brought the case (the plaintiff in a civil case, the prosecutor in a criminal matter) must decide whether to take the case to court again. A mistrial has no legal effect; it is as if no trial took place.

HUNG JURIES

In criminal cases, jurors must reach a unanimous decision. Jurors in a civil case may also be required to reach a verdict that is unanimous or nearly so—for example, five out of six votes. (Jury trials in civil cases are increasingly rare.)

If all the members of a jury cannot agree, they will notify the presiding judge. The judge may then remind the jury of the importance of reaching a verdict, due to the time, effort, and expense involved in trying the case. If the jurors remain deadlocked, the judge will be forced to declare a mistrial and the jury will be discharged.

OTHER GROUNDS

A judge may also declare a mistrial if there is a serious error in the trial proceedings that cannot be corrected; or if, during the trial, he or one of the jurors realizes that he is related to one of the key witnesses, or that he may have an interest in the outcome.

Lawyers may ask for a mistrial because of biased behavior by the judge, jury tampering, the sudden death or severe illness of the judge or one of the lawyers, or a natural calamity, such as a flood, that interrupts the trial.

In 1993, a murder trial was halted because the judge, the Hon. Henry Steinberg of the Superior Court of Quebec, was appointed to the Appeal Court. The witnesses refused to testify at a new trial, so the accused was released. Tragically, he later murdered another person—an 11-year-old girl. This time he was tried and received a life sentence.

See also JURY DUTY; JURY TAMPERING.

MITIGATING CIRCUM-STANCES

Events or facts that can reduce the level of blame for a person's act, but that are not enough to excuse it, are known as mitigating circumstances.

Suppose that when Jeff was having a tooth extracted, the procedure went awry and Jeff spent six weeks in hospital fighting a life-threatening infec-tion. When he recovered, he complained to the provincial board of dentistry.

Although Jeff's dentist did not dispute that the procedure had been mishandled, he claimed that personal problems at the time—including his mother's death and the serious illness of his daughter—had impaired his professional skills. He said he had undergone psychological counseling to help him overcome these problems and pointed out that Jeff's complaint was the only one brought against him in more than 20 years of practice.

By introducing this information, Jeff's dentist was able to reduce the severity of the punishment that the board of dentistry imposed upon him, and instead of being suspended from practice, he was merely reprimanded.

Mitigating circumstances are not enough to exonerate a defendant in court, but they may convince a judge to reduce his punishment to smaller money damages, a reduced fine, or a shorter prison sentence.

See also HEAT OF PASSION.

MOBILE HOME

With the cost of a traditionally constructed house averaging from about $80,000 in the East to some $250,000 in the West, some Canadians choose instead to buy less-expensive mobile homes (sometimes referred to as manufactured homes). Although mobile homes have come a long way since the original 14-foot-wide trailer modcls, thcrc arc still some disadvantages to buying one.

Unlike a traditional house, a mobile home generally depreciates in value over time. Because mobile homes tend to suffer significant damage from fire and high winds, insurance rates are generally quite high. Interest rates on loans to buy mobile homes are usually higher, too—in fact, loans for mobile homes generally resemble automobile loans rather than standard mortgages.

BUYING YOUR HOME

Provisions of provincial consumer protection laws and sale of goods acts offer the purchaser of a mobile home protection from certain abuses. Nevertheless, if you decide to buy a previously owned mobile home, have it inspected first. See HOME BUYING AND SELLING. If you purchase a new mobile home, get these documents:

◇ A certificate from the manufacturer declaring that the home conforms to Canadian Standards Association norms for mobile homes.

◇ The manufacturer's written warranty on the home.

◇ A bill of sale and copies of any manufacturer's warranties for plumbing, heating, and air-conditioning fixtures.

◇ A title (which is much like the title to an automobile).

◇ Copies of all documents regarding your loan.

FINDING A HOMESITE

When you buy a mobile home, you will probably put it either on your own lot or on a lot in a mobile-home community. Before installing the home on

a lot of your own, check local zoning laws; some areas prohibit mobile homes. Your costs will include fees for constructing a pad or foundation, having utilities installed, and putting in a septic tank or a connection to community sewer lines.

In a mobile-home community, you will pay a monthly fee for the lot and perhaps for maintaining common areas, charges for connecting utilities, and the cost of installing a skirt around the base of your home. You may also be prohibited from owning pets, holding garage sales, or receiving visitors for more than a few days.

MONEY MARKET ACCOUNT

A money market account is a type of mutual fund that invests in highly liquid assets, such as short-term corporate bonds, bank certificates of deposit, and Treasury bills and notes. You can write cheques on a money market account, although some funds require that cheques be above a certain dollar amount (such as $500) or that you write no more than a specified number per month.

At one time, only stockbrokers and investment companies offered these accounts, but today they are available from most banks and trust companies. Because of their minimum balance requirements and limitations on withdrawals, bank money market accounts usually pay higher interest rates than savings accounts in the same institution. By and large, money markets make a good short-term investment.

Although there is no legal minimum deposit, banks and brokerage houses normally require an initial deposit of $1,000 or more. Then, if you keep a minimum balance, you will probably not have to pay a monthly fee or service charge. Many banks now also give their money market account customers an automated teller machine (ATM) card to facilitate deposits and withdrawals.

Because certain money market funds amortize their earnings, the net asset value of the investment is not reflected on a daily basis. Consequently, some money market funds may appear to be as stable and safe as a regular savings account, when in reality they are subject to changes in interest rates. Recent guidelines from the Investment Funds Institute of Canada state that money market funds promotional materials must indicate that these funds have fluctuating yields and do not guarantee a fixed net asset value. Money market accounts are not protected by the Canada Deposit Insurance Corporation.

See also BANK ACCOUNT; CHEQUE; MUTUAL FUND.

MORTGAGE

A mortgage is a loan agreement by which your home serves as the security for the money you borrowed to buy it. Because very few families have the financial resources to pay cash for a home, nearly everyone who wishes to buy a house is obliged to seek a mortgage, and the sale of a home is usually dependent on the buyer's receiving this financing.

A home buyer can obtain a mortgage from a friend, a family member, or even the seller of the house, but most often the lender is a bank, trust company, *caisse populaire*, or credit union. Because there are a bewildering number of home-financing options available, you should take the time to shop around.

All mortgages, however, work in essentially the same way. The mortgage holder agrees to make regular payments for a specified time. For the first several years, these payments cover interest and a very small amount of principal; only gradually does the amount of principal repaid begin to increase. A mortgage holder may, of course, make additional payments to reduce the principal and shorten the life of a mortgage. (If you decide to do this, make sure your lender permits prepayments without charging a penalty fee.) If a homeowner cannot meet his mortgage payments, the lender can take possession of the property by foreclosure.

There are two basic types of mortgages. With a conventional mortgage, available from banks and trust companies, buyers may borrow up to 75 percent of the home's purchase price, or value, whichever is less. This necessitates at least a 25 percent down payment. The second type is the insured or high-ratio mortgage, which allows the buyer to borrow up to 90 percent of the value or purchase price of the home, with a down payment of as low as 10 percent. Since this type of mortgage provides additional protection to lenders, it contains insurance-related clauses not found in conventional mortgage contracts.

One Canada Mortgage and Housing Corporation (CMHC) program currently allows first-time homeowners to obtain a mortgage with only a 5 percent down payment.

In Quebec, mortgages are called hypothecs, and mortgage deeds must be drawn up and registered by notaries. Hypothecs, although not identical to mortgages, operate in much the same way. See also CANADA MORTGAGE AND HOUSING CORPORATION; FORECLOSURE; HOME BUYING AND SELLING.

FIXED-RATE MORTGAGES

The traditional fixed-rate mortgage is still a popular option for many home buyers. Although the initial interest rate is usually higher than for other mortgages, you have the security of knowing that it will not fluctuate over the life of the loan. Fixed-rate loans are offered for a variety of time periods, most commonly 1- to 5-year terms. The shorter the term, the larger the monthly payments, but you will save many thousands of dollars in interest charges with a shorter term—and you will own your home sooner.

A fixed-rate loan is a good choice if you are planning to stay in your home for more than a few years because it provides you with stable payments and protection against the possibility of rising interest rates. But interest rates can also decline, as occurred in the early 1990s. If they fall far enough, you may wish to refinance your mortgage.

VARIABLE-RATE AND CONVERTIBLE MORTGAGES

The constantly changing Bank of Canada interest rate is the basis for the variable- or floating-rate mortgage. It usually begins with a lower interest rate than a fixed-rate loan, and in some case the interest can increase by no more than a stated amount (6 or 8 percent) above the initial rate.

For example, a variable-rate mortgage that starts out at 7 percent may be "capped" at 14 percent—you will never pay more than 14 percent interest. Your payments can be adjusted every year to reflect interest-rate changes (although usually the interest rate can go up no more than one time per year). Ask your lender to explain how new payments are calculated. Your lawyer or real estate broker may be able to give you the name of a company that will double-check the calculations for a small fee.

If you have a variable-rate mortgage and interest rates go

ABC's

OF APPLYING FOR A MORTGAGE

Applying for a home mortgage requires more than simply filling out a form and giving authorization for a credit report check. To complete a mortgage application, you will need the following items, many of which the lender will help you obtain.

■ A current appraisal of the property, made by a certified appraiser.

■ A credit report from a reputable credit-reporting firm.

■ Verification of bank accounts and investments.

■ Verification of employment and your annual salary.

■ If you are self-employed: signed financial statements, statements of income and expenses, and federal tax returns for the past two years.

■ Approval of any government or private mortgage insurer.

■ The sales contract.

■ The preliminary title report or title insurance commitment.

■ If you are buying a condominium or a cooperative apartment, copies of any financial statements of the condo or co-op association.

---

up significantly, try to refinance your loan and obtain a long-term fixed-rate mortgage.

Many lenders now offer convertible mortgages, which combine the benefits of a variable-rate mortgage (a low initial rate for the buyer and adjustability for the lender) with the option to convert to a fixed-rate loan in the future. The chief benefit of a convertible loan is that the conversion usually costs a flat fee of several hundred dollars and involves very little paperwork. By contrast, refinancing expenses may come to 4 to 6 percent of the borrowed amount, and the volume of paperwork involved is typically the same as it was for the original financing.

PORTABLE MORTGAGES

Portable mortgages are a very flexible option, in that they allow the borrower to transfer her mortgage to her new home, or to the purchaser of her old home if the lending institution approves. This is advantageous if the interest rate on the mortgage is lower than the current rate, and also eliminates the need to requalify for a new mortgage.

CONDOMINIUM MORTGAGE

A condominium mortgage differs from a regular mortgage in a number of ways:

◇ Your agreement with the lender specifies that you will abide by all condo bylaws. Noncompliance with a bylaw would therefore be a default under the terms of the mortgage;

◇ Usually the lender, not the condo owner, has the right to vote in the condominium corporation;

◇ The lender usually reserves the right to pay for common area costs if the owner defaults. These costs are then added to the principal owed under the mortgage and charged to the borrower with interest.

BUYDOWNS

A popular mortgage option, especially for buyers of newly constructed homes, is the so-called buydown. With a buydown, you receive a fixed-rate loan, but the first and second years of the loan carry an interest rate one or two percentage points lower than the institution's current fixed rate, while from the third year onward you are charged a slightly higher rate. As an incentive to buyers, home builders often make arrangements with lenders to provide this kind of loan. The lower interest rate (and consequent lower monthly payments) during the initial years makes it easier for a home buyer to qualify for a loan. A buydown can also be a good choice if you expect your income to grow significantly within a few years.

BIWEEKLY MORTGAGES

With a biweekly mortgage, you finance your home over a 15- or 30-year period, but instead of making 12 payments each year, you make 26 payments, one every two weeks. These payments are equal to one-half a standard monthly payment; so you actually make an extra monthly payment each year.

A biweekly mortgage can save you thousands of dollars in interest charges over the life of your mortgage, because by making the extra payments you can sharply reduce the length of the loan. In the case of a 30-year loan, the length would be reduced by nearly a third. Depending on the interest rate on your loan, you could save up to $80,000 or more in interest on a $100,000 mortgage.

A biweekly mortgage is attractive, but you can accomplish the same purpose with a traditional monthly mortgage by making an extra payment each year or by making an additional payment of principal to reduce the length of your loan. Either way, you are not locked into a series of higher payments at times when you might not be able to afford them.

Beware of companies that offer to help you shorten your mortgage if you make biweekly payments to them, which they then forward to your lender. Most of these companies capitalize on consumer confusion by making the process seem more complicated than it is, and they almost always charge a fee for doing something that you can easily do yourself.

DOWN PAYMENTS

If you purchase a home with money obtained from a conventional mortgage, you will most likely have to make a down payment of at least 25 percent of the home's total price. For many families, that kind of money is hard to come by.

Fortunately, there are public and private mortgage payment insurance plans which may be of help. You may be able to insure your mortgage through the Canada Mortgage and Housing Corporation (CMHC), for example. Alternatively, mortgage payment insurance is available from private companies that cover loans which CMHC does not. With such insurance, a lender may accept a down payment of as little as 5 percent. There may be other programs available through provincial and local governments. A mortgage loan officer at a bank, trust company or mortgage company can give you more information.

Many young home buyers rely on the generosity of their parents to give them some or all of the down payment for a home. If you opt for this, the mortgage lender will probably ask your parents to sign an affidavit that the amount they gave you is in fact a gift and not a loan. A loan would affect your total debt and you might not qualify for the mortgage.

OTHER COSTS

Apart from your down payment, there are a fair number of other costs related to getting a mortgage and purchasing a house. These are called transaction, settlement, and closing costs, and they can add up to thousands of dollars. They include fees for the mortgage application, credit report, property appraisal, inspections, title search, and a survey of the house and land. There are also lawyers' fees and provincial transfer taxes.

QUALIFYING FOR A MORTGAGE

In order to qualify for a mortgage, your monthly payments—which include the mortgage payment, property taxes, and home insurance—cannot exceed about 30 percent of your gross monthly income. The mortgage lender will also examine your credit history for any record of missed payments or excessive debt.

A mortgage application may be rejected because the lender thinks your property is worth less than the price you are paying or because you are asking to borrow more than you can repay. If your mortgage application has been turned down, you have the right to know the reason. If an inaccurate credit report or other mistake is to blame, you can correct it and then ask the lender to reconsider your application. If your credit rating is the reason, you can look for a lender who will assume the risk by charging you a higher interest rate.

REVERSE MORTGAGE

A reverse mortgage is a loan that is intended to help homeowners, particularly the elderly, remain in their homes even as their incomes drop.

Suppose, for example, that Ruby owns her home outright, but has only a small monthly income from investments made by her late husband. Fearing that Ruby's income is not adequate to cover her living expenses, and knowing that she does not want to move, her neighbor Josephine suggests that she obtain a reverse mort-

gage from a local bank. With this type of mortgage, Ruby will receive either monthly payments or a line of credit to draw against as needed, and she never has to repay the loan. When she moves or dies, the mortgage is repaid through the sale of the home. It is also possible for either Ruby or her relatives to repay the bank and reclaim the home.

Reverse mortgages are not yet widely available in Canada. Only Ontario and British Columbia financial institutions offer this type of loan.

STEPS TO TAKE

Applying for a mortgage can be stressful and time-consuming. Here are ways to make the process a little easier:

1. Plan ahead. Before you apply for your mortgage, get a copy of your credit report and check it for any errors or information that could affect your ability to get a mortgage. See CREDIT BUREAU AND CREDIT RATING.

2. Before you begin house hunting, check with several lenders to learn how much they would be willing to lend you. Many banks, mortgage companies, and trust companies will "prequalify" borrowers. When you know how much you can borrow, you are in a better position to negotiate. You will also avoid the disappointment of choosing a home, then learning later you cannot afford to buy it.

3. Once you have made an application, keep tabs on its progress. In most instances you can expect several weeks to elapse before you find out

whether your loan has been approved. Meanwhile, do not call the mortgage lender or broker every day to find out what is happening.

4. Do not try to hide credit problems or make false statements about your income or work record. It is a crime to attempt to obtain a mortgage under false pretenses.

See also HOME EQUITY LOAN; REAL ESTATE AGENT AND BROKER.

MORTGAGE LIFE INSURANCE

Mortgage life insurance is not the same as mortgage payment insurance offered by Canada Mortgage and Housing Corporation (CMHC) to home buyers making a down payment of less than 25 percent of the purchase price. Mortgage life insurance works like this. If the borrower dies, the proceeds of the policy go to the lender to pay the remainder of the mortgage. Mortgage life insurance is similar to a term life insurance policy in that no cash value builds up. But although the face value of an ordinary term policy stays the same, the face value of an ordinary mortgage insurance policy declines as the total amount of the mortgage declines, even though the premiums do not.

Mortgage life insurance may be purchased either through the lending institution with which you have your mortgage, or from a life insurance company. Buying it from your bank or trust company may be simpler because you will not have to undergo a medical examination or extensive personal investigation. However, proceeds from policies issued through lending institutions may be used only to pay off the mortgage, whereas with life insurance companies the beneficiary of the policy may either pay off the mortgage or purchase additional investments.

If you do not have mortgage life insurance, make sure that your regular life insurance policy will cover the mortgage payments in the event of death. In families where both spouses work and help to pay the mortgage, each should have insurance so that survivors do not face the loss of their home.

MOTOR VEHICLE BUREAU

Your provincial motor vehicle bureau, or department of motor vehicles, is authorized by the provincial legislature to enforce regulations regarding the operation of private motorized vehicles on provincial roads. Generally, provinces require the following documents if you own or operate a motor vehicle:

◇ *A valid driver's license.* To obtain a driver's license, you must be the legally required age, meet minimum vision standards, and pass a written examination on the rules of the road and a test of driving skills. See also DRIVER'S LICENSE.

◇ *A valid certificate of registration for the vehicle you own.* To obtain this certificate, you must pay a fee, which often varies according to the value of the vehicle being registered. You may also have to prove that the vehicle has passed safety and pollution inspections.

◇ *Proof of liability insurance for your vehicle.* When you register your car, most provinces require you to sign an affidavit stating that you have at least the minimum amount of insurance required by law. Other provinces may not require such proof until you are actually involved in an accident or the police stop you for a traffic violation. If you get into an accident without insurance, you will have to pay for any damages out of your own pocket, and you can also be charged with an offense which may result in a fine and/or imprisonment.

See also AUTOMOBILE INSURANCE.

MOVING

Most Canadians move several times during their lifetime. Whether across town or across the country, moving can present problems with legal ramifications, including delays in pickups and deliveries, damage to property, and overcharging by movers.

Friends and co-workers may be able to recommend a reli-able mover. Before you sign a contract with any company, check its reputation with your local Better Business Bureau and your provincial consumer protection agency. Avoid a company with a history of consumer complaints.

Make sure the company you choose is licensed and insured. If your move is within the province, the movers should be licensed by the provincial transportation department. If you are moving out of the province, the mover should be certified by Transport Canada.

ESTIMATES

Get two or three written estimates for the move. A low initial estimate does not always turn out to be cheaper in the long run. Some moving companies will give a free, but artificially low, estimate and then charge more money later.

If you get an estimate and choose to move with a particular company, the actual cost of the move will be determined when your possessions are weighed and loaded into the truck. Some companies offer an estimate guaranteed to within 10 percent; others, a fixed price, also known as a binding estimate or quote.

THE CONTRACT

Make sure your contract with the mover (your bill of lading) contains the following information: the pickup and delivery dates; the total cost (including any extras, such as having the movers do the packing and unpacking and the cost of containers); an inventory of possessions being moved; and the amount of liability insurance. The bill of lading should also note any existing damage to furniture or other items and set out the terms of the mover's responsibility. It should state, for example, whether the mover will be responsible for storing your goods, or if the company will allow someone other than you to accept delivery if you are not at the destination. Be sure to keep the contract and take a copy with you when you move.

Under Transport Canada rules, movers may limit their responsibility for damage to your property to 60 cents per pound per article. Most provinces set similar limits. Therefore, if the mover drops your valuable, 80-pound, antique grandfather clock, you will only be entitled to $48 reimbursement. You can, however, buy additional insurance from the mover.

Recently, the Ontario Court of Appeal found a mover responsible for damages amounting to $54,000, even though the insurance contract limited the mover's liability to 10 cents a pound. The court's decision was based on the fact that the customer was not advised of the limitation clause before the contract was made.

Insurance rates vary depending on the company and the amount of the deductible. Ask the mover's agent for a quote.

MOVING DAY

If you are making a local move, you may be able to pay the moving company with a personal cheque, but interprovincial movers demand payment

ABC's

OF MOVING

Moving can be costly, time-consuming, and stressful. By following these tips, you can help reduce the difficulties you are otherwise likely to encounter.

■ Get at least three written estimates before selecting a moving company. Try to get a binding estimate to prevent the mover from adding charges before your belongings are unloaded.

■ Do not schedule your move for the day your lease expires or the day the buyer of your current home takes possession of it. Bad weather, auto breakdowns, or other unforeseen events could delay your move. Likewise, avoid moving into your home the same day the previous occupants are moving out.

■ Check your homeowners' insurance policy to see if it covers your possessions during the move. If not, talk to your insurance agent about buying coverage that may be less expensive than that offered by the mover.

■ When the driver picks up your items, carefully check his inventory sheets. All entries should be legible. If you disagree about the condition of an item, make a note on the inventory sheet about the difference of opinion.

■ Make sure the mover can reach you while your goods are in transit. You are entitled to know about any delays or problems, but if the mover cannot find you, your possessions could end up in storage at an additional cost.

■ If you do have a claim for damage, file it within one month of the day your goods were delivered. Keep complete records of any correspondence or telephone calls made concerning the problem. Transport Canada rules require the mover to acknowledge receipt of your claim within 30 days and either to deny or settle the claim within 60 days.

in cash or by certified cheque, traveler's cheques, or perhaps a credit card. And with an interprovincial move, you may have to pay the full amount before the movers will unload a single piece of furniture.

When moving day arrives, go over the bill of lading with the movers. You will also have to be ready for the movers at the new house, or pay added charges if they have to store

your furniture and boxes temporarily. As the movers unload, check each item off the inventory list on your bill of lading and note any obvious new damage. Do not sign a release until all damage has been noted by both you and the movers.

If you discover hidden damage after the movers have left—such as a television set that no longer works—you may not be compensated unless the movers packed the item. If they did, the company is generally responsible unless their contract states otherwise.

If you have a claim for damage, file it as soon as possible. The maximum time period for filing a claim should be indicated on your contract. In many instances it will be 30 days.

MOVING TO A NEW JOB

If you are moving because of a job transfer, your employer may cover most of the moving expenses as well as transportation, meals, and temporary-housing costs for you and your family. Your employee handbook or human resources department will tell you which costs the company will reimburse. You may have to negotiate with your employer for any extras you want, such as reimbursement for house-hunting trips or your real estate agent's commission.

If your employer does not pay all costs, or if you are moving to a new job, you may still be able to recover some of your expenses. Revenue Canada gives a tax deduction to some people who must move to a new job location and residence. If you qualify, nearly all your unreimbursed direct moving expenses may be deductible, even a percentage of the restaurant and hotel costs your family incurs during the move. You may also be able to deduct some indirect moving costs, such as the cost of canceling a lease or legal costs involved in purchasing a new residence. To qualify, you must meet the following requirements.

First, your move must be for the purposes of starting a job or business in the new location. Second, your new residence must be at least 40 kilometers closer to your new place of business or employment than was your former home.

You may also claim a tax deduction if you are moving in order to attend a university or other post-secondary educational institution, even if you will be studying outside Canada.

Moving expenses must be deducted in the year of the move, but may not exceed the claimant's earned income for that year. However, if the claimed amount does exceed your total earned income, any leftover amount may be deducted the following year. You will need income tax form T1-M in order to claim this deduction.

MURDER

The killing of one human being by another, under any circumstances, is a homicide.

Some homicides are non-culpable (not blameworthy) because they are either justifiable or excusable. A homicide will be justified if authorized by law, such as when a police officer kills an attacking criminal. Someone who kills in self-defense would be committing an excusable homicide.

Killing without such legal justification or excuse is known as culpable homicide. Depending on the circumstances, culpable homicide ranges from criminal negligence (the least serious offense) to first-degree

murder (the most serious). The traditional definition of murder is the killing of one human being by another with intent. See also HOMICIDE; MANSLAUGHTER; SELF-DEFENSE.

In determining whether a murder occurred, Canadian criminal law looks for the intention to kill, rather than malice. Intent is the element that distinguishes murder from manslaughter, for example. If the evidence proves beyond a reasonable doubt that the intent to kill existed, a murder conviction will follow unless there exists a valid legal reason (such as self-defense), and without any extenuating circumstances (such as extreme provocation). See also HEAT OF PASSION.

The legal notion of intent can be quite wide in the context of a murder. For example, suppose that Fred and Macka fight, and during the fight Macka beats Fred so badly that he dies. Although Macka may not have been attempting to cause Fred's death, if the evidence at his trial shows that he knew death was likely to result from his actions and he nevertheless acted with disregard for Fred's life, the law would find him guilty of murder.

MURDER IN THE FIRST DEGREE

The combined elements of planning and deliberation differentiate the degrees of murder: first degree and second degree. First-degree murder is premeditated—a planned and deliberate act. It is considered a heinous crime and punished with great severity.

The premeditation or deliberation necessary for murder in the first degree does not require that the killer mulled over his plan for a long time. It simply means that he intended to kill another person and that he had sufficient time to think about the act before committing it. In fact, a very brief time may elapse between premeditation (conceiving the thought or desire to kill a victim) and the actual time when the murderer puts his plan into action.

Suppose Walt decides he wants to kill Fred, and immediately draws a gun and does so. Many courts have held that there need not be any significant length of time between Walt forming his intent to kill Fred and carrying out that intent.

In the eyes of the law, the identity of certain victims is considered as seriously as the requirements of planning and deliberation. According to the Criminal Code, any murder that results in the death of a law enforcement official, such as a police officer or prison guard, in the course of his duties, is automatically classified as first-degree murder. Similar reasoning applies to murders carried out in conjunction with certain serious offenses. For example, a murder, whether premeditated or accidental, that occurs during a kidnapping will be considered first-degree murder.

Quite apart from the elements that distinguish them from each other, first- and second-degree murder also differ in terms of the sentences that may be handed down by the courts. The punishment for second-degree murder is life imprisonment with no parole for at least 10 years. In the case of first-degree murder, there is no possibility of parole for 25 years.

MURDER IN THE SECOND DEGREE

A killing committed impulsively, and without the element of provocation that would reduce the charge to manslaughter, is considered to be murder in the second degree. Second-degree murder is not premeditated but results from the murderer's extreme recklessness and a heartless indifference to human life. Someone who intentionally fires a rifle into the stands at a crowded baseball game without regard for the lives of those sitting there would be guilty of murder in the second degree.

DEFENDING A MURDER CHARGE

The defenses to a charge of either first- or second-degree murder include self-defense and the defense of another person. But if you kill a person to protect yourself or someone else from death or serious bodily harm, you may still be in trouble, as you may use only the force necessary for your protection. You could not plead self-defense if you used deadly force against someone who had given up his attack and was attempting to escape, or if you killed someone in "mutual combat" (a fight in which both people agreed to participate), or if you provoked the assault in the first place.

It is not a defense to a murder charge to claim that the victim consented to his own death or that the killing was necessary in order to relieve the victim's suffering.

Mental disorder, duress or compulsion by threats, and the defense of your property are additional defenses to a murder charge. A most unusual defense, non-insane automatism, was successfully invoked in 1992 before the Supreme Court of Canada in the case of *Regina* v. *Parks*. The accused in the case, while in a somnambulant state, drove a considerable distance to the home of his wife's parents. Once there, he stabbed and beat both of them, killing his mother-in-law. The accused was acquitted after expert witnessess testified that sleepwalkers often have no control over their behavior.

"Voluntary" states of mental disorder, such as those that accompany the deliberate use of drugs or alcohol, are not normally defenses to murder. However, the level of drunkenness may influence the court's finding on "planning and deliberation," thus bringing about a reduction from first- to second-degree murder.

Involuntary intoxication—if, for example, you go to a party and drink some punch that someone had surreptitiously spiked with a hallucinogen—can be a defense to a charge of murder. See also INSANITY PLEA.

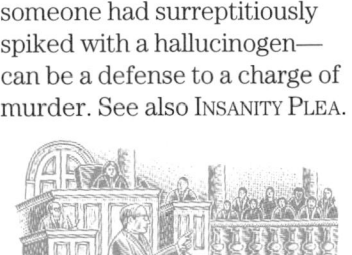

MUTUAL FUND

A mutual fund is a means by which you can invest money in a variety of different securities selected and managed by professional investment managers. The money you invest buys shares in the fund, which in turn invests your money in the stocks and bonds of other companies. A well-managed mutual fund will usually give you returns that exceed those you can get elsewhere (at a bank or trust company, for example). But not all funds are well managed. You could end up earning less interest and even losing some of your initial investment if the fund's managers make unwise investment decisions.

One kind of mutual fund that will provide higher rates than passbook savings accounts and yet is relatively safe is a money market fund offered by many banks and trust companies. See also MONEY MARKET ACCOUNT.

HOW MUTUAL FUNDS WORK

Different mutual funds have different objectives and therefore different risks. For example, some funds seek high returns by investing in the stocks of small companies, which they hope will grow quickly, but which also have a higher risk of failure. Other funds are designed to provide steady, reliable income by investing in stocks or bonds of large, stable companies or in government securities.

Mutual funds may be open-or closed-end. Most are opened funds—that is, they can issue shares in unlimited numbers as investors buy into the fund. Closed-end funds have a fixed number of shares.

Many sources of information are available to help you choose the mutual fund that best suits your investment needs. Financial magazines report regularly on the performance of the various mutual funds. In addition, your local library may subscribe to one of the detailed mutual fund reports, such as the *Mutual Fund Sourcebook* of the *Financial Times of Canada*.

COMMISSION AND FEES

Before you invest in any mutual fund, read its prospectus—the document that describes the fund's investment objectives, identifies its managers, and discloses its charges. A "no-load" mutual fund charges no up-front sales commission, whereas a "front-end load" fund gives the salesperson a commission of about 5 percent, which is deducted from your initial investment.

It is also a good idea to contact the company that manages the fund. Some companies will sell you shares directly without charging a commission.

Some mutual funds charge a redemption fee, or a "back-end load," when you sell your fund shares. Generally, the longer you hold the shares in the fund, the lower this fee will be. Be wary of a mutual fund that charges additional sales commissions when you reinvest the dividends you earned through the fund; such fees can greatly reduce your investment.

One of the least expensive ways to buy a load fund is through discount brokers, who usually charge a 2 percent "front-end" load. The disadvantage of this method is that discount brokers do not give investment advice, although they may provide you with research material explaining their products.

Every mutual fund charges a management fee to compensate its managers and to pay administrative costs. In most companies this fee is approximately 1 to 2 percent annually. You should be aware that there may also be costs associated with registration, cancellation, early redemption, and switching from one fund to another, as well as costs for advertising and marketing the fund which may be passed on to the consumer. Be sure to inquire about these fees when purchasing units in a fund.

TAX CONSIDERATIONS

When you sell your mutual fund shares and make a profit, you have realized capital gains, on which you must pay income taxes. But you can offset capital gains taxes by taking a tax deduction when you sell investments at a loss. You must also pay income taxes on dividends or interest you receive from your investment.

See also CAPITAL GAINS TAX; INCOME TAX.

N

FROM
NAME CHANGE
TO
NURSING HOME

NAME CHANGE

You might wish to change your surname for any number of reasons. You may have just married or divorced, converted to a new religion, or entered show business. In most provinces, the standard procedure for legally changing names is set out in the Change of Name Act, or Name Act, as the case may be. In general, you must have resided in the province for three months, although Ontario has a one-year residency requirement. The minimum age for a legal name change ranges from 16 years in Ontario to 19 years in British Columbia. In some provinces, name changes may be granted to people under the minimum age if they are married, divorced, or are parents with custody of children.

Applications to change a name are made to your provincial registrar-general or direc-tor of vital statistics, or to the courts (in Quebec). Alberta and British Columbia require you to publish a notice of your intention to change your name in order to inform those who may be affected by the change. As a rule, your application must show your present and future names, your address, and age, and must be accompanied by copies of birth certificates and previous change of name cer-tificates, as well as the pre-scribed fee. If you require the consent of another person—a divorced spouse, for example, if you are applying to change a child's surname—you will have to provide proof that the consent has been obtained.

Only changes made accord-ing to statutory procedure are recognized by law. Therefore, stage names, noms de plume, or names adopted by people who join religious orders have no legal status. Courts in the past have said that using such a name is not illegal unless the alias is being used to defraud or mislead.

If you change your name, you should notify your em-ployer, the post office, banks, and other financial and credit institutions, and any businesses with which you deal. Govern-ment agencies, such as Medicare, Old Age Security, Canada (Quebec) Pension Plan, and Revenue Canada should also be notified. Simply send a letter stating that you have changed your name and include a copy of your name change certificate. Tell them you would like all future trans-actions and correspondence delivered to your new name.

APPEAL PROCEDURE

It is possible that a request to change your name might be denied. However, each prov-ince has an appeal procedure. If you live in Ontario or Man-itoba, you ask the court to reverse the decision; in Alberta and British Columbia you appeal to the appropriate provincial minister.

In general you can choose any name you like, and you can choose any number of words in your name (a name is legally defined as the words that iden-tify a person). However, you cannot choose a name that is obscene or consists merely of numerals. If a judge or public official believes that you are changing your name in order to commit fraud or to confuse people, he may refuse to allow the change. Suppose you want-ed to take on the name of a well-known politician and then run for office using your new name. The judge might refuse to grant you the name change on the grounds that voters could be confused by the name.

MARRIAGE

Traditionally, a woman who married would voluntarily change her maiden name to that of her husband. However, many women now keep their maiden names or use a hyphen-ated form of both surnames.

In some provinces, a woman may adopt the surname of her spouse without any legal for-mality; in others, such as Ontario, the woman must fol-low the standard name-change procedures. The requirements in the case of divorce vary from province to province. In Alberta, Ontario, and Saskatchewan, for example, a divorced woman must follow the standard legal procedure if she wishes to revert to a previously used surname. In British Columbia, she may ask the divorce court to order that her name be changed. In Quebec, a woman keeps her original surname for all legal purposes. She may, however, use her husband's surname for social reasons.

CHILDREN

Children also have reasons for having their names changed. A child's name may be changed when he is adopted or when he wishes to take the name of a new stepparent. The requirements for changing a child's name depend on provincial law, but approval is always required from one or both parents. A child cannot petition for his own name change; it must be done by one of his parents or his legal guardian. If there is a dispute between the parents about the child's name, the courts consider the child's welfare as the primary factor when ruling on the name change.

Suppose Susan and Anthony divorce, and Susan receives custody of their 14-year-old son, Joshua. When Susan remarries, Joshua decides to change his name to that of his stepfather, with whom he has developed a close relationship. The father, Anthony, has seen very little of his son since the divorce, but when he is notified of Joshua's desire to change his name, he objects. Nevertheless, the court decides that Joshua

has a right to change his name, given his relationship with his father and stepfather.

However, if Susan wanted Joshua to change his name just so that he would have the same surname as her new husband, the court would probably not consider this a sufficient reason to approve the change, especially if Anthony opposed it. See also ADOPTION.

NARCOTIC CONTROL ACT

The Narcotic Control Act gives police wider powers to search for illegal drugs than those allowed under the Criminal Code. As a result, most drug offenses, such as possession for the purpose of trafficking, fall under the Narcotic Control Act. This act enables police to enter any building or structure, except a private residence, without a warrant, and to search any person found there.

Since a vehicle is not a private dwelling, police looking for drugs may search a boat or car without a warrant. If drugs are found in the vehicle, a court may order that it be forfeited to the state. However, the owner of such a vehicle has a right to appeal the seizure. His chances of winning the appeal are related to whether or not he is involved in the drug offense.

Before conducting a search without warrant, police must have reasonable grounds for the action. Mere suspicion or conjecture would probably not be sufficient.

The Narcotic Control Act also permits police to enter

a dwelling, with a warrant, or other places such as commercial buildings, without a warrant, without first announcing themselves. They may do so if they think evidence might be destroyed, or violence is likely if the inhabitants know of the raid. In a drug search, police are allowed to break open any door, window, lock, fastener, floor, wall, ceiling, plumbing fixture box, or any other thing in the pursuit of evidence.

The act also permits the courts to confiscate all monies or property obtained through illegal drug offenses, and to impose severe sentences, including a life sentence for importing and exporting drugs. See also FOOD AND DRUG LAWS.

NATIVE PEOPLE'S LAW CODE

The Kaianere'ko:wa, or The Law of the Great Peace, the oldest constitution of Canadian native peoples, is said to be the oldest constitution still in use in the world. Formed in about 1390, when the five founding nations, or tribes, of northeast North America unified into the Haudenosaunee (The People of the Long House), also known as the League of the Five Nations or Iroquois Confederation, its traditions are still recognized by six Iroquois tribes. (The Haudenosaunee became a six-nation confederacy when the Tuscarora joined the league early in the 18th century.)

The law was transmitted in the symbolic beaded designs on the wampum belts held by the female chiefs. Particular laws and paragraphs were encoded on beaded strings. Any of these laws or regulations could be recited from the designs by the sachems, or chiefs. Such recitations were common during Long House rituals or whenever the peoples' representatives met to settle a dispute serious enough to warrant calling them together. Such a confederacy was in effect a parliament.

The original five-nation treaty was forged by Dekanawida and the better-known Haiyentwatha (Hiawatha), his interpreter. The confederate council consisted of 50 rodiyaner (civil chiefs), divided into three brotherhoods: the older brothers (the Mohawk and Seneca); the younger brothers (the Cayuga and Oneida); and the fire-keepers (the Onondaga). Each brotherhood debated a question separately and reported to the fire-keepers, who referred the matter back and ordered a unanimous decision. If the two brotherhoods disagreed, the fire-keepers had the casting vote. If, however, the brotherhoods agreed but their decision was not in accord with that of the fire-keepers, the decision had to remain, for absolute unanimity among the Mohawk, Seneca, Cayuga, and Oneida was the law. The council could convene to consider any question put to it, acting in effect as a supreme court.

The 50 civil chiefs were nominated by certain noble women who carried a hereditary title in their family. The nominations were confirmed by popular councils made up of men and women, and then by the confederate council. As well as having the power to nominate rulers, the noble women could also depose them for incompetency in office.

There is no mention of private property in the native peoples' code of law. Since the concept of private ownership of land did not exist, land was considered to exist in itself and was part of the public domain—it did not confer special privileges on a particular individual. Territory held in common was inherent in the notion of a people or nation. (Even today, each time a council meeting is convened, homage is made to the land and respect expressed for its bounty.) By contrast, land in Europe was first considered a common national resource during the course of the English revolution of the mid-1600s, when Crown lands came to be regarded as common land.

The principle of federation in Canada's constitution has affinities with the territorial autonomy of the united nations of the Iroquois Confederation.

NECESSARIES

The items needed to maintain a minimum standard of living— such as food, clothing, and shelter—are known as necessaries. Depending on the circumstances, medical care and burial expenses can also be considered necessaries.

Parents, foster parents, and guardians have a legal duty to provide the necessaries of life for children under the age of 16. Spouses have the same duty toward each other. Similar obligations apply to those who have charge of people unable to care for themselves, such as the elderly, or physically or mentally ill adults.

Necessaries most often become a legal issue when a couple gets divorced or separated. Depending on the financial circumstances of those involved, the extent to which items are considered necessaries can vary. For example, a young working couple with no children might be considered to have few requirements, so that a modest apartment, hot dogs and beans in the refrigerator, and clothes from discount stores might meet the legal requirements for necessaries. At the other extreme, some courts have required a divorcing spouse to provide for the other spouse such things as maid service, luxury automobiles, and a lavish entertainment budget, if the couple have been accustomed to them while married.

When a couple gets divorced, child-support payments fulfill the noncustodial parent's obligation to provide necessaries for the minor children. Interestingly, several courts have held that paying for a child's university education falls within the category of the necessaries of life.

Until November 1993, a bankrupt person was required to pay debts for goods considered to be necessaries of life.

However, this stipulation was removed and a person discharged from bankruptcy is now free of all debts, except for fines, alimentary pension, or debts incurred through fraud.

See also CHILD SUPPORT; DIVORCE; GARNISHMENT.

NEGLIGENCE

If someone injures another person or his property by breaching his duty of care—by taking an unreasonable action or failing to take a reasonable one, for example—he is guilty of negligence. Although negligence is often difficult to determine, it is the decisive factor in most personal-injury and property-damage lawsuits.

NEGLIGENT BEHAVIOR

To win a lawsuit against someone for negligence, you must show that the person failed to meet the standard of care that a reasonably prudent person would have met under the same circumstances. This usually means that the negligent person was inattentive, careless, or thoughtless, and that his actions caused you injury or distress.

Negligent behavior is neither deliberate nor accidental. If Sam injures Elizabeth when he knocks her down while trying to steal her purse, he has willfully committed a criminal act, not a negligent one. Likewise, if Sam accidentally makes Elizabeth fall, his behavior would not necessarily be considered negligent unless he failed to act in a reasonably prudent manner. If he was

barreling along the sidewalk on roller skates and knocked Elizabeth down, Sam might be found negligent, since a reasonably careful adult would not roller-skate fast on the sidewalk. See RECKLESSNESS; TORT.

In some circumstances, you can be found negligent even if you did not participate directly in the incident that led to the charge of negligence. For instance, the owner of a car with faulty brakes can be found negligent if he lends his car to someone who then causes an automobile accident. See also ACCIDENTS; AUTOMOBILE ACCIDENTS; FAMILY-CAR DOCTRINE.

DETERMINING NEGLIGENCE

Suppose Richard and Carolyn decide to go out to dinner on a Friday night. They arrive at a restaurant named *Chez Pierre* and park in the restaurant's rear parking lot. The lot is dark and the pavement is in poor condition. As Richard gets out of the car in the dark, he stumbles over a crack in the asphalt, spraining his ankle and tearing his slacks. If Richard sues *Chez Pierre*, the restaurant's management could be found negligent for failing to provide proper lighting and repair the pavement, and Richard could

REAL LIFE, REAL LAW

The Case of the Alpine Accident

On Christmas Day 1970, Jack joined family members and friends for some downhill skiing at the Blue Mountain Resort. Skiing down a relatively straight run, with which he was unfamiliar, Jack veered to the left to avoid a group of skiers who had stopped to the right further down the hill. He was unaware that he was approaching a steep gully, and before he could react he flew off the gully's edge and crashed into the streambed below. Jack's right leg was seriously injured in the fall and he subsequently sued the Blue Mountain Resort for $20,000.

At the trial, the ski resort put forward the defense that the back of the lift ticket stated, albeit in small print, that the ticket holder assumed all risks of personal injury. Jack admitted he had not read the fine print.

The court rejected the ski resort's defense, stating that the ski lift disclaimer had little effect unless the notice was brought to the attention of the skier. Furthermore, the court held that the danger posed by the gully was not obvious and should have been marked. However, because Jack was new to the run and so should not have veered off the main track, the court found he was partly responsible for his misfortune. As a result, the Blue Mountain Resort was found to be only 75 percent to blame, and consequently was ordered to pay Jack the sum of $15,000.

probably recover monetary damages for his injured ankle.

After Richard picks himself up and limps into the restaurant, he finds they have to wait for a table, so he and Carolyn decide to have a drink at the bar. While they are enjoying their cocktails, another restaurant patron knocks over his beer glass, and a shard of glass cuts Carolyn's hand. In this case *Chez Pierre* probably would not be found guilty of negligence, since no restaurant employee failed to exercise reasonable care. But if the counter was slippery or the beer glass had a crack in it, the bartender (and the restaurant) might be considered at fault. Or the restaurant might be held responsible if the customer was obviously intoxicated when the bartender served him. Had the other patron in fact been negligent and Carolyn seriously injured, she could have sued him for monetary compensation for her injury.

After Richard and Carolyn are escorted to their table, they order spaghetti primavera as a first course. When their pasta arrives, Richard is dismayed to find a large dead insect in the sauce. In this situation the restaurant is negligent, since it has clearly failed to do what a reasonably careful restaurant would do—that is, serve insect-free food. Richard might be able to sue *Chez Pierre* for the distress he suffered when he found the insect.

Their meal having ended prematurely, Richard and Carolyn leave the restaurant, find their car, and drive out of the parking lot. Because they are discussing the evening's horrors, Richard is distracted and collides with the rear fender of the car ahead.

As a driver, Richard did not exercise reasonable care when he chatted with Carolyn while leaving the parking lot. As a consequence, his negligence caused damage to the other car, and Richard will probably have to cover the cost of repairing the damaged fender.

ASSIGNING BLAME

Sometimes a person who is accused of negligence argues that the victim's negligence was the cause of the injury and that the defendant is therefore not responsible.

In such a case, most relevant provincial legislation follows the rule of contributory negligence, by which a plaintiff's compensation is reduced by the degree to which his own negligence contributed to his injuries. Suppose Richard seeks $10,000 in damages from *Chez Pierre*. The jury decides he should have been more careful and that he was 40 percent responsible for his fall. They award him $6,000.

If the judge or jury cannot determine the extent to which each party is negligent, jurisprudence states that the plaintiff and defendant are equally responsible. See LAST CLEAR CHANCE RULE.

You may not be awarded damages for injuries if you have voluntarily assumed a certain risk, particularly if you participate in a hazardous activity. For example, when Natalie decides to go horseback riding in Alberta, she signs a consent form releasing the stable of any liability for injuries she might suffer. Natalie assumes a risk, and if her horse throws her, she will probably be unable to get any compensation from the stable.

However, even a person who assumes a risk by knowingly engaging in dangerous activities may still collect damages if her injuries result from another person's carelessness. In such cases, the court must decide whether or not the injury occurred in the ordinary course of the activity. Suppose a stable employee sets off firecrackers and frightens Natalie's horse. The horse throws her and she breaks her leg. Because Natalie could not have anticipated such an event, she would be entitled to compensation from the riding stable for her fractured limb. See also SPORTING EVENT.

NEGLIGENCE BY PROFESSIONALS

When you pay someone to perform a service in exchange for money, he has a particular duty to you. If you are injured as a result of a professional's negligence, you may be entitled to sue the person for malpractice. In general, courts try to determine whether the person acted according to accepted standards of professional behavior and competence.

Professionals subject to malpractice suits include people such as physicians, lawyers, dentists, pharmacists, architects, engineers, and accountants. See CONSENT FORM; LAWYER; MEDICAL MALPRACTICE.

Businesses have a duty to their customers and the public in a number of ways. A business that is open to the public, such as a store or hotel, has an obligation to maintain its property so that customers or passersby are not hurt.

In addition, employers are responsible for the negligent actions of their employees. See ACCIDENTS IN PUBLIC PLACES; LIABILITY.

The various levels of government are responsible for maintaining the areas under their jurisdiction in reasonably safe condition. For instance, the transport department is usually required to repair potholes on highways; local government offices are required to keep their floors safely uncluttered; and Parks Canada is responsible for maintaining safe conditions in national parks. If you are injured in an accident involving government property, you may, in some cases, be able to bring a lawsuit against the government. See ACCIDENTS ON GOVERNMENT PROPERTY; ACCIDENTS ON PUBLIC TRANSPORTATION; ROADS AND HIGHWAYS.

NEGLIGENCE AND MINORS

Because children may not be able to recognize the dangers inherent in a situation, they are often not held responsible for their negligent acts. This is especially true of very young children. Furthermore, the law holds that adults have a greater responsibility to children than to other adults.

Suppose two-year-old Andrew is playing with a cigarette lighter in his neighbor's garage.

If he sets the garage on fire, he will not be responsible for the cost of rebuilding it. On the contrary, the garage might be considered an attractive nuisance (dangerous property that attracts children), and if Andrew were hurt, the owner might be held responsible. See ATTRACTIVE NUISANCE.

However, the negligent acts of older children are treated differently. For example, if Andrew had been 16 years old, a court might require him to pay for the damage he caused. Because court judgments remain enforceable for many years, Andrew could end up paying for his negligence once he gained sufficient assets or began working.

In some instances parents can be held liable for their children's negligent acts. See PARENTAL LIABILITY LAWS; TORT.

INSURANCE

You can buy liability insurance to protect you if you are sued for negligent behavior. Homeowners' liability insurance protects you from a lawsuit by anyone who is injured on your property; likewise, automobile liability insurance covers you if you are responsible for a car accident.

Businesses should also carry liability insurance to protect them against claims made by customers or employees. See AUTOMOBILE INSURANCE; CASUALTY INSURANCE; HOME BUSINESS; HOMEOWNERS' INSURANCE; LAWSUIT; LIABILITY INSURANCE.

CRIMINAL NEGLIGENCE

In some cases a person's behavior can be so negligent that

it becomes criminal. For example, a parent who fails to provide adequate care for his children may be charged with failing to provide the necessaries of life or abandoning a child. If the child dies as a result of such abuse, the parent can be prosecuted for criminal negligence causing death.

Or suppose that Stewart is involved in an automobile accident that results in the death of several people. Witnesses to the accident testify that they saw Stewart speeding and weaving his car from lane to lane on the highway without signaling. It is apparent that Stewart's reckless driving caused the accident and subsequent deaths. Stewart is convicted of criminal negligence causing death and sentenced to several years' imprisonment.

NEGOTIABLE INSTRUMENT

Cheques, drafts, traveler's cheques, bills of exchange, postal notes, money orders, postal orders, promissory notes, and other similar written documents are instruments, which can be transferred (negotiated) from one person to another by endorsement (signing one's name on the back). Such endorsement allows the instrument holder to acquire the money indicated in the document. The originator of the document, or any subsequent endorser (except those who make restrictive endorsements), must pay the bearer the full amount of the document, with interest if applicable. (To avoid being liable to subsequent holders, a holder of a negotiable instrument may write "without recourse" on the back immediately after his signature. This is known as a restrictive endorsement.)

Because of electronic banking, negotiable instruments are becoming increasingly rare.

NEIGHBOR

Although there is no strict legal definition of who your neighbors are, anyone who lives near you, or who owns or lives on property adjoining yours, is considered your neighbor. Neighbors have a responsibility to each other that must be balanced with their own enjoyment and use of their property. For instance, you cannot store dilapidated cars, garbage, or other unsightly material that lowers the value of the surrounding property. Any construction work or landscaping you do to your property should not adversely affect a neighbor's property or her enjoyment of it. Neighbors must also respect the boundary lines separating them. And although light and a view are pleasant, you are not automatically entitled to them. If your neighbor wants to build a new extension that will block your view of the sea, there may be nothing you can do to prevent him. See also BOUNDARY LINE; FENCE BUILDING; NUISANCE; QUIET ENJOYMENT; TRESPASS.

Problems between neighbors can vary from the relatively insignificant (such as a neighbor who lets his fallen leaves blow into your yard) to the extremely serious (someone who sells drugs from the house next door). Many of the disputes that occur between neighbors involve local ordinances or regulations. In a planned community, condominium complex, or an area with a homeowners' association, your deed or lease may have additional prohibitions. It is a good idea to find out early what restrictions there are. Some of the following are likely to apply:

◇ In addition to being a public nuisance, making excessive noise is often against the law. See NOISE.

◇ In many places, homeowners are expected to keep their property in good repair so that it does not constitute either a danger or an eyesore to others in the neighborhood.

◇ Many communities forbid homeowners to accumulate refuse that is hazardous or smelly, or that may attract vermin. In some cities, you can be fined for putting your garbage out at any time other than on collection day.

◇ Pets may be prohibited or, if they are permitted, you may be required to keep them enclosed or otherwise restrained. You may also be required to clean up after them. See also ANIMALS; DOG LAW; PETS.

◇ You may be required to keep your lawn and garden free of excessive growth. If your trees overhang public property, the local utility company or the municipality may require you to trim the branches or may do the trimming themselves.

◇ You may be responsible for keeping the sidewalk in front of your house in good repair and free of snow and ice. See also SIDEWALK.

STEPS TO TAKE TO RESOLVE DISPUTES

If you have a problem with a neighbor, try the steps below. Sometimes a simple solution can be found.

1. If you are not sure whether your neighbor is violating a city bylaw, consult your municipal clerk's office. Then, before doing anything else, talk to your neighbor. He may not know that he is breaking the law, and you may be able to work out a solution. Keep a record of your conversations or correspondence in case the matter ends up in court.

2. If this does not work, explain the problem to your landlord, tenants' or homeowners' association, or condominium board. Such organizations often help mediate disputes between neighbors.

3. If your neighbor is violating a zoning law or a bylaw, report the violation to the municipal government. It then becomes the city's responsibility to persuade your neighbor to correct the problem.

4. If you are seeking a small amount of money damages from your neighbor, file a suit in the small-claims court.

5. If none of these measures works, hire a lawyer.

6. If you believe your neighbor is carrying out criminal activity from her home, report the problem to your local police department.

See also SMALL-CLAIMS COURT; ZONING.

NO-FAULT INSURANCE

Under the traditional fault system, the driver who causes an auto accident and his insurance company must reimburse the other driver for such expenses as lost wages. No-fault automobile insurance on the other hand requires anyone who is involved in an accident to seek compensation for his injuries and sometimes for property damage from his own insurance company or from his provincial automobile accident plan. In Quebec, for example, all bodily injuries are paid for by the provincial automobile insurance board.

The no-fault system was established to ensure that accident victims were compensated for their injuries without delay. Suppose, for instance, that Marlene is driving to work, obeying all the traffic laws, when another driver swerves into her lane. The resulting collision leaves her with an $1,800 dental bill and costs her $800 in lost wages. The damage to her car is $4,000. Under a pure no-fault scheme, Marlene can ask her own insurance company to reimburse her these expenses, rather than waiting for the other driver's insurance company to decide upon her claim. However, she would not be able to receive any compensation for pain and suffering.

If an accident causes serious injury, no-fault laws may allow the injured person to sue the negligent driver for personal injury. This is the case in Ontario, for example.

Ask your insurance agent whether your no-fault insurance policy applies in all cases. If Marlene's accident occurs while she is in another province, for example, her coverage might be limited.

See also AUTOMOBILE INSURANCE.

NOISE

Noise that disturbs you and deprives you of the use or enjoyment of your own property, or that diminishes its value, is considered a private nuisance. You have the right to call the police to have such noise reduced or halted. Anyone who creates noise that exceeds specified legal limits can be found to have created a public nuisance and can be fined.

Many communities have laws that limit the amount of noise permitted in residential areas or around such facilities as hospitals or nursing homes. Not only is the level of noise regulated, but also the type of noise and the time of day when it occurs. For instance, letting your son's rock group practice in the garage may be acceptable at 4 p.m. on Saturday, but not at 2 a.m. on Friday. The law often specifies a decibel level that is considered acceptable, and the police may measure it with noise meters.

If you live in a city, you are likely to need a higher tolerance for noise than if you reside in a quiet suburban neighborhood. In every community, however, there are people and agencies charged with creating or enforcing legislation against excessive noise. Landlords, co-op, condominium, and rental boards, homeowners' and tenants' associations, and the municipal government may all impose penalties on violators of noise regulations.

Barking dogs, yowling cats, and other raucous pets often prompt complaints. If a dog barks continuously, the owners may be ordered to muzzle it or keep it indoors, and they may also be subject to fines. See also DOG LAW; PETS.

DEALING WITH NOISE

Suppose the peace and quiet of your suburban neighborhood has been diminished greatly in the past few weeks by a new neighbor's late-night tuba practice. Together with several of your neighbors, you have already asked him to restrict his playing to a more reasonable hour, but he refuses. You call the police and ask them to visit your neighbor and order him to stop. Nevertheless, the next night your neighbor plays his tuba again. The police will once more come if you call them, but this time they may issue your neighbor a summons to appear in court. There he can be fined and ordered to cease his musical annoyance.

If you plan to have a party, do construction work on your house, or otherwise create excessive noise for a limited time, tell your neighbors. If they are forewarned, they may be less likely to call the police or file a complaint against you. See also NUISANCE.

NO-KNOCK LAWS

Police procedure requires law enforcement officers to "knock and announce" their presence before entering a residence. Even if police have a search warrant, it is illegal for them to enter a dwelling without first identifying themselves as police officers and then giving the occupants time to open the door. Police may only break open a door or window if they are refused admittance. If knock-and-announce procedures are not followed, the officers' entry is considered unlawful, and any evidence seized in the home may not be admissible in court.

However, knocking and announcing are not necessary in some instances, such as when the building or residence is unoccupied, or when the announcement would allow a suspect to escape or destroy pertinent evidence. Such "no-knock" searches often take place in drug arrests, because it is relatively easy for a suspect to dispose of evidence if the police are required to knock and wait for admittance. See also SEARCH AND SEIZURE; SEARCH WARRANT.

NONCONFORM-ING USE

Nonconforming use is a legal exception to zoning laws, which dictate how particular areas of land can be used—typically for residential, agricul-tural, industrial, or commercial purposes. If you notice a small tailor shop operating in an area that is zoned for residential use, it may be that the shop was there before the residential zoning ordinance was passed and that it has obtained a non-conforming use.

A nonconforming use runs with the land. This means that the use is not a personal right but transfers with a change in ownership. Thus if the tailor sold his store to another tailor, the second tailor could con-tinue to operate the store.

A municipality has the right to cancel a nonconforming use if the owner substantially changes the existing use of the business (if the tailor shop becomes a video store, for instance), or if the building is damaged or destroyed (so that the tailor has to rebuild). See also VARIANCE; ZONING.

NONPROFIT CORPORATION

A nonprofit corporation does not distribute any of its income to shareholders but instead donates it for charitable or benevolent purposes. In most provinces, a nonprofit corpora-tion can be established and licensed for one of many rea-sons. It may be organized for public education; for agricul-tural, medical, or scientific, research; for civic or political purposes; or to serve the mem-bers of a profession or trade.

Revenue Canada grants some nonprofit organizations tax-exempt status. Donors to such organizations may claim tax deductions for their gifts. To achieve this status, a non-profit corporation must meet strict guidelines. Always ask about an organization's tax-exempt status before making a donation. You should also ask to see its financial statement, which will tell you how much of its income is used for such things as administrative expenses. See also CHARITABLE DONATIONS.

Setting up a nonprofit corpo-ration is similar to setting up a regular corporation. Govern-ment agencies monitor non-profit corporations and can take away their status for such abuses as using funds for pur-poses other than those stated in their corporate charter.

See also CORPORATION.

NOTARY PUBLIC

A notary public (sometimes simply called a notary) is some-one authorized by provincial law to administer oaths and attest to the authenticity of documents and signatures. Notaries public and commis-sioners of oaths perform similar tasks, although in some cases a document being sent from one province to another can be authenticated only by a notary public.

Most lawyers in the nine common-law provinces are notaries public. In Quebec, the only province not to practice common law, the legal profes-sion has two categories: lawyers and notaries. Quebec notaries draft and authenticate certain acts and contracts, but are not involved in disputes before the courts. All Quebec lawyers are automatically commissioners for oaths.

To become a notary public, you must be an adult and you are usually required to pass an examination. When you receive permission to practice in your town or within a certain area, you may be asked to post a bond to protect the public in case you fail to perform your duties. You can charge fees for your services at rates set by the province; however, apart from Quebec, notaries rarely make a living from their services.

A notary is not responsible for the accuracy of documents she notarizes; she merely verifies the identity of the person who presents them to her. Suppose Walter buys a car from a stranger. The seller signs the bill of sale before a notary public, who puts her seal on it—no questions asked. Later Walter learns that the signature on the ownership papers is a forgery. In fact, the car was stolen, and the police tell Walter that he must return the car to its original owner. Walter can sue the notary public because she should have required identification from the seller to prove that he was the person named on the title to the automobile.

NOTICE

In legal usage, a notice (*mise en demeure* in Quebec) is the warning given to someone to inform him of a legal proceeding in which he has an interest, such as a lawsuit for breach of contract or a divorce.

Actual notice occurs when you give information to the opposing party or when he is made aware that the information is available. For example, before taking your former husband to court in a child-custody dispute, you must notify him of the impending legal action so that he will have the opportunity to respond in his own defense. The notice may be hand-delivered, mailed, or published in a newspaper, depending on whether you know your ex-spouse's whereabouts.

Without actual notice, a person's constitutional guarantee of due process of law is violated. If, for instance, one party to a lawsuit does not appear in court to defend himself, a default judgment may be brought against him. However, if he can show that he did not receive notice of the court proceedings, the judgment may be invalidated. See also DEFAULT JUDGMENT; DUE PROCESS OF LAW.

Another type of legal notice, constructive notice, is the knowledge that you can reasonably be expected to have. If you are sued for climbing over a fence and trespassing upon someone's property, you cannot claim the charge should be dismissed because the owner failed to post a "No trespassing" sign. The court presumes that any reasonable person knows or should know that trespassing is illegal. In other words, you have had constructive notice that trespassing on the property is not allowed, even though there was no sign that specifically prohibited it.

In contract law, if one party breaches the terms of the con-

tract, no notice is usually necessary since each party should be aware of his obligations.

NUISANCE

Any activity or condition that is unreasonable or illegal, or inconveniences, offends, or annoys another person, may be called a nuisance. A nuisance is also an activity or condition that causes damage to property. And anything that interferes with another's peaceful enjoyment of his property, home, or life can also be a nuisance. For example, unreasonable noise, foul odors, and disorderly conduct are all nuisances. Certain dangerous conditions that are especially tempting to children are called attractive nuisances. See also ATTRACTIVE NUISANCE.

Nuisances are usually classified as either public or private, or a combination of both.

PUBLIC NUISANCES

A public nuisance is a recurring or continuous activity or condition that is deemed to be harmful to the health, morals, or peace of the community. The harm must be substantial, but it does not have to affect every person in the community. For instance, a garbage heap where flies and vermin breed and generate disease can be a public nuisance (as well as a violation of sanitation laws).

The classic example of a public nuisance is a "bawdy house" where illegal gambling, drinking, and prostitution occur. A current example is a "crack house," maintained for the illegal sale of drugs, which has a continuing deleterious effect on the community. Many public nuisances are also violations of the law and are punishable by fines. A person who is maintaining a public nuisance may also be prosecuted under the Criminal Code. See also DISORDERLY HOUSE.

PRIVATE NUISANCES

A private nuisance is one that interferes with another person's private rights to the use and enjoyment of his own property. Maintaining a private nuisance is not a crime, but someone who is affected by a private nuisance may sue to end the activity or to change the condition. For example, it is not illegal to put up elaborate Christmas light displays on your property and play Christmas carols, nor is this offensive or dangerous to the public at large. However, suppose that by Thanksgiving, Graham's neighbor William has decorated his house for Christmas with such a tremendous number of Christmas lights that the sky is illuminated and Graham's bedroom is brilliantly lit all night. In addition, William plays *The Twelve Days of Christmas* continuously over a loudspeaker. Cars from surrounding communities are starting to drive up and down Graham's street, admiring the lavish display. Graham has grounds to sue William to end this private nuisance, though he should first try to convince William to end it of his own accord. See also NEIGHBOR.

To sue someone for a private nuisance, you must show both that the person committing the nuisance intended to do it and that his behavior substantially interferes with your enjoyment of your property. The judge will also be asked to decide whether his behavior conforms to a standard of reasonableness. For instance, if you want to prevent the women who live next door from sunbathing in bikinis because you find it offensive, you will probably not win your case. Sunbathing with appropriate attire is reasonable behavior.

NURSING HOME

Advances in medical technology and an improved standard of living have resulted in an ever increasing elderly population. Canada's current 3 million seniors are estimated to number 7.5 million, or 22 percent of the population, by 2013.

Some 8 percent of older Canadians now live in nursing homes or similar institutions. At best, nursing homes are pleasant places run by competent, caring staff. At worst, they can be depressing, lonely institutions staffed by unqualified employees. So before entering a nursing home or committing a relative to one, thoroughly evaluate the home.

DETERMINING YOUR NEEDS

The term "nursing home" describes several kinds of facilities, some government run, others private businesses. What are known as nursing homes in Alberta, New Brunswick, New-foundland, Nova Scotia, and Prince Edward Island are called special-care homes in Saskatchewan, personal-care homes in Manitoba, and reception centers (*centres d'accueil*) in Quebec. The organization and regulation of these institutions also vary from province to province.

Levels of care vary considerably. Extended-care homes are a good choice if you need professional nursing care following hospitalization or an accident. Such facilities provide 24-hour nursing care, rehabilitative therapy, and diet supervision. A physician is on call and available for emergency care.

Intermediate-level nursing homes, or residential-care facilities, provide supportive care and nursing services for people who suffer from chronic conditions but do not require the level of professional care of an extended-care facility. Rather than having registered nurses on staff, these institutions may have nurses' aides, and physicians may not be on call.

Unlike Manitoba, where all types of institutions for the elderly are called personal-care homes, a personal-care home in British Columbia offers no nursing care but caters to residents who may require help with daily activities, such as bathing or dressing.

Often a physician will be the first to recommend a nursing home. But be aware that there are other options for care and housing of the elderly—home health-care and senior-citizen housing among them. If you are unsure whether to enter a nursing facility, ask a profes-

CHECKLIST

Nursing Home Residents' Rights

Provincial regulations require all licensed nursing homes to guarantee residents certain rights. These include your right:

■ To know your medical condition and participate in decisions about your medical treatment.

■ To manage your own financial affairs (unless a guardian is appointed).

■ To be informed of services available in the facility and any extra charges for them.

■ To have a safe, clean, comfortable environment.

■ To be free from physical, sexual, or mental abuse, including corporal punishment, isolation, or restraints.

■ To send and receive personal mail unopened.

■ To associate and communicate privately with others.

■ To participate in social and religious activities.

■ To receive advance notice if you are to be moved to another room or facility, or if you will be getting a new roommate.

◇ Are you ill or planning to undergo surgery that will disable you for a period of time?

◇ Are you making a permanent living arrangement, or do you merely need a place to stay during a convalescence?

◇ Do you have relatives and friends near the home who will be able to visit you?

◇ Do you live alone? If not, do you have a family member who depends on you for care?

◇ Can you cook for yourself at home and organize your own finances and other household affairs?

◇ Do you have financial resources that are sufficient to pay for a nursing home? Are you eligible for any financial assistance that would provide you with alternative care?

If someone is under your guardianship, such as an elderly parent, you have the authority to place her in a nursing home. It is a good idea, however, to discuss this option with your relative before she becomes incapable of making the decision herself. See also GUARDIAN AND WARD.

SELECTING A FACILITY

To find a nursing home, ask your public health authority for a list of the facilities in your area. For information on long-term care, ask your provincial agency on aging. Get recommendations from your doctor, the social services departments of local hospitals, friends, church groups, and seniors' associations.

Then visit several homes to get an idea of their services and general character. Make a checklist of important criteria, and compare the different homes to see which offers the best combination of services.

◇ Is the home equipped with a fire alarm system and a sprinkler system? Has it posted an evacuation plan in case of an emergency ?

◇ Is the facility homey? Are residents allowed to decorate their rooms and bring in personal belongings?

◇ Do the residents seem to enjoy their surroundings, and would they recommend the nursing home to others?

◇ Is the staff courteous and cheerful?

◇ Does the facility specialize in certain conditions or illnesses, such as Alzheimer's disease? Would you feel comfortable around other residents who are suffering from such a condition?

◇ Is there a schedule of daily activities in which you can choose to participate?

◇ Does the food look appetizing and nourishing? Are the kitchen and dining areas clean?

◇ Are you allowed to have a stove, refrigerator or extra heater in your room?

FINANCIAL CONSIDERATIONS

Living in a nursing home costs about $15,000 per year, which is usually payable in monthly installments. Ask the administrative staff which services are included in the basic fee and whether there are extra fees. Find out whether you must give the nursing home an initial deposit, and what procedure must be followed to get it back.

Almost all provinces provide

sional, such as a hospital social worker, about the level of care you may need. In determining the best level of care, consider the following:

insurance coverage, which subsidizes the cost of staying in a nursing home for certain individuals. Nursing home care is not part of the regular health insurance in the Maritimes, but financial assistance is granted to those in need. People residing in privately run institutions anywhere in Canada may not be eligible to receive any financial assistance.

Elderly people with no income apart from the Old Age Pension and the Guaranteed Income Supplement are ordinarily required to direct a significant portion of these payments toward the cost of staying in a facility. However, they are entitled to keep a small percentage for their personal use.

Your children cannot be forced to pay the expenses of your medical care unless they have agreed to do so—for example, by signing a contract with a nursing home.

RESIDENTS' RIGHTS

Nursing home licenses are issued by the provincial regulatory agency, usually the health department, to facilities that meet the minimum standards for construction, staffing, diet, and nursing procedures. Provincial legislation, such as Ontario's Nursing Home Act, sets standards for the treatment of residents, in some cases even establishing a bill of rights for their protection.

When you enter a nursing home, you sign a contract. If you are mentally competent, you should be able to leave the nursing home at any time. The home may reserve the right to remove a resident under certain specific circumstances (such as violent behavior).

NEGLECT AND ABUSE

Even with laws that prohibit abuse, residents of nursing homes are at times placed in restraints, medicated unnecessarily, or neglected to the point where they suffer from malnutrition, bedsores, and other illnesses. If you have a complaint about nutrition, sanitation, or the health or safety of a resident, notify the nursing home administrator at once.

Provincial laws may require licensed medical professionals to report suspected cases of abused nursing home patients. If you suspect abuse that has not been reported, contact the nursing home ombudsman at your province's agency for aging and department of health. If the accusations are warranted, the licensing agency can fine the home or take away its license. For cases of abuse that present an immediate threat to the patient's safety or well-being, or that involve theft of a patient's money, Old Age Security benefits, or personal property, call the local police. In extreme cases, if battery, abuse, or assault has taken place, criminal charges may be filed against the nursing home. If you feel that the nursing home has been negligent, you (or your guardian) can file a lawsuit against the home.

OATH AND AFFIRMATION

You could be asked to give an oath in a number of different situations. You may have to take an oath before you are admitted into a particular profession, such as medicine or law, or before you assume public office. You will be asked to give an oath or a solemn affirmation if you testify in court, or you may have to sign documents under oath or solemn affirmation.

When you give an oath you are swearing to tell the truth. Although the oath given for legal purposes has its root in religious traditions, you no longer have to place your hand on the Bible and swear to tell the truth. Section 14 of the Canada Evidence Act permits you to choose instead a solemn affirmation to tell "the truth, the whole truth and nothing but the truth." The Ontario Court of Appeal overturned the decision of a trial judge who refused the solemn affirmation of a Satanist. The appeal court ruled that, even though the Satanist could not swear on the Bible, he was still competent to testify by solemn affirmation.

The courts have also allowed people to give oaths according to their own religious traditions, rather than by swearing on the Bible. In a criminal trial arising from the 1990 Oka confrontation in Quebec between the Mohawks and the Quebec Provincial Police, members of the Mohawk tribe were allowed to give an oath according to their native rituals.

At one time, only sworn testimony was accepted by the courts, so only those who could take an oath to tell the truth by placing their hand on the Bible could testify in court. Young children were allowed to testify only in exceptional circumstances, for instance where there was corroborating evidence. Today, however, children are allowed to testify more often, and their testimony is often very important in cases such as child abuse.

You will often have to have certain legal documents signed and stamped by a commissioner of oaths. By doing so, you are swearing to the truth of the facts in the documents. If you cannot go to court to testify in a certain case, for instance, you may prepare a statement that you then sign and have sworn in by a commissioner of oaths. This affidavit can then be used in court, and would have more weight than an "unsworn" document, such as a signed letter.

Under the Criminal Code, anyone who knowingly tells a lie in oral testimony or in a sworn document, such as an affidavit, commits perjury.

See also PERJURY.

OBJECTION

In its most common legal sense, an objection is a motion made by one of the parties to a lawsuit or criminal prosecution, protesting that some testimony or ruling of the court is improper and should not be allowed. Questions by lawyers, testimony on the stand, or rulings of the court may all be cause for an objection. When a judge agrees with the objection being made, it is said to be sustained; an objection that is not accepted by the judge is said to be overruled.

An objection can serve as the basis for an appeal, provided it is made during the course of the trial. Suppose a witness testifies about something he heard another person say. An objection that the testimony is hearsay must be raised at once. Otherwise, the party injured by this testimony cannot later claim in an appeal that it should have been excluded.

See also EVIDENCE.

OBSCENITY

Defining obscenity in legal terms (in order to pass laws prohibiting it) is a challenge that has eluded lawmakers for decades. In its broadest sense, obscenity is any material that appeals to a prurient interest in sex, nudity, genitalia, or excretion and that has no socially redeeming literary, political, scientific, or artistic value when judged by an average person against community standards.

CORRUPTING PUBLIC MORALS

Section 163 of the Criminal Code is designed to protect the public from exposure to obscene materials. The section makes it an offense to "corrupt morals" by publishing, distributing, advertising, or selling obscene materials, pictures, and recordings. A person who makes or distributes publications which are too sexually explicit or which depict too much horror or violence—a video store owner who rents such videos, for instance— could be charged with violating the Criminal Code. Chances are, however, if you are simply watching obscene movies in your own home, even rented movies, you are not in violation of the code. In one case, where an obscene film was played at a stag party for friends and relatives of the bridegroom, the accused was acquitted. The court accepted that it was a "private" viewing.

In determining if a film is obscene, for instance, the courts will examine the producer's purpose in making the film, look at its artistic merit, then consider whether the general public would tolerate the material. If the court thinks that the majority of the public would be very offended by the material and would not watch it, then the material might be considered obscene.

Ruling on a video store owner charged with distributing obscene material, the Supreme Court of Canada has said the material's potential harm to society should also be considered in determining if an offense has been committed. Degrading, dehumanizing material, or material which encourages antisocial behavior, could also be considered obscene, the court said.

Many people charged under section 163 of the code argue that their freedom of expression, guaranteed by the Charter of Rights and Freedoms, has been violated. The courts have often agreed that this is true, but point out that the restriction on individual rights serves a purpose to society as a whole, which is more important than the individual's rights. In other words, your individual right to read and write what you choose is important, but protecting the public from the negative effects the material might have is more important.

See CENSORSHIP; CHARTER OF RIGHTS AND FREEDOMS.

OBSTRUCTION OF JUSTICE

The orderly resolution of disputes in our civil courts and the fair administration of justice in our criminal courts are of fundamental interest to everyone. Acts that undermine people's confidence in the justice system are therefore prohibited by a variety of provincial and federal laws. Anyone guilty of witness tampering or intimidation, giving false information such as a false name, fabricating evidence, hindering or impersonating a police officer, or even offering to compensate a victim, can be charged with obstructing justice.

YOUR PROTECTION AND DUTY AS A WITNESS

It is essential for people with information relevant to an issue before the court to present that information to the judge or jury. If you are or may be a witness, you should immediately report:

◇ Any effort to influence your testimony through bribes, threats, entreaties, or intimidation, including offers of money or threats of violence aimed at persuading you to commit perjury (lie under oath) at a court proceeding.

◇ Any request that you hide or destroy documents or other objects that are, or may become, evidence in a case.

◇ An attempt to convince you to fail to appear in court, to leave the court's jurisdiction, or to hide to avoid being served with a subpoena.

◇ Acts or threats of retaliation after you have given your testimony.

Anyone convicted of obstructing justice by paying or accepting bribes, or threatening people is liable to two years' imprisonment. The bribe does not have to be accepted, nor the threat carried out for a charge to be laid. A jailed man who wrote to his brother asking that he threaten a witness who was to testify against the imprisoned man was convicted, even though his brother never got the letter: prison authorities had intercepted it.

A Quebec lawyer was recently refused permission to appeal his conviction for obstructing justice to the Supreme Court of Canada. He had been convicted of trying to convince a client to make a statement that would get a gang leader off the hook for a bombing that claimed the lives of four people.

JUDGES AND JURORS

Judges and jurors are also protected from interference. It is an obstruction of justice to attempt to influence a juror by bribing or threatening him. Similarly, communications with judges will be scrutinized closely. Judges are allowed to solicit expert information or opinion regarding a case, provided such information is entered into the court record, and people involved in a case may ask to speak with the judge if they think they have some information that he requires. However, unsolicited communication that is off the record is not allowed. Accepting money or other favors from someone in return for using your personal influence with a judge is also an obstruction of justice.

POLICE

When a police officer is performing his official duties, it is illegal to try to prevent him from carrying them out. The following acts are all considered obstructions of justice and are punishable by law:

◇ Giving false information or concealing or withholding

information to help someone avoid detection or arrest.

◇ Using or threatening to use force against a police officer.

◇ Refusing to provide identification when an officer has reason to request it—if your car is involved in an accident, for example.

◇ Running away or hiding from a police officer. That means, for example, that you must stop your car when directed to do so.

You have the right to question an officer, but use moderate language. It is not illegal to criticize a police officer, but you are obstructing justice if your language hinders the officer in the performance of his duties—for example, if you incite an angry crowd of bystanders to interfere with him.

Similarly, you are allowed to observe the arrest of another person as long as your activities do not interfere with the police officer's ability to carry out his official duties.

OCCUPATIONAL HEALTH AND SAFETY LAWS

Up to the 1970s, work safety was governed by a multitude of laws dealing with particular industries—mining, construction, industrial establishments, logging, and so on. Some workplaces were covered by several laws, whereas other work situations were not covered by any legislation.

In 1972, Saskatchewan enacted the first Canadian occupational health and safety statute. Other provinces followed its lead—Alberta, Manitoba, New Brunswick, and Ontario (1976), Newfoundland (1978), and Quebec (1979). Today, every province and territory has laws guaranteeing the right to work in an environment that meets legal and safety requirements, the right to know of hazards in the workplace, the right to be free of employer reprisals, and the right to bargain for future protection that the law provides.

In the Northwest Territories, the relevant law is a general safety ordinance. The Workers' Compensation Board is responsible for implementing occupational health and safety in British Columbia, Prince Edward Island, and Yukon.

British Columbia, Manitoba, and Newfoundland have separate laws for the mining industry. Elsewhere mining is governed by occupational, health, and safety laws.

People who work for the federal government or in industries under federal jurisdiction are covered for the most part by the Canada Labour Code. In some industries—aeronautics, petroleum exploration and production, policing, public hospitals, railways and shipping, and highway transportation—because of their special nature, separate federal statutes apply.

COMMON ELEMENTS

Although names of occupational health and safety statutes may vary from one province to another, the laws generally have common elements.

◇ In most cases, they cover the three major sectors—mining, construction, and manufacturing.

◇ They are regulated by a government department or commission, usually run by the labor minister. In Manitoba, Ontario, and Quebec, the Occupational Health and Safety Commission (OHSC) is an independent agency. (Even self-employed persons are governed by OHS laws in Ontario.)

◇ Joint management-labor committees have to be established.

◇ Employees have the right to information that may affect them. In most cases, the OHSC inspectors' reports are available to employees.

◇ Standards governing accident prevention and exposure to environmental hazards are reviewed and updated.

◇ Workers have the right to refuse hazardous work without retribution from the employer.

ENFORCEMENT

Occupational health and safety inspections may be carried out on the inspectors' own initiative, or following a complaint. Usually, complaints to the OHSC are kept confidential. In some provinces, the worker has to ask for confidentiality; in Ontario and Quebec, confidentiality is the rule.

If you are going to make a complaint concerning work conditions in your place of employment, ask the OHSC inspector whether your name will be kept confidential. In some cases, the union representative will make the complaint for you.

An employer who disregards the recommendations and orders of an OHSC inspector is liable for fines and even criminal charges.

OCCUPIER'S LIABILITY

Occupiers of a premises, whether owners or tenants, have a duty to make sure that people who come onto their property will not be injured. You must take all the steps that any reasonable person would take to ensure that the property is safe. Otherwise, you could be responsible for the injury suffered by someone, or the damage caused to the property of another person, and have to compensate that person accordingly.

There is insurance for this kind of liability. As well, many homeowners' policies and tenants' policies allow a certain amount of coverage for personal liability.

RESPONSIBILITY VARIES

The measures that owners and tenants are expected to take to ensure a property is safe will vary according to individual circumstances. If, for instance, there is a pool on your property and you fail to fence it, you may not have acted irresponsibly if you have no neighbors for several miles. The same could not be said if you live in an area where there are a number of young children. In such surroundings, a reasonable person would put up a fence. If you fail to do so, you could be liable if a child is hurt in your pool area.

You are unlikely to be liable, for instance, if you own a hockey arena, and during a game a fan is hit in the face by a puck that flies into the stands. Stray pucks are an everyday risk in hockey games and people who attend such an event are assuming the risk that they may be hit by a puck. A person who enters a premises knowing there is a risk is said to have assumed the risk, so ordinarily the owner will not be responsible for any injuries if the risk materializes.

Should the occupier be liable if a trespasser is injured on the premises? By and large, the degree of care owed depends on the nature of the trespass—whether the trespasser was an adult or a child, a door-to-door salesperson or an intruder.

Ontario's Occupier's Liability Act makes a distinction between trespassers: those who trespass with the intent to commit a criminal act cannot recover damages for any injuries they suffer on the premises. Other trespassers may be able to recover compensation for their damages, but they might not be owed as high a standard of care as people who are not trespassing.

If somebody uses your land for recreational activities and you have not been paid for that use, the users are considered to have assumed all risks. Even if you had invited them, chances are you will not be held responsible for any injuries they suffer unless there are hidden dangers, such as debris-covered open pits, of which they were not warned.

On the other hand, if you charge a fee for the recreational activities, you must take reasonable steps to ensure your guests' safety. In certain businesses, such as hotels, an even higher standard of care would be expected.

These rules apply only to land use—structures, vacant lots, and private roads. You are also expected to take reasonable steps to ensure that buildings on your land are safe. If someone is hurt in one of your buildings, you could be liable, whether he has paid to be there or not. If people stop by to see your horses, and they are hurt when the barn collapses, you will not be able to say they had assumed any risks.

If there is a dangerous area on your property, post signs to this effect. Thus it should be clear that anyone who passes the signs is assuming the risk.

RECOURSE AGAINST TRESPASSERS

A trespasser is someone who does not have the right to be on your property, or who has not been authorized to be there. In Ontario, it is up to trespassers to show that they have the right, or the authorization, to be on the property.

People can trespass even when they have permission to be on a particular property. If, for instance, you give Patrick permission to hike on your land, which is clearly posted "No hunting," and Patrick spends the afternoon hunting, he is a trespasser. So are you, if you enter the "Employees Only" section of a restaurant. If you are in a bar and you are asked to leave, you must do so whether you think it fair or not. Otherwise, you could be charged with trespassing. Even in a movie theater, if you are asked to leave for making too much noise, you must do so even if you do not agree with the usher, and even if you have paid for a ticket.

As a tenant or owner, you have the right to post signs prohibiting trespassers and such activities as hunting and fishing. Certain people, such as land surveyors, meter readers, and health inspectors, are allowed on your property with or without your permission, so long as they are performing their duties.

If you have a trespasser on your land, you should avoid confrontation. You can call the police, or ask the person politely to leave. If you know the identity of the person, you can arrange to press charges after he has left. Trespassers can be fined, and you may be able to recover money for any damage they cause.

ODOMETER STATEMENT

Jovida was reading the classified ads one Saturday when an ad caught her eye. A 1965 Mustang was being offered for sale at a very reasonable price, especially since the ad claimed that the car had been driven only 20,000 miles. She arranged to see the car at a used-car lot. The car did look in reasonably good shape, but even so she still found it hard to believe the low mileage.

Jovida was wise to be skeptical, since many used cars are sold with false odometer readings. To combat this problem, consumer protection laws now require sellers of used cars to provide purchasers with an odometer statement, which must say whether the mileage is accurate, whether it has been altered, or that the seller is unsure about its accuracy.

Anyone who deliberately misrepresents the mileage on an odometer can be held liable to the buyer for the loss in the car's value due to the higher actual mileage. For example, if Jovida is told that a car has only 20,000 miles on it, but a mechanic finds that it has been driven over 100,000 miles, she can recover the resulting difference in the value of the car. Of course it is also a crime to disconnect or tamper with an odometer with the intention of defrauding a buyer.

If you are selling a used car, complete an odometer statement. In many provinces this is printed on the back of the title to your automobile.

STEPS TO TAKE

If you are buying a used car, take these steps to check the odometer reading.

1. Examine the brake and gas pedals for wear. The more worn they are, the higher the mileage is likely to be.

2. Check the odometer. The numbers on altered odometers are often misaligned.

3. Have the car inspected by a qualified mechanic who is not associated in any way with the seller. He can tell you if the wear and tear on the engine

and transmission are consistent with the mileage shown.

4. If you believe that you have bought a car with an illegally altered odometer, report it to your consumer affairs bureau or to the police. If you bought the car from a dealer, also file a complaint with the board that licenses dealers in your province.

OFFICIAL LANGUAGES ACT

The Official Languages Act came into force in September 1988, replacing an act of the same name passed in 1969. A federal statute, it declares that French and English are Canada's official languages, and it obliges all federal institutions to provide services in English and French at the individual's choice.

PUBLIC SERVICES

The act provides that all federal institutions and departments—the post office, Transport Canada, Health Canada, and so on—be bilingual. All employees need not be bilingual, but any member of the public may demand to be served in either English or French. If you write to any federal institution in the official language of your choice, you have a right to be answered in that language. Any member of the public also has the right to services in either English or French where there is a "significant demand" for services in that language or where the "nature of the office" is such that it would be reasonable for services to be available in both languages.

All federal legislation, proclamations, and treaties must be drawn up in both languages. Government notices must be published in both English and French publications. If there are only one-language publications in the area, the notices must appear in bilingual form.

IN THE COURTS

An accused in a criminal trial anywhere in Canada has the right to plead his case in either English or French. In addition, the accused and his lawyer have the right to use either English or French at the preliminary hearing, trial, and for all oral and written pleas. Witnesses, too, may testify in either official language.

At a preliminary hearing, the accused has the right to have the prosecutor and presiding justice speak his language. Any record of proceedings at the preliminary hearing or at trial, and all court judgments, must be made available in the language of the accused.

Where the federal government is party to a civil case before a federal court, the other party has the right to choose the language in which the trial will be held. All summonses and subpoenas from federal courts must be bilingual. So, too, must be final decisions from these courts if the proceedings were conducted even partly in one of the official languages.

Anyone testifying before a federal court may use either English or French, and any party to proceedings before such a court may request simultaneous translation.

Except for the Supreme Court of Canada, the presiding judge in every federal court must be able to understand both English and French without the help of an interpreter.

COMPLAINTS

If the act is violated—for example, if a federal regulation is published in only one language—any person or group may complain to the Commissioner of Official Languages. If the complaint is not resolved within six months, and it is clear that the commissioner has had sufficient time to investigate and find a remedy, the complainant may bring the matter before the Federal Court (Trial Division), which will hear such cases quickly.

BILINGUALISM GAINING GROUND

The Charter of Rights and Freedoms entrenches the equality of our two official languages in all federal institutions. Some provinces— Ontario and New Brunswick, for example—also take pains to provide services in both French or English to their residents. So even if Canada is not yet completely bilingual, more and more Canadians are learning both English and French. This is evident from the popularity of French immersion courses in Western Canada and elsewhere, and the success of English classes among French speakers in Quebec.

OMBUDSMAN

Canada's provinces have been world leaders in adopting the office of ombudsman, an independent public protector who investigates complaints from the public. Prince Edward Island is the only province without one.

This public protector can intervene when you get the runaround from government agencies, or when you feel a government body has treated you unfairly. Yet many people are unaware that this office exists to guide them when they no longer know where to turn.

There are limits to what the public protector's office can do, however. It can investigate a complaint, and make recommendations, but it cannot force an agency to act on its recommendations. Also, it cannot investigate all government agencies. In Quebec, for instance, the public protector cannot intervene with school boards, universities, legal aid offices, or health-care agencies.

OTHER OPTIONS

Consumer protection offices, rental boards, and human rights commissions all exist to ensure the consumer is treated fairly. Contact them if you have a problem with a business or a government department. They will investigate your complaint if they feel there are grounds to do so. Some of these agencies can enforce their decisions; others can only put pressure on the investigated body to change its ways.

OPTION CONTRACT

Ray sees an antique dining room set advertised, looks at it, likes it, but wants a few days to think about it. How can he ensure that nobody else buys the set before he decides?

One way is for Ray to offer the seller, Thuy, a small sum of money in exchange for her promise not to sell the set to anyone else for a given time. If she agrees, Thuy and Ray have created an option contract—a legally enforceable agreement under which one party promises to honor an offer to buy or sell something for a specific price within a set time. In exchange, the second party pays a sum of money, or option fee. The second party then has the option to complete the deal within the specified time but is not obliged to do so. If Ray decides not to buy the furniture, Thuy can keep the option fee because she upheld her part of the agreement.

On the other hand, if Ray decides to purchase the dining set and then finds out that Thuy has sold it to Charles, he is entitled to get the money back. Depending on the circumstances, the holder of an option contract may also be able to sue for breach of contract and recover any financial losses he suffered because of the breach. In rare instances—when the item for sale cannot be duplicated, for example—it may be possible to file a lawsuit to have the sale rescinded.

Option contracts are also used in the sale of real estate. See also BREACH OF CONTRACT; CONTRACT.

ORDER OF PROTECTION

An adult victim of domestic violence may seek protection against her abuser. The court may issue an order of protection, stating that the abuser must keep away from his victim. Unlike a temporary restraining order, an order of protection applies only to cases of domestic violence—that is, abuse by a spouse, boyfriend, or girlfriend. If the abuser violates the order, he will be immediately jailed for contempt. See also BATTERED WOMEN.

RESTRAINING ORDERS

To get a restraining order, you must either call the police to your house or file a complaint at a police station. The court will likely issue the order if there are grounds, and if the terms are reasonable and do not cause undue inconvenience to the person being restrained. There are several different types of restraining orders. Some prohibit:

◇ Contact or communication with you and members of your family;

◇ The person to come within a certain vicinity (usually the home, or your workplace);

◇ The person from entering a certain road or neighborhood.

The type of order issued will depend on the types of charges and the circumstances of the case. If, for instance, the person being restrained works in your office, it is unlikely he could be ordered to stay away unless the circumstances were very serious.

Many people mistakenly believe that a restraining order will protect them from the person named in the order. The police usually intervene and make an arrest only when the order is actually violated. You might protect yourself better by changing your phone number or moving to a new address.

Note, however, that under antistalking legislation that went into effect Aug. 1, 1993, persistent following, watching, contacting, or otherwise harassing a victim is a crime. A "stalker" is liable to up to five years' imprisonment.

"ORDINARILY RESIDENT"

You are required to file income tax returns in Canada only if you "ordinarily reside" here. According to the Income Tax Act, a resident is somebody who has spent 183 days or more of the calendar year here. This doesn't mean that you must spend 183 consecutive days of the year in Canada, just 183 days of the year in total.

There are exceptions to this general rule: Canadian Armed Forces staff and ambassadors, for instance, continue to be considered "ordinarily resident" even though they may be out of the country for the better part of the year.

ORGAN AND TISSUE TRANSPLANTS

Within the last 25 years, medical science has advanced dramatically so that transplanting hearts, kidneys, eyes, and other organs has become almost commonplace. The ability to extend life, or to dramatically improve a patient's life through transplant techniques must be among medicine's greatest achievements. This has come about through improved surgical techniques, a greater understanding of the body's immune system, and the discovery and development of new drugs such as cyclosporine. No longer is tissue or organ rejection the main problem, but rather the chronic shortage of organs, which are of use only for a very short time after the donor's death.

POSTMORTEM DONATIONS

Today, all provinces have legislation enabling people to donate their organs once they have died (postmortem). All that is required is that you sign an organ donation consent form (often found on the reverse side of a driver's license), or carry such a consent form in your wallet or purse. Family members—a spouse, parents, or an adult child, brother, or sister—may also consent to having the organs of a deceased relative transplanted. Such consent follows hierarchical lines: a widow's consent to the removal of her husband's kidney, for example, would override an objection by a child of the deceased. Similarly, the consent of the deceased's child would override an objection by the deceased's brother or sister. However, it is doubtful that a hospital would remove an organ if there was any opposition from the family.

Quebec is the only province where postmortem organ removal is legal without the signed consent of the donor, or family consent. According to Quebec's new Civil Code: "Consent is not required where two physicians attest in writing to the impossibility of obtaining it in due time, the urgency of the operation, and the serious hope of saving a human life or of improving its quality to an appreciative degree."

Under the federal Uniform Human Tissue Act, a person in his or her last illness may also consent to donating organs for therapeutic, educational, or research purposes. In this case, the consent must be given in the presence of two witnesses.

INTER VIVOS DONATIONS

Even though tissue and organs are mostly transplanted after the donor's death, some may be given while the donor is alive (*inter vivos*). This occurs, for example, when one family member donates a kidney, or bone marrow, to another.

The various provincial human tissues acts permit *inter vivos* donation of all regenerative tissue, such as blood, bone, skin, or other tissue replaceable by natural process or repair. Kidney donation is the only non-regenerative organ donation allowed in all provinces.

Article 19 of Quebec's new Civil Code reads: "A person of full age who is capable of giving his consent may alienate a part of his body 'inter vivos,' provided the risk incurred is not disproportionate to the benefit that may be reasonably anticipated . . . and only if that part is capable of regeneration and provided that no serious risk to his health results." But to avoid a market in organs, article 25 of the code states: "The alienation by a person of a part or product of his body shall be gratuitous; it may not be repeated if it involves a risk to his health." (This article of the code would also prohibit surrogate mothers from charging for their services.)

DONATIONS BY MINORS

All adults capable of giving their consent may donate tissue or organs at age 18 (19 in British Columbia). The law also provides for the donation *inter vivos* of tissues or organs by minors in certain cases in all provinces other than Quebec. In Quebec, a minor or an adult not capable of giving his consent may not donate a kidney while alive, although he may do so with the consent of his tutor after death. In Manitoba, a minor under 18 but over 16 may donate tissue or a kidney provided he understands the "nature and effect of the procedure authorized by the consent," the recipient is of the same immediate family, and his informed consent is obtained from the donor's parents or guardian.

OVERTIME

If you are an employee of the federal government, there are specific regulations which apply to overtime pay. For employees not regulated by federal law, the rules governing payment of overtime in your province will apply.

In some provinces, you will be entitled to overtime if you work more than a certain number of hours a day or a week. In others, you are not even allowed to work once you have been on the job for a certain number of hours in a day or in a week. For instance, Yukon miners are not allowed to work more than 40 hours a week.

In some provinces, once you have worked the maximum number of hours in a standard workweek, you will be entitled to overtime pay, but you may nonetheless refuse the additional work. In other words, you cannot be forced to work overtime. In other provinces, you may may not have that choice; you may only refuse overtime if you have not been given sufficient notice or if you have a personal emergency.

In most provinces, the maximum allowable hours in your workweek may be increased if your work is necessary to ensure the life, health, or safety of other people, or when an essential service is interrupted.

Overtime is paid at an hourly rate of 1½ times the minimum wage rate in New Brunswick, Newfoundland, and Nova Scotia. Elsewhere, you are entitled to time and a half of your regular rate of pay. In British Columbia, you are entitled to twice your regular wages if you work more than 11 hours in a day or 48 hours in a week.

Usually, the maximum number of hours in a workweek is reduced if there is a public holiday. For instance, if the maximum length of your workweek is 40 hours, and there is a public holiday during the week, then you have to work only 32 hours, after which you will be entitled to overtime pay.

Employees are normally entitled to at least one day off a week, and to time off for meals once they have worked five hours straight. This amounts to half an hour in Alberta, British Columbia, New Brunswick, Northwest Territories, Ontario, Prince Edward Island, Quebec, and Yukon, but one hour in Manitoba and Newfoundland. However, in Newfoundland, the terms of some collective agreements can stipulate otherwise.

In most provinces, employers can deviate somewhat from the standard workweek, as long as they respect the terms of the federal or provincial labor codes. There are also other laws governing certain industries, such as the construction industry in Manitoba and Quebec, and the garment industry in Ontario and Quebec. For example, the standard workweek for garment workers in the latter two provinces is only 35 hours.

British Columbia also has 30 different categories of employees that are excluded from these general provisions. Most provinces exclude managerial staff, agricultural workers, public employees, members of certain professions such as doctors and lawyers, and those who provide essential services from these general rules.

EMPLOYMENT OF CHILDREN

Most provinces also have laws respecting the employment of children. Children must be of a certain age before they can be employed at all, and there are laws respecting the number of hours they are allowed to work in a day or in a week.

To obtain more information on employment standards legislation in your province, contact the Canada Communication Group—Publishing in Ottawa. See USEFUL ADDRESSES at back of book.

See also CHILD EMPLOYMENT; EMPLOYEE WORKING CONDITIONS.

P

FROM

PALIMONY

TO

PYRAMID SALES SCHEME

PALIMONY

Canadian law does not recognize the concept of "palimony," support paid to a former live-in partner, as opposed to a common-law spouse. Nevertheless, if you happen to live with a friend (of the opposite sex) with whom you split the rent and other household expenses —even if the relationship falls somewhat short of common-law marriage in that you have no desire to have children together or to live openly as husband and wife—take precautions now against future problems.

To avoid a possible lawsuit in the event of a future breakup, you and your partner should draw up a cohabitation agreement, a written contract that spells out your obligations to one another during the relationship, as well as each person's rights if the relationship ends. Such an agreement will minimize disputes and protect you from unfounded claims of an embittered ex-partner.

A cohabitation agreement is especially important if one of you has substantial assets, or if the living arrangement requires one of you to make a major sacrifice, such as giving up a job or moving a long distance away.

See EVERYDAY LEGAL FORMS at back of book. See also LIVING TOGETHER.

PARALEGAL

A paralegal is someone with some legal training who provides a supplementary or auxiliary legal service to a fully qualified lawyer. Independent paralegal services can substantially reduce the cost of certain minor court cases. When paralegals are hired by lawyers for research, investigating facts, and interviewing witnesses, the saving involved will also be reflected in the client's bill.

Because paralegals can often deal with simple legal matters at a much lower cost than lawyers, more and more people have been turning to them for help. But since paralegals can practice without a license, there are no regulatory mechanisms for monitoring their professional conduct or the quality of their services. However, a University of Windsor study concluded that many paralegals are quite competent and that most clients were pleased with their work.

Paralegals' greatest obstacle is the lack of guidelines on what exactly they can and cannot do.

British Columbia will not permit paralegals to represent clients in provincial courts, but Manitoba amended its law so that paralegals can represent clients in highway traffic offenses. Alberta not only allows paralegals to represent clients in traffic offenses and minor criminal offenses, but it has hired paralegals to prosecute these cases. In Ontario and Newfoundland, paralegals were permitted to represent clients in minor traffic offenses, highway traffic offenses, and some summary conviction offenses. But the matter was before the Supreme Court of Canada at the time of writing.

A former policeman opened a successful franchise paralegal service in Ontario called POINTTS (Provincial Offences Information and Traffic Ticket Service) in 1984. The Law Society of Upper Canada challenged the operation, but the Ontario District Court as well as the Ontario Court of Appeal ruled in the former policeman's favor. Today, POINTTS has 32 offices in Ontario, Manitoba, and Alberta, which handle up to 25,000 cases a year.

PARDON

Once you have been convicted of an offense, the record of your crime remains on file. A pardon gives you a chance to make a fresh start.

The governor-general can grant either free or conditional pardons. With a free pardon, you are exonerated of the offense for which you were convicted: you are given a clean slate. The more common conditional pardon will not erase your criminal record, but your record will be accessible only by special permission from the solicitor general.

With a pardon, some human rights laws can safeguard you from discrimination, and you will be eligible for employment in the federal and some provincial public services. However, you must still say that you have been convicted of a crime if asked.

To obtain an application kit for a pardon, write to the Clemency and Pardons Division of the National Parole Board in Ottawa. The kit is free and contains everything needed for your application. It even includes instructions for getting a copy of your criminal record from the RCMP and provides a specially treated tape for your fingerprints. Both must be submitted with your application, which is investigated by the RCMP. The process generally takes eight months to a year.

If you were convicted on a summary conviction offense, you can apply for a pardon two years after your sentence is completed. In the case of an indictable offense, you must wait five years. If you received a conditional discharge or an absolute discharge, you can apply one year after the sentence in the case of a summary offense, three years if the offense was indictable.

A pardon can be revoked if your behavior is not good, or if it is discovered that your application contained a false statement.

PARENTAL LIABILITY LAWS

When a minor injures someone or maliciously damages or destroys property, most provinces impose some financial responsibility on the child's parents. Without parental liability laws, people injured by a child's actions must wait until the child becomes an adult to claim his wages or property.

Parental liability laws usually do not apply if the child is very young. For example, the parents of most six-year-olds are not responsible if the child injures another person or willfully destroys someone's property. The situation may be different if parents can foresee that a child may act in a certain way.

The British Columbia Supreme Court held that the parents of a young boy with behavioral problems were liable for bodily injuries to a six-year-old girl the boy shoved off a balcony. The girl suffered a badly broken arm and possible brain damage. The boy, who had been living in a residence for children with behavioral problems, was visiting his parents when the incident occurred. He had a history of unprovoked attacks and because he was known to be physically aggressive often required extra supervision. The parents therefore had a duty to supervise their son and take reasonable steps to avoid foreseeable loss, Mr. Justice C. Ross Lander said.

Parental liability usually ends when a child reaches 18.

See also LIABILITY; NEGLIGENCE; TORT.

PARKING GARAGE

You drive your brand-new car into town one morning and park it at Fred's Friendly Garage. But when you return to pick it up, you learn that it has been stolen. What should you do, and who is responsible for your loss?

Before you do anything else, you should report the theft to the police and to your insurance company, as you would do with any other kind of theft.

The way in which the car was parked will determine who is responsible for its being stolen. If you parked the car yourself and kept the keys, the garage owner will probably not be held responsible, since he just rented you the space. If you were required to give your keys to an attendant, however, you created what is known as a bailment— that is, you entrusted your property to another person's care. In that case, the garage owner would be required to exercise reasonable care to safeguard your car while it is in his possession. If he failed to do so, he would be held liable. See BAILMENT.

If a car parked by an attendant is damaged, the garage owner is responsible. But if the damage occurs in a garage where you park your car yourself, the owner will probably not be liable.

If your car is insured against theft or damage, and your insurance company determines that your car was stolen or damaged as a result of the garage owner's carelessness, the company will pay your claim and then take action against the garage owner for reimbursement. But if you do not have the appropriate insurance, you will have to sue the garage on your own.

If you leave your car at a garage that requires attendant parking, make sure that the person you give your keys to is actually an employee. Ask to see identification, especially if the garage is one you do not use regularly. There have been a number of instances of car owners accepting receipts from young men dressed in official-looking jackets, only to discover later that the receipts were counterfeit and the "attendants" were members of a car-theft ring. See also AUTOMOBILE ACCIDENTS; AUTOMOBILE INSURANCE; LAWSUIT.

PAROLE

A person who has served part of his sentence may be eligible for parole, or conditional release. For many offenses, you can be paroled after serving only one-third of the sentence.

Persons sentenced to life imprisonment for murder will not be eligible for parole for 25 years, in the case of a first-degree conviction (10 years, if second-degree). If the person sentenced to life for second-degree murder has a previous murder conviction, he will not be eligible for parole for 25 years. Persons deemed dangerous offenders and sentenced to indefinite prison terms can have their cases reviewed by the parole board after three years' detention, and every two years thereafter. Dangerous offenders convicted before October 1977 are entitled to have their cases reviewed every year.

BILL C-36

Parole reform was the subject of Bill C-36, which was passed by the House of Commons in May 1992. It encourages the "accelerated review" of parole applicants convicted of non-violent crimes, since their release poses no risk to society. The societal risk becomes the central question in determining whether to grant parole. The parole board must consider the offense, the age of the offender, previous criminal offenses, the offender's marital status, and how many dependants he has.

Bill C-36 also gives trial judges the power to delay parole eligibility for those being sentenced for violent acts, such as robbery, assault, sexual assault, and manslaughter, for serious drug offenses, and for money-laundering offenses.

Although many Bill C-36 reforms were instituted to address public concerns about violent criminals, the early parole of nonviolent offenders —four to five months earlier in most cases—has also come under fire. Without proper rehabilitation, many of these parolees are likely to repeat their car theft, burglary, and fraud offenses.

FUNDAMENTAL JUSTICE

On Nov. 1, 1992, the Parole Act was replaced by the Corrections and Conditional Release Act. The following May, the Supreme Court of Canada unanimously ruled that refusing early release to a man serving 12 years for manslaughter did not infringe on the Charter of Rights and Freedoms.

Under the Parole Act, the man would have been eligible for supervised release after serving two-thirds of his sentence. But the parole board decided to keep him in prison for his full term because the community feared he would still be dangerous if drunk. He had been convicted of killing a New Brunswick man with 120 blows of an axe.

"While the amendments of the Parole Act to eliminate automatic release on mandatory supervision restricted the appellant's liberty interest, it did not violate the principles of fundamental justice," wrote Madame Justice Beverly McLachlin. "The principles of fundamental justice are concerned not only with the interest of the person who claims his liberty has been limited, but with the protection of society."

See also PROBATION.

PARTNERSHIP

A partnership is an association of two or more persons, known as general partners, who act as co-owners of a business and operate it for profit. Two other main forms of business are sole proprietorship and a corporation. See also CORPORATION; SOLE PROPRIETORSHIP.

Each province has specific laws on the formation and dissolution of partnerships, as well as laws regarding the legal responsibilities of each partner. Business owners are well advised to consult a lawyer and a tax accountant before establishing a partnership.

ADVANTAGES AND DISADVANTAGES

A partnership is relatively simple to establish and does not require the same amount of record-keeping as a corporation. Another advantage is that income is taxed only once. By contrast, most corporations are taxed twice—taxes are paid on the corporation's dividends.

Partnerships need only file an information return (a form indicating the partnership's income, expenses, and profits or losses) with Revenue Canada, but the partnership itself does not pay taxes. Each partner pays federal, provincial, and local taxes on their income from the partnership as if it were personal income. See also STOCKS AND BONDS.

The chief disadvantage of being a general partner is that you can be held personally responsible for another partner's negligence or carelessness. This means that if your partnership is unable to meet its financial obligations, you may have to use your personal assets to pay off debtors, even though you personally may not be at fault. If the partnership defaults on a loan, for example, the bank has the right to sue any general partner to collect this debt. If you own a car or a home, the court may order you to sell that property and turn the proceeds over to the bank. (If you and your spouse own the property jointly, the bank is entitled to only half of the proceeds).

Another disadvantage is that if one partner decides to sever the business relationship, then the partnership generally dissolves. The bankruptcy or death of a partner usually results in the end of the partnership.

Often partnerships take out life insurance on each partner's life. Then, in the event of one partner's death, the others would have the financial means to buy his share. Thus his interest would not go to his heirs.

PARTNERSHIP AGREEMENT

Once you and another person have decided to form a partnership, you should prepare a written agreement. It should include the following:

◇ The name of the partnership and the names of each of the partners.

◇ A general description of the type of business that will be conducted.

◇ The powers and duties of the partners, including any limitations or restrictions.

◇ The financial contributions each partner will make.

◇ How profits and losses are to be divided.

◇ How partners can leave the business and how new partners can be added.

◇ What steps must be taken to dissolve the partnership.

SILENT PARTNERSHIPS

A person who invests money in a partnership, but who does not take part in its day-to-day activities, is known as a "silent partner." He is not personally responsible to the partnership's creditors except for the amount of money he has invested. He is entitled to a share of the profits according to whatever terms have been agreed on, and he has the right to be informed of the activities of the general partners. If the silent partner begins making decisions concerning the partnership, he may lose his special status, and be liable to third parties.

ENDING A PARTNERSHIP

After a partnership is dissolved, the partners are no longer authorized to conduct business together. They must discharge all business obligations to creditors and divide all assets and any remaining profits among themselves.

PART-TIME WORK

If you are employed as a part-time worker—one who works on a limited schedule—you will probably not be eligible for the benefits given to full-time employees, and you may not be covered by laws regarding unemployment benefits.

MINIMUM WAGE

Before you accept a part-time job, check both provincial and federal minimum wage laws to find out if part-time employees are entitled to the minimum wage. Some employment standards laws not only exclude certain categories of work but also permit a lower-than-minimum wage for trainees, apprentices, or students in certain work programs. Your right to be paid the minimum wage, therefore, may depend on your job category rather than the number of hours you work. See also MINIMUM WAGE LAWS.

COMPANY BENEFITS

Part-time workers may also be ineligible for participation in group health, life, or disability insurance plans. An employer's contract with his insurance company defines "eligibility" or "employee." It also states the minimum number of hours per week and the number of days of continuous service a person must work to qualify for coverage. A typical policy may limit coverage to employees who work at least 20 or 30 hours per week with 90 days of continuous service.

Ask your prospective employer about the kind of insurance he offers. You may be eligible for group health coverage but not for long-term disability, for example.

PENSIONS

As with insurance plans, pension plans require that part-time employees work a certain number of hours before they can qualify for plan participa-

tion. If the plan specifies 1,000 hours, therefore, those who work 25 or more hours per week become eligible for coverage after 40 weeks.

WORKERS' COMPENSATION

One benefit available to both full-time and part-time employees is workers' compensation. If you are injured on the job, the laws in your province will determine how much compensation you will receive and for how long. The amount of compensation will be affected by whether you worked full- or part-time, since one factor used in calculating your benefit is how much you would earn if you could continue working. See WORKERS' COMPENSATION.

UNEMPLOYMENT COMPENSATION

Eligibility for unemployment benefits is determined by the Unemployment Insurance Act and Regulations. Under the act, workers who work less than 15 hours a week and whose cash earnings are less than 20 percent of the maximum weekly insurable earnings (that is, 20 percent of about $42,000 subject to change by regulation) are not eligible for unemployment insurance benefits.

If you are fired from a part-time job, you may not be eligible for unemployment compensation, or the benefits you receive may be reduced. In some cases, benefits are calculated according to your base pay. If your compensation is less than the minimum amount, you will not qualify.

DISCRIMINATION

Your protection against job discrimination is determined not by the number of hours you work, but by the federal Charter of Rights and Freedoms, provincial human rights legislation, and federal and provincial employment standards legislation, which prohibit discrimination on the basis of race, color, national origin, sex, or religious beliefs.

In some provinces, legislation protects against discrimination on the basis of sexual orientation, criminal record, social class, and mental or physical disability.

PASSPORT

A Canadian passport certifies to other countries that you are a citizen of Canada and guarantees your admittance to Canada on your return. To get one, you must have proof of Canadian citizenship, such as a previous Canadian passport, birth certificate or a certificate of identity issued in the last five years, and you must have evidence of Canadian citizenship and custody documents for any children you wish to include on the passport. You must have original documents to prove your citizenship: photocopies will not do.

You must include two signed standard passport-size photos with your application. One photo must be signed by a guarantor—a minister of religion, judge, police officer, lawyer, veterinarian, doctor, or bank manager who has known you for at least two years and can confirm your identity. Otherwise, you will have to obtain a special form from the passport office.

The name on your passport application must be the same as that on your proof of citizenship or your marriage certificate. If not you will have to provide appropriate legal documents explaining your name change. You can request that your place of birth not be indicated on your passport if you wish.

Passports are valid for five years only. If your children under 16 years of age travel with you, they can be included on your passport. If you wish to get a passport for children previously included on yours, you must apply to have their names deleted from your passport. Only a parent who has custody of the child can apply for a passport.

You can obtain a passport by applying in person at one of the regional passport offices, or you can write to the main Passport Office in Hull, Que. See USEFUL ADDRESSES at back of book.

PROTECTING YOUR PASSPORT

Canadian passports are highly prized on the foreign black market, so guard yours carefully. Before your trip, make two photocopies of your passport; leave one at home and put the other in a separate section of your luggage. To avoid theft, carry your passport separate from your money—preferably in a front inside coat pocket or in a document pouch strapped under your shirt or blouse. Never leave your passport in a hotel room; carry it with you or store it in the hotel's safe-deposit box and get a receipt.

REPLACING A LOST PASSPORT

If you lose your passport while traveling abroad, immediately notify the local police and the nearest Canadian embassy or consulate. These offices can help you obtain replacement documents that will allow you to continue your travels and return home. If your passport is lost, stolen, or destroyed in Canada, call the police and notify the Passport Office at the Department of Citizenship and Immigration.

See also CITIZENSHIP; IMMIGRATION.

PATENT

Patents are a form of intellectual property, just as are copyrights, industrial designs, trademarks, and planters' rights to particular strains of fruits and vegetables.

Patents are issued by the Canadian Intellectual Property Office on application by the original inventor. Applications must be accompanied by a detailed description, drawings, and pictures, and you must show why your invention is different from others. You cannot patent inventions such as scientific principles, ideas, and medical methods for treating the human body.

A patentable invention must work and be useful: it cannot be something that someone

ABC's OF APPLYING FOR A PATENT

You or your lawyer will need to write to the Canadian Intellectual Property Office and ask for complete instructions and application materials. Address your request to the Commissioner of Patents in Hull, Que. (See USEFUL ADDRESSES at back of book.) Your completed application will generally consist of:

■ a petition executed by the applicant or a patent agent on the applicant's behalf
■ a specification, including claims of the invention, as well as a full description of the best way of using the invention
■ a drawing or drawings of the invention done according to regulation
■ the filing fee.

else could have dreamed up just as easily. A registered patent agent can help with your application, and make sure that a similar invention has not already been patented.

You must apply for a patent within two years of the first time the invention is published or used publicly. It is therefore wise to apply as soon as the invention is completed. Remember, however, that if you change anything substantial later, you will probably have to submit a new application.

Once patented, you can prevent other people from making, using, or selling your invention for 17 years. Anyone who does so in that time, without your permission or without a license, can be sued. Other inventors may be able to improve on it, however, although they may need your permission to do so. Once the 17-year term is up, the patent cannot be extended. Anyone can make, use, or sell the product afterward.

All patented inventions must be marked, and stamped "patented" with the year the patent was issued. Otherwise the holder could be subject to a fine or even imprisonment. Marking an article "patented" when it is not is also illegal.

An inventor can sell his patent to another person, and that person is entitled to the same privileges as the original inventor. A patent can also be taken away from inventors who do not use their inventions or who abuse their privilege.

If you obtain a patent in Canada, the patent is not valid in other countries. To patent your invention abroad, contact the Commissioner of Patents for information. See USEFUL ADDRESSES at back of book.

A joint industrial research assistance program (IRAP) of Industry Canada and the National Research Council can help inventors with research and development. Even with such assistance, most inventors do not have adequate financial resources to bring their creations to market; they usually sell or license their patents to companies. Generally, before a company agrees to a licensing or purchase agreement, it will ask for a prototype—a working model. Creating a prototype can be costly, so before invest-

ing a lot of money, you may want to have your patent evaluated for marketability. Some universities may critique inventions for little or no charge and, for a fee, private companies, such as the Canadian Industrial Innovation Centre in Waterloo, Ont., will assess the commercial potential of inventions and recommend what steps the inventor should take. Be wary of companies that offer "development contracts," promising to market your invention for a large evaluation fee.

See also COPYRIGHT; TRADEMARK.

PATERNITY LEAVE

Nowadays, in homes where both spouses are employed, it is increasingly common for a husband to want "paternity leave" to take care of newborn children while his wife continues to work.

At one time, the Unemployment Insurance Act allowed 15 weeks of maternity benefits to biological mothers and 15 weeks of parental benefits to adoptive parents, but made no provision for biological fathers. The act was challenged by a father whose wife returned to work while he stayed home to take care of their baby. Citing section 15 of the Charter of Rights and Freedoms, which guarantees equality on the basis of sex, he claimed he was being treated differently just because he was male. The Federal Court rejected this argument as did the Court of Appeal. In 1992, however, the

Supreme Court of Canada allowed the man's appeal. By this time, the Unemployment Insurance Act had already been amended to allow all new parents 10 weeks of parental leave.

PATERNITY SUIT

An unmarried mother can compel the father of her child to provide financial support for the child by bringing a paternity suit against him. Generally, the evidence—which often includes blood tests of the mother, child, and alleged father, as well as testimony about their relationship at the time of conception—must show that the defendant is more likely than not to be the child's father. This is called establishing a preponderance of evidence.

See also BLOOD TESTING; BURDEN OF PROOF; CHILD SUPPORT; ILLEGITIMACY.

PATIENTS' RIGHTS

When you are sick or injured, you generally must trust in physicians or hospitals to give you the proper care. However, you should recognize that you are in charge of the treatment you receive and, as a patient, you have certain rights.

CONSENT

Your most basic right is that of consent. Your physician must fully inform you of all the options available for treatment and the risks and benefits associated with each. This is known as the doctrine of informed consent. A doctor who explains only the treatment she wants to provide has not fulfilled her responsibility, and the patient's consent will therefore not be valid. In some instances, a doctor may be allowed to limit the amount of information she gives to the patient. For example, she may withhold information that could have an adverse effect on the patient, or the patient himself may not want to know the truth about his condition. In these situations, the physician may keep family members fully informed about the patient's illness.

Before medical personnel begin any form of treatment—from a simple laboratory test to major surgery—they must obtain your consent. If they do not, you may be able to sue them for assault and battery. If you are too ill to give consent, they must ask the permission of a family member before beginning any procedures, unless a delay would be life threatening. See CONSENT FORM; INFORMED CONSENT.

RIGHT TO REFUSE TREATMENT

Apart from minors and adults who are unable to give their consent because of mental problems, a patient is always entitled to refuse medical treatment, even if the refusal would result in death. In such cases, the state's interest in preserving life is outweighed by the patient's greater right to control his or her own body and destiny.

It is often a good idea to make a living will or durable power of attorney to ensure your wishes are followed. In such a document, you may stipulate that you do not wish to be kept alive by artificial means, if your chances of recovering are very slim.

You should also always feel free to ask your doctor about the risks involved in certain procedures, and about alternative forms of treatment. It is never a bad idea to see a second or even a third doctor for another opinion when you are faced with a serious medical condition.

In May 1993, the Supreme Court of Canada ruled that a patient has the right to withdraw consent to a medical procedure, even if such procedure is under way, unless the termination would be either life threatening or pose immediate serious problems to the patient's health.

See also LIVING WILL.

CONFIDENTIALITY

As a patient, you have a right to confidentiality. Unless you agree to have medical information released, your doctor is not permitted to give it to anyone—even family members who may want to know about your condition. If you have a communicable disease, however, your doctor is obliged by law to notify the public health department and, in some cases, anyone close to you who might be at risk.

The issue of confidentiality is often raised when the patient is a child. Generally a parent must grant permission for medical treatment, because the child is not considered mature

enough to make such a decision. In some cases, however, teenagers are allowed to consent to treatment for pregnancy, drug abuse, alcoholism, or emotional problems without notifying their parents.

Depending upon the age of the young patient and her degree of maturity, the physician must decide whether or not to inform the parents. Usually at about the age of 14 or 15 the doctor may keep medical information confidential. However, a doctor should not consent to certain procedures such as a vasectomy or tubal ligation on a young person without a court order. The Ontario Hospitals Act Regulation prohibits surgery on a minor over 16 years of age without her consent.

See ABORTION; CHILDREN'S RIGHTS.

A PATIENT'S BILL OF RIGHTS

Some provinces and hospitals now have patients' rights associations, most of which subscribe to some form of the following list of rights.

◇ A proper standard of care.

◇ Within limits to choose your own doctor. For example, if you are injured at work you may choose to be treated by your doctor rather than one named by your employer.

◇ Sufficient information to give informed consent.

◇ Information about hospital rules and regulations that apply to you.

◇ Complete, up-to-date information about your condition, treatment, and prognosis.

◇ Information about any experimental procedures that are performed on you.

◇ Considerate and respectful care.

◇ Privacy during consultations, examinations, and treatments.

◇ Confidential treatment of your medical records.

◇ Information about how care will be provided after you have been discharged.

◇ Protection of your property.

STEPS TO TAKE IF YOUR RIGHTS ARE VIOLATED

If you believe that your rights as a patient have been violated by your caregiver, consider taking the following actions:

1. Express your concern to the doctor, nurse, or other caregiver. A frank discussion will usually resolve what may be a simple misunderstanding.

2. Call the hospital administrator, who may investigate the problem and order corrective action.

3. Write to or call the provincial licensing authority (usually the department of health).

4. You may also want to notify the nursing board or board of medical examiners if you have a complaint about a nurse or doctor.

5. If the problem persists, call a lawyer.

6. If you are not satisfied with the results obtained by the department of health or the nursing or medical examiner's board, you may apply for help to the provincial ombudsman.

PAWNBROKER

A pawnbroker is someone who makes loans using personal property as collateral. Pawnbrokers differ from banks in that they charge higher interest, are willing to lend smaller sums of money, and are more flexible about what they will accept as collateral. Borrowers pledge items of personal property, such as jewelry, musical instruments, electronic equipment—even automobiles—to secure their loans.

Because pawnbrokers are often lenders of last resort, used primarily by people with poor credit ratings who cannot get loans elsewhere, they lend their customers only a fraction of the value of their collateral—10 to 50 cents on the dollar is not unusual. For this reason, and because of the high interest rates, you should consider other avenues for borrowing the money you need before you go to a pawnbroker.

Collateral that you leave with a pawnbroker remains your property as long as you meet the terms of the loan agreement. The pawnbroker is prohibited from using the property or doing anything that would diminish its value. But if you fail to repay the loan, the pawnbroker can legally sell your property to recover the amount of your loan, plus interest (and sometimes insurance and storage fees). Whether he must return any remaining money to you depends on your agreement with him and the laws in your province.

Because pawnbrokers were once commonly used by burglars to obtain cash for stolen goods, every province now has laws that strictly regulate pawnbrokers' activities and require them to keep careful records of their clients' identities. If a pawnbroker knowingly or unknowingly accepts stolen property and the true owner can prove it is hers, the pawnbroker must return it without being compensated for his loss.

PEDESTRIAN

A pedestrian is a person walking or standing on a public thoroughfare. The legal definition includes people in wheelchairs, on roller skates, on crutches—even on stilts.

Under most highway safety legislation, when a vehicle and a pedestrian are involved in an accident there is a presumption that the motorist was at fault. This is so because the pedestrian is the weaker party and the motorist has the greater duty of care because of the inherent danger an automobile poses. This presumption can be rebutted by proof—that the pedestrian crossed the street between two parked cars, for example. Even if a pedestrian crosses on a red light, the motorist could be liable for damages if he could have avoided the accident, but did not because of inattention or some other carelessness.

PENSION PLAN

A program that provides retirement income for wage earners is called a pension plan. It may be sponsored by government, such as the Canada (Quebec) Pension Plan, or by private corporations, unions, the employee himself, or combinations of these. Although many corporations offer pensions so that they can attract and keep good employees, corporations are not legally required to provide such plans. Both employers and employees are, however, required by law to make contributions to the Canada (Quebec) Pension Plan.

Pension plans are regulated by both the federal and provincial governments. The federal Income Tax Act provides tax-exempt status to income earned by pension funds that are registered with Revenue Canada and operate within the limits of Revenue Canada's rules on maximum pension benefits allowed in a registered pension plan. Such rules govern permissible methods of funding plans, definitions of normal retirement date, and the extent of employer contributions.

Most provinces also have comprehensive pension benefit regulation covering the terms, operations, and funding of pension plans. In provinces with such legislation, pension plans must be registered with the provincial pension commission in addition to Revenue Canada. Joint federal-provin-cial agreements assure the portability of pensions and a relative uniformity of rules.

A wave of pension legislation was passed by the provinces in the late 1980s. Among the reforms were:

◇ Flexible retirement age, requiring employers to allow for early retirement.

◇ Survivor benefits to the employee's spouse or estate in the event that the employee dies before retirement, or a continuation of pension payments at a reduced rate to the surviving spouse of an employee who has already retired.

◇ Part-time employee's eligibility: generally required after 24 months' continuous service.

◇ Portability, by which pension entitlements can be transferred to an employee's subsequent pension plan or a registered retirement savings plan.

◇ Minimum employer pension contribution: 50 percent in most jurisdictions.

◇ Early vesting and locking in, by which the employer's contributions are locked in to the employee's pension fund after two to five years of employment.

◇ Investments and funding, requiring minimum funding levels and restricting investment to the types of investment available to insurance companies.

GOVERNMENT PENSIONS

The federal government offers two different types of retirement benefits: the universal Old Age Security pension and the earnings-related Canada Pension Plan (CPP). In Quebec, the CPP is replaced by the virtually identical Quebec Pension Plan, the investment funds for which are directly controlled by that province.

The Old Age Security pension is a monthly benefit payable to all persons aged 65 or over who meet the residency requirements. For 1994, the basic monthly Old Age Security pension was $385.81, and the maximum Guaranteed Income Supplement (GIS) was $458.50 for a single person, $298.65 for a person whose spouse was receiving a spouse's allowance.

You have to apply to receive the Old Age Security pension; the application should not be submitted more than 12 months before the date of eligibility. To be eligible, you must be a Canadian citizen or legal resident in Canada (or, if applying from outside the country, you must have been a citizen or legal resident just prior to departure). A full pension is payable at age 65 to people who have resided in Canada for a total of 40 years after age 18. A full pension is also payable to those who were at least 25 years old and resident in Canada on July 1, 1977, and who have resided in Canada for the 10 years immediately before their pension was approved.

People aged 65 who cannot qualify for a full pension, but have resided in Canada for a minimum of 10 years (20 years, if applying from abroad) after the age of 18, can receive a partial pension equal to 1/40th of the full pension for each year residency in Canada (after reaching the age of 18).

As well, a 60- to 64-year-old spouse of an Old Age Security pensioner may be eligible for a spouse's allowance. These benefits also must be applied for and eligibility is based on the combined income of the couple and/or the length of the spouse's residency in Canada.

Another potential benefit which must be applied for is the GIS, which is payable to Old Age Security pensioners who have little other income. Low-income widows and widowers between the ages of 60 and 64 can receive the Widowed Spouse's Allowance, if they meet the residency requirements. Application for the GIS must be made every year.

The Canada (Quebec) Pension Plan is based on the mandatory contributions of all employers and employees (including the self-employed). Both the contributions and the benefits paid are relative to the level of earnings of the individual employee. The benefits include a retirement pension, which can begin any time between the ages of 60 and 70, with the rate of payment being adjusted to reflect the age at which the pension begins.

The Canada (Quebec) Pension Plan also provides disability pensions and survivor benefits for spouses and orphans. At age 60, the pension is 70 percent of the maximum; at age 70, it would be 130 percent of the maximum pension given at age 65. The maximum Canada Pension Plan benefit for 1994 was $694.44 per month, indexed quarterly.

Disability pensions are available to individuals under the age of 65 who are suffering from a severe and prolonged mental or physical impairment. The disability must seriously affect the person's ability to earn money and must be likely to do so for more than a temporary period. The benefit payments consist of a flat-rate portion (such as the Old Age Security pension) and an earnings-related portion (such as the Canada [Quebec] Pension Plan). This pension is payable beginning the fourth month after a person becomes disabled, and you should apply as soon as the permanent disability seriously affects your earning ability. The disability pension is 75 percent of the retirement pension plus a flat rate. As of Jan. 1, 1994, the maximum amount was $839.09 per month, which included the flat-rate portion of $318.26 and 75 percent of the contributory retirement pension. A death benefit could also be paid to the surviving spouse or the deceased's estate. In 1994 the maximum death benefit was $3,440.

PRIVATE PENSIONS

Private pension plans are divided into two categories: defined benefit or defined contribution.

Defined-benefit plans

A defined-benefit plan pays participants a fixed income from the day they retire until the day they die. The amount is related to the employee's length of service and earnings. Defined-benefit plans are the most common type of plan in Canada, except for plans favored by members of trade unions, who typically subscribe to defined-contribution plans.

Executive plans

Sometimes senior executives have their own pension plans in addition to or instead of the employer's regular pension plan. The benefits of such plans are generally much more generous than the regular plan. Pension plans may be restricted to particular select groups of employees unless such restrictions are based on such criteria as race or sex or age (in which cases, the restrictions would be illegal).

Defined-contribution plans

Under a defined-contribution plan, your employer agrees to put a specified sum into your retirement fund every year. Unlike a defined-benefit plan, it does not promise you a fixed income at retirement. Rather, it offers a fixed annual contribution to your retirement fund. The contributions are invested, and your retirement income will depend on how well those investments do. The investments must be reasonable and prudent, and the employer (or the plan's trustee) is legally responsible for managing the funds wisely. You can choose among several investment options in some defined-contribution plans.

With a defined-contribution plan, when you retire, you can take the pension either in monthly installments or in a lump sum.

WHEN YOU WILL GET YOUR PENSION

You will begin to receive benefits when you reach the age

specified in your plan. This is usually age 65, but each plan contains its own specified age. Check the summary description of your plan, available from your employer. Some pension plans allow participants to retire before age 65, if they have worked a given length of time. If you retire early, your monthly benefit will be lower, since the pension will be paid out over a longer period. Some plans pay an employee retiring at age 55 half of what a 65-year-old retiree would receive.

EARLY RETIREMENT

In recent years, some employers have offered early retirement to employees to reduce overstaffing in general or in specific job categories. In these instances, the employer may offer employees nearing retirement age financial incentives to retire, such as bonuses or pension payments larger than those due to the employee. These offers are legal, unless certain employees are singled out to receive such offers because of their age, sex, or for other prohibited reasons.

Before accepting an offer of early retirement, weigh such factors as your ability to obtain other employment, whether you will lose company-sponsored medical insurance, and the length of time between early retirement and your eligibility for Old Age Security and Canada Pension Plan benefits.

MONTHLY PAYMENTS VERSUS A LUMP SUM

Suppose you are about to retire with $100,000 in your pension fund, which is a defined-benefit plan. You are told that you can take the money either in monthly payments or as a lump sum. What should you do?

Monthly payments

If you do not want the responsibility of handling a large sum of money, you may prefer to take your pension in monthly installments. But before you make this choice, be sure that your company is financially stable and that your pension plan is insured.

You can also find out about your company's financial stability by reviewing its quarterly and annual reports if the company is publicly traded. Other valuable sources of fiscal information are the trade journals, newspaper reports, and your company's own communications to its employees.

Lump sum

Some retirees take their pension in a lump sum because they want to use the money for a specific purpose, such as purchasing a new home, or because they want to reinvest it themselves. Keep in mind that you will pay income taxes on the lump sum in the year you receive it.

PLAN TERMINATIONS

If a corporation closes down, the law requires that its pension plan be closed down as well. All the benefits earned by active plan members become vested as of the date of closure. A partial shut down of a corporation can trigger a partial termination of a pension plan, but employers try to avoid such situations because of the complexities involved.

If a business is sold and its employees become employees of the buyer, generally the seller remains responsible for all pension benefits accrued to the date of the sale. The buyer is not obliged to provide any pension benefits for the future under pension law. However, if the pension is part of a collective agreement, the new owner must honor its terms (as he must honor the entire collective agreement) under labor relations law.

When a corporation is purchased by the acquisition of a majority of shares, the corporation itself remains unchanged and so do its pension obligations. The purchaser takes over all the rights, duties, assets, and liabilities. The buyers in effect replace the seller in this situation.

PENSIONS AND DIVORCE

There is a great variation between the provinces as to how such marital assets as pension benefits acquired during the marriage are treated at the dissolution of the marriage.

Changes to the Canada Pension Plan in 1991 may benefit spouses who signed away their rights to half their spouse's pension benefits. These amendments give the federal Minister of Health the power to place a claimant, denied a division of CPP benefits by a spousal agreement or court order made prior to June 4, 1986, in the same position as one who did not sign away her rights. If you were divorced or separated after January 1987, but signed a spousal agreement before June 4, 1986, renouncing any future claim on your spouse, contact the Canada Pension Plan office in your area to see if you are eligible for a share in your spouse's benefits. In some cases, retroactive benefits may be as high as $20,000. (The amendments do not seem to apply to people divorced before January 1987, but since the law is unclear they should apply anyway.) Common-law or married couples who stopped living together or got a divorce from Jan. 27, 1992 have 36 months from the date of their judgment to apply for CPP benefits to be split.

FURTHER INFORMATION

The best way to find out what your pension will be is to check the summary of your plan's annual report. There you will find general information, such as the amount by which your benefit is reduced if you are married and elect to take a joint-and-survivor benefit, or what will happen if you take a leave of absence and return at a later date.

For more specific information about your pension, you can turn to your annual statement, which companies provide for each employee.

See also SOCIAL SECURITY.

PEREMPTORY CHALLENGE

A peremptory challenge will allow a lawyer who is in the process of jury selection to refuse a potential juror without giving a reason for dismissing him. If a juror reveals that he has a bias for or against one side, the lawyer for either party can remove him "for cause." But if a lawyer wants to remove a juror but does not have a legally acceptable cause, he can make a peremptory challenge.

NUMBER OF CHALLENGES

The number of peremptory challenges either side can make varies with the seriousness of the charge. The prosecutor and the accused are entitled to 20 peremptory challenges each when the charge is high treason or first-degree murder; 12 challenges each for any other crime that carries a possible prison term of more than five years; and four challenges each for any other offense.

If two or more charges are tried at the same time, each side is entitled to only the number of peremptory challenges permitted for whichever charge allows the greatest number of challenges. But if two or more accused are tried together, each accused is entitled to the same number of peremptory challenges as he would have if he were tried alone, while the prosecution is entitled to the total number of peremptory challenges available to all the accused.

Peremptory challenges play a vital role in the selection of juries. In nearly all cases neither of the opposing lawyers will make any objection to peremptory challenges made by the other.

See also JURY.

PERJURY

Perjury is the crime of intentionally lying under oath. Sometimes known as false swearing, perjury can occur in any proceeding in which witnesses are required to give sworn testimony, or in any legal document signed under oath. The central elements of the criminal offense are that a sworn statement be false, that the person making the statement knows it to be false and that the statement be made with the intention of misleading.

Because perjury can result in a serious obstruction of justice, courts tend to view charges of perjury very seriously. An indictable offense, it carries a maximum penalty of 14 years' imprisonment. However, a person who commits perjury in order to procure the conviction of someone for an offense punishable by death (as is still the case for a few offenses under the National Defence Act) is liable to life imprisonment.

Some common examples of perjury are:

◇ Deliberately lying on the witness stand in a trial or other judicial hearing such as an inquest or judicial inquiry.

◇ Lying while giving a deposition (a procedure for conducting discovery or collecting evidence for a trial). See also DEPOSITION.

◇ Swearing a false affidavit to be used in a judicial proceeding. See AFFIDAVIT.

If your religious convictions prevent you from taking an oath and you affirm that you will tell the truth, this does not affect your duty to tell the truth under the perjury laws. See OATH AND AFFIRMATION.

EXCEPTIONS

In some situations false statements that are made under oath are not considered to be perjury. Such instances fall into the following categories.

Ignorance

If you make a false statement under oath but do not know or believe it to be false, you have not committed perjury. False statements due to a mistake, forgetfulness, or misunderstanding the question are not considered perjury.

Irrelevance

To qualify as perjury, a false statement must be about the matter at issue, whether in a court or on a document. For example, if a witness testifying at a murder trial lies about her age, she would probably not be prosecuted for perjury.

Opinion

A mistake or an incorrectly held opinion is not perjury. If you say, "I thought that the driver was drunk," when in fact the driver was having a fainting spell, you are not committing perjury because you are testifying to your opinion, not fact.

PERJURY IN WRITTEN FORM

The crime of perjury is not limited to courtroom testimony. You can be prosecuted for perjury if you sign your name to a legal document that you know deliberately contains a false statement. You will be guilty of perjury:

◇ If you sign false pleadings—written statements regarding a lawsuit.

◇ If you make a false statement when applying for a marriage license or passport.

◇ If you sign a false affidavit in connection with a lawsuit or with an application for a professional license or permit.

◇ If you sign your income tax return knowing that it contains fraudulent information.

PERMIT

A permit is a document issued by a government agency that authorizes a person or entity to carry out certain activities. For example, you may need a permit from the local building department to add a deck to your home. Likewise, the piece of paper a customs official gives you after inspecting your baggage is a permit that allows you to remove your property from the customs area.

See also HOME IMPROVEMENT AND REPAIR; LICENSE.

PERSONAL RECORDS

From the moment of birth, Canadians begin to accumulate documents and personal records. Many of these, such as birth certificates, marriage licenses, real estate deeds, and insurance policies, should be retained for legal reasons.

WHAT TO THROW AWAY

Good record-keeping means not only putting papers you

need to save in places where they can easily be retrieved, but also discarding papers that are no longer useful. There is no need to keep the following:

◇ Passbooks or cheque books from bank accounts that you have closed, after you have reconciled them with your final bank statements. (Be sure to tear up or shred any unused cheques, so that they do not fall into the wrong hands and so that you cannot accidentally write a cheque on an account that is closed.)

◇ Warranties from products you no longer own.

◇ Paycheque stubs (once you have received your annual T-4 form from your employer and have compared it to the amount shown on the stubs).

◇ Credit card agreements for cards that you no longer hold.

◇ Expired passports (once you have received a new one).

WHAT TO KEEP

Certain records should be kept for a limited time.

◇ Canceled cheques and bank statements that provide substantiation for income tax deductions and credits should be retained for seven years to protect you in case of an income tax audit.

◇ Credit card statements provide proof of the price you paid for major items and can bolster your case for certain tax deductions (such as business gifts) and should be kept for seven years, in case your tax return is audited by Revenue Canada.

◇ Statements of the sale of investments from your brokerage firm should be held for seven years. If you are audited and you have misplaced these documents, your broker can probably duplicate them.

For a list of records you should keep permanently, such as wills or deeds—and where you should keep them—see the Personal Records Inventory in EVERYDAY LEGAL FORMS at back of book.

See also FINANCIAL RECORDS.

PET

Along with the rewards and pleasures of owning a pet, you assume certain responsibilities when you take a dog, cat, or other animal into your home.

SELECTING A PET

Before you buy a pet, make sure that you are allowed to own it. If you live in a town or city, you need to find out about restrictions on the types of animals allowed within city limits. Most municipalities prohibit what they call dangerous animals, such as wolves or poisonous snakes. Your city bylaws may limit ownership to domesticated dogs and cats, canaries and other birds, rabbits, hamsters, and gerbils.

Provincial laws place further limitations on the animals that can be kept as house pets. For example, some people like to adopt animals they find in the wilderness and domesticate

them. Since animals living on public property are generally considered to belong to the Crown, simply taking home a wild animal (even one that is not dangerous) may be a violation of the law. Your provincial conservation department or the department of wildlife, fish, and game can give you information about the status of wild animals that may live in your area.

LICENSING

Provinces and municipalities may have licensing requirements for pet ownership, usually for dogs. A typical municipal ordinance requires owners to obtain a license each year and pay a small fee.

CARE AND LIABILITY

You are responsible by law for taking care of your pet. If you leave a pet unattended without adequate food or water, you may be reported to the local police for cruelty to an animal. If found guilty, you could face a fine or several months in jail.

Most cities and towns have leash laws that prohibit owners from allowing dogs to run around at large. If you do not keep your dog properly restrained, it may be impounded. At the pound, the dog may be put up for adoption or destroyed if it is not reclaimed within a specified period. In addition, you may face penalties for violating the leash law, as well as a civil lawsuit if your pet causes an accident or injures someone while running around loose.

The general rule in most provinces is that you are not

responsible for your pet's actions unless you were already aware the pet had anti-social tendencies. For example, if you know that your cat will not tolerate being handled by children, you can be held liable if it scratches or bites a toddler. Owners are usually not held responsible for a pet's action if its behavior was unpredictable. See also ANIMALS; DOG LAW; VETERINARIAN.

PET CUSTODY

Because people become attached to their pets, a beloved dog or cat can become an issue in a divorce case. Couples who quarrel over the custody of a pet should keep in mind that it is in their interests to settle the matter between themselves, just as they should try to agree about sentimental keepsakes, or furniture, or cars. They can take the matter to court and the judge will make a decision, but judicial intervention will cost both parties a good deal of time and money.

WILLS

Suppose you leave $1 million to your dog, Hogie, and only $1,000 to your only child, Sue. Sue could contest your will successfully, because you cannot leave property to property (legally, that is what a pet is). Sue would have less success if you made what is called a conditional gift to another person—for example, "I give my friend Jeff $1 million, provided he cares for Hogie as long as Hogie lives." Or you could put the money in trust for Hogie's care, designating a beneficiary for any money that remains when Hogie dies. Sometimes a pet owner requests in his will that upon his death his pets be destroyed. Most courts would probably find that this provision violates public policy.

One recent case in Nova Scotia provoked a national letter-writing campaign to save the lives of several beautiful horses whose owner had willed that they be put to death lest they might be mistreated by a subsequent owner. The judge in the case said it was a letter from a nine-year-old that convinced him to set aside that provision in the will.

PETITION

A formal written application requesting that specific action be taken is known as a petition and is the first step in civil litigation. For instance, a spouse seeking a divorce must first file a petition with the court in order to begin the divorce proceedings.

Legal proceedings are often divided into two forms: actions and petitions. For example, you may take an action or suit to sue someone, say for damages or for breach of contract. But you may petition a court to change custody or reduce alimentary pension.

A petition is generally supported by an affidavit and is meant to be heard in a quicker manner than an actual action or suit. However, this is not always the case, since, in many cases, the facts to be judged in a petition may be more complicated than those of an action or suit in law.

Another common form of petition is a request made to a public official or government body, such as a request to preserve an historic site, to prevent the development of woods or green space, or to stop pollution. For example, environmentalists may circulate a petition to be signed by members of the community and later presented to the municipal council seeking to force a local factory to stop polluting the atmosphere.

PHARMACIST

A pharmacist is a health-care professional who has been trained to prepare and dispense medicines, known as ethical drugs, which require a doctor's prescription.

RESPONSIBILITIES

The pharmacist's responsibilities are not limited to putting the prescribed number of pills or amount of liquid into a bottle and handing it to the customer. She must certify the prescription order by deciding whether the dosage is correct and the medication appropriate for that patient. The pharmacist checks the safety of the dosage as well as legal requirements for dispensing the drug. Finally, she must make a record of the prescription, price charged, and the date dispensed.

Pharmacists are regulated by the provinces. Each province has a code of ethics for its own pharmacists. In all cases, pharmacists are not permitted to take back medication for resale to other patients, and must

keep careful records of certain drugs such as narcotics and stimulants. It is not that unusual for an alert pharmacist to discover errors in a physician's prescription.

Some codes of ethics require pharmacists to inquire about other medications their customers may be taking in order to avoid adverse drug interactions and other potential problems. The pharmacist should also counsel customers on the safest use of a prescribed drug—for example, that it must be taken on a full stomach or with a glass of water.

If you have questions about a prescription, ask your pharmacist before you have it filled. She can tell you about possible side effects, how and when to take the medication, whether generic drugs can be substituted to save money, how to store the medication at home, and whether the prescription is refillable.

POTENTIAL LIABILITY

Dispensing prescription drugs requires a high degree of care, because mistakes can result in injury or even death. If a pharmacist fills a prescription with the wrong medication or the wrong dosage or refills a prescription that was written by the physician as nonrefillable, the pharmacist can be subject to a lawsuit for negligence. A pharmacist may have her license suspended or revoked for a serious breach of professional duty.

Pharmacists also must comply with laws and regulations about storage, record-keeping, and other administrative duties related to prescriptions. Failing to keep drugs in their original containers, which indicate lot numbers and expiry dates, or selling drugs that have been marked as professional samples "not to be sold," can lead to the pharmacist's license being revoked. Also, a pharmacist is required by federal law to keep complete and accurate records of his stock of "controlled substances," such as codeine, phenobarbital, and amphetamine. These are drugs that have such a strong potential for abuse that the government has established guidelines to monitor their use.

See also DRUG.

PHYSICIAN AND SURGEON

Individuals who have received the required professional training and who have been licensed to practice medicine are called physicians, or doctors. Those physicians who perform operations on the human body are called surgeons.

LICENSING

Physicians are regulated provincially by corporations of physicians. The corporations can temporarily suspend or permanently bar a physician from practicing in a province in the event of professional misconduct.

A physician is held to a standard of care of a reasonable practitioner in the same field. In the event of malpractice, you can seek damages through a civil court action.

CONFIDENTIALITY

The doctor-patient relationship is based on trust and a doctor generally cannot be required to reveal any communication she has had with a patient during the course of treatment. In the matter of court testimony, however, the legal system does not regard the doctor-patient privilege in the same way it does that of lawyer and client.

In most provinces, the law requires physicians to notify health authorities when a patient has certain infectious diseases, such as tuberculosis, which could pose a problem to the community's health. Doctors may also be subpoenaed to testify in court concerning insurance and personal injury suits. Psychiatrists are obliged to warn potential victims if a patient threatens to harm them or otherwise cause mischief.

See also PRIVILEGED COMMUNICATION.

PICKETING

When people gather in an area in order to publicly announce a dispute or to gain support for a cause, the practice is known as picketing. Picketers usually carry signs or voice slogans related to their cause. Picketing is most often associated with labor disputes, but it also occurs when there are marches and rallies espousing particular political causes or views.

The Supreme Court of Canada has recognized picketing as a form of expression protected under article 2(b) of the Charter of Rights and Freedoms. The Court, however, has also upheld laws and court orders limiting the right to picket when these limitations could be justified as "reasonable limits prescribed by law" under article 1 of the charter. Avoiding the spread of an industrial dispute, facilitating access to a public facility, and reducing the risk of violent confrontation have all been accepted by the courts as grounds for restricting the right to picket under certain circumstances. For instance, an injunction prohibiting striking workers from picketing the place of business of a firm that was not their employer was upheld as was an injunction prohibiting striking employees from picketing the Vancouver Courthouse. See also LABOR UNION; SPEECH, FREEDOM OF.

Picketers who interfere with people who want to go to work or who harass them by threats of violence can be charged with false imprisonment or assault and battery. An employer can ask the court to order a stop to this kind of picketing. Likewise, if picketers make untrue or defamatory statements about an employer, a court may order them to stop.

Picketing is not limited to labor disputes. Political figures are often confronted by pickets at rallies and other public gatherings, and even outside their homes. As long as these picket lines are on public property, they will generally be permitted. But just as in a labor dispute, the picketers can be subject to arrest and prosecution if they interfere with or threaten those who wish to cross their line.

See also Labor Union; Speech, Freedom of.

PLEA

A plea is an accused's response to a criminal charge brought against him by the Crown. An accused can generally choose between two pleas: guilty or not guilty. Under particular circumstances, there are also several special pleas that may apply. These are *autrefois acquit, autrefois convict*, and pardon; or, in a case of defamatory libel, justification.

Contrary to popular opinion, a defendant cannot plead "innocent," because the purpose of a criminal trial is to find out whether the defendant is either "not guilty" or "guilty beyond a reasonable doubt." A "not-guilty" verdict does not necessarily mean that the defendant is innocent, although he may be, but rather that the Crown has failed to meet the burden of proof that is required for a conviction.

By entering one of the special pleas of *autrefois acquit, autrefois convict*, or pardon, the accused is claiming to have already either been acquitted, convicted, discharged, or pardoned for the offense. If he can show that this claim is true, by indicating where and when the matter was dealt with previously, he will not be tried again for the same offense.

When an accused who has been charged with publishing a defamatory libel enters a plea

of "justification," he is claiming that the matter published, notwithstanding that it may be defamatory, was true and should have been published for the public benefit.

The plea of justification is only available in a case of defamatory libel. In other situations where the accused believes his apparently criminal actions to have been justified, he would plead "not guilty" and attempt to use the justification as a defense in order to secure an acquittal.

See also Criminal Law.

PLEA BARGAINING

The vast majority of criminal charges filed in courts across the country are never tried before a judge or jury. Most are

resolved through a process called plea bargaining. The bargain is that the defendant is treated more leniently, while the prosecutor gets a conviction without having to spend the time and money needed to conduct a trial.

Although plea bargaining is the subject of much criticism, especially from the victims of crimes and from victims'-rights groups, it is essential to the orderly administration of criminal justice. If every accused exercised his constitutional right to a trial, the criminal justice system would collapse under the weight of the constant litigation, because there are not enough judges, prosecutors, or courtrooms to handle the number of trials that would be required. Plea bargains are also used to encourage criminal defendants to cooperate with

---

REAL LIFE, REAL LAW

The Case of the Amazed Attorneys

As a young lawyer, Ross was representing a man accused of stealing a car. The man had just been released from prison in Manitoba, and was returning to his home in Nova Scotia. While in Montreal the accused decided that it would be more comfortable to return home by car rather than by bus, so he stole a car.

The prosecutor was also a young lawyer and both he and the defense lawyer decided that a six-month sentence would be fair in the circumstances. The accused was happy with this development. Ross and the Crown made a deal and both parties asked the judge to hand down a six-month sentence. The judge was not amused. After reading the accused's lengthy record of convictions that dated back many years, he addressed the defendant: "Sir! you are a thief who has learned nothing. I sentence you to two years in prison." Both lawyers were shocked, but learned that a plea bargain made between the Crown and the defense does not always tie the hands of the judge.

---

law enforcement officials in the investigation and prosecution of other crimes.

Sometimes prisoners who enter into plea bargains and then receive harsh jail sentences claim that they were coerced into accepting the plea bargain because of the threat of more severe punishment if they asked for a trial. Such attempts to undo the bargain are usually unsuccessful. But if a prisoner can show that he was misinformed about the consequences of the plea bargain, that he was tricked into accepting it, or that the prosecutor did not keep his promise, then the prisoner may have grounds to appeal his sentence and ask that his guilty plea be set aside and the case go to trial.

PLEADING

A pleading is a formal written statement made to a court by the parties to a lawsuit that spells out not only the issues, but also the positions of the parties to the lawsuit. Pleadings consist of the plaintiff's declaration, bill of particulars, or statement of claim, the defendant's answer to the complaint, and the answers to any counterclaims and cross-claims. If a third party is named in the lawsuit, a third-party statement of claim and answer will be included, too. Normally, pleadings limit the issues that will be contested during the lawsuit. For example, a spouse filing for divorce cannot raise the issue of his spouse's cruelty unless he first made such a claim in the pleadings.

POLICE

Since criminal law falls under the exclusive jurisdiction of the federal government, but the provinces also play a role in administering justice, both levels of government have the power and responsibility for establishing police forces.

Quebec and Ontario each have their own provincial force and, in the large metropolitan areas, municipal forces have been set up under provincial laws. The remaining eight provinces have contracted with the federal government for provincial policing by the federal force—the Royal Canadian Mounted Police, or RCMP. Most small municipalities in those eight provinces also have contracts with the RCMP for municipal police services. The smaller communities in Ontario and Quebec have similar contracts with their respective provincial police. All policing in Yukon and the Northwest Territories is by the RCMP.

Regardless of whether they be federal, provincial or municipal, all police are responsible for protecting the safety, health and morals of the public and enforcing the law. Today, some communities prefer to use the terms "public safety officer" or "law enforcement officer" when referring to a police officer.

Police departments usually require recruits to pass physical and written examinations. Because of the rigorous physical demands of police work, disabled persons may be refused a job with a police

department. However, a woman may not be denied a job because of her gender. Although the physical requirements (for instance, the minimum height and weight) for female police officers differ from those of male officers, once on the force there are no duties from which female police officers are exempt.

The methods of training police officers vary, but they almost always include learning the use of firearms, criminal investigative techniques, and some aspects of the law, such as the rights of the accused and the extent of police powers. Increasingly, police officers are required to take interpersonal training programs to increase their sensitivity toward minorities and women.

POLICE PROCEDURES

Because of their duty to protect the public, police officers are granted a wide range of powers. If they have sufficient cause, for example, they may temporarily deprive people of their rights, as when they take someone into custody. For the most part, however, in the course of their job, they must protect the constitutional rights of all people. To this end, police officers must follow proper procedure when they stop a car, make an arrest, or conduct a search of private property.

Because police work is dangerous and events often happen quickly, police officers are not always able to follow procedure to the letter. Nevertheless, they must observe it as closely as possible. For example, when a police officer sees a person committing a crime, he has the right to give chase and apprehend him, using reasonable force if necessary. Once he has apprehended him, the officer may disarm and search the suspect. But before questioning him, the officer must notify him of his constitutional rights. If the officer fails to give these warnings, any statements made by the suspect may not be used as evidence against him in court. See also ARREST.

Similarly, during a criminal investigation, police officers must follow certain procedures when obtaining evidence. If they do not, any evidence they acquire may be inadmissible in court. Telephone wiretaps, searches, entering a suspect's home, and other intrusions of a suspect's privacy must first be authorized by a judge in the form of search warrants.

In a Supreme Court of Canada case heard in June 1993, the court ruled that the police have the right to enter residential premises without a warrant when they are in "hot pursuit" of an alleged offender, in order to make an arrest. This right to enter premises in hot pursuit applies to persons suspected of having committed indictable offenses or even for infractions of provincial highway traffic acts.

Body searches must be conducted properly too. A woman who is suspected of concealing a weapon or drugs on her person usually can be subjected to a strip search only by a female police officer. Conversely, a female police officer is not allowed to strip-search a male suspect. However, if a male or

female police officer has reason to believe that a suspect of either sex is concealing a weapon, the officer may perform a "pat down," or frisk—a quick, external search of the suspect. See also SEARCH AND SEIZURE.

USE OF FORCE

An officer may, and often must, use force to defend himself or to apprehend and secure a suspect, but he may not use unnecessary or unreasonable force. If a suspect does not resist arrest, the officer has no right to use violence. If the suspect is resisting arrest, the officer may use only enough force as is necessary to overcome the resistance.

Police officers may use deadly force—that is, any force that could cause a life-threatening injury—when necessary and reasonable to apprehend and secure a person who is believed to have committed a serious crime, or indictable offense. Deadly force cannot be used against a person suspected of committing a less serious crime, or summary conviction offense. However, if a police officer feels his life is threatened, he may use whatever force is reasonably necessary, including deadly force, in self-defense. See also POLICE BRUTALITY.

A ROUND-THE-CLOCK JOB

When a person becomes a police officer, he takes an oath to protect the public at all times. Essentially this means that police officers are on duty 24 hours a day. They are generally permitted to carry their weap-

ons at all times and to use them if necessary.

Suppose that Doris and her husband Mike, both police officers, attend a hockey game on a day when they are both off duty. While sitting in the stands, they notice that several spectators are becoming rowdy. If the rowdiness turns to violence, with the spectators taking swings at each other, then Doris and Mike are legally required to break up the conflict. In doing so they must identify themselves as police officers. They can make arrests and hold the rowdy spectators in custody until police reinforcements arrive.

YOUR DUTY TO THE POLICE

The public has an obligation to cooperate with the police during criminal investigations. If you refuse, you can be charged with a summary conviction offense. For example, if you are a witness to a crime and the police question you, you must answer their questions to the best of your ability or possibly face obstruction of justice charges.

POLICE BRUTALITY

A police officer can be held responsible in civil and criminal courts if he uses unnecessary or excessive force against a citizen in the performance of his duties. He can be prosecuted as a criminal or sued for any injury or harm he caused.

A Saskatchewan policeman, for example, was ordered to pay $4,545 in damages for having kicked an impaired driver in the knee. In another case, a policeman was ordered to pay damages to an accused whose hand was broken by the policeman's nightstick.

EXAMPLES OF EXCESSIVE FORCE

Courts have found that the following acts exceed a police officer's authority to use necessary and reasonable force:

◇ Shooting and killing a motorist who refused to stop for an officer who wanted to arrest him for drunk driving.

◇ Handcuffing and forcibly placing a citizen in a police car during an unlawful arrest. (Since the arrest was illegal, any force used to effect it was unreasonable.)

◇ Using "third-degree" techniques, such as beating or punching, in order to extract a confession from a suspect.

TAKING LEGAL ACTION

If you feel that you have been the victim of police brutality, you should call the police department and ask to speak with the person who handles civilian complaints against officers. The department will investigate and, if necessary, will take disciplinary action, such as reprimanding, suspending, or even dismissing the officer.

Criminal charges

In addition, you can ask the local prosecutor to file criminal charges against the officer for excessive force. If she feels there is sufficient evidence, she will indict the officer. The charge may be assault and battery or aggravated assault.

Civil lawsuits

You may sue an officer in civil court for assault and battery or for wrongful death (for example, if you believe the police wrongfully killed a relative). At the time of writing, the Montreal Urban Community and one of its officers are being sued by the common-law spouse of Marcellus François, who was shot to death by police who mistook him for another man. In September 1993, the Supreme Court ordered the policeman to undergo a new trial. He was acquitted at trial, but the Supreme Court overruled the verdict claiming the trial judge made an error in instructing the jury.

Your lawyer may suggest that you also file a suit against the police department, as well as the municipality or province that employed the officer. As a result of your lawsuit, you may receive compensatory damages for lost wages, pain and suffering, disability, and the like, as well as punitive damages (monetary awards in excess of the actual harm you suffered). See also DAMAGES; LAWSUIT.

If a police officer uses excessive force against you, he may be violating your human rights.

FACTORS THE COURTS CONSIDER

Each instance of alleged police brutality is considered individually. In reaching its decision, a judge and jury will take the following questions into account:

◇ Was the victim committing an offense at the time of the purported assault, and if so, was the offense, such as a rape or armed robbery, inherently dangerous to the victim, the public, or the police officer, or was it a minor offense, such as shoplifting or vandalism?

◇ Did the suspect resist arrest, and if so, how? Did he threaten the officer with a weapon or shoot at him? Or did he simply have words with the officer?

◇ Was the officer's life or that of anyone else in danger, or did he have reason to believe it was? If a suspect, for instance, reached into his jacket and pulled out a gun, the officer may have believed his life was in danger, even if the gun later turned out to be a toy.

◇ Did the officer give the suspect a chance to surrender peacefully?

◇ Was there any way other than the use of force to apprehend or subdue the suspect?

PONZI SCHEME

Named after Charles Ponzi, a swindler and confidence man who operated in Boston during the 1920s, a Ponzi scheme is a type of investment scam. It purports to offer big returns to investors, when in fact no investments are ever made.

Typically, the swindler recruits participants through social contacts, seminars, or church activities. He offers large returns on a specific investment, such as an oil well or a diamond mine. The first investors receive some money the swindler collects from the next investors, and the swindler pockets the rest. These investors in turn receive money from newer investors, and so on. Eventually, Ponzi schemes collapse, since the number of people whom the swindler can persuade to invest is finite. If no more new investors can be enlisted, then there is no more money to pay to participants.

A warning signal of a Ponzi scheme is an investment that shows high initial returns. For instance, one Ponzi scheme was based on selling shares in a nonexistent oil drilling operation. For every $1,000 invested, the promoter's clients received $500 in interest every three months—a 200 percent annual return. Before long, hundreds of people had invested large sums of money in the supposed oil drilling company. But then the investors stopped receiving their interest cheques. Calls to the promoter went unreturned. Finally, a group of investors visited the promoter's office, only to discover that it was vacant, and that he and their money had disappeared.

In a recent Ponzi scheme involving investors in Montreal and Miami, a company called Premium Sales Ltd. claimed it made money buying large quantities of food products in areas where they were cheap, and selling them wholesale in other areas at considerable profit. The company promoted itself so convincing that it lured hundreds of highly sophisticated professionals and business people, Montrealers among others, into investing about

US$425 million. The company promised a return on investment of about 60 percent, and in fact the early investors received this exaggerated profit.

The company, currently under investigation by U.S. authorities, collapsed in 1993. By then, much of the investors' money had disappeared into the promoters' bank accounts in the Cayman Islands and other offshore banks, where it is immune from seizure by U.S. or Canadian authorities. It is unlikely that more than a small fraction of the money will ever be recovered.

STEPS TO TAKE TO AVOID BEING SWINDLED

Even financially sophisticated investors such as brokers, lawyers, and accountants have been duped by Ponzi schemes. To avoid becoming a victim, consider the following advice:

1. Look into the background of the person making the offer. Call his previous employers to verify his employment claims; check his claims to membership in professional organizations; contact your provincial securities commission or your provincial attorney general's office about his previous investment offerings. Ask your local police department to see if there are any outstanding warrants against him.

2. Be wary of odd or exotic investments in precious metals, oil or gas leases, diamonds, or commodities, especially when they promise you enormous returns. Any investment offer that sounds "too good to be true" probably is.

3. Get the advice of an independent attorney or accountant before you put money in an unfamiliar investment. See also LAWYER; STOCKBROKER.

PORNOGRAPHY

Pornography consists of erotic depictions, either in words or visuals, that are intended to produce sexual excitement or arousal on the part of the reader or viewer. Generally speaking, pornography is not, itself, illegal unless it is deemed to be obscene, or involves the use of children. The Criminal Code defines material as obscene if its dominant characteristic is "the undue exploitation of sex" or of sex and crime, horror, cruelty, or violence. However, the courts must determine what the community will tolerate when deciding what constitutes "undue exploitation" in any individual case.

The Supreme Court has attempted to develop criteria for deciding where to draw the line. It found that there are three categories of pornography: depictions of explicit sex with violence, depictions of explicit sex which are degrading but do not include violence, and depictions of explicit sex which are neither degrading nor include violence.

Pornography in the first category will almost always be considered obscene. Pornography in the second category will sometimes be considered obscene and sometimes not, depending on the degree of degradation depicted. Pornog-

ABC's

OF BATTLING PORNOGRAPHY

If you are concerned about sexually explicit material being spread in your community, here are a few suggestions on how to control it:

■ Find out if there are municipal bylaws that govern adult bookstores, nightclubs, and movie theaters. Ask if they are being enforced. Many cities have zoning laws that prohibit such businesses from operating within a specified distance from homes, churches, or schools. Others require that nearby businesses and residents consent to the opening of a business that sells pornography.

■ If you have heard or seen obscene or pornographic materials over radio or television, including cable television stations, write a letter of complaint to the station and send a copy to the the Canadian Radio-Television and Telecommunications Commission in Hull, Que. See USEFUL ADDRESSES at back of book.

■ To prevent an unwanted channel from being broadcast to your home by your cable television service, ask the cable company to block reception or to provide a blocking device that you can install.

■ If you receive offensive materials in the mail, tell your local post office. At your request, Canada Post is legally required to order anyone who sends you such mail to stop.

raphy in the third category will generally be tolerated unless it includes children.

In an attempt to discourage pedophilia and stop the flow of child pornography being produced and distributed in an underground network of pedophiles, Parliament has recently enacted tough new laws banning the production, distribution or possession of "kiddie porn." The new laws make it a crime to depict explicit sexual activities involving children under 18. The law prohibits, as well, material counseling sexual activity with children. While the general obscenity provisions do not prohibit the private possession of obscene materials, the new law banning child pornography does criminalize private possession. See also OBSCENITY.

"LIVE" PORNOGRAPHY

A September 1993 decision by the Supreme Court of Canada set a new standard of what constitutes acceptable and legal "live" pornography. The owners of the Pussy Cat Club in Montreal were charged with keeping a bawdy house. For a fee of $40 to $50, clients were given a book featuring several models, one of which they could chose to "perform" for them. The "performances" took place in a small private room where, for 20 minutes, the nude dancer would appear "in a variety of suggestive positions while caressing herself in simulated or actual masturbation" on a mattress. Clients were encouraged to undress and masturbate while watching the show. Touching the dancers was strictly forbidden.

In a 3-2 decision, the Court ruled that such activities were legal and within the "community standards of tolerance." The standard to apply is not what the community would "applaud, appreciate or even accept" but what it will tolerate, said the Hon. Mr. Justice Peter Cory.

The judge noted that the performances were carried out in private behind closed doors, and both customers and dancers knew what the activities entailed. He characterized the performances as "acts of voyeurism and exhibitionism that did not cause harm to anyone." The judge went on to say that "in these times when so many sexual activities can have a truly fatal attraction, these acts provided an opportunity for safe sex with no risk of infection."

The club's owners pointed out that in the several years of operation, they never received any complaints from neighbors.

POWER OF ATTORNEY

A power of attorney is a written document stating that one person (known as the principal) delegates authority to another person (called an agent or attorney in fact). The agent undertakes to perform certain functions on behalf of the principal, such as handling financial matters, making decisions on medical care, or standing in for the principal during a legal proceeding. (In Quebec, a power of attorney is also known as a mandate, and the person who acts as the agent is known as the mandatory.)

GENERAL AND SPECIAL AUTHORITY

The authority granted to the agent may be very broad or quite specific. Broad authority is given through a "general power of attorney." This kind of document may, for example, designate your spouse to make all financial or medical decisions for you should you become incapacitated.

A "special power of attorney," in contrast, is used to authorize a particular person to take action in one or more specific ways. Suppose Martha is about to go on a long-awaited trek in Nepal. A few days before she is due to leave for the airport, her real estate agent calls to inform her that the couple who wish to buy her house have finally agreed to her price. Despite Martha's protestations, the closing will have to take place while she is out of town. Martha's real estate agent suggests that she designate someone to sign the papers on her behalf. Martha then gives her sister Anne specific power of attorney to attend the closing and sign all necessary papers on Martha's behalf. Anne's signature is as legally binding as if Martha had signed the papers herself.

Combinations of general and special powers of attorney are also possible. For instance, if Martha had not yet found willing buyers for her house, she could create a power of attorney authorizing Anne to handle only those negotiations necessary to achieve the sale of her house while she was away. Thus Anne could act on Martha's behalf to a great extent, including reaching an agreement on the price and conditions of sale, and even closing the sale, without consulting Martha at any point. But she would not have a general power of attorney over all of Martha's financial affairs.

Obviously, you must be very careful how you word a specific power of attorney, because allowing someone to make important decisions for you can have significant consequences. In addition to making clear the kind of authority granted, a power of attorney should also state when the power goes into effect and when it ends. For instance, Martha may give power of attorney to Anne to be her agent in a real estate closing effective upon the date of her departure to Nepal and ending on the day she returns home. Or she may strictly limit her sister's authority to the particular day when the buyers plan to close the sale.

DURABLE POWER OF ATTORNEY

Generally a power of attorney expires automatically when the principal becomes mentally incompetent, under the theory that the agent can act only to the extent that the principal

could act for himself. However, an individual may appoint an agent to act on his behalf in the event that he becomes incompetent or incapacitated. This special grant of authority is known as a "durable power of attorney." It ends only when the principal dies or again becomes legally competent.

A durable power of attorney may give the agent the immediate authority to act on the principal's behalf, or it may be designed to take effect at a specified time, such as upon the incapacitation of the principal. The latter case is known as a "springing power of attorney," because it "springs" into effect only when a specified event takes place—for example when an agent has medical corroboration that a principal can no longer make decisions about his medical care.

A common springing power of attorney is the "durable power of attorney for health care," which authorizes the agent to make decisions on the principal's behalf concerning the principal's medical treatment, including the administration of life-sustaining procedures. This power of attorney is often used in conjunction with a living will and authorizes your agent to make decisions consistent with your living will. See EVERYDAY LEGAL FORMS at back of book.

See also LIVING WILL.

REVOCATION

To revoke a power of attorney, you can write "revoked" across the document or simply tear it up. You should also notify the agent that you are revoking his

ABC's

OF PREPARING A POWER OF ATTORNEY

Suppose you have decided to give your power of attorney to an agent who has agreed to act on your behalf. Now you have to draft the document so that it will be legally valid. If you carefully follow the advice below, your power of attorney should be free of problems.

■ For legibility, write the document on a typewriter or word processor, although a handwritten version will probably be valid. If you prefer, you can obtain a blank power-of-attorney form from your stationery store or bank. For samples of various power of attorney forms, see EVERYDAY LEGAL FORMS, at back of book.

■ Clearly identify yourself and your agent (or agents), using full legal names and addresses. Note any relevant information about your relationship to the agent—for example, whether she is your spouse or a sibling.

■ Describe, in plain but precise language, the authority that you have conveyed. Indicate whether the power is general or special. State any limitations on the agent's authority.

■ If you intend to give a power of attorney that will take effect in the future, indicate what event will put it into effect—for example, if you become incapacitated by illness and you wish the power of attorney to continue during your incapacity.

■ If you are granting the power to take part in a real estate transaction, include a legal description of the property on the power-of-attorney document. A simple description of the property may be sufficient, but some provinces and financial institutions require the standard legal description that is used in drawing up deeds.

■ Specify when the power of attorney is to become effective and when it will end. State how and when the power of attorney may be revoked, such as by notifying the agent in writing that you are terminating the agreement and tearing up the original.

■ Both you and your agent should sign and date the document. If you have designated more than one agent, each agent should sign and date the document. The signatures should be notarized.

■ Some provinces require two witnesses to be present at the signing. If so, be sure the witnesses are of legal age.

■ Before you have signed, notarized, and recorded your draft, you may wish to have a lawyer review it (even though this is not required by law). Unless major changes are required, the lawyer's review should be relatively inexpensive.

■ Some provinces may require a power of attorney to be recorded at the local courthouse. This is advisable even if it is not required by law, because it strengthens the authenticity of your power of attorney.

power of attorney. Agents may also relinquish their authority to act under the power of attorney. If there is any disagreement over ending the power of attorney, see a lawyer.

If any interested party wants to challenge a power of attorney, he can do so in court. For instance, if the family members of a principal feel that she was coerced or misled into granting a power of attorney, they can ask a court to revoke it.

PROS AND CONS

By selecting whom you wish to stand in your stead, you can avoid the need for a government or court to choose an agent for you in an emergency. Since you can designate the amount of authority you wish to convey and the circum-

stances under which the power should be revoked, you will have a greater degree of control over your affairs than you would otherwise.

Never underestimate the magnitude of the power of attorney. Once in effect, the right of the agent to act on your behalf is virtually absolute, and you are legally bound by the actions of the agent. As principal, you should choose your agent very carefully. It must be someone who has your complete trust and enough knowledge of your affairs to handle them competently.

You should not accept a power of attorney without first understanding what may be expected of you. Just as the law recognizes the authority granted by a power of attorney, so does it impose a duty on the agent to be careful and judicious in upholding the wishes of the principal. You can be held financially responsible to the principal for any mistakes you make as the principal's agent. Bear in mind that you are under no obligation to accept the authority of power of attorney granted to you. You can simply decline to sign the form that authorizes it.

PRELIMINARY HEARING

When a person is accused of a serious crime, a preliminary hearing is held in court to decide whether there is strong enough evidence for the case to go to trial. The hearing is a procedural safeguard against a person's being subjected to a criminal prosecution based on insufficient or improperly obtained evidence.

At the hearing the prosecutor must show that he has reasonable grounds, or "probable cause," to believe that a crime has been committed and that the suspect committed it. The prosecutor is not required to prove his case beyond a reasonable doubt. In fact, at this point if there is any doubt that there is sufficient proof of a crime, the doubt works against the accused, so that a trial would be ordered. Of course, if there appears to be a reasonable doubt as to the accused's guilt, he will be acquitted.

The defense will try to counter the prosecution's claims or will raise arguments about whether the evidence is sufficient or was properly obtained by the police or the prosecutor. If the judge determines that there is no probable cause, the case will be dismissed and the prosecution terminated, at least until the prosecutor and police can obtain enough evidence to show probable cause, which may result in another hearing.

See also CRIMINAL PROCEDURE.

PREMEDITATION

The plan or decision to commit a crime before it is actually carried out is known as premeditation. The plan does not have to be elaborate, and the decision does not have to be made far in advance of the criminal act. Suppose a husband sees his wife standing at the top of a long flight of stairs. The couple had been arguing and it occurs to the husband that if he pushes his wife down the stairs she will be killed. If he acts on his thought, even just a moment later, his act is premeditated. Premeditated crimes carry greater penalties than identical crimes committed without premeditation.

See also MANSLAUGHTER; MURDER.

PRENUPTIAL AGREEMENT

A prenuptial (or antenuptial) agreement is a contract, entered into by a couple planning to be married, which specifies their individual property rights throughout the marriage and if their marriage should end. The agreement must be in writing, signed by both parties, and in some provinces, signed before witnesses and entered into the court records.

All provinces have laws that give a widow or widower a minimum interest in the other's property when his or her spouse dies, regardless of what the will says. But when a couple enter into a prenuptial agreement, they do so before either of them has a legal claim to the other's property by virtue of marriage. They are therefore not subject to provincial laws governing the division of property when the marriage ends, whether by death or divorce.

A prenuptial agreement takes effect when the parties marry. It may be revoked or altered at any time, provided both parties agree. Although the courts are reluctant to set aside the terms of a prenuptial agreement, they will not hesitate to do so if one of the parties concealed assets at the time the agreement was made, if one of the parties was "forced" to sign the agreement and therefore did not give a free and informed consent to the agreement, or if the terms of the agreement are such that one of the parties would be grossly cheated if the agreement were honored. This is sometimes known as unconscionability.

DECIDING WHETHER YOU NEED A PRENUPTIAL AGREEMENT

A prenuptial agreement may be a wise choice if you find that your situation is similar to any one of the following:

◇ If you have children from a previous marriage and are entering a new marriage with assets that you wish to keep for them. A prenuptial agreement can stipulate that your spouse may make no claim to those assets in the event of a divorce or upon your death.

◇ If your spouse has substantial assets. A prenuptial agreement can ensure that you receive support during the marriage and in the event of your spouse's death. Your prenuptial agreement may provide that certain property be transferred to you upon the marriage or left to you in a will when your spouse dies. It may also provide that your spouse carry life insurance for your benefit. And it may arrange for support, or limitations on support, in the event of divorce.

◇ If you have inherited property or expect to do so. A prenuptial agreement can stipulate that your spouse shall make no claim on these assets and will allow you to give them to other family members or to whomever you choose.

OTHER CONSIDERATIONS

If you are considering writing a prenuptial agreement with your future spouse, or if you are asked to sign one, note that the law does not condone such agreements as a method of avoiding marital duties. Both parties, therefore, must fully inform each other of the nature and value of their property. A prenuptial agreement is not valid without such disclosure. For that reason, many prenuptial contracts contain a list of the property that each party is bringing to the marriage.

Make quite sure that you and your future spouse understand the meaning and the terms of the agreement. A prenuptial agreement that is signed through coercion, ignorance, or trickery can be declared invalid. Both parties are required to act in good faith. If one party is at a disadvantage because of youth, inexperience, or other circumstances, a court may not enforce the agreement. To be on the safe side, have your lawyer review the agreement.

Make sure that your future spouse will be adequately provided for whenever the marriage ends (whether through death or divorce). The courts do not favor one-sided prenuptial agreements that leave one spouse destitute or encourage divorce or dissension by unduly enriching one partner if the marriage ends. See Everyday Legal Forms at back of book.

PREPAID LEGAL SERVICES

If you are looking for a lawyer, you may want to consider a prepaid legal-services plan. Still relatively rare in Canada, such plans are common in the United States, where independent marketing companies and law firms provide a menu of basic legal services for an annual fee of several hundred dollars. With a prepaid legal plan, you will be able to get legal advice over the phone as well as in a lawyer's office. Most plans also offer the services of a lawyer to review legal documents like wills and real estate contracts before you sign them. In addition, some plans provide a lawyer to write letters on your behalf, represent you in traffic court or in criminal cases, and draft contracts and leases. These services are often free once you have paid the annual fee, but some plans require you to pay additional fees for special services.

Some plans provide coverage in the event of a lawsuit, regardless of whether you are the defendant or plaintiff. A prepaid plan serves its members best, however, when their legal problems are simple and straightforward. It may not be suitable for complicated cases such as contested divorces or bankruptcies, which may need more time than the plan's lawyers can provide.

Some employers now offer a prepaid plan as an employee benefit.

PRESS, FREEDOM OF

Journalists have the same freedom of expression as any other member of the public, but they do not have free rein to gather information and report whatever they wish to report. Section 2(b) of the Charter of Rights and Freedoms protects the freedom of "thought, belief, opinion and expression, including freedom of the press and other media of information." However, there is some controversy about whether the charter protects the right to gather news from various sources or whether it protects only the right to report the news.

This is an important distinction, since if the freedom does not include the right to gather information, then it is easier to justify barring the media from attending certain events. In other words, if a journalist does not have the right to gather information, then he or she can be prevented from gathering it.

For many years, most cases involving freedom of the press concerned the press's right to be in the courtroom during trial, and the press's right to publish information gathered at trial. In most cases, the press is allowed to attend the trial and publish information from the trial. This is based on the premise that the court process should be open and available to the public. In a number of cases, however, particularly criminal trials, courts have found that the individual rights of the accused outweighed the freedom of the press. For instance, if the disclosure of information during a criminal trial might cause a great deal of public debate and speculation, then the court could order that the information not be published until the trial is over. These publication bans are usually allowed because the accused's right to a fair trial could be compromised if the facts of the case are leaked out before the trial is concluded. Many courts have said that publication bans do not really violate the press's freedom because the press will eventually be allowed to publish the information, once a verdict has been rendered in the case.

In civil cases, the same problem exists: is the freedom of the press and the public's right to know more important than the privacy of the parties involved in the case? This will often depend on the kind of case in question. It would be easier to get a publication ban in a divorce case or a custody case, for instance, than it would be to ban the publication of information from a civil trial involving a manufacturer's defective product.

Some years ago, *The Globe and Mail* challenged a decision by Victoria, B.C., to bar all news boxes from city streets on the grounds that the boxes adversely affected the tourist trade. But the court decided the city's action did not violate the freedom of the press.

During the Oka crisis in 1990, Canadian Armed Forces cut off the food supply and telephone communications of reporters on the scene. When the media challenged the army's action, the court dismissed their complaints, stating that the media's rights had not been violated and that the army was permitted to handle the crisis as it saw fit.

At the time of writing, two cases are before the Supreme Court of Canada concerning the right to have television cameras in a provincial legislature and a courthouse. In the latter case, the Canadian Broadcasting Corporation (CBC) is contesting the constitutionality of the law prohibiting cameras inside and outside a courtroom. (Television cameras are permitted in courts in 45 U.S. states.) In March 1993, the Supreme Court of Canada allowed television cameras to cover one of its cases, as an experiment. The Court is considering whether to permit regular television coverage of its proceedings.

INVASION OF PRIVACY AND UNNAMED SOURCES

A free press is vital to democracy, but the press does not have the right to invade a person's privacy. Although publishing the truth about a person's private life is not considered libel, it can be an invasion of privacy, which may be grounds for a lawsuit. Such cases are hard to prove, however, because the right of the press to print true and accurate information usually far outweighs the right of a person to keep the same information private.

If a reporter writes about a crime using information from

an unnamed source, a court of law can compel him to reveal the name of his source. If he refuses to reveal his sources or to hand over notes that are pertinent to a case, he may be found in contempt of court and fined or imprisoned.

PREVENTIVE DETENTION

Prisons and other places of detention are not occupied just by persons convicted of a crime. Some men and women are detained there without being found guilty of anything. Held under what is called preventive detention, these people fall into two categories: those awaiting trial who are denied bail because they pose a threat to the public, and those who are involuntarily committed to psychiatric hospitals because they are a threat to themselves or to others.

PRISONERS

Most subjects of preventive detention are people who have been denied bail. Under section 515(10) of the Criminal Code, there are two grounds for denying bail to someone accused of committing an offense. The first is to ensure the person will attend his trial where, for instance, the authorities have reason to believe the person may leave the country or go into hiding if released on bail. The second is where the accused's release may compromise the public's safety, when the accused is likely to commit another offense, or attempt to obstruct justice by, for exam-

ple, trying to convince certain witnesses not to testify.

In one bail hearing, the court stated that the evidence against the accused, the probability of conviction, and the seriousness of the crime should be considered to determine if the accused should be released on bail. The judge must be careful not to try and convict the accused at the bail hearing, keeping in mind that the accused has the right to be presumed innocent.

Just recently, the Supreme Court of Canada struck down a portion of the Criminal Code that states bail may be denied if it is in "the public interest" to have the accused detained. The Court said that the term was too broad.

When an alleged criminal is released on bail, he can remain on bail as long as he respects the conditions of his release. The conditions of bail must also be "reasonable." For example, the accused will not necessarily have to leave a cash deposit to guarantee his bail, but if a deposit or surety is required it cannot be so high that it would be impossible for the accused to satisfy the condition.

A judge can impose a variety of conditions on the accused's bail, as long as they are reasonable and in some way related to the crime of which the person has been accused. In one case, a man who was accused of entering a brothel was ordered to get treatment for a venereal disease as a condition of his bail. The condition was later struck down because it was not related to the charge. (The court said that if the man had

been accused of communicating a venereal disease to another person the condition may have been allowed.)

According to the Charter of Rights and Freedoms, if someone is arrested for allegedly committing an offense, he has the right "not to be denied reasonable bail without just cause." The Crown prosecutor has the burden of proving that the accused should not be released on bail. With certain offenses, especially those related to drugs, the burden of proof is on the accused to show that he should be released on bail. Section 515(6) of the Criminal Code specifically states that those charged with an offense under the Narcotic Control Act must be detained unless the accused shows that he should be released.

Many of the bail-related rules have often been challenged as a violation of the charter, including its guarantee of the presumption of innocence. But, depending on the charge, the courts have held that, in bail hearings, the reversal of the burden of proof is justified. Even though the accused's rights may be infringed, the provisions are often not struck down because they serve an important purpose to our society. For instance, it is acceptable to make it more difficult for a person charged with a drug-related offense to get bail because our society is so threatened by drug trafficking.

THE MENTALLY ILL

Some mentally ill persons may be forced into a hospital against their will through civil commitment proceedings. Only those who the court finds are a danger to themselves or others can be forced into preventive detention in this way.

In a civil commitment procedure, a petitioner—usually a friend, family member, doctor, or law enforcement official—presents evidence to the court that someone is likely to cause harm to himself or others because of his mental illness. In some cases, a person suffering from alcoholism or drug addiction may be the subject of a civil commitment.

The petitioner must prove that the person she is seeking to have committed poses a "clear and present danger to self or others." The fact that he was dangerous in the past or might become dangerous in the future will not justify a preventive detention through civil commitment proceedings.

PRICE FIXING

When businesses in the same industry agree upon a price that they will all charge for the same product, they are engaged in price fixing, a practice that is prohibited by the federal Competition Act. A company that requires retailers to sell its products at a set price is also guilty of price fixing.

Price fixing is difficult to prove. The mere fact that companies charge the same price for the same goods or services is not enough to prove a charge of price fixing.

Sometimes you may notice that all the service stations in town appear to be charging the same price for gasoline, and you may wonder whether the station operators are engaging in price fixing. When service station operators are accused of this, they reply that the practice is "price leadership," not price fixing. This means that one operator sets a price, and the others independently adopt that price in order to compete. As long as there is no agreement among the operators to stick to a uniform price, the law upholds their contention that there has been no price fixing.

PRIOR RESTRAINT

When the government prevents the publication or dissemination to the public of books, movies, or other materials, it is using prior restraint. Such an action contravenes the Charter of Rights and Freedoms' guarantee of freedom of expression: the right to speak and write is worthless unless there is also an opportunity to be heard and published. Thus, any provincial or federal law that requires a person to submit materials to a government agency for approval before publication, that denies a person the right to speak out on public issues, or that prevents a person from distributing handbills is unconstitutional and therefore unenforceable.

However, the government can use prior restraint if it can show that the materials in question (1) present a clear and present danger to the country, (2) are obscene, or (3) unduly invade a person's privacy—causing, for example, irreparable harm.

Private individuals, publishers, and distributors who refuse to publish, distribute, or sell certain materials are not guilty of prior restraint. See also CENSORSHIP; PRESS, FREEDOM OF; SPEECH, FREEDOM OF.

PRISON

A prison is a place where persons accused of crimes are kept until trial, and where convicted criminals are confined until they serve the sentence imposed upon them.

There are several types of prisons. A maximum-security prison is one that holds criminals who are likely to try to escape or who are guilty of violent crimes such as rape or murder. A medium-security prison is one in which burglars and nonviolent thieves are confined. A person who is convicted of a nonviolent crime such as embezzlement or forgery is usually placed in a minimum-security prison. The prison board evaluates each prisoner before assigning him to a particular facility.

Maximum-security prisons have high walls and heavily armed guards. Medium-security prisons may allow the prisoners more access to visitors. A minimum-security prison may resemble a college campus and may not even be fenced in.

Prisons are built by the federal government and most are federally operated. Prisons where people serve sentences of less than two years are run by the provinces and are usually referred to as jails. The federal prisons, where convicts with longer sentences are sent, are known as penitentiaries. Canada's only women's penitentiary is in Kingston, Ont.

PRISON SENTENCE

When a defendant is found guilty at the end of a criminal trial, the court imposes its punishment, or sentence. This may consist of a specified period of time in prison, or a fine, or both. Sentencing must take place within a reasonable time of the verdict. There is currently great concern in Canada about crime prevention, and increasingly this is reflected in the sentences handed down by our courts.

Today, the criminal justice system is trying to put more emphasis on rehabilitating criminals so that they can return to society as productive and law-abiding citizens. The goal is to separate offenders from society only when it is necessary—in other words, only when society would be threatened if the offender were released. The Canadian Criminal Justice Association—which is made up of police officers, judges, lawyers, academics, and former offenders—is among individuals and groups that believe deterrence and rehabilitation of offenders are more effective than imprisonment is in preventing crime. The association recommends "intermediate sanctions"—community service, intensive supervision, drug rehabilita-

REAL LIFE, REAL LAW

The Case of the Prisoner's Prerogative

Some recent court rulings have recognized certain rights that everyone, even prisoners, should enjoy. A prisoner challenged a section of the Canada Elections Act, which prohibited him from voting. The prisoner was successful at trial and was granted permission to vote by the Federal Court. The Crown appealed to the Federal Court (Appeal Division), claiming among other grounds that the section of the Canada Elections Act that denied prisoners the vote was meant to sanctify the franchise in Canada.

The Honorable Mr. Justice James Hugessen of the Federal Appeal Court disagreed, however. He felt that that part of the Canada Elections Act had as its objective "to satisfy a widely held stereotype of a prisoner as a 'no-good almost subhuman form of life to which all rights should be indiscriminately denied.'" Furthermore, the judge said the right to vote was so fundamental in our democracy that it was enshrined in the charter, which guaranteed the vote to "every citizen," prisoners included.

In another case, the British Columbia Supreme Court ruled that even a prisoner had the right to a private telephone conversation, which could not be intercepted by prison authorities unless they first obtained a warrant to do so. If prison security was not at stake, the court ruled that a prisoner has the charter right to be free of unreasonable search and seizure, and listening in to a prisoner's personal telephone conversation infringed on this right.

tion, therapy, and requiring the offender to compensate the victim—instead of prison terms. The financial saving would also be considerable. In 1991, for example, supervised probation of one offender cost about $1,200 for the year compared with $50,400 to keep a single inmate in a federal penitentiary, and about $41,890 to keep one in a provincial jail.

PRESENTENCE REPORTS

Many factors influence the judge's decision regarding the length of the sentence. The circumstances surrounding the

wrongdoing, past criminal record, the person's character, economic situation and social standing, the seriousness of the crime, and the threat that person may pose to the public are all important factors. In some cases, a judge may ask a probation officer to prepare a presentence report. Such a report gives the judge a personal profile of the offender and helps him decide on the most appropriate sentence. The presentence report can be challenged by the offender, and the Crown has the burden of proving the truth of its contents.

The judge can also have the victim prepare a victim impact statement about the harm or loss suffered as a result of the crime.

CRUEL AND UNUSUAL PUNISHMENT

If a person is sentenced to prison, the term must be proportionate to the offense. The Charter of Rights and Freedoms guarantees offenders protection from "cruel and unusual punishment," and a sentence "grossly disproportionate" to the appropriate sentence or "so excessive as to outrage the public's standard of decency" would contravene the charter.

Under the Criminal Code, dangerous offenders can be sentenced to serve an indeterminate prison term. In other words, they will be imprisoned for an indefinite period of time. These sentences have been unsuccessfully challenged under section 12 of the charter. The Supreme Court of Canada has decided that this type of sentence does not violate the section because the offenders have the opportunity for parole at regular intervals. The Court is of the same opinion regarding offenses that carry a minimum sentence of life imprisonment.

If, however, someone is incarcerated for an unusually long period of time and has been refused parole repeatedly without good reason, the court may decide that the offender has been subject to cruel and unusual punishment. On these grounds, the Supreme Court of Canada ruled in favor of a man who had been convicted of attempted rape in 1953 at age 18. For 37 years he had been unable to get parole until, in 1990, the Supreme Court ordered his release.

YOUNG OFFENDERS

The Supreme Court has ruled that young offenders should not be subject to the same sentencing procedure as adults. When sentencing a youth, the courts should consider the seriousness of the offense and the protection of society, but should also consider the needs of the youth and how to provide the guidance and support such offenders need. The Court also stated that, when sentencing, courts should not use the

---

ABC's
OF PRISONERS' RIGHTS

Prisoners' rights have been especially recognized since the Charter of Rights and Freedoms came into effect. Bill C-36, which amended the Corrections and Conditional Release Act, states that prisoners have the same rights and privileges as any citizen, with the exception of those who are necessarily restricted because of their conviction. Many of the following rights have been upheld by the courts:

■ The right to make private phone calls and to send and receive letters without undue restrictions or unnecessary invasion of privacy. But in the interest of security, prison officials may censor a prisoner's mail.

■ The right to privacy when talking with a lawyer or spouse, and probably anyone else.

■ The right (in some provinces) to private conjugal visits with a spouse or other person.

■ The right to medical care and to sue if they are the victims of medical malpractice.

■ The right to regular periods of exercise, wholesome food, clean clothing, and showers.

■ The right to bring a complaint and file a lawsuit against the prison when a prisoner believes his constitutional rights have been violated. To that end, he has the right to consult legal books and, in most cases, to have a lawyer assist him.

■ The right not to be strip-searched by guards of the opposite sex. However, female guards are allowed to "frisk" or "pat down" clothed male prisoners, but male guards may not do so to female prisoners. The right not to be psychologically intimidated or physically abused by prison guards. But, guards have the right to use necessary force to protect themselves and to preserve order.

■ The right to practice one's religion, to have access to religious books and other materials, and to be visited by a member of the clergy.

■ The right to vote.

---

young offender as an example to other youths.

SENTENCING RESTRICTIONS

The judge must decide upon the punishment within a reasonable time, ordinarily within about two months. Before passing sentence, one judge gave a young offender five months to see how he would respond to probation. The Ontario Court of Appeal found that the judge's objectives were valid and upheld his decision. But when another judge gave an adult offender seven months to overcome his drug problem before imposing a sentence, the Nova Scotia Appellate Court found the judge had abused his discretion and ruled his decision inappropriate.

When sentencing, the judge must also respect the jury's conclusions. In one case, a man had been accused of dangerous driving causing death, but the jury convicted him only of dangerous driving. In imposing a sentence, the judge took the death into consideration. The Supreme Court of Canada said that since the jury had not found the man guilty of causing death, the death could not be a factor in the sentence.

If someone is convicted of more than one offense, the judge can order that the sentences be served consecutively (one after the other). In other words, if someone is sentenced to three years for theft and three years for fraud, he must serve six years. If a person has already been convicted of an offense and is in jail, he can still be convicted of a second offense, and the second sentence will be added to the first.

The time served usually begins when a sentence is imposed, but there are several exceptions. If a person was detained before trial, for instance, the time may count as time served, but not if it amounts to less than the minimum sentence stipulated for the offense.

If a prisoner escapes, and is gone for three months before he is caught, the three months will not count as time served. In one case, a prisoner was accidentally released before his sentence had been served. Although the prison authorities had made the error, the court said the offender could be re-arrested and forced to serve the remainder of his sentence.

TYPES OF SENTENCE

The judge has a great deal of discretion in imposing a sentence, and can choose from several different forms of punishment. He can order the offender to pay a fine, or to serve a sentence, or to do both, or to return stolen property. If a new Criminal Code provision becomes law, the judge will be able to order the offender to compensate the victim for injuries suffered or property lost as a result of the crime.

There are "minimum" and "maximum" sentences for certain offenses, but nothing is stipulated for others. If no minimum or maximum sentence is stipulated for an indictable offense, the maximum term of imprisonment is five years.

A person accused of an offense that carries a minimum five-year sentence is entitled to a trial by jury if he so chooses.

A person sentenced to two years or more must be imprisoned in a penitentiary. The judge cannot order otherwise. In a case where a judge wanted an offender, who had been sentenced to more than two years, to receive treatment at a provincial institution, the Ontario Court of Appeal ordered that the offender be sent to a penitentiary. The appeal court noted that the most the trial judge could do was recommend that the offender receive treatment at the penitentiary.

Offenders sentenced to less than two years must serve their sentence in a provincial jail or similar institution.

Conditional discharge and absolute discharge
If someone is found guilty of an offense which does not have a minimum sentence, the court can grant the offender an absolute or conditional discharge. With an absolute discharge, it will be as if he had never been found guilty. A conditional discharge usually carries certain conditions, such as having to report to a probation officer periodically.

Suspended sentence
The court can suspend or postpone sentencing when putting an offender on probation.

Life imprisonment
Anyone convicted of high treason or found guilty of first-degree murder must serve a minimum of 25 years without parole. A person sentenced to life imprisonment for second-degree murder who has been

convicted of murder on a previous occasion must also serve a minimum of 25 years. A person sentenced to life imprisonment for second-degree murder will have to serve only 10 years of his sentence before becoming eligible for parole, unless the court decides that the period should be longer.

Indeterminate sentences

The court can order that a sentence be indeterminate. In other words, the court will not fix a term. It will do this if the offender has a history of aggressive behavior that amounts to a threat to the public's safety, or if the offender is unable to control his sexual impulses which could cause personal injury to other people.

Enhanced sentences

Crime does not pay, especially for repeat offenders. The Criminal Code allows sentences to be increased for offenders with a "record." For example, if a defendant with previous convictions is found guilty of an offense punishable by up to five years, he could be sentenced to the full five years, whereas a person convicted on a first offense might receive a one-year sentence only.

Mandatory sentences

Some crimes carry mandatory sentences. Regardless of the circumstances under which the crime was committed, the judge is required to issue the sentence as laid down by law. For example, if someone is convicted of an offense during which he used a firearm, he must serve a minimum sentence, even if it was a first offense.

♦ Many provinces have passed mandatory sentencing laws for drunk driving. There are federal mandatory sentences for certain crimes, such as trafficking in illegal drugs. The parole boards can sometimes shorten mandatory sentences if circumstances permit.

PRIVACY RIGHTS

Although there is no mention of the right to privacy in the Charter of Rights and Freedoms, it is implied nonetheless since the charter guarantees freedom of association and prohibits unreasonable searches and seizures. The right to be let alone is a cherished one, but some aspects of this right continue to be hotly debated.

INVASION OF PRIVACY

Invasion of your privacy by private individuals or companies is a tort, or civil wrong, and you can sue for any damages you suffer. In order for an action to be considered an invasion of privacy, one of the following must have occurred:

◇ *Public disclosure of private information about you that is offensive or objectionable.* Suppose you are late in making your car payment and the lender sends you a letter of reminder. But on the outside of the envelope the phrase "PAY UP, DEADBEAT" is printed in large red letters for anyone to read. Your privacy has been invaded, and you may sue for any damages that happen to result, such as pain and suffering, humiliation, or some other misfortune.

◇ *Being portrayed in a false light.* Suppose your local television station decides to do a story about insurance swindlers. To illustrate the story, it uses a videotape of you at your insurance office. The implication is that you are one of the swindlers talked about in the broadcast. This puts you in a false light.

◇ *Use of your name or likeness for a commercial purpose without permission.* For instance, a cosmetics company cannot use your picture in a magazine advertisement without obtaining your permission in advance. If it does, you may sue for compensation based on company profits from using your picture.

◇ *Unreasonable intrusion into your private life.* You do not have to endure people peeking in your windows, tapping your telephone lines, or going through your personal belongings without the legal authority to do so.

PRIVACY LAWS

Part VI of the Criminal Code enumerates many offenses dealing with invasions of privacy. The code specifically prohibits a person from "intercepting" a "private communication" without the permission of the party in question. In other words, it would be illegal to record a conversation between two parties without their permission. If they are suspected of being involved in criminal activities, however, police with a special warrant can intercept without the parties' authorization. The conversation of a lawyer and a client, for instance, cannot be recorded even with a warrant, even in a criminal investigation. In one case, however, where a conversation between a lawyer and a client in a police cell block was overheard, the information was allowed in court, because the conversation took place in an area that was not ordinarily used for discussions between lawyers and their clients.

The Supreme Court of Canada has stated that section 8 of the charter, which guarantees the right to be secure from unreasonable search and seizure, is meant to protect individuals from unjustified intrusions upon their privacy. If you are subjected to an unreasonable search and seizure by the police, for instance, the court may not allow evidence obtained by the police to be used against you at trial.

Search warrants

A search warrant may be issued where there are "reasonable grounds to believe that there is in a building, receptacle or place" anything that was used or will be used in committing an offense. In other words, there must be reasonable and probable grounds that a crime has been or will be committed. A police officer cannot search your home just because he suspects you may have committed a crime. However, authorization for search and seizure can some-

times be obtained after the fact. For instance, this might apply if a police officer had reasonable and probable grounds to believe a crime had been committed or was about to be committed and did not have the time to get a proper warrant. If you are arrested, police also have the right to search you and seize whatever you have in your possession if it could be used as evidence against you. They can also seize objects such as knives, which could put them at risk.

In short, the police cannot search your person or enter your home unless they have very good reason to do so. In one case, the police suspected a man of growing marijuana in his home, and peered through his windows to confirm their suspicions. The Supreme Court of Canada ruled that the police needed a search warrant to do so, and found that the man's rights had been violated by a search based only on suspicion.

The Supreme Court also acquitted a couple of cocaine trafficking because the evidence against them had been obtained in violation of their rights. The police had walked into their hotel room through an open door during a firearm search and discovered the couple packaging cocaine.

Your right to privacy also extends to your car and your office. The police may conduct a search only when they have reasonable grounds to believe that you may be preparing to commit a crime or that you have already committed one. In some cases, the police may search your car—if you have

been arrested under provincial traffic laws, for example. Police also have the right to stop you in your car to check your driver's license and registration.

Wiretaps

Electronic surveillance (wiretapping) can be carried out only when the police have a warrant to do so. This is a controversial area of the law: because it involves eavesdropping on private conversations, many regard it as the worst form of invasion of privacy.

Blood samples

The police cannot order a blood sample, or order a physician to turn over a blood sample, unless they have proper authorization. They must either have a warrant or get your consent.

Border crossings

At border crossings, customs officials can search your bags and your clothing. If you are asked to strip for a search, however, you may ask to see a lawyer to inform you of your rights. In one case, for example, the court held that a man's rights had been violated when he had to submit to a rectal examination simply because the police suspected he might be carrying drugs.

Waived rights

If you allow the police to search your home when they do not have a warrant, the court may find that you waived your right against unreasonable search and seizure. If you were not aware of your right or you were unaware of the effects of waiving your right, the court will probably not consider your consent to the search as a waiver of your right.

More questions

This area of the law is constantly evolving as new factors come into play. Cellular phone communications, pagers, video cameras, and other new technologies all raise more questions about privacy rights.

PRIVATE COURTS

Because the public courts are swamped with cases, thereby forcing parties to wait sometimes years before their cases are heard, an alternative dispute resolution (ADR) service, a private court, is becoming more prevalent.

Ontario has had a private court since 1988 and it has proven to be a great success. Seven retired judges sit as arbitrators, and the court functions in much the same way as public courts do. A major difference is that parties may choose to have the private court's rulings binding or not binding. By using sections of the Ontario Arbitrations Act, the court can compel witnesses to appear, and it can enforce the arbitrator's orders. Rules of evidence can be set by mutual consent of the parties, who also agree whether to allow an appeal. If there is an appeal, it is heard by three members of the private court or by a judge of the Ontario Court of Justice.

Pleadings are similar to those in regular courts, though simplified: a statement of claim is called a "claim," and the defendants' document is called a "response." The discovery process is similar to that of the regular courts.

As a rule, private court costs are less than the regular court's, and clients appreciate the flexibility, informality, and privacy of the proceedings. A major advantage is that cases are heard and disposed of much more quickly than they would be in the regular courts.

If the parties want to use the private court for nonbinding arbitration, they can avail themselves of mediation, a mini trial, and a settlement conference. The parties are encouraged to cooperate in many details so as to speed up the process.

Private courts deal with many matters, ranging from small domestic disputes and commercial disagreements to major complicated matters such as the restructuring of the huge Olympia and York company. Certain proceedings, such as divorce and custody matters, as well as all criminal matters, are outside its jurisdiction.

Private courts may be too expensive for typical consumer or landlord-tenant disputes. For alternatives, see ARBITRATION; MEDIATION; SMALL-CLAIMS COURT.

PRIVATE INVESTIGATOR

Private investigators offer a number of services, from looking into the backgrounds of prospective employees to locating missing persons. Some provinces require investigators to be licensed. Others require them to complete law enforcement training courses or to have experience with a law enforcement agency.

If you decide to hire an investigator, bear in mind that you could be held responsible for any misconduct on his part committed during the course of his investigation. For example, if a private investigator breaks into your neighbor's house and removes an item he believes is yours, you could be held liable for any damage he does. You might also be charged as an accessory to burglary if you knew about the investigator's action before it took place.

Quebec's new Civil Code, which came into force on Jan. 1, 1994, reads: "The following acts, in particular, may be considered as invasions of the privacy of a person . . . keeping his private life under supervision." This prohibition may complicate the work of private investigators in Quebec.

STEPS TO TAKE WHEN HIRING A PRIVATE INVESTIGATOR

Before hiring a private investigator, be sure to inquire into his background and expertise. Consider the following:

1. Find out whether the investigator is licensed and check his credentials with the provincial licensing board. You might be charged with invasion of privacy if you use an unlicensed investigator in a province that requires licensing.

2. Ask whether the investigator carries liability insurance. Get the name of his insurance company and check to be sure his policy is in effect.

3. Inquire about the investigator's background. Ask about his training, experience, and whether he has ever been sued as a result of an investigation.

4. Check references. Do not be fooled by an investigator who says he cannot reveal the names of current or former clients out of respect for his clients' privacy. A client can always waive confidentiality. If the investigator refuses to give you references, look elsewhere.

5. Get a written agreement about fees and request that all bills for services or expenses be submitted in writing. Private investigators usually charge by the hour, and their fees vary widely. To be safe, draw up an agreement limiting the number of hours the investigator can spend on your case without obtaining additional approval from you.

PRIVILEGED COMMUNICATION

In recent years there have been many developments in the law concerning privileged communications—namely, what kinds of information are privileged and cannot be disclosed. There are a number of different situations in which you could communicate information believing it would not be disclosed to another party, and this may not be the case.

Medical records and psychiatric records, for example, are not supposed to be released to anybody who requests them, yet in some situations, they may be. If the information would promote public health or safety, for instance, someone may be able to access your medical records. The police may also be authorized to access your personal records.

INFORMATION HELD BY PUBLIC BODIES

Many provinces now have legislation making government documents and records accessible to the public. In British Columbia, Nova Scotia, Ontario, and Quebec, such laws are also designed to protect individual privacy. For example, British Columbia's Freedom of Information and Protection of Privacy Act states that court records, court documents, court notes, and archives of public bodies should be open to the public, and that public bodies must disclose "without delay" any information they have about environmental risks which may adversely affect a group of people, but it bars disclosure of personal information when disclosing it would amount to an "unreasonable invasion" of the individual's privacy. The information can usually be used only for the purpose for which it was obtained. Also, the public cannot access records pertaining to cabinet confidences, personal privacy, trade secrets, labor relations, and commercial relations. There are also restrictions on documents relating to legal advice, law enforcement, intergovernmental relations, conservation of heritage sites, and public safety.

REQUIRED BY LAW

Certain information may have to be disclosed because it is required by law. The Income Tax Act, for instance, may provide that certain financial information be disclosed.

REVENUE CANADA

When you complete your tax return, you may be asked for information about your business, your suppliers, your clients, your accountants, or your lawyers. Similarly, Revenue Canada could ask them to provide information about you.

The type of information Revenue Canada may ask for could concern transactions, or your range of assets. There are few documents that you are allowed to refuse to disclose. Among them are documents held by your lawyer. Revenue Canada may even be able to ask your auditor or accountant to turn over his working papers.

JOURNALISTS

The courts have not yet recognized the reporters' right to keep their sources confidential, and it is very possible that reporters will be required to reveal their sources to prove the truth of their stories. Often, people who give information to the press will ask that their names remain confidential. If a journalist reports a story whose validity is later challenged in court, the journalist may be in a difficult position.

In 1986, *The Ottawa Citizen* reported that a minister of defense had been seen at a strip club overseas while on government business. The newspaper refused to identify the source of the information, because the informant had asked that his identity not be revealed. The court decided that the informant's identity need not be revealed, in the interest of the public's right to be informed and to ensure that reporters' sources feel that their confidence will be respected. The court believed the press's role in uncovering the truth would be hampered if a confidential source feared his identity would be revealed. Nonetheless, the court ordered that three corroborating sources of the story be named.

CLERICS

When you confide something to your priest or minister you might expect that your confidence will never be revealed because you believe that it is a privileged communication. This is not the case. There have been a number of instances where members of the clergy have had to disclose information confided to them. This has put the clergy, as well as those eager to relieve their conscience, in a delicate position.

BANK RECORDS

Historically, the dealings between a bank and its customer could not be disclosed. Over time, exceptions to the rule developed and the bank's records could be divulged if required by law, if it was in the public interest, if it was in the bank's interest, or if the customer consented to the disclosure. These exceptions are still recognized in Canadian law.

In one case, decided in 1983, Amphana went to her bank manager to arrange financing for a restaurant she thought

she could pick up at a good price. The bank manager apparently agreed that it was a good deal, and within weeks the restaurant had been sold—but to the bank manager's wife. Amphana took the matter to court and won her case. The bank manager had breached his obligation to keep the information confidential.

Banks are also required to report suspicious transactions that suggest the customer may be involved in criminal activities. New laws oblige banks, as well as cooperatives, credit unions, loan companies, financing companies, insurance companies, and exchange bureaus to report large cash transactions, usually transactions in excess of $10 000.

MEDICAL RECORDS

As a patient, you have the right to have your medical records kept confidential. Without your consent, they cannot ordinarily be disclosed. If a person is not competent to give her consent, a doctor must nonetheless get the consent of a family member or another person who is able to decide on the patient's behalf.

However, there are laws in place that also make it mandatory for doctors to disclose what would otherwise be confidential information. In Ontario, for instance, if a physician treats somebody who, in his opinion, is not fit to drive a car, he must report it, with or without the patient's permission. If you have been diagnosed with one of a number of communicable diseases, a doctor may also have to report it. The same

applies to cases of suspected child abuse, and cases where the doctor feels the patient may threaten others' safety.

Psychiatrists may also have to disclose information revealed to them by a patient, and in this area of the law psychiatrists are put in a very delicate situation. If a patient confesses to wanting to harm someone or confesses to have committed a crime, a psychiatrist must decide whether the case should be reported to the authorities. This could be a difficult decision for the physician to make, given that if he is wrong, he could be sued for malpractice.

See also LAWYER; MEDICAL RECORDS; PRIVACY RIGHTS.

PROBABLE CAUSE

Simple suspicion that is not corroborated by facts or circumstances is not enough to support an arrest or to justify most searches and seizures. Police officers and judges must have probable cause—that is, reasonable grounds to believe that a person has committed a crime or is about to commit one—before they can take serious action against a suspect. The proper use of probable cause is vital to good law enforcement, and is applicable at several stages in the course of criminal proceedings.

SEARCH WARRANTS

The Charter of Rights and Freedoms protects citizens and their possessions from random, unjustified searches. Thus law enforcement officials may not search civilians or their homes without a search warrant. To obtain a search warrant for a home, office, garage, barn, storage facility, or car, the police must convince the judge that they have probable cause—sufficient information from other sources—to believe that a crime has been or is about to be committed and that evidence of it may be found at the place to be searched.

Before physically searching, or "frisking," a suspect, a police officer must have probable cause to believe that the suspect has the "fruits or instrumentalities of crime"(such as illegal drugs or a gun) on his person. If such an item is in plain view, an officer can arrest a suspect without a warrant. And once a person has been placed under arrest, the police officer has the right to search him for other evidence.

ARREST WARRANTS

A similar procedure must be followed before a law enforcement officer can obtain an arrest warrant. The officer cannot just tell the judge that she believes that the suspect is guilty. She must state the facts and sources of information that led her to that belief and thus provide probable cause.

Warrants are issued for specific places and persons. If it turns out that a warrant for a search or an arrest was not based on probable cause, or that the search or arrest was improperly conducted, then any evidence obtained in the search or arrest cannot be used in court. In the case of

an arrest, the charges will be dismissed and the person will be allowed to go free.

See PRELIMINARY HEARING; SEARCH AND SEIZURE.

PROBATE

Probate, which comes from a Latin word meaning "prove," is the process that establishes the validity of a person's last will and testament. It is also the legal term for settling a deceased's estate. Probate allows for the transfer of assets from the deceased to his heirs, as stipulated in his will. But if the transfer of ownership was made before the person died— for example, by placing property in joint tenancy, naming a beneficiary to a life insurance policy, or establishing a living trust—then those assets do not have to be probated.

The will certifies the transfer of assets from the deceased to his heirs. The person in charge of handling this process is the executor, who is named in the will. The executor's first duty is to present the will to the probate court. Once the will and probate petition are filed with the probate court, the will becomes public record. The court issues a notice of the filing to interested parties and arranges for a hearing. In some instances, the date of the hearing is published in the local newspapers so that creditors can come forward to make their claims.

The probate hearing provides a chance for anyone to contest the validity of the will. There are only two grounds on

which to do so: (1) that the will does not comply with provincial law, or (2) that the person who wrote it was legally incompetent (unable to make rational decisions about the disposition of his property). See COMPETENCY.

At the probate hearing, the witnesses to the will may be asked to swear that they witnessed the signing of the will by the deceased and the other witnesses. (In Quebec, a will is often drawn up by a notary. These notarial wills do not have to be probated.) See WILL.

Depending on the size of the estate, probate can be expensive and time-consuming. The total cost will include lawyers' fees, court fees, and money paid to other professionals, such as appraisers and accountants. From start to finish, probate can take as long as a year or more.

Living trusts, life insurance trusts, and joint tenancy accounts eliminate or reduce the assets transferred through a will so that, in some cases, probate costs may be reduced, if not avoided altogether.

PROBATION

If someone is convicted of an offense, and that person does not pose a threat to society, instead of imposing a prison term, the court may order that the person be put on probation. Even though an offender may not have to go to prison, he will nonetheless have to respect certain conditions of the probation, such as meeting a probation officer regularly, keeping out of trouble, and appearing at court when asked to do so.

If the offender does not respect the conditions, his sentence will be reviewed, in which case either new conditions may be imposed or the probation may be replaced by a prison term.

See also PAROLE; PRISON SENTENCE.

PROCEEDS OF CRIME

Until 1989, the Criminal Code did not have specific offenses for being involved in organized crime or money laundering, or benefiting from the "proceeds of crime." Today, these are offenses and, with drug crimes, make up what are known as "enterprise crime offenses."

Part XII.2 of the Criminal Code, which came into force in 1989, allows police to obtain special search warrants and restraint orders, which they can use to seize property and freeze liquid assets when it is likely that they are proceeds of crime. If the person charged with one of these offenses is eventually convicted, the court can order that the property, and the money, be forfeited. In other words, the criminal could lose the property and the money.

PROMISSORY NOTE

A written document by which one or more persons (known as the "makers") unconditionally promise to pay a specific sum of money to another person or persons (the "payees") at a specified time is called a promissory note. It is used when the payee has lent money or given something valuable to the maker in return for the promise of repayment. When you borrow money from a bank to purchase a car or a home, you will have to sign a promissory note.

Promissory notes are strongly advised when you lend or borrow large sums of money. A promissory note protects the maker from an unscrupulous payee who may demand more money than was originally loaned. The maker is obliged to pay back only the amount set down in writing. To be effective, a promissory note must state the amount to be paid, including the interest rate, if any, and when payment is due, and be signed by the maker. If the note is written to be payable on demand, the payee may redeem it at any time. If the note has a specific date for payment, the payee can collect only on this date.

If the maker dies, a promissory note serves as evidence of the debt, and the maker's estate is obliged to pay it. See EVERYDAY LEGAL FORMS at back of book. See also FAMILY LOAN.

PROPERTY TAX

If you own a home or other real estate, you must pay property taxes imposed by the town or county, and province in which you live. Some provinces and municipalities impose a property tax on personal property, such as automobiles and boats.

These taxes help finance schools, roads, and other public services.

Generally, property taxes are determined by the tax rate (set by the municipality or province) and the assessed value of the real estate. Property assessments are made by an official local body —the board of assessors. To arrive at a value for a property, the board evaluates the home's size, age, acreage, condition, and the value of comparable property in the area.

Depending on law, real estate is reassessed regularly, sometimes as often as once a year, and when it is sold. Whenever your property is assessed, the board must tell you what the assessment is and how it was determined. If you do not agree with the assessment, you can challenge it.

FAILURE TO PAY

If you fail to pay your property taxes, the government can place a lien, or claim, on the property. A lien requires you to pay all past-due taxes and penalties before you can sell it. If you do not pay for several years, the government can foreclose on its lien and force the sale of your property to recover the money owed. See also FORECLOSURE.

PAYING TAXES

Homeowners with mortgages often do not pay their taxes directly to the government. Instead, a portion of the tax is included in their mortgage payments and placed in a tax reserve or escrow account. The bank or lender then forwards

ABC's

OF CHALLENGING PROPERTY TAX ASSESSMENTS

The amount of property tax you pay on your home or other real estate is based on a subjective evaluation of what your property is worth. If you believe this assessment is too high, you have the right to challenge it. To increase your chances of a successful appeal, here are some tips to follow:

■ When you receive an assessment you believe is too high, initiate your appeal right away. In some provinces, instructions for making an appeal are on the tax bill itself; in other cases, you must ask your municipality for instructions.

■ Follow the instructions to the letter. If you must make your appeal in person, do so. If there are forms you need to complete, fill them out.

■ Look for obvious mistakes in the appraisal of your property. For example, your home may have been listed as having three bedrooms and two baths when it actually has two bedrooms and one bath.

■ Assemble the evidence you need to support your case. This may mean securing a private appraisal of your property or obtaining information about comparable properties that have been sold in your neighborhood recently. In some places, an appraiser's affidavit is sufficient evidence; in others, the appraiser may have to appear before the board.

■ If your property is not in excellent shape, obtain estimates of repairs and necessary renovations from reputable contractors. For example, if your house needs a new roof or extensive plumbing or electrical work, submit this information.

■ Attend a hearing before your own case is scheduled. You will learn not only about the board's procedures but also the kinds of arguments that persuade the board.

■ Tell the board in advance what evidence you intend to present, such as photographs of your property and comparable properties nearby, maps of your local area, and the names of witnesses who will appear on your behalf. You may also want to provide copies of your original sales contract to show the price you paid for the property.

■ Present your case briefly and clearly. Do not get argumentative. Claiming you do not have the money to pay your taxes will not help your case.

■ If you are still not satisfied, consider making a further appeal. The board of assessors must tell you what your appeal rights are and how much time you have to file an appeal. You will probably need a lawyer at this stage of the process.

the payments to the tax office. The amount you pay for property taxes may be indicated on your mortgage coupon. If it is not, the lender will tell you what it is.

See also MORTGAGE.

PROSTITUTION

Prostitution, or the exchange of sexual relations for money, remains a serious social problem despite strict laws that make it illegal. In the past, law enforcement efforts were aimed at arresting prostitutes and sending them to prison. Today many communities arrest the customers too.

Prostitutes are at high risk of contracting and transmitting the human immunodeficiency virus (HIV), which causes AIDS.

The Criminal Code makes it an offense to buy or sell sexual services, or to live on the avails of prostitution. The maximum sentence for this offense ranges from five to 14 years.

The code states that a person who lives with or is habitually in the company of prostitutes is presumed to be living off the avails of prostitution. In a case that went before the Supreme Court of Canada in 1992, a man working for an escort service was charged under this section. The man was aware that the agency escorts often received money for sexual activities, though his only role was to answer the telephone and handle the banking and deposits. He did not actually receive any portion of the money earned by the

435

escorts for their sexual activities. He argued that the section of the Criminal Code under which he was charged violated his right to be presumed innocent. Four of the court's seven judges found this was true but said the violation was justified because the law served a greater purpose to the interest of society as a whole.

PUBLIC NUISANCE

Until 1985, when the offense of prostitution was added to the Criminal Code, prostitutes, pimps, and their clients could be charged with running or frequenting a "bawdy house," and prostitutes were often charged with vagrancy. The Fraser Committee report of 1983 had concluded that criminalization would not reduce prostitution but might get prostitutes off the street. It recommended that prostitutes be charged with causing a public nuisance rather than with prostitution.

Some people feel it would be more effective to deal with the social realities that give rise to prostitution—women's poverty and runaway youths, for example—rather than to punish the victims of those realities. Studies have shown that the majority of prostitutes embark on their particular lifestyle when they are young. The Brannigan and Freischmann study, which was based on statistics for 1986-87, estimated the number of youths involved in prostitution ranged from 80 in Halifax to 5,000 in Toronto. Their average age was 15 to 16 years. A large number were victims of physical and/or sexual abuse at home.

PSYCHIATRIST

A psychiatrist is a physician who specializes in the study, diagnosis, treatment, and prevention of mental illness.

Psychiatrists are in a special position of trust and confidence with their patients, who may be in a precarious emotional state. Consequently, psychiatrists often face ethical challenges that other kinds of doctors rarely encounter. For example, when a patient confides his secrets, the psychiatrist cannot ethically reveal them to others without the patient's consent. Because the psychiatrist knows a patient's most private thoughts and weaknesses, he is in a position to exploit the patient and to cause significant psychological harm as a result. One American study discovered that 70 percent of therapists reported that they had treated at least one patient who had had a relationship with a former therapist.

A psychiatrist who engages in sexual relations with a patient can be charged with sexual assault, but prosecution can often be difficult because it can often appear that the victim consented to the act. If you have been abused by a therapist, you must report the incident within a certain period of time if you want to take legal action. In Ontario, for instance, the incident must be reported within a year.

The psychiatrist-patient communication is not as privileged as that of the lawyer-client. A psychiatrist can be subpoenaed in certain cases. If a psychiatrist finds out that one of his patients is about to harm another person, it is his duty to inform the potential victim.

OTHER MENTAL-HEALTH PRACTITIONERS

In addition to psychiatrists, there are other qualified therapists, namely psychologists and social workers, who practice in the mental-health field and are subject to provincial licensing procedures and laws.

In some provinces, however, almost anyone, regardless of training or background, can set up a "counseling" or "therapy" practice. Few, if any provinces, for example, have recognized the occupation of "psychotherapist" as one of the regulated professions. Thus, in most places, anyone—regardless of lack of training—can advertise himself as a psychotherapist. To protect yourself from untrained counselors, be sure to check their credentials and membership in professional organizations. Be aware also that most health insurance companies do not cover counseling from therapists who are not licensed. Call or write to your provincial department of health and the provincial board of medical examiners to find out whether the therapist is licensed and whether any complaints have been lodged against him.

See MEDICAL MALPRACTICE; PRIVILEGED COMMUNICATION.

PYRAMID SALES SCHEME

Employment ads for Koskot Interplanetary, Inc., sounded too good to be true. No experience was required, and the ad assured prospective salespeople that within a year they would make $100,000 annually. When eager candidates dialed the number of Koskot Interplanetary, they learned that they only had to pay a one-time fee of $5,000, which entitled them to distribute Koskot products and earn a 40 percent commission on each sale. Moreover, if a salesperson recruited other salespeople, he would receive $3,000 of their $5,000 start-up fees, as well as a percentage of their sales.

In a classic pyramid scheme, such as the one offered by Koskot, the first participants are paid with money from those who buy in later. In order for the later salespeople to make money, they have to recruit more distributors and so on, until millions of people must be made distributors in order for the previous distributors to make their profits. Those at the bottom of the pyramid will never get their money back. In fact, from the first level of the pyramid to the sixth, the program must have 5,461 participants in order to meet the profits already promised to the first through the fifth level.

Not all sales programs that resemble pyramid schemes are against the law. Many reputable companies use a form of the concept, which they call multilevel marketing. As long as a marketing program's primary goal is to sell products and not distributorships, multilevel marketing is legal.

Koskot Interplanetary Inc. was eventually forced out of business by government prosecutors, but similar pyramid sales schemes continue to surface.

Canada's Competition Act and some provincial consumer protection legislation outlaw all pyramid and referral selling schemes. This includes any multilevel marketing plan that features "head hunting" fees, required purchases as a condition of entry into the plan, inventory loading, or the lack of a buy-back guarantee on reasonable commercial terms. Furthermore, an operator or participant in such a plan cannot advertise or mention the amount of money you can make unless he discloses the compensation received by a typical participant.

Some companies make their money by selling large lots of inventory to participants and then leave the participant on his own to sell the product. Never buy a large amount of inventory and make sure that you can be reimbursed for unsold inventory you did buy. Before embarking on one of these types of selling schemes, write to the Director of Investigation and Research at Industry Canada's Bureau of Competition Policy for an opinion on the legality of the enterprise.

If it is an illegal pyramid selling scheme, the government will investigate and prosecute. You can also find out about the company by getting in touch with your provincial consumer protection commission.

STEPS TO TAKE

Do not buy into a pyramid or multilevel marketing plan before you take the following measures:

1. Ask how much you can expect to earn. In reputable distributing companies, most participants earn $200 to $300 per month or less.

2. Investigate the company's product. Is the price reasonable when compared with similar products sold elsewhere? Does the company stand behind its products with a warranty? Will you be liable if a customer is harmed by the product?

3. Ask whether the company will require you to buy large quantities of their products, and whether you will be able to return unsold products. What out-of-pocket expenses will you incur as a distributor? What expenses will the company pay for?

4. Evaluate the company's payment schedule. If it has sales quotas, ask what yours will be. Find out how many distributors you will have to recruit in order to earn bonuses.

See also PONZI SCHEME; SCAMS AND SWINDLES.

FROM
QUASI-CRIMINAL OFFENSE
TO
QUO WARRANTO

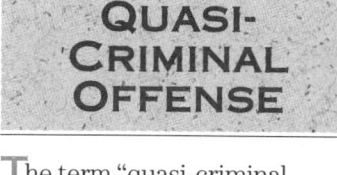

QUASI-CRIMINAL OFFENSE

The term "quasi-criminal offense" typically refers to minor infractions of such regulatory provincial legislation as highway traffic acts, liquor license acts, environmental protection acts, securities acts, motorized snowmobiles acts, trespassing acts, and game and fish acts.

About 95 percent of the offenses involving these laws that end up in court are very minor indeed. Most carry a maximum fine of a few hundred dollars and can be processed by "ticketing," as in the case of a speeding ticket. The alleged offender is given a certificate of offense which contains all the pertinent information, such as the time, location, and names. The set fine for the offense also appears on the ticket.

PLEA OPTIONS

Often, the defendant will have three plea options: guilty, not guilty, or guilty with a reason. The last would apply if, say, a defendant admits to having gone through a red light but attributes part of the fault to bad weather conditions. In such cases, the judge may reduce the penalty, though not the charge itself. This is important: if you plead guilty with a reason, your fine may be reduced but your car insurance premiums will go up, since you will still lose points from your driver's license.

Serious provincial offenses, such as polluting contrary to environmental protection laws, can carry fines of up to $50,000 and/or imprisonment for up to five years. Most likely the accused in such a case will be summoned before the court.

Proceedings are started by laying an information. Any person, though this is usually a provincial offense officer, may provide information under oath attesting that an offense has been committed. If the judge is satisfied that there are sufficient grounds for a case, then a summons, or alternatively, an arrest warrant may be issued. However, it is rare that an alleged offender will be imprisoned awaiting trial for provincial offenses. Most are not serious enough to justify denying the defendant's pretrial liberty.

If you have been charged and fail to show for your court hearing, an automatic conviction may be recorded against you. However, if you can later show,

under oath, that forces beyond your control prevented you from learning of the court date (if the summons was delivered to the wrong address, for example), the judge may strike out the conviction, or grant a new trial. Another alternative is to plead guilty with reason, on the spot. If you lie about the information you swear, you could be liable to fines of up to $1,000, depending on the province.

COURT PROCEDURES

If the prosecution does not appear for the trial, the judge may either dismiss the case or set another trial date. In some cases, you may plead guilty to a lesser offense in court, if the prosecutor so consents (for example, you might plead guilty to following too close rather than to careless driving).

You are allowed to represent yourself or have an agent or lawyer represent you. If the certificate of offense you received is fundamentally flawed, then the judge may quash it: new charges would have to be laid if the prosecution wished to proceed with the case. Often, the judge will allow defective documents to be amended in open court, if both parties are present to have their say, and if doing so would not prejudice the defendant's case.

If you are convicted and fined, you will have a short grace period to pay the fine. In cases where immediate payment would cause undue hardship, the court will sometimes explore alternative payment options. With pensioners, for example, the court may impose a suspended sentence rather than a fine. If you are not satisfied either with your conviction or your sentence, either or both may be appealed in the Provincial Court or the court of appeal of your province.

QUEEN'S COUNSEL

This honorary title is conferred upon distinguished lawyers for years of meritorious conduct. Traditionally, Queen's counselors wear different court robes from ordinary lawyers and are accorded greater respect by their peers than junior lawyers would expect to receive.

QUEEN'S PRIVY COUNCIL FOR CANADA

Commonly referred to as the Privy Council, the Queen's Privy Council is appointed by the governor-general on the prime minister's advice. Its primary role is to aid and advise the governor-general on government matters.

In practice, this work is carried out by the Cabinet, which acts formally as the Privy Council. As a condition of office, all cabinet members must first be sworn into the Privy Council.

The Cabinet exercises formal authority through legal instruments called orders-in-council. These are submitted for approval by the governor-general, who acts as the governor-in-council.

Privy Council membership is for life and is typically extended to provincial premiers, the chief justice of the Supreme Court of Canada, speakers of the House of Commons and Senate, and other distinguished Canadians. Members are given the title "Honorable," and may use the initials "P.C." after their names.

QUIET ENJOYMENT

The right to use and enjoy your home without being disturbed is called quiet enjoyment. It protects you not only from trespassers but from nuisances such as loud music or foul smells, created by neighbors. To enforce this right, you can bring a lawsuit against the offending neighbors. See BREACH OF THE PEACE; NOISE; NUISANCE; TENANT'S RIGHTS.

QUITCLAIM DEED

A quitclaim deed transfers whatever interest the grantor (or owner) has in a piece of property but does not guaran-

tee that no one else has an interest in it. A quitclaim deed offers a buyer the least protection of any form of deed and allows the possibility that his ownership will be challenged later on. Before accepting such a deed, consult a lawyer experienced in real estate law.

QUO WARRANTO

As a legal action, quo warranto has its historical roots in old English common law. Traditionally, it was used to challenge the validity of administrative decisions by government agencies. The person bringing the action was essentially asking "by what warrant" or "by what authority" the administrative agency had made its decision.

A quo warranto writ enabled a litigant to question before a court whether the government agency possessed the necessary legal qualifications for exercising powers of office.

Although quo warranto relief still exists in most Canadian jurisdictions, the remedies of prohibition or injunction are now normally used to settle complaints of this kind. The writ of quo warranto is now mainly used to challenge an elected official's right to assume his office or to continue in office once his mandate has expired.

R
FROM
RAFFLE
TO
ROYAL
CANADIAN
MOUNTED
POLICE

RAFFLE

A raffle is a kind of lottery, a game of chance in which you purchase a ticket for a chance at winning something much more valuable than the price of the ticket. Lotteries and raffles are generally illegal under the Criminal Code. However, the law makes exceptions for provinces setting up lottery schemes, such as Wintario or Loto Quebec.

Charitable and religious organizations, as well as fair or exhibition administrators, may also get licenses to operate a raffle for a given event or period of time. In addition, as long as the bets required do not exceed $200 and the prize $500, anyone may apply for a license to operate a raffle at a place of amusement.

When you buy a raffle ticket, be sure that the raffle is sponsored by a legitimate charity. Keep your ticket stub, because you may not be able to claim the prize without it. If you belong to an organization that wants to hold a raffle, look in the Blue Pages of the phone book for the lotteries commission or other possible raffle licensing agencies in your province.

See also GAMBLING; LOTTERY.

RAPE

Rape occurs if a man has sexual intercourse with another person without obtaining consent. A woman can be considered the victim of rape even if she does not resist her assailant, especially if resisting him would put her in danger of physical harm or death. The crime of "rape" in Canada has been submerged under the newer, broader offense of "sexual assault."

STEPS TO TAKE IF YOU ARE RAPED

By taking these steps and precautions in the event of rape, you will help law enforcement agencies prosecute the rapist:

1. Report the crime to the police as soon as possible. In most communities, a female police officer or victim's advocate will be available when you make your statement.

2. If possible, do not shower or bathe until after you have been examined by a doctor. A physical examination can provide crucial evidence to support your contention that you have been raped and may help identify your assailant.

3. Give the police the clothing you were wearing at the time of the rape.

4. Answer questions from the police truthfully and carefully. However, if an officer should suggest to you that you instigated the attack, ask for a victim's advocate or ask that the officer's supervisor be present. Then answer no more questions until your request is granted.

5. Call a rape victim hotline or community health center for counseling and emotional support. Early counseling can help you to resume a normal life.

See also DATE RAPE; SEXUAL ASSAULT.

REAL ESTATE

The term "real estate," also known as real property and realty, refers not only to land but to everything permanently below it (such as minerals, gas, and oil) and permanently above it (such as trees and buildings). As is the case with all property, real estate may be bought, sold, inherited, leased, or given to someone as a gift.

Provincial laws regulate the manner in which real estate may be obtained or transferred. In all provinces, specific documents must be completed and filed with the appropriate local government agency in order to record a change in real estate ownership.

See also DEED; GIFT; HOME BUYING AND SELLING; LEASE; MORTGAGE.

REAL ESTATE AGENT AND BROKER

The terms "real estate agent," "realtor," or "real estate broker" all refer to people involved in selling and purchasing land. A realtor is someone who is a member of the Canadian Real Estate Association, a nation-wide trade organization. Provincial real estate associations represent realtors' interests at the provincial level. There are also municipal real estate boards. Often these provide a multiple listing service (MLS) which may enhance your chance of selling your property. Not all real estate agents are board members, however, and nonmembers' fees are typically less than those of members.

All real estate agents must undergo professional training and be licensed in order to sell real property. Laws such as Ontario's Real Estate and Business Brokers Act set ethical as well as professional standards. At one time, real estate agents' commissions were set at about 5 percent for "exclusive listings" and 7 percent for "multiple listings" (see below). This regulation has recently been abandoned, but commissions have remained roughly the same. The real estate agent's commission usually is paid by the person selling the property.

LISTING AGREEMENTS

There are three types of listing agreements, or contracts. These set out the respective rights between the seller and the real estate agent.

An open listing. This allows the seller to deal with several real estate agents at once. It is a kind of free-for-all in which the first agent to sell the house gets the commission. One advantage is that potentially many agents and their clients will view the property. The disadvantages are a higher commission and the fact that there is little incentive for a given agent to find buyers. After Agent A has done all the work, agent B can collect the rewards.

Exclusive listing. For a limited time (say, six months), one agent has the sole right to sell a given property. Thus your agent has more incentive to sell the land in question and the commission is usually less than for an open listing.

Co-operative listing. These listings are essentially exclusive contracts that allow the principal agent to employ subagents to sell the property. This is often the quickest way to sell a property, but it can also be more expensive than an exclusive listing.

IF YOU ARE SELLING REAL ESTATE

When you enter into a listing agreement, it should specify:

◇ The property that you are authorizing the agent to sell,

REAL LIFE, REAL LAW

The Case of the Exclusive Estate

While exclusive listings generally entitle real estate agents to the sole right to commission on a given property, the issues can become so complicated that they wind up before the courts.

In one case, John sold his house to Evelyn on condition that if she later sold the property, John could have the first option to purchase. When Evelyn eventually tried to sell her house, she listed it exclusively with Marilyn. As it turns out, John exercised his option to buy back his old house, but Marilyn wanted her commission from Evelyn. The court found that the old buyback option predated, and therefore trumped, the exclusive listing agreement between Marilyn and Evelyn.

In another instance, Carine was engaged as exclusive agent by Emily. Bill made an offer and deposit on the land, which were accepted by Emily. However, just before closing the sale, Bill backed out of the deal. Carine wished to keep a portion of the deposit in her escrow account in order to pay for her commission on the aborted sale. The Supreme Court of Canada held that since the terms of the listing agreement clearly stated that it was Carine's duty to sell, not merely to introduce the vendor and buyer, then no commission was due since no sale had been closed.

as well as any items not included in the sale, such as your antique chandelier or built-in microwave oven.

◇ The period of time for which the agent has the right to list the property.

◇ The amount of the commission. (The average rate is 6 percent of the selling price.)

◇ The listing price of the property.

In some provinces, a listing agreement will be invalid if it does not specify an expiry date; if it has more than one expiry date; or if a copy of the agreement is not delivered to the vendor by the agent immediately the agreement is concluded. Some provinces, Ontario for example, forbid real estate agents from basing their commission upon the difference between listing and selling prices. Instead, the commission must be given a percentage of the sale price or a lump sum. Where there was no payment agreement, the court will fix a reasonable price based on prevailing industry standards.

Market analysis

One reason you pay an agent a commission is to benefit from her expertise in pricing property. Ask her for a market analysis that shows what other property comparable in size, condition, and location is selling for. This will help you to establish a selling price for your home that is in keeping with current market conditions.

Seller's rights

As a seller, you have the following rights:

◇ You do not have to list your property at the price suggested by the agent.

◇ Your agent is required to bring you all offers, whether or not she thinks they are acceptable. Unless you specifically authorize her to accept or reject offers, that decision rests with you. However, if the agent brings you a buyer ready to pay the full listing price at the time and place specified by your agreement, you may be obliged to pay her the commission, even if you reject the offer.

◇ Although most agents prefer an exclusive listing, you may request modifications. For example, you can have a provision stating that if you find the buyer yourself, the commission is reduced or eliminated.

◇ You are not required to show your home at times that are inconvenient for you, to place a "for sale" sign on your property, or to conduct an open house.

◇ Your agent must actively search for buyers—by advertising the property, putting it in multiple listings, or holding open houses. If she does not, you have the right to terminate your agreement.

IF YOU ARE BUYING REAL ESTATE

If you give a real estate agent a deposit on a home, she must keep those funds in an escrow account and must follow your instructions regarding their use. Keep in mind that, in most instances, the real estate agent works for the seller, and that is the person to whom she owes her loyalty.

The courts allow some flexibility in the interpretation of exclusive listing agreements in order to ensure fairness to all

parties. In one case, the defendant seller had agreed to pay commission to the real estate agent up to two months after the listing expired, so long as it could be shown that it was through the agent's previous efforts that the vendor sold the property. Even though the sale technically took place beyond this grace period, the court gave the agent his commission nonetheless, as it found that he was the "real cause" of the sale. The court felt it would be especially unfair to deprive him of his money, since the vendor had entered into a secret agreement with the buyer in order to avoid paying the agent's commission.

See also HOME BUYING AND SELLING.

REBATE

As a way to boost sales, the manufacturers of everything from aspirin to automobiles often offer a rebate—a refund of part of an item's purchase price. When you respond to a rebate offer, you enter into a contract with the company offering the rebate. Like other contracts, a rebate offer is legally binding and can be enforced by a court; but since rebate amounts are usually small, they are seldom worth the expense of pursuing a court action. Nevertheless, there are measures you can take to persuade a company to honor its rebate contract.

Companies that offer rebates are permitted to place restrictions on their offers, but these restrictions must be clearly stated in advance. For example, a rebate offer may require you to buy more than one product or to send the company a copy of your sales receipt as proof of purchase. The company can limit the rebate offer to one per household or to a specified period of time.

Rebates for automobiles and other expensive items may be sent either to the consumer or to the dealer, who uses it to reduce your purchase price. Although the dealer cannot require you to assign your rebate to the dealership, you may not qualify for financing without it, since your down payment will be lower.

STEPS TO TAKE TO COLLECT A REBATE

If you are entitled to a rebate, do the following:

1. Be sure to read the terms of the rebate offer carefully and comply with all the proof-of-purchase requirements.

2. Keep a copy of the rebate coupon and your proof of purchase, and record the date on which you responded to the rebate offer.

3. If you do not receive your rebate payment within the time period indicated by the manufacturer, write to the company at the rebate address. Be sure to include a copy of the original documentation.

4. If you still do not receive a response, write to the president or chief executive officer of the company at its headquarters. You can find the address at the public library or by calling the company. Be sure to indicate a date by which you expect a response.

5. If all else fails, write a letter to the consumer protection agency of your province. Send a copy to the company's president.

RECEIVERSHIP

A court order that places someone's property under the control of an independent person charged with preserving it for the benefit of concerned parties is known as a receivership. When a lawsuit is under way to determine the rightful owner of property, or when a person appears to be unable to meet his obligations as the owner of a business, the court may appoint an independent person, or receiver, to manage the property so that its value is not unduly reduced during that period. Suppose Hector is seriously injured in an accident, and as a result his business falls into debt. Hector's creditors could file a lawsuit asking the court to appoint a receiver.

Courts are usually reluctant to appoint a receiver, because the action takes property out of private ownership and places it under a court's supervision. The receiver does not serve as the representative of the property owner but as an officer of the court, and he must obey the court's instructions in running the business.

Receivers are accountable to the court only and not to the owners of an indebted business put into receivership. In the case of *Acme Ltd.* v. *X Corporation*, the receiver decided to sell off the indebted company to the highest bidder, an action which the court approved. Acme's previous owners sought an order preventing the sale, to allow a last-minute attempt to get the company out of debt. The application was refused and the sale withstood challenge. The court stood behind the receiver's decision to sell because it was a sound business decision.

A receiver who fails to preserve the property entrusted to him can be liable for any losses and can be removed and replaced by another person.

RECEIVING STOLEN PROPERTY

"Hey, buddy," a stranger calls from an alley. "Wanna buy a watch? Only 15 bucks." He shows you an array of expensive-looking wristwatches. You ask where he got them and how he can sell them for such a low price. "They're hot," he replies, using the street term for stolen merchandise.

If you buy a watch and get caught, can you get into trouble? The answer is yes. Possessing property obtained by crimes makes you liable for a variety of charges, including summary conviction offenses punishable by fines of up to $1,000, and indictable crimes punishable by imprisonment terms ranging up to six months, and some up to 10 years.

RECIPROCITY

When provinces extend privileges to each other, they are said to engage in reciprocity. For example, reciprocity may be given in regard to driver's licenses. A driver with a valid license who relocates to another province may obtain a license without having to pass another driving test. Similarly, a person whose license has been revoked in one province may be prevented from obtaining a license in another.

RECKLESSNESS

Rash, irresponsible, or uncaring behavior that shows disregard for the possibility of injuring another person or damaging property is known as recklessness. The Supreme Court of Canada recently defined recklessness as existing where the accused is aware that there is a risk that his conduct may involve results that are prohibited by criminal law, but persists in that activity, despite the risk.

Criminal recklessness is different from simple, civil negligence. In the first case, the defendant must have subjectively known about the risk. In the second, the defendant will be liable even if he didn't in fact know of the risk, but objectively should have.

In the *Hundel* case of 1993, the Supreme Court ruled that, in driving a vehicle, the intent of the driver is not that important. He could be found guilty of dangerous driving even if the intention to drive dangerously was absent. An objective driving standard was felt to be more in keeping with the purpose of the law, which is to promote safe driving.

Prior to this Supreme Court ruling, proving the accused's subjective intent to commit a crime (the *mens rea*) was crucial for the Crown in order to obtain a conviction. For some crimes, the Crown need not show that the accused had a clear intent to commit the crime in question, but rather that there was a form of legally recognized intent, such as "willful blindness," "criminal negligence," or "recklessness." If any of these are shown, then the required intent is inferred by the court. See NEGLIGENCE.

REFERENCE, EMPLOYEE

An employment reference is a statement about the qualifications of a former employee. If you are seeking a reference from a former employer, you may find that he will verify only your dates of employment, your salary range, and your job title. Information that is not requested by the new employer may not be included.

Your former employer may refuse to give information on the telephone and insist that inquiries be written on your prospective employer's letterhead. If an employer gives out a false or defamatory reference that causes you to lose a job opportunity, you may be able to sue him. Suppose you are laid off at your company because of a slump in sales. When you ask the reason for your dismissal, you are told that it is due to your "insubordination" to your supervisor. You may be able to sue your employer for defamation, even if he never gave the false reason for your firing to anyone but you.

In certain cases, employers are allowed a good deal of latitude when making statements about the conduct of past employees. Take the case of Janice, who was dismissed from her welding job for alleged misconduct. Following the dismissal, her employer posted a notice visible to nearly 300 employees that she had been fired for being "dishonest" and "deceitful" as well as creating a disturbance on the job site. Janice sued her employer and was successful in showing that he had made defamatory statements. However, the court found that, since it was in the interests of both management and labor to have full disclosure of facts surrounding this incident, then the employer should enjoy a "qualified privilege" relieving him from liability.

Most companies ask departing employees to sign a form giving their consent to release accurate and truthful information to prospective employers. Be aware that by signing such a form you waive your right to sue the employer when this information is released.

Employers in sectors such as the health industry and the securities field are legally bound to ask a job applicant about many aspects of his background. If they fail to do

CHECKLIST

If You Are Asked to Give a Reference

If you are an employer or manager, sooner or later you will be asked to give a reference for a former employee. You will want to consider the following before you agree to do so.

■ **BE TRUTHFUL.**
When firing an employee, give the reason for her dismissal. If the reason is her poor job perfor- mance, do not say that it is a downturn in the company's sales.

■ **OBTAIN PERMISSION.**
Have the employee sign a form giving her consent for you to release accurate and truthful information to the personnel department of a company where she applies for work.

■ **PUT IT IN WRITING.**
Do not transmit uncomplimenta- ry references by facsimile or tele- phone; you cannot be sure who else may have access to the fax machine or who may be listen- ing on another extension.

■ **ENSURE PRIVACY.**
Be careful that no one sees the reference except the person for whom it was intended. Address

the envelope to the person mak- ing the inquiry, and seal it your- self. Do not leave it in an "out" box or anywhere that someone else could pick it up

■ **BE CIRCUMSPECT.**
Do not divulge any information not requested by the new employer.

■ **FOLLOW THE RULES.**
If you are a manager, follow your company's policy if you are asked to give a reference. Failing to give references in the manner set out in company guidelines could jeopardize your own position.

■ **GIVE AN ATTESTATION.**
If you have nothing good or bad to say about an employee, you can always give an attestation, which is a letter that simply says employee A worked for you from one date to another in such and such a position.

so, they could be found guilty of negligence in hiring a person unsuited or unfit for a particu- lar job. For example, a nursing home that fails to check the background of a newly hired orderly who was dismissed from his previous job for physi- cally abusing patients can be held legally responsible for any injuries the orderly inflicts at his new workplace. See also BLACKLISTING; WHISTLE-BLOWER.

REGISTERED RETIREMENT SAVINGS PLANS

In order to have enough money to retire comfortably and independently, many Canadians invest in Registered Retirement Savings Plans (RRSPs). An RRSP is a govern- ment-approved plan which

allows you to accumulate tax- sheltered savings. At the time of writing, Canadians had approximately $200 billion invested in RRSPs.

There are two main advan- tages to RRSPs. First, the con- tributions you make to the plan are tax deductible, resulting in tax savings. Second, as long as the money remains in the RRSP, there will be no tax on the investment income, whether it results from interest, dividends, or capital gains. An additional advantage applies to first-time home buy- ers. If you are buying your first home, you may make a down payment of up to 20 percent of the house price, using funds withdrawn tax-free from an RRSP. These funds must be repaid into the RRSP within 15 years.

You may start an RRSP at any bank, trust company, *caisse populaire*, credit union, treasury branch or other finan- cial institution. Alternatively, you can make arrangements with an investment dealer or broker.

TYPES OF RRSP

There are two basic categories of RRSPs: those offering a guaranteed rate of return, and those whose rate depends on the value of assets held by the plan.

Guaranteed plans, chosen by most people, may allow you to opt for either a fixed or a vari- able rate of return. The interest rate in a fixed plan remains unchanged for anywhere from one to five years, while with a variable plan the rate fluctuates according to the prime lending rate. Under a guaranteed plan, the money will normally be invested in Guaranteed Investment Certificates, available at banks, trust companies, *caisses populaires* and credit unions. However, it may even be placed in a daily-interest savings account.

Mutual funds are a typical vehicle for the second type of RRSP. Although riskier, they have the potential to greatly increase your investment. A mutual fund is a portfolio of investments such as stocks, bonds, treasury bills, and mortgages, which is managed by professional investors. Because the rates of return from these RRSPs can vary widely from one year to the next, they tend to be popular with people investing over the longer term.

Another type of speculative RRSP is the self-directed plan, where you choose the investments that make up the fund. These plans are generally recommended for experienced investors with substantial RRSP savings. In the case of mutual funds and self-directed RRSPs, you may have to pay administrative fees.

CONTRIBUTION LIMITS

The Income Tax Act specifies the amount you may contribute to an RRSP in a given year: the limits for 1994 and 1995, for example, are $14,500 and $15,500 respectively. In general, earned income includes either gross employment income (minus dues and some expenses) or net business income. However, also included are research grants, net rental income, royalties, disability payments from the Canada (Quebec) Pension Plan and taxable maintenance, alimony, and child support payments which you have received. In addition, your maximum allowable contribution will be further reduced if you earned benefits from a deferred profit-sharing plan or a company pension plan.

Contributions to an RRSP must be made within 60 days of the end of the taxation year, which is normally March 1 (February 29 if it is a leap year). However, if you make your contributions as early in the taxation year as possible, the money will begin compounding right away. If you forget or if you are unable to make a contribution for a given year, any unused deduction may be carried forward for up to seven years.

SPOUSAL PLANS

You may not exceed your personal contribution limit when contributing to your spouse's plan. If funds are withdrawn from a spousal RRSP within three years of the time they were contributed, the contributing spouse will have to pay tax on them. Special rules may apply to those receiving retirement income.

If you contribute to your spouse's RRSP, he or she becomes the owner of the assets. This may be problematic for common-law couples when a relationship ends. (Recent changes to the Income Tax Act allow common-law couples to take advantage of these plans.)

RELEASE

A release is a contract under which one person agrees to give up a legally enforceable claim against another. Like other contracts, a release must be supported by consideration—something of value given up by the party obtaining the release in exchange for the other party's giving up a claim. Once a release is signed and goods or money are exchanged, no more claims can be brought.

You are most likely to encounter a release when you are involved in an accident and your insurer or the insurer of the other party asks you to sign a form before paying you a settlement.

Before you sign a release form, be sure to read it carefully. If you do not understand what it says, get the advice of a lawyer. If you think that the amount the insurer will pay will not cover your injuries or damage to your property, do not sign the release or accept the insurer's cheque.

Sometimes medical problems may linger or not even show up until weeks or months after an accident occurred. If you sign a release form before you find out the full extent of your injuries, you may be barred from seeking further payment that you would otherwise have been entitled to receive. See EVERYDAY LEGAL FORMS at back of book.

See also ACCIDENTS IN PUBLIC PLACES.

RELIGION, FREEDOM OF

The fundamental right to freedom of conscience and religion is recognized as such by the Charter of Rights and Freedoms. Therefore no federal, provincial, or local government can pass laws hindering any individual's freedom of religious worship, unless such laws are reasonably justifiable in a free and democratic society.

One of the most famous of religious freedom cases in recent history was the court challenge to the old Lord's Day Act, which prohibited shopping and other forms of commercial activity on Sundays. Interestingly, the challenge came not from a concerned individual but from a corporation. The Supreme Court of Canada struck down the law because it infringed on the religious freedoms of non-Christians who were forced to observe the Sunday Sabbath. However, the courts have upheld some provincial Sunday closing laws on the grounds that they serve a secular, not a religious, purpose which is justifiable in a democratic society.

RENT CONTROL

In an attempt to make rental housing more affordable, many provinces have passed rent control legislation of some form or another. Under the Manitoba Residential Rent Regulation Act, for example, a landlord is generally prevented from raising rent more than once in a 12-month period. Under Saskatchewan's Residential Tenancies Act, any landlord wishing to increase rent must get approval from the rentalsman (the clerk of the rent control office) and the tenant must be given at least one month's notice before the increase takes effect.

Your province's rental board or a local tenant rights advocacy group can tell you about rent control laws in your area.

RENT STRIKE

Suppose you and the other tenants in your apartment building have spent months trying to get the landlord to maintain your building, all to no avail. The garbage is piling up. The hallway lights have burned out and need replacement. Some tenants want to stage a rent strike, but this makes you uneasy. You are not sure that a rent strike is legal.

Your concern is reasonable. For years, all rent strikes were unlawful, and a tenant was obliged to pay rent even if the landlord failed to keep the premises in good repair or to provide such services as water and electricity.

Today, however, the courts are more understanding of tenant's problems and have permitted damage awards against landlords who fail to honor their obligations to their tenants. In one case, where renovations by the landlord caused damage to the tenant's goods—thus breaching the latter's right to quiet enjoyment of the rental property—the court awarded the tenant damages equal to three months' rent. In another case, where the landlord's failure to fix a leaky roof caused water damage to the tenant, the court ordered the tenant's rent reduced.

STRICT REQUIREMENTS

The fact that your apartment needs a paint job or that the appliances are old does not justify a rent strike. Nor can you stage a rent strike if you or the other tenants created the objectionable conditions, by breaking the windows, for example, or piling garbage in the hallways rather than in the receptacles provided. Conditions must be such that the apartment or building is not fit to live in.

If a rent strike is justified and permitted by law where you live, tenants still must pay rent, usually into a court-supervised fund or to a court-specified receiver. The landlord will get the money only after all necessary repairs are made, or the court may order that the money be spent to make the repairs. After the apartment building is brought into a habitable condition, rent payments to the landlord must be resumed.

STEPS TO TAKE BEFORE A RENT STRIKE

A rent strike should always be a last resort. Before beginning one, you should be sure to take the following steps:

1. Provide the landlord with a clear written statement of your complaints, and give him a chance to correct them. Keep copies of all correspondence you send or receive.

2. Keep a careful record of the dates and times of any telephone conversations you have with the landlord, and make notes about what he said.

3. Photograph or videotape the problem. Nothing could be more effective in helping you make your case than a video of mice scurrying around.

4. Ask your local housing department to inspect the building. If inspectors find that the premises are not up to minimum standards, the department can declare the building a public nuisance, and the city will order the landlord to correct the problems.

5. If the problems pose a threat to tenants' health, get in touch with the local health department, which can start legal action against the landlord.

6. Make sure you have solid legal advice that a rent strike is permitted in your community. If you cannot afford to hire a lawyer, contact the legal aid office in your area. Some communities have tenant organizations that can also provide legal help.

7. Since it is always illegal to just stop paying rent without court or rental control board permission, apply to your rent control board or commission or to the courts for permission to withhold the rent or to pay the rent into court until the repairs are done. You may also request that the accumulated rent be used for repairs.

See also LANDLORD; LEGAL AID; TENANT'S RIGHTS.

REPAIR SHOP

Since almost anyone can open a repair shop, finding a business qualified to repair your appliances or electronic equipment can be a daunting task. Moreover, many appliances today are designed to be disposable. It is often cheaper to replace a broken hair dryer, shaver, or coffeemaker, for example, than to repair it. In fact, many companies do just that when you send an item in for service under warranty. The decision whether to repair or replace an item under warranty belongs to the manufacturer, not you. See also AUTOMOBILE REPAIR; CONSUMER PROTECTION; WARRANTY AND GUARANTEE.

STEPS TO TAKE WHEN CHOOSING A REPAIR SHOP

Here are some suggestions on choosing and dealing with repair shops.

1. Look for shops that have been authorized to repair major brand-name appliances. Manufacturers will have already checked to be sure that the shop's repair staff meets their minimum standards. You may pay a little more, but you will have fewer problems, and you may be able to get the manufacturer on your side in the event of a dispute.

2. Ask about the shop's policy regarding estimates. Some shops provide free estimates, while others charge a fee. Either way, be sure you know in advance whether the estimate is binding, and tell the shop to obtain your approval before undertaking any additional work beyond the estimate.

3. Find out what warranties the shop provides. Ask for warranties in writing, and be sure you learn whether they cover parts, labor, or both.

4. Always get a written receipt or claim check, and check any terms it contains before you leave the premises. Some claim checks may give you a time limit for claiming your merchandise, after which the shop will not be responsible for it. If you do not like the terms, take your item elsewhere.

5. Get a date by which the repair will be completed. If there is going to be a delay in getting parts or diagnosing the problem, make sure that the shop will notify you and give you a new completion date.

6. When your repair is complete, get an itemized receipt that shows the charges for parts and labor.

7. If the repair is defective, return the item to the shop and give it a chance to make good on its warranty. But if repeated efforts to fix the item fail, you may want to take it elsewhere. If the item can be repaired at another place, ask the first shop to reimburse you for additional costs. If it refuses, you can seek reimbursement in the small-claims court.

REPOSSESSION

You are a few months late on your car payments, but you expect to pay them off by next week. As you are getting ready for bed one night, you look out the window and see your car being hooked up to a tow truck. You race downstairs and tell the tow truck operator that you are going to make all your overdue payments next week. He takes your car just the same.

Repossession of items that are collateral for a loan is governed by provincial law. In some provinces the lender does not have to notify you of your default or tell you that he plans to repossess your car. When you sign your loan agreement, your car is pledged as collateral. This gives the lender a security interest in your car; if you default, he can repossess it without giving you the chance to pay what you owe. In other provinces, lenders must give you notice and the opportunity to pay your debt.

In British Columbia and Ontario, repossession is not permitted when two-thirds of the debt has already been paid off, unless the creditor has obtained a court order. In Quebec, it is illegal if 50 percent is paid. It is also illegal for a bailiff or repossessor, often called a "repo man," to break down garage doors or force open windows in order to take possession of the car. However, once a court order has been issued, the bailiff may use any means, even picking locks, to repossess your property. (Ontario law states that bailiffs must be polite, and must avoid confrontation at all costs.) Not surprisingly, most repossessions take place at night, when the delinquent borrower is likely to be asleep.

Once the car or other item is repossessed, the lender has the right to sell the item to pay off the loan. If what he gets is less than the outstanding amount of the loan and repossession costs, he can seek a deficiency judgment against the borrower for the remainder of the money. In the unlikely event that the lender sells the item for more than the borrower owes, the excess goes to the borrower.

In general, seized property must be held for a certain period of time before it is sold, during which you can arrange to get it back. In some provinces, you will be required to make all missed payments and pay for the expenses incurred by the creditor in seizing your goods. In other provinces, it may be necessary to pay off the entire debt before your goods can be reclaimed. It is important to ensure that the options available to the creditor are stipulated in the original contract. In Alberta, British Columbia, Manitoba, Newfoundland, Quebec, Yukon, and the Northwest Territories, once the seller has repossessed the item the contract is canceled and you owe nothing more to the seller.

See also COLLATERAL; COLLECTION AGENCY; DEFICIENCY JUDGMENT; SECURITY AGREEMENT.

RESCISSION

Rescission is the cancellation of a contract by the mutual agreement of both parties or by one party who has the proper grounds to cancel (such as breach of contract). Suppose you buy an expensive gold necklace for your wife's birthday at a jewelry store that offers a money-back guarantee. Later, when you discover that your wife likes silver better than gold, you return the necklace, and get a refund. You have rescinded your contract.

But suppose the store refuses to honor its money-back guarantee. You can go to court to seek a rescission, since the store has breached one of the terms of the contract, giving you proper grounds. If you win, the court will order the store to return your money and take the necklace back.

Besides breach of contract, other grounds for rescission include fraud, duress, a mistake in the contract, and the mental incapacity of one of the parties. See also BREACH OF CONTRACT; CONTRACT.

RESIDENCY LAW

A provincial or local residency law, or requirement, determines where you can vote and pay taxes, go to school, or go to court, and it requires you to live in a certain area for a specific length of time before you can do so.

ACCESS TO THE COURTS

Where you live and how long you have lived there can determine your access to the courts.

If you wish to file for divorce, for example, a court in the province where you or your spouse has lived for a year immediately preceding the petition will have jurisdiction to hear your case. Should both you and your spouse file for divorce in different provinces, the court in the province where the first proceeding was started will have exclusive jurisdiction to hear the case.

If you are involved in a dispute over child custody, you may be subject to either federal or provincial residency requirements. If custody is to be determined in conjunction with a divorce, the residency rules under the Divorce Act will apply. However, if the case is being heard in a province to which the child has little connection, the court may order that the case be transferred to the court in the province where the child resides. If the petition for divorce is dismissed or if divorce is not an issue, provincial legislation will apply. Under provincial law, a court in a province will normally have jurisdiction to hear an application for custody if the child is habitually resident in the province. A determination of custody under the Divorce Act will supersede any custody order issued at the provincial level. See also CHILD CUSTODY.

If you enter into guardianship proceedings, you must do so in the judicial district where the proposed ward lives. See also GUARDIAN AND WARD.

PUBLIC RIGHTS AND DUTIES

Provincial and local governments can set reasonable residency requirements. The following are typical:

◇ A province may require proof of residency when you register to vote.

◇ A municipality may require its employees to live within the city limits.

◇ A school district may limit enrollment to students who reside in the district.

◇ A province may require candidates for provincial and local office to have resided in the province or municipality for a specified period of time.

◇ Colleges and universities may set higher tuition rates and stricter entrance requirements for foreign students.

DETERMINING YOUR DOMICILE

"Domicile" is a legal term that is often used interchangeably with "residence." However, the two are not exactly synonymous. A residence can be a permanent, temporary, or part-time abode—a house from which you commute to work, a summer cottage, or even a hotel room you are using on a business trip. But a domicile is the one place that you consider your permanent home. You may have several residences, but you can have only one domicile.

A domicile is generally defined as the place where you normally reside and to which you intend to return when you are away. If you have more than one residence, a court may be called upon to determine which one is your domicile. In doing so, the court will consider the following factors:

◇ Where you pay personal property taxes.

◇ Where you go to church.

◇ Where you are a member of civic or social organizations.

◇ Where your spouse and children live.

◇ Where you vote.

◇ Where you have maintained a residence for the longest period of time.

◇ Where your job is located. The court's decision about the location of your domicile may have important legal consequences. For example, it may determine the province in which you must pay taxes or the province in which your will is administered.

See also DOMICILE.

RESTAURANT

A restaurant is a business that serves prepared food and drink to the public for immediate consumption, and as such it is subject to federal, provincial, and local regulations.

Provincial laws prohibit restaurants from discriminating against their patrons on the basis of race, color, national origin, sex, or religion. They also require restaurants to make reasonable accommodations for handicapped customers and employees. Provincial and local laws regulate sanitation and food-handling procedures, the serving of alcoholic beverages, and other details of day-to-day operations.

CONTAMINATED FOOD

All provinces have laws that prohibit selling contaminated or unwholesome food, but what constitutes contamination varies. If you are served food that you believe is contaminated (food that is spoiled or contains foreign matter), you will have to show that you were actually injured in order to collect damages.

KEEPING CUSTOMERS SAFE

Restaurants have an obligation to maintain reasonably safe premises by keeping the floors and stairs clean and free of debris and the tables and chairs in good repair.

A patron who suffers an injury because there was a dangerous condition on the premises may be awarded compensation if he can show that the condition was created by the restaurant operator, or that the operator knew or should have known about it. For example, if a restaurant employee wet-mops a floor without letting customers know that the floor may be slippery, a patron who slips and hurts himself can sue the restaurant operator. But suppose a customer drops an ice cream cone on the floor and another customer slips on it immediately afterward. In this instance the restaurant is not responsible, since it did not cause the spill and had no time to clean it up before the accident occurred.

Restaurants are also obliged to keep their patrons reasonably safe from the actions of other patrons. For example, if a restaurant operator allows unruly or drunken patrons to remain on the premises and they injure another customer, the operator may be held responsible for that customer's injuries.

See also ACCIDENTS IN PUBLIC PLACES; ALCOHOL.

RESTRAINING ORDER

A restraining order is a court order prohibiting a party from taking some action until a hearing can be held to determine whether the action is lawful. For example, a historic preservation committee can seek a restraining order to keep an owner from razing his building until a court can determine whether the building should be saved. Restraining orders are also known as temporary restraining orders, or TROs.

RESTRICTIVE COVENANT

A provision in a deed to real estate that puts certain restrictions on the owner's use of the property is known as a restrictive covenant or—in real estate jargon—CC&R, which stands for covenants, conditions, and restrictions.

Restrictive covenants are not the same as zoning regulations, which are created by the government. Covenants are often put in a deed by the seller when he sells a part or all of his property. Enforcement of restrictive covenants is generally left up to the owners of neighboring land, whose property values, as well as the enjoyment of their own real estate, are affected by violations of the covenant.

Suppose you own 1,000 acres of farmland, and a developer wants to buy half of it. A restrictive covenant prohibiting him from creating lots smaller than five acres can help to preserve your remaining property's value and to maintain the rural nature of the area.

Restrictive covenants are often found in deeds for residential real estate. Typically, they limit the use of property to a specified purpose—a single-family home, for example. In some situations, they may also do the following:

◇ Limit the height of fences.

◇ Restrict the construction of outbuildings, unless they meet certain standards.

◇ Limit the types of construction materials used.

◇ Limit the number and types of animals kept on the property.

◇ Prohibit planting trees that block a neighbor's view.

◇ Require landscaping and mowing.

◇ Prohibit basketball backboards and hoops.

◇ Prohibit parking on the street.

◇ Require garage doors to be closed.

◇ Regulate interior lighting and exterior paint colors.

Restrictive covenants are usually created by the seller as a part of the new owner's deed; therefore, your neighbor may not have the same kinds of covenants in his deed as you do, or any at all. To find out, you have a couple of options.

FINDING OUT ABOUT YOUR NEIGHBOR'S COVENANTS

If you and your neighbor both live in a planned subdivision with a homeowners' association, you can check with the association's office to find out which covenants apply to your neighbor's property.

Another way to discover the covenants in your neighbor's deed is to visit the land registry or land titles office, where deeds are recorded. You will need to provide the address of the property and the owner's name, if possible, because most deeds are filed by name. If you do not have the owner's name, the recorder may be able to locate the deed by the address. In any event, call the registry office before you go to find out exactly what you will need in order to get a copy of the deed.

ENFORCING A NEIGHBOR'S COVENANT

Trying to enforce a restrictive covenant in your neighbor's deed by filing a lawsuit against him can be difficult and expensive. Before you consider taking legal action, you should do whatever you can to avoid such a confrontation.

It is possible that your neighbor is simply not aware that he is violating a covenant, and bringing it to his attention may be all it takes to resolve the problem. If you live in an area with a homeowners' association, chances are that the association can provide mediation services or will help you to enforce the covenant. If your neighbor refuses to cooperate, and the issue is important enough to you, a lawsuit may be your only recourse.

See also HOME BUYING AND SELLING; HOMEOWNERS' ASSOCIATION; NEIGHBOR; ZONING.

RETIREMENT PLANNING

Too many Canadians find themselves approaching retirement with inadequate financial security. Old Age Security benefits alone were not meant to cover all retirement needs, and retirees should not count on them exclusively. Planning for retirement should begin early in your working life.

Of course, working Canadians pay into the Canada (Quebec) Pension Plan, which provides benefits upon retirement, death, or disability. Companies and institutions may also establish pension plans for their employees which enable retirees to collect annuities. There are also registered retirement savings plans and registered retirement income funds which allow you to build up tax-deferred savings. Many entries in this book will be useful to people who are approaching retirement or who have already retired.

See also AGE DISCRIMINATION; ESTATE PLANNING; FINANCIAL PLANNER; LIVING TRUST; PENSION PLAN; REGISTERED RETIREMENT SAVINGS PLANS; TRUST; WILL.

REAL LIFE, REAL LAW

The Case of the Disputed Development

Sylviane owned property bordering Shuswap Lake in British Columbia. It contained a single family home which Sylviane transformed into a licensed dining room. The venture was quite successful, so Sylviane then added a pub with a deck and live entertainment, and later she added a mini mart. However, the property was subject to a building scheme containing a restrictive covenant stipulating that only dwellings for one family or household unit could be constructed on the lot. Neighboring property owners petitioned the court to declare Sylviane's use of her property a breach of the restrictive covenant.

The court found that the commercial development undertaken by Sylviane was indeed a clear violation of the restrictive covenant. However, counsel for Sylviane argued that the neighbors had waited too long to complain. Since they did not react at the outset of the development, they should not be able to halt the business enterprise this late in the day.

Even though the judge declared that the covenant had been breached, he asked lawyers for both sides to help their clients resolve the dispute in a manner that would enable Sylviane to continue some commercial activity. In the judge's opinion, the neighboring residents had accepted the presence of the initial development; it was the continuing expansion of the commercial enterprise they found unacceptable.

REWARD

A reward is sometimes offered by a person, organization, or law enforcement agency for information leading to the arrest and conviction of a suspected criminal or for the return of stolen or lost property. The reward may be offered to a particular individual or to the general public by posting or publishing an announcement.

OFFER

An offer to pay a reward is like any other contract offer, in that it may be withdrawn at any time before it is accepted. Generally, an offer of a reward is accepted when a person knowingly performs the steps required to collect it, unless a government agency or official has offered the reward. Suppose you provide information to the police that leads to the arrest and conviction of a drug dealer and later find out about the reward. Depending on the way the reward was authorized, you may be entitled to collect even though your actions were not prompted by the reward offer.

TIME LIMIT

If a reward offer does not specify when it will expire, it will generally be considered to remain open for a "reasonable period of time." But what constitutes a reasonable time varies from case to case. Suppose a reward is offered for information leading to the identification, arrest, and conviction of a person who committed an armed robbery or a murder. Because there is no time limit for indictable offenses, the reward might remain open indefinitely. However, proceedings in respect of summary conviction offenses must be instituted within six months of the alleged crime, so that it would be reasonable for a reward in such a case to expire after six months.

ADVERTISING A REWARD

Keep in mind that if you want to advertise a reward for something you have lost, it is usually a good idea not to specify the amount you will pay. For example, if you say "generous reward offered," a person who finds your property cannot keep it if he happens to disagree with you about what constitutes a generous reward.

Sometimes a person offers a reward for the return of a lost or stolen item, and states that no questions will be asked if the thing is returned. However, making such a statement is an offense under the Criminal Code, punishable on summary conviction. It is also an offense for a victim of fraud or theft to threaten the alleged criminal with criminal proceedings in order to be repaid.

See ABANDONED PROPERTY; LOST AND FOUND PROPERTY; STATUTE OF LIMITATIONS.

RIGHT-OF-WAY

The term "right-of-way" applies to situations involving both real estate and automobile traffic. In real estate, an easement, or right, granted by a property owner allowing another person to travel over a portion of the property is a right-of-way. For example, a property owner might grant a right-of-way to the city allowing it to construct a road over his or her land. See EASEMENT.

In traffic situations, right-of-way applies to a person's or vehicle's right to proceed, to which others must yield. Emergency vehicles, such as ambulances, fire trucks, and police cars, for example, have the right-of-way over all other vehicles while they are responding to an emergency with their lights and sirens on. If you are driving and become aware of an emergency vehicle approaching, you must pull your car over to the right side of the road, if possible, and stop until the vehicle passes.

A vehicle traveling on a highway has the right-of-way over cars entering the highway from an on-ramp, and a car traveling on a through street has the right-of-way over cars entering or crossing the street from a side street or driveway. At an intersection with no traffic light or stop sign, or one with four-way stop signs, the right-of-way belongs to the car that reaches the intersection first; if two cars reach it at the same time, the right-of-way belongs to the car on the right.

Pedestrians have the right-of-way when they are crossing a road at a crosswalk, provided they have started to cross before any traffic light or walk signal has changed against them.

See also AUTOMOBILE ACCIDENTS; PEDESTRIAN; ROADS AND HIGHWAYS.

RIGHTS, INDIVIDUAL

Your individual rights, or civil liberties, consist of certain fundamental rights to which you are entitled by virtue of your existence as a human being, and numerous powers and privileges bestowed on you by various Canadian statutes. For example, you hold certain civil rights because of your citizenship or legal residence in Canada—the right to marry and divorce; to enter into contracts; to buy, sell, and own property; and to choose your own religion. These and other rights are recognized in many ways under various laws. Foremost is the federal Charter of Rights and Freedoms, which protects individuals from the actions of federal and provincial governments.

The charter acknowledges that certain freedoms—freedom of conscience, religion, thought, belief, opinion, expression, peaceful assembly, and association—are fundamental rights. It also guarantees citizens certain political rights, such as the right to vote in elections and to run for political office. Concerning legal rights, the charter proclaims that everyone has the right "to life, liberty and security of the person" and to "equal protection and equal benefit of the law without discrimination."

However, because the charter does not apply to relations between private persons, you may have to turn elsewhere to secure your individual legal rights. If you believe that you were discriminated against when applying for a job with a private firm, for example, you might file your complaint under a provincial human rights code, or you might attempt to enforce it in the courts by means of a tort, or an action under family, contract, property, or labor law as the case might be.

SELF HELP

In extreme situations, you have the right to defend your life and the lives of others when they are threatened. So if a robber points a pistol at you, the law does not require you to go to court to obtain an injunction prohibiting him from pulling the trigger. Instead, the law allows you to take immediate steps to protect yourself. Such steps may include disarming the gunman or even shooting him first. See SELF-DEFENSE.

In situations that do not pose an immediate danger, however, the courts frown on self-help solutions. For example, if you rent an apartment to a tenant who refuses to pay the rent when it is due, the law does not let you forcibly remove him, throw his possessions into the street, and change the locks on his door unless you first obtain a court's permission to do so. Similarly, if you enter into a contract with your neighbor to sell him your lawn mower for $100, and he then fails to pay you, you cannot simply take the money from his wallet or bank account. A court must hear the case, and if it rules in your favor, it will order him to make payment.

Despite all its imperfections and delays, the Canadian system of civil and criminal justice provides a workable method for enforcing individual rights with a minimum of disorder.

See also CHARTER OF RIGHTS AND FREEDOMS; CIVIL RIGHTS.

RIOT

In 1986 and 1993, downtown Montreal erupted in riots following Stanley Cup victories by the Montreal Canadiens. What began as a joyous tribute to local heroes soon turned into mass acts of vandalism and looting, resulting in millions of dollars of damage.

The Criminal Code defines a riot as "an unlawful assembly that has begun to disturb the peace tumultuously." A person who takes part in a riot, or a peace officer who fails to take all reasonable steps to suppress a riot, is guilty of an indictable offense punishable by up to two years' imprisonment.

READING THE RIOT ACT

Local and provincial governments have the legal responsibility to suppress riots as quickly as possible. The Criminal Code provides that a justice, mayor or sheriff (or a lawful deputy of the latter two) who receives notice that 12 or more persons are riotously assembled shall go to the place indicated. If he is satisfied that a riot is in progress, he must command silence and, in a loud voice, "read the riot act." This is a proclamation ordering the rioters to disperse or risk being found guilty of an offense for which they may be imprisoned for life. Peace officers, military personnel, and even civilians may legally use as much force as is reasonable in order to suppress a riot. Under the National Defence Act, a provincial attorney general may call upon the Chief of Defence Staff to send the Canadian Armed Forces to help suppress a riot.

If you are charged with rioting, it is not a defense to claim that not everyone who rioted was arrested. The very nature of riots allows many participants to escape prosecution.

UNLAWFUL ASSEMBLY

An unlawful assembly occurs when three or more persons assemble and cause others in the neighborhood to worry that a disorderly and chaotic situation is imminent. When a group of people assemble to commit an unlawful act, for example, they are guilty of unlawful assembly, which is a summary conviction offense.

Protesters who block the entrances to women's health clinics or the offices of foreign countries are often charged with unlawful assembly when they refuse to follow police orders to disperse. Although the protesters have a legal right to express their opinions, they do not have a right to physically prevent anyone from entering the clinic or office building.

ROADS AND HIGHWAYS

Roads and highways are the responsibility of local, provincial and federal governments, which both build and maintain them and make the laws for driving on them.

RULES OF THE ROAD

Because traffic laws are enacted by provincial and local governments, they may vary in minor ways from one place to another, but they are essentially the same throughout the country, as are the penalties for violating them. For example, the law in every province requires drivers to stay on the right side of the road, and in the right-hand lane of multilane highways, except when passing another vehicle or while preparing to make a left turn.

PASSING

Passing on the right is permitted when a vehicle in the left-hand lane is preparing to make a left turn, or it may be permitted on a multilane highway. Passing or driving on the shoulder of a highway is prohibited. You may not pass another vehicle on a two-lane road when you are within 30 metres of an intersection, bridge, tunnel, or railroad crossing. Nor may you pass a vehicle when doing so would require you to cross a solid center line on your side of the road or when passing is prohibited by a highway sign.

You may not pass a school bus in either direction when it is loading or unloading passengers and its red lights are flashing. Even after the bus door closes and the red lights are off, you must wait until the children have crossed the street before you resume driving.

STOPPING

You are required to come to a complete stop at a stop sign or at a red traffic signal. When the light turns green, you may proceed after being sure that cross traffic has stopped or is able to stop. A yellow (or amber) light means "caution." If a traffic light turns from green to amber when you are within an intersection, you may continue through the intersection. If it turns yellow before you enter the intersection, you should prepare to stop if you cannot clear the intersection before the light turns red.

SPEED LIMITS

You must obey all posted speed limits, and you are presumed to know the maximum legal speed even in areas where no speed-limit signs are posted. Although speed limits vary, generally you may drive no more than 50 kilometres per hour in residential areas, 80 kilometres per hour on rural two-lane highways and major urban roads, and 100 to 110 kilometres per hour on major highways. In some provinces, the speed limit in school zones is 30 kilometres per hour. See also SPEEDING TICKET.

TURNING

When making a turn, you must signal your intention at least 30 metres before reaching

OF CONTRIBUTORY NEGLIGENCE ON THE ROAD

If you are injured or suffer property damage on a public highway or road, your claim could be reduced or even denied if your actions contributed to the accident. This is known as contributory negligence, and it includes:

■ Driving too fast for conditions, as on a wet or snow-covered road or during fog.

■ Driving without your headlights on at dawn or dusk, or whenever conditions would require them.

■ Driving on the shoulder of the road, except in emergencies.

■ Driving a vehicle that is overloaded.

■ Driving a vehicle with defective brakes.

■ Driving on the wrong side of the road.

■ Driving on a road when signs indicate it is closed for repairs.

the intersection, giving other drivers sufficient time to react. You must make a right turn from the extreme right-hand lane and a left turn from the lane closest to the center line unless a sign permits use of another lane.

If traffic signals indicate that you may turn on a green arrow, you may do so only if oncoming traffic has stopped and it is safe to proceed. At some intersections, you may be permitted to make a left turn only when the left-turn arrow is green; at others, a left turn is allowed either on a green arrow or a green straight-ahead signal, provided you can do so safely. In most provinces, it is now legal to make a right turn after coming to a complete stop at a red light, but this may not apply in some cities or at certain intersections. See TRAFFIC TICKET.

HIGHWAY CONSTRUCTION AND MAINTENANCE

The building and maintenance of public roads are financed through federal and provincial taxes on gasoline and diesel fuel, through license and registration fees, and revenues and fines from street parking. Provincial and local governments may also issue bonds to help finance road construction and maintenance of bridges, roads, and highways.

Provincial and local governments have a duty to maintain roads, highways, and other public thoroughfares in a reasonably safe condition. If your car is damaged or you are injured because of a poorly designed or maintained street, you can usually sue the government. Quebec, however, has legislation limiting the liability of the province for damages caused to your car because of poor road maintenance.

◆ You must act quickly and follow the steps required by law in filing a claim against the government. In some areas, the local government must have received written notice of a dangerous condition before it can be held responsible for resulting damages. So if you hit a pothole and break a wheel bearing, you may not be able to collect any compensation unless the city was already notified that the pothole existed. In other areas, however, the law holds the city responsible if it should have known about the pothole because the hole had been there for a long time. Under these laws, knowledge of the pothole is not necessary.

You may also be required to file a written notice or claim of damage with a government agency within a specified number of days after the accident.

STEPS TO TAKE

If your automobile is damaged or you are injured because of a poorly maintained or designed road, you can take these steps:

1. As soon as possible, contact the government agency responsible for maintaining the road, and report the incident. If you were on an interprovincial or provincial highway, contact the province's highway department; in a city, the department of streets.

2. Ask the agency to send you any forms that are required for filing your claim.

3. Meanwhile, send the agency a letter confirming the incident. Include the date and time of your initial contact with the agency, the name of the person you spoke to, and the name of the person who agreed to send you the claim forms.

4. Obtain at least two estimates for repairing the damage to your car. For personal injuries, obtain a medical report from your doctor.

5. Complete the claim forms promptly. Send them by certified mail, return receipt requested, so that you can prove that your claim was delivered to the agency.

6. You may want to consult a lawyer about proceeding further if your claim is denied.

See ACCIDENTS ON GOVERNMENT PROPERTY; AUTOMOBILE ACCIDENTS.

ROBBERY

Robbery is a crime against property because it is a type of theft, but it is also a crime against a person, because it involves violence, either threatened or real. A robbery occurs when someone takes or intends to take property by using force or threatening to use force.

Robbery is considered more serious than other types of theft because of the use or threat of violence. The property may be on the person, such as a wallet or a piece of jewelry, or it may be in the person's presence, such as money in a safe. If the robber ties up a person in another room or locks her up while he takes the property, his action is considered a theft in the person's presence, although it occurs elsewhere. See also ASSAULT AND BATTERY.

The property taken in a robbery may be almost anything—money, credit cards, keys, even dentures. It does not have to be something of intrinsic value, as long as it has value to the person from whom it is taken. Nor does it have to belong to that person. Taking property that belongs to you or that you honestly believe is yours is not robbery, but you could still face charges of assault if you use force when you take it.

For a robbery to occur, a theft must be against the victim's will, by violence or intimidation. Suppose a thief steals property from your house while you are asleep. In the legal sense, he has not robbed you, because you were not subject to violence or the threat of violence. Instead, he has committed the crime of theft.

Whether pickpockets and purse snatchers are robbers depends on the circumstances. If someone is able to steal your property without your knowledge and without using force, he is a thief but not a robber.

REAL LIFE, REAL LAW

The Case of the Terrified Tellers

On Jan. 23, 1990, three tellers at a Montreal bank were startled when a man who called himself Claude jumped over the counter into the area where they worked. He then screamed at the manager to come out of his office. Understandably frightened, the tellers promptly backed away from their wickets in order to allow Claude to empty their cash drawers.

Claude was not wearing a mask, was unarmed, and did not use physical violence against any bank employee. However, when he encountered difficulty opening one of the cash drawers, he became frustrated and threw it on the floor.

Claude was subsequently charged with robbery. At his trial, the defense lawyer argued that Claude could not have committed robbery. Under the Criminal Code, a person can only be convicted of robbery if, during the act of stealing, he uses violence or threats of violence. Claude's lawyer suggested that the accused's actions and words did not amount to threats of violence. Consequently, the lawyer argued, Claude should have been charged with theft, not robbery.

Despite the defense arguments, the trial judge convicted Claude of robbery. However, the case was appealed. The deciding issue for the appeal court was whether Claude's conduct could have reasonably created a feeling of apprehension on the part of the three tellers. The court found that at the very least Claude's actions were intimidating, and constituted an implicit threat of violence. The court also stated that due to the nature of their work, it is normal that bank tellers would be frightened by such conduct. Claude's appeal was dismissed.

ROOMMATE

When you decide to share your home with another person, you run the risk of winding up in serious disputes, especially over money. This is true whether you found your roommate through an ad in the newspaper or she has been your best friend since kindergarten. When a roommate does not meet his obligations, the dispute can end up in court.

RESPONSIBILITY FOR BILLS

Perhaps the most common problems that arise between roommates involve responsibility for household bills.

Your rent or mortgage

When you and your roommate sign a lease, it probably will not specify how the rent is to be apportioned between you. It will merely state that each of you has agreed to see that the entire amount due is paid each month. If your roommate does not pay her share, you will have to pay the entire amount to avoid eviction. See also LEASE.

If you own a house or condominium and are paying a mortgage, you are, in effect, your roommate's landlord. You are obliged to make the full monthly payment, whether your roommate pays or not, but you can evict her if she refuses to pay. Similarly, if the lease is in your name alone, the responsibility for paying the rent is yours. Check that your lease even permits you to have a roommate.

If you and your roommate own the property jointly, you are both responsible for seeing that the entire payment is made each month. If you pay your share but your roommate does not, the bank or other lender can foreclose.

Utilities

Bills for electricity, gas, water, cable TV, and telephone service will probably be addressed to only one of you. Even if the utility company puts both your names on the bill, be sure that the entire amount is paid each month. If a bill is in your name and goes unpaid, the service will be cut off, your credit rating may suffer, and you might have a problem obtaining utility service in the future.

Deposits

You may be required to make a deposit before moving into your apartment or to start utility services. Your landlord or the utility company is required to return the deposit to the person who signed the cheque or is named on the receipt, even if some of the money came from someone else. If the deposit is returned to your roommate and part of the money is yours, you—and not the landlord or utility company—are responsible for getting your share from her. Also, in some provinces, the landlord can apply the deposit to money he is due for damages to the apartment, or the utility can apply the money to an unpaid bill, no matter which roommate originally failed to pay it.

Getting what you are owed

If your roommate leaves you holding the bag for a telephone bill or more than your share of the rent, or if she departs with your share of the security deposit, you can take her to the small-claims court. To do so, be aware of the following:

◇ When you file your claim, be sure you know where your roommate can be found. The clerk will need to arrange for your complaint to be mailed or delivered to the defendant.

◇ When you go to court to argue your case, take a copy of the lease, the rental agreement with your roommate, copies of unpaid bills, canceled cheques, and receipts showing what you paid, and any written agreement you had with your roommate about paying bills. If anyone else can give the court information about your claim, ask him to come with you.

◇ If you win your case and the court gives you a judgment against your former roommate, you may enforce that judgment by garnisheeing her wages or bank account. See COMMON-LAW MARRIAGE; GARNISHMENT; LIVING TOGETHER; PALIMONY.

STEPS TO TAKE TO KEEP THE PEACE

Before problems arise, you can minimize the potential for conflict over money matters by taking the following steps:

1. Make a written agreement with your roommate regarding responsibility for bills.

2. Keep accurate records of payments made by all the roommates on all the bills.

3. Make a fair arrangement for buying household supplies, such as food and cleaning products, as by taking turns.

4. Try to keep personal bills separate whenever possible—for example, by buying your own snacks and toiletries.

ROYAL CANADIAN MOUNTED POLICE

From some 700 detachments nationwide, the 20,000-member Royal Canadian Mounted Police (RCMP) enforces federal law across Canada, and provincial and municipal legislation in all provinces and territories outside Ontario and Quebec. RCMP officers also serve as Canadian liaison officers in some 30 foreign capitals. Established in 1873 as the North West Mounted Police (NWMP), the force's mission was to bring law and order to the West, then terrorized by the whisky trade. Organized like a cavalry regiment—but headed by a commissioner, and armed with pistols and small artillery—the red uniformed NWMP routed the whisky traders and mediated between the Indians and the settlers.

In 1919, the force merged with the Dominion Police, which had been established to guard government buildings and enforce government statutes. The following year, the merged force was renamed the RCMP and its headquarters moved from Regina to Ottawa. The RCMP has been Canada's federal police force ever since.

Commonly known as the "Mounties," the RCMP no longer requires its recruits to take mounted training on horses. However, the distinctive red tunics are still part of the dress uniform, even though daily wear is dark blue.

FROM SAFE-DEPOSIT BOX TO SWIMMING POOL

SAFE-DEPOSIT BOX

The best place to store many hard-to-replace documents and small valuables is in a safe-deposit box at your bank.

When you rent a safe-deposit box, you create what is known as a bailment—that is, you entrust your property to the care of another person. In exchange for a rental fee, the bank provides a safe place for your valuables. Because each party in this relationship receives something of value, the bailment is considered to be of mutual benefit. The bank is therefore required to exercise only ordinary care—such as minimizing the risk of theft or damage—in safeguarding your property. See BAILMENT.

The bank's level of responsibility, however, depends on your contract with the institution. Some agreements state that the provider of the safe-deposit box is responsible only for willful acts, such as theft by its employees or agents, but not for ordinary negligence, such as failing to identify someone properly before giving him access to the box. Before signing the agreement, read it carefully. If the terms are not acceptable, ask to have them changed. If your request is denied, you may want to go somewhere else.

In addition to terms regarding liability, the rental agreement should include the following: (1) the names of the bank and the renter, (2) the rental fee, (3) an explanation of how to terminate the agreement, and (4) the rules for access.

ACCESS

If you rent a safe-deposit box in your name only, no one else will be allowed to open it. To gain access to the box, you must bring your key (which is used in conjunction with another key held by the bank) and proper identification. For further protection, you will be asked to sign an access ticket.

Because there may be times when you cannot go to the bank personally to deposit or retrieve items, it may be a good idea to authorize a member of your family to have access as well. It is not enough simply to give your key to that person or write a note to the bank granting your permission. The bank requires a signature from each authorized co-renter. But having two or more names on the rental agreement does not always mean that a co-renter has access to the box if another co-renter dies. In most cases, a safe-deposit box is sealed upon the death of a co-renter. Even though the bank must seal the safe-deposit box when it learns that the box's owner has died, wills, life insurance policies, and other private papers may be removed in the presence of a bank official who will make an inventory of which documents were taken away. Jewelry, bank notes, stocks and bonds, and other articles or documents of value must remain until the deceased's estate has been settled. When a certificate of disposal from the government (showing that all taxes have been paid) and a letter of transmission have been given to the bank, the rightful owner of these valuables, or the executor of the estate, may have access to the safe-deposit box contents.

CONTENTS

All your important documents can go into a safe-deposit box: birth, adoption, marriage, divorce, and death certificates; citizenship papers; mortgages and real estate deeds; stock, bond, and savings certificates; military service records; automobile and homeowners' insurance policies; a copy of your will; and an inventory of your personal property. Make a list of the contents of the box and give a copy to a relative or trusted friend. Update the list periodically.

If you have seldom-used jewelry or a valuable stamp or coin collection that you want to keep in your safe-deposit box, first check that your homeowners' insurance policy covers items stored in this way. If not, see if the bank will insure the contents.

When you rent a safe-deposit box, title to (ownership of) the contents remains with you. If you fail to pay the rental, you may risk losing them. Strict procedures dictate that the bank send you a written notice to remove the contents or pay your back rent. Typically, one or two years must pass before the bank can sell the contents.

SALE PRICE

You can barely believe your eyes. According to the newspaper ad, a $395 cappuccino machine is on sale at the local department store for only $49.99. Before you race to the store, there are some things you should know about the sale prices.

SUGGESTED RETAIL PRICES

According to the ad, the cappuccino machine's "suggested retail price" is $395. Suggested retail prices are set by manufacturers, but they usually bear little relationship to the price the retailer will charge. Almost the only time you will pay a suggested retail price is when you shop at a very exclusive store or order from certain mail order catalogs.

ERRONEOUS ADS

What if the salesclerk informs you that the $49.99 was a typographical error? The advertised price should have read $249.99. Can you compel the store to sell you the item at the advertised price?

Probably not. If the price in the ad was an honest error, the store would not be required to honor it. If, however, you can show that the ad was a lure to bring customers into the store, a court might order the store to honor the sale price. To prove your case, you would probably need to show that the store has a history of deceptive practices or that its management knew of the error and took no action to correct it. But if the store required the newspaper to run a correction or posted a corrective notice in the store, you would have a hard time proving that the low price was an intentional misrepresentation. See also BAIT AND SWITCH; FALSE ADVERTISING.

A similar situation exists when merchandise is tagged incorrectly. Suppose you find a designer dress with a price tag of $24.99. When you take the dress to the register, however, the clerk tells you that the actual price is $249.99. Because anyone can make an honest mistake, you cannot force the store to sell you the dress at the lower price, unless you can show that the tag price was an intentional deception.

STEPS TO TAKE

If you think a store is engaging in deceptive sales practices, this is what you should do:

1. Complain to the manager. A reputable merchant will appreciate being told about a mistake in its advertising or an item that is tagged incorrectly.

2. If an ad contains an incorrect price, check with the advertising department of the newspaper to see whether the store filed a correction. If merchandise is incorrectly tagged, visit the store again later on the same day to see if the price has been corrected.

3. If you suspect that the store is intentionally misrepresenting its prices, notify the Director of Investigation and Research of Industry Canada's Bureau of Competition Policy, or your provincial consumer protection office. You may be asked to file a written complaint; if possible, provide copies of ads and the names of store personnel with whom you spoke.

SALES TAX

Though once challenged in the courts as being unconstitutional, sales taxes on goods and services have become important revenue sources for federal and provincial governments. Up to 1991, when the federal government introduced its Goods and Services Tax (GST), sales taxes were levied solely by the provinces.

Alberta is the only province without a general retail sales tax. Ironically, it was the first province to introduce one. However, the 1936 measure proved so unpopular that it was repealed the following year.

To be constitutionally valid, property subject to provincial sales tax must have a substantial presence within the province. The Supreme Court of Canada recently held that

---

CHECKLIST
How to Avoid Scams and Swindles

A healthy dose of skepticism is the best vaccination against a scam or swindle. Here are some tips:

■ **BE WARY OF PEOPLE WHO CLAIM TO BE POLICE OFFICERS, BANK EXAMINERS, OR OTHER OFFICIALS.**
Don't be fooled by swindlers who **give** you a telephone number to call to verify their identity. The call will, of course, be answered by an accomplice. If you are suspicious, call the police or your bank at the number listed in the directory, not the number the alleged official provides.

■ **DESTROY UNUSED OR INCORRECTLY COMPLETED CHEQUES AND BANK SLIPS.**
If you spoil a deposit or withdrawal slip at the bank, take it home and dispose of it there.

■ **REMEMBER THAT IF AN OFFER SEEMS TOO GOOD TO BE TRUE, IT PROBABLY IS.**
It is better to take a little time to investigate and ask questions than to fall victim to a swindler.

■ **BE WARY OF STRANGERS WHO ASK YOU ABOUT MONEY.**
If you are approached by someone who claims to need your advice about found money, a winning lottery ticket, or some other windfall, chances are you are being set up for a swindle. Call the police immediately.

■ **BE WARY OF BYSTANDERS WHO STAND TOO CLOSE TO YOU IN LINE AT THE BANK.**
Con artists can obtain information from your deposit slips and cheques that will help give them credibility later on.

■ **NEVER GIVE YOUR CREDIT CARD NUMBER OVER THE PHONE.**
Do so only if you were the person initiating the call, and the seller is a well-known company. Beware of "charity" scams or promises to publish ads in unknown periodicals.

♦ Manitoba could not collect a sales tax from Air Canada. Although the airline sold services—meals and liquor—during its flights over the province, the Court did not consider this to be "consumption within the province."

SCAMS AND SWINDLES

Thousands of con artists are waiting to prey on the unwary, with perhaps just as many types of scams and swindles. This entry discusses some common confidence games, but you should also refer to the following: EMPLOYMENT AGENCY; FRAUD; HEALTH CLUB; HOME

IMPROVEMENT AND REPAIR; MAIL ORDER SALES; PONZI SCHEME; PYRAMID SALES SCHEME.

THE PIGEON DROP

The most frequent targets for the pigeon drop are elderly people and newly arrived immigrants. The scam works like this: Harriet is walking down a busy street when she is approached by a younger woman who holds up a bulging billfold and asks her if she has dropped her wallet. Harriet says that the wallet is not hers, and the two women start talking about what they should do, since the billfold does not contain any identification.

At this point, an accomplice enters the scene—Roger, a well-dressed man who offers to help the flustered women. When the con woman, Barbara, shows Roger the wallet, he claims to work for a lawyer and offers to ask his boss what the women should do. Roger disappears for a while, then returns with an elaborate plan. The money, he suggests, should be put in a safe-deposit box at a local bank, and an ad should be placed in the lost-and-found column of the local newspaper. If no one claims the money in 30 days, he says, Harriet and Barbara will be able to keep it. But there is one catch. As a "sign of good faith," each of the women must put up a sum of money (usually $1,000 or more) and store their funds in the safe-deposit box along with the found money.

The swindlers accompany Harriet to her bank, where she withdraws the necessary amount. The man then takes the money from Harriet and Barbara and places it with the found money "for safekeeping." At about this time, Roger excuses himself to make a telephone call to his boss to set up the safe-deposit box. He promises to return in a few minutes. After a while Barbara, pretending concern, goes to look for Roger. Of course, neither she nor her accomplice ever returns, and by the time Harriet realizes she has been tricked, the two swindlers have disappeared for good.

THE DEAD MAN'S BIBLE

For the scam known as the dead man's Bible, a con artist reads newspaper obituaries to find the name of a recently deceased person. Then he visits the home of the grieving family and claims to be delivering a box with merchandise that the deceased person had ordered to be paid on delivery. (In one common version of this scam, the merchandise is an inexpensive Bible which the con artist says is very valuable.) Because the family is usually too upset to ask questions, the con artist walks away with cash or a cheque for the "merchandise." Sometimes the box contains only a brick and newspapers.

THE BANK EXAMINER

In the bank examiner swindle, the con man stands behind his potential victim in a teller's line to learn her address, or he takes a peek at someone's mail to learn where she keeps her bank accounts.

The con artist then telephones or visits the person, identifying himself as a bank examiner who is investigating a bank teller suspected of dishonesty, and asks for the victim's help. All she has to do, he says, is withdraw some money from her account (again, usually around $1,000), place it in an envelope, and take it outside to the "bank examiner," who will then inspect the money for fingerprints or suspicious serial numbers. He promises that the money will be returned as soon as the investigation is completed, but of course it never is.

THE LONG-LOST RELATIVE

The long-lost-relative scam is often carried out by mail or telephone, although it can also be done in person. The victim is notified that he may be the only living relative of a person who recently died without a will in a faraway place, leaving an estate worth millions of dollars. In order to investigate further, however, the con artist asks for a fee of $50 or more to cover the expense of the investigation, process the necessary paperwork, and protect the victim's claim to the estate. The con artist may even provide some information about the victim's background that helps lend credibility to his story.

The victim mails the "fee" to a post office box in another city, possibly in another province. Several weeks pass, and when the victim calls or writes to the "investigator," he learns that the telephone has been disconnected (or never existed under that name) or that the post office box has been closed.

If you are swindled, here are some actions you can take:

◇ Notify the police immediately. Too many victims never report the crime because they are embarrassed about having been so gullible. The sooner you tell the police about the swindle, the greater their chance of recovering some of your losses, and the sooner they can protect others from the same scheme.

◇ If you believe that you were the victim of a business scam, contact your local consumer protection office or Better Business Bureau. They may be able to tell you if the person's actions are within the law, or if other complaints have been lodged against him.

SCHOOL ATTENDANCE

Most Canadians take the right to a free education for granted, and indeed all provinces and territories have laws establishing public schools funded by the taxpayers. As a rule, a student is required to attend the public school in his district. The student's parents do not have the right to choose which school he will attend; only the school board has the authority to assign students in the district to particular schools. A school district may deny a student admission if he is not living in the district with a parent or legal guardian. A child may be denied admission if he is not of school age or has a contagious disease. Unwed mothers may not be denied admission to school solely because they are unwed mothers.

COMPULSORY ATTENDANCE

All provinces have laws regarding compulsory school attendance. The parents or guardians of school-age children are required by law to see that their children attend school. However, the provincial legislation does not require students to go to public schools. As a parent, you have the right to enroll your child in a private school, and in most provinces you may have your child "home schooled"—that is, educated at home. If you do not send your child to a public school, however, you must make sure that the education provided by the private school or tutor (such as yourself) meets the minimum standards set by your local school board and provincial authorities. See also HOME SCHOOLING.

If you fail to enroll your child in school or otherwise provide for his education, you may face prosecution under provincial education acts. Furthermore, provincial welfare authorities may charge you with neglect in a youth or family court. You can be fined, and your child may be placed in foster care.

A child may be excused from attending school because of illness, dangerous conditions in the school, bad weather, or lack of transportation. But if your child refuses to attend school, he may be charged with truancy in a youth court. If the child is found to be a truant, the court may impose restrictions on him or remove him from your home and place him in a foster or group home. See also SCHOOL PRAYER; YOUNG OFFENDER.

MINORITY LANGUAGE EDUCATION RIGHTS

In an effort to protect minority language rights, the Canadian Charter of Rights and Freedoms requires that Canadian citizens be permitted to choose whether their children be educated in English or French. This protection is not absolute, however, and depends on a variety of circumstances.

One set of criteria relates to the parents' mother tongue and the language of their primary school instruction in Canada. For example, the children of a francophone parent living in Saskatchewan have the right to go to a school where the language of instruction is French. Similarly, a Quebec resident who attended a primary school in Newfoundland, where the language of instruction was English, may choose to have her children educated in English. Canadian citizens who have a child that has already received some primary or secondary instruction in English or French in Canada have the right to have all their children educated in that language.

The minority language education rights section of the charter contains some important qualifications. The right to minority language education will be protected only where numbers warrant. This means that there must be a sufficient number of eligible students to justify the expense of special treatment. However, where the number of students is sufficient, the instruction must be paid for out of public funds.

In 1984, the Supreme Court of Canada struck down a section of the Quebec law that denied citizens who had received their English education in other provinces the right to have their children educated in English. The court stated that the law was a direct violation of the minority language section of the charter. The Alberta Court of Appeal relied on the same charter provision to strike down a section of the Alberta School Act, which did not grant francophone Albertans sufficient control over French-language instruction for their children.

School Expulsion and Suspension

Provincial legislatures, school boards, and teachers have broad powers to establish reasonable rules and regulations for primary and secondary school students. These rules generally cover such behavior` as truancy, tardiness, plagiarism, inappropriate language, alcohol and drug use, and weapon possession. The rules may also extend to off-campus events, such as class trips.

A student may not be suspended or expelled for refusing to perform actions that violate his religious beliefs, such as dancing in a coed gym class.

SCHOOL AUTHORITY

If a student refuses to abide by the rules, school authorities may take disciplinary measures. Usually the school will try to counsel a student who misbehaves, but for major transgressions, or in cases of consistently disruptive behavior, the authorities may be compelled to suspend or expel the child. Suspension is a temporary punishment, but expulsion is permanent; both suspension and expulsion are entered on the student's permanent school record.

In most public school systems the principal has the right to suspend or expel students, but the school board or the district superintendent of schools may review and overturn her decision. A student who is expelled may be assigned to a special school, or if the matter is brought to a family court, a judge may order him to live in a group home or other facility.

Private schools are not subject to the same due process requirements as public schools and so have greater latitude to suspend or expel students.

STUDENTS' RIGHTS TO DUE PROCESS

In matters of suspension and expulsion, all students have the protection of the Canadian Charter of Rights and Freedoms and provincial human rights legislation. Moreover, laws such as the Ontario Statutory Powers Procedure Act guarantee students a right to a lawyer and a full hearing. This would include the right to call, examine, and cross-examine witnesses under oath. Usually, school board members would preside over the hearing to decide whether to confirm or overturn a principal's expulsion or suspension of a student.

Even though the hearing procedure can be flexible, a certain level of procedural fairness must be observed. If not, then the case may be subject to an appeal. For example, suppose Richard, who is facing a two-week suspension from his high school, is not permitted to cross-examine a witness testifying against him. In such an instance, it would be manifestly unfair to allow judgment against him.

The appeal process varies from province to province. For example, in Manitoba and Ontario, there is no appeal beyond the school board, but appeals may be made to the education minister in Alberta and New Brunswick. Students who disagree with a school board decision can appeal to the courts. If you are contemplating legal action over an expulsion or suspension, you are best advised to contact a lawyer who specializes in this area of the law.

SCHOOL PRAYER

Debate over the proper place of religion in our public school system is not new. However, the decision to exclude mandatory religious rituals such as prayer or Bible readings from the school system is a relatively recent development. Until the late 1980s, Ontario's Education

Act required readings from the Scriptures and reading of the Lord's Prayer or other "suitable" ceremonies. Eventually, this was challenged on the grounds that it violated the religious freedom of certain students. Even though the act allowed students to refrain from participating in religious exercises, the Ontario Court of Appeal found that peer pressure rendered this right effectively useless in the classroom.

Since the Ontario Court of Appeal's decision, courts in other provinces have used the Charter of Rights and Freedoms to strike down mandatory school prayers as well.

See also HOME SCHOOLING; RELIGION, FREEDOM OF.

SCOUTING

For many children, part of growing up involves belonging to clubs and organizations, including the Boy Scouts and Girl Guides, or their junior counterparts, the Cubs and Brownies. Unlike most other youth groups, these organizations were established through federal legislation.

STRUCTURE AND AIMS

The scouting movement originated in England in 1907 through the labors of Robert Baden-Powell. The roots of scouting in Canada date to early 1908. In 1914, the federal government passed legislation which incorporated the Canadian General Council of the Boy Scouts Association, the highest organization body of the Scouts. The original stated aims of this organization involved the teaching of discipline, loyalty, and good citizenship, among others, to boys involved in the movement.

The Girl Guides of Canada began operating in 1910 and were incorporated by federal law in 1917. Guides seek to teach girls to "serve God, monarch and country." As of the late 1980s, there were 280,000 boys and 211,172 girls involved in the activities of the Boy Scouts, Girl Guides, and other branches of the movement, such as Brownies and Cubs.

Both the Boy Scouts and Girl Guides have the exclusive right to the emblems, badges, descriptive marks, and words or phrases used in the scouting program, including the terms "Scout," "Boy Scout," or "Girl Scout." This means that the Scouts can sue anyone who tries to use material proprietary to the Scouts.

Regional scouting councils across the country set qualifications for the men and women who run individual Scout troops.

LIABILITY

If a Scout is injured during a scouting activity, he has the right to sue the national or regional council. But to win his case, he has to show that the council had some direct control over the activity.

If the Scout's injury was due to the leader's negligence, the lawsuit should be filed against him personally, unless the organization was negligent in selecting him as a Scout leader.

Suppose your son Bobby's Scout troop goes on an overnight hike in the Laurentian Mountains. During the hike the Scouts become separated, and Bobby falls and hurts himself. If you find out that the Scout leader had no wilderness hiking experience, you could probably sue the scouting council, arguing that it had the duty to make sure that the leader was qualified to take children on such a trip.

SEARCH AND SEIZURE

The Charter of Rights and Freedoms states that everyone has the right to be free from unreasonable search or seizure by the government or its agents. Moreover, the Supreme Court of Canada has held that before seeking a search warrant from a justice, the police must have reasonable and credible grounds for making such an application. They cannot do so just because someone claims that his neighbor has stolen merchandise in his basement. The police cannot immediately race out to conduct a search—they must further investigate the situation first. See SEARCH WARRANT.

WHERE THE CHARTER APPLIES

The charter protects citizens and noncitizens alike in areas generally considered private — not only in their homes but in offices, hotel rooms, automobiles, and in some cases the grounds surrounding a building. But it does not apply to public places, such as restaurants or shopping malls, or places where no privacy can reasonably be expected, such as in a prison, military barracks, or hospital.

Sealed mail in transit within Canada cannot be opened by law enforcement officials, nor can mail that is sent over international boundaries into Canada. For example, if customs officials want to open a piece of mail because they suspect it contains drugs or other illegal items, they must either obtain the permission of the addressee or get a search warrant. If a package appears to present an imminent danger—for instance, if customs or law enforcement officials believe it contains explosives—they do not need to obtain a search warrant before attempting to dismantle or destroy it.

The charter does not apply to items that are discarded. Moreover, the police may seize illegal items or evidence of wrongdoing that is in plain view, provided that the officers had a right to be on the premises.

Electronic surveillance also falls within the purview of the charter. Law enforcement officials cannot "bug" your office, rooms in your house, or your telephone unless they have a legal warrant to do so.

UNREASONABLE SEARCH AND SEIZURE

To obtain a search warrant, a law enforcement officer must give a judge or other magistrate information that gives her probable cause to believe that the search or seizure will produce evidence of wrongdoing. Judges decide upon these requests as they are made, determining whether a reasonable person would find the information convincing.

WITHOUT A WARRANT

In some cases, the police may search a person or premises without a warrant. To avoid contravening the charter, there must be reasonable and probable grounds for the search. The Criminal Code expressly allows warrantless searches for offenses involving weapons, gambling, impaired driving (Breathalyzer test), suspected stolen timber, cockfights, and counterfeit money—crimes where time is of the essence for successful police operations. In some situations, warrantless searches preceding arrest or following it are also possible. For example, if a man with a gun is arrested by police, they have reasonable grounds to search him for any other weapons, even without a warrant. If there are no reasonable grounds for a search, any evidence found must be excluded.

Suppose Fred, a police officer who has held a grudge against his high school classmate Tom for many years, goes to Tom's home, demands entrance, and searches the premises. Fred has no reason to believe he will find evidence of a crime, and he does not have a search warrant. Tom does not consent to the search but is afraid to protest. When Fred finds a plastic bag full of marijuana in a bedroom drawer, he arrests Tom.

At the preliminary hearing, Tom's lawyer asks that the evidence be suppressed on the grounds that it was found during a search that violated the charter. The judge agrees, and orders that the marijuana be excluded from evidence, leading to the dismissal of the case because there is no other evidence against Tom.

When illegally obtained evidence leads to the discovery of still more incriminating evidence, that evidence could also be deemed inadmissible. Suppose Fred had found a hotel key when he searched Tom's home. He took the key and went to the hotel, where he found a stash of stolen money. Most likely neither the key nor the money could be used as evidence in Tom's trial for robbery.

BODY SEARCHES

A strip search, for which a suspect is required to remove his clothes, or a complete body search, which involves probing his hair or body cavities, cannot be conducted without lawful authority. Exactly what amounts to such authority is the matter of numerous legal decisions which have dealt with a variety of different sets of facts.

Before the charter was created, police officers in the process of an arrest had much more power to search suspects' bodies. In one 1949 case, a suspected drug dealer was arrested in public and a struggle ensued. The arresting officer tried to put his hand in the suspect's mouth to find drugs. None were found there. The drugs ultimately turned up in the suspect's car. However, in light of the circumstances and given the nature of the crime, the judge found that the mouth search was justified.

Faced with a similar set of facts in 1987, the Supreme Court of Canada ruled in favor of the accused. In this case, an RCMP officer approached a suspected drug dealer in a bar, announced himself, then immediately grabbed the suspect by the throat to prevent her swallowing any drugs, and threw her to the floor. As it turned out, the woman had a balloon filled with heroin in her hand, not her mouth. Because the officer originally had little evidence to go on, the whole search process was held to be illegal. As such, the evidence found in the woman's hand had to be excluded at her trial.

Canadian courts have generally refused police applications for the surgical removal of evidence from suspected criminals. Such a search would be considered too intrusive and would violate the bodily integrity of the suspect. In a case where an accused was in a car accident, blood taken to prove intoxication was ruled a violation of the charter's guarantees against unreasonable searches.

Not only is the evidence obtained during an illegal body or strip search not admissible at a trial, but the victim can file a civil rights lawsuit against the officer who performed it.

CHECKLIST

When a Search Warrant Is Not Required

Most searches are conducted only after the police have obtained a search warrant, but the police can legally conduct a search without a warrant in the following situations:

■ **IF AN OBJECT IS IN PLAIN VIEW.** No warrant is needed if a piece of evidence or an illegal item is easily visible. For instance, if the police walk by a car and see a sawn-off shotgun lying on the backseat, they may seize the weapon.

■ **IF AN INDIVIDUAL CONSENTS.** The police can conduct a search without a warrant if a person voluntarily gives permission, but they may not coerce or trick someone into consenting. The person who gives consent must be authorized to give it—a landlord, for instance, may allow a search of public areas in his building but not of private apartments—and he may withdraw his permission at any time.

■ **DURING AN ARREST.** When a suspect is lawfully arrested, the police may conduct a search without her consent. The search is limited to the suspect and the areas within her immediate vicinity, however.

■ **TO SEARCH A VEHICLE.** Because cars, boats, trucks, and other vehicles could be moved while the police obtain a search warrant, they may be searched on the spot if the police have probable cause to believe evidence of a crime will be found.

■ **DURING AN IMPOUNDMENT.** Police may conduct a warrantless search of a vehicle or other property they have seized during the commission of a crime. An inventory is taken both to protect the owner's property and to alert the police to dangerous items, such as explosives.

■ **WHEN A PERSON IS A SUSPECT.** A police officer may temporarily detain someone whom he suspects of committing or planning a crime. If the officer suspects danger, he may conduct a pat-down search of the suspect for weapons.

■ **IN AN EMERGENCY.** Police may follow suspects into a building and search for contraband or weapons immediately if there is a risk that the evidence will be destroyed or hidden.

■ **IF THE POLICE ARE IN PURSUIT.** Suppose an officer arrives at a crime scene, sees someone running into a house, and is told by witnesses, "That's the guy who knifed that woman." The officer does not need a warrant before demanding entry to the home and searching the suspect.

■ **AT A BORDER CROSSING.** At an international border crossing, you and your luggage and vehicle may be subject to a complete search. However, customs officials must have strong suspicions before they can subject you to a body or strip search, even at a border crossing.

The Supreme Court of Canada has ruled that, despite the principles of equality upheld in the charter, female prison guards may search clothed male inmates, even if the converse is not true.

EXCEPTIONS

Evidence that is inadmissible in court can sometimes be used to determine whether a suspect should be indicted or whether a witness or defendant is perjuring himself. For example, if a defendant in a burglary trial denies that he ever met his codefendant, the prosecution could use his address book, containing the codefendant's name, to cast doubt on his credibility.

SEARCH WARRANT

Before a law enforcement officer can search you or your home or car, he generally must have a search warrant issued by a judge or magistrate. When applying for a warrant, an officer must make an affidavit, or sworn statement, that he has probable cause to believe that he will find a suspect or evidence of a crime at the location to be searched. Mere suspicion of criminal activity is not enough to convince a judge to issue a warrant—there must be facts or convincing circumstantial evidence. Secondhand information, such as statements from a reliable informant, may be enough.

Because warrants are sometimes needed urgently, the procedure for getting one is not complicated. In an emergency

a warrant can be issued almost immediately, even if a law enforcement official must rouse a judge from bed. In some urgent cases, involving serious crimes, police may submit an information on oath by telephone or other telecommunications to a justice who could authorize the issuance of a telewarrant.

A search warrant must be bilingual and describe in detail the person or the place to be searched and the type of evidence that is being sought. Also, the police must limit their search to the scope of the warrant. For instance, if a warrant authorizes the police to look for a rifle at a specific address, they may open closets, cabinets, drawers, and other areas in the house where a rifle could potentially be concealed—but not a purse or shoe box. Under certain circumstances, however, evidence not specified on the warrant may be obtained during the search. For an example of these circumstances, see the checklist on page 467. See also No-KNOCK LAWS; SEARCH AND SEIZURE.

SEAT BELT LAWS

For many years, automobile manufacturers have been required to install seat belts for as many passengers as a given car can carry. In the past decade, so-called passive restraints, such as air bags and gravity shoulder belts, have also been mandated. But in spite of these regulations and the mounting evidence that

seat belts save lives, many Canadians still neglect to buckle up.

Today, seat belt use is mandatory in all provinces. Several people charged under seat belt laws have taken the government to court claiming that such laws violate their charter rights to life, liberty, and security of the person. The argument goes something like this: seat belts themselves may cause injuries, therefore it should be up to the individual to decide whether or not to wear them.

Several courts have recognized that there is evidence that seat belts can cause or aggravate injuries in certain cases. However, the courts also acknowledge the overwhelming proof that, in the vast majority of cases, seat belts save lives or reduce injuries. Thus, seat belt laws have been found constitutional over and over again.

Courts in some provinces have held that failure to wear a seat belt amounts to contributory negligence in a car accident. If you live in one of these provinces and are injured in an automobile accident, you may have any potential compensation reduced or denied if you were not wearing your seat belt when the accident occurred. See also NEGLIGENCE.

Passenger seat belts are not usually required for public transportation vehicles, such as buses, trains, and subway cars. Airport shuttle buses and taxicabs usually must have them, although the driver is normally not responsible for seeing that passengers use them.

One immediate advantage to owners of cars equipped with the passive-restraint systems is that insurance companies may charge them lower premiums. If your car has a gravity shoulder belt or an air bag, ask your insurer whether you are eligible for a discount. See also AUTOMOBILE ACCIDENTS; AUTOMOBILE INSURANCE.

SECOND MARRIAGE

Remarriages of widowed or divorced men and women can proceed more smoothly if both parties are prepared to deal with such legal issues as financial responsibility, adoption, and estate planning.

People who are marrying for the second time often own substantial amounts of property. To avoid disputes arising when the marriage ends, whether through death or divorce, it is advisable for both parties to enter into a prenuptial, or premarital, agreement. This contract defines how the couple's property will be divided, and states how spousal- or child-support payments will be determined. See PRENUPTIAL AGREEMENT.

SPOUSAL AND CHILD SUPPORT

A divorced person who is receiving support from a previous spouse generally loses it when she remarries. If a person paying alimentary pension remarries, he may be able to have the payments reduced if he can prove that his new marriage reduces his ability to pay.

Child support is generally not affected by the remarriage of either parent. However, a judge may decide to revise child-support payments if the financial circumstances of either parent change. See also CHILD SUPPORT.

ADOPTION

A new stepparent may wish to adopt the children from his spouse's former marriage. If both biological parents are alive, generally both must consent to the adoption. An exception can be made if a biological parent is unfit or has not acted upon his parental rights. Suppose Darlene's former husband, Stewart, has failed to pay support for their two children, never visits them, and shows no interest in their welfare. Darlene has remarried, and her new husband wants to adopt the children. Stewart is notified that there will be a hearing to decide whether he should continue to have parental rights. He fails to appear at the hearing and, after listening to the facts of the case, the family court terminates Stewart's parental rights. The court no longer needs to obtain Stewart's consent for the adoption. See also ADOPTION.

If a stepparent adopts a stepchild, he is responsible for supporting that child. Moreover, even if a stepparent has not adopted a child, but has acted as if the child was his own, then a support obligation may arise. For example, suppose that Philomena (a teacher) marries Patrick (an unpublished writer), who has a child by a previous marriage.

Over a couple of years, Philomena develops a loving relationship with Patrick's child. She plays with, teaches and feeds the child, who calls her "Mommy." In such a case, Philomena may be obliged under the law to continue such support even if her relationship with Patrick someday ends.

See also ALIMENTARY PENSION; STEPPARENT.

ESTATE PLANNING

Remarriage will affect the distribution of your estate. You and your new spouse should review your wills and specify what property you want to leave to each other and what should go to children or other relatives and friends. See DYING WITHOUT A WILL.

Your new spouse has inheritance rights, but your stepchildren will generally have no claim to your estate if you do not adopt them. If you want them to inherit, you will have to so specify in your will. If you do adopt your stepchildren, they will be treated in the same way as biological children and have the same rights to a share of your estate.

SECURITIES REGULATION

Arguably, the stock market crash of 1929 and the ensuing Great Depression provided an impetus for governments to regulate the issuing, buying, and selling of stocks, bonds, and other securities. For decades, the Toronto and Montreal stock exchanges have been under the watchful eye of such government agencies as the Ontario Securities Commission (OSC) and the Commission des valeurs mobilières du Québec (CVMQ).

The importance of such regulation cannot be understated. In one recent year, for example, new bonds issued for trading by the federal and provincial governments totaled over $30 billion and new securities of private corporations exceeded $27 billion. Trading in already existing shares for the same year was valued at $104 billion for the Toronto Stock Exchange alone. With sums this large in play, it is important for investors to have a certain amount of market stability insured by means of a public regulatory body.

Unlike the United States, security regulation in Canada is done at the provincial rather than the federal level. Despite the absence of federal involvement, there is a degree of cooperation between various provincial organizations through Canadian Securities Administrators. This body meets once yearly to adopt national policies on a wide range of subjects. One example of success in interprovincial cooperation was the harmonization of all provincial legislation dealing with takeover bids. Another example is a national policy for reviewing prospectuses in different jurisdictions.

BOND ISSUES

When a corporation or a government wishes to issue new shares or bonds to raise money from investors, the securities regulators in that province often require a prospectus, a set of documents which shows the bond issuer's financial health. Moreover, the share or bond issuer is typically under continuous obligation to disclose its dealings to the securities commission of the province where the shares are being traded. In this way, worthless securities are best kept off the market.

STOCK MARKET

Securities regulators also have a say in how the stock market functions, including which types of business may trade on the market, and the levels of competence they must show. They can exempt certain businesses from particular rules, often on a discretionary basis. In short then, the business of securities regulation involves licensing businesses to trade on the stock market and maintaining ethical and business standards in this trade.

See also BLUE-SKY LAW; CHURNING; STOCKBROKER; STOCKS AND BONDS.

SECURITY AGREEMENT

When you borrow money to make an expensive purchase, such as an automobile, jewelry, or a major appliance, you will almost certainly be asked to give the lender what is known

CHECKLIST

Property That May Be Subject to a Security Agreement

All provinces now have some form of register for recording a security interest on personal property. Any of the following can be subject to a security interest.

■ Consumer goods used for family or household purposes.

■ Farm products.

■ Business inventory held for sale to others.

■ Business equipment, such as office and manufacturing machinery.

■ Financial instruments, such as stocks, bonds, and promissory notes.

■ Bills of lading, warehouse receipts, and other business documents.

■ Leases on personal property, known as chattel paper.

■ Accounts receivable.

■ General intangibles, such as trademark, copyright, and royalty interests.

as a security agreement. The agreement is usually a part of your sales contract, although it is sometimes a separate document.

The agreement states that if you do not adhere to the terms

of your sales contract, the lender can repossess your purchase and sell it to recover any money you owe. The agreement creates what is known as a secured transaction—the lender's money is "secured" by his right to the property if you default on your payments. If the lender has to resort to this procedure, and the sale of the item does not pay off your entire debt, in some provinces you can be held responsible for the balance. See also DEFAULT JUDGMENT; DEFICIENCY JUDGMENT; REPOSSESSION.

RECORDING A SECURITY INTEREST

Under various provincial laws, lenders are required to register a record of security interests in another's property. This is done on forms which are essentially the same but vary in name from jurisdiction to jurisdiction. For example, security agreements affecting personal property (that is not real estate) in Ontario are done on a Form 1C. In Alberta, the proper document is a Financing Statement, Form AG1767.

Different provinces allow security agreements to remain valid for varying periods of time. For instance, in Ontario, registered security agreements are good for up to five years, depending on the financing agreement. In Alberta, the duration may be up to 25 years.

The registration of security agreements provides many benefits. Creditors have an official record of what they are owed. Possible lenders can see how indebted those applying for credit are. Lastly, when a

debtor with several creditors defaults on several debts, then the registration system plays a part in sorting out who gets what of the debtor's secured property.

SECURITY DEPOSIT

When a landlord rents an apartment or house to a tenant, he assumes a risk that the tenant may damage the property or move out without paying all the rent. To guard against this possibility, landlords sometimes require tenants to pay a sum of money, called a security deposit, before they move in.

AMOUNT

Security deposits are legal in some provinces, illegal in others. Where they are permitted, the amount a landlord can demand may be controlled by provincial law. Typically, he can ask for one month's rent if the dwelling is unfurnished, more if it is furnished. Where security deposits are allowed, landlords are required to pay tenants interest on that money at the end of the lease.

Purposes
The rental agreement as well as provincial law will specify the purposes for which a security deposit can be used. Sometimes the landlord will designate separate portions for a cleaning deposit, or a default on the rent. The lease may also specify that some portion of the deposit is nonrefundable. These stipulations are important, because they regulate the landlord's use of the money.

For example, if your lease says that a sum of money is to be used in the event that you do not pay your rent, but your landlord later attempts to deduct routine cleaning expenses when you move out, you may be able to challenge this deduction and get it back.

RETURN OF THE DEPOSIT

To get your security deposit back when you move from the apartment, make sure you have complied with all the conditions in your lease. First, note whether the lease specifies that you must give notice of your intent to move, and how far in advance the notice must be given. Second, make sure that your dwelling is clean. Walk through it with the rental manager so that he can inspect its condition, and ask for a checklist indicating the condition of each room. If you have any reason to believe that you may not get all of your security deposit back, take pictures of the premises.

Some provinces require landlords to return a security deposit within a specified time after a tenancy has ended, usually from one to four weeks. If the landlord is going to keep some of the deposit, provincial law may require him to send you an itemized list of his deductions. If he fails to do so, he may lose the right to keep any of the money.

SMALL-CLAIMS COURT

If you and your landlord cannot come to an agreement about the amount withheld from your deposit, you can pursue the matter in the small-claims court or through your local rent control board. Copies of your lease; check-in and check-out lists of the rooms, appliances, fixtures, and their condition; and pictures of the apartment or house will be useful when you present your case to the judge or commissioners.

See SMALL-CLAIMS COURT.

SELF-DEFENSE

Late one night Harold and Maude were awakened by the sound of glass breaking downstairs. Harold grabbed the baseball bat he kept under the bed and headed down the darkened staircase. In the front hallway he encountered a burly figure, who swung a crowbar at him. Harold ducked, the crowbar missed, and Harold struck the intruder on the knees with the bat. The man fell to the ground, and Harold stood watch over him until the police arrived and took him away.

Under other circumstances Harold might have faced a charge of battery and been held financially responsible for the injuries he caused. But the law recognizes that people have a right to protect themselves when they are in danger. Because Harold acted in self-defense, he was not subject to criminal charges.

The law allows people to use reasonable force to defend themselves and others when they believe they are in jeopardy. Generally, what constitutes reasonable force depends on the circumstances of each case. Suppose that Harold had armed himself not with a base-ball bat but with a gun, and the figure he encountered was busy loading the family silver into a cloth bag. Harold would not be justified in shooting the burglar, since neither his nor any family member's life was threatened. See also BURGLARY.

Suppose Harold is not at home, but at the local mall, when he sees a man running toward him with a large knife. Harold wrests the knife from the man, who during the struggle falls to the pavement and cracks his skull. Under these circumstances Harold could reasonably believe that the attacker was attempting to kill him (or someone else) and has the right to use as much force as necessary to prevent this from happening. Even if the man died from the fall, Harold would not be guilty of murder.

SELF-EMPLOYMENT

At one time or another in your life, you have probably dreamed about "being your own boss" some day. But turning that dream into reality requires some careful planning. Important decisions must be made—not only about the type of product or service you will offer, but also about such matters as licensing, zoning, insurance, financing, taxes, and retirement planning.

LICENSING AND ZONING

People who decide to go into business for themselves often find that they cannot simply set up shop and begin selling a product or service. For exam-ple, if you want to start a bakery, you will probably find that you must have a permit for handling food.

You should also check your local zoning laws. If you plan to operate a business out of your home, you could be violating a zoning law that prohibits business enterprises in residential areas. See also HOME BUSINESS.

LIABILITY INSURANCE

Many small businesses start out as sole proprietorships because they are easy to set up. But as a sole proprietor, you may be held personally responsible if someone is harmed by your product or injured on your premises. All your personal property, bank accounts, and other assets are in jeopardy if someone sues you and is awarded a large amount of money. Check with your insurance agent about adequate coverage for your business. You might consider, too, forming a corporation, also known as a limited-liability company. See CORPORATION; LIABILITY INSURANCE; PARTNERSHIP; SOLE PROPRIETORSHIP.

LOANS

There are several sources of financing if you need start-up capital for your small business. Apart from banks, there are several government programs designed to help fledgling businesses. Check your local branch of the Federal Business Development Bank to see if you meet its lending requirements. Check also the various provincial ministries dealing with industry, small business, tourism and the like.

CANADA PENSION

If you have worked for an employer in the past, you will know that a percentage of your gross salary is deducted to pay into the Canada (Quebec) Pension Plan. For the current rate of deduction, contact Revenue Canada.

Unlike an employee, who has money deducted from each pay for this purpose, when you are self-employed you pay into your Canada (Quebec) Pension Plan only once a year.

UNEMPLOYMENT AND RETIREMENT BENEFITS

If you are self-employed and operating as a sole proprietor or in a partnership, you do not have to contribute funds under the Unemployment Insurance (UI) Act. Only people who hire workers must do this, and even then there are some exceptions. The downside to this, of course, is that you will not be entitled to unemployment insurance benefits in the event that your business fails. Taxi drivers (who do not own their taxis), and hairdressers who operate independently in a place of work owned by another person, can and should pay UI premiums.

It is therefore a good idea that you plan for a financial cushion of some sort to help through hard times. One method is plain old-fashioned savings. However, various types of business insurance are available as well. Some policies cover business interruptions (due to shortage of materials, fire and so on), the bad debts of creditors, and so forth.

TAXES

When you start your own business, the number of tax forms will increase. You will still fill out your personal income tax forms as always, but you will have to file a number of other forms as well, depending on the type of business you have. If you have incorporated your business, you will have to file corporate tax forms, either with the federal or provincial government, depending on the Business Corporations Act under which you have set up shop. If you are a sole proprietor or in a partnership, you should order (free) one of the following guides (forms) from Revenue Canada: Business and Professional Income, Capital Gains, Farming Income, Fishing Income, or Rental Income.

In a nutshell, depending on the type of business you run, you enter the various expenses you have run up over the year (advertising, rent, supplies, utilities, wages and so on) and deduct these from gross revenues as per the form. This will give you the resulting profit or loss, which you enter on your personal income tax form under the appropriate section of "Calculation of Total Income."

In some cases, you cannot deduct all of one year's expense in one taxable year. Instead, you are granted a "Capital Cost Allowance" (CCA). This enables you to deduct a percentage of a given business asset's value as it depreciates over the years. Suppose Nat buys a truck for

$10,000 and uses it exclusively for his painting business. Assume that this year's rate of capital cost allowance for vehicles happens to be 10 percent. Thus, as a business expense for this year, Nat can deduct $1,000 for the truck purchase. Keep in mind that this leaves $9,000 to be deducted in future years until the whole vehicle has been "written off." Some items, such as computer software, are 100 percent deductible under CCA in the year they were bought. The CCA rates are listed in the Revenue Canada guides mentioned earlier.

SEPARATION

When married people decide they can no longer live together, they usually go to court to get a divorce. But some couples decide that although they do not wish to stay together, they are not ready to take the final step of dissolving the marriage. Such couples have two options: they can agree to separate voluntarily and draw up a formal separation agreement that covers spousal and child support, or one or both spouses can petition the court for a legal separation (sometimes called a judicial separation), and the court will enforce the separation agreement.

A court-ordered separation is common when one spouse

refuses to leave the family home voluntarily. In such instances, a judge may set the terms of the separation regarding use of the family residence, as well as spousal and child support.

AFTER A SEPARATION IS GRANTED

Whether the separation is voluntary or involuntary, the people involved are still considered legally married and are therefore prohibited from marrying again—unless, of course, they get divorced. Nevertheless, both spouses are free from the duties and rights of cohabitation. The couple will remain legally separated until: (1) one of the spouses dies; (2) there is a reconciliation; or (3) they divorce to end their marriage.

If they reconcile, the parties must notify the court in writing to have their court-ordered separation agreement set aside. Couples who have made their own informal separation agreement should tear up the document when they reconcile.

LEGAL ENFORCEMENT

A voluntary separation agreement is legally binding, but it does not have the force of a judicial order—that is, if one party does not honor a voluntary agreement, the other can sue only for breach of contract. But if a spouse violates a court-ordered separation agreement, he or she may be found in contempt of court and subject to fines, imprisonment, or both. Spousal support may be automatically canceled if a couple resumes marital relations after a court-ordered separation.

TERMS OF THE AGREEMENT

Often the separation agreement is quite similar to the agreement reached in a divorce case. It can entail the payment of a lump sum or periodic payments by one spouse to support the other spouse, any or all children of the marriage, or both spouse and children as the case may be.

When such a court order is made, fairness is supposed to be uppermost in the judge's mind. She will usually not consider the fault of either spouse in the marriage in declaring any support order. The needs of the spouse and children seeking support and the means of the other spouse to pay must be considered. In addition, a range of other factors must be pondered: how long did the couple live together? what contributions did each make to the household? how can the order facilitate the reestablishment of the self-sufficiency of the spouses? and so on. The order that the court ultimately makes can be set for a given period of time (for example, until one of the parties has finished college, or until one spouse gets a job), and may be modified to fit new circumstances.

STEPS TO TAKE TO OBTAIN A COURT-ORDERED SEPARATION

Prior to obtaining a legal separation, couples are often advised to try marriage counseling. If that fails and separation is advised, either or both spouses may hire a lawyer (preferably one specializing in family law) and apply to the court for corollary relief.

1. Do not move out of the marital home without a legal agreement. Your spouse could claim desertion, change the locks, and refuse you permission to collect your personal belongings. To gain access to your belongings, you would have to file a petition in the district or family court, in addition to filing for a legal separation.

2. Through your lawyer or on your own, negotiate the terms of your separation. The terms should address the division of property and debts; child custody, visitation rights, and support; and spousal support. Either party may waive spousal support, but if you do not claim the right to support at the time of the separation, you sometimes cannot ask the court to award it later.

3. You or your spouse must petition the court for a permanent order of separation.

4. The court will review the terms of the agreement and, if it decides that they are unfair, may insist upon further negotiation or impose its own terms. See also ALIMENTARY PENSION; CHILD CUSTODY; CHILD SUPPORT; DIVORCE.

SERVICE CONTRACT

You have shopped carefully for your new washing machine. You have read the consumer guides and compared prices at a number of local dealers. You are especially pleased with the manufacturer's warranty, which covers all parts and repairs for the first year of owner-ship, and parts for another three years. You are just about to write your cheque when the salesperson murmurs: "Of course, you will want to buy our super service contract, won't you?"

Today an extended service contract is available for almost every expensive appliance or piece of electronic equipment. Such a contract may provide for periodic inspections and cleaning and pay for repairs after the manufacturer's war-ranty expires. Depending on the cost of the item and the time period that the contract covers, the fee for this addi-tional protection may range from a few dollars to several hundred dollars or more. Extended service contracts on automobiles can cost thousands of dollars.

How important is it to pur-chase an extended service con-tract? Despite the claims of salespeople (who earn a com-mission for each contract they sell), most service contracts are not necessarily good value. A good warranty from a rep-utable manufacturer will cover all the costs of repair or replacement for a reasonable time. For example, typical warranties for personal appli-ances such as hair dryers and shavers provide for free repairs or replacement for 90 days to one year. For major appliances, a one-year warranty is often the standard, and some manu-facturers will guarantee the most expensive components for much longer periods. (For example, most refrigerator manufacturers will guarantee

the compressor for five years.) Typical automobile warranties provide bumper-to-bumper coverage for 12 months or 20,000 kilometres, whichever comes first. Many now offer this coverage for three years or up to 60,000 kilometres.

Most service contracts mere-ly extend the coverage of the original warranties, and some of them begin to run from the time of purchase, essentially duplicating your free warranty protection for that period.

Although much is made of the preventive maintenance features of these contracts, people who buy them seldom take advantage of the inspec-tions and cleanings. Further-more, the cost of a service contract is often disproportion-ate to the cost of the item itself. Buying a $200 service contract on a $300 VCR makes little financial sense.

Problems often arise when you try to file a claim. Most ser-vice contracts on automobiles and major appliances exclude coverage for problems caused by owner misuse, and many service-contract companies routinely reject claims on the basis of this exclusion. When that happens, the burden of proof shifts to you. Unless you have kept careful records of all maintenance procedures and can show that the item was never used in a way for which it was not intended, you will probably not win your case.

Some credit card companies will extend the manufacturer's warranty for an extra year if you purchase the object using their card, usually a "Gold Card."

SEX DIS-CRIMINATION

Provincial and federal laws prohibit discrimination based on gender in many settings, from the classroom to the workplace.

EDUCATIONAL OPPORTUNITIES

All children in public schools are entitled to equal education-al opportunities, regardless of their gender. Students cannot be excluded because of preg-nancy, childbirth, or for having an abortion. Voluntary pro-grams for pregnant students or programs designed to benefit those who have traditionally suffered sex discrimination would not contravene provi-sions of the Charter of Rights and Freedoms.

School sports
At the very least, schools must provide equal opportunity for students of both sexes to enjoy school sports. In some cases, schools may have to allow girls to play on boys' teams in order to bring policies into line with the charter. If Eva wants to play hockey, it would be dis-criminatory not to let her play on the boys' hockey team when she is as good as any other player and in no more danger of injury than the other players.

Higher education
Except for equal opportunity programs, gender cannot be a factor in admissions to univer-sities, colleges, and other post-secondary educational institutions that are subject to the charter.

REAL LIFE, REAL LAW

The Case of the Muzzled Man

Shay was reading a feminist newspaper, when an article caught his attention. It argued that men should never get custody or access rights to children in separation or divorce settlements. The paper had a policy not to allow men to contribute to its publication in any way, and printed this fact in its paper. Shay submitted a response to the article anyway, but he was refused publication on the grounds of his gender. He brought an action against the paper before his province's human rights commission, but lost his case. The commission held that the exclusion of men from the activities of certain women-only organizations is justified in some cases. It said that such exclusion is a necessary counterbalance for women to achieve equality in a society in which they are often not treated equally with men.

Social clubs and organizations

Sororities and fraternities are among private clubs that may exclude women or men from their membership without contravening the Charter of Rights and Freedoms. However, under the human rights legislation of some provinces and territories, private organizations may not discriminate on the basis of sex in providing certain services to the public. The law is not totally settled in this area, however, as this example from Yukon shows. A historical society there refused membership to a woman on the basis of her gender. The purpose of the society was to preserve the history of Yukon and of the society itself. This meant keeping the society membership exclusively male.

The Yukon courts agreed there was discrimination, but noted that the service the society offered the public was not membership but rather access to its documented works. At the time of writing, it was unclear if the case would be appealed to the Supreme Court of Canada.

EMPLOYMENT

In many different ways, federal and provincial human rights legislation, as well as labor and employment laws, seek to prohibit sexual discrimination in the workplace.

Women cannot be refused hiring or be fired for being pregnant, planning to have an abortion or having children, so long as none of these things unduly interfere with performance of the job (absence from work is allowed under maternity leave sections of provincial labor standards legislation).

A Saskatchewan businessman who, fearing for her safety, refused to employ a woman for the "graveyard shift" in his convenience store was fined $1,000 for the humiliation and suffering caused by his discriminatory attitude. In another case, a woman working for a lumber company was let go after being told that women cannot operate machines as well as men. She ended up successfully suing for nearly $30,000 in lost wages and damages for the humiliation.

See also EMPLOYEE HIRING AND FIRING; EMPLOYMENT AGENCY.

SEXUAL ABUSE

The term "sexual abuse" can be applied to a wide variety of situations, but the common denominator is that one person is forced into having unwanted sexual contact with another. Typically, victims of sexual abuse cannot defend themselves because their abuser is physically stronger or holds a position of trust, as does a family member, babysitter, or professional caregiver.

The victims of sexual abuse are entitled to bring criminal charges against their abuser and can sue in civil court for money damages as well. If the abuse took place in an institutional setting, such as a nursing home or psychiatric hospital, the abuser's employers can also be sued.

See also CHILD ABUSE AND NEGLECT; INCEST; RAPE.

SEXUAL ASSAULT

This assault is one that is committed in circumstances of a sexual nature and which violates the sexual integrity of the victim. It need not always entail the act of rape, but can also exist where there is fondling or unwanted touching. The nature of the contact, the circumstances of the alleged assault, and the relationship between assaulter and victim are among factors that would help indicate whether there was a violation.

In the past, women in sexual assault cases often suffered during court proceedings from a form of "victim blaming." Defendants could attempt to discredit the testimony of the victim by portraying her as a sexually permissive person, or by requiring corroboration of her testimony—despite the fact that most rapes occur with only the assailant and victim present. Women also suffered under the law since husbands, at one time, could not be found guilty of raping their wives. Parliament has attempted to remedy these traditional injustices by passing special amendments to the Criminal Code.

Now, the new and controversial "rape shield" law permits only certain types of evidence to be presented about a complainant's past sexual history. In some cases, it may be shown that the victim had sexual conduct with people other than the accused, but such proof can be used only for the purpose of showing that the accused could not have committed the crime.

Bias or motive on the part of the complainant can also be presented. Evidence that the accused knew of the victim's prior sexual conduct can

REAL LIFE, REAL LAW

The Case of the Felonious Fathers

Alfred's three-year-old son, Billy, had the embarrassing habit of touching the private parts of friends, neighbors and family members when over for visits. One day, Alfred "snapped" when Billy touched his father's friend. To "teach Billy a lesson," Alfred did a little grabbing of his own and caused some damage to Billy's genitals. In spite of the fact that there was no evidence that Alfred wished to gain sexual satisfaction from this punishment, the Supreme Court of Canada in September 1993 ruled that his actions constituted sexual assault.

In another case, Susan was awarded roughly $180,000 in an action she brought against her sexually abusive father, Rex. Rex began to fondle Susan at the age of 6. Between the ages of 10 and 14, he forced her to have sex with him two to three times a week telling her to "keep it secret." While criminal sexual assault charges failed in court, the civil suit did not, having a lower standard of proof.

also be relevant in proving that the alleged offender believed the victim consented to sexual acts.

The victim's past sexual history may also be raised by the defense, but only to rebut any claims by the prosecution. Such evidence is conditional, in that it is first presented to the court behind closed doors. The judge then decides whether the evidence is admissible in open court. Moreover, no evidence of this kind may be introduced merely to show that the victim is untrustworthy or that she indeed consented to the act complained of.

That the accused is the victim's husband is no longer a defense against sexual assault. Generally, drunkenness is no defense either. However, the Supreme Court of Canada recently ruled that in some

cases extreme drunkenness may be considered akin to insanity or automatism, which are allowed as a defense.

Sexual assault with a weapon, threats, or causing bodily harm, carries more serious penalties than simple sexual assault. Moreover, where the sexual assault is accompanied by wounding, maiming, disfiguring or endangering the life of the victim, prison sentences of 25 years are a possibility.

SEXUAL HARASSMENT

There is no catchall definition for sexual harassment in Canadian law. The Supreme Court of Canada has stated that workplace sexual harassment can be "broadly defined as unwelcome conduct of a sexual nature that detrimentally affects the work environment or leads to adverse job-related consequences for the victims of the harassment." The courts have also likened sexual harassment to sexual discrimination.

Thus, sexual harassment is not just when a supervisor refuses to promote a woman who has rejected his sexual advances. It can also include the more subtle "poisoning" of the workplace atmosphere with sexist jokes, statements, and so on. Below are just a few examples of what would be illegal sexual harassment under Canadian law. Any of the following kinds of behavior are considered to create a hostile work environment:

◇ Making graphic or degrading comments about an employee's dress, appearance, or anatomy.

◇ Displaying sexually suggestive objects or pictures in the workplace.

◇ Telling dirty jokes or making indecent gestures.

◇ Using such familiar terms as "honey," "dear," or "baby."

◇ Asking questions about an employee's sex life.

◇ Offering descriptions of the harasser's own sexual conduct or experiences.

◇ Giving leering looks, whistles, or catcalls.

◇ Making unsolicited and unwelcome sexual advances or propositions.

◇ Making unwelcome physical contact, such as patting, pinching, touching, hugging, and kissing.

◇ Exposing genitalia.

◇ Committing physical or sexual assault, including rape.

Sexual harassment may be a much bigger problem in the workplace than many employers realize. Victims are often reluctant to file a complaint because they fear reprisals and ridicule. And in the majority of sexual-harassment cases the victim receives little more than job reinstatement and back pay, despite the fact that the law sometimes allows victims to sue for punitive damages.

WHEN YOU ARE THE EMPLOYER

Employers are well advised to establish a clearly stated policy concerning sexual harassment. You should circulate a written list of unacceptable behavior and outline the steps an employee can take to bring a harassment complaint to your attention. Every employee should know what punishment your company will administer to anyone who commits sexual harassment.

Employers should be cautioned that they cannot merely make token efforts to rid their workplace of sexism. The Supreme Court of Canada has recently ruled that there is a positive duty on employers to create a "harassment-free" environment. This seems to imply that the courts will expect results and not just talk in the future.

IF YOU ARE ACCUSED OF HARASSMENT

The burden of proof in sexual harassment cases lies with the person who brought the complaint. If she has little or no documentation or corroborating testimony, the case may become a "swearing contest"—

one person's word against the other's. The best defense against a sexual-harassment charge is to make sure your behavior toward your employees always is above reproach and to have witnesses who will testify that this is true.

STEPS TO TAKE IF YOU ARE HARASSED

First of all, try to confront the offender directly and insist that he (or she) end the harassing behavior. He may not realize that you find the behavior offensive. Or write him a letter explaining your objection to his actions. If this approach fails, do the following:

1. Tell your supervisor. If the supervisor is the offender, take your complaint to his superior or your employer's director of personnel or human resources.

2. If the behavior continues, or if you are not satisfied with your employer's remedy, call your provincial labor standards or human rights commission. You can find the telephone number in the blue pages of your telephone book.

3. Be sure to document any instances of harassment. Keep a log of the dates and times that they took place. If other employees are being harassed or have witnessed your harassment, ask for their assistance in pursuing your claim.

4. If the harassment has caused you financial loss or great distress, consider filing a lawsuit against your harasser and employer. You should have the advice of a lawyer experienced in labor law.

See also DATE RAPE; EMPLOYEE RIGHTS.

SHOPLIFTING

Jennifer was working at her part-time job as a salesclerk for a department store when she noticed a nervous-looking man near the jewelry counter. Jennifer was astonished to see the man place several pieces of costume jewelry in his jacket pocket. She quickly alerted a co-worker, who notified the store's security staff. But before the security guards could arrive, the man headed for the exit.

Jennifer ran to the exit and closed the door to prevent him from leaving. Moments later the security guards escorted the man to the manager's office and Jennifer called the police. Despite the man's protests that he had intended to pay for the items, the police charged him with shoplifting.

While the Criminal Code allows store owners or their employees to arrest those they have seen committing theft (so long as they immediately involve the police), it is always better to have the assistance of the police, both for the safety of the store employees and to minimize or prevent later claims of false imprisonment or assault.

See FALSE ARREST; FALSE IMPRISONMENT.

SIDEWALK

When a public sidewalk adjoins privately owned real estate, the private-property owner usually has several legal

---

ABC's
OF SPOTTING A SHOPLIFTER

If you are a shopkeeper or employee, be aware that the most effective way to combat shoplifting is through good customer service. Approaching as many customers as you can in a friendly way reduces theft, because shoplifters hate to be noticed. To spot a potential shoplifter, keep an eye out for shoppers who:

■ Wander aimlessly around the store or drop merchandise on the floor. These "browsers" may be looking for an opportunity to conceal merchandise when no one is looking.

■ Avoid sales personnel and other shoppers. It is easier to shoplift in isolated areas, and many shoplifters choose a time when customer traffic is slow and clerks are distracted by other duties, such as taking inventory.

■ Wear loose-fitting garments or carry oversize packages. Be especially wary of shoppers wearing long or heavy overcoats on a summer day. Shoplifters may also use packages with spring-loaded false bottoms, which they can place over an item and carry out of the store. You can cut down on the use of these ploys by asking customers to leave their packages at the checkout area.

■ Seem especially nervous. Shoplifters are always on the lookout for sales personnel, store detectives, and other shoppers. A shopper who spends more time watching others than examining merchandise may be a shoplifter.

---

responsibilities. For example, she must report any damaged sections of the sidewalk to the city as soon as she notices them. She must also bear at least some of the cost of the repair, because the sidewalk benefits the property owner more than it does the public at large. In fact, homes in areas with sidewalks are usually valued somewhat higher than those in areas without them.

If you have a private sidewalk, such as a paved path that leads from the street or driveway to your front door, you must keep it in good repair. If you know that your private

sidewalk is cracked or broken, you can be held responsible for any injuries a visitor may suffer, unless you put up a warning sign or place a barricade around the broken area.

SNOW REMOVAL

Homeowners are responsible for clearing snow and ice from private sidewalks and walkways that are used by the public. If an owner takes too long to do the work or does a poor job and someone slips on her sidewalk, she will be held liable, even if she was out of town when it snowed. If you own property that is adjacent to a public walkway, it is a good idea to arrange for a neighbor or a hired helper to clear your sidewalk in your absence. See also ACCIDENTS IN THE HOME.

SIMULTANEOUS DEATH LAW

An airplane or automobile crash, an explosion, or a natural disaster may result in the death of a husband and wife or an entire family at the same time. One of the legal problems created by these situations is how to distribute their estates.

For example, if a couple dies in a sailing accident with no surviving witnesses and no other evidence that one of them died after the other, the court must decide who died first in order to determine whose will takes effect first. If the husband left his estate to his wife and the court rules that he died before she did, his estate would pass to his deceased wife, and her estate would then be passed along according to the terms laid out in her will.

Several provinces have enacted provisions to cover situations of simultaneous deaths. Ontario's Succession Law Reform Act states that where two or more people die simultaneously, the property of each person is to be disposed of as if he had survived the others. For example, suppose John

and Mary were killed together in an automobile crash. They had prepared wills leaving the bulk of their estates to each other, but like most people they had made no special provision for what would happen if they died at the same time. Thus, the court would apply the law as follows: since John was presumed to have survived Mary and Mary was presumed to have survived John, their individual property and one-half of their jointly owned property were distributed to other legatees designated in their wills. See also COMMUNITY PROPERTY.

To avoid any legal confusion or misunderstanding among family members, you can include a provision specifying what should happen to your property should you and your spouse die simultaneously. Similar provisions should be included in insurance policies, living trusts, and deeds.

See also PROBATE; WILL.

SMALL BUSINESS

More and more Canadians are working for small businesses or establishing their own. Whether you are an entrepreneur or work for a small business, you will find the following entries useful and informative: EMPLOYEE; HOME BUSINESS; INCOME TAX; INDEPENDENT CONTRACTOR; JOB DISCRIMINATION; LICENSE; REGISTERED RETIREMENT SAVINGS PLANS; SELF-EMPLOYMENT; SMALL-CLAIMS COURT; SOCIAL SECURITY.

SMALL-CLAIMS COURT

Small-claims courts were created to help people with relatively minor disputes avoid long and costly litigation. The maximum amount of money a small-claims court can award is $3,000 to $10,000, depending on the province (see map, page 483). From time to time, these limits are increased; you can find out the limits in your province by calling the court. If your claim is only slightly above the maximum, consider reducing it to fit within the legal limit rather than hiring a lawyer and incurring the extra expense of bringing suit in another court.

Because the procedures in a small-claims court are far less complex than in regular courts, the parties to a lawsuit usually represent themselves. A decision is rendered after one short hearing, typically completed in 15 minutes or less. Appeal rights are limited, and judges tend to base their decisions on what seems fair in the individual case and not on legal technicalities or precedents. The following problems are typical of those that could be resolved in a small-claims court:

◇ Your landlord fails to return your security deposit after you move.

◇ The attendant in a parking garage damages your car.

◇ A store will not replace a defective product you bought.

◇ A company owes you money for freelance work you did and will not pay you.

CHECKLIST

Alternatives to the Small-Claims Court

Before you decide to file a small-claims lawsuit, consider some of the following alternatives. If none of these methods resolves your dispute, a small-claims lawsuit is appropriate.

■ **ARBITRATION.**
Arbitration programs have become the standard way of resolving lawyer-fee disputes and claims against dry cleaners, stock-brokers, and others. The decision of the arbitrator may or may not be binding on either party. Today, many business contracts require any disputes that arise to be submitted to arbitration first.

■ **PRIVATE COURT.**
In Toronto, the Private Court offers an alternative to traditional litigation. Composed of retired judges and senior lawyers, the court operates like a traditional court if the parties to a dispute so choose. The Ontario Arbitration Act grants judges in the Private Court the power to issue injunctions and apply procedural rules as in a normal court. However, it is the parties who choose whether Private Court arbitration is to be binding or not. The court's philosophy is toward conciliation rather than competition, and it offers a quicker settlement than the courts.

■ **BCIAC.**
Originally a forum for arbitrating matters between countries, the British Columbia International Arbitration Centre now deals mainly with domestic commercial disputes, mostly about insurance. It takes about one-third the time to settle matters in the BCIAC as in the regular courts.

■ **CONSUMER ACTION AGENCIES.**
The automobile industry is about to establish a national arbitration board, which will be free to the consumer and will attempt to settle disputes involving automobile purchasers and manufacturers.

■ **MEDIA PROGRAMS.**
Some television and radio stations and newspapers have consumer hotlines. These programs prefer to feature problems that have dramatic potential, and although they are unable to investigate all the cases brought to their attention, they can be of great help if they decide to report on your problem. The threat of adverse publicity can change a merchant's attitude about a consumer problem very quickly.

■ **MEDIATION.**
Mediation programs are run by courts, nonprofit groups, and private profit-making organizations. A mediator tries to get the opposing parties to reach a solution between themselves. The fact that the parties themselves, and not an outsider, make the final agreement is especially advantageous when the parties must continue dealing with each other.

■ **COURT PROGRAMS.**
Many small-claims courts offer optional arbitration and mediation programs as alternatives to a full-fledged lawsuit.

◇ You paid for auto repairs, but your car is still not fixed.

◇ You want your dry cleaner to pay for the suede jacket she ruined.

◇ You were bitten by the neighbor's dog and you want reimbursement for medical treatment.

JURISDICTION

Small-claims courts can usually order people to pay only money damages. They cannot order "specific performance"—that is, they cannot order the person you are suing to give you a particular piece of property or perform a particular act. Nor can small-claims courts grant injunctions forbidding an action. For these types of judgments, you must file a lawsuit in a superior court.

FILING AND SERVING YOUR COMPLAINT

To initiate a small-claims action, you must file a complaint, which you can obtain from the small-claims court clerk. The form is usually short and fairly straightforward. It asks for your name and address, the name and address of the defendant, the amount of your claim, and a brief explanation of your complaint.

If you have questions about completing the form, the court clerk can probably help you. Since small-claims cases are usually handled without lawyers, clerks are accustomed to dealing with questions about procedures.

File your claim as soon as possible, especially if you are bringing witnesses to testify for you. Every province sets limits on the period of time in which you can file a lawsuit, and if you exceed it, your claim may be dismissed.

SERVICE OF PROCESS

An essential step in filing any lawsuit is notifying the defendant about the case so that he has the opportunity to defend himself. The notification consists of the complaint and a summons to appear in court at a specified time.

The rules about service vary considerably from province to province, so be sure to follow carefully whatever procedures apply in your court. You should be aware of some general rules:

◇ You must have the defendant served within a certain number of days before your trial is to be held. If the defendant gets less than the minimum notice, he is entitled to a postponement.

◇ It is best to serve the defendant directly. However, each province has its own rules on alternative procedures. Some provinces allow service at a defendant's home or place of business to be made on any reasonable person. Other provinces allow service by mail to defendants under special circumstances.

◇ If the defendant is a corporation, service must typically be made to an officer of the corporation or to someone in charge of the office at the time of service.

◇ There will usually be rules regarding when valid service can be made. For example, making service at 3 a.m. would be illegal out of respect for the rights of the defendant.

◆ Usually, service can be made between 7 a.m. and 10 p.m.

◇ If the defendant lives in another province, the rules of service there may be different from where you live.

IF YOU ARE THE DEFENDANT

When you are served with a complaint, usually all you have to do is show up in court at the specified day and time, prepared to defend yourself. A few provinces require you to file a simple answer stating whether you plan to contest the case and why.

As part of your response to the plaintiff's charges, you may wish to file a counterclaim, especially if you suffered any injury or loss in the same accident or other incident cited by the plaintiff. If you do not file a counterclaim, you may lose your right to sue your opponent at some later date. Be aware that if your counterclaim is for an amount larger than the limit for the small-claims court, it may move the whole case to a higher court.

OUT-OF-COURT SETTLEMENTS

The defendant may offer a settlement just before your case is scheduled to be heard. This frequently happens when you are suing a business. If you decide to accept the settlement, be sure to obtain your money on the spot or get a written settlement statement from the defendant. A signed settlement agreement is a legally enforceable contract. If you are unable to collect the money as promised by the

◆ defendant, you can sue for it in the small-claims court without having to prove your original case. All you need to prove is that the defendant has breached his written promise to pay you. Aside from listing the terms of the settlement, the statement should also say that if your opponent defaults, he will pay for your collection expenses. Then, if you have to use a lawyer to collect, your opponent will have to reimburse you for the lawyer's fees.

STATING YOUR CASE

If your case goes to trial, arrive early so that you can familiarize yourself with the court's procedures and make an assessment of the judge's personality. In most courts the clerk will call the roll of cases being presented that day, and you can get an idea of the time the judge will hear your case.

You do not have to wear business attire at a small-claims court, but being neat and conservatively dressed is an asset.

Remember that the judge and your opponent may want to question you or your witnesses. Be sure your witnesses are familiar with your claims and are prepared for whatever counterclaims you think the defendant might make. When your turn comes, state your case clearly and succinctly. Nobody expects you to be an expert on the law or have the presentation skills of a trial lawyer. The judge will ask you questions and guide you along to elicit the information she needs.

When you have presented ◆ your case, introduce any pertincnt documents or witnesses that support it. Do not insist on covering points with which the judge already appears to be familiar. Be polite and do not interrupt the defendant or his witnesses. Be especially careful not to interrupt the judge.

Some judgment awards are taxable (see below). Awards for personal injury, however, are tax free.

JUDGMENT

In many small-claims courts, a decision is not announced immediately. Instead, the parties are notified by mail within a few days. Most judgments are tax-free except for awards of lost wages, which are not. If the judge makes her decision in your presence and you are found at fault, you can petition her to be allowed to pay the plaintiff in installments. If the decision is to come in the mail and you fear that you will lose, you can ask the judge to let you pay the plaintiff over a period of time.

APPEALS

Decisions in small-claims courts are rarely appealed. Usually, when small-claims court judges have made an error in the law or in an assessment of the facts, an appeal is possible. For example, in one case, a small-claims judge participated too much in the examination of witnesses and denied the right of cross-examination to one of the parties. His decision was thus overturned on appeal. In another example, a judge accepted the defense that the legal issue before him had already been

decided in another court without carrying out proper investigation procedures designed to protect the plaintiff. This error in law allowed the plaintiff to appeal successfully.

Some provinces do not allow appeals at all, whereas other provinces allow only limited rights to appeal. An appeal usually results in a new trial in a county or district court.

Since there are no written transcripts in small-claims courts, and since judges usually do not write opinions explain-

ing their decisions, it is very difficult to appeal on a matter of law. See APPEAL; COURTS; JUDGMENT.

SMALL-BUSINESS CLAIMS

The small-claims court is not just for individuals. Increasingly, small businesses such as painting contractors and retail shops are turning to the small-claims courts as a way to speed collections from customers who default on their bills. If you own a small business, you may want to consider using the

SMALL-CLAIMS COURT LIMITS

The maximum amount for which you can file suit in a small-claims court is established by provincial law. To find out whether any of the limits listed below have changed, check with the clerk at your local courthouse.

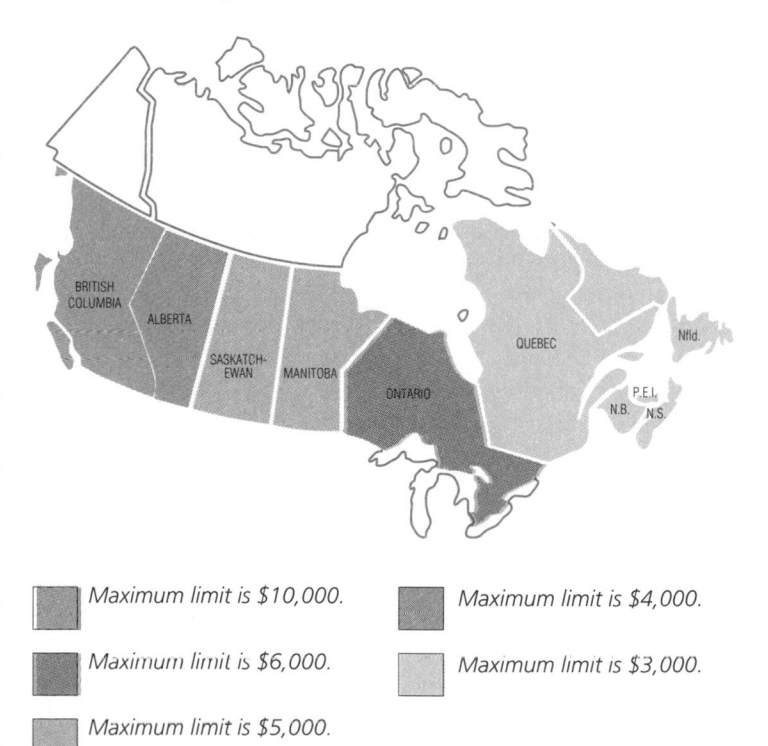

Maximum limit is $10,000.

Maximum limit is $6,000.

Maximum limit is $5,000.

Maximum limit is $4,000.

Maximum limit is $3,000.

small-claims court as a way to reduce lawyer's fees and avoid the delays of filing suit in district court. However, if your business is incorporated, some provinces require that you have a lawyer represent you, and some provinces limit the number of small-claims actions you can bring in a single year. Check with your small-claims court clerk for your province's specific rules for small businesses.

SMOKING

As medical research continues to expose the health risks of smoking, both to smokers and to people around them, the legal restrictions on smoking have multiplied. Every province prohibits minors from purchasing tobacco products. People who are found guilty of selling or giving tobacco products to minors may be fined. Transport Canada has banned smoking on all commercial domestic and international flights. Most provinces prohibit smoking in government office buildings, elevators, public libraries, and theaters. Many employers now prohibit smoking in the workplace.

Legally, smokers are not a "protected class," and the employer's right to limit or forbid smoking in the workplace does not violate constitutional guarantees against discrimination. Some courts have upheld employers who fired workers for refusing to obey a company ban on smoking. See EQUAL PROTECTION OF THE LAWS.

◆ Some employers have even begun to require employees to give up their smoking habit altogether. Courts have held that employers may refuse to hire a smoker who will not quit without fear of being sued for unlawful discrimination.

SOBRIETY CHECKPOINT

As part of their efforts to curb drunk driving, many provincial law enforcement agencies set up sobriety checkpoints, or roadblocks, usually on weekends and holidays. Sometimes the police announce that checkpoints are being set up without saying where they will be. Officers stop vehicles at the checkpoint area ostensibly to check driver's licenses and vehicle registration papers. While so doing, an officer can observe the driver's behavior for signs of intoxication. Stopping cars at roadblocks, however, raises the question of unreasonable search and seizure.

In reviewing sobriety checkpoint cases, courts look at such factors as how long each motorist was detained, whether the location and time interfered with the regular flow of traffic or created hazards for motorists, whether motorists were given advance warning that checkpoints were being set up, whether there were signs at the checkpoint explaining its purpose, and whether the police chose to stop the vehicles arbitrarily or according
◆ to a predetermined pattern,

◆ such as every second, third, or fourth approaching car.

Generally, most courts will admit evidence of drunk driving obtained from a sobriety checkpoint if the procedure to stop motorists was minimally intrusive.

See also DRUNK DRIVING.

SOCIAL SECURITY

Canada has an array of social services to help those in need. Canada's Old Age Security pension provides monthly benefits to everyone 65 and over who meets residency requirements. Some pensioners are also eligible for the Guaranteed Income Supplement, and Spouses' Allowances are available to spouses of pensioners when the couple has little income. The Canada (or Quebec) Pension Plan provides monthly benefits to retired contributors, and Unemployment Insurance provides up to one year's benefits for out-of-work contributors.

Each province designs and administers its own welfare or social assistance program, which the federal government partly funds. Welfare payments are provided for food, shelter, fuel, clothing, and other essential items. Various programs for veterans and native peoples are offered by the
◆ federal government. See also

MEDICARE; PENSION PLAN, UNEMPLOYMENT INSURANCE; WEL-FARE;WORKERS' COMPENSATION.

SOLE PROPRIETORSHIP

If you own your business, the simplest form of ownership is a sole proprietorship, even if you have employees. All you have to do to start a sole proprietorship is to obtain the licenses or permits required of any business by provincial and municipal laws. Then you must report business income and expenses to Revenue Canada, where they will be subject to personal income tax. You will have to complete the T1 form and attach Schedule 8. It should be noted that the personal tax rate is normally higher than the rate applicable to corporations.

When you operate your business as a sole proprietorship, you assume personal liability, or responsibility, for all the activities of the business. For instance, if you borrow money for your business and cannot repay it, the lender will be able to obtain a judgment against you personally for the unpaid amount—that is, he may be able to attach your personal bank account or put a lien on your house. Similarly, if the goods or services you sell harm someone or damage his property, you may end up forfeiting your personal assets to compensate him. For this reason, it is important that people who own a sole proprietorship have sufficient liability insurance.

To avoid this kind of liability, you may choose to form a corporation or limited-liability company. Keep in mind, however, that these business entities require more complex accounting and reporting procedures than a sole proprietorship.

See CORPORATION; HOME BUSINESS; INDEPENDENT CONTRACTOR; PARTNERSHIP; SELF-EMPLOYMENT.

SPEECH, FREEDOM OF

The Charter of Rights and Freedoms states that "everyone has the fundamental freedom of expression, including freedom of the press and other media of communication." As a result, Canadians may speak freely without fear of reprisal or censorship by federal or provincial governments. For instance, if a person gives a speech condemning the federal government's foreign policy regarding developing countries, he is within his rights to do so.

Because the charter applies only to federal and provincial governments and agencies, private companies, foundations, and other nongovernmental bodies may restrict the free speech of others without violating the charter. For example, if a corporation fires an employee for publicly speaking out against corporate policy, it is within its rights. Private companies can also require employees and contractors to sign confidentiality agreements as a condition of employment. See also WHISTLE-BLOWER.

EXCEPTIONS

The right to free expression is not absolute. Just as the government may legitimately prohibit the distribution of printed matter that is obscene, violates national security, or libels another person, it may also place restrictions on oral statements that people can make in public. See also DEFAMATION.

Students and prisoners, for example, are permitted freedom of speech only as long as their speech does not interfere with discipline and order in their respective institutions. Statements that slander another person are punishable under the law. Similarly, the government can prohibit speech that is obscene or that expresses a sedition intention.

For instance, a speaker at a public gathering who urges the crowd to attack the police there can be arrested. If, however, the speaker merely rails against police brutality, he is protected by the guarantee of free speech.

Individuals do not have the right to make statements that harm the welfare of a nation, such as those that breach national security or advocate concrete steps to overthrow the government, although they may support revolution in an abstract way.

The government may also restrict its own employees' right to speak to some extent. A government worker with access to sensitive documents—such as those concerning national security or containing trade secrets—can be prohibited from disclosing the contents of those documents in public. And an agency such as the Canadian Security Intelligence Service, which deals with issues of national security, can require former employees to refrain from discussing or publishing information they obtained during the course of their employment without the agency's approval.

In 1990, the Supreme Court of Canada heard the case of two members of a white supremacist group which had published and distributed material containing statements that denigrated other races. The two had been charged under the Criminal Code provision relating to the promotion of hatred against identifiable groups. The Court found that the law violated the charter's guarantee of free expression, but that it was a justifiable limit given the nature of the message conveyed.

See also PRIOR RESTRAINT.

TEACHERS

A public schoolteacher's right to free speech is limited in some respects. In general, teachers may express their views on political or historical events. However, a teacher cannot, in a classroom, present views that deny known facts. He may not teach that the Holocaust never happened or that Canada was the first country to send a satellite into orbit, for example. In addition, a teacher may not make statements that disrupt the running of the school or interfere with the educational process.

COMMERCIAL SPEECH

Provincial and federal governments can place reasonable limitations on commercial speech, such as that in television or radio commercials. For example, by virtue of its Tobacco Products Control Act, the federal government has banned television and radio advertisements for cigarettes and liquor.

However, unreasonable regulation is not permitted. For instance, an Ontario law unduly restricting dentists from advertising their services was held to be unconstitutional. In order to promote professional conduct, the law in question prohibited dentists from advertising their office hours and languages spoken. The Supreme Court of Canada found that this provision was an unreasonable infringement on the freedom of expression, because such information was useful for the public and did not threaten professionalism. The court found that the public's right to this information outweighs the province's right to prohibit professionals from advertising, provided the advertisements are truthful.

SYMBOLIC SPEECH

The constitutional protection of freedom of speech is not limited to the spoken word.

Indeed, the charter refers to freedom of "expression," which encompasses a broader range of concepts than freedom of "speech." According to the Supreme Court of Canada,

"activity is expressive if it attempts to convey meaning." Therefore, a meaning conveyed by a work of art such as a novel, play or painting would also receive constitutional protection.

See also CENSORSHIP; FLAG, CANADIAN; LIBEL AND SLANDER; PRESS, FREEDOM OF.

SPEEDING TICKET

You have had a terrible morning. Your alarm clock did not go off, and you overslept. Then, to make up for lost time, you drove 80 km an hour in a 50-km-per-hour zone on your way to work, and soon saw a flashing light in your rearview mirror. The speeding ticket you got is going to cost you three demerit points on your driver's license and a $100 fine.

CALCULATING SPEED

Police officers calculate a car's speed using a radar instrument or a speed trap. A car's speed obtained by a radar instrument is considered reliable evidence by the courts, so if such evidence indicates you exceeded the speed limit, you will probably be found guilty of speeding.

In a speed trap, the police time cars as they enter and exit a measured section of road. By knowing the length of the section of road and the time the car took to travel across it, they can calculate the car's speed. Courts consider this method to be less reliable than radar.

CONSEQUENCES OF SPEEDING

The consequences of speeding vary from province to province, but they can be severe— particularly if you have a record of repeated offenses or have greatly exceeded the speed limit. At the very least, you will probably be fined, the offense will be entered into your permanent driving record, and you will have demerit points assessed against your driver's license. Your insurance rates can also be raised, and eventually your insurer may cancel your coverage. See also DRIVER'S LICENSE.

If you are caught speeding repeatedly or have accumulated a certain number of demerit points on your license, the judge may order you to attend driving school, or he may suspend or revoke your license. In addition, most provinces have reciprocity agreements, whereby out-of-province speeding violations are entered on your driving record in your home province.

When you receive a speeding ticket, you may either contest it or pay the fine. If you do neither, the fine will be increased and you will receive a summons to pay it. If you choose to ignore the summons, your car may be towed away and impounded, and a warrant may be issued for your arrest.

Finally, speeding or otherwise driving recklessly may increase your liability in an accident. See also NEGLIGENCE.

CHALLENGING A TICKET

It is seldom easy to challenge a speeding ticket, especially if you have no witnesses. An officer's word is more likely than yours to have credibility with the court. Challenges to speeding tickets are heard in a traffic court by a judge, rather than a jury. You do not need a lawyer if you are challenging a ticket for the first time, but if you face the revocation of your license or a large increase in your insurance rates, you should hire one.

One way to challenge a ticket is to discredit the way the police determined your speed. If the police officer used radar, for example, your lawyer might ask him about his training in using radar equipment, the working condition of the radar equipment, and whether there was other traffic between the radar beam and your car.

If your defense is that your car's speedometer was not operating properly, you should have it repaired before you go to court and present the mechanic's receipt to the judge. Although having a faulty speedometer is not a valid defense against speeding, you may be able to convince the judge to be more lenient. See also TRAFFIC TICKET.

RADAR DETECTORS

If you are tempted to install a radar detector in your car, be sure you know your provincial laws. In some provinces— Manitoba, Ontario, and Quebec for example—you may be fined if you are caught with a radar detector.

SPORTING EQUIPMENT

The manufacturers of sporting goods have been held responsible for players' injuries when their products proved defective. For example, a manufacturer of lenses was held to be liable in negligence for the plaintiff's eye injury after a lens broke during a game of touch football. The manufacturer did not supply hardened lenses as it had undertaken to do. In this case, the optometrist who ordered the lenses was also held to be liable. The court found that both the manufacturer and the optometrist were negligent in failing to test the lenses.

If the coach or organizer of a sports event knew that the equipment used was inadequate, he too may be held liable for any resulting injuries. Today, most sports equipment carries labels with extensive warnings about proper use.

SPORTING EVENT

When you are a spectator or a participant in a sport, you have certain rights and you assume certain risks.

SPECTATOR SPORTS

Jack has bought a good seat for a professional basketball game. Just as he is settling down, one of the players chasing a loose ball bounds into the crowd and crashes into Jack, who suffers a broken leg. Can Jack sue the arena operator? Probably not, nor can he sue the player who crashed into him. The law presumes that when spectators attend sporting events they are assuming the risk of being injured at the game. This is especially true in Jack's case, since he bought a courtside seat.

When you attend a sporting event, the operator of the arena is not obliged to ensure your absolute safety from a game-related injury, but he is liable for injuries you suffer if reasonable precautions could have prevented them. That is why screens are erected behind home plate at baseball stadiums and shatterproof glass barriers are put up at hockey rinks. If the arena operator fails to provide such protection and you are injured, you can sue. See ACCIDENTS IN PUBLIC PLACES.

When you buy a ticket for a reserved seat at a sporting event, you have an enforceable contract. If someone else is sitting in your seat and refuses to leave, you can ask the arena management to move her. But if the management does not respond, you are entitled only to a refund of the price printed on the ticket, even if you bought it from a ticket broker at a premium. The same refund policy applies in the event that the game is canceled.

You should be aware that scalping—selling tickets for more than the box office price—may be illegal where you live. Ontario's Ticket Speculation Act, for example, provides that anyone selling or buying tickets at an inflated price is liable to a $5,000 fine.

PARTICIPATING IN SPORTS

When you participate in a sport, you assume the risk of being injured during the normal course of play. Therefore you cannot sue the operators of your neighborhood softball league if you break your ankle while sliding into second base, nor can you sue the outfielder of the other team if his throw to the second baseman hits you in the head. But if the second baseman goes into a rage and punches you because your hit drove in the winning run, you can file suit against him for your injuries, since his behavior is not a natural consequence of participating in the game, or one you could reasonably have expected.

MINORS

When young people participate in sports, their parents are asked to sign a waiver excusing the sports operators from liability. Generally, these waivers have no real legal effect except to put the parents on notice of the potential injuries that their children could suffer. Coaches, operators, or sponsors are responsible for an injury only if it resulted from their negligence.

REAL LIFE, REAL LAW

The Case of the Defensive Defenseman

On the evening of Sept. 21, 1969, the Boston Bruins and the St. Louis Blues met in a National Hockey League (NHL) exhibition game at the Ottawa Civic Centre. About halfway through the first period, there was an altercation involving Ted Green of the Bruins and Wayne Maki of the Blues. The evidence showed that during a skirmish along the boards behind the Boston net, Green punched Maki in the face. Maki retaliated by spearing his opponent, which resulted in Green slashing Maki across his shoulder. Green was subsequently charged under the Criminal Code with common assault.

After hearing the evidence, the trial judge held that Green was not guilty of the offense. In the first place, the judge found that NHL players consent to being assaulted by virtue of their participation in the game. That is, all players assume the risk of being hit by an opposing player. Second, the court found that the most serious blow struck during the scuffle was the spearing of Green by Maki. Green's subsequent retaliatory slash was held to be an act of self-defense and warning, and did not constitute an assault in the circumstances.

The judge concluded that, due to hockey's permissiveness and the risks involved with the game, it was unlikely that a charge of common assault could ever stand based on events arising during the course of a hockey game such as the one in question.

Suppose your child tells his coach that he has sprained his ankle, but the coach sends him back onto the field anyway and the sprain is aggravated. The league and the coach could be held liable, because no reasonably prudent person would knowingly let a child continue playing with a sprained ankle. Even if you had signed a waiver of liability, neither the coach nor the league would be relieved of responsibility.

PROHIBITED SPORTS

The Criminal Code prohibits certain so-called sports such as pit bull fighting and cockfighting because these events violate public policy against cruelty to animals and birds. Those who encourage, aid, or assist at the fighting or baiting of animals or birds can be subject to a fine, imprisonment, or both. The Criminal Code also outlaws prizefighting between members of society, based on concerns about good order and the public interest. However, the code permits provincial authorities to sanction boxing matches as long as the combatants wear gloves, with each glove having a mass of at least 140 grams. It should be noted that attendance at an outlawed event is also a crime, and spectators may be punished.

STATUTE OF LIMITATIONS

The provinces and the federal government have laws known as statutes of limitations or prescriptions, which limit the time period within which a civil lawsuit or criminal charge must be filed. Failure to comply with a statute of limitations means that a plaintiff loses her right to file suit or that the government may lose its right to prosecute a criminal suspect in some offenses.

With a few exceptions, there is no limitation period for indictable offenses under the Criminal Code. Proceedings relating to summary conviction offenses must be started within six months of the alleged criminal act.

Every civil offense has its own statute of limitations. For example, a civil lawsuit in relation to a simple contract must be brought within six years. This rule applies in most Canadian jurisdictions. Claims for criminal injuries compensation must be brought within one year, except in Manitoba where the limitation period is two years. In most provinces, lawsuits for personal injury arising from motor vehicle accidents must be brought within two years (three years in Quebec, but 12 months in Saskatchewan). The limitation period for actions against hospitals varies from province to province. In Ontario and Nova Scotia, it is two years, whereas in Alberta it is one year. Note that the statute of limitations may be different for physicians than for hospitals.

Ontario is in the process of revising the limitations provisions, which are scattered throughout a variety of provincial statutes. The goal is to make limitation periods easier to find and apply. One significant area of the reform deals with the victims of sexual assault. If the sexual assault was carried out by a person in a position of trust or authority, no limitation period will apply to a civil action against that person. This aspect of the legislation is in keeping with a 1992 judgment by the Supreme Court of Canada.

One purpose of the statutes of limitations is to prevent potential plaintiffs from "sitting on their rights" while memories surrounding the controversy grow dim and witnesses move away or die. They also allow potential defendants to go on with their lives without having to worry indefinitely that a lawsuit may be filed as the result of some long ago occurrence.

In the area of criminal law, the statute of limitations prevents prosecutors from conducting open-ended investigations of people whom they suspect of committing a crime, but whom they cannot formally accuse because there is insufficient evidence.

STEPPARENT

Paul married Donna about a year after the death of his first wife. He had two small children, both under four years of age when they married, and Donna quit her job in order to be a full-time mother to them. Seven years later, when Paul filed for divorce, he told Donna she would have no visitation or custody rights over the children whom she had come to love as her own. Donna was devastated. Did she have any legal rights?

STEPPARENTS' RIGHTS AND DUTIES

Although there are thousands of stepparent-stepchild relationships in Canada, many stepparents have no rights regarding their stepchildren if their marriages end, either by death or divorce.

When stepparents divorce, in the majority of cases the legal parent is automatically granted custody of the children. If the legal parent abandoned the children or proved to be an unfit parent, the court might award custody to a stepparent, because that would be in the best interests of the children. However, it is not an easy task to prove that a parent is unfit, and the courts generally prefer to keep children with their biological parents to maintain the integrity of the family.

Similarly, a stepparent may lose custody of her stepchildren when her spouse dies and the surviving natural parent comes forward to claim custody. In such a case, the stepparent must show that the surviving natural parent is unfit or has abandoned the children. Naming your spouse (the stepparent of your children) in your will as the children's legal guardian will have little effect if their surviving biological parent claims custody.

In the event of death or divorce, stepparents may have more success when seeking visitation rights. All provinces have legislation which permits a stepparent to apply for rights of access. However, a court will only grant such a request if it is in the best interests of the child.

Depending on the circumstances of each case, a stepparent may also be obliged to provide monetary support to a stepchild upon divorce or separation. This obligation will be determined by examining the role of the stepparent during the marriage. If a husband, for example, helps to provide for the financial needs of his stepchildren and assumes a fatherly role when dealing with the children, it is likely that a court would order him to pay support once the marriage ends. See ALIMENTARY PENSION.

ADOPTION

Many stepparents adopt their stepchildren. When an adoption is final, the stepparent assumes all the legal rights and responsibilities of the relationship. If the noncustodial biological parent is still alive, the adoption ends his or her parental rights and responsibilities. The adoptive parent has a duty to support the child, even if the marriage later ends in divorce. See also ADOPTION.

WILLS AND PROBATE

Many stepparents have close and loving relationships with their stepchildren and wish to provide for them upon their death. If you are in this situation, you should be sure to specify what portion of your estate you wish to leave to your stepchild or stepchildren in your will. If you die intestate (without a will), your estate will be divided among your "heirs at law," and because stepchildren do not fall into this category, they cannot inherit from you. See also DYING WITHOUT A WILL; WILL.

CANADA PENSION PLAN AND VETERANS' BENEFITS

When a parent dies leaving minor children, the children are usually entitled to government payments, such as Canada (Quebec) Pension Plan survivor benefits and veterans' benefits. If you have stepchildren who reside in your household and depend upon you for support, they may be eligible to receive these benefits also. See SOCIAL SECURITY.

STOCKBROKER

If you want to buy stocks or bonds, you will probably have to use the services of a stockbroker—someone who acts as an intermediary for your purchases and sales of securities.

Before you do any business with a broker, check with your province's office of securities regulation to find out how long she has been licensed; how long she has been employed at her current firm; whether she or her firm has ever been sued or disciplined by a provincial regulatory body; and whether her firm is facing any financial troubles that might influence her to sell you higher-risk investments or churn your account. It is advisable to do this even if the broker is working for a large, reputable brokerage house. See CHURNING.

Stockbrokers receive commissions on the sales and purchases of stock made through their services. Their fees range from about 1 to 5 percent. One way to pay lower fees is to use a discount broker instead of a full-service broker. Full-service brokers will advise you about market conditions, suggest when to buy or sell particular investments, and have a staff of analysts to help manage your portfolio. Discount brokers merely follow your instructions for buying and selling.

COMPLAINTS ABOUT STOCKBROKERS

Even if you choose a stockbroker carefully, problems may arise, especially if the broker's "sure thing" turns out to be a loser. In most cases, any losses you suffer as a result of a broker's recommendation are yours to bear. But if the broker has violated the law or neglected his professional responsibility, you may be able to get some or all of your money back.

For example, if your broker has traded securities in your account without your permission or intentionally misrepresented an investment by failing to disclose information about a potential risk, she may be liable for your losses. Similarly, if your broker puts your money in high-risk investments when your investment needs dictate a safer, less risky portfolio, the broker might also be held responsible.

Stockbrokerage agreements may require you to use arbitra-tion to resolve disputes with your broker. Although you do not need a lawyer to represent you in an arbitration hearing, if the amount of money at stake is considerable, you should probably hire a lawyer experienced in alternative dispute resolution. Many lawyers accept such cases on a contingent-fee basis.

STEPS TO TAKE

If you have a complaint about the way your stockbroker has handled your account, follow these steps.

1. Talk to the broker immediately and notify her of your complaint. Keep detailed notes about the telephone conversation you have with her and any follow-up conversations about the complaint. Ask her to put her explanation in writing.

2. Follow up with a letter of your own summarizing your discussion. State the actions you expect her to take to remedy the situation, such as making good on any losses created by unauthorized trading in your account. Include a deadline for a response, such as two weeks, and send a copy of the letter to the broker's manager.

3. If you do not get a reply, write to the president of the firm. Restate your complaint and the actions you want taken, and include copies of your previous correspondence.

4. If you still do not receive a response, or if you are dissatisfied with the response you do receive, contact your provincial office of securities regulation. Enclose copies of your correspondence with all the parties involved.

STOCKS AND BONDS

Buying stocks and bonds is a traditional way of diversifying an investment portfolio. But before you make any purchases, you should be aware of the legal, as well as the monetary, considerations of these financial instruments.

STOCKS

When you buy stock in a corporation, you become, in effect, a part owner of the business. That is why stocks are often called equities; when you buy them, you obtain equity, or ownership, in the company. As a stockholder, you participate in the company's success or failure in proportion to your investment. Most stockholders own only a minute interest, or share, in the business. Nevertheless, all stockholders of voting shares are entitled to vote (in proportion to the amount of stock they hold) on major issues that affect the company's management. They may also receive a portion of the company's profits in the form of a dividend.

Common stock
Corporations may issue two kinds of stock: common and preferred. When you buy common stock, you are entitled to receive a proportionate share of any dividends the company may pay, but you are not guaranteed any specific return on your investment.

Many profitable companies pay regular dividends to their common-stock holders, but they are not legally required to do so. The decision to pay dividends is made annually by the company's board of directors. If the company has had a bad year, it may decide to reduce dividends or eliminate them entirely. Even if business is booming, the directors may decide to reinvest the company's profits rather than pay them out as dividends.

Preferred stock

Sometimes a company may try to attract investors by offering preferred stock, which entitles shareholders to dividends at a specified rate. Holders of preferred stock will receive their dividends before any are paid to the holders of the company's common stock. Furthermore, if the company should fail, the holders of preferred stock can receive—ahead of those who own common stock—any assets that may remain after the company's debts have been paid. Sometimes preferred stock is "called" by the company. See the discussion about called bonds on page 494.

Buying stocks

Although a few companies sell their stock directly to the public, most make their shares available through a stockbroker who works for a brokerage house. When you buy stock, the corporation will issue a stock certificate, which can be held either by you or by your stockbroker. See STOCKBROKER.

The stocks of publicly traded companies are bought and sold on five different Canadian stock exchanges. The largest is in Toronto; others are in Montreal, Vancouver, Calgary, and Winnipeg. There is also a market for unlisted stocks, called the over-the-counter (OTC) market, which lists the stock offerings of small, new companies.

The larger stock exchanges have a central exchange board, which posts the asking and selling prices of their various stocks. OTC stocks are not

---

CHECKLIST

Stocks, Scams, and Swindles

Although the vast majority of stockbrokers and brokerage firms are honest and diligent in serving their customers, some brokers take advantage of an investor's trust. The following stock scams and swindles might affect you:

■ **FALSIFYING YOUR NET WORTH.** When you open your brokerage account, you will be asked to provide personal financial information. If your net worth—that is, all the assets you have free of debts—is low, ethical brokers will not consider investing your money in risky investments such as junk bonds, options, or penny stocks. Be sure to fill in all the blank spaces on your new-account form. It is possible that a dishonest broker could falsify your net worth on your new-account form, and could put your limited funds into risky investments, which often earn him a higher commission. Be sure to review your new-account form for inaccuracy.

■ **STEALING FROM YOUR ACCOUNT.** A broker who is in personal financial trouble may succeed in circumventing the many security safeguards to gain access to your account. Be sure that you carefully read your account statement each month and bring any discrepancies to the attention of the branch manager of the brokerage firm immediately.

■ **CHURNING—MAKING FREQUENT, UNNECESSARY TRADES.** Brokers earn a commission whenever they buy or sell a stock. Therefore, the more stock trades they make, the greater their commission. Beware of brokers who call frequently advising you to make trades, particularly if they will generate little profit for your account. See CHURNING.

■ **OTC PRICE MANIPULATION.** Because over-the-counter (or OTC) stocks are owned by broker-dealers, it is possible that a dishonest broker-dealer could create intentional increases or decreases in an OTC stock price by aggressively trading it. If he convinces you to buy at the inflated price, the broker-dealer can take his profit, then sit back and watch as the stock value falls back to its real worth. He may then begin the process all over again. If you suspect a broker-dealer of manipulating the price of a stock, contact your provincial office of securities regulation for information about filing disciplinary proceedings against the broker.

traded through a central exchange, but by registered dealers who create a market for these stocks for resale to other broker-dealers or to brokerage houses. In Ontario and Quebec, trades in unlisted stocks are reported each day.

Legal protection

As an investor, you are protected from unscrupulous stock market dealings by both federal and provincial governments. All companies offering stock for sale to the public nationwide must register the offering under the relevant provincial securities act. Companies must disclose information that enables a purchaser to evaluate the stock's worth and stability.

The securities act also requires publicly traded companies to publish financial information about their operations on a quarterly and annual basis. These reports, which are available from your broker, give investors a detailed accounting of the corporation's activities and financial performance. Be sure to review them carefully before investing in a company.

Provincial regulatory agencies enforce what are known as blue-sky laws, which set out the requirements that must be met for issuing and selling stocks within a given province.

Investors are further protected by the self-regulation of those involved in the stock market, such as the Investment Dealers Association of Canada and the Investment Funds Institute of Canada. The Criminal Code also contains provisions dealing with securities transactions. See BLUE-SKY LAW; SECURITIES REGULATION.

BONDS

Another way to invest in a company (or a government or governmental agency) is to buy its bonds. When you buy a bond, the issuer promises to pay you back the money you have invested in it, along with a specified rate of interest. As a bondholder, you are a creditor. If the issuer is a corporation, it must pay the interest it owes you before it makes any payments of dividends to stockholders. Also, if the issuer should go bankrupt, you as a bondholder have priority over stockholders in receiving your share of any assets.

Canada Savings Bonds

The best-known government bonds, Canada Savings Bonds are issued by the federal government, generally in the fall, and sold through banks and other financial institutions. They can be purchased with cash or through employee payroll deductions. They must be registered in your name, or in the name of a deceased person's estate. They may also be registered in the name of a trust set up for an individual. Purchasers must be Canadian citizens (or residents) with a Canadian address.

Savings bonds are a good investment for several reasons: (1) they are guaranteed by the Canadian government and can be replaced without charge should they be lost or stolen; (2) you can purchase them in installments through your employer; (3) you can redeem them at any time after six months.

Once a Canada Savings Bond has reached maturity, no more interest is paid. At that point, it should be reinvested in a newer issue.

Provincial and municipal bonds

Provincial and local governments and their agencies also issue bonds. Like Canada Savings Bonds, provincial and municipal bonds are available in many denominations. The interest they bear is related to prevailing interest rates and to the safety of the bonds, which depends on the fiscal health of the province or municipality that issues them. For an evaluation of bond safety, you should consult such publications as *The Bond Buyer*, *Credit Week*, and *Moody's Bond Survey*—all available at the public library.

Corporate bonds

Many corporations sell bonds—usually in denominations of $1,000—to raise money for expansion or to spread their existing debt among a greater number of buyers. Although they are riskier than Canada Savings Bonds, they promise regular interest income twice a year and may be redeemed for their full face value upon maturity.

How bonds are valued

The face value, or par value, of a bond is the amount you will be paid when the bond matures. But the amount that you actually pay for the bond (known as its market price) may be different from the face value. For example, a bond with a face value of $10,000 may be sellable for only $9,000 if interest rates have risen sharply since the bond was issued. On the other hand, if interest rates have fallen since then, the bond will usually sell for more than its original issue price. The market price can fluctuate widely from the time a bond is issued until the day it matures. As a rule, a bond with a high interest rate is a riskier investment than a comparable one with a lower rate.

When bonds are called

When interest rates drop, businesses and municipalities often call, or redeem, bonds before their maturity dates. (Canada Savings Bonds are not callable.) Essentially, a call means that the issuer has decided to redeem its older bonds paying high interest rates and refinance its debt through new bonds issued at lower rates. To attract and keep investors, some bond issuers promise not to call their bonds for a given period of time, such as five years. The earliest date at which a bond can be called is specified in the bond contract.When a call is issued, you have no choice but to surrender the bond. You will receive its face value and perhaps a small bonus, plus the accrued interest owed on the bond.

STRIKE

A strike is a work stoppage staged by the employees of a company or industry in order to pressure the management into granting concessions, such as higher wages or benefits. At one time, strikes were illegal, and an employee's only recourse against an employer was his freedom to quit his job.

It was not until the late 1800s that it became legal to establish a trade union, the formation of which was previously viewed as a criminal attempt to restrict trade. A series of strikes around 1900 prompted Parliament to enact legislation designed to promote conciliation between employers and workers. Strikes are now dealt with under provincial labor legislation, although the federal government still has authority over federal matters such as aviation and shipping.

In British Columbia and New Brunswick, the law specifically states that a legal refusal to work based on health and safety concerns is not considered to be a strike. Because it is necessary that there be a common understanding among employees, courts and labor relations boards have held that it is not strike action when individual employees refuse to cross picket lines out of fear. On the other hand, it has been held that a refusal to perform overtime work constitutes a strike, as does a refusal to work until the reinstatement of a union representative.

THE LABOR TRILOGY

The right to strike is not guaranteed by the constitution. This was determined by the Supreme Court of Canada in a series of 1987 cases known as the Labor Trilogy. The Court held that while individuals enjoy freedom of association, an association such as a trade union does not possess the right to strike, even though this may be one of the union's essential objectives. According to the Court, giving a union the right to strike would grant it greater rights than those enjoyed by individuals.

Non-unionized employees may also go on strike. But the Supreme Court's decision in the Labor Trilogy means that strike action may not be permitted to all workers. For example, the Court sanctioned Alberta legislation prohibiting certain classes of government employees from striking, based on the public need for government services and the fact that a strike by public employees can cripple, or even paralyze, government operations and endanger public safety.

LEGAL STRIKES

Although not explicitly stated in Canadian labor legislation, employees may legally strike under certain circumstances. For example, the Ontario Labour Relations Act prohibits strikes as long as a collective agreement is in force. Once the agreement expires, and certain procedures including attempts at conciliation have been followed, a legal strike can take place.

The legislation also provides that employees who participate in lawful strikes may not be refused continued employment for having taken part in such activities. Thus the employer-employee relationship is held to remain in force during a strike. For a strike to be considered legal, most provinces require that the employees vote beforehand on whether a strike should take place.

Alberta, British Columbia, and Ontario guarantee that employee pension benefits will continue during strikes, and Saskatchewan guarantees that benefits such as sick or holiday pay and vacations will continue. In other provinces, these rights are determined during collective agreement negotiations.

The safeguards built into the various labor laws may not apply to employees who participate in an unlawful strike.

On the matter of replacement workers, labor statutes in British Columbia, Ontario, and Quebec prohibit employers in those provinces from hiring such workers. Permanent replacement workers may not be hired in Manitoba.

OTHER TYPES OF STRIKES

There are certain types of strikes that relate to unionized companies only. A wildcat strike, for example, is one that the union has not authorized. Suppose the United Auto Workers Union enters into a national agreement with all the nation's auto manufacturers, but the workers at a single plant refuse to abide by the terms of the agreement and stage a walkout. Their action is called a wildcat strike, and their jobs would not be legally protected since wildcat strikes are prohibited by most union contracts.

A sympathy strike is conducted by workers to lend support to a strike being waged by a related union. Suppose a glassmakers' union strikes for a pay raise. Workers in the same plant who belong to the pipefitters' union may decide to stage a sympathy strike. Unless sympathy strikes are prohibited by their collective-bargaining agreement, they may do so.

UNEMPLOYMENT BENEFITS AND STRIKING WORKERS

Strikers are not entitled to receive unemployment benefits while on strike, since technically they are not unemployed. However, if you want to go to work but fear for your safety if you cross the picket line, you may be entitled to receive unemployment benefits.

Usually, a portion of union members' dues is placed in a special fund for workers who participate in a strike authorized by the union. Your union representative can give you the details about your union's strike fund.

See also LABOR UNION.

STUDENT LOAN

The costs of studying full-time at a post-secondary institution away from home are between $8,000 and $11,000 per year. Even with income from summer jobs and part-time work during the school year, many students simply cannot afford to pay for their education. For this reason, students must often depend on government financial assistance in the form of student loans.

The Canada Student Loans Plan was established in 1964 to provide funds for needy students. Under the plan, the federal government will guarantee a loan to students who can demonstrate that they do not have access to sufficient resources. The program is administered through the provincial and territorial governments.

Applications for student financial aid are available at universities, community colleges, technical schools, and in certain high schools. Once completed, they should be sent to your nearest provincial or territorial office of higher education. For students requesting funds for September study, many provinces suggest that loan applications be made before the end of May.

The information you must provide varies from one province to another. You will have to give a detailed list of expenses for the school year, as well as a list of your own resources, including money saved from summer jobs, parental contributions, and scholarships. In certain cases, your parents may have to provide a list of their assets and liabilities. Each province and territory is required to offer an appeal service for students whose applications are refused.

Once you receive a student loan, it will have to be stamped by your educational institution. You may then deposit it at any financial institution which negotiates these loans. If, during future years of study, you do not apply for a loan, be sure to advise your financial institution that you are still a student. Otherwise, it will be assumed that you are no longer eligible for the repayment exemption and you will be expected to begin making payments.

Apart from Canada Student Loans, there are also loan programs funded by the provincial and territorial governments. They may also offer grants, bursaries, and special assistance to target groups such as the disabled and workers undergoing retraining. It is not uncommon for a student to receive funds from both the federal and provincial levels of government.

REPAYMENT AND DEFAULT

Students are required to begin repaying their loans immediately upon graduation, with the payment schedule extending no further than 10 years. The rate of interest is set annually.

In cases of economic hardship, repayment of student loans may sometimes be postponed or even forgiven. To obtain a postponement, however, the borrower must appeal to the lender. If you simply stop making payments, you may be subject to severe penalties, such as having your income tax refund withheld by Revenue Canada or Revenue Quebec. A loan payment default may also jeopardize your credit rating, making it difficult to obtain future loans.

Alberta, New Brunswick, and Quebec offer remissions on provincially funded loans.

Canada Student Loans, however, are completely repayable. See also COLLEGE ADMISSIONS; COLLEGE SCHOLARSHIP; CREDIT BUREAU AND CREDIT RATING.

STUDENT RIGHTS

Canadians place a high value on individual freedom as well as the right to a good education. Occasionally, however, these two rights clash. For example, a school may claim that it must interfere with a student's freedom of speech in order to maintain classroom discipline. The fact that this type of conflict can arise has taken on new contours since the arrival of the Charter of Rights and Freedoms. The courts have been increasingly called upon to decide on questions of the rights of some students against those of schools to maintain order, discipline, and provide a high-quality education to other students.

FREEDOM OF EXPRESSION AND ASSOCIATION

The charter guarantees all individuals the freedoms of expression and association. Generally, the government is required to respect these rights. So one would expect that students have a right to speak their mind in class. However, the courts would likely not deny schools the authority to make and enforce rules prohibiting language which disrupted normal classroom activities. For example, even though a student may have the freedom to disagree

with a teacher, he likely cannot do it in mocking or abusive language. To allow otherwise could potentially interfere with the rights of other students to a quality education. Similarly, if a school prohibited carving graffiti in a desk or otherwise destroying school property, the courts would likely consider this to be a reasonable limit on student freedoms. It is most likely, too, that a school's administration would be within its rights to ban or control student associations on school grounds if the associations' activities interfered with the education of the student body.

While corporal punishment is allowed in some school districts in the United States, legal opinion in Canada has argued that it offends our charter. Indeed, in a number of Canadian jurisdictions, corporal punishment in schools is outlawed by school-board policy. The Criminal Code currently allows schoolteachers the right to use force to correct their students. That is to say, physical punishment is not allowed for its own sake. It can be applied only for the correction of the child. If the force used by the teacher exceeds what is reasonable in the circumstances, then he may find himself open to assault charges. See also CORPORAL PUNISHMENT.

DUE PROCESS

Students facing suspension or expulsion for breaking school rules are entitled to be notified of the infraction and the proposed punishment. They are also entitled to a hearing, at which they may try to refute the allegations. See SCHOOL EXPULSION AND SUSPENSION.

SEARCH AND SEIZURE

The charter also states that no one may be subject to unreasonable search or seizure. While this has been held to apply to students and teachers in a school context, the courts have so far been willing to ignore student's charter rights out of deference to school authorities and their duties.

For example, in Ontario, a principal received a tip from one student that another had drugs in his socks. Based on the tip, the principal asked the suspected student to remove his socks. The student complied, drugs were found, and the police were called. The student argued that an unreasonable search, violating his charter rights, had taken place. However, the Ontario Court of Appeal held that the principal had acted reasonably in view of his duty to maintain a safe school atmosphere. Requiring the student to remove his socks was not too intrusive on his privacy, the court said.

A Quebec principal searched a student's locker on a tip that it contained stolen school property. The property was found and the student arrested. The judge found that the student's rights had been violated since the principal should have got permission from the student or a judge before entering the locker. However, this violation was accepted on the grounds that it was not arbitrary or unreasonable, since the evidence was found in the locker.

SUBLEASE

Four months after moving into a new apartment in Toronto, you find out that your employer is sending you to Vancouver for a three-month-long assignment. You signed a one-year lease and would like to keep your apartment, but you do not want to pay rent while you are away. One option you may have is to sublease (or sublet) your apartment to someone else during your absence.

A sublease is a contract between the original tenant and a second tenant that gives the second tenant part of the rights granted in the lease. The original tenant may sublet the entire premises for a specified period of time, or he may continue to live there and rent out part of his leased space. For example, a restaurant may rent space in a mall and sublet part of it to an ice cream shop. Or a person might rent a house and sublet a basement room to another tenant in most cases.

If a tenant sublets, usually the landlord's only legal recourse for rent owed or damages caused by the subtenant is against the original tenant, because the landlord is not a party to the sublease. But the tenant can sue the subtenant for any expenses he incurs.

ASSIGNMENT

If you transfer your entire lease to another person—that is, the new tenant "takes over" the lease—the transaction is not a sublease but an "assignment." Thus, the new tenant assumes

ABC's

OF CHOOSING A SUBTENANT

Because you are responsible for property you sublease, you should select a subtenant very carefully. Essentially, you are the landlord to the subtenant, and you should follow the same procedure your landlord uses in renting to tenants. Before agreeing to let anyone become your subtenant, you should be sure to:

■ Obtain a copy of the subtenant's credit history from a credit bureau.

■ Call the subtenant's current employer to verify his employment and salary.

■ Ask the subtenant's previous landlord to verify his length of residence.

■ Put the sublease in writing. State the length of the sublease, the amount of security deposit, and the amount of the rent and when it is to be paid, as well as fees for late payment. Include a clause specifying responsibility for damages and the length of time required for notice to terminate the sublease.

all the rights and responsibilities that were stated in your lease.

When there is an assignment of the lease, the landlord can sue the subtenant if the property is damaged or the subtenant does not pay the rent. In addition, the landlord

497

may insist upon maintaining the right to sue you, as the assignor, for unpaid rent or damage, even if he consented to the assignment.

RIGHT TO SUBLEASE

If you are thinking about subletting your apartment, be sure to check the terms of your lease. Landlords frequently include a provision that either prohibits subletting or requires the landlord's approval. In some provinces, however, a landlord cannot unreasonably refuse a subtenant, provided she is financially responsible and meets the appropriate criteria. Even if your lease or the law in your province does not require the landlord's written approval, it is best to get it.

If the landlord denies you permission, do not sublease the apartment. The subtenant may then be considered a trespasser, and the landlord could begin eviction proceedings against both you and the subtenant. If the subtenant has not moved in, the landlord may get a court order prohibiting her from doing so.

Because you are legally responsible when you sublet property, you should be careful when choosing a subtenant. Ask for employer's references, and check the person's financial record. For more tips on choosing a subtenant, see box on preceding page. See also CREDIT BUREAU AND CREDIT RATING; LEASE; TENANT'S RIGHTS.

SUBORDINATION

In real estate law, establishing priorities in the payment of mortgages, liens, or other claims placed on property is known as subordination. Suppose you want to buy a house for $200,000. You have $20,000 in cash for the down payment, but your bank will give you a mortgage for only $160,000, leaving you $20,000 short. The seller agrees to help you out by lending you the remaining $20,000. The bank, in order to protect its status as your major creditor, will require that the seller's loan include a subordination clause, which states that the bank's loan must be repaid first if you default.

In provinces that use the Land Titles, or Torrens System of land registry, subordination may not be an issue. In such a system, the priority of creditors is determined on a first-come, first-served basis. A bank would not, therefore, grant you such a loan unless it was assured of registering ahead of the seller.

SUBROGATION

You are driving home from work one Friday afternoon when a van comes speeding out of a side street and slams into your car. Although you are unhurt, the car is badly damaged. When you find out that the person at fault is uninsured, you notify your insurer of the accident, and the insurance company agrees to pay for the repairs to your car. Before the insur-

ance adjuster sends you a cheque, he asks you to sign a document called a subrogation agreement, which allows your insurer to attempt to collect from the other driver (by getting a court judgment to garnishee his wages, for example). The proceeds may reimburse some or all of the amount your insurer paid to you.

A subrogation agreement is a standard part of most automobile insurance policies. Under certain circumstances, as in the case above, you may also be asked to sign an additional subrogation agreement.

SUPREME COURT OF CANADA

The nation's highest court, the Supreme Court of Canada, was established by Parliament under the Supreme and Exchequer Courts Act of 1875. Even so, it has been the court of last resort only since 1949. Before then, the Judicial Committee of the Privy Council in England was the final court of appeal for Canada and the other British colonies.

The Court hears both civil and criminal appeals from the various provincial appeal courts. Permission (leave to appeal) must be obtained for most civil appearances before the Court, but the majority of criminal cases it hears are automatic appeals (appeals of right). Since it is the final appeal court for all Canada, decisions by the Supreme Court have a unifying influence on the country's laws.

THE JUSTICES

The Supreme Court Act provides that the Court be composed of nine judges, called justices, three of whom must come from Quebec. Current practice is that three other judges come from Ontario, that two be from the Western provinces, and one from Atlantic Canada. One judge is designated the Chief Justice.

Five judges constitute a quorum, which is the minimum number required to hand down a judgment. A full bench of nine judges is often present for important cases.

Supreme Court justices are appointed by the federal cabinet on the recommendation of the Prime Minister. Those appointed must have been either a judge of a provincial superior court, or a lawyer who has been a member of a provincial bar association for at least 10 years. Supreme Court justices stay in office until age 75, unless removed for lack of good behavior.

The Supreme Court sits in Ottawa—for three sessions each year. The justices are required to maintain residences either in or within 40 kilometres of the National Capital Region.

CASES

The Supreme Court has what is known as appellate jurisdiction, meaning the cases it hears must have previously been dealt with at the provincial appeal courts, or at the Federal Court of Appeal. An exception is made for references—issues that the federal government asks the Court to rule upon. In practice, most references are questions of a constitutional nature.

References from provincial governments go to provincial courts of appeal. Of course, decisions by the provincial appeal courts may be appealed to the Supreme Court.

HOW APPEALS ARE MADE

In most cases, appeals to the Supreme Court begin with a party asking for leave to appeal, and submitting a factum outlining the arguments in the case. A panel of three judges then hears oral arguments from both sides in the dispute. Each party is allowed 15 minutes to present his case, with the applicant receiving a further five minutes to reply to the other side's arguments.

Hearing applications for leave to appeal occupies a great deal of the Court's time. It has recently begun hearing satellite-transmitted applications, so that the parties need not travel to Ottawa.

Once an appeal has been granted, or comes about as of right, the appellant and respondent submit written factums to the Court and to each other. Factums must set out concisely the facts giving rise to the appeal, the legal issues, the party's arguments, and the nature of the order the Court is asked to make.

On the date of the hearing, the parties present oral arguments to the Court. There is no specific time limit at this stage. Because the Court will have already read the factums, oral arguments serve only to emphasize key points and difficulties. Appeals generally last for half a day, although complete cases may require three or four days of argument. It is extremely rare for the Supreme Court to hear witnesses.

DECISIONS

If the Court deems that a full bench is not necessary, the Chief Justice will appoint five or more judges to hear the case. The judges are often appointed based on their province or region of origin. This is especially so when cases are from Quebec. The three Quebec judges are naturally more familiar than their fellow justices with the principles of that province's civil law.

All judges need not agree on the outcome of a particular case. The majority opinion is often composed of separate concurring opinions, in which various judges arrive at the same result, but adopt slightly different reasoning. It is common, however, for only one or two judges to write majority opinions, with the remaining judges simply expressing their agreement. Judges who disagree with the result of the majority submit dissenting opinions.

The Court has several options. It can affirm the lower court's decision, reverse it, or send the case back to a court of original jurisdiction for a new trial. The Court may also modify the lower court's decision, for example by reducing the amount of damages awarded. However, a decision by the Supreme Court of Canada is final.

SURROGATE MOTHER

"**W**oman gives birth to own grandchildren!" It may sound like a bizarre tabloid headline, but such a phenomenon is now possible and has occurred in at least one highly publicized American case in which a woman agreed to be a surrogate mother for her infertile daughter.

TYPES OF SURROGACY

There are two different kinds of medical procedures for becoming a surrogate mother: artificial insemination and in vitro fertilization.

The typical surrogate mother is a woman who agrees to be artificially inseminated with a man's sperm in order to bear a child for someone else. When the child is born, she gives it up for adoption to the biological father and his wife. In this arrangement, the surrogate mother is considered both the biological and the genetic mother of the child. See ARTIFICIAL INSEMINATION.

In another procedure, known as in vitro fertilization, a woman's egg is fertilized with her husband's sperm in a petri dish. The fertilized egg is then implanted in the womb of the surrogate mother, who bears the child and then relinquishes custody. In this arrangement, the surrogate mother has no genetic link with the baby but is legally considered the biological mother.

See IN VITRO FERTILIZATION.

SURROGACY CONTRACTS

Arrangements for surrogate mothers are sometimes handled in an informal way—that is, without fees, lawyers, or contracts—between close friends or family members who want to help a loved one have a child. Usually, however, the surrogate mother has a contract with the infertile couple whose child she will bear. A typical contract provides that the surrogate will relinquish her rights to the child upon birth. She may also be required to refrain from smoking, drinking, or using drugs during her pregnancy. The couple agree to cover all expenses related to the pregnancy and to pay the mother a fee.

THE LEGALITY OF SURROGACY CONTRACTS

Because the issue of surrogate motherhood is so recent, few provinces have made laws regarding the legality of such an arrangement. However, under ordinary contract law, such an arrangement would seem to be illegal if money is charged for such a "service," since a human being, and also most probably a fetus, cannot be the object of a contract. Under Quebec's Civil Code, charging money for being a surrogate mother is illegal. Article 25 of the new Civil Code reads: "The alienation by a person of a part or product of the body shall be gratuitous; it may not be repeated if it involves a risk to his health." Doubtless, other provinces will also soon pass legislation in this area.

REPRODUCTIVE TECHNOLOGIES

After years of research, and some $28.2 million in expenditures, the Royal Commission's report on new reproductive technologies was completed in November 1993. The commission cited the need for legislation and for a permanent 12-member National Reproductive Technologies Commission to regulate and license the new techniques.

Among the report's other recommendations were:

◇ That legislation be enacted to prohibit human zygote-embryo research related to cloning and animal-human hybrids; the sale of human eggs, sperm, zygotes, fetuses, and fetal tissues; and advertising for a surrogate mother, or receiving or making payments for arranging surrogacy.

◇ That expectant parents not be allowed to choose the sex of their child.

◇ That only women with blocked fallopian tubes receive in vitro fertilization treatment.

◇ That a national sperm collection and distribution system be set up to ensure that donated sperm is free from the AIDS virus and other diseases.

◇ That artificial insemination and in vitro fertilization should be provided only by licensed facilities following national standards.

◇ That the idea of profit be excluded from the context of conceiving and bearing children.

◇ That prenatal testing to determine the sex of a child

be banned unless there is a medical reason.

◇ That research to correct genetic diseases be allowed, but not to enhance characteristics such as height, intelligence, and longevity.

◇ That adoption proceedings be reviewed to better meet the needs of children and adoptive parents.

SWEEPSTAKES

"You may already be a winner." That message and similar ones arrive in mailboxes across the country several times a year, as magazine subscription services and catalog companies offer prizes large and small to those who respond to the mailing. Sweepstakes are popular promotional devices.

SWEEPSTAKES LAWS

Sweepstakes are governed by such laws as the Criminal Code, the Combines Investigation Act, and the Quebec Lotteries Act. Since winners may not be selected on the basis of pure chance, you may have to answer a skill-testing question to be eligible for a prize. It is also illegal to require participants to purchase something or to pay to enter a sweepstakes, so some contest promoters get around this stipulation by permitting you to send in a proof of purchase or a reasonable facsimile thereof.

Sweepstakes must disclose the odds of winning as well as any regional distribution of prizes. Contest rules and all winners' names must also be disclosed. Quebec law requires

sweepstakes promoters to provide a security deposit to ensure that prizes are allocated in the proper manner. See LOTTERY.

SWEEPSTAKES SCAMS

Although many sweepstakes are legal and aboveboard, various scams and swindles masquerade as sweepstakes. They typically work as follows:

You receive a postcard in the mail announcing that you have won a sweepstakes prize, but that the sponsor has not been able to reach you. This seems very peculiar, since you have a telephone answering machine, but you read on, tempted by the thought of winning a valuable prize.

To claim your prize, you are instructed to call the company at its 900 number. Just because you can dial the number, do not be misled into thinking it must be a Canadian number. It is not. In small print you notice—or perhaps you do not—that you will be charged for the call. When you call, you learn that you have won a "major prize," but in order to get it you will have to pay a fee for shipping it or buy some merchandise, such as vitamins or office supplies. When you receive the merchandise, it is generally overpriced and of poor quality, as is the "prize." You may be asked to provide a credit card number, "just to verify that you are indeed the winner." If you should be so naive as to do so, your next statement may reflect purchases you did not make or charges for a "membership fee" you did not agree to.

CAUTIONS

If you ever receive offers like those mentioned above, call the Marketing Practices Branch of Industry Canada immediately.

Never give your credit card number to verify your identity to anyone who calls you over the telephone. Never call a 900 number (one that charges a fee) to collect a prize. A legitimate sweepstakes will not ask you to do either of these.

Never agree to buy anything to obtain a sweepstakes "prize." If you did not mail an entry to a sponsor, it is not a true sweepstakes and you have not won anything. A "prize notification" from an unfamiliar company is probably a fraud. See FRAUD.

SWIMMING POOL

Swimming pools can be a source not only of fun but also of anguish—injuries, fatalities, and lawsuits. If you own one, you should know about your legal rights and responsibilities.

A swimming pool is known in legal terms as an "attractive nuisance"—something on your property that attracts children and may be harmful to them. By law, you must take special precautions to protect children—even those trespassing on your property—from injuring themselves in or around your pool. The best way to do this is to erect a tall and sturdy fence around the pool area, and keep the gate locked so that children will not be able to get in easily. If a child does climb over the fence and injures himself or drowns, you will usually not be held responsible.

When children or adults are using the pool with your permission, you must carefully supervise their activities. Prohibit rough horseplay, beverages in bottles or glasses, and diving (unless restricted and carefully supervised). Ask those who refuse to comply with your rules to leave. Limit or prohibit the use of alcohol; if a swimmer is injured or drowns, and evidence shows that you knew or should have known that she was intoxicated, you may be held liable.

GETTING INSURED

Notify your homeowners' insurance carrier when you install a pool. Most standard policies do not protect you from liability claims unless you have added a special provision, called an endorsement, and have paid an additional premium. Also, since pool injuries and deaths can lead to large court awards, you should consider buying an umbrella insurance policy. See also UMBRELLA INSURANCE.

USING POOLS

In most situations, pool operators do not have to supply lifeguards, provided that a sign clearly notifies swimmers that no lifeguard is on duty and that swimmers use the pool at their own risk. Most public pools have clearly posted rules governing their use. If you violate one of these rules—for example, by swimming after the pool has officially closed—you may not be able to collect damages if you are injured.

FROM TAXICAB TO TRUSTEE

TAXICAB

Because taxicabs are a form of public transportation, provincial and local governments are permitted to regulate taxicab owners and drivers. They can require drivers to take special tests and pay special fees in order to be licensed, and they can require taxicab owners to post bond, carry adequate insurance, and submit their vehicles to periodic safety inspections. Governments may also set maximum fares and limit the number of available taxi licenses. Taxicab companies and drivers that fail to meet provincial or local regulations may be fined or prohibited from operating.

If a taxi driver has acted improperly—for example, by overcharging you or using an indirect route to reach your destination—you can file a complaint. Before you leave the cab, make a note of the driver's name and license number—usually posted in the cab. Then write to the taxicab company explaining what happened and asking for a response. Suggest a remedy that the company can take, such as refunding your fare or disciplining the driver. Keep a copy of your letter.

If you do not receive an answer or are not satisfied with the answer you get, write to your local taxicab licensing agency and include copies of your correspondence with the company. The agency will make its own inquiries, and if the company refuses to respond or has a history of dissatisfied customers, its license may be suspended or revoked.

Taxicab companies are legally obliged to ensure the safety of their passengers. For example, they may require their employees to submit to periodic tests for drug or alcohol use, and they can require passengers to enter and leave taxis on the curbside only.

If you drive a taxi for someone, and you are working under a service contract, you may be entitled to unemployment insurance (UI). To qualify for UI, the person you work for must own the taxi you drive, and operate the business. You must also work at least 15 hours a week or earn a certain amount of money per week—the amount varies from province to province. Contact your local taxation office to see if you qualify. To claim UI benefits, contact any Canada Employment Centre.

TAX PREPARATION

Despite the federal government's attempts to simplify its tax forms, many Canadians remain confused and intimidated when it comes to completing their income tax returns. Fortunately, there are some tax-preparation aids available.

FINDING HELP

The least expensive and most basic assistance consists of books and personal-computer programs designed to help you complete your return.

Revenue Canada publishes a number of booklets that deal with specific tax problems such as paying tax by instalments, tax information for people with disabilities, tax consequences of separation and divorce, students and income tax, among others. For more information concerning tax information booklets, write to the nearest Revenue Canada district office.

In many communities, volunteer groups prepare simple tax returns for senior citizens at little or no cost. To find out if such programs exist in your community, ask your local senior-citizens center.

If you are willing to pay someone to prepare a simple return, consider an individual tax preparer or a large tax-preparation firm. Their fees start at $50 to $75, but can be much higher depending on the complexity of your return. If you need help with a complicated return (for example, if you have capital gains or losses or depreciation or amortization deductions), you can use a chartered accountant (CA), who will either charge you by the return or by the hour (at a rate comparable to a lawyer's). Ask for referrals from friends with tax situations similar to yours. Lawyers and bankers may be good sources too, because they often deal with accountants.

YOUR LEGAL RESPONSIBILITIES

Be aware that you (not your tax preparer) are legally responsible for the accuracy of your income tax return.

Accuracy

If your income is understated or your deductions are overstated, Revenue Canada may assess back taxes, interest, and penalties, and you will have to pay them. If anything on your return seems questionable, ask your preparer to explain it. If you do not understand the explanation, you may want to have the forms reviewed by another preparer. If a tax preparer promises to pay interest and penalties incurred by any errors on your return, ask for a written guarantee. Note also that although some preparers say they will accompany you to an audit, they may lack the qualifications to help you at higher-level proceedings with Revenue Canada.

You can call Revenue Canada for advice about your return. Note the date and time you called and the name of the agent who helped you. Remember that Revenue Canada advice may be inaccurate. If your return is audited or additional taxes are assessed, the fact that you consulted Revenue Canada may not be a defense.

Filing

You are responsible for seeing that your tax return reaches the appropriate Revenue Canada office on time or that your application for an extension (in order to file a late return) is mailed before the April 30 deadline. Always keep photocopies of the records that you give your preparer. The Federal Tax Court has ruled that a taxpayer is responsible for substantiating his deductions, even if his preparer loses his records.

See also INCOME TAX; INCOME TAX AUDIT; TAX REFUND.

TAX REFUND

Perhaps the only redeeming aspect of the tax season is the refund cheque you may get from Revenue Canada. But if the refund is large, it means that you have either had too much withheld from your paycheque or overpaid your estimated taxes. Either way, you have given the government an interest-free loan of money that could have been earning money for you in a savings account or investments.

CONSEQUENCES OF OVERPAYMENT

Under certain circumstances, overpaying income taxes may affect you adversely. Revenue Canada can withhold all or part of a refund for any number of reasons. For example, if you owe child support, defaulted on a federally guaranteed business or student loan, or owe back taxes, penalties, or interest for a previous year, you may not get a refund at all.

To avoid overpayment, find out from your employer how many exemptions you now claim and ask for a new T-4 form. If you take additional exemptions, you will reduce the amount of tax withheld from your paycheques.

WHEN YOUR REFUND IS OVERDUE

Generally, the earlier you file your return, the sooner you will receive your refund. For example, if you file in early February, you will probably get your refund within three or four weeks. If you file your return by April 30 and do not receive your refund by June 1, Revenue Canada must start paying you interest.

TEACHER

To teach in the public school system, a teacher must obtain a teaching certificate or license from the province. The province can establish minimum requirements for the education and student-teaching experience of its teachers, and local school boards may impose additional standards. Some provinces require licenses for schoolteachers in private as well as public schools.

The criteria for becoming a teacher vary from one province or community to another. Applicants can be rejected if they have been convicted of a violent crime or are known to

---

CHECKLIST
Choosing a Tax Preparer

Before you entrust an accountant or tax preparer with your return, you should interview him carefully. Here are some questions you should ask.

■ WHAT KINDS OF CLIENTS DO YOU HAVE?
A preparer who mainly does simple returns based solely on T-4 forms is not a good choice if you have a complicated return with many itemized deductions, investment income, or other complex matters.

■ WILL YOU DO ALL THE WORK ON MY RETURN YOURSELF?
Some firms divide returns among several preparers. It is preferable, however, to have one preparer do the entire return. A single preparer can better answer any questions you may have.

■ WHAT KIND OF TRAINING AND EXPERIENCE DO YOU HAVE?
The most desirable background is a degree in accounting, but college credits and on-the-job training with a tax-preparation company can be adequate for straightforward returns.

Be skeptical of anyone who does not ask questions about your basic financial situation, such as if you have a Registered Retirement Savings Plan , own your home or rent it, or have a home office. Beware of preparers who promise a refund or ask for a percentage of your refund as their fee.

---

abuse drugs or alcohol, but physical characteristics, such as obesity, have been challenged as discriminatory and have been overturned in the courts.

REPORTING CHILD ABUSE

Many school boards have implemented programs to educate students, staff, and the community about child abuse, to encourage people to report cases, and to help those who have been or who might be abused. All provinces and the Northwest Territories have laws which oblige teachers to report suspected cases, and make them potentially liable

to a charge of negligence if they fail to do so. (In Yukon, suspected child abuse is reported at the teacher's discretion.) Depending on the province, this obligation—and liability— extends to school administrators, and even to the school board.

In some provinces, the abuse need not be reported if the student has reached the age of majority. Teachers in Newfoundland and Nova Scotia, for example, need not report cases involving anyone 17 years and older since laws in these provinces define "a child" as someone under the age of 16.

Most child protection and welfare statutes stipulate that

an educator must report an incident even if the child has reported it in confidence. Reportable abuse includes physical and sexual abuse, emotional maltreatment, and even physical and emotional neglect. The abuse should be reported whether the suspected abuser is a member of the school's staff, a parent, or even another pupil.

Many educators may hesitate about reporting suspected abuse because they fear their suspicions are unfounded, or that they may be open to a lawsuit if their suspicions are incorrect. Some teachers may fail to report suspected abuse because they fear retaliation from the parents, or worry that the complaint may have serious repercussions for the child. None of these reasons justify failing to report the abuse.

For the protection of those who seek to help the abused child, many provinces stipulate that a person cannot be sued for reporting suspected abuse, unless he does so maliciously or without reasonable grounds. Manitoba, New Brunswick, Prince Edward Island, and Quebec guarantee anonymity to anyone who reports a case of child abuse.

The penalties for educators who do not report child abuse vary among provinces, from fines of $200 to $500 in Quebec, to fines of up to $1,000 and/or one year in prison in New Brunswick. Under the Criminal Code, an educator who fails to report a case of child abuse, particularly one that involves a child under 10 years of age, could be charged

either with exposing the child to a situation that could compromise her health or safety, or he could be charged with criminal negligence. His position as a teacher could also be affected.

TELEPHONE CALL

Unwanted telephone calls have long plagued homeowners, and the problem is receiving attention from lawmakers and law enforcement officers.

OBSCENE CALLS

Making an obscene, harassing, or threatening telephone call is illegal. If you receive such a call, hang up immediately. If the caller persists, record the date and time of each call and notify the police. Some telephone companies provide a service that enables the recipient to identify the caller's number by entering a special code on a touch-tone phone after the call has been received. New models of telephone display the number of the caller. Report the call, and the number where it was dialed, to the police or the telephone company. A sharp blow into the speaker with a whistle may also discourage your harasser.

See also MAIL ORDER SALES.

TEMPORARY RESTRAINING ORDER

A temporary restraining order (also known as a temporary injunction) is an order

issued by a court, often without a formal hearing, that forbids someone from performing a certain act until the court can obtain more information and make a decision.

A judge issues the order or injunction to maintain the current state of events, out of concern that if a change were made, it would permanently affect the petitioner in a way that could never be fully rectified. Ignoring a temporary restraining order may result in a charge of contempt of court, which is punishable by a fine, or imprisonment, or both.

Suppose Lumbermill Inc. planned to cut down several acres of a forest that is home to a rare species of deer. An environmental action group, fearing that the destruction of the animals' habitat would threaten the species, steps in and files a petition in court for a temporary restraining order to halt the felling of the trees. If the judge decides that the evidence in the group's petition shows that the deer would be endangered by Lumbermill's proposed forest clearing, he will issue a temporary restraining order against the company.

After such an order has been issued, a hearing is held, during the course of which both sides can present their cases. The judge then rules whether to lift the temporary restraining order or make it permanent. See also ORDER OF PROTECTION.

TENANCY IN COMMON

In a tenancy in common, two or more people hold a separate and undivided interest in the same property. This means that each tenant has the right to the use of all the property, and no tenant has an exclusive right to a particular part of it. Property owned by more than one person is generally presumed to be owned as a tenancy in common unless the deed or other proof of ownership states otherwise.

A tenant in common must share the cost of maintaining the property, but he does not have to pay for unnecessary improvements—such as central air-conditioning—unless he specifically authorizes them. All parties must refrain from actions that would diminish the property's value, or risk being sued by the other tenants.

Tenancy in common can be ended when one tenant abandons his interest or sells it to a cotenant or someone else, or when the tenants in common reach an agreement to divide the property among themselves. Also, an heir may inherit the interest of a tenant in common through a will or the laws of intestate succession.

See COMMUNITY PROPERTY; EQUITABLE DISTRIBUTION.

TENANCY BY THE ENTIRETY

In most provinces, a married couple who want to own property jointly can use a form of ownership called tenancy by the entirety. Under this arrangement, neither spouse may sell or dispose of the property without the permission of the other. If you and your spouse hold a savings account as tenants by the entirety, for example, neither of you may close the account without the other's knowledge and consent.

Should one spouse die, his or her share goes automatically to the survivor without going through probate court. Moreover, the surviving spouse owns the entire property regardless of any contrary provisions in the deceased spouse's will.

With the passage of statutes in all provinces and territories giving married women full legal rights, and with the introduction of the concept of family property, the whole concept of tenancy by the entirety has become somewhat redundant.

See also JOINT TENANCY; MARITAL PROPERTY.

TENANT'S RIGHTS

You moved into your apartment three months ago after signing a one-year lease. A month later, Hiram moved in across the hall. He works from 3 P.M. to 11 P.M., and when he comes home he plays his stereo so loudly that dishes on your kitchen shelf rattle. You have asked Hiram to turn down the stereo, but he refuses to do so. What recourse do you have?

USE AND ENJOYMENT

At the time you moved into the apartment, you probably signed a lease that spelled out your obligations regarding rent, security deposits, use of the premises, and the like. Your lease may also have restricted the hours of noise and stated that a violation of this rule constitutes a breach of the lease. If it does, you can notify your landlord that a fellow tenant is violating his lease.

Even if the lease does not contain specific rules against noise, the landlord-tenant laws of your province define your basic rights and responsibilities as a tenant, including your right to the "quiet enjoyment" of your home. If your landlord makes no attempt to help you, and you have to move out, you can sue him for not fulfilling his obligations under provincial law. You may be able to recover money for your moving expenses as well as any increase in your rent for a new apartment. See QUIET ENJOYMENT.

HABITABILITY

In many provinces, another major right you have as a tenant is called the warranty of habitability, which means that a dwelling must be fit for human occupancy. It should meet the local building and sanitary codes, and it should have adequate plumbing, lighting, and heating. The windows, walls, floors, and ceilings must be in good repair. You also have the right to expect that common areas of an apartment building or complex, such as hallways, stairs, basements, sidewalks, and clubhouse areas, will be kept clean and safe. Many leases also make the landlord responsible for pest control, garbage collection, and security measures, including locks and keys that work.

TENANT ORGANIZATIONS

Landlord-tenant law varies significantly from province to province. Often there is a tenants' organization or office that can advise you about your rights and obligations. For instance, in Ontario there is the Rent Control Board, New Brunswick has a Rentalsman, in British Columbia there is the Residency Tenancy Branch, in Nova Scotia there is the Residential Tenancy Board, and Quebec has the Régie du logement.

Not only can these organizations inform you of your rights, many can also help you enforce them if you and your landlord are unable to settle a dispute. British Columbia and Quebec have special arbitration boards to hear your complaints and to decide what should be done. In Ontario, however, you will have to get a private mediator or go to court if you are unable to settle a dispute with your landlord.

SECURITY DEPOSITS

Security deposits are allowed in most provinces, but are illegal in others. Where they are legal, there is usually a limit on the amount. The maximum allowable security deposit is one month's rent in Ontario, but the maximum in British Columbia is only half a month's, and you cannot be asked for a deposit after you have already signed the lease, even if a new landlord takes over the premises.

In some provinces, Alberta for example, the deposit is kept by the landlord and must be returned to you with interest when you leave. In New Brunswick, security deposits must be turned over to the Rentalsman, who will release the money when the lease is terminated. A landlord has seven days in which to deliver the deposit to the rentalsman. Failure to do so in that time is punishable by fines ranging from $100 to $7,500.

RENT INCREASE

Some provinces limit the amount by which your rent can be increased and specify how much advance notice you must have of the increase.

There is no fixed limit on increases in British Columbia, but if you have a one-year lease your landlord must give you a minimum of three months' notice of any increase. In that province, a landlord may not ask you to pay for something that was not agreed upon when the lease was signed. For instance, he cannot decide in the middle of your lease that you should pay extra for your parking spot.

An Ontario landlord can raise your rent once a year only but the increase must be within the maximum allowable figures set by the Ministry of Housing. If the apartment required major renovations during the year, or if heat, hydro, water, or property taxes were extraordinarily high, the landlord may ask for more, but this additional amount must be approved by the Rent Control Board.

STEPS TO TAKE

Depending on the nature of the violation and on provincial and local laws, there are various actions you can take if you think your landlord is violating the law or the terms of your lease:

1. If the problem affects the immediate health or safety of the tenants, contact building inspectors or health-department officials.

2. If your dispute is over repairs, always put your request in writing. Keep a copy of your letters and send them by certified mail, return receipt requested, as proof that you have notified the landlord. Take photographs of the defects in question; they may later serve as evidence if legal action becomes necessary.

3. Give the landlord a reasonable amount of time to take care of the problem.

4. If the allotted time passes and the landlord ignores your requests, you may either move out if the lack of repairs poses a health or safety danger to you or your family (be sure a public inspector has seen the condition of your dwelling before you leave), or you can sue him.

5. In your suit, you can ask for a reduction of rent, or permission to apply the rent toward doing the necessary repairs your landlord neglects to do. The court or rental tribunal has a large discretion in granting what it feels is the appropriate remedy. See also LANDLORD; LEASE; RENT STRIKE.

ABC's

OF CHOOSING A VACATION TIME-SHARE

Before signing a contract to buy or lease a time-share, take a close look at the details and discuss the following issues with the salesperson and your lawyer.

■ Does the time-share contract offer a cooling-off period? If it does, how can you cancel the contract?

■ What amenities are included? Do you have to bring your own linens, for instance, or arrange for maid service?

■ Is the time-share property still under construction? If so, has the developer posted a bond for its completion?

■ Are you able to trade your time-share unit with another owner for use of his unit in a different resort?

■ Does your contract permit you to sell the time-share at a later date?

■ What extra expenses, such as maintenance fees and taxes, will add to your total cost?

■ If there is a monthly maintenance fee, are there limits on how much the fee can rise?

■ Will you need to buy additional liability insurance in order to cover you for accidents that occur while you have guests on the property? (If the salesperson is unsure, ask your insurance agent.)

■ Will you have to bear the cost of making repairs or improvements to the property?

■ Are there restrictions as to children, pets, or the number of guests you may have?

TIME-SHARE

Sara and Barry, who live in Toronto, are considering buying a ski chalet in Banff, Alta. But they are dismayed at the high cost of property there. Then they learn they might be able to purchase a time-share at that location. A time-share is the ownership or use of real estate for a specific period. By purchasing or leasing this period of time, each buyer or renter gains the exclusive right to use the property during that designated time.

Developers make large profits from time-shares. Since the cost of a single property is borne by a number of people, they are able to get a greater price for the property than if they sold it to one buyer.

Although time-shares may enable buyers to enjoy a vacation property that they could not afford to buy on their own, they should not be viewed as investments. They are rarely resold at a profit.

HOW TIME-SHARES WORK

Most time-share units are in vacation resorts. A unit may be an apartment of any size, a cottage, a chalet, a studio, or even a full-size house. Typically, the developer of the property owns the entire community or complex of units. He may also have arrangements with developments in other areas so that owners in his complex can trade their time-share for a stay in a unit located elsewhere.

Before you sign a contract, you should have a lawyer who

TENURE

Tenure is the legal right to hold a job or public office for a specified or unlimited period of time. Tenure protects many teachers and certain government employees from arbitrary dismissal. For example, judges have tenure, contingent upon their good behavior.

Tenure allows professors to retain their academic standing and job security even if their personal views are unpopular. A professor cannot be dismissed for his political views unless he expresses them in a way that is disruptive to the school—for example, organizing a student strike. Once a professor has obtained tenure, he can usually be dismissed only for incompetence or serious misconduct, such as physical abuse of a student or conviction of an indictable offense.

See also SPEECH, FREEDOM OF; TEACHER.

specializes in real estate review the developer's proposal. The terms of time-share ownership differ from one developer to another, and you should know what type of interest you are being offered in the property.

Some developers require you to buy your time-share property outright. Although the ownership arrangements differ slightly from one company to another, you will probably receive a deed and possibly a separate agreement that establishes your right to use the property between specific dates. For example, you might buy the right to occupy Unit 25 every year during the third week in July.

Other time-share developers make similar provisions but do not convey any interest in real estate to the buyer. Instead, they offer you one of the following options:

◇ A *vacation license*, which entitles you to use a particular unit for a specified period of time each year for a certain number of years.

◇ A *vacation lease,* which is like a vacation license, but also enables you to rent or transfer your time-share rights.

◇ A *club membership,* which allows you to stay at the resort at a particular time each year, but not at a specific unit. Sometimes, a club membership offers you a flexible arrangement, whereby you can stay at different residences at different times each year.

COMPLAINTS

If the developer who sold you a time-share misled you about the terms, you may be able to break your contract. A lawyer can tell you which laws apply to your situation. The provincial office of consumer protection may be able to give you the names of developers who unfairly or misleadingly advertise time-share opportunities.

See also VACATION HOME.

TITLE INSURANCE

Among the closing costs you pay in a real estate transaction is a lump-sum premium for title insurance. This type of insurance, which is usually required by mortgage lenders, protects you if someone else claims ownership of your new property, or if there are any outstanding liens or debts against it. Such claims create what are known as defects in the title.

When you buy title insurance, the insurer agrees to defend your title to the property if someone challenges your ownership in court or makes a claim against it arising from a previous owner's debts.

Title insurance usually costs about 1 percent of the property's purchase price, and the coverage lasts as long as you own the property. In some instances the mortgage lender purchases the title insurance. Most policies will insure you for loss up to the full purchase price of the house.

Title insurance will not protect you against any defects in the title that occur after you own the property. For instance, if you fail to pay the roofer for his work and he puts a lien on the house, you alone are responsible for the debt.

The title insurance policy will specify how and when you must notify the insurer about a claim. When you make a claim, you are entitled to be reimbursed only for your actual loss. For instance, if a subcontractor has a lien against the property you purchase, which the previous owner did not pay, your title insurance will cover the amount owed to the subcontractor. Or, if an undisclosed easement reduces the value of the property, your title insurer may pay you the difference between what you paid for the property and what it is actually worth.

Even when a title search indicates that the title is clear, someone may still challenge your ownership rights. For instance, Stella bought a house from Stanley without realizing that he was a minor, and thus not old enough to transfer the ownership of the property to another person. Stanley's older brother took Stella to court to invalidate the sale, and the court returned the house to Stanley's brother. Stella's title insurer reimbursed her for her down payment and for other expenses that she had incurred in buying the house.

See also EASEMENT; HOME BUYING AND SELLING; LIEN.

TORT

A tort is a civil wrong committed by one person against another person. A tort occurs when someone injures another person or causes damage to his property, whether intentionally or through negligence.

Torts form the basis for most lawsuits. In a tort case, the individual who has been harmed in some way (the plaintiff in the civil lawsuit) seeks some sort of redress or compensation from the wrongdoer (the defendant). If the plaintiff sues the defendant, a judge or jury decides whether the case has merit and determines the amount of monetary damages to be awarded.

The element of injury or damage is important, for without it there are no grounds for a lawsuit. Suppose Jeff uninten-

tionally bumps into Laurie on a crowded bus. Technically, Jeff has committed the tort of battery (the unauthorized touching of another), but because Laurie has suffered no injury, she cannot sue Jeff.

Since a corporation or government body is considered to be a person in the eyes of the law, it can be either the plaintiff or the defendant of a tort. See also DAMAGES; LAWSUIT; NEGLIGENCE.

INTENTIONAL AND NEGLIGENT TORTS

Any tort that is willfully committed is known as an inten-

tional tort. There are dozens of such torts, among them false arrest and false imprisonment, battery, assault, invasion of privacy, theft, interference with property rights, defamation (including libel and slander), infliction of emotional distress, damaging or destroying someone else's property, embezzlement, extortion, trespass, and malicious prosecution.

Unintentional torts are generally referred to as torts of negligence. The standard for determining negligence is whether the wrongdoer took care to act as a reasonably prudent person would in similar circumstances.

Suppose Lucy slips and falls on a store's recently mopped floor. Since there is no question that the store owner did not set out to harm its customers, Lucy would have to prove that the store had not taken reasonable care to keep the floor dry. See also NEGLIGENCE.

Courts usually award damages to the plaintiff based on her injuries. A victim of an intentional tort may also receive a further award, called punitive damages.

STRICT LIABILITY

In some situations, a plaintiff in a tort lawsuit does not have to show that the defendant was negligent or that he acted intentionally. A person or business who creates or maintains any product or property that is inherently dangerous may be held strictly liable for injuries caused by that product or property. For example, the operator of a nuclear power plant, the owner of a pet

REAL LIFE, REAL LAW

The Case of the Harmful Helmet

In 1990, a young Ontario man brought an action in damages against Cooper Canada Ltd. for injuries suffered during a hockey game. The young man became a quadriplegic when he slid into the boards head first, suffering a compression fracture of his neck. He sued the maker of the helmet he was wearing, claiming that the shape of his helmet had caused his injury. The plaintiff claimed that if the crown of his helmet had been round instead of flat, the blow would have been deflected. Instead, the flat crown caused the helmet to rotate, giving rise to the injury. He also alleged that the manufacturer should have taken the possibility of compressive fractures into consideration when designing the helmet.

The manufacturer countered by stating that the helmet met the standards set by Canadian Standards Associations and was meant to protect only the head and not other parts of the body.

Unfortunately for the young man, the court ruled in favor of the manufacturer. Mr. Justice R. C. Rutherford of the Ontario Supreme Court held that the helmet was not inherently dangerous and that there was no flaw in its design. The manner of hitting the boards head first was the cause of the injury and no helmet could have protected the young man from this injury. Had the company been held liable, the young man would have received $7.1 million in compensation.

python, or the makers of a poisonous chemical could all be found strictly liable for an injury someone suffers due to their premises, pet, or product. See also Dog Law; Liability; Pet.

MINORS

Minors can be held responsible for their torts, depending on the age of the child. In determining whether a child who committed a civil wrong did so intentionally, a court must decide whether the child knew that his behavior was improper. All provinces have specific ages below which a child is considered to be incapable of committing an intentional tort.

In all provinces, parents may be held responsible for the torts of their children, whether intentional or not, if the party who suffers damages can show that the parents were negligent in their surveillance of their minor children, or did not exercise parenthood in a responsible and reasonable manner while raising their children. For example, if it could be shown that a child was often causing trouble and the parents ignored this behavior and did not try to discipline or otherwise teach their child to abstain from harmful behavior, the parents may be sued successfully.

Suppose 10-year-old Darlene and her friends are standing on a bridge throwing snowballs at the cars passing below, and one of the snowballs shatters the windshield of an automobile. In her province, Darlene has reached the age at which she can be held personally accountable for her actions. However, because she is still a minor, her parents may also be liable for the cost of the windshield and any injuries suffered by the occupants of the car. See Parental Liability Laws.

Of course, minors usually do not have assets or insurance to compensate a person for his injuries or damages. But provincial laws generally allow a winning plaintiff to keep his judgment in force for many years. Therefore, the person who was injured by Darlene's negligent snowball-throwing and was awarded monetary damages in court might be able to enforce his judgment years later, when Darlene is a legal adult who is earning income or has acquired assets. See also Judgment.

INCOMPETENT PERSONS

Incompetent people are not legally responsible for the torts they commit. However, if the guardian or person in charge of the incompetent person was lax in his duty to look after his ward, the guardian may be sued. See also Incompetency.

TOUR OPERATOR

A tour operator organizes travel arrangements for vacationers in a "package" that usually includes transportation, accommodation, and meals for one inclusive price. Typically, these packages are sold by travel agents.

Although the vast majority of tour operators are honest and conscientious, some make promises that they fail to keep: first-class hotels turn out to be rundown, the airline is in fact a small-time charter organization, or an "experienced" guide may know little more about the destination than you do. Since there is minimal government regulation of tour operators, protect yourself against such mishaps by careful shopping and investigation. See also Airline Charter; Travel Agency.

STEPS TO TAKE

Before signing up for a tour, do the following:

1. Get recommendations from your travel agent and people you trust who have had direct experience with the tour operator.

2. To determine the financial stability of a tour operator, ask if he is bonded or is a member of a recognized provincial tour operator association. In addition, ask the tour operator how long he has been in business and make sure that he deals only with reputable air carriers and hotel chains.

3. Ask your provincial or local office of consumer affairs if there have been past complaints about the operator and whether they were resolved satisfactorily.

4. Find out exactly what is included in the price of the trip and whether you will have to pay extra for meals, tips, agent's fees, insurance, or transfers between hotels and airports.

5. Pay the smallest deposit you can, and use a credit card. If you do not receive all the services you were promised, or if you are dissatisfied with the quality of the travel arrangements, your credit card company may intercede on your behalf. For more information, see CREDIT CARD AND CHARGE ACCOUNT.

6. Read the terms and conditions of your tour carefully. Find out the tour operator's refund policy in the event that the company cancels the tour or revises the itinerary in an unacceptable way. Inquire also about the operator's policy if you cancel. You may have to purchase cancellation insurance to cover yourself in the event that you become ill or otherwise have to cancel the trip. Most operators will refund only a portion of your money, and if you cancel on very short notice you may not receive a refund at all.

TOY

Like the manufacturers of other products, toy makers are subject to product-liability laws when a poorly made or defectively designed toy causes an injury to someone.

Suppose you buy your young nephew a string of wooden beads—the kind designed to hang in a crib. Unknown to you, the beads are strung in such a way that a child could pull them off the string. While playing with the beads, your nephew pulls one off, swallows it, and chokes. Fortunately, his mother is able to dislodge the bead, but the child still requires medical treatment.

In this example, the manufacturer of the beads has violated the warranty of merchantability—the promise made to a consumer that the product is safe for intended use. Because your nephew suffered an injury due to the faulty design of the beads, his parents could sue the manufacturer for compensation for medical costs related to the injury and for additional damages for your nephew's pain and suffering. If the merchant misrepresented the age at which a child could safely play with the toy, the parents could sue him for damages too. Keep in mind that you will have no basis to sue if you give your child a toy that is inappropriate for his age or if you do not adequately supervise him when he plays with it. See CONSUMER PROTECTION.

SAFETY STANDARDS

Acting under provisions of legislation such as the Hazardous Products Act, the Product Safety Bureau of Health Canada monitors the advertising, sale, and importation of toys in an effort to keep dangerous products off the market.

All toys sold here must meet standards set by the Canadian Standards Association (CSA) or the Underwriters Laboratories of Canada (ULC) as well as the following requirements:

◇ Toys must not be packaged in flexible film bags.

◇ Toys must not be made partly or wholly with glass.

◇ Toys to be used by children under three years old should not have a folding mechanism, exposed metal edges, or have embedded in them a wire frame or structure.

◇ Toys intended for children under three years old must be unbreakable and free of small parts that could present a choking hazard. Certain toys, including crayons, chalk, and balloons, are exempt from this provision, however.

◇ Toys must not contain toxic chemicals or materials.

◇ Electrical toys must be constructed in a way that prevents the possibility of electrical shock or burn.

◇ Toys made for children under eight years old must not contain any heating elements, nor may they have any sharp points or edges.

If the Product Safety Bureau receives a complaint about a poorly made or defective toy, or learns of injuries caused by the toy, it can order the manufacturer to recall the product and refund the purchaser's money. You can find out about product recalls by writing to or calling the Product Safety Bureau of Health Canada. See USEFUL ADDRESSES at back of book.

AGE AND SAFETY LABELS

When you buy a toy, check the packaging for the manufacturer's name and address, and for labels about safety and the age range the toy was designed for. The toy industry has established voluntary age and safety labeling standards for manufacturers. For instance, a cloth toy should have a label stating that it is flame-resistant, and a toy oven should have a label indicating that it is intended for use only by children over eight years old. Some manufacturers offer toll-free customer-service lines to answer questions about their products.

TRADEMARK

Trademarks are words, symbols or designs used by companies, individuals, partnerships, trade unions, and other organizations to distinguish their goods or services in the marketplace. Once a trademark is registered in Canada, you are granted exclusive right to its use in this country for 15 years. To protect your trademark abroad, you must register it in those countries where you wish to use it.

A trade name is sometimes used to identify a company or business. It also can be registered as a trademark if used in this way.

You will have to pay $150 just to apply for a trademark, and a further $200 for the first certificate of registration, as well as for any subsequent registration after your 15-year term expires. Trademarks need not be registered—there is no legal requirement to do so— but it may be difficult to stop others from using the trademark without your permission if it is not registered.

You can sell or assign the rights in a trademark to another person or company, provided you inform the Registrar of Trade Marks of the transaction. That person or company can then become a registered user by filing an application and paying a fee. Registered users can use the trademark for as long as the owner lets them.

REGISTRATION

If you are planning to register a trademark, you would be wise to consult a trademark agent, especially if you plan to register in other countries. Applications are available from the Registrar of Trade Marks (see USEFUL ADDRESSES at back of book). If your trademark is a symbol, you will need a drawing of it to send with your application.

Applications take about a year to process. If two or more people apply for the same trademark, the registrar will decide which application has priority and register it. Someone may oppose your use of the trademark, or you may wish to oppose the registration of someone else's. Either way, this is done by lodging an objection with the registrar's office, which charges about $250 to open such proceedings.

If your trademark application is refused, you can appeal the decision of the registrar to the Federal Court.

PROHIBITED MARKS

Section 9(1) of the Trade Marks Act specifies certain marks you may not use in your trademark, and marks that are so similar to prohibited marks that they might lead to confusion. Your trademark may not contain official government symbols such as the Canadian flag; the coat of arms of the Royal Family, or of provinces or cities; badges and crests of the armed forces or the RCMP, emblems and names of the Red Cross, Red Crescent or the United Nations; or flags or symbols of other countries.

The act also prohibits the use of portraits or signatures of living persons or persons who have died less than 30 years ago, unless the appropriate permission was obtained. Thus, you cannot use a picture of Prince Charles to sell a cologne, for example.

FILING A SUIT

The Registrar of Trade Marks does not enforce trademarks, but the holder of a trademark can bring a lawsuit to stop someone from using a trademark. If a person or company successfully sues someone for trademark infringement, the court may issue an injunction against the infringing party to halt its use of the trademark. It may also award monetary compensation, or damages, to the trademark holder. The damages may be based on the profit and goodwill lost by the trademark holder as a result of the infringement.

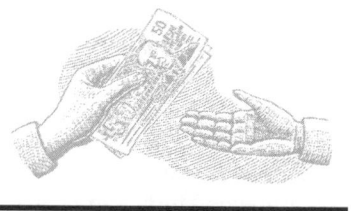

TRADE SCHOOL

Trade schools provide career training in a variety of fields, such as truck driving, auto mechanics, bartending, cosmetology, medical technology, carpentry, printing, computer programming, and secretarial work. In general, the course of study lasts up to two years.

Trade schools may vary widely in the training and opportunities they offer. Some make claims about their students' job prospects that are unrealistic or simply false. Furthermore, they may ask students to sign contracts that require them to pay large tuition fees. Even if a student does not finish the course of study, he will often be obliged by law to pay the full amount stated in the contract. For this reason alone, students should take care when choosing a trade school.

ACCREDITATION

Although trade schools are licensed by the province in which they are located, the licensing requirements may be relatively easy to meet. In some provinces a trade school needs little more than a name, a permanent address, and a few instructors. Your department of education can tell you the licensing requirements for trade schools in your province and whether a particular school has a past record of complaints.

Teacher-student ratio or the number and variety of classes are often good indications of a school's quality.

INFLATED CLAIMS

Some trade schools try to attract students by advertising that their students are eligible to receive provincial or federal loans and grants. They do not mention, however, that finan-cial aid programs are generally available to students at any licensed trade school and are no indication of the quality of a school. A student's ability to obtain this aid will depend primarily on his own financial need.

Find out whether the school has a placement office and whether or not prospective employers regard the school's programs as adequate prepara-tion for the field. Note that many junior colleges and vocational-technical schools offer similar training programs, often at lower cost, and do not require you to sign a long-term contract.

CHECK REFUND POLICY BEFORE YOU SIGN

Review the school's admis-sions contract carefully. Some schools expect you to sign up for a full program of study; oth-ers will let you pay for courses as you take them. Be sure you know the school's refund policy in case you change your mind after you sign up.

Do not let an admissions representative pressure you into signing a contract. Many of these representatives are actually commissioned sales-people whose income depends on getting you to sign on the dotted line. If you do not understand something in the contract, do not rely on the admissions representative for an explanation. Instead, con-sult a lawyer. Also, ask school officials for the names and addresses of former students, and be extremely wary of a school that will not divulge them.

TRAFFIC TICKET

Because Sharon was late for an appointment, she drove faster than the posted speed limit. A police officer pulled her over and, while writing up the speeding ticket, informed Sharon that one of her car's brake lights was not working and included a citation for that violation as well. Sharon finally made it downtown and found a metered parking space. When she returned three hours later, there was a parking ticket on her windshield; the meter had expired one half-hour before.

Sharon has been the unfor-tunate recipient of the three types of traffic tickets: a mov-ing violation, an equipment vio-lation, and a parking violation. A traffic ticket is considered a summons, and if Sharon does not pay the fine or appear in court to contest the charge, the court may issue a warrant for her arrest. She may also be unable to renew the registra-tion on her car if she has out-standing traffic tickets.

MOVING VIOLATIONS

Speeding is the most common moving violation for which drivers are ticketed. Other violations include failure to yield the right-of-way, not restraining a young child in a car seat, and failing to obey a traffic signal.

If a police officer signals you to pull over, you must do so. You should remain seated in your car with your hands in plain view, unless the officer

CHECKLIST

How to Fight a Traffic Ticket

When you receive a traffic ticket, the province bears the burden of proving your guilt. In some provinces your guilt must be proved "beyond a reasonable doubt," whereas in others the government need show your guilt only by a preponderance of the evidence. In any case, if the province cannot meet the burden of proof, you will not have to pay the ticket. For this reason, some experts suggest that you always contest a traffic ticket in court and require the province to prove its case against you. A traffic ticket can be dismissed for the following reasons:

■ **FAILURE TO MAKE PROOF.**
Suppose you are charged with speeding. If you can cast doubts on the reliability of the radar instrument used by the police you may be acquitted. You may, in your cross-examination of the police officer, ask him what degree of error the machine generally shows—5 percent is not rare. Also ask him to tell the court when the machine was last calibrated and tested and how it works. If the policeman is not accompanied by a radar technician, he may be unable to answer your questions adequately and you may have created an element of reasonable doubt which may get your charge dismissed.

■ **MISTAKEN IDENTITY.**
A classic instance of mistaken identity occurs when you receive a parking ticket in the mail from a town that you have never been in. The reason for the error usually is that the police officer miscopied letters or numbers on the

offender's license plate. In this situation you can often have the ticket canceled simply by notifying the police department that issued the ticket.

■ **LACK OF JURISDICTION.**
Suppose you are stopped for running a red light by a city police officer, but the ticket shows that the light is in an unincorporated area of the county. You would argue that the officer was not authorized to write the ticket and that the court has no jurisdiction over the matter.

■ **LACK OF PROSECUTION.**
This situation occurs when the city is not ready to present its case at the time of your court appearance. It happens most often when the police officer who wrote the ticket fails to appear in court to testify. The first time he does not appear, the court is likely to grant a continuance. But if he fails to show up a second time, the charges are more likely to be dismissed.

---

while intoxicated, you may be asked to take a roadside sobriety or breath test and be taken into custody. See also DRUNK DRIVING; SPEEDING TICKET.

EQUIPMENT VIOLATIONS

When you operate a vehicle on public streets and highways, the law expects it to be in proper working order and in compliance with all the required safety standards. If your vehicle does not meet these standards, you may be given a ticket. Headlights, taillights, brake lights, and turn signals that do not work are safety hazards that could prompt a police officer to issue you a ticket. If you have the necessary repairs made before your court date, the judge may be willing to waive the fine if you can prove that the repair was made.

Depending on provincial law, other equipment violations include not having a windshield made out of approved safety glass, having materials or objects that obstruct the driver's view, or not having a muffler or tail pipe. Tickets issued for these violations usually order the driver to make repairs within a reasonable period of time or pay a fine.

PARKING VIOLATIONS

Your vehicle may be ticketed for being illegally parked on a local street or on a highway. Among the violations found in most cities are parking in restricted areas, such as spaces for the handicapped; parking during hours prohibited by a posted sign; and parking in a space after the meter has expired. Your city may also

---

orders you out of the car. The officer will ask to see your driver's license and, in some instances, proof of vehicle registration. Being pulled over

♦ does not necessarily mean that you will be given a traffic ticket. The officer may decide to give you a warning. For more serious offenses, such as driving

prohibit you from parking dismantled or unregistered cars in your yard and may limit the number of registered cars you can park outside your garage over a long period.

If you find a ticket on your windshield, read the instructions carefully. You may have the option of paying the fine by mail or appearing in traffic court to contest the ticket. Ignoring a ticket can lead to further trouble. You may find a "boot" on your car—a metal device that locks around the tire to prevent you from driving the car away. You may also be arrested, especially if you have other outstanding tickets.

TRAFFIC COURT

Before you decide to contest a ticket in court, look at the facts of your case objectively. Do you have a valid reason for violating traffic laws, or just an excuse? Being late for an important appointment will never be accepted by a traffic court judge as justification for exceeding the speed limit.

Your case will also be weak unless you have objective evidence and impartial witnesses to support it. Suppose you are ticketed for having defective taillights. You may avoid a fine if you can give the judge a receipt showing that you recently had the car in for that particular repair, but the mechanic apparently did not do his work properly.

If the potential penalty is serious, such as suspension of your license, you may want to have a lawyer accompany you to court. For most other traffic violations, where you face only the prospect of a small fine, you can generally appear without counsel. The judge will ask you whether you want to plead guilty or not guilty. If you plead guilty, you may be given the opportunity to offer an explanation.

If you plead not guilty, the case proceeds with the presentation of the evidence against you by a lawyer representing the prosecuting lawyer's office. The police officer who issued the ticket will be questioned to establish that you did, in fact, violate the Highway Traffic Code. You will then be given the opportunity to cross-examine the officer. If he is the only witness for the prosecution, the lawyer will rest his case. At that time you may present any witnesses or evidence to support your own version of the facts. Once all the evidence has been heard, each side may make closing remarks.

Even though traffic court is not as formal as other court proceedings, you should dress appropriately and be neatly groomed. Your appearance can help make a good impression with the court. Be respectful of the judge and any witnesses, such as the officer who issued the ticket, and be courteous when asking questions. Practice your presentation before you go to court to help you organize your thoughts and present a clearer explanation of your case.

PENALTIES

Whether you plead guilty, or not guilty and lose your case, the judge will impose a sentence, which may be a fine or imprisonment. A serious violation, such as driving under the influence of alcohol, could result in both a fine and imprisonment. If the violation is not an extremely serious one, some judges will give the offender the option of attending a driver education or improvement program. Other possible penalties are suspension or revocation of driving privileges and community-service work. If the judge imposes a fine, you must pay it on time or the judge could issue a warrant for your arrest and have you put in jail.

TRAVEL AGENCY

Travel agencies make travel arrangements for their customers. They make their living from commissions paid by the companies that provide the travel services, such as airlines, hotels, and cruise operators. Few, if any, laws specifically regulate travel agencies or their employees. Nonetheless, agencies have a legal duty to be honest and fair in their dealings with you. For example, a travel agent who intentionally overcharges you for a ticket can be sued for damages, and an agent who takes money from his customer but fails to forward it to the airline or hotel can be charged with fraud.

If a travel agent makes a mistake on your reservation, you may be able to sue him for breach of contract. Some travel agencies try to limit their liability for such mistakes by printing disclaimers on ticket envelopes and itineraries, but an agent might still be liable for civil charges.

Many of the issues that arise when a travel agency fails to fulfill its promises were addressed in one recent case before the Superior Court of Quebec. During the winter holiday season, Elite Tours booked many passengers on a return Montreal to Paris flight with Minerva Airlines. Unable to get authorization either to land in Paris on the arrival date, or to take off from Paris on the departure date, the airline scheduled its landing and later takeoff in Brussels. The passengers, who were bussed to and from Paris, sued both the travel agency and the airline for the lost time, aggravation and inconvenience, as well as exemplary damages.

The court found the tour agency was at fault for failing to check that the airline was able to get authorization for the flight, and for not informing passengers of the change in plans. It found the airline at fault for allowing tickets to be sold before it had authorization to land and take off in Paris.

Tickets for the flight had a clause exonerating the airline from liability for damages. However, Quebec's Loi sur le transport aérien stipulated that an airline cannot exonerate itself from damages caused when a plane is late, unless the airline can show that it took all possible measures to ensure that it would not be late and that the delay was impossible to prevent. In other words, the airline should have made sure the flight got its authorization before selling the tickets.

In the end, the passengers were each awarded $300 in general damages for their fatigue, aggravation, and inconvenience, and $100 in exemplary damages. They qualified for exemplary damages because of Quebec's Consumer Protection Act, which stipulates these are payable when a consumer has been guided into a contract under a false statement or a significant omission by the merchant.

See also AIRLINE CHARTER; TOUR OPERATOR.

TREASON

Treason is defined in the Criminal Code as using force or violence for the purpose of overthrowing the government of Canada or a province or, without lawful authority, communicating or making available to an agent of another country any military or scientific information that you know or should know would be used by that state to the detriment of Canada.

High treason is the killing or the attempt to kill Her Majesty the Queen. Levying war against Canada or assisting an enemy at war with Canada would also be acts of high treason.

The key component of treason is a person's willingness to betray his allegiance to his country. For example, a Canadian citizen who willfully encourages Canadian troops fighting in an enemy country to surrender is committing an act of treason. However, merely speaking out against the government's policy toward its enemies or its conduct of a military action is not an act of treason.

Charges of treason are laid under the National Defense Act. The highest crime in the nation, it is punishable by imprisonment and even death. This is so even though the death penalty has been abolished in Canada.

TREE

George was annoyed when he saw that branches from his neighbor's tree were extending so far over the property line that they could scratch his new car. George asked his neighbor to trim the tree, but his neighbor refused. What action can George take?

First, George should find out whether his community has a homeowners' association that can provide mediation services. If the covenants in his neighbor's deed require the neighbor to keep his trees trimmed, the association might be able to take action on George's behalf. If this fails, and if George's province allows a lawsuit to be brought against someone whose tree is extending onto a neighbor's property, he might want to take his neighbor to court.

If George prefers to take matters into his own hands, he has a legal right to trim the tree branches back as far as the boundary line between his property and his neighbor's. He would also be allowed to cut back or block the roots of his neighbor's tree if they extend onto his property. But in most cases, George would not be allowed to trim the tree simply because it blocked his view or cast shade on his lawn. Before doing any major trimming, he should first check with his city's building or parks department to see if a permit is required.

Under the Trees Act of Ontario, any trees planted on the boundary of two properties are said to be the common property of the owners of the properties. If a tree is planted by one owner to decorate the property or to give shade, a person who injures the tree may have to pay a fine. However, in a recent case the Supreme Court of Ontario decided that if the tree is injured by the other co-owner, he cannot be fined. The court reasoned that one co-owner has as much right to cut down a tree on his property as the other does. The court said it would be different if the tree had been planted with the consent of both owners.

At one time, a tree growing on a boundary could not be removed unless both owners consented. This does not appear to be the case any longer in Ontario.

If a tree is planted on your neighbor's property and branches and roots of the tree encroach on your property, you can remove the branches and/or the roots, even if the tree may die as a result.

Some municipalities have bylaws that forbid tree removal, even if the tree is on your land. One Ontario resident

was fined $3,000 for cutting down 750 trees on his property, thus contravening a bylaw forbidding the removal of trees from "environmentally sensitive areas." The outcome might have been different had he proven that he cut the trees for "his own use," or "in accordance with good forestry practices." The Trees Act specifies that people who have owned a property for two years can remove trees on their land for their own use.

See also HOMEOWNERS' ASSOCIATION; NEIGHBOR; VIEW.

TRESPASS

Entering another person's property without permission or interfering with an owner's use and enjoyment of her property constitutes trespassing. Trespassers can be subject to both civil and criminal charges.

You can be guilty of trespassing even if you do not step onto the property. Suppose you are hunting on public land when you see a deer in a privately owned field. If you decide to shoot, bear in mind that the moment your rifle's bullet crosses the boundary of the private land, you

REAL LIFE, REAL LAW

The Case of the Punished Punter

An Ontario woman, who won substantial sums of money at racetracks owned by the Ontario Jockey Club, was surprised one day to be served with a written notice to leave a racetrack. The notice, served under the Trespass to Property Act, gave no reason for the action. The skilled bettor went to court, where she argued that since such betting was legal, and since trespassing connoted an unjustified invasion of another's privacy and property, she could not be guilty of trespassing. She also argued that her rights to be treated equally, guaranteed by the Charter of Rights and Freedoms, were violated, since a racetrack is a quasi-public place.

To the lady's chagrin, the Ontario Supreme Court sided with the racetrack owner and ruled that the racetrack could lawfully exclude this person. The court also ruled that, under statute and common law, the owner of land could exclude whomever he wanted from his land without giving reasons, and that a privately owned racetrack was not a "person" engaged in a public calling at common law. Thus, the charter argument could not avail. The judge said this rule applied to the owner of a home as well as the owner of a shopping mall, exhibition or racetrack.

are guilty of trespassing. This is true even if no harm is done.

If your trespassing results in damage to property, you can be held financially responsible for it, even if the damage was unintentional. Suppose your shot had found its mark and you enter the private land to collect the deer carcass. In doing so, you inadvertently trample on a garden planted with rare flowers. You are responsible for compensating the owner for the damage to his plants.

Trespassing can be caused by objects as well as people. For example, if your neighbor's unsecured garbage cans blow into your yard and ruin your tulip beds, your neighbor is guilty of trespassing and may be held liable for damages.

PROTECTING TRESPASSERS

Although trespassing is illegal, a property owner may not use force to remove a trespasser who poses no threat of violence. If he does, he could be subject to civil and criminal charges. Instead, the property owner should call the police to have the trespasser removed.

A property owner could also be held liable if he sets a trap for trespassers and someone is injured by it. For example, if you dig a hole in your yard solely for the purpose of injuring trespassers and someone falls in the hole and breaks his leg, the trespasser might be able to sue you for his injuries.

You may have different responsibilities to children who trespass. The law extends special protection to children if something on your property might cause them harm but is too tempting for them to stay away from, such as an unfenced swimming pool.

See ATTRACTIVE NUISANCE; TORT.

CRIMINAL TRESPASS

Criminal charges can be made only when a trespasser enters someone's property with the intention of actually committing a crime, such as burglary or arson.

POSSESSION VERSUS OWNERSHIP

In cases between owners and tenants, most courts rule that the party in physical possession of the property has the right to keep out everyone else, including the owner. For example, if your landlord enters your apartment without notice or without obtaining your approval beforehand, he may be guilty of trespassing.

See also ADVERSE POSSESSION; EASEMENT; EVICTION; LANDLORD.

TRUST

A trust is a legal arrangement by which the assets of one person are transferred to another person or institution for the benefit of a third party. In a trust, the person with the assets (the settlor) transfers ownership of his property to someone (the trustee) who promises to administer the property for a third party (the beneficiary) according to the settlor's wishes.

TYPES OF TRUSTS

Essentially, all trusts fall into one of two basic categories: living or testamentary.

Living trusts

In a living, or *inter vivos,* trust the settlor transfers ownership of his property to a trustee who manages it throughout the settlor's lifetime. Upon the death of the settlor, the trustee distributes the trust to the beneficiaries in accordance with the settlor's instructions.

In most cases, the settlor of a living trust reserves the right to modify or revoke the trust as long as he lives. This type of living trust is known as a revocable trust. If you are creating a revocable living trust, you can name yourself as the trustee, but you will have to name a successor trustee to manage your estate if you become incapacitated and to distribute your assets when you die.

A major reason for creating a revocable trust is to pass property without the delay and expenses involved in probating a will. Living trusts do not have to be probated. See PROBATE.

To create an irrevocable trust, the settlor signs away the right to make any changes to the trust. Be careful if you are considering establishing an irrevocable trust. If your financial conditions change, for example, you cannot cancel the trust or amend it to obtain more of the trust's income or principal for your own support. Never make an irrevocable trust without the advice of a lawyer who is experienced in trust and estate law. See LIVING TRUST.

Testamentary trusts

A testamentary trust is a provision of your last will and testament. It instructs a trustee regarding the use or sale of property that the creator of the will, or testator, has left to his heirs. In effect, it allows the testator to extend control over property after his death. Since a testamentary trust is part of a will, it must be probated.

WHAT TRUSTS CAN DO

Apart from the fact that it sometimes prevents probate expenses, trusts are established to serve a variety of worthwhile purposes. The trusts described below can be either living or testamentary.

◇ In a *spendthrift trust* the beneficiary receives income from the trust, but the trustee is prohibited from distributing any of the principal. As its name implies, a spendthrift trust is a good way to keep an irresponsible son or daughter from squandering his or her inheritance on foolish investments or luxury purchases.

◇ An *accumulation trust* is designed to provide a nest egg for a beneficiary. To build the nest egg, the trustee keeps adding the interest and dividends from the principal to the trust until it is distributed to the beneficiary at the designated time.

◇ To create a *life insurance trust* the settlor names an adult trustee as the beneficiary of his life insurance. Upon the settlor's death, the trustee distributes the proceeds of the life insurance policy in accordance with the settlor's instructions. A life insurance trust is advis-able if you have large amounts of life insurance coverage, minor children whom you have named as beneficiaries, and an ex-spouse whom you do not want to have control of the money. See LIFE INSURANCE.

◇ A *charitable trust*, unlike other kinds of trusts, which must by law eventually terminate, may continue indefinitely. It can thus provide benefits to a charitable organization on an ongoing basis.

In the Civil Code of Jan. 1, 1994, Quebec adopted many of the principles and rules of trusts that had long existed in the common-law provinces.

TRUSTEE

A trustee is a person who is authorized by another person (known as the settlor of the trust) to take possession of and manage some or all of the settlor's property on behalf of and in the best interests of a third party, known as the beneficiary, and in accordance with the terms of the trust.

NAMING A TRUSTEE

Although the law generally permits any legally competent person to serve as a trustee, not everyone is able or willing to accept the responsibility. Trustees are entitled to be paid for their services out of the trust's assets, although family and friends who agree to act as trustees may waive this right.

In some situations a settlor may want to consider using a corporate trustee—a trust company or other financial institution that is authorized by the province to manage trusts. Most corporate trustees, however, rarely take on trusts that are valued at less than $250,000, and they will charge a fee for their services based on a percentage of the estate's value, up to the limit set by law.

If you do not know whom to select as a trustee, your lawyer can probably help you find a qualified person.

DUTIES AND POWERS

A trustee is a fiduciary—that is, he has a legal duty to act in the best interest of the beneficiary and abide by the provisions of the trust, as described in the checklist on the facing page.

A trustee's powers are extensive. They may be either express or implied, mandatory or discretionary. Powers that are specifically stated in the trust document are express powers. For example, a written authorization given by the settlor to sell or lease trust property is an express power.

Implied powers are ones that are not stated explicitly, but that are necessary to carry out the trustee's duties. Suppose your trust requires the trustee to manage your business on behalf of your beneficiaries. The trust may not specifically authorize the trustee to pay rent for the business's warehouse or buy insurance for its assets, but the trustee's authority to do so is implied, since without it the trustee cannot fulfill his responsibility to manage the business.

Mandatory powers are ones that the trust document requires the trustee to exer-

CHECKLIST

Your Duties as a Trustee

Serving as a trustee is a difficult task, which has legal and financial consequences if you do not perform your duties properly. Think very carefully before agreeing to serve as one. A trustee's responsibilities include:

■ **THE DUTY TO FOLLOW THE EXPRESS INSTRUCTIONS OF THE SETTLOR OF THE TRUST TO THE BEST OF YOUR ABILITIES.**
If you fail to fulfill this obligation—for example, by not selling property as required by the trust—you could be sued by the trust's beneficiaries.

■ **THE DUTY TO ADMINISTER THE TRUST SOLELY FOR THE BENEFIT OF THE BENEFICIARIES, RATHER THAN FOR PERSONAL PROFIT.**
If you invest trust property in your own business, for example, you may be guilty of a breach of fiduciary duty and even criminal theft.

■ **THE DUTY TO PROTECT THE TRUST PROPERTY.**
You must take reasonable steps to ensure that the value of the property is not diminished through unwise investments or mismanagement. You must also make necessary repairs, and buy insurance for tangible property such as automobiles and real estate.

■ **THE DUTY TO FOSTER GROWTH OF THE TRUST PROPERTY.**
It is not enough to keep the trust property as it is when you receive it. You have an obligation to manage, invest, and reinvest trust property in the best interests of the beneficiaries. In most provinces, statutes prohibit trustees from making risky investments, and some provinces even set forth the kinds of investments a trustee can make. Failing to follow these legal requirements can make you personally responsible for any losses.

■ **THE DUTY TO MAKE PAY-MENTS TO THE TRUST'S BENEFI-CIARIES ACCORDING TO THE PROVISIONS IN THE TRUST.**
For example, if a trust orders the trustee to make payments only of income, you cannot pay with both income and principal. If you do, a beneficiary could sue you for the amount you spent.

■ **THE DUTY TO KEEP TRUST PROPERTY SEPARATE FROM YOUR OWN PROPERTY AND FROM OTHER PROPERTY THAT YOU MANAGE.**
For example, trust accounts must be kept separate from your own bank accounts, and you cannot commingle funds from more than one trust unless you receive prior approval from the settlors.

assets to beneficiaries. For example, a trustee would be permitted to distribute a portion of the principal or interest of the trust if he felt that it was in the best interest of the beneficiary to do so. Unless the trustee acts irresponsibly or in bad faith, a court will not interfere in his exercise of discretionary powers. However, the actions of a trustee are subject to review by the beneficiaries, who can sue for restitution of any lost value.

TRUSTEES FOR NON-PROFIT ORGANIZATIONS

Colleges, churches, hospitals, and other nonprofit or charitable organizations often turn over the management of their business affairs to a board of trustees. A board of trustees for a nonprofit organization serves much the same function as the board of directors of a profit-making corporation, making decisions about the management of the organization's finances.

Like the trustees of a trust created by an individual, the trustees of a nonprofit organization manage the property entrusted to them for the benefit of others. For example, a church's board of trustees manages property for the benefit of the church's members, in accordance with the authority granted to them by the church. Unlike the trustees of a private trust, who may serve for the life of the trust, trustees for a nonprofit organization usually serve for a limited period. Like other trustees, they have the responsibilities outlined in the checklist above.

cise. For example, if a trust instructs the trustee to sell a piece of vacation property and deposit the proceeds from the sale in a certificate of deposit, the trustee has both the right and the duty to do so.

Discretionary powers require the trustee to use his own judgment in distributing

FROM
UMBRELLA
INSURANCE
TO
UNORDERED
MERCHANDISE

UMBRELLA INSURANCE

Most insurance protects its owners against the everyday risks of life. But sometimes people may want to extend their coverage beyond the limits of standard automobile and homeowners' policies. Umbrella insurance, which offers protection against almost every contingency, provides the most comprehensive coverage available. An umbrella policy provides two types of extended protection.

First, it covers risks that other insurance policies usually exclude. Most homeowners' insurance provides personal liability protection if someone is injured on your property. But an umbrella policy insures you against risks not covered by homeowners' insurance—

for example, if you are sued for invasion of privacy, false arrest, libel, or slander.

Second, an umbrella policy pays for losses that exceed the limits of your basic insurance policies. Suppose you have automobile liability insurance that pays up to $500,000 to anyone injured as a result of your negligence. You can buy an umbrella policy that will insure against awards or settlements above that amount. The typical limit for an umbrella policy ranges from $1 million to $10 million.

An umbrella policy is a particularly wise investment for people who have extensive personal assets and therefore run the risk of substantial losses if they are sued successfully. See also AUTOMOBILE INSURANCE; HOMEOWNERS' INSURANCE.

UNCONSCIONABILITY

When a legal contract is blatantly one-sided and unfair in its terms, it is said to be unconscionable. The legal doctrine of unconscionability allows courts to undo such unconscionable contracts that would otherwise be binding. Supporters of absolute contractual freedom argue that this doctrine creates instability in the marketplace. They say that no one can ever be assured that a contract is binding if the doctrine of unconscionability exists. Their fears have not been borne out in the many years the doctrine has existed, possibly because the courts apply the principle only in the clearest cases.

Anyone seeking to have an unconscionable contract set aside by the courts must prove that the terms were arrived at through a combination of inequality in bargaining power and inexperience of the party asking for the contract to be canceled. Typically, the doctrine seeks to protect the elderly, the infirm, and those inexperienced in business.

Unconscionability will not protect all people who make imprudent bargains. The disproportionate power between the bargaining parties is the key. So, if John, a car salesman, pays $10,000 for a car which is actually worth $2,000, he will have a hard time convincing the court that this bargain was unconscionable. John may have made a bad deal, but his experience would indicate that he knew what he was doing and that his actions were voluntary.

However, a Manitoba judge set aside a contract by which an elderly widow agreed to sell property worth $17,000 for $10,000. The 85-year-old woman, who resided in a nursing home, was not very knowledgeable in real estate matters and had received no independent advice before agreeing to sell her land. The court found the plaintiffs had taken advantage of her in an unconscionable manner and declared the contract unenforceable.

The doctrine of unconscionability does not merely protect the old. When a 21-year-old Ontario man approached a motorcycle company about setting up a motorcycle dealership, he was told that this was possible provided his wife and father guaranteed collateral in the event that the business failed. Neither the young man, nor his wife, nor his father had any experience in this line of business, whereas the company did. Yet the company offered no advise about the viability of the dealership, nor gave any hints that motorcycle sales lasted for only a few months each year. Neither did it make any effort to keep the enterprise afloat. When the dealership failed, the motorcycle company sought to make good on the promises made by the wife and the father. The court refused to allow this given the combination of unequal bargaining power between the parties, the lack of information given to the young man and his relatives, and the company's failure to take any steps to prevent the dealership from folding.

UNDERWRITER

In the early days of international shipping, wealthy businessmen sometimes used their own money to insure a shipment against loss of goods in transit. Before a voyage, each man who accepted a share of the risk would write his name under the amount he invested, thus becoming an "underwriter." If the goods were delivered safely, each investor was paid a premium.

If not, the underwriter lost his investment.

The term *underwriter* is still used to describe someone who subsidizes a venture involving risk. Insurance companies employ underwriters to determine whether to accept applications for insurance and the terms and conditions under which each individual policy will be offered. In the securities industry, an underwriter insures the sale of stocks and bonds to the public by promising to buy all those that remain unsold.

See also INSURANCE; STOCKS AND BONDS.

UNDUE INFLUENCE

When your uncle dies, you learn that a year earlier he had signed a power of attorney authorizing his neighbor to withdraw funds from his bank account. But what really seems odd is that the account had a balance of $25,000 when the power of attorney was granted, and now it contains less than $200. Could your uncle have been subject to undue influence when he signed the power of attorney?

Undue influence occurs when someone tries to benefit himself by persuading another person to do something that person would not ordinarily do. Charges of undue influence are most often made in cases involving deeds, contracts, and wills. To determine whether undue influence has been used, the court considers: (1) the age, health, or mental capacity

of the person who was supposedly influenced; (2) whether there was an opportunity or motive for someone to influence him; and (3) whether there is evidence to suggest such influence.

Suppose your uncle gave his power of attorney to the neighbor while she nursed him through a long-term illness. If so, all three determining factors were present: your uncle was in a frail and dependent condition; the neighbor had much to gain by being granted power of attorney; and a large sum of money suddenly disappeared from your uncle's bank account. Under these circumstances, a court might hold that the neighbor exercised undue influence on your uncle.

UNEMPLOYMENT INSURANCE

If you lose your job through no fault of your own, unemployment insurance (UI) is your safety net. Anyone who leaves a job voluntarily or is fired is not eligible.

In order to be eligible for UI benefits, you must have accumulated a sufficient number of insurable weeks of employment in the 52 weeks before becoming unemployed. For a job to be insurable, there must be an employee-employer relationship between you and your boss. This relationship will likely exist if you receive orders from a superior, do not own your own tools, do not share in a company's profits and so on. The law also requires that in any given workweek, you must have worked 15 hours or have earned at least 20 percent of the maximum weekly earnings, as determined by the UI Commission. You can find out the current maximum insurable amount by calling the commission. Holders of certain jobs are excluded from collecting UI, so you should check this out as well.

For UI purposes, your job has legally ended when you pass seven consecutive days without work and without payment. This can be frustrating for some since, by this definition, you cannot receive UI until you have used up all your vacation pay, severance pay, company departure bonuses and similar payments.

For a first claim, you will need 20 insurable weeks in the previous 52 weeks. However, if you have less than 20 insurable weeks, but more than 12, in that period, and you can show that in the previous 104 weeks you accumulated 14 weeks in the "labor force attachment," you may still get UI. The "labor force attachment" includes those who worked, were denied benefits because they were on strike, were in a government training program, and so on. The number of weeks required will vary in this case according to the level of unemployment in your region.

APPLYING FOR BENEFITS

You will need your record of employment from your employer (who is required by law to give it to you) when you apply for UI benefits. You will also need to fill out short forms explaining how long and why you are without work, what sort of job you would be willing to take, where you would be willing to work, and so on. You will have a minimum two-week wait before you see any money from the commission and this wait could be extended in certain circumstances. You will receive roughly 55 percent of your previous wage in UI payments for between 17 to 50 weeks before your payments will end. The length of time you can get UI depends on the level of unemployment in your area and the number of insurable weeks you had before making a claim.

REASONABLE EXPECTATIONS

When you apply for UI benefits, be very careful in what you declare and which documents you sign. Always set high (but reasonable) expectations on your application form with regard to what salary you would work for. If you do not, the commission will use this against you. You would be wise to consult a lawyer in your local legal aid clinic, or to talk to one of a number of community groups that seek to defend the rights of the unemployed, before handing in your application forms. Making a mistake in your application, even an innocent one, could cost you thousands of dollars in UI benefits and unnecessary delays.

ACTIVE JOB SEARCH

While you receive UI, you must maintain an active job search and be ready and available for work. When you first file for benefits, you are allowed some degree of choosiness as to the jobs you are willing to take. For example, if you were a construction worker making $15 an hour, you would not have to immediately accept a job at McDonald's for minimum wage. As time goes on, however, the commission will usually require that you lower your expectations to maintain your benefits. You should consult a lawyer or an unemployment insurance counseling group to find out what a safe plan of action would be. It is always a good idea to keep a written record of where you applied for work—get an employee to sign that you visited, at what time, and which position you applied for. In this way, you can always prove to the commission that you maintained your job search.

SPECIAL CASES

If you are a student, you may receive UI at the same time that you study. However, just like anyone else, you must be able and available to work. If you have a history of working and studying simultaneously, the commission will be less likely to cut your benefits. Similarly, if there is no obvious conflict between school and work (that is, if all your classes are after working hours or if you previously worked night shift or would be willing to now), you stand a better chance of getting UI as a student. If you are on strike, you are not entitled to UI.

There are also circumstances, too, where the regular

UI requirement of being able to work may not apply. For example, you can get 15 weeks' benefits for sickness or maternity leave, and 10 weeks for parental absence—but no more than 30 weeks combined—if you have 20 insurable weeks. Maternity leave, for example, will often rule out the possibility of being ready to take any job that comes along, and it is likely that, after having your baby, you will be returning to your old job. Maternity benefits must be taken between the eighth week before expected delivery and the seventeenth week after birth.

CONTESTING UNFAVORABLE ASSESSMENTS

Despite much media hype about fraudulent claims being made by unemployed people, the truth is that only a very small portion of UI claims are bogus. Many of the so-called frauds subsequently turn out to have been legal claims, once a decision of the commission makes its way through the appeals process. If you feel that you have been unfairly dealt with in the processing of your claim, you may lodge an appeal to the commission. You must do this within 30 days of receiving notice of a decision unfavorable to you. It may be a good idea to have a lawyer or a member of an unemployment advisory group assist in your appeal; however, you may carry out the process yourself.

To start an appeal, write a letter indicating which decision you wish to appeal and deliver this letter (preferably in person) to the commission office that made the decision. You will be notified where and when your appeal will take place. The appeal will take place in front of three referees (independent of the commission). You will receive a decision within a week of your hearing.

It is a good idea to do some research on what the state of the law is if you are appealing yourself. The letter the commission sent you will state the relevant provisions of law on which it based its decision. See if your local library or UI office has an annotated copy of the Unemployment Insurance Act. This will show you how the courts have interpreted the law in the past. With this information and the testimony of yourself and other witnesses, you can build your case. If you are overwhelmed by the task of research, explain your situation to the librarian and ask for help.

For example, if you were sexually harassed by your boss to the point where you had to leave your job, you could be denied UI since, on first sight, the commission will think you left your job voluntarily. However, research will show that the courts have interpreted such situations in the past to be not voluntary departures but "constructive dismissals"— where the boss essentially forced you to leave. If you can prove a constructive dismissal (with a therapist's note, your testimony, co-worker's testimony, etc.), then your appeal will succeed.

UNFAIR COMPETITION

Until the mid-1980s, the government regulated competition under the Combines Investigation Act. However, this act had become outdated so a new Competition Act was passed by Parliament in 1986. It is designed to maintain and encourage competition in order to promote the efficiency and adaptability of our economy. While attempting to respect the rights of foreign investors and larger corporations, it also tries to protect the interests of the "little guy" in business.

Underlying all these objectives is a concern for the welfare of the consumer who is assumed to benefit from the workings of a competitive economy in the form of greater choice in products and services along with lower prices overall.

The Competition Act provided for a competition tribunal to replace the role formerly filled by the criminal courts in competition law. As a form of administrative "court," the tribunal offers the advantage of specialization and efficiency that comes from doing only one very specific type of law. The tribunal is empowered to hear all civil matters contained in the Competition Act, including such issues as abuse of dominant position (monopoly), mergers, and price-fixing. Appeals from this administrative body are made to the Federal Court of Appeal.

UNITED FAMILY COURT

Ontario and Prince Edward Island have introduced united family courts in an attempt to have one court deal with all issues concerning the family. Matters such as divorce, custody, guardianship, visiting rights, property claims between spouses, and matters arising from the Young Offenders Act are handled by united family court judges, who are specialists in family law. Ordinarily, such cases are heard in Youth, Superior, Supreme, or Provincial courts.

UNJUST ENRICHMENT

The law of unjust enrichment (also called restitution) in Canada is relatively new, officially dating to the 1950s. The idea behind it is that someone who has been unjustly enriched at the expense of another should have to make restitution to the other. Typically, unjust enrichment claims are also seen as subsidiary to the more common branches of private law—contract and tort. A claim in unjust enrichment usually arises because there is no legal action available in these other branches of the law.

For example, Amphana and Gary lived together in a common-law relationship. Gary had once asked Amphana to marry him, but she simply replied "later on." They lived on a farm owned by Gary, a traveling salesman. Because this was his principal occupation, Amphana was left with much of the farm work over the years. In 1971, she asked Gary for a legal part-interest in the land to be registered in her name, but he refused. Several years later, due to their deteriorating relationship and her bad health, Amphana moved into a senior citizens' home and sued Gary under the doctrine of unjust enrichment. The Supreme Court held in her favor. It found that Gary had indeed been enriched over the years by Amphana's work on the farm. Amphana had likewise been deprived of the fruits of her labor by the fact that she was denied an interest in the land by Gary, despite her great efforts to improve and maintain it. Lastly, it was found that Gary's enrichment was unjust in that he had no legal claim to the work that Amphana had done. Since they were not married, Amphana never really owed Gary the work that she performed. Moreover, there was no other contractual agreement by which she had agreed to do the work.

UNLAWFUL ASSEMBLY

According to the Criminal Code, an unlawful assembly occurs when three or more people, with intent to carry out a common purpose, assemble in such a manner that other people have reason to fear they will disturb the peace or cause others to disturb the peace in a tumultuous manner.

Such a tumultuous assembly is called a riot and if more than 12 people are involved, a justice of the peace, mayor, sheriff, or a deputy chosen by one of them may read the Riot Act. Unlawful assembly is punishable by six months in jail ,or a $2,000 fine, or both.

See also RIOT.

UNORDERED MERCHANDISE

If you receive merchandise that you did not order, you are legally entitled to keep it and treat it as a gift. If the company attempts to bill you for the merchandise, notify your local consumer protection office.

A company that sends unordered merchandise through the mail must clearly mark the package "Free Sample." Provincial legislation prohibits such a company from billing the consumer for the merchandise.

Recognized charitable organizations are legally permitted to send you small items—such as pins, address labels, or note cards—and request a donation. But even in these cases you are under no obligation either to return the items or to make a contribution.

These legal protections apply to individual consumers, not necessarily to businesses. If you are a business owner, you should closely monitor the products you receive and refuse merchandise sent by companies with whom you do not do business.

See CONSUMER PROTECTION; SCAMS AND SWINDLES.

V

FROM

VACATION HOME

TO

VISA

VACATION HOME

A vacation home can be a valuable investment as well as a personally enjoyable possession, but it can also be burdensome and expensive. If you decide to rent your vacation home (or "second" home) for part of the year to trim expenses and to take advantage of tax benefits, you should know the tax rules for second homes in order to avoid pitfalls.

TAX CONSIDERATIONS

If you have a vacation home that you sometimes rent out to others, Revenue Canada would probably consider it a business and you would be subject to tax on the income. In fact, any revenue that you obtain from renting your vacation home is technically taxable, but you would also be able to claim deductions for certain expenses, such as fuel, mainte-

nance, repairs, and insurance. Contact Revenue Canada or your accountant to make sure you are fairly assessed and that you claim for all expenses to which you are entitled.

PROPERTY INSURANCE

Because a vacation home may stand empty for much of the year, it is an easy target for break-ins, thefts, and vandalism. You may therefore find it more expensive to insure than a primary home of equal value.

If you rent the house to others, your liability insurance rates will also be higher. Be sure that you keep your rental property in top condition and make regular inspections and repairs. Failing to do so can lead to costly claims for injuries. You may want to buy an umbrella insurance policy to enhance your liability coverage. See also HOME-OWNERS' INSURANCE; UMBRELLA INSURANCE.

FINANCING

Just as insurance rates on second homes are higher, the cost of financing a vacation home itself is often higher too. Many banks require larger down payments and tack on extra interest points on mortgages for vacation homes, because the rate of default on these mortgages tends to be higher than on mortgages for primary residences.

Sometimes the seller of a home may be willing to "carry the paper" on the property—that is, provide the financing for you. If the owner offers such an arrangement, you should hire a lawyer to draw up

the mortgage papers or review the documents created by the seller, since a homeowner who provides financing to a buyer is usually not required to make the same disclosures to you as are banks and mortgage companies. See also HOME BUYING AND SELLING; MORTGAGE.

VACCINATION

Most Canadian provinces do not have mandatory school immunization laws. The health departments of provinces without vaccination legislation have traditionally relied on more voluntary methods. Education on the beneficial aspects of immunization programs has provided a sufficiently high rate of success in the school system to protect the entire population from various harmful diseases.

In provinces where vaccinations are compulsory, strict procedures must be followed lest those responsible for administering the immunizations find themselves acting outside the law. The courts will consider forced immunization a form of battery, subject to legal action.

VAGRANCY

The term vagrancy typically conjures up images of people who spend their time wandering from place to place with no visible means of support. Criminal law, however, has a more precise meaning.

The crime of vagrancy is committed in one of two ways. A person who has no lawful job and who supports himself or herself wholly or in part by gaming or crime is guilty of vagrancy. So, too, is anyone who has already been convicted of one of a variety of sexual offenses and who is found loitering in or near a school ground, playground, public park, or bathing area.

One cannot be charged with vagrancy merely for hanging around. There must be some malicious aspect to loitering, as set out above, before it becomes criminal. A summary offense, vagrancy is punishable by up to six months in jail, or a $2,000 fine, or both.

VANDALISM

In A.D. 455 the Vandals, a tribe of nomadic people, overran and sacked Rome. Their appalling acts of wanton and senseless destruction earned them a permanent place in our vocabulary. In the Canadian Criminal Code, acts of vandalism come under the offense of "mischief." There are many ways in which mischief can be committed, and each way carries a different punishment, according to the severity of the crime.

Willful vandalism, which destroys or damages property—by throwing a stone through a window, for example—carries a maximum penalty of two years' imprisonment if tried by indictment, or six months in jail if tried summarily. Fines of up to $2,000 may also be imposed. Vandalism of electronic data carries more serious penalties—up to 10 years in prison.

It is unlikely that criminal legislation against vandalism violates the guarantee of freedom of expression in the Charter of Rights and Freedoms. For example, Fred, a peace activist, cannot spray-paint political messages on the front of an army recruitment office without breaking the law. Moreover, drunkenness is no defense of this crime.

VARIANCE

Generally, a community's zoning laws are enacted in accordance with a comprehensive plan designed to ensure orderly and predictable development. In some situations, however, the local zoning board may allow an exception to a zoning law, known as a variance. Suppose you want to operate a home-based business, but the zoning laws in your community prohibit you from doing so. Or you want to keep a horse or a cow in an area where the zoning prohibits farm animals. To obtain a variance, you would apply to the local zoning board, which is responsible for enforcing zoning laws. The board will review your application and schedule a public hearing, at which you will be permitted to make your case for the variance. Other members of the community will also be heard. If there are few objections or none at all, your application will probably be approved.

If your application is denied, you can appeal, but keep in mind that appeals can be costly and time-consuming. Local zoning authorities are given considerable latitude in the decisions they make. Unless the board failed to follow its own rules, or its actions were clearly arbitrary and unsupported by the facts, its decision will probably stand. See also NONCONFORMING USE; ZONING.

VENUE

The place where a trial or other legal proceeding is held is called its venue. Venue is not the same as jurisdiction, which is the authority of a particular court to hear a case. For example, the provincial superior courts will have jurisdiction over most personal injury cases involving large sums of money.

Suppose the plaintiff in such a case lives in one county, while the defendant lives in another, hundreds of miles away. The court in either county may have jurisdiction over the case, but the venue will depend on such factors as convenience to the parties and the potential for getting a fair trial. Usually, the venue is in the defendant's county. However, the plaintiff can petition for a "change of venue" if, for example, publicity in the defendant's county or a friendship between the defendant and the local judge would make a fair trial unlikely.

See COURTS; JURISDICTION.

VERBAL AGREEMENT

"A verbal contract isn't worth the paper it's written on." The quip, attributed to the legendary Hollywood mogul Samuel Goldwyn, underscores a popular misconception that verbal agreements are not enforceable. However, the law views them as contracts that, even unwritten, are valid as long as they do not concern real estate and other contracts which by law must be in writing. See also CONTRACT.

COURT JUDGMENTS

Verbal contracts involving millions of dollars have been held to be valid by Canadian courts. In one case, an Ontario judge awarded $7 million in damages to a Rhode Island packaging company after another company breached a verbal agreement to deliver a machine worth only $425,000.

The large amount awarded was to compensate for the lost profits the plaintiff would have received if the defendant had lived up to his oral promise. The court was told that although there was no written contract, several meetings had taken place between the two companies, and that they had reached an agreement in principle over the sale of the machine. The court held that the breach of this agreement should thus be treated the same as if the contract had been written and then broken.

The problem with lawsuits over verbal agreements is the matter of proof. Suppose you make a verbal contract with a handyman, who agrees to paint your porch for $200. You give him half the money in cash up front, but he never does the job. If you take him to small-claims court and he denies

making the agreement, it will be your word against his. Unless you have a witness, the judge will have to make a decision based on two conflicting stories, each of which may seem credible. Because the burden of proof is on you as the plaintiff, chances are you may lose your lawsuit. See also BURDEN OF PROOF; EVIDENCE.

Unless the amount of money in question is very small, it is a good idea to put all agreements in writing. Contracts do not necessarily have to be formal; a simple letter signed by both parties will usually suffice. For more costly projects or purchases, however, a formal written contract is advisable.

VETERANS' BENEFITS

Canada has numerous programs to meet the special needs of its military veterans, whether they be regular duty personnel, veterans of the Korean or the two world wars, or veterans of active peace-keeping/peacemaking duty in various war zones around the world.

The Department of Veterans Affairs oversees such services as disability pensions, widows' pensions, prisoner of war compensation, war veterans' allowances, medical treatment, counseling, advocacy, the

Veterans Independence Program, educational assistance to the children of the war dead, and commemorative ceremonies to honor those who gave their lives in the service of their country.

DISABILITY PENSIONS

The Pension Act and the Civilian War Pensions and Allowances Act provide compensatory pensions for death and injury of veterans and those who served in civilian organizations closely linked to the military—the Merchant Navy for example. For the most part, these acts are administered by the Canadian Pension Commission, which administers the pensions of employees of other government agencies such as the RCMP.

Check with your nearest veterans affairs office for information on your eligibility for benefits. Counselors there will advise you, and assist you with any application you may have. You may also wish to consult a lawyer or the Bureau of Pensions Advocates. The latter is an independent agency set up to provide legal aid to pension applicants in the preparation and presentation of their claims.

Once you apply for a disability pension, the Canadian Pension Commission will decide whether you are entitled to an award. If the decision is unfavorable, you may appeal to the Entitlement Board. Beyond that, further appeal can be made to the Review Board and, lastly, you may appeal to the courts to review the agency's decision.

In addition to pension benefits, you may also be granted compensation to cover certain special expenses arising from service-related injuries. For example, some programs cover the cost of special clothing and medical treatment for amputees. Moreover, survivor benefits are available to the spouse and children (within a certain age) of deceased veterans where the death can be attributed to military service.

Pensions are not affected by the pensioner's place of residence: they are payable anywhere in the world. Paid by cheque, in Canadian dollars, they typically arrive at the end of the month.

HEALTH CARE

People receiving a disability pension from the Canadian Pension Commission, a war veterans allowance or a civilian war allowance, and those who are only denied the above benefits because of other forms of government income such as the Old Age Pension, may qualify for one of many health-care programs designed to benefit veterans. Services available include dental treatment, prescriptions, travel and out-of-pocket expenses, as well as special equipment where circumstances warrant. For further information, you should contact your local veterans affairs office.

In certain cases, medical expenses incurred out of Canada may not be covered by the above plan. Again, for further information, contact your local veterans affairs office.

VETERANS' INDEPENDENCE PROGRAM

The Veterans' Independence Program (VIP) helps veterans maintain their independence and quality of life in a number of ways. Every effort is made to help even those who have become somewhat dependent on others to recover their self-sufficiency.

The program is primarily concerned with helping veterans who want to remain in their own homes and communities, rather than move into an institution.

Counseling and referral services are geared to determining the needs of a given veteran, and finding ways of helping him or her meet these needs. The help provided may involve: ambulatory health care, having the home adapted to the veteran's particular needs, transportation, home care, and adult residential care.

COUNSELING AND TUITION SERVICES

The Department of Veterans Affairs also provides counseling for veterans to help them adapt to changing, social, economic, and health conditions. Moreover, training and education assistance are available under the Pensioners' Training Regulations. These regulations allow for the disbursement of funds for tuition fees and other related costs.

FUNERALS, BURIALS, AND GRAVE MARKERS

Within limits, financial assistance toward funeral and burial expenses is available to certain eligible persons. Additional information may be obtained from Veterans Affairs or the Canadian Pension Commission. An alternative, nongovernmental source of covering burial costs is the Last Post Fund, which may be reached through the Canadian Legion, the Department of Veterans Affairs, or by writing to the Fund itself. See USEFUL ADDRESSES at back of book.

REMEMBRANCE

The Commonwealth War Graves Commission, established in 1917, maintains the graves and the funeral records of members of the Forces of the Commonwealth who died in either of the two world wars. Each of the dead is commemorated individually by a name on a headstone or monument. There is no distinction as to rank. Among the war dead it commemorates are 110,000 Canadians in 74 different countries.

Those who have given their lives for Canada in military service are also commemorated in volumes on public display in the Peace Tower of the Parliament Buildings in Ottawa. Each day, a different set of the names of the fallen is placed in view. A copy of these books is also open to public viewing in each of the provincial capitals.

VETERINARIAN

A veterinarian is a person licensed to diagnose and treat sick and/or injured animals. Canada's some 6,000 practicing veterinarians have completed at least two years of university preveterinary training followed by four years of professional instruction. They are licensed and regulated by provincial professional corporations that typically seek to increase the knowledge and skills of their members.

In the eyes of the law, a pet is considered the personal property of its owner. A veterinarian is therefore responsible for the pet while it is in his custody. This means that the animal must be properly fed, sheltered, exercised, cleaned, and protected from other animals.

Although veterinarians are not subject to the same malpractice laws that apply to physicians, they can be held responsible for the suffering, injury, or death of an animal if it results from: (1) a negligent diagnosis, (2) unskillful surgery, (3) unsafe or inadequate food or shelter, (4) neglect or abandonment, or (5) actions by an unskilled or negligent employee. If a veterinarian is found guilty of negligence, he may be suspended from his practice and subjected to civil penalties, such as a fine. However, a pet owner who successfully sues a veterinarian can usually recover no more than the dollar value of the animal.

If your pet happens to injure a veterinarian or one of his assistants while it is under his care, you generally cannot be held responsible for the injuries, because veterinarians treat animals with full knowledge of the risks of being scratched or bitten. If your pet is unusually vicious, however, and you fail to warn the veterinarian, you might be held liable for any injuries the animal inflicts on him or his employees.

VICTIM IMPACT STATEMENT

Since 1985, crime victims may prepare a written "victims impact statement" for presentation to the court before judgment is rendered. Such a statement may describe the harm done to the victim and may be considered by the judge in sentencing the offender.

When the victim was killed, the victim impact statement may be prepared by the victim's spouse or other relative.

VICTIMS' RIGHTS

Under the Charter of Rights and Freedoms, a criminal defendant is guaranteed certain rights to ensure that he is not unjustly convicted. Until relatively recently, however, courts and provincial and federal legislatures gave little or no consideration to the rights of victims of crimes.

Nowadays, thanks to strong advocacy by victims' rights groups, the law protects not only the defendant but the victim as well.

On request from the crime victim, the sentencing judge can order the accused to compensate the victim for any loss or damage to her property resulting from the crime in question. The judge may also order that any monies seized at the time of the arrest be used for this purpose, assuming no other person has a legal claim to that money. If the restitution of the victim's property is not made immediately, the sentencing order is enforceable in the same way in which a civil judgment would be. A criminal's wage could also be subject to garnishment or his property subject to seizure and judicial sale in order to compensate the victim. However, the law will not allow double compensation for the victim (which would also be double punishment for the criminal). So, if restitution has already been made in a civil lawsuit, or if she has received compensation from an insurance company, then a criminal court cannot award further compensation, and vice versa.

If the victim prefers that restitution be made to an organization, such as a charity, the court can order this. Restitution may sometimes be done through service, rather than money. For example, a court may order a convicted vandal to spend a certain number of hours performing cleanup work in his community.

ABC's

OF VICTIM'S RIGHTS

Even though Canada has no formal victim's bill of rights, there have been several legislative changes in recent years, all designed to ensure that the rights of the victims of crime are not forgotten. The following are some of the rights due to a victim:

■ The right to be treated with respect and courtesy.

■ The right to be provided with quick and appropriate medical attention, if needed.

■ The right to get back stolen property within three months of the offense, unless the property is needed for evidence at trial. In some cases, photographs of stolen property may be used, in which case there may be no need to withhold items for long periods.

■ The right to have the case dealt with promptly.

■ In property crimes, such as theft, fraud, breaking and entering, and false pretense—provided the Crown and defense lawyers agree—the right to prepare an affidavit, describing the circumstances of the crime and the nature and value of the property. This affidavit may then be used at trial instead of having you appear to testify.

■ The right to be informed of the progress of the investigation.

■ The right to attend the trial.

■ The right to receive compensation for bodily injury from your provincial or territorial crime injury indemnity fund.

■ The right to prepare and present to the court a written victim's impact statement that informs the court of the harmful effects the particular crime had on your life and state of health.

■ In sexual or extortion offenses, you have the right to request that the judge issue a non-publication order. Witnesses at such trials may also request the same. The court has the discretion, however, to grant such an order or not when the victim or witness is 18 years of age or older.

VICTIM COMPENSATION PROGRAMS

All provinces and territories have programs for compensating victims of crime. Moreover, these programs are more comprehensive than the remedies available under the Criminal Code, in that they seek to cover personal injuries as well as some property damage.

Victim compensation programs vary substantially. Some provinces allow compensation for pain and suffering, others do not. As well as compensating for injuries or death caused by crime, Ontario also seeks to help those who have suffered while attempting a citizen's arrest or otherwise helping the police perform their duties.

A victim should apply for relief as soon as possible after the crime took place and fulfill any requirements set by his province's compensation board. In some instances, illegal or imprudent behavior on the part of the claimant may lessen the award. For example, suppose Brian, Michael, and Bernard commit armed robbery. Afterward, Brian decides he wants all the loot and shoots his two accomplices. Michael and Bernard survive the shooting, a clearly criminal act. But even though they are both victims of attempted murder, their plight was in part linked to the crime they had committed, so their claim for compensation is weak at best.

See also CRIMINAL INJURIES COMPENSATION.

VIEW

When Pierre bought his home, one of its most appealing features was the spectacular mountain view it afforded. But he has just heard from a neighbor that developers are planning to build a tall commercial complex on the property directly across the road. The result, of course, is that his breathtaking vista will soon become only a dim memory.

Is there anything he can do to stop the construction?

Probably not. Under common law, a property owner has no legal right to a view—scenic or otherwise. As long as his neighbors do not act maliciously—by putting up a fence just to spite him, for example—Pierre has no recourse when his view becomes obstructed.

In some areas, however, local laws protect landowners from having their views blocked. And in a number of development communities, covenants in landowners' deeds prevent them from erecting buildings or planting vegetation that would obstruct their neighbor's view. To find out whether you are protected by local laws, ask your city clerk's office. Your homeowners' association will be able to help you determine whether your view is protected by a covenant in your neighbor's deed.

See FENCE BUILDING; HOMEOWNERS' ASSOCIATION; TREE.

VISA

A visa is an endorsement, usually in the form of a stamp, placed by a foreign government on a Canadian passport to permit the bearer to visit that country. Some countries, such as Italy and Great Britain, allow you to stay several months without a visa, while others, such as Australia, require visitors to secure a visa in advance.

If you are planning to visit a foreign country, find out well beforehand whether a visa is required. For visa information, call the nearest consulate of the country you wish to visit or go to an experienced travel agency.

See also IMMIGRATION; PASSPORT.

FROM
WARRANTY AND GUARANTEE
TO
WRONGFUL LIFE

WARRANTY AND GUARANTEE

A warranty, also known as a guarantee, is a legally binding contract in which the seller or manufacturer of a product promises the buyer that the statements he makes about the quality of his merchandise are true and that he will stand by them. Most consumer legislation requires the manufacturer or vendor to guarantee that the goods bought will serve the purpose for which they were made, for a reasonable period of time. Any ambiguity concerning a written guarantee is interpreted in favor of the consumer.

EXPRESS WARRANTY

An express warranty may be either full or limited. A full warranty obliges the manufacturer either to repair a defective item within a reasonable period of time without charge or, if he cannot do so, to give the consumer the choice between a no-cost replacement or a full refund of the purchase price. If a full warranty is restricted to a specified period of time (such as 90 days or one year), the manufacturer must state this at the top of the warranty.

A limited warranty gives the consumer less protection. It may cover only selected parts or require the consumer to pay shipping and handling or labor costs in order to obtain repairs.

IMPLIED WARRANTY

An implied warranty is one that the law presumes to exist, even if it is not expressed in writing. For example, when a furniture manufacturer sells a sofa to a consumer, the law presumes an "implied warranty of merchantability." This means that the consumer has the right to assume that the sofa will be of the same general quality as similarly priced sofas made by other manufacturers. If the sofa falls below this standard—for example, if the frame cracks prematurely with ordinary use—the consumer has a right to have it repaired or replaced.

Implied warranties represent the minimum standards imposed by law, whereas express warranties allow merchants and manufacturers to proclaim their high standards and obtain a competitive advantage. Suppose two manufacturers offer similarly priced 19-inch color television sets. If one offers a 90-day parts and labor warranty and the other offers full coverage for a year, whose set are you likely to choose?

Another kind of implied warranty is the warranty of suitability for a particular purpose. Suppose that your car requires a new engine. If you tell the auto parts supplier the make and model of your car but he sends you the wrong engine by mistake, he has breached the implied warranty of suitability for a particular purpose. See also SERVICE CONTRACT.

In some cases, an implied warranty can be excluded, but only if you are told of the exclusion in advance. However, some provinces prohibit or severely limit these exclusions. Your provincial consumer-protection office can advise you.

WEAPON

Just about any object or substance, from a hatpin to a can of lighter fluid, can be used as a weapon. Since the law cannot control everything that could potentially be used to commit a crime, it concerns itself primarily with items that are most commonly recognized as dangerous (likely to produce death or severe bodily harm) and criminal (likely to be used in a criminal manner).

Unlike the United States, no one in Canada has a right to own a firearm. Prior to obtaining a firearm here, you must obtain a firearm acquisition certificate (FAC), which indicates which firearm you can own, and where you must keep it. Except for police, security guards, and a few other special cases, no one is allowed to carry a firearm in a city or town.

PROHIBITED WEAPONS

Weapons are divided into two categories: those that are prohibited and those that are restricted.

Prohibited weapons include certain assault pistols and carbines, such as the UZI, the Sterling MK-6 carbine, the Partisan Avenger Auto pistol, and the Ingram type pistol. People who owned such weapons as of July 27, 1992, may keep them, but may not sell or otherwise dispose of them. Upon the death of the owner, such items automatically become prohibited weapons.

Other prohibited weapons include assault pistols, combat shotguns, 50-caliber sniper rifles and other military type firearms, and the "stinger," a firearm designated to look like a fountain pen.

Certain types of ammunition such as armor-piercing handgun cartridges, explosive or incendiary ammunition, as well as shotgun cartridges containing flechettes instead of pellets are also prohibited.

RESTRICTED WEAPONS

Restricted weapons are legal if you have a special permit and the weapon is properly registered. Included are some semiautomatic rifles such as the AK-47 family and variants, Beretta AR 70 and variants, Thompson Submachine 6 (semiautomatic version), and Bushmaster Auto rifle and variants. Other restricted weapons include stun guns such as the "Taser public defender," tear gas, mace, or "any liquid, spray, powder or other substance that is capable of injuring, immobilizing or otherwise incapacitating any person." This restriction is so vague it may even cover the popular self-defense pepper spray sold widely in the United States.

Certain martial arts weapons, such as "nunchaku" (two hard sticks joined by a short chain or wire), shuriken (sharp star-shaped throwing devices), as well as spiked wristbands, blowguns capable of shooting small arrows or darts, "brass knuckles," or spring- or gravity-operated switchblade knives, are also restricted by law or order-in-council. For more information about weapons, contact your local RCMP office or Justice Canada.

WELFARE

Welfare, also known as social welfare assistance or income security, is a last resort measure whereby the provincial government will give people and families in financial distress a certain amount of money each month to cover basic needs. How much a person or family receives is set out in schedules prepared by the provincial social affairs ministries, and is based on need.

Typically, between $500 and $600 may be given to an eligible individual and about $1,000 to $1,200 per month may be given to a family of four.

For those who are eligible for welfare, receiving financial aid is a right and not a privilege. In most provinces, welfare is given to citizens and permanent residents in need. It could be refused to sponsored immigrants who must first sue their sponsor for support, before being allowed to claim welfare.

Welfare payments vary from province to province and from one individual's case to another. Payments are based on the assets of the applicant, the size of her family, special needs of family member (such as certain medical devices or medications they may need), as well as whether the applicant is able and willing to participate in various educational, retraining, or work programs. Under some welfare programs, people are entitled to welfare if they are studying in programs approved by the minister, and some programs allow people to work and keep part of their earnings while still qualifying for welfare benefits.

Under most provincial plans, people do not have to be totally destitute to receive welfare—in fact, many people on welfare live in homes that they own and some even have modest savings. In some cases, welfare payments may be granted on a conditional basis (that is, the recipient must reimburse the welfare authorities). This could happen, for example, when a person has no assets or revenue and is waiting for her unemployment insurance benefits to come into effect.

In the last recession, many people who never thought that they would ever apply for welfare have been obliged to do so because of job loss, illness, or other unforeseen events.

RECIPIENTS' RIGHTS AND DUTIES

When a person applies for welfare, there is usually a conflict between his rights to privacy and confidentiality and his rights to receive benefits. For example, the welfare application obliges you to disclose a lot of personal information and to supply various documents concerning your private life.

Typically, you have to provide birth certificates for each member of the family; their social insurance numbers; proof of status, such as a passport, or certificate of landing; proof of earnings; income tax returns; lists of assets; copies of leases or deeds of sale for your home; bank statements, and so on. You could also be obliged to allow welfare officers into your home so that they may check to see who is living there. This requirement, however, which many consider to be an infringment of one's charter right to be free from unreasonable search and seizure, may yet be decided by the courts.

Welfare recipients may be penalized if they refuse to participate in certain educational or work programs sponsored by the welfare authorities.

Any change in the family situation, such as a family member leaving the home, or getting a job, should always be reported to the welfare authorities.

Despite the occasional massive welfare fraud that usually receives a lot of publicity, the overwhelming number of people on welfare are honest citizens who would much prefer to work if they could find employment. The vast majority are working hard at keeping their self-respect and optimism despite circumstances that conspire against them.

Welfare payments are not seizable by creditors, and you cannot sign away or assign your welfare benefits.

See FRAUD.

WHISTLE-BLOWER

An employee who witnesses a crime, a health or safety hazard, or a breach of employment rules by other employees or by management, and who brings that activity to the attention of the employer, the media, or government officials, is called a whistle-blower.

Until recently, whistle-blowers were not shielded from reprisals. Now federal and provincial laws provide some protection. For example, an employee who reports a safety violation to the Occupational Health and Safety Commission in good faith cannot be fired for doing so.

STEPS TO TAKE

If you have reason to believe that your employer is engaged in unethical or illegal business practices, consider taking the following steps:

1. Make sure your allegations are well-founded. Before

making accusations to anyone, check with a reliable source to confirm that a particular activity is, in fact, taking place and that it is unethical or illegal.

2. Record your observations and your conversations with fellow employees and supervisors. Keep a journal listing the day and time of each activity, as well as the management's response to each complaint.

3. Ask your provincial bar association for the name of a lawyer experienced in employment law. Discussing your concerns with a lawyer is not whistle-blowing; you are protected by lawyer-client privilege.

4. If you do decide to blow the whistle, protect yourself by carefully following the steps required by law and outlined by your lawyer. This may mean informing your employer of the wrongdoing in writing.

5. Do not talk to the media without your lawyer's permission. By doing so, you could risk being sued by your employer for defamation.

WILL

A will is a legal document that states how your property is to be distributed after your death. Many people do not make wills, thinking that to do so is either complicated, expensive or both. In fact, the opposite is true. If your will is not too complicated, a lawyer can draw one up for about $100 to $150.

For a will to be valid, it must be made by a competent person, that is a person of legal age (18 in most provinces, 19 in

Nova Scotia and British Columbia), and who is of "sound mind"—she must understand the purpose of the will and must clearly name the person or persons who will inherit her property.

All provinces except Quebec, which has a Civil Code, have dependent relief legislation which allows the courts to order that a deceased's estate pay an allowance, or a lump sum, or even transfer property to a surviving spouse who was not adequately provided for in a deceased's will. In Alberta, Manitoba, Newfoundland, Ontario, Prince Edward Island, and Saskatchewan, the courts are empowered through legislation such as Alberta's Family Relief Act, Saskatchewan's Dependent Relief Act, Ontario's Succession Law Reform Act, and so on, to increase the share due to the surviving spouse, when the deceased dies intestate (without leaving a will). In cases of intestacy, the deceased's property is distributed according to the laws of the province. In most cases, the property is divided between the surviving spouse and the children, usually in a ratio of 50-50, but sometimes in a ratio of 1-3 to the surviving spouse and 2-3 to the children.

Provincial intestacy laws also take into account other scenarios, such as what happens when the deceased had no children, no surviving spouse, or a spouse and parents but no children, for example.

To prevent your property from being distributed according to law rather than according to your wishes, all you have to do is make a will and the property will be distributed according to your instructions.

Life insurance payments are paid directly to the named beneficiary and do not normally become part of the deceased's estate.

FORM OF WILL

In Canada, three types of wills are generally recognized as valid: 1) holograph wills; 2) English form wills; and 3) notarial wills. The international form of will, recognized by Alberta, Manitoba, Ontario, and Newfoundland, has not yet gained wide acceptance.

A holograph will is a document that is entirely written by the hand of the testator. To be valid, no other person may write or type on this will, not even to put on a date. Holograph wills are recognized as valid in all provinces except British Columbia, Prince Edward Island, and Nova Scotia.

An English form will is perhaps the most popular. To be valid, it must be signed by the testator in the presence of two competent witnesses who must also sign the will. English form wills may be typed, printed, or handwritten, but must bear the three requisite signatures.

Form is very important in drawing up a will, as some wills have been set aside because the testator did not sign in the presence of the witnesses as required by law (the witnesses signed the will while the testator was not present), or because the testator signed at the beginning or in the margin of the will instead of at the end.

A notarial will is valid in Quebec if signed before two notaries, or before one notary and two witnesses. Unlike other wills, notarial wills do not have to be probated, as they are drawn up by a judicial official (a notary) and the original is kept in his file. It is signed after the will was read out before the testator who then signs his name.

UNDUE INFLUENCE

Among the grounds for contesting a will are the lack of proper form, the incapacity of the testator, or undue influence. Undue influence may arise in cases where a person in a position of trust or confidence with the testator uses his position or influence to obtain a part of the testator's estate. To establish undue influence, it must be shown that fraud or coercion was used on the testator when he drew up his will, taking into account the fragile health, age, and mental capacity of the testator, if these elements are relevant.

In Ontario, the will of an 81-year-old man who left his farm to a 29-year-old female friend was contested by the man's family. Evidence at the trial showed that, though eccentric, the testator was alert and independent. Futhermore, the will was drawn up by a lawyer's secretary upon the testator's instructions, and was signed by him in the presence of the secretary and the 29-year-old woman. The court held that the will was valid as no undue influence could be proved. See also JOINT TENANCY; LIVING TRUST.

NAMING YOUR EXECUTOR

To guide your estate through probate court and carry out the provisions of your will, you will need to name an executor. Most people choose a spouse, relative, or friend, but you can name almost anyone of legal age, even your accountant or lawyer. Whoever the person is, he or she should be someone you can trust to carry out your wishes. Since your executor will be required to attend local court hearings and administer your estate, it is best to choose someone who lives nearby.

Serving as an executor requires a considerable amount of time and effort. Therefore, before naming someone, you should get her permission. You should also name an alternate executor in the event your first choice is unwilling or unable to serve when you die; otherwise, the court will have to name an executor. See also EXECUTOR AND ADMINISTRATOR; PROBATE.

NAMING A GUARDIAN

If you die while your children are minors, their other parent remains the legal guardian—unless he or she has been declared unfit for custody. If the children's other parent has died, or to protect against the possibility that he dies at the same time you do (or shortly thereafter), you should name a guardian in your will.

The guardian should be someone who can offer your children the kind of care and upbringing you yourself would give them. Usually, you will want to name a relative or close

---

CHECKLIST

Property You Cannot Will to Others

The law prevents some kinds of property from being passed to others in your will. The most common examples are:

■ **LIFE INSURANCE PROCEEDS.** Proceeds are paid directly to the beneficiary named in the policy. However, if you fail to name a beneficiary, the proceeds become part of your estate.

■ **FAMILY ASSETS.** In most provinces, certain property such as the matrimonial home and furnishings devolve to the surviving spouse and cannot be given to a third party.

■ **ASSETS HELD BY A TRUST.** Trust assets are distributed according to the terms of the trust.

■ **PROPERTY UNDER CONTRACT.** Suppose you have a contract to sell your car, but die before the paperwork is completed. The buyer can enforce the contract, and the car will not be included in your estate. However, the amount of money received from the buyer as payment will be included.

friend who is willing to accept the responsibility. You should also name an alternate guardian in case your first choice cannot or will not serve. See GUARDIAN AND WARD.

DISINHERITING A FAMILY MEMBER

If you want to disinherit a child, you should specify the child by name. If you fail to mention a child in your will, the law in most provinces assumes that this was an oversight, and the court may award the child the same share that she would have received if you had died without a will. See also DISINHERITANCE; PRENUPTIAL AGREEMENT.

SPECIFIC BEQUESTS

When you make a will, you can list specific bequests—gifts of clearly designated property, such as jewelry, furniture, specific amounts of cash, real estate, or just about anything else you own. However, if you no longer own the property at the time of your death, your designated beneficiary cannot claim the bequest. Suppose you leave your coin collection to your cousin Jim. Forgetting that you have made this bequest, you sell the collection. When you die, your cousin Jim cannot claim its monetary value.

YOUR RESIDUARY ESTATE

Your will should contain a clause relating to your residuary estate—that is, the remainder of your property after specific bequests have been made and the taxes and expenses of administering your estate have been paid.

♦ You must name a beneficiary for your residuary estate. If you fail to do so, your remaining property may be distributed as if you had died without a will, or it might even go to the state.

REVISING YOUR WILL

You cannot revise a will by altering it. Corrections, erasures, or deletions can invalidate it entirely. There are only two ways to revise an existing will legally. One is to create a document known as a codicil— an amendment to a will that must be prepared, signed, and witnessed in the same manner as a will. See also CODICIL.

The other way is to create a new will, which automatically revokes any previous wills and codicils. To avoid the possibility that your outdated will may be mistaken for a revised one, either tear it up, burn it, or write the word *revoked* or *canceled* across each page. It is also a good idea to state in your new will that it revokes all previous wills.

WHEN SHOULD YOU WRITE A NEW WILL?

Review your will at least once a year to make sure that it still reflects your property and wishes.

You should consider making a new will if one of the following happens:

◇ If you marry.

◇ If a child is born to you or if you adopt one.

◇ If you get divorced.

◇ If there is a change in your financial condition or that of your beneficiaries.

◇ If your spouse or some other beneficiary dies.

DOING IT YOURSELF

If your estate is relatively small, and if you plan to distribute it in a fairly straightforward manner, such as to your spouse and children, you may want to use a do-it-yourself will kit, available at many book and stationery stores, rather than hire a lawyer. Keep in mind, however, that if laws change, or if you complete the forms incorrectly, your self-made will could be invalid, and your estate could be treated as if you had died without making a will. See the EVERYDAY LEGAL FORMS section of this book.

See also ESTATE PLANNING; HOLOGRAPHIC WILL; TRUST.

WIRETAPPING

Wiretapping refers to the electronic surveillance of a person and his activities, without the person being aware that this is being done. The Protection of Privacy Act as well as the Criminal Code permit wiretapping by police, provided they have a judge's authorization for the search.

This precondition was set by the Supreme Court of Canada in 1984 after it had come to light that police wiretaps had been used not just on people suspected of having committed a crime or who were thought to be preparing to commit one, but also against political dissenters.

Once police have obtained appropriate prior authorization, they may intercept any type of private conversation. With the advance in audio-technology, conversations can now be recorded not only from phone calls, but from private offices (police may not wiretap lawyers' offices), jails, and automobiles. With the help of hyperbolic microphones, some conversations may be recorded from great distances.

Small, high-resolution video cameras, disguised as innocuous objects or otherwise hidden, are also used by police in electronic surveillance. Since suspects can now most likely legally refuse to take part in traditional lineups, the police have taken to making secret videotapes of certain suspects, so that a "video lineup" may be prepared. In October 1993, the Saskatchewan Court of Appeal declared such a secret videotape legal even though the suspect did not consent. Based on that ruling, a video lineup can be used instead of actually having the suspects physically present.

Police may get wiretap authorization from a superior court judge. Authorization can also be given by a county or district court judge if the application is signed by the attorney general of the province or the Solicitor General for Canada. An application must be supported by an affidavit of the police officer or prosecutor and must describe the offense being investigated, the facts that justify such a belief, what the police plan to monitor, and where and how this will take place.

A wiretap authorization is valid for up to 60 days and subject to renewal for a further 60 days.

Wiretapping is permitted only for serious offenses— murder, robbery, fraud, arson, perjury, drug trafficking, and assault causing bodily harm. It would not be considered for driving offenses, or summary conviction offenses such as common assault.

CHARTER IMPACT

Until relatively recently, no judicial authorization was required if one of the parties to a conversation consented to be wiretapped. An undercover policeman, pretending to be a friend or accomplice of a suspect, was free to tape any conversation between himself and the suspect.

This changed following a 1993 ruling by the Supreme Court of Canada. It declared it was unconstitutional to wiretap a suspect without his knowledge. Such an action was a violation of the Charter of Rights and Freedoms' guarantee that a person accused of a crime has the right to remain silent and not to incriminate himself.

The subject of a wiretap must be informed by the provincial attorney general or the Solicitor General for Canada that he was wiretapped. However, such notice need not be given for three years after the deed was done. At the end of each year, the Solicitor General and each provincial attorney general must publish or report all wiretap authorizations.

Even if the police have obtained the right to intercept your private conversations, you also have the right to take

whatever means are necessary to find and destroy any such wiretapping devices in your house, car, or phone. For a fee, a number of private companies will "sweep" your house or car for hidden microphones or other devices.

Interception of private conversations by the police, or by anyone else without proper authority, is punishable by up to five years' imprisonment. The victim of an illegally intercepted communication may be eligible for up to $5,000 in damages.

It is also illegal to possess, buy, or sell any device whose primary purpose is to intercept unauthorized private communications.

WOMEN'S RIGHTS

Although women have made a great deal of progress in their fight for equality with men in the last 100 years, much has yet to be accomplished. Pay equity legislation, guaranteed maternity leave, and special programs to hire women in formerly "men's jobs" such as in the construction industry and the armed forces are helping to improve the position of women in the workplace. Discrimination against women on the basis of their sex is also clearly prohibited under section 15 of the Charter of Rights and Freedoms and under many provincial human rights acts. Yet an equal-oppportunity society remains elusive.

IN THE WORKPLACE

Admittedly many women now are employed in what were once considered male trades and professions, but in the workplace overall, women tend to fill a disproportionate number of low-paid clerical, sales, and service occupations, while the better-paying, more attractive jobs remain largely male-dominated. The male-dominated professions usually pay better wages and offer better employment security.

Women, who are often subordinate to male employees and employers, earn 60 to 75 percent of the average male wage.

Women make up a larger percentage of the unemployed. Less than one in four women benefits from union protection.

Women's progress in the workplace has also been hampered by employment plans and policies that discriminate against them. In one case that went all the way to the Supreme Court of Canada, a woman pointed out that Canada Safeway Ltd.'s accident and sickness plan discriminated against her on the basis of sex. She had been denied full benefits under the company's health insurance plan when she had to take time off because of her pregnancy. The plan stipulated that the benefits would be reduced for pregnant women. The Court found this was discriminatory against women.

SEXUAL HARASSMENT

Women's fight for equality is also hindered by the fact that sexual harassment is still common in the workplace. This perpetuates the stereotype of women as sexual objects, rather than recognizing them as competent employees willing and able to do the job.

The courts have treated sexual harassment as a form of discrimination on the basis of sex, but the judgments have not been consistent. In the case of *Canada Post Corporation* v. *The Canadian Union of Postal Workers*, the court found that a woman who had been the victim of a single incident of sexual touching had been sexually harassed. But in the case of *Watt* v. *The Regional Municipality of Niagara*, the court dismissed the claim of a woman who had her legs forced open by her supervisor, who told her that she had an unpleasant smell between her legs. The court ruled that this was only an "isolated incident."

A 1993 study of Canada's legal system found that female law professors and lawyers still face obstacles their male counterparts do not.

WORKERS' COMPENSATION

Wadad was delivering bakery goods when her van was hit, and she suffered a broken arm. Thomas operates a punch press at a manufacturing plant and lost two fingers when the machine malfunctioned. And

Marilyn had surgery on her wrist to correct an injury resulting from her continual use of a computer keyboard at work. Since all three workers were injured on the job, they can apply for workers' compensation benefits.

Workers' compensation is a system set up in every province and territory to provide money awards to employees or their families when a worker is injured, becomes ill, or dies from a work-related activity. In the past, employees had to sue their employers in order to be compensated for job-related injuries. As plaintiffs, it was up to them to prove that the injury was the employers' fault. Employers often argued that employees assumed the risk of injury by taking the job, and the courts generally accepted this defense. Such rulings often left injured workers destitute.

Ontario was the first province to establish a worker's compensation act. It went into effect on Jan. 1, 1915, and its legislation is the basis of most workers' compensation laws across Canada. The act was based on seven important points.

◇ Workers' compensation should be universal in coverage.

◇ Employees should be entitled to compensation without regard to fault.

◇ Compensation should cover a worker's loss of earnings because of injury but not pain and suffering (pain and suffering are now covered in most jurisdictions).

◇ Most employers should bear the costs of the program

by paying into a central insurance fund.

◇ Compensation should be administered by an independent body and not the courts.

◇ Compensation should be secure, speedy, and last as long as the disability.

◇ Compensation should be paid for accidents as well as for industrial diseases.

Under workers' compensation, an employer must compensate an injured worker regardless of how his injury occurred. Generally, the only determinations to be made are whether the injury was work-related and the amount of compensation.

WHEN YOU CAN SUE

In return for workers' compensation, which is essentially a no-fault arrangement between workers and employers, injured workers generally forfeit the right to sue their employers. Quebec is the only province that allows an injured employee to sue an employer over a work-related injury. The employee may sue if the employer intentionally violated a safety standard or deliberately failed to inform workers about hazardous conditions.

In some cases, injured workers who are eligible for workers' compensation may sue a third party to the accident—the manufacturer of defective equipment, for example. Once the suit is launched, the employee cannot receive benefits from the workers' compensation board (WCB). It is advisable to get a ruling from the WCB before taking legal action, to find out if in fact you

---

ABC's

OF HIRING A LAWYER FOR A WORKERS' COMPENSATION CLAIM

If you have been harmed at the workplace and are filing a claim for workers' compensation, you have the right to be represented by a lawyer. You should consider hiring a lawyer familiar with workers' compensation legislation under any of the following circumstances:

■ If your claim for benefits is rejected.

■ If your claim has been accepted, but you believe you are not receiving the correct amount of compensation.

■ If you are fired, suspended, or otherwise disciplined for filing a workers' compensation claim.

■ If you are asked to participate in a vocational-rehabilitation program, despite the fact that you believe you are not physically able to do so.

■ If you are not satisfied with the medical treatment you are receiving from a doctor provided by the workers' compensation carrier.

■ If you are released from medical care and ordered to return to work before you believe you are able to do so.

---

can sue a third party in the particular circumstances of your case. Once you ask for a ruling, you cannot sue until the WCB responds.

Even though prohibited by workers' compensation rules from suing your employer, you may be able to sue one or more of your company's executives if you were injured because of a decision, act, or omission of one or more of the executives.

ELIGIBILITY

By law, employers either purchase workers' compensation insurance or contribute to a fund out of which benefits are paid to eligible employees. The various workers' compensation laws determine which employees are covered by

workers' compensation. Farm workers and household or domestic help are often excluded. Some employees are not covered because their companies have fewer than the minimum number of workers designated by the statute.

Other categories of workers who may be excluded include temporary or seasonal employees, highly paid workers, executives, and management personnel.

Depending on provincial law, volunteers and independent contractors (individuals who work for themselves) may also be ineligible.

FILING A CLAIM

When you are injured on the job, notify your supervisor or

employer promptly. Later you will have to fill out a claim form that asks for information about when, where, and how the accident happened and the extent of your injuries. You will then receive notification accepting or rejecting your claim. If the claim is accepted, weekly or monthly benefit cheques will be sent to you.

If your claim is rejected or partly denied, you can appeal the decision. If the appeal board rules against you, the decision can be appealed to a panel of WCB commissioners. In most cases, when the issue involved is the degree of incapacity, the question is settled by medical arbitration. In Alberta, Ontario, and Quebec , an injured worker can also seek help from the provincial ombudsman's office.

BENEFITS

Every province has adopted an extensive schedule that is used to determine the amount and length of benefits per injury. When reviewing an application for compensation, the Workers' Compensation Board looks at the severity of the injury, the prognosis for a full recovery, and the worker's salary. If you sprain your wrist, for example, your injury would be classified as a temporary partial disability, and you would receive benefits for the number of weeks allowed for that injury.

An accident that leaves you blind in one eye is considered to be a permanent partial injury. Benefits for permanent disabilities are paid out until you have received the maxi-

mum amount set by provincial law. If the accident leads to your death, your family will receive compensation.

Receiving workers' compensation benefits does not disqualify you from getting benefits from other private pension and disability insurance programs.

INJURIES NOT COVERED

An employee may be denied workers' compensation benefits if she lied about the condition of her health on her employment application. For example, if you lie about your bad back and the condition contributes to an accident, you may not receive compensation.

Accidents or injuries that are due to the willful misconduct of an employee are generally denied compensation. If you deliberately injure yourself, ignore safety instructions, fail to use safety equipment, or otherwise engage in willful misconduct, the employer may be released from any obligation to provide benefits. For example, if you remove a safety guard from a piece of dangerous equipment in violation of company policy and then injure yourself, you probably will not receive workers' compensation.

At one time, claims based on pranks or practical jokes were not recognized, but today the laws are more lenient. An employee might receive compensation for injuries if his employer knew he had no part in the prank.

Fights between co-workers may be excluded by provincial law, depending on the reason for the dispute. For example, if

the fight was related to personal matters and had nothing to do with the workplace, the claim is likely to be rejected.

INJURIES OUTSIDE THE WORKPLACE

Workers' compensation provides coverage for injuries that occur "in the course of employment." Does that include going to and from work?

The "coming and going rule" holds that an accident that occurs while a worker is traveling to work is work-related. If a salesperson is injured while combining business and personal errands, the workers' compensation board determines the primary reason for the trip. If it is business, the injury will be covered; if personal, it will be denied.

An injury that occurs during lunch hour may be covered only if the injured worker is on the company's premises. Injuries at company social gatherings and athletic activities are covered in some provinces if the events are part of the job, and especially if attendance is mandatory. Other provinces consider sports activities outside the scope of workers' compensation, and thus a worker may have to sue his employer to collect for any injuries.

WRONGFUL DEATH

When one person's intentional or negligent actions result in the death of another, a wrongful death has occurred. The spouse, children, or parents of the deceased may bring lawsuits for wrongful death against the wrongdoers to compensate for the loss of wages or other support they would have received had the person lived.

WHO CAN SUE

A plaintiff in a wrongful-death suit does not have to prove that he or she was completely dependent on the deceased for support, but only that the death results in a financial loss. For example, a woman whose husband dies in an automobile accident may have her own means of support, such as a job or an inheritance. But if she can show that her husband's income was put into a joint account and shared by them equally, she can recover for that loss. To help determine the deceased's potential income, the court will hear expert testimony from economists and statisticians.

To win a wrongful-death action, the plaintiff must prove that the defendant's actions were the "proximate," or immediate, cause of the death. Suppose you carelessly run into a man with your car and knock him to the pavement. He picks himself up, dusts himself off, and continues on his way. Two weeks later, he dies of a heart attack. To find you liable for his wrongful death, a court would have to be convinced that the incident on the street was the cause of the heart attack, a connection that would be hard to make.

But suppose that after getting up, the man fell down, struck his head on the pavement, and was knocked unconscious. He is ultimately revived, but dies from a brain injury several days later. In this case, the plaintiff would have a greater chance of proving the connection between the accident and the cause of death. See also JUDGMENT; LAWSUIT; LIABILITY; NEGLIGENCE; TORT.

FILING A SUIT

Wrongful-death suits are often taken on a contingency basis—that is, the lawyer will take the case for a percentage of the damages awarded. But first the lawyer will determine whether the defendant has assets or liability insurance that he can use to pay any damages the court may order. Some people who are responsible for wrongful deaths are "judgment proof"—that is, they have no assets or insurance that can be used to pay compensation. See also DAMAGES.

WRONGFUL LIFE

"I wish I'd never been born." Most people who say this do not really mean it, but some people have sued persons who, they claim, wrongfully allowed them to be born. These lawsuits, sometimes referred to as wrongful-life cases, are usually brought by or on behalf of severely disabled or disfigured children against physicians who allegedly were negligent in failing to prevent their birth.

Wrongful-life lawsuits are generally disallowed by the courts. Most courts have found that no person has a right not to be born, and therefore no person has grounds to sue anyone for not preventing his birth. Likewise, many courts have found that no one has the right to be born without defects. Thus, even a child born with severe abnormalities may not sue a doctor for his birth and the pain and suffering caused by his disability.

However, a British Columbia woman and her seven-year old daughter were awarded almost $900,000 because the child was born severely disfigured as a result of a bungled abortion. But in a case from the Maritimes, in which a doctor was sued by the mother of a child born after the doctor had performed a tubal ligation to prevent pregnancy, the court dismissed the case. It ruled that the doctor did not guarantee results. Also, the court could not find that the birth of a child was a "fault," or tort.

WRONGFUL PREGNANCY

In some cases, parents may bring an unwanted-pregnancy suit against doctors or hospitals, when negligence results in an unplanned and unwanted pregnancy. When the botched performance of a sterilization procedure, such as a tubal ligation or a vasectomy, results in the conception of a child, some courts will allow the parents to sue the doctor who made the mistake.

In these cases, the parents may be compensated for the cost of the pregnancy and birth, the pain and suffering associated with the pregnancy and birth (as well as the failed surgical procedure), and the loss of the mother's wages due to the pregnancy and birth.

X MARK

An X mark serves as a signature for someone who cannot write because he is either illiterate or physically disabled. This type of signature must usually be witnessed by a competent person who can testify that it is authentic.

X-RATED MATERIAL

In response to concerns about the language, violence, and sexual content of movies, the motion-picture industry established a rating system to indicate the suitability of films for certain age groups. Films are rated G (suitable for audiences of all ages), PG (parental guidance required), PG-13 (contains matter unsuitable for children under age 13), R (restricted to people age 17 or older unless accompanied by an adult), and NC-17 (no one under 17 admitted).

Although the X rating used for adult films has no legal definition, a theater or video store that allows minors to view or purchase X-rated materials may be charged with contributing to the delinquency of a minor or distributing obscene materials to a minor.

See also OBSCENITY; PORNOGRAPHY.

YOUNG OFFENDER

Prior to 1984, young people in conflict with the law were dealt with under the provisions of the Juvenile Delinquents Act. At its inception in 1908, this legislation was seen as a progressive development in the treatment of children involved in crime. It was based on the idea that delinquent behavior reflected a troubled social environment. Consequently, until 1984, the juvenile justice system worked closely with the child welfare system in order to rehabilitate troubled youth.

Children found to be delinquents were often committed to children's aid societies, industrial schools, or foster homes. Juvenile court judges and custodial officials were granted wide discretion to make decisions concerning a child's best interests. As a result that punishment for a similar offense could vary greatly from case to case. The system was also very informal, and concepts such as the right to counsel and the right to bail were often disregarded.

Eventually, as youth crime continued to be a problem, it was perceived that the Juvenile Delinquents Act was ineffective in reforming troubled children. So, in 1984, the act was repealed and replaced by the Young Offenders Act. Under its provisions, treatment of young offenders now resembles more closely the criminal justice system to which adults are subject. Rights, responsibility and accountability are now the underlying concepts.

For this reason, children must be at least 12 years old to be convicted of an offense, under the Young Offenders Act, whereas the Juvenile Delinquents Act dealt with wrongdoers as young as seven. While concerns for child welfare continue to be important, the present legislation is primarily concerned with imposing criminal sanctions.

Despite these reforms, the treatment of young offenders continues to elicit public criticism. At the time of writing, a federal discussion paper had been released outlining possible changes to the Young Offenders Act. Lowering the minimum and maximum age at which a young person may be charged under the act, automatic transfers to adult court in certain cases, longer sentences, and the right to publish the names of young offenders are among the proposals.

LEGAL RIGHTS

Just as is the case with adults confronted by the justice system, the Young Offenders Act entitles young accused to all the rights and freedoms guaranteed to Canadians under the Charter of Rights and Freedoms. For example, teenagers have the right to counsel and to legal aid. Young people have the right to be informed of their rights and freedoms when they come into contact with the justice system and to participate in court matters which concern them. The act specifies that "young persons should have special guarantees of their rights and freedoms," which may be interpreted as requiring police officers and other judicial officials to take extra steps to ensure that a teenager's rights are respected.

In 1991, an Ontario court held that a pretrial delay for cases involving teenagers must not exceed four months. This is significantly less than the maximum delay accepted by courts in adult cases.

PUNISHMENT

Although young offenders are responsible for their actions, the law chooses to treat them differently from adults. This is illustrated by the principle of limited accountability, which is central to the Young Offenders Act. The maximum punishment for an adolescent found guilty of a crime in youth court is a $1,000 fine, or five years' imprisonment. (Three years was the maximum possible sentence up to 1992, when the act was amended in response to public concern that young offenders were being treated too softly.) Monetary compensation to victims, community service work, and probation are other forms of punishment possible under the act.

ADULT COURT

In certain cases, the law permits a young offender to be tried in adult court. This can occur only when the accused is at least 14 years of age and is charged with a serious offense, such as murder.

A transfer hearing will be held to determine whether the move to adult court is appropriate. The hearing will focus on the seriousness of the offense; the child's age, character, and background; previous situations in which the child was guilty; what treatment facilities are available; and statements by the accused and the public prosecutor.

A teenager found guilty of murder in adult court may receive a life sentence. Nevertheless, he will be eligible for parole after 5 or 10 years. An adult receiving the same sentence would not be eligible for parole for 10 to 25 years.

ALTERNATIVE MEASURES

In certain cases, young offenders may be offered an alternative to the formal process of going to court for trial. The Young Offenders Act includes provisions for certain alternative measures, such as participating in treatment programs.

The opportunity to enter into such a program often hinges on how the prosecutor or the police perceive the offender—whether they believe admission to the program is appropriate, given the evidence as well as society's interests. If they approve, the young person will be interviewed by social workers or government personnel. They, in turn, may make recommendations based on the young person's needs and his willingness, or otherwise, to take part.

Participation in an alternative measures program involves a young offender acknowledging that he accepts responsibility for his acts. He may be required to perform community service work, or to write essays or letters of apology.

The exact nature of these programs varies widely from province to province. Each one has a great deal of latitude in how they are set up. In fact, the Supreme Court of Canada has ruled that a province is not even required to have such programs.

Experts agree, however, that where these programs exist, they should not be viewed as a simple way of avoiding court, nor are they equivalent to having the charge withdrawn. The judge must be told if a young offender before the court had previously participated in an alternative measures program. The courts also regard accepting responsibility—the primary requirement for participation in alternative measures—as equivalent to admitting legal guilt.

PARENTS

The Young Offenders Act aims to encourage parental involvement in young offender proceedings. Parents must be notified when their child is detained in custody, or when the child had been charged and released pending a court date. Before making statements, young persons must be given a reasonable opportunity to consult with a parent, lawyer, or other appropriate adult. Otherwise, the statements will be inadmissible as evidence in court.

Parents have the right to be heard at hearings to determine a young offender's punishment, and before a young person's case is transferred to adult court. In some cases, the child may be released into a parent's custody before or after the trial.

RECORDS

The Young Offenders Act is concerned with safeguarding the privacy and reputation of young offenders. Therefore, court documents and transcripts contain only the initials of those involved. Young per-

sons found guilty of an offense receive a youth court record and not a criminal record, and public access to these documents is restricted. There are, however, instances where the records may be consulted by a person having a valid interest. For example, in the case of a job which involves working with children, the employer would probably have a valid interest in finding out if the young person has ever been found guilty of the sexual assault of a child.

Once the punishment has been served, the young person is considered not to have been found guilty of any offense. In addition, five years from the time the punishment is completed, he or she is deemed not to have committed the offense, and records relating to the incident are destroyed.

It should be noted, however, that if a young offender commits a crime as an adult, reference may be made to the fact that he was a young offender.

Z MARK

A Z mark is used to fill in blank spaces on a legal document, such as a contract, to prevent an unauthorized person from filling in those spaces at a later time, thereby changing the terms of the contract.

ZONING

Virtually every city has zoning ordinances to regulate real estate use. By prohibiting industrial development in a residential area, the city can minimize traffic and pollution overall. By prohibiting or restricting the development of shopping malls, a municipality can help preserve both the appearance and ambience of a community. Limiting the use of property in a particular area to agricultural, residential, industrial, or commercial uses, or to some combination thereof, can help maintain property values.

Zoning regulations may be general or specific. General regulations may prohibit buildings whose designs are inconsistent with the area's existing architecture. Specific regulations may establish a minimum number of off-street parking spaces for each newly constructed building.

Certain uses of property that do not conform to current zoning plans may be allowed. If the property was used a certain way before current zoning regulations were enacted, that use may be allowed to continue under the "nonconforming use" exception. Another exception may be made when a property owner wants to alter his property in a way that is not permitted by local zoning regulations. In this event, he may apply for a "variance"—official permission to use the property in a way that would normally violate the zoning laws. See also NONCONFORMING USE; VARIANCE.

The mailing addresses listed here are for agencies, organizations, and companies mentioned throughout the A-to-Z portion of the book. Addresses appear in the same order as in the text, so look under A for any mentioned in the A entries, and so on. When an organization is cited in more than one section, you will be referred to the letter under which the address is given. For example, Industry Canada's Bureau of Competition Policy is included in the entries for Bait and Switch and Pyramid Sales Scheme. You will find the address under B, and a cross-reference under P. For easy reference, addresses have been alphabetized under each letter.

A

Air Transport Association of America
1301 Pennsylvania Ave.,
   Suite 1100
Washington, D.C. 20004-7017

Canadian Bar Association
50 O'Connor St., Suite 902
Ottawa, Ont. K1P 6L2

Canadian Red Cross Society
1800 Alta Vista Dr.
Ottawa, Ont. K1G 4J5

International Committee of the Red Cross (ICRC)
17, avenue de la Paix
CH-1202 Geneva, Switzerland

International Social Service
10, rue Alfred-Vincent
CH-1201 Geneva, Switzerland

International Social Service Canada
55 Parkdale Ave.
Ottawa, Ont. K1Y 1E5

Missing Children's Network Canada
828 Decarie Blvd., Suite 201
St. Laurent, Que. H4L 3L9

Royal Military College Canada
Kingston, Ont. K7K 5L0

B

Canadian Bankers' Association
Commerce Crt. W., Suite 3000
Toronto, Ont. M5L 1G2

Canadian Transfer Association
688 Mapleview Dr. E.
Stroud, Ont. L0L 2M0

◆ **Director of Investigation and Research**
Bureau of Competition Policy
Industry Canada
Place du Portage, Phase I,
   21st Floor
50 Victoria St.
Hull, Que. K1A 0C9

Superintendent of Financial Institutions Canada
255 Albert St., 16th Floor
Ottawa, Ont. K1A 0H2

C

Associated Credit Bureaus of Canada
80 Bloor St. W., Suite 900
Toronto, Ont. M5S 2V1

Canada Development Investment Corporation (CDIC)
Scotia Plaza, Suite 2730
P.O. Box 320
Toronto, Ont. M5H 3Y2

Canada Mortgage and Housing Corporation
700 Montreal Rd.
Ottawa, Ont. K1A 0P7

Canadian Security Intelligence Service (CSIS)
P.O. Box 9732, Stn. T
Ottawa, Ont. K1G 0H8

Copyright and Industrial Design Branch
Industry Canada
Place du Portage, Phase I
50 Victoria St.
Hull, Que. K1A 0C9

Crime Compensation Board
J.E. Brownlee Bldg., 7th Floor
10365–97th St.
Edmonton, Alta. T5J 3W7
◆

◆ **Criminal Injuries Compensation Board**
439 University Ave., 4th Floor
Toronto, Ont. M5G 1Y8

Criminal Injury Compensation
6951 Westminster Hwy.
Richmond, B.C. V7C 1C6

Criminal Injury Compensation Board
763 Portage Ave.
Winnipeg, Man. R3G 0N3

Debtor Assistance Branch
Ministry of Housing, Recreation
   and Consumer Services
1019 Wharf St.
Victoria, B.C. V8V 1X4

Department of Citizenship and Immigration
Phase IV, Place du Portage
Ottawa, Ont. K1A 0J9

Department of Justice
Justice Building
Wellington and Kent Sts.
Ottawa, Ont. K1A 0H8

Disnat
2020 University, 9th Floor
Montreal, Que. H3A 2A5

Green Line Service (TD Bank)
Box 1, Toronto Dominion Centre
Toronto, Ont. M5K 1A2

Marathon Brokerage
(See **Green Line Service** above.)

National Library of Canada
395 Wellington St.
Ottawa, Ont. K1A 0N4

Ontario Association of Credit Counseling
5 Mountain St.
◆ Grimsby, Ont. L3M 4G5

Permissions Officer
Canadian Government
  Publications Centre
45 Sacré-Cœur Blvd.
Hull, Que. K1A 0S9

**Quebec Deposit Insurance
Board/Régie de l'Assurance-
dépôts du Québec**
800, Place d'Youville
Quebec, Que. G1R 4Y5

Registrar of Citizenship
Department of Citizenship
  and Immigration
Phase IV, Place du Portage
Ottawa, Ont. K1A 0J9

E/F

**Bristish Columbia Securities
Commission**
865 Hornby St. Suite 1100
Vancouver, B.C. V6Z 2H4

**Canadian Association of
Financial Planners**
60 St. Clair Ave. E., Suite 510
Toronto, Ont. M4T 1N5

**The Law Society of Upper
Canada**
Osgoode Hall
130 Queen St. W.
Toronto, Ont. M5H 2N6

**Ontario Securities
Commission**
20 Queen St. W., Suite 800
Toronto, Ont. M5H 3S8

**Quebec Securities
Commission/Commission
des valeurs mobilières
du Québec (CVMQ)**
800 Square Victoria, 17th Floor
P.O. Box 246
Stock Exchange Tower
Montreal, Que. H4Z 2K1

**Superintendent of Financial
Institutions Canada**
See under **B**

G

Registrar of Divorces
161 Elgin St., 2nd Floor
Family Division
Ottawa, Ont. K2P 2K1

◆ H/I

**Canadian Chamber of
Commerce**
55 Metcalfe St., Suite 1160
Ottawa, Ont. K1P 6N4

**Canadian Federation of
Independent Business**
414 Yonge St., Suite 401
Toronto, Ont. M2P 2A6

**Federal Business
Development Bank**
800 Victoria Sq.
Montreal, Que. H4Z 1L4

**Immigration and Refugee
Board**
240 Bank St.
Ottawa, Ont. K1A 0K1

Insurance Bureau of Canada
181 University Ave.
13th Floor, Suite 1300
Toronto, Ont. M5H 3M7

**Ontario Development
Corporation**
56 Wellesley St. W.
Toronto, Ont. M7A 2E7

L

Canadian Bar Association
See under **A**

**Lobbyists Registration
Branch**
Industry Canada
Place du Portage, Phase II,
  4th Floor
165 Hôtel de Ville St.
Hull, Que. K1A 0C9

M/N

**Canadian Direct Marketing
Association**
1 Concord Gate, Suite 607
Don Mills, Ont. M3C 3N6

**Canadian Medical Protective
Association**
P.O. Box 8225
Ottawa, Ont. K1G 3H7

◆ Legal Advisory Division
Department of Foreign Affairs
  and International Trade
125 Sussex Dr.
Ottawa, Ont. K1A 0G2

O/P

**Canada Communication
Group**
45 Sacré-Cœur Blvd.
Hull, Que. K1A 0S7

**Canadian Industrial
Innovation Centre/Waterloo**
156 Columbia St. W.
Waterloo, Ont. N2L 3L3

**Canadian Intellectual
Property Office**
Commissioner of Patents
Industry Canada
Place du Portage
50 Victoria St.
Hull, Que. K1A 0C9

**Canadian Radio-Television
and Telecommunications
Commission (CRTC)**
Terrasses de la Chaudière
1 Promenade du Portage
Central Building
Hull, Que. K1A 0N2

**Clemency and Pardons
Division**
National Parole Board
Sir Wilfrid Laurier Bldg.
340 Laurier Ave. W.
Ottawa, Ont. K1A 0R1

**Director of Investigation and
Research**
Bureau of Competition Policy
Industry Canada
See under **B**

National Research Council
Headquarters, Building M-58
Montreal Road
Ottawa, Ont. K1A 0R6

Passport Bureau
Place du Centre, 6th Floor
200 Promenade du Portage
Hull, Que. J8X 4B7

Q/R

Canadian Real Estate Association
Place de Ville, Tower A
320 Queen St., Suite 2100
Ottawa, Ont. K1R 5A3

Royal Canadian Mounted Police
Headquarters
1200 Vanier Parkway
Ottawa, Ont. K1A 0R2

S

British Columbia International Arbitration Centre
670-999 Canada Place
Vancouver, B.C. V6C 2E2

Commission des valeurs mobilières du Québec (CVMQ)
See under **E/F**

Director of Investigation and Research
Bureau of Competition Policy
Industry Canada
See under **B**

Investment Dealers Association of Canada
Standard Life Bldg.
121 King St. W., Suite 1600
Toronto, Ont. M5H 3T9

Investment Funds Institute of Canada
80 Bond St., Main Floor
Toronto, Ont. M5B 1X8

Ontario Securities Commission
See under **E/F**

The Private Court
150 King St. W., Suite 2512
Toronto, Ont. M5H 3T9

T

BC Residential Tenancy Branch
5021 Kingsway, 4th Floor
Burnaby, B.C. V5H 4A5

◆ **Canadian Standards Association**
178 Rexdale Blvd.
Rexdale, Ont. M9W 1R3

New Brunswick Rentalsman's Office
300 St. Mary St.
Fredericton, N.B. E3B 5H1

N.S. Residential Tenancy Board
5151 Terminal Rd., 1st Floor
P.O. Box 998
Halifax, N.S. B3J 2X3

Ontario Ministry of Housing
777 Bay St.
Toronto, Ont. M5G 2E5

Ontario Rent Control Programs
415 Yonge St., 19th Floor
Toronto, Ont. M5B 2E7

Product Safety Bureau
Health Canada
Place du Portage, Phase I,
17th Floor, Zone 4
50 Victoria St.
Hull, Que. K1A 0C9

Régie du logement du Québec
1, rue Notre-Dame est, 11ᵉ étage
Montréal, Qué. H2Y 1B6

Registrar of Trade Marks
50 Victoria St.
Hull, Que. K1A 0C9

Underwriters' Laboratories of Canada
7 Crouse Rd.
Scarborough, Ont. M1R 3A9

U

Competition Tribunal
Royal Bank Centre
90 Sparks St.
P.O. Box 1899, Stn. B
Ottawa, Ont. K1P 5R5

Unemployment Insurance Office
Over 450 offices across Canada.
Call your local Canada employment office for assistance.

◆ **V**

Army Benevolent Fund
284 Wellington St.
Ottawa, Ont. K1A 0P4

Canada Pension Commission
Daniel J. MacDonald Bldg.
P.O. Box 9900
Charlottetown, P.E.I. C1A 8V6

Last Post Fund
685 Cathcart St., Suite 902
Montreal, Que. H3B 1M7

Old Age Pension
Income Security Programs
Branch
Place Vanier, 355 River Rd.
Vanier, Ont. K1A 0L1

RCMP
See under **Q/R**

Royal Canadian Air Force Benevolent Fund
424 Metcalfe St.
Ottawa, Ont. K2P 2C3

Royal Canadian Navy Benevolent Fund
P.O. Box 505
Ottawa, Ont. K1P 5P6

The Royal Canadian Legion
359 Kent St.
Ottawa, Ont. K2P 0R7

Veterans' Affairs Canada
Daniel J. MacDonald Bldg.
161 Grafton St.
P.O. Box 7700
Charlottetown, P.E.I. C1A 8M9

W

Canadian Centre for Occupational Health and Safety
250 Main St. E.
Hamilton, Ont. L8N 1H6

Consumer Bureau
Industry Canada
Place du Portage, Phase I
50 Victoria St.
Hull, Que. K1A 0C9
(Each province has its own consumer protection office.)

The terms included in this glossary should be regarded as supplementary to those that already appear as entry titles in the A-to-Z text. If you cannot find a word in the glossary, look for it in the index or in the text itself. To help the reader, many glossary entries include cross-references to articles in the main text. But note that, in order to keep the main text free of legal jargon, terms that appear in the glossary do not necessarily appear in the main text. The stressed parts of the words are indicated in capital letters.

Ab initio (*ab in-ISH-ee-oh*) A Latin phrase meaning "from the beginning." For example, to say that a marriage was unlawful ab initio means that the marriage was never valid in the first place.

Abate To decrease, reduce, remove, or destroy. For example, to abate a bequest (a gift made to someone through a will) is to reduce it because there are not enough funds in the estate to pay the full amount. To abate a nuisance is to remove or destroy whatever causes it.

Abrogate To abolish. A statute is abrogated, for example, if the legislature repeals it or a court declares it unconstitutional.

Abscond To flee from a court's area of authority, or to hide within it to avoid prosecution.

Abstract of title A short history of the ownership of a piece of real estate, recording all its sales and transfers, its previous owners, the liens and other liabilities against the property, and any other information a prospective buyer would need to know to be sure of its rightful owner. See CLOSING, REAL ESTATE; TITLE INSURANCE.

Act of God An unforeseeable event, such as a tornado or an earthquake, which is due to natural causes. Also known as *force majeure*. If a person is unable to fulfill the terms of a contract because of an act of God, he will usually be relieved of his contractual obligations.

Action A legal proceeding, such as a civil lawsuit or criminal trial, held to enforce or protect someone's right, to redress or prevent a wrong, or to punish a crime. See CRIMINAL PROCEDURE; LAWSUIT.

Ad damnum (*add DAM-num*) A Latin phrase meaning "to the damage," referring to the clause in a civil complaint that states the amount of damages, or money, demanded by the plaintiff. See DAMAGES.

Ad hoc (*add HOCK*) A Latin phrase meaning "for this," that is, for a particular purpose. For example, an ad hoc committee is created for one specific purpose.

Addendum An item or list of items added to a document.

Ademption An act by which a person who has made his will sells, gives away, or uses up a bequest he has made to someone, so that it is no longer part of the will. Suppose your uncle leaves you his 1988 Buick in his will, but then sells it. This is an ademption and when he dies you cannot claim the car or anything else to replace it. See WILL.

Adjudication The judgment or decree of a court and the legal process by which the decision is reached.

Advocate A person who assists, advises, or pleads the cause of another person in court; a lawyer or counselor. See LAWYER.

Affiant A person who makes statements in an affidavit, and swears to the truth of those statements. See AFFIDAVIT.

Aggravated Severe; intensified. For example, someone who attacks another person with a dangerous weapon can be charged with aggravated assault. It is a more serious charge than simple assault, which involves simply striking another person.

Aka An abbreviation for "also known as." Often used by police to indicate a criminal's alias, or alternate name.

Alibi From the Latin word for "elsewhere," referring to a defense by which an accused person tries to establish his innocence by showing that he was somewhere else at the time of the crime.

Allegation An accusation made by either party to a lawsuit, indicating what that party intends to prove. See LAWSUIT.

Amicus curiae (*ah-MEE-kus CURE-ee-eye*) A Latin term meaning "friend of the court," referring to a person or organization that, although not involved in a lawsuit, may be affected by the court's decision and is therefore permitted to point out information that might be helpful to the court in making a decision.

Amortization The payment of a mortgage or other debt in installments over a specified period. Amortization is calculated by adding the amount owed (the principal) to the amount of interest that will be paid over the life of the loan, and then dividing the total by the number of payments to be made. See MORTGAGE.

Appurtenant Belonging or attached to something else more important. For example, a garage is appurtenant to the main house. See HOME BUYING AND SELLING.

Arbitrary and capricious A term used to describe a decision of an agency or a court that is made with willful disregard for the facts and circumstances of the case and that is cause for an appeal to a higher court.

Attest To affirm that something, such as a signature or document, is either authentic or true.

Barratry The offense of repeatedly provoking quarrels or unnecessary lawsuits. A lawyer who tries to generate lawsuits for his own profit is guilty of barratry and may be disbarred. See *Champerty*.

Bearer A person who is in possession of a negotiable document, such as a bill, note, or cheque, that is payable to the person who holds it. See BOND; CHEQUE; COMMERCIAL PAPER.

Bench warrant An order issued by a sitting judge (hence the word *bench*) permitting law enforcement officials to arrest someone in order to compel him to appear in court. A bench warrant may be issued for a witness who has been subpoenaed, a suspect who has been indicted, or a person charged with contempt of court. See ARREST.

Beneficiary A person or organization designated to receive certain property or money, such as the proceeds from an estate or a life insurance policy. See LIFE INSURANCE; WILL.

Bequest A gift of money or other personal property (but not real estate) left to someone through a will. See WILL.

Bill of lading A receipt issued by a railway, trucker, or other transport company showing which goods have been received for shipment; terms of the contract may also be included.

Bill of particulars A document listing the details of charges being brought against a defendant in a lawsuit. See CRIMINAL PROCEDURE; LAWSUIT.

Binding authority The relevant statutes and legal precedents a judge must follow when he rules on a case.

Bona fide (*bone-uh fide*) A Latin phrase meaning "in good faith," referring to an action performed honestly, with no intent to deceive or defraud. See BAD FAITH; CONTRACT; GOOD FAITH.

Brief A lawyer's written summary of the facts, arguments, and legal precedents he intends to use to support his case. See CRIMINAL PROCEDURE; LAWSUIT.

Bylaws A set of rules adopted by a corporation or other organization, which governs the way it does business. See COOPERATIVE APARTMENT; CORPORATION.

Canon law The body of rules and religious doctrines adopted by a church to govern the institution and its members. It is not related to civil or common law, which affect the public at large.

Capacity The qualifications, such as age or competency, that are necessary for a person's actions to be legally permitted and recognized. Testamentary capacity, for example, refers to someone's legal ability to make a will. See COMPETENCY; WILL.

Causa mortis (*COW-za MORE-tis*) A Latin phrase meaning "because of death," referring to a gift given by someone because he believes he is near death. If the person dies, the gift takes effect; if he recovers, it may be revoked. See GIFT.

Caveat emptor (*KAV-ee-at EMP-tor*) A Latin phrase meaning "let the buyer beware." It refers to the risk a consumer assumes when purchasing goods and his responsibility to be cautious. See CONSUMER PROTECTION.

Cease and desist order An order issued by a court or government administrative agency directing a person or business to discontinue an illegal practice. See FALSE ADVERTISING.

Certiorari (*sir-shee-er-RAH-ree*) A Latin term meaning "to be informed of," referring to a writ, or order, from a higher court to a lower one demanding a certified record of its proceedings in a case that is under review.

Chain of title The succession of transfers of a particular piece of real estate from its original source to its present owner.

Champerty (*CHAM por too*) An arrangement in which one person, such as a lawyer, agrees to pay another person's expenses in a lawsuit in exchange for part of the settlement. Champerty is generally prohibited because it leads to unnecessary litigation. See also CONTINGENT FEE.

Chattel An article of personal property which is not real estate, such as money, stocks, jewelry, or cars. See CHATTEL MORTGAGE.

Civil law A system of law based on a legislated code rather than individual statutes and previous cases (precedents), which form the basis of common law. In Canada, Quebec is the only province that uses civil law, which is derived from Roman law.

Claim A request or demand for some right or supposed right. Also, the thing that is requested, such as a piece of land.

Closed shop A business that hires only union members. See LABOR UNION.

Codification The act or process by which the laws of a state or country are systematically collected and organized into a body of rules, called a code.

Coinsurance A system of insurance that divides risk between the insurer and the insured. For example, if you have a property insurance policy that pays only 80 percent of your loss up to a specified amount, the 20 percent you pay is the coinsurance. See HOMEOWNERS' INSURANCE.

Comity The principle that the courts of one province or locality will give full acceptance to the judicial decisions of another, not because of any obligation, but out of mutual respect. When a provincial court refuses to hear a law suit because the parties to it are involved in an identical suit in another province, for example, it is acting through comity.

Complainant The party that petitions the court to commence a legal action. In civil suits the complainant, or person who brings suit, is often called the plaintiff. In criminal cases the complainant is the Crown and is called the prosecution. See CRIMINAL PROCEDURE; LAWSUIT.

Concealment The act of hiding or withholding information. A party to an insurance contract is guilty of concealment if he fails to disclose or tries to suppress facts that he has a legal duty to reveal.

Confiscate To seize property from someone because he is using it illegally or does not own it.

Consanguinity The kinship, or blood relationship, between people who share a common ancestor. Consanguinity is a consideration in inheritance rights and in eligibility for marriage (which is forbidden between parent and child, brother and sister, and grandparent and grandchild). See also MARRIAGE.

Consortium The right of each spouse to the care, affection, companionship, and cooperation of the other. If one spouse is unable to provide these essentials because he is killed or injured by a third person, the other spouse can sue the third party for loss of consortium.

Contingent Dependent on a future event whose outcome is unknown. A gift left in a will, for example, may be contingent on certain actions or conditions, or a lawyer's fee may be contingent on the outcome of the case. See CONTINGENT FEE.

Contraband Goods that are illegal to import or export over national borders, such as narcotics.

Convey To transfer the title to (ownership of) property from one person to another, usually by deed. See DEED.

Coroner A city or county official who conducts investigations of unexplained or violent deaths and takes charge of unclaimed bodies. See AUTOPSY.

Corpus delicti (*CORE-pus di-LICK-tie*) Latin for "the body of the crime," referring to the physical evidence that indicates that a crime was committed, such as a body with a gunshot wound or a cache of stolen goods.

Curfew A regulation issued by public authorities forbidding people to be on the streets at designated hours. See ASSEMBLY, RIGHT OF.

Curtesy The right by which a man is entitled to a share in his wife's property after her death. See DOWER AND CURTESY.

Cy pres (*sigh PRAY*) A French phrase meaning "as nearly as possible," referring to the doctrine by which a gift or trust that cannot be administered according to the exact wishes of the deceased may be administered as closely as possible to those wishes. See EXECUTOR AND ADMINISTRATOR; WILL.

De facto (*day FACK-toe*) A Latin phrase meaning "in fact," referring to a government, corporation, or situation that is not legitimate. A de facto government, for example, is one that attains power by an illegal overthrow of the legitimate government. The term is the opposite of *de jure*.

De jure (*day JOOR-ay*) A Latin phrase meaning "by right," "legal," or "legitimate." The government of Canada, which was established according to a constitution and abides by it, is a de jure government. *De jure* is the opposite of *de facto*.

De minimis (*day MIN-i-mis*) A Latin phrase meaning "concerning minor things." The term is used to refer to a violation so insignificant that it should be overlooked in the interest of justice.

Debenture A document, such as a bond or promissory note, which acknowledges that a debt is owed and will be paid, usually without any collateral.

Deceit A trick, false statement, or pretense by which one person

intentionally misleads another, who then suffers injury or damage as a result. See FRAUD.

Declarant A person who makes a declaration, particularly someone who makes a living will. See LIVING WILL.

Declaratory judgment A judgment that formally states the duties, responsibilities, rights, or status of the parties involved in a lawsuit without ordering any action to be taken. For example, a court may issue a declaratory judgment stating that a particular person is the true and rightful owner of a piece of real estate when its ownership is disputed.

Decree The decision of a court in a matter of equity, divorce, or probate. The terms *decree* and *judgment* are often used interchangeably.

Dedication A landowner's donation of private property for public use, as when he sets aside several acres of his land for a park.

Defendant A person or organization that is being prosecuted for a crime or sued in a lawsuit.

Defraud To cheat, trick, or swindle a person; to deprive a person of his property, interest, or estate by deceit. See FRAUD; SCAMS AND SWINDLES.

Demurrer A statement by the defendant in a lawsuit claiming that even though the plaintiff's accusations are true, they are not sufficient to compel the defendant to come to court to answer them. See LAWSUIT.

Dictum An incidental comment by a judge that is not directly relevant to the case at hand.

Dismissal without prejudice The cancellation of an action or proceeding in a way that does not prevent the plaintiff from bringing another lawsuit for the same reason. See LAWSUIT.

Docket The list of cases scheduled to be tried before a court.

The term is used interchangeably with *calendar*. See CALENDAR.

Ejectment The name of a lawsuit initiated to determine who owns a particular piece of land. The plaintiff claims ownership of the property even though the defendant currently possesses it.

Eminent domain Also known as expropriation. The power vested in the government to take private property for public use, without the consent of the owner, but the owner must be paid just compensation.

En banc (*on BONK*) A French phrase meaning "by the full bench (court)," referring to a court session attended by a full complement of judges. For example, a routine Supreme Court of Canada case might be heard by three judges out of a possible nine; but in an en banc hearing all nine judges would participate. En banc proceedings are usually reserved for important cases that establish far-reaching precedents.

Encumbrance Any outstanding claim on real estate that lessens its value or bars its sale, such as a mechanic's lien, or unpaid tax. See HOME BUYING AND SELLING.

Estate Everything a person owns or has a financial interest in; the property and possessions of a deceased or bankrupt person.

Estoppel (*es-TOP-el*) A legal prohibition that prevents a person from denying a statement previously made or changing an action already taken if it will cause loss or injury to another person who relied on that statement or action. Suppose that an insurance agent sends a policy application and fee to the company, which accepts them and issues a policy. The company later refuses to honor a legitimate claim, arguing that the agent was not authorized to sell that kind of policy. The company is estopped from making such a claim by its prior acceptance of the agent's actions.

♦ **Et al.** (*et AHL*) An abbreviation for the Latin phrase *et alii*, meaning "and others." It is often used to indicate a number of defendants in a lawsuit, as in "the Crown v. Williams et al."

Ex parte (*ex PAR-tay*) A Latin phrase meaning "from one party only." The term describes a legal proceeding that takes place without the adversary party being present. For example, if one party does not answer to the demand of another in a lawsuit, a judgment may be rendered against him "ex parte."

Ex post facto Latin for "after the fact," referring to a law that makes an act punishable as a crime even though the act was committed before the law was passed. Ex post facto laws are unconstitutional.

Excise tax A tax imposed on certain types of goods, such as liquor and tobacco.

Executory Designed to occur or be put into effect in the future. An executory contract is an agreement between two parties requiring one to perform a service for the other at a later date.

Expatriation The voluntary giving up of citizenship in one's native country to become a citizen of another.

Expert witness Someone who, because of his or her special knowledge of a certain trade, science or activity, may give opinion testimony in court to interpret or explain a fact or other evidence.

Expropriation The taking of private property for public use, such as to build a park or railway.

Eyewitness A person who is able to give testimony about an act or event because he saw it take place.

Face value The amount printed on a bond, insurance policy, or note, representing its value at maturity, or when it is due. See STOCKS AND BONDS.

♦ **Fee simple** Absolute ownership of real estate, giving the owner complete authority to sell or otherwise dispose of the property during his lifetime and to pass this authority to whomever he wishes upon his death.

Fiduciary A person, such as an executor, or institution, such as a bank or trust company, that has a duty to act for the benefit of another person. This duty arises because the fiduciary is in a position of trust or confidentiality.

Firm offer A written offer to enter into a contract, such as that made by a merchant who buys and sells goods. Such an offer usually states that it will remain open for a fixed period of time, during which it cannot be revoked. See CONTRACT.

Fixed asset Property (such as land, buildings, or machinery) that is held for the purpose of conducting business but is not used up in the operation of the business or sold for cash. Lenders consider the value of a company's fixed assets when deciding whether or not to grant credit. See SECURITY AGREEMENT.

Floating lien An agreement between a debtor and a creditor in which collateral offered by the debtor as security for a loan will serve as security for any future loans from the creditor to the debtor. See LIEN; MECHANIC'S LIEN.

Forcible entry Taking possession of someone else's house or land without his permission and by means of violence or terror. The phrase is often used when a landlord tries illegally to evict a tenant. See EVICTION.

Foreman The member of the jury who is elected by the jury or the court to speak for the jury, preside over its deliberations, and communicate with the court on its behalf. See JURY.

Futures Contracts that promise to buy or sell standard commodities, such as grain, at a set price on a future date.

Garnishment A court order that allows a judgment creditor to seize a portion of a debtor's salary while it is in the hands of the debtor's employer. The employer is bound to give to the creditor the employee's seizable portion of salary or other monies until the amount of the judgment is fully paid. An employer who refuses or neglects to do so may become personally liable for the debt.

Grace period The brief period of time specified in a contract that allows a payment to be made after the due date. Generally, the term refers to the length of time an insurance policyholder has to pay the premium after its due date.

Hold over To remain in possession after the end of a term, as an officeholder or a tenant. See EVICTION; LANDLORD; LEASE.

Holder A person in legal possession of a cheque, promissory note, or bill of exchange who is entitled to receive payment. See PROMISSORY NOTE.

Housebreaking Breaking into and entering a home for the purpose of committing a crime inside. See BURGLARY.

Illusory promise A statement that appears to be the basis for a contract, but in fact is so vague that it promises nothing that is legally binding. A contract based on an illusory promise cannot be enforced. Suppose you buy an appliance with a service contract stating that the manufacturer will "replace or repair the item if, in the company's sole judgment, such action is within the terms of this warranty." With this type of wording, the company—not you—decides whether your appliance merits repair or replacement. Because there is no real warranty or promise, you cannot obtain satisfaction unless you take the company to court.

Impound To confiscate personal property, such as an automobile or document, as evidence or for safekeeping.

In camera A Latin phrase meaning "in chambers," referring to a case or portion of a case heard in a judge's chambers or in a private courtroom from which spectators are barred.

In loco parentis (*in LO-co pa-REN-tis*) A Latin phrase meaning "in the place of a parent," referring to the parental rights and obligations that are granted to a person or institution temporarily entrusted with a child, such as a teacher or school.

In re (*in ray*) A Latin phrase meaning "in the case (or matter) of," used in the title of lawsuits or other legal proceedings in which there are no opposing parties. For example, an uncontested divorce might be identified as "In re the marriage of Smith and Smith."

In rem A Latin phrase meaning "against the thing," referring to an act or proceeding that involves a specific thing rather than opposing parties. For example, a probate court has "in rem" jurisdiction, or authority, over a deceased person's estate.

Inalienable right A right, such as freedom of speech, that cannot be bought, sold, forfeited, or transferred to another person. Someone cannot agree to become another person's slave, for example, because personal liberty is an inalienable right.

Inchoate Begun but not finished. For example, a contract that has not been executed by both parties is inchoate until both parties have signed it.

Indenture A deed, contract, or other written agreement between two or more parties that sets forth a certain mutual obligation.

Information An accusation similar to an indictment, presented by a prosecutor or an arresting officer. See CRIMINAL PROCEDURE.

Inquest A court-ordered inquiry by a coroner into the cause and circumstances of a sudden or unexplained death. See AUTOPSY.

Insolvency The inability to pay one's debts as they become due, or the situation in which one's liabilities exceed one's assets. See BANKRUPTCY.

Instrument A formal, written, legally binding document, such as a contract, will, lease, or promissory note.

Insurable interest An interest in the life of a person, or a property, that gives someone reason to want to preserve that life or property. A husband has an insurable interest in his wife's life, for example, and can buy a life insurance policy on it, but a stranger who stands to benefit financially from the death probably would not. See LIFE INSURANCE.

Inter alia (*in-ter AH-lee-ah*) A Latin phrase meaning "among other things."

Inter vivos (*IN-ter VEE-vos*) A Latin phrase meaning "between living persons." An inter vivos gift, for example, is one that is given while the donor is still alive. See GIFT.

Interlocutory Temporary or provisional. An interlocutory divorce decree, for example, does not become final until a specified period has elapsed. See DIVORCE.

Interpleader A legal procedure used to decide the rights of rival claimants to money or property held by a third person who has no interest in it. Insurance companies often use interpleader proceedings when there are multiple claims upon a policy—for example, if the deceased person's heirs are fighting among themselves for the proceeds.

Interrogatory A written question, usually designed to obtain basic factual information, that is given by one party to the opposing party to a lawsuit before the trial begins. An interrogatory must be answered under oath. See DISCOVERY.

Intestate (*in-TES-tate*) The condition of having died without a valid will. The property of a person who dies intestate is distributed according to provincial law. See DYING WITHOUT A WILL.

Ipso facto (*IP-so FACK-toe*) A Latin phrase meaning "by the fact itself." When a person signs an insurance claim form, he gives up his right ipso facto to seek further damages (money).

Joinder The joining of two or more legal proceedings; the uniting of two or more persons (who are pursuing individual lawsuits) as plaintiffs or defendants in a single lawsuit.

Judgment-proof A person or company that claims insolvency or bankruptcy, and is therefore unable to pay the money damages that are awarded by a court. See JUDGMENT.

Judicial review The power of a court to review and revise the decision of a public administrative agency, such as the CRTC, if someone affected by that decision petitions the court.

Laches (*LATCH-ez*) A defense raised by the defendant in a lawsuit alleging that the plaintiff has waited so long to file suit that the defendant can no longer defend himself.

Lapse The forfeit of a right or privilege due to a failure to perform some necessary act. For example, a lapse of insurance may occur if the policy owner fails to make premium payments.

Larceny Criminal theft; the act of taking someone's property without his consent.

Latent defect A defect that is not visible or apparent. A latent defect in merchandise or in the title to land, for example, is one that cannot be discovered by reasonably careful inspection.

Leasehold The property or land governed by a lease. If you sign a lease on a two-bedroom apartment, for example, the apartment is a leasehold for the time and conditions specified by the contract. See LEASE.

Legacy A bequest, or gift, of personal property left to someone through a will. Technically, the term refers only to personal property; real property is given by devise. However, when a will fails to make this distinction, the term legacy is usually understood to refer to both.

Legitimate Authorized or sanctioned by law; legal.

Lessee A person who is granted a lease. See LEASE.

Lessor A person who grants a lease; a landlord. See LANDLORD.

Letters of administration Documents issued by a probate court authorizing one or more persons to administer the estate of a person who has died without a will. See DYING WITHOUT A WILL.

Letters testamentary Documents issued by a probate court authorizing the executor of a will to perform the duties required by law and the terms of the will. See EXECUTOR AND ADMINISTRATOR.

Levy To impose or collect, such as a tax or fine.

Lewdness, public An act, such as removing one's bathing suit on a public beach or looking into women's bedroom windows, that offends the community's standard of decency.

Lex The Latin word for law; a collection or body of laws.

Licensee Someone who has been granted a license; also, a person, such as a mail carrier or delivery person, who enters someone's house or property with the owner's permission but without an invitation. See ACCIDENTS IN THE HOME.

Liquid asset Cash or anything else of value that can easily be converted into cash, such as stocks, bonds, or jewelry.

Liquidate To pay and settle a debt or estate. To liquidate a business, for example, is to pay off all creditors and put the company out of business. See PARTNERSHIP.

Litigation A lawsuit; a judicial contest.

Maim To injure seriously, as by mutilating or crippling.

Malfeasance The commission of a wrongful act, especially one that prevents a public official from performing his duties.

Malice aforethought The intention to commit an unlawful act, in particular when the act results in the serious injury or death of another. Malice aforethought does not necessarily imply ill will or hatred toward the victim, but rather a conscious disregard for the life of another. See PREMEDITATION.

Malpractice Professional misconduct; the failure of a professional, such as a doctor, lawyer, or accountant, to follow the accepted standards of his profession in providing services to his clients. A lawyer who neglects to file a lawsuit before the time period allowed by law, for example, or a doctor who prescribes a medicine without first asking whether the patient is allergic, is guilty of malpractice. See LAWYER; MEDICAL MALPRACTICE.

Malum in se (*MAH-lum in SAY*) A Latin phrase meaning "wrong in itself," referring to an act, such as cheating on a test, that is inherently wrong or immoral even though it is not prohibited by law.

Malum prohibitum (*MAH-lum pro-HIB-i-tum*) A Latin phrase meaning "a wrong prohibited," referring to an act, such as driving faster than the speed limit, that is prohibited by law even though it is not inherently wrong.

Mandamus (*man-DAY-mus*) A Latin word meaning "we command." A writ of mandamus is a court order directing public officials to do or not do something that is ordinarily within the scope of their official duties. If, for example, a city refuses to issue a parade permit when the law requires it to do so, the group seeking the permit could ask the court for a writ of mandamus ordering the city to issue the permit.

Marital misconduct Actions such as adultery, cruelty, or desertion that are grounds for marriage breakdown. See DIVORCE.

Mayhem The crime of intentionally maiming, disabling, or disfiguring someone.

Meeting of the minds The point at which both parties forming a contract come to an agreement on its terms. See CONTRACT.

Mens rea Latin for "guilty mind," and the requisite intention or mental component of a crime. When coupled with an *actus reus* (wrongful act), a crime is committed. In most serious crimes, such as murder, failure by the prosecutor to prove *mens rea* could result in a murder charge being reduced to manslaughter or lead to an acquittal.

Mental anguish The fear, anxiety, depression, or emotional pain and suffering that may accompany a physical injury or result from a traumatic experience. If the plaintiff can prove mental anguish, she may be awarded money damages in addition to those awarded for her physical injury. See DAMAGES; LAWSUIT.

Metes and bounds The precise boundary lines of a tract of land, usually measured and determined by a surveyor. See BOUNDARY LINE.

Mill levy An amount used by county treasurers to calculate a homeowner's annual property tax. To calculate the tax, the assessed value of the property is multiplied by the mill levy. A "mill" is one tenth of one cent.

Thus, if the mill levy is 6.5 mills, the tax rate for each dollar's worth of property is $0.0065, and if your home is assessed for $100,000, your mill levy would be $650. See PROPERTY TAX.

Minor A person below the age (usually 18) at which he or she is legally entitled to the rights and privileges of an adult. See CHILD EMPLOYMENT; CHILDREN'S RIGHTS.

Misfeasance The commission of an act that is wrong or improper but legal. For example, if a judge makes insulting remarks about a defense lawyer during a trial, he is guilty of misfeasance.

Mistrial A trial terminated by the judge because of legal errors, disruptive behavior in the courtroom, or the failure of the jury to reach a verdict. See APPEAL.

M'Naughten rule A standard used by courts to determine whether a person was legally insane (that is, unable to understand the difference between right and wrong) when he committed a crime, and therefore not legally responsible for his actions. See INSANITY PLEA.

Monopoly The exclusive right or power to control the production, sale, or supply of a particular item. Monopolies are usually against the law because they are harmful to the general welfare by preventing competition and increasing prices.

Moot Open to discussion; undecided; debatable. A moot point of law is one that has not been settled by a judicial decision.

Moral turpitude An action or form of conduct, such as bribery or prostitution, that is viewed as highly dishonest or immoral because it is contrary to the accepted rules of society.

Motion A request made to a judge by one of the parties to a lawsuit asking for some action to be taken. For example, a defendant may make a motion to dismiss the case, claiming that the

plaintiff has no grounds for a lawsuit. See LAWSUIT.

Motive The cause, reason, or incentive for a person's action or behavior, used most often in the context of committing a crime. See INTENT.

Mutuality of contract The principle that each party must take some action or make some promise in order to create a legally binding contract, since neither one is bound unless both are. See CONTRACT.

N.B. An abbreviation for nota bene (*no-tah BEN-ay*), a Latin phrase meaning "note well." It is used in footnoting legal briefs and writings.

Necessaries Things that are essential, proper, or useful for daily life, such as food, clothing, and shelter.

Nolle prosequi (*NOL-lay PROSS-ekwee*) A Latin phrase meaning "will not further prosecute," referring to the decision of a plaintiff or prosecutor not to proceed any further with his case.

Nominal Existing in name only; minor or trivial. For example, nominal damages are a small sum of money awarded by a court to compensate the plaintiff for a violation of his legal rights, even though he may not have suffered a significant loss or injury. See DAMAGES.

Non compos mentis (*non compus MEN-tis*) A Latin phrase meaning "not of sound mind," referring to a claim by a defendant in a criminal or civil case that he was mentally incompetent when he committed a certain act and should therefore not be held responsible. See INCOMPETENCY.

Note A written promise to pay a certain amount of money to a particular person at a specified time. See PROMISSORY NOTE.

Novation The substitution of a new debt or obligation for an old one, or of one debtor or creditor for another.

Nunc pro tunc (*noonqk pro toongk*) A Latin phrase meaning "now for then," referring to an act that is given the legal consequences it would have had if it had been done at an earlier time. For example, a child born out of wedlock is not considered illegitimate if the parents get married.

Objection A formal statement used in court by a lawyer, calling the court's attention to testimony, evidence, or a procedure that he considers improper or illegal.

Offer A proposal to make a contract that contains all the terms of the contract and becomes legally binding if the terms are accepted. See CONTRACT.

Officer of the court A court employee, such as a judge, bailiff, or attorney, who must obey court rules and regulations. See CONTEMPT OF COURT; JUDGE; LAWYER.

Ombudsman (*OM-boodz-mun*) A government-employed investigator who resolves citizens' complaints against government agencies.

Open shop A company that hires both union and nonunion members. See LABOR UNION.

Opinion The official statement of a court after the completion of a case. It announces the court's decision, outlines the facts of the case, and explains the laws and reasoning that were applied.

Order in council An assent by the governor-general (federal) or lieutenant governor (provincial) to an order of the cabinet which has the effect of law but is not a law passed by parliament.

Ordinance A law enacted by a city government or other municipality. Ordinances regulate local affairs, such as traffic, parking, and business licensing.

Original jurisdiction The authority of a court to consider cases for the first time; distinguished from *appellate jurisdiction*, which is the authority to review cases on appeal. See JURISDICTION.

Overrule To reverse or reject. For example, for various reasons a judge may overrule a lawyer's objection during a trial or an appeal court may overrule the decision of a lower court.

Par value The value at which a stock, bond, or other security sells on the market. See BOOK VALUE.

Parens patriae (*Parenz PAY-tree-eye*) A Latin phrase meaning "parent of the country." It also refers to a province's power to serve as guardian for someone who is legally incompetent, such as a mentally ill person.

Parol Oral; expressed in speech rather than in writing.

Parol evidence Oral evidence; testimony presented by a witness before a court. Under the parol evidence rule, a written contract takes precedence over any previous oral promise or agreement about the same matter. If Bob and Sue have a written contract that Sue will paint Bob's house and Bob claims in court that Sue had also agreed to "throw in" a paint job for the garage, Bob would not win his case under this rule. See EVIDENCE.

Party A person who takes part in a contract, transaction, or legal proceeding. In a trial, the parties are the plaintiff, or petitioner, and the defendant, or respondent. In an appeal, the parties are the appellant and the respondent.

Pauper A person who is so poor that he is legally entitled to receive public charity or to prosecute or defend a lawsuit at no cost to himself.

Pendente lite (*pen DEN-tay LEE-tay*) A Latin phrase meaning "pending or during suit," referring to an event that takes place while a lawsuit is in progress. For example, a court may require that a business be placed in receivership, pendente lite.

Pending Begun but not yet finished. For example, a pending legal action is one that is underway but is awaiting a court's final judgment, or decision.

Per capita A Latin phrase meaning "by heads" (by individual persons), referring to a method used to divide something into equal shares, such as the estate of a deceased person. See DYING WITHOUT A WILL.

Per curiam (*per CURE-ee-ahm*) A Latin phrase meaning "by the court," referring to an opinion rendered by an entire appeal court rather than one judge.

Per stirpes (*per STER-pays*) A Latin term meaning "through the roots," referring to a method used by lawyers to divide someone's estate when a beneficiary or heir has died before him. For example, suppose Jim's will names his sons, Tom and Peter, to inherit equal shares of his estate, but Tom dies before his father and is survived by two daughters. If Jim's estate is distributed per stirpes, each of Tom's daughters will receive half of their father's share of the estate. See WILL.

Peremptory challenge The right of the prosecuting lawyer and defense lawyer in a jury trial to reject a certain number of prospective jurors without having to give a reason. See JURY.

Permission slip A consent form used by schools to obtain permission from parents to have their child participate in some school-related activity. It does not release the school from responsibility for its own negligence. See CONSENT FORM.

Personal property Anything a person can own other than real estate (known as real property).

Plaintiff The party that initiates a civil lawsuit or criminal prosecution. In criminal cases, the plaintiff is a government entity, such as the Crown.

Police power The authority of government to make and enforce all laws and regulations it deems necessary for the good and welfare of the state and its citizens.

Post mortem A Latin phrase meaning "after death," referring to an autopsy or examination of a body made by medical authorities to determine the cause of death. See AUTOPSY.

Precedent A decision made in an earlier, similar case that a court uses as a guide in deciding the case at hand. Prosecuting and defense lawyers try to find precedents favorable to their case and present them in court.

Premeditation Prior consideration of a criminal act and the determination to commit it. A person who commits premeditated murder is subject to a higher penalty than a person who kills someone in the heat of passion, because he had enough time to consider the consequences of his actions. See MURDER.

Prenuptial agreement Also known as a marriage contract, a document prepared by a couple with the help of a lawyer (or notary in Quebec) prior to marriage, that outlines how property is to be divided in the event of divorce, separation, or death of a spouse.

Presentment A grand jury's written statement alleging that a crime has been committed and that there is adequate evidence to charge one or more persons with the crime. See GRAND JURY; INDICTMENT.

Pretermitted heir An adult or minor child who has been omitted from his parent's will. See HEIR.

Prima facie (*PRIME-uh FAY-shuh*) A Latin phrase meaning "on first sight," referring to evidence in favor of the plaintiff that is sufficient to present a convincing case against the defendant.

Primogeniture A common-law tradition (no longer valid) that the first-born son inherits all the real estate owned by his parent or other ancestor.

Principal A person who authorizes someone (called an agent) to act on his behalf. Also, an amount of money borrowed, not including interest and other charges. See AGENT.

Private property Any property that is owned by a person, association, or corporation rather than by the government.

Privity A relationship of mutual interest, such as that between a buyer and a seller or two parties who make a contract.

Pro bono (*pro BONE-oh*) A shortened form of the Latin phrase *pro bono publico* ("for the public good"), referring to work performed by lawyers free of charge for clients who cannot afford their services. See LAWYER; LEGAL AID.

Pro rata (*pro RAY-tuh, or RAH-tuh*) A Latin phrase meaning "according to a given rate, proportion, or percentage." Property taxes, for example, may be assessed pro rata between the buyer and the seller of a home at closing.

Pro se (*pro SAY*) A Latin phrase meaning "for oneself," referring to a person who represents himself without a lawyer in a legal proceeding.

Process server A person authorized to serve a summons or subpoena to the defendant in a lawsuit. See LAWSUIT.

Prosecutor The public official, such as a Crown attorney, who files charges against a person suspected of committing a crime and acts on behalf of the government to get the person convicted. See CRIMINAL PROCEDURE.

Provocation Action or behavior by one person that invites another person to take some action in response. For example, if one man insults another man's wife, causing the husband to throw a punch, the man who made the insulting remark would be guilty of provocation.

Proximate cause The direct, primary cause of an injury or loss, without which the injury or loss would not have occurred. See LAWSUIT.

Proxy A document signed by one person authorizing another to act on his behalf in a specific circumstance, such as voting for officers of a club or corporation. Also, the person to whom such authorization is granted.

Public defender A lawyer employed by the government to represent criminal defendants who cannot afford to hire a lawyer.

Public domain Belonging to the general public rather than an individual. A creative work whose copyright has expired is considered in the public domain, as is publicly owned land. See COPYRIGHT.

Quasi (*KWAY-sigh or KWAH-see*) A Latin term meaning "as if," referring to a thing or situation that resembles something else even though there are essential differences between the two. For example, an administrative agency, such as the Environmental Protection Directorate of Environment Canada, acts in a quasi-judicial capacity when, like a court, it holds hearings and issues rulings.

Quid pro quo A Latin phrase meaning "this for that," referring to the mutual exchange of benefits that makes a contract valid and legally binding.

Ransom A sum of money demanded or paid for the release of a hostage.

Reasonable and prudent person An adult without any physical or mental disabilities who is careful but not overly cautious. In negligence cases, the concept of a reasonable and prudent person is used as a standard against which the actions of the defendant can be judged. See LAWSUIT; NEGLIGENCE; TORT.

Recidivist A habitual criminal; one who continues to commit crimes even after being caught and convicted repeatedly.

Recognizance A written promise by a criminal defendant to appear in court at a later date, without posting bail, to answer charges against him. See BAIL.

Recourse A person's right to seek payment on a cheque from anyone who has previously endorsed it, even if the original issuer refuses to honor it. See CHEQUE.

Referendum The submission of a proposed law, such as one for a tax increase, to voters for ratification.

Reformation The revision of a contract by the court in a situation where the terms of the contract do not represent what was originally agreed upon due to a mutual mistake by the parties.

Registrar A government official responsible for maintaining public records, such as deeds.

Regulation A rule or order issued by a public administrative agency, such as the Canadian Radio Television and Telecommunication Commission (CRTC), to supervise or control the operation of a business that affects the general public.

Remainder The assets of a deceased person's estate after all specific gifts have been made and all taxes and administrative expenses have been paid. Also, an interest in a piece of real estate that takes effect only after another's interest in the property ends. For example, suppose your father dies and leaves a life estate in the family home to your mother, allowing her to live there until she dies. The will also states that upon her death, you will become the owner of the home. Your interest in the house is known as a remainder. See WILL.

Remand To return. For example, a criminal defendant may be remanded to jail after a preliminary hearing, or a case may be remanded to a lower court for retrial after being heard by a court of appeal.

Remedy The method by which a court compensates someone for a wrong that has been done to him, such as by awarding him money damages. See DAMAGES.

Renounce To abandon a right or privilege without transferring it to someone else. For example, when an immigrant becomes a Canadian citizen, he may renounce his allegiance to his former country.

Repeal The cancellation of an earlier law by a later one.

Replevin (*ri-plev-in*) A type of lawsuit used to recover property that has been taken illegally or borrowed and not returned.

Repudiate To reject or refuse a right, privilege, or duty. For example, a party to a contract repudiates the contract if he decides not to honor his part of the agreement. See BREACH OF CONTRACT.

Res (*raze*) A Latin word meaning "thing," referring to the object of, or the subject matter of, a lawsuit. The res of a foreclosure proceeding, for example, is the property secured by the mortgage being foreclosed on.

Res ipsa loquitur (*raze IP-sah LOW-kwi-toor*) A Latin phrase meaning "the thing speaks for itself," referring to circumstantial evidence presented by the plaintiff in a lawsuit that indicates an event was probably caused by the negligence of the defendant. See EVIDENCE.

Res judicata (*raze JOO-di-KAH-tuh*) A Latin phrase meaning "the thing judged," referring to a rule of law stating that when a court with authority over a matter renders its final decision, that judgment is conclusive, even though it may later be appealed.

Residuary clause The provision in a will that disposes of the remainder of a person's estate after all specific gifts have been made

and all taxes and expenses have been paid. See WILL.

Respondeat superior (*res-PON-dee-at soo-PEER-ee-ore*) A Latin phrase meaning "let the master answer," referring to an employer's responsibility for any actions performed by his employees in the course of their work, including ones that may injure or harm another person.

Restitution Restoring something to its rightful owner; returning someone to the position he would have held if a contract had not been broken. For example, a court may order a convicted con man to make restitution to his victims by refunding the money he swindled from them.

Retainer The fee a client pays a lawyer in order to hire him; the act by which a client employs a lawyer and gives him the authority to represent him. See LAWYER.

Reversion A legal interest in real estate that a person keeps after transferring ownership of the property to someone else, which he may exercise at some point in the future. For example, suppose Fred sells property to Jeff, but includes a provision that if Jeff uses the property for anything other than a farm, it will be returned to Fred. Fred has retained a reversion in the property.

Riparian rights The rights of a person to use the water of a river or stream on the borders of his property. See FISHING RIGHTS.

Rogatory commission A person or group authorized by a court to take evidence from witnesses living in a foreign jurisdiction. The evidence would be used by the commissioning court in legal proceedings.

Sanction A penalty imposed for violating a law or regulation.

Sealed verdict A signed jury verdict that is placed in a sealed envelope and secured until it can be delivered. It allows jurors to separate temporarily if they have reached a verdict when the court is not in session.

Seizure The forcible taking of property by a law enforcement official from someone who is suspected of having violated the law or someone who has neglected to pay a court-ordered debt. See SEARCH AND SEIZURE.

Service of process The delivery, either in person or by mail, of a summons to the person designated to receive it.

Setoff A counterdemand made by a defendant to reduce or defeat a plaintiff's demand in a lawsuit. It is unconnected with the plaintiff's cause of action, or basis for suing. See LAWSUIT.

Severability The ability of one party to a contract to force the other party to honor some of its provisions even though others have been found to be illegal or unenforceable. The unenforceable parts of the agreement are said to be severable (or separatable) from the whole.

Sheriff The chief law enforcement officer of a county, responsible for serving summonses and enforcing court orders.

Sine die (*SEE-nay DEE-ay*) A Latin phrase meaning "without a day," referring to the final adjournment (with no day specified for readjournment) of a court or legislative body.

Sine qua non (*SEE-nay kwah non*) A Latin phrase meaning "without which not," referring to a thing or condition that is essential or indispensable.

Solicitation The crime of asking or enticing another person to commit a criminal act. For example, a prostitute who approaches men on the street is engaging in solicitation.

Solvency The ability to pay one's debts as they become due.

Specific performance A legal means of carrying out a contract exactly as the terms are written.

It is ordered by a court when a contract has been broken and when money damages would be inadequate, as in the case of a broken agreement to sell a one-of-a-kind work of art.

Spousal support Regular payments made by one spouse to another during a separation or after a divorce. See ALIMENTARY PENSION.

Squatter A person who trespasses upon or occupies land that does not belong to him without the owner's permission. See ADVERSE POSSESSION.

ss. An abbreviation of the Latin word *scilicet*, meaning "to wit," or "namely." It is used in a legal document to state the venue (place) in which the document is executed.

Stare decisis (*STAH-ray di-SIGH-sis*) A Latin phrase meaning "to stand by the decided," referring to the policy of courts to base their decisions on those of similar previous cases, or precedents. See COMMON LAW.

Status offender Someone whose behavior is unacceptable to society but who has not committed a crime, such as a disobedient child or a truant.

Statute A law enacted by a legislature (such as parliament), as opposed to the common law, which is based on court decisions and precedents. Statutes prescribe and proscribe conduct, define crimes, levy taxes, create government agencies, and the like.

Statute of frauds A law requiring certain types of contracts, such as those for the sale of real estate, to be in writing because they would be vulnerable to fraud if they were agreed upon orally. See CONTRACT.

Stay The use of a court order to stop a judicial proceeding or prevent a judgment from being carried out.

Stipulation An agreement between the parties to a lawsuit that is designed to speed up the settlement or reduce the costs. See LAWSUIT.

Sua sponte (*SOO-uh SPON-tay*) A Latin phrase meaning "of its own accord," referring to a court order made in the best interest of the court or of justice. For example, a court may move sua sponte to dismiss a criminal case if it believes there is not enough evidence to convict the defendant.

Subcontractor Someone, such as a plumber, who forms an agreement with a general contractor, such as a construction company, to do part of the job the general contractor was hired to do. See CONTRACTOR; HOME IMPROVEMENT AND REPAIR.

Subornation of perjury The attempt to persuade someone to lie under oath, which becomes a crime only if the person actually does lie under oath.

Subpoena (*suh-PEEN-uh*) A Latin word meaning "under penalty," referring to a court order commanding someone to testify in court on a designated date.

Subpoena duces tecum (*suh-PEEN-uh DOO-ches TAY-koom*) A Latin phrase meaning "under penalty, take with you," referring to a court order that commands a witness to bring to court a document that is relevant to a lawsuit.

Subsidiary A corporation controlled by another corporation which owns at least a majority of the shares—enough to control the subsidiary.

Sue To bring legal proceedings against a person, company, or the government in order to enforce one's rights or obtain compensation for some wrongdoing. See LAWSUIT.

Summary conviction offense A lesser offense punishable by a fine or less than two years in prison. A person convicted of a summary conviction offense does not have the right to a preliminary inquiry. More serious crimes are called indictable offenses in Canada, or felonies in the U.S.

Summons A document that notifies someone that he is being sued and specifies a date by which he must appear in court to answer the charges against him. See LAWSUIT.

Surety A person who agrees to be responsible for someone else's debt if she does not pay.

Surrogate court A court that presides over the execution of wills and estates. Also called probate court. See PROBATE.

Sustain To uphold, grant, support, or approve. For example, a judge in a criminal trial may sustain a lawyer's objection to evidence if he believes it is correct and appropriate.

Tariff A duty, or fee, that must be paid when merchandise is imported into Canada.

Tax sale The sale of a delinquent taxpayer's property by the government to collect payment for his unpaid taxes.

Tender A formal, unconditional offer of money or other property to satisfy someone's claim.

Tender offer An attempt by one or more investors to gain control of a corporation by offering to buy a certain amount of its stock at a specified price.

Testamentary Relating to, established in, or based on someone's will, such as a testamentary trust. See TRUST; WILL.

Title Ownership of property, entitling the owner to use, sell, lease, donate, or even destroy it. Also, the document that serves as proof of ownership for property.

Title search An examination of registered deeds to make sure that a piece of real estate can be sold without anyone else claiming a right to it. See HOME BUYING AND SELLING; TITLE INSURANCE.

Treason The crime of attempting to overthrow the legitimate government to which one owes his allegiance.

Treaty A formal, legally ratified agreement between two or more nations.

Truant A child who deliberately and repeatedly misses school without justification.

Ultra vires (*UL-truh vee-rez*) A Latin phrase meaning "beyond the powers," referring to an act by a corporation that exceeds the powers granted by its charter.

Uniform law A law intended for general adoption by all provinces.

Unlawful assembly A gathering of three or more people for the purpose of committing a crime or disturbing the peace. See ASSEMBLY, RIGHT OF.

Usufruct In Quebec civil law, the right of a person or persons to have the use and the fruits of an object for a specified time or during their lifetime. After this time, the object must be given over to a third person who would have the full power of the object, including the right to dispose of it. Similar to a life interest in the common-law provinces.

Usury The crime of charging an illegally high interest rate on a loan.

Variance An official permit to use land or property in a way that does not conform to zoning regulations. See ZONING.

Video piracy The crime of making unauthorized copies of commercial copyrighted videotapes

for sale to the public. See COPYRIGHT.

Voir dire (*vwahr deer*) A French phrase meaning "to speak the truth," referring to the process by which prospective jurors are questioned by lawyers to determine whether they are qualified to serve on a case. See JURY; JURY DUTY.

Volenti non fit injuria (*Vo-LEN-ti non feet in-JOOR-ee-ah*) A Latin phrase meaning "damages cannot be claimed by one who has assumed the risk." So, a hockey player injured when checked into the boards by a member of the opposite team cannot sue for injuries, as he has assumed the risk of injury by participating in a game which has body contact as a natural part of the game.

Waiver The voluntary relinquishment of a known legal right or claim. An express waiver is one that is stated, such as the statement on a ticket to a sporting event that informs you that the facility cannot be held responsible for any injuries you might suffer. An implied waiver is one that is not stated, as when you allow someone to cross your property as a shortcut on a regular basis.

Warrant A written order directing someone to perform a specific act. For example, an arrest warrant issued by a judge authorizes a law enforcement officer to take a suspect into custody. See ARREST; SEARCH AND SEIZURE.

Writ A written order issued by a court that directs the person to whom it is addressed to take a specified action. A writ of habeas corpus, for example, orders government officials to present someone being held in prison so that the court can determine whether his imprisonment is lawful. See HABEAS CORPUS.

Everyday Legal Forms

Contracts, deeds, notices, applications, wills, affidavits—the world of law is a world of paper. Designed to make something official by putting it in writing, these forms are often long and technical, and they can be daunting to the layman. But to lawyers they serve a valuable purpose: they simplify and standardize the legal process. On the following pages you will find some common legal forms, 36 samples covering a wide variety of everyday situations, from buying a car to writing a will. Each form uses traditional legal terminology and is accompanied by clear instructions on how to fill it out and put it to use. Also, each form includes cross-references to related articles in case you need more information.

Although you can adopt some of these forms for your own use, you should do so with caution. Laws vary widely across the country, and the exact language required in your province may not match that in the sample provided. Moreover, some financial institutions will not honor forms that are not their own. For example, if you want to authorize someone to gain access to your bank account, your bank may require you to use its own power of attorney form. If a document has far-reaching consequences, such as a prenuptial agreement, be sure to consult a lawyer before signing it.

Whether you use these forms as working models or simply for reference, they will save you time and money. They will not only acquaint you with the language and content of formal legal documents, but will alert you to the information you will need in order to fill in the blanks. If you fill out a form before you see a lawyer, you will reduce the time he must spend explaining it to you and asking you questions, and you will therefore save money.

Perhaps most important of all, these forms will help you tidy up your legal life. If you are a tenant or a landlord, for example, you should know what information should be contained in a residential lease. If you are concerned about your credit rating, you should know how to check it and correct any errors. If you are considering granting someone a power of attorney, you should know about the different kinds that exist, and about the rights and duties of each. Filling out forms can be tedious and time-consuming, but the ones provided here will make the task much easier.

CONTENTS

An inventory of personal records can help you to keep track of important documents. It can also be invaluable to family members if certain items must be located in your absence.

My Personal Records

_____your name_____

Funeral Instructions: _location of documents_

Letters of Final Bequest: _location_

Anatomical Gift Form: _location; who has copies_

Will and Trust(s): _location; who has copies_

Living Will: _location; who has copies_

Power of Attorney: _location; name and address of appointee_

Insurance Policies: _location; names of insurance companies and beneficiaries_

Safe-Deposit Box Keys: _location of keys; name and address of bank_

Bank Passbooks and Chequebooks: _location; account numbers; names and addresses of banks_

Business Papers: _location; description_

Deeds to Real Estate: _location; list of property_

Mortgage Documents: _location; list of mortgaged property_

Stock Certificates: _location; name and address of brokerage firm; account number(s)_

Other Investment Certificates: _location; list of profit-sharing, pension, and retirement plans_

Social Insurance Number: _location; Social insurance number_

Tax Returns: _location_

Birth Certificate: _location_

Marriage Certificate(s): _location; date and place of marriage(s)_

Prenuptial Agreement: _location_

Divorce Decree(s): _location; date and place of divorce(s)_

Death Certificates: _location; names of deceased_

Passport: _location; passport number_

Citizenship Papers: _location; date of issue_

Military Discharge Papers: _location; date of discharge_

Warranties: _location; description_

Other: _location; description_

■ **Note:** Funeral instructions list the funeral arrangements you want. Letters of final bequest give instructions on the disposition of personal property not mentioned in your will. Update your personal records inventory periodically and keep it in an accessible place that is known to family members. For more information, see FINANCIAL RECORDS; PERSONAL RECORDS.

ACKNOWLEDGMENT

Sometimes a court may require that a person who wrote a will or other legal document make a formal declaration that the document is authenti- cally his. Such a declaration, called an acknowledg- ment, is usually made in the presence of a notary public or officer of the court, such as a lawyer.

PROVINCE OF_____*your province*_____

COUNTY OF_____*your county*_____

Before me personally appeared _____*your name*_____, the Testator, and _____*first witness's name*_____, and _*second witness's name*_____, as Witnesses, known by me to be the persons whose names are subscribed to this document, and having first been sworn, declared that the Testator signed and executed this document as his/her Last Will and Testament and did so as his/her free and voluntary act, and that each of the Witnesses, in the presence of the Testator and in each other's presence, signed their names to the aforesaid documents as Witnesses. The Witnesses declare under oath that to the best of their knowledge, the Testator was of full legal age, of sound mind, and under no undue restraint or influence.

Subscribed and sworn to before me this_____, _____ day of _____, 19___,

[SEAL]

_____
NOTARY PUBLIC

My commission expires: _____

■ **Note:** Fill in the blanks for your name and those of the witnesses. The notary will sign the acknowl- edgment and affix his seal to it. Then be sure to staple the acknowledgment to your will. For further information, see ACKNOWLEDGMENT; NOTARY PUBLIC; WILL.

A SIMPLE WILL

This simple will is suitable for a married person with children. You should regularly review your will, and amend it by means of a codicil if needed. If you marry or become divorced, however, or after the birth or adoption of a child, you should execute an entirely new will.

Last Will and Testament

I, _____*your full legal name*_____, a resident of __*your address*__, in the Province of __*your province*__, being of sound mind and memory, and under no duress, hereby make, publish, and declare this to be my Last Will and Testament, revoking and canceling all previous wills and codicils made by me. It is my intention to dispose of all property, whether real, personal, or mixed, and wherever located, which I own or which I have the right to dispose of by will.

I. I am married to _____*your spouse's name*_____, and all references to my spouse in this document are to the person named in this paragraph. I have __*number*__ children, whose names are:

[list names of children]

II. I direct my Executor to pay all of my just debts and the expenses of my funeral as soon as is reasonably possible after my death, and authorize my Executor to settle, compromise, and discharge any claims against my estate in his or her absolute discretion. I give my Executor full right, power, and authority to do any act in regard to my estate which I could do if living.

III. I hereby make and appoint _____*your executor's name*_____ as Executor of this, my Last Will and Testament, to serve without bond, and if my Executor is for any reason unable or unwilling to serve, then I make and appoint ____*your alternate executor's name*____ to serve as Executor, also to serve without bond.

IV. I give, devise, and bequeath to my spouse, ___*your spouse's name*___, my entire estate. In the event that my spouse dies before I do, or fails to survive me by thirty (30) days, then I give, devise, and bequeath my entire estate to my children in equal shares, per stirpes. If neither my spouse nor any children survive me, then I give, devise, and bequeath my entire estate to ___*name(s) of your alternate beneficiary (beneficiaries)*___.

V. If I am survived by minor children, their other parent shall serve as Guardian. If the other parent dies before I do, I appoint _____*guardian's name*_____ as Guardian. If the person named herein to serve as Guardian shall be unable or unwilling to serve, then I appoint _____*alternate guardian's name*_____, instead, to serve as Guardian. No person named in this paragraph to serve as Guardian shall be required to post bond.

IN WITNESS WHEREOF, I have signed and published this Last Will and Testament on this _*date*_ day of _____*month*_____, 19___ at _____*city*_____, _____*province*_____.

_____*your name signed as it appears above*_____
Testator

On the date written above, the foregoing document was signed in our presence by the Testator named therein, who declared it to be his/her Last Will and Testament, and at the same time, at the request of the Testator, in the Testator's presence and in the presence of each other, we have signed our names as witnesses. We attest that at the time of executing this Last Will and Testament, we believe the Testator to be of sound mind and memory, and under no duress, and that said Testator executed the foregoing Last Will and Testament as his/her free act and deed.

_____*witness's signature*_____   _____*witness's address*_____
Witness   Address

_____*witness's signature*_____   _____*witness's address*_____
Witness   Address

Affidavit

The declarant is personally known to me, and I believe the declarant to be of sound mind. I saw the declarant sign the declaration in my presence, freely and voluntarily, and I signed the declaration as a witness in the presence of the declarant. I did not sign the declarant's signature above for or at the direction of the declarant. At the date of this declaration, I am not entitled to any portion of the estate of the declarant according to the laws of intestate succession, or, to the best of my knowledge and belief, under any will of the declarant or other instrument taking effect at the declarant's death. I am not related to the declarant by blood or marriage. I am not the declarant's attending physician, nor an employee of the attending physician, nor am I an employee of or patient in the health care facility in which the declarant is a patient. I am not directly financially responsible for the medical care of the declarant. I am of sufficient legal age to serve as a witness to this declaration under the laws of the province of _____ *your province* _____.

_____ *witness's signature* _____
Witness

_____ *witness's address* _____
Address

_____ *witness's signature* _____
Witness

_____ *witness's address* _____
Address

NOTARY'S STATEMENT

PROVINCE OF _____

COUNTY OF _____

I, _____, a notary public in and for the province and county named above, hereby certify that on the _____ day of _____, 19___, personally appeared the declarant, and _____ and _____, as witnesses, and having first been duly sworn, each of them signed the above declaration in my presence and in the presence of each other, freely and voluntarily, and for the purposes described therein.

_____

[SEAL]   NOTARY PUBLIC

                                 My commission expires: _____

■ **Note:** The statement in the affidavit referring to intestate succession means that the witness is not someone who would be entitled to share in the declarant's estate if he were to die without having made a final will. This ensures that the witness is not likely to be someone who has an interest in the declarant's death.

A codicil is an amendment to an existing will. You can use a codicil when you want to make small changes in your will. However, if you want to make extensive changes, such as when you marry, or if you have already made one or two codicils previously, you should execute a new will.

Codicil to Last Will and Testament of

_____*your full legal name*_____
Testator

I, _____*your name*_____, residing at _____*your address*_____, in the City of _*your city*_, County of _____*your county*_____, Province of _____*your province*_____, being of sound mind and memory, hereby make, publish, and declare this to be the first Codicil to my Last Will and Testament dated _____*date of your will*_____, 19__.

I give, devise, and bequeath to _*your beneficiary's name*_, the following described property:

[description of bequest]

IN WITNESS WHEREOF, I have signed and published this Codicil on this _date_ day of _*month*_, 19__.

_____*your name signed as it appears above*_____
Testator

The foregoing document, consisting of _number_ pages including this page, was signed, published, and declared by the Testator named therein as the first Codicil to his/her Last Will and Testament dated _date of your will_, 19__. At the same time, in the Testator's presence and in the presence of each other, and at his/her request, we subscribed our names as witnesses this _current date_ day of _current month_, 19__.

_____*witness's signature*_____ residing at _____*witness's address*_____
Witness   Address

_____*witness's signature*_____ residing at _____*witness's address*_____
Witness   Address

■ **Note:** This codicil adds a bequest, of either personal property or real estate, to a will. You can use codicils in other ways, such as to revoke a gift, name a new executor, or add another beneficiary to your estate. A codicil must be signed and witnessed just like a will. It should be stapled to your original will. For more information, see CODICIL; WILL.

569

LIVING WILL

A living will informs your family, doctors, and hospitals of your desire not to be kept alive by artificial means. It can be revoked at any time. Living wills are recognized in Nova Scotia and Quebec, but are also useful in other provinces. A living will should be signed in the presence of two witnesses.

Living Will Declaration and Directive to Physicians

Declaration made this ___*date*___ day of ___*month*___, 19__.

I, ___*your full legal name*___, a resident of ___*your address*___, in the Province of ___*your province*___, being an adult of sound mind, and emotionally and mentally competent to make this declaration, willfully and voluntarily make known my desires that my death shall not be artificially postponed, and hereby declare:

If at any time I should be diagnosed by at least two (2) physicians who have personally examined me, one of whom shall be my attending physician, as having an incurable and irreversible injury, disease, or illness, and that my death is imminent, where the application of life-sustaining procedures would serve only to artificially prolong the moment of my death, I direct that such procedures be withheld or withdrawn, and that I be permitted to die naturally, with only the administration of medication, food, or fluids or the performance of medical procedures deemed necessary to alleviate suffering and provide comfort care.

In the absence of my ability to give directions regarding the use of such life-prolonging procedures, it is my intention that this declaration shall be honored by my family and physicians as the final expression of my legal right to refuse medical or surgical treatment, and I accept the consequences of such refusal.

If I have been diagnosed as pregnant and that diagnosis is known to my attending physician, this directive shall be without force or effect during the term of my pregnancy.

I, my estate, and my heirs and successors will hold harmless any person, organization, or institution from any and all liability that may be incurred as a result of following the instructions contained in this declaration.

This declaration shall remain in effect unless and until it is revoked by me. I understand that I may revoke this declaration at any time. This declaration shall be governed by the laws of the province of ___*your province*___.

Signed ___*your name signed as it appears above*___
Declarant

___*witness's signature*___ ___*witness's address*___
Witness Address

___*witness's signature*___ ___*witness's address*___
Witness Address

FUNERAL INSTRUCTIONS

Funeral instructions should state whether you wish to be buried or cremated, as well as where you want to be buried or where your ashes are to go. On either form, you can also include detailed instructions for the kind of burial or memorial service you would like.

Instructions for Funeral and Burial

I, _____*your name*_____, hereby direct that upon my death my mortal remains be disposed of as follows:

1. It is my wish to be buried in ___*name and address of cemetery*___, Section No. ____, Plot No. ____ [if plot has been purchased]. The deed to this plot is with the original of these funeral instructions.

2. It is my wish that my funeral [or memorial] service be conducted at _____*name and address of church or funeral home*_____. It is my wish that the following arrangements for my funeral [or memorial] service be honored:

> *[Instructions for service. For example, "I wish to have my funeral service conducted by the Reverend Peter Smith or one of his assistants."]*

The fully executed original of my last will and testament can be found in _____*exact location*_____.

_____*your signature*_____
Signature

Instructions for Cremation

I, _____*your name*_____, hereby direct that upon my death my mortal remains be disposed of as follows:

It is my wish that my remains be cremated at ___*name and address of funeral home*___ and that my ashes be disposed of in accordance with the desires of my next of kin [or other instructions].

The fully executed original of my last will and testament can be found in _____*exact location*_____.

_____*your signature*_____
Signature

■ **Note:** Even if your will contains funeral instructions, prepare a separate document describing the funeral arrangements you want—a will often is not read before the deceased's funeral. Keep the instructions in a safe place and give copies to your family, executor, and lawyer. For more information, see EXECUTOR AND ADMINISTRATOR; FUNERAL AND BURIAL; WILL.

EMPLOYMENT AGREEMENT

An employment contract should spell out such things as the employee's duties, hours of work, rate of pay, and annual vacation days. It should also specify the period of time for which the contract is in force, such as six months, one year or, as in this example, an indefinite period.

This employment agreement is made in two original copies between

(1) _____ *employer's name* _____
     Employer

and

(2) _____ *employee's name* _____
     Employee

It is agreed as follows:

1. The Employer agrees to employ the Employee and the Employee agrees to work for the Employer as a _____ *specify the position* _____
for an indefinite period of time commencing _____ *date* _____

2. Subject to reasonable direction by the Employer, the Employee shall perform the following duties and have the following responsibilities:

(This should enumerate tasks the employee will have to perform. For example,
  * *Transfer files from MacIntosh to Windows environment*
  * *set up travel arrangements*
  * *type visual presentations*
  * *prepare purchase orders*
  * *complete data entry for time sheets, and so on.)*

However, it is understood and agreed that these duties and responsibilities are not exhaustive and may be changed with the Employer's changing circumstances; in this regard, the Employee may not refuse any reasonable employment request by the Employer.

3. Subject to statutory holidays and ordinary vacation, the Employee shall work from _____ a.m. to _____ p.m., Monday through Friday in each week of employment.

4. In addition to statutory holidays, the Employee is entitled to ___ *specify how many* ___ weeks' ordinary, paid, non-cumulative vacation in each calendar year of employment but the Employee may not take any ordinary vacation until after ___ *specify how many* ___ months of employment.

5. It is understood and agreed that any ordinary vacation is subject to reasonable control over scheduling by the Employer.

6. Subject to statutory deductions, the Employer shall pay the Employee a gross cash salary, inclusive of any statutory vacation pay to which the Employee may be entitled, equivalent to _____ dollars ($_____) per annum in weekly installments not in advance.

7. The Employer shall also reimburse the Employee for all authorized business expenses incurred by the Employee in the course of employment. However, the Employee shall repay the Employer all amounts paid by the Employer to the Employee under this paragraph that are disallowed, in whole or in part, as deductible to the Employer for income tax purposes.

8. The Employee is also entitled to _____ days' paid, sick leave for each complete _____*time period*_____ worked for the Employer.
However, in order to qualify for any given period of sick leave, the Employee must provide the Employer with a doctor's certificate of the Employee's medical incapacity to work for the period claimed. It is understood and agreed that unused sick leave is lost and will not be compensated for on termination of the Employee's employment with the Employer for any reason.

9. The Employer may terminate the employment of the Employee without cause on ____*specify how many*____ *(Note that the length of time may not be less than that provided by statute)* weeks' notice to the Employee. However, the Employer reserves the right to terminate the Employee's employment without notice for cause, including but not limited to death, incapacitating illness, incompetence, or failure to follow reasonable employment requests, at any time.

10. The Employee promises to keep the Employer's business secrets confidential during and after the term of employment and the Employee also promises that, on the termination of the Employee's employment with the Employer for any reason, the Employee will not operate a _____*specify which kind*_____
business or in any way aid and assist any other person to operate such a business in _____*geographical area*_____ for a period of _____*time period*_____ from the date of termination of the Employee's employment.

11. If any provision or part of any provision in this agreement is void for any reason, it shall be severed without affecting the validity of the balance of the agreement.

12. Except for increases in salary or extension of employment benefits, the terms of this agreement remain in force until amended in writing and signed by both parties.

13. There are no representations, warranties, conditions, terms, or collateral contracts affecting the employment contemplated in this agreement except as set out in this agreement.

14. The Employee acknowledges ample opportunity and advice to take independent legal advice in connection with the execution of this employment agreement.

15. This agreement is governed by the laws of the Province of _____.

Executed on _____ *date* _____ at _____ *employer's address* _____ in the Province of _____ *employer's province* _____.

___ *Employer's signature* ___
Employer

___ *Employee's signature* ___
Employee

■ **Note:** For a contract to be enforceable, there must be mutual agreement between the two parties on the details. Clear and precise wording is impor-tant in a written contract. One that contains confusing or ambiguous wording cannot be enforced. For more information, see AGE DISCRIMINATION; BREACH OF CONTRACT; CIVIL RIGHTS; CONTRACT; EMPLOYEE; EMPLOYEE HIRING AND FIRING; INDEPENDENT CONTRACTOR; JOB DISCRIMINATION; OCCUPATIONAL HEALTH AND SAFETY LAWS.

INDEPENDENT CONTRACTOR AGREEMENT

An independent contractor, also called a free-lance worker, provides a service or product for specific clients in exchange for money. Such contractors provide their own place of work and determine their own working hours. A company that hires an independent contractor does not have to contribute to his Canada (Quebec) Pension Plan, unemployment insurance, or workers compensation insurance, or provide such benefits as paid vacations.

This contract for services is made in two original copies between
(1) _____ *the hirer* _____
and
(2) _____ *the contractor* _____
It is agreed as follows:

1. The Contractor shall provide the Hirer with the following services as an independent contractor:

_____ *For example, such research, writing, art, and translation services as required* _____
_____ *for the company's annual report in English and French* _____

2. The Contractor shall commence the Work on ____ *date* ____ and substantially complete it by no later than ____ *date* ____ .

3. The total contract price ___ *the contract price* ___ payable by the Hirer to the Contractor for doing the Work, exclusive of any Authorized Extras, is _____ dollars ($_____).

4. Subject to a statutory holdback of 15% under any applicable construction or mechanics lien legislation, the Hirer shall pay the Contract Price as follows:
_____ *terms and time of payment* _____

5. The Contractor is only liable to perform and the Hirer is only liable to pay for extra services, in addition to the Work, that are authorized in writing setting out the price of the extra services and signed by both parties _____ *authorized extras* _____ .

6. The Contractor is entitled to interest at the rate of ____% per annum on any overdue payments for doing the Work and any Authorized Extras under this agreement.

7. The Contractor shall indemnify and save the Hirer harmless from any and all claims against the Hirer arising out of the performance of the Contractor's services under this agreement.

8. Time is of the essence of this agreement.

9. The terms of this agreement may only be amended in writing signed by both parties.

10. This agreement is governed by the laws of the Province of _____ .

Executed on ____ *date* ____ at _____ *address* _____ in the Province of____ *date* ____ .

____ *Employer's signature* ____
Employer

____ *Contractor signature* ____
Independent Contractor

REQUEST FOR CREDIT INFORMATION

If you want to see the information in your credit file, you can write a letter such as this to make your request. Insert whichever paragraph in parentheses applies to your situation.

_____current date_____

credit reporting agency
street address_____
city_____province_____postal code_____

Re: Request for Credit Report

As provided for under the consumer protection legislation of ___your province___, I hereby request that you send me a full disclosure of my credit file. This should include the sources of information contained in my file, as well as the name and address of any person or organization that has received my credit report in writing, orally, or by any other means.

(As I have been denied credit in the last 30 days, I request that you provide me with this report free of charge in accordance with provincial law.)

or

(I enclose my cheque for $ _____amount_____ as full payment for this request.)

If my report is written wholly or partly in code, please provide code explanation.

Please feel free to contact me at the telephone number below with any questions you may have. Thank you for your prompt attention.

Sincerely,

your social insurance number   _____your signature_____
your area code and telephone number   _____your name printed_____
_____your street address_____
city_____province_____postal code_____

_____any previous names or recent previous addresses_____

_____your firm name_____
as required, until further notice.

Dated _____.
_____Witness' signature_____   _____Applicant's signature_____
Witness   Credit Applicant

FORM 801

■ **Note:** Before mailing your request, call the credit bureau to ask what it charges for a report and whether it has any special instructions. If you have recently changed your name—because you married for instance—or if you have been at your current address less than three years, provide the bureau with your previous name and address. See CREDIT BUREAU and CREDIT RATING.

CORRECTION TO CREDIT REPORT

If you find that your credit record contains inaccuracies, notify the credit bureau immediately. You can use this form letter to be sure you have included all the necessary information.

_____ _current date_____

_credit reporting agency_____

_street address_____

_city_____ _province_____ _postal code_____

Dear Sir or Madam:

A review of my credit file reveals the following erroneous or incomplete information:

_____ _incorrect information as presented on your credit report_____
_____

This information is erroneous or incomplete because:

_____ _facts explaining why information is wrong_____
_____

In accordance with the terms of the provincial consumer protection legislation, I hereby request that you correct the erroneous information contained in my file.

Sincerely,

_your signature_____

_your name printed_____
_your Social Insurance Number_____
_your street address_____
_city_____ _province_____ _postal code_____

■ **Note:** When you send this letter to the credit bureau, include copies of any documents that prove a mistake was made. You can also write to the source of the erroneous information (for example, the store that failed to credit your payment) to clear up any misunderstanding that caused the error. For more information, see CREDIT BUREAU AND CREDIT RATING.

AFFIDAVIT

An affidavit is a document in which someone, who is called an affiant, makes a statement of facts under oath. Affidavits are used in business transactions and in legal proceedings and are sometimes required with applications for employment or for certain kinds of licenses.

PROVINCE OF ___*your province*___

COUNTY OF ___*your county*___

HAVING FIRST BEEN DULY SWORN, ___*your full name*___, the undersigned affiant, does hereby depose and say as follows:

1.[Your statement, for example: That on Jan. 3, 1994, I was employed as the Vice President of Corporate Communications for the Temper Metals Company, and that the copy of the memorandum attached is a true and accurate copy of the memorandum that I wrote to John Jameson, President of Temper Metals Company, on that date.]
2.
3. etc.

FURTHER AFFIANT SAYETH NOT.

Witness my hand under the penalties of perjury this ___*date*___ day of ___*month*___, 19___.

___*your signature*___
Affiant

NOTARY'S STATEMENT

PROVINCE OF _____

COUNTY OF _____

On this day personally appeared _____, who, having first been sworn, acknowledged the foregoing before me.

_____

[SEAL]

NOTARY PUBLIC
(or Commissioner for Oaths)
My commission expires:_____

■ **Note:** When making an affidavit, state the facts as you know them in a clear and precise way. If you believe something to be true but you are not positive, you should write in the affidavit that the statement is true "to the best of my knowledge and belief," but it is best to avoid statements of which you are not sure. Do not sign the affidavit until you have sworn before a notary or other qualified official that the statements you made are true. After you have signed it, the notary fills out the statement below your signature and affixes her seal. See AFFIDAVIT.

ACCESS TO INFORMATION REQUEST

The federal government and several provinces now have access to information legislation that gives individuals the right to examine unpublished records compiled by public institutions and agencies. To obtain a copy of records you want to see, send a written request such as the one below.

_____current date_____

Access to Information Request Staff

name of government agency

street address

city   *province*   *postal code*

Re: Access to Information request

Pursuant to the _____*federal or name of province*_____ access to information legislation, I hereby request a copy of all records held by _____*name of agency*_____ pertaining to _____*information you are requesting*_____.

I will pay all reasonable costs associated with this request. However, if costs are expected to exceed $_*amount*_, please let me know the amount in advance.

Sincerely,

your signature

your name printed

your street address

city   *province*   *postal code*

■ **Note:** Your request should be as specific as possible. An agency can reject a request that is so unclear or broad that it would take an unreasonable amount of time to fulfill. The cost will depend on how difficult it is to find the records you want and how many pages must be copied. For further information, see ACCESS TO INFORMATION.

GENERAL RELEASE

A general release is signed when one party agrees to give up all claims against another that resulted from a broken contract or an accident. For example, if you sign a contract to buy a home, and the seller later has a change of heart, you may be willing to accept monetary compensation from him rather than suing him for breach of contract. When the seller gives you the amount of money you both agreed upon, he will ask you to sign a general release like the one below.

Release

FOR GOOD AND VALUABLE CONSIDERATION, receipt of which is hereby acknowledged, the undersigned jointly and severally release, discharge, acquit, and forgive ___*name of person receiving the release*___ now and forevermore, from any and all claims, actions, suits, demands, agreements, liabilities, and proceedings of every nature and description, whether at law or in equity, arising from the beginning of time to the date of this release and more particularly related to an incident or claim that arose out of:

[Description of the accident or contract that is the cause of the dispute.
For example: "A contract dated March 6, 1994, by and between the parties for the pur-
chase of real property located at 1234 Confederation Road, Regina, Sask."]

This release shall be binding upon and inure to the benefit of the parties, their heirs, successors, assigns, and personal representatives.

Signed this _____*date*_____ day of _____*month*_____, 19___.

At _____*address*_____ in the Province of _____.

_____*witness's signature*_____	_____*signature of first party*_____
Witness	Signature
_____*witness's signature*_____	_____*signature of second party*_____
Witness	Signature

■ **Note:** For a general release to be valid, you must receive some kind of consideration, or compensation, in return for relinquishing your legal rights. Unless you are certain that you have been adequately compensated, do not sign a release of this type without first consulting a lawyer. For more information, see ACCIDENTS IN PUBLIC PLACES; RELEASE.

DOOR-TO-DOOR SALES THREE-DAY*
CANCELLATION NOTICE

Anyone who buys merchandise sold door-to-door, or at other than the seller's place of business, has a right to cancel the transaction within two to 10 days, depending on the province. The seller must inform the buyer of this right as well as provide him with two copies of a cancellation notice.

You, the buyer, may cancel this transaction at any time prior to midnight of the third business day after the date of this transaction. See the accompanying notice of cancellation form for an explanation of this right.

NOTICE OF RIGHT TO CANCEL

date of transaction , 19 ___

You may cancel this transaction, without any penalty or obligation, within three (3) business days from the above date.

If you cancel, any property traded in, any payment made by you under the contract of sale, and any negotiable instrument [such as a cheque] executed by you will be returned within ten (10) business days following receipt by the seller of the cancellation notice, and any security interest arising out of the transaction will be canceled.

If you cancel, you must make available to the seller at your residence, in substantially as good condition as when received, any goods delivered to you under this contract of sale; or you may, if you wish, comply with the instructions of the seller regarding the return shipment of the goods at the seller's expense and risk.

If you do make the goods available to the seller and the seller does not pick them up within twenty (20) days of the date of your notice of cancellation, you may retain or dispose of the goods without any further obligation. If you fail to make the goods available to the seller, or if you agree to return the goods to the seller and fail to do so, then you remain liable for performance of all obligations under the sales contract.

To cancel this transaction, mail or deliver a signed and dated copy of this cancellation notice or any other written notice, or send a telegram to the seller, _name of company_ , at _____ _address_ _____ not later than midnight of _date_ , 19__.
I hereby cancel this transaction.

_____ _your signature_ _____ **Date:** _____, 19 ___
Buyer

■ **Note:** The notice may be part of the sales contract or a separate document. The seller fills in the transaction date, seller's or company's name and address, and expiry date; you sign and date the notice. Make a copy for your records. Send cancellation forms by certified mail, return receipt requested.

*The delay for canceling door-to-door sales varies from two to 10 days. See COOLING-OFF PERIOD.

A bill of sale is used when a seller transfers ownership of personal property (property other than real estate) to a buyer. It gives the buyer proof of ownership, and can be useful in obtaining insurance coverage for expensive items, such as electronic equipment or jewelry.

Bill of Sale

FOR GOOD AND VALUABLE CONSIDERATION, and in payment of the sum of $ _purchase price_ , receipt of which is hereby acknowledged, the undersigned Seller hereby sells and transfers to _____ _buyer's name_ _____, Buyer, and his/her successors and assigns forever, the following described personal property:

[description of property]

The Seller warrants to Buyer that he/she has good and marketable title to and full authority to sell said property, and that said property is sold free of all liens, encumbrances, liabilities, and claims of every nature and description whatsoever.

The Seller warrants to Buyer that he/she will defend, protect, indemnify and hold harmless the Buyer and its lawful successors and assigns from any adverse claim made against the property.

The property is otherwise sold in "as is" condition and where presently located, and no warranties either express or implied are made regarding the condition of the property or its suitability for any particular purpose.

Signed this _date_ day of _month_ , 19__ at _____ _address_ _____ in the Province of ____.

_____ _witness's signature_ _____
Witness

_____ _seller's signature_ _____
Seller

_____ _witness's address_ _____
Address

_____ _seller's address_ _____
Address

■ **Note:** The seller should not give the buyer a bill of sale until the buyer has paid the full purchase price. The bill of sale should include a full description of the property, including any model, serial, or identification numbers. A bill of sale may or may not include warranties of title, or ownership ("The Seller warrants to Buyer..."). When they are included it means that the seller declares that he owns the property free and clear, has the right to sell it, and promises that he will defend the buyer's right to the property against anyone who may claim to be the owner. However, in this example, the seller is selling the property in its present condition ("as is") and at its present location (he does not have to deliver it to the buyer), and makes no promise (warranty) regarding its condition. For further information, see BILL OF SALE.

BILL OF SALE FOR MOTOR VEHICLES

This bill of sale transfers the ownership of a motor vehicle from a seller to a buyer. The seller should give the bill of sale to the buyer along with an odometer statement. Many provinces require a bill of sale; some have special forms that can be obtained from the provincial motor vehicle bureau. In many provinces the official transfer of a vehicle is valid only when done by the provincial motor vehicle bureau. The buyer must pay the appropriate sales tax.

Bill of Sale

FOR GOOD AND VALUABLE CONSIDERATION, and in payment of the sum of $ _purchase price_ , receipt of which is hereby acknowledged, the undersigned Seller hereby grants, sells, and transfers to _____ buyer's name _____ ("Buyer"), his/her/its successors and assigns, the following described motor vehicle:

Make: _____ manufacturer of automobile [e.g., Ford] _____

Model: _____ name of model [Taurus] _____

Year: _____ model year [1993] _____

Color: _____ [blue] _____

Vehicle Identification Number: ___ [number stamped on metal plate visible _____ through windshield on driver's side] _____

Seller warrants that he/she/it is the legal owner of said vehicle; that the vehicle is sold free and clear of all adverse claims, liens, and encumbrances; that Seller has full right, power, and authority to sell and transfer said vehicle; and that Seller will protect, defend, indemnify, and hold Buyer harmless from any adverse claims made against the vehicle.

Said vehicle is being sold "as is" and "where is," and no express or implied warranty is made as to its condition.

Signed this _date_ day of _____ month _____, 19___.

_____ seller's signature _____
Seller 1

_____ seller's signature _____
Seller 2

_____ seller's address _____
Address

_____ seller's address _____
Address

■ **Note:** As with the general bill of sale, this bill of sale includes warranties of title but not of the vehicle's condition. The phrase "where is" means that the seller need not deliver the vehicle to the buyer. For more information, on buying and selling vehicles, see AUTOMOBILE PURCHASE; ODOMETER STATEMENT.

CONSIGNMENT SALES AGREEMENT

A consignment agreement allows one person to place items for sale with another while retaining ownership of them until they are sold. The terms of the agreement are negotiable. While this one favors the consignor, another may favor the consignee. See also CONSIGNMENT; SECURITY AGREEMENT.

Consignment Agreement

AGREEMENT made this __date__ day of __month__, 19__, at __address__ in the Province of _____, between __name of consignor__ with its principal place of business at _____ address _____ (hereinafter "Consignor"), and ___name of consignee___, with its principal place of business at __address of business__ ("Consignee").

1. Property consigned: _____ description of property _____.

2. Property value: $__dollar estimate of value__.

3. Consignee shall hold the property consigned for the term of consignment in Trust for Consignor and for the sole purpose of selling the property. Consignor shall at all times retain title to the property consigned. Consignee agrees not to pledge, mortgage, assign, rent, lend, or otherwise encumber the property consigned.

4. Consignee shall pay to Consignor the value set forth above, within _____ days of selling the property consigned. A security interest in the proceeds of such sale shall vest in Consignor until Consignor is paid proceeds or the property consigned is returned to Consignor.

5. Consignor warrants that he/she/it has title to the property consigned, has the right to convey title to said property, and that the property consigned is free of all liens except those here noted: _____. Consignor agrees to hold Consignee harmless for damages, including lawyer's fees and court costs arising from any breach of said warranty.

6. The term of consignment for the property consigned shall be for _____ days/months from the date of this Agreement. When this period ends, each party may terminate this Agreement by giving the other party _____ days' notice of the intent to terminate, in which case the property shall be made available to Consignor by Consignee.

7. Consignee shall insure the property against fire, theft, or other casualty loss during the term of consignment. Consignee agrees that he/she/it shall be fully liable for the above stated value of the property consigned if it is lost, damaged, or destroyed while in Consignee's possession. Possession of the property by Consignee shall begin at the time when the property consigned is physically delivered to Consignee or Consignee's employee or agent.

8. This agreement is evidence of the debt that Consignee is obligated to pay Consignor upon sale of the property consigned, and which is secured with a continuing security agreement in accordance with the laws of the Province of _____. Consignee shall have a priority interest in the property consigned, or the proceeds from the property consigned, in preference to any other claims or security interests of other creditors of Consignor.

IN WITNESS WHEREOF, the parties have executed this Agreement on the date first written above.

_____ consignor's signature _____
Consignor

_____ consignee's signature _____
Consignee

When one person lends money to another, a promissory note is used to record the terms of the loan. A demand promissory note requires the borrower (the maker) to repay the full amount of the loan to the lender upon the lender's request. One person must witness the maker's signature.

Promissory Note

FOR VALUE RECEIVED, the undersigned Maker(s) of this note promises (promise) to pay to the order of ____*name of lender*____, residing at *lender's address*____, the sum of ____*written amount of loan*____dollars ($ _*amount in figures*_), with annual interest at ___*amount of interest*__% on the unpaid balance. The full unpaid principal and any earned interest shall be fully due and immediately payable UPON DEMAND of any holder of this note. Upon failure to make payment within _*number of days*_ days of demand, and should this note be turned over for collection, the Maker(s) shall pay all reasonable legal fees and costs of collection.

The parties waive the requirement for presentation for payment, notice of non-payment, protest, and notices of protest in connection with this note.

If this note is signed by more than one Maker, then each of them shall be jointly and severally liable under this note.

Signed this ___*date*___ day of ____*month*____, 19___ at _____*address*_____ in the Province of _____

_____*maker's signature*_____
Maker

_____*witness's signature*_____
Witness

_____*maker's signature*_____
Maker

■ **Note:** In this sample, the borrower (the payee) is responsible for expenses the lender incurs while collecting a late payment. "Jointly and severally" means that each person who signs this note is responsible for paying the entire amount. The lender keeps the original document; the borrower should have a copy. When the loan has been repaid, the lender writes "Paid in Full" on the original, dates it, signs it, and gives it to the borrower. For more information, see PROMISSORY NOTE.

This type of promissory note is used to define the terms of a loan that is to be repaid in equal payments (installments) of principal and interest, in contrast to the due date note on facing page.

Promissory Note

FOR VALUE RECEIVED, the undersigned Maker(s) promises (promise)to pay to the order of _____*name of lender*_____, or any subsequent holder of this Note, the sum of _____*written amount of loan*_____ dollars ($_*amount in figures*_), together with annual interest of _*amount of interest*_ % on any unpaid balance.

Payments shall be made in _*number*_ installments of $ _*amount*_ each, with a first payment due _____*date*_____, 19___, and the same amount on the same day of each _*day/month*_ thereafter until the entire principal amount of this note and earned interest are fully paid. All payments and prepayments shall be applied first to accrued interest, and then to principal.

If there is a default in making the monthly payments on this note, at the option of its holder, its unpaid principal and accrued interest shall immediately become due and payable.

For value received, if there is a default in making any payment on this note, the undersigned also promises to pay _____*payee*_____ on demand all reasonably incurred costs of enforcing payment on the note, including but not necessarily limited to, legal costs.

The undersigned waives presentation for payment, notice of nonpayment, protest, and notices of protest in connection with this note.

Made this _*date*_ day of _____*month*_____, 19___ at _____*address*_____ in the Province of _____

_____*witness's signature*_____
Witness

_____*maker's signature*_____
Maker

_____*maker's signature*_____
Maker

■ **Note:** Although it is similar to the other promissory notes in this section, this installment note gives the lender the right to demand repayment of the entire loan if a payment is late. A detailed payment schedule to which the parties have agreed should be attached to this document. For further information, see PROMISSORY NOTE.

COSIGNER'S GUARANTY

A guaranty is an agreement in which a third party (the guarantor) promises a lender in writing that he will pay the borrower's debts if the borrower fails to do so.

street address

city   *province*   *postal code*

date

Guaranty

FOR VALUE RECEIVED, and in consideration of and as an inducement for _____ *lender's name* _____ (hereinafter "Lender") to extend credit to _____ *borrower's name* _____ ("Borrower"), the undersigned jointly and severally and unconditionally guarantee to Lender the prompt and full payment, when due, of each and every claim hereinafter due Lender from Borrower.

The undersigned agree to remain fully bound on this guaranty notwithstanding any extension, forbearance, waiver, or release, discharge, or substitution of any party, collateral, or security for the debt, and hereby consent to and waive all notice of same. In the event of default, the Lender may seek payment directly from the undersigned without need to proceed first against the Borrower.

The undersigned further agree to pay all reasonable lawyers' fees and costs of collection necessary for the enforcement of this guaranty.

This guaranty is unlimited as to amount or duration, except that any guarantor hereto may terminate his/her obligations in regard to future credit extended after delivery of notice of termination of this guaranty to the Lender by certified mail, return receipt requested. Said termination notice shall not discharge guarantor's obligations regarding debts incurred up to the date said termination notice is received.

_____ *witness's signature* _____
Witness

_____ *witness's signature* _____
Witness

_____ *guarantor's signature* _____
Guarantor

_____ *guarantor's signature* _____
Guarantor

◼ **Note:** You should not guarantee a loan for someone unless you are confident of her ability to repay it. "Jointly and severally" means that each guarantor is responsible for paying all the borrower's debts. If anything in the borrower's loan agreement is changed, each guarantor is still obligated by the terms in this document. If the borrower misses a payment, the lender can demand repayment of the debt from the guarantor. Because it is "unlimited as to amount or duration," each guarantor is responsible for all future debts owed to this lender until the guaranty is revoked. If a formal revocation of the guaranty is sent to the lender, the guarantor is absolved from future debts, but not from debts the borrower owed before the revocation. For further information, see COSIGNING.

A security agreement is signed when a borrower gives a lender collateral (a secured interest in personal property) of equal value to the borrower's debt. If the borrower (debtor) fails to repay the loan, the lender (secured party) can take possession of the borrower's personal property. The lender may either keep such property for his own use or sell it to recover the money he is owed.

Security Agreement

NOTICE: THIS SECURITY AGREEMENT OR OTHER REQUIRED FINANCING STATEMENTS MUST BE FILED IN THE APPROPRIATE PROVINCIAL REGISTRY OFFICE TO PROTECT YOUR RIGHTS IN THE COLLATERAL AGAINST CLAIMS BY THIRD PARTIES.

BE IT KNOWN that, for good and valuable consideration, _*borrower's name*_ whose address is ____*borrower's address*____ (hereinafter "Debtor"), grants to ____*lender's name*____, whose address is ____*lender's address*____ ("Secured Party"), his/her/its successors and assigns, a security interest in the following property ("the collateral"), which shall include all after-acquired property of a like nature and description and the proceeds and profits thereof:

[description of personal property offered as collateral]

This security interest is granted to secure payment and performance on the following obligations now or hereinafter owed to Secured Party by Debtor:

[amount and date of loan]

Debtor hereby acknowledges to Secured Party that:

1. The collateral shall be kept at Debtor's above address and shall not be moved or relocated without the prior written consent of Secured Party.

2. Debtor warrants to Secured Party that he/she/it owns the collateral; that it is free from any other lien, encumbrance, and security interest or adverse interest; and that Debtor has full right, power, and authority to grant this security interest in the above-described collateral.

3. Debtor agrees to execute such financing statements as are reasonably required by Secured Party to perfect this security agreement in accordance with provincial law.

4. In the event of any default in payment or performance of any obligation for which this security interest is granted, or upon breach of any term of this

security agreement, Secured Party may declare all obligations immediately due and payable and shall have all remedies of a secured party available under provincial law. Such rights shall be cumulative and not necessarily successive with any other rights or remedies.

5. This security agreement shall further be in default upon the death, insolvency, or bankruptcy of any party who is an obligor* to this agreement, or upon any material decrease in the value of the collateral or adverse change in the financial condition of Debtor.

6. In the event of default, Debtor shall pay all reasonable lawyers' fees and costs of collection necessary to enforce this agreement.

7. Debtor agrees to maintain adequate insurance coverage on the collateral as Secured Party may reasonably require, and Secured Party shall be named as loss payee.

8. Any waiver, express or implied, of any breach of this Agreement, shall not be deemed a waiver of any subsequent breach.

IN WITNESS WHEREOF, this agreement is executed this ___*date*___ day of _____*month*_____, 19____, at ___*town*___ in the province of ___*province*___.

_____*debtor's signature*_____
Debtor

___*secured party's signature*___
Secured Party

■ **Note:** This agreement may accompany any loan agreement if the debtor agrees to put up collateral for the loan. The debtor declares that she is the owner of the collateral, and that no one else has an interest or claim in the property (it is free from lien, encumbrance, and security or adverse interest). She also agrees to complete the forms that are required by provincial law. These forms are filed with the provincial officials where the debtor lives, and they ensure (perfect) the secured party's interest in the collateral by making it a matter of public record. If any of the terms of this agreement are not met (default of payment or performance of any obligation), the secured party has the right to demand payment of the debt (declare all obligations due). Further, he can demand payment if the debtor becomes insolvent, declares bankruptcy, or dies. For more information, see COLLATERAL; SECURITY AGREEMENT.
*An obligor is a person who is bound by a legal obligation.

GENERAL ASSIGNMENT

An assignment is a contract that transfers property, rights, or responsibilities from one person (the assignor) to another (the assignee). Usually it is property, or an interest in it, that is transferred.

Assignment

FOR VALUE RECEIVED, the undersigned hereby unconditionally and irrevocably assigns and transfers unto _____ *name of person receiving property (assignee)* _____, all right, title, and interest in and to the following:

[description of property]

The undersigned hereby warrants that he/she has full right, power, and authority to enter into this assignment and transfer, and that the rights and benefits assigned hereunder are free and clear of any lien, encumbrance, adverse claim, or interest.

This assignment shall be binding upon and inure to the benefit of the parties, their heirs, successors, assigns, and personal representatives.

Signed this _____ *date* _____ day of _____ *month* _____, 19___.at _____ *address* _____ in the Province of _____

_____ *assignor's signature* _____
Assignor

_____ *witness's signature* _____
Witness

_____ *witness's signature* _____
Witness

NOTARY'S STATEMENT

PROVINCE OF _____

COUNTY OF _____

On this _____ day of _____, 19___, before me, a Notary Public, personally appeared _____, known to me to be the individual described in and who executed the foregoing Assignment, and duly acknowledged it to me as his/her free act and deed.

[SEAL]

_____
NOTARY PUBLIC

My commission expires: _____

■ **Note:** Provincial laws vary regarding witnesses for assignments. Where they are required, the assignor signs the document in the presence of the witnesses, who also sign it. Assignments may also be acknowledged by the assignor in the presence of a notary, who completes the statement and puts his seal on it. If real estate is being transferred, the assignee must record the assignment with the registry office for the county where the property is held. For more information, see ACKNOWLEDGMENT; ASSIGNMENT.

MECHANIC'S LIEN

A mechanic's lien is a claim placed by a contractor (the lienholder) on a customer's property to collect any unpaid fees. Such a lien is on the entire property, not just the contractor's improvements to it.

Notice of Mechanic's Lien

Notice is hereby provided that the lienholder named below provided labor and/or materials relative to the construction and/or improvements on that real estate commonly known as:

_____ *address of property* _____

_____ *city or town* _____

_____ *province* _____ *postal code* _____

said real estate being more particularly described in Book or Volume ___ *volume number* ___, page ___ *page number* ___, of the ___ *county where property is located* ___ County Register of Deeds.

The owner of record of said property is: _____ *property owner's name* _____.

This lien is filed to secure the balance of $ ___ *amount owed* ___, plus such additional amounts as may be due lienholder in accordance with state law.

Dated: ___ *date* ___, 19___ _____ *lienholder's signature* _____
Lienholder
_____ *lienholder's address* _____
Address
city _____ *province* _____ *postal code* _____

PROVINCE OF _____

COUNTY OF _____

Subscribed and sworn to before me this _____ day of _____, 19__.

_____

[SEAL]   NOTARY PUBLIC

My commission expires: _____

■ **Note:** To obtain a mechanic's lien, a contractor must show that he supplied materials or labor for home construction or other service but was never paid for them. Once a lien is placed, it will remain with the property until the property's current or future owner pays the debt or the contractor drops the claim. A mechanic's lien is usually recorded at the county clerk's office or the registry of deeds so that anyone interested in buying the property can find out whether there are any claims against it. For more information, see LIEN; MECHANIC'S LIEN.

Prenuptial agreements—also called antenuptial agreements—are made by couples before they marry. While these agreements can cover almost any matter, they are most frequently concerned with the way that property would be divided if the marriage ends either by divorce or death.

Prenuptial Agreement

THIS AGREEMENT is entered into this _date_ day 19___, at _____address_____ in the Province of _____, between _____name of fiancé_____ and _____name of fiancée_____ .

WHEREAS, the undersigned parties contemplate marriage under the laws of the Province of _province where marriage will take place_; and whereas it is their desire to enter into this agreement so that each of them will continue to own and exercise control over his/her own property; and whereas neither of them desires that their present separate financial interests should be changed by his/her marriage or the laws of this state regarding the division of property;

NOW, THEREFORE, THE PARTIES AGREE AS FOLLOWS:

1. All property, whether real, personal, or mixed, which belongs to each of the above parties shall be, now and forever, their personal and separate property, including all interest, rents, and profits that may accrue from such property, and such property shall remain forever free of claim by the other.

2. The parties shall continue to have the full right, power, and authority, in all respects the same as each would have if not married, to enjoy, use, sell, lease, give, and convey all property as may presently belong to him or her.

3. In the event of a separation or divorce, the parties shall have no right against each other by way of claims for spousal support, maintenance, alimentary pension, compensation, or division of any separately owned property in existence as of the date of this Agreement.

4. In the event of separation or divorce, marital property acquired after marriage shall nevertheless remain subject to division, either by agreement or judicial determination.

5. In the event of the death of either party, the other party hereby waives now and forever any claim or interest in the deceased's property granted by statute, and agrees that the distribution of all such property shall be governed solely by the Last Will and Testament of the deceased party.

6. This Agreement shall be binding upon and inure to the benefit of the parties, their heirs, successors, assigns, and personal representatives.

7. Additional provisions:

[list any additional provisions here]

8. The parties acknowledge that they have entered into this Agreement after full disclosure of the property owned by each of them, and that each of them has been afforded the opportunity to have this Agreement reviewed by independent counsel.

9. This Agreement shall be enforced in accordance with the laws of the Province of _*province where couple will reside*_. If any part or provision of this Agreement shall be found invalid or unenforceable, then the rest of this Agreement shall remain in full force and effect to the extent practicable.

Signed this _*date*_ day of _*month*_, 19___.

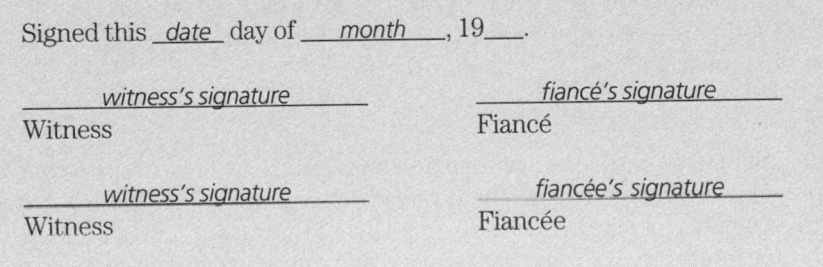

____*witness's signature*____   ____*fiancé's signature*____
Witness   Fiancé

____*witness's signature*____   ____*fiancée's signature*____
Witness   Fiancée

■ **Note:** A prenuptial agreement should be written in easily understandable language so that the parties cannot claim later they did not understand what they were signing. However, no one should sign a prenuptial agreement without consulting a lawyer. Each party should sign and keep a copy of the agreement. Each spouse should also write a last will and testament clearly stating how his or her property should be divided in the event that one spouse dies before the other. For more information, see MARRIAGE; PRENUPTIAL AGREEMENT.

Cohabitation, or living-together, agreements are useful for couples who share a home and expenses, whether or not they plan to marry. By putting their rights and duties in writing, they can avoid disputes over property or children if they separate. This sample is a typical agreement.

Cohabitation Agreement

THIS AGREEMENT is made this _date_ day of ___month___, 19___, by and between ___first party's name___ and _____second party's name_____, who presently reside in the County of ___name of county___, Province of ___name of province___.

WHEREAS, the parties wish to live together, but do not wish to be bound by the statutory or common-law provisions relating to marriage, it is hereby agreed that the parties to this Agreement shall live together for an indefinite period of time subject to the following terms and conditions:

1. Property: Any real or personal property acquired by either of us during the relationship shall be considered to be our separate property. All property listed on the pages attached is incorporated in this Agreement by reference. The property now and hereinafter belongs to the party under whose name it is listed prior to the making of this Agreement. All listed property is and shall continue to be the separate property of the person who owns it. All property received by either of us by gift or inheritance during our relationship shall be the separate property of the one who receives it.

2. Income: All income earned or accumulated during the existence of our relationship shall be maintained in one fund, and all debts and expenses arising during the existence of our union shall be paid out of this fund. Each of us shall have an equal interest in this fund, and equal right to its management and control, and each of us shall be equally entitled to any surplus that remains after payment of all debts and expenses.

3. Termination: Our relationship may be terminated at the sole will and decision of either of us, expressed by a written notice given to the other.

4. Modification: This Agreement may be modified by an agreement in writing signed by both parties, with the exception that no modifications may decrease the obligations that may be imposed regarding any children born of our union.

5. Application of Law: The validity of this Agreement shall be determined solely under the laws of the Province of ___*name of province where parties reside*___. If any portion of this Agreement is held invalid or unenforceable in a court of law, then the rest of this Agreement shall remain in full force and effect to the extent practicable.

6. Claims Waived: Neither of us shall maintain any action or claim against the other for support, alimentary pension, compensation, or for rights to any property existing prior to this date, or acquired on or subsequent to the date of termination.

7. Free Act of Parties; Full Disclosure: The parties enter into this Agreement of their own will and accord without reliance on any other inducement or promise, and with full disclosure of the interest each holds in any and all property, real, personal, or mixed.

8. Captions: The use of captions in this Agreement is for convenience only, and shall have no bearing on the interpretation of the contents of the section to which they refer.

9. Right to Independent Counsel: Each party to this Agreement has had the opportunity to have this Agreement reviewed by independent counsel.

Signed this ___*date*___ day of ___*month*___, 19___.

_____*first party's signature*_____
First Party

_____*second party's signature*_____
Second Party

■ **Note:** Cohabitation agreements should cover property rights, management of income, provisions for the termination of the relationship, and responsibility for any children that the couple have. Agreements can also include other topics that couples wish to add. Captions—the wording at the beginning of each numbered paragraph—make the agreement easier to read. A couple can usually write their own agreement, but it is a good idea for each party to have it reviewed by a lawyer before signing it. The couple should sign and date two copies, and each party should keep one copy. For further information, see LIVING TOGETHER.

A general durable power of attorney is granted by someone who wants to place the management of her property and financial affairs in the hands of a person whom she trusts. This type of power of attorney remains in effect when the person granting it (the principal) becomes incapacitated.

Durable Power of Attorney (General)

NOTICE: THIS LEGAL DOCUMENT GIVES THE PERSON NAMED AS ATTORNEY-IN-FACT BROAD POWERS OVER THE PROPERTY OF THE GRANTOR, UNLESS LIMITED BY THE TERMS OF THE DOCUMENT ITSELF. THESE POWERS MAY EXIST FOR AN UNLIMITED TIME PERIOD UNLESS LIMITED BY THE TERMS OF THE DOCUMENT ITSELF. THE GRANTOR MAY REVOKE THIS POWER OF ATTORNEY AT ANY TIME. DO NOT SIGN THIS POWER OF ATTORNEY UNLESS YOU UNDERSTAND ALL ITS TERMS. CONSULT WITH A LAWYER FOR ADVICE AND ASSISTANCE.

I, _name of person giving authority_, the undersigned Principal, hereby grant this General Power of Attorney to _name of person receiving authority_, as my attorney-in-fact.

My attorney-in-fact shall have full power and authority to do any and all acts on my behalf that I could do personally including but not limited to:

the right to sell, deed, buy, trade, lease, mortgage, assign, rent, or dispose of any of my present or future real or personal property;

the right to execute, accept, undertake, and perform any and all contracts in my name;

the right to deposit, endorse, or withdraw funds to or from any of my bank accounts, depositories or safe-deposit boxes;

the right to borrow, lend, invest, or reinvest funds on any terms;

the right to initiate, defend, commence, or settle legal actions on my behalf;

the right to vote any shares or beneficial interest in any entity;

and the right to retain any accountant, lawyer, or other adviser deemed necessary to protect my interests generally or relative to any foregoing unlimited power.

The real estate covered by this Power of Attorney is commonly known as:

[list real estate covered under the general durable power of attorney]

My attorney-in-fact hereby accepts this appointment subject to its terms and agrees to act and perform in a fiduciary capacity consistent with my best interests as he/she in his/her best discretion deems advisable, and I affirm and ratify all acts so undertaken.

This power of attorney may be revoked by me at any time, and shall automatically be revoked upon my death, provided any person relying on this power of attorney before my death shall have full rights to accept the authority of my attorney-in-fact until in receipt of actual notice of revocation. It is my intention that this instrument be construed as a Durable Power of Attorney, and that it shall not be affected by my subsequent disability or incapacity.

A photocopy of this Power of Attorney shall be deemed an original for all purposes permitted by law.

NOTICE: DELETE POWERS THAT DO NOT APPLY

Signed this _____*date*_____ day of _____*month*_____, 19___, at _____*address*_____ in the Province of _____

_____*principal's signature*_____
Principal

I accept appointment as attorney-in-fact as granted by this Power of Attorney.

_____*attorney-in-fact's signature*_____
Attorney-in-Fact

NOTARY'S STATEMENT

PROVINCE OF _____   _____, 19___.

COUNTY OF _____

Before me personally appeared _____ and _____, who, having first been sworn, acknowledged the foregoing instrument as their free and voluntary acts, and signed the above instrument in my presence.

_____

[SEAL]   NOTARY PUBLIC

                                      My commission expires: _____

Note: The principal may delete any of the powers granted to the attorney-in-fact in this sample form. You can draft a power of attorney on your own, but never sign one without first consulting a lawyer. Provincial laws vary on such issues as who may serve as an attorney-in-fact and whether special forms are required. The attorney-in-fact and principal should each keep several copies and give them to banks or other institutions with which the attorney-in-fact will be dealing on the principal's behalf. A power of attorney can be revoked at any time by means of a notarized letter. For further information, see POWER OF ATTORNEY.

A springing durable power of attorney goes into effect only if the person granting it (the principal) becomes incapacitated. With this type of durable power of attorney, the principal retains full control over his own financial affairs until he is unable to do so any longer.

Durable Power of Attorney
(Springing)

I, ___name of person giving authority___, the undersigned Principal, do hereby grant a Durable Power of Attorney to ___name of person receiving authority___, as my attorney-in-fact.

My attorney-in-fact shall have full right, power, and authority to do all acts on my behalf that I could do personally, including but not limited to:

The right to sell, deed, buy, trade, lease, mortgage, assign, rent, or dispose of any real or personal property; the right to execute, accept, undertake, and perform all contracts in my name; the right to deposit, endorse, or withdraw funds to or from any of my bank accounts or safe-deposit boxes; the right to borrow, collect, lend, invest, or reinvest funds; the right to initiate, defend, commence, or settle legal actions on my behalf; the right to vote (in person or by proxy) any shares or beneficial interest in any entity; and the right to retain any accountant, lawyer, or other adviser deemed necessary to protect my interests relative to any foregoing unlimited power. My attorney-in-fact shall have full power and authority to execute, deliver, and accept all documents and undertake all acts consistent with the powers granted herein.

This Power of Attorney shall become effective upon and remain in effect only during such time periods as I may be mentally or physically incapacitated and unable to care for my own needs or make competent decisions as are necessary to protect my interests or conduct my affairs.

My attorney-in-fact hereby accepts this appointment and agrees to act in said capacity consistent with my best interests as he/she in his/her sole discretion deems advisable, and I hereby affirm and ratify all such acts as if they were my own.

This Power of Attorney may be revoked by me at any time, and shall automatically be revoked upon my death. Any person relying on this power of attorney shall have full rights to accept the authority of my attorney-in-fact until in receipt of actual notice of revocation.

IN WITNESS WHEREOF, I have executed this Power of Attorney this ___*date*___ day of ___*month*___, 19___, at _____*address*_____, in the Province of _____ as my free act and deed.

_____*principal's signature*_____
Principal

I accept the duties of attorney-in-fact as described in the above Power of Attorney.

_____*attorney-in-fact's signature*_____
Attorney-in-Fact

____*witness's signature*____   _____*witness's address*_____
Witness   Address

____*witness's signature*____   _____*witness's address*_____
Witness   Address

NOTARY'S STATEMENT

PROVINCE OF _____   _____, 19___.

COUNTY OF _____

Before me personally appeared _____ and _____, known to me personally as the Principal and Attorney-in-Fact in the Power of Attorney above, and having first been sworn, signed the above power of attorney as their free act and deed, in my presence, and for the purposes described therein.

[SEAL]   _____
                                       NOTARY PUBLIC

                                       My commission expires: _____

■ **Note:** Not every province recognizes a springing durable power of attorney. In provinces that do, it should be signed and notarized in the same way as a general power of attorney.

Delete any powers in this document that do not apply, and review it periodically to be sure it still reflects your wishes. Since a springing power of attorney does not go into effect immedi-

ately, the principal should keep the original document in a safe place that is accessible to the attorney-in-fact. See POWER OF ATTORNEY.

DURABLE POWER OF ATTORNEY
FOR HEALTH CARE

A durable power of attorney for health care is used by someone (the principal) to give another (the attorney-in-fact) the authority to make medical decisions for him. This document helps ensure that if the principal becomes incapacitated, his health care wishes will still be carried out.

Durable Power of Attorney (Health Care)

I, _name of person giving authority_, the undersigned Principal, do hereby grant a Durable Power of Attorney for health care to _name of person receiving authority_, as my attorney-in-fact.

I hereby grant to my attorney-in-fact full power and authority to make health care decisions for me to the same extent that I could make such decisions for myself if I had the capacity to do so. In exercising this authority, my attorney-in-fact shall make health care decisions that are consistent with my desires as stated in this document or which I otherwise make known to my attorney-in-fact, including, but not limited to, my desires concerning obtaining, withholding, or withdrawing life-prolonging care, treatment, services, and procedures.

I hereby authorize all physicians and psychiatrists who have treated me, and all other providers of health care, including hospitals, to release to my attorney-in-fact all information contained in my medical records that my attorney-in-fact may request. I hereby waive all privileges attached to the physician-patient relationship, and to any verbal or written communication arising out of such a relationship. My attorney-in-fact is hereby authorized to receive and review any information, whether verbal or written, pertaining to my physical or mental health, including medical and hospital records, and to execute any releases, waivers, or other documents that may be required in order to obtain such information, and to disclose such information to such persons, organizations, and health-care providers as my attorney-in-fact shall deem appropriate. My attorney-in-fact is authorized to employ and discharge health-care providers including physicians, psychiatrists, dentists, nurses, and therapists as shall be deemed appropriate for my physical, mental and emotional well-being in my attorney-in-fact's sole discretion. My attorney-in-fact is hereby authorized to pay all reasonable fees and expenses for the provision of such services.

My attorney-in-fact is hereby authorized to apply for my admission to any medical, nursing, or residential, institution, or other similar facility; execute any consent or admission forms required by such facility; and enter into any and all agreements for my care at such facility or elsewhere during my lifetime. My attorney-in-fact is authorized to arrange for and consent to medical, therapeutic, and surgical procedures for me including the administration of drugs. The power to make health-care decisions on my behalf shall include the power and authority to give, refuse, or withdraw consent to any care, treatment, service, or procedure to maintain, diagnose, or treat a physical or mental condition.

I reserve the right to revoke the authority granted to my attorney-in-fact to make health-care decisions for me by notifying the treating physician, hospital, or other health-care provider orally or in writing. Notwithstanding any provision herein to the contrary, I retain the right to make medical and other health-care decisions for myself so long as I am able to give informed consent with respect to any such decision. No treatment shall be given to me over my objection, and no treatment or care necessary to keep me alive may be stopped if I object.

This Power of Attorney shall not be affected by my subsequent disability or incapacity. Notwithstanding any provision herein to the contrary, my attorney-in-fact shall take no action under this instrument unless I am deemed to be disabled or incapacitated as defined herein. My incapacity shall be deemed to exist when so certified in writing by two (2) licensed physicians not related by blood or marriage to either me or to my attorney-in-fact. Such certification shall state that I am incapable of caring for myself and that I am physically and mentally incapable of managing my financial affairs. The certificate of the physicians described above shall be attached to the original of this instrument, and if this instrument is filed or recorded among public records, then such certificate shall be similarly filed or recorded as required or permitted by applicable law.

My attorney-in-fact shall be entitled to reimbursement for all reasonable costs actually incurred and paid on my behalf under the authority granted in this instrument.

To the extent permitted by law, I nominate and appoint my attorney-in-fact to serve as my guardian, conservator, and/or in any similar representative capacity. If I am not permitted by law to so nominate and appoint my attorney-in-fact, then I request any court of competent jurisdiction that may be petitioned by any person to appoint a guardian, conservator, or similar representative for me to give due consideration to this request.

IN WITNESS WHEREOF, I have signed this Durable Power of Attorney this ___*date*___ day of
*month*___, 19___.

_____*principal's signature*_____
Principal

NOTARY'S STATEMENT

PROVINCE OF _____

COUNTY OF _____

Before me appeared _____, known to me personally to be the Principal named in the above Power of Attorney, and who, having first been sworn, signed the foregoing document as his/her free act and deed, voluntarily and under no duress, and for the purposes described therein, this _____ day of _____, 19___.

_____

[SEAL]   NOTARY PUBLIC
                              My commission expires: _____

Note: To make sure that you receive the health care you want, you can create both a living will and a power of attorney for health care. A living will contains instructions on the specific type of medical care you want. A durable power of attorney for health care authorizes someone to make decisions based on those instructions. You must be competent and of legal age to sign a power of attorney—otherwise it will be considered invalid and a court will appoint a guardian or conservator to act on your behalf. Many provinces require very specific language for a durable power of attorney for health care; ask a lawyer or your doctor about the form recognized in your province. This document should be signed and notarized in the same manner as a general power of attorney. The attorney-in-fact for health care should keep the original in a safe, accessible place. Both the principal and the attorney-in-fact should have several copies to give to the principal's medical care practitioners and facilities. For further information, see LIVING WILL; POWER OF ATTORNEY.

SPECIAL POWER OF ATTORNEY

A special, or limited, power of attorney is used when one person gives another the authority to perform one or more specific acts. For example, parents can use a special power of attorney to give a babysitter the authority to consent to medical care for their child in an emergency.

Power of Attorney (Special)

I, ___name of person giving authority___, as Principal, hereby grant a limited and specific Power of Attorney to ___name of person receiving authority___, as my attorney-in-fact. My attorney-in-fact shall have full right, power, and authority to undertake and perform the following acts on my behalf to the same extent as if I had done so personally:

[Description of acts for which authority is granted. For example, "To authorize medical treatment for my son, Ezra, and to obligate me for the cost of such treatment."]

The authority granted herein shall include such acts as are reasonably required or necessary to carry out and perform the specific duties granted to my attorney-in-fact. My attorney-in-fact agrees to accept this appointment subject to its terms, and agrees to act in said capacity consistent with my best interests as he/she in his/her sole discretion deems advisable, and I hereby ratify all acts so carried out. This Power of Attorney may be revoked by me at any time, and shall automatically be revoked upon my death, provided any person relying on this Power of Attorney before or after my death shall have full rights to accept the authority of my attorney-in-fact consistent with the powers granted herein until in receipt of actual notice of revocation.

Signed this ___date___ day of ___month___, 19__ at ___address___ in the Province of _____

_____
principal's signature
Principal

I, _____, hereby accept appointment as attorney-in-fact for the above-named Principal, and for the purposes described.

_____
attorney-in-fact's signature
Attorney-in-Fact

NOTARY'S STATEMENT

PROVINCE OF _____

COUNTY OF _____

Before me personally appeared _____ and _____, known to me personally as the Principal and Attorney-in-fact named in the above Power of Attorney, and having first been sworn, signed the above document as their free act and deed, voluntarily and under no duress, and for the purposes described therein, this ___ day of _____, 19___.

_____
[SEAL]   NOTARY PUBLIC
                          My commission expires: _____

■ **Note:** This document should be signed and notarized. The attorney-in-fact should keep the original, and the principal should keep a copy. A special power of attorney can be re- voked by a written letter from the principal. For more information, see BABYSITTER; POWER OF ATTORNEY.

RESIDENTIAL RENTAL APPLICATION

Residential rental applications help landlords to determine who might make a good tenant. By asking applicants for information about such matters as family, pets, employment history, and income, and by checking references, landlords can minimize their chances of renting to tenants who are irresponsible or unable to pay their rent. For more information, see LANDLORD; TENANT'S RIGHTS.

Rental Application

Name _____ *applicant's name* _____ Telephone _____

Present Address _____ *street address* _____

City, Province, Postal Code _____

How long at present address? _____

Social Insurance No. _____ Driver's License No. _____

Birth Date _____

Co-applicant's Name _____

Co-applicant's Social Insurance No. _____

Co-applicant's Driver's License No. _____

Co-applicant's Birth Date _____

How many in your family? Adults _____ Children _____ Any pets? _____

Name, breed, and weight of pet(s), if any _____

_____

Current landlord _____ Telephone _____

Employer _____ Position _____

Number of years with current employer _____ Phone _____ Salary _____

Co-applicant's employer _____ Position _____

Number of years with current employer _____ Phone _____ Salary _____

Name of bank _____

_____ Chequing   Account No. _____

_____ Savings   Account No. _____

Personal References

Name and Address	Relationship	Telephone

I represent that the information provided in this application is true and correct to the best of my knowledge. You are hereby authorized to verify my credit and references in connection with the processing of this application. I acknowledge receipt of a copy of this application.

Dated: _____ *current date* _____, 19___   _____ *applicant's signature* _____

at _____ *address* _____   Applicant

in the Province of _____   _____ *co-applicant's signature* _____

          Co-applicant

RESIDENTIAL LEASE

This sample lease contains the terms most commonly found in rental contracts. As with other contracts, a lease can be modified as long as both landlord and tenant agree to the changes.

Lease Agreement

LEASE AGREEMENT, entered into by and between ___*property owner's name*___ ("Landlord") and _____*renter's name*_____ ("Tenant").

For good and valuable consideration the parties agree as follows:

1. Landlord hereby leases and lets to Tenant the premises described as follows:

[address of rental property]

2. This Lease shall be for a term of _____*length of lease*_____, beginning on _____*date lease begins*_____, 19___, and ending on _____*date lease ends*_____, 19___.

3. Tenant shall pay to Landlord rent in the amount of $ ___*amount of rent*___ per month during said term, payable on the _*day rent is due*_ day of each month in advance. Tenant shall pay a security deposit of $ _*amount of deposit*_, to be kept by Landlord in accordance with provincial law, and to be returned upon termination of this Lease and the payment of all rents due and performance of all other obligations. (*Note that security deposits are not legal in all provinces.*)

4. Tenant shall at his/her own expense provide the following utilities:

[list utilities tenant must pay for in addition to rent]

5. Tenant further agrees that:

   a) Upon the expiry of the Lease, Tenant will return possession of the leased premises to Landlord in its present condition, except for reasonable wear and tear. Tenant shall commit no waste to the leased premises.
   b) Tenant shall not assign or sublet the premises or allow any other person to occupy the leased premises without Landlord's prior written consent.
   c) Tenant shall not make any material or structural alterations to the premises or change locks on the premises without Landlord's prior written consent.
   d) Tenant shall comply with all building, zoning, and health codes and other applicable laws for the use of said leased premises.

c) Tenant shall not conduct on premises any activity deemed by Landlord in its sole discretion hazardous, a nuisance, or requiring an increase in fire or hazard insurance premiums.

f) Tenant shall not allow pets on the premises without the prior written consent of Landlord.

g) In the event of any breach of the payment of rent, or any other breach of this Lease, Landlord shall have full rights to terminate this Lease in accordance with provincial law and re-enter and reclaim possession of the premises, in addition to such other remedies which are available to Landlord as a result of said breach.

h) Each tenant shall be jointly and severally liable for all rent due.

6. This Lease shall be binding upon and inure to the benefit of the parties, and their respective successors, agents, personal representatives, and assigns.

7. This Lease shall be subordinate to all present or future mortgages against the property.

8. Additional Lease terms:

[list any other terms to which tenant and landlord agree]

Signed this _____*date*_____ day of _____*month*_____, 19___.

_____*witness's signature*_____   _____*landlord's signature*_____
Witness   Landlord

_____*witness's signature*_____   _____*tenant's signature*_____
Witness   Tenant

                                             _____*co-tenant's signature*_____
                                             Co-tenant

                                             _____*co-tenant's signature*_____
                                             Co-tenant

Note: Both landlord and tenant must initial any changes they make to the terms of the lease. The landlord and the tenant should both sign two original documents, with each keeping one of the originals. For more information, see LANDLORD; LEASE; SECURITY DEPOSIT; TENANT'S RIGHTS.

LEASE CANCELLATION

In most cases, a landlord is entitled to three-months' notice, if you do not plan to renew your lease. If you wish to cancel your lease before the term expires, he may let you sublet the premises, or cancel the lease for, say, three months' rent. Your cancellation notice should specify the terms.

Notice of Intention to Vacate

CERTIFIED MAIL—RETURN RECEIPT REQUESTED

_____ *street address* _____
_____ *city   province   postal code*
_____ *date* _____, 19____

TO: _*landlord's name*_____
     _*street address*_____
     *city   province   postal code*

Whereas

_____*landlord's name*_____ (the "Landlord") and _____*tenant's name*_____
(the "Tenant") executed a lease dated _____*the lease*_____ of certain premises
located at _____*address*_____
_____*the premises*_____
but the parties now wish to cancel the Lease.

It is agreed as follows:

1. In return for the Tenant vacating the Premises on or before __*the termination date*__,
and _____*specify cancellation terms, if any*_____ the Lease is canceled effective that date
and the parties will have no further obligation to each other under the Lease.

2. Nothing in this agreement operated to discharge obligations and liabilities accrued under the Lease up to the date of its cancellation.

3. If the Tenant does not vacate the Premises on or before the Termination Date, this agreement is null and void.

4. This agreement binds and benefits the parties and their respective heirs, executors, administrators, personal representatives, successors, and assigns.

_____*tenant's signature*_____
Tenant

_____*landlord's name printed*_____
Landlord's Name

■ **Note:** The tenant should send his notice to the landlord by certified mail, with a return receipt requested. By doing so, he will have proof that the landlord received the notice. For further information, see LANDLORD; TENANT'S RIGHTS.

REAL ESTATE ESCROW AGREEMENT

Once a real estate sales contract is signed, the buyer's down payment is deposited in an escrow account. This agreement informs the escrow agent when the down payment can be released.

Escrow Agreement

AGREEMENT between _____ *seller's name* _____ (name, hereinafter "Seller"), _____ *buyer's name* _____ ("Buyer"), and _____ *escrow agent's name* _____ ("Escrow Agent"), made this __*date*__ day of __*month*__, 19___ at __*address*__ in the Province of _____.

Simultaneously with the making of this Agreement, Seller and Buyer have entered into a contract ("the Contract") by which Seller will sell to Buyer the following property:

[address of property]

The closing will take place on the __*date*__ day of __*month*__, 19___, at __*hour*__ a.m./p.m, at the offices of _____ *name of law firm, bank, etc.* _____, whose address is _____ *address of law firm, bank, etc.* _____, or at such other time and place as Seller and Buyer may jointly designate in writing. As required by the Contract, Buyer must deposit $ _____ *amount of down payment* _____ as a down payment to be held in escrow by Escrow Agent.

The down payment referred to above has been paid by Buyer to Escrow Agent, and Escrow Agent acknowledges receipt of $ _____ *amount of down payment* _____ from Buyer. If paid by cheque, receipt is subject to collection.

If closing takes place as stated in the Contract, Escrow Agent at the time of closing shall pay the amount deposited with him/her to Seller, or as instructed by Seller in writing.

If no closing takes place under the Contract, Escrow Agent shall continue to hold the amount deposited until receipt of a written authorization for its disposition signed by both Buyer and Seller. In the event of any dispute as to whom Escrow Agent is to deliver the amount deposited, Escrow Agent shall hold the sum until the parties' rights are finally determined in an appropriate action or proceeding, or until a court orders Escrow Agent to deposit the down payment with it. If Escrow Agent does not receive a proper written authorization from Seller and Buyer, or if an action or proceeding to determine Seller's and Buyer's rights is not begun or diligently prosecuted, Escrow Agent is under no obligation to bring an action or proceeding to deposit the sum held by him/her in court, but may continue to hold the deposit. Escrow Agent assumes no liability except as that of a stakeholder.

Escrow Agent's duties are limited to those specifically set forth in this Agreement, and Escrow Agent shall incur no liability to anyone except as a result of willful misconduct or gross negligence so long as the Escrow Agent acts in good faith. Seller and Buyer hereby release Escrow Agent from liability for any act done or omitted in good faith in the performance of Escrow Agent's duties.

_____ *seller's signature* _____
Seller

_____ *escrow agent's signature* _____
Escrow Agent

_____ *buyer's signature* _____
Buyer

■ **Note:** An escrow agreement can be a separate document or it can be a clause within the sales contract. The escrow agent can be a bank, a lawyer, or any third party who agrees to hold the down payment. However, the home buyer's lawyer is usually prohibited from serving as an escrow agent. For more information, see Escrow.

A binder is an offer to purchase real estate. It can be converted into a sales contract when the seller accepts the offer, as in the sample below, or it can require the seller and buyer to draw up a sales contract at a later date. For more information, see BINDER; HOME BUYING AND SELLING.

Binder

1. The undersigned _____*purchaser's name*_____, herein called the Purchaser, having inspected the real property described as _____*description of property*_____ on the ___ day of __*month*__, 19__, herein agrees to and with _____*vendor's name*_____, herein called the Vendor, to purchase the said real property at the price of _____ dollars ($_____) of which the sum of _____ dollars ($_____) the Purchaser pays to and is received by _____*vendor's name*_____ as a deposit on account of the purchase price.

2. The purchase price is payable as ☐ all cash on completion; or ☐ $ _____ cash on completion with the balance as follows: _____

3. This offer is made subject to the following conditions: *(for example: These terms are for the benefit of the Purchaser and may be waived by the Purchaser alone:*
a) The dwelling on the real property being purchased has been constructed in accordance with and presently complies with all relevant municipal, provincial and federal requirements.
b) The heating system, plumbing system, electrical system are not in need of repair.
c) The property does not contain urea formaldehyde foam insulation.
d) That the purchaser be able to obtain proper financing to complete the purchase.)

4. The balance of cash is to be paid by ___*date*___, 19__, and the sale completed by ___*date*___, 19__.

5. Provided the sale is completed, the Purchaser is to have vacant possession of the property (subject to existing tenancies) at __ o'clock __ a.m/p.m. on ___*date*___, 19__.

6. Purchaser will assume and pay taxes, water and sewer rates and continuing charges, and adjustments shall be made as of ___*time and date*___, 19__.

7. A conveyance by way of a deed, mortgage or agreement for sale on the terms set out herein and in registerable form shall be delivered to the Purchaser or the Purchaser's solicitor on or before the date set for completion.

8. The property shall be at the risk of the Vendor until 12 o'clock noon on the adjustment date and thereafter at the risk of the Purchaser and in the event that buildings or improvements thereon are destroyed or substantially damaged prior to that time, either party may at his option cancel this agreement and all monies paid under this agreement shall be returned.

9. Title is subject to restrictive covenants, statutory building schemes, reservations and exceptions contained in the original grant from the Crown, easements in favor of utilities, public authorities, and adjacent land, building, zoning and other municipal or governmental restrictions, and also to be subject to existing tenancies and the Purchaser is satisfied as to the legality of any suites on the property.

10. The purchase price includes any buildings, improvements, fixtures, appurtenances, and attachments and all television antennae, blinds, swings, screen doors and windows, storm windows, curtain rods, tracks and valences, fixed mirrors, fixed carpeting, electrical, plumbing, and heating fixtures and appurtenances and attachments thereto, present on the date of inspection, except the following: _____ *list of exceptions. For example, dining room chandelier, dishwasher, front porch swing*_____.

11. The Vendor is to clear the title of all charges, encumbrances and judgments not assumed herein by the Purchaser, unless the parties arrange for deduction and discharge of same from the sale proceeds. Purchaser will pay all costs of conveyancing and arranging any mortgage, if applicable.

12. There are no representations, warranties, guarantees, promises or agreements other than those contained in this agreement, and words importing the singular, masculine and neuter shall mean and include the plural, feminine or body corporate wherever the context or parties to this agreement require.

13. The offer, when accepted, shall constitute a binding contract of purchase and sale and time shall be of the essence.

14. The Vendor represents and warrants to the Purchaser that:
(a) he is not now, nor will be 60 days after the possession date, a non-resident of Canada within the meaning of the Income Tax Act of Canada.
(b) he is not the agent or trustee for anyone with an interest in this property who is or will be 60 days after the possession date a non-resident of Canada within the meaning of the Income Tax Act of Canada.

15. This offer shall be held open for acceptance by the Vendor until __ o'clock __ a.m./p.m. on ___ *date* ___ , 19___ .

16. If the offer is not accepted by the Vendor within this time, the offer shall become null and void and the deposit shall be returned to the Purchaser without interest.

OFFER: I hereby agree and offer to purchase the property at the price and on the terms and conditions herein set out.

_____ *purchaser's signature* _____
Purchaser
_____ *purchaser's name printed* _____
Purchaser's Name

_____
Address

_____
City   Province   Postal Code

SELLER'S ACCEPTANCE OF OFFER

ACCEPTANCE: I hereby accept the above offer on the terms and conditions contained therein.

_____ *seller's signature* _____
Seller

FULL COVENANT AND WARRANTY DEED

A real estate transaction is not complete until the seller (grantor) has signed a written description of the property (deed) and given it to the buyer (grantee). There are several types of deed; a full covenant and warranty deed offers the buyer the best guarantee against legal problems that might arise in the future as a result of judgments or claims by others against the property. If faced with such claims, the holder of a full covenant and warranty deed has the right to sue the seller.

Full Covenant and Warranty Deed

BE IT KNOWN, that _____ *seller's name* _____, Grantor, of
_____ *seller's address* _____,
County of _____ *seller's county* _____, Province of _____ *seller's province* _____,
hereby bargains, deeds, and conveys to _____ *buyer's name* _____,
Grantee, of _____ *buyer's address* _____,
County of _____ *buyer's county* _____, Province of _____ *buyer's province* _____,
and his heirs and assigns, for the sum of $ _____ *selling price* _____, the following
described real estate in _____ *name of county* _____ County, Province of
_____ *name of province* _____, in fee simple:

[legal description of property]

along with all the tenements, hereditaments, and appurtenances belonging to
the above property.

Grantor, for himself, his heirs and successors, hereby covenants with Grantee,
Grantee's heirs and assigns, that Grantor is lawfully seized in fee simple of
the above-described property and that he has the right to convey it; that the
property is free from all encumbrances, except those listed in Schedule A
attached to this document and incorporated herein by reference; that Grantor
and his heirs, and all persons acquiring any interest in the property granted,
through or for Grantor, will, on demand of and at the expense of the Grantee,
or his heirs or assigns, execute any additional instrument necessary for the further assurance of the title to the property that may be reasonably required;
and that Grantor and his heirs will warrant and defend forever title to all of the
property so granted to Grantee, his heirs and assigns, against every person
lawfully claiming the same or any part thereof.

Grantor obtained title to the above-described property by deed of _____*previous owner*_____, dated _____*date of seller's deed*_____, 19___, and recorded in the office of the Recorder of Deeds for ___*name of county*___ County in Book or Volume _*number*_ at Page _*number*_.

IN WITNESS WHEREOF, the Grantor has signed this deed this _*date*_ day of _*month*_, 19___at _____*address*_____ in the Province of_____.

_____*seller's signature*_____
Grantor

NOTARY'S STATEMENT

PROVINCE OF _____

COUNTY OF _____

The foregoing instrument was acknowledged before me this _____ day of _____, 19 ____, by _____, as Grantor.

_____
[SEAL]   NOTARY PUBLIC

My commission expires: _____

■ **Note:** All deeds contain a legal description of the property, which precisely defines its boundaries. In this deed the land, as well as any houses, buildings, or structures ("tenements, hereditaments, and appurtenances"), is conveyed to the buyer. The seller swears that he is the sole owner of the property ("is lawfully seized in fee simple"), that there are no encumbrances (liens or judgments) against the property, and that he and his heirs will defend the buyer's and his heirs' rights to the property if anyone challenges their ownership. If there are any encumbrances against the property, they should be listed on a separate page (here called Schedule A). The buyer should keep the property deed in a safe place, such as a safe-deposit box. For more information, see DEED.

QUITCLAIM DEED

A quitclaim deed gives a real estate buyer (grantee) the least amount of protection from any claims by others on the property. In a quitclaim deed, the seller (grantor) gives the buyer his interests or rights to the property, but gives no assurances that he has sole claim to the property.

Quitclaim Deed

BE IT KNOWN, that _____ seller's name _____ (Grantor), of _____ seller's address _____, County of _____ seller's county _____, Province of _____ seller's province _____, hereby QUIT-CLAIMS and transfers to _____ buyer's name _____, of_____ buyer's address _____, County of _____ buyer's county _____, Province of _____ buyer's province _____, for the sum of $ _____ selling price _____, receipt of which is hereby acknowledged, the following described real property located in ___ name of county County, Province of _____ name of province ___:

[legal description of property]

Grantor does not covenant that he/she is the lawful owner of any estate in the above-mentioned property, nor does he/she make any covenant regarding encumbrances, liens, or his/her right to convey the above-mentioned property. Nor does Grantor make any covenant, representation, or warranty regarding the quality or condition of the above-mentioned property. Grantor intends this deed to convey only whatever interest he/she may now have in the property.

IN WITNESS WHEREOF, I have signed this Deed this _date_ day of___ month ___, 19___.

_____ seller's signature _____
Grantor

NOTARY'S STATEMENT

PROVINCE OF _____

COUNTY OF _____

Before me personally appeared _____, who acknowledged the foregoing as his/her free act and deed, this ____ day of _____, 19__.

_____
NOTARY PUBLIC

[SEAL]

My commission expires: _____

■ **Note:** A legal description of the property precisely defines its boundaries. The seller makes no promise (covenant) that she has lawful title to the property she is selling, or that there are no claims or judgments against it. Nor does she make any promises regarding the property's condition. Before accepting a quitclaim deed, consult a lawyer about the possible problems you can encounter with this type of deed. You should keep a quitclaim deed in a safe place, such as a safe-deposit box. For further information, see DEED; QUITCLAIM DEED.

For a quick guide to LEGAL PROBLEM SOLVER entries relating to major subject areas of everyday interest, use this handy thematic index to locate topics that might not immediately come to mind.

INDEX

X

Y

Z